FOOD AND DRUG LAW

FEDERAL REGULATION OF DRUGS, BIOLOGICS, MEDICAL DEVICES, FOODS, DIETARY SUPPLEMENTS, PERSONAL CARE, VETERINARY AND TOBACCO PRODUCTS

CONTAINS ALL 12 VOLUMES

ROSEANN B. TERMINI, ESQ.

TENTH EDITION
FORTI PUBLICATIONS®

www.FortiPublications.com | Info@FortiPublications.com

FORTI Publications
info@fortipublications.com
www.fortipublications.com

NOTE: Nothing contained in this book is considered rendering legal advice or other professional services. This publication was not necessarily developed by persons licensed to practice law in a specific jurisdiction. Obtain the services of an attorney or professional if legal advice or professional advice is so desired.

Tenth Edition

www.fortipublications.com

info@fortipublications.com

Library of Congress Cataloging-in-Publication Data

ISBN: 978-0-9843561-8-8

Printed in the United States of America

Preface

Purpose of this Book

This comprehensive food and drug law resource, "Food and Drug Law: Federal Regulation of Drugs, Biologics, Medical Devices, Foods, Dietary Supplements, Personal Care, Veterinary and Tobacco Products Regulation," is organized for ease of reading in order to comprehend a complex area of law. This easy to navigate treatise is well-ordered into separate volumes with a concise introduction to provide a particular focus for the reader. This reference contains a distinct volume for each subject based on regulation under the United States Federal Food, Drug and Cosmetic Act (FDCA) and related law. This entire work serves as an inclusive resource for:

> The regulated industry such as legal counsel and regulatory affairs professionals searching for concise explanations of relevant portions of the Food, Drug and Cosmetic Act (FDCA);

> Legal practitioners whose practice involves food, medical devices, drugs, biologics, personal care, veterinary, dietary supplements and tobacco products regulatory law;

> Government personnel—federal, state and local involved in these topics;

> Attorneys in related disciplines who find themselves in the crosshairs of the FDCA; and

> The academic community including professors and students searching for a clear resource.

The titles of each volume all contained in this book are as follows:

Volume I: The "Why" of the United States Food and Drug Administration, Landmark Legislation, and Court Decisions

Volume II: Food and Drug Law Administrative Primer

Volume III: The Food and Drug Administration—Criminal and Civil Enforcement Strategies

Volume IV: Medical Device and Radiation Emitting Products Regulation

Volume V: Human Drug Regulation—Approvals, Promotion, Marketing, Warnings, Accountability, and Post-market Surveillance

Volume VI: Biotechnology and Biologic Products Regulation

Volume VII: Veterinary Products Regulation

Volume VIII: Personal Care Products Regulation—Safety, Product Classification and Enforcement

Volume IX: Food Regulation—Food Safety, Recalls, Claims, Additives, Allergens and Biotechnology

Volume X: Dietary Supplements, Herbs and Botanicals Regulation

Volume XI: Tobacco Products Regulation

Volume XII: Professionalism, Politics, Foreign Corrupt Practices, Product Classification, Globalization and the Future

NOTE: _Each volume is available as a separate E-book._

About the Author

Roseann B. Termini, B.S., Ed. M., J.D. has over thirty years of extensive experience in food and drug law. These 12 volumes, all contained in this new tenth edition, emanate from her comprehensive food and drug regulatory law books. Ms. Termini has frequently presented food and drug law topics as a featured international and national speaker. Further, she has published a broad array of specialized food and drug law issues such as corporate accountability, criminal liability, enforcement, health claims, dietary supplements, safety, duty to warn, preemption, regulation, promotion, tobacco, stem cells, risk assessment, right-to-try and globalization. She was the inaugural recipient of the Plain English Award by the Pennsylvania Bar Association. Her expertise includes an appellate clerkship, sole corporate counsel, regulatory attorney and senior deputy attorney general at the Pennsylvania Office of Attorney General (OAG). While at the OAG, she prosecuted cases at the trial and appellate levels and was in charge of implementation procedures for the Pennsylvania Plain Language Act. Ms. Termini designed and developed the inaugural online food and drug law courses at Delaware Law School of Widener University, Johns Hopkins University, the University of Georgia, Drexel University and pharmaceutical promotion courses at St. Joseph's University's Executive Program. Ms. Termini has also taught food and drug law courses at Temple University's Quality and Regulatory Affairs Graduate Program and Dickinson School of Law. She was appointed to Immaculata University President's Council. Ms. Termini has been active in professional associations for numerous years, including her service as Academic Chair of a Food and Drug Law Committee and Vice Chancellor of the Justinian Society. She is Vice Chair of the Pennsylvania Bar Association Health Law and Disability Rights Committees, Board member of the St. Thomas More Law Society and is involved in the Central Atlantic States Association of Food and Drug Law Officials. In 2018, Ms. Termini was admitted to the Bar of the United States Supreme Court.

Acknowledgments

A Look Back at DSHEA—Over 25 Years Later the Dangers of a Reactionary Approach to Dietary Supplement Regulation, (co-authored), Quinnipiac Health Law Journal, Vol. 22 Issue 2 (2019).

The Latest "Federal Movement" in the Food and Drug Law Arena: The Federal Right-to-Try or Rather Right-to-Know and Thus Request Investigational Therapies for Individuals with a Life-Threatening Disease or Condition, Indiana Health L. Rev., Volume XVI, Issue I (2018).

Right-to-Try or Right-to-Ask, 38 *Pennsylvania Lawyer* 45, PA Bar Assn. (2016).

What is the Role of FDA—Watchdog, Regulator, Facilitator or All of the Above, 7 N.C. Cent. Biotech. & Pharm. L. Rev. (2014).

Sex, Politics, and Lessons Learned from Plan B: A Review of the FDA's Actions and Future Direction, (co-authored) Oklahoma L. Rev. Vol. 36, No. 2 (2011).

Food Advertising and Childhood Obesity: A Call to Action for Proactive Solutions, (co-authored) Minnesota J. of Law, Science and Technology, 12 (2) 619-651 (2011).

Should Congress Pass Legislation to Regulate Child-Directed Food Advertising? (co-authored) Vol. 1, No. 9 Food and Drug Law Institute Policy Forum (2011).

Does "Political" Science Exist Anymore? Embryonic Stem Cell Research in This New Political Climate, 5 J. of Health & Biomedical Law 249 (2009).

The Influence of Culture, Government and the Law on the Use of Antidepressants for Children in the United States and Pakistan, (co-authored) 63 Food and Drug Law J. 713 (2008).

American Beauty: An Analytical View of the Past and Current Effectiveness of Cosmetic Safety Regulations, (co-authored) 63 Food and Drug Law J. 257 (2008).

The Legal Authority of the United States Federal Food and Drug Administration to Regulate Tobacco: Calling on Congress, 74 ST. JOHN'S LAW REV. 63 (2000).

Pharmanex v. Shalala, A Wake-Up Call for Congress and a Not so Bitter Pill for FDA, 26 OHIO N.U. LAW REV. 269 (2000).

The Pharmacist Duty to Warn Revisited: The Changing Role of Pharmacy in Health Care and the Resultant Impact on the Obligation of a Pharmacist to Warn, 24 OHIO N.U. LAW REV. 551 (1998).

The Prevention of Misbranded Food Labeling— The Nutrition Labeling and Education Act of 1990 and Alternative Enforcement Mechanisms, 18 OHIO N.U. LAW REV. 77 (1991).

Who Should Mind the Internet Drugstore? 2 PHARMACEUTICAL & MEDICAL DEVICE BULL. 1 (2002).

Dedication

I dedicate this book to the memory of my parents who fostered values that afforded the opportunity to fulfill this passion, to the memory of my mentor, Alan H. Kaplan, Esquire; and to my beloved collies, who have spurred my interest in veterinary products regulation.

Special Appreciation

With special appreciation to Abby Foster, J.D. for her support, encouragement, and exceptional suggestions; to Janet Lindenmuth, M.S., of Delaware Law School, for her excellent research, to Phyllis Pilla for her tireless editing, *phyllispilla@comcast.net*; and to Stan Termini, B.S., for the excellent formatting and cover designs, *stan.termini@gmail.com.*

Table of Contents

Table of Contents

Table of Selected Cases

Cases

Table of Selected Cases

Table of Selected Cases

VOLUME I

Volume I: The "Why" of the United States Food and Drug Administration, Landmark Legislation and Court Decisions

Why is there an "FDA" today? Reviewing the evolution of food and drug law legislation and events reveals the answer. The mission of the United States Food and Drug Administration (FDA), a federal agency within the United States Department of Health and Human Services, is that of public protection which is in keeping with the evolution of food and drug related laws. FDA protects the public health by assuring the safety, effectiveness, and security of human and veterinary drugs, vaccines and other biological products for human use, medical devices, food, cosmetics, dietary supplements, electronic radiating products and for regulating tobacco products. Volume I centers on significant legislation and legal decisions in food and drug law including United States Supreme Court cases that have impacted on the practice of food and drug law.

Chapter 1 details significant legislative enactments originating from the early English influence. Chapter 2 details landmark legislation and court decisions starting with 2000. For example, the decision of Washington Legal Foundation (WLF) v. Henney, decided in 2000 and Thompson v. Western States decided in 2002, invalidated portions of the Food and Drug Administration Modernization Act (FDAMA). The Bioterrorism Act of 2002 provided FDA with increased regulatory authority to safeguard the food and drug supply. Also, in 2002, specific legislation that focuses on the use of pediatric pharmaceuticals was enacted. User fees continue in the pharmaceutical arena and have been extended to the medical device industry with the enactment of the Medical Device User Fee and Modernization Act (MDUFMA) of 2002. The Medicare Modernization Act of 2003 and its application to patent issues and generic drug products has had a far-reaching impact in terms of patent reforms and more expedient entry of generic drug products into the marketplace. Known as the Best Pharmaceuticals for Children Act, this is a safety-based law about drugs for children. The 2003 Pediatric Research Equity Act was approved to complement and comport with the Best Pharmaceuticals for Children Act by explicit authorization for FDA to require pharmaceutical manufacturers to conduct pediatric clinical trials and studies. This chapter contains significant highlights of the Food and Drug Administration Amendments Act of 2007 (FDAAA). Notable United States Supreme Court decisions pertaining to the duty of a drug manufacturer to warn included Wyeth v. Levine and Pliva v. Mensing with the result dependent on whether the pharmaceutical was a generic or brand name drug. Nearly ten years after the Brown v. Williamson Tobacco Supreme Court decision, Congress enacted the historic Family Smoking Prevention and Tobacco Control Act. The 2011 Food Safety Modernization Act, the 2012 FDA Safety and Innovation Act, the 2013 Drug Quality and Security Act, the 2014 Sunscreen Innovation Act, the 2015 CURES Act, the 2018 Right-to-Try Act and the 2018 Opioid legislation are all highlighted.

Chapter 3 details the "why" of FDA. Finally, Chapter 4 focuses on the United States Food and Drug Administration (FDA) and other noteworthy agencies. The mission of FDA, as stated, in accordance with the Federal Food, Drug and Cosmetic Act (FDCA), is to protect the public health and safety. Each chapter contains critical analysis issues to explore.

Chapter 1: The Evolution of Food and Drug Law
Key Web site: *www.fda.gov*

Public protection, a vital factor in food and drug law legislation, has remained steadfast over the years. The mission of the United States Food and Drug Administration (FDA) stems from key historical enactments detailed below. This chapter details key legislation enactments originating from the early English influence. Significant landmark law and legal court cases that have affected the regulation of foods, drugs, medical devices, dietary supplements, biologics and cosmetics are emphasized. During the latter part of the 19th century, Congress considered endorsing federal food regulation statutes as part of a growing public concern over adulteration. Over 100 years ago, Congress authorized the first Food and Drugs Act in 1906. Later, in 1938, Congress enacted the Federal Food, Drug and Cosmetic Act (FDCA). The purpose of the FDCA included the prohibition of any false or misleading statements. The FDCA contained provisions that extended control to cosmetics and therapeutic devices, required safety of new drugs prior to marketing, provided safe tolerance levels for pesticides, preservatives and additives, authorized factory inspections and added court injunctions as a remedy for violations.

The 1967 Federal Meat Inspection Act focused on inspection, adulteration and misbranding. A highlight of the 1970s included the passage of the Medical Device Amendments of 1976 to ensure the safety and efficacy of medical devices including diagnostic products. Much of the 1980s focused on drug regulation. Laws passed included the Orphan Drug Act, the Drug Price Competition and Patent Term Restoration Act, the AIDS test for blood, the Childhood Vaccine Act, the Prescription Drug Marketing Act, and the Generic Animal Drug and Patent Term Restoration Act.

The 1990s started out with enactment of major food legislation. The Nutrition Labeling and Education Act of 1990 created parameters for food labeling and certain health claims. Additional Medical Device legislation passed in the 1990s included the Safe Medical Device Act and the Medical Device Amendments. The 1990s ended with passage of milestone legislation—The Food and Drug Administration Modernization Act of 1997 (FDAMA), which mandated the most reforms since the Food, Drug and Cosmetic Act of 1938.

Regulation in the 1800s—Food Law, USP, Federal Regulation

First English Food Laws: Initially, food laws in the United States approximated those of England. The Assize of Bread prohibited adulteration of bread and instituted weight measures.[1] Regulation of food in the United States dates from early colonial times.[2] The laws of colonial Virginia pertained to weight and measures of food.[3] Massachusetts enacted the first general food law aimed toward protecting consumers against adulteration.[4]

The United States Pharmacopeia (USP) was the first compendium of standard drugs for the United States. Congress passed the Drug Importation Act in 1820. This law required United States Customs Service inspection to stop the entry of adulterated drugs from overseas. In 1862, President Lincoln appointed chemist Charles M. Wetherill to serve in the United States Department of Agriculture. Known as the Bureau of Chemistry, it was the predecessor of the United States Food and Drug Administration. Even before the unsanitary conditions in the Chicago stockyards were exposed in Upton Sinclair's book *The Jungle*, there was concern aimed toward food safety. In 1880, Peter Collier, chief chemist at the United States Department of Agriculture, recommended the passage of a national food law. Although the bill was defeated, more than 100 food and drug bills were introduced in Congress during the next 25 years.

In 1883, Dr. Harvey W. Wiley, successor to Peter Collier, expanded food adulteration studies started by Collier and campaigned for a federal law. Dr. Wiley was known as the "Crusading Chemist" and "Father of the Pure Food and Drugs Act." During this time, Congress did pass the Tea Importation Act, which pertained to adulterated tea.[5] In 1886, Congress passed a federal law concerning the manufacture of oleomargarine.[6] The oleomargarine law authorized the Internal

Revenue Service Commissioner to determine if the "imitation" butter contained deleterious ingredients and, if so, the product was forfeited. The 1800s ended with establishment of the 1898 Food Standards Committee for states to incorporate standards.

Regulation Throughout the 20th Century

Early 1900s—The Biologics Control Act enacted in 1902 was passed to ensure purity and safety of serums, vaccines and other products used to prevent or treat diseases. In 1903, Collier established a "poison squad" of volunteers who ate foods with chemical preservatives for determining whether the foods were harmful. Other events that spurred the passage of the 1906 Food and Drugs Act[7] (1906 Act) and the Meat Inspection Act[8] included Industrialization and New Nationalism.[9] The Meat Inspection Act resulted from shocking disclosures of unsanitary conditions in meat packing industries.[10] The 1906 Act aimed toward the prohibition in interstate commerce of misbranded and adulterated foods and drugs established the necessity of government intervention to protect both the public and the honest manufacturer. In 1911, the Supreme Court ruled in *United States v. Johnson*[11] that the 1906 Act did not prohibit false therapeutic claims but only false and misleading statements about the ingredients or identity of a drug. However, in 1912, Congress enacted the Sherley Amendment[12] to overcome the ruling in *United States v. Johnson*. It prohibited labeling medicines with false therapeutic claims intended to defraud the purchaser.

The Gould Amendment, enacted in 1913, required food package contents be plainly and conspicuously marked on the outside of the package in terms of weights and measures.[13] As early as 1914, the United States Supreme Court, in *United States v. Lexington Mill Elevator Co.*,[14] set forth the purpose of the 1906 Act. The Court stated that "[t]he consumer should know that an article purchased was what it purported to be; that it might be bought for what it really was and not upon misrepresentations as to character and quality."[15] Ten years later, in *United States v. 95 Barrels, More or Less, Alleged Apple Cider Vinegar*,[16] the Court emphasized that the aim of the 1906 Act was to prohibit every statement, design and device which may mislead or deceive and to prevent ambiguity.[17] FDA celebrated the 100th anniversary of the 1906 Act on June 30, 2006.

1930s—Tragedy Leads to Enactment of "The 1938 Act"—In 1933, FDA recommended a complete revision of the 1906 Act, a recommendation strengthened in 1937 with the Elixir of Sulfanilamide tragedy. The elixir contained the poisonous solvent diethylene glycol and killed 107 people including children, demonstrating the need for drug safety before marketing. Finally, the Federal, Food, Drug and Cosmetic Act of 1938 (FDCA) was passed.[18]

The FDCA contained provisions which extended control to cosmetics and therapeutic devices; required safety of new drugs prior to marketing; eliminated the Sherley Amendment requirement to prove intent to defraud in drug misbranding cases; provided safe tolerance levels for pesticides, preservatives and additives; authorized standards of identity, quality, and fill of container for foods; authorized factory inspections; and added court injunctions as a remedy for violations. During the same year, passage of the Wheeler-Lea Act[19] provided the Federal Trade Commission the regulatory authority over advertised products otherwise regulated by FDA with the exception of prescription drugs. Issuance of the first food standards occurred in 1939.

1940s—Corporate Accountability and *United States v. Dotterweich*—In 1943, the Supreme Court in *United States v. Dotterweich*[20] held that responsible corporate officials as well as the corporation might be prosecuted. The Supreme Court followed the FDCA and permitted the imposition of strict liability. Proof that the officials intended or even knew of the violations was not required. The following year, the Public Health Services Act[21] was passed, which covered a wide spectrum of health concerns, including the regulation of biological products and the control of communicable diseases. In 1945, the Penicillin Amendment required FDA to test and certify the safety and effectiveness of all penicillin products. *Kordel v. United States*,[22] decided in 1948, clarified the definition of labeling. The 1940s ended with the Miller Amendment, which affirmed that the FDCA applied to goods regulated by FDA that were transported from state to state.

1950s—Drug Label, Delaney, Pesticides, Additives, GRAS, and Poultry—The 1950s showed a stronger commitment toward prohibiting misleading information. For instance, in *Alberty Food Products Co. v. United States*, [23] the court ruled that the directions for use on a drug label must include the purpose for which the drug is offered. The Oleomargarine Act was passed, requiring prominent labeling to distinguish oleomargarine from butter. The Delaney Committee started Congressional investigation of the safety of chemicals in foods and cosmetics and established the foundation for the 1954 Miller Pesticide Amendment[24] and the 1958 Food Additives Amendment.[25] In 1957, the Poultry Products Inspection Act was enacted.[26] The 1950s concluded with publication of the first list of Substances Generally Recognized As Safe (GRAS).

1960s—Color Additives, Thalidomide Tragedy, the Kefauver-Harris Amendments, Fair Packaging, and Drug Defined—The 1960 Color Additive Amendment required manufacturers to establish the safety of color additives in foods, drugs, and cosmetics.[27] Color additives cannot be approved if shown to induce cancer in humans or animals. The Thalidomide tragedy that caused thousands of birth defects in babies born in Western Europe was averted in the United States due to the efforts of FDA medical officer Dr. Frances Kelsey. In 1962, the Kefauver-Harris Drug Amendments[28] were passed to ensure drug efficacy and greater drug safety. This meant that drug manufacturers were required to prove efficacy or effectiveness prior to marketing. The Fair Packaging and Labeling Act[29], enacted during this time period, pertained to unfair and deceptive packaging and labeling; that is, packaging and labeling must be accurate, fair and informative.

In 1966, FDA contracted with the National Academy of Sciences/National Research Council (NAS/NRC) to evaluate the effectiveness of 4,000 Drugs approved based on safety alone between 1938 and 1962. In 1968, FDA formed the Drug Efficacy Study Implementation (DESI) to implement the National Academy of Sciences recommendations. In 1968, The Animal Drug Amendments[30] made approval of animal drugs and medicated feeds more efficient by placing all regulation of new animal drugs under section 512 of the Food Drug and Cosmetic Act. The Federal Meat Inspection Act, [31] passed in 1967, focused on inspection, adulteration and misbranding. The Radiation Control for Health and Safety Act[32] of 1968 gave the Food and Drug Administration the responsibility for regulating products that emit radiation. *United States v. An Article...Bacto-Unidisk*,[33] reiterated the theme of public protection in deciding that an antibiotic sensitivity disk was a drug under the FDCA. The 1960s ended with the White House Conference on Food, Nutrition, and Health, which recommended a systematic review of GRAS substances because of the FDA's ban of the artificial sweetener cyclamate.

1970s—Corporate Accountability, Drug Effectiveness, and the Medical Device Amendments—In *Upjohn v. Finch*,[34] the court of appeals upheld the enforcement of the 1962 drug effectiveness amendments and held that commercial success alone does not constitute substantial evidence of drug safety and efficacy. In 1970, FDA required the first patient package insert for oral contraceptives to contain information for the patient about specific risks and benefits. Over-the-Counter Drug Review was started in 1972 to enhance the safety, effectiveness and appropriate labeling of drugs sold without a prescription. The Medical Device Amendments of 1976[35] were passed to ensure the safety and effectiveness of medical devices.

The 1970s ended with passage of the Saccharin Study and Labeling Act,[36] to prevent FDA from banning the chemical sweetener yet requiring a label warning that it was found to cause cancer in laboratory animals. The decision of *United States v. Park*,[37] focused on accountability and the use of criminal sanctions for corporate officials.

1980s—Product Tampering, Orphan Drugs, Drug Price Competition and Patents, Vaccines, and the Prescription Drug Marketing Act—Much of the 1980s focused on drug regulation. The Tamper-Resistant Packaging Regulations issued by FDA to prevent product tampering in response to what occurred when cyanide was placed in Tylenol® capsules. The Federal Anti-Tampering Act[38] of 1983 classifies package tampering of consumer products as a crime. The

Orphan Drug Act[39] passed in 1983, allows FDA to promote research and marketing of drugs necessary for treating rare diseases.

Another milestone in drug law was passage of the Drug Price Competition and Patent Term Restoration Act[40] to expedite the availability of generic drugs. It allows FDA to approve applications to market generic versions of brand-name drugs without repeating the research done to prove them safe and effective. Original manufacturers can apply for up to five additional years of patent protection for newly developed medicines to compensate for time expended in the FDA approval process. In its first major step to protect patients from infected donors, FDA approved an AIDS test for blood. The Childhood Vaccine Act[41] of 1986 requires patient information about vaccines, gives FDA the authority to recall biologics and authorizes civil penalties.

The 1987 revised investigational drug regulations expanded access to experimental drugs for patients with serious diseases without alternative therapies. The Prescription Drug Marketing Act,[42] enacted in 1988, banned the diversion of prescription drugs, bans the sale, trade or purchase of drug samples, and restricts re-importation from other countries. This Act required drug wholesalers to be state licensed. The Generic Animal Drug and Patent Term Restoration Act[43] of 1988 extends to veterinary products benefits given to human drugs under the 1984 Drug Price Competition and Patent Term Restoration Act. The 1980s ended with the Food and Drug Administration Act,[44] that officially established FDA as an agency of the Department of Health and Human Services with a Commissioner of Food and Drugs appointed by the President of the United States with the advice and consent of the Senate.

1990s—Drugs, Device Safety, Food Labeling, and FDA Modernization Act— Legislation during the 1990s focused on drug legislation. Regulations were passed in 1991 to accelerate the review of drugs for life-threatening diseases. The Generic Drug Enforcement Act[45] of 1992 imposed debarment and other penalties for illegal acts involving abbreviated drug applications. The 1992 Prescription Drug User Fee Act[46] requires drug and biologics manufacturers to pay fees for product applications and supplemental materials. This Act also allows FDA to use these funds to hire additional reviewers to evaluate applications. Major laws enacted for veterinarians included the Animal Medicinal Drug Use Clarification Act[47] concerning extra-label use of veterinary drugs for animals under specific conditions. Licensed veterinarians may prescribe human drugs for use in animals under certain circumstances. The Animal Drug Availability Act[48] provides for flexible labeling and direct communication between drug sponsors and FDA.

Several food laws were enacted during the 1990s. One major food law was enacted starting in 1990, with the Nutrition Labeling and Education Act (NLEA)[49]. NLEA requires all packaged foods to contain standardized nutrition labeling and certain health claims. NLEA preempts state requirements about nutrition labeling and health claims. Other food related legislation included the Federal Tea Tasters Repeal Act[50] that repealed the Tea Importation Act of 1897 and eliminated the Board of Tea Experts and user fees for FDA testing of imported tea. However, FDA still regulates tea itself. The Saccharin Notice Repeal Act of 1996[51] repealed the saccharin notice requirements. The Food Quality Protection Act of 1996[52] amended the Food Drug and Cosmetic Act by eliminating the application of the Delaney amendment to pesticides. The Dietary Supplement Health and Education Act of 1994[53] establishes specific labeling requirements, provides a regulatory framework, and authorizes FDA to develop good manufacturing practice regulations. *Pearson v. Shalala*[54] has influenced health claims authorization concerning dietary supplements.

The Safe Medical Devices Act[55] requires nursing homes, hospitals, and other facilities that use medical devices to report to FDA incidences of death, serious injury or serious illness.[56] The Medical Device Amendments[57] followed in 1992. *Medtronic v. Lohr*,[58] decided in 1996, concerned state court remedies for federally approved medical devices. The Court held that that statutory language of the Medical Device Amendments of 1976 did not preempt state common law tort remedies. The Mammography Quality Standards Act[59] requires all mammography facilities in the United States to be both accredited and certified.

In 1997, one of the most aggressive landmark legislative reforms in food and drug law history occurred with passage of the Food and Drug Administration Modernization Act (FDAMA) (Public Law No. 105-115).[60] Hailed as one of the most sweeping reforms since the 1938 FDCA, FDAMA mandated specific timeframes for FDA to complete regulations, guidance documents, regulatory notices and reports. Significant FDAMA initiatives include the reauthorization of prescription drug user fees, risk-based regulation of medical devices, food safety, pharmacy compounding, biologic modernization and product standards for medical products. Yet, *Washington Legal Foundation v. Henney*[61] invalidated the requirements in FDAMA concerning promotion of off-label uses and the First Amendment.[62] Overall, FDAMA affords industry a larger role in the regulatory decision-making process by promoting better communication with FDA.

---

[1] Wallace F. Janssen, America's First Food and Drug Laws, 30 FOOD DRUG COSM. L.J. 665, 666 (1975). Janssen related that the 1646 General Court of Massachusetts Bay Colony regulation required bakers to use a distinct mark for bread. Id.

[2] Wallace F. Janssen, America's First Food and Drug Laws, 30 FOOD DRUG COSM. L.J. 665, 666 (1975). Janssen related that the 1646 General Court of Massachusetts Bay Colony regulation required bakers to use a distinct mark for bread. Id

[3] L. Va. 1623-1624 , Act 22 l Hening 126. See Peter Barton Hutt & Peter Barton Hutt II, A History of Government Regulation of Adulteration and Misbranding of Food, 39 FOOD DRUG COSM. L. J. 2, 36-37 (1984).

[4] L. Mass. 1785, reprinted in Wallace F. Janssen, America's First Food and Drug law, 31 FOOD DRUG COSM. L. J. 246 (1976).

[5] Act of Mar. 2, 1883, ch. 64, 22 Stat. 451 (1883) (amended in 1897 to require "uniform standards of purity, quality and fitness for consumption of all kinds of tea imported into the United States"). See Act of Mar. 2, 1897, ch. 358, 29 Stat. 604, 605 (1897) (codified as amended at 21 U.S.C. § 41 (1988).

[6] Act of Aug. 2, 1886, ch. 840, 24 Stat. 209, 212 (1886) (superceded by the Oleomargarine Act of 1959, Act of Mar. 16, 1950, ch.61, 64 Stat. 20 (1950)).

[7] Pure Food and Drugs Act, ch. 3915, 34 Stat. 768, P. L. 59- 384 (1906) (repealed).

[8] Provisions for Meat Inspection in Pub. L. 59-242, appropriation act for the Department of Agriculture, approved March 4, 1907, 34 Stat. 1260, as amended.

[9] Richard C. Litman and Donald S. Litman, Protection of the American Consumer: The Muckrakers and the Enactment of the First Federal Food and Drug Law in the United States, 36 FOOD DRUG COSM.L. J. 647, 659 (1981).

[10] Publication of *The Jungle* provided additional support for passage of the Meat Inspection Act. *The Jungle* detailed the unsanitary conditions and employee abuse in the Chicago meat packing industry during this era. Upton Sinclair, *The Jungle* (1906).

[11] United States v. Johnson, 221 U.S. 488 (1911).

[12] 37 Stat. 416 (1912).

[13] 37 Stat. 732 (1913).

[14] 232 U.S. 399 (1914).

[15] Id. at 409.

[16] 265 U.S. 438 (1924).

[17] Id. at 44.

[18] Federal Food, Drug and Cosmetic Act of 1938, ch.675, 52 Stat. 1040 (1938) (codified as amended at 21 U.S.C. § 301 et seq.)

[19] See Jackson, FOOD AND DRUG LEGISLATION IN THE NEW DEAL (1970); Cavers, The Food, Drug and Cosmetic Act of 1938: Its Legislative History and Its Substantive Provisions, 6 Law & Contemp. Probs. 2 (1939).

[20] 320 U.S. 277 (1943).

[21] 58 Stat.682, 702 (1944), codified at 42 U.S.C. § 262.

[22] 335 U.S. 345 (1948).

[23] 185 F.2d 321 (1950).

[24] Superseded by the Pesticide Monitoring Improvements Act 102 Stat.1411 (1988), 21 U.S.C. §§ 1401, 1401 note, 1402-03.

[25] 72 Stat. 1784 (1958), codified at 21 U.S.C. § 348.

[26] 71 Stat. 441 (1957, codified at 21 U.S.C. § 457.

[27] 74 Stat. 397 (1960), codified at 21 U.S.C. § 376.

[28] Senator Kefauver pursued this legislation for several years before it was revived by the thalidomide tragedy in 1962.

[29] 80 Stat. 1296 (1966), codified at 15 U.S.C. § 1451 et seq.

[30] 82 Stat. 342 (1968), codified at 21 U.S.C. § 351 et seq.

[31] 34 Stat. 1260 (1967), codified at 21 U.S.C. § 601 et seq.

[32] 82 Stat. 1173 (1968), codified at 21 U.S.C. § 530 et seq.

[33] 394 U.S. 784 (1969).

[34] 422 F.2d 944 (6th Cir. 1970).

[35] 90 Stat. 539 (1976), codified at 15 U.S.C. § 55; 21 U.S.C. §§ 31, 331, 334, 351, 352, 358, 360, 374, 379, 381.

[36] 92 Stat. 1451 (1977), codified at 21 U.S.C.§ 343 (o) (1).

[37] 421 U.S. 658 (1975).

[38] 97 Stat. 831 (1983), codified at 18 U.S.C. § 1365.

[39] 96 Stat. 2049 (1983), codified as amended at 21 U.S.C. §360 aa et seq.

[40] 98 Stat. 1585 (1984), codified at 15 U.S.C.§§ 68b-c, 70b;§ 21 U.S.C. 301 note et seq., § 28 U.S.C. 2201, 35 U.S.C. §§ 156, 271, 282.

[41] 100 Stat. 3743 (1986) codified at 42 U.S.C. §300aa et seq.

[42] 102 Stat. 95 (1987) codified at 21 U.S.C.§ 301 note et seq.

[43] 102 Stat 3971 (1988) codified at 21 U.S.C.§ 301 note et seq.; §28 U.S.C. 2201; §§ 35 U.S.C. 156,271.

[44] 102 Stat. 3120 (1988) codified at 5 U.S.C. §§ 5315-16; § 21 U.S.C. 301 note et seq.

[45] 106 Stat. 149 (1992) codified at 21 U.S.C. §§ 301 note et seq.

[46] 106 Stat. 4491 (1992) codified as amended at 21 U.S.C. §§ 321 et seq.

[47] 108 Stat. 4153 (1994) codified at 21 U.S.C. §§ 301 note et seq.

[48] 110 Stat. 3151 (1996) codified at 21 U.S.C.§§ 301 note et seq.

[49] 104 Stat. 2353 (1990) codified at 21 U.S.C.§ 301 note et seq.

[50] 110 Stat. 1198 (1996) codified at 21 U.S.C. § 41 et seq.

[51] 110 Stat. 882 (1996) codified at 21 U.S.C. §343 (p).

[52] 110 Stat. 1489 (1986) codified at 7 U.S.C. §136 et seq.

[53] 108 Stat. 4325 (1994) codified at 21 U.S.C.§321 et seq.

[54] 164 F.3d 650 (1999).

[55] 104 Stat. 4511 (1990) codified at 21 U.S.C. §301 note et seq.

[56] 104 Stat. 4511 (1990) codified at 21 U.S.C. §301 note et seq.

[57] 106 Stat. 238 (1992) codified at 21 U.S.C. §301 note et seq.

[58] 518 U.S. 470 (1996).

[59] 106 Stat. 3547 (1992) codified at 42 U.S.C.§ 201 note et seq.

[60] 111 Stat. 2296 (1997) codified at 21 U.S.C.§360 bbb-1.

[61] 56 F.Supp.2d 81 aff 'd 202 F.3d 331 (2000).

[62] Id.

Critical Analysis: Evaluate legislation in the 19ᵗʰ and throughout the 20ᵗʰ century from a public protection stance.

Chapter 2: Legislative Hallmarks 2000s–Safety and Emerging Trends

Regulation in the 21st Century

Starting with 2000, this chapter details landmark legislation and court decisions. As an example, *Washington Legal Foundation v. Henney*, decided in 2000, and *Thompson v. Western States* decided in 2002, invalidated portions of FDAMA. The 2002 Bioterrorism Act provided FDA with increased regulatory authority to safeguard the food and drug supply. Further, in 2002, specific legislation that focused on the use of pediatric pharmaceuticals was enacted. User fees continue in the pharmaceutical arena and have been extended to the medical device industry with the enactment of the Medical Device User Fee and Modernization Act (MDUFMA) of 2002. The Medicare Modernization Act of 2003 and its application to patent issues and generic drug products has had a far-reaching impact in terms of patent reforms and more expedient entry of generic drug products into the marketplace. Known as the Best Pharmaceuticals for Children Act, this is a safety-based law about drugs for children. The 2003 Pediatric Research Equity Act was approved to complement and comport with the Best Pharmaceuticals for Children Act by explicit authorization for FDA to require pharmaceutical manufacturers to conduct pediatric clinical trials and studies. This chapter contains significant highlights of the Food and Drug Administration Amendments Act of 2007 (FDAAA). Notable United States Supreme Court decisions, namely *Wyeth v. Levine* and *Pliva v. Mensing* pertain to a drug manufacturer's duty to warn with the result dependent on whether a generic or brand name drug. Nearly ten years after the *Brown v. Williamson Tobacco* Supreme Court decision, Congress enacted the historic Family Smoking Prevention and Tobacco Control Act. The 2011 Food Safety Modernization Act, the 2012 Food and Drug Administration Safety and Innovation Act, Biosimilar legislation, Drug Quality and Security Act, Opioid legislation and the Federal Right-to-Try Act are highlighted.

Medicine Equity and Drug Safety Act—On October 28, 2000 the Medicine Equity and Drug Safety Act was enacted.[63] The intent of the legislation is to lower costs associated with pharmaceuticals and address reimportation. Yet, this remains in flux. Legislation that allows the reimportation of prescription drugs has many opponents. According to some drug manufacturers, the potential for counterfeit medicines exists. Drug reimportation remains debatable.

Best Pharmaceuticals for Children Act—On January 4, 2002, the Best Pharmaceuticals for Children Act (BPCA) became law.[64] The intent of the BPCA is to improve the safety and efficacy of pharmaceuticals for children and provide an additional six months of market exclusivity. In 2003, the Pediatric Research Equity Act (Equity Act) of 2003 was enacted to complement and comport with the BPCA to provide FDA with the legal authority to require pharmaceutical manufacturers to conduct pediatric studies on suitable drugs and biologics.[65] The Equity Act resulted from a prior court decision that held that the FDA lacked sufficient statutory authority to require pediatric studies. The Equity Act represents a milestone in narrowing the gaps that exist for pediatric testing and this law was reauthorized by the 2007 FDAAA, 21 U.S. C. sec. 355(c). The BPCA was reauthorized by the 2007 FDAAA and includes a requirement for submission of adverse event reporting along with the pediatric study reports.

Pharmacy Compounding—The United States Supreme Court settled First Amendment issues associated with promotion of pharmacy compounding in the decision of *Thompson v. Western States Medical CenterPharmacy*.[66] Due to problems including deaths associated with compounded products, the Drug Quality and Security Act was enacted in 2013.

Public Health Security and Bioterrorism Preparedness and Response Act—Notably, with bioterrorism in the forefront, the Public Health Security and Bioterrorism Preparedness and Response Act of 2002 was enacted.[67]

Medical Device User Fee and Modernization Act—Medical device user fee legislation was enacted as the Medical Device User Fee and Modernization Act of 2002.[68] Significant provisions concern user fees for device reviews; third party establishment inspections; and reprocessed single-use devices regulatory requirements.

Rare Diseases Orphan Product Development Act—Issues surrounding medication for rare diseases were addressed in the 2002 "Rare Diseases Orphan Product Development Act".[69]

Animal Drug User Fee Act—Similar to the Prescription Drug User Fee Act and the Medical Device User Fee and Modernization Act, the Animal Drug User Fee Act, enacted in 2003, authorizes the collection of annual user fees.[70] This legislation affords FDA the ability to hire additional reviewers and to initiate programs to accelerate and improve new animal drug reviews.

Medicare Prescription Drug Improvement and Modernization Act—The enactment of the 2003 Medicare Prescription Drug Improvement and Modernization Act amended the FDCA in terms of patent and exclusivity issues for both brand or innovator drug companies and generic firms.[71]

Anabolic Steroid Control Act—The Anabolic Steroid Control Act of 2004 was enacted to address the problems associated with steroids.[72]

Food Allergen Labeling and Consumer Protection Act—In response to the consumer's right to know concerning specific food labeling and food allergens, the Food Allergen Labeling and Consumer Protection Act of 2004 was enacted.[73] However, debates continue about the consumer's right to know concerning genetically altered foods. Different viewpoints of European countries and the United States certainly influence international trade issues.

Contact Lenses Non-Corrective—In 2005, a law that requires FDA's Center for Devices and Radiological Health to regulate all contact lenses whether corrective or cosmetic was enacted.[74] Previously, non-corrective contact lenses were regulated as cosmetics. However, due to eye injury concerns, FDA regulates all types of contact lenses, non-corrective and corrective as medical devices. The Food, Drug, and Cosmetic Act (21 U.S.C. 360j) was amended by adding: *(n)(1) All contact lenses shall be deemed to be devices under section 201(h) [21 U.S.C. 321 (h)].* This comports with the "2003 Fairness to Contact Lens Consumers Act" and subsequent FTC Contact Lens Rule which requires a prescription or proper fitting by a qualified eye care professional.

Adverse Event Reporting Dietary Supplement and Nonprescription Drug Act—Adverse event reporting for FDA regulated products remains a priority. Consequently, in 2006, the Dietary Supplement and Nonprescription Drug Consumer Protection Act became law for reporting of serious advent events.[75]

Pandemic and All-Hazards Preparedness Act—BioShield II Title IV—The Bio-Shield Act pertains to efforts by the federal government to develop pharmaceutical and other medical countermeasures for responding to chemical, biological, radiological and nuclear attacks.[76]

Food and Drug Administration Amendments Act—Considered the most comprehensive milestone legislation since FDAMA, the Food and Drug Administration Amendments Act of 2007[77] (FDAAA) was signed into law September 27, 2007 (Pub. L. No. 110-85). There are 11 separate titles and the first five titles address reauthorization of user fees for drugs and medical devices and pediatric programs.

Highlights include user fees reauthorization; post approval studies for high risk drugs; clinical trial database collaboration with the National Institutes of Health; pediatric research and labeling; and conflict of interest issues. Titles VI-VIII addresses public-private partnerships. Title IX, perhaps the most far reaching in terms of reform, addresses post market drug safety issues. Title X concentrates on food safety. Title XI focuses on miscellaneous provisions such as antibiotic access and tropical disease treatment. Overall, the impact of FDAAA is significant in terms of industry accountability, consumer safety and FDA for post-market safety surveillance. Significant provisions are as follows.

Title I—Prescription Drug User Fees (PDUFA IV) reauthorization— *Of particular note is the authorization of "Fees Relating to Advisory Review of Prescription-Drug Television Advertising" (DTC) that establishes a voluntary user fee program for FDA to both assess and collect fees for the pre-broadcast review of DTC. Any DTC advertisement that is subject to required pre-dissemination review is not subject to the user fees.*

NOTE: See *Volume V: Human Drugs*, Chapter 5. User fee program for review of direct-to-consumer television advertisements was not implemented due to lack of allocation in the consolidated Appropriations Act of 2008 (Pub. L. No. 110-161).

Title II—Medical Device User Fees Increased to Support Improved Safety Reviews and Testing
Reauthorizes device user fees established under the Medical Device User Fee and Modernization Act (MDUFA) Pub. L. No. 107-250 116 Stat. 1588 (2002).

Title III—Pediatric Medical Device Safety and Improvement Act-Encourages pediatric medical device product development (companion to Titles IV and V)
Requires FDA to work with the National Institutes of Health to establish clinical trial databases including adverse event information.

Title IV—Pediatric Research Equity Act —*Reauthorizes and amends the Pediatric Research Equity Act (PREA) Pub. L. No. 108-155 117 Stat. 1936 (2003). FDAAA impact is that of increased accountability for agreed upon evaluations. For example, FDAAA requires applicants to provide an annual update as to progress in conducting pediatric studies.*

Title V—Best Pharmaceuticals for Children Act—*Reauthorizes and amends the Best Pharmaceuticals for Children Act (BPCA) Pub. L. No. 107-109, 115 Stat. 1408 (2002). Similar to the Pediatric Research Equity Act, the FDAAA impact is that of increased accountability for agreed upon pediatric studies.*

Title VI—Reagan-Udall Foundation— *The FDAAA under Title V amends the FDCA by establishing a non-profit corporation the purpose of which is to advance FDA's Critical Path Initiative in terms of modernization. Specifically, FDA may collaborate with other researchers to promote newer testing techniques necessary to evaluate newer technologies.*

Title VII—Advisory Committee Conflicts of Interest—*Requires disclosure of financial interests by those who are under consideration for an FDA Advisory Committee Appointment that would be affected by specific committee actions.*

Title VIII—Clinical Trial Data Bases—*FDAAA expands the current clinical trial registry database and establishes a new clinical trial results database. The new clinical trials database accounts for trials for all diseases and conditions and increases the information available about the trial. Clinical trials of medical devices are included. The results database consists of results on all trials that form the main basis of an efficacy claim or are conducted after a drug or a device is approved. FDAAA section 801(d) includes a preemption provision that applies to the registry and results databases.*

Title IX—Enhanced FDA Authority Regarding Postmarket Safety of Drugs
Broadens FDA's authority to monitor and improve drug and biologics safety and includes penalties for violations. Postmarket Studies and Clinical Trials—Requires some drug sponsors to conduct postmarket studies and clinical trials; Requires FDA to "develop methods to access disparate data sources." 21 U.S.C. section 505(k) (3) (B)-(C). Requires FDA to develop and implement a "postmarket risk identification and analysis system" 21 U.S.C. section 505(k) (3) (B)-(C).

Safety Labeling Changes—*FDA can require postmarket safety labeling changes if it becomes aware of new safety information that should be included in the drug or biologic labeling. The NDA or BLA holder must submit a supplement to FDA within 30 days of the proposed labeling changes to reflect the new safety information; otherwise provide a comprehensive basis as to why the NDA* *or BLA holder does not believe the new labeling changes are warranted.*

DTC Television Advertising—Creates a process for FDA to "Pre-review Television Advertisements"

The FDAAA provides FDA with the authority to pre-review television advertisements. Upon review, FDA might provide recommendations as well as require an amendment if it addresses a serious drug risk.

> *The following statement is required to be included in all DTC ads for human drugs that are published: "You are encouraged to report negative side effects of prescription drugs to FDA. Visit www.fda.gov/medwatch or call 1-800-FDA-1088."*

Risk Evaluation and Mitigation Strategy (REMS)—*Required if FDA determines that the REMS is essential to make certain that the benefits outweigh the risks.*

Generic Drug Approvals—*Prohibits delaying approval of a generic drug application based on a citizen's petition with the exception of protection of public health.*

Title IX—Food and Dietary Supplement Application—*Adds a new section 21 USC section 321 (II) "Prohibition Against Food to Which Drugs or Biological Products Have Been Added". See Sec. 912. This provision impacts on the development of functional food ingredients. There are exemptions to this provision such as a drug or biological product marketed as food prior to FDA approval of the drug or biologic or prior to the commencement of any substantial clinical investigations of the drug or biologic.*

Title X—Food Safety—*Requires a registry to track all adulterated foods. Pet Food Safety—Requires the establishment of pet food safety standards.*

Title XI—Miscellaneous Provisions
FDA Review and Clearance of Employee Scientific Articles.
Transferable Priority Review System for Products that Treat Tropical Diseases.
Genetic Test Safety and Quality Antibiotic Access and Innovation.

Consumer Product Safety Improvement Act—In 2008, former President Bush signed the Consumer Safety Improvement Act (CPSIA) Pub. L. 110-314[78], which amended the Consumer Product Safety Act to add new section 6A. The relevancy for food and drug law concerns a database about the following: Reports of harm; Manufacturer/Importer or Private Labeler comments regarding reports of harm and information from mandatory recall notices and notices of voluntary corrective action by manufacturers.

The Family Smoking Prevention and Tobacco Control Act—Hailed as landmark and milestone legislation, the Family Smoking and Tobacco Prevention Control Act (FSTPCA)[79] of 2009 provides explicit authority to FDA to regulate tobacco products. In the past, FDA tried to regulate tobacco by assuming jurisdiction; however, the United States Supreme Court in *Brown & Williamson,* 120 S. Ct. 1291(2000) determined that FDA did not have the legal authority to regulate tobacco. Formerly, Congress had rejected proposals to give FDA the authority to regulate tobacco and FDA, at one time, determined they did not have the legal authority to regulate tobacco. Yet, the position of FDA altered due to scientific data related to the effects of tobacco. Congress revisited this issue to authorize this specific legislation that provides the agency with jurisdiction. **See Volume XI for further discussion.**

Biologics Price Competition and Innovation Act—The Biologics Price Competition and Innovation Act of 2009[80] within the Patient Protections and Affordable Care Act provides an exclusivity period of 12 years for innovator biologic products. This law was a result of years of debate and compromise. See: *Natural Res. Def. Council v. U.S. Food & Drug Admin.,* 11 CIV. 3562 JCF, 2012 WL 3229296 (S.D.N.Y. Aug. 8, 2012)

Sunshine Payment Provisions—Patient Protection and Affordable Care Act—
Section 6002[81] of the Patient Protection and Affordable Health Care Act contains provisions for annual disclosure of payments to physicians and teaching hospitals by drug, device, biologic and medical supply manufacturers.

Nutrition Disclosure—Patient Protection and Affordable Care Act—The Patient Protection and Affordable Care Act[82] of 2010 (Affordable Care Act) established changes for fast food menus and vending machines. Nutrition disclosure on menus is required for those fast food establishments with 20 or more locations nationwide. The "menu disclosure law" preempts state and local requirements. The Affordable Care Act was upheld in *Nat'l Fed'n of Indep. Bus. v. Sebelius*, 132 S. Ct. 2566, 183 L. Ed. 2d 450 (2012). **See Volume IX** *Food Regulation*.

Food Safety Modernization Act—Hailed as another example of landmark legislation, the FDA Food Safety Modernization Act (FSMA) signed into law by former President Obama in early January 2011. The FSMA, Public Law 111-353 (January 4, 2011), 124 Stat. 3885[83] represents landmark legislation and an overall of food safety regulation. **See Volume IX** *Food Regulation* for the detailed overview of key mandates.

Food and Drug Administration Safety and Innovation Act—Brand Name and Generic Drugs, Biosimilars, and Medical Devices

On July 9, 2012 former President Obama signed into law Senate Bill 3187, Pub. L. No. 112-144, the Food and Drug Administration Safety and Innovation Act (FDASIA).[84] This law reauthorized the Prescription Drug User Fee Act (PDUFA). It is the fifth authorization of PDUFA that includes Title I of FDASIA and the performance goals and procedures for PDUFA V. This legislation includes user fees of $6 billion over five years for medical devices, brand name drug approvals, generic drugs and biosimilars. The FDASIA includes the Medical Device User Fee Amendments of 2012 (MDUFA III).

Drug Quality and Security Act—This necessary and milestone legislation (H.R. 3204)[85] enacted towards the end of 2013, addresses federal regulatory authority over pharmacy compounding. Unfortunately, this legislation was enacted in response to the many deaths associated with large scale compounding. This law establishes parameters associated with compounding in terms of greater federal regulatory oversight. Additionally, Title II of the DQSA contains the *Drug Supply Chain Security Act*, (DSCSA) the "track and trace" provisions throughout the drug supply chain.

Sunscreen Innovation Act—This landmark milestone legislative enactment occurred in late 2014. The Sunscreen Innovation Act pertains to a more consumer protection initiative and provides for timeframes for FDA rulemaking. [86]

Designer Anabolic Steroid Control Act—Pub. L. 113-260 113th Congress. This 2014 law designated 25 ingredients familiar to federal regulators as controlled substances and simpler for other compounds to be also categorized as controlled substances in the future. [87]

Cures Act—The 21st Century Cures Act[88] is intended to accelerate drug and medical device approvals and address the opioid crisis. The Act strengthens mental health services, includes $1 billion for opioid abuse prevention and $4.8 billion for biomedical research funding and $1.8 billion for cancer research.

Comprehension Addiction and Recovery Act[89]—authorized spending to combat the opioid crisis. Funding was not appropriated in Fiscal Year 2018; however, the Bipartisan Budget Act authorized $3 billion for FY 2018 and $3 billion for FY 2019.

Food and Drug Administration Reauthorization Act (FDARA) [90]—reauthorized the Prescription Drug User Fee Act PDUFA VI: Fiscal Years 2018 – 2022 .

Federal Right-to-Try Act[91]—Trickett Wendler, Frank Mongiello, Jordan McLinn and Matthew Bellina Right to Try Act of 2017 enacted in 2018 which addresses the right of the individual to request and try investigational drugs.

Opioid Epidemic[92]—Substance Use Disorder Prevention that Promotes Opioid Recovery and Treatment for Patients and Communities Act (SUPPORT) in 2018.

Emerging Initiatives

Overall safety issues should remain the focus of future food and drug related legislation. This comports with the intent of the FDCA that is, to protect the public health and welfare. Post market drug and medical device safety is paramount. Food safety issues affording federal, state, local and tribal authorities with more stringent enforcement authority remain in the forefront. An ongoing debate persists regarding the feasibility of creating a unified system for food safety with a single federal agency being responsible. Other types of food and drug law legislation will focus on accountability and disclosure especially in this era of public and private responsibility. Increased safety monitoring, risk assessment, clinical trials to support claims on products, dietary supplement safety and efficacy, product classification, foodborne pathogens, food safety, generic biotech products, fast track human drug approvals, Internet promotion of food and drug regulated products, global harmonization remain in the forefront.

Stakeholder responsibility will increase, as should cooperative efforts between industry and the regulators. Future legislation should protect the public safety and health in accordance with the stated purpose of the Food, Drug and Cosmetic Act.

[63] 114 Stat, 1549 (2000); See also: Prescription Drug Import Fairness Act, 114 Stat. 1549 (2000) Title VII sec. 746(a).

[64] 115 Stat, 1408 (2002).

[65] 117 Stat. 1936 (2003).

[66] 122 S.Ct.1497 (2002).

[67] Pub.L.107-188 (2002), 116 Stat. 594.

[68] 116 Stat, 1588 (2002).

[69] 116 Stat, 1992 (2002).

[70] 117 Stat, 1361 (2003); Pub. L. 113-14 (Animal Drug and Animal Generic Drug User Fee Reauthorization Act 2013).

[71] Pub. L. 108-173 (2003)

[72] 118 Stat, 1661 (2004).

[73] 118 Stat, 891 (2004).

[74] 109-96 109th Congress (1st. Sess. 2005).

[75] 109-462 109th Congress (2nd. Sess. 2006).

[76] 109-417 109th Congress, 120 Stat. 2831 (2nd. Sess. 2006).

[77] 110-085 110th Congress, 121 Stat. 823 (2nd. Sess. 2007).

[78] Pub. L. 110-314 (2008).

[79] P. L. 111-31, Stat. 1776. (June 22, 2009)

[80] Pub.L. 111–148, Title VII, Subtitle A, Mar. 23, 2010, 124 Stat. 804 Short title, see 42 USCA § 201 note Enacting law: Pub.L. 111–148, Title VII, Subtitle A, Mar. 23, 2010, 124 Stat. 804 (21 §§ 355, 355a, 355c, 379g; 28 § 2201; 35 § 271; 42 §§ 201 note, 262, 284m) Public law Pub.L. 111–148 is the PATIENT PROTECTION AND AFFORDABLE CARE ACT passed March 23, 2010.

[81] Id.

[82] Id.

[83] P. L. 111-353 (January 4, 2011), 124 Stat. 3885.

[84] P. L. No. 112-144 (2012).

[85] P. L. No. 115-4 (2013).

[86] P. L. No. 113-195 (2014).

[87] P. L. No. 113- 260 (2014).

[88] P. L. No. 114-255 (2016).

[89] P. L. No. 114-198 (2016).

[90] P. L. No. 115-52 (2017).

[91] P. L. No. 115-1769 (2018).

[92] P. L. No. 115-271 (2018).

CRITICAL ANALYSIS: Review the legislative landmarks in the 21st century and evaluate from a public protection stance. What amendments to current laws would provide further protections? Include a discussion about future progressive legislative and regulatory initiatives.

Chapter 3: The Role and Mission of the United States Food and Drug Administration

The mission of the FDA is the promotion of the public health through prompt and efficient review of clinical research and taking appropriate action on the marketing of regulated products in a timely manner. Is the FDA a regulatory agency? Is the FDA a watchdog agency? Is the FDA a facilitating agency? The relationship between the multi-functional role of the FDA and the question of whether or not FDA regulated companies would comply if the agency did not exist provides the basis for this article. What would transpire if the United States Federal Food and Drug Administration (FDA) did not exist? The charge of this inquiry is to analyze whether or not FDA regulated companies would comply with the Federal Food, Drug and Cosmetic Act if this administrative agency did not exist. The mission of the FDA is the promotion of the public health through prompt and efficient review of clinical research and taking appropriate action on the marketing of regulated products in a timely manner. The expanse of FDA regulation is all encompassing. That is, FDA regulatory authority extends to several types of products such as foods, human and veterinary drugs, medical devices, cosmetics, dietary supplements, biologics, and tobacco. An overview will provide the origin to explain the need, foundation, and development of regulation geared toward drug law regulation as it exists in the United States today. Whether the United States even needs an FDA will be analyzed into its functions as regulator, watchdog and facilitator. A look back at history, case law, and the expansive reach of the FDA strongly suggests that while many, if not most FDA regulated companies, would comply or attempt to comply with federal law, a climate without a strong administrative agency to oversee the regulated industry would simply be too precarious to the public health to justify.

A Look Back Unravels the Current Regulatory Environment

Determining whether or not FDA regulated companies would comply with Congressional mandates requires an understanding of why Congress was compelled to establish a regulatory agency aimed at the drug industry. History provides the starting point for discussion. This section discusses not only when and why the federal government established this regulatory agency, but will highlight why, how and at what points Congress and the judicial system broadened the scope and ultimately the regulatory power of what today is well known as the "FDA".

The Food and Drug Administration is the oldest comprehensive consumer protection agency in the United States federal government.[1] At the turn of the 20th century, Dr. Harvey Washington Wiley, Chief Chemist of the Bureau of Chemistry in the Department of Agriculture spearheaded an investigation into widespread adulteration of syrup in the United States marketplace.[2] The author Upton Sinclair,[3] drew public attention to the deplorable conditions in the United States meat packing industry with his novel, *The Jungle*. Pressure and public outrage over these circumstances as well as the determination of Dr. Wiley to provide consumer protection through federal regulatory intervention drove the passage of the Pure Food and Drugs Act of 1906.[4] The law prohibited the interstate transport of unlawful food and drugs under penalty of product seizure and/or criminal prosecution.[5] Yet, the Supreme Court of the United States held in *United States v. Johnson,* that

---

[1] John P. Swann, Ph.D., *About FDA: History,* http://www.fda.gov/AboutFDA/WhatWeDo/History/default.htm (last accessed July 1, 2012).

[2] *Id.*

[3] Upton Sinclair was a novelist and social crusader from California who pioneered what is called 'muckraking journalism,' which is reform-oriented, investigative reporting. 'The Jungle' was an expose on the substandard conditions in the meatpacking industry in the early 20th century.

Social Security History, http://www.ssa.gov/history/sinclair.html (last accessed July 1, 2012).

[4] Pure Food and Drug Act of 1906, 34 Stat. 768, 59 Cong. (1906) *repealed by* Act of June 25, 1938, 52 Stat. 1059 (1938).

[5] *Id.*

false or misleading therapeutic claims as to remedial effects on drug labels were not "misbranded" within the meaning of the Food and Drugs Act of June 30, 1906.[6] In 1912, Congress reacted to *United States v. Johnson* by enacting the Sherley Amendment to explicitly state that false therapeutic claims are prohibited under the 1906 Act.

In 1927, Congress formed the Food, Drug, and Insecticide Administration, and then, in 1930, changed the name to the Federal Food and Drug Administration.[7] The FDA was transferred from the Department of Agriculture to the Federal Security Agency (later known as the Department of Health, Education and Welfare) then to the Public Health Service, which is incorporated into the Department of Health and Human Services.[8] Pending legislation to overhaul the 1906 Act stagnated in Congress for nearly five years until 1937, due to the "Elixir Sulfanilamide" tragedy.[9] The chief chemist of the S. E. Massengill Co. was not aware that DEG was poisonous to humans yet, at the time it was known in the industry. The company chemist added raspberry flavoring to the sulfa drug which dissolved in DEG and the company marketed the product.[10] This incident and the subsequent public outcry propelled Congressional action to enact the Food, Drug and Cosmetic Act of 1938 (FDCA). The FDCA not only provided public protections against potentially dangerous drugs, but also stimulated medical research and progress generally.

The FDA quickly enforced the recently enacted FDCA by distinguishing over-the-counter drugs from those drugs requiring prescription. The Durham-Humphrey Amendment of 1951 mandated that the manufacturer provides adequate directions for use.[11] In 1960, due to the astute intervention of Dr. Frances Kelsey, M.D., the thalidomide tragedy was averted in the United States. Congress took note of the questionable state of science in supporting drug effectiveness and the claims made in labeling and advertising by passing the Kefauver-Harris Drug Amendments of 1962.[12]

Public protection continued throughout the 1990s with legislative mandates for over the counter drug products, tamper resistant packaging, biologics, food additives, food packaging and labeling as a few illustrations. The Drug Price Competition and Patent Term Restoration Act of 1984 (also known as the Hatch-Waxman Act) amended the FDCA to expedite the availability of less costly generic drugs by permitting FDA to approve applications to market generic versions of brand-name drugs without repeating the research done to prove them safe and effective.[13] The Hatch-Waxman Act also permitted brand-name companies to apply for up to five years additional patent protection for the new medicines they developed to compensate for time lost while their products were undergoing the FDA approval process. In the late 1990s Congress enacted the landmark Food and Drug Administration Modernization Act (FDAMA).[14]

Fast forward ten years from FDAMA and Congress enacted the Food and Drug Administration Amendments Act (FDAAA) of 2007.[15] FDAs focus on youth contributed to the enactment of the Family Smoking Prevention Tobacco Act (FSPTA), passed in 2009 after nearly 10 years of controversy in the judicial system. The Biologics Price Competition and Innovation Act was enacted as part of the Patient Protection and Affordable Care Act.[16] Former President Obama signed the Food and Drug Administration Safety and Innovation Act (FDASIA), into law on July 9, 2012.[17]

---

[6] *United States v. Johnson*, 221 U.S. 488 (1911).

[7] *Significant Dates in U.S. Food and Drug Law History*, http://www.fda.gov/aboutfda/whatwedo/history/milestones/ucm128305.htm (last accessed July 1, 2012).

[8] *Id.*

[9] Steven Gilbert, *Elixir Sulfanilamide*, http://toxipedia.org/display/toxipedia/Elixir+Sulfanilamide (last accessed July 1, 2012).

[10] *Id.*

[11] Durham-Humphrey Amendment of 1951, Pub. L. No 82-215, 65 Stat. 648.

[12] Harris Kefauver Act of 1962, Pub. L. 87-781, 76 Stat. 780.

[13] Hatch-Waxman Act of 1984, Pub. L. 98-417, 98 Stat. 1585.

[14] Food and Drug Administration Modernization Act of 1997, Pub. L. 115-105, 111 Stat. 2296

[15] 110-085 110th Congress, 121 Stat. 823(2nd Sess.).

[16] Patient Protection and Affordable Care Act of 2010, Pub. L. No 111-148, 124 Stat. 119. See: Nat'l Fed'n of Indep. Bus. v. Sebelius, 132 S. Ct. 2566, 183 L. Ed. 2d 450 (2012)

[17] Senate Bill 3187, Pub. L. No. 112-144.

The Drug Quality and Security Act of 2013 was enacted to address supply chain issues and pharmacy compounding.

The point is that Congress enacted the FDCA and created the Food and Drug Administration to promulgate its mandates. The resultant climate is one where the private sector and the federal government should both be fully invested in ensuring that only safe and effective products make their way to the American consumer and patient. Striking a balance between a stagnant bureaucracy and a profit driven market will most probably remain a challenge.

Regulator, Watchdog, and Facilitator

The Food and Drug Administration simultaneously acts as a regulator of federal law, a watchdog and facilitator. Ultimately, it would be next to impossible for FDA regulated companies to comply with federal laws enacted to protect the public health in a manner that would fully effectuate that mission without the influence of the FDA. In several respects the FDA serves as constant reminder to companies that although they do exist to profit, their profits must always be tempered by an overall consciousness of their duty to provide safe and effective products to the consumer.

The Food and Drug Administration as Regulator—The Food, Drug, and Cosmetic Act (FDCA), the principal statute authorizing the FDA to promulgate Congressional mandates, enumerates prohibited acts.[18] The Code of Federal Regulations provides clarification for compliance with the FDCA.[19] The FDCA delegates authority to the FDA to conduct inspections and investigations of potentially noncompliant conduct.[20] Further, the FDA is also authorized to issue warning letters which serve as written notice by the FDA that a firm and or person is believed to be in violation of laws or regulations enforced by the FDA.[21] Warning letters exemplify the regulatory and watchdog functions of the agency providing the regulated industry proactive compliance prior to FDA enforcement action. Even media press coverage impacts on industry compliance.

The Food and Drug Administration as "Watchdog"—Every regulatory function that Congress delegates to the Food and Drug Administration through the Food, Drug, and Cosmetic Act could technically be labeled 'watchdogging' because each function is driven by this singular directive; to ensure the safety of the American public through food and drug consumer protection.[22]

The Food and Drug Administration as Facilitator—As stated previously, the FDA does not develop or manufacture products. By way of illustration, it is the express responsibility of drug firms to conduct research and clinical trials in order to gain FDA approval for a new drug,[23] investigational new drug,[24] or generic drug.[25] Rather FDA serves as a facilitator. A 'facilitator' is one that helps to generate an outcome (as learning, productivity, or communication) by providing indirect or unobtrusive assistance, guidance, or supervision.[26]

The FDA Transparency Initiative

Pursuant to the Open Government Initiative[27] of the Obama Administration, the FDA released its Transparency Initiative with the express goal of improving communication with both stakeholders and the public.[28] These initiatives include the improvement of data quality and more timely data

---

[18] 21 U.S.C. § 331 (2012).

[19] Food and Drug Administration General Labeling Provisions, 21 C.F.R. § 201(2012).

[20] 21 U.S.C. § 374 (2012).

[21] FDA Administrative Enforcement, § 6:2 (2011).

[22] 21 U.S.C. § 393 (2012).

[23] New drug substance means any substance that when used in the manufacture, processing, or packing of a drug, causes that drug to be a new drug, but does not include intermediates used in the synthesis of such substance. 21 C.F.R. § 310.3 (2012).

[24] Investigational new drug means a new drug or biological drug that is used in a clinical investigation. 21 C.F.R. § 312.3 (2012).

[25] Authorized generic drug means a listed drug, as defined in this section, that has been approved under section 505(c) of the act and is marketed, sold, or distributed directly or indirectly to retail class of trade with labeling, packaging (other than repackaging as the listed drug in blister packs, unit doses, or similar packaging for use in institutions), product code, labeler code, trade name, or trademark that differs from that of the listed drug. 21 C.F.R. § 314.3 (2012).

[26] "facilitator" Merriam-Webster Online Dictionary. 2012. http://www.merriam-webster.com (last accessed June 25, 2012).

[27] *Open Government Initiative*, http://www.whitehouse.gov/open (last accessed October 1, 2013).

[28] *FDA Transparency Initiative*, http://www.fda.gov/AboutFDA/Transparency/TransparencyInitiative/default.htm (last accessed October 1, 2013).

disclosure, the improvement of inspection database webpages, and improved graphic presentation of FDA compliance and enforcement data.[29] This exemplifies FDA recognition of communication with the regulated community. In keeping with the "Open Government" philosophy, FDA has aimed to become more transparent by providing the public with greater information and by communicating with FDA regulated industry. The following provides a capsule summary of the initiatives:

FDA Basics—FDA launched a web-based resource which provides the public with basic information;

Public Disclosure—Also in 2010, the FDA Task Force released the Phase II Transparency Report, which focused on disclosing certain information about FDA regulated products and firms. See: Summary of Phase II Progress Report of Phase II; and

Transparency to Regulated Industry—The FDA Task Force released the Phase III Transparency Report in 2011, which focused on increasing the transparency of FDA operations and decision making.

Conclusion

Congress enacted the Food, Drug, and Cosmetics Act to, among other objectives, ensure that food and drug related companies conduct themselves in a manner focused at all times on the safety of the American public. Most firms would in fact conduct themselves in this manner with or without the threat of government intervention. Even if the single goal of the regulated industry is understandably profits, the most cynical would concede that the goal would be impossible to achieve without providing safe and effective products. The regulated industry should comply with Congressional mandates toward public safety without FDA oversight. They should self-regulate toward consumer safety without Congressional mandates; their financial stability depends on it. Yet this does not relieve Congress, expressly empowered to provide for the public welfare, from legislating and delegating regulatory power to the FDA to that end.

Striking the appropriate balance between free enterprise principles and obligatory government intervention is the most debated component of FDA regulation. Irrespective of individual frame of reference, an unrelenting focus on safety and efficacy from both the federal government and the private sector is the only acceptable standard by which FDA regulated products can be marketed and sold to the American patient and consumer. The conclusion reached, at this juncture, is that the FDA remains critical and vital for safe and effective drug products and the overall mission of protecting the American public. That is why "calling on Congress" to enact legislation in keeping with these innovative technological era remains paramount.

CRITICAL ANALYSIS: What would transpire if the United States Federal Food and Drug Administration (FDA) did not exist? Include a discussion of the role and mission of the FDA.

---

[29] *Report on Exploratory Program to Increase Access to the Agency's Compliance and Enforcement Data*
http://www.fda.gov/AboutFDA/Transparency/TransparencyInitiative/ucm289638.htm (last accessed October 2, 2013);
http://www.fda.gov/NewsEvents/Newsroom/PressAnnouncements/2011/ucm274201.htm (last accessed Feb. 3, 2014).

Chapter 4: Key Regulatory Agencies

The United States Federal Food and Drug Administration
10903 New Hampshire Ave., Silver Spring, MD 20993-0002
1-888-INFO-FDA (1-888-463-6332) *www.fda.gov*

Did you know that the FDA regulates 25% of the United States economy? The products that FDA regulates in interstate commerce account for about 25 percent of every consumer dollar spent. What does interstate commerce mean for regulated products? Interstate commerce pertains to every part in the manufacture, packaging, and distribution of a product. The mission of FDA, in keeping with the mandate of the Food, Drug and Cosmetic Act (FDCA) is that of public protection and FDA utilizes a science-based approach to its regulatory activities. FDA had a $5.1 billion budget for fiscal year (FY) 2018, an increase of 10% from FY 2017 and in FY 2019 an increase as well. Adequate resources remains critical especially with the global environment.

Originally, FDA was called the Food, Drug, and Insecticide Administration and was renamed in 1931. Eventually, FDA was transferred from the U.S. Department of Agriculture to the Federal Security Administration (FSA). The FSA became the Department of Health, Education and Welfare now known as the Department of Health and Human Services. Regarded as one of the most respected federal consumer protection agencies, FDA responsibility entails administering food, drug, dietary supplement, cosmetic and medical device laws and ensuring that only beneficial products travel through interstate commerce. FDA maintains broad authority and responsibility ranging from pre-market approval for some products to ongoing regulatory surveillance of other products. FDA's regulatory approach depends on the law that FDA enforces. For instance, new drug and various medical devices must be proven safe and effective prior to entry into the marketplace. Other products such as dietary supplements and cosmetics do not require prior approval before marketing.

FDA has the legal authority or jurisdiction to regulate a wide variety of products such as animal feed and drugs and the safety of the United States blood supply. Investigators routinely monitor blood bank operations that range from record keeping to testing for contaminants. FDA regulates the effectiveness and purity of biologics, that is, medical preparations made from living organisms, for instance vaccines and insulin. Besides conducting investigations at facilities within FDA's legal authority, the agency can use various legal sanctions if a company does not voluntarily comply. For example, FDA can seek the court remedy of an injunction if the agency demonstrates public harm and the likelihood of injury. Scientists, chemists and microbiologists prepare the scientific evidence necessary for FDA's legal cases. FDA scientists review test results submitted by companies for agency approval of drugs, vaccines, food additives, coloring agents and medical devices. FDA operates the National Center for Toxicological Research that investigates the biological effects of widely used chemicals. FDA as well operates an Engineering and Analytical Center, which tests medical devices, radiation-emitting products and radioactive drugs. A "Beyond Our Borders" initiative instituted by FDA involves the placement of FDA staff in foreign countries such as China, India, Latin America, Europe and eventually the Middle East. This involved requisite approval from the Department of States as well as authorization from the foreign governments. The intent is to safeguard food, drugs and medical devices that are imported into the United States.

FDA is divided into regions and districts throughout the United States. FDA headquarters include the Commissioner and central administration staff and several product based "Centers". Each Center has the responsibility to confirm that the specific industry it regulates meets specified regulatory requirements. The specific names of each FDA Center include:

> ➢ *Center for Biologics Evaluation and Research (CBER);*
> ➢ *Center for Drug Evaluation and Research (CDER);*
> ➢ *Center for Food Safety and Applied Nutrition (CFSAN);*
> ➢ *Center for Devices and Radiological Health (CDRH);*
> ➢ *Center for Tobacco Products (CTP); and*
> ➢ *Center for Veterinary Medicine (CVM).*

Each center contains Offices and Divisions such as the: Office of Food Labeling; Office of Pre-Market Approval; Office of Plant and Dairy Foods and Beverages; Office of Seafood, Office of Special Nutritionals; Office of Cosmetics and Colors; Office of Drug Evaluation; Office of Pharmaceutical Quality; Office of New Drug Chemistry; Office of Scientific Analysis and Support; Office of Field Programs; Office of Prescription Drug Promotion; and Division of Labeling and Nonprescription Drug Compliance.

FDA Transparency Initiatives—FDA has aimed to become more transparent by providing the public with greater information and by communicating with FDA regulated industry. In keeping with the "Open Government" philosophy the Phases are as follows: Phase I: FDA Basics, Phase II: Public Disclosure and Phase III: Transparency to Regulated Industry.

Strategic Priorities and Government Accounting Office Review—The Government Accounting Office (GAO) conducted a review of FDA's strategic planning and management. The GAO found inconsistent progress with strategic endeavors and recommended several types of actions. Recommendations included development of a strategic human capital plan as well as a results-based performance measures. FDA remains committed to strategic planning and management and agreed with the GAO recommendations. See: GAO-1-279. FDA issued "Strategic Priorities 2014-2018" detailing five strategic priorities: regulatory science, globalization, safety and quality, smart regulation, and stewardship. FDA stressed that regulatory science remains essential and influences any actions taken involving the other priorities. The priorities set forth FDA's core mission goals and objectives which include improving and safeguarding access to and informed decision making about the products FDA regulates. The 2018-2020 Strategic Priorities are detailed as follows:

https://www.fda.gov/downloads/AboutFDA/CentersOffices/OfficeofMedicalProductsandTo-bacco/CDRH/CDRHVisionandMission/UCM592693.pdf

CRITICAL ANALYSIS: Evaluate the 2018-2020 FDA Strategic Priorities (link above) and recommend any additional priorities in keeping with the mission of the Food, Drug and Cosmetic Act.

Other Notable Federal Agencies

FDA is the primary agency responsible for food and drug law regulation. However other federal agencies such as the U.S. Department of Agriculture (USDA), the Federal Trade Commission (FTC), the Consumer Product Safety Commission, the Drug Enforcement Administration, U.S. Department of Commerce, the U.S. Department of the Treasury, the U.S. Customs Service, the U.S. Department of Justice and the Environmental Protection Agency work along with FDA. For example, the Centers for Disease Control and Prevention (CDC) contribute a major role in investigating sources of food-borne disease outbreaks. Even state and local agencies coordinate activities with FDA and other federal health agencies to implement standards, to enforce certain laws and for example to investigate food-borne disease outbreaks.

NOTE: *Determining the proper agency for regulatory purposes is complicated. FDA and USDA recognize the jurisdiction confusion that could result over which agency has the legal authority to regulate certain food products that contain cheese, meat and or poultry. Recommendations from a working group included FDA regulation of food products that contain meat and/or poultry as ingredients for the purpose of accentuating flavor only and do not contribute to the identity of the food product, such as dried poultry soup mixes, flavor bases, pizza with a slight amount of meat, salad dressings, breads, cheese products and flavors. FSIS would regulate food products that primarily contain meat and poultry ingredients, such as bagel dogs, meat and poultry-based sandwiches and natural casings.*

Department of Agriculture: USDA
1400 Independence Ave. S.W., Washington, DC 20250   202-720-2791
http://www.usda.gov/wps/portal/usda/usdahome   http://www.fns.usda.gov/fns/food_safety.htm
USDA, pursuant to the Federal Meat Inspection Act, Poultry Products Inspection Act, and the Egg Products Inspection Act, is responsible for the inspection and regulation of meat, poultry, dairy products and eggs (shell eggs include joint responsibility with FDA). USDA also retains jurisdiction for meat and most meat products labeling. In accordance with the Meat Inspection Act and the Poultry Inspection Act, USDA is involved in the inspection and regulation of meat and poultry products at all production stages. In addition to inspection, USDA approves new plant construction and equipment, develops and supervises plant sanitation standards and trains inspection personnel. USDA is organized by service organizations such as the Farm and Foreign Agricultural Services; Food, Nutrition and Consumer Services; Food Safety and Inspection Service; Marketing and Regulatory Programs; Rural Development; Natural Resources; and the Environment and Research, Education and Economics Service.

Drug Enforcement Administration: DEA Office of Diversion Control
8701 Morrissette Drive Springfield, VA 22152; 202-307-100—The *Drug Enforcement Administration* (DEA) enforces the United States controlled substances laws and regulations specific to the manufacture, distribution, and dispensing of legally produced controlled substances.

Federal Trade Commission: FTC *https://www.ftc.gov*
600 Pennsylvania Ave., N.W Washington, DC 20580 202-326-2222—The *FTC* has jurisdiction over most advertising except for prescription drug promotion, which is retained by FDA. FTC has jurisdiction over food advertising and FDA maintains jurisdiction over food labeling. However, FDA and FTC jurisdiction may overlap. For example, FTC may regulate false or misleading labeling if it constitutes an unfair business practice as it is used in advertising. FDA may regulate advertising to the extent that it also becomes labeling. FTC can issue cease and desist orders and injunctions against those responsible for false labeling. FTC issued its enforcement principles in 2015 pertaining to Section 5 of the FTC Act. Section 5 declares "unfair methods of competition in or affecting commerce" to be unlawful, 15 U.S.C. § 45(a)(1).
https://www.ftc.gov/system/files/documents/public_statements/735201/150813section5enforcement.pdf

Consumer Product Safety Commission: CPSC *http://www.cpsc.gov*
Logan Building, 1111 18 St., N.W. Washington, DC 20207 800-638-2772—The *CPSC* is responsible for protecting the public against unreasonable risk of injury associated with consumer products. CPSC regulates mechanical hazards caused by food contaminants such as jagged edges or exploding bottles and refrigerators or freezers that do not perform at the correct temperature.

Environmental Protection Agency: EPA *www.epa.gov* **Ariel Rios Bldg. 1200 Pennsylvania Ave., N. W. Washington, DC 20460 202-272-0167**—The *EPA* establishes safe water drinking standards, assists states in monitoring water quality, determines safety of new pesticides, pesticide tolerance levels and residues in foods, and directions on the safe use of pesticides.

Centers for Disease Control and Prevention: CDC *www.cdc.gov*
1600 Clifton Rd., N.E. Atlanta, GA 30333 1-800-311-3435   —The *CDC* is part of the United States Department of Health and Human Services. CDC investigates sources of food-borne disease outbreaks and maintains a nationwide system of food-borne disease surveillance. Other responsibilities of the CDC concern the development of public health policies to prevent food-borne diseases and ongoing research to help prevent food-borne illness.

National Institutes of Health: NIH *www.nih.gov* **9000 Rockville Pike Bethesda, MD 20892 301-496-4000**— Part of the United States Department of Health and Human Services, NIH is the medical research agency for the United States and serves as the primary research federal agency.

United States Department of Commerce *http://www.seafood.nmfs.noaa.gov*
Seafood Inspection Program, 1315 East-West Highway
Silver Spring, MD 20910 1-800-422-2750—The National Oceanic and Atmospheric Administration Commerce Department inspects and certifies fishing vessels, seafood processing plants, and retail facilities for sanitation standards.

Alcohol and Tobacco Tax &Trade Bureau *http://www.atf.gov/*
Market Compliance Branch, 650 Massachusetts Ave., N.W., Rm. 5200, Washington, DC 20226 202-927-8130—The United States Department of Treasury, Alcohol and Tobacco Tax and Trade Bureau (TTB) is responsible for all inquiries with respect to the regulation of alcohol and tobacco industries. TTB oversees alcoholic beverages except wine beverages containing less than 7 percent alcohol, which are under the jurisdiction of FDA. TTB enforces laws that govern the production and distribution of alcoholic beverages and investigates adulterated alcoholic products. Wine is defined in the Federal Alcohol Administration Act (FAA Act) as containing not less than 7 and not more than 24 percent alcohol by volume, 27 U.S.C. 211(a)(6). The labeling regulations are applicable only to wines containing alcohol within the stipulated range. Dealcoholized wines are made by removing alcohol from wine. Dealcoholized wine products contain less than 7 percent alcohol by volume, 27 CFR 4.21. Therefore, they are not covered by the FAA Act and are subject to the labeling provisions of the Federal Food, Drug, and Cosmetic Act. The term "malt beverage" is defined in the FAA Act as a beverage made by alcoholic fermentation of specific materials, 27 U.S.C. 211(a)(7). Malt beverages are not characterized by specific alcohol content. Therefore, malt beverages that meet the definition under FAA Act are within the jurisdiction of the TTB statute, regardless of the alcohol content. Title 27 of the Code of Federal Regulations (CFR), Part 7 contains the regulations that pertain to the labeling of malt beverages.
Guidance for Industry: Labeling of Certain Beers Subject to the Labeling Jurisdiction of the Food and Drug Administration (December 2014).
http://www.fda.gov/Food/GuidanceRegulation/GuidanceDocumentsRegulatoryInformation/LabelingNutrition/ucm166239.htm
CPG Sec. 510.400 Dealcoholized Wine and Malt Beverages – Labeling
http://www.fda.gov/ICECI/ComplianceManuals/CompliancePolicyGuidanceManual/ucm074430.htm
CRITICAL ANALYSIS: Discuss jurisdiction and labeling issues associated with "beer" and "dealcoholized wine".

United States Customs Service and Border Protection *www.customs.ustreas.gov*
1300 Pennsylvania Ave. N.W.; Washington, DC 20229 202-5728700—The U.S. Customs Service works in cooperation with federal regulatory agencies to ensure that all goods enter the United States in accordance with U.S. laws and regulations.

United States Department of Justice *www.usdoj.gov*
950 Pennsylvania Avenue, NW, Washington, DC 20530-0001 202-514-2000—The U.S. Department of Justice prosecutes companies and individuals suspected of violating food and drug related laws. The U.S. Marshals Service as ordered by courts can lawfully seize unsafe products.

State, Local and Tribal Governments

Coordination and communication with state, local and federal agencies is crucial. Therefore, state, local and tribal governments work with FDA and other federal agencies to implement, for example, food safety standards and inspect restaurants, grocery stores and other retail food establishments. These governmental entities inspect dairy farms and milk processing plants, grain mills and food manufacturing plants within local jurisdictions. Coordination and communication with state, local and federal agencies is crucial in terms of public protection.

CRITICAL ANALYSIS: How should the confusion about jurisdiction be addressed? For example, should there be a "coordinating" agency designated to guide stakeholders?

VOLUME II

Volume II: Food and Drug Law Administrative Primer

The focus of Volume II is federal administrative law and agencies, particularly the United States Food and Drug Administration (FDA) and United States Department of Agriculture (USDA). The role of FDA is discussed and analyzed from an administrative law stance. The importance of understanding the impact of the administrative process concerning federal agencies cannot be overstated.

Recognized as due process requirements under the Administrative Procedures Act (APA), agencies such as FDA and USDA must adhere to exact legal procedures in publishing proposed rules. These agencies must follow all the requirements under the APA, since they are both administrative agencies. The creation and powers of administrative agencies are included along with the administrative process.

What is the Federal Register? Think of the Federal Register as the daily newspaper of the Federal government. It is a legal newspaper and published every single business day by the National Archives and Records Administration (NARA). The Federal Register serves the official daily publication for rules, proposed rules, and notices of federal agencies that includes FDA and USDA.

What is the Code of Federal Regulations or CFR? The CFR is a compilation of the general and permanent rules published in the Federal Register by agencies of the federal government such as FDA and USDA. The regulations are organized by subject area and assigned a Title number. For example, Title 21 CFR concerns Food and Drugs. Every title is divided into chapters and each chapter is further subdivided into parts that cover specific regulatory areas. Practical food and drug law related examples from the Federal Register and the CFR are listed. Both the Federal Register and the CFR are important in the practice of food and drug law.

Volume II contains an administrative law backgrounder that details the nuts and bolts of administrative law. The Food and Drug Administration simultaneously acts as a regulator of federal law, a watchdog and facilitator. Finally, this resource imparts a comprehensive review of key administrative law topics. Other administrative law topics include comment submission, the increased use of guidance documents and key agencies in food and drug law regulation. Each chapter contains critical analysis issues to explore. Suffice it to state, the APA preserves the requisites of due process.

Chapter 1: Federal Administrative Law Backgrounder
Key web site: *www.fda.gov* has direct links to administrative law sites.

This chapter details federal administrative law and agencies, particularly the United States Food and Drug Administration (FDA) and United States Department of Agriculture (USDA) in their administrative roles. The creation and powers of administrative agencies are included along with the administrative process. Legislative, executive and judicial powers are analyzed and agency limitations noted. Specific terminology important to understanding the authority of FDA and USDA is detailed. For example, FDA enforces the Federal Food, Drug and Cosmetic Act (FDCA) under Title 21 of the United States Code. The Code of Federal Regulations (CFR) under Title 21 for food and drug law is a compilation of rules and regulations that carry out the FDCA. A notice and comment period is required in the *Federal Register* before a rule becomes final. The *Federal Register* is the official daily publication for rules, proposed rules, and notices of federal agencies.

Recognized as due process requirements under the Administrative Procedures Act (APA), agencies such as FDA and USDA must adhere to exact legal procedures in publishing proposed rules. These agencies must follow all the requirements under the APA, since they are both administrative agencies. Courts review whether the proper administrative procedures were adhered to prior to the promulgation of rules and regulations. Courts analyze these rules and notices for due process requirements. For example, a court will inquire whether the agency violated any of the administrative procedures that they were required to follow. Usually, a court will not usually delve into the specific nature of the rule and the underlying principles of the rules and regulations, because an agency like FDA or USDA is considered expert in this area of law. Generally, questions of public health and safety are decided in favor of the agency. Other administrative topics include comment submission, the increased use of guidance documents and key agencies in food and drug law regulation.
NOTE: See *Volume III Enforcement*—Warning Letters and Final Agency Action.

Legislative Backgrounder

This chapter focuses on the administrative process; however, a parallel is useful. Forms of Congressional action include Bills, Joint Resolutions, Concurrent Resolutions and Simple Resolutions. After a Bill is introduced in Congress, there is much debate in the form of public hearings and markup sessions. Understandably, consideration in the House of Representatives might range from a simple debate to a very complex discussion. Once differences are resolved in the House, the Bill moves to the Senate for consideration. Then, the process of back and forth negotiation between the Senate and the House begins. For example, if the Senate changes the language, the Bill is sent to the House for concurrence or other changes. Once the measure is finally passed, it is deemed "enrolled". The President may sign the measure into law, veto it, send it back to Congress, let it become law without any signature or perhaps pocket veto it at the end of a session.

The Legislative Process

http://thomas.loc.gov/home/lawsmade.toc.html

"All Legislative Powers herein granted shall be vested in a Congress of the United States, which shall consist of a Senate and House of Representatives." United States Constitution: Article I, Section 1. The chief function of Congress is the making of laws. The following brief overview outlines the legislative process within the House of Representatives.

Principal Forms of Congressional Action include: Bills, Joint Resolutions, Concurrent Resolutions, and Simple Resolutions.

Bills: A bill is the form used for most legislation, whether permanent or temporary, general or special, public or private. The letters "H.R.", signifying "House of Representatives", followed by a number that it retains throughout all its parliamentary stages designate a bill originating in the House of Representatives. Bills are presented to the President for action when approved in identical form by both the House of Representatives and the Senate.

Joint Resolutions: Joint resolutions may originate either in the House of Representatives or in the Senate. There is little practical difference between a bill and a joint resolution. Both are subject to the same procedure, except for a joint resolution that proposes a Constitutional amendment. On approval of such a resolution by two-thirds of both the House and Senate, it is then sent directly to the Administrator of General Services for submission to the individual states for ratification. It is not presented to the President for approval. A joint resolution originating in the House of Representatives is designated "H.J.Res." followed by its individual number. Joint resolutions become law in the same manner as bills.

Concurrent Resolutions: Matters affecting the operations of both the House of Representatives and Senate are usually initiated by means of concurrent resolutions. A concurrent resolution originating in the House of Representatives is designated "H.Con.Res." followed by its individual number. On approval by both the House of Representatives and Senate, the Clerk of the House and the Secretary of the Senate sign them. They are not presented to the President for action.

Simple Resolutions: A matter concerning the operation of either the House of Representatives or Senate alone is initiated by a simple resolution which is not presented to the President. A resolution affecting the House of Representatives is designated "H.Res." followed by its number.

Introduction and Referral to Committee: Any Member in the House of Representatives may introduce a bill at any time while the House is in session by simply placing it in the "hopper" provided for the purpose at the side of the Clerk's desk in the House Chamber. The sponsor's signature must appear on the bill. A public bill may have an unlimited number of co-sponsoring Members. The bill is assigned its legislative number by the Clerk and referred to the appropriate committee by the Speaker, with the assistance of the Parliamentarian. The bill is then printed in its introduced form. An important phase of the legislative process is the action taken by committees. It is during committee action that the most intense consideration is given to the proposed measures; this is also the time when the people are given their opportunity to be heard. Each piece of legislation is referred to the committee that has jurisdiction over the area affected by the measure.

Consideration by Committee: Public Hearings and Markup Sessions: Usually the first step in this process is a public hearing, where the committee members hear witnesses representing various viewpoints on the measure. Each committee makes public the date, place and subject of any hearing it conducts. Public announcements are also published in the Daily Digest portion of the Congressional Record. A transcript of the testimony taken at a hearing is made available for inspection in the committee office, and frequently the complete transcript is printed and distributed by the committee. After hearings are completed, the bill is considered in a session that is popularly known as the "mark-up" session. Members of the committee study the viewpoints presented in detail. Amendments may be offered to the bill, and the committee members vote to accept or reject these changes. This process can take place at either the subcommittee level or the full committee level, or at both. Hearings and markup sessions are status steps noted in the Legislative Action portion of the Bill Status.

Committee Action: At the conclusion of deliberation, a vote of committee or subcommittee members is taken to determine what action to take on the measure. It can be reported, with or without amendment, or tabled, which means no further action on it will occur. If the committee has approved extensive amendments, they may decide to report a new bill incorporating all the amendments. This is known as a "Clean Bill," which will have a new number. If the committee votes to report a bill, the Committee Report is written. This report describes the purpose and scope of the measure and the reasons for recommended approval. House Report numbers are prefixed with "H. Rpt." and then a number indicating the Congress.

House Floor Consideration: Consideration of a measure by the full House can be a simple or very complex operation. In general, a measure is ready for consideration by the full House after it has been reported by a committee. Under certain circumstances, it may be brought to the Floor directly. The consideration of a measure may be governed by a "rule." A rule is itself a simple resolution, which must be passed by the House, that sets out the particulars of debate for a specific bill—how much time will be allowed for debate, whether amendments can be offered, and other matters. Debate time for a measure is normally divided between proponents and opponents. Each side yields time to those Members who wish to speak on the bill. When amendments are offered, these are also debated and voted upon. After all debate is concluded and amendments decided upon, the House is ready to vote on final passage. In some cases, a vote to "recommit" the bill to committee is requested. This is usually an effort by opponents to change some portion or table the measure. If the attempt to recommit fails, a vote on final passage is ordered.

Resolving Differences: After a measure passes in the House, it goes to the Senate for consideration. A bill must pass both bodies in the same form before it can be presented to the President for signature into law. If the Senate changes the language of the measure, it must return to the House for concurrence or additional changes. This back-and-forth negotiation may occur on the House floor, with the House accepting or rejecting Senate amendments or complete Senate text. Often a conference committee will be appointed with both House and Senate members. This group will resolve the differences in committee and report the identical measure back to both bodies for a vote. Conference committees also issue reports outlining the final version of the bill.

Final Step: Votes on final passage, as well as all other votes in the House, may be taken by the electronic voting system, which registers each individual Member's response. These votes are referred to as Yea/Nay votes or recorded votes, and are available in House Votes by Bill number, roll call vote number or words describing the reason for the vote.

Votes in the House may also be by voice vote, and no record of individual responses is available. After a measure has been passed in identical form by both the House and Senate, it is considered "enrolled." It is sent to the President who may sign the measure into law, veto it and return it to Congress, let it become law without signature, or at the end of a session, pocket-veto it.

Administrative Law Backgrounder

William J. McDevitt, Esquire

In 1887, Congress faced a dilemma. The railroad industry emerged after the Civil War as one of the most powerful and wealthy industries in the land. Crisscrossing the country and linking the coasts, railroads moved the products of merchants and the produce of farmers throughout the nation. Despite the large number of railroad companies, the industry itself was essentially monopolistic, since routes and branches of one did not often compete directly with those of another. This unique setup led to exploitation of businesses that needed raw material brought in and finished goods sent out, and of farmers who needed their food products transported to market. While many states had railroad commissions that attempted to control rates and routes, their authority ended at the state line. What was needed was one, central authority with national scope to regulate this powerful industry that was exerting such great influence on economic development and the lives of ordinary people.

Only the federal government had the power to pass laws that could regulate the railroad industry on an interstate basis. Congress' dilemma, however, was that it faced a major shortcoming; it had neither the time nor expertise to create the complex laws that were required to establish a uniform, nationwide rate and route system. Other pressing issues faced the nation, and few in Congress were experts on railroad matters. Eventually, Congress came up with a brilliant solution. Article I, Section 8, of the U.S. Constitution empowers Congress to regulate commerce "among the several states." The last clause of that section also gives Congress the power "to make all Laws which shall be necessary and proper for carrying into Execution the foregoing Powers." These powers included the power to regulate interstate commerce. Why not, it was proposed, use Congress' power under the "necessary and proper" clause to establish a governmental body and delegate to it: (a) the power to make regulations which would have the same force and effect as statutes passed by Congress; (b) the power to enforce those regulations; and (c) the power, subject to review by the courts, to adjudicate disputes between the governmental body and the regulated person or business? The idea was one whose time had come. Accordingly, in 1887, Congress passed the Interstate Commerce Act, an enabling act that established the first modern federal administrative regulatory agency – the Interstate Commerce Commission.

From this inauspicious beginning, other administrative agencies followed. In 1906, Congress passed the Pure Food and Drug Act, which established the Bureau of Chemistry (later to become the Food and Drug Administration) for the purpose of regulating the safety of food products and various medicinal concoctions. In 1914, Congress passed the Federal Trade Commission Act, which established an agency by the same name. The FTC was initially created to prevent unfair methods of competition in commerce as part of the battle to "bust the trusts." Later laws and amendments expanded the FTC's power to limit unfair trade practices in business.

Congress created several more administrative agencies throughout the Twentieth Century. The Great Depression spawned a number of these governmental bodies, many designed to reign in the power of businesses, such as the Securities and Exchange Commission and the National Labor Relations Board. The "cultural revolution" of the 1960s saw another period of rapid administrative agency growth, this time focused on social issues such as the Equal Employment Opportunity Commission and the Environmental Protection Agency. The net effect of Congress' use of the "necessary and proper clause" to delegate legislative, executive and judicial power to its legislatively created "agents" was the creation of a "fourth branch" of government and the emergence of a new source of law—administrative agency law.

The Nature of an Administrative Agency

An administrative agency is a governmental body created by the legislature with legislative, executive, and judicial power. Its main purpose is to regulate the conduct and activities of businesses and individuals within the parameters set by the legislature that created it. Both the federal government and the state governments have created administrative agencies. Administrative agencies are sometimes referred to as the fourth branch of government, or mini-governments. Just as the Constitution of the United States created a federal government with legislative (Congress), executive (President) and judicial powers (The Courts), many administrative agencies also possess these same three powers. However, unlike the government where the powers are divided among the three branches of government within a framework of checks and balances, many federal administrative agencies exercise these traditional powers of government under one roof. In other words, the same administrative regulatory agency that adopts a regulation also enforces the regulation against violators, and it adjudicates disputes between the agency and those accused of failing to comply or meet the regulatory standard. At first glance, it would appear that administrative agencies are extremely powerful entities. However, due to the authority that the President, the courts, and especially Congress have, the power of administrative agencies is significantly curbed.

Administrative Law Sources

Each administrative agency can trace its existence to a statute that created it. This statute is called an "enabling act." This act sets forth the purpose of the agency, delegates to the agency its powers, and marks the limits of those powers. Examples include:

- ✓ *Interstate Commerce Commission (ICC)–Interstate Commerce Act (1887);*
- ✓ *Food and Drug Administration (FDA)–Pure Food and Drugs Act (1906);*
- ✓ *Federal Trade Commission (FTC)–Federal Trade Commission Act (1914);*
- ✓ *National Labor Relations Board (NLRB)–National Labor Relations Act (1935);*
- ✓ *Equal Employment Opportunity Commission (EEOC)–Civil Rights Act of 1964; and the*
- ✓ *Occupational Safety and Health Administration (OSHA)–Occupational Safety and Health Act (1970).*

These agencies, like all agencies, can only exercise those powers that Congress specifically delegates to them under their specific enabling act. While enabling acts can be amended from time to time, expanding or contracting an agency's power, agencies are never permitted to act beyond the scope of their authority. A second source of administrative law is the Administrative Procedures

Act of 1946 (APA). During the Great Depression, there was an explosion of growth in the number of federal administrative agencies, as citizens demanded that the federal government take a more active role in regulating business. The various agencies each established their own procedures for rule making and challenging administrative decisions and actions. This labyrinth of different administrative procedures created difficulties for persons dealing with or appearing before administrative agencies, as well as to abuses of power. The APA standardized many of the procedures that administrative agencies use. As a result, all federal administrative agencies now function and perform their tasks in essentially the same way.

The third source of administrative law is case law; that is, opinions handed down by the court in resolving disputes involving administrative agencies. Congress passes the enabling act that establishes an agency's power, and agencies promulgate rules and regulations that businesses and individuals must follow. However, this is only part of substantive administrative law. As with the Constitution and any statute, it is not enough to know what the words say. Rather, it is important to know how the courts have interpreted those words and applied the underlying concepts in order to fully understand the document. The same is true in administrative law. How the courts interpret enabling acts and regulations and apply them to specific cases (case law) constitutes another source of administrative law.

Types of Administrative Agencies

There are two types of administrative agencies—executive and independent. Executive agencies are actually part of the executive branch of government. They are subject to direct presidential authority through the executive department under which they operate. The departments themselves are also executive agencies. Examples include:

✓ *Department of Health and Human Services—Food and Drug Administration (FDA);*
✓ *Department of Labor—Occupational Safety and Health Administration (OSHA);*
✓ *Department of Treasury—Internal Revenue Service (IRS); and the*
✓ *Department of Transportation—Federal Highway Administration (FHA).*

Common to all executive administrative agencies is the fact that one person heads them, and that person serves at the pleasure of the president, that is, he or she can be replaced at any time. Contrasted to executive administrative agencies are independent agencies. These agencies operate outside of the executive branch of government. They are not headed by a single individual, but rather by a commission or board. The members serve not at the pleasure of the president, but rather for fixed, staggered terms. Whereas a new president can replace all of the heads of executive administrative agencies, he or she can only gradually replace the members of independent administrative agencies as their terms expire. Well known independent agencies include the Federal Reserve Board, the Federal Trade Commission, the Securities and Exchange Commission and the Equal Employment Opportunity Commission.

The Administrative Process

An agency's ability to exercise the three traditional powers of government that is, legislative, executive and judicial, is known as the "administrative process." An agency exercises its legislative power by making "rules" or "regulations." It exercises its executive power by investigating and enforcing compliance with those rules. Finally, its judicial powers are found in its ability to adjudicate disputes that arise in the execution of its rules.

Rulemaking—The Legislative Power

Agencies have the power to make, or promulgate, rules that are also known as regulations. Congress' delegation of its authority to make laws to administrative agencies under the "necessary and proper" clause of the Constitution is the essence of "administrative law" referred to as the delegation doctrine. There are three types of rules or regulations. The first are substantive rules. These are rules that create, define or describe the legal obligations and rights of those who are subject to the agency's authority. Substantive rules have the same status and effect as statutes that are passed by the legislature and signed into law by the executive. Violating a substantive rule can result in fines and punishment akin to violating a statute. Because substantive rules are crafted in exacting language to assure compliance with the agency's enabling act, substantive rules can be difficult for the agency's staff, let alone the general public, to understand. To assist those who must comply with or enforce a substantive rule to better comprehend the true intent of the substantive rule, agencies frequently issue interpretive rules, also known as guidance. Unlike substantive rules, interpretive rules have no legal effect.

The final type of rule is a procedural rule. Although the Administrative Procedures Act of 1946 prescribes most of the procedures that administrative agencies must follow, each agency still has some discretion in controlling its own internal processes and procedures. Rules of this nature are known as procedural rules. Agencies cannot unilaterally adopt rules. Rather, the Administrative Procedures Act dictates a strict process that an agency must follow in order to adopt a substantive rule. The steps include:

1) Notice of Proposed Rulemaking,
2) Comment Period,
3) Public Hearings, and
4) Adoption of the Final Rule.

Before an agency can adopt a rule, it must give the public the opportunity to convey its thoughts and reactions to the rule. The process begins, therefore, with the agency giving notice to the public of the proposed rule, known as "Notice of Proposed Rulemaking." Under the APA, such notice must appear in the *Federal Register* which is tantamount to the "Daily News" of the federal government. Most industries in this country have trade associations. One of the key functions of these trade associations is to review the *Federal Register* every day for notice of rules that may affect the industry. The trade association then alerts the members to the proposed rules so that they can react to them.

The Notice of Proposed Rulemaking will include information on a comment period. This is the second stage of the rulemaking process. The comment period is normally 60 days, during which time the public – usually members of the industry that the proposed rule will affect – can express their views, both positive and negative, in writing on the necessity and practicality of the rule. For example, the USDA could propose a rule tightening the requirements of processing beef in order to reduce the chance of E. coli contamination. Industry, which would initially bear the costs of the new procedures, would be expected to criticize the proposed rule as unnecessary and not cost effective. Consumer groups, on the other hand, would probably complain to the USDA that the new rule does not go far enough in assuring food safety.

At the conclusion of the comment period, the agency's next step depends on whether it is using the formal or informal rulemaking process. In formal rulemaking, the agency will hold one or more public hearings that follow most of the evidentiary and procedural rules of a trial in court. In informal rulemaking, the agency will rely on the written comments received during the comment period and may hold an open hearing that merely serves as a forum for the public to express its opinions. If the comments and hearings do not substantially alter the agency's attitude toward its proposed rule, it will adopt it as a final rule. If the agency materially alters the rule, it may have to begin the rulemaking process anew. Although notice of the adoption of a final rule is initially published in the *Federal Register*, its permanent embodiment is a set of books known as the Code of Federal Regulations, or CFR for short. The CFR, updated in published form annually, is the repository of all of the rules and regulations of all of the federal administrative regulations. The U.S. Constitution, the United States Code, which contains the statutes passed by Congress and signed by the President, and CFR constitute the vastness of federal law in this country.

Investigative—The Executive Power

Not only do agencies make rules, but they also investigate compliance with the rules and enforce them against those who fail to comply. Just as the FBI investigates crimes for the Justice Department whenever our federal criminal statutes are broken, many administrative agencies have investigators to assure that the agency's regulations are followed.

Agencies tend to investigate in three ways. The first is direct observation. FDA investigators will inspect plants for adherence to rules and the USDA will send investigators into meat packing plants to assure that procedures dictated by agency regulations are followed. In the case *Marshall v. Barlow's, Inc.*, the Supreme Court held that the Fourth Amendment's protection against unreasonable searches and seizures apply to investigators from administrative agencies. Accordingly, except in a few heavily regulated industries like food processing and pharmaceutical manufacturing where there is no expectation of privacy from government regulators, most agency investigators must obtain a warrant in order to enter the premises of a business if the owner does not voluntarily consent. While the agent does not have to demonstrate to a judge that there is evidence of wrongdoing as in criminal cases, the agent must still obtain a warrant in order to enter a premise to conduct an investigation.

A second method of investigation is self-reporting, that is, the regulated business or individual must report to the agency periodically, or when incidents occur that are subject to regulation. Failure to make a self-report usually results in severe penalties. The final common method by which agencies investigate compliance with regulations is the use of subpoenas. A subpoena is an order from a judicial body to appear and answer questions under oath. A subpoena is frequently accompanied with a demand to produce documents or things. Persons served with a subpoena must appear at the agency with the requested material and be prepared to answer the agency's questions. If the answers to the questions could implicate the individual in criminal activity, he could invoke his Fifth Amendment right against self-incrimination and refuse to answer.

The other part of the executive power is enforcement. The manner in which agencies enforce their rules and regulations varies. Frequently, agencies will assess fines against violators, like OSHA. Where agencies issue licenses, like the Federal Communications Commission (FCC), enforcement can take the form of revocation or non-renewal of a license. Other agencies, such as the FDA, may enforce their rules by filing a lawsuit against violators in court to seek injunctions or criminal penalties.

Adjudication—The Judicial Power

When a business or individual disagrees with an administrative agency's action or decision, most agencies have a mechanism within their framework to resolve the dispute. This is known as the agency's adjudicatory or judicial power. Either the aggrieved party or the agency may initiate the adjudicatory process. The matter is assigned to an administrative law judge (ALJ) for resolution. On the federal level, there are approximately 1300 ALJs. Although the federal ALJ is usually an employee of the agency, more than half of the states have unbundled the judicial power from the agency by creating a separate, independent agency, which hears appeals from all of the state's administrative agencies. The ALJ will conduct a hearing, at which the agency and the regulated entity or individual can submit evidence in the form of testimony or documents. At the conclusion of the hearing, the ALJ will enter an order. If the regulated entity or individual loses, it can appeal the decision to the board or commission that heads the agency by filing a "request for reconsideration." The commission or board then issues the agency's final order. At that point, the aggrieved party is said to have "exhausted the administrative remedies." An appeal of the agency's decision can then be taken to a court of competent jurisdiction for ultimate resolution by court order.

Most disputes between an agency and the regulated entity or individual do not end up before ALJs. Agencies frequently negotiate alleged violations of the regulations and settle the claims amicably. Even if the matter is referred to an ALJ, most defendants enter into a Consent Decree, which is a form of settlement of the dispute at hand. For example, a business that is charged with false advertising may enter into a Consent Decree with the FTC to cease using the offensive ad without acknowledging any wrongdoing or fault.

Limitations of Agency Powers

With legislative, executive and judicial power concentrated in one body, agencies appear to be an omnipotent governmental entity. They are not, however. The courts, the executive branch and, particularly, the legislature exercise considerable control, both directly and indirectly, over the power of administrative agencies.

Judicial Control

Virtually every decision and action taken by an administrative agency is subject to review by the courts. Whether it is the adoption of a new regulation under its rulemaking power or a decision by an ALJ, parties who disagree with the agency can seek judicial review. The scope of review, that is, how much deference the court will give to the agency's decision depends on what issue is being appealed to the court. When an agency makes a substantive determination in the rulemaking process, such as certain material in packaged meat, the courts give great deference to the decision of the administrative agency. Only if the substantive determination is arbitrary or capricious, constitutes an abuse of discretion, or lacks substantial evidence will a court substitute its judgment for that of the agency. On the other extreme of judicial review is a procedural requirement. Appeals based on this ground attract the court's strictest scope of review. Unless the agency adheres strictly to each and every procedural step and requirement, the court will automatically void the agency action. Thus, advertising on February 1 that all written comments to a proposed rule are due on March 1 when the procedural rules require a 30-day notice period will cause a court to void the rule if challenged on procedural grounds. Other common grounds for challenging an agency's action in the court are that it misinterpreted its enabling statute, that it exceeded its authority, or that it acted in a way that violated the Constitution.

Executive Controls

The President, or governor on the state level, exercises significant control over executive agencies, that is, those agencies that are part of executive departments. Since the heads of executive agencies and departments serve at the pleasure of the executive, they can be dismissed at any time for no reason or virtually any reason at all. An agency whose work displeases the executive will have a new administrative hierarchy in short order. While the executive exercises less control over independent administrative agencies, it is still considerable. First, the president has the power to appoint the members of the boards and commissions, subject to advice and consent of Congress, as their terms expire. A president who is in office long enough can eventually replace an entire commission or board. Second, the president can veto enabling acts that establish new administrative agencies or that expand or reduce the authority of existing agencies. A president, therefore, who is opposed to a cleaner environment or safer food products, can frustrate Congressional efforts to achieve these goals by vetoing legislation to expand an agency's power or increase its budget.

Legislative Controls

Since administrative agencies are devised by the legislature, it follows that the legislature exercises the greatest control of the three branches of government over them. The legislature's power on the federal level is both direct and indirect.

Direct Controls

Congress exercises direct control over administrative agencies in several ways. First, since it is Congress that drafts the enabling act, which creates an administrative agency, Congress controls the scope of the agency's power. For example, Congress expanded the authority of the Equal Employment Opportunity Commission, which it established under the Civil Rights Act of 1964, to handle disability issues when it passed the Americans with Disabilities Act of 1990. Congress holds the "power of the purse" under the scheme of government devised by the U.S. Constitution. The power to appropriate money, or reduce such an appropriation, is another direct control that Congress exercises over administrative agencies.

Another direct control that Congress uses against administrative agencies is reporting requirements. Every administrative agency is designed to regulate some sort of activity. The failure of an agency to carry out its purpose can result in increased Congressional scrutiny. The passage of "sunset laws" is another direct control of Congress over administrative agencies. For many years, Congress created administrative agencies with an indefinite life span. Over the years, some agencies became obsolete due to the changing business environment. Nevertheless, each year there was a line in the federal budget to fund the agency despite its uselessness. In order to redress this oversight, Congress began to place fixed terms on the life spans of some federal agencies. Unless Congress takes affirmative action to pass legislation renewing its term, the agency will fade into the sunset and cease to exist.

Indirect Controls

Congress has enacted several laws that, while not directly controlling administrative agencies, still exert a significant influence on their operations. The first is the Freedom of Information Act (1966). Under this law, the public is entitled to obtain copies of virtually all records of an administrative agency. The realization that members of the news media in particular can review most of an agency's documents tends to dissuade agencies from engaging in improper conduct. Another law that limits the power of federal agencies is the Privacy Act (Act). This law protects businesses and individuals about whom the government has information. Agencies are prohibited, with certain exceptions such as criminal investigations, from sharing information collected on an individual with other agencies without the consent of the person from whom the information was collected. The Act requires agencies to provide safeguards against misuse of the information and a means for individuals to correct erroneous information in the agency's records.

The Government-in-the-Sunshine Act (Sunshine Act), is a major factor in assuring that agencies do not abuse their powers. Under this Act, virtually all substantive actions that an agency takes must be done in the open. Thus, the agency must give the public notice of all of its meetings, the meetings must be open to the public, and deliberation by an agency on substantive matters must occur in public. The act contains certain exceptions to its open door policy, such as meetings to investigate possible criminal activity and meetings that discuss potential or pending litigation. In 1980, Congress passed the Regulatory Flexibility Act, which also has the effect of limiting an agency's power. Under this act, agencies are required to conduct a cost/benefit analysis of its proposed rules when those rules will have a "significant impact upon a substantial number of small entities." This law tries to assure that overzealous regulators use common sense when drafting regulations that place burdens on businesses and individuals. Finally, Congress can actually "freeze" new regulations that it opposes. Under the Small Business Regulatory Enforcement Fairness Act of 1996, Congress can block the implementation of a regulation if it passes a joint resolution of disapproval within 60 days of adoption. The regulation is then sent to the appropriate legislative committee for further review.

State Administrative Agencies

The same forces that drove the federal government to create administrative regulatory agencies have also been at work among the states. Frequently, the state agencies mirror their federal counterparts in purpose and operation. Sometimes, regulations promulgated by state agencies conflict with those of federal agencies. The "default" mode for resolving such conflicts is applying the Supremacy Clause of the U.S. Constitution. Under Article VI, the Constitution of the United States and the laws made by the federal government, which includes administrative agencies, "shall be the supreme Law of the Land." Unless Congress specifically allows states to adopt regulations different from that of the federal government, state regulations that conflict with federal regulations are generally preempted and void.

Administrative Law and Politics

An inherent tension between administrative agencies and businesses; between the regulators and the regulated. Business strives for a *laissez-faire* environment in which they are left alone to pursue their profits, arguably for the good of society. The public, on the other hand, often fear and mistrust big business and the power that they possess and consequently seek to have the government reign in the financial and social power of business through rules and regulations that protect and foster areas of concern such as product safety, worker safety and food and drug safety.

The conflict between business and regulators, or the public whom they represent, over power and control is fought continuously before the regulatory agencies, in the halls of Congress, in court rooms and on the campaign trail for elected office. Business and its allies rail against "big government," which, in essence is a code name for administrative agencies. They also assail "job killing government regulations" which, in their opinion, prevent American companies from competing effectively and from achieving the level profits that will lead to full employment. The public, however, points to the social benefits of regulations and the abuses that occur, from personal injury to the collapse of the entire economy, in the absence of effective regulation.

Administrative agencies can find themselves under significant pressure. First, lobbyists can attempt to persuade Congress to repeal the enabling act that created the agency, thus terminating its existence. More common is tinkering with an agency's enabling act by shrinking its powers or removing matters which it is authorized to regulate. The most common method, however, of crippling an agency is to slash its budget. Attempts are made periodically to gut the budget of agencies like the FDA, which would hobble it from enforcing its regulations. Another tactic to combat agency power is to infiltrate it with decision-making level employees who are sympathetic to the industry which they are charged with regulating. Even neutral Commissioners can be influenced to consider business' interests more favorably with offers of lucrative employment in the industry at the end of their appointed terms. Political interference at times, does influence administrative agency decision making. Notably, the *Tunmmino* "Plan B" and "Plan B One-Step" decisions illustrate the reluctance of FDA to approve an emergency contraceptive for over-the-counter or OTC availability, despite recommendations from an FDA panel to do so. The court determined that the delay in approval was not safety or science based. Rather, the delay was a result of political pressure. This is not to say that administrative agencies are perfect. There are many examples of overzealous regulators who propose truly onerous regulations that add little or nothing to the health, safety or welfare of the public or its institutions. Congress recognizes this problem, and it enacted the Regulatory Flexibility Act and Small Business Regulatory Enforcement Fairness Act, mentioned above, to give it more control over agencies' actions.

The tug of war between business, whose main goal is maximizing profits, and regulators, who are interested in promoting fairness and safety on behalf of the public, will continue as long as there is a free market economy. Who has the upper hand at any one time is a function of politics; that is, who has the power and control.

NOTE: See *Volume XII-Tummino v. Torti* and *Tummino v. Sebelius* decisions. See also: Roseann B. Termini and Miranda Lee, *Sex, Politics, and Lessons Learned from Plan B: A Review of the FDA's Actions and Future Direction*, Oklahoma L. Rev. Vol. 36, No. 2 (2011).

CRITICAL ANALYSIS: Review the above article—*Administrative Law Backgrounder*. Analyze how FDA has authority at all levels, that is, legislative, regulatory and judicial. Does FDA have overly broad powers? Incorporate a discussion about political influence.

Chapter 2: The Federal Register and Code of Federal Regulations

Federal Register—Comments, Petitions, Proposed and Final Rules

Congress delegated more responsibility to federal agencies in the 1930s, permitting them to develop and issue detailed regulations. This was the result of the New Deal legislation. However, no centralized system existed. Ultimately, Congress passed the *Federal Register* Act (Act), enacted on July 26, 1935 (44 U.S.C. Chapter 15). The Act instituted a uniform system for handling agency regulations including the filing of documents with the Office of the *Federal Register*; posting of documents for public inspection; publication of documents in the *Federal Register* and after a 1937 amendment, a permanent codification of rules in the Code of Federal Regulations. The legal effect of publication in the *Federal Register* consists of giving official notice of a document and its contents; establishing the text as the copy of the original document; providing the date when the regulation was issued and providing evidence of the document acceptable to a court of law commonly known as *prima facie* evidence. One of the most important additions to the *Federal Register* system was through the Administrative Procedures Act (APA). Enacted in 1946 (5 U.S.C. section 551 et seq.), the APA permits public participation in the rulemaking process by submitting comments about a proposed rule.

The *Federal Register* is the official daily publication for Rules, Proposed Rules, and Notices of Federal agencies and organizations, as well as Executive Orders and other Presidential documents. Documents in the *Federal Register* are cited or referenced by volume and page number. Proposed rules and final rules are drafted as agency documents and submitted to the Office of the *Federal Register*. The documents are then edited to conform to a specific style and are then published in the *Federal Register*. The *Federal Register* includes any announcements related to agency matters such as the request for comments on particular issues. The *Federal Register*, as indicated, contains notices of proposed rules. Even proposed amendments to an initially proposed rule must appear, as well as any notices about a comment period extension.

Submission of Comments and Petitions

http://www.fda.gov/RegulatoryInformation/Dockets/Comments/default.htm (edited and modified in part)

As a regulatory agency, FDA publishes rules that establish or modify the manner in which the agency regulates foods, drugs, biologics, cosmetics, radiation-emitting electronic products, tobacco products, dietary supplements, and medical devices. FDA rules have considerable impact on the nation's health, industries and economy. These rules are not created arbitrarily or in a vacuum. FDA gathers public comments mainly through proposed rules and petitions.

Proposed Rules—When FDA plans to issue a new regulation or revise an existing regulation, it places an announcement in the *Federal Register* on the day the public comment period begins. Published every weekday, the *Federal Register* is available at many public libraries and colleges, and on the FDA Web site. Issues open to public comment often are reported by the news media and can be found at ***regulations.gov***. Instructions for finding *Federal Register* documents and submitting comments are found on the Federal Dockets Management System Instruction Sheet. In the *Federal Register*, the "notice of proposed rulemaking" describes the planned regulation and provides background on the issue. It also gives the address for submitting written comments and the name of the person to contact for more information. Also noted is the "comment period," which specifies how long the agency will accept public comments. Usually, the file or docket stays open for comments at least 60 days, though some comment periods are longer and some comment periods are extended.

Comment Submission—Recommendations to consider for comment submission include:
- ✓ *Clearly indicate your position about the proposed rule and why. FDA regulatory decisions are based largely on law and science, and agency reviewers look for reasoning, logic, and good science in comments they evaluate.*
- ✓ *Refer to the docket number, listed in Federal Register notice.*

✓ *Include a copy of articles or other references that support your comments. (Electronic attachments will not be forwarded if the "Comment" box is left empty.)*

✓ *Only relevant material should be submitted. If an article or reference is in a foreign language, it must be accompanied by an English translation verified to be accurate. A copy of the original publication should accompany translations.*

✓ *To protect privacy when submitting medical information, delete names or other information that would identify patients.*

✓ *Comments must be postmarked, electronically submitted or delivered in person by the last day of the comment period. When a comment is received, it is logged in, numbered, and placed in a file for that docket. It then becomes a public record and is available for anyone to examine at regulations.gov.*

Petitions—Another way to influence the way FDA does business is to petition the agency to issue, change or cancel a regulation, or to take other action. The agency receives hundreds of petitions on an annual basis. Petitions require careful preparation by the submitter. FDA expends considerable resources processing petitions. Individuals sometimes submit petitions; however, most come from regulated industry or consumer groups. For example, a drug company might request a change in labeling for one of its products; a food company might ask that its product be exempted from some provision of a regulation; or a consumer group might petition FDA.

Submission of Petitions

✓ *Action requested—What rule, order, or other administrative action does the petitioner want FDA to issue, amend or revoke?*

✓ *Statement of grounds—The factual and legal grounds for the petition, including all supporting material, as well as information known to the petitioner that may be unfavorable to the petitioner's position.*

✓ *Environmental impact—This information is generally required if the petition requests approval of food or color additives, drugs, biological products, animal drugs, or certain medical devices, or for a food to be categorized as GRAS (generally recognized as safe). Procedures for preparing environmental impact statements can be found in Title 21, Part 25 of the Code of Federal Regulations. If an environmental impact statement is not required, petitions should include a statement to that effect.*

✓ *The following official certification statement—"The undersigned certifies that, to the best knowledge and belief of the undersigned, this petition includes all information and views on which the petition relies, and that it includes representative data and information known to the petition which are unfavorable to the petition."*

✓ *Identifying information—The petition must be signed and include contact information.*

NOTE: An economic impact statement may be required.

Ultimately, FDA management decides whether to grant a petition. Agency staffers evaluate it, a process that may take several weeks to more than a year, depending on the issue's complexity. After FDA grants or denies the petition, the agency will notify the petitioner directly. If not satisfied, the petitioner can take the matter to court. See: Title 21 of the Code of Federal Regulations, Sections 10.30, 10.33, and 10.35. Besides accepting public comments and petitions, FDA also schedules public meetings and hearings to discuss and explain its proposals. These usually are held with industry representatives or consumer groups; however, anyone may attend and, with advance notice, may comment on a proposal. Meetings are held in the Washington, D.C., area, and throughout the country. Public meetings are announced in the *Federal Register*.

CRITICAL ANALYSIS: Submit a petition or a comment to a proposed FDA regulation.
https://www.fda.gov/RegulatoryInformation/Dockets/ucm379450.htm
https://www.regulations.gov

Proposed Rule: Banned Devices—Powdered Surgeon's Gloves

81 FR 15173 (March 22, 2016). Agency: Food and Drug Administration, HHS.
Action: Proposed rule. *Banned Devices; Proposal To Ban Powdered Surgeon's Gloves* (21 CFR 878.4460), *Powdered Patient Examination Gloves* (21 CFR 880.6250),, *and Absorbable Powder for Lubricating a Surgeon's Glove* (21 CFR 878.4480).
https://www.federalregister.gov/articles/2016/03/22/2016-06360/banned-devices-proposal-to-ban-powdered-surgeons-gloves-powdered-patient-examination-gloves-and
Proposed Rule Summary—FDA issued a proposed rule (March 22, 2016) to ban the following devices: *Powdered Surgeon's Gloves, Powdered Patient Examination Gloves, and Absorbable Powder for Lubricating a Surgeon's Glove.* The proposed rule would apply to all powdered gloves except powdered radiographic protection gloves. The reason for the proposed rule to ban these medical device products is because of the unreasonable and substantial risk of illness or injury and that the risk cannot be corrected or eliminated by labeling or a change in labeling. The gloves include: Powdered Natural Rubber Latex Surgeon's Gloves, Powdered Synthetic Latex Surgeon's Gloves, Powdered Natural Rubber Latex Patient Examination Gloves, Powdered Synthetic Patient Examination Gloves, and Absorbable Powder for Lubricating a Surgeon's Glove. Under 21 U.S.C. sec. 360f authorizes FDA to ban by regulation any device any device intended for human use if FDA finds, based on all available data and information, that such device presents a "substantial deception" or an "unreasonable and substantial risk of illness or injury," which cannot be, or has not been, corrected or eliminated by labeling or a change in labeling.
NOTE: Non-powdered gloves are not included in this proposed ban and FDA is unaware of any powdered radiographic protection gloves currently in the marketplace.

Code of Federal Regulations—Rule Codification

Once published in the *Federal Register*, the regulation is codified as a final rule in the Code of Federal Regulations (CFR). The CFR is the codification of the general and permanent rules published in the Federal Register by the executive departments and agencies of the federal government such as FDA and USDA. The CFR is divided into "Titles" which represent broad subject areas of federal regulation. For example, food and drug matters appear under Title 21 of the CFR. The USDA regulations appear under Titles 7 and 9.

In terms of codification, it is helpful to make a parallel comparison of the publication process by Congress and regulations created by Federal agencies. Legislation is initially published as slip law. This means the Office of the Federal Register prints the law in pamphlet form on an annual basis. The United States statutes at large are a compilation in chronological order of all private and public laws of a Congressional session. The law is then codified in the United States Code and arranged by subject matter. Proposed and final rules are submitted to the Office of the Federal Register and published in the Federal Register. Volume 1 started in 1936 and there are changes with each calendar year.

Final Rules under Section 4205 Vending Machines and Restaurant Menus

Food Labeling; Calorie Labeling of Articles of Food in Vending Machines. A final rule was issued December 1, 2014 to assist consumers by requiring the availability of point of purchase nutrition caloric information prior to purchasing the food item. (Proposed Rule April 6, 2011).
Food Labeling; Nutrition Labeling of Standard Menu Items in Restaurants and Similar Retail Food Establishments. The purpose of the final rule also published December 1, 2014 is to implement the menu labeling provisions of the Affordable Care Act.

CRITICAL ANALYSIS: Discuss the timeframe from when the rule was initially proposed in 2011 to the eventual compliance date in 2018. Include the impact both on stakeholders and consumers. CRS Report link and NOTE as follows.
See: *https://fas.org/sgp/crs/misc/R44272.pdf*

NOTE: Compliance for caloric disclosure restaurants delayed until May 7, 2018 and July 26, 2018 for vending machines. Trade associations requested an extension due to front-of-package font size requirements for certain foods sold from glass-front vending machines.

Direct Final Rule

Similar to other administrative agencies, FDA has resorted to companion publication of a direct final rule along with the proposed rule. Recognized as a "direct final rule", this procedure is usually reserved for rules, which the agency views as noncontroversial. In theory, the concept is a sound policy if it works because it could be more efficient. Yet, as the example below illustrates, this is not always the situation. Sometimes a rule can be withdrawn due to adverse comments. In this situation, the direct final rule was published at the same time as the proposed rule.

Section 920 of FDAAA added new section 505(t) to the Federal Food, Drug, and Cosmetic Act (FDCA) (21 U.S.C. 355(t)) (P.L. 110-85, 121 Stat. 823, Sept. 27, 2007). This section mandated that FDA: *Publish on its Internet site a complete list of all authorized generic drugs and included in an annual report submitted to the agency after January 1, 1999, consisting of the drug trade name, the brand company manufacturer, and the date the authorized generic drug entered the market.* FDA amended its regulations in a direct final rule, requiring the holder of a new drug application (NDA) to provide information regarding authorized generic drugs in an annual report. However, the direct final rule was withdrawn due to significant adverse comments received. (74 Fed. Reg. 6541, 2/10/09). **See *Volume V Human Drugs Regulation*—Authorized Generics.**

Similarly, the Center for Tobacco Products Regulation announced that FDA withdrew the following direct final rule.

AGENCY: Food and Drug Administration, HHS.

ACTION: Direct final rule; withdrawal.

SUMMARY: The Food and Drug Administration (FDA) published in the **Federal Register** on August 8, 2016, a direct final rule regarding procedures for refusing to accept premarket tobacco product submissions. The comment period closed October 24, 2016. FDA withdrew the direct final rule because the Agency received significant adverse comment. FDA intends to consider the comments received on the direct final rule to be comments on the companion proposed rule published at 81 FR 52371 (August 8, 2016).

DATES: The direct final rule published at 81 FR 52329 (August 8, 2016), withdrawn effective November 16, 2016.

https://www.federalregister.gov/documents/2016/11/16/2016-27456/refuse-to-accept-procedures-for-premarket-tobacco-product-submissions-withdrawal?source=govdelivery&utm_campaign=ctp-refusetoaccept&utm_content=20161115-twictp&utm_medium=email&utm_source=govdelivery

CRITICAL ANALYIS: Review the direct final rule pertaining to premarket tobacco submissions. Evaluate whether FDA was correct in withdrawing the direct final rule.

Chapter 3: Freedom of Information Act and Guidance Documents

Freedom of Information Act

http://www.fda.gov/RegulatoryInformation/foi/ElectronicReadingRoom/default.htm

The Freedom of Information Act (FOIA) has provided public access to records from federal agencies such as FDA and USDA. The Office of Information Policy at the Department of Justice (DOJ) issues guidance to agencies on the FOIA for compliance purposes. According to DOJ:

"The basic function of the Freedom of Information Act is to ensure informed citizens, vital to the functioning of a democratic society."

The regulatory administrative process involves the Freedom of Information Act, 5 U.S.C. Section 552 (FOIA). Section 552 focuses on how to obtain public information. FDA and USDA must follow the mandates of FOIA, which means that certain "records" must be given to "any person" when requested. The FOIA makes available many unpublished documents about FDA's regulatory activities. Documents such as press releases, consumer publications, speeches, and congressional testimony are available from FDA without having to file a Freedom of Information Act (FOIA) request. The following list contains categories of documents available from the Food and Drug Administration's electronic reading room.

- ✓ *Center for Drug Evaluation and Research (CDER)*
- ✓ *Center for Biologics Evaluation and Research (CBER)*
- ✓ *Center for Devices and Radiological Health (CDRH)*
- ✓ *Center for Food Safety and Applied Nutrition (Includes Cosmetics) (CFSAN)*
- ✓ *Center for Veterinary Medicine (CVM)*
- ✓ *Center for Tobacco Products (CTP)*
- ✓ *Division of Dockets Management Branch (DMB)*
- ✓ *Office of Regulatory Affairs (ORA)*

FOIA allows written requests of copies of existing records not normally prepared for public distribution. Failure to comply with a request under FOIA for information under FOIA may be challenged in federal district court. Public accessible information could include regulatory letters informing a company of a violation discovered during an FDA inspection, product recall notices, enforcement records and safety and effectiveness data.

Electronic Freedom of Information Act

Enacted in 1996, the Electronic Freedom of Information Act (EFOIA) expanded the flow of information in a timelier manner. The EFOIA amendments attempt to improve public access to agency records and information. The FOIA is a valuable tool for industry. It is an excellent way for industry to obtain information from the federal government. However, obtaining information under the FOIA and the EFOIA amendments depends on the type of information requested. For example, the information might be classified as commercial and therefore exempt from disclosure. Such exemptions include:

- ✓ *FDA's internal rules and practices;*
- ✓ *Trade secret and confidential commercial or financial information;*
- ✓ *Interagency and intra-agency information;*
- ✓ *Individual personnel and medical information where disclosure would constitute an invasion of privacy; and*
- ✓ *Records and information collected for law enforcement purposes and such disclosure would interfere with the enforcement matter.*

Commercial requesters wishing to keep their identity confidential should consider that all requests become part of the public record; therefore, third party requests can be made. For example, attorneys may place requests on behalf of their client.

CRITICAL ANALYSIS: According to the Department of Justice "The basic function of the Freedom of Information Act is to ensure informed citizens, vital to the functioning of a democratic society." See: https://www.foia.gov. How does a federal agency such as FDA comply with the above statement? Include a discussion about timeliness, proprietary information and provide examples. https://www.foia.gov/about.html

Guidance Documents

http://www.fda.gov/RegulatoryInformation/Guidances/default.htm

Ever since the United States Supreme Court decision in *Abbott Laboratories v. Gardner*, 387 U.S. 136 (1967), FDA has used the rulemaking process. The Court in *Abbott* held that notice and comment regulations issued by FDA under section 701(a) had the force and effect of law. Over the years, the rulemaking process has become increasingly complex, time consuming and costlier for industry and government. Federal agencies such as FDA and USDA have increasingly issued guidance documents (GDs). GDs are a less formal method for announcing FDA and USDA regulatory expectations. GDs have existed for quite some time; however, they were not used as frequently as they are today. **However, it is significant to note that GDs are not legally binding on either the agency or the public. (emphasis added).** Although GDs are not legally binding, they explain how the agencies interpret or apply relevant laws and regulations. They are significant because they allow the regulated industry to recognize what is expected in a wide variety of contexts such as permissible filth levels in food or the requisite design of clinical studies for new drug approvals. See: FR vol.65, no. 182 9/19/2000 pgs. 56468-56480 GDs documents should:

    ✓ Relate to the processing, content, evaluation and approval submissions;
    ✓ Pertain to the design, production, manufacturing and testing of regulated products;
    ✓ Describe the agency's policy and regulatory approach to an issue; and
    ✓ Establish inspection and enforcement policies and procedures.

Legal Effect: Guidance documents are not legally binding documents. That is, guidance documents do not legally obligate the FDA or the public. In other words, they do not create legally enforceable rights. GDs explain how the FDA interprets or applies relevant laws and regulations. In so doing, the FDA aims to guarantee that FDA staff follows guidance documents. GDs can be analogized to Good Manufacturing Practices, Good Laboratory Practices and Good Clinical Practices that FDA regulated industries must follow. Guidance documents are very significant to the regulated community by allowing industry to recognize what is expected in a wide variety of contexts such pre-market submissions for pharmaceuticals, bio-equivalence studies for generic drugs, compliance and inspection issues, financial disclosure, regulatory procedures manual, food labeling, sanitation ratings of milk supplies, shellfish sanitation, and label declaration of allergenic substances in foods.

Procedures: FDA created two categories for guidance documents. The exact procedure for forming a guidance paper depends on whether it is "Level 1" or "Level 2".

Level 1 Documents encompass directives aimed to those in the regulated industry such as applicants/sponsors that establish regulatory interpretations, modifications in policy, particularly complicated scientific issues or extremely contentious issues. A good example of a "Level 1" document is an explanation of how to comply with a new regulation. Usually, the FDA will ask for public comment before a guidance document is implemented unless:

    1. Public health reasons exist for immediate implementation;
    2. A new statutory requirement, executive order, or court order exists that necessitates immediate implementation; or
    3. The guidance document presents a less burdensome policy compatible with public health.

FDA seeks public feedback by issuing a notice of availability in the *Federal Register*. The FDA may use one *Federal Register* notice to obtain comments on more than one draft guidance. The FDA designates its availability on the applicable FDA home page. Guidance document notices and or drafts are posted on the FDA home page. Besides comment submission, FDA may hold public workshops to review a draft or present a draft to an advisory panel.

Level 2 Documents include all other guidance documents. A good example of a "Level 2" document is an FDA update without substantive impact such as advising the regulated industry about the FDA home page availability. FDA permits an opportunity for public comment when a Level 2 guidance is issued.

Basic Components*:* All guidance documents include standard information. For example, all guidance documents contain basic terminology such as the word "guidance" and the specific FDA Center or Office and the regulatory activity to which the document applies. All guidance documents contain a statement of non-binding effect. This means that words like "shall" and "must" are inappropriate. Other standard elements consist of issuance dates, latest revisions, and whether the guidance document is a draft.

Availability*:* FDA publishes a quarterly list in the *Federal Register* of guidance documents issued and withdrawn on the FDA homepage at *http://www.fda.gov*. Examples include the following:

> ➢ *Animal and Veterinary;*
> ➢ *Cosmetics;*
> ➢ *Drugs;*
> ➢ *Food;*
> ➢ *Medical Devices;*
> ➢ *Radiation-Emitting Products;*
> ➢ *Vaccines, Blood and Biologics; and Tobacco Products.*

Handling Controversies*:* Perhaps there are times when the GDs were not followed or the GDs fail to accomplish the intended purpose. FDA affords the opportunity for appeal to FDA. Generally, a person with a controversy about a guidance document should start with the supervisor of the person who issued or applied the guidance document. The dispute should then be brought through the chain of command or the Center's Ombudsman. *Ombuds@oc.fda.gov*

NOTE: See the following link for Guidance, Compliance, & Regulatory Information.
http://www.fda.gov/Drugs/GuidanceComplianceRegulatoryInformation/default.htm

CRITICAL ANALYSIS: Choose a "Popular Item" (see above link) and evaluate in terms of stakeholder information and reliance by industry.

VOLUME III

Volume III: The Food and Drug Administration—Criminal and Civil Enforcement Strategies

This volume focuses on regulatory issues and legal court cases in Food and Drug Law pertaining to enforcement. The United States Food and Drug Administration (FDA), the Federal Trade Commission (FTC) and the United States Department of Agriculture (USDA) are charged with the responsibility of enforcement in accordance with the particular statute that each agency or Commission regulates. Public protection and public trust remain paramount.

This volume contains enforcement terminology, FDA enforcement mechanisms and strategies such as seizure, warning letters, detention and debarment as well as criminal sanctions and strict criminal liability. FDA utilizes other enforcement tools not detailed in the FDCA. For example, FDA utilizes advisory letters, known as "Titled" and "Untitled" warning letters as an enforcement tool. Warning letters serve as a "caveat" for the potential of legal action. Economic harm is covered. "Off-label" enforcement is included in this Volume and in Volume V: Human Drugs.

The Food Drug and Cosmetic Act enumerates prohibited acts under 21 U.S.C. section 331 that includes criminal misdemeanor and felony provisions. The Office of Criminal Investigations focuses on the submission of false information and criminal activity related to product safety. The Office of General Counsel assumes a major role in enforcement activities by advising FDA employees and reviewing materials related to enforcement activities such as product withdrawals, inspections and search warrants.

The FDCA contains criminal sanctions and over the years, FDA has pursued what is termed a "Park" prosecution. A Park prosecution stems from a case back in 1975 concerning individual criminal liability; that is, prosecution of a corporate official. United States v. Park, a Supreme Court decision changed the landscape in terms of individual corporate accountability and is still followed today as this volume details in several decisions. United States v. Dotterweich was the precursor to the Park decision. Fast-forward to today and the "Park" doctrine remains viable as illustrated in this Volume. Prosecution of corporate executives remains a constant deterrent as illustrated in the misdemeanor Jensen Farms and Quality Egg convictions of corporate officials and the felony conviction of the Peanut Corporation of America executives.

Warning Letters, import refusals, seizures, recalls and injunctions remain important regulatory enforcement tools. The FDA, FTC and USDA continue to use enforcement mechanisms to protect the public in keeping with the underlying statutes.

Chapter 1: Food and Drug Administration Enforcement Mechanisms

Prohibited Acts and Violations

Key websites: *http://www.fda.gov* and *http://www.fsis.usda.gov/wps/portal/fsis/home*

The United States Food and Drug Administration (FDA), the Federal Trade Commission (FTC) and the United States Department of Agriculture (USDA) enforcement mechanisms are for compliance purposes, in keeping with public protection and public trust. The United States Department of Agriculture (USDA) and the Food and Drug Administration (FDA) use specific enforcement mechanisms. The FDCA enumerates prohibited acts under 21 U.S.C. section 331 that includes criminal misdemeanor and felony provisions. Examples include:

> **Misbranding, Adulteration, Refusal to permit entry or inspection, False guarantees, Forging, Counterfeiting, and Falsification.**

The FDA's Office of Enforcement is responsible for managing FDA's compliance activities and supervising compliance actions. The Office of Criminal Investigations focuses on the submission of false information and criminal activity related to product safety. The Office of General Counsel assumes a major role in enforcement activities by advising FDA employees and reviewing materials related to enforcement activities such as product withdrawals, inspections and search warrants. FDA enforcement methods are contained in the Food, Drug and Cosmetic Act (FDCA), Chapter III: Title 21 United States Code. For example, FDA has the authority to seize a misbranded or adulterated product under 21 U.S.C. section 334. Seizure is a specific legal action to remove a product from the marketplace through the court process. An injunction, 21 U.S.C. section 332, is a specific legal civil action against an individual or company to cease production and or distribution of a product that violates the FDCA. Condemnation proceedings against a company may be sought as well.

However, FDA utilizes other enforcement practices not enumerated in the FDCA. For example, FDA utilizes advisory letters, known as *"Titled"* and *"Untitled"* warning letters as an enforcement tool. Usually, "titled" letters are sent to the company president and an "untitled" letter is addressed to the head of a regulatory affairs department. Warning letters do not necessarily commit the agency to take enforcement action. Rather, the intent of a warning letter is for compliance by a firm prior to FDA instituting an enforcement action.

Company initiated recalls and field corrections are usually conducted on a voluntary basis. Yet, the landmark FDA Food Safety Modernization Act provides for recall authority in the food arena and additionally FDA's recall authority includes section 360h (e), which pertains to medical devices. Company initiated recalls and field corrections are usually conducted on a voluntary basis. Condemnation proceedings against a company may be sought as well. Companies sometimes enter into consent decrees in order to settle a pending litigation matter and avoid a lengthy and costly court proceeding. See: *Volume V: Human Drugs.*

The FDCA provides for both court-ordered civil and criminal penalties. FTC and USDA have similar enforcement methods. A prosecution involves criminal action taken against an individual or company charged with violating the FDCA. Penalties under the FDCA are enumerated under 21 U.S.C. section 333. The seminal United States Supreme Court decisions of *United States v. Dotterwiech* and *United States v. Park* pertained to individual corporate accountability and the absence of a *mens rea* requirement for certain violations. That is, the government did not have to prove the element of criminal intent in its prosecution or that the defendant knew of or participated in the illegal activity.

CRITICAL ANALYSIS: Evaluate the prohibited acts and penalties under the Federal Food, Drug and Cosmetic Act (FDCA). See 21 U.S.C. Sections 331, 332, 333, 334 and 335(a) (b) (c) and 336. Discuss additional proscribed acts and penalties for Congress to address.

Besides the FDCA, there are other pertinent statutes and respective violations. These include the following.

Title 18 Violations

Title 18, USC § 287 — False, Fictitious or Fraudulent Claims
Title 18, USC § 371 — Conspiracy to Commit Offense or to Defraud the United States
Title 18, USC § 1001—False Statements to the Government
Title 18, USC § 1035—False Statements Relating to Health Care Matters
Title 18, USC § 1341—Mail Fraud
Title 18, USC § 1343—Wire Fraud
Title 18, USC § 1347—Health Care fraud
Title 18, USC § 1365—Federal Anti-Tampering Act (FATA)
Title 18, USC § 1505—Obstruction of Proceedings before Departments /Agencies
Title 18, USC § 1518—Obstruction of Criminal Investigation of Health Care Offenses
Title 18, USC § 2314—Interstate Transportation of Stolen Property, or Articles used in Counterfeiting
Title 18, USC § 2315—Sale or Receipt of stolen goods moved interstate
Title 18, USC § 2320—Trafficking in Counterfeit Goods

Title 42 Violations

Title 42—Medicaid False Claims Act—prohibits false statements in connection with applications, benefits or assets. See 42 U.S.C. section 1320a-7b(a).

Title 42—Anti-Kickback Statute—prohibits solicitation or the receipt of remuneration in connection with Medicare or Medicaid activities. See 42 U.S.C. section 1320a-7b(b)(1).

Title 42—Civil False Claims Act—prohibits the filing of false claims for payment by the federal government. See 31 U.S.C. section 3729(a); 28 U.S.C. section 2461.

Enforcement Terminology

http://www.fda.gov/ICECI/EnforcementActions/default.htm

COMPLIANCE ACHIEVEMENT: The observed repair, modification, or adjustment of a violative condition, or the repair, modification, adjustment, relabeling, or destruction of a violative product when either the product or condition does not comply.

CIVIL MONEY PENALTY: A monetary penalty that is assessed by FDA or the courts for violations of the Federal Food, Drug, and Cosmetic Act or the Public Health Service Act.

DISPOSITON: A final order entered by a court to conclude cases involving prosecutions or injunctions. Prosecutions may conclude with the entry of a plea, a verdict, and, if guilty, conviction and sentencing. Injunctions are resolved when a court imposes an order on a firm or declines to issue the order.

INDICTMENT: A formal accusation by a grand jury that sets forth charges against a defendant and states when the alleged crime occurred. An indictment is not a finding of guilt. Guilt can only be determined by a judge or jury after a trial.

INFORMATION: A formal accusation by a U.S. attorney similar to an indictment except that the charges usually are not presented to a grand jury. A criminal information alleges a misdemeanor rather than a felony except when consented to by the proposed defendant.

INDUSTRY SURVEILLANCE: The total number of establishment inspections, sample collections, field examinations and wharf examinations conducted by FDA personnel.

INJUNCTION: A civil process taken against an individual or a firm initiated to stop continued production or distribution of a violative product. See 21 U.S.C. 332; Rule 65, Rules of Civil Procedure.

PROSECUTION: A criminal action against a company or individual charging a violation of law.

RECALL AND FIELD CORRECTION: Action taken by a firm either to remove a product from the market or to conduct a field correction. Recalls may be conducted on a firm's own initiative, by FDA request, or by FDA order under statutory authority. A Class I recall is a situation in which there is a reasonable probability that the use of or exposure to a violative product will cause serious adverse health consequences or death. A Class II recall is a situation in which use of or exposure to a violative product may cause temporary or medically reversible adverse health consequences or where the probability of serious adverse health consequences is remote. A Class III recall is a situation in which use of or exposure to a violative product is not likely to cause adverse health consequences.

SEIZURE: An action taken to remove a product from commerce because it is in violation of the law. FDA initiates a seizure by filing a complaint with the U.S. District Court where the product is located. A U.S. Marshal then takes possession of the goods until the matter is resolved.

WARNING LETTER: An informal advisory to a firm communicating the agency's position on a matter but does not commit FDA to taking enforcement action. Warning Letters should be issued for violations that are of regulatory significance in that failure to adequately and promptly take corrections may be expected to result in enforcement action should the violation(s) continue.

Other Agencies and Private Actions

Federal agencies such as the Federal Trade Commission (FTC) may institute enforcement actions. State Attorneys General may join FTC or institute enforcement with other states under state consumer protection laws such as unfair practices.

- ➢ Federal—U.S. Department of Agriculture and the Federal Trade Commission;
- ➢ State Enforcement;
- ➢ Private Action—Lanham Act; and
- ➢ Self-Regulation—National Advertising Division (NAD) Better Business Bureau

As illustrated below, the Lanham Act permits a cause of action for unfair competition through misleading labeling or advertising. The Lanham Act does not permit a federal court to determine how a federal agency will interpret and enforce its own regulations. See: *PhotoMedex v. Irwin*, 601 F.3d 919 (9th Cir.2010). *PhotoMedex* concerned a medical device and clearance claims. (Court dismissed and denied motion for reconsideration). Nos. 04-CV-24 JLS (CAB), 06-CV-1479 JLS (CAB) Sept. 27, 2010. Yet, see below *POM Wonderful LLC v. Coca-Cola Co.* (Juice named "Pomegranate Blueberry" and allegations that product contained minimal of either pomegranate or blueberry juice).

Lanham Act Lawsuit—*POM Wonderful LLC*

POM Wonderful LLC, v. The Coca–Cola Co., 134 S. Ct. 2228 (2014)

This case concerned the intersection of two federal statutes that is, the Lanham Act which permits one competitor to sue another for unfair competition resulting from false or misleading product descriptions, 15 U.S.C. § 1125 and the Federal Food, Drug, and Cosmetic Act (FDCA) which prohibits the misbranding of food and drink 21 U.S.C. §§ 321(f), 331. The Lanham Act lawsuit against the Coca–Cola Company, alleged that the name, label, marketing, and advertising of one of Coca–Cola's juice blends misled consumers into thinking the product consisted primarily of pomegranate and blueberry juice. However, actually it consisted mainly of apple and grape juices. The District Court ruled that the FDCA and its regulations preclude Lanham Act challenges to the name and label of Coca–Cola's juice blend. The Ninth Circuit affirmed in relevant part. The Supreme Court held that competitors may bring Lanham Act claims such as the challenge by POM regarding food and beverage labels despite regulation by the FDCA.

NOTE: The above is, in part, from the syllabus that constitutes no part of the opinion of the Court and has been prepared by the Reporter of Decisions for the convenience of the reader. See: *United States v. Detroit Timber & Lumber Co.*, 200 U.S. 321, 337, 26 S.Ct. 282, 50 L.Ed. 499.

Opinion Justice KENNEDY delivered the opinion of the Court. POM Wonderful LLC makes and sells pomegranate juice products, including a pomegranate-blueberry juice blend. App. 23a. One of POM's competitors is the Coca–Cola Company. Coca–Cola's Minute Maid Division makes a juice blend sold with a label that, in describing the contents, displays the words "pomegranate blueberry" with far more prominence than other words on the label that show the juice to be a blend of five juices. In truth, the Coca–Cola product contains but 0.3% pomegranate juice and 0.2% blueberry juice. Alleging that the use of that label is deceptive and misleading, POM sued Coca–Cola under § 43 of the Lanham Act. 60 Stat. 441, as amended, 15 U.S.C. § 1125. That provision allows one competitor to sue another if it alleges unfair competition arising from false or misleading product descriptions. *** There is no statutory text or established interpretive principle to support the contention that the FDCA precludes Lanham Act suits like the one brought by POM in this case. *** Quite to the contrary, the FDCA and the Lanham Act complement each other in the federal regulation of misleading food and beverage labels. ***

I. A. Congress enacted the Lanham Act nearly seven decades ago. See 60 Stat. 427 (1946). *** Section 45 of the Lanham Act provides: "The intent of this chapter is to regulate commerce within the control of Congress by making actionable the deceptive and misleading use of marks in such commerce; to protect registered marks used in such commerce from interference by State, or territorial legislation; to protect persons engaged in such commerce against unfair competition; to prevent fraud and deception in such commerce by the use of reproductions, copies, counterfeits, or colorable imitations of registered marks; and to provide rights and remedies stipulated by treaties and conventions respecting trademarks, trade names, and unfair competition entered into between the United States and foreign nations." 15 U.S.C. § 1127. ***

The FDCA statutory regime is designed primarily to protect the health and safety of the public at large. See *62 Cases of Jam v. United States,* 340 U.S. 593, 596, 71 S.Ct. 515, 95 L.Ed. 566 (1951); FDCA, § 401, 52 Stat. 1046, 21 U.S.C. § 341 (agency may issue certain regulations to "promote honesty and fair dealing in the interest of consumers"). The FDCA prohibits the misbranding of food and drink. 21 U.S.C. §§ 321(f), 331. A food or drink is deemed misbranded if, *inter alia,* "its labeling is false or misleading," § 343(a), information required to appear on its label "is not prominently placed thereon," § 343(f), or a label does not bear "the common or usual name of the food *** " § 343(i). *** See 21 C.F.R. § 102.33 (2013). One provision of those regulations is particularly relevant to this case: If a juice blend does not name all the juices it contains and mentions only juices that are not predominant in the blend, then it must either declare the percentage content of the named juice or "[i]ndicate that the named juice is present as a flavor or flavoring," *e.g.,* "raspberry and cranberry flavored juice drink." § 102.33(d). *** Unlike the Lanham Act, which relies in substantial part for its enforcement on private suits brought by injured competitors, the FDCA and its regulations provide the United States with nearly exclusive enforcement authority, including the authority to seek criminal sanctions in some circumstances. 21 U.S.C. §§ 333(a), 337. Private parties may not bring enforcement suits. § 337. ***

B. POM Wonderful LLC is a grower of pomegranates and a distributor of pomegranate juices. Through its POM Wonderful brand, POM produces, markets, and sells a variety of pomegranate products, including a pomegranate-blueberry juice blend. POM competes in the pomegranate-blueberry juice market with the Coca–Cola Company. Coca–Cola, under its Minute Maid brand, created a juice blend containing 99.4% apple and grape juices, 0.3% pomegranate juice, 0.2% blueberry juice, and 0.1% raspberry juice. Despite the minuscule amount of pomegranate and blueberry juices in the blend, the front label of the Coca–Cola product displays the words "pomegranate blueberry" in all capital letters, on two separate lines. Below those words, Coca–Cola placed the phrase "flavored blend of 5 juices" in much smaller type. And below that phrase, in still smaller type, were the words "from concentrate with added ingredients"—and, with a line break before the final phrase—"and other natural flavors." The product's front label also displays a vignette of blueberries, grapes, and raspberries in front of a halved pomegranate and a halved apple. *** POM alleged that the name, label, marketing, and advertising of Coca–Cola's juice blend mislead consumers into believing the product consists predominantly of pomegranate and blueberry juice when it in fact consists predominantly of less expensive apple and grape juices. *** The District Court granted partial summary judgment to Coca–Cola on POM's Lanham Act claim, ruling that the FDCA and its regulations preclude challenges to the name and label of Coca–Cola's juice blend. *** Like the District Court, the Court of Appeals reasoned that Congress decided "to entrust matters of juice beverage labeling to the FDA"; the FDA has promulgated "comprehensive regulation of that labeling"; and the FDA "apparently" has not imposed the requirements on Coca–Cola's label that are sought by POM. 679 F.3d 1170, 1178 (2012).

II. A. First, this is not a pre-emption case. *** This case, however, concerns the alleged preclusion of a cause of action under one federal statute by the provisions of another federal statute. *** Second, this is a statutory interpretation case and the Court relies on traditional rules of statutory interpretation. That does not change because the case involves multiple federal statutes. See *FDA v.*

Brown & Williamson Tobacco Corp., 529 U.S. 120, 137–139, 120 S.Ct. 1291, 146 L.Ed.2d 121 (2000). *** Even assuming that Coca–Cola is correct that the Court's task is to reconcile or harmonize the statutes and not, as POM urges, to enforce both statutes in full unless there is a genuinely irreconcilable conflict, Coca–Cola is incorrect that the best way to harmonize the statutes is to bar POM's Lanham Act claim.

B. Beginning with the text of the two statutes, it must be observed that neither the Lanham Act nor the FDCA, in express terms, forbids or limits Lanham Act claims challenging labels that are regulated by the FDCA. *** In consequence, food and beverage labels regulated by the FDCA are not, under the terms of either statute, off limits to Lanham Act claims. *** This absence is of special significance because the Lanham Act and the FDCA have coexisted since the passage of the Lanham Act in 1946. 60 Stat. 427 (1946); ch. 675, 52 Stat. 1040 (1938). If Congress had concluded, in light of experience, that Lanham Act suits could interfere with th

e FDCA, it might well have enacted a provision addressing the issue during these 70 years. See *Wyeth, supra,* at 574, 129 S.Ct. 1187 ("If Congress thought state-law suits posed an obstacle to its objectives, it surely would have enacted an express pre-emption provision at some point during the FDCA's 70–year history"). Congress enacted amendments to the FDCA and the Lanham Act, see, *e.g.,* Trademark Law Revision Act of 1988, § 132, 102 Stat. 3946, including an amendment that added to the FDCA an express pre-emption provision with respect to state laws addressing food and beverage misbranding, § 6, 104 Stat. 2362 *** Perhaps the closest the statutes come to addressing the preclusion of the Lanham Act claim at issue here is the pre-emption provision added to the FDCA in 1990 as part of the Nutrition Labeling and Education Act. See 21 U.S.C. § 343–1. *** This pre-emption provision forbids a "State or political subdivision of a State" from imposing requirements that are of the type but "not identical to" corresponding FDCA requirements for food and beverage labeling. It is significant that the complex pre-emption provision distinguishes among different FDCA requirements. *** A holding that the FDCA precludes Lanham Act claims challenging food and beverage labels would not only ignore the distinct functional aspects of the FDCA and the Lanham Act but also would lead to a result that Congress likely did not intend. ***

C. Coca–Cola says that the FDCA's delegation of enforcement authority to the Federal Government shows Congress' intent to achieve national uniformity in labeling. But POM seeks to enforce the Lanham Act, not the FDCA or its regulations. ***

D. The Government assumes that the FDCA and its regulations are at least in some circumstances a ceiling on the regulation of food and beverage labeling. But, as discussed above, Congress intended the Lanham Act and the FDCA to complement each other with respect to food and beverage labeling. *** In addition, *Geier v. American Honda Motor Co.*, 529 U.S. 861, 120 S.Ct. 1913, 146 L.Ed.2d 914 (2000), does not support the Government's argument. In *Geier,* the agency enacted a regulation deliberately allowing manufacturers to choose between different options because the agency wanted to encourage diversity in the industry. *** The Court concluded that the action was barred because it directly conflicted with the agency's policy choice to encourage flexibility to foster innovation. *Id.,* at 875, 120 S.Ct. 1913. Here, by contrast, the FDA has not made a policy judgment that is inconsistent with POM's Lanham Act suit. ***

The judgment of the Court of Appeals for the Ninth Circuit is reversed. *It is so ordered.* Justice BREYER took no part in the consideration or decision of this case.

NOTE: A California jury found that "The Coca Cola Company" did not falsely advertise its Minute Maid pomegranate juice thus effectively ending POM Wonderful's lengthy $77 million Lanham Act lawsuit against "The Coca Cola Company". Coca Cola defense included "unclean hands" doctrine. *POM Wonderful LLC v. The Coca Cola Co.*, 166 F.Supp.3d 1085 (C.D. Cal.); Case No. 2:08-cv-06237 (Feb. 19, 2016).

CRITICAL ANALYSIS: Evaluate the Court's analysis in terms of the federal FDCA and a private right of action by a competitor under the federal Lanham Act.

Chapter 2: Inspection, Seizure, Recalls, Warning Letters, Debarment, Detention and Application Integrity Policy

Inspection "482" and "483"

Under 21 U.S.C. section 374, FDA has authority to conduct an inspection. A "482 Notice of Inspection" is provided to the firm and afterward, "Form 483 Observations" by FDA during the inspection is provided. The following serves as a guide for inspection purposes.

➢ Develop Standard Operating Inspection Compliance Procedures (SOICP) in writing.
➢ Involve key personnel such as legal, quality and regulatory affairs, management, operations in drafting the SOICP.
➢ Identify staff written in the SOICP to speak and correspond with FDA inspectors.
➢ Assess the SOICP before an FDA inspection such as through audits, "trial runs".
➢ Respond to FDA inspectors within scope of staff knowledge.
➢ Deliver on corrective actions that the company pledges and within the timeframe promised.

CRITICAL ANALYSIS: Detail strategic considerations in preparation for an inspection.

Photographs During an Inspection

http://www.fda.gov/ICECI/Inspections/IOM/ucm122531.htm#5.3.4

The use of photographs by an FDA inspector during an inspection has become more common. Two key legal decisions provide some guidance. *Dow Chemical Co. v. United States,* 476 U.S. 227 (1986) (Court held aerial photographs of a Dow Chemical Plant permissible after the Environmental Protection Agency was refused entry to conduct an on-site inspection and *United States v. Acri Wholesale Grocery Co. v. United States,* 409 F. Supp. 529 (S.D. Iowa 1976) (inspection photographs of rodent infestation deemed admissible); See: *United States v. Chung's Products* Civil Action NO. H-10-759, (April 3, 2013).

5.3.4.1 - In-Plant Photographs (FDA Investigations Operations Manual)—Do not request permission from management to take photographs during an inspection. Take your camera into the firm and use it as necessary just as you use other inspectional equipment. If management objects to taking photographs, explain that photos are an integral part of an inspection and present an accurate picture of plant conditions. Advise management the U. S. Courts have held that photographs may lawfully be taken as part of an inspection. If management refuses, obtain name and contact information for the firm's legal counsel, and advise your district management immediately. If the firm does not have legal counsel on retainer, collect the name and contact information for the most responsible individual. District management will inform their ORA Regional Counselor in the Office of Chief Counsel (OCC) of the situation, and OCC will then contact the firm's legal counsel or most responsible individual to discuss FDA's legal right to take pictures during inspections. If you have already taken some photos do not surrender film to management. Advise the firm it can obtain copies of the photos under the Freedom of Information Act.

CRITICAL ANALYSIS: Review 5.3.4.1 concerning photographs by an FDA inspector. How should you advise your client?

FDA Enforcement Statistics Fiscal Year 2017

https://www.fda.gov/downloads/iceci/enforcementactions/ucm592790.pdf

Enforcement Type	Count
Seizures	3
Injunctions	12
Warning Letters	15,318
Recall Events	2,945
Recalled Products	9,199
Debarments (Drugs)	5
Food Importation Debarments	0

Seizure Example—Kratom

https://www.fda.gov/NewsEvents/PublicHealthFocus/ucm584952.htm
https://www.fda.gov/NewsEvents/Newsroom/PressAnnouncements/ucm480344.htm

U.S. Marshals seized nearly 90,000 bottles of dietary supplements labeled as containing kratom. The product, manufactured for and held by Dordoniz Natural Products LLC, located in South Beloit, Illinois, is marketed under the brand name RelaKzpro and worth more than $400,000. *Mitragyna speciosa*, commonly known as kratom, is a botanical substance that grows naturally in Thailand, Malaysia, Indonesia and Papua New Guinea. Serious concerns exist regarding the toxicity of kratom in multiple organ systems. Consumption of kratom can lead to a number of health impacts, including, among others, respiratory depression, vomiting, nervousness, weight loss and constipation. Kratom has been indicated to have both narcotic and stimulant-like effects and withdrawal symptoms may include hostility, aggression, excessive tearing, aching of muscles and bones and jerky limb movements.

CRITICAL ANALYSIS: Why did FDA seize the product? Discuss any safety issues associated with Kratom. See also: *Volume X* **for further discussion of Kratom.**

FDA Recall Policy

FDA has recall policies and procedures in place; however, the FDCA does not specifically authorize FDA to order recalls for all FDA regulated products with exceptions stipulated under 21 U.S.C. section 360h (e) for recall authority of medical devices and the recall authority for foods under the Food Safety Modernization Act of 2011. Generally, the product manufacturer or distributor conducts the majority of recalls voluntarily. In other situations, FDA will inform a company that a product is defective and will request a recall. In general, a company will comply; however, if the company objects and fails to do so, FDA can then seek a court order enforcing its legal authority under the FDCA to seize the product and/or obtain a court ordered injunction.

FDA guidelines under 21 CFR Part 7 specifies procedures for companies to follow in recalling defective products that fall within its authority. These procedures detail that FDA expects a firm to take full responsibility for product recalls, including subsequent checks to ensure that the recall was successful. Firms are responsible for notifying FDA when recalls are initiated and to provide progress reports to FDA. Manufacturers and distributors must develop contingency plans. FDA monitors recalls and assesses the adequacy of the action taken by a firm. FDA ensures the product is destroyed or reconditioned depending on the nature and recall classification.

Classification

> **Class I Recalls** cover dangerous or defective products that could cause serious health problems or even death. Examples include food that contains botulinal toxin, a labeling error on a "life-saving drug," or a defective artificial heart valve.
> **Class II Recalls** concern products that might cause a temporary health problem, such as a sub-potent drug used to treat a life-threatening condition.
> **Class III Recalls** pertain to products that are unlikely to cause any adverse health consequences. For example, an aspirin bottle that contains 90 tablets instead of 100 tablets stated on the label would be misbranded and necessitate a Class III recall.

Usually, FDA only seeks publicity about a recall when the agency believes the public needs to be alerted about a serious health problem. For example, if a canned food product purchased by a consumer is found to contain botulinal toxin, then a press release by FDA would alert consumers of the danger. FDA may post a press release about a firm-initiated recall.

CRITICAL ANALYSIS: The number of recalled products remains problematic. How should a company prevent a recall? How should a company respond to an FDA initiated recall request?

Warning Letters—Traditional and Cyber

FDA issues warning letters for violations deemed of "regulatory significance". Warning letters are not enumerated as an enforcement action under the FDCA; yet, the purpose of an FDA issued warning letter is to alert the regulated entity of violations that if not promptly and sufficiently corrected, could lead to enforcement action. It was not until the late 1960's that FDA increased the use of warning letters. A proposed regulation in 1978 recommended two specific types of warning letters: Notice of Adverse Findings Letters and Regulatory Letters. However, in 1980, the proposed regulation was subsequently withdrawn, and FDA eventually instituted the single Warning Letter system in 1991.

FDA may issue either a "Titled letter or "Untitled letter". A titled letter, known as a warning letter, is an advisory sent by certified mail usually to the president or chief executive of a company. Warning letters do not necessarily commit the agency to take an enforcement action. Rather, the intent is for firm compliance prior to FDA instituting an enforcement action. Do warning letters constitute a "final agency action"? In *Cody Laboratories, Inc. v. Sebelius,* No. 10-CV-1475 (2010), the district court determined that the warning letter at issue did not constitute a final agency action and the Court of Appeals affirmed. The Appeals Court opined that every court determined that a warning letter does not constitute a "Final Agency Action". Warning letters have served as a deterrent to the regulated industry in the belief of possibly avoiding legal action by FDA. FDA "untitled letters" address matters that do not necessarily rise to the level of "regulatory significance". Untitled letters are sometimes sent to an entire industry. An untitled warning letter to a specific company or firm is typically addressed to the head of regulatory affairs.

FDA issues "cyber" letters to domestic and foreign-based Internet sites, which are electronic versions comparable to traditional warning letters. The letters are transmitted through the Internet to operators of Internet based sites who offer to sell online FDA regulated products and to domain owners whose legality is questionable under the FDCA. Hard copies are sent to the U.S. Customs Service and the regulatory officials in the country where the operator is headquartered. For example, prescription drugs may be offered for sale without a valid prescription or any prescription at all.

Responding to Warning Letters
- ✓ Determine and assess the extent of the problem.
- ✓ Respond within the time period specified–usually 15 days.
- ✓ Provide a comprehensible compliance and corrective action plan.
- ✓ Implement the procedures detailed in the compliance program.
- ✓ Detail timeframes for compliance.
- ✓ Present supporting documentation.
- ✓ Specify a proactive plan for prevention.

CRITICAL ANALYSIS: Choose a "Recently Posted" warning letter (link below). Prepare a response to FDA.
See: *http://www.fda.gov/ICECI/EnforcementActions/WarningLetters/default.htm#recent*

Application Integrity Policy
https://www.fda.gov/ICECI/EnforcementActions/ApplicationIntegrityPolicy/ucm134453.htm (list)

FDA may utilize "Refusal to Review Data" such as drug applications as another enforcement tool. This means FDA defers substantive scientific review of one or more of the firm's applications and/or is proceeding to withdraw the approved applications. In effect, this precludes a company from getting drugs approved until violations are corrected. **See:** ***This Volume and Volume V: Human Drugs*** **for** ***Ranbaxy*** **enforcement.**

Exclusion and Debarment
Succinctly stated, individual debarment has serious repercussions and essentially precludes any involvement. Mandatory and Permissive Exclusion under the Social Security Act (SSA) precludes payment from Federal health care programs. A final rule effective May 30, 2012 expanded the scope of clinical investigator disqualification to any FDA regulated product.

Misconduct in Drug and Device Development
http://www.fda.gov/ICECI/EnforcementActions/ucm321308.htm

FDA increased the agency's efforts to prevent non-compliant investigators and others from participating in new product development. Procedures for debarment and disqualification have been enhanced to better protect participants in clinical studies and for ensuring the safety and effectiveness of the medical products marketed to the American public. Compliance with the FDA's statutes and regulations is crucial to protecting clinical study participants and the public. The debarment and disqualification procedures ensure that sponsors of clinical studies do not unknowingly use individuals who potentially may be debarred or disqualified by the FDA. The FDA can ban or debar individuals known to have broken the law from working for companies with approved or pending drug applications. The agency can also disqualify researchers conducting clinical testing of new drugs and devices, when the FDA determines that they have not followed the rules intended to protect study subjects. Further, the FDA can disqualify a clinical investigator who has, for example, manipulated data to inaccurately report study findings.

OIG Mandatory Exclusion: The Office of Inspector General (OIG) is required to order mandatory exclusion for a five year minimum period when an individual is convicted of a program related crime, a felony related to health care fraud, a crime related to abuse or neglect or a felony related to controlled substances and permanent exclusion for individual convictions of three or more offenses. See 42 U.S.C sec. 1320a-7(a),(c).

OIG Permissive Exclusion: OIG, under the SSA, has the discretion to issue "Permissive Exclusion" for a three-year minimum period if an individual is convicted of a misdemeanor relating to fraud, theft, embezzlement, breach of fiduciary responsibility or other financial misconduct; obstruction of investigation concerning a health care program or an offense concerning controlled substances. See 42 U.S.C sec. 1320a-7(b).

FDA Mandatory Debarment: Permanent or mandatory debarment is required under the FDCA if the individual is convicted of a felony for conduct that pertains to the development or approval process or regulation of any drug product. See 21 USC sec. 335a(a)(2).

FDA Permissive Debarment: FDA has discretion to order "Permissive Debarment" for a five-year maximum period if an individual was convicted of a federal misdemeanor or felony under a state law for conduct relating to drug approval and or drug regulation or a felony such as obstruction of justice or bribery and which does not necessarily have to relate to drug regulation. See 21 U.S.C. sec. 335a(b)(2)(B).

CRITICAL ANALYSIS: See above link for the Application Integrity Policy List. Discuss the implications as well as debarment below in *United States v. Lam.*

Debarment Example—*United States v. Peter Xuong Lam*
http://www.federalregister.gov/articles/2009/12/14/E9-29715/peter-xuong-lam-debarment-order#p-14
Summary: The Food and Drug Administration (FDA) issu[ed] an order under the Federal Food, Drug, and Cosmetic Act debarring Peter Xuong Lam for a period of 20 years from importing articles of food or offering such articles for importation into the United States. FDA bases this order on a finding that Mr. Lam was convicted of four felonies under Federal law for conduct relating to the importation into the United States of an article of food. Mr. Lam's failure to request a hearing constitutes a waiver of his right to a hearing concerning this action.

I. Background: Section 306(b)(1)(C) of the act (21 U.S.C. 335a(b)(1)(C)) permits FDA to debar an individual from importing an article of food or offering such an article for import into the United States if FDA finds, as required by section 306(b)(3)(A) of the act (21 U.S.C. 335a(b)(3)(A)), that the individual has been convicted of a felony under Federal law for conduct relating to the importation into the United States of any food. On October 29, 2008, Mr. Lam was convicted in the United States District Court for the Central District of California of one count of conspiracy, in violation of 18 U.S.C. 371, for conspiring to violate 18 U.S.C. 545 (importation contrary to law) and 21 U.S.C. 331(a) and (c) and 21 U.S.C. 333(a)(2) (felony delivery and receipt of misbranded food) and of three counts of violating 18 U.S.C. 545 and 18 U.S.C. 2(b) (trafficking in fish contrary to 18 U.S.C. 541 and 21 U.S.C. 331(a)). The factual basis for those convictions is as follows: From

May 2004 until on or about October 2006, Mr. Lam conspired to falsely identify, mislabel, and fraudulently declare certain imports of frozen fillets of *Pangasius hypophthalmus*, commonly referred to as "Vietnamese catfish" or "basa," in order to evade antidumping duties and to then market them, still falsely labeled. Mr. Lam sold the imported frozen Vietnamese catfish fillets in the United States, mislabeled as other types of fish, for a lower price than would have been necessary if the antidumping duties had been paid. He told purchasers who had specifically ordered Vietnamese catfish, and who questioned the subsequently received boxes of fish labeled as other species, or invoices identifying the fish as other species, that, among other things, the names used were alternative names for what the purchasers had ordered, or that the factory had made an error with the boxes, but the contents of the box were in fact the Vietnamese catfish that the purchasers had ordered. On or about November 17, 2004, Mr. Lam filled an order for 800 cases of "catfish fillet (Basa)" with 800 cases of "conger pike fillet," and then represented to the purchaser that "conger pike fillet" was the scientific name for basa and that the product sold to the purchaser was basa. The documents and labels identified the fish as "common carp," "sole," and "conger pike," though Mr. Lam knew the fish was Vietnamese catfish that had been transported in foreign commerce and imported with intent to sell.

II. Findings and Order: Mr. Lam is debarred for a period of 20 years from importing articles of food or offering such articles for import into the United States.

NOTE: See Chapter 5 in this *Volume* for the *Lam* decision.

Product Importation and Detention

The Food Safety Modernization Act of 2011 (FSMA) has addressed the unique challenges associated with food importation as the United States imports food from over 150 countries. FDA conducts inspections of imported products, can refuse entry of foods into the United States with the ultimate goal of public protection. Even prior to the FSMA, 21 USC section 381, authorized FDA to examine foods, drugs, biologics, dietary supplements, cosmetics and medical devices, and electronic products that emit radiation and are offered for entry into United States. USDA regulates most meat and poultry products.

The Public Health Security and Bioterrorism Preparedness and Response Act (Bioterrorism Act) was enacted on June 12, 2002 to provide greater enforcement authority. Important aspects of the Bioterrorism Act include administrative detention, debarment proceedings, facility registration and record keeping. The Import for Export amendment allows importation of unapproved drug and medical device components, food additives, color additives, and dietary supplements intended for further processing into products and then ultimately exported from the United States.

The following laws and regulations apply to imported products:
- Food Safety Modernization Act (FSMA);
- Public Health Security and Bioterrorism Preparedness and Response Act;
- Federal Food, Drug, and Cosmetic Act;
- Fair Packaging and Labeling Act;
- Nutrition Labeling and Education Act (NLEA);
- Import Milk Act/Filled Milk Act;
- Federal Caustic Poison Act;
- Radiation Control for Health and Safety Act;
- Public Health Service Act, Part F, Subpart 1, Biologic Products;
- Title 21 CFR Subpart E - Imports and Exports 1.83 *et alia.*;
- Title 19 CFR Customs Duties (authority to sample delegated by Custom Regulations); and
- The FDA Export Reform and Enhancement Act of 1996 (PL 104-134 and 104-180) which amended the FDCA by adding Section 801(d)(3) ("Import for Export").

Imported products must meet the same standards as domestic goods. An importer must file an entry notice and bond with the U.S. Customs Service. FDA has agreements with foreign governments called Memorandum of Understanding (MOUs). MOUs specify an agreement by the foreign government that their products are manufactured under sanitary conditions and meet U.S. standards for quality. Imported foods must be pure, wholesome, safe to eat, and produced under sanitary conditions. Drugs and medical devices must be safe and effective. Cosmetics must also be safe and effective and made from approved ingredients. Inspectors look for signs of filth, spoilage or contamination and for mislabeling. Further, all labeling and packaging must be informative and truthful. For example, in examining medical and radiation emitting devices, inspectors examine labeling certifications or declarations. When a product appears to be adulterated or misbranded, the importer is given an opportunity to bring the product into compliance through reconditioning or re-labeling. Drug shipments present unique challenges. Inspectors check packaging for possible tampering and verify labeling.

Certain products that violate regulations cannot be reconditioned and must either be exported or destroyed. These include products that appear to be manufactured, processed or packaged under unsanitary conditions and drugs or devices that have not been produced in accordance with good manufacturing practices. Products or articles that are temporarily detained can be entered into the United States if brought into compliance. However, products can be refused entry or seized if they fail to meet compliance requisites. A product may be detained without physical evidence based on prior problems. The importer has the responsibility to ensure that foreign goods comply with United States regulations. Products that consistently violate regulations or are suspected of health hazards are automatically detained.

Similar to FDA policies and procedures, USDA's Food Safety and Inspection Services is responsible for inspection of meat, poultry, and egg products for safety, wholesomeness and label accuracy. FSIS performs audits of foreign inspection systems to ensure that the foreign entities have equivalent systems. In addition, FSIS re-inspects meat and poultry at the port-of-entry. Before a country is permitted to export a product, foreign countries undergo a rigorous review process. The process involves a document review and on-site audit. Mandatory country of origin labeling and eligibility is required. If a country is found eligible, certain requirements must be fulfilled. For instance, foreign inspection certificates are required for all meat, poultry and egg products. Filing entry forms with the U.S. Customs Service are required. Other documentation for meat and poultry shipments includes the original certificate from the country of origin and an import inspection application and report. The U.S. Customs Service requires the importer to post a bond to cover the value of the shipments along with other fees. All meat and poultry products are re-inspected at a United States port of entry prior to United States entry. Microbial testing such as for listeria and *E.coli 0157:H7* is performed on imported meat and poultry products. Pasteurized egg products are tested for food borne pathogens such as *salmonella*. FSIS conducts audits on a regular basis to ensure that they are equal to the United States system. Suspension of eligibility occurs for a number of reasons including sanitation and unsatisfactory documentation. Permanent withdrawal of eligibility must go through rulemaking procedures to comport with due process.

FDA'S Import Refusal Report (IRR)

https://www.accessdata.fda.gov/scripts/importrefusals/

The Import Refusal Report (IRR), formerly known as the Detention Report, provides a more detailed history from the initial action to the ultimate disposition. FDA, through its District Office issues a "Notice of FDA Action" which details the nature of the violation to the owner or consignee. However, the owner or consignee is entitled to an informal hearing to provide testimony concerning the admissibility of the product. If the owner fails to submit evidence that the product is in compliance or fails to submit a plan to bring the product into compliance, FDA will issue another "Notice of FDA Action" Refusing admission to the product.

The IRR is developed from data collected by FDA's Operational and Administrative System for Import Support (OASIS). Types of reports are by country and by product based on the industry code. Industry codes are the first two characters of FDA's product code. For example, all fishery/seafood products are coded 16. **NOTE: See also *Volume IX: Food Safety Modernization Act* and the *Bioterrorism Act*.**

Chapter 3: Criminal Liability and Corporate Accountability

Criminal Strict Liability

The Food Drug and Cosmetic Act is a public protection statute and provides for strict criminal liability. Therefore, corporate officials could be held criminally liable even if they had no knowledge or notice of the wrongdoing. The decision of *Dotterweich* concerned misbranded and adulterated drugs. The Supreme Court held that responsible corporate officials definitely could be prosecuted for violations and that strict liability applies under the Food Drug and Cosmetic Act. This means that the Court dispensed with a *mens rea* requirement or criminal intent usually requisite to sustain a criminal conviction. The jury, at the trial court level, found Mr. Dotterwiech, president and general manager, guilty of shipping misbranded drugs in interstate commerce and for shipping an adulterated drug. The Court of Appeals reversed the conviction and concluded that only the corporation was the 'person' subject to prosecution. Then, the United States Supreme Court reversed the Court of Appeals judgment and reinstated the conviction of the individual.

United States v. Park is another landmark decision that involved criminal liability of corporate officials. The United States Supreme Court affirmed the imposition of criminal sanctions against a corporate official. That is, corporate officials can be held criminally accountable for failure to exercise authority and responsibility. The Court determined that a corporate official has a duty to remedy violations and implement measures so that violations do not repeatedly occur. In this case, the president of a national food chain was held criminally liable for violations of the FDCA.

Today, courts continue to rely on *Park* and *Dotterweich* for authority to impose criminal sanctions on high-level corporate officials. For example, the former chief executive officer of Inter-Mune, Inc., W. Scott Harkonen, M.D., was convicted of wire fraud and was sentenced in 2011 to a three-year term of probation, with six months of home confinement concerning the dissemination of false and misleading statements about clinical trial results of InterMune's drug Actimmune. Additionally, Dr. Harkonen was ordered to pay a $20,000 fine and to perform 200 hours of community service. His conviction was based on the false and misleading information about the efficacy of Actimmune (Interferon gamma-1b) as a treatment for idiopathic pulmonary fibrosis (IPF), a fatal disease. On appeal, Dr. Harkonen's conviction was affirmed. (*United States v. Harkonen*, 9th Cir., No. 11-10209, 3/4/13). The United States Supreme Court declined to hear the case (Cert. denied Dec. 16, 2013). However, in 2018, another petition was filed *Harkonen v. United States*, U.S., No. 18-417 (Oct. 1, 2018). Interestingly, the majority of Actimmune sales were for the unapproved, off-label use of treating IPF. Yearly costs of IPF per patient were approximately $50,000. Back in 2006, InterMune agreed to enter into a deferred prosecution agreement and to pay nearly $37 million to resolve criminal charges and civil liability in connection with the illegal promotion and marketing of its drug Actimmune and entered into a five-year Corporate Integrity Agreement. *http://www.justice.gov/opa/pr/2011/April/11-civ-475.html*

The *Purdue* case provides another illustration of corporate accountability. *Purdue* involved a $600,000.00 settlement of civil and criminal charges of top executives who entered guilty pleas even though there was no evidence that the executives had knowledge of the marketing and promotional conduct. In *United States v. Norian-Synthes,* executives were sentenced to terms of imprisonment based on criminal strict liability due to the use of unapproved bone cement. The *Jensen Farms* and *Peanut Corporation of America* 2014 convictions of the executives both illustrate continued criminal enforcement. Most recently, *Quality Egg* two corporate executives each received three-month prison sentences.

"A *Park* Prosecution" and FDA Considerations

FDA revised its Regulatory Procedures Manual (RPM) 1 to include nonbinding "considerations" that FDA uses to determine whether to recommend to the Department of Justice (DOJ) to prosecute misdemeanors under the *Park* Doctrine. The *Park* doctrine means that a responsible corporate official can be charged under the FDCA even though there is no proof that the individual acted with intent or negligence or that the corporate official had knowledge of the prohibited acts. The Justice Department issued a memo in 2015 related to Individual Accountability for Corporate Wrongdoing. The memo has been referred to as the Yates memo because it was written by Deputy Attorney General Yates. See link below.

https://www.justice.gov/dag/file/769036/download

The following FDA considerations are set forth in the RPM:

- ✓ Individual's position in the company;
- ✓ Relationship to the violation;
- ✓ Whether the corporate official had authority to correct or prevent the violation;
- ✓ Whether the violation involves actual or potential harm to the public;
- ✓ Whether the violation is obvious;
- ✓ Whether the violation reflects a pattern of ignoring prior warnings;
- ✓ Whether the violation reflects a pattern of illegal behavior;
- ✓ Whether the violation is serious;
- ✓ Whether the violation is widespread;
- ✓ Whether the proposed prosecution is a prudent use of agency resources; and the
- ✓ Quality of the legal and factual support for the prosecution.

http://www.fda.gov/ICECI/ComplianceManuals/RegulatoryProceduresManual/ucm176738.htm#SUB6-5-

CRITICAL ANALYSIS: Analyze individual executive responsibility and potential criminal and or civil liability. Integrate due diligence and the "impossibility" defense in your analysis. How would you advise your client?

United States v. Dotterweich,
320 U.S. 277, 64 S.Ct. 134, 88 L.Ed. 48 (1943)

Mr. Justice FRANKFURTER delivered the opinion of the Court. This was a prosecution begun by two informations, consolidated for trial, charging Buffalo Pharmacal Company, Inc., and Dotterweich, its president and general manager, with violations of the Act of Congress of June 25, 1938, c. 675, 52 Stat. 1040, 21 U.S.C. §§ 301-392, 21 U.S.C.A. §§ 301- 392, known as the Federal Food, Drug, and Cosmetic Act. The Company, a jobber in drugs, purchased them from their manufacturers and shipped them, repacked under its own label, in interstate commerce. (No question is raised in this case regarding the implications that may properly arise when, although the manufacturer gives the jobber a guaranty, the latter through his own label makes representations.) The informations were based on § 301 of that Act, 21 U.S.C. § 331, 21 U.S.C.A. § 331, paragraph (a) of which prohibits 'The introduction or delivery for introduction into interstate commerce of any *** drug *** that is adulterated or misbranded'. 'Any person' violating this provision is, by paragraph (a) of §303, 21 U.S.C. § 333, 21 U.S.C.A. § 333, made 'guilty of a misdemeanor'.

The jury disagreed as to the corporation and found Dotterweich guilty on all three counts. The Circuit Court of Appeals, reversed the conviction on the ground that only the corporation was the 'person' subject to prosecution. *** The statute (§303) makes 'any person' who violates § 301(a) guilty of a 'misdemeanor'. It specifically defines 'person' to include 'corporation'. § 201(e). But the only way in which a corporation can act is through the individuals who act on its behalf. *New York Central & H.R.R.R Co. v. United States*, 212 U.S. 481, 29 S.Ct. 304, 53 L.Ed. 613. And the historic conception of a 'misdemeanor' makes all those responsible for it equally guilty, *United States v. Mills*, 7 Pet. 138, 141, 8 L.Ed. 636, a doctrine given general application in §332 of the Penal Code, 18 U.S.C. § 550, 18 U.S.C.A. § 550. If, then, Dotterweich is not subject to the Act, it must be solely on the ground that individuals are immune when the 'person' who violates § 301(a) is a corporation, although from the point of view of action the individuals are the corporation. As a matter of legal development, it has taken time to establish criminal liability also for a corporation and not merely for its agents.

Section 12 of the Food and Drugs Act of 1906, 21 U.S.C. § 4, provided that, 'the act, omission, or failure of any officer, agent, or other person acting for or employed by any corporation, company, society, or association, within the scope of his employment or office, shall in every case be also deemed to be the act, omission, or failure of such corporation, company, society, or association as well as that of the person.' By 1938, legal understanding and practice had rendered such statement of the obvious superfluous. To hold that the Act of 1938 freed all individuals, except when proprietors, from the culpability under which the earlier legislation had placed them is to defeat the very object of the new Act. Nothing is clearer than that the later legislation was designed to enlarge and stiffen the penal net and not to narrow and loosen it. This purpose was unequivocally avowed by the two committees which reported the bills to the Congress. The House Committee reported that the Act 'seeks to set up effective provisions against abuses of consumer welfare growing out of inadequacies in the Food and Drugs Act of June 30, 1906'. ***

If a guaranty immunizes shipments of course it immunizes all involved in the shipment. But simply because if there had been a guaranty it would have been received by the proprietor, whether corporate or individual, as a safe-guard for the enterprise, the want of a guaranty does not cut down the scope of responsibility of all who are concerned with transactions forbidden by §301. *** To read the guaranty section, as did the court below, so as to restrict liability for penalties to the only person who normally would receive a guaranty—the proprietor—disregards the admonition that 'the meaning of a sentence is to be felt rather than to be proved'. *United States v. Johnson*, 221 U.S. 488, 496, 31 S.Ct. 627, 55 L.Ed. 823. It also reads an exception to an important provision safeguarding the public welfare with a liberality, which more appropriately belongs to enforcement of the central purpose of the Act. ***

For present purpose it suffices to say that in what the defense characterized as 'a very fair charge' the District Court properly left the question of the responsibility of Dotterweich for the shipment to the jury, and there was sufficient evidence to support its verdict. *** Judgment reversed. [Ct. of Appeals Judgment reversed and conviction reinstated].

CRITICAL ANALYSIS: Why did the Supreme Court reverse and reinstate the verdict. Include a discussion of "person" and corporate accountability.

United States v. Park,
95 S.Ct. 1903 (1975)

Mr. Chief Justice BURGER delivered the opinion of the Court. We granted certiorari to consider whether the jury instructions in the prosecution of a corporate officer under § 301(k) of the Federal Food, Drug, and Cosmetic Act, 52 Stat. 1042, as amended, 21 U.S.C. § 331(k), were appropriate under *United States v. Dotterweich*, 320 U.S. 277, 64 S.Ct. 134, 88 L.Ed. 48 (1943).

Acme Markets, Inc. is a national retail food chain with approximately 36,000 employees, 874 retail outlets, 12 general warehouses, and four special warehouses. Its headquarters, including the office of the president, respondent Park, who is chief executive officer of the corporation, are located in Philadelphia, Pa. In a five-count information filed in the United States District Court for the District of Maryland, the Government charged Acme and respondent with violations of the Federal Food, Drug and Cosmetic Act. Each count of the information alleged that the defendants had received food that had been shipped in interstate commerce and that, while the food was being held for sale in Acme's Baltimore warehouse following shipment in interstate commerce, they caused it to be held in a building accessible to rodents and to be exposed to contamination by rodents. These acts were alleged to have resulted in the food's being adulterated within the meaning of 21 U.S.C. §§ 342(a)(3) and (4), in violation of 21 U.S.C. § 331(k).   ***

Acme pleaded guilty to each count of the information. Respondent pleaded not guilty. The evidence at trial demonstrated that in April 1970 the Food and Drug Administration (FDA) advised respondent by letter of insanitary conditions in Acme's Philadelphia warehouse. In 1971, the FDA found that similar conditions existed in the firm's Baltimore warehouse. An FDA consumer safety officer testified concerning evidence of rodent infestation and other insanitary conditions discovered during a 12-day inspection of the Baltimore warehouse in November and December 1971. He also related that a second inspection of the warehouse had been conducted in March 1972. On that occasion, the inspectors found that there had been improvement in the sanitary conditions, but that 'there was still evidence of rodent activity in the building and in the warehouses and we found some rodent-contaminated lots of food items.'

The Government also presented testimony by the Chief of Compliance of the FDA's Baltimore office, who informed respondent by letter of the conditions at the Baltimore warehouse after the first inspection. There was testimony by Acme's Baltimore division vice president, who had responded to the letter on behalf of Acme and respondent and who described the steps taken to remedy the insanitary conditions discovered by both inspections. The Government's final witness, Acme's vice president for legal affairs and assistant secretary, identified respondent as the president and chief executive officer of the company and read a bylaw prescribing the duties of the chief executive officer. He testified that respondent functioned by delegating 'normal operating duties,' including sanitation, but that he retained 'certain things, which are the big, broad, principles of the operation of the company,' and had 'the responsibility of seeing that they all work together.' *** At the close of the Government's case in chief, respondent moved for a judgment of acquittal on the ground that 'the evidence in chief has shown that Mr. Park is not personally concerned in this Food and Drug violation. The trial judge denied the motion, stating that *United States v. Dotterweich*, 320 U.S. 277, 64 S.Ct. 134, 88 L.Ed. 48 (1943), was controlling. He testified that, although all of Acme's employees were in a sense under his general direction, the company had an 'organizational structure for responsibilities for certain functions' according to which different phases of its operation were 'assigned to individuals who, in turn, have staff and departments under them.' He identified those individuals responsible for sanitation, and related that upon receipt of the January 1972 FDA letter, he had conferred with the vice president for legal affairs, who informed him that the Baltimore division vice president 'was investigating the situation immediately and would be taking corrective action and would be preparing a summary of the corrective action to reply to the letter.' *** On cross-examination, respondent conceded that providing sanitary conditions for food offered for sale to the public was something that he was 'responsible for in the entire operation of the company,' and he stated that it was one of many phases of the company that he assigned to 'dependable subordinates.' *** The rule that corporate employees who have 'a responsible share in the furtherance of the transaction which the statute outlaws' are subject to the criminal provisions of the Act was not formulated in a vacuum. *Cf. Morissette v. United States*, 342 U.S. 246, 258, 72 S.Ct. 240, 96 L.Ed. 288 (1952). Cases under the Federal Food and Drugs Act of 1906 reflected the view both that knowledge or intent were not required to be proved in prosecutions under its criminal provisions, and that responsible corporate agents could be subjected to the liability thereby imposed. *See, e.g., United States v. Mayfield*, 177 F. 765 (ND Ala.1910). Moreover, the principle had been recognized that a corporate agent, through whose act, default, or omission the corporation committed a crime, was himself guilty individually of that crime. The principle had been applied whether or not the crime required 'consciousness of wrongdoing,' and it had been applied not only to those corporate agents who themselves committed the criminal act, but also to those who by virtue of their managerial positions or other similar relation to the actor could be deemed responsible for its commission. In the latter class of cases, the liability of managerial officers did not depend on their knowledge of, or personal participation in, the act made criminal by the statute. *** The requirements of foresight and vigilance imposed on responsible corporate agents are beyond question demanding, and perhaps onerous, but they are no more stringent than the public has a right to expect of those who voluntarily assume positions of authority in business enterprises whose services and products affect the health and well-being of the public that supports them. *** The Act does not, as we observed in Dotterweich, make criminal liability turn on 'awareness of some wrongdoing' or 'conscious fraud.' The duty imposed by Congress on responsible corporate agents is, we emphasize, one that requires the highest standard of foresight and vigilance, but the Act, in its criminal aspect, does not require that which is objectively impossible. The theory upon which responsible corporate agents are held criminally accountable for 'causing' violations of the Act permits a claim that a defendant was 'powerless' to prevent or correct the violation to 'be raised defensively at a trial on the merits.' *United States v. Wiesenfeld Warehouse Co.*, 376 U.S. 86, 91, 84 S.Ct. 559, 563, 11 L.Ed.2d 536 (1964). *** Congress has seen fit to enforce the accountability of responsible corporate agents dealing with products which may affect the health of consumers by penal sanctions cast in rigorous terms, and the obligation of the courts is to give them effect so long as they do not violate the Constitution. *** Our conclusion that the Court of Appeals erred in its reading of the jury charge suggests as well our disagreement with that court concerning the admissibility of evidence demonstrating that respondent was advised by the FDA in 1970 of insanitary conditions in Acme's Philadelphia warehouse. [T]he Act imposes the highest standard of care and permits conviction of responsible corporate officials who, in light of this standard of care, have the power to prevent or correct violations of its provisions. ***

Section 402 of the Act, 21 U.S.C. § 342, provides in pertinent part:
A food shall be deemed to be adulterated—

(a) . . . (3) if it consists in whole or in part of any filthy, putrid, or decomposed substance, or if it is otherwise unfit for food; or (4) if it has been prepared, packed, or held under insanitary conditions whereby it may have become contaminated with filth, or whereby it may have been rendered injurious to health . . .

Section 301 of the Act, 21 U.S.C. § 331, provides in pertinent part: 'The following acts and the causing thereof are prohibited:

(k) The alteration, mutilation, destruction, obliteration, or removal of the whole or any part of the labeling of, or the doing of any other act with respect to, a food, drug, device, or cosmetic, if such act is done while such article is held for sale (whether or not the first sale) after shipment in interstate commerce and results in such article being adulterated or misbranded.

Sections 303(a) and (b) of the Act, 21 U.S.C. §333(a) and (b), provide:
(a) Any person who violates a provision of section 331 of this title shall be imprisoned for not more than one year or fined not more than $1,000, or both.

(b) Notwithstanding the provisions of subsection (a) of this section, if any person commits such a violation after a conviction of him under this section has become final, or commits such a violation with the intent to defraud or mislead, such person shall be imprisoned for not more than three years or fined not more than $10,000, or both.

CRITICAL ANALYSIS: Why did United States Supreme Court affirm the imposition of criminal sanctions against a corporate official in *Park*. Analyze individual executive responsibility and potential criminal and or civil liability. Integrate due diligence and the "impossibility" defense in your analysis.

United States v. Norian Corp. [*Synthes*],
No. 09-cr-403 (E.D. Pa. July 20, 2009)

In *United States v. Norian Corp.* [*Synthes*], the Department of Justice issued a 52-felony count indictment against Synthes, Inc. and its Norian company subsidiary and the corporate executives because of failure to disclose to any of the patients that they were participating in experimental surgery. Synthes executives were charged with a misdemeanor related to the labeling of Norian XR. Further, the indictment alleged that the company executives made false statements to FDA about whether they tested the product for unapproved uses. FDA approved Norian XR as filler for bony voids or defects in some parts of the body; however, it was not approved for use in the spine and FDA required clinical testing prior to spine use. According to the indictment, clinical trials were not conducted. Further, the indictment detailed that Synthes convinced surgeons to test Norian XR in patients with spinal fractures.

Synthes and its Norian company subsidiary entered a plea of guilty. They agreed to pay a fine, which totaled $23.2 million dollars and agreed to enter into what is termed a corporate integrity agreement. Synthes pled guilty to shipping a mislabeled product, a misdemeanor. Norian pled guilty to conspiracy to impede federal safety standards, which is a felony. Thereafter, the former Synthes executives were then sentenced.

The Synthes executives were sentenced in late 2011 to terms of imprisonment and $100,000 fines for their roles in the medical-device maker's promotion of a bone cement for unauthorized uses. The officers were indicted back in June 2009 over claims they conspired to conduct unapproved clinical trials of Norian-branded cements from May 2002 to late 2004. The cement was used in the spines of 200 patients with fractured vertebrae and three patients died. Each defendant pled guilty to misdemeanor counts of violating the FDCA known as the "Park" or Corporate Officer doctrine. U.S. District Court Judge Legrome Davis sentenced Michael D. Huggins, former chief operating officer of Synthes and Thomas B. Higgins, former president of the Synthes spine division, to nine months in federal prison. John Walsh, head of regulatory affairs, received a five-month term of imprisonment. The fourth executive, Huggins challenged his eight-month sentence of imprisonment. His sentence was upheld. See: *United States v. Huggins.* Criminal Action No. 09–403–3 (Dec. 13, 2011).

CRITICAL ANALYSIS: How *is Synthes* the same and how is *Synthes* different from *Park* and *Dotterweich*?

Purdue Pharma Company

In 2017 and continuing, the United States Department of Justice (DOJ) has again investigated Purdue Pharma for improper marketing. However, back in 2007, Purdue Frederick Company (Purdue Pharma) pled guilty to felony charges and three Purdue officials pled guilty to strict liability misdemeanor charges as "responsible corporate officers". Purdue agreed to settle allegations by FDA's Office of Criminal Investigations and the DOJ of improper marketing in terms of sales and promotion of its pain reliever product OxyContin. The improper marketing concerned superiority claims that the product was less addictive and less subject to abuse than other pain medications. The defendants agreed to pay $634,515,475. Of this amount, the individuals agreed to pay over $34 million. Purdue agreed to pay $600 million, forfeiture of over $276 million as well as a criminal fine of $500,000. In the 2007 sentencing, Judge Jones imposed the sentences agreed upon; however, there was no order of restitution nor incarceration.

United States v. Purdue Frederick Co., Inc.,
495 F. Supp.2d 569 (W. D. Va. 2007)

Opinion and Order James P. Jones Chief United States District Judge. The Purdue Frederick Company, Inc. ("Purdue") has pleaded guilty to misbranding OxyContin, a prescription opioid pain medication, with the intent to defraud or mislead, a felony under the federal Food, Drug, and Cosmetic Act. 21 U.S.C.A. §§ 331(a), 333(a)(2) (West 1999). The individual defendants, Michael Friedman, [former President and CEO] Howard R. Udell, [executive vice president and chief legal officer] and Paul D. Goldenheim, [former chief scientific officer] have pleaded guilty to the misdemeanor charge of misbranding, solely as responsible corporate officers. 21 U.S.C.A. § 333(a)(1) (West 1999); *see United States v. Park,* 421 U.S. 658, 676, 95 S. Ct. 1903, 44 L. Ed. 2d 489 (1975). The individual defendants are not charged with personal knowledge of the misbranding or with any personal intent to defraud. *** Beginning on or about December 12, 1995, and continuing until on or about June 30, 2001, certain PURDUE supervisors and employees, with the intent to defraud or mislead, marketed and promoted OxyContin as less addictive, less subject to abuse and diversion, and less likely to cause tolerance and withdrawal than other pain medications as follows:

a. Trained PURDUE sales representatives told some health care providers that it was more difficult to extract the oxycodone from an OxyContin tablet for the purpose of intravenous abuse, although PURDUE's own study showed that a drug abuser could extract approximately 68% of the oxycodone from a single 10mg OxyContin tablet by crushing the tablet, stirring it in water, and drawing the solution through cotton into a syringe;

b. Told PURDUE sales representatives they could tell health care providers that OxyContin potentially creates less chance for addiction than immediate-release opioids;

c. Sponsored training that taught PURDUE sales supervisors that OxyContin had fewer "peak and trough" blood level effects than immediate-release opioids resulting in less euphoria and less potential for abuse than short-acting opioids;

d. Told certain health care providers that patients could stop therapy abruptly without experiencing withdrawal symptoms and that patients who took OxyContin would not develop tolerance to the drug; and

e. Told certain health care providers that OxyContin did not cause a "buzz" or euphoria, caused less euphoria, had less addiction potential, had less abuse potential, was less likely to be diverted than immediate-release opioids, and could be used to "weed out" addicts and drug seekers.

Purdue has agreed that these facts are true, and the individual defendants, while they do not agree that they had knowledge of these things, have agreed that the court may accept these facts in support of their guilty pleas. *** Under the law, Purdue is subject to a penalty of five years of probation and a fine of up to $500,000. In its plea agreement, Purdue has agreed to substantial additional monetary sanctions totaling $600 million, reported to be one of the largest in the history of the pharmaceutical industry. The amount includes the following:

1. $100,615,797.25 payable to federal government health care agencies under a Civil Settlement Agreement;

2. $59,384,202.75 in escrow for those states that elect to settle their claims against Purdue. These civil settlements to the federal and state government total $ 160 million, of which the federal government is receiving sixty percent;

3. $3,471,220.68 to Medicaid programs for improperly calculated rebates;

4. $500,000 fine to the United States;

5. $20 million in trust to the Commonwealth of Virginia for operating the Virginia Prescription Monitoring Program;

6. $5.3 million to the Virginia Medicaid Fraud Control Unit's Program Income Fund;

7. $276.1 million forfeiture to the United States;

8. $130 million to settle private civil claims related to OxyContin; and

9. $4,628,779.32 to be expended by Purdue for monitoring costs in connection with a Corporate Integrity Agreement with the U.S. Department of Health and Human Services.

The individual defendants are subject to a punishment of twelve months imprisonment and a fine of up to $100,000. In their plea agreements, they have agreed to pay a total of $34.5 million to the Virginia Medicaid Fraud Unit's Program Income Fund. In return, the government has agreed to sentences for them without any imprisonment.

There have been several reasons suggested why the court should reject the plea agreements. Lack of Restitution. *

Purdue agrees to pay at least $130 million to settle private claims, but no maximum limit is imposed. I do not find that the plea agreements are inherently unfair in this regard. Accordingly, in spite of the arguments by putative victims, I agree that the restitution process would unduly complicate and prolong the sentencing process. In order to prove causation, litigation over many months, if not years, would be required before final judgment in this case could be entered. Such delay would be contrary to the basic principles of our criminal justice system. I would have preferred that the plea agreements had allocated some amount of the money for the education of those at risk from the improper use of prescription drugs, and the treatment of those who have succumbed to such use. *** On the other hand, I am forbidden by law to participate in plea discussions, Fed. R. Crim. P. 11(c)(1), and I will not reject these agreements simply because they do not contain provisions that I would have preferred. ***

Political Interference. *** I have had long experience with the United States Attorney for this district, and I am convinced that neither he nor the career prosecutors who handled this case would have permitted any political interference. ***

Lack of Incarceration. The plea agreements provide for no incarceration for the individual defendants. The government points out that a sentence of incarceration under the federal sentencing guidelines would be unusual based on the facts of the case. The government is also convinced that the nature of the convictions of the individual defendants—based on strict liability for misbranding—will send a strong deterrent message to the pharmaceutical industry. *** However, while the question is a close one, I find that in the absence of government proof of knowledge by the individual defendants of the wrongdoing, prison sentences are not appropriate.

Summary. In summary, I find that the plea agreements are supported by the facts and the law and impose adequate punishment on the defendants and I accept them. ***

NOTE: The Office of Inspector General (OIG) in the Department of Health and Human Services (HHS) excluded the three former Purdue executives in 2007 from federal healthcare programs due to their convictions for misbranding under FDCA responsible corporate officer (RCO) doctrine. Originally, the individuals were excluded for 20 years and through administrative appeals the exclusion was reduced to 12 years. In 2012, in *Friedman v. Sebelius*, (11-5028) the Court of Appeals upheld their exclusions; however, the Court of Appeals remanded the case back to the district court concerning the length of the exclusion because there was no explanation as to the length imposed. That is, HHS failed to explain why the penalty was much longer (three times) than comparable cases and longer than the presumptive baseline in the statute (four times).

CRITICAL ANALYSIS: This case has resurfaced due to the opioid epidemic. Were the plea agreements supported by the facts and law as the court determined? Include a discussion of whether the defendants should have received a sentence of incarceration.

Corporate Liability Pharmaceuticals Forest Laboratories

Forest Pharmaceuticals, Inc., a wholly owned subsidiary of Forest Laboratories, Inc., entered into a guilty plea in 2010. The sentencing occurred in 2011 for the following criminal offenses: (1) distributing a misbranded drug (Celexa); (2) distributing Levothroid, an unapproved new drug and (3) felony obstruction of an agency proceeding, that is, an FDA inspection relating to Levothroid. Additionally, Forest Pharmaceuticals and its corporate parent settled civil False Claims Act allegations related to improper drug marketing and distribution. Forest paid $313 million to resolve the criminal and civil cases. *http://www.justice.gov/opa/pr/2011/March/11-civ-270.html*

Executive and Manager Liability Pharmaceuticals
Valeant-Philidor Rx and Pharmacia

Valeant-Philidor Rx—Former Valeant Pharmaceuticals International Inc. executive Gary Tanner and Andrew Davenport, the ex-CEO of mail-order pharmacy Philidor Rx Services LLC, each received sentences of one year and a day in prison for planning a $9.7 million kickback strategy linked to a possible acquisition transaction. The convictions included honest services wire fraud and conspiracy to commit money laundering. Both defendants were ordered to forfeit approximately $9.7 million.

Pharmacia & Upjohn Company, Inc.—A regional sales manager, Mary Holloway was sentenced to pay a $75,000 fine and twenty-four months of probation after she pled guilty to a Criminal Information that charged her with distribution of a misbranded drug Bextra for promoting uses and dosages unapproved by the FDA. According to the charging documents, Holloway trained and encouraged her sales teams to promote Bextra by obtaining protocols from doctors that instructed that Bextra be used for the pain of surgery, an unapproved use, and at 20 mgs, an unapproved dose. Holloway also instructed her staff to market Bextra for use before, during and after surgery to reduce the risk of deep vein thrombosis, which is a form of life threatening blood clots, even though she knew there were no studies showing that Bextra was safe and effective for this use. The charges detailed that Holloway encouraged her staff to make false safety claims about Bextra for sales purposes. (March 30, 2009 edited).

https://wayback.archive-it.org/7993/20170406213409/https://www.fda.gov/ICECI/CriminalInvestigations/ucm261211.htm

NOTE: Bextra was withdrawn from the market in 2005. The proposal (Jan. 20, 2010) to disbar Holloway was revoked. See (83 FR 23469 (May 21, 2018)). *https://www.federalregister.gov/documents/2018/05/21/2018-10685/mary-c-holloway-order-revoking-a-proposed-order-of-debarment*

CRITICAL ANALYSIS I: Discuss whether the corporate officers in Forrest Laboratories should have been prosecuted. Incorporate the individual executive and management liability in Valeant, Philidor Rx and Bextra.

CRITICAL ANALYSIS II: Discuss whether the corporate executives in Valeant and Philidor Rx Services should have received longer sentences.

Corporate Executive Liability Food Safety—Peanut Corp., Jensen, and Quality Egg
Peanut Corporation of America—Felony Convictions

http://www.justice.gov/opa/pr/peanut-corporation-america-former-officials-and-broker-convicted-criminal-charges-related

http://www.justice.gov/opa/pr/former-peanut-company-president-receives-largest-criminal-sentence-food-safety-case-two

Former Peanut Corporation of America (PCA) President and Owner Stewart Parnell received a criminal prison sentence of 28 years in connection with the 2009 salmonella poisoning outbreak of 700 reported cases in 46 states. See: *United States v. Parnell*, et al, No. 15-14400 (11th Cir. Jan. 23, 2018 (affirmed)). There were nine deaths linked to PCAs tainted products. Parnell's brother Michael received a 20-year prison sentence. The Quality Assurance employee received a five-year sentence. They were sentenced based on their roles at PCA by shipping salmonella-positive peanut products and by falsifying microbiological test results. A federal jury convicted the Parnell brothers in September 2014 on several counts of conspiracy, mail and wire fraud as well as selling misbranded food. Stewart Parnell was also convicted for introducing adulterated food into interstate commerce. Stewart Parnell and Quality Assurance Manager Mary Wilkerson were also convicted of obstruction of justice. Other former PCA employees previously pled guilty to multiple charges. The prosecutors alleged that PCA defrauded customers as well as defrauded several national food companies by failing to inform them about the presence of food-borne pathogens in laboratory tests, including salmonella. According to prosecutors, in some instances, despite these results, PCA officials totally falsified lab results, maintaining peanut products were safe for consumption. Further, at times, PCA failed to even perform testing.

For years corporate executives have been charged with misdemeanor offenses under the strict criminal liability theory known as the *Park* doctrine, this case is distinguishable. The PCA prosecution represents a felony prosecution under the Federal Food, Drug and Cosmetic Act.

NOTE: Judgment Affirmed (No. 15-14400,11th Cir. January 23, 2018).

PCA filed for Chapter 7 bankruptcy protection weeks after the outbreak began.

CRTICAL ANALYSIS: How is this case different from the misdemeanor cases below?

Jensen Farms and Executive Criminal Liability—Misdemeanor Convictions
United States v. Jensen et al., Docket No. 1:13-mj-01138 (D. Colo. Jan. 2014)

The owners of Jensen Farms, Eric and Ryan Jensen, were sentenced in 2014 because their Colorado based cantaloupe farm, was linked to a deadly Listeria outbreak in 2011. There were 30 deaths associated with the listeria outbreak and also sickened 147 people. Each owner was charged with introducing an adulterated food in interstate commerce under 21 U.S.C. secs. 331 (a), 333 (a) (1) and aiding and abetting under 18 U.S.C. sec. 2. Each owner was sentenced to a five-year term of probation, six months home detention, and $150,000 each in restitution fees to victims. The Jensens could have received a maximum of six years in jail and $1.5 million each in fines on six counts of introducing contaminated food into interstate commerce. The Jensens filed a lawsuit against food safety auditor Primus Labs, which gave the farm's processing facilities a safety rating of 96% shortly prior to when the outbreak occurred.

CRITICAL ANALYSIS: Postulate why the Jensens did not receive a jail sentence.

Quality Egg and Executive Criminal Liability—Misdemeanor Convictions

In *United States v. Quality Egg, LLC* there were 2,000 cases of a *Salmonella* poisoning outbreak. The company fine amounted to $6.79 million and $7.8 million in compensation for damages caused by the contaminated eggs shipment. The two former executives, Jack DeCoster and Peter DeCoster, who pled guilty, received prison sentences (three months each) and a $100,000 criminal fine, restitution and probation. Court deemed prison sentences appropriate due to company's prior problems of disregard for food safety standards and practices, bribery of a government inspector and disregarded high positive *Salmonella* test results. This case is an illustration of a "Park" prosecution. The DeCosters appeal centered on the allegation of "cruel and unusual punishment". The 8th Circuit Court of Appeals affirmed the three-month term of imprisonment.

United States v. Austin DeCoster and United States v. Peter DeCoster, Nat'l Assn. of Manufacturers; Cato Institute; Washington Legal Foundation, Amici on Behalf of Appellant(s) No. 15-1890, No. 15-1891 (July 6, 2016)

Austin "Jack" DeCoster and Peter DeCoster both pled guilty, as "responsible corporate officers" of Quality Egg, LLC, to misdemeanor violations of 21 U.S.C. § 331(a) for introducing eggs that had been adulterated with salmonella enteritidis into interstate commerce. The district court sentenced Jack and Peter to three months imprisonment. The DeCosters appeal, arguing that their prison sentences and 21 U.S.C. § 333(a)(1) are unconstitutional, and claiming in the alternative that their prison sentences were procedurally and substantively unreasonable. We affirm.

Jack DeCoster owned Quality Egg, LLC, an Iowa egg production company. Jack's son Peter DeCoster served as the company's chief operating officer. *** Other than conducting the single egg test in April 2009, Quality Egg did not test or divert eggs from the market before July 2010 despite receiving multiple positive environmental and hen test results. *** The FDA inspected the Quality Egg operations in Iowa from August 12–30, 2010. Investigators discovered live and dead rodents and frogs in the laying areas, feed areas, conveyer belts, and outside the buildings. They also found holes in the walls and baseboards of the feed and laying buildings. The investigators discovered that some rodent traps were broken, and others had dead rodents in them. In one building near the laying hens, manure was found piled to the rafters; it had pushed a screen out of the door which allowed rodents into the building. Investigators also observed employees not wearing or changing protective clothing and not cleaning or sanitizing equipment. The FDA concluded that Quality Egg had failed to comply with its written plans for biosecurity and salmonella prevention. *** The investigation revealed that Quality Egg previously had falsified records about food safety measures and had lied to auditors for several years about pest control measures and sanitation practices. ***

The elimination of a *mens rea* requirement does not violate the Due Process Clause for a public welfare offense where the penalty is "relatively small," the conviction does not gravely damage the defendant's reputation, and congressional intent supports the imposition of the penalty. The three-month prison sentences the DeCosters received were relatively short. *** Moreover, the DeCosters' three month prison sentences fell at the low end of the prescribed statutory range of 21 U.S.C. § 333(a) (one year maximum), and we have "never held a sentence within the statutory range to violate the Eighth Amendment," *United States v. Vanhorn* 740 F.3d 1166, 1170 (8th Cir. 2014). We decline to do so here as well. We conclude that the district court's sentences in this case do not violate the Eighth Amendment.

CRITICAL ANALYSIS: *DeCoster (Quality Egg), Jensen Farms, Peanut Corporation of America* serve as a warning and wake up call to the food industry in terms of executive liability. Assess the best practices for a company to adhere to. Include an analysis of why in *DeCoster* the sentences did not violate the 8th Amendment.

NOTE: Interestingly, in the ConAgra case, company executives were not charged. The ConAgra company agreed in 2015 to pay $11.2 million to settle federal charges from a 2007 salmonella

outbreak due to the tainted peanut butter produced in a plant in Georgia. Over 600 people in 47 states became ill which triggered a massive recall. The misdemeanor charge against the Omaha, Nebraska, based company was due to shipping adulterated food. The company agreed to pay $8 million in criminal fines, as well as an additional $3.2 million in forfeitures to the federal government.

CRITICAL ANALYSIS: Discuss whether the ConAgra executives should have been charged.

Bogus Sleep Studies

https://www.fda.gov/ICECI/CriminalInvestigations/ucm598957.htm

U.S. Department of Justice Press Release (edited)

Doctors Omidi and Zarrabi were arrested on federal fraud charges stemming from more than $250 million in allegedly fraudulent bills related to the 1-800-GET-THIN Lap-Band surgery business. (February 28, 2018). Two corporations controlled, in part, by Omidi – Surgery Center Management, LLC (SCM), and Independent Medical Services, Inc. (IMS) – are also named in the 37-count superseding indictment. The indictment contains charges of mail fraud, wire fraud, false statements, money laundering and aggravated identity theft.

The purpose of the sleep studies was to find a second reason – a "co-morbidity," such as sleep apnea – that GET THIN would use to convince the patient's insurance company to pre-approve the Lap-Band procedure. After patients underwent sleep studies – often with little indication that any doctor had ever determined the study was medically necessary – GET THIN employees, acting at Omidi's direction, allegedly often falsified the results to reflect that the patient had moderate or severe sleep apnea, and that they suffered from severe daytime sleepiness. Omidi then caused those falsified sleep study reports to be used in support of GET THIN's pre-authorization requests for Lap-Band surgery. Relying on the false sleep studies – as well as other false information, including patients' heights and weights – insurance companies authorized payment for some of the proposed Lap-Band surgeries. The indictment alleges that GET THIN received at least $38 million for the Lap-Band procedures. Even if the insurance company did not authorize the surgery, GET THIN still was able to submit bills for approximately $15,000 for each sleep study, receiving millions of dollars in payments for these claims, according to the indictment. The insurance payments were deposited into bank accounts associated with the GET THIN entities.

Zarrabi allowed his electronic signature to be used by GET THIN to make it falsely appear that he had reviewed and interpreted the falsified sleep studies, even though he knew the reports were being altered, according to the indictment. Zarrabi also allegedly demanded to be paid for the use of his electronic signature on hundreds of prescriptions for devices to treat sleep apnea. Zarrabi allegedly did not review the prescriptions, which were sent with the falsified sleep study reports to durable medical equipment providers that billed for sleep apnea equipment that patients often did not need. ***

CRITICAL ANALYSIS: Suppose you represent one of the physicians. Provide arguments in support of the defendant physician. Predict how the prosecution would respond.

Chapter 4: Off-Label Promotion, False Claims Act, Consent Decrees, and Global Settlements

Consent Decrees and Global Resolutions

A consent decree is a legally binding agreement between a regulatory agency and a company stipulating specific action a company will undertake for compliance purposes. Over the years, companies regulated by FDA have entered into consent decrees to settle a pending litigation matter and to avoid a lengthy and costly court proceeding. Consent decrees are subject to court approval. Significant elements include:

- ➢ *Voluntary agreement with the government;*
- ➢ *Detailed action required for compliance purposes;*
- ➢ *Payments to the United States government;*
- ➢ *Possible reimbursement to the government for inspection and other follow-up;*
- ➢ *Third party expert certification;*
- ➢ *Specific due dates for compliance; and*
- ➢ *Penalties for noncompliance.*

One of the earliest consent decrees was *Abbott Laboratories* in 1999. The *Abbott* decree involved a monetary amount of $100 million, other costs and agreed upon compliance measures. In a 2002 consent decree, *Schering Plough* was required to disgorge $500 million. The consent decree with *Schering Plough Corporation, Schering Plough Products, LLC* and individual corporate officers agreed to procedures to ensure that the drug manufacturing practices comply with FDA's current good manufacturing practices (CGMP's). The violations related to the manufacturing, quality assurance, equipment, laboratories, packing and labeling. Since then, there have been other consent decrees that have escalated to billions of dollars.

Generic Drug Safety Settlement—Ranbaxy

In one of the largest drug safety settlements with a generic drug manufacturer, Ranbaxy USA Inc., a subsidiary of Indian generic pharmaceutical manufacturer Ranbaxy Laboratories Limited, pleaded guilty in 2013 to felony charges relating to the manufacture and distribution of certain adulterated drugs made at two of Ranbaxy's manufacturing facilities in India. Ranbaxy also agreed to pay a criminal fine and forfeiture totaling $150 million and to settle civil claims under the False Claims Act and related state laws for $350 million. A federal district court denied Ranbaxy Laboratories Ltd.'s motion for a temporary restraining order seeking to prevent the Food and Drug Administration's decision to withdraw its tentative approvals of Ranbaxy Laboratories, Inc.'s generic versions of the anti-viral drug Valcyte (valganciclovir) and the heartburn tablet Nexium (esomeprazole magnesium) from taking effect (*Ranbaxy Laboratories, Ltd. v. Burwell*, D.D.C., No. 14-cv-01923-BAH, motion for temporary restraining order denied, 11/19/14).

Consent Decree Example—*Medtronic, Inc.*

The following is an example of FDA entering into a consent decree with Medtronic, Inc. *http://www.fda.gov/NewsEvents/Newsroom/PressAnnouncements/ucm444690.htm*

Consent decree filed against Medtronic, Inc., and two of the company's officers—S. Omar Ishrak and Thomas M. Tefft —for repeatedly failing to correct violations, related to the manufacture of Synchromed II Implantable Infusion Pump Systems, medical devices that deliver medication to treat primary or metastatic cancer, chronic pain and severe spasticity. The consent decree cites violations of the quality system regulation for medical devices, which requires manufacturers to have processes in place to assure that the design, manufacture and distribution of a device allows for its safe use. The legal action requires the company to stop manufacturing, designing and distributing new Synchromed II Implantable Infusion Pump Systems except in very limited cases, such as when a physician determines that the Synchromed II Implantable Infusion Pump System is medically necessary for a patient's treatment. The consent decree also requires Medtronic to retain a third-party expert to help develop and submit plans to the FDA to correct violations. The consent decree will remain in effect until the FDA has determined that Medtronic has met all the provisions listed in the consent decree. Once Medtronic receives permission from the FDA to resume the design, manufacture and distribution of these products, the company must continue to submit audit reports so the agency can verify the company's compliance. The FDA first approved the Synchromed II Implantable Infusion Pump Systems in 2004, and first identified problems with the manufacture of these pumps in 2006. These problems can result in over or underinfusion or a delay in therapy for patients. Between 2006 and 2013, FDA investigators conducted five inspections at Medtronic's Neuromodulation facilities, resulting in three warning letters notifying the company of major violations. The violations included inadequate processes for identifying, investigating, and correcting quality problems with the Synchromed II Implantable Infusion Pump Systems; failure to document design changes; and failure to ensure that finished products meet design specifications (April 27, 2015).

CRITICAL ANALYSIS: Evaluate the ramifications of the consent decree.

False Claims Act

Under the False Claims Act (FCA), 31 U.S.C. section 3729, lawsuits brought by private citizens are commonly referred to as *qui tam* actions to address allegations of violations under federal law such as the FDCA (Food, Drug and Cosmetic Act). *Qui tam* actions, are lawsuits by a private party for money damages where part of the monetary recovery is awarded to the "whistleblower" and part to the United States government. Frequently, whistleblower actions are filed by current or former employees. The initial lawsuit filed by the "whistleblower" is not served on the defendant. However, the plaintiff "whistleblower" must give notice to the government and then the government determines whether to take over the case. Violations of the FDCA and related law such as the False Claims Act in connection with "off-label promotion" can have a far-reaching effect in terms of company liability. Illustrated below are examples of multistate and federal settlements that involved off-label promotion deemed illegal. **See also:** *Volume V.*

Off-Label Enforcement—Impact of *Caronia* and *Amarin*

Federal compliance requires that a drug label must reveal "all conditions, purposes or uses for which a drug is intended, including suggested [uses] in oral, written, printed or graphic advertising." 21 C.F.R. section 201.5(a). FDA approves prescription drug labeling. The use of a drug for any purpose(s) other than that stated on the label is known as an "off-label" use and hence prohibited. However, physicians are not prohibited from prescribing drugs for "off-label" use.

In the *Amarin Pharma* (No. 15 Civ. 3588 2nd Cir. 2015) and *Caronia* (No. 09-5006 2nd Cir. 2012) decisions, the same district court applied First Amendment protections to "off-label" promotion; that it is permissible to engage in truthful and non-misleading speech promoting the off-label use. Yet, the Justice Department along with FDA continue to aggressively combat health fraud. In *Amarin*, a settlement was reached with FDA where the company can engage in truthful and non-misleading speech promoting the off-label use of Vascepa®. *Amarin* had filed a complaint against FDA proactively; that is, prior to disseminating the off-label information relating to its hypertriglyceridemia drug, Vascepa®, indicated for the decrease of triglyceride levels in adults with severe hypertriglyceridemia. The settlement provides an optional preclearance provision where the company may submit to FDA "up to two proposed communications per calendar year about the off-label use of Vascepa before disseminating the promotion to doctors to determine if FDA has concerns. FDA has 60 days to respond with any concerns.

NOTE: See 21 U.S.C. section 396 of the FDCA "Practice of Medicine".

Federal Off-Label Settlement Examples

Abbott Laboratories—25 million to end a whistleblower's False Claims Act case alleging off-label promotion of triglyceride drug TriCor and unlawful kickbacks in gift baskets and gift cards. *U.S. ex rel. Bergman v. Abbott Laboratories*, **2:09-cv-04264, (D. C. Eastern District PA).**

Celgene—$280 million settlement in 2017. Former sales manager alleged that Celgene promoted the cancer drugs Thalomid and Revlimid for unapproved off-label uses.

Shire Subsidiaries—global resolution under the civil FCA with federal and state governments in 2017 for $350 million. Allegations concerned that the companies marketed Dermagraft® for off-label uses and kickbacks the companies paid to physicians.

Genentech and OSI Pharmaceuticals LLC—civil FCA settlement in 2016 with the federal and state governments for $67 million in connection with a qui tam lawsuit; alleged Genentech made misleading statements to health care providers about effectiveness of the cancer drug Tarceva.

Genzyme Corp. (*U.S. v. Genzyme Corp*, U.S. District Court, Middle District of Florida, No. 15-cr-00352) (acquired by Sanofi in 20111) agreed to pay $32.59 million in 2015, admit wrongdoing and enter a two-year deferred prosecution agreement to resolve criminal charge under the FDCA from 2005-2011 over its marketing of the surgical implant Seprafilm, a clear film used in laparotomies to reduce abnormal scarring; however, it was promoted as a "slurry" for laparoscopic surgery. sales representatives trained surgeons how to turn Seprafilm into "slurry", an unapproved use.

NOTE: Genzyme reached a $22.28 million civil agreement (2013) to resolve claims related to Seprafilm under the federal False Claims Act.

Johnson & Johnson—**$2.2 Billion** settlement in 2013 Johnson & Johnson (J&J) and its subsidiaries a $2.2 billion settlement to resolve criminal and civil liability arising from allegations relating to the prescription drugs Risperdal, Invega and Natrecor for off-label marketing of uses not approved as safe and effective by FDA and payments of kickbacks to physicians and pharmacists. The settlement included criminal fines and forfeiture totaling $485 million and civil settlements with the federal government and states totaling $1.72 billion.

Wyeth Pharmaceuticals—**$490.9 Million** settlement in 2013 to resolve its criminal and civil liability arising from the unlawful marketing of the prescription drug Rapamune for unapproved uses. Rapamune is an "immunosuppressive" drug that prevents the body's immune system from rejecting a transplanted organ.

Par Pharmaceuticals—**$45 Million** settlement in 2013 where Par Pharmaceutical Companies, Inc. pleaded guilty in 2013 and agreed to pay $45 million to resolve its criminal and civil liability in promotion of its prescription drug Megace ES for uses not approved as safe and effective by FDA. Chief Executive Officer Paul V. Campanelli pleaded guilty on behalf of the company. Par was fined $18 million and $4.5 million in criminal forfeiture. Par also agreed to pay $22.5 million to resolve its civil liability. *http://www.justice.gov/opa/pr/2013/March/13-civ-270.html*

GlaxoSmith Kline—**$3 Billion** settlement in 2012 where GlaxoSmithKline pled guilty and agreed to pay $3 billion to resolve criminal and civil allegations involving off-label marketing the diabetes medication, Avandia and other medications, failure to report safety data and false price reporting. Additionally, GlaxoSmithKline agreed to pay $90 million to settle claims by 37 states and the District of Columbia concerning the illegal promotion of Avandia.

NOTE: Glaxo announced in December 2013 the company would stop paying physicians to attend medical meetings or to speak about its drugs and the diseases that Glaxo drugs treat.

GlaxoSmithKline Plc was fined 37.6 million pounds ($54.3 million) by the U.K. antitrust over pay-for-delay deals that stymied sales of cheaper, generic versions of its anti-depressant Seroxat.

Abbott Laboratories—**$1.5 Billion** settlement in 2012 concerning the off-label marketing of the anti-seizure drug Depakote. The allegations involved misbranding and the settlement resolved criminal and civil allegations involving misbranding the drug to the elderly.

Merck, Sharp & Dohme—**$950 Million** settlement in 2012 to resolve criminal charges and civil claims related to its promotion and marketing of the painkiller Vioxx® (rofecoxib). Vioxx®, approved by FDA in 1999 was subsequently withdrawn from the marketplace in 2004. *http://www.justice.gov/opa/pr/2011/November/11-civ-1524.html*

NOTE: In 2016, a settlement was reached in *Merck & Co., Inc. Securities Litigation*, D.N.J., MDL-1651, 1/15/16) where the company agreed to pay $830 million to settle investor litigation alleging

misleading statements about safety. This means over $8.5 billion in total payments including lawsuits and government.

Cypress Pharmaceuticals, Inc., Hawthorn Pharmaceuticals Inc.—**$2.8 Million** settlement in 2012 along with CEO Max Draughn to resolve civil allegations under the False Claims Act. The government alleged that between 2003 and 2009, Cypress, Hawthorn and Draughn were responsible for marketing three pharmaceutical products that were not approved as safe and effective by (FDA). The products were Hylira, a gel used for the treatment of dry skin, Zaclir, an acne treatment and Zacare, another acne treatment. The settlement resolves a False Claims Act lawsuit filed by Robert Heiden, a former district sales manager for Hawthorn. The whistleblower, or *qui tam*, provisions of the False Claims Act permitted the relator, Heiden, to receive over $300,000 which was a portion of the proceeds obtained by the federal government.

http://www.justice.gov/opa/pr/2012/March/12-civ-389.html

AstraZenecaLP and AstraZeneca Pharmaceuticals **LP**—**$520 Million** settlement in 2010 for off-label promotion of the antipsychotic drug Seroquel (quetiapine). The company signed a civil settlement to resolve allegations that by marketing Seroquel for unapproved uses, the company caused false claims for payment to be submitted to federal insurance programs. The whistleblower, James Wetta, received over $45 million from the federal share of the civil recovery. The resolution included a five Corporate Integrity Agreement (CIA) between AstraZeneca and the Office of Inspector General which requires: annual review; certification of compliance by a board of directors committee; managers annual certification compliance; notification to physicians by AstraZeneca about the settlement; company website information about payments to doctors, such as honoraria, travel or lodging. AstraZeneca is subject to exclusion from Federal health care programs, including Medicare and Medicaid, for a material breach of the CIA and subject to monetary penalties for less significant breaches.

NOTE: Multistate settlement of $68.5 Million in 2011 involving 36 states.

U.S. ex rel. Cheryl Eckard v. GlaxoSmithKline—**$750 Million** settlement of which $150 million dollars was for criminal fines and forfeitures and the remaining account was to settle civil claims. Cheryl Eckard, a former GSK employee, brought this whistleblower action. The allegations stemmed from Good Manufacturing Practices (GMP) compliance at a GDK plant in Puerto Rico. **See: Gardener Harris and Duff Wilson, *Glaxo to Pay $750 Million for Sale of Bad Products*, N.Y. Times, Oct. 26, A1 (2010).**

Novartis—**$422.5 Million** in 2011 to pay both the federal government and whistleblowers to resolve both criminal and civil charges concerning how Trileptal, (oxcarbazepine), a drug to treat epilepsy along with five other drugs were marketed. Trileptal, an epilepsy drug, is approved only to treat partial seizures; however, it was marketed to treat psychiatric and pain uses. Four separate whistleblower actions were filed against Novartis as follows: *United* States *ex rel. Garrity v. Novartis Pharmaceuticals Corp.*, E.D. Pa., No. 08-CV-2588); *United States ex rel. McKee v. Novartis Pharmaceuticals Corp., E.D. Pa., No. 06-1664; United States ex rel. Copeland v. Novartis Pharmaceuticals Corp., E.D. Pa., No. 06-1630 and United States ex rel. Austin v. Novartis Pharmaceuticals Corp., M.D. Fla., No. 8:03-CV-1551.*

Criminal Violations and Forfeiture—**$185 million** for marketing Trileptal for unapproved or "off-label" uses, in violation of the FDCA. The FDCA does not prohibit "off-label" use by health care providers yet does so for manufacturers.

Civil Settlement—Novartis paid **$237.5 million** to settle contentions that it illegally promoted Trileptal and five other drugs Diovan (valsartan), Exforge (amlodipine and valsartan), Sandostatin (octreotide), Tekturna (aliskiren), and Zelnorm (tegaserod) for various unapproved or off-label uses which resulted in false claims submissions to both federal and state health care programs. The civil settlement resolves accusations that Novartis paid kickbacks to doctors.

Accountability—*Corporate Integrity Agreement* Novartis executed a five-year corporate integrity agreement with the Office of Inspector General, Department of Health and Human Services. Novartis senior executives must certify on an annual basis departmental compliance.

Pfizer—**$14.5 Million** settlement in 2011 of a *qui tam* lawsuit that alleged False Claims Act violations by marketing the urinary incontinence drugs Detrol and Detrol LA for unapproved uses. **$142 Million** settlement in 2010 for the illegal off-label marketing of Neurontin.

NOTE: The U.S. Supreme Court declined to review the RICO case against Pfizer related to its allegedly deceptive marketing of Neurontin.

$2.3 Billion settlement in 2009 to settle civil and criminal charges about how the company marketed some of its drugs including the arthritis drug Bextra withdrawn in 2005. Other drugs involved in the settlement included the cholesterol drug Lipitor, Lyrica treatment for nerve pain, and Zoloft, an antidepressant. This amount surpassed the $1.42 billion dollars Eli Lilly and Company settlement agreement to resolve allegations of off-label promotion of the antipsychotic drug Zyprexa to the elderly for unapproved uses.

Forest Laboratories—**$313 Million** in 2010 for off-label promotion of Celexa and Lexapro.

Eli Lily—**$1.4 Billion** settlement agreement in 2009 with the United States Department of Justice for the off-label promotion of Zyprexa®. In 2005, Lily agreed to a **$36 million** settlement which involved both criminal fines and civil liabilities along with implementation of training programs for the off-label marketing of Evista®.

Cephalon—**$425 Million** 2008 settlement off-label marketing of Actiq, Provigil and Gabitril.

Purdue—**$634.5 Million** settlement in 2007 for off-label marketing of Oxycontin.

Bristol Myers Squibb—**$515 Million** settlement in 2007 for off-label marketing of Abilify.

Schering Plough—**$435 Million** settlement in 2006 to settle charges concerning "off-label" marketing. The Justice Department alleged that Schering illegally promoted drugs for certain types of cancer that had not been approved by FDA.

Parke Davis Company—**$430 Million (Warner Lambert parent company) (acquired by Pfizer Corporation)** *Franklin v. Parke Davis* settlement in 2004, a whistleblower action by an employee due to non-compliance with FDA regulations for off-label promotion. The basis of the action alleged that the company engaged in unlawful activities such as an aggressive illegal marketing plan, kickbacks and questionable research related to the promotion of "off-label uses" such as bi-polar disorder and other illnesses for Neurontin, an anti-convulsant drug approved to treat epilepsy. The company agreed to enter a plea of guilty and pay a fine.

NOTE: *Parke Davis* **served as the catalyst for several lawsuits for off-label marketing of neurontin. See: The Neurontin Legacy—Marketing through Misinformation and Manipulation,** *Seth Landefeld, Michael A. Steinman,* **360 The New England Journal of Medicine. 103 (Jan. 8, 2009). For an example of how other countries regulate "off-label" see Feng Ma and Nan Lou,** *Chinese Regulation of Off-Label Use of Drugs,* **68 Food and Drug Law J. 189 (2013).**

Multistate and State Off-Label Settlements
State Consumer Protection Laws and Claims under state unfair trade practice laws.
Bristol-Myers Squibb (BMS)—In 2016, BMS agreed to pay $19.5 million to resolve a consumer protection investigation that BMS improperly marketed the antipsychotic drug Abilify.

Amgen $71 million settlement—In 2015, Amgen agreed to settle claims with 48 states and the District of Columbia concerning the promotion of the anemia drug Aranesp and psoriasis treatment Enbrel. Allegations involved that Amgen marketed Aranesp for dosing frequencies that surpassed the FDA approved levels and for non-approved conditions. The multistate allegations claimed Enbrel was marketed to patients with mild plaque psoriasis when it was only approved for moderate to severe cases.

Pfizer (Wyeth Pharmaceuticals)—**35 million Multistate settlement**—In 2014, Pfizer agreed to pay $35 million to 41 states and Washington, D.C. to settle claims that its Wyeth unit illegally marketed the drug Rapamune® and encouraged doctors and hospitals to prescribe it for off-label uses. Rapamune® is an "immunosuppressive" drug that prevents the body's immune system from rejecting a transplanted organ.

GlaxoSmithKline (GSK)—In June 2014, the District of Columbia along with 44 states shared $105 million that GSK agreed to pay to resolve improper marketing allegations under state consumer protection laws concerning its asthma drug Advair® and its antidepressants Paxil® and Wellbutrin® for unapproved off-label uses. The states alleged that GSK promoted the antidepressant Wellbutrin® for weight loss and sexual dysfunction and that Advair® was promoted for mild asthma when the FDA approved was for severe asthma. Further, the states alleged that GSK concealed studies of teen suicidal thoughts concerning Paxil®.

NOTE: West Virginia GSK $22 million settlement—The lawsuit alleged that GSK failed to disclose the side effects of Avandia, Avandamet and Avandaryl when it was marketing the medicine as a product to lower patients' blood sugar and reducing diabetics' cardiovascular risks.

Johnson & Johnson (J&J) Ortho-McNeil-Janssen Pharmaceuticals—Risperdal®

In 2012, the District of Columbia along with 36 states shared $181 million that Johnson & Johnson (J&J) Ortho-McNeil-Janssen Pharmaceuticals agreed to pay to resolve improper marketing allegations concerning Risperdal®, an antipsychotic drug. The state complaints alleged that J&J and Janssen used "unconscionable business practices and deception", in violation of state Consumer Fraud Acts. The alleged off-label promotion activities occurred from 1994-2004. North Carolina Example—In 2013, there was a $38.8 million recovery as part of a multi-state and federal settlement with Johnson & Johnson and its subsidiary Janssen Pharmaceuticals, Inc. to resolve allegations of improper drug marketing of the atypical antipsychotic drugs Risperdal® and Invega. North Carolina and the other states alleged Johnson & Johnson and Janssen promoted and marketed Risperdal® and Invega for uses not approved by FDA including the treatment of hyperactive children and elderly dementia patients.

Individual State Jury Decision Illustrations—Risperdal®

Pennsylvania—In 2016, a $70 million verdict in Philadelphia where the jury found that the antipsychotic drug Risperdal® had caused an adolescent boy to grow female breasts. *A.Y. v. Janssen Pharm., Inc.*, Pa. Ct. Com. Pl., No. 130402094, verdict7/1/16).

South Carolina—In 2011, jurors found that J&J Ortho-McNeil-Janssen Pharmaceuticals engaged in "unfair and deceptive acts" when the company sent a letter in 2003 to over 7,000 physicians in South Carolina claiming that Risperdal®, an antipsychotic drug, was superior to and safer than competing drugs. Johnson & Johnson was ordered to pay, in 2011, $327 million in penalties for deceptively marketing the medicine. Court reduced amount to $136 million due to a three-year statute of limitation and then further reduced to $124.3 million due to a mathematical error.

NOTE: See: *State ex rel. Wilson v. Ortho-McNeil-Janssen Pharm., Inc.*, S.C., No. 27502, 7/8/2015.

Louisiana—Similarly, a Louisiana jury in 2011 ordered Janssen to pay $257.7 million in damages for misleading claims about Risperdal® as well as $73.3 million in attorney's fees and costs. The court of appeals upheld the jury verdict of $257.7 million 2012.

Arkansas—In 2015, Johnson & Johnson agreed to pay $7.8 million to settle Arkansas's claims the company illegally marketed its Risperdal® antipsychotic medicine. In 2014, the Supreme Court in Arkansas had reversed the $1.26 billion judgment against J&J Ortho-McNeil-Janssen Pharmaceuticals (***Arkansas v. Ortho-McNeil-Janssen Pharm. Inc.*, Ark. Cir. Ct., No. CV07-15345, settlement 5/21/15).**

CRITICAL ANALYSIS: The United States Department of Justice continues to prosecute off-label promotion. Evaluate the federal and multistate off-label settlements above despite the decisions in *Amarin* and *Caronia*.

Chapter 5: Anti-Dumping, Restitution and Disgorgement

Economic Harm—"Honeygate", "Catfish" and "Cod"

Enforcement related to anti-dumping escalated due to the economic harm to United States industries. "Honey dumping" culminated in convictions and fines in 2013 as detailed below for individuals and companies. The practice, dubbed "Honeygate", started in 2001 and involved both economic harm and adulteration. The duties were as high as 221 percent of the declared value, and later were assessed against the entered net weight, currently at $2.63 per net kilogram, in addition to a "honey assessment fee" of one cent per pound of all honey. In 2002, the Food and Drug Administration issued an import alert for honey containing the antibiotic Chloramphenicol, a broad-spectrum antibiotic that is used to treat serious infections in humans, but which is not approved for use in honey. Honey containing certain antibiotics is deemed "adulterated" under the FDCA. In 2008, federal authorities began investigating allegations involving circumventing antidumping duties through illegal imports, including transshipment and mislabeling, on the "supply side" of the honey industry. Similarly, in 2003, anti-dumping duties went into effect on frozen fillets of sutchi, basa and swai because the fish product was being sold in the United States at less than fair value and were economically harming domestic catfish producers.

Honey Broker Sentenced and Debarment—Tariff Avoidance of $39.2 Million
http://www.justice.gov/usao/iln/pr/chicago/2013/pr0930_01.html
http://www.fda.gov/RegulatoryInformation/FOI/ElectronicReadingRoom/ucm418356.htm
Hung Yi Lin pleaded guilty to violating U.S. importation laws by falsely declaring that the honey shipments contained sugars, syrups, and apple juice concentrate to avoid $39.2 million in anti-dumping duties. She was sentenced to three years in prison and ordered to pay restitution of $512,852 in unpaid tariffs for illegally transporting hundreds of container loads of Chinese-origin honey. Between 2009 and 2012, Lin schemed to falsify the importation documents for hundreds of containers of Chinese-origin honey by misrepresenting the contents as sugars and syrups. FDA issued a debarment order for 12 years from importing or offering food articles for import into the United States, 80 FR 8664 (Feb. 18, 2015).

United States Honey Suppliers—The other investigation involved the illegal buying, processing, and trading of honey that illegally entered the U.S. on the "demand side" of the industry. Groeb Farms, Inc., one of the largest suppliers of processed honey, accepted criminal responsibility for fraudulently entered Chinese honey that had avoided $79 million in duties. The court, in 2013, approved deferred prosecution agreements; however, Groeb Farms was fined $2 million. Texas based Honey Holding I, Ltd. (dba Honey Solutions), agreed to pay $1 million in fines.
https://www.justice.gov/usao-ndil/pr/two-companies-and-five-individuals-charged-roles-illegal-honey-imports-avoided-180
NOTE: See *Volume IX* for the draft guidance regarding the proper labeling of Honey.

Economic Harm—Misbranded "Catfish"
United States v. Peter Xuong Lam
http://www.justice.gov/opa/pr/2008/October/08-enrd-967.html (edited)
Peter Xuong Lam (Lam) was found guilty of conspiring to import mislabeled fish to avoid federal import tariffs. Peter Xuong Lam was convicted of three counts of selling illegally imported fish, in violation of 18 U.S.C. § 545; introducing misbranded fish into interstate commerce with intent to defraud, in violation of 21 U.S.C. §§ 331(a), (c); and conspiracy to commit these offenses, in violation of 18 U.S.C.§ 371. Several individuals and companies, including Lam and Yavelberg, a co-conspirator, were convicted for criminal offenses concerning a scheme to avoid paying tariffs by falsely labeling fish for import and then selling it in the United States at below market price, a practice known, as "dumping". At trial, evidence was presented that two Virginia-based companies,

Virginia Star Seafood Corp., of which Lam became president, and International Sea Products Corporation, illegally imported more than ten million pounds, or $15.5 million worth, of frozen fish fillets from Vietnamese companies Binh Dinh, Antesco and Anhaco between May 2004 and March 2005. These companies were affiliated with Cafatex, one of the largest producers in Vietnam of a fish called Pangasius hypophthalmus. The imported fish was labeled as sole, grouper, flounder, snakehead, channa and conger pike, a type of eel; however, DNA tests revealed that the frozen fish fillets were in fact Pangasius hypophthalmus. The Pangasius hypophthalmus fish in the catfish family and marketed under approved trade names including swai or striped pangasius. An anti-dumping duty or tariff was placed on Pangasius hypophthalmus imports from Vietnam in January 2003. Catfish farmers of the United States had filed a petition, which alleged that this fish was being imported from Vietnam at less than fair market value. None of the species names the defendants used to label the imported fish were subject to any federal tariffs. *** According to the prosecution, Lam then knowingly marketed and sold millions of dollars worth of the falsely labeled and illegally imported fish to seafood buyers in the United States as basa, a trade name for a more expensive type of Vietnamese catfish, Pangasius bocourti, and also as sole. *** The jury convicted Yavelberg of marketing the fillets, without necessarily knowing they had been mislabeled. *** Henry Yip, T.P. Company, David Wong, True World Foods, Inc., David Chu, Dakon International, Du Sa Ngo, Southern Bay, Joseph Xie and Agar Supply all entered guilty pleas related to their participation in these transactions. Lam faced a statutory maximum of five years in jail and fines of up to $250,000 for each of the counts on which he was convicted. Yavelberg faced a statutory maximum of up to one year in prison and $100,000 fine.

NOTE: The Court of Appeals affirmed the convictions and remanded for resentencing due to a procedural error in determining the amount of tax loss to assess against defendant Lam. Upon remand, Lam was sentenced to 41 months of imprisonment. Lam was ordered to forfeit 267,570 pounds of fish and $12.58 million. Lam appealed the forfeiture order to the Court of Appeals for the 9th Circuit (D.C. No. 2:07-cr-00449-PSG-6). The Court of Appeals vacated the forfeiture order and remanded to the District Court to consider whether the forfeiture order was unconstitutionally excessive in violation of the Eighth Amendment. Upon remand, by Order dated October 10, 2013, the District Court affirmed the original order.

Economic Harm— "Codfish and Grouper"
False Labeling, Smuggling and Misbranding
Codfish—*United States v. Rafael* et al, 1:16CR10124 (2016), 17-2109 (2017)

Dubbed the "Codfather", Carlos Rafael pleaded guilty in federal court (Boston) in 2017 to one count of conspiring to commit offenses against the United States, 23 counts of false labeling and fish identification, two counts of falsifying federal records to evade federal fishing quotas, one count of bulk cash smuggling the proceeds to Portugal, and one count of tax evasion. The court ordered Rafael to forfeit four boats and 34 fishing licenses worth roughly $2.3 million and was sentenced to a four-year prison sentence for evasion of taxes and fish quotas. (Appealed).

Grouper—Falsely Labeled Fish, Smuggling and Misbranding of Seafood Products
http://www.justice.gov/opa/pr/2011/May/11-enrd-577.html (edited)

Karen L. Blyth and David H. M. Phelps were sentenced May 5, 2011 in federal court in Mobile, Ala., to 33 months and 24 months in prison, respectively and each were fined $5,000 and barred for three years from working in the seafood industry or owning any seafood related business for their roles in purchasing and selling farm-raised Asian catfish and Lake Victoria perch falsely labeled as grouper, selling foreign farm-raised shrimp falsely labeled as U.S. wild caught shrimp, selling shrimp they falsely claimed to be larger, more expensive shrimp than they actually were, and for buying fish they knew had been illegally imported into the United States.

CRITICAL ANALYSIS: Evaluate the economic harm and consumer deception in the above "Honeygate" and "Seafood" cases.

Equitable Remedies—Restitution and Disgorgement

Are equitable remedies such as restitution and disgorgement viable remedies under the FDCA? FDA has successfully pursued equitable remedies such as disgorgement and restitution. Disgorgement pertains to unjust enrichment, whereby the wrongdoer gives up the ill-gotten gains or profits. However, the FDCA does not contain a specific provision for disgorgement. Rather, this remedy is one of equitable relief determined by the court and has evolved through case law. See: *Universal Management*, 999 F. Supp. 974 (N.D. Ohio 1997), aff'd, 191 F. 3d 750 (6th Cir. 1999) (disgorgement applied). FDA has pursued other cases involving restitution and disgorgement of profits such as *Lane Labs*, a court case that concerned dietary supplements and *RxDepot,* a legal decision that involved drug reimportation. Corporate compliance programs are essential for accountability reasons. Although debatable, the Sarbanes-Oxley Act (Sarbanes-Oxley) may apply to FDA related prosecutions. Sarbanes-Oxley imposed obligations to report potential misconduct internally and to conduct thorough investigations. FDA and the Securities and Exchange Commission (SEC) have collaborated to identify potentially misleading statements by publicly traded entities. The FDCA does not specifically provide for these equitable remedies and FDA does not have a written policy statement as to when these remedies are appropriate. The FTC developed a Policy Statement on *Monetary Equitable Remedies in Competition Cases.* The following serves as a guide in deciding whether to seek disgorgement or restitution:

> ➤ **The underlying violation must be clear;**
> ➤ **There must be a reasonable basis for calculating the amount of a remedial payment; and the**
> ➤ **Value of seeking monetary relief.**

Restitution—United States v. Lane Labs

The FDCA does not specifically provide for restitution; though, courts have ordered restitution as an equitable remedy. *Lane Labs* provides a good illustration of an appellate court upholding a district court's order of restitution.

United States v. Lane Labs,
417 F.3d 219 (3rd Cir. 2005)

OPINION OF THE COURT RENDELL, Circuit Judge. In this case, we are called upon to decide whether a district court has the power under the Federal Food, Drug and Cosmetic Act, 21 U.S.C. § 301, *et. seq.* ("FDCA"), to order a defendant found to be in violation of the Act to pay restitution to consumers. Because a district court's equitable powers in such a situation are broad, we hold that an order of restitution is properly within the jurisdiction of the court. Appellant Andrew Lane formed Lane Labs ("Labs") to manufacture and supply health products. Andrew Lane is the president, director, and sole shareholder of Labs. Labs sells its products in several different ways: directly to consumers, through its CompassioNet Division, and through third-party distributors. Three products are the subject of this action: (1) BeneFin, sold in powder or tablet form as a dietary supplement and containing shark cartilage; (2) SkinAnswer, a skin cream containing glycoalkaloid; and (3) MGN-3, a dietary fiber produced by the hydrolysis of rice bran with the enzymatic extract of Shiitake mushroom, and whose main ingredient is arabinoxylan.

At a convention in 1997, FDA first observed Labs distributing materials promoting BeneFin to treat cancer. The FDA informed Labs through letters and telephone conversations that such conduct violates the FDCA. The FDA also inspected Cartilage Consultants, Inc. ("CCI"), a company founded by Dr. I. William Lane, Ph.D., Andrew Lane's father. *** Through this inspection, the FDA discovered that Dr. Lane actively promoted BeneFin and SkinAnswer as potential treatments for cancer and that he was a "paid consultant" to Labs. *** For instance, in a letter to health professionals, Labs touted Dr. Lane as "the world's foremost authority on shark cartilage [who] has directed the development of BeneFin Shark Cartilage." On the SkinAnswer packaging itself, Labs placed both Dr. Lane's photograph and his endorsement of the product. Appellants marketed their products in several different ways. They sent monthly catalogs of their products to a mailing list they maintained. They also advertised in magazines and maintained several websites. They operated a network of companies, including their CompassioNet Division, which acted as a sales agent for the products. Appellants used CCI and paid researcher spokesmen, such as Dr. Lane and Mamdooh Ghoneum, Ph.D, to promote the products. *** Dr. Lane's Volumes and writings are available for sale through several avenues, such as Amazon.com. Health newsletters, such as *Alternatives,* included claims for the products and the television show "60 Minutes" aired a story featuring Dr. Lane about shark cartilage as a cancer therapy. Investigations revealed that Appellants specifically promoted the products to treat diseases. Employees answering calls to Appellants' toll-free telephone number referred callers to an employee of CCI, who then promoted the products as cancer and HIV treatments. Appellants sent mass mailings to customers, including order forms and articles promoting the products as disease treatments, some of which were written by Drs. Lane and Ghoneum. *** In 1998, Appellants asserted that Dr. Lane had previously worked with Labs, but was no longer employed or consulting for Labs. Discovery showed that Dr. Lane was continuing to receive large consulting fees from Labs.

FTC Action—The FTC filed a complaint against Labs, Andrew Lane, Cartilage Consultants, Inc. and Dr. Lane, contending that they inappropriately advertised and promoted BeneFin and SkinAnswer as effective in the prevention, treatment, and cure of cancer. *** Labs and Andrew Lane entered into a Consent Decree with the FTC and judgment was entered against Labs (but not Andrew Lane) in the amount of $1 million. A permanent injunction was also ordered, prohibiting defendants from representing that BeneFin or any other shark cartilage product "prevents, treats or cures cancer unless, at the time the representation is made, defendants possess and rely upon competent and reliable scientific evidence that substantiates the representation."

FDA Action—FDA filed a Complaint for Permanent Injunction, alleging that Labs' promotional claims brought their products under 21 U.S.C. § 321(g)(1)(B)'s definition of "drugs" and that they were "new drugs" within the meaning of § 321(p) being distributed without requisite FDA approval in violation of 21 U.S.C. § 331(d) and § 355(a). It also alleged that the products were misbranded within the meaning of § 353(f)(1) because they lacked adequate directions for use and were being distributed and held for sale in violation of § 331(a) and (k). ***

District Court's Disposition—[T]he District Court granted the government's motion for summary judgment, issued a permanent injunction against the future sales of the products until a new drug application was approved for them, and ordered restitution to all purchasers of the products since September 22, 1999. *** the Court found that Labs' violations had been recurring, noted that Appellants did not appear to recognize the wrongful nature of their conduct, and had not voluntarily ceased the challenged practices. *** Though the FDCA does not specifically authorize restitution, such specificity is not required where the government properly invokes a court's equitable jurisdiction under this statute. *** We agree that protecting consumer health and safety is a primary purpose of the FDCA. *See* 21 U.S.C. § 321(p) (defining a "new drug" as a drug "not generally recognized among experts ... as safe and effective for use"); 21 U.S.C. § 393(b) (establishing the FDA's mission to promote and protect public health). *** One of the FDCA's explicit mandates to the Secretary of Health and Human Services is to "promote honesty and fair dealing in the interest of consumers." 21 U.S.C. § 341. *** Whether or not Congress specifically contemplated restitution under the FDCA, the ability to order this remedy is within the broad equitable power granted to the district courts to further the economic protection purposes of the statute. Restitution also serves a deterrent function embodied in the district court's authority to "restrain violations of section 331." 21 U.S.C. § 332(a). ***

Nearly fifty years ago, in *United States v. Parkinson* 240 F.2d 918 (9th Cir.1956), the Court of Appeals for the Ninth Circuit rejected the government's request to collect restitution under the FDCA. ****Parkinson* does not survive *Porter* and *Mitchell*. First, it was based on the premise that "[t]he use of the extraordinary remedies of equity in governmental litigation should never be permitted by the courts unless clearly authorized by the statute in express terms." *Id.* This proposition is at odds with the Supreme Court's reasoning in these cases. In addition, *Parkinson* predates *Mitchell*, which expanded the reasoning of *Porter* to a statutory grant of equitable power *identical* to the grant included in the FDCA. *** More recently, the Court of Appeals for the Sixth Circuit rejected the reasoning in *Parkinson* and ordered a party to pay restitution under the FDCA, *Universal Mgmt. Servs., Inc.,* 191 F.3d at 764. In that case, the defendant sold electric gas grill lighters equipped with finger grips as pain relieving devices without obtaining FDA approval. The court held that the grant of equitable power in § 332(a) was so broad that it was within the district court's authority to order restitution. *** In 1999, just two months after *Universal Management* was decided, Abbott Laboratories agreed to pay $100 million to the government as part of a consent decree. *** Most recently, Schering-Plough paid $500 million for equitable disgorgement as part of the consent decree. *** Given the breadth and open-ended nature of § 332(a), and the direct correlation between the language of that provision and the directives in *Porter* and *Mitchell,* we hold that the District Court here did have the power to grant restitution. We will therefore AFFIRM its order.

Disgorgement—*United States v. RxDepot*

Does a federal district court have the power to order a defendant to disgorge profits? Courts have ordered disgorgement as an equitable remedy as illustrated in the *RxDepot* decision.

United States v. RxDepot,
438 F.3d 1052 (10th Cir. 2006)

OPINION: MURPHY, Circuit Judge.

Introduction: Appellees Rx Depot, Inc., Rx of Canada, LLC, Carl Moore, and David Peoples (collectively "Rx Depot") facilitated the sale of prescription drugs from Canada to customers in the United States. The United States brought suit against Rx Depot, alleging its business practices violated provisions of the Federal Food, Drug and Cosmetic Act ("FDCA"), 21 U.S.C. §§ 301-397. Rx Depot admitted to violating the Act and entered into a consent decree of permanent injunction. Subsequently, the United States sought disgorgement of Rx Depot's profits. The district court denied disgorgement, concluding it was not an available remedy under the FDCA as a matter of law. *** Because the FDCA invokes courts' general equity jurisdiction and does not prohibit disgorgement by clear legislative command or necessary and inescapable inference, we reverse.

Background: Rx Depot helped consumers in the United States obtain prescription drugs from Canada at reduced prices. A customer with a prescription from an American physician could download forms from Rx Depot's website or visit one of Rx Depot's storefront affiliates to order medications. Rx Depot then transmitted the customer's forms, prescription, and payment information to cooperating Canadian pharmacies. A Canadian physician would rewrite the prescription, which was then filled by a Canadian pharmacy and sent directly to the customer in the United States. Rx Depot received a ten to twelve percent commission for each sale they facilitated. The United States filed a civil action alleging Rx Depot's activities violated provisions of the FDCA. Specifically, the Government alleged Rx Depot violated § 381(d)(1) by reimporting prescription drugs originally manufactured in the United States and § 355(a) by introducing new drugs into interstate commerce without FDA approval. *** In the consent decree, Rx Depot admitted to violating the FDCA and agreed not to resume its business operations. *** Subsequently, the district court denied restitution, reasoning Rx Depot's customers did not lose money in their transactions because they purchased medications at reduced prices. ***

Discussion: Section 332(a) of the FDCA invokes the equity jurisdiction of courts using the same statutory language the Supreme Court construed in *Mitchell* to authorize all traditional equitable remedies. *Compare* 21 U.S.C. §332(a) ("district courts . . . shall have jurisdiction, for cause shown to restrain violations"), *with* 29 U.S.C. §217 ("district courts . . . shall have jurisdiction, for cause shown, to restrain violations"); *** Thus, disgorgement is available under the FDCA unless (1) there is a clear legislative command or necessary and inescapable inference prohibiting disgorgement or (2) disgorgement is inconsistent with the purposes of the FDCA. *** In addition to general equity jurisdiction, the FDCA explicitly provides for criminal, civil, and administrative remedies.

See 21 U.S.C. §333 (providing for criminal fines and imprisonment and civil monetary penalties); *id.* § 360h(b) & (e) (authorizing Secretary of Health and Human Services ("Secretary") to order recall, repair, replacement, or refund of purchase price for medical devices); *id.* §350a(e)(1)(B) (authorizing Secretary to recall adulterated or misbranded infant formula); *id.* § 360pp(a) & (b) (granting district courts equity jurisdiction and providing for civil monetary penalties for violation of statutory provisions relating to electronic products). *** Finally, Rx Depot argues the legislative history of the FDCA, which indicates that Congress intended seizure to be the harshest remedy available under the Act, precludes disgorgement. *** *See United States v. Universal Mgmt. Servs., Inc.*, 191 F.3d 750, 762 (6th Cir. 1999) (concluding restitution is not necessarily harsher than seizure). *** Disgorgement, on the other hand, is only permitted after a party is found by a court to be in violation of the Act and only at the court's discretion. Additionally, seizure is not necessarily harsher than disgorgement in terms of monetary loss to a company. *** Thus, even if Congress intended seizure to be the harshest remedy available under the statute, it does not follow that Congress necessarily and inescapably intended to preclude disgorgement in all circumstances. *** In sum, the FDCA invokes courts' general equity jurisdiction by authorizing courts "to restrain violations" of the Act. *** Moreover, disgorgement furthers the purposes of the FDCA by deterring future violations of the Act, which may put the public health and safety at risk. Therefore, according to the analysis established in *Porter* and *Mitchell*, we conclude disgorgement is permitted under the FDCA in appropriate cases. Our determination that disgorgement is authorized by the FDCA is supported by decisions in several other circuits. Although we are the first circuit to address disgorgement under the FDCA, two circuits have held recently that restitution is authorized by the Act. *** In *Universal Management*, the Sixth Circuit upheld an order of restitution requiring a party who sold adulterated medical devices to provide refunds to its customers. 191 F.3d at 762. The court relied on *Porter* and *Mitchell* in refusing to interpret the FDCA as limiting the equitable jurisdiction of federal courts because it found no clear congressional intent to impose such a limit. *** The Third Circuit similarly upheld the authority of courts to order restitution under the FDCA in a case involving misbranding of and failure to obtain FDA approval for dietary supplements and skin cream purported to prevent and treat cancer. *United States v. Lane Labs-USA, Inc.*, 427 F.3d 219, 220 (3d Cir. 2005). Applying *Porter* and *Mitchell*, the court determined that a district court sitting in equity may order restitution unless the statute clearly limits the court's equitable jurisdiction or restitution does not further the purposes of the statute. *Id.* at 225. Moreover, the court determined restitution furthered the purposes of the statute because it protected the financial interests of consumers and deterred individuals from violating the Act. *Id.* at 227, 229. *** In *Mitchell*, the Court reaffirmed *Porter* in holding equitable remedies need not be expressly authorized by a statute; rather, a grant of general equity jurisdiction is sufficient to enable a court to exercise all traditional equitable powers absent explicit or implicit evidence to the contrary. *Mitchell*, 361 U.S. at 290-292. *** Because *Parkinson*'s reasoning was later rejected by *Mitchell*, it is not persuasive. *See Lane Labs*, 427 F.3d at 233-34 (rejecting reasoning of *Parkinson*).

Conclusion: For the foregoing reasons, this court REVERSES the district court's denial of disgorgement.

NOTE: FDA does not always seek disgorgement of profits as illustrated in the *Baxter Healthcare Corp.* consent decree. The intent of the consent decree was to resolve the GMP and Quality System requirements concerning infusion pumps that revealed manufacturing violations despite previous warning letters.

CRITICAL ANALYSIS: Determine whether the court correctly ordered restitution in *Lane Labs* and disgorgement in *RxDepot* even though there is no specific grant of authority to do so under the FDCA. See: Penalties under the FDCA starting with 21 U.S.C. section 332(a) through section 335. Should the FDCA be amended to include equitable remedies such as restitution and disgorgement and any additional penalties and enforcement mechanisms?

VOLUME IV

Volume IV: Medical Devices and Radiation Emitting Products Regulation

Originally, medical devices were regulated under the United States Postal Statutes; however, that changed with the enactment of the Food, Drug and Cosmetic Act of 1938. The 1906 Pure Food and Drugs Act did not provide regulatory authority for devices. Instead, regulation of fraudulent medical devices occurred pursuant to the 1872 Postal Fraud Statute through the United States Post Office and the Postmaster General. Today, thousands of medical devices exist in the marketplace. Further, approximately half of all medical devices used in the United States are imported. The Center for Devices and Radiological Health (CDRH) regulates medical devices. CDRH has the authority and responsibility for regulating companies who manufacture, repackage and relabel medical devices. This includes medical devices that are imported and sold in the United States. This responsibility and authority extends to radiation-emitting electronic products both medical and non-medical such as lasers, x-ray systems, ultrasound equipment, microwave ovens and color televisions. The goals of this volume are to:

> ➤ *Discuss the historical foundation for medical device legislation as well as current pertinent legislation;*
> ➤ *Explain how the Center for Devices and Radiological Health functions;*
> ➤ *Provide information about medical device fundamentals including classifications and submissions;*
> ➤ *Provide significant landmark United States Supreme Court decisions;*
> ➤ *Specify personalized medicine endeavors;*
> ➤ *Evaluate liability and preemption issues; and*
> ➤ *Detail postmarket surveillance and enforcement mechanisms.*

Landmark cases involving medical devices and the legal concept of preemption are included as well. Preemption is a legal term of art that emanates from the Supremacy Clause (Article VI, clause 2) of the United States Constitution. Article VI, clause 2 prohibits states from enacting laws that conflict with federal law. Radiation emitting products regulation is also included. Each chapter within this volume contains critical analysis issues to explore.

Medical devices are approved differently than human drugs. The distinction of how medical devices are approved is significant. There are two main types of approval processes as follows: Premarket Notification generally known as a "510(k)", involves "substantial equivalence to a device already in the marketplace. The 510 (k) pre-clearance approval mechanism has not been without controversy. Yet, to that end, FDA has stepped up enforcement. The other submission type is a Premarket Application process that involves a complex review process. How a device is approved, that is whether by a Premarket Application or a Premarket Notification submission impacts the ability of a plaintiff to seek redress in state court. Legislation had been introduced to correct the inconsistency; yet it has not been enacted.

Chapter 1: Center for Devices and Radiological Health—CDRH and Legislative Hallmarks

CDRH Priorities and Responsibilities

Key website: *https://www.fda.gov/MedicalDevices/default.htm*

Medical devices range from a simple tongue depressor to a complex pacemaker. The Center for Devices and Radiological Health (CDRH) strategic priorities include the following: Establish a National Evaluation System for Medical Devices; Promote a Culture of Quality and Organizational Excellence; and Partner with Patients. CDRH responsibilities include the following:

> ➢ *Ensure the safety and effectiveness of medical devices;*
> ➢ *Eliminate exposure to radiation from medical, occupational and consumer products;*
> ➢ *Review requests for medical device approvals;*
> ➢ *Collect, analyze and act on information about injuries and other adverse events;*
> ➢ *Enforce and establish good manufacturing practice regulations and performance standards;*
> ➢ *Monitor compliance surveillance programs for medical devices; and*
> ➢ *Provide technical and other assistance to all manufacturers of such devices.*

Legislative Foundation and Landmarks

Regulation of fraudulent medical devices occurred through the 1872 Postal Fraud Statute and regulated by the United States Post Office and the Postmaster General. The 1906 Pure Food and Drugs Act did not provide for regulatory authority for devices. Subsequently, the 1938 Food, Drug and Cosmetic Act (FDCA) contained separate definitions for the terms "drugs" and "devices." By 1947, there were over 460 manufacturers of surgical, medical and dental instruments and supplies, eventually giving rise to a need for strengthened authority. Dr. Theodore Cooper, Director of the National Heart and Lung Institute, headed the Health Education and Welfare study group on medical devices in the late 1960s and early 1970s. The Cooper Committee, recommendations included: a different regulatory approach; an inventory of devices in the market; classification scheme; and good manufacturing processes with concomitant enforcement, inspection and record keeping. Debates regarding these recommendations continued in Congress until the mid 1970s. In 1976, the Medical Device Amendments (1976 Amendments) were enacted and incorporated in the FDCA. Devices were then categorized into three classes: Class I, Class II and Class III. Congress established the legal definition of device under 21 U.S.C. § 321(h) of the FDCA. Legislative landmarks include the following:

> ➢ *1976 Medical Device Amendments*
> ➢ *1990 Safe Medical Devices Act*
> ➢ *1992 Medical Device Amendments*
> ➢ *1996 510(k) Quality Review Program*
> ➢ *1997 Food and Drug Administration Modernization Act*
> ➢ *2002 Medical Device User Fee and Modernization Act*
> ➢ *2005 Contact Lens Legislation*
> ➢ *2007 Food and Drug Administration Amendments Act*
> ➢ *2012 Food and Drug Administration Safety and Innovation Act*

1976 Amendments—The 1976 Amendments detailed the required device notification to FDA prior to marketing. The submission process involves either a Premarket Notification, "510(k)", for a "substantially equivalent" device or a Pre-market Application (PMA) for a new or Class III device. Premarket application and premarket notification or 510(k) filings could impact on state tort claims and the federal preemption doctrine is discussed in the United States Supreme Court landmark decisions of *Riegel v. Medtronic* and *Medtronic v. Lohr*. "Fraud on the FDA" is examined in *Buckman v. Plaintiffs Legal Committee*. Drawbacks of the 1976 Medical Device Amendments included poor post-market surveillance, limited enforcement and difficult reclassification. Several pre-1976 Amendments devices slipped through the system under substantial equivalence and by "grandfathering."

1990 and 1992 Medical Device Amendments—Enacted in 1990, the Safe Medical Device Amendments addressed safety and adverse event reporting by healthcare professionals. The 1992 Medical Device Amendments focused on post marketing surveillance. Section 360h(e), under the FDCA, pertains to FDA recall authority specific to devices. Recognized as marketplace corrections or removals, these recalls are necessary for public health and safety reasons. Medical device manufacturers and importers have 10 days from the time a firm initiates a recall to file a report with FDA if the device correction or removal involves a "risk to health." See: 21 CFR 806.

2002 Medical Device User Fee and Modernization Act—Modeled after user fees for new drugs, the Medical Device User Fee and Modernization Act (MDUFMA) of 2002 provides for user fees. MDUFMA authorizes FDA to collect fees related to devices including 510(k)'s, premarket applications, supplements and premarket reports. The user fee program includes measurable performance goals and FDA accountability such as review times. The aim of the MDUFA is to reduce review times, improve timeliness of premarket inspections, greater use of outside consultants and additional training. In fiscal year (FY) 2019, the standard premarket application (PMA) fee was $322,147 and the 510(k) fee for FY 2019 was $10,953.

Premarket Reviews: pertain to certain applications such as a Premarket Approval Application (PMA), product development protocol, premarket report or PMR for reprocessed devices and application supplements related to the manufacture of medical devices.

Third Party Accredited Persons Inspections: for Class II and Class III manufacturers affords FDA the ability to concentrate on higher risk inspections. Third party review permits global firms a more efficient multiple inspection schedule. The company that decides to use third party inspection pays for the cost of third-party inspections to the accredited person. Due to the potential for conflict of interest, federal government employees; owners or those affiliated with a medical device manufacturer, supplier or vendor including consultants; those with a financial interest pertaining to any FDA regulated product; and anyone engaged in the design, manufacture, sale or promotion of FDA regulated products are precluded from third party establishment accreditation.

Reprocessed Medical Devices: MDUFMA applies to reprocessed medical devices as well. Prior to enactment of the MDUFMA, the regulatory requirements were based on the medical device class. Changes under MDUFMA include validation data requirements, 510(k) submissions with validation data and pre-market reports for Class III devices.

Post Market Surveillance: MDUFMA authorizes additional funding for post-market surveillance through Congressional appropriations and requires FDA to submit reports to Congress about postmarket surveillance effectiveness.

2005 "Contact Lens" Regulation—CDRH regulates corrective and non-corrective contact lenses due to the 2005 "contact lens" law. Previously, non-corrective contact lenses were regulated as cosmetics. This comports with the 2003 "Fairness to Contact Lens Consumers Act" and the subsequent FTC Contact Lens Rule which requires a prescription or fitting by a qualified eye care professional.

NOTE: See: *FTC Settlement Requires Internet Marketer to Stop Selling Cosmetic Contact Lenses without Prescriptions (07/20/2011).*

2007 FDA Amendments Act Application to Medical Devices—Key highlights include the following: reduced user fees; the addition of clinical trials to a public registry; and incorporation of the Pediatric Medical Device Safety and Improvement Act that requires descriptions of pediatric populations in product marketing applications to FDA.

2010 Patient Protection and Affordable Care Act—includes mandatory annual reporting by device manufacturers of every payment or transfer of value in excess of $10.00 or $100.00 in the annual aggregate made to physicians and teaching hospitals. According to the Centers for Medicare and Medicaid Services' Open Payments program reported that 1,444 drug and device companies made $8.40 billion in payments to physicians and teaching hospitals in 2017. See: P.L. 111-148

2012 Food and Drug Administration Safety and Innovation Act—Device companies are projected to pay $595 million in user fees over five years through fiscal year 2017. Other applicable sections include: performance goals; a new *de novo* pathway for risk-based classification; a process change for how devices are reclassified; and postmarket surveillance expansion.

NOTE: Taxable Medical Device— Despite strong lobbying by the medical device industry, a 2.3% excise tax was imposed on medical device manufacturers under the Affordable Care Act. Yet, there was a stay of this tax for two years which was then extended through December 31, 2019.

Chapter 2: Medical Device Regulation Fundamentals—Definitions, "Medical Apps", Classifications, Expanded Access, Personalized Medicine and Reuse

Medical Device Defined

http://www.fda.gov/MedicalDevices/DeviceRegulationandGuidance/HowtoMarketYourDevice/default.htm

In order market a device, a manufacturer first needs to determine if the product meets the definition of a medical device under the FDCA, 21 U.S.C. section 321(h) as follows:

(h) The term "device" . . . means an instrument, apparatus, implement, machine, contrivance, implant, in vitro reagent, or other similar or related article, including any component, part, or accessory, which is. . . . (2) intended for use in the diagnosis of disease or other conditions, or in the cure, mitigation, treatment, or prevention of disease, in man or other animals, or (3) intended to affect the structure or any function of the body of man or other animals, and which does not achieve its primary intended purposes through chemical action within or on the body of man or other animals and which is not dependent upon being metabolized for the achievement of its primary intended purposes.

Medical devices are subject to controls detailed in the final procedural regulations in Title 21 of the Code of Federal Regulations (CFR), Parts 800-1200, which are the fundamental prerequisites essential for marketing, proper labeling and monitoring the device performance once marketed. It is important to determine if the product is in fact a medical device as it could fall into another category entirely, such as a biologic or a drug under the FDCA, which would result in very different approval requirements. Additionally, the product could still be a medical device and an electronic radiation-emitting product as well with additional premarket considerations. Combination products present complex issues. Mandated by MDUFA, the Office of Combination Products (OCP) was established.

http://www.fda.gov/MedicalDevices/DeviceRegulationandGuidance/Overview/default.htm

Mobile Medical Applications—"Apps"

https://www.fda.gov/MedicalDevices/DigitalHealth/MobileMedicalApplications/default.htm

The 21st Century Cures Act (Cures Act) (12/13/2016) both clarified FDA's **regulation of medical software** and amended the definition of "device" in the Food, Drug and Cosmetic Act by excluding selected software functions. According to FDA, mobile medical apps are medical devices that are mobile apps and serve as an accessory to a regulated medical device or transform a mobile platform into a regulated medical device. "Mobile apps" are software programs that run on mobile communication devices such as smartphones. According to FDA, mobile medical apps are medical devices that are mobile apps, meet the definition of a medical device and serve as an accessory to a regulated medical device or transform a mobile platform into a regulated medical device. In 2018, approximately 50 percent of smartphone and tablet users downloaded mobile health applications.

FDA has cleared some mobile medical Apps for use by healthcare professionals and patients. For example, the National Institutes of Health's LactMed app provides nursing mothers with information about the effects of medicines on breast milk and nursing infants. See also: the AgaMatrix's iPhone Glucose Meter which connects to the iPhone and iPod touch. Users are able to view information and send data to their health care professional. As with other FDA products, intent, safety and efficacy are important considerations. However, for numerous mobile apps that meet the regulatory definition of a "device" and pose minimal risk to patients and consumers, FDA exercises enforcement discretion. Under these circumstances, FDA will not require manufacturers to submit premarket review applications or to register and list their medical apps. An example of such a mobile app is one that automates simple tasks for health care providers.

NOTE: Due to the 21ˢᵗ Century Cures Act, FDA is revising the guidance the *Mobile Medical Applications Guidance for Industry and Food and Drug Administration Staff* issued February 9, 2015 and which superseded the September 25, 2013 issued guidance was updated for consistency with the guidance document *Medical Devices Data Systems, Medical Image Storage Devices, and Medical Image Communications Devices* issued Feb. 9, 2015. See:
https://www.fda.gov/MedicalDevices/DigitalHealth/default.htm
https://www.fda.gov/downloads/MedicalDevices/.../UCM263366.pdf

CRITICAL ANALYSIS: Discuss the implications of the 21ˢᵗ Century Cures Act concerning "Mobile Medical Apps".

Combination Products—*Prevor v. FDA*

http://www.fda.gov/CombinationProducts/default.htm

Primary Mode of Action—Determining the *primary mode of action of* (PMOA) of a product presents complex issues and at times, a combination product could have two modes of action and can fall within several FDA Centers. Combination products, that is, device-drug; or device-biologic present complex issues in terms of the FDA Center with primary regulatory authority. The Office of Combination Products (OCP) was established as required under the MDUFA of 2002. The main thrust of OCP eliminates the complex issues and confusion in the regulatory industry concerning product classification and FDA review. OCPs involvement emanates from the initial stages of FDA review through postmarket review. Principal responsibilities include: determining which FDA Center reviews a combination product; assigning each combination product to the FDA Center with primary jurisdiction; coordinating product reviews that consist of more than one FDA Center; deciding disagreements about the time involved in premarket product review; managing FDA guidance document policies; ensuring the uniformity concerning post market combination product regulation; and annual reporting to Congress.

A final rule published (November 23, 2005) defines *"mode of action"* and *"primary mode of action"*. See: 21 CFR Part 3. If the OCP determines that the principal or primary mode of the product is a medical device, then CDRH will have primary jurisdiction. However, if the primary mode of the product is a drug, then the Center for Drug Evaluation and Research will have primary regulatory authority. Similarly, if the principal mode is that of a biologic, the Center for Biologics Evaluation and Research has primary regulatory oversight.

Skin Wash Example—*Prevor v. Food and Drug Administration*

The case of *Prevor I v. Food and Drug Administration*, 895 F. Supp. 2d 90, 92, 100-01 (D.D.C. 2012) D.D.C., *Prevor II v. FDA* No. 1:13-cv-01177 (D.D.C. Sept. 9, 2014) provides a significant example. The core issue concerned whether the product, Diphoterine® Skin Wash (DSW), should be classified as a drug, medical device or combination. The form of Diphoterine® Skin Wash (DSW) is a liquid substance in a canister propelled by pressurized gas. The court, in *Prevor I*, stated that the FDA "could find that DSW should be classified as a drug-device combination product with a drug mode of action if it also adopts a plausible construction of the relevant statutory language." Upon remand, on May 24, 2013, FDA issued a detailed conclusion that the combination product was a drug device and primary mode for the skin wash product was a drug. Chemical action and intent remain critical as the court set forth that classification is dependent on whether its chemical action will prevent and minimize chemical burns. Therefore, the court "left open" and remanded the designation decision to the FDA. The court in *Prevor II*, remanded back to FDA (*Prevor II v. FDA* No. 1:13-cv-01177 (D.D.C. Sept. 9, 2014)). On remand to FDA, the agency again determined that the primary mode for the combination product was a drug. This case has spanned several years as Prevor vigorously argued that the primary mode for the product should be a medical device.

CRITICAL ANALYSIS: Do you agree with the FDA determination in *Prevor* (link below)?
https://www.fda.gov/downloads/CombinationProducts/JurisdictionalInformation/RFDJurisdictionalDecisions/RedactedDecisionLetters/UCM479168.pdf

Investigational Device Exemptions

Investigational device exemptions (IDE) permit the use of a device on human subjects in clinical trials. An approved IDE stipulates the maximum number of clinical sites and the maximum number of human subjects that may be enrolled in a study. FDA has the authority to exempt investigational use devices from particular requirements that other devices must abide by. An approved IDE application permits shipment of a device, otherwise subject to marketing clearance. An approved IDE permits use in a clinical trial to gather safety and efficacy data necessary to substantiate some 510(k) submissions and for PMA's. Clinical studies requisite for a PMA and in some instances a 510(k) and require: an approved IDE by an institutional review board (IRB); informed consent from patients; labeling that details investigational use only; and records and reports. See: 21 CFR Part 812, Investigational Devices; 21 CFR Part 50, Protection of Human Subjects; Part 54, Financial Disclosure by Clinical Investigators; Part 56, Institutional Review Boards and Part 820, Subpart C, Design Controls of the Quality System Regulation.

Expanded Access-Emergency, Treatment, Humanitarian or Compassionate Use

http://www.fda.gov/MedicalDevices/DeviceRegulationandGuidance/HowtoMarketYourDevice/InvestigationalDeviceExemptionIDE/ucm051345.htm#treatment

Some patients might not be eligible for an investigational device clinical trial. Fortunately, there are methods available to those patients who have a life-threatening disease for which there are no currently approved medical device treatments. These include the following:

➢ **Emergency Use,**
➢ **Treatment Use, and**
➢ **Compassionate or Humanitarian Use.**

Emergency Use of Unapproved Medical Devices

An unapproved device may provide the single potential life-saving alternative. However, what happens when there is no IDE or perhaps the proposed use is not approved under an existing IDE? Additionally, the physician or institution may not be approved under the IDE. FDA will use enforcement discretion, if a physician utilizes an unapproved device on an emergency basis. FDA prior approval is not required as long as the following criteria for emergency use are met:

✓ The patient is in a life-threatening condition that needs immediate treatment;
✓ No generally acceptable alternative for treating the patient is available; and
✓ No time to use existing procedures to get FDA approval for the use.

Informed Consent—The investigator is obligated to obtain informed consent of the subject or the subject's legally authorized representative unless both the investigator and a physician who is not otherwise participating in the clinical investigation certify in writing all of the following [21 CFR 50.23(a)]: *Subject is confronted by a life-threatening situation necessitating the use of test article; Informed consent cannot be obtained because of an inability to communicate with, or obtain legally effective consent from, the subject; Time is not sufficient to obtain consent from the subject's legal representative; and No alternative method of approved or generally recognized therapy is available that provides an equal or greater likelihood of saving the subject's life.*

Physician Responsibilities include the following— Report to the IRB within five days [21 CFR 56.104(c)] and comply with provisions of the IRB regulations [21 CFR part 56]; Evaluate the likelihood of a similar need for the device occurring again, and if future use is likely, immediately initiate efforts to obtain IRB approval and an approved IDE for the device's subsequent use; and if an IDE for the use does exist, notify the sponsor of the emergency use, or if an IDE does not exist, notify FDA of the emergency use (CDRH Program Operation Staff 301-594-1190) and provide FDA with a written summary of the conditions constituting the emergency, subject protection measures, and results.

Treatment Use of Investigational Devices— Treatment use means that an IDE trial may be expanded to include additional patients with life-threatening or serious diseases if the data indicates that the device is effective. This is called treatment use. The following parameters apply:

✓ Device intended to treat or diagnose a serious or immediately life-threatening disease or condition;

- ✓ No comparable or satisfactory alternative device available to treat or diagnose the disease or condition in the intended patient population;
- ✓ Device is under investigation in a controlled clinical trial for the same use under an approved IDE, or all clinical trials have been completed; and
- ✓ The sponsor of the controlled clinical trial is pursuing marketing approval/clearance of the investigational device with due diligence.

Humanitarian or Compassionate Use Devices

A humanitarian device, (HUD) also referred to as a compassionate use device, provides patients with a method to use an investigational device not yet approved. Submission of a humanitarian device exemption application is necessary and the approval rate is approximately 99%. The format and content of a HUD application is similar to that of a PMA; however, with one major distinction. The HUD submission application is exempt from the effectiveness requisites required for a PMA. 21 CFR 814 Subpart H - Humanitarian Use Devices. See: 21 U.S. C. § 360bbb (Expanded access to unapproved therapies and diagnostics) (2019).

NOTE: The Federal Right-to-Try Act became law on May 30, 2018; however, it does not expressly include medical devices as prior proposed legislation. Trickett Wendler, Frank Mongiello, Jordan McLinn and Matthew Bellina Right-to- Try Act of 2017. P. L. No. 115-176 9 (May 30, 2018); 21 U.S. C. § 360bbb (Expanded access to unapproved therapies and diagnostics).

Classification and Reclassification

http://www.fda.gov/MedicalDevices/DeviceRegulationandGuidance/Overview/ClassifyYourDevice/default.htm

The Medical Device Amendments (1976 Amendments) grouped devices into Class I, Class II, and Class III. Classification is based on the amount of control necessary for both product safety and effectiveness and depends on intended use and indications for use and risk. The product class determines the type of pre-marketing submission necessary for FDA clearance. The 1976 Amendments contain device classifications specifying those devices requiring pre-market notification, known as a 510(k). A 510(k) is a pre-marketing submission to FDA to demonstrate safety and effectiveness or substantially equivalent to a legally marketed device. FDA may reclassify a device due to "new information" based on valid scientific evidence as defined under section 513 (21 U.S. C. 360c). FDA may initiate reclassification or an interested person may file a petition with safety and efficacy substantiation data to reclassify a device.

Class I General Controls: Class I devices are subject to the least amount of regulation; that is, "general" control requirements apply. Registration is by the manufacturer and a 510(k) may be required; however; some well-established devices are exempt from 510(k) requirements.

Examples: *Surgeon's Gloves* and *Microscope*

Class II General and Special Controls: Class II devices pose a greater health-market threat and therefore, "general" control requirements are alone insufficient to ensure safety and effectiveness. There must be sufficient data available to establish performance standard. Post-market surveillance and patient registries may be required.

Examples: *Surgical Drapes* and *Powdered Wheelchair*

Class III Premarket Approval: Class III devices have the greatest rigorous controls. A Class III device requires an approved premarket approval application (PMA) with safety and efficacy data prior to marketing. Class III devices that require a PMA include devices regulated as new drugs prior to May 28, 1976, known as transitional devices; devices not substantially equivalent to devices marketed prior to May 28, 1976 and pre-amendment Class III devices listed under 21 CFR require a PMA. Contents of a (PMA) include a complete description of the device, functional components or ingredients, devices properties relevant to preventing the respective disease, the principles of operation and "methods used in manufacture." Requirements include reference to performance standards, results of non-clinical and clinical studies and labeling.

Examples: *Hip Joint Prosthesis* and *Pacemaker*

Labeling and Symbols

http://www.fda.gov/MedicalDevices/DeviceRegulationandGuidance/Overview/DeviceLabeling/default.htm

The term "label", under 21 U.S.C. 321 (k), is defined in part, as: *The term 'label' means a display of written, printed, or graphic matter upon the immediate container of any article..."*

The term "labeling", under 21 U.S.C. 321 (m), is defined in part, as: *"The terms labeling means all labels and other written, printed, or graphic matter (1) upon any article or any of its containers or wrappers, or accompanying such article."* 21 CFR Part 801 details general labeling requirements that vary depending on the type of device. Over-the-counter or non-prescription medical devices must use very specific labeling to allow accurate use by the consumer including intended use, adequate directions and prominence. Applicable regulations are: General Device Labeling 21 CFR Part 801; In Vitro Diagnostic Products (known as reagents, instruments and systems) 21 CFR Part 809; Investigational Device Exemptions 21 CFR Part 812; Good Manufacturing Practices 21 CFR Part 820; General Electronic Products 21 CFR Part 1010. Some devices require labeling requirements specific to the device itself such as: Denture repair or refitting kits 21 CFR 801.405; Impact resistant lenses 21 CFR 801.410; Hearing aids 21 CFR 801.420; Menstrual tampons 21 CFR 801.430; and Latex condoms 21 CFR 801.435. These devices require additional requirements such as informational literature, patient release forms, performance testing and or specific tolerances or prohibitions on particular ingredients.

FDA issued a final rule, effective on September 13, 2016, to permit the optional use of standalone symbols or graphical representations of information in labeling (including labels) without adjacent explanatory text. The final rule details that the use of symbols, accompanied by adjacent explanatory text is still permissible. Additionally, FDA revised its prescription device labeling regulations to permit the use of the symbol "Rx only" or "℞ only" in the labeling for prescription devices. See: 81 FR 38911 (June 25, 2016).

Device Advertising

http://www.fda.gov/NewsEvents/Testimony/ucm096272.htm

The Federal Trade Commission (FTC) regulates the advertising of most medical devices except restricted devices. Sections 12-15 of the Federal Trade Commission Act prohibit false or misleading advertising of certain products that FDA regulates. See: 15 U.S.C. section 52-55.

However, FDA regulates the advertising of restricted devices and has specific authority to do so under 21 U. S. C. sections 352(q) and 352(r). Specifically, 21 U.S. C. section 352(r) states that restricted devices are not subject to sections 12-15 of the Federal Trade Commission Act. The majority of restricted devices are Class III premarket approval devices restricted as a condition of approval, under 21 U. S. C. sections 360e(d)(1)(B)(ii). A few Class I and II devices are restricted by regulation such as hearing aids or as part of a performance standard requirement that sale and distribution of a device be restricted. See 21 U. S. C. section 360 (d)(a)(2)(b)(v).

Reprocessed Single-Use Devices

http://www.fda.gov/MedicalDevices/DeviceRegulationandGuidance/ReprocessingofSingle-UseDevices/ucm121093.htm (edited)

The reuse of medical devices labeled or intended for "one-time use" started in the late 1970s. Prior to that time, the majority of medical devices were considered "reusable". Most of these medical devices were composed of glass, rubber or metal. However, in response to market demand for disposable devices, manufacturers started selling "single-use" devices (SUDs). The terminology "single-use device" connotes the impression that the device will be used one time. Yet, an industry of third party reprocessors evolved to decontaminate and sterilize devices that are more complicated. In 2015, FDA issued a guidance aimed toward infection prevention and safety. Titled *"Reprocessing Medical Devices in Health Care Settings: Validation Methods and Labeling",* the guidance for industry includes recommendations medical device manufacturers should follow pre-market and post-market for the safe and effective use of reprocessed devices.

http://www.fda.gov/downloads/MedicalDevices/DeviceRegulationandGuidance/GuidanceDocuments/UCM253010.pdf

Prior to the MDUFMA, the regulatory requirements for manufacturers of reprocessed single use devices were dependent upon the device class. For example, unless exempt from a 510(k), manufacturers of reprocessed Class I and Class II single use devices were required to have a 510(k). Under MDUFMA, some reprocessors who are exempt still must submit validation data. Validation data is required as well for those reprocessors whose devices have cleared 510(k)'s. Reprocessors of Class III devices must submit premarket reports. The MDUFMA imposes different requirements dependent on whether the device is exempt from a 510(k) submission, non-exempt or premarket application (PMA) status. See: *Pub.Med.* for articles on this topic. The Ethics of reusing single-use devices *https://www.ncbi.nlm.nih.gov/pmc/articles/PMC3153512/*

Examples of Reprocessed devices: Surgical saw blades; Surgical drills; Laparoscopy scissors; Electrophysiology catheters; Biopsy forceps; Ophthalmic knife; Respiratory therapy and anesthesia breathing circuits; and Balloon angioplasty catheters.

Definitions Applicable to Reuse

Single-use device: "The term 'single-use device' means a device that is intended for one time use or on a single patient during a single procedure."

Reprocessed: "The term 'reprocessed', with respect to a single-use device, means an original device that has previously been used on a patient and has been subjected to additional processing and manufacturing for the purpose of an additional single use on a patient.

Original device: "The term 'original device' means a new, unused single-use device."

Critical reprocessed single-use device: "The term 'critical reprocessed single-use device' means a reprocessed single-use device that is intended to contact normally sterile tissue or body spaces during use."

Semi-critical reprocessed single-use device: "The term 'semi-critical reprocessed single-use device' means a reprocessed single-use device that is intended to contact intact mucous membranes and not penetrate normally sterile areas of the body."

Non-critical: a reprocessed device that only makes topical contact and does not penetrate the skin.

Validation Data: Critical and semi-critical reprocessed single use devices: Validation data is required for non-exempt 510(k) devices. The MDUFMA requires validation data for some single use reprocessed devices that are already cleared, that is, devices that are not 510(k) exempt. Notification is placed in the Federal Register and updated as necessary as to those cleared 510(k) single use reprocessed devices where validation is required. Finally, MDUFMA requires premarket reports for Class III PMA reprocessed single use devices.

Labeling Requirements—Mandated by the MDUFMA, the following statement is required for reprocessed single-use devices both "prominently and conspicuously".

> *"Reprocessed device for single use. Reprocessed by [name of manufacturer that reprocessed the device]."*

The 2005 Medical Device User Fee Stabilization Act amended section 352(u) of the FDCA to apply only to SUD reprocessors regarding the labeling requirement of the manufacturer's name.

Enforcement Priorities— FDA requires hospitals that reprocess SUDs to meet the same regulatory requirements as the original manufacturer of the product. FDA enforces these requirements for hospitals just as for medical device manufacturers. For example, under the FDCA, regulatory actions FDA may take against non-compliant hospitals include:

➢ Public health alerts and notifications; Warning Letters; Mandatory recalls;

➢ Seizure actions; Injunctions; Civil monetary penalties; and Prosecutions.

CRITICAL ANALYSIS: Discuss the issues of patient safety, informed consent and ethics. See: PubMed for articles about reprocessed single use devices. See: PubMed for articles on this topic.
https://www.ncbi.nlm.nih.gov/pmc/articles/PMC3153512/

Personalized Medicine—Guidance and Diagnostic Device Approvals

FDA has recognized personalized approaches to medicine by and issued a guidance in 2014 that addresses the use of diagnostic devices and approvals of testing kits. The intent of the guidance is: "to assist (1) sponsors who are planning to develop a therapeutic product (either a novel product or an existing product with a new indication) for which the use of an in vitro companion diagnostic device (or test) is essential for the therapeutic product's safe and effective use and (2) sponsors planning to develop an in vitro companion diagnostic device that is intended to be used with a corresponding therapeutic product."

https://www.fda.gov/downloads/MedicalDevices/DeviceRegulationandGuidance/GuidanceDocuments/UCM262327.pdf

Prior to the 2014 guidance, in 2013, FDA issued a warning letter to the CEO of *23andMe*, Inc., due to marketing the *23andMe* Saliva Collection Kit and Personal Genome Service (PGS) without clearance or approval. Ultimately, *23andMe*, Inc. submitted a revised 510(k) application for its direct-to-consumer genetic testing service focusing on a single rare inherited condition. In 2015 (Feb.) FDA authorized marketing of *23andMe*'s Bloom Syndrome carrier test, a direct-to-consumer (DTC) genetic test to determine whether a healthy person has a variant in a gene that could lead to their offspring inheriting the serious disorder. FDA classified carrier screening tests as class II and exempts these devices from premarket review.

A $1.3 million NIH grant was awarded in 2014 to support further development of its Web-based database and research engine to stimulate genetic discoveries. According to *23andMe*, the funding enabled the company to use its stored genetic data on thousands of diseases and traits for over 400,000 people to pursue research endeavors and detect novel and rare genetic associations with health conditions. In 2018 (March) FDA permitted *23andMe* to conduct new direct-to consumer testing of three mutations in a gene that are associated with higher risks of breast, ovarian and prostate cancer. The test can identify three of more than 1,000 known BRCA gene mutations; however the specific mutations affect a very slight percentage of the population. According to FDA said in a statement. The three mutations affect about 2 percent of Ashkenazi Jewish women, and between 0 percent and 0.1 percent of other populations. FDA emphasized that the tests are intended to be informative but not definitive and should not influence treatment decisions. According to *23andMe* if the test detects a mutation, a woman would have between a 45 percent and 85 percent chance of developing breast cancer by age 70. Yet, along with genetics there are other factors that impact such as obesity and the environment.

NOTE: *Davis-Hudson and Diaz v. 23andMe, Inc.*, Case No. 74-20-1400-0032, before the American Arbitration Association. See settlement. *http://www.23andmesettlement.com*

CRITICAL ANALYSIS: Review the *23andMe, Inc.* settlement noted above. Consumers alleged in the lawsuit that they were misled about the types of health information they would receive from the home DNA testing kits. Discuss the fairness of the recovery.

Chapter 3: Medical Device Submissions—Premarket Notification 510(k), Premarket Approval, Liability, and Preemption

Submission Types—510(k) Premarket Notification or Premarket Approval

Medical device submission procedures range from a premarket notification, referred to as a "510(k) clearance" to premarket approval or PMA. The PMA process is quite complex in comparison to a 510k submission. In fiscal year (FY) 2019, the standard premarket application (PMA) fee was $322,147 and the 510(k) fee for FY 2019 was $10,953. However, the majority of medical devices sold in the United States, are through the 510(k) premarket notification and are less costly in terms of FDA clearance.

Premarket Notification—510(k)

The 510(k) process, applicable to most Class I and II and some Class III devices, require a premarket notification submission by the manufacturer prior to marketing. A "510(k)" is a pre-marketing submission to demonstrate that the device is safe and effective or substantially equivalent to a legally marketed device. A legally marketed device or predicate device means a device that was marketed before the 1976 Amendments. A device is substantially equivalent if it has the same intended use and the same technological characteristics as the predicate device. Alternatively, even if the proposed device has different technological characteristics, a device could be substantially equivalent as long as it is as safe and effective as the legally marketed device. Descriptive data must be submitted and performance data, if necessary, to demonstrate substantial equivalence. FDAMA created the opportunity for third party review by accredited persons.

Submission Types—*Traditional, Special, or Abbreviated*

Submission Categories—*Domestic manufacturers, Specification Developers, Exporters, Foreign manufacturers or U.S. representatives of foreign manufacturers who intend to introduce a device into the United States market;*

and

Repackers or relabelers who make labeling modifications or whose operations considerably alter the device;

Substantial Equivalence Determination Factors

Sec. 513 of the FDCA (i)(1)(A): For purposes of determinations of substantial equivalence under subsection (f) and section 520(l), the term "substantially equivalent" or "substantial equivalence" means, with respect to a device being compared to a predicate device, that the device has *the same intended use as the predicate device and the device*
(i) has the same technological characteristics as the predicate device,

or

(ii)(I) has different technological characteristics and the information submitted that the device is substantially equivalent to the predicate device contains information, including appropriate clinical or scientific data if deemed necessary ..... that demonstrates that the device is as safe and effective as a legally marketed device, and (II) does not raise different questions of safety and effectiveness than the predicate device.

Guidance—Evaluating Substantial Equivalence

FDA issued a final guidance document titled, *"The 510(k) Program: Evaluating Substantial Equivalence in Premarket Notifications [510(k)]"* (July 28, 2014). The FDA developed this document to provide guidance to industry and FDA staff about current review practices for premarket notification (510(k)) submissions. The intent of the guidance is to identify, explain, and clarify each of the critical decision points FDA utilizes to determine substantial equivalence. Further, the purpose of the guidance is to enhance predictability, consistency, and transparency of the 510(k) program by providing better detail of the regulatory framework, policies, and practices underlying FDA's 510(k) review.

The FDA 510(k) premarket notifications process has become controversial. The Institute of Medicine (IOM) issued a report in 2011, "Medical Devices and the Public's Health: The FDA 510(k) Clearance Process at 35 Years" IOM determined that the current 510(k) process is faulty. The IOM recommended development of a premarket and postmarket regulatory framework. *http://www.iom.edu/Reports/2011/Medical-Devices-and-the-Publics-Health-The-FDA-510k-Clearance-Process-at-35-Years.aspx*

In 2015, the Government Accounting Office (GAO) examined FDA's actions involved with the controversial power morcellator. In 2014, FDA issued a guidance document and safety communication: ***Laparoscopic Uterine Power Morcellation: Product Labeling for Laparoscopic Power Morcellators Guidance***
https://www.gpo.gov/fdsys/pkg/FR-2014-11-25/html/2014-27857.htm?source=govdelivery&utm_medium=email&utm_source=govdelivery
Laparoscopic Uterine Power Morcellation in Hysterectomy and Myomectomy: FDA Safety Communication *http://www.fda.gov/MedicalDevices/Safety/AlertsandNotices/ucm424443.htm https://www.fda.gov/MedicalDevices/ProductsandMedicalProcedures/SurgeryandLifeSupport/ucm584463.htm https://www.fda.gov/downloads/MedicalDevices/DeviceRegulationandGuidance/GuidanceDocuments/UCM284443.pdf?source=govdelivery&utm_medium=email&utm_source=govdelivery;*
Benefit-Risk Factors to Consider When Determining Substantial Equivalence in Premarket Notifications [510(k)] with Different Technological Characteristics: Draft Guidance for Industry and Food and Drug Administration Staff (July 15, 2014);
http://www.fda.gov/medicaldevices/deviceregulationandguidance/guidancedocuments/ucm282958.htm

CRITICAL ANALYSIS: Evaluate the 510(k) process in terms of patient safety. See for example: *Laparoscopic Uterine Power Morcellator* **above.**

Premarket Approval PMA

Unlike a 510(k) submission, a premarket approval submission involves a more complex process. A PMA application submission is a request to market a device or to continue the marketing of a Class III device. PMA requirements apply to almost all Class III devices marketed or to be marketed in the United States. Transitional, pre-amendment, or not substantially equivalent post-amendment Class III devices all require a PMA. Unlike a 510(k), a PMA approval is based on a determination by FDA that the submission contains adequate scientific evidence that the device is safe and effective for its intended use. The review period for a PMA submission is 180 days; however, the review time usually takes longer. An advisory committee reviews the PMA and makes a recommendation as to whether FDA should authorize the submission.

Preemption Doctrine

Preemption is a legal term of art that emanates from the Supremacy Clause (Article VI, clause 2) of the United States Constitution. Article VI, clause 2 prohibits states from enacting laws that conflict with federal law unless the federal law contains explicit preemption language. Unlike most other products that FDA regulates, the Medical Devices Amendments contain express preemptive language. The Medical Amendments of 1976 under section 521 of the FDCA, 21 U.S.C §360(k), prohibits a state from promulgating any "requirement regarding a medical device intended for human use" that is "different from or in addition to" any requirement of the FDCA. Preemption is discussed in *Riegel v. Medtronic, Inc.* and *Medtronic, Inc. v. Lohr.*

Riegel concerned a PMA and common law state negligence action against the manufacturer of an allegedly defective catheter and the ability to bring a legal action in state court. The United States Supreme Court in *Riegel v. Medtronic* was faced with the issue of preemption concerning a

PMA and determined that makers of medical devices that go through the arduous PMA process are immune from liability for personal injuries under state law. That is, the Supreme Court in *Riegel* held that lawsuits involving devices that went through the PMA approval process under the Medical Device Amendments (MDA) are preempted from state law tort claims. The ruling applies to PMA devices based on the language in the MDA under §360 (k)(a)(1).

Similarly, in *Horn v. Thoratec Corp.* 376 F.3d 163 (3rd Cir. 2004) the court held that where the device received premarket approval, the Medical Device Amendments of the FDCA preempts state common law tort claims for PMA approved devices. Conversely, a device under 510(k) pre-market clearance such as in the *Lohr* case concerned a common law negligence action against the manufacturer of an allegedly defective pacemaker lead and the ability to bring a lawsuit in state court. The Supreme Court in *Lohr* held that the FDCA did not preempt lawsuits involving devices that granted premarketing clearance under section 510(k). In terms of preemption, does it matter if the device was granted premarket clearance under a 510(k), 21 U.S.C. §360 (k), or premarket approval under a Premarket Application (PMA)? Apparently, it matters if there was an approval based on a "510 (k)" submission or a premarket application. The United States Supreme Court in *Riegel* and *Lohr* addressed this issue.

Premarket Application and Preemption of State Claims—*Riegel*
Riegel v. Medtronic, 128 S. Ct. 999 (2008)

SCALIA, J., delivered the opinion of the Court, joined by ROBERTS, C. J., and KENNEDY, SOUTER, THOMAS, BREYER, and ALITO, JJ., and also joined by STEVENS, J., except for Parts III-A and III-B. STEVENS, J., filed an opinion concurring in part and concurring in the judgment. GINSBURG, J., filed a dissenting opinion.

Scalia, J. We consider whether the pre-emption clause enacted in the Medical Device Amendments of 1976, 21 U.S.C. § 360k, bars common-law claims challenging the safety and effectiveness of a medical device given premarket approval by the Food and Drug Administration (FDA). *** The Federal Food, Drug, and Cosmetic Act (FDCA), 52 Stat. 1040, as amended, 21 U.S.C. § 301 *et seq.*, has long required FDA approval for the introduction of new drugs into the market. Until the statutory enactment at issue here, however, the introduction of new medical devices was left largely for the States to supervise as they saw fit. See *Medtronic, Inc. v. Lohr,* 518 U.S. 470, 475-476, 116 S.Ct. 2240, 135 L.Ed.2d 700 (1996). The regulatory landscape changed in the 1960's and 1970's, as complex devices proliferated and some failed. Most notably, the Dalkon Shield intrauterine device, introduced in 1970, was linked to serious infections and several deaths, not to mention a large number of pregnancies. *** Congress stepped in with passage of the Medical Device Amendments of 1976(MDA), 21 U.S.C. § 360c *et seq.*, which swept back some state obligations and imposed a regime of detailed federal oversight. The MDA includes an express pre-emption provision that states: *"Except as provided in subsection (b) of this section, no State or political subdivision of a State may establish or continue in effect with respect to a device intended for human use any requirement—*

"(1) which is different from, or in addition to, any requirement applicable under this chapter to the device, and *"(2) which relates to the safety or effectiveness of the device or to any other matter included in a requirement applicable to the device under this chapter."§ 360k(a).*

The exception contained in subsection (b) permits the FDA to exempt some state and local requirements from pre-emption. The new regulatory regime established various levels of oversight for medical devices, depending on the risks they present. Class I, which includes such devices as elastic bandages and examination gloves, is subject to the lowest level of oversight: "general controls," such as labeling requirements. § 360c(a)(1)(A); Class II, which includes such devices as powered wheelchairs and surgical drapes, *ibid.,* is subject in addition to "special controls" such as performance standards and postmarket surveillance measures, § 360c(a)(1)(B).The devices receiving the most federal oversight are those in Class III, which include replacement heart valves, implanted cerebella stimulators, and pacemaker pulse generators.

Although the MDA established a rigorous regime of premarket approval for new Class III devices, it grandfathered many that were already on the market. Devices sold before the MDA's effective date may remain on the market until the FDA promulgates, after notice and comment, a regulation requiring premarket approval. §§ 360c (f)(1), 360e(b)(1). A related provision seeks to limit the competitive advantage grandfathered devices receive. A new device need not undergo premarket approval if the FDA finds it is "substantially equivalent" to another device exempt from premarket approval. § 360c(f)(1)(A) [§ 510(k)]. The agency's review of devices for substantial equivalence is known as the § 510(k) process, named after the section of the MDA describing the review. Most new Class III devices enter the market through § 510(k). ***

Premarket approval is a "rigorous" process. *Lohr,* 518 U.S., at 477, 116 S.Ct. 2240. A manufacturer must submit what is typically a multivolume application. It includes, among other things, full reports of all studies and investigations of the device's safety and effectiveness that have been published or should reasonably be known to the applicant; a "full statement" of the device's "components, ingredients, and properties and of the principle or principles of operation"; "a full description of the methods used in, and the facilities and controls used for, the manufacture, processing, and, when relevant, packing and installation of, such device"; samples or device components required by the FDA; and a specimen of the proposed labeling. § 360e(c)(1). *** After completing its review, the FDA may grant or deny premarket approval. § 360e(d). It may also condition approval on adherence to performance standards, 21 CFR § 861.1(b)(3), restrictions upon sale or distribution, or compliance with other requirements, § 814.82. The agency is also free to impose device-specific restrictions by regulation. § 360j(e)(1). ***If an applicant wishes to make such a change, it must submit, and the FDA must approve, an application for supplemental premarket approval, to be evaluated under largely the same criteria as an initial application. § 360e(d)(6); 21 CFR § 814.39(c). After premarket approval, the devices are subject to reporting requirements. § 360i. *** The FDA has the power to withdraw premarket approval based on newly reported data or existing information and must withdraw approval if it determines that a device is unsafe or ineffective under the conditions in its labeling. § 360e(e)(1); see also § 360h(e) (recall authority). ***

The device at issue is an Evergreen Balloon Catheter marketed by defendant-respondent Medtronic, Inc. It is a Class III device that received premarket approval from the FDA in 1994; changes to its label received supplemental approvals in 1995 and 1996. Charles Riegel underwent coronary angioplasty in 1996, shortly after suffering a myocardial infarction. His right coronary artery was diffusely diseased and heavily calcified. Riegel's doctor inserted the Evergreen Balloon Catheter into his patient's coronary artery in an attempt to dilate the artery, although the device's labeling stated that use was contraindicated for patients with diffuse or calcified stenoses. The label also warned that the catheter should not be inflated beyond its rated burst pressure of eight atmospheres. Riegel's doctor inflated the catheter five times, to a pressure of 10 atmospheres; on its fifth inflation, the catheter ruptured. Riegel developed a heart block, was placed on life support, and underwent emergency coronary bypass surgery. *** The United States Court of Appeals for the Second Circuit affirmed these dismissals. 451 F.3d 104 (2006). The court concluded that Medtronic was "clearly subject to the federal, device-specific requirement of adhering to the standards contained in its individual, federally approved" premarket approval application. *Id.,* at 118. ***

Premarket approval, in contrast, imposes "requirements" under the MDA as we interpreted it in *Lohr.* Unlike general labeling duties, premarket approval is specific to individual devices. And it is in no sense an exemption from federal safety review—it *is* federal safety review. *** While devices that enter the market through § 510(k) have "never been formally reviewed under the MDA for safety or efficacy," *ibid.,* the FDA may grant premarket approval only after it determines that a device offers a reasonable assurance of safety and effectiveness, § 360e(d). *** For the foregoing reasons, the judgment of the Court of Appeals is *Affirmed.*

CRITICAL ANALYSIS: Since the *Riegel* decision, Congressional attempts to enact legisla-

tion that would permit state common law actions for PMA approved devices have been unsuccessful. Assess why these attempts have failed.

Premarket Clearance §510(k) State Claims Not Preempted—*Lohr*

Medtronic v. Lohr, 116 S. Ct. 2240 (1996)

OPINION: JUSTICE STEVENS announced the judgment of the Court. Congress enacted the Medical Device Amendments of 1976, in the words of the statute's preamble, "to provide for the safety and effectiveness of medical devices intended for human use." 90 Stat. 539. The question presented is whether that statute pre-empts a state common-law negligence action against the manufacturer of an allegedly defective medical device. Specifically, we must consider whether Lora Lohr, who was injured when her pacemaker failed, may rely on Florida common law to recover damages from Medtronic, Inc., the manufacturer of the device. *** In response to the mounting consumer and regulatory concern, Congress enacted the statute at issue here: the Medical Device Amendments of 1976 (MDA or Act). ***

Before a new Class III device may be introduced to the market, the manufacturer must provide the FDA with a "reasonable assurance" that the device is both safe and effective. See 21 U.S.C. § 360e(d)(2). Despite its relatively innocuous phrasing, the process of establishing this "reasonable assurance," which is known as the "premarket approval," or "PMA" process, is a rigorous one. Manufacturers must submit detailed information regarding the safety and efficacy of their devices, which the FDA then reviews, spending an average of 1,200 hours on each submission. *** Not all, nor even most, Class III devices on the market today have received premarket approval because of two important exceptions to the PMA requirement. First, Congress realized that existing medical devices could not be withdrawn from the market while the FDA completed its PMA analysis for those devices. The statute therefore includes a "grandfathering" provision which allows pre-1976 devices to remain on the market without FDA approval until such time as the FDA initiates and completes the requisite PMA. See 21 U.S.C. § 360e(b)(1)(A); 21 CFR § 814.1(c)(1). Second, to prevent manufacturers of grandfathered devices from monopolizing the market while new devices clear the PMA hurdle, and to ensure that improvements to existing devices can be rapidly introduced into the market, the Act also permits devices that are "substantially equivalent" to pre-existing devices to avoid the PMA process. See 21 U.S.C. § 360e(b)(1)(B).

Although "substantially equivalent" Class III devices may be marketed without the rigorous PMA review, such new devices, as well as all new Class I and Class II devices, are subject to the requirements of § 360(k) [§ 510(k)]. That section imposes a limited form of review on every manufacturer intending to market a new device by requiring it to submit a "premarket notification" to the FDA (the process is also known as a "§ 510(k) process," after the number of the section in the original Act). *** The § 510(k) notification process is by no means comparable to the PMA process; in contrast to the 1,200 hours necessary to complete a PMA review, the § 510(k) review is completed in an average of only 20 hours. *** As have so many other medical device manufacturers, petitioner Medtronic took advantage of § 510(k)'s expedited process in October 1982, when it notified the FDA that it intended to market its Model 4011 pacemaker lead as a device that was "substantially equivalent" to devices already on the market. (The lead is the portion of a pacemaker that transmits the heartbeat-steadying electrical signal from the "pulse generator" to the heart itself.) On November 30, 1982, the FDA found that the model was "substantially equivalent to devices introduced into interstate commerce" prior to the effective date of the Act, and advised Medtronic that it could therefore market its device subject only to the general control provisions of the Act, which could be found in the Code of Federal Regulations. *** In 1993 Lohr and her husband filed this action in a Florida state court. *** Medtronic removed the case to Federal District Court, where it filed a motion for summary judgment arguing that both the negligence and strict-liability claims were pre-empted by 21 U.S.C. § 360k(a). That section, which is at the core of the dispute between the parties in this suit, provides:

> *"§ 360k. State and local requirements respecting devices"* (a) General rule *"Except as provided in subsection (b) of this section, no State or political subdivision of a State may establish or continue in effect with respect to a device intended for human use any requirement*
>
> *"(1) which is different from, or in addition to, any requirement applicable under this chapter to the device, and*
>
> *"(2) which relates to the safety or effectiveness of the device or to any other matter included in a requirement applicable to the device under this chapter."*

In essence, the company argues that the plain language of the statute pre-empts any and all common-law claims brought by an injured plaintiff against a manufacturer of medical devices. *** The legislative history also confirms our understanding that § 360(k) simply was not intended to pre-empt most, let alone all, general common-law duties enforced by damages actions. ***

Design Claim: The Court of Appeals concluded that the Lohrs' defective design claims were not pre-empted because the requirements with which the company had to comply were not sufficiently concrete to constitute a pre-empting federal requirement. Medtronic counters by pointing to the FDA's determination that Model 4011 is "substantially equivalent" to an earlier device as well as the agency's continuing authority to exclude the device from the market if its design is changed. *** The design Model 4011, as with the design of pre-1976 and other "substantially equivalent" devices, has never been formally reviewed under the MDA for safety or efficacy. ***

Identity of Requirements Claims: The Lohrs next suggest that even if "requirements" exist with respect to the manufacturing and labeling of the pacemaker, and even if we can also consider state law to impose a "requirement" under the Act, the state requirement is not pre-empted unless it is "different from, or in addition to," the federal requirement. § 360k(a)(1). *** At least these claims, they suggest, can be maintained without being pre-empted by § 360k, and we agree. *** The regulations promulgated by the FDA expressly support the conclusion that § 360k "does not preempt State or local requirements that are equal to, or substantially identical to, requirements imposed by or under the act."

Manufacturing and Labeling Claims: *** The Lohrs' theory is supported by the FDA regulations, which provide that state requirements are pre-empted "only" when the FDA has established "specific counterpart regulations or . . . other specific requirements applicable to a particular device. " 21 CFR § 808.1(d) (1995). They further note that the statute is not intended to pre-empt "State or local requirements of general applicability where the purpose of the requirement relates either to other products in addition to devices . . . or to unfair trade practices in which the requirements are not limited to devices." § 808.1(d)(1). *** The legal duty that is the predicate for the Lohrs' negligent manufacturing claim is the general duty of every manufacturer to use due care to avoid foreseeable dangers in its products. Similarly, the predicate for the failure to warn claim is the general duty to inform users and purchasers of potentially dangerous items of the risks involved in their use. *** These state requirements therefore escape pre-emption, not because the source of the duty is a judge-made common-law rule, but rather because their generality leaves them outside the category of requirements that § 360k envisioned to be "with respect to" specific devices such as pacemakers. As a result, none of the Lohrs' claims based on allegedly defective manufacturing or labeling are pre-empted by the MDA. *** Accordingly, the judgment of the Court of Appeals is reversed insofar as it held that any of the claims were pre-empted and affirmed insofar as it rejected the pre-emption defense. ***

CRITICAL ANALYSIS: What did the *Riegel* decision hinge on? Assess the legal ramifications of precluding state common law negligence claims. Distinguish *Riegel* and *Lohr*.

Fraud on the FDA and State Claims—*Buckman*

The United States Supreme Court unanimously held that state-law tort claims alleging "fraud on the FDA" were preempted due to the inherent conflict with FDA's administrative procedures. In distinguishing *Buckman* from *Medtronic*, the fraud claims in *Buckman* existed due to violation of the FDCA disclosure requirements. Additionally, the *Buckman* decision was consistent with previous cases that have held that there is no right of private action under the FDCA.

Buckman v. Plaintiffs' Legal Committee, 121 S. Ct. 1012 (2001)

CHIEF JUSTICE REHNQUIST delivered the opinion of the Court.

Respondent represents plaintiffs who claim injuries resulting from the use of orthopedic bone screws in the pedicles of their spines. Petitioner is a consulting company that assisted the screws' manufacturer, AcroMed Corporation, in navigating the federal regulatory process for these devices. Plaintiffs say petitioner made fraudulent representations to the Food and Drug Administration (FDA or Agency) in the course of obtaining approval to market the screws. Plaintiffs further claim that such representations were at least a "but for" cause of injuries that plaintiffs sustained from the implantation of these devices. Had the representations not been made, the FDA would not have approved the devices, and plaintiffs would not have been injured. Plaintiffs sought damages from petitioner under state tort law. We hold that such claims are pre-empted by the Federal Food, Drug, and Cosmetic Act (FDCA), 52 Stat. 1040, as amended by the Medical Device Amendments of 1976 (MDA), 90 Stat. 539, 21 U.S.C. § 301. ***

The MDA separates devices into three categories: Class I devices are those that present no unreasonable risk of illness or injury and therefore require only general manufacturing controls; Class II devices are those possessing a greater potential dangerousness and thus warranting more stringent controls; Class III devices "present a potential unreasonable risk of illness or injury" and therefore incur the FDA's strictest regulation. § 360c(a)(1)(c)(ii)(II). It is not disputed that the bone screws manufactured by AcroMed are Class III devices. Class III devices must complete a thorough review process with the FDA before they may be marketed. *** Among other information, an application must include all known reports pertaining to the device's safety and efficacy, see § 360e(c)(1)(A); "a full statement of the components, ingredients, and properties and of the principle or principles of operation of such device," § 360e(c)(1)(B); "a full description of the methods used in, and the facilities and controls used for, the manufacture, processing, and, when relevant, packing and installation of, such device," § 360e(c)(1)(C); samples of the device (when practicable), see § 360e(c)(1)(E); and "specimens of the labeling proposed to be used for such device," § 360e(c)(1)(F). ***

An exception to the PMA requirement exists for devices that were already on the market prior to the MDA's enactment in 1976. See 21 U.S.C. §360e(b)(1)(A). The MDA allows these "predicate" devices to remain available until the FDA initiates and completes the PMA process. *** Demonstrating that a device qualifies for this exception is known as the "§ 510(k) process," which refers to the section of the original MDA containing this provision. Section 510(k) submissions must include the following: "Proposed labels, labeling, and advertisements sufficient to describe the device, its intended use, and the directions for its use," 21 CFR §807.87(e) (2000); "[a] statement indicating the device is similar to and/or different from other products of comparable type in commercial distribution, accompanied by data to support the statement," § 807.87(f); "[a] statement that the submitter believes, to the best of his or her knowledge, that all data and information submitted in the premarket notification are truthful and accurate and that no material fact has been omitted," § 807.87(k); and "any additional information regarding the device requested by the [FDA] Commissioner that is necessary for the Commissioner to make a finding as to whether or not the device is substantially equivalent to a device in commercial distribution," § 807.87(l). In 1984, AcroMed sought §510(k) approval for its bone screw device, indicating it for use in spinal surgery. See In re Orthopedic Bone Screw Products Liability Litigation, 159 F.3d 817, 820 (CA3 1998). The FDA denied approval on the grounds that the Class III device lacked substantial equivalence to a predicate device. In September 1985, with the assistance of petitioner, AcroMed filed another § 510(k) application. "The application provided additional information about the . . . device and again indicated its use in spinal surgery. The FDA again rejected the application, determining that the device was not substantially equivalent to a predicate device and that it posed potential risks not exhibited by other spinal-fixation systems." In December 1985, AcroMed and petitioner filed a third § 510(k) application. The FDA is empowered to investigate suspected fraud, see 21 U.S.C. § 372; 21 CFR § 5.35 (2000), and citizens may report wrongdoing and petition the agency to take action, § 10.30. In addition to the general criminal proscription on making false statements to the Federal Government, 18 U.S.C. § 1001, (1994 ed., Supp. IV), the FDA may respond to fraud by seeking injunctive relief, 21 U.S.C. § 332, and civil penalties, 21 U.S.C. § 333(f)(1)(A); seizing the device, § 334(a)(2)(D); and pursuing criminal prosecutions, § 333(a). The FDA thus has at its disposal a variety of enforcement options that allow it to make a measured response to suspected fraud upon the Agency. ***

State-law fraud-on-the-FDA claims inevitably conflict with the FDA's responsibility to police fraud consistently with the Agency's judgment and objectives. As a practical matter, complying with the FDA's detailed regulatory regime in the shadow of 50 States' tort regimes will dramatically increase the burdens facing potential applicants—burdens not contemplated by Congress in enacting the FDCA and the MDA. *** In the present case, however, the fraud claims exist solely by virtue of the FDCA disclosure requirements. Thus, although Medtronic can be read to allow certain state-law causes of actions that parallel federal safety requirements, it does not and cannot stand for the proposition that any violation of the FDCA will support a state-law claim. The judgment of the Court of Appeals is reversed.

CRITICAL ANALYSIS: Evaluate whether the Supreme Court rule correctly? Determine whether federal or state law should control in *Buckman*.

Chapter 4: Postmarket Surveillance, Compliance, Tracking, MedWatch, MedSun and Open Payments

Key website: *http://www.fda.gov/Safety/MedWatch/SafetyInformation/default.htm*

Postmarket covigilance involves complex issues. These issues involve a cost benefit analysis in terms of a "best approach" to postmarket co-vigilance. FDA remains the gatekeeper for safety of all medical products in the United States whether manufactured in the United States or abroad. Oversight of medical device products was added to the Government Accounting Office (GAO's) "High-Risk" list in 2009 due to evolving safety issues in foreign establishment inspection, post-market monitoring and clinical trial oversight. The GAO recommended that FDA:

➢ Develop performance-based standards that are results oriented on public safety;
➢ Respond effectively to globalization;
➢ Expand the scope of postmarket safety; and
➢ Establish a timetable for implementation of the Safe Medical Devices (1990) concerning re-classification of high-risk devices to enter the marketplace with premarket approval rather than pre-notification.

FDA has specified programs in terms of postmarket risk prevention. Post approval requirements include "continuing evaluation and periodic reporting on the safety, effectiveness, and reliability of the device for its intended use." 21 CFR 814.82 (a)(2). The 1976 Medical Device Amendments, the 1990 Safe Medical Devices Act and 1992 Medical Device Amendments have served as milestones in medical device legislation, resulting in a system in which manufacturers must track the device from manufacture through distribution to assure accurate tracing in the event of problems. The regulations for tracking are found in 21 CFR Part 821. The FDA Modernization Act of 1997 and in 2007 the FDA Amendments Act legislated a medical device surveillance network for adverse events. The 2012 FDA Safety and Innovation Act went even further in terms of enhanced surveillance capabilities. The FDCA provides authority to order postmarket surveillance studies in several instances:

➢ Class II or Class III products intended to be implanted for more than one year;
➢ Life sustaining or life supporting and used outside of a user facility; or
➢ Failure would most likely result in serious health consequences.

The FDA MedWatch program provides a concise reporting process and the overall goal is product safety. MedSun pertains to user reporting of medical device related events. MedSun is an ongoing endeavor to provide FDA with data pertaining to medical device adverse events. The ultimate goal is to improve the health and safety of patients. Once an adverse event is identified, the agency could initiate any of the following:

➢ *Medical alerts; Labeling changes; Boxed warnings; and Product withdrawals.*

➢ "FDA Safety Information Summaries" posted on the Internet include:
➢ *"Dear Health Professional" letters; Public Health Alerts Notifications; and Talk Papers.*

Tracking Guidance

http://www.fda.gov/MedicalDevices/DeviceRegulationandGuidance/GuidanceDocuments/ucm071756.htm

Manufacturers must track certain devices from manufacture through the distribution chain when an FDA order is received to put into effect a tracking system for a certain type of device. The purpose of device tracking is to ensure that manufacturers of certain devices establish tracking systems that will enable them to promptly locate devices in commercial distribution. Tracking information may be used to facilitate notifications and recalls ordered by FDA in the case of serious risks to health presented by the devices. Manufacturers must adopt a method of tracking devices whose failure would be reasonably likely to have serious, adverse health consequences; or which is intended to be implanted in the human body for more than one year; or are life-sustaining or life-supporting devices used outside of a device user facility. Types of devices subject to a tracking order may include any Class II or Class III device as follows:

> Failure would be reasonably likely to have serious adverse health consequences;
> Intended to be implanted in the human body for more than one year; and
> Intended as a life sustaining or life-supporting device used outside a device user facility.
> FDA uses discretion as to whether to order tracking for devices that meet the statutory requirements or to release devices from tracking based on additional guidance factors and other relevant information that comes to the agency's attention. The following additional guidance factors may be considered to determine whether a tracking order should be issued:
> Likelihood of sudden, catastrophic failure;
> Likelihood of significant adverse clinical outcome; and
> Need for prompt professional intervention.

MedWatch and MAUDE Adverse Event Reporting Database

http://www.fda.gov/MedicalDevices/DeviceRegulationandGuidance/PostmarketRequirements/ReportingAdverseEvents/ucm127891.htm

Inaugurated in 1993, MedWatch provides a comprehensive and streamlined postmarket reporting program. MedWatch depends on collaboration with health professionals and trade organizations. For instance, FDA MedWatch has partnered with ePocrates, an organization of physicians, to disseminate critical drug safety alerts to health care professionals. The Medical Device Reporting (MDR) database maintained by FDA contains both mandatory and voluntary reports.

The Manufacturer and User Facility Device Experience (MAUDE) database contains voluntary reports, user facility reports, distributor reports and manufacturer reports. The data consists of voluntary reports since June 1993, user facility reports since 1991, distributor reports since 1993, and manufacturer reports since 1996. MAUDE may not include reports made according to exemptions, variances, or alternative reporting requirements granted under 21 CFR 803.19.

MedWatch Objectives

The following are strategic goals of MedWatch:

> Explanation of what should and should not be reported;
> Improved awareness of serious reactions caused by drugs or medical devices;
> Enhanced feedback to the health community; and a
> Less complicated reporting system.

This large-scale monitoring of products is multifaceted; that is, there is both voluntary and mandatory reporting. Reports of serious adverse reactions or problems with products can be made directly to the manufacturer who is legally required to report the adverse information to FDA. Understanding the definition of adverse event is paramount. A serious adverse event consists of:

> Death from use of the medical product;
> A life-threatening hazard such as failure of an intravenous IV pump that could result in disproportionate drug dosing;
> Hospitalization due to the serious reaction;
> Disability such as a permanent change in physical activities; birth defects, miscarriage, stillbirth, or birth with disease; and
> Intercession to avoid permanent damage.

Voluntary Reporting Form FDA 3500—Health professionals, consumers and patients use the voluntary Form 3500 to report adverse events or problems related to medical products.

Consumer Voluntary Reporting Form FDA 3500B—FDA issued a voluntary consumer reporting form in 2015 and is a consumer-friendly version of Form 3500.

http://www.fda.gov/downloads/AboutFDA/ReportsManualsForms/Forms/UCM349464.pdf

Mandatory Reporting Form FDA 3500A: Manufacturers, importers, distributors, IND reporters, and health professionals who work in a user facility such as a hospital, nursing home, ambulatory surgical facility, outpatient treatment facility and outpatient diagnostic facility have mandatory reporting requirements. Risk managers and other personnel within the user facility are legally required to report suspected medical device-related deaths and serious injuries. However, physician's offices are excluded from the user facility definition and are therefore exempt from mandatory reporting requirements as are dentists, nurses, optometrists and nurse practitioners. See: 21 CFR 803, 807 Reporting requirements.

REPORTING REQUIREMENTS
Summary of Reporting Requirements for Manufacturers

REPORTER	WHAT TO REPORT	REPORT FORM #	TO WHOM	WHEN
Manufacturer	30-day reports of deaths, serious injuries and mal-functions	Form FDA 3500A	FDA	Within 30 calendar days from becoming aware of an event
Manufacturer	5-day reports on events that require remedial action to prevent an unreasonable risk of substantial harm to the public health and other types of events designated by FDA	Form FDA 3500A	FDA	Within 5 work days from becoming aware of an event
Manufacturer	Baseline reports to identify and provide basic data on each device that is subject of an MDR report. At this time, FDA has stayed the requirement for denominator data requested in Part II, Items 15 and 16 on Form 3417.	Form FDA 3417	FDA	Within 30 calendar, and 5 work day reports when device or device family is reported for the first time. Interim and annual updates are also required if any baseline information changes after initial submission.
Manufacturer	Annual Certification	Form FDA 3381	FDA	Coincide with firm's annual registration dates.

http://www.fda.gov/medicaldevices/deviceregulationandguidance/guidancedocuments/ucm094529.htm#whomust

Summary of Reporting Requirements for User Facilities

REPORTER	WHAT TO REPORT	REPORT FORM #	TO WHOM	WHEN
User Facility	Death	Form FDA 3500A	FDA & Manufacturer	Within 10 work days
User Facility	Serious injury	Form FDA 3500A	Manufacturer. FDA only if manufacturer unknown	Within 10 work days
User Facility	Annual reports of death & serious injury	Form FDA 3419	FDA	January 1

Summary of Mandatory Reporting Requirements for Importers

REPORTER	WHAT TO REPORT	REPORT FORM #	TO WHOM	WHEN
Importers*	Reports of deaths and serious injuries 21 CFR 803.10 and 21 CFR 803.40	Form FDA 3500A	FDA and the manufacturer	Within 30 calendar days of becoming aware of an event
	Reports of malfunctions [21 CFR 803.10 and 21 CFR 803.40].	Form FDA 3500A	Manufacturer	Within 30 calendar days of becoming aware of an event

http://www.fda.gov/MedicalDevices/DeviceRegulationandGuidance/PostmarketRequirements/Report-ingAdverseEvents/default.htm (Mandatory)

Importer Defined: *An "importer" is any person who imports a device into the US and who furthers the marketing of the device from the original place of manufacture to the person who makes final delivery or sale to the ultimate user of the device. However, a person who repackages or otherwise changes the container, wrapper, or labeling of the device or device package is considered to be a manufacturer of the device [21 CFR 803.3]. Importers are also required to:

> ➢ Develop, maintain and implement written MDR procedures [21 CFR 803.17]; and
> ➢ Maintain files related to medical device adverse events [21 CFR 803.18].

Summary of Reporting Requirement for Distributors
Distributor Defined: A "distributor" is any person, other than the manufacturer or importer, who furthers the marketing of a device from the original place of manufacture to the person who makes final delivery or sale to the ultimate user [21 CFR 803.3]. It should be noted, however, that, as is the case with importers, a person who repackages or otherwise changes the container, wrapper, or labeling of the device is considered to be a manufacturer of the device. Distributors are only required to establish and maintain device complaint records (files) [21 CFR 803.18(d)]. That is, distributors are no longer required to report device related adverse events involving death, serious injury and malfunction to the FDA and or the device manufacturer. However, distributors must maintain records of complaints and provide them to FDA if requested.
NOTE: The above summary for importers and distributors are relevant excerpts from Appendix "A" of the final guidance titled: *Medical Device Reporting for Manufacturers*, issued November 2016.
http://www.fda.gov/downloads/MedicalDevices/DeviceRegulationandGuidance/GuidanceDocments/ucm359566.pdf?source=govdelivery&utm_medium=email&utm_source=govdelivery

MedSun Medical Product Surveillance Network
http://www.fda.gov/MedicalDevices/Safety/MedSunMedicalProductSafetyNetwork/default.htm

The Medical Product Surveillance Network, known as MedSun, was launched 2002 in response to the FDA Modernization Act of 1997 (FDAMA) mandate. Section 213 of FDAMA legislated a change to universal user reporting of device related adverse events by mandating implementation of a system involving a "subset of user facilities that constitutes a representative profile of user reports" for device related deaths and serious illnesses or injuries. This means implementation of a national surveillance network to provide critically important data on medical devices. Critical design aspects include: confidentiality through the use of a neutral third party; incentives for participation; and communicating timely feedback to the participants.

Patterned and mirrored after Mandatory Reporting Form 3500A, MedSun provides options for recording additional information to help improve the safety and design of medical devices. Hospitals, nursing homes and other healthcare facilities that participate receive several benefits including feedback and experience sharing among the other participating facilities; special database analyses as well as dispensing with the requirement to complete a paper Form 3500A. Confidentiality remains a priority in terms of protecting the identity of both the person who submits the report as well as the reporting facility.

Postmarket Surveillance —Endoscopes, Surgical Mesh Trans-Vaginal
http://www.fda.gov/MedicalDevices/Safety/AlertsandNotices/ucm434871.htm

ERCP Endoscopes (Duodenoscopes) Investigation—Preventable Tragedies: Superbugs and How Ineffective Monitoring of Medical Device Safety Fails Patients (Senate report)
Manufacturers of *ERCP Endoscopes* also called duodenoscopes must conduct postmarket surveillance studies to better ascertain how these devices are reprocessed. The reason for the FDA order is due to infection transmission associated with this device. FDA ordered the manufacturers to submit postmarket surveillance plans. There are no alternative devices for endoscopic retrograde cholangiopancreatography procedures (ERCP). Over 500,000 ERCP are performed annually and is the least invasive way of draining fluids from pancreatic and biliary ducts blocked by cancerous tumors, gallstones or other conditions. The outcome of the post market studies could entail label amendments with different reprocessing instructions.

Surgical Mesh Trans-Vaginal—Reclassification—FDA issued two final orders to reclassify the surgical mesh for trans-vaginal pelvic organ prolapse repair from Class II to Class III and to require a Premarket Application. 81 Fed. Reg. 353 (Jan. 5, 2016) 21 CFR Part 884).

See: *http://www.fda.gov/NewsEvents/Newsroom/PressAnnouncements/ucm479732.htm*

See: *https://www.gpo.gov/fdsys/pkg/FR-2016-01-05/html/2015-33165.htm?source=govdelivery&utm_medium=email&utm_source=govdelivery*

FDA Reclassification—FDA issued two final orders to reclassify the surgical mesh for trans-vaginal pelvic organ prolapse repair from Class II to Class III and to require a Premarket Application. 81 Fed. Reg. 353 (Jan. 5, 2016) 21 CFR Part 884).

See: *http://www.fda.gov/NewsEvents/Newsroom/PressAnnouncements/ucm479732.htm*

See: *https://www.gpo.gov/fdsys/pkg/FR-2016-01-05/html/2015-33165.htm?source=govdelivery&utm_medium=email&utm_source=govdelivery*

NOTE: Court Decisions—Boston Scientific, has faced over 26,000 liability lawsuits alleging that the device for urinary incontinence is defective and causes complications and the company was ordered to pay $100 million including $75 million in punitive damages (appealed to the Delaware Supreme Ct.), $18.5 million (West Virginia) and $26.7 million (Florida). Other verdicts against J&J's Ethicon subsidiary include: in 2017, a $57.1 million award which includes $50 million in punitive damages and $7.1 million in compensatory damages. *Ebaugh et al. v. Ethicon Inc et al.*, (Ct. Common Pleas Phila., PA, No. 130700866, 9/07/2017); a $20 million verdict in 2017 *Engleman v. Gynecare et al.*, (Phila. Court of Common Pleas No. 140305384) a trans-vaginal tape product; in 2016, a $13.5 million verdict, which included $10 million in punitive damages (Pennsylvania) (increased to $13,738,119 for delay damages *Carlino v. Ethicon, Inc.* Phila. Ct. Common Pleas June Term 2013No. 03470 Jan. 3, 2017); a $12.5 million jury verdict in 2015, including $7 million in punitive damages; however, See: *Adkins v. Ethicon, Inc. et al.*, No. 130700919 (2017), (Ct. Common Pleas Philadelphia Cty. PA) (Jurors agreed that pelvic mesh defectively designed, yet concluded plaintiff not injured by device); (2018 jury award of $35 million in punitive damages and $33 million in compensatory damages against C.R. Bard, Inc.

Implantable Forms of Sterilization—**Essure® Permanent Birth Control**

http://www.fda.gov/MedicalDevices/ProductsandMedicalProcedures/ImplantsandProsthetics/EssurePermanentBirthControl/ucm452254.htm?source=govdelivery&utm_medium=email&utm_source=govdelivery

<u>Postmarket Surveillance</u>—FDA ordered Bayer to conduct a postmarket surveillance study to obtain additional data to better describe and understand events and effects linked to Essure®.

<u>Final guidance</u>—"*Labeling for Permanent Hysteroscopically-Placed Tubal Implants Intended for Sterilization*" Manufacturers of permanent hysteroscopically-placed tubal implants intended for sterilization must include key information in-patient and physician labeling. See link below.

http://www.fda.gov/downloads/MedicalDevices/DeviceRegulationandGuidance/GuidanceDocuments/UCM488020.pdf?source=govdelivery&utm_medium=email&utm_source=govdelivery

<u>Boxed Warning</u>—FDA now requires a boxed warning and *Patient Decision Checklist* as part of the labeling to help confirm that a woman obtains and comprehends information concerning both the benefits and risks of this type of device. (October 2016).

CRITICAL ANALYSIS: Using the above examples, evaluate whether postmarket programs are functioning as intended. What additional safeguards would you recommend?

Compliance—*Utah Medical*

FDA sought an injunction against the Utah Medical company for alleged violations of the Quality System Regulation, 21 C.F.R. Part 820. Ultimately, the federal court ruled against FDA and determined that product safety was not at issue. The court determined that, although the company might have chosen a different method in its validation process, there was no violation.

***United States vs. Utah Medical Products, Inc.*, 404 F. Supp. 2d 1315 (D. C. Utah 2005)**

On behalf of the Food and Drug Administration ("FDA"), the United States seeks a permanent injunction against Utah Medical under the Federal Food, Drug, and Cosmetic Act, 21 U.S.C. §

332(a), regarding alleged violations of the Quality System Regulation ("QSR"), 21 C.F.R. Part 820 (2004). *** Defendant Kevin L. Cornwell is the Chairman and Chief Executive Officer of Utah Medical. Mr. Cornwell is involved in the day-to-day operations of Utah Medical and has authority over all of the Company's operations, including the design, manufacture, packing and storage of Utah Medical's devices. Defendant Ben L. Shirley is the Vice President of Quality Assurance and Product Development at Utah Medical and is involved in the day-to-day activities.

Utah Medical develops, manufactures, and markets a broad range of disposable and reusable specialty medical devices. Utah Medical's current product line includes devices for labor and delivery, neonatal intensive care, gynecology, urology, electrosurgery and blood pressure monitoring. Utah Medical regularly manufactures devices from components that it receives in interstate commerce and introduces finished devices into interstate commerce. Utah Medical also manufactures "components," as defined at 21 C.F.R. § 820.3(c) (2004), because it manufactures parts or subassemblies that are intended to be included as part of finished, packaged and labeled medical devices. *** Utah Medical asserts that it has a comprehensive quality system, intended to comply with all Quality System Regulations provisions. *** The FDA has inspected Utah Medical several times since 2001. During certain inspections, the FDA has issued written observations by FDA inspectors on Forms FDA-483. A Form FDA-483 is a list of concerns observed by an FDA inspector during the course of an inspection. The specific questions before the court are three:

Issue No. 1(a): Whether Utah Medical properly validated extrusion and injection molding processes?

Issue No. 1(b): Whether Utah Medical properly validated the software programs used as part of production or the quality system?

Issue No. 2: Whether Utah Medical properly processes complaints with look backs and failure codes?

21 C.F.R. § 820.75 Process validation.

(a) Where the results of a process cannot be fully verified by subsequent inspection and test, the process shall be validated with a high degree of assurance and approved according to established procedures. The validation activities and results, including the date and signature of the individual(s) approving the validation and where appropriate the major equipment validated, shall be documented.

(b) Each manufacturer shall establish and maintain procedures for monitoring and control of process parameters for validated processes to ensure that the specified requirements continue to be met.

  (1) Each manufacturer shall ensure that qualified individuals perform validated processes.

  (2) For validated processes, the monitoring and control methods and data, the date performed, and, where appropriate, the individual(s) performing the process or the major equipment used shall be documented.

(c) When changes or process deviations occur, the manufacturer shall review and evaluate the process and perform revalidation where appropriate. These activities shall be documented.

21 C.F.R. § 820.70(i) reads in pertinent part as follows: (i) Automated processes. When computers or automated data processing systems are used as part of production or the quality system, the manufacturer shall validate computer software for its intended use according to an established protocol. All software changes shall be validated before approval and issuance.

21 C.F.R. § 820.198 reads in pertinent part as follows: § 820.198 Complaint files.

(a) Each manufacturer shall maintain complaint files. Each manufacturer shall establish and maintain procedures for receiving, reviewing, and evaluating complaints by a formally designated unit.

21 C.F.R. § 820.250 Statistical techniques.

(a) Where appropriate, each manufacturer shall establish and maintain procedures for identifying valid statistical techniques required for establishing, controlling, and verifying the acceptability of process capability and product characteristics.

(b) Sampling plans, when used, shall be written and based on a valid statistical rationale. Each manufacturer shall establish and maintain procedures to ensure that sampling methods are adequate for their intended use and to ensure that when changes occur the sampling plans are reviewed. These activities shall be documented. ***

Since about 2001, there has been an ongoing interplay between the agency and Utah Medical through the FDA oversight process of inspections, written observations by inspectors, responses by Utah Medical, review by District Directors and others, disagreements with the observations, purported "corrective actions" by the Utah Medical, and the gathering and furnishing of documents of various kinds to satisfy the FDA.

1.Utah Medical Adequately Validates its Manufacturing Process in accordance with the Quality System Regulations. *** The United States generally contends that there is insufficient documentation demonstrating: (a) a proper installation of the extrusion and injection molding equipment; (b) proper calibration of the extrusion and injection molding equipment; (c) proper establishment of process parameters for the extrusion and injection molding processes; (d) adequate monitoring of critical dimensions of products manufactured through the extrusion and injection molding processes; (e) adequate inspection and testing of products manufactured through the extrusion and injection molding process; and (f) "edge of failure" testing of its processing parameters. The United States' experts stated that, according to industry standards, "process validation requires three separate elements known as "installation qualification" (IQ), "operational qualification" (OQ), and "performance qualification" (PQ). *** First, as to installation validation, the machines used for injection and extrusion have been in place and producing product for many years. *** Though done years after actual installation, the in-house engineers checked out the installation over a period of months and documented what they did over a period of months. They determined that the machines were properly installed. To the Court, that seems perfectly adequate. *** Utah Medical establishes its processing parameters in part during the design phase of its manufacturing process. *See* 21 C.F.R. 820.75(b). Utah Medical identifies critical dimensions for all of its extruded and injection molded products. Utah Medical calibrates its extrusion and injection molding equipment on a regular, periodic basis, following established, documented procedures. This calibration work is done periodically and regularly by outside vendors. Utah Medical employs a statistical process control procedure to monitor and control its extrusion and injection molding process, by which samples of component parts are inspected at regular intervals. Process parameters are established and followed, and inspection occurs. All steps are documented. For the reasons stated above, the Court finds that Utah Medical has adequately validated its manufacturing processes in accordance with the Quality System Regulations.

2. Utah Medical Adequately Validates its Software in compliance with the Quality System Regulations. Utah Medical presented substantial testimony and documentary evidence that it validates its software for the software's intended use. Date discrepancies of a trivial nature and Y2K matters were easily explained by later drafts, interlineations, or typographical errors unrelated to validation. The undisputed hands-on testimony confirmed that the intended use of the software used by Utah Medical is adequately documented and the software is tested properly.

3. Utah Medical Has a Uniform Complaint Handling Process in compliance with the Quality System Regulations. Utah Medical has established uniform procedures for implementing corrective and preventive action in accordance with 21 C.F.R. § 820.100(a). The company employs a detailed and uniform procedure that it follows for receiving, reviewing, and evaluating complaints. Utah Medical has documented its complaint-handling procedure. Utah Medical uses "failure codes" merely as an internal general trending tool. The Company groups complaints not by failure codes, but by a corrective action number, allowing people to review similar complaints, if any, according to the corrective action number. The company holds regular weekly meetings to discuss complaints. In addition, the Chief Executive Officer, Kevin Cornwell, periodically reviewed complaints. Utah Medical complies with Quality System Regulations as to complaint handling under 21 C.F.R. § 820.90(a) and § 820.198(a). The question here is whether the processes and procedures used by Utah Medical to currently produce products comply with the applicable regulations. The answer is yes, they do. *** It seems to me that a recurring problem in this extended and in some instances "nitpicking" case is a failure of the regulator and the regulated to communicate. It appears to me they have often talked past each other and, while using the same words, have meant entirely different things. This seems to be a common characteristic of both, arising in part because of the general nature of the regulations themselves, which have the virtue of generality and the vice of imprecision. *** Utah Medical in times past may have lacked documentation of the particular kinds they now say are readily available, such as injection molding manuals and drawings. Utah Medical may well have applied an incorrect electronic label to a complaint, but the complaint process itself was both uniform and effective. *** "Validation" is the key word, and has often been noted, "many roads lead to Rome." The fact that the road chosen by Utah Medical may be different in degree than that thought to be appropriate by a regulator, does not mean that it is wrong, or in violation of the regulations. *** Without a doubt, the United States captured Utah Medical's attention in the past, and whatever modest deviations from *regulations* may have occurred in times past no longer exist at present. It makes no sense for the court to order Utah Medical to do something they are already doing. Petition DENIED, and case DISMISSED.

NOTE: Following this decision, the United States Department of Health and Human Services denied the claim by Utah Medical of abuse of process allegations by FDA workers during inspections, review and enforcement actions. Utah Medical requested reconsideration of the decision as well as removal of a press release from FDAs website about the court injunction in the case and purging of FDAs administrative file including 483s related to the 2001 through 2004 inspections and permanent injunction recommendations.

CRITICAL ANALYSIS: Compare and contrast *Prevor* (Chapter 2 Combination Product) and *Utah Medical*. Evaluate what led to the litigation in both of these cases.

Open Payments Disclosure
https://openpaymentsdata.cms.gov

The Centers for Medicare and Medicaid Services' Open Payments for program year 2017 reported that applicable manufacturers and group purchasing organizations (GPOs) totaled $8.40 billion in payments and ownership investment interests to physicians and teaching hospitals.

See Tom Avril, *Study: Most Patients are Treated by Industry-Paid Docs*, Phila. Inq. G1 (March 19, 2017); 65 percent of patients in the United States were treated by doctors who received industry money.

CRITICAL ANALYSIS: What impact does the payment disclosure have on physicians and the regulated medical device and pharmaceutical industries? Include a discussion about conflict of interest.

Chapter 5: Medical Device Enforcement Strategies

Enforcement Mechanisms

Enforcement actions are either administrative in nature where FDA acts on its own or judicial in nature where FDA acts in coordination with, for example the U.S. Department of Justice for prosecution. Enforcement actions include:

> ➤ *Administrative Detention; Recalls; Warning Letters; Injunction; Criminal Prosecution; Import Detention; Seizure; and Civil Actions.*

Recalls and Field Corrections

Unlike some FDA regulated products, the FDCA provides FDA with explicit regulatory authority to order "field corrections" or recalls. Recalls, also known as corrections or removals from the marketplace, are sometimes necessary for public health and safety reasons. Medical device manufacturers and importers have 10 days from the time the firm initiates the recall to file a report with FDA if the device correction or removal involves a "risk to health." Recall authority or field corrections for medical devices with serious adverse health consequences or death is specifically authorized under the FDCA section 518(e), 21 U.S.C. section 360(h)(e). The accompanying regulations under 21 CFR 7.3(g), 806 and 810 apply to recalls or field corrections and removals of a marketed medical device product. Manufacturers and importers are required to file a report with FDA. Listed below are recall classifications, market withdrawal and safety alert information.

- ✓ **Class I Recall:** a situation in which there is a reasonable probability that the use of or exposure to a violative product will cause *serious adverse health consequences or death*.
- ✓ **Class II Recall:** a situation in which use of or exposure to a violative product may cause temporary or medically reversible adverse health consequences or where the probability of *serious adverse health consequences is remote*.
- ✓ **Class III Recall:** use of or exposure is *unlikely to cause adverse health consequences*.
- ✓ **Field Correction and Removal:** occurs when a product has a minor violation that would not be subject to FDA legal action. The firm removes the product from the market or corrects the violation. A product removed from the market due to tampering, without evidence of manufacturing or distribution problems, would be a market withdrawal.
- ✓ **Medical Device Safety Alert:** issued in situations where a medical device may present an unreasonable risk of substantial harm. **NOTE: Considered recalls in some instances.**

Class I Recall—Medtronic Recalls Cardiac Resynchronization Therapy Implantable Cardioverter Defibrillators Due to Manufacturing Error Preventing Electrical Shock Delivery
https://www.fda.gov/MedicalDevices/Safety/ListofRecalls/ucm598198.htm
The FDA has identified this as a Class I recall, the most serious type of recall. Use of these devices may cause serious injuries or death.

- ✓ Recalled Product(s): Medtronic Cardiac Resynchronization Therapy with Defibrillation (CRT-Ds) and Implantable Cardiovert-Defibrillators (ICDs)
- ✓ Product Codes: NIK, LWS
- ✓ Serial Numbers: See Complete List
- ✓ Manufacturing Dates: July 13, 2013 to August 8, 2017
- ✓ Devices Recalled in the U.S.: 48 units nationwide

Device Use: Implantable Cardioverter Defibrillators (ICDs) and Cardiac Resynchronization Therapy Defibrillators (CRT-Ds) are devices that provide pacing for slow heart rhythms, and electrical shock or pacing to stop dangerously fast heart rhythms.

ICDs and CRT-Ds are both implanted under the skin in the upper chest area with connecting insulated wires called "leads" that go into the heart. Patients need an ICD or CRT-D if their heartbeat is too slow (bradycardia), too fast (tachycardia), or needs coordination to treat heart failure.

Reason for Recall: Medtronic is recalling certain ICDs and CRT-Ds due to a defect in the manufacturing process. This defect causes an out of specification gas mixture inside the device and may prevent the device from delivering the electrical shock needed to pace a patient's heartbeat or revive a patient in cardiac arrest.

The delay or inability to deliver a shock to a patient in cardiac arrest or pace a patient's heart whose heartbeat is too slow could result in serious injury and/or death.

Who is affected? Patients with an affected Medtronic ICD or CRT-D device

What to Do? On January 22, 2018 Medtronic sent an Urgent Medical Device Recall notice to affected customers. The notice asked customers to: Consider Prophylactic device replacement for patients who have been implanted with one of the affected devices.

    ✓   Contact their Medtronic sales representative for terms and conditions for device warranties.

    ✓   Review the recall notice and ensure appropriate staff is aware of the notice.

    ✓   Medtronic will offer a supplemental device warranty for affected devices.

CRITICAL ANALYSIS: Review the above recall. What procedures should a company have in place to address a recall possibility?

Warning Letters

FDA utilizes warning letters as an enforcement tool with follow up enforcement action if warranted. FDA launched a Medical Device Warning Letter Pilot (MDWLP) in 1999, which permitted manufacturers the opportunity to deal with FDA concerns about quality system, premarket 510(k) and labeling issues prior to issuance of a warning letter. FDA terminated the MDWLP because the agency did not find that compliance measurably increased in comparison to the traditional warning letter approach. FDA utilizes the traditional warning letter approach, as notice to a company, of FDA listed violations and needed corrective action for compliance purposes.

Injunction—Investigational and Custom Devices: *Endotec*

FDA does seek court injunctions when the agency deems it a necessity. For example, FDA sought a permanent injunction against *Endotec,* a medical device manufacturer and its owners. FDA alleged they manufactured and distributed adulterated ankle, knee, and jaw devices and that they went beyond the scope of an approved clinical study of ankle devices. The United States District Court enjoined the manufacturing and distributing of the knee devices; however, the District Court rejected the other claims. Both parties appealed and eventually the case was remanded to the District Court. *United States v. Endotec*, 563 F.3d 1187 (11th Cir.2009).

Criminal Corporate Liability—*Norian* and *Caputo*

United States v. Norian Corp. [Synthes] No. 09-cr-403 (E.D. Pa. July 20, 2009)

Is there individual criminal liability for failure to disclose to patients that they were participating in experimental surgery? In *United States v. Norian Corp. [Synthes]*, the Department of Justice issued a 52-felony count indictment against Synthes, Inc. and its Norian company subsidiary and the corporate executives because of the failure to disclose to any of the patients that they were participating in experimental surgery. Synthes executives were charged with a misdemeanor related to the labeling of Norian XR. Further, the indictment alleged that the company executives made false statements to FDA about whether they tested the product for unapproved uses. FDA approved Norian XR as filler for bony voids or defects in some parts of the body; however, it was not approved for use in the spine and FDA required clinical testing prior to spine use. According to the indictment, clinical trials were not conducted. Further, the indictment detailed that Synthes convinced surgeons to test Norian XR in patients with spinal fractures.

Synthes and its Norian company subsidiary entered a plea of guilty. They agreed to pay a fine, which totaled $23.2 million dollars and agreed to enter into what is termed a Corporate Integrity Agreement. Synthes pled guilty to shipping a mislabeled product, a misdemeanor. Norian pled guilty to conspiracy to impede federal safety standards, which is a felony. The former Synthes executives were sentenced in late 2011 to terms of imprisonment and $100,000 fines for their roles in the medical-device maker's promotion of a bone cement for unauthorized uses. The officers were indicted back in June 2009 over claims they conspired to conduct unapproved clinical trials of Norian-branded cements from May 2002 to late 2004. The cement was used in the spines of 200 patients with fractured vertebrae and three patients died. Each defendant pled guilty to misdemeanor counts of violating the FDCA known as the *"Park"* or Corporate Officer doctrine. U.S. District Court Judge Legrome Davis sentenced Michael D. Huggins, former chief operating officer of Synthes and Thomas B. Higgins, former president of the Synthes spine division, to nine months in federal prison. John Walsh, head of regulatory affairs, received a five-month term of imprisonment. The fourth executive, Huggins challenged his sentence of eight months imprisonment. His challenge proved unsuccessful. See: *United States v. Huggins.* Criminal Action No. 09–403–3 (Dec. 13, 2011).

NOTE: OtisMed (acquired by Stryker) and its former chief executive officer entered a guilty plea in 2014 to intentionally distributing knee replacement surgery cutting guides used in surgeries. Their application for marketing clearance had been rejected by FDA. The corporation agreed to pay over $80 million to resolve its related criminal and civil liability. See also, *Volume III.*
http://www.justice.gov/usao/nj/Press/files/Otismed%20News%20Release.html

United States v. Caputo

Similarly, in *United States v. Caputo,* the former chief executive of the now defunct medical device firm AbTox was sentenced to 10 years imprisonment and ordered to pay restitution along with the defendant vice president for selling an unapproved sterilizer to hospitals, which was reported to have caused blindness to patients undergoing eye surgery. The Court of Appeals affirmed the lower court decision except with respect to restitution, which was remanded, to the District Court for recalculation. This case illustrates the imposition of criminal sanctions when a device company time after time knowingly violates the Food Drug and Cosmetic Act.

United States v. Caputo, 517 F.3d 935 (7th Cir. 2008)

EASTERBROOK, Chief Judge An autoclave sterilizes medical instruments quickly and cheaply. But some instruments can't stand the high temperatures and pressures of an autoclave, so there is a demand for sterilizers that use lower temperatures and non-aqueous sterilants. One system in widespread use relies on ethylene oxide gas as the sterilant. That gas is toxic and hard to handle, however, and Ross Caputo saw a business opportunity in these drawbacks. He designed a low-temperature system using a plasma of peracetic acid as the sterilant and in 1990 asked FDA to approve this device, which his company AbTox, Inc. called the Plazlyte. *** The Medical Device Amendments to the Food, Drug, and Cosmetic Act have a grandfather clause covering devices that had been lawfully sold on or before May 28, 1976, or are "substantially equivalent" to them. 21 U.S.C. § 360c(f)(1)(A)(ii). AbTox asked the FDA to approve sales of a Plazlyte as "substantially equivalent" to units that employ ethylene oxide as the sterilant. *** The first [small Plazlyte] had an interior volume of one cubic foot and used 10% peracetic acid made by mixing water with a solution of 30% peracetic acid. *** The second model [large Plazlyte] had an interior volume of approximately five cubic feet, used 5% peracetic acid from a single bottle (no dilution with water from a second bottle), and ran just one cycle, at a different pressure from the first model. AbTox submitted the small Plazlyte for approval in 1990. It also submitted only those tests that favored the device's effectiveness; others, less helpful to AbTox, were concealed (or so a jury could conclude; we recount the evidence in the light most favorable to the verdict). *** When the FDA signed off on the small Plazlyte in 1994, it approved the device only for use with solid stainless-steel instruments. *** A new and expensive machine (Plazlytes sold for about $100,000) for sterilizing solid instruments made of stainless steel had no prospect in the market. Autoclaves are cheaper and do not require the handling of acids. *** Instead they immediately began promoting the large Plazlyte as a replacement for ethylene-oxide devices, and thus as suitable for general-purpose sterilization. It had begun selling the large Plazlyte outside the United States in 1993; thus, long before receiving the FDA's approval to sell the small Plazlyte, it knew that the small device would never be marketed and that the large Plazlyte would be promoted for use with many kinds of instruments—though it did not tell the FDA these things when negotiating the details of the limited use that would be allowed to the small Plazlyte. The Plazlyte left a blue-green residue on some of these instruments—and, although the instruments were sterile, the residue (copper and zinc acetate) was harmful to patients' eyes. Some patients experienced corneal decomposition, a severe condition that entails loss of vision. In May 1995, the FDA found out what AbTox was telling customers and reminded it about the limitations on the scope of approval. AbTox then sought the FDA's approval to sell the large Plazlyte to sterilize a wider class of instruments; when the FDA rejected AbTox's request for expedited decision and told AbTox that it "may not market this device until you have received a letter from the FDA allowing you to do so", AbTox went on promoting the large Plazlyte as before. On September 27, 1996, the FDA sent AbTox another instruction to stop selling the large Plazlyte; AbTox failed to comply (though it did not tell the FDA so). The agency never authorized AbTox to sell the large Plazlyte for any use. *** Meanwhile, in January 1998, the FDA inspected AbTox's facilities and discovered that it was still selling the large Plazlyte. The inspectors told AbTox to desist; it didn't. In April 1998, the FDA issued a warning to all hospitals, telling them that the large Plazlyte was not an approved device and at all events must not be used with any instruments containing solder, copper, or zinc, or for any ophthalmic instruments. The FDA directed AbTox to recall the devices; U.S. marshals seized its inventory; this criminal prosecution eventually followed. *** The indictment charged them with conspiring to defraud the United States, 18 U.S.C. § 371, mail fraud, 18 U.S.C. § 1341, wire fraud, 18 U.S.C. § 1343, lying to federal agents, 18 U.S.C. § 1001, and the delivery of misbranded devices, 21 U.S.C. §§ 331(a) and 333(a)(1). Caputo has been sentenced to 120 months' imprisonment and Riley to 72 months. Both were ordered to make restitution of $17.2 million, the list price of all Plazlyte units ever sold. *** The jury concluded not only that Caputo and Riley had lied to the agency when seeking approval of the small Plazlyte but also that the large Plazlyte differed enough from the small one that new approval was essential. Once the FDA certifies a medical device under the grandfather clause, the seller may make modifications to that device without obtaining fresh approval. The line between a "modification" (no approval needed) and a new device (which must be submitted independently for approval) is drawn in 21 C.F.R. § 807.81. *** There remains the rule that a "major change or modification in the intended use of the device" requires fresh approval. Promoting the large Plazlyte as suitable for use with all medical instruments is a major change in intended use, compared with using it for solid stainless-steel instruments alone. This expansion of use caused the copper and zinc acetates that injured patients. So the large Plazlyte, with its expanded "intended use", was not covered by the FDA's approval of the small Plazlyte and could not lawfully be sold *at all*. *** The FDA gave AbTox notice. *** It sent letters, which AbTox ignored. It sent an inspection team, whose directions AbTox spurned. *** The agency comprehensively alerted AbTox, Caputo, and Riley to its view of their legal obligations, and an agency's interpretation of its own regulations, no less than a judicial opinion, may disambiguate them. *** The district court calculated the loss at roughly $17 million, the list price for all Plazlyte devices that AbTox delivered. *** What of the machines that remained in service after the recall? Some hospitals returned their Plazlyte machines; others junked them; but a few kept them and continued using them, even purchasing extra sterilant from AbTox to extend their lives. *** These customers evidently believed that the machines were valuable—and, if hospitals took care to avoid certain kinds of instruments, they continued to be safe. We think that no restitution is owed to customers that, with full knowledge, continued to operate Plazlyte machines for longer than was necessary to replace them. *** The judgment of the district court is affirmed except with respect to restitution. The award of restitution is vacated and the case remanded for calculation, using the principles in this opinion, of the amount that defendants owe to each of AbTox's customers.

CRITICAL ANALYSIS: Evaluate *Caputo* and *Norian* and discuss why the individuals were charged.

Off-Label Settlements

Genzyme Corp. (*U.S. v. Genzyme Corp.*, U.S. District Court, Middle District of Florida, No. 15-cr-00352) agreed to pay $32.59 million in 2015, admit wrongdoing and enter a two-year deferred prosecution agreement to resolve criminal charge under the FDCA from 2005-2011 over its marketing of the surgical implant Seprafilm, a clear film used in laparotomies to reduce abnormal scarring; however it was promoted as a "slurry" for laparoscopic surgery. Sanofi acquired Genzyme in 2011. According to the Justice Department, sales representatives trained surgeons how to turn Seprafilm into a "slurry", an unapproved use.

NOTE: Genzyme reached a $22.28 million civil agreement in 2013, to resolve claims related to Seprafilm under the federal False Claims Act.

False Claims Allegations—*Medtronic, Inc.* and *Olympus*

https://www.justice.gov/opa/pr/minnesota-based-medtronic-inc-pay-99-million-resolve-claims-company-paid-kickbacks-physicians

United States ex rel. Schroeder v. Medtronic, Inc., E.D. Cal., No. 2:09-cv-0279 (5/28/14)

Medtronic, Inc. agreed to pay $9.9 million to resolve allegations under the False Claims Act (FCA) concerning payments to induce physicians to implant Medtronic's pacemakers and defibrillators. (*United States ex rel. Schroeder v. Medtronic, Inc.*, E.D. Cal., No. 2:09-cv-0279 WBS EJB, settlement 5/28/14). The complaint by a former employee of Medtronic, was under the *qui tam* provisions of the FCA. The whistleblower received approximately $1.73 million.

According to the Justice Department, Medtronic caused the submission of false claims to Medicare and Medicaid by allegedly encouraging physicians to use the company's products. The allegations included compensating the physicians to speak at events intended to increase referral business, creating marketing and business development plans for physicians at no cost and providing tickets to sporting events.

Illegal Payments to Physicians and Hospitals—Olympus Corporation

Olympus Corp. (Americas), the United States' largest distributor of endoscopes and related equipment agreed in 2016 to pay $623.2 million to resolve criminal charges ($312.4 million criminal penalty) and civil ($310.8 million) claims relating to a kickback scheme to doctors and hospitals. Further, a subsidiary agreed to pay $22.8 million to resolve criminal charges relating to the Foreign Corrupt Practices Act (FCPA) in Latin America.

CRITICAL ANALYSIS: Review the *Olympus* and *Medtronic* settlements and advise how these companies could have prevented what happened.

https://www.justice.gov/opa/pr/medical-equipment-company-will-pay-646-million-making-illegal-payments-doctors-and-hospitals

NOTE: See earlier discussion in this Chapter and *Volume V* Open Payments Disclosure—Drug Companies.

Enforcement Besides FDA

> ➤ Federal Trade Commission actions;
> ➤ States Attorney Generals actions;
> ➤ Lanham Act actions; and
> ➤ Better Business Bureau National Advertising Division (NAD) involvement.

Besides FDA, the Federal Trade Commission (FTC) may institute enforcement actions. State Attorneys General may join FDA or FTC or institute enforcement along with other states under state consumer protection laws such as prohibitions on unfair and deceptive practices. A company may bring an action in federal court under the Lanham Act, which authorizes a plaintiff to initiate a legal action pertaining to false or misleading advertising. Finally, NAD, is a type of self-regulation where advertising is reviewed due to a competitor's complaint or by NADs initiative.

Chapter 6: Electronic Products Radiation Control

http://www.fda.gov/Radiation-EmittingProducts/default.htm

The Center for Devices and Radiological Health (CDRH) has authority to enforce the Electronic products radiation provisions of the Federal Food, Drug and Cosmetic Act (FDCA). The goal is to protect the public from hazardous and unnecessary exposure to man-made radiation from medical, occupational and consumer products. The Mammography Quality Standards Act (MQSA) enacted in 1992 established national standards for accreditation, certification, and inspection of mammography facilities throughout the United States. This means that most if not all mammography facilities use national standards, which have enhanced radiation doses, and overall improvement of equipment devices. The goal, since enactment over 20 years ago, remains the same; that is to improve the quality of mammography services. The Division of Mammography Quality Standards within CDRH oversees the regulation of MQSA in maintaining this goal.

Examples of radiation-emitting devices that are regulated by CDRH include both medical and non-medical products such as medical ultrasound and x-ray machines, microwave ovens, video display terminals and cellular phones. Legally, FDA cannot review the safety of radiation-emitting consumer products such as cell phones and similar wireless devices prior to their being sold as it does with new drugs or medical devices. However, if cell phones emit radiofrequency energy (RF) at a level that is hazardous to the consumer, FDA could require cell phone manufacturers to notify users and to repair, replace or recall the phones. See:

https://www.gpo.gov/fdsys/pkg/USCODE-2010-title21/html/USCODE-2010-title21-chap9-subchapV-partC-sec360ii.htm

Definition

Manufacturers and distributors of products meeting the definition of "electronic product radiation" may be subject to certain stipulations under the FDCA. The terms electronic product radiation and electronic product are defined under 21 U.S.C. section 360hh of the FDCA:

"(1) the term 'electronic product radiation' means—
> *(A) any ionizing or non-ionizing electromagnetic or particulate radiation, or*
> *(B) any sonic, infrasonic, or ultrasonic wave, which is emitted from an electronic product as the result of the operation of an electronic circuit in such product;"*

"(2) the term "electronic product" means
> *(A) any manufactured or assembled product which, when in operation,*

>> *(i) contains or acts as part of an electronic circuit and*
>> *(ii) emits (or in the absence of effective shielding or other controls would emit) electronic product radiation, or*

> *(B) any manufactured or assembled article which is intended for use as a component, part, or accessory of a product described in clause (A) and which when in operation emits (or in the absence of effective shielding or other controls would emit) such radiation".*

The following diagram, with product examples, depicts the specific enabling legislative authority of FDA.

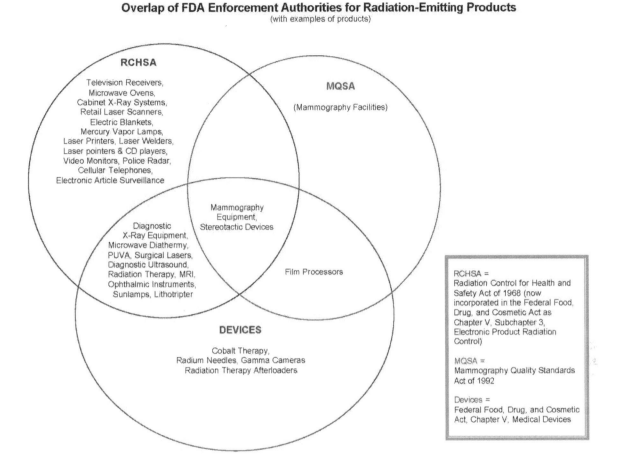

Overlap of FDA Enforcement Authorities for Radiation-Emitting Products
(with examples of products)

Radiation Emitting Electronic Product Examples

The regulations for electronic product radiation, including product requirements, record keeping and reporting, are contained under 21 CFR Parts 1000-1299. Examples of radiation emitting electronic products subject to the provisions of the FDCA include:

- **Medical:** diagnostic x-ray or ultrasound imaging devices, microwave or ultrasound diathermy devices, microwave blood warmers or sterilizers, laser coagulators, ultrasound phacoemulsifiers, x-ray or electron accelerators, sunlamps, ultraviolet dental curing devices;
- **Non-medical:** microwave ovens, televisions receivers and monitors (video displays), entertainment lasers, industrial x-ray systems, cordless and cellular telephones, industrial RF sealers of plastics and laminates, laser CD players.

https://www.fda.gov/downloads/Radiation-EmittingProducts/RadiationEmittingProductsandProcedures/UCM183653.pdf

CRITICAL ANALYSIS: Radiation emitting devices have increased due to technological advances. How would you advise your client as to appropriate action in bringing a product to market? See link as follows:

https://www.fda.gov/radiation-emittingproducts/electronicproductradiationcontrolprogram/gettinga-producttomarket/default.htm#5

The chart below illustrates the types of radiation emitting products and use.

Examples of Radiation-Emitting Electronic Products

Use \ Radiation	Ionizing (x-ray)	Optical (visible, UV, IR, laser)	RF, Microwave, VLF/ELF, magnetic	Acoustic (sonic, ultrasonic)
Medical: Diagnostic	• General radiography • Dental radiography • Fluoroscopy • Computed tomography • Mammography	• Slit lamp • Retinal acuity • Fluorescence spectroscopy • Transilluminator	• Magnetic resonance imaging	• Ultrasonography • Doppler ultrasound • Color doppler ultrasound
Medical: Therapeutic	• Medical accelerator (Rad therapy)	• Wound healing • Low-level laser therapy • PUVA therapy	• Hyperthermia • Diathermy • Bone healing • Wound healing • Prostate therapy	• Hyperthermia • Diathermy/physical therapy • Bone healing • Lithotripsy
Medical: Surgical	• Intra-operative electron beam	• Surgical laser • Ophthalmic, PRK laser • Dental laser	• Electrocautery	• Phacoemulsifier • Needle guide
Medical: Other	• Bone density measurement • Cabinet x-ray • Veterinary imaging	• Germicide lamps • Dental resin curing • Operating lights • Patient positioning • X-Ray indicator light field	• Blood warmers (microwave) • Sterilizer (plasma) • Telemetry	• Bone density measuring • Geriatric bath (ultrasound) • Hearing aid
Scientific, Other	• Analytical x-ray • Oscilloscope	• Research lasers • UV/IR research, uses	• Many scientific uses • Nuclear magnetic resonance • Weather doppler	• Many scientific uses
Industrial	• Cabinet x-ray • Industrial x-ray • Check weld/metal integrity	• Ranging & detection • Alignment, surveying • Laser welder • Laser material processing • Process control/ machine vision • UV curing	• Dielectric heater, sealer • Food processing • Dryer • Air traffic control	• Nondestructive tests • Gauging • Detect motion/occupancy • Cleaner • Welder
Business, Commercial, Security	• People (contraband) scanner • Baggage x-ray	• Suntan parlors • Fluorescent lamp • IR detector or security • Fiberoptic communication • Reprographics • Mercury vapor lamp • UPC readers • Laser pointer • IR data transmit/control	• Police radar • Pest controllers • EAS, metal detector • Security system (microwave) • Walkie-talkie • Clothes dryer • Communication • Microwave LAN • RF-excited lighting	• Jewelry cleaners • Motion detector • Security system • Humidifier
Consumer (household, entertainment, sports)	• Television receiver • Video monitor • Night vision scope	• Halogen lamp • Laser light shows • Laser printer • Suntan bed, lamps • CD and CD-ROM player • Laser toys/novelties • Laser gunsight • Remote controller • Autofocus camera • Digital display/monitor	• Cellular telephone • Microwave oven • Electric blanket • CB/amateur radio • Intrusion/anti-theft • Remote controller • Video monitor	• Ultrasonic toothbrush • Pest repeller • Intrusion alarm/security • Audio system/radio • Massager • Humidifier • Autofocus camera • Telephone ringer

Performance Standards

The following performance standards under 21 CFR are product specific.

http://www.accessdata.fda.gov/scripts/cdrh/cfdocs/cfcfr/CFRSearch.cfm?CFRPart=1010

21 CFR 1020.10. Television Receivers

- Applies to receivers and monitors that receive and convert a signal to display a "television picture"; and
- Limits radiation at 5 cm from the surface to 0.5 mR/hr during conditions of maximized user and service controls and a single worst-case component fault.

21 CFR 1020.20. Cold-cathode Discharge Tubes

- Limits radiation at 30 cm to 10 mR/hr; and
- Requires user precautions labeling.

21 CFR 1020.30. Diagnostic X-Ray Systems and their Major Components

- Applies to tube housings, generators and controls, film changers; fluoroscopic assemblies; spot film and image intensifiers; cephalometric devices; image receptor support devices for mammographic systems; diagnostic systems; CT systems (in part);
- Limits leakage at 1 meter from the source to 100 mR in 1 hr and at 5 cm from any other components to 2 mR in 1 hr; and
- Specifies beam limitations and beam quality criteria; user and assembler instructions and technical information.

21 CFR 1020.31. Radiographic Equipment

- Requires control and indication of technique factors; timer termination conditions; accuracy and re-producibility specifications; indication and limits on field size and alignment, etc.; and

- Limits transmission through mammographic image support system at 5 cm to 0.1 mR for each tube activation.

21 CFR 1020.32. Fluoroscopic Equipment

- Requires primary protective barrier; field limitation; continuous pressure control; source to skin distance; timer and
- Limits entrance exposure rates to 5 R/min (or 10 R/min with automatic exposure rate control).

21 CFR 1020.33. Computed Tomography (CT) Equipment

- Specifies user information on dose, imaging performance and quality assurance and
- Requires indication prior to initiation of scan, timer control to terminate or shutter the beam, indication of plane and alignment; beam on and shutter status indicators.

21 CFR 1020.40. Cabinet X-Ray Systems

- Applies to systems with x-ray tube installed in an enclosure, including carry-on baggage inspection systems;
- Limits radiation at 5 cm to 0.5 mR/hr under maximized operating conditions and door positions; restricts human access to the primary beam and
- Requires 2 interlocks on each door with 1 resulting in physical disconnection of energy to the generator; key control; 2 independent x-ray on indicators; warning indicators and labels; and user instructions.

21 CFR 1030.10. Microwave Ovens

- Applies to ovens for heating and cooking food (household or commercial; not industrial food processing);
- Limits radiation at 5 cm to 1 mW per sq cm prior to purchase and 5 mW per sq cm throughout useful life under conditions of allowable door positions and primary interlock failure, or with conducting wire;
- Limits access by human body to energy-containing space and to 1 of 2 required interlocks; at least 1 interlock must be "monitored" to disable the source and
- Requires user caution label and user and service manuals.

21 CFR 1040.10. Lasers and Laser Systems

- Applies to lasers, products containing lasers, and products intended to contain lasers;
- Specifies classification and user logotype with precautions based on radiation accessible during use; limits radiation from viewing optics, ports and displays to less than Class I; specifies interlocks/labels based on radiation accessible during maintenance and service;
- Requires, based on increasing hazard class, radiation indicators and safety: aperture label, beam attenuator, emission indicator (some with time delay), remote door interlock, key control, scanning safeguards, etc. and
- Requires user, maintenance and service manuals.

21 CFR 1040.11. Specific Laser Products

- Requires indication of power levels on medical lasers with +/- 20% accuracy;
- Limits radiation to less than Class IIIa for surveying, leveling and alignment lasers; and
- Limits radiation to less than Class IIIa for demonstration lasers, including display or entertainment (NOTE: Variances, with extensive human access limitations, are often granted for laser light shows.).

21 CFR 1040.20. Sunlamps and Sunlamp Products

- Applies to products intended to produce skin tanning;
- Limits levels of UV-C radiation and ratio of UV-A/ UV-B; requires specification of compatible lamps; and
- Requires maximum exposure time based on ultraviolet levels, timers with +/- 10% accuracy, protective eyewear, and user labeling and instructions.

21 CFR 1040.30. High-intensity Mercury Vapor Discharge Lamps

- Requires self-extinguishing lamps to cease operating after breakage or removal of 3 sq. cm of the outer envelope; and

- Specifies lamp packaging and advertisement information.

21 CFR 1050.10. Ultrasonic Therapy Products
- Applies to applicators or generators operating above 16 kHz for physical therapy;
- Provides indication of radiation parameters: average and temporal peak power and/or intensity; pulse duration, pulse repetition rate; effective radiating area; beam non-uniformity and spatial distributions, etc.; and
- Requires power accuracy of +/- 20% and timer accuracy +/- 10%.

Reporting Requirements
21 CFR 1010.4, 1010.5. Variances; Exemptions
- Manufacturers may request variances (i.e., an individual standard) for alternate, or equivalent, safety; and
- Manufacturers may request exemption from a performance standard for reason of national security, investigations, etc.

21 CFR 1002.20. Accidental Radiation Occurrences
- Documents any actual or possible unexpected exposure during manufacturing, testing or use of ANY electronic product; and
- Reports are due immediately after the event is known (MDR may be substituted, if applicable).

21 CFR 1002.10, 11, 12. Product Reports (also Supplements, Abbreviated)
- Applies to products listed in Table 1 of 1002.1 (most are subject to performance standards), unless excluded by 1002.1 or 1002.50;
- Documents information on manner of conformity to standards, labeling, test instrumentation, test procedures, quality control, etc.; submitted prior to family of products being introduced into commerce; and
- Abbreviated reports were added in Oct 1995 to reduce burdens.

21 CFR 1002.13. Annual Reports
- Applies to products as listed in Table 1; and
- Documents results of testing and user safety concerns; annually or quarterly updates contain model listings.

21 CFR 1003.20. Notice of Defect or Noncompliance
- Applies to ALL radiation-emitting electronic products; and
- Documents safety concerns, corrective actions, and information to users for safe use.

Imported Devices Under IDE and Performance Standards
Imported devices into the United States under an FDA approved Investigational Device Exemption (IDE) which are exempt from complying with performance standards under the Radiological Health program are not exempt from complying with applicable radiation standards. Medical devices that are also radiation-emitting products must comply with both medical device regulations and electronic product regulations. Electronic product regulation 21 CFR 1010.1 states the standards listed in that subchapter are prescribed pursuant to performance standards under section 534 of the Food, Drug, and Cosmetic Act. Therefore, although an IDE would provide exemptions from section 514 (medical device performance standards), it does not exempt manufacturers from section 534 (electronic product performance standards). This means those regulations in 21 CFR 1000 - 1050 must still be followed for radiation emitting products used in clinical studies following an approved IDE. It is essential that the product comply with the applicable standard(s), be certified, and a completed and accurate product report must be submitted to CDRH before the product is

released to the importer and clinical investigators, as required by 21 CFR 1002.10. (edited in part). See the following link.

Other Radiation Control Regulations

21 CFR 1003.2 Defect in an Electronic Product

- Applies to products not subject to performance standards and to products subject to standards if the standard does not address the specific safety issue; and
- Exists, for products that USE radiation to accomplish the purpose of the product and emissions are intended, when radiation.
  (1) Fails to meet design specifications, or
  (2) is unnecessary and creates a risk of injury, or
  (3) fails to accomplish its intended purpose.
- Exists, for products that DO NOT USE radiation to accomplish the purpose and do not intend to emit radiation, when radiation
  (1) is emitted that creates a risk of injury, or
  (2) fails to meet its design specifications.

21 CFR 1003.10/.11. Determination of Noncompliance or Defect

- FDA or manufacturer informs the other of safety concern based on product testing, inspection, research, or review of reports or other data; and
- Manufacturer notifies purchasers, dealers and distributors of the hazard and appropriate use until corrected (per 1003.21).

21 CFR 1003.30/.31. Exemption from Notification

- Based on data to show there is no significant risk of injury as a result of the defect or failure to comply and
- Granted by FDA on own initiative or in response to a written request from the manufacturer.

21 CFR 1004.1/.2/.3. Repurchase, Repair, and Replacement

- Correction of noncompliance or defect which is neither successfully refuted nor granted an exemption; and
- Plan, including (draft) notification to users, documented by the responsible firm and approved by FDA (usually prior to implementation); may include one or more of the options to repair, replace or refund as needed.

21 CFR 1005.3/.10. Importation Requirements

- Form FDA 2877 is filed by importer for entry (19 CFR 12.90); and
- FDA samples and tests products to verify compliance if necessary products failing to meet applicable standards are refused entry by U.S. Customs.

21 CFR 1005.21 / .22 / .23 / .24 / .25. Bringing Imported Products into Compliance

- Under a U.S. Customs term bond, importer submits written application (usually Form FDA 766) for approval by FDA; and
- FDA supervises activities and the importer pays fees for such supervision.

21 CFR 1010.2/.3. Certification and Identification Labels

- Label(s) on each product subject to a standard identifying the name and address of the manufacturer and date of manufacture; and
- Label on each product subject to a standard of the manufacturer's statement that the product complies with DHHS radiation standards or similar language.

Compliance Actions for Radiation Control Act Violations

A. FDA Administrative Actions

- ➢ Recall Products (corrective actions are approved and substantiated);
- ➢ Disapprove Quality Control and Testing Program (i.e., embargo products); and
- ➢ Import Alert, Automatic Detention and Refusal (with U.S. Customs Service).

B. Actions through U.S. District Courts

> ➢ Injunction from shipping in interstate commerce or to require reporting and certification requirements; and
> ➢ Civil (money) penalties for failure to report, failure to certify, failure to comply with standards.

CRITICAL ANALYSIS: Detail which laws, including specific sections and pertinent regulations a company must follow to import an investigational device that is a radiation-emitting product. Incorporate a discussion about the ramifications for non-compliance.

Labeling Requirements

http://www.fda.gov/MedicalDevices/DeviceRegulationandGuidance/Overview/DeviceLabeling/LabelingRequirementsforRadiationEmittingDevicesandProducts/default.htm

Radiation-emitting products that discharge sonic, infrasonic, or ultrasonic radiation are subject to specific labeling requirements. Radiation emitting devices embody electronic products that emit radiation by design such as X-ray equipment or because of operation such as a television set. These labeling requirements include:

> ➢ A statement that the product complies with the applicable performance standard.
> ➢ The full name and address of the manufacturer of the product. Alternately, the product may contain the full name and address of a company or individual other than the manufacturer, provided that the full name and address of the actual manufacturer has been previously identified to the Director of the Center for Devices and Radiological Health (CDRH). (This alternative is necessary so that CDRH can identify manufacturers of particular models of devices in those instances where the listed distributor uses different manufacturers for each model.) Abbreviations such as Co., Inc., or their foreign equivalents, and the initial of the first and middle names of individuals may be used.
> ➢ The place, month, and year of manufacture. The place of manufacture may be expressed in a code if the code has been previously supplied to the Director of CDRH. The month and year of manufacture cannot be coded or abbreviated. The month and a four digit number for the year must appear as follows:

"MANUFACTURED: (Insert Month and Year of Manufacture)"

Specific labeling requirements exist for specific types of radiation emitting products such as ionizing radiation emitting products; microwave and radio frequency emitting products; ultrasonic radiation emitting products and light emitting products.

Laser "Pointers"

http://www.fda.gov/AboutFDA/Transparency/Basics/ucm302664.htm (edited)

FDA regulates all laser products, even handheld, battery-powered lasers available for purchase from manufacturers, importers, assemblers, dealers or distributors in the United States and its territories. Manufacturers of these lasers must limit the laser light power to **5 milliWatts** (often abbreviated as "mW") or less. Mandatory labeling or packaging requirements must detail laser power, hazard class (**Class I, Class IIa, Class II, Class IIIa or Class 1, Class 2 or Class 3R**) and wavelength prior to purchase. Wavelength is a number that describes the color of the beam.

Online labeling and advertisements must disclose this information as well. Size does not matter as even the smallest handheld, battery-powered lasers can emit laser light at hazardous powers. Larger models (small flashlight size) have the potential to burn skin and pop balloons. Any size handheld battery-powered laser not directly controlled has the potential to blind or permanently affect eyesight.

CRITICAL ANALYSIS: Discuss further regulatory oversight regarding lasers.

VOLUME V

Volume V: Human Drug Regulation—Approvals, Promotion, Off-Label, Warnings, Accountability, and Postmarket Surveillance

This volume imparts information about the drug development process, from test-tube to new drug application review as well as the investigational drug review process and experimental treatments. In 2018, FDA Commissioner Gottlieb announced a modernization of the drug review process. Volume V imparts an across-the-board analysis of drug law topics and significant legislation. FDA approval mechanisms for new and generic drugs as well as biosimilars, investigational drugs, direct-to-consumer advertising, "off-label" enforcement, corporate accountability, drug reimportation, and post market surveillance are covered. The impact of copyright infringement is discussed in the decision of Smithkline Beecham Consumer Health Care, L.P. v. Watson Pharmaceuticals. Other important topics include bioequivalence, the MedWatch program, user fees and over-the-counter product labeling. This volume contains information on direct-to-consumer promotion, includes a discussion of off-label promotion, and legal decisions. For example, in Washington Legal Foundation v. Henney, the court invalidated the restrictions imposed by FDA on off-label uses because of First Amendment violations. The decisions of Perez, Schering Plough, Centocor and Johnson distinguish the impact of direct-to-consumer promotion on the learned intermediary doctrine. Thompson v. Western States Medical Center invalidated Section 127 of FDAMA concerning promotion of pharmacy compounding. Duty to warn issues that involve the manufacturer, physician and pharmacist are included.

This volume contains landmark United States Supreme Court legal decisions that have impacted on the practice of pharmaceutical regulatory law. Preemption is a legal term of art that emanates from the Supremacy Clause (Article VI, clause 2) of the United States Constitution. Article VI, clause 2 prohibits states from enacting laws that conflict with federal law unless the federal law contains explicit preemption language. Today preemption in failure to warn cases presents a complex dilemma between federal and state tort actions. The 2009 landmark United States Supreme Court decision, Wyeth v. Levine, concerned a brand name drug and the ability to bring a lawsuit in state court. Conversely, another United States Supreme Court case decided in 2011, Pliva v. Mensing involved a generic drug and held preemption prevailed. Finally, the United States Supreme Court in the 2011 Sorrell decision determined that a State regulation precluding the sale of data violated the First Amendment. Similarly, First Amendment principles prevailed in the off-label cases of Amarin and Caronia, both Federal 2nd Circuit decisions and fact specific. Yet off-label issues remain controversial.

The Supreme Court set forth in the landmark Actavis decision that the Federal Trade Commission can review settlements between brand and generic companies commonly referred to as pay-for-delay. The Court in Mutual Pharmaceutical set forth a demarcation between generic and brand name drugs and the right to recovery in state court. Rulemaking proceedings to overcome the brand and generic discrepancy were initiated in 2013 and remains stalled.

FDA approved the first drug using 3-D technology in 2015. In 2018, FDA approved three drugs to prevent migraines. Furthermore, in 2018, the first botanically extracted cannabis product, Epidiolex was approved. The future holds promise for further innovation in development, approvals and post marketing surveillance.

Chapter 1: Major Legislation and the Center for Drug Evaluation and Research—CDER

Significant Legislation

Key website *http://www.fda.gov/AboutFDA/CentersOffices/OfficeofMedicalProductsandTobacco/CDER/default.htm*

Initially, back in the 1800s, regulation of pharmaceuticals centered on the prevention of imported adulterated drugs. Originally, most medicines were sold without having to obtain a prescription from a physician. That changed due to several enactments including the 1938 Food, Drug and Cosmetic Act and the 1951 Humphrey-Durham Amendment designating a prescription drug as one that is habit forming, harmful without physician intervention or those under the 1938 FDCA designation. Since that time, drug legislation has evolved with safety and efficacy issues as paramount. For example, the 1962 Drug Amendments required proof of effectiveness by substantial evidence. In response to this legislation, the Drug Efficacy Program commonly referred to as the DESI program, was implemented to review products already on the market. OTC products were handled by the 1972 Drug Monograph approach and today it remains ongoing.

The focus has been on a range of human drug-related areas such as prescription drugs, generic drugs, drug price competition, orphan drugs, investigational drugs and promotion. The Supreme Court landmark decision of *Bacto-Unidisk* distinguished the term drug from medical device in furtherance of public protection. The Food and Drug Administration Modernization Act (FDAMA) in 1997 imposed requirements for pediatric studies, fast track products and radiopharmaceuticals. Ten years later, the Food and Drug Administration Amendments Act (FDAAA) of 2007 focused on several key drug related provisions such as pediatric safety and postmarket surveillance. Since 2007 FDA has enacted legislation such as the following:

Cures Act

The 21st Century Cures Act is intended to accelerate drug and medical device approvals and address the opioid crisis. The Act strengthens mental health services, includes $1 billion for opioid abuse prevention, $4.8 billion for biomedical research and $1.8 billion for cancer research.

Drug Quality and Security Act

This necessary and milestone legislation 113th Congress (H.R. 3204) enacted towards the end of 2013, addresses federal regulatory authority over pharmacy compounding. Unfortunately, this legislation was enacted in response to the many deaths associated with large scale compounding. Additionally, Title II of the Drug Quality and Security Act (DQSA) contains the *Drug Supply Chain Security Act*, (DSCSA) the "track and trace" provisions throughout the drug supply chain. The DSCSA outlines critical steps to construct an electronic, interoperable system to ascertain and trace certain prescription drugs as they are distributed.

http://www.fda.gov/Drugs/DrugSafety/DrugIntegrityandSupplyChainSecurity/DrugSupplyChainSecurityAct/ucm376829.htm

Food and Drug Administration Safety and Innovation Act—Brand Name and Generic Drugs, Biosimilars, and Medical Devices

The Food and Drug Administration Safety and Innovation Act (FDASIA), enacted July 9, 2012 (Senate Bill 3187, Pub. L. No. 112-144) reauthorized the Prescription Drug User Fee Act (PDUFA). It is the fifth authorization of PDUFA that includes Title I of FDASIA and the performance goals and procedures for PDUFA V. The FSASIA includes user fees of $6 billion over five years for medical devices, brand name drug approvals, generic drugs and biosimilars.

The Food and Drug Administration Amendments Act (FDAAA)

Title I—Prescription Drug User Fees (PDUFA) Reauthorization—"Fees Relating to Advisory Review of Prescription Drug Television Advertising" (DTC), establishes a voluntary user fee for the pre-broadcast review of DTC. NOTE: Any DTC advertisement that is subject to required pre-dissemination review is not subject to user fees. See Title IX below.

Title III—Pediatric Medical Device Safety and Improvement Act—Requires FDA to work with the NIH to establish clinical trial databases including adverse event information.

Title IV—Pediatric Research Equity Act of 2007—Reauthorizes and amends the Pediatric Research Equity Act (PREA) Pub. L. No. 108-155 117 Stat. 1936 (2003); Increased accountability for agreed upon evaluations; and annual update as to progress in conducting pediatric studies.

Title V—Best Pharmaceuticals for Children Act of 2007—Reauthorized and amended the Best Pharmaceuticals for Children Act (BPCA) *Pub. L. No. 107-109, 115 Stat. 1408 (2002)—Impact is increased accountability for agreed upon pediatric studies.*

Title VI— Reagan-Udall Foundation—Establishes a non-profit corporation to advance FDA's Critical Path Initiative.

Title VII—Advisory Committee Conflicts of Interest—Requires disclosure of financial interests.

Title VIII—Clinical Trial Data Bases—Expanded clinical trial registry database.

Title IX— Enhanced FDA Authority Regarding Postmarket Safety of Drugs—Broadened authority to monitor and improve drug and biologics safety and includes penalties for violations.

Postmarket Studies and Clinical Trials—Requires FDA to develop and implement a "postmarket risk identification and analysis system" 21 U.S.C. section 505(k) (3) (B)-(C).

Safety Labeling Changes—FDA can require postmarket safety labeling changes if warranted. The NDA or BLA holder must submit a supplement to FDA within 30 days of the proposed labeling changes to reflect the new safety information; otherwise provide a comprehensive basis as to why the NDA or BLA holder does not believe the new labeling changes are warranted.

Television Advertising—Created a process for FDA to "Pre-review Television Advertisements".

DTC Advertising Statement—Required statement all published DTC ads for human drugs—
"You are encouraged to report negative side effects of prescription drugs to the FDA. Visit www.fda.gov/medwatrch or call 1-800-FDA-1088." **NOTE: See This Volume, Chapter 5.**

Risk Evaluation and Mitigation Strategy—Required if FDA determines that the REMS is essential to make certain that the benefits outweigh the risks.

Generic Drug Approvals—Prohibits delaying approval of a generic drug application based on a citizen's petition with the exception of protection of public health.

The Center for Drug Evaluation and Research

Identified as CDER, the Center for Drug Evaluation and Research is the largest of FDA's Centers, has responsibility for brand name and generic prescription and over-the-counter drugs; affirming product safety and effectiveness prior to market approval. Additionally, CDER regulates other types of products considered drugs such as fluoride toothpaste, antiperspirants, dandruff shampoos and sunscreens. FDA has a separate center for biologics and blood safety; however, biological product reviews are conducted by CDER.

CDER Responsibilities include the following:

➢ Premarket drug review;
➢ Surveillance for drug problems;
➢ Drug information and advertising monitoring;
➢ Drug quality protections; *and*
➢ Applied research.

CDER does not test drugs, though the Office of Testing and Research does conduct limited research in the areas of drug quality, safety and effectiveness. It is the responsibility of the manufacturer to ensure that a pharmaceutical is tested and to support the drug application with safety and effectiveness data. A team of CDER physicians, statisticians, chemists, pharmacologists and other scientists review new drug applications (NDAs) submitted by a manufacturer. NDAs contain the data and the proposed labeling for the new drug product. New drug reviewing divisions of CDER are grouped into several offices of drug evaluation. Each office oversees drugs for certain medical conditions. The Office of Drug Evaluation I, for example, is responsible for neuropharmacological, oenological, and cardiorenal drug products. The Office of Drug Evaluation V reviews OTC drugs. Each review division works with reviewers in the Office of New Drug Chemistry, Office of Clinical Pharmacology and Biopharmaceutics and the Office of Epidemiology and Biostatistics to evaluate the drug for safety and efficacy. A listing of new and generic drug approvals is available at Drugs@FDA.

Drug promotion continues to spiral, and FDA has the regulatory authority to oversee the advertising of prescription drugs. Specifically, CDER's Office of Prescription Drug Promotion monitors prescription drug advertising to ensure that it contains a truthful summary of information about effectiveness, side effects, and circumstances when use is not advisable. The Federal Trade Commission regulates the advertising of OTC drugs.

CDER Achievements, Accomplishments, Approvals

The following denote across the board accomplishments at CDER:

➢ *Modernization of Drug Development Review Processes;*
➢ *Overhaul of professional package inserts;*
➢ *Medication Guides; Drug approvals both new drugs and generic equivalents;*
➢ *Good manufacturing practices (cGMP) critical initiatives;*
➢ *Domestic and foreign inspections;*
➢ *Counterterrorism programs against chemical, biological and nuclear weapons; Advertising and promotion review;*
➢ *Increased communications through the Internet; and*
➢ *Postmarketing initiatives.*

Drug approvals have benefited people with cancer, HIV, diabetes, heart disease and circulatory and nerve systems disorders and children with asthma. Median total approval time for new drugs has been shortened considerably to approximately one year or less. In 2018 (Oct. 2018) there were 47 novel drug approvals. In prior years there 46 drug approvals in 2017, 22 drug approvals in 2016 and 45 novel drug approvals in 2015 New Molecular Entity (NME) and New Therapeutic Biological Product Approvals.

https://www.fda.gov/Drugs/DevelopmentApprovalProcess/DrugInnovation/ucm537040.htm
https://www.fda.gov/Drugs/DevelopmentApprovalProcess/DrugInnovation/ucm483775.htm
https://www.fda.gov/Drugs/DevelopmentApprovalProcess/DrugInnovation/ucm430302.htm

Outsourcing

Previously, the regulatory pharmaceutical arena centered on smaller pharmaceutical companies with most activities done in-house. That has changed dramatically in terms of outsourcing both in and outside of the United States and suffice it to state, that contract manufacturers abound. Yet, compliance with FDA regulatory requisites remains critical.

CRITICAL ANALYSIS: How has outsourcing changed the regulation of pharmaceuticals? Evaluate outsourcing in terms of advantages and disadvantages and patient privacy.

Drug Shortages

Drug scarcities in the United States have received considerable attention. Former President Obama issued an Executive Order in 2011 to address this problem including requesting Congressional action that would change reporting to FDA from voluntary to mandatory. FDA helped thwart 282 drug shortages in 2012. The FDA Safety and Innovation Act (Pub. L. 112-144) (FDASIA) codified the Executive Order and significantly amended provisions in the FD&C Act related to drug shortages. The FDASIA amended section 506C of the FD&C Act (21 U.S.C. 356c) to require all manufacturers of certain drugs to notify FDA of a permanent discontinuance or an interruption in manufacturing of these drugs 6 months in advance of the permanent discontinuance or interruption in manufacturing, or as soon practicable. The FDASIA also added section 506E to the FDCA (21 U.S.C. 356e) requiring FDA to maintain a current list of drugs that are determined by FDA to be in shortage in the United States, and to include on that public list certain information about those shortages. The FDASIA permits FDA to apply section 506C to biological products by regulation. In accordance with FDASIA, FDA issued a final rule (January 9, 2014) to improve FDA's ability to identify potential drug shortages.

NOTE: Does it really cost $2.7 billion to develop and bring a drug to market? According to the Tufts Center for Drug Development, costs have escalated. However, See:
https://jamanetwork.com/journals/jamainternalmedicine/article-abstract/2653012

(discusses research and development costs of cancer drugs) and Matthew Herber, The Cost Of Developing Drugs Is Insane. That Paper That Says Otherwise Is Insanely Bad,
https://www.forbes.com/sites/matthewherper/2017/10/16/the-cost-of-developing-drugs-is-insane-a-paper-that-argued-otherwise-was-insanely-bad/#7a2d32512d45

See also: Ed Silverman, Can It Really Cost $2.6 Billion to Develop a Drug? Wall St. J. B3 (Nov. 21, 2014).

CRITICAL ANALYSIS: Review the note above concerning costs. In your analysis, consider resources required to develop a new drug as well as how the issue of drug shortages was addressed in the FDA Safety and Innovation Act. Explore viable solutions.

Patient Package Inserts and Medication Guides

http://www.fda.gov/downloads/AdvisoryCommittees/CommitteesMeetingMaterials/RiskCommuni-cationAdvisoryCommittee/UCM150262.pdf

The revamping of the FDA regulated patient package inserts (PPI) is a major accomplishment in terms of detailing risks and benefits in an easy to read format including the following:
 ➢ Immediate access to the most important prescribing information about benefits and risks;
 ➢ Table of Contents for easy reference to safety and efficacy information;
 ➢ Date of initial product approval; and
 ➢ Internet information and a toll-free number for adverse event reporting.

The FDA Medication Guide is part of the labeling and is required by regulation for certain drugs. Manufacturers notify pharmacists about the Medication Guides and pharmacists, in turn, are required to distribute them. Typically, the Medication Guides are utilized for certain drug and biological products that present serious and significant public health issues. Approximately 250 products have medication guides and are required when FDA determines that:
 ➢ Certain information is necessary to prevent serious adverse effects;
 ➢ Patient decision-making should be informed by information about a known serious side effect with a product; or
 ➢ Patient adherence to directions for the use of a product is essential to its effectiveness.

Medication guides provide answers to critical questions such as:
 ➢ What is this drug and what does it do?
 ➢ What is the most important information that I need to know about the medication?
 ➢ What are the risks involved in taking this?
 ➢ What are the possible side effects?
 ➢ Who should not take the drug?
 ➢ What ingredients are in this medication?

http://www.fda.gov/Drugs/DrugSafety/ucm085729.htm

Consumer Medication Information

A Consumer Medication Information Sheet (CMI) includes important information about the prescription medicine such as "how to take it, how to store it, and how to monitor improvement". Although not under FDA jurisdiction, FDA *encourages the private sector to provide CMI; provides guidance to the companies that write CMI; and evaluates pharmacies' progress in providing CMI information.* FDA regulates prescription drug labels written for health care professionals and Medication Guides and Patient Package Inserts written for consumers, FDA does not regulate the CMI leaflets. Details on precautions and warnings, and serious or frequent adverse event symptoms are included. Compared to the Medication Guide, the CMI offers more general information on how to properly use a medicine. Typically, CMIs are purchased by pharmacies from outside companies that use the FDA approved professional labeling as the basis for the CMI.

Postmarket Surveillance

Despite efficient, high-quality reviews, postmarket surveillance activities remain an important function within CDER. Monitoring the quality of drugs once marketed remains a top priority for CDER. Called MedWatch, health professionals and consumers can report serious adverse reactions. CDER's Office of Epidemiology and Biostatistics collects information from MedWatch and conducts statistical evaluations on drug usage, adverse reactions, poisonings, safety, and effectiveness. Congress affirmatively addressed this issue with post market surveillance legislative measures through the *Food and Drug Administration Amendments Act* (2007) and other legislation such as the *Food and Drug Administration, Safety and Innovation Act* (2012) and the *Drug Quality and Security Act* (2013).

NOTE: See This *Volume*, Chapter 10 Adverse Events and Postmarket Surveillance.

Drug Interactions

http://www.fda.gov/drugs/resourcesforyou/ucm163354.htm#top
http://www.fda.gov/ForConsumers/ConsumerUpdates/UCM096386#supplements (edited)
There are three main types of drug interactions: *Drugs with Food and Beverages; Drugs with Dietary Supplements;* and *Drugs with Other Drugs.*

Drugs with Food and Beverages—Concerns of drug interactions with food and beverages may include delayed, decreased, or enhanced absorption of a medication. Food can affect the bioavailability (the degree and rate at which a drug is absorbed into someone's system), metabolism, and excretion of certain medications. Examples of drug interactions include:

Alcohol: Alcohol can increase or decrease the effect of many drugs.

Grapefruit juice: Grapefruit juice should not be taken with certain blood pressure-lowering drugs or cyclosporine for the prevention of organ transplant rejection. The juice can also interact to cause higher blood levels of the anti-anxiety medicine Buspar (buspirone); the anti-malaria drugs Quinerva or Quinite (quinine); and Halcion (triazolam), a medication used to treat insomnia.

Licorice: Lanoxin is used to treat congestive heart failure and abnormal heart rhythms. Some forms of licorice may increase the risk for Lanoxin toxicity. Licorice may also reduce the effects of blood pressure drugs or diuretic (urine-producing) drugs, including Hydrodiuril (hydrochlorothiazide) and Aldactone (spironolactone).

Chocolate: MAO inhibitors should not be consumed with excessive amounts of chocolate. Caffeine in chocolate can interact with stimulant drugs. Ritalin can (methylphenidate), increase their effect, or decrease the effect of sedative-hypnotics such as Ambien (zolpidem).

Drugs with Dietary Supplements—Research has revealed that over 50 percent or more of American adults use dietary supplements regularly.

St. John's Wort (Hypericum perforatum): This herb is considered an inducer of liver enzymes, which means it can reduce the concentration of medications in the blood. St. John's Wort can reduce the blood level of medications such as Lanoxin, the cholesterol-lowering drugs Mevacor and Altocor (lovastatin), and the erectile dysfunction drug Viagra (sildenafil).

Vitamin E: Taking vitamin E with a blood-thinning medication such as Coumadin can increase anti-clotting activity and may cause an increased risk of bleeding.

Ginseng: This herb can interfere with the bleeding effects of Coumadin. In addition, ginseng can enhance the bleeding effects of heparin, aspirin, and nonsteroidal anti-inflammatory drugs such as ibuprofen, naproxen, and ketoprofen. Combining ginseng with MAO inhibitors such as Nardil or Parnate may cause headache, trouble sleeping, nervousness, and hyperactivity.

Ginkgo Biloba: High doses of the herb Ginkgo biloba could decrease the effectiveness of anticonvulsant therapy in patients taking the following medications to control seizures: Tegretol, Equetro or Carbatrol (carbamazepine), and Depakote (valproic acid).

Drugs with Other Drugs—Nearly, 40 percent of the United States population receive prescriptions for four or more medications. The rate of adverse drug reactions increases dramatically after a patient is on four or more medications. Examples of drug interactions include:

Cordarone (amiodarone): FDA issued an alert in August 2008, warning patients about taking Cordarone to correct abnormal rhythms of the heart and the cholesterol-lowering drug Zocor (Simvastatin). Patients taking Zocor in doses higher than 20 mg while also taking Cordarone run the risk of developing a rare condition of muscle injury called rhabdomyolysis, which can lead to kidney failure or death. According to Dr. Huang, Cordarone also can inhibit or reduce the effect of the blood thinner Coumadin (warfarin).

Lanoxin (digoxin): "Lanoxin has a narrow therapeutic range. So other drugs, such as Norvir (ritonvair), can elevate the level of Lanoxin," says Huang. "And an increased level of Lanoxin can cause irregular heart rhythms." Norvir is a protease inhibitor used to treat HIV.

Antihistamines: Over-the-counter (OTC) antihistamines are drugs that temporarily relieve a runny nose, or reduce sneezing, itching of the nose or throat, and itchy watery eyes.] The sedating effect of some antihistamines combined with a sedating antidepressant could strongly affect concentration level. Antihistamines taken in conjunction with blood pressure medication may cause a person's blood pressure to increase and may also speed up the heart rate.

Drug Defined—*United States v. Bacto-Unidisk*

The FDCA under Section 201(g) or (21 U.S.C sec. 321(g)) defines the meaning of "Drug". The *United States v. Bacto-Unidisk* decision, decided by the United States Supreme Court, is an important case for understanding the parameters of this definition. The case centered on whether an antibiotic screening disc used as a screening test for help in deciding the correct amount of antibiotic drug to administer was a drug. Ultimately, the Court determined the product was a drug and therefore subject to pre-market approval.

United States v. Bacto-Unidisk, 89 S. Ct. 1410 (1969)

Mr. Chief Justice WARREN delivered the opinion of the court. At issue here is the scope of the statutory definition of drug contained in the Federal Food, Drug, and Cosmetic Act and the extent of the Secretary of Health, Education, and Welfare's regulatory authority under that definition. The specific item involved in this definitional controversy is a laboratory aid known as an antibiotic sensitivity disc, used as a screening test for help in determining the proper antibiotic drug to administer to patients. If the article is a 'drug' within the general definition of section 201 of the Federal Food, Drug, and Cosmetic Act (52 Stat. 1040, 21 U.S.C. § 321 (1964 ed., Supp. II)), then the Secretary can subject it to pre-market clearance. The regulations require batch certification of any antibiotic product which also meets the general drug definition of § 201. If, on the other hand, the article is merely a 'device' under the Act, it is subject only to the misbranding and adulteration proscriptions of the Act and does not have to be pretested before marketing; and, of course, if the disc does not fall under either definition, the Act itself is totally inapplicable.

When the discs were marketed without complying with the certification regulations of the Secretary, the Government condemned them pursuant to § 334 of the Act (21 U.S.C. § 331) on the assumption that the discs were drugs and thus validly subject to pre-market regulation. In this action following the condemnation, however, the United States District Court for the Eastern District of Michigan held that the discs were not drugs within the meaning of the Act, suggesting that, if anything, they were devices. *** The Court of Appeals for the Sixth Circuit affirmed on the same reasoning. We reverse. *** With the proliferation of the various types of antibiotics, doctors found a need for a screening test to help choose which antibiotic to use in treating a particular infection. *** In this test, a round paper disc, which has been impregnated with a specific antibiotic, is placed in contact with sample cultures, or isolates, of a patient's virus, grown in a special culture medium (agar) from a specimen of the patient's fluid (blood, spinal fluid, sputum, urine, etc.). The disc is used, in conjunction with a patient's specimen, in laboratory work exclusively, and never comes in contact with any part of the patient's body itself. *** The discs had been in general use for some four years when, in 1960, the Secretary of Health, Education, and Welfare determined to regulate them pursuant to § 507. *** The Commissioner's action, the regulations noted, followed 'numerous complaints by the medical profession, hospitals, and laboratory technicians' and a resulting extensive survey of the use of the discs. That study found the discs unreliable in their statements of potency with resulting loss of safety and efficacy, and thus found it 'vital for the protection of the public health' to adopt the regulations (25 Fed.Reg. 9370). Section 502, as set forth in 21 U.S.C. § 352, reads, in part, as follows:

'A drug or device shall be deemed to be misbranded—

'(l) If it is, or purports to be, or is represented as a drug composed wholly or partly of any kind of penicillin, streptomycin, chlortetracycline, chloramphenicol, bacitracin, or any other antibiotic drug, or any derivative thereof, unless (1) it is from a batch with respect to which a certificate or release has been issued pursuant to section 357 of this title, and (2) such certificate or release is in effect with respect to such drug: Provided, That this subsection shall not apply to any drug or class of drugs exempted by regulations promulgated under section 357(c) or (d) of this title.'

'(g) (1) The term 'drug' means (A) articles recognized in the official United States Pharmacopoeia, official Homoeopathic Pharmacopoeia of the United States, or official National Formulary, or any supplement to any of them; and (B) articles intended for use in the diagnosis, cure, mitigation, treatment, or prevention of disease in man or other animals; and (C) articles (other than food) intended to affect the structure or any function of the body of man or other animals; and (D) articles intended for use as a component of any article specified in clauses (A), (B), or (C) of this paragraph; but does not include devices or their components, parts, or accessories.' 21 U.S.C. § 321 (1964 ed., Supp. II). If, on the other hand, the product was a 'device,' only the misbranding, adulteration, and labeling provisions of § 501 and 502 applied, and the Secretary's disc certification regulations were invalidly promulgated.

'The term 'device' *** means instruments, apparatus, and contrivances, including their components, parts, and accessories, intended (1) for use in the diagnosis, cure, mitigation, treatment, or prevention of disease in man or other animals; or (2) to affect the structure or any function of the body of man or other animals.' 21 U.S.C. § 321(h). ***

Thus, the essential question for our determination is whether Congress intended the definition of drug to have the broad coverage the courts below and the parties agree its words allow. Viewing the structure, the legislative history, and the remedial nature of the Act, we think it plain that Congress intended to define 'drug' far more broadly than does the medical profession. *** At the outset, it is clear from § 201 that the word 'drug' is a term of art for the purposes of the Act, encompassing far more than the strict medical definition of that word. *** The historical expansion of the definition of drug, and the creation of a parallel concept of devices, clearly show, we think, that Congress fully intended that the Act's coverage be as broad as its literal language indicates— and equally clearly, broader than any strict medical definition might otherwise allow. *** At the outset, it must be conceded that the language of the statute is of little assistance in determining precisely what differentiates a 'drug' from a 'device': to the extent that both are intended for use in the treatment, mitigation and cure of disease, the former is an 'article' and the latter includes 'instruments,' 'apparatus,' and 'contrivances.' *** In upholding the Secretary's determination here, without deciding the precise contours of the 'device' classification, we need only point out that the exception was created primarily for the purpose of avoiding the semantic incongruity of classifying as drugs (1) certain quack contraptions and (2) basic aids used in the routine operation of a hospital—items characterized more by their purely mechanical nature than by the fact that they are composed of complex chemical compounds or biological substances. *** Our holding here simply involves an obvious corollary to that principle that we must take care not to narrow the coverage of a statute short of the point where Congress indicated it should extend. Reversed.

Mr. Justice DOUGLAS, [dissented] being of the view that an antibiotic sensitivity disc used by physicians to aid them in determining what antibiotic drug, if any, to give to a patient, is a 'device' as defined in §201(h) of the Act, not a 'drug' as defined in § 201(g), would affirm.

CRITICAL ANALYSIS: Would the Court have reached the same decision if this was decided today? Include the ramifications of how the product is classified: drug, device or combination.

Practice of Medicine or Drug/Biologic—*Regenerative Sciences*

Regenerative Sciences, LLC vigorously defended its position that FDA could not regulate the practice of medicine in its Regenexx™ treatment or Regenexx-C™ cultured treatment which uses Mesenchymal adult stem cells (MSCs) that originate primarily from bone marrow. The majority of shareholders of Regenerative Sciences, LLC are physicians and the company promotes the Regenexx™ treatment as a "non-surgical" treatment option for joint or bone pain in the hip, knee, shoulder, back or ankle as well as non-union fractures. Regenerative Sciences filed an injunction to prevent FDA from regulating the product as a drug. However, the court dismissed the matter as FDA has not yet taken regulatory action.

Subsequently, the court granted FDA's motion for summary judgment and issued a permanent injunction against the use of the Regenexx™ procedure and deemed the product a drug. *United States v. Regenerative Scis., LLC*, 878 F. Supp. 2d 248 (D.D.C. 2012). The Court of Appeals affirmed. (Feb. 4, 2014 No. 12-5254) (Docket Mandate Aff'd). April 7, 2014 and the decision is below. See: *http://www.regenexx.com* and *http://fortipublications.com/blog/*

United States v. Regenerative Sciences, LLC, 741 F. 3d 1314 (D.C. Cir. 2014)

GRIFFITH, Circuit Judge: In this civil enforcement action, we must decide whether the appellants—three individuals and a related corporate entity—violated federal laws regulating the manufacture and labeling of drugs and biological products by producing, as part of their medical practice, a substance consisting of a mixture of a patient's stem cells and the antibiotic doxycycline. Because we conclude that they did, we affirm the district court's judgment and the permanent injunction it entered against appellants.

I. A. This case involves two statutes under which the Food and Drug Administration (FDA) regulates the healthcare industry: the Federal Food, Drug & Cosmetic Act (FDCA), 21 U.S.C. § 301 *et seq.*, and the Public Health Service Act (PHSA), 42 U.S.C. § 201 *et seq.* Those statutes promote the safety of drugs and biological products, respectively, by setting forth detailed requirements for how such substances are to be manufactured and labeled. ***

B. The substance at issue in this case is produced by appellants Dr. Christopher Centeno, Dr. John Schultz, Michelle Cheever, and Regenerative Sciences, LLC, as part of a medical therapy that they market as the "Cultured Regenexx Procedure" (the Procedure). Drs. Centeno and Schultz, who practice medicine together at the Centeno–Schultz Clinic in Colorado, jointly developed the Procedure to treat patients' orthopedic conditions. *** The Procedure begins with the extraction of a sample of a patient's bone marrow or synovial fluid. From that sample, Regenerative Sciences isolates mesenchymal stem cells (MSCs), which are capable of differentiating into bone and cartilage cells. The MSCs are then placed in a solution to culture them—that is, to cause them to divide and proliferate. *** When the MSCs are sufficiently numerous for re-injection, they are combined with doxycycline, an antibiotic obtained in interstate commerce and used to prevent bacterial contamination of the MSCs. The resulting mixture (the Mixture) is injected into the patient from whom the stem cell sample was initially taken, at the site of the damaged tissue. Appellants promote the

Procedure as an alternative to surgery for various orthopedic conditions and diseases. In court filings, they have described the Procedure as a "treatment [for] orthopedic injuries and arthritis" and for "musculoskeletal and spinal injury." Their promotional materials recommend the Procedure for treatment of osteoarthritis, non-healing bone fractures, chronic bulging lumbar discs, and soft tissue injuries. In August 2010, the government filed this action for a permanent injunction against appellants, alleging that the Mixture is both a drug and a biological product that is adulterated and misbranded in violation of § 331(k) of the FDCA and § 262(j) of the PHSA, which incorporates § 331(k) by reference. *** The district court granted the government's motion for summary judgment and dismissed appellants' counterclaims, holding that they had violated the FDCA and the PHSA. *United States v. Regenerative Scis., LLC,* 878 F.Supp.2d 248, 263 (D.D.C.2012). Finding a "cognizable danger of a recurrent violation," the district court entered a permanent injunction prohibiting appellants from committing further violations. ***

II. Appellants' principal argument is that the Mixture is not subject to regulation under the FDCA or PHSA because it is neither a drug nor a biological product but is, rather, a medical procedure. Equally untenable is appellants' contention that because the Procedure occurs entirely within the state of Colorado, the Mixture lacks a sufficient connection to interstate commerce to permit federal regulation under the Commerce Clause. It is simply impossible to square this argument with the last seventy years of Commerce Clause jurisprudence, which, in recognition of Congress's authority to regulate even "purely local activities that are part of an economic 'class of activities' that have a substantial effect on interstate commerce," *Gonzales v. Raich,* 545 U.S. 1, 17 (2005) [.]

III. A. Appellants next advance two arguments why the Mixture is exempt from the FDCA's manufacturing and labeling requirements even if it is otherwise subject to federal regulation. *** Appellants concede that culturing MSCs affects their characteristics and offer no evidence that those effects constitute only minimal manipulation, they fail to carry that burden as a matter of law. ***

B. Alternatively, appellants contend that the Mixture is exempt from the FDCA's manufacturing and labeling requirements because it is a compounded drug. *See* 21 U.S.C. § 353a(a). A compounded drug must be produced using certain types of "bulk drug substances," one of which is "bulk drug substances ... that ... are components of drugs approved by the [government]." *Id.* § 353a(b)(1)(A). ***

IV. A. The FDCA provides that a drug "*shall be deemed to be adulterated* ... if ... the methods used in, or the facilities or controls used for, its manufacture, processing, packing, or holding do not conform to or are not operated or administered in conformity with current good manufacturing practice." 21 U.S.C. § 351(a) (emphasis added). *** Here, it is undisputed that appellants' facilities, methods, and controls for processing the Mixture violated federal manufacturing standards.

B. The FDCA also provides that a drug "shall be deemed to be misbranded" if its label omits certain information. As relevant here, the FDCA requires that a drug's label provide "adequate directions for use," 21 U.S.C. § 352(f)(1), and, in the case of prescription drugs, bear the symbol "Rx only," *id.* § 353(b)(4)(A). Appellants admit that the Mixture's labeling satisfies neither of these requirements. *** Both exemptions require that the label bear the symbol "Rx only," *see* 21 U.S.C. § 353(b)(4)(A); 21 C.F.R. § 201.l00(b)(1), and it is undisputed that the Mixture's label does not. Because its label fails to provide the minimum information necessary to qualify for either exemption from § 352(f), the Mixture is misbranded. ***

V. *** Appellants also admit that they did not improve their manufacturing process even after receiving FDA warnings. Such conduct is sufficient to warrant the permanent injunction.

VI. For the foregoing reasons, we affirm the district court's orders granting summary judgment to the government, dismissing appellants' counterclaims, and permanently enjoining appellants from committing future violations of the FDCA's manufacturing and labeling provisions.

CRITICAL ANALYSIS: Discuss whether the court erred in this case and perhaps this falls under the "Practice of Medicine" as opposed to regulation as a drug (see 21 U.S. C. Sec. 321 (g)(1)(D)) and biologic (see 42 U.S. C. Sec. 262(i)).

Chapter 2: New Drug Development, Investigational Drugs, Botanicals and Clinical Trials

New Drug Development

FDA Commissioner Gottlieb vowed in 2018 to modernize the drug development review process from test-tube to the new drug application (NDA) review process. New drug applications have been required since the 1938 FDCA. According to FDA, the documentation required in an NDA reports the "entire story" including what happened during clinical tests, results of animal studies, drug ingredients, how the drug acts in the body, and the manufacturing process including quality control, labeling and packaging. The clinical trial results are critical for FDA to evaluate effectiveness and assess proper product labeling. Today, broader policies permit broader use of some investigational new drugs (IND) prior to marketing. This occurs while still studying the drug and at the same time providing treatment for people who have no other viable alternative. The time-frame for approval varies; however, the average is ten years from the time an IND is filed until a company receives a New Drug Application (NDA) or Biological License Application (BLA) approval. To overcome the time involved, brand-name drug companies receive:

> ➤ Patent exclusivity under the Hatch-Waxman Act;
> ➤ Orphan drug exclusivity *and*
> ➤ Pediatric exclusivity.

A drug developer can apply for fast track designation if the compound will meet an unmet medical need. The fast track status involves meetings with FDA beforehand so that the developer knows ahead of time the requisites for the clinical trial designs. Fast track status affords the opportunity to file the NDA in segments rather than all at once. Priority review and accelerated approval programs are also available. Accelerated approval means FDA granting conditional approval of a drug based on its ability to show that the drug reduces disease and will most likely lengthen survival. Priority review status is given for an NDA or BLA when there is currently no adequate therapy. This means FDA review is shortened to six months rather than 10 months.

Ultimately, the decision as to whether or not to approve a product involves issues of efficacy and safety. Is the drug effective, that is; do the results of the studies conducted demonstrate effectiveness? Another question that FDA needs to answer is whether the results demonstrate that the drug is safe under the conditions of use specified in the proposed labeling. The issues regarding manufacturing processes used to maintain the quality of the drug is another important consideration. Safety, effectiveness, and risks versus benefits remain constants for FDA in the drug approval process. All drugs present certain risks and the ultimate determination as to whether to approve a drug application hinges on safety, effectiveness and a risk benefit analysis. Drugs@FDA is a searchable Web site within CDER where information about approved and tentatively approved prescription, over-the-counter, as well as discontinued drugs along with links to drug approval letters, labels, and review packages are covered.

https://www.fda.gov/NewsEvents/Newsroom/PressAnnouncements/ucm609647.htm

Drug Development Glossary

http://www.fda.gov/Drugs/InformationOnDrugs/ucm079436.htm

Abbreviated New Drug Application (ANDA)—An Abbreviated New Drug Application (ANDA) contains data that, when submitted to CDER's Office of Generic Drugs, provides for the review and ultimate approval of a generic drug product. Generic drug applications are called "abbreviated" because they are generally not required to include preclinical (animal) and clinical (human) data to establish safety and effectiveness. Instead, a generic applicant must scientifically demonstrate that its product is bioequivalent (i.e., performs in the same manner as the innovator drug). Once approved, an applicant may manufacture and market the generic drug product to provide a safe, effective, low cost alternative.

Abbreviated New Drug Application (ANDA) Number—This six-digit number is assigned by FDA staff to each application for approval to market a generic drug in the United States.

Active Ingredient—An active ingredient is any component that provides pharmacological activity or other direct effect in the diagnosis, cure, mitigation, treatment, or prevention of disease, or to affect the structure or any function of the body of man or animals.

Approval History—Chronological list of all FDA actions involving one drug product with an FDA Application number (NDA). There are over 50 kinds of approval actions including changes in the labeling, a new route of administration, and a new patient population for a drug product.

Approval Letter—Official communication from FDA to a new drug application (NDA) sponsor that allows the commercial marketing of the product.

Biologic License Application (BLA)—Biological products are approved for marketing under the provisions of the Public Health Service (PHS) Act. The Act requires a firm who manufactures a biologic for sale in interstate commerce to hold a license for the product. A biologics license application is a submission that contains specific information on the manufacturing processes, chemistry, pharmacology, clinical pharmacology and the medical effects of the biologic product. If the information provided meets FDA requirements, the application is approved, and a license is issued allowing the firm to market the product.

Biological Product—Includes a wide range of products such as vaccines, blood and blood components, allergenics, somatic cells, gene therapy, tissues, and recombinant therapeutic proteins. Biologics can be composed of sugars, proteins, or nucleic acids or complex combinations of these substances, or may be living entities such as cells and tissues. Biologics are isolated from a variety of natural sources human, animal, or microorganism and may be produced by biotechnology methods and other cutting-edge technologies. Gene-based and cellular biologics, for example, often are at the forefront of biomedical research, and may be used to treat a variety of medical conditions for which no other treatments are available. In general, the term "drugs" includes therapeutic biological products.

Brand Name Drug—Marketed under a proprietary, trademark-protected name.

Chemical Type Represents the newness of a drug formulation or a new indication for an existing drug formulation. For example, Chemical Type 1 is assigned to an active ingredient that has never before been marketed in the United States in any form.

Company—The company (also called applicant or sponsor) submits an application to FDA for approval to market a drug product in the United States.

Discontinued Drug Product—Listed in Drugs@FDA as "discontinued" are approved products that have never been marketed, have been discontinued from marketing, are for military use, are for export only, or have had their approvals withdrawn for reasons other than safety or efficacy after being discontinued from marketing.

Dosage Form—Physical form in which a drug is produced and dispensed, such as a tablet, a capsule, or an injectable.

Drug A drug is defined as:
- ✓ A substance recognized by an official pharmacopoeia or formulary.
- ✓ A substance intended for use in the diagnosis, cure, mitigation, treatment, or prevention of disease.
- ✓ A substance (other than food) intended to affect the structure or any function of the body.
- ✓ A substance intended for use as a component of a medicine but not a device or a component, part or accessory of a device.

✓ Biological products are included within this definition and are generally covered by the same laws and regulations, but differences exist regarding their manufacturing processes (chemical process versus biological process).

Drug Product—The finished dosage form that contains a drug substance, generally, but not necessarily in association with other active or inactive ingredients.

FDA Action Date—The action date tells when an FDA regulatory action, such as an original or supplemental approval, took place.

FDA Application Number—This number, also known as the NDA (New Drug Application) number, is assigned by FDA staff to each application for approval to market a new drug in the United States. One drug can have more than one application number if it has different dosage forms or routes of administration

Generic Drug—Is the same as a brand name drug in dosage, safety, strength, how it is taken, quality, performance, and intended use. Before approving a generic drug product, FDA requires many rigorous tests and procedures to assure that the generic drug can be substituted for the brand name drug. The FDA bases evaluations of substitutability, or "therapeutic equivalence," of generic drugs on scientific evaluations. By law, a generic drug product must contain the identical amounts of the same active ingredient(s) as the brand name product. Drug products evaluated as "therapeutically equivalent" can be expected to have equal effect and no difference when substituted for the brand name product.

Label—The FDA approved label is the official description of a drug product which includes indication (what the drug is used for); who should take it; adverse events (side effects); instructions for uses in pregnancy, children, and other populations; and safety information for the patient. Labels are often found inside drug product packaging.

Marketing Status—Indicates how a drug product is sold in the United States. Drug products in Drugs@FDA are identified as: Prescription; Over-the-counter; Discontinued; and None—drug products that have been tentatively approved.

Medication Guide—Contains information for patients on how to safely use a drug product.

New Drug Application (NDA)–When the sponsor of a new drug believes that enough evidence on the drug's safety and effectiveness has been obtained to meet FDA's requirements for marketing approval, the sponsor submits to FDA a new drug application (NDA). The application must contain data from specific technical viewpoints for review, including chemistry, pharmacology, medical, biopharmaceutics, and statistics. If the NDA is approved, the product may be marketed in the United States. For internal tracking purposes, all NDA's are assigned an NDA number.

New Drug Application (NDA) Number—This six-digit number is assigned by FDA staff to each application for approval to market a new drug in the United States. A drug can have more than one application number if it has different dosage forms or routes of administration. In Drugs@FDA, you can find the NDA number under the column named "FDA Application."

New Molecular Entity (NME)—Is an active ingredient that has never before been marketed in the United States in any form.

Over-the-Counter Drugs (OTC)—FDA defines OTC drugs as safe and effective for use by the general public without a doctor's prescription.

Patient Package Insert (PPI)—Contains information for patients' understanding of how to safely use a drug product.

Pharmaceutical Equivalents—FDA considers drug products to be pharmaceutical equivalents if they meet these three criteria:

✓ Same active ingredient(s);

Same dosage form and route of administration; and

✓ Identical in strength or concentration.

Pharmaceutically equivalent drug products may differ in characteristics such as: Shape,

✓ Release mechanism,

   ✓ Labeling (to some extent),
   ✓ Scoring, and
   ✓ Excipients (including colors, flavors, preservatives).

Prescription Drug Product—Requires a doctor's authorization to purchase.

Product Number—Is assigned to each drug product associated with an NDA (New Drug Application). If a drug product is available in multiple strengths, there are multiple product numbers.

Review—A review is the basis of FDA's decision to approve an application. It is a comprehensive analysis of clinical trial data and other information prepared by FDA drug application reviewers. A review is divided into sections on medical analysis, chemistry, clinical pharmacology, biopharmaceutics, pharmacology, statistics, and microbiology.

Review Classification—The NDA and BLA classification system provides a way of describing drug applications upon initial receipt and throughout the review process and prioritizing their review.

RLD (Reference Listed Drug)—Is an approved drug product to which new generic versions are compared to show that they are bioequivalent. A drug company seeking approval to market a generic equivalent must refer to the Reference Listed Drug in its Abbreviated New Drug Application (ANDA). By designating a single reference listed drug as the standard to which all generic versions must be shown to be bioequivalent, FDA hopes to avoid possible significant variations among generic drugs and their brand name counterpart.

Route—A route of administration is a way of administering a drug to a site in a patient. A comprehensive list of specific routes of administration appears in the CDER Data Standards Manual.

Strength—Reveals how much of the active ingredient is present in each dosage.

Supplement—An application to allow a company to make changes in a product that already has an approved new drug application (NDA). CDER must approve all important NDA changes (in packaging or ingredients, for instance) to ensure the original conditions are still met.

Supplement Number—Is associated with an existing FDA New Drug Application (NDA) number. Companies are allowed to make changes to drugs or their labels after they have been approved. To change a label, market a new dosage or strength of a drug, or change the way it manufactures a drug, a company must submit a supplemental new drug application (sNDA). Each sNDA is assigned a number which is usually, but not always, sequential, starting with 001.

Supplement Type—Companies are allowed to make changes to drugs or their labels after they have been approved. To change a label, market a new dosage or strength of a drug, or change the way it manufactures a drug, a company must submit a supplemental new drug application (sNDA). The supplement type refers to the kind of change that was approved by FDA. This includes changes in manufacturing, patient population, and formulation.

Tentative Approval—If a generic drug product is ready for approval before the expiration of any patents or exclusivities accorded to the reference listed drug product, FDA issues a tentative approval letter to the applicant. The tentative approval letter details the circumstances associated with the tentative approval. FDA delays final approval of the generic drug product until all patent or exclusivity issues have been resolved. A tentative approval does not allow the applicant to market the generic drug product.

Therapeutic Biological Product—Is a protein derived from living material (such as cells or tissues) used to treat or cure disease.

Therapeutic Equivalence (TE)—Drug products classified as therapeutically equivalent can be substituted with the full expectation that the substituted product will produce the same clinical effect and safety profile as the prescribed product. Drug products are considered to be therapeutically equivalent **only** if they meet these criteria:

   ✓ They are pharmaceutical equivalents (contain the same active ingredient(s); dosage form and route of administration; and strength).
   ✓ They are assigned the same therapeutic equivalence codes starting with the letter "A ".

✓ To receive a letter "A", FDA designates a brand name drug or a generic drug to be the Reference Listed Drug (RLD) and assigns therapeutic equivalence codes based on data that a drug sponsor submits in an ANDA to scientifically demonstrate that its product is bioequivalent (i.e., performs in the same manner as the Reference Listed Drug).

Therapeutic Equivalence (TE) Codes—The coding system allows users to determine whether FDA has evaluated a particular approved product as therapeutically equivalent to other pharmaceutically equivalent products (first letter) and to provide additional information on the basis of FDA's evaluations (second letter). Sample TE codes: AA, AB, and BC.

✓ FDA assigns therapeutic equivalence codes to pharmaceutically equivalent drug products. A drug product is deemed to be therapeutically equivalent ("A" rated) only if:

✓ Drug company's approved application contains adequate scientific evidence establishing through in vivo and/or in vitro studies the bioequivalence of the product to a selected reference listed drug. Those active ingredients or dosage forms for which no in vivo bioequivalence issue is known or suspected.

✓ Some drug products have more than one TE Code.

✓ Those products which the FDA does not deem to be therapeutically equivalent are "B" rated.

✓ Over-the-counter drugs are not assigned TE codes.

User Fees

http://www.fda.gov/ForIndustry/UserFees/PrescriptionDrugUserFee/default.htm

The time involved in obtaining FDA approval for new prescription drugs has considerably shortened due to the Prescription Drug User-Fee Act (PDUFA). In 1992, PDUFA I provided authority for FDA to collect fees from industry that afford FDA to accelerate its drug evaluation process. This Act requires drug companies to pay fees when submitting new drug applications (NDAs) to the agency. PDUFA covers three categories of user fees as follows:

✓ Fees for drug and biologic applications and supplements;

✓ Annual establishment fees; and

✓ Annual product fees.

In 1997, after the success of PDUFA I, Congress reauthorized PDUFA II for an additional five years. The main goal of the Center for Drug Evaluation and Research (CDRH) is to ensure that reviews are maintained on a high-quality basis yet accomplished within a shorter time frame. PDUFA II has helped achieve this goal because review times have been reduced significantly. Of significance to PDUFA is that the goal of shortened decision times has been attained as well as a decrease in approval times. According to FDA, total approval time, the time from the initial application submission to the approval letter issuance, has decreased from a pre-PDUFA of a median of 23 months to 12 months. Total approval time for priority applications for products that offer important therapeutic gains has dropped to 6 months. PDUFA III, reauthorized in 2002, amended sections 736(b) of the FDCA, 21 U.S.C. Section 379(h) concerning the authority to assess and use drug fees, and fulfills the goal for CDER to maintain its high-quality reviews yet do so within a shorter time frame. PDUFAs III objectives included identification of risk management strategies. Section 735 and 736 of the FDCA or 21 U.S.C. sections 379(g) and 379(h) established the different types of fees for certain types of applications and supplements for approval of drug and biological products, certain establishments where such products are made and certain products. PDUFA IV was reauthorized in 2007 under the Food and Drug Administration Amendments Act (FDAAA) for fiscal years 2008-2012. The Congressional hearings for PDUFA V reauthorization resounded with safety and efficacy objectives. Former President Obama signed into law the Food and Drug Administration Safety and Innovation Act (FDASIA) of 2012 on July 9, 2012, which reauthorized PDUFA V (Pub. L. No. 112-144) for fiscal years 2013-2017. The *Food and Drug Administration Reauthorization Act* (FDARA) (Pub. L. 115-52) reauthorized the Prescription Drug User Fee Act PDUFA VI: Fiscal Years 2018 – 2022. This law provides FDA with the necessary resources to maintain a predictable and efficient review process for human drug and biologic products.

https://www.fda.gov/forindustry/userfees/prescriptiondruguserfee/ucm446608.htm

The following charts detail Pre-Clinical Research to New Drug Application (NDA) review.

New Drug Development Process

Test Tube to New Drug

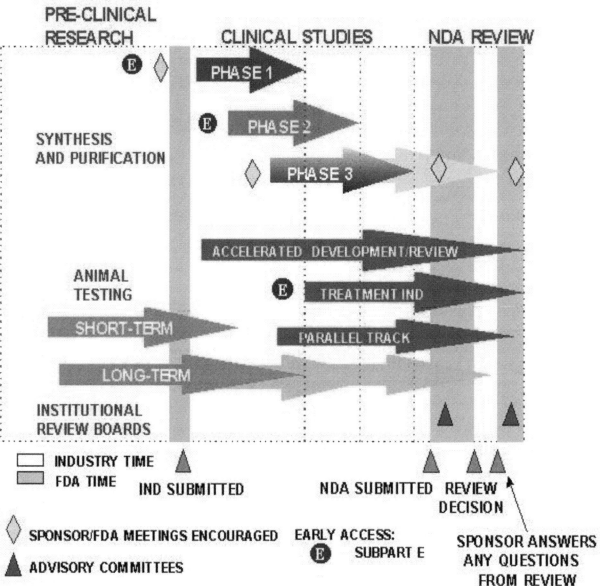

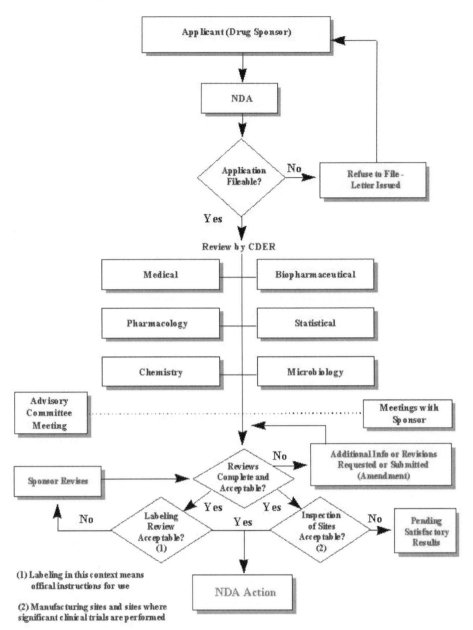

CRITICAL ANALYSIS: FDA Commissioner Gottlieb declared a drug modernization plan in 2018. Review the plan and evaluate the feasibility.
https://www.fda.gov/NewsEvents/Newsroom/PressAnnouncements/ucm609647.htm

Clinical Trials

ClinicalTrials.gov contains information about publicly and privately funded trials concerning safety and efficacy studies for Phase II, Phase III and postmarket Phase IV. FDA will not disclose certain information such as trade secrets and confidential commercial information and certain inter-or-intra government agency memoranda. See: final rule concerning informed consent. See Fed. Reg. 256 (Jan.4, 2011). *ClinicalTrials.gov* lists over 288,395 studies with locations in all 50 States and in 205 countries (2018).

FDA regulations require disclosure as follows:

✓ New Drug Applications—once approved summaries are publicly disclosed;

✓ Postmarketing of adverse drug events—15-day alert reports, annual and periodic reports;

✓ New use treatment information;

✓ Pediatric clinical trials—summaries made public; and
✓ Serious or Life-threatening conditions clinical trials.

Access to unapproved drugs includes participation in a clinical trial. A sponsor of an investigational New Drug or IND will probably want to ship the investigational drug to clinical investigators in many states; therefore, it must seek an exemption from the legal requirement of an approved marketing application. The IND provides a method for a sponsor to ship an investigational drug to clinical investigators without an approved NDA. The IND application includes informed consent from the research subjects and review of the study by an institutional review board (IRB). Once a sponsor submits an IND application, there is a 30-day waiting period before commencing any clinical trials for safety reasons.

The following regulations apply to the IND application process:

21CFR Part 312	Investigational New Drug Application
21CFR Part 314	INDA and NDA Applications for FDA Approval to Market a New Drug
21CFR Part 316	Orphan Drugs
21CFR Part 58	Good Lab Practice for Nonclinical Laboratory [Animal] Studies
21CFR Part 50	Protection of Human Subjects
21CFR Part 56	Institutional Review Boards
21CFR Part 201	Drug Labeling
21CFR Part 54	Financial Disclosure by Clinical Investigators

The following final rules apply to the IND process for patient safety and access:

Final Rule: Investigational New Drug Safety Reporting Requirements for Human Drug and Biological Products and Safety Reporting Requirements for Bioavailability and Bioequivalence Studies in Humans (issued 9/28/2010).

Final Rules for Expanded Access to Investigational Drugs for Treatment Use and Charging for Investigational Drugs (8/12/2009).

http://www.fda.gov/Drugs/DevelopmentApprovalProcess/HowDrugsareDevelopedandApproved/ApprovalApplications/InvestigationalNewDrugINDApplication/default.htm

Investigational New Drugs (IND)

Types of IND's include the following:

➢ Investigator IND,
➢ Emergency Use IND, *and a*
➢ Treatment IND.

Investigator IND—submissions are by a physician who commences and performs an investigation. The investigation is under direct control of the physician. For example, a physician could propose a research IND to suggest studying an unapproved drug. A physician could also propose a research IND for a new indication or for a new patient population.

Emergency Use INDs—permits use of an experimental drug in an emergency situation. This means that there is insufficient time for submission of an IND in keeping with 21CFR sections 312.23 or 312.34. An emergency IND can be used for those patients who do not satisfy the conditions of an existing study protocol or possibly if there is no approved study protocol.

Treatment INDs—for experimental drugs showing potential in clinical testing for serious or life-threatening conditions and conducted during the final clinical work and during FDA review.

IND Application Information

➢ Animal pharmacology and toxicology studies;
➢ Manufacturing information—relating to composition, manufacturer, stability, and manufacturing controls; **and**
➢ Clinical protocols and investigator information consisting of comprehensive protocols for proposed clinical studies to evaluate any exposure to unnecessary risks.

http://www.fda.gov/drugs/developmentapprovalprocess/howdrugsaredevelopedandapproved/approvalapplications/investigationalnewdrugindapplication/default.htm

Fast Track, Priority Review, Accelerated Approval, and Breakthrough Therapy

Once an IND is filed, several years transpire prior to full approval. Programs that facilitate and expedite development and review of new drugs that address unmet medical needs in the treatment of serious or life-threatening conditions are as follows:

> ➢ **Fast track:** unmet medical need must be established;
> ➢ **Priority review:** 6-month review time period where no sufficient therapy exists;
> ➢ **Accelerated approval:** initial clinical trials disclose disease reduction and survival lengthened;
> ➢ **Breakthrough therapy designation:** part of FDA Safety and Innovation Act (2012).

FDA issued a final guidance on expedited development and review programs for drugs and biologics in 2014. The guidance provides direction for industry to establish if their products qualify for faster review as designated above. *http://www.fda.gov/downloads/Drugs/GuidanceComplian-ceRegulatoryInformation/Guidances/UCM358301.pdf* (May 21014).

Right-to-Try Legislation and FDA "Compassionate Use"

Congress enacted the *Trickett Wendler, Frank Mongiello, Jordan McLinn and Matthew Bellina Right-to-Try Act* (Federal Right-to-Try Act) in 2018 (P. L. 115-176) (May 30, 2018). Further, prior to the Federal Right-to-Try Act, approximately 41 states enacted legislation that addresses investigational drug access by the terminally ill. Despite such legislation, a patient who is ineligible to obtain an experimental therapy through a clinical trial can apply to FDA for "compassionate use". That is, even if the eligibility criteria in a study protocol is not appropriate for a specific patient treatment, it may be possible as a special exception. Expanded access, also referred to as "*compassionate use*," is the use outside of a clinical trial of an investigational medical product. The FDA approval rate for compassionate use therapy is 99 percent. Treating a patient as a special exception entails modifying the informed consent form, sending the request to FDA, and acquiring permission from the Institutional Review Board (IRB). The FDA published a final version on June 2, 2016, entitled *"Individual Patient Expanded Access Applications - Form FDA 3926"*, along with patient and physician information sheets and related guidances for expanded access for experimental drugs. The revised procedure, which also specifically applies to biologics, streamlines the application process for physicians. The Federal-Right-to-Try does not remove this FDA pathway for an individual to request an investigational therapy. The Federal-Right-to-Try Act details that it gives the individual the right to request.

NOTE: In *Abigal Alliance for Better Access to Developmental Drugs and Washington Legal Foundation v. von Eshenbach*, 469 F.3d 129 (D.C. Cir. Nov. 21, 2006; Rehearing *en banc* 495 F.3d 695 (D.C. Cir. August 7, 2007), U.S. No.07-444, *cert. denied* Jan. 14, 2008 the Court of Appeals held that terminally ill patients do not have a constitutional right to attain investigational drugs prior to FDA approval. Yet, see above Federal Right-to-Try Act (2018).

See: Alison Bateman-House and Arthur Caplan, *Drug-right Bills Give Patients False Hope*, Philadelphia Inquirer, B1 (Nov. 16, 2014). (Authors conclude that state "right to try" laws could actually harm a terminally ill patient). See also: Janet Lis and Roseann B. Termini, *Right-to-Try or Right-to-Ask*, 38 PA Lawyer 45, (2016) (authors conclude "right-to-ask" provides autonomy); See also: Roseann B. Termini, *The Latest "Federal Movement" in the Food and Drug Law Arena: The Federal Right-to-Try or Rather Right-to-Know and Thus Request Investigational Therapies for Individuals with a Life-Threatening Disease or Condition*, Indiana Health Law Review, Vol. XVI, Issue I (2018).

CRITICAL ANALYSIS: Why did Congress enact a federal law when under the FDCA there is compassionate use? Include a discussion about informed consent, patient safety, and costs.

Investigational New Drug Application (IND) Process
The chart on the next page illustrates the steps involved in the investigational new drug application process.

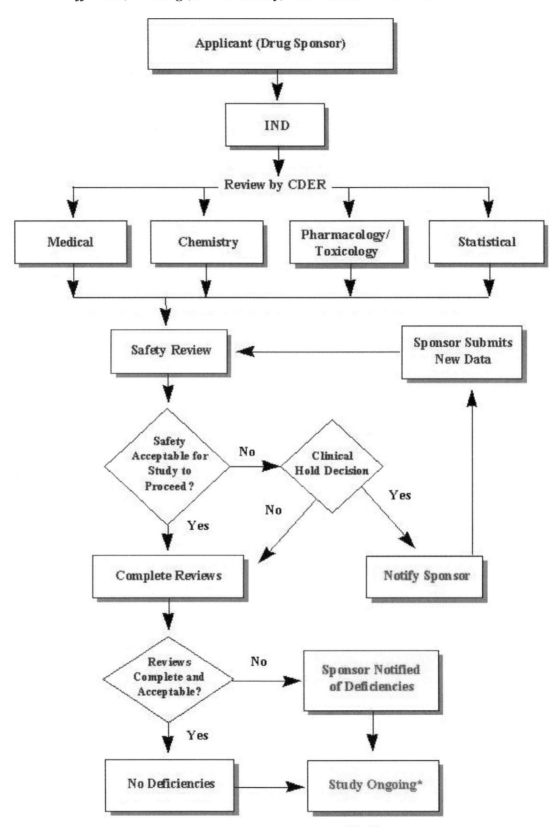

*While sponsor answers any deficiencies

Botanical Drugs

http://www.fda.gov/AboutFDA/CentersOffices/OfficeofMedicalProductsandTo-
bacco/CDER/ucm090983.htm

A botanical drug's unique features require special consideration during the FDA review process. The Center for Drug Evaluation and Research (CDER) issued a Guidance titled "Botanical Drug Products" to facilitate expansion of new therapies from botanical sources. The Botanical Guidance applies to only botanical products intended to be developed and used as drugs. There must be published data establishing a general recognition of safety and effectiveness, as well as results of adequate and well-controlled clinical studies for a botanical drug substance to be included in an OTC monograph. The guidance applies only to finished, labeled products that contain vegetable matter as ingredients. The guidance explains when a botanical drug may be marketed under an over-the-counter (OTC) monograph and when FDA approval of a new drug application (NDA) under 21 U.S.C. section 355(b) is required. The guidance gives information to sponsors on submitting investigational new drug applications (INDs) for botanical drug products. According to the guidance, "botanical products are finished labeled products that contain vegetable matter as ingredients". As with other FDA regulated products, intended use determines whether the botanical product is a food; dietary supplement; a drug including a biological drug; a medical device, or cosmetic. Labeling claims, advertising, oral, and written statements are factors used in deciding product classification under the FDCA.

The first botanical prescription drug, Veregen (sinecatechins), a treatment for external genital and perianal warts was approved in 2006. In 2012, FDA approved Fulyzaq (crofelemer) to relieve symptoms of diarrhea in HIV/AIDS patients taking antiretroviral therapy, a combination of medicines used to treat HIV infection. Fulyzaq, originates from the red sap of the Croton lechleri plant.

Homeopathic Product Regulation

https://nccih.nih.gov/health/homeopathy
https://www.federalregister.gov/documents/2017/12/20/2017-27157/drug-products-labeled-as-homeo-
pathic-draft-guidance-for-food-and-drug-administration-staff-and (Federal Register Vol. 82, No. 243, December 20, 2017, Notices 60403)
https://www.fda.gov/downloads/Drugs/GuidanceComplianceRegulatoryInformation/Guid-
ances/UCM589373.pdf

The definition of "drug" in section 201(g)(1) of the Federal Food, Drug, and Cosmetic Act (the FDCA) (21 U.S.C. 321(g)(1)) includes articles recognized in the Homeopathic Pharmacopoeia of the United States (HPUS) or any supplement to it. Therefore, homeopathic drugs are subject to the same regulatory requirements as other drugs. Interestingly, Senator Royal Copeland was a physician trained in homeopathy and a major sponsor of the 1938 FDCA.

Although FDA regulates homeopathic remedies, enforcement has lagged especially in comparison with the popularity and increased use. Finally, in late 2017, FDA issued a draft guidance entitled "***Drug Products Labeled as Homeopathic.***" The draft guidance explains how FDA expects to prioritize enforcement and regulatory action with respect to drug and biological products, labeled as homeopathic and marketed in the United States without the required FDA approval. Compliance Policy Guide (CPG) 400.400, "*Conditions Under Which Homeopathic Drugs May be Marketed*", issued back on May 31, 1988 will be withdrawn when the guidance if finalized.

The guidance defines homeopathy as follows:

"*Homeopathy is an alternative medical practice that has an historical basis in theory and practice first systematized in the late 1700s. Homeopathy is generally based on two main principles: (1) A substance that causes symptoms in a healthy person can be used in diluted form to treat symptoms and illnesses (known as "like-cures-like") and (2) the more diluted the substance, the more potent it is (known as the "law of infinitesimals").*"

FDA applies apply a risk-based enforcement approach to the manufacturing, distribution, and marketing of drug products labeled as homeopathic. Categories include:

Products with reported safety concerns;

Products that contain or purport to contain ingredients associated with potentially significant safety concerns;

Products for routes of administration other than oral and topical—For example, unapproved injectable drug products and unapproved ophthalmic drug products pose a greater risk of harm to users due to their routes of administration;

Products intended to be used for the prevention or treatment of serious and/or life- threatening diseases and conditions;

Products for vulnerable populations; and

Products deemed adulterated under the Food, Drug and Cosmetic Act.

See: Federal Register Vol. 82, No. 243 (December 20, 2017) Notices 60403.

NOTE: A 2012 National Health Interview Survey (NHIS), estimated 5 million adults and 1 million children used homeopathy in 2011. However, only 0.2 percent of children went to a homeopathic practitioner. Out-of-pocket costs for adults were $2.9 billion for homeopathic medicines and $170 million for visits to homeopathic practitioners.

Warning Homeopathic Teething Products Containing Belladonna

https://www.fda.gov/Drugs/DrugSafety/InformationbyDrugClass/ucm523936.htm

https://www.fda.gov/Drugs/DrugSafety/InformationbyDrugClass/ucm538669.htm

FDA issued a warning about homeopathic teething products that contain belladonna due to the risk to infants and children. FDA tested homeopathic teething tablets labeled as containing belladonna and other ingredients marketed by Hyland's, Inc. FDA found a lack of consistency in the belladonna alkaloids (atropine and scopolamine) content and coffea cruda (caffeine). FDA analysis established the levels of atropine and scopolamine in some of the CVS tablets and the levels of scopolamine in some of the Hyland's tablets far exceeded the amount stated on the products' labels. Hyland whose parent company is Standard Homeopathic, ceased product production and CVS voluntarily removed the product from its store shelves. Raritan Pharmaceuticals (November 2016) had recalled three teething products that contained belladonna.

See: *https://www.fda.gov/Drugs/DrugSafety/InformationbyDrugClass/ucm538669.htm*

CRITICAL ANALYSIS: The definition of "drug" in section 201(g)(1) of the Federal Food, Drug, and Cosmetic Act (21 U.S.C. 321(g)(1)) includes articles recognized in the Homeopathic Pharmacopoeia of the United States (HPUS) or any supplement to it. Is regulation of homeopathic products sufficient or too lax?

Innovation—Digital, 3-D Produced and Cannabis-Based Drugs

Digital—In 2017, FDA approved a digital pill which monitors whether and when a patient takes the medication. For example, the Otkusa Pharmaceutical company received approval for a sensor where the drug sends signal to a smartphone app.

3-D—FDA approved the drug Spritam manufactured by Aprecia Pharmaceuticals using a 3-D printer. It is intended to treat seizures in people who suffer from epilepsy. The benefits of using the 3-D printing technology permits the drug to dissolve more quickly which means it is easier to swallow. Further, the 3-D technology affords delivery of up to 1,000 mg in a single dose.

Cannabis-Based Drugs—FDA approved in 2018the first botanically extracted cannabis product, Epidiolex (cannabidiol) for rare forms of epilepsy. According to GW Pharmaceuticals, drug cost is approximately $32,000.00 annually per patient. See: Wall St. J. B3 Aug. 9, 2018.

CRITICAL ANALYSIS I: Could the digital sensor technology be applied to other products and perhaps alert physicians about patient abuse of opioids?

CRITICAL ANALYSIS II: Several states and the federal government are in conflict regarding the legalization of medical marijuana. How should this be resolved?

Chapter 3: Generic Drugs—Approvals, Copyright Infringement, Pay-for-Delay, Authorized Generics and Biosimilars

Generic Drugs and Abbreviated New Drug Applications

The generic drug industry has spurred competition with the net result of lower drug prices especially when a second generic competitor enters the marketplace. In fiscal year 2018 there were 971 approvals. (See: FDA Activities Report; See also, Wall St. J. B12 Aug. 10, 2017). This could be attributed to the 2017 Food and Drug Administration Reauthorization Act (FDARA), which reauthorized the Generic Drug User Fee Amendments (GDUFA) through 2022.

Once the patent for a brand-name drug expires, the Office of Generic Drugs perhaps will approve a generic copy if bioequivalence is demonstrated. "Bioequivalent" means that its active ingredient acts in the same mode and in the same amount of time as the brand-name drug. A generic drug must be bioequivalent and have identical dosage form; safety; strength; route of administration; quality; performance characteristics and intended use as the innovator drug. A generic drug must contain the same active ingredients and indications as the innovator or brand drug.

FDA Requirements for Generic Drugs

➢ Generic drugs must have the same active ingredients and the same labeled strength as the brand-name product.

➢ Generic drugs must have the same dosage form (for example, tablets, liquids) and must be administered in the same way.

➢ Generic drug manufacturers must show that a generic drug is bioequivalent to the brand-name drug, which means the generic version delivers the same amount of active ingredients into a patient's bloodstream in the same amount of time as the brand-name drug.

➢ Generic drug labeling must be essentially the same as the labeling of the brand-name drug.

➢ Generic drug manufacturers must fully document the generic drug's chemistry, manufacturing steps, and quality control measures.

➢ Firms must assure FDA that the raw materials and finished product meet specifications of the U.S. Pharmacopoeia, the organization that sets standards for drug purity in the United States.

➢ Firms must show that a generic drug will remain potent and unchanged until the expiration date on the label before it can be sold.

➢ Firms must comply with federal regulations for good manufacturing practices and provide the FDA a full description of facilities they use to manufacture, process, test, package, and label the drug. The FDA inspects manufacturing facilities to ensure compliance.

An ANDA applicant must submit data from all bioequivalence (BE) studies the applicant conducts on a drug product formulation submitted for approval. This means submission of both passing and non-passing bioequivalence data. 74 Fed. Reg. 2849 (Jan. 16, 2009)

The Drug Price Competition and Patent Term Restoration Act of 1984 (Hatch Waxman Act or Waxman Hatch), created an abbreviated approval process for generic prescription drugs under section 505(j) of the FDCA, 21 U.S.C section 355(j) and extended patent terms for innovator drugs. The intent of Hatch Waxman is to balance two competing objectives by encouraging competition in generic drugs with a result of less costly generic drugs while keeping incentives to invest in developing innovator drugs through patent extension to compensate for the time it takes the innovator products to go through the approval process. The Medicare Modernization Act amended aspects of the Hatch Waxman Act with the intent of expedient access to generic drugs.

An abbreviated new drug application or ANDA contains data for review by CDER's Office of Generic Products. The term "abbreviated" applies because the application does not have to include preclinical and clinical data to establish safety and efficacy. The ANDA process does not entail that the sponsor repeat animal and clinical research on ingredients or dosage forms already permitted.

This is applicable to drugs first marketed after 1962. However, the crucial element is that of bioequivalence. That is, a generic drug applicant must scientifically prove that the generic drug product performs in the same manner as the innovator drug. A method for determining bioequivalence is to measure the time it takes the generic drug to reach the bloodstream in healthy volunteers. This method gives absorption rate, known as bioavailability, allows for comparison to the innovator drug. In terms of bioavailability, the vital element is that the generic drug must deliver the same amount of active ingredients in the bloodstream of a person in the exact amount of time like the innovator drug. Guidance documents, although not legally binding, serve as an ANDA resource for ANDA submissions. ANDAs may be submitted in electronic format as permitted under 21 CFR Part 11. Regulations applicable to the ANDA process include 21 CFR Part 314; Applications for FDA Approval to Market a New Drug or Antibiotic Drug; 21 CFR Part 320 Bioavailability and Bioequivalence Requirements. The review of ANDAs focus on "First Cycle" drugs to meet priority health needs rather than "first-in, first reviewed". The FDA considers safety of paramount importance for both brand name and generic drugs. The settlement below is a prime example.

Generic Drug Safety Settlement—Ranbaxy

Ranbaxy USA, Inc., a subsidiary of Indian generic pharmaceutical manufacturer Ranbaxy Laboratories Limited, pled guilty in 2013 to felony charges relating to the manufacture and distribution of certain adulterated drugs made at two of Ranbaxy's manufacturing facilities in India. Ranbaxy also agreed to pay a criminal fine and forfeiture totaling $150 million and to settle civil claims under the False Claims Act and related State laws for $350 million. A federal district court denied Ranbaxy Laboratories Ltd.'s motion for a temporary restraining order seeking to prevent the Food and Drug Administration's decision to withdraw its tentative approvals of Ranbaxy Laboratories, Inc.'s generic versions of the anti-viral drug Valcyte (valganciclovir) and the heartburn tablet Nexium (esomeprazole magnesium) from taking effect (*Ranbaxy Laboratories, Ltd. v. Burwell,* D.D.C., No. 14-cv-01923-BAH, motion for temporary restraining order denied, 11/19/14). The Ranbaxy settlement was one of the largest drug safety settlements to date.

CRITICAL ANALYSIS: Recommend action Ranbaxy should take to avoid any future FDA temporary drug approval withdrawals.

"Generic Changes Being Effected" Proposed Rule
Supplemental Applications Proposing Labeling Changes for Approved Drugs and Biological Products

The proposed rule would enable generic drug application holders to promptly update product labeling to reflect certain types of newly acquired information related to drug safety, irrespective of whether the revised labeling differs from that of the corresponding brand drug. A generic drug application holder would be required to send notice of the labeling change proposed in the CBE-0 supplement, including a copy of the information supporting the change, to the application holder ("new drug application (NDA)" holder) for the corresponding brand drug at the same time that the supplement to the generic drug application is submitted to FDA, unless approval of the brand drug application has been withdrawn. This would ensure that the brand drug application holder for the corresponding brand drug is promptly advised of the newly acquired information that was considered to warrant the labeling change proposed for the drug in the CBE-0 supplement.

CRITICAL ANALYSIS: The "Generic Changes Being Effected Rule" proposed in 2013 has met with resistance. The final rule was scheduled for publication towards the end of 2015; yet this did not occur and despite an amended projected publication date of July 2016 this did not occur. See: 78 FR 67985. Discuss reasons why this proposed rule has not been finalized.

Abbreviated New Drug Application (ANDA) Process
See the chart on the following page.

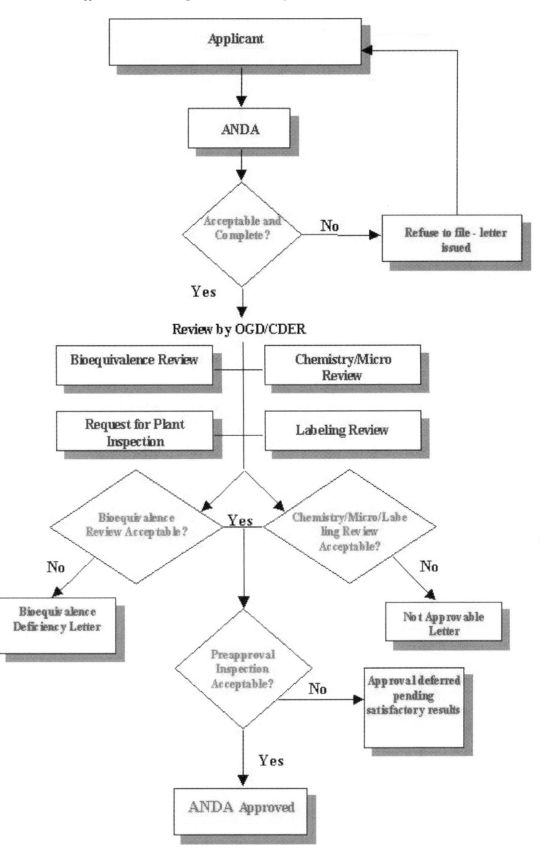

Copyright infringement and FDA Compliance—*Smithkline*

What ensues when compliance with FDA product labeling requirements by a generic company could infringe on the brand product? *Smithkline Beecham* resolves the copyright infringement action in favor of FDA compliance.

Smithkline Beecham v. Watson Pharmaceuticals,
211 F. 3d 21 (2nd Cir. 2000) Cert. Denied, 121 S.Ct. 173 (2000)

WINTER, Chief Judge: This appeal arises out of a copyright action alleging infringement of appellant's copyright in a user's guide and audiotape developed for its Nicorette-brand gum. Appellees [Watson Pharmaceuticals], in obtaining approval to sell a competing generic nicotine gum product, were directed by the Food and Drug Administration ("FDA") to use labeling almost identical to appellant's copyrighted guide and tape. *** Appellees cannot be liable for copyright infringement because the Hatch-Waxman Amendments require generic drug producers to use the same labeling as was approved by the FDA for, and is used by, the producer of the pioneer drug. We therefore affirm.

Appellant SmithKline Beecham Consumer Healthcare, L.P. ("SmithKline") manufactures and sells Nicorette nicotine polacrilex gum ("Nicorette"), an over-the-counter ("OTC") product designed to help smokers overcome the cigarette habit. On January 13, 1984, SmithKline obtained FDA approval to sell 2 mg strength Nicorette for prescription-only use. Later, on June 8, 1992, the FDA approved prescription-only use of 4 mg Nicorette. Finally, on February 9, 1996, the FDA approved both 2 mg and 4 mg Nicorette for OTC sale. Pursuant to 21 U.S.C. § 355(c)(3)(D)(iv), SmithKline obtained a three-year period of exclusivity—essentially an extension of the effective term of SmithKline's Nicorette patent based on additional clinical testing—for OTC sale of Nicorette. SmithKline's user's guide and audiotape were developed in the course of its research into producing a method of, and product for, quitting smoking. To obtain approval for the OTC sale of Nicorette, SmithKline submitted various versions of the guide and tape to the FDA for review. *** Between July 1993 and February 1996, SmithKline made approximately 70 changes to the guide and the tape at the FDA's request. Most of the changes related to factual matters, safety, and efficiency. The tape and guide were ultimately included as part of Nicorette's FDA-approved OTC labeling. On April 21, 1998, SmithKline registered a federal copyright for the guide and audiotape script. On February 9, 1999, the day when its exclusivity period for Nicorette expired, SmithKline registered a copyright for the words and music on the tape.

Shortly thereafter, appellees Watson Pharmaceuticals, Inc., Watson Laboratories, Inc., and Circa Pharmaceuticals, Inc. (collectively "Watson") obtained FDA approval for the OTC marketing of a generic version of nicotine gum intended to compete directly with Nicorette. To obtain that approval from the FDA, Watson had to comply with the requirement imposed by the Hatch-Waxman Amendments that "the labeling proposed for [its] new drug [be] the same as the labeling approved for Nicorette." 21 U.S.C. § 355(j)(2)(A)(v); see also 21 C.F.R. § 314.127(a)(7) ("FDA will refuse to approve an abbreviated application for a new drug under section 505(j) of the act [if] .... [i]nformation submitted in the abbreviated new drug application is insufficient to show that the labeling proposed for the drug is the same as the labeling approved for the listed drug...."). Thus, Watson's generic nicotine gum was "accompanied by a user guide and audio tape that [we]re virtually identical to SmithKline's." SmithKline I, 63 F.Supp.2d at 469.

Before Watson could sell its product to the public, SmithKline initiated the present copyright action, alleging willful infringement of its guide and tape. *** The district court relied on a March 1999 FDA letter recounting that the agency had explained to Watson that "the 'same labeling' requirement d[oes] not require that the generic's behavioral support materials be identical to the innovator's materials" and indeed that "generic sponsors, like all other sponsors of nicotine-based smoking cessation aids, have discretion to design their own audio support materials." Id. at 470.

137

*** Subsequently, the FDA altered its position. In the face of the preliminary injunction, Watson revised its guide and tape to render them "comparable, but not identical, to SmithKline's." Id. However, on November 23, 1999, the FDA rejected the revised user guide. The FDA "advised Watson that it would approve a revised version of Watson's 'previously approved labeling,' i.e., the virtually identical user's guide previously approved by the FDA." Id. To assist Watson, the FDA "marked up a copy of the previously approved user guide" and bracketed certain portions of text which could be in appropriate cases deleted or "substituted with new text .... similar to the original in tone, content and length." Id. Nevertheless, the bracketed guide gave Watson "very little leeway to deviate from the previously approved user guide." Id. In essence, therefore, the FDA "determined that Watson had to copy verbatim substantially all of the text used in the SmithKline" user's guide. *** With specific regard to labeling, the Hatch-Waxman Amendments require that an ANDA "show that the labeling proposed for the [generic] drug is the same as the labeling proposed for the [pioneer] drug ... except for changes required because of [approved] differences [between the pioneer and generic drug] or because the [generic] drug and [pioneer] drug are produced or distributed by different manufacturers." 21 U.S.C. § 355(j)(2)(A)(v). The FFDCA defines "label" and "labeling" for these purposes as "a display of written, printed, or graphic matter upon the immediate container of any article" or "accompanying such article," 21 U.S.C. § 321(k) & (m), which the FDA has broadly interpreted to include "[b]rochures, booklets, sound recordings, and similar pieces of printed, audio, or visual matter descriptive of a drug." 21 C.F.R. § 202.1(l)(2). Applying the Hatch-Waxman Amendments to the present appeal, SmithKline's copyright claim fails. First, its copyrighted user's guide and audiotape constitute "labeling" for purposes of the Hatch-Waxman Amendments. SmithKline has not contended otherwise and understandably so. The guide and tape clearly fall within the statutory and regulatory definitions quoted immediately above. Moreover, they were submitted to the FDA as part of SmithKline's quest for administrative approval of OTC sales of Nicorette. The guide and tape were approved only after more than two years of administrative consideration and after that consideration had led to some 70 changes in the guide and tape at the FDA's request. As noted, the [Hatch-Waxman] Amendments require that the labeling for the generic drug be the "same" as the labeling for the pioneer drug. See 21 U.S.C. § 355(j)(2)(A)(v).

*** Third, if SmithKline's copyright claim has merit, then Watson cannot realistically use the ANDA process to sell its generic nicotine gum because it will either have to change the label and lose FDA approval or be enjoined from using a label that infringes SmithKline's copyright. We are thus faced with a conflict between two statutes. The Hatch-Waxman Amendments require generic drug producers to use labeling that will infringe upon copyrights in labels of pioneer drugs. *** The Amendments were intended to facilitate the introduction of generic competitors once a pioneer drug's patent term and exclusivity periods had ended by allowing the generic producer to piggyback upon the pioneer producer's successful FDA application. *** Even though such an owner cannot enforce its copyright against generic drug manufacturers who are required by the Hatch-Waxman Amendments to copy labeling and who do no more than that, it still retains a copyright, if otherwise valid, in the label and might well pursue copyright claims against potential infringers in other circumstances, e.g., use of the copyrighted material in non-labeling advertisements. Because recognition of SmithKline's claim here would severely undermine the Hatch-Waxman Amendments while its dismissal would not impair the copyright laws, we affirm and direct dismissal of SmithKline's complaint for failure to state a claim.

CRITICAL ANALYSIS: Assess competing issues regarding FDA compliance and copyright protection under Hatch-Waxman and brand company protections from infringement.

NOTE: See Roseann B. Termini and Amy Miele, *Copyright and Trademark Issues in the Pharmaceutical Industry—Generic Compliance or Brand Drug Imitation— "Copycat or Compliance"*, **Vol. LXXXIV PA Bar Assn. Qtrly., 34 (2013) (article discusses generic drug labeling, shape and color similarity to a brand name or innovator drug without infringement).**

Paragraph IV Certification and the 30 Month Stay

A generic applicant may seek FDA approval to market a generic drug prior to the patent expiration of a brand name product. This is referred to as a "Paragraph IV Certification", under 21 U.S.C. section 355 (2)(j)(A)(vii). The generic drug applicant must certify in its ANDA that the patent in question is invalid or is not infringed by the generic product and notify the patent holder of the ANDA submission. Under 21 CFR 314.94 (a)(12)(i)(A)(4), the applicant must provide the patent number and certify that the patent is invalid, unenforceable, or not be infringed by the manufacture, use, or sale of the drug product for when the abbreviated application is submitted. The first generic company to get the ANDA approved under a "Paragraph IV Certification" has market exclusivity for 180 days.

Over the years, the delay in access to generic drugs has been attributed to increased litigation pertaining to patent issues. The ANDA process allows approval of generic drugs and market timing depends on patent protections for the innovator drug. All ANDAs must contain a certification for each listed patent in what is known as the "FDA Orange Book". The FDCA enumerates four possible types of certifications, 21 U.S.C section 355(j)(2)(A) (vii); however, only a "Paragraph IV Certification" is eligible for exclusivity. The Medicare Prescription Drug Improvement and Modernization Act attempted to provide greater generic drug access.

Prescription Drug Improvement and Modernization Act

The Medicare Prescription Drug Improvement and Modernization Act of 2003 (MPDMA), P.L.108-173 108th (2003) included the same 30-month rule issued by FDA regulation August 18, 2003 and additional important aspects. Generic drug makers may file counterclaims in patent infringement lawsuits. The MPDMA does not contain a "court trigger" for the 180-day period. Instead, the MPDMA contains forfeiture provisions. That is, the MPDMA clarified the conditions under which the 180-day marketing exclusivity can be granted. Generic drug makers could forfeit the 180-day exclusivity if they fail to market the drug within 75 days of FDA approval or within 75 days after a "non-appealed" federal District Court decision. Specifically the MPDMA:

➢ Limits the NDA holder to one 30-month stay* (*See NOTE next page) per product;
➢ Permits the stay only to those patents listed in the Orange Book as of the date the ANDA and Patent IV Certification were filed;
➢ Provides that if a federal district court decides that the patent at issue is invalid or otherwise not infringed, the ANDA approval is effective on the date the district court decision is entered;
➢ ANDA Applicants must provide notice to the NDA holder of the ANDA and Paragraph IV Certification within 20 days of the postmark date on the FDA notice advising the ANDA applicant of the ANDA filing date with FDA;
➢ ANDA Applicants must provide notice of a Paragraph IV Certification to the NDA holder upon a submission of an amendment or supplement to the original ANDA;
➢ Grants one 180-day exclusivity period;
➢ Provides for forfeiture of the 180-day exclusivity period for failure to market within 75 days;
➢ Permits a declaratory judgment action by the ANDA applicant seeking a finding that the patent is invalid or will not be infringed by the drug for which the applicant seeks approval if the 45-day notice period for filing a lawsuit for patent infringement has expired;
➢ Allows the ANDA applicant, if sued for patent infringement, to file a counterclaim concerning the "Orange Book" listing; and
➢ Gives authority to the Federal Trade Commission to review agreements between generic and innovator companies.

NOTE: A stay is a legal term of art. It is the delay in a generic drug approval that occurs when a brand-name company files a patent infringement lawsuit.

Citizen Petition for Delay

http://www.fda.gov/downloads/Drugs/GuidanceComplianceRegulatoryInformation/Guid-
ances/UCM079353.pdf

The Food and Drug Administration Amendments Act (FDAAA) enacted a provision that addresses the delay in ANDA approvals due to the filing of a citizen petition.

Section 505(q)(1)(A) provides: The Secretary shall not delay approval of a pending application submitted under subsection (b)(2) or (j) because of any request to take any form of action relating to the application, either before or during consideration of the request, unless–

> (i) the request is in writing and is a petition submitted to the Secretary pursuant to section 10.30 or 10.35 of title 21, Code of Federal Regulations (or any successor regulations); and
> (ii) the Secretary determines, upon reviewing the petition, that a delay is necessary to protect the public health. In section 505(q)(5), the term application is defined as an application submitted under section 505(b)(2) or 505(j) of the Act and the term petition is defined as a request described in 505(q)(1)(A)(i).

NOTE: The FDA Safety and Innovation Act of 2012 (FDASIA) shortened the review time by FDA of a citizen petition to 130 days.

CRITICAL ANALYSIS: The reforms are in place yet have they provided for improved availability of generic drug products in the marketplace?

Pay-for-Delay or Reverse Payment Agreements

https://www.ftc.gov/news-events/press-releases/2014/12/ftc-staff-issues-fy-2013-report-branded-drug-firms-patent

FTC is required to review brand and generic drug company agreements for anticompetitive outcomes under the Medicare Prescription Drug, Improvement and Modernization Act of 2003 (MPDMA). According to FTC, brand name companies and generic drug companies continue to formulate agreements to pay generic companies in order to keep them from entering the marketplace. In Fiscal Year 2014 (FY) there were 160 patent settlements filed with the FTC with 21 potential "Pay-for-Delay" agreements and in FY 2013 companies filed a total of 145 final patent dispute settlements, of which 29 created potential "Pay-for-Delay" agreements between branded and generic drug companies, according to a Federal Trade Commission report. Although the number of potential Pay-for-Delay settlements was less than FY 2012 (40 potential "Pay-for-Delay" settlements), it is similar to FY 2010 and 2011 (28 potential "Pay-for-Delay" settlements).

What are the costs to consumers? FTC projections of future costs to the consumer for these types of "Pay-for-Delay" are $3.5 billion per year; that is, FTC estimates that "Pay-for-Delay" agreements between brand and generic companies will cost consumers approximately $35 billion over the next ten years. The FTC "Pay for Delay" Report recommends Congressional action though not to necessarily ban pay-for-delay settlements outright. Such legislation could be tailored to mandate that companies could legally prove by "clear and convincing evidence" that such pay-for-delay settlements do not hinder competition. The Supreme Court in the 2013 decision of *Actavis,* established that these types of agreements are subject to review.

CRITICAL ANALYSIS: Evaluate whether "Pay-for-Delay" settlement agreements deny entry into the marketplace or perhaps benefit the consumer by avoiding costly litigation.

Pre-*Actavis* Historical Foundation—*Andrx and K-Dur Delay*

Andrx Pharmaceuticals, Inc. v. Biovail Corp. In *Andrx,*

The court in *Andrx* ruled that Biovail pleaded sufficient facts to support its allegation that Andrx and the patent holder Hoechst Marion Roussel, Inc. (Aventis) misused the Hatch-Waxman Act to delay the entry of Biovail's generic version of Cardizem CD, used to treat angina and other heart problems. *Andrx Pharmaceuticals, Inc. v. Biovail Corp*. 256 F.3d 799 (DC Cir.2001) *cert. denied,* 535 U.S. 931 (2002). Furthermore, Andrx and Hoeschst Marion Roussel entered into a consent agreement with the FTC. The consent agreement barred the companies from entering into agreements with the purpose or effect of delaying the entry of generic pharmaceuticals into the marketplace. *In the Matter of Hoeshst Marion Roussel, Inc.; Carderm Capital L.P.; and Andrx Corporation* Docket No. 9293. See: *In re Cardizem CD Antitrust Litigation*, 332 F.3d 896 (6ᵗʰ Cir. 2003), cert. denied by *Andrx Pharmaceuticals, Inc. v. Kroger Co.*, 543 U.S. 939 (2004); See also, *Valley Drug v. Geneva Pharmaceuticals, Inc.*, 344 F3d 1294 (11ᵗʰ Cir. 2003); *In re: Terazosin Hydrochloride Antitrust Litigation*, 352 F. Supp. 2d 1279 (Jan. 5, 2005).

K-Dur 20— Schering-Plough Corp., Upsher-Smith Laboratories, Inc. v. FTC
Administrative Action Dismissed-2005

The FTC determined in the K-Dur case that the agreements between the pharmaceutical companies and a generic company that delayed the market entry of a generic potassium supplement for high blood pressure in exchange for cash payments of $10 million and $60 million violated antitrust laws. The active ingredient of K-Dur 20, a potassium supplement was not patentable; however, Schering held a patent on the drug's time-release formulation. According to FTC, the agreements contradicted the legislative intent for low cost availability of generic products. An administrative law judge dismissed the FTC allegations against *Schering-Plough Corporation* where the FTC asserted that an agreement between *Schering-Plough* and *Upsher-Smith Laboratories*, a generic drug company, was anticompetitive. The court ruled that the agreement between *Schering-Plough* and *Upsher* was reasonable and did not raise anticompetitive practices. *Schering-Plough Corp., Upsher-Smith Laboratories, Inc. v. FTC* 402 F.3d 1056 (11ᵗʰ Cir. 2005).

In Re: K-Dur- Case No. 149 (D.C. NJ)
Consumer Action Settled-2017

In 2017, a $60.2 million settlement effectively closed the protracted litigation among Merck & Co. Inc., *Upsher-Smith Laboratories, Inc.* and direct purchasers of the potassium supplement K-Dur. The case stems back to 2011 when consumers who purchased the blood pressure medication brought suit for anticompetitive reasons. Purchasers of K-Dur 20, alleged that Schering's settlement agreements with Upsher and ESI violated the Sherman Act.

The background of this litigation involves several rulings. The district court granted defendants' motions for summary judgment and on appeal to the 3ʳᵈ Circuit, the court applied the "quick look test". The "quick look" rule specifies "the finder of fact must treat any payment from a patent holder to a generic patent challenger who agrees to delay entry into the market as prima facie evidence of an unreasonable restraint of trade, which could be rebutted by showing that the payment (1) was for a purpose other than delayed entry or (2) offers some pro-competitive benefit." *In re K-Dur Antitrust Litigation*, 3d Cir. No. 10-2077, 686 F.3d 197 (3ʳᵈ Cir. 2012). Subsequently, the Court of Appeals Judgment was VACATED and the case was REMANDED for further consideration in light of *FTC v. Actavis*, Inc., 133 S. Ct. 2223 (2013) which established that pay-for-delay or reverse payment agreements are not *per se* illegal; yet are subject to the "scope of patent test" and not the "quick look" test as the United States Supreme Court addressed below.

Pay-for-Delay Landmark U. S. Supreme Ct. Decision—*Actavis*

The United States Supreme Court in *Federal Trade Commission v. Actavis, Inc.* (Docket No. 12-416), issued a landmark ruling concerning drug patent settlement agreements referred to as "reverse payment agreements" or "pay-for-delay agreements". The Court granted certiorari to hear the Eleventh Circuit decision which affirmed in April 2012, a February 2010 decision by the U.S. District Court for the Northern District of Georgia fundamentally dismissing multidistrict litigation brought by the FTC as well as private plaintiffs who challenged certain drug patent settlement agreements in which Solvay Pharmaceuticals, Inc. ("Solvay") allegedly paid some generic drug companies to delay generic competition to Solvay's testosterone gel drug product, Androgel. The Eleventh Circuit followed previous holdings in *Valley Drug Co. v. Geneva Pharm., Inc.*, 344 F.3d 1294, 1296 (11th Cir. 2003), *Schering-Plough Corp. v. FTC*, 402 F.3d 1056 (11th Cir. 2005), and *Andrx Pharmaceuticals, Inc. v. Elan Corp.*, 421 F.3d 1227 (11th Cir. 2005), and held that "absent sham litigation or fraud in obtaining the patent, a reverse payment settlement is immune from antitrust attack so long as its anticompetitive effects fall within the scope of the exclusionary potential of the patent."

The *Actavis* Court held that these types of agreements are subject to antitrust scrutiny; yet, the Court did not hold that reverse payment settlement agreements are presumptively unlawful; the *Actavis* Court set forth that "Courts reviewing such agreements should proceed by applying the 'rule of reason,' rather than under a 'quick look' approach." Further, the Court held that the FTC should have been given the opportunity to prove its antitrust claims and that the exclusionary potential of a patent does not immunize a drug patent settlement agreement from antitrust attack. In summary, the Supreme Court in *Actavis* settled that pay-for-delay or reverse payment agreements are subject to scrutiny and the applicable test is the "scope of the patent test" and not the "quick rule of reason" analysis.

Federal Trade Commission v. Actavis, Inc., 133 S. Ct. 2223 (2013)

Syllabus—The syllabus constitutes no part of the opinion of the Court but has been prepared by the Reporter of Decisions for the convenience of the reader. See United States v. Detroit Timber & Lumber Co., 200 U.S. 321, 337, 26 S.Ct. 282, 50 L.Ed. 499. *** Solvay Pharmaceuticals obtained a patent for its approved brand-name drug AndroGel. Subsequently, respondents Actavis and Paddock filed applications for generic drugs modeled after AndroGel and certified under paragraph IV that Solvay's patent was invalid and that their drugs did not infringe it. Solvay sued Actavis and Paddock, claiming patent infringement. See 35 U.S.C. § 271(e)(2)(A). The FDA eventually approved Actavis' generic product; however, instead of bringing its drug to market, Actavis entered into a "reverse payment" settlement agreement with Solvay, agreeing not to bring its generic to market for a specified number of years and agreeing to promote AndroGel to doctors in exchange for millions of dollars.

The Federal Trade Commission (FTC) lawsuit alleged that respondents violated § 5 of the Federal Trade Commission Act by unlawfully agreeing to abandon their patent challenges, to refrain from launching their low-cost generic drugs, and to share in Solvay's monopoly profits. The District Court dismissed the complaint and the Eleventh Circuit affirmed the dismissal and determined that as long as the anticompetitive effects of a settlement fall within the scope of the patent's exclusionary potential, the settlement is immune from antitrust attack.

Held: The Eleventh Circuit erred in affirming the dismissal of the FTC's complaint.

(a) Although the anticompetitive effects of the reverse settlement agreement might fall within the scope of the exclusionary potential of Solvay's patent, this does not immunize the agreement from antitrust attack. *** Here, the paragraph IV litigation put the patent's validity and preclusive scope at issue, and the parties' settlement—in which, the FTC alleges, the plaintiff agreed to pay the defendants millions to stay out of its market, even though the defendants had no monetary claim against the plaintiff—ended that litigation. ***

(b) First, the specific restraint at issue has the "potential for genuine adverse effects on competition." *FTC v. Indiana Federation of Dentists,* 476 U.S. 447, 460–461, 106 S.Ct. 2009, 90 L.Ed.2d 445. *** Second, these anticompetitive consequences will at least sometimes prove unjustified. Third, where a reverse payment threatens to work unjustified anticompetitive harm, the patentee likely has the power to bring about that harm in practice. The size of the payment from a branded drug manufacturer to a generic challenger is a strong indicator of such power. Fourth, an antitrust action is likely to prove more feasible administratively than the Eleventh Circuit believed. It is normally not necessary to litigate patent validity to answer the antitrust question. *** Fifth, the fact that a large, unjustified reverse payment risks antitrust liability does not prevent litigating parties from settling their lawsuits.

(c) This Court declines to hold that reverse payment settlement agreements are presumptively unlawful. Courts reviewing such agreements should proceed by applying the "rule of reason," rather than under a "quick look" approach.

Opinion—Justice BREYER delivered the opinion of the Court.

Company A sues Company B for patent infringement. The two companies settle under terms that require (1) Company B, the claimed infringer, not to produce the patented product until the patent's term expires, and (2) Company A, the patentee, to pay B many millions of dollars. Because the settlement requires the patentee to pay the alleged infringer, rather than the other way around, this kind of settlement agreement is often called a "reverse payment" settlement agreement. And the basic question here is whether such an agreement can sometimes unreasonably diminish competition in violation of the antitrust laws. See, *e.g.,* 15 U.S.C. § 1 (Sherman Act prohibition of "restraint[s] of trade or commerce"). *** In our view, however, reverse payment settlements such as the agreement alleged in the complaint before us can sometimes violate the antitrust laws. We consequently hold that the Eleventh Circuit should have allowed the FTC's lawsuit to proceed.

I. A. Apparently most if not all reverse payment settlement agreements arise in the context of pharmaceutical drug regulation, and specifically in the context of suits brought under statutory provisions allowing a generic drug manufacturer (seeking speedy marketing approval) to challenge the validity of a patent owned by an already-approved brand-name drug owner. *** First, a drug manufacturer, wishing to market a new prescription drug, must submit a New Drug Application to the Federal Food and Drug Administration (FDA) and undergo a long, comprehensive, and costly testing process, after which, if successful, the manufacturer will receive marketing approval from the FDA. See 21 U.S.C. § 355(b)(1). Second, once the FDA has approved a brand-name drug for marketing, a manufacturer of a generic drug can obtain similar marketing approval through use of abbreviated procedures. The Hatch–Waxman Act permits a generic manufacturer to file an Abbreviated New Drug Application specifying that the generic has the "same active ingredients as," and is "biologically equivalent" to, the already-approved brand-name drug. *Caraco Pharmaceutical Laboratories, Ltd. v. Novo Nordisk A/S,* 132 S.Ct. 1670, 1676, (2012) (21 U.S.C. §§ 355(j)(2)(A)(ii), (iv)). *** Third, the Hatch–Waxman Act sets forth special procedures for identifying, and resolving, related patent disputes. It requires the pioneer brand-name manufacturer to list in its New Drug Application the "number and the expiration date" of any relevant patent. See 21 U.S.C. § 355(b)(1). And it requires the generic manufacturer in its Abbreviated New Drug Application to "assure the FDA" that the generic "will not infringe" the brand-name's patents. The generic can provide this assurance in one of several ways. See 21 U.S.C. § 355(j)(2)(A)(vii). It can certify that the brand-name manufacturer has not listed any relevant patents. It can certify that any relevant patents have expired. It can request approval to market beginning when any still-in-force patents expire. Or, it can certify that any listed, relevant patent "is invalid or will not be infringed by the manufacture, use, or sale" of the drug described in the Abbreviated New Drug Application. See § 355(j)(2)(A)(vii)(IV). Taking this last-mentioned route (called the "paragraph IV" route), automatically counts as patent infringement, see 35 U.S.C. § 271(e)(2)(A) (2006 ed., Supp. V), and often "means provoking litigation." *Caraco, supra,* at, 132 S.Ct., at 1677. If the brand-name patentee brings an infringement suit within 45 days, the FDA then must withhold approving the generic, usually for a 30–month period, while the parties litigate patent validity (or infringement) in court. If the courts decide the matter within that period, the FDA follows that determination; if they do not, the FDA may go forward and give approval to market the generic product. See 21 U.S.C. § 355(j)(5)(B)(iii).

Fourth, Hatch–Waxman provides a special incentive for a generic to be the first to file an Abbreviated New Drug Application taking the paragraph IV route. That applicant will enjoy a period of 180 days of exclusivity (from the first commercial marketing of its drug). See § 355(j)(5)(B)(iv) (establishing exclusivity period). During that period of exclusivity no other generic can compete with the brand-name drug. If the first-to-file generic manufacturer can overcome any patent obstacle and bring the generic to market, this 180–day period of exclusivity can prove valuable, possibly "worth several hundred million dollars." *** The 180–day exclusivity period, however, can belong only to the first generic to file. Should that first-to-file generic forfeit the exclusivity right in one of the ways specified by statute, no other generic can obtain it. See § 355(j)(5)(D).

B. 1. In 1999, Solvay Pharmaceuticals, a respondent here, filed a New Drug Application for a brand-name drug called AndroGel. The FDA approved the application in 2000. In 2003, Solvay obtained a relevant patent and disclosed that fact to the FDA, 677 F.3d, at 1308, as Hatch–Waxman requires. See § 355(c)(2). Later the same year another respondent, Actavis, Inc. (then known as Watson Pharmaceuticals), filed an Abbreviated New Drug Application for a generic drug modeled after AndroGel. Subsequently, Paddock Laboratories, also a respondent, separately filed an Abbreviated New Drug Application for its own generic product. Both Actavis and Paddock certified under paragraph IV that Solvay's listed patent was invalid and their drugs did not infringe it. A fourth manufacturer, Par Pharmaceutical, likewise a respondent, did not file an application of its own but joined forces with Paddock, agreeing to share the patent litigation costs in return for a share of profits if Paddock obtained approval for its generic drug.

Solvay initiated paragraph IV patent litigation against Actavis and Paddock. Thirty months later, the FDA approved Actavis' first-to-file generic product, but, in 2006, the patent-litigation parties all settled. Under the terms of the settlement Actavis agreed that it would not bring its generic to market until August 31, 2015, 65 months before Solvay's patent expired (unless someone else marketed a generic sooner). Actavis also agreed to promote AndroGel to urologists. *** And Solvay agreed to pay millions of dollars to each generic—$12 million in total to Paddock; $60 million in total to Par; and an estimated $19–$30 million annually, for nine years, to Actavis. *** According to the FTC the true point of the payments was to compensate the generics for agreeing not to compete against AndroGel until 2015.

2. On January 29, 2009, the FTC filed this lawsuit against all the settling parties, namely, Solvay, Actavis, Paddock, and Par. The FTC's complaint (as since amended) alleged that respondents violated § 5 of the Federal Trade Commission Act, 15 U.S.C. § 45, by unlawfully agreeing "to share in Solvay's monopoly profits, abandon their patent challenges, and refrain from launching their low-cost generic products to compete with AndroGel for nine years." *** The District Court held that these allegations did not set forth an antitrust law violation. *In re Androgel Antitrust Litigation (No. II),* 687 F.Supp.2d 1371, 1379 (N.D.Ga.2010).

The Court of Appeals for the Eleventh Circuit affirmed the District Court. It wrote that "absent sham litigation or fraud in obtaining the patent, a reverse payment settlement is immune from antitrust attack so long as its anticompetitive effects fall within the scope of the exclusionary potential of the patent." 677 F.3d, at 1312. *** The FTC sought certiorari. Because different courts have reached different conclusions about the application of the antitrust laws to Hatch–Waxman–related patent settlements, we granted the FTC's petition. Compare, *e.g., id.,* at 1312 (case below) (settlements generally "immune from antitrust attack"); *In re Ciprofloxacin Hydrochloride Antitrust Litigation,* 544 F.3d 1323, 1332–1337 (C.A.Fed.2008) (similar); *In re Tamoxifen Citrate Antitrust Litigation,* 466 F.3d 187, 212–213 (C.A.2 2006) (similar), with *In re K–Dur Antitrust Litigation,* 686 F.3d 197, 214–218 (C.A.3 2012) (settlements presumptively unlawful).

II. A. Solvay's patent, if valid and infringed, might have permitted it to charge drug prices sufficient to recoup the reverse settlement payments it agreed to make to its potential generic competitors. *** The FTC alleges that in substance, the plaintiff agreed to pay the defendants many millions of dollars to stay out of its market, even though the defendants did not have any claim that the plaintiff was liable to them for damages. That form of settlement is unusual. ***

For another thing, this Court's precedents make clear that patent-related settlement agreements can sometimes violate the antitrust laws. In *United States v. Singer Mfg. Co.,* 374 U.S. 174, 83 S.Ct. 1773, 10 L.Ed.2d 823 (1963), for example, two sewing machine companies possessed competing patent claims; a third company sought a patent under circumstances where doing so might lead to the disclosure of information that would invalidate the other two firms' patents. *** Rather, emphasizing that the Sherman Act "imposes strict limitations on the concerted activities in which patent owners may lawfully engage," *id.,* at 197, 83 S.Ct. 1773, it held that the agreements, although settling patent disputes, violated the antitrust laws. *Id.,* at 195, 197, 83 S.Ct. 1773. *** Finally in *Standard Oil Co. (Indiana),* the Court upheld cross-licensing agreements among patentees that settled actual and impending patent litigation, 283 U.S., at 168, 51 S.Ct. 421, which agreements set royalty rates to be charged third parties for a license to practice all the patents at issue (and which divided resulting revenues). In reverse payment settlements, in contrast, a party with no claim for damages (something that is usually true of a paragraph IV litigation defendant) walks away with money simply so it will stay away from the patentee's market.

B. *** Rather, five sets of considerations lead us to conclude that the FTC should have been given the opportunity to prove its antitrust claim. [T]he specific restraint at issue has the "potential for genuine adverse effects on competition." *Indiana Federation of Dentists,* 476 U.S., at 460–461, 106 S.Ct. 2009 *** But settlement on the terms said by the FTC to be at issue here—payment in return for staying out of the market—simply keeps prices at patentee-set levels, potentially producing the full patent-related $500 million monopoly return while dividing that return between the challenged patentee and the patent challenger. The patentee and the challenger gain; the consumer loses. ***

First, under Hatch–Waxman only the first challenger gains the special advantage of 180 days of an exclusive right to sell a generic version of the brand-name product. ***

Second, these anticompetitive consequences will at least sometimes prove unjustified. *** Where a reverse payment reflects traditional settlement considerations, such as avoided litigation costs or fair value for services, there is not the same concern that a patentee is using its monopoly profits to avoid the risk of patent invalidation or a finding of non-infringement. ***

Third, where a reverse payment threatens to work unjustified anticompetitive harm, the patentee likely possesses the power to bring that harm about in practice. *** At least, the "size of the payment from a branded drug manufacturer to a prospective generic is itself a strong indicator of power"—namely, the power to charge prices higher than the competitive level. ***

Fourth, an antitrust action is likely to prove more feasible administratively than the Eleventh Circuit believed. *** An unexplained large reverse payment itself would normally suggest that the patentee has serious doubts about the patent's survival. And that fact, in turn, suggests that the payment's objective is to maintain super competitive prices to be shared among the patentee and the challenger rather than face what might have been a competitive market—the very anticompetitive consequence that underlies the claim of antitrust unlawfulness. ***

Fifth, *** If the basic reason is a desire to maintain and to share patent-generated monopoly profits, then, in the absence of some other justification, the antitrust laws are likely to forbid the arrangement.

In sum, a reverse payment, where large and unjustified, can bring with it the risk of significant anticompetitive effects; one who makes such a payment may be unable to explain and to justify it; such a firm or individual may well possess market power derived from the patent; a court, by examining the size of the payment, may well be able to assess its likely anticompetitive effects along with its potential justifications without litigating the validity of the patent; and parties may well find ways to settle patent disputes without the use of reverse payments. ***

III. The FTC urges us to hold that reverse payment settlement agreements are presumptively unlawful and that courts reviewing such agreements should proceed via a "quick look" approach, rather than applying a "rule of reason." We decline to do so. *** That is because the likelihood of a reverse payment bringing about anticompetitive effects depends upon its size, its scale in relation to the payor's anticipated future litigation costs, its independence from other services for which it might represent payment, and the lack of any other convincing justification. *** These complexities lead us to conclude that the FTC must prove its case as in other rule-of-reason cases. *** We reverse the judgment of the Eleventh Circuit. And we remand the case for further proceedings consistent with this opinion. *It is so ordered.*

Chief Justice ROBERTS, joined by Justice SCALIA and Justice THOMAS, dissenting.

I. The point of antitrust law is to encourage competitive markets to promote consumer welfare. The point of patent law is to grant limited monopolies as a way of encouraging innovation. *** *Walker Process Equipment, Inc. v. Food Machinery & Chemical Corp.,* 382 U.S. 172, 177, 86 S.Ct. 347, 15 L.Ed.2d 247 (1965) (" 'A patent ... is an exception to the general rule against monopolies' "); *** Solvay paid a competitor to respect its patent—conduct which did not exceed the scope of its patent. ***

II. *** The majority points to *no* case where a patent settlement was subject to antitrust scrutiny merely because the validity of the patent was uncertain. ***

III. The majority's rule will discourage settlement of patent litigation. ***

IV. Even if a subsequent generic would not be entitled to this additional incentive, it will have as much or nearly as much incentive to challenge the patent as a potential challenger would in any other context outside of Hatch–Waxman, where there is no 180–day exclusivity period. ***

V. The majority today departs from the settled approach separating patent and antitrust law, weakens the protections afforded to innovators by patents, frustrates the public policy in favor of settling, and likely undermines the very policy it seeks to promote by forcing generics who step into the litigation ring to do so without the prospect of cash settlements. *** I respectfully dissent.

Post *Actavis* Pay-for-Delay—$1.2 Billion *FTC v. Cephalon, Inc.* and *Apotex, Inc. v. Cephalon*

In 2017, the trial occurred in this antitrust case which spanned nearly 10 years. *Apotex Inc. v. Cephalon Inc.,* E.D. Pa., 06-cv-2768, (6/12/17) challenged the reserve payment settlement agreements entered into by Cephalon, Inc., manufacturer of Provigil (modafinil), a narcolepsy drug. The plaintiffs alleged that Cephalon, Inc. conspired with four generic drug makers to delay generic competition.

Teva Pharmaceutical Industries Ltd. (Teva) agreed to pay $1.2 billion in a settlement with the Federal Trade Commission. *http://1.usa.gov/1I53LfD* Teva acquired Cephalon, Inc. in 2012. The settlement resolves claims that Cephalon, Inc., hindered generic drug competition.

NOTE: See: *FTC v. Cephalon,* E.D. Pa.No. 2:08-cv-2141 (May 28, 2015). See also: *In Re: K-Dur- Case No. 149* (D.C. NJ) (above).

CRITICAL ANALYSIS: Based on the analytical test articulated in *Actavis*, assess whether the agreements in *Actavis* delayed entry of the generic drug into the marketplace. Incorporate the K-Dur $62 million settlement, the Teva $1.2 billion settlement with FTC and the Endo settlement.

FTC v. Endo Settlement 2017 and Complaint Other Pharmaceutical Companies

https://www.ftc.gov/news-events/press-releases/2017/01/endo-pharmaceuticals-inc-agrees-abandon-anticompetitive-pay-delay (settlement and refiling)

https://www.ftc.gov/news-events/press-releases/2016/03/ftc-sues-endo-pharmaceuticals-inc-others-illegally-blocking-lower (original complaint)

FTC filed a lawsuit against several drug companies in 2016, including Endo International Plc, Allergan Plc, and Impax Laboratories, Inc. over allegedly illegal patent litigation settlements that delayed generic drug competition (*FTC v. Endo Pharms. Inc.,* E.D. Pa., No. 2:16-cv-01440-PD, complaint 3/30/16 and was settled with *Endo* January 23, 2017. FTC alleged that Endo and the other companies violated antitrust laws by entering into pay-for-delay settlements over the shingles treatment Lidoderm (lidocaine) and the painkiller Opana ER (oxymorphone hydrochloride extended-release).

FTC refiled charges against Watson Laboratories, Inc., and its former parent, Allergan plc, for illegally blocking a lower-cost generic version of Lidoderm when it entered into a pay-for-delay agreement with Endo. Further, FTC also issued an administrative complaint against Impax Laboratories, Inc. for engaging in similar conduct with regard to Opana ER.

See: *https://www.ftc.gov/news-events/press-releases/2017/01/endo-pharmaceuticals-inc-agrees-abandon-anticompetitive-pay-delay*

Marketplace Delay—Citizen Petitions and "Authorized Generics"

Delay of Generic Entry into the Marketplace—Use of Citizen Petitions

FTC filed a complaint against Shire PLC, a unit of ViroPharma Inc., concerning the attempts to delay generic versions of its brand-name antibiotic Vancocin by the vast number of public filings which included 24 citizen petitions. FTC characterized the filings as "Serial, Sham Petitioning to Delay Generics and Maintain its Monopoly over Vancocin HCl Capsules". See: *Federal Trade Commission v. Shire Viropharma, Inc.* Case 1:17-cv-00131-(Filed 02/07/17)

Delay of Entry into Marketplace Due to Authorized Generics

Authorized generics are generic drugs sold under a license from the patent holder. The Drug Price Competition and Patent Term Restoration Act and the FDCA do not prohibit authorized generics. Former President Bush signed into law FDAAA (Public Law 110-85, 121 Stat. 823). Section 920 of FDAAA added new section 505(t) to the Federal Food, Drug, and Cosmetic Act (FDCA) (21 U.S.C. 355(t)). A final rule effective January 25, 2010 amended FDA's postmarketing reporting requirements to add 21 C.F.R. § 314.81(b)(2)(ii)(b) to require NDA holders to include in annual reports the date the authorized generic drug entered the market. The Hatch Waxman provides that the first generic company to obtain ANDA approval under a "Paragraph IV Certification" has the exclusive right to market the generic drug for 180 days. "Authorized Generics", also known as brand generics or branded generics, are marketed by the NDA holder or authorized by the NDA holder including through a third-party distributor at a lower price than the brand drug during the 180-exclusivity period thereby in effect eliminating the exclusivity period. The court in *Mylan* opined that the issue of marketing authorized generics during the 180-day exclusivity period is a Congressional issue. Ultimately, Congress needs to address this issue by amending the FDCA with a specific legislative enactment.

Mylan v. FDA, 454 F.3d 270 (4th Cir. 2006)

MICHAEL, Circuit Judge: The Food and Drug Administration (FDA) approved Mylan Pharmaceuticals, Inc.'s application to sell a generic version of a drug that Procter & Gamble Pharmaceuticals, Inc. sold under the brand name Macrobid. Just as Mylan began selling its generic drug, a third party under license from Procter & Gamble started selling a competing generic version. Sales of the generic authorized by Procter & Gamble crimped revenues from Mylan's version. Mylan petitioned the FDA for a ruling that under a provision of the Federal Food, Drug, and Cosmetic Act (FFDCA or Act) the authorized generic could not be sold until Mylan's drug had been on the market for 180 days. We affirm the dismissal, concluding that the statute does not grant the FDA the power to prohibit the marketing of authorized generics during the 180-day exclusivity period afforded to a drug company.

I. A. *** The first applicant to file a paragraph IV ANDA enjoys a unique advantage. For 180 days it may sell its drug without competition from later ANDA applicants. The 180-day period starts to run on the earlier of two dates: (1) the date the FDA receives notice "of the first commercial marketing of the drug under the previous application" (the commercial marketing trigger) or (2) the date a court decides that the patent is either invalid or not infringed (the patent litigation trigger). *See* 21 U.S.C. § 355(j)(5)(B)(iv) (preventing the FDA from making effective a later paragraph IV ANDA earlier than 180 days after one of these two triggering events). *** By selling an authorized generic during the exclusivity period enjoyed by the first paragraph IV ANDA applicant, the pioneer drug maker prevents that applicant from winning all of the customers who want to switch from the branded drug to a cheaper generic form. *** The question before us is whether § 355(j)(5)(B)(iv) empowers the FDA to prohibit sale of authorized generics during the exclusivity period.

B. This dispute began when Mylan filed a paragraph IV ANDA seeking authorization to produce nitrofurantoin, a generic version of a drug to treat urinary tract infections. Procter & Gamble held the approved NDA for the drug and sold it under the brand name Macrobid. The FDA approved Mylan's application on March 22, 2004. Mylan began commercial marketing of nitrofurantoin on

March 23, the same day that Watson Pharmaceuticals began selling the authorized generic version of Macrobid under a license from Procter & Gamble. Mylan lost sales worth "tens of millions" of dollars as a result of this competition.

II. Mylan concedes that the language of § 355(j)(5)(B)(iv) is plain. The provision makes no mention of drugs under approved NDAs. It speaks only about the rights of the paragraph IV ANDA applicant who files first as against all subsequent paragraph IV ANDA applicants [emphasis added]. Indeed, the statute describes the 180-day exclusivity period entirely from the point of view of a later-filing paragraph IV ANDA applicant. *** Nothing in the statute restricts the established right of such companies to make ordinary licensing agreements with third parties. ***

III. Although the introduction of an authorized generic may reduce the economic benefit of the 180 days of exclusivity awarded to the first paragraph IV ANDA applicant, § 355(j)(5)(B)(iv) gives no legal basis for the FDA to prohibit the encroachment of authorized generics on that exclusivity. The denial of Mylan's petition therefore was not "arbitrary, capricious ... or otherwise not in accordance with law," and the district court correctly dismissed the case. Affirmed.

CRITICAL ANALYSIS: How do "authorized" generics thwart generic drugs from entering the marketplace? Review the Endo FTC settlement above and complaint refiling against Watson Laboratories, Inc., and its former parent, Allergan plc, for illegally blocking a lower-cost generic version of Lidoderm when it entered into a pay-for-delay agreement with Endo. FTC also issued an administrative complaint against Impax Laboratories, Inc. for engaging in similar practices concerning Opana ER. See link below.

https://www.ftc.gov/news-events/press-releases/2017/01/endo-pharmaceuticals-inc-agrees-abandon-anticompetitive-pay-delay

NOTE: Legislation was introduced *Creating and Restoring Equal Access to Equivalent Samples Act of 2017 or* **CREATES with the stated purposes as follows:** *To promote competition in the market for drugs and biological products by facilitating the timely entry of lower-cost generic and biosimilar versions of those drugs and biological products.* **However, it was not enacted.**

https://www.congress.gov/bill/115th-congress/senate-bill/974
https://www.congress.gov/bill/115th-congress/house-bill/2212

Biosimilars or Follow-on Biologics

NOTE: See Volume VI Biotechnology

http://www.fda.gov/Drugs/DevelopmentApprovalProcess/HowDrugsareDevelopedandApproved/ApprovalApplications/TherapeuticBiologicApplications/Biosimilars/

Generic versions of biotech drugs referred to as biosimilars or follow-on biologics, present an interesting and complex issue for both industry and FDA. The biotech industry is relatively new and has not faced competition from generic companies. Biotech drugs are used to treat a variety of serious illness such as cancer and autoimmune diseases. Biosimilar drugs are more expensive and complex than traditional chemical drugs because they are composed of living organisms. Ultimately, Congress passed the Biologics Price Competition and Innovation Act (BPCI or Biosimilars Act) , included as Title VII of the Patient Protection and Affordable Care Act of 2010 Pub.L. 111-148 as amended by the Health Care and Reconciliation Act of 2010 (Healthcare Reform Act or Affordable Care Act). The Affordable Care Act was upheld in: *Nat'l Fed'n of Indep. Bus. v. Sebelius*, 132 S. Ct. 2566, 183 L. Ed. 2d 450 (2012).

The BPCIA provides an abbreviated pathway for obtaining Food and Drug Administration (FDA) approval of a drug that is biosimilar to a licensed biological product known as the reference product. The Biosimilars Act established a 12-year exclusivity period before biosimilars can be approved for marketing in the United States. Additionally, section 351 of Public Health Services Act, 42 U.S.C. section 262 was amended to include a new abbreviated licensure approval pathway for biosimilar biological products. FDA will only accept a Biosimilar Biological Product Application (BBPA) 4 years after the referenced product was approved. Significant elements include a pathway for biosimilar products that permits manufacturers to gain approval without duplicating the innovator's safety and efficacy data in a Biosimilar Biological Product Application (BBPA). The biosimilar pathway application is dependent on existing data on the brand biologic.

Proposed products must have the same—Mechanism of use; route of administration; dosage form; and strength as the referenced products.

Exclusivity Provisions are as follows—Innovator Exclusivity—12 years of exclusivity after the reference product was originally approved; and Generics—1 year after commercial launch.

Timely Infringement suits and forfeiture provisions—FDA approval 18 months after final court decision or dismissal; and if litigation persists, 42 months following approval of first interchangeable product. See: Biosimilars Act, § 351(k)(6)(C)(i)

Guidance Documents—FDA issued several guidance documents for "biosimilar" drugs which detail what a company must do in order to obtain approval. Examples include: *Scientific and Quality Considerations in Demonstrating Biosimilarity to a Reference Product. Biosimilars: Additional Questions and Answers Regarding Implementation of the Biologics Price Competition and Innovation Act of 2009* (Draft) (2015).
http://www.fda.gov/downloads/Drugs/GuidanceComplianceRegulatoryInformation/Guidances/UCM273001.pdf
Clinical Pharmacology Data to Support a Demonstration of Biosimilarity to a Reference Product (2014).

FDA evaluation has focused on biotech drugs that replace or supplement natural human proteins rather than more complicated biotech drugs such as antibody-based cancer treatments. A critical issue that remains is what constitutes "bioequivalence". Apparently, the type of the protein impacts and this might necessitate clinical evidence of the therapeutic qualities of a final product. Perhaps a comparability assessment might suffice. Yet, the basic concerns for generic biosimilars remain the same; that is, safety and efficacy are paramount and generic follow-on biologics must be held to those standards. Regulatory guidance from FDA continues to evolve and undoubtedly necessitates a lengthy process due to the complexity involved. The European Union spearheaded a regulatory framework for approval of biosimilars. See: Committee for Medicinal Products for Human Use, Guideline on Similar Biological Medicinal Products, CHMP/437/04 Oct. 30, 2005 (EU Guidelines).

Biosimilar Approvals, Nonproprietary Naming and Labeling

Sandoz, Inc. v. Amgen, Inc.,
137 S. Ct. 1664 (2017)

Syllabus (edited)—The Biologics Price Competition and Innovation Act of 2009 (BPCIA or Act) provides an abbreviated pathway for acquiring FDA approval of a drug that is biosimilar to an already licensed biological product termed the reference product. 42 U.S.C. § 262(k). Under § 262(*l*)(2)(A), an applicant seeking FDA approval of a biosimilar must provide its application and manufacturing information to the sponsor within 20 days of the date the FDA notifies the applicant that it has accepted the application for review. There are two levels of patent litigation. First, the parties collaborate to identify patents on the lists for immediate litigation. The second phase is triggered when the applicant, under § 262(*l*)(8)(A), gives the sponsor notice at least 180 days before commercial marketing the biosimilar. *** Under § 262(*l*)(9)(C), if an applicant fails to provide its application and manufacturing information to the sponsor under § 262(*l*)(2)(A), then the sponsor may immediately bring an action "for a declaration of infringement, validity, or enforceability of any patent that claims the biological product or a use of the biological product."

Sandoz sought FDA approval to market a biosimilar filgrastim product under the brand name Zarxio, with Neupogen as the licensed reference product. A day after the FDA informed Sandoz that its application had been accepted for review, Sandoz notified Amgen that it had submitted an application and that it intended to market Zarxio immediately upon receiving FDA approval. It later informed Amgen that it did not intend to provide the application and manufacturing information required by § 262(*l*)(2)(A) and that Amgen could sue immediately for infringement under § 262(*l*)(9)(C). Amgen sued Sandoz for patent infringement and also asserted that Sandoz engaged in "unlawful" conduct in violation of California's unfair competition law. Subsequently, FDA licensed

Zarxio, and Sandoz provided Amgen further notice of commercial marketing. The District Court subsequently granted partial judgment on the pleadings to Sandoz on its BPCIA counterclaims and dismissed Amgen's unfair competition claims with prejudice. *** The [Federal Circuit] court affirmed the dismissal of Amgen's state-law claim based on Sandoz's alleged violation of § 262(*l*)(2)(A), holding that Sandoz did not violate the BPCIA in failing to disclose its application and manufacturing information and that the BPCIA provides the exclusive remedies for failure to comply with this requirement. The court also held that under § 262(*l*)(8)(A) an applicant must provide notice of commercial marketing after obtaining licensure, and that this requirement is mandatory. It thus enjoined Sandoz from marketing Zarxio until 180 days after the date it provided its second notice.

(a) Section 262(*l*)(2)(A)'s requirement that an applicant provide the sponsor with its application and manufacturing information is not enforceable by an injunction under federal law. The Federal Circuit reached the proper result on this issue. *** Another provision, § 262(*l*)(9)(C), provides a remedy for an applicant's failure to turn over its application and manufacturing information. It authorizes the sponsor, but not the applicant, to bring an immediate declaratory-judgment action for artificial infringement ***. The presence of this remedy, coupled with the absence of any other textually specified remedies, indicates that Congress did not intend sponsors to have access to injunctive relief, at least as a matter of federal law, to enforce the disclosure requirement.

(b) The Federal Circuit should determine on remand whether an injunction is available under state law to enforce § 262(*l*)(2)(A). The court on remand should determine whether California law would treat noncompliance with § 262(*l*)(2)(A) as "unlawful," and whether the BPCIA pre-empts any additional state-law remedy for failure to comply with § 262(*l*)(2)(A).

(c) An applicant may provide notice of commercial marketing before obtaining a license. Section 262(*l*)(8)(A) states that the applicant "shall provide notice to the reference product sponsor not later than 180 days before the date of the first commercial marketing of the biological product licensed under subsection (k)." [T]he applicant may provide notice either before or after receiving FDA approval. 794 F.3d 1347, vacated in part, reversed in part, and remanded.

***Key Holdings*: Section 262(*l*)(2)(A) is not enforceable by injunction under federal law, but the Federal Circuit on remand should determine whether a state-law injunction is available. An applicant may provide notice under § 262(*l*)(8)(A) prior to obtaining licensure.**

Opinion—THOMAS, J., delivered the opinion for a unanimous Court. BREYER, J., filed a concurring opinion. These cases involve 42 U.S.C. § 262(*l*), which was enacted as part of the Biologics Price Competition and Innovation Act of 2009 (BPCIA), 124 Stat. 808. The BPCIA governs a type of drug called a biosimilar, which is a biologic product that is highly similar to a biologic product that has already been approved by the Food and Drug Administration (FDA). Under § 262(*l*), an applicant that seeks FDA approval of a biosimilar must provide its application materials and manufacturing information to the manufacturer of the corresponding biologic within 20 days of the date the FDA notifies the applicant that it has accepted the application for review. The applicant then must give notice to the manufacturer at least 180 days before marketing the biosimilar commercially.

I. A. A biologic is a type of drug derived from natural, biological sources such as animals or microorganisms. Biologics thus differ from traditional drugs, which are typically synthesized from chemicals. A manufacturer of a biologic may market the drug only if the FDA has licensed it pursuant to either of two review processes set forth in § 262. Under that subsection [§ 262(a)], the FDA may license a new biologic if, among other things, the manufacturer demonstrates that it is "safe, pure, and potent." § 262(a)(2)(C)(i)(I). *** To obtain approval through the BPCIA's abbreviated process, the manufacturer of a biosimilar (applicant) does not need to show that the product is "safe, pure, and potent." Instead, the applicant may piggyback on the showing made by the manufacturer (sponsor) of a previously licensed biologic (reference product). See § 262(k)(2)(A)(iii). *** An applicant may not submit an application until 4 years after the reference product is first licensed, and the FDA may not license a biosimilar until 12 years after the reference product is first licensed. §§ 262(k)(7)(A), (B). As a result, the manufacturer of a new biologic enjoys a 12–year period *** without competition from biosimilars.

B. The BPCIA facilitates litigation during the period preceding FDA approval so that the parties do not have to wait until commercial marketing to resolve their patent disputes. *** Specifically, it provides that the mere submission of a biosimilar application constitutes an act of infringement. §§ 271(e)(2)(C)(i), (ii). We will refer to this kind of preapproval infringement as "artificial" infringement. Section 271(e)(4) provides remedies for artificial infringement, including injunctive relief and damages.

C. The BPCIA sets forth a carefully calibrated scheme for preparing to adjudicate, and then adjudicating, claims of infringement. See 42 U.S.C. § 262(*l*). When the FDA accepts an application for review, it notifies the applicant, who within 20 days "shall provide" to the sponsor a copy of the application and information about how the biosimilar is manufactured. § 262(*l*)(2)(A). *** These disclosures enable the sponsor to evaluate the biosimilar for possible infringement of patents it holds on the reference product ***. § 262(*l*) (1)(D). ***

Amgen alleged that Sandoz engaged in "unlawful" conduct when it failed to provide its application and manufacturing information under § 262(*l*)(2)(A), and when it provided notice of commercial marketing under § 262(*l*)(8)(A) before, rather than after, the FDA licensed its biosimilar.

While the case was pending in the District Court, the FDA licensed Zarxio, and Sandoz provided Amgen a further notice of commercial marketing. ***

III. The first question we must answer is whether § 262(*l*)(2)(A)'s requirement that an applicant provide the sponsor with its application and manufacturing information is enforceable by an injunction under either federal or state law.

A. We agree with the Federal Circuit that an injunction under federal law is not available to enforce § 262(*l*)(2)(A), though for slightly different reasons than those provided by the court below. *** A separate provision of § 262, however, does provide a remedy for an applicant's failure to turn over its application and manufacturing information. When an applicant fails to comply with § 262(*l*)(2)(A), § 262(*l*)(9)(C) authorizes the sponsor, but not the applicant, to bring an immediate declaratory-judgment action for artificial infringement as defined in § 271(e)(2)(C)(ii). Section 262(*l*)(9)(C) thus vests in the sponsor the control that the applicant would otherwise have exercised over the scope and timing of the patent litigation. *** The remedy provided by § 262 (*l*)(9)(C) excludes all other federal remedies, including injunctive relief. Where, as here, "a statute expressly provides a remedy, courts must be especially reluctant to provide additional remedies." *Karahalios v. Federal Employees,* 489 U.S. 527, 533, 109 S.Ct. 1282, 103 L.Ed.2d 539 (1989). The BPCIA's "carefully crafted and detailed enforcement scheme provides strong evidence that Congress did *not* intend to authorize other remedies that it simply forgot to incorporate expressly." *Great–West Life & Annuity Ins. Co. v. Knudson,* 534 U.S. 204, 209, 122 S.Ct. 708, 151 L.Ed.2d 635 (2002) (internal quotation marks omitted). The presence of § 262(*l*)(9)(C), coupled with the absence of any other textually specified remedies, indicates that Congress did not intend sponsors to have access to injunctive relief, at least as a matter of federal law, to enforce the disclosure requirement.

B. We decline to resolve this particular dispute definitively because it does not present a question of federal law. *** If the applicant failed to provide that information, then the sponsor, but not the applicant, could bring an immediate declaratory-judgment action pursuant to § 262(*l*)(9)(C). The parties in these cases agree—as did the Federal Circuit—that Sandoz failed to comply with § 262(*l*)(2)(A), thus subjecting itself to that consequence. *** Whether Sandoz's conduct was "unlawful" under the unfair competition law is a state-law question, and the court below erred in attempting to answer that question by referring to the BPCIA alone.

IV. The second question at issue in these cases is whether an applicant must provide notice *after* the FDA licenses its biosimilar, or if it may also provide effective notice before licensure. Section 262(*l*)(8)(A) states that the applicant "shall provide notice to the reference product sponsor not later than 180 days before the date of the first commercial marketing of the biological product licensed under subsection (k)." *** The applicant must give "notice" at least 180 days "before the date of the first commercial marketing." "[C]ommercial marketing," in turn, must be "of the biological product licensed under subsection (k)." § 262(*l*) (8)(A). Because this latter phrase modifies "commercial marketing" rather than "notice," "commercial marketing" is the point in time by which the biosimilar must be "licensed." ***Accordingly, the applicant may provide notice either before or after receiving FDA approval. *** In sum, because Sandoz fully complied with § 262(*l*)(8)(A) when it first gave notice (before licensure) in July 2014, the Federal Circuit erred in issuing a federal injunction prohibiting Sandoz from marketing Zarxio until 180 days after licensure. ***We accordingly reverse the Federal Circuit's judgment as to the notice provision.

For the foregoing reasons, the judgment of the Court of Appeals is vacated in part and reversed in part, and the cases are remanded for further proceedings consistent with this opinion. *It is so ordered. https://www.supremecourt.gov/opinions/16pdf/15-1039_1b8e.pdf*

NOTE: On remand the federal Court of Appeals Court held it had discretion to address the preemption issue; field preemption barred the sponsor's state law unfair competition claims; and conflict preemption barred sponsor's state law unfair competition claims.

Other Approvals—Besides Zarxio, FDAs approvals of biosimilars continue. In 2017 five additional biosimilars were approved and several in 2018. A novel gene therapy was approved for the treatment of hereditary retinal disorder. Another approval CAR T-cell is indicated to treat blood cancers. Pfizer, Inc. and Celltrion, Inc. received FDA approval to market Inflectra, a low-cost biosimilar to Johnson & Johnson's arthritis treatment, Remicade. FDA approved the intravenous infusion for seven conditions treated by Remicade, including rheumatoid arthritis and plaque psoriasis. FDA approved the biosimilar Erelzi, (2016) (etanercept-szzs) for multiple inflammatory diseases. Enbrel (etanercept) was originally licensed in 1998. Erelzi is administered by injection for the treatment of moderate to severe rheumatoid arthritis. Amgen Inc.'s Amjevita, was approved 2016 a biosimilar of AbbVie, Inc.'s immunosuppressant Humira.

Naming—The active ingredient in Neupogen is filgrastim and FDA determined that Zarxio's name is filgrastim-sndz. FDA issued a guidance titled: "Nonproprietary Naming of Biological Products, 80 FR 52296-01." The nonproprietary name includes a suffix of four lowercase letters, applicable to biological products previously licensed and newly licensed under sections 351(a) and 351(k) of the Public Health Services Act (PHS).

Label Statement—Biosimilar product labels must include a statement that the product is a biosimilar and may rely on the data submitted for FDA approval by the originator biologic maker.

Biosimilars Future—The market for biosimilars suggests vast possibilities and is a multi-billion-dollar industry. The biosimilars market is expected to reach 23.63 billion by 2023. Examples of the top biologics and their sales (2017) include: Humira rheumatoid arthritis, $18.4 billion; Rituxan $9.2 million; Enbrel rheumatoid arthritis, $7.9 billion; Herceptin breast cancer, $7.4 billion; Remicade rheumatoid arthritis, $7.1 billion; Avastin cancers, $7.1 billion; Lantus, $5.7 billion; Neulasta chemotherapy infections, $4.7 billion; Avonex $2.1 billion; Lucentis $1.5 billion. *https://www.thebalance.com/top-biologic-drugs-2663233*

NOTE: See also *Volume VI: Biotechnology and Biologics Regulation*. The Biologics Price Competition and Innovation Act, incorporated into the Patient Protection and Affordable Care Act mandated the creation of an abbreviated biosimilars approval pathway. See: *Nat'l Fed'n of Indep. Bus. v. Sebelius*, 132 S. Ct. 2566, 183 L. Ed. 2d 450 (2012).

CRITICAL ANALYSIS: Discuss the future of biosimilars. Does the Biosimilars Act adequately protect both innovator and biosimilar companies?

Chapter 4: Over-the-Counter Drug Products
Nonprescription Drug Products

Due to escalating health costs including prescription drugs, the use of nonprescription over-the-counter (OTC) drug products has risen considerably Other contributing factors include the vast array of OTC product availability along with the switch from Rx to OTC medications. OTC drugs marketed in the United States have been estimated at between 100,000 to 300,000 products. Consequently, the potential for adverse reactions has increased. The Office of Nonprescription Products within CDER is responsible for the regulation of OTC nonprescription drug products. OTC products are marketed in the United States under the OTC Drug Review Monograph system or by an approved new drug application. Launched in 1972, OTC Drug Review analyzes safety and efficacy for intended use.

Standards for safety, effectiveness and labeling for OTC products are detailed under 21 CFR 330.10 (a) (4). OTC safety means a low incidence of adverse reactions under adequate directions for use, a low probability for harm and inclusion of warnings against unsafe use. Monographs for OTC drug classes have been developed through the OTC Drug Review. For example, topical anti-fungal drugs are designated as a drug class. Each specific class of drugs describes the active ingredients predetermined for safety and efficacy along with the specifications for dosage amount and formulation requirements. Over 80 categories of OTC drugs exist with therapeutic categories that range from acne drugs to weight control drug products.

OTC Monograph products do not require any further FDA pre-clearance. However, drugs not covered under the OTC Drug Review Monograph system may be marketed as an OTC product under an approved new drug application. This means that a new drug application must be filed if there is no OTC Monograph. Usually, these products have already been marketed as prescription drugs and sufficient scientific and post marketing safety data demonstrates that the product can safely be "switched" to OTC status. Specific examples of product "switches" include antidiarrheals, acid reducers and antihistamines. At times, the dose of a "switched" product may be lower than the original prescription drug product. Other considerations prior to FDA approval to "switch" a prescription product to OTC may involve the potential for product abuse, potential harm from abuse, drug interactions, and need for further safety and efficacy data.

Drug Facts Labeling

Prior to 2002, the design, format and location of mandatory labeling varied widely among OTC products and consumers had difficulty in both reading and understanding OTC label information. In response, FDA established uniform labeling of (OTC) drug products that has involved a major overhaul of OTC labeling by pharmaceutical manufacturers. The "Drug Facts" labeling rule of 2002 provides for improved understanding of product information. The "Drug Facts" rule covers over 100,000 nonprescription products. A standardized arrangement allows for improved legibility, clarity and easier comparison.

First, drug product labels now include standardized headings, subheadings, and graphics in a uniform way. Second, manufacturers, distributors or packers are permitted to remove specific terms as long as the meaning of the information would not be changed. Third, the list of "interchangeable terms" is expanded to simplify the labeling. Fourth, specific warning language such as "keep out of reach of children", the pregnancy-nursing label and the overdose/accidental ingestion warning is standardized to make the warnings easier to understand and more succinct. The OTC format and content requirements apply to OTC applications, OTC products marketed under an existing final OTC drug monograph, and OTC drug products marketed under an approved application. Active ingredient is defined as follows:

"Any component that is intended to furnish pharmacological activity or other direct effect in the diagnosis, cure, mitigation, treatment, or prevention of disease, or to affect the structure of any

function of the body of humans or other animals. The term includes those components that may undergo chemical change in the manufacture of the drug product and be present in the drug product in a modified form intended to furnish the specified activity or effect."

FDA established minimum standards for reasons of consumer readability and comprehension. For example, type size, type style, letter and line spacing, contrast print and background color all perform an essential role in the readability of the OTC label. The rule established minimum type size for the title, headings, text and subheadings and a clear, easy-to-read style. Undoubtedly, the labeling changes enhanced appearance and readability. The following chart illustrates the standardized OTC label format.

Labeling Amendment Example—Acetaminophen Tylenol®

At times, it is necessary to amend the labeling of OTC products. Acetaminophen provides an excellent example. Over 600 OTC and prescription products contain acetaminophen. Studies have revealed that acetaminophen overdoses in the United States have led to approximately 80,000 visits to hospital emergency rooms. According to FDA and the CDC, there are approximately 500 deaths each year attributed to acetaminophen overdoses. Acetaminophen, is the nation's leading cause of sudden liver failure. To that end, Johnson & Johnson's Extra Strength Tylenol® bottles now contain a red warning label on the cap. The message on the cap states: "CONTAINS ACETAMINOPHEN" and "ALWAYS READ THE LABEL." *http://livertox.nih.gov/Acetaminophen.htm*

http://www.fda.gov/drugs/drugsafety/informationbydrugclass/ucm165107.htm

Over-the-Counter Recalls—Novartis and J&J

Novartis—There are recalls of OTC products and an example is the voluntary recall by Novartis Consumer Health, Inc. (Novartis). The voluntary recall involved all lots of select bottle packaging of Excedrin® and NoDoz® products as well as Bufferin® and Gas-X Prevention® products. Novartis issued the recall due to the possibility of stray tablets, capsules, or caplets from other Novartis products, and/or broken or chipped tablets.

See: *http://www.fda.gov/safety/recalls/ucm286240.htm*

J&J Criminal Fine—One of the largest product recalls involved OTC drugs of over 140 million bottles of children's medicines (2010) by McNeil Consumer Healthcare, a subsidiary of the Johnson & Johnson company. The OTC products included Tylenol®, Motrin®, Zyrtec®, and Benadryl® and necessitated closure of the McNeil facility (Fort Washington, PA) that manufactured these products. The recall involved quality, purity or potency issues. A recall of this magnitude is deemed serious especially due to the target population of children. Congressional hearings held in 2010 focused on the significant delay in the recall of the eight pill vials of Motrin® manufactured in the Puerto Rico facility.

Further, according to Congressional investigators, McNeil found out there was a problem with Motrin in the eight-vial packet because it did not dissolve properly. Dubbed a "phantom recall" by Congressional investigators, the Motrin problem was not deemed a recall by the company; rather "mystery shoppers" were used to purchase back the vials. However, this changed in 2009 when FDA insisted a formal recall be conducted. In 2015, Johnson & Johnson's McNeil Consumer Healthcare pled guilty and was fined $20 million and $5million forfeiture.

http://www.justice.gov/usao-edpa/pr/mcneil-ppc-inc-pleads-guilty-connection-adulterated-infants-and-childrens-liquid

CRITICAL ANALYSIS Using J&J as an example, detail specific enforcement FDA should exercise over OTC products.

Sunscreen Drug Products

https://www.congress.gov/bill/113th-congress/senate-bill/2141/text

The Sunscreen Innovation Act (SIA (Public Law No: 113-195 Nov. 26, 2014) established a new process for the review and approval of over-the-counter sunscreen active ingredients. The SIA provides FDA with explicit, expedited deadlines for review. The SIA is a major improvement as, for example, some sunscreen ingredients have been under review for numerous years.

Back in 1999, FDA established a monograph that specifies conditions under which over-the-counter (OTC) sunscreen drug products are generally recognized as safe, effective, and not misbranded. See: *Federal Register*, 64 FR 98 (May 21, 1999); See: *Federal Register,* 65 FR 111, June 8, 2000). The final sunscreen monograph, December 31, 2002, addressed formulation, labeling and testing requirements for ultraviolet B (UVB) and ultraviolet A (UVA) radiation protection and is applicable to all OTC sunscreen drug products under 21 CFR Parts 310, 352 and 700. Final Monograph (21 CFR part 352) *Sunscreen Drug Products for Over-the-Counter Human Use,* 68 FR 33381, June 4, 2003, part 352 was stayed effective June 4, 2004. In 2007, FDA issued a proposed rule to amend the final monograph for over-the-counter (OTC) sunscreen drug products. The amendment addressed formulation, labeling, indications, ingredients, directions and testing requirements for both ultraviolet B (UVB) and ultraviolet A (UVA) radiation protection. See: *Sunscreen Drug Products for Over-the-Counter Human Use; Proposed Amendment of Final Monograph*; Proposed Rule Federal Register Vol. 72, No. 165 (August 27, 2007). Then, in 2011, FDA issued a final rule effective June 18, 2012 (effective date extended to Dec. 17, 2012): *Labeling and Effectiveness Testing; Sunscreen Drug Products for Over-the-Counter Human Use,* which lifted the delay of implementation for sec. 201.66. Besides, the "Sunscreen Rule", FDA issued other important measures. See: 77 FR 27591-01, 21 CFR Parts 201 and 310.

Sunscreen Rule *http://www.fda.gov/ForConsumers/ConsumerUpdates/ucm258416.htm* **Labeling and Effectiveness Testing; Sunscreen Drug Products for Over-the-Counter Human Use. 21 CFR Parts 201 and 310 (June 9, 2011).** The final regulations establish standards for testing the effectiveness of sunscreen products and require labeling that accurately reflects test results. Key elements include: **Standard Test:** Establishes a standard test for over-the-counter sunscreen products that will determine which products are allowed to be labeled as "Broad Spectrum". Products that pass this test will provide protection against both ultraviolet B radiation (UVB) and ultraviolet A radiation (UVA). **Labeling:** Under the new regulations, sunscreen products that protect against all types of sun-induced skin damage are labeled **"Broad Spectrum" and "SPF 15"** (or higher) on the front. Informs consumers on the back of the product that sunscreens labeled as both "Broad Spectrum" and "SPF 15" (or higher) not only protect against sunburn, but, if used as directed with other sun protection measures, can reduce the risk of skin cancer and early skin aging. For these broad spectrum products, higher SPF (Sun Protection Factor) values also indicate higher levels of overall protection. By contrast, any sunscreen not labeled as "Broad Spectrum" or that has an SPF value between 2 and 14, has only been shown to help prevent sunburn. **Warning:** Sunscreen products that are not broad spectrum or that are broad spectrum with SPF values from 2 to14 must be labeled with a warning that reads: **"Skin Cancer/Skin Aging Alert: Spending time in the sun increases your risk of skin cancer and early skin aging. This product has been shown only to help prevent sunburn, not skin cancer or early skin aging."** **Claims:** Water resistance claims on the product's front label must tell how much time a user can expect to get the declared SPF level of protection while swimming or sweating, based on standard testing. Two times are permitted on labels: 40 minutes or 80 minutes. Manufacturers cannot make claims that sunscreens are "waterproof" or "sweatproof", or identify their products as "sunblocks." In addition, sunscreens cannot claim protection immediately on application (for example, "instant protection") or protection for more than two hours without reapplication, unless they submit data and get FDA approval. *Enforcement Guidance* FDA issued an Enforcement Draft guidance at the same time as the "Sunscreen Rule" for sunscreen manufacturers on how to test and label their products in light of these new measures.	Rule Issued: June 9, 2011 Compliance Date of June 18, 2012 delayed until December 17, 2012. Compliance date of June 17, 2013 delayed until December 17, 2013 with annual sales less than $25,000.
Sunscreen Sprays An **Advanced Notice of Rule Making** was issued at the same time as the "Sunscreen Rule". The Notice concerns a data request for safety and effectiveness information for sunscreen products formulated in certain dosage forms (e.g., sprays).	Notice Issued: June 9, 2011.
Proposed Regulation SPF 50+ FDA proposed a regulation that would limit the maximum SPF value on sunscreen labeling to "SPF 50+". The FDA proposed Rule sets forth that the maximum labeled SPF value for over the counter (OTC) sunscreen products would be "50&plus". The proposed rule comes after a data review showed that there is not currently sufficient data to indicate that there is additional clinical benefit above SPF 50. There was not adequate data that demonstrated that a sunscreen product with an SPF value over 50 provided an increase in clinical benefit over a sunscreen product with an SPF value of over 50. Written or electronic comments were due by Sept. 15, 2011.	Proposed Rule Issued: June 9, 2011.

Sunscreen Drug Products: Original Active Ingredients and Labeling

Advance Notice Of Proposed Rulemaking	**Date**	*FR* **Citation**
Advance Notice of Proposed Rulemaking	8/25/1978	43FR38206

Extension of Comment Period	12/1/1978	43FR56249	
Correction	12/12/1978	43FR58097	
Correction	12/29/1978	43FR60957	
Reopening of Administrative Record	3/21/1980	45FR18403	
Public Meeting: SPF testing	9/4/1987	52FR33598	
Extension of Comment Period: SPF testing	12/4/1987	52FR46095	
Reopening of Administrative Record: SPF testing	5/4/1988	53FR15853	
Proposed Rule	**Date**	***FR* Citation**	
Tentative Final Monograph	5/12/1993	58FR28194	
Extension of Comment Period	10/15/1993	58FR53460	
Reopening of Comment Period	2/11/1994	59FR6606	
Notice: Public meeting	8/15/1996	61FR42398	
Final Rule	**Date**	***FR* Citation**	
Final Monograph	5/21/1999	64FR27666	
Extension of Effective Date	6/8/2000	65FR36319	
Partial Stay of Effective Date	12/31/2001	66FR67485	
Delay of Drug Fact Implementation	9/3/2004	69FR53801	
Technical Amendment: Incorporates 4 U.S.P. name changes	6/20/2002	67FR41821	
Notice: Guidance on 4 U.S.P. name changes	6/3/2003	68FR33164	
Sunscreen Drug Products: Time and Extent Applications			
Advance Notice Of Proposed Rulemaking	**Date**	***FR* Citation**	
Request for Data: Amiloxate, enzacamene, and octyl triazone	7/11/2003	68FR41386	
Request for Data: Bisoctrizole and bemotrizonol	12/5/2005	70FR72449	
Request for Data: Diethylhexyl butamido triazone	7/26/2006	71FR42405	
Request for Data: Terephthalylidene dicamphor sulfonic acid (ecamsule)	9/12/2008	73FR53029	
Request for Data: Drometrizole Trisiloxane [PDF]	6/2/2010	75FR30838	
Sunscreen Drug Products: Avobenzone			
Proposed Rule	**Date**	***FR* Citation**	
Proposed Rule [PDF]	9/16/1996	61FR48645	
Correction [PDF]	10/11/1996	61FR53340	
Correction [PDF]	2/26/1997	62FR8663	
Enforcement of Policy: Allows avobenzone marketing [PDF]	4/30/1997	62FR23350	
Final Rule	**Date**	***FR* Citation**	
Final Monograph [PDF]	5/21/1999	64FR27666	
Extension of Effective Date [PDF]	6/8/2000	65FR36319	
Partial Stay of Effective Date [PDF]	12/31/2001	66FR67485	
Delay of Drug Fact Implementation [PDF]	9/3/2004	69FR53801	

Technical Amendment: Incorporates 4 U.S.P. name changes [PDF]	6/20/2002	67FR41821
Sunscreen Drug Products: UVA Protection		
Advance Notice Of Proposed Rulemaking	**Date**	**FR Citation**
Notice: Public Meeting	4/5/1994	59FR16042
Proposed Rules	**Date**	**FR Citation**
Proposed Rule: UVA Testing and Labeling	8/27/2007	72FR49070
Extension of Comment Period	11/28/2007	72FR67264
Sunscreen Drug Products: Zinc Oxide		
	Date	**FR Citation**
Proposed Rule	10/22/1998	63FR56584
Final Rule	**Date**	**FR Citation**
Final Monograph	5/21/1999	64FR27666
Extension of Effective Date	6/8/2000	65FR36319
Partial Stay of Effective Date	12/31/2001	66FR67485
Delay of Drug Fact Implementation	9/3/2004	69FR53801
Technical Amendment: Incorporates 4 U.S.P. name changes	6/20/2002	67FR41821
Notice: Guidance on 4 U.S.P. name changes	6/3/2003	68FR33164

http://www.fda.gov/Drugs/DevelopmentApprovalProcess/DevelopmentResources/Over-the-Coun-
terOTCDrugs/StatusofOTCRulemakings/ucm072134.htm

CRITICAL ANALYSIS I: Evaluate the following: The "Sunscreen Rule", "sprays" from a safety and effectiveness standpoint and the proposed regulation "SPF 50+" SPF maximum value to sunscreen labeling.

CRITICAL ANALYSIS II: Review the SIA link below. Devise a legal plan that addresses consumer confusion with sunscreen products. Assess whether the SIA provides a realistic plan considering due process yet undue delay.

https://www.congress.gov/bill/113th-congress/senate-bill/2141/text

Warning Statement: Tanning Products Without Sunscreen

http://www.fda.gov/Cosmetics/ProductandIngredientSafety/ProductInformation/ucm134252.htm

Suntan products that do not contain sunscreen ingredients must include a warning statement on the label that the product does not contain sunscreen ingredients and does not protect against sunburn. All suntan preparations that do not contain sunscreen ingredients are required to carry the following warning statement on the label pursuant to Title 21 CFR Section 740.19):

> *"Warning—This product does not contain a sunscreen and does not protect against sunburn. Repeated exposure of unprotected skin while tanning may increase the risk of skin aging, skin cancer, and other harmful effects to the skin even if you do not burn."*

Suntan preparations include gels, creams, liquids, and other topical products that are intended to provide cosmetic effects on the skin while tanning through exposure to ultraviolet (UV) radiation (such as moisturizing or conditioning products) or to give the appearance of a tan by imparting color to the skin through the application of approved color additives, such as dihydroxyacetone, without the need for exposure to UV radiation.

CRITICAL ANALYSIS: Evaluate the above warning statement in terms of consumer protection. Recommend improvements to the warning statement.

Chapter 5: Direct-to-Consumer Promotion and Marketing
http://www.fda.gov/AboutFDA/CentersOffices/OfficeofMedicalProductsandTobacco/CDER/ucm090142.htm

It is indeed difficult to imagine a "moratorium" on direct-to-consumer promotion. Yet, a moratorium did occur in 1983 so that FDA could evaluate this issue. The moratorium was withdrawn in 1985 and this effectively opened the floodgates to this type of advertising. See: 50 FR 36677 (September 9, 1985). Prior to the early 1980's, product sponsors disseminated materials for patients through health care professionals and not directly to the consumer. Direct-to-Consumer Promotion (DTC) for prescription drugs started in the early 1980's and focused on consumer concerns about certain medical conditions, for instance, pneumonia and arthritis. In the 1990's, advertisements directed toward consumers greatly increased both in print and television media. In the 2000s, social media is utilized to promote drug products. Besides New Zealand, the United States is the only other country in the world that advertises directly to consumers. Suffice it to state, drug advertising expenditures have escalated to billions of dollars.

Consumers are inundated with DTC advertisements by the Internet, print media, television, radio and other social media methods. Billions of dollars are spent on an annual basis. According to FDA, surveys have indicated that DTC encourages patients to inquire about a medical condition that they might not have asked their physician previously.

Advantages: Greater consumer knowledge; Increased responsibility in the decision-making process; and Improved communication and dialog between patients and physicians.

Disadvantages: Overall, opponents assert that direct-to-consumer promotion diminishes and hinders the role of the physician. Some courts have recognized an advertising exception to the learned intermediary doctrine. See *e.g., Perez v. Wyeth Laboratories,* 734 A.2d 1245 (N.J. 1999), where the court determined that the advertising about a contraceptive product interfered with and diminished the doctor patient relationship. The *Perez* Court determined that a drug manufacturer that advertises directly to the public cannot rely on the learned intermediary doctrine. In contrast, just prior to the *Perez* decision, the court, *In re Norplant Contraceptive Products Liability Litigation,* 165 F.3d 374 (5th Cir. 1999) reached an opposite result and held that direct marketing to consumers did not abrogate the learned intermediary doctrine thereby preserving the learned intermediary doctrine intact. See *State Ex Rel. & Johnson,* 647 S.E.2d 899 where the court refused to adopt the learned intermediary doctrine because of direct-to-consumer promotion.

Another disadvantage could entail confusion to the consumer in terms of either insufficient or excessive information. The advertisement must present the major risk information; however, an open question remains as to whether this can be effectively accomplished through social media, television or print advertising. Finally, other disadvantages include prescription overuse and promotion of costlier treatments. Yet, direct-to-consumer promotion continues to flourish.

NOTE: See Direct-to-Consumer Pharmaceutical Advertising Therapeutic or Toxic?
C. Lee Ventola, MS *http://www.ncbi.nlm.nih.gov/pmc/articles/PMC3278148/*

CRITICAL ANALYSIS I: Should drug companies who use direct-to-consumer promotion be required to include the suggested retail price in the advertisement?

CRITICAL ANALYSIS II: Discuss the ethics of using "celebrity or well-known figures" as spokespeople in drug promotion.

Office of Prescription Drug Promotion Oversight and Enforcement
http://www.fda.gov/AboutFDA/CentersOffices/OfficeofMedicalProductsandTobacco/CDER/ucm090142.htm

The Office of Prescription Drug Promotion (OPDP), formerly the Division of Drug Marketing, Advertising and Communications (DDMAC) regulates prescription drug promotion. The mission of the Office of Prescription Drug Promotion (OPDP) within FDA is to: *"To protect the public health by ensuring that prescription drug information is truthful, balanced, and accurately communicated. This is accomplished through a comprehensive surveillance, enforcement, and education program, and by fostering better communication of labeling and promotional information to both healthcare professionals and consumers."*

To accomplish this mission FDA aims to conduct comprehensive surveillance, enforcement and education, and communication of labeling and promotional information to healthcare professionals and consumers. For example, the "Bad Ad" program, initiated in 2010, aims to educate health care providers about how they can assist in ferreting out misleading and or untruthful drug promotion. Further, Section 906 of FDAAA mandated that published direct-to-consumer advertisements for prescription drugs include the following statement printed in conspicuous text:

"You are encouraged to report negative side effects of prescription drugs to the FDA.
Visit www.fda.gov/medwatch, or call 1-800-FDA-1088."

The OPDP monitors prescription drug advertising to ensure the advertisement contains a truthful summary of information about effectiveness, side effects, and circumstances of when the product should not be used. OPDP reviewers have responsibility for assessing prescription drug advertising and promotional labeling to ensure that the information contained in these promotional materials is not false or misleading. They engage in a variety of tasks to perform this responsibility, including: providing written comments to pharmaceutical sponsors on proposed promotional materials to ensure clear and unambiguous communication of the laws and regulations relating to prescription drug promotion; reviewing complaints about alleged promotional violations; initiating enforcement actions on promotional materials that are false or misleading; comparing the product labeling and promotional materials of various closely related products to ensure that the regulatory requirements are consistently and equitably applied; traveling to major medical meetings and pharmaceutical conventions to monitor promotional exhibits and activities; and acting as a liaison between OPDP and other divisions within the FDA on promotional issues. FDA may require a corrective advertisement. The FDAAA contains a provision for direct-to-consumer promotion submissions. The issuance of warning letters by the OPDP continues to increase.

Oversight Besides FDA

Other government and private oversight besides FDA includes the following: FTC, States Attorneys General, Lanham Act action, and the National Advertising Division (NAD). The Federal Trade Commission (FTC) regulates advertising of OTC nonprescription products. Advertisements must be truthful, non-deceptive and not misleading in any material respect. FTC requires that advertisers must have evidence to support advertising claims. FTC considers representations made or suggested and the extent to which the advertisement fails to reveal material facts. FTC evaluates the advertisement using a "reasonable consumer" standard. The context of the advertisement, that is, words, pictures and phrases are all considered. Express claims are examined as well as implied or indirect claims.

A company may bring an action in federal court under the Lanham Act, which authorizes a plaintiff to initiate a legal action pertaining to false or misleading advertising. See: for example, *PhotoMedex v. Irwin*, 601 F.3d 919 (9th Cir.2010). Finally, NAD, of the Better Business Bureau, is a voluntary and industry supported type of self-regulation where advertising is reviewed on NAD's initiative or due to a complaint by a competitor.

NOTE: State Attorneys General may join the FTC, the United States Department of Justice or institute enforcement along with other states under state consumer protection laws such as prohibitions on unfair and deceptive practices. See this Volume Chapter 7 for examples.

Legal Authority Under the FDCA

The pertinent section under the FDCA, 502(n), 21 U.S.C. section 352(n), applies to prescription drug advertisements. Section 352(n) requires that advertisements for prescription drugs and biological products include a true statement of information in brief summary that relates to the side effects, contraindications, and effectiveness. The prescription drug advertising regulations under

21 C.F.R. section 202.1 (e)(3)(iii) specify that risks must cover each specific side effect and contraindication from the drug product's approved labeling. FDA uses its regulatory authority and has issued, for example, regulatory action letters to companies for prescription drug promotions determined to be false, misleading or lacking in fair balance of risks and benefits.

What Constitutes Advertising—Accompanying regulations under 21 C.F.R. 202.1(l) (1)(2) state that advertisements encompass those published in journals, magazines, other periodicals, and newspapers; and broadcast through media such as radio, television, videotapes and telephone communications systems. FDA regulates advertising conducted by sales representatives, advertising on computer programs, through fax machines, or on electronic bulletin boards. Other examples of the types of promotional materials or labeling are booklets, brochures, bulletins, calendars, catalogs, mailing pieces, exhibits and motion picture films.

General Requirements—Under section 502(n), 21 U.S.C. 352(n), of the FDCA, advertisements must include: the established name, the brand name if any, the formula showing quantitatively each ingredient, and a "brief summary". A "brief summary", detailed in 21 C.F.R. 202.1(e)(1) and (e)(3)(iii), means information that relates to side effects, effectiveness and contraindications. The prescription drug advertising regulations, 21 CFR 202.1, differentiate between print and broadcast advertisements. Print advertisements must include the "brief summary", which generally contains each of the risk concepts from the product's approved package labeling. Broadcast advertisements through media such as television, radio, or telephone communications systems must disclose the product's major risks in either the audio or audio and visual parts of the presentation. This is described as the "major statement". Crucial principles for all types of prescription drug advertisements are that the advertisement must not be false or misleading, the advertisement must present a fair balance and the advertisement must include material facts.

Specific Terminology—"FDA approved", "New", "Drug of Choice"

"FDA Approved"—FDAMA eliminated the FDCA prior prohibition on the use of any representation or suggestion that the product was approved. Therefore, if a manufacturer or sponsor has received an approval letter stating the product has been approved, then the advertising may include the phrase "FDA approved".

"New"—OPDP considers the word "New" an accurate description for marketing purposes for six months from the time a product is initially marketed not the time the product is cleared by FDA for marketing.

"Drug of Choice"—Terminology implies superiority and the advertisement or labeling would require substantiation to support the claim.

Adverse Event Reporting—Section 906 of FDAAA mandated that published direct-to-consumer advertisements for prescription drugs include the following statement printed in conspicuous text:
> *"You are encouraged to report negative side effects of prescription drugs to the FDA.*
> *Visit www.fda.gov/medwatch, or call 1-800-FDA-1088."*

Required Pre-Dissemination Review of Promotional Materials

Previously, FDA only required pre-dissemination review under limited circumstances. For example, FDA required "pre-approval" of direct-to-consumer advertising for accelerated products for serious and life-threatening illnesses. However, the Food and Drug Administration Amendments Act of 2007 (FDAAA) gave FDA the authority to require pre-dissemination review of any television advertisement for a drug not later than 45 days before dissemination of the television advertisement. 21 U.S.C. sec. 353 (b).

The draft guidance below specifies the pre-dissemination categories that FDA intends to require sponsors in submitting TV advertisements. The categories were developed in accordance to a risk-based approach. The goal in adhering to the public protection mandate of the FDCA and FDAAA amendments is to review advertisements for products that present a high risk as well as efficacy statements related to specific populations such as the elderly, children, and racial and ethnic minorities.

Direct-to-Consumer Television Advertisements—FDAAA DTC Television Ad
Pre-Dissemination Review Program Draft Guidance (March 2012).
http://www.fda.gov/downloads/Drugs/GuidanceComplianceRegulatoryInformation/Guid-
ances/UCM295554.pdf

> ➢ Category 1: The initial TV ad for any prescription drug or the initial TV ad for a new or expanded approved indication for any prescription drug.
> ➢ Category 2: All TV ads for prescription drugs subject to a Risk Evaluation and Mitigation Strategy (REMS) with elements to assure safe use (see section 505-1(f) of the FDCA).
> ➢ Category 3: All TV ads for Schedule II controlled substances.
> ➢ Category 4: The first TV ad for a prescription drug following a safety labeling update that affects the Boxed Warning, Contraindications, or Warnings & Precautions section of its labeling.
> ➢ Category 5: The first TV ad for a prescription drug following the receipt by the sponsor of an enforcement letter (i.e. a Warning or untitled letter) for that product that either cites a TV ad or causes a TV ad to be discontinued because the TV ad contained violations similar to the ones cited in the enforcement letter.
> ➢ Category 6: Any TV ad that is otherwise identified by FDA as subject to the pre-dissemination review provision.

Expedited review is given to materials used in newly approved products or products with new indications. Television and radio advertisements receive expedited review as well. OPDP reviews promotional materials at exhibits and professional meetings as well as complaints about promotion from competitors, health care professionals and consumers. The OPDP may still issue advisory letters on proposed advertisements and labeling prior to dissemination. The regulations apply to all holders of NDA, ANDA and antibiotic applications.

NOTE: User Fees and Submission of Promotional Materials—The FDA Amendments Act (FDAAA) had legislated a voluntary direct-to-consumer (DTC) television advertisement user fee program for pre-broadcast review. "Fees Relating to Advisory Review of Prescription-Drug Television Advertising". However, the user program was not implemented due to lack of Congressional authorization. See: User Fee Program for Advisory Review of Direct-to-Consumer Television Advertisements for Prescription Drug and Biological Products; Program Will Not Be Implemented (73 FR 2924-01).

Product Claim Advertisements—Full Requirements

Full advertising requirements apply to product claim promotion about a prescription drug. "Product claim" advertisements must include a fair balance of the risks and benefits and all risk information in the FDA-approved labeling.

Disclosure Requirements for Product Claim Advertisements

Print Advertisements—Disclosure of Risks in "Brief Summary" requirement of product's labeling and fair balance and material facts and not false or misleading.

Brief Summary-Disclosing Risk Information in Consumer-Directed Print Advertisements Draft Guidance—Issued in January 2004, the draft guidance details compliance for print advertisements in a more "user consumer friendly manner". Previously, print advertisements usually included a reprinting of the risk related section of the product's labeling, known as the full prescribing information or the package insert. The advertising text itself usually includes the non-risk related information such as dosage information, the quantity of drug in each pill and how the product works. In 2009, FDA issued a draft guidance related to how to present risk information in a more user-friendly format as follows.

Presenting **Risk Information** *in Prescription Drug and* **Medical Device** *Promotion Draft Guidance* was issued in May 2009. According to FDA, manufacturers fulfill the brief summary requirement by including the complete risk-related sections of the FDA-approved professional labeling in the ad in small type. Although risk information presented in this format technically complies with applicable regulations, the information presented in this manner is not user friendly. The purpose of the draft guidance is to encourage manufacturers to impart the information in a more user friendly manner as follows:

http://www.fda.gov/downloads/drugs/guidancecomplianceregulatoryinformation/guidances/ucm155480.pdf

Reprinted as Approved—FDA approved patient labeling as long as the labeling is reprinted in full and includes information from the advertised product's of FDA-approved professional labeling that address certain risks including:

> ➤ All contraindications;
> ➤ All warnings;
> ➤ Major precautions; and
> ➤ Adverse reactions (3-5 most common non-serious).

Reprinted Risk Information Only—FDA approved patient labeling even if the labeling is modified to contain only risk information by deleting instructions for use and includes information from the advertised product's of FDA-approved professional labeling that address certain risks:

> ➤ All contraindications;
> ➤ All warnings;
> ➤ Major precautions; and
> ➤ Adverse reactions (3-5 most common non-serious).

Broadcast Advertisements—"Major Statement" of contraindications and side effects *and a* "Brief Summary" or "Adequate Provision" directing consumers to labeling information.

***Consumer Directed Broadcast Advertising Guidance for Industry* (Final Guidance 1999)**.
http://www.fda.gov/RegulatoryInformation/Guidances/ucm125039.htm

Television advertisements present unique challenges in terms of compliance and consumer understanding of the "brief summary". In short, the "brief summary" listing of adverse events and other product information, used in television advertisements, ended up being confusing to consumers rather than consumer friendly; therefore, product sponsors resorted to the use of "reminder" advertisements because "reminder" advertisements are not required to contain a "brief summary". The guidance is intended to assist sponsors who are interested in advertising their prescription human and animal drugs, including biological products for humans, directly to consumers through broadcast media, such as television, radio, or telephone communications systems. For prescription drugs and biologics, the FDCA requires advertisements to contain information in brief summary relating to side effects, contraindications, and effectiveness (21 U.S.C. 352(n)). See: 21 CFR 202.1. The resulting information disclosure is commonly called the brief summary.

Broadcast advertisements have the following two specific requirements:

"Major statement" requirement which means including all of the major risk information related to the product in the audio or audio and visual part of the advertisement; **and a**

"Brief summary" requirement **or "Adequate Provision"** requirement. Fulfilling the adequate provision can be accomplished in several ways. Disclosure can be accomplished by reference to the following:

1. Disclosure of a toll-free telephone number for consumers to call to have approved labeling mailed or read by selecting a prerecorded topic;
2. Disclosure that a healthcare provider such as physician or pharmacist may provide additional product information;
3. Reference in the advertisement to concurrently available print information;
4. Reference to an Internet web page address, URL that provides access to the package labeling.

The Broadcast Guidance assumes that such advertisements:

> ➤ Are not false or misleading in any respect. For a prescription drug, this would include communicating that the advertised product is available only by prescription and that only a prescribing healthcare professional can decide whether the product is appropriate for a patient;
> ➤ Present a fair balance between information about effectiveness and information about risk;
> ➤ Include a thorough major statement conveying all of the product's most important risk information in consumer-friendly language; and

> ➢ Communicate all information relevant to the product's indication (including limitations to use) in consumer-friendly language.

Exceptions to the Full Advertising Requirements

Exemptions from the advertising regulations are detailed under 21 CFR 202.1(e)(2) and include reminder and help seeking advertisements, advertisements of bulk-sale drugs and advertisements of compounded drugs. The following lists the types of advertisements that are exemptions from the "brief summary" requirement:

Advertisements of Bulk-sale drugs promote sale of the drug in bulk packages to be processed, manufactured, labeled, or repackaged and contain no claims for the therapeutic safety or effectiveness of the drug are also excluded.

Advertisements of prescription-compounding drugs promote sale of a drug for use as a prescription chemical or other compound for use by registered pharmacists are excluded as well.

Reminder advertisements usually do not have the same requirements for disclosure as product claim(s) advertisements unless the advertisement is deemed a "Bookend advertisement" discussed later in this chapter. Reminder advertisements that call attention to the *name* of the drug product but do not include indications or dosage recommendations for use of the product or any other representation are exempt. Reminder advertisements include the proprietary name of the drug and the established name of each active ingredient. The name of the company, price, or dosage form may be included. However, the "reminder ad" exception does not apply to products with black box warnings in their approved product labeling nor is the exception applicable if the advertisement is a "Bookend advertisement".

Help seeking advertisements discuss a disease or condition and advise the viewer to "see your doctor" and do not mention or imply a drug product are similarly exempt unless deemed a "Bookend advertisement".

Promotional messages for specific treatments for a disease are usually subject to FDA regulation as advertising or promotional labeling. However, exceptions are as follows:

1. *A "reminder" piece, which includes the name of a drug or device but makes no safety or effectiveness claims or a full product promotional piece.*
2. *Disease awareness or "help seeking" message, which encourages consumers to seek health care practitioner assistance or practitioners to provide such assistance in identifying and treating a particular health condition but does not mention any product by name.*

The FDA rules for risk disclosure are inapplicable if the disease awareness and reminder communications are presented alone. However, "when reminder and disease awareness or full product and disease awareness pieces that use similar themes, story lines or other presentation elements are taken together", FDA will regulate the advertisements as product claims requiring risk disclose. The guidance clarifies the term "Bookend" advertisements in print or broadcast formats. The draft guidance above imparts advice to manufacturers on the standards FDA uses in determining whether such disease awareness messages are subject to regulation as advertisement or labeling. These criteria assess whether the two components are perceptually distinct and whether they are separated in space or time. FDA recommends the following content for Disease Awareness Communications:

> ➢ *Disease or health condition specific;*
> ➢ *Enhance consumer or health practitioner education;*
> ➢ *Clear and specific;*
> ➢ *Identify the population at risk or affected by the disease or health condition and*
> ➢ *Contain a responsible public health message; and*
> ➢ *Refer consumers to a qualified healthcare practitioner and discourage self-treatment.*

Guidance Documents Related to Promotion

Over the years, FDA has issued several other guidance documents related to direct-to-consumer promotion as follows:

https://www.fda.gov/AnimalVeterinary/GuidanceComplianceEnforcement/GuidanceforIndustry/ucm123607.htm

➤ *Presenting Quantitative Efficacy and Risk Information in Direct-to-Consumer Promotional Labeling and Advertisements; Draft Guidance for Industry, 83 FR 52484-01, 2018.*

➤ *"Help Seeking and Disease Awareness Communications by or on Behalf of Drug and Device Firms"http://www.fda.gov/downloads/Drugs/GuidanceComplianceRegulatoryInformation/Guidances/UCM070068.pdf. This draft guidance, issued in 2004, "clarifies the criteria that FDA will use to distinguish manufacturer communications that provide information about the importance of recognizing that certain signs and symptoms may be evidence of a treatable disease from manufacturer promotional messages for particular treatments for a disease."*

➤ *Brief Summary and Adequate Directions for Use: Disclosing Risk Information in Consumer-Directed Print Advertisements* Revised Draft Guidance (Feb. 2015) Revised Aug. 5, 2015 to incorporate prescription animal drugs) (original draft guidance issued 2004).

➤ *Fulfilling Regulatory Requirements for Postmarketing Submissions of Interactive Promotional Media for Prescription Human and Animal Drugs and Biologics Draft (2014). http://www.fda.gov/downloads/Drugs/GuidanceComplianceRegulatoryInformation/Guidances/UCM381352.pdf*

➤ *Distributing Scientific and Medical Publications on Risk Information for Approved Prescription Drugs and Biological Products—Recommended Practices (2014)*

➤ *Distributing Scientific and Medical Publications on Unapproved New Uses — Recommended Practices - Revised Guidance (2014).*

➤ *Internet/Social Media Platforms: Correcting Independent Third-Party Misinformation About Prescription Drugs and Medical Devices (2014).*

➤ *Product Name Placement, Size, and Prominence in Advertising and Promotional Labeling Draft (2013).*

➤ *Direct-to-Consumer Television Advertisements—FDAAA DTC Television Ad Pre-Dissemination Review Program* Draft Guidance (2012);

➤ *Presenting* Risk Information *in Prescription Drug and* Medical Device *Promotion* Draft Guidance (2009);

➤ *"Help-Seeking" and Other Disease Awareness Communications by or on Behalf of Drug and Device Firms* Draft Guidance (2004); and

➤ *Consumer Directed Broadcast Advertising Guidance for Industry Final Guidance (1999).*

CRITICAL ANALYSIS: Europe utilizes unbranded advertisements about disease awareness and permits a company to use a logo. Similarly, companies in the United States have used disease awareness communications as well. Discuss the advantages and disadvantages of disease awareness communications by drug companies.

Social Media Platforms and FDA Guidance

The social media market boom continues to escalate. Today, the phrases "Follow us on Facebook" and "We're on Twitter" remain common everyday marketing techniques. Even FDA regulated companies have joined in the social media foray. Interestingly, in the past, Facebook permitted a request by a pharmaceutical company to block the public's ability to openly comment on a page Wall. However, that changed in 2011, as public comments are not prevented anymore.

The Internet is a constant in society and today, more than ever, consumers may resort to self-medication by using the Internet because "going to the neighborhood doctor or neighborhood pharmacy" has decreased. Yet, the cost of health care continues to escalate. At times, consumers cannot rely on physicians for their medical advice and expertise. Rather, in our high-tech society, the Internet replaces the person-to-person contact in medicine today. FDA noted benefits include access and convenience whereas risks include unapproved drugs; drugs dispensed without a prescription and fraudulent products. Now, there is Web 1.0 through Web 4.0. The simplest explanation is that Web 1.0 is company controlled in a read only format. Web 2.0 is not company controlled and anyone can post commentary and "conversate" which is a term coined by the social media field as "conversation". Web. 3.0 pertains to computer execution and Web 4 is a linkage with other devices such as a mobile telephone. There are also Web Blogs and examples of Web Blogs (Blogs) include Blogger, WordPress and TypePad. Twitter is an example of a micro Blog. Nearly everyone is aware of YouTube, a video sharing website. Finally, "Wiki" is another popular website where anyone with access can modify. Popular Wikis include Wikipedia and Sidewiki. Does FDA regulate social media? FDA's Office of Prescription Drug Promotion indeed regulates social media use by pharmaceutical companies. Warning letters were sent about a YouTube video, "banner ads", sponsored links and webcasts.

The Code of Federal Regulations does not define "social media". Online advertising and sales of prescription drugs through the Internet continues to proliferate. FDA solicited comments and held a public hearing in 2009 on how companies use the web and social media tools to promote their products. The FDA Center's involved included FDA's Center for Drug Evaluation and Research (CDER), in collaboration with FDA's Center for Biologics Evaluation and Research (CBER), Center for Veterinary Medicine (CVM), and Center for Devices and Radiological Health (CDRH). FDA sought participation and comments from: consumers, patients, caregivers, health care professionals, patient groups, Internet vendors, advertising agencies, and the regulated industry. Two years later, in 2011, a draft guidance was issued, titled: *"Responding to Unsolicited Requests for Off-Label Information About Prescription Drugs and Medical Devices."* Yet, the draft guidance is limited to off-label issues and does not address social media issues such as for promotion purposes by the regulated community.

The Food and Drug Administration Safety and Innovation Act of 2012 (FDASIA) required FDA to address the social media issues in the form of a guidance document(s) by July 9, 2014. In accordance with the FDASIA, FDA issued two draft guidances in 2014 as detailed below. Despite the issuance of Guidance Documents, FDA has not issued new regulations about social media and admittedly the definition of labeling under 21 CFR sec. 201.1 (*l*)(1) remains outdated (lantern slides were introduced in 1849 and have not been used since 1950). Now that industry has some guidance will FDA enforce social media use? According to FDA's Office of Prescription Drug Promotion with the issuance of the two guidances in 2014 that pertain to electronic and digital media there will be enhanced scrutiny. In so doing, FDA is communicating expectations to the regulated industry. Yet, these draft guidances have met with controversy. The guidance below discusses space limitations such as Twitter and the guidance that follows concerns correcting misinformation from third parties.

http://www.fda.gov/downloads/Drugs/GuidanceComplianceRegulatoryInformation/Guidances/UCM285145.pd

Internet/Social Media Platforms with Character Space Limitations—Presenting Risk and Benefit Information for Prescription Drugs and Medical Devices

http://www.fda.gov/downloads/Drugs/GuidanceComplianceRegulatoryInformation/Guidances/UCM401087.pdf

This draft guidance, 79 FR 34759, issued June 2014 explains how manufacturers, packers and distributors of prescription drugs and devices should present both benefit and risk information within advertising and promotional labeling on electronic/digital platforms that are associated with character space limitations, specifically on the Internet and through social media or other technological venues. Internet/social media platforms with character space limitations include online microblog messaging (Twitter messages or "tweets," changed from 140 to 240-character spaces per tweet) and online paid search ("sponsored links" on search engines such as Google and Yahoo, which have limited character spaces). Major points:

Product claims—Benefit information and indicated use must be accurate and non-misleading and disclose material facts within each individual character-space-limited communication (e.g., each individual message or tweet).

Risk information—Must be disclosed within each individual character-space-limited communication.

Character Space Limitations such as Twitter—Risk information should be presented together with benefit information within each individual character-space-limited communication (e.g., each individual message or tweet). Risk information content presented within each individual character-space-limited communication should, at a minimum, include the most serious risks associated with the product.

Risk information prominence should be comparable to the benefit information within each individual character-space-limited communication, taking into consideration any formatting capabilities available on the specific Internet/social media platform. A hyperlink, for example, should also be provided within each individual character space limited communication to permit direct access to a more complete discussion of risk information.

NOTE: According to the guidance, if a company determines that adequate benefit and risk information, including other required information, cannot all be communicated within the same character-space-limited communication, then a company should reexamine using that platform for the intended promotional message.

CRITICAL ANALYSIS: Fair Balance and Twitter—Twitter now permits 240 characters "tweets". How can fair balance including risk information be achieved on Twitter based on the FDA issued (draft) guidance (see above)?

Internet/Social Media Platforms—Correcting Independent Third-Party Misinformation About Prescription Drugs and Medical Devices

http://www.fda.gov/downloads/Drugs/GuidanceComplianceRegulatoryInformation/Guidances/UCM401079.pdf

This draft guidance, also issued in June 2014, describes how drug and device manufacturers, packers, and distributors should respond, if they choose to respond, to misinformation created and disseminated by independent third parties on the Internet or through social media platforms. According to FDA appropriate corrective action by a company should be as follows:

> ➢ *Relevant and responsive to the misinformation;*
> ➢ *Limited and tailored to the misinformation;*
> ➢ *Non-promotional in nature, tone, and presentation;*
> ➢ *Accurate;*
> ➢ *Consistent with the FDA-required labeling for the product;*
> ➢ *Supported by sufficient evidence, including substantial evidence, when appropriate, for prescription drugs;*
> ➢ *Either be posted in conjunction with the misinformation in the same area or forum (if posted directly to the forum by the firm) or should reference the misinformation and be intended to be posted in conjunction with the misinformation (if provided to the forum operator or author) (see section IV.B); and*
> ➢ *Disclose that the person providing the corrective information is affiliated with the firm that manufactures, packs, or distributes the product.*

CRITICAL ANALYSIS: Assess whether a drug company who becomes aware via a social media post of an adverse event (Blog, Twitter, Facebook) has a legal duty to track, investigate and report the adverse event(s) to FDA.

Social Media Data Mining and Reportable Adverse Events

Mining of social media sites such as Twitter and Facebook for consumer buying behavior and adverse events by drug companies and health-care providers is on the rise. FDA has indicated that if a company chooses to monitor a site and becomes aware of adverse event information they are required to review the information and if necessary, report it to FDA. According to FDA, an adverse experience from an Internet source is considered to be a spontaneously reported event. A spontaneously reported adverse event, such as a post on Twitter or Facebook, must have an:

> ➢ Identifiable reporter;
> ➢ Identifiable patient;
> ➢ Adverse experience; and
> ➢ A suspect drug or biological product.

Who Should Mind the Internet Drugstore?

Used with permission: Copyright © American Law Media, (updated and modified 2018)

How and who should the advertising of medicines over the Internet be monitored? The regulation and enforcement of health care product sales over the Internet presents a challenging opportunity for regulatory agencies to function as a unified team. Advertising and sales of prescription drugs through the Internet has become more widespread especially due to health care costs. Today, more than ever, consumers may resort to self-medication because health care costs continue to escalate. In our high-tech society, the Internet replaces the person-to-person contact in medicine today. The Internet has changed consumers purchasing habits, including how medical products are obtained. Several trends indicate future growth of Internet provided health care services and products. Although reports of Internet drug sales growth vary, it is clear that with easy access to the Internet, anyone with a credit card can purchase prescription drugs, controlled substances and unapproved drugs not available in the United States.

The sale or dispensing of a prescription drug without a valid prescription is illegal and misbrands the drug under 21 USC section 353(b). The teams responsible in terms of Internet "watches" include Federal, State and Local agencies and Licensing Boards. Federal agencies include the U.S. Food and Drug Administration, Drug Enforcement Administration, Federal Trade Commission, U.S. Customs, and the U.S. Department of Justice. For example, the FDA has primary responsibility to regulate labeling and advertising of prescription drugs as well as the authority to prosecute unapproved, adulterated and misbranded products. The U.S. Customs can stop entry into the United States of unapproved, misbranded or adulterated products. The FTC regulates the advertising of nonprescription drug products. The FTC ensures that only true and fair representations are posted on the web site. They oversee deceptive practices relating to the collection and use of personal consumer information, including improper billing to an insurance company for a drug purchase or online physician consultation, particularly when these consist of a questionnaire.

State agencies and licensing boards play a role as well. States have jurisdiction over licensing requirements for health care providers such as physicians and pharmacists. States have primary jurisdiction over pharmacies and physicians. Each state has laws and regulations for pharmacy and medical licensure, patient confidentiality and consumer protection. FDA's concern with Internet drug sales includes unproved drug sales; use of the internet to circumvent FDA regulation. FDA implemented specific steps to curb illegal prescription drug marketing on the Internet.

Pangea X International Police Organization Interpol—In 2017, Pangea X a global operation targeted illegal websites of millions potentially dangerous unapproved and counterfeit prescription drugs and medical devices worth over $51 million with over 400 arrests worldwide.

https://www.fda.gov/ICECI/CriminalInvestigations/ucm577828.htm
https://www.interpol.int/News-and-media/News/2017/N2017-119

Criminal Prosecution—The president of Pharmalogical, Inc., who operated Internet sites known as Medical Device King and Taranis Medical Corp., was sentenced to five years in prison for his role in an Internet sales operation that distributed misbranded prescription drugs (*United States v. Scully*, E.D.N.Y., No. 1:14-cr-00208 (2016)); (Judgement vacated and remanded Docket No. 16-3073-cr Dec. 2017) (error to exclude evidence related advice of counsel defense).

***Warning Letters*—Gilead Sciences and Citius Pharmaceuticals**

Gilead Sciences Incorporated's (Gilead) sponsored link on the internet search engine, Google.com, for VIREAD® (tenofovir disoproxil fumarate) tablets and powder, for oral use

(Viread). According to FDA, the sponsored link provides evidence that Viread is intended for a new use for which it lacks approval, and for which its labeling did not provide adequate directions for use. In addition, according to FDA, the sponsored link was misleading because it makes representations and/or suggestions about the efficacy of Viread. FDA determined that Gilead failed to communicate any risk information associated with the use of this product.

Citius Pharmaceuticals, LLC (Citius)— In Citius Pharmaceuticals, LLC (Citius) and Akrimax Pharmaceuticals, LLC (Akrimax), agent for SuprenzaTM (phentermine hydrochloride) orally disintegrating tablet CIV (Suprenza) NDA 202088, FDA reviewed the homepage (webpage) of a website for Suprenza. FDA determined that the webpage is false or misleading because it omits risk information, includes unsubstantiated efficacy claims for Suprenza, and omits material facts.

http://www.fda.gov/Drugs/GuidanceComplianceRegulatoryInformation/EnforcementActivities-byFDA/WarningLettersandNoticeofViolationLetterstoPharmaceuticalCompanies/ucm380323.htm

Other examples of enforcement actions against Internet fraud and abuse include seizures, recalls, domestic Warning Letters, Cyber Letters, Injunctions and Voluntary destruction of violative products. Enforcement actions have been taken against websites in the United States that have been found to sell drugs without a valid prescription or without meaningful interaction with a healthcare practitioner. Sites have been shut down and their owners fined. Cyber letters have been sent to site owners when therapeutic claims are made that establish the product as a drug under the FDCA 21 USC section 321 (g). At the same time, these products may also be considered new drugs under section 21 USC section 321(p) of the FDCA and thus cannot be legally marketed without FDA approval under 21 USC section 355 (a). Advertisements for prescription drugs must contain certain requirements such as a brief summary of the side effects, contraindications, and effectiveness under 21 U.S. C. section 352 (n) as required by the regulations. The regulations under 21 C.F.R. section 202.1 mandate both benefit as well as risk disclosure. The question remains whether promotional materials on the Internet are considered labeling, advertising, both labeling and advertising or perhaps a completely different grouping. The FTC has taken on sites for false or deceptive advertising, as well as unauthorized credit card processing. *Operation CureAll* represents a successful FTC program in cooperation with FDA and other enforcement agencies including state Attorneys General and Health Canada aimed toward combating health fraud on the Internet. The companies targeted include those that promote dietary supplements and herbal products to cure life-threatening diseases such as cancer. The Internet has no boundaries. It does not recognize the same borders that Federal and State agencies are bound to, in terms of jurisdiction. This creates jurisdictional issues, since several federal agencies as well as states have the authority to regulate or enforce laws. "People" and or "Entities" to prosecute can be complicated to locate. When they are found, which state should respond? There have been situations where an individual in state "A" reviews a questionnaire and prescribes a drug that is shipped from a location in state "B", to the consumer living in state "C". To complicate matters, the prescription drug may be manufactured outside of the United States. Internet regulation is a significant challenge on the international front. Federal agencies have limited jurisdiction over prescription drugs manufactured outside the United States or foreign-based Internet sites. Does an online interaction result in a valid prescription under 21 USC 353(b)?

The FDA and its partners are increasing enforcement efforts of unapproved new drugs, health fraud and prescription drugs sold without a valid prescription. The focus center on significant risk to the consumer. As a result, the Online Sales of Drugs and Medical Products Interagency Working Group was formed and consists of DOJ, DEA, FBI, FDA, Customs, Postal Inspection Service, Dept. of HHS, Dept. of Defense, Defense Criminal Investigation Service, and the National Association of Attorneys General. FDA, Customs and DEA collaborate to clarify and strengthen personal import policies of controlled substances. Electronic access to the FCC API database is now available to district offices. This database contains label images and packaging information for foreign APIs. This will assist in determining if a product is counterfeit. The DEA contends that online questionnaires do not meet requirements for valid prescriptions of controlled substances. To control foreign sites, FDA's office of Criminal Investigations maintains an ongoing liaison with government agencies in Canada, UK, Spain, Germany, Belgium, Netherlands, Ireland, Brazil, Singapore and others.

Perhaps a solution to government regulation is industry self-regulation. One successful example is the VIPPS program. The Verified Internet Pharmacy Practice Sites or VIPPS program is a voluntary certification program. VIPPS functions as a verification site of the National Association of Boards of Pharmacy or NABS. VIPPS certification requires maintenance of all state licenses in good standing; inspection of operations by NABS; display of the VIPPS seal with the VIPPS website link and specific information about the pharmacy on the VIPPS website. Vigilant enforcement from multiple agencies, consumer education and awareness remain key parameters. Consumers perusing the FDA website are warned by the "Buying medicines and medical products online". Consumer education, improving technology, and acquiring enforcement resources remain priorities for enforcement. States have taken legal action against physicians and web sites. The risks of using counterfeit, unapproved, outdated, adulterated or misbranded prescription drugs to treat illness can be life threatening. Federal and State agencies must continue to collaborate to eliminate these risks.

NOTE: See the following link for a list of current warning letters:
http://www.fda.gov/Drugs/GuidanceComplianceRegulatoryInformation/EnforcementActivities-byFDA/WarningLettersandNoticeofViolationLetterstoPharmaceuticalCompanies/default.htm

CRITICAL ANALYSIS: Design an effective system for monitoring and enforcing promotion of pharmaceuticals on the Internet. Include a discussion of *Pangea X International* above.

Internet Drug Sales and Shipper Liability
United Parcel Service, Inc.—Non-Prosecution Agreement

Does a shipper such as FedX or United Parcel Service, Inc. (UPS) have a legal duty to refuse to ship drug products to United States customers who obtain controlled substances and prescription drugs without a prescription from "Internet Pharmacies"? UPS agreed in 2013 to a "Nonprosecution Agreement" with the United States Department of Justice in which the company agreed to forfeit $40 million in payments it received from illicit online pharmacies.

UPS agreed to institute a compliance program to assure that illegal online pharmacies will not be able to use UPS for shipment. For example, an online pharmacy compliance officer position is responsible to implement, monitor and provide regular reports to UPS's chief executive officer. According to FDA and the Department of Justice, UPS was on notice since 2004 that Internet pharmacies were illegally shipping prescription through common carriers such as UPS. Despite a compliance program instituted in 2004, it was deemed ineffective.

See: *https://www.justice.gov/usao-ndca/pr/ups-agrees-forfeit-40-million-payments-illicit-online-pharmacies-shipping-services*

United States v. FedEx Corp., **N.D. Cal., No. 3:14-cr-00380, (N.D. Cal. 7/17/14)** (grand jury indictment regarding FedEx accepting shipments from illegal online "pharmacies"). However, by order dated June 17, 2016, the charges were dismissed. A conviction could have entailed fines, penalties, forfeiture and mandatory compliance parameters.

CRITICAL ANALYSIS: The cases above proved opposite outcomes. How would you advise your client if you represented a shipper or carrier?

First Amendment Issues and Marketing Practices

Promotion to health providers and consumers by pharmaceutical companies remains controversial. Federal regulators have increased scrutiny of pharmaceutical marketing. For example, Forest Laboratories agreed to a criminal fine and civil settlement. The Purdue Frederick Company (Purdue) agreed to settle allegations of improper marketing of its pain reliever product OxyContin. First Amendment principles were preserved in the United States Supreme Court decision of *Sorrell v. IMS Health.* The government and industry have issued codes of conduct.

PhRMA Code

http://www.phrma.org/about/principles-guidelines/code-interactions-healthcare-professionals

The Pharmaceutical and Manufacturers Association of America (PhRMA), a trade association for research based pharmaceutical and biotech companies, issued a voluntary marketing code for its members titled: *"Code on Interaction with Healthcare Professionals"* (Code). The Code, originally published in 2005 and updated in 2009, applies to actions of pharmaceutical representations in the marketing of health care items and focuses on the following marketing practices: informational presentations, educational and or professional meetings, consultants, scholarships and educational funds, speaker training meetings and educational and practice related items. The Code addresses "limits" on payments to physicians for speaking appointments as well as meals offered to physicians and health care staff. The "guiding principles" in the Code do not specifically limit direct-to-consumer advertising. Instead, the "guiding principles" direct the industry in improved communication of risks and benefits.

CRITICAL ANALYIS: Evaluate Pharma's self-regulation and whether this is a viable solution or perhaps government regulation should remain the focus for compliance purposes. Assess the feasibility of a hybrid approach. Discuss the impact of eliminating for example, the prohibition of paying for restaurant meals by pharmaceutical companies. See also: Prescription Drug Promotion Involving Payments and Gifts: Physicians' Perspective.
http://oig.hhs.gov/oei/reports/oei-01-90-00481.pdf

Office of Inspector General's Compliance Program Guidance
Guidance for Pharmaceutical Manufacturers
https://oig.hhs.gov/authorities/docs/03/050503FRCPGPharmac.pdf

The Office of Inspector General (OIG) issued *"Office of Inspector General's Compliance Program Guidance for Pharmaceutical Manufacturers"*, guidance assist companies that develop, manufacture, market and sell pharmaceutical drugs or biological products in devising and implementing internal controls and procedures that foster compliance with applicable statutes and regulations. 68 Fed Reg. 23731 (May 5, 2003). The guidance stresses that cooperation of senior management is crucial. The goal of the guidance is for pharmaceutical manufacturers to have a compliance program in place that addresses fraud and abuse. The intent of the guidance is to provide direction in terms of compliance programs that improve health care services and reduce health care costs. Compliance should alleviate the submission of false or inaccurate pricing or rebate information to any federal health care program and illegal marketing activities. The OIG Compliance specifically enumerates seven elements for an effective compliance program as follows:

> ➢ Implementation of written policies and procedures;
> ➢ Designation of a compliance officer and compliance committee;
> ➢ Implementation of effective training and education;
> ➢ Development of effective channels of communication;
> ➢ Management of internal monitoring and auditing;
> ➢ Enforcement of standards through disciplinary guidelines; and
> ➢ Handling problems and taking corrective action in an expedient manner.

Significant factors addressed in the OIG Compliance include—a code of conduct, data used to establish government reimbursement, kickbacks and other illegal remuneration and relationships with physicians and other health care professionals.

Data Mining and Commercial Free Speech—*Sorrell*

First Amendment Commercial Free Speech principles were preserved in the 2011 United States Supreme Court decision of *Sorrell v. IMS Health.* In *Sorrell*, the Court struck down a Vermont state law that prohibited pharmaceutical sales representatives from using data mining sales information for the purpose of detailing information to physicians. The Vermont state law banned the use of prescription data for detailing by sales representatives of drug companies; however, it was permitted for use by law enforcement, insurance companies and journalists. Detailing by pharmaceutical sales representatives means that a pharmaceutical sales representative targets doctors known to be prescribing a certain drug with information about other drugs. Data mining companies purchase the prescription sales information without patient identifiers from pharmacies and drug companies purchase the information from the data mining companies.

Sorrell v. IMS Health, Inc. et al., 131 S.Ct. 2653 (2011)

KENNEDY, J., delivered the opinion of the Court, in which ROBERTS, C.J., and SCALIA, THOMAS, ALITO, and SOTOMAYOR, JJ., joined. BREYER, J., filed a dissenting opinion, in which GINSBURG and KAGAN, JJ., joined.

Justice KENNEDY delivered the opinion of the Court. Vermont law restricts the sale, disclosure, and use of pharmacy records that reveal the prescribing practices of individual doctors. Vt. Stat. Ann., Tit. 18, § 4631 (Supp.2010). Subject to certain exceptions, the information may not be sold, disclosed by pharmacies for marketing purposes, or used for marketing by pharmaceutical manufacturers. Vermont argues that its prohibitions safeguard medical privacy and diminish the likelihood that marketing will lead to prescription decisions not in the best interests of patients or the State. *** Speech in aid of pharmaceutical marketing, however, is a form of expression protected by the Free Speech Clause of the First Amendment. As a consequence, Vermont's statute must be subjected to heightened judicial scrutiny. The law cannot satisfy that standard.

I. A. Pharmaceutical manufacturers promote their drugs to doctors through a process called "detailing." This often involves a scheduled visit to a doctor's office to persuade the doctor to prescribe a particular pharmaceutical. Detailers bring drug samples as well as medical studies that explain the "details" and potential advantages of various prescription drugs. Interested physicians listen, ask questions, and receive follow-up data. Salespersons can be more effective when they know the background and purchasing preferences of their clientele, and pharmaceutical salespersons are no exception. Knowledge of a physician's prescription practices—called "prescriber-identifying information"—enables a detailer better to ascertain which doctors are likely to be interested in a particular drug and how best to present a particular sales message. Detailing is an expensive undertaking, so pharmaceutical companies most often use it to promote high-profit brand-name drugs protected by patent. ***

Pharmacies, as a matter of business routine and federal law, receive prescriber-identifying information when processing prescriptions. See 21 U.S.C. § 353(b); see also Vt. Bd. of Pharmacy Admin. Rule 9.1 (2009); Rule 9.2. Many pharmacies sell this information to "data miners," firms that analyze prescriber-identifying information and produce reports on prescriber behavior. Data miners lease these reports to pharmaceutical manufacturers subject to nondisclosure agreements. Detailers, who represent the manufacturers, then use the reports to refine their marketing tactics and increase sales. In 2007, Vermont enacted the Prescription Confidentiality Law. The measure is also referred to as Act 80. It has several components. The central provision of the present case is § 4631(d). *"A health insurer, a self-insured employer, an electronic transmission intermediary, a pharmacy, or other similar entity shall not sell, license, or exchange for value regulated records containing prescriber-identifiable information, nor permit the use of regulated records containing prescriber-identifiable information for marketing or promoting a prescription drug, unless the prescriber consents .... Pharmaceutical manufacturers and pharmaceutical marketers shall not use prescriber-identifiable information for marketing or promoting a prescription drug unless the prescriber consents ...."* ***

The District Court found that "[p]harmaceutical manufacturers are essentially the only paying customers of the data vendor industry" and that, because detailing unpatented generic drugs is not "cost-effective," pharmaceutical sales representatives "detail only branded drugs." *Id.*, at 451, 442. *** The United States Court of Appeals for the Second Circuit reversed and remanded. It held that § 4631(d) violates the First Amendment by burdening the speech of pharmaceutical marketers and data miners without an adequate justification. *** In any event, § 4631(d) cannot be sustained even under the interpretation the State now adopts. As a consequence this Court can assume that the opening clause of § 4631(d) prohibits pharmacies, health insurers, and similar entities from selling prescriber-identifying information, subject to the statutory exceptions set out at § 4631(e). Under that reading, pharmacies may sell the information to private or academic researchers, see § 4631(e)(1), but not, for example, to pharmaceutical marketers. *** It prohibits pharmacies, health insurers, and similar entities from disclosing or otherwise allowing prescriber-identifying information to be used for marketing. And it bars pharmaceutical manufacturers and detailers from using the information for marketing. ***

II.A. 1. On its face, Vermont's law enacts content and speaker-based restrictions on the sale, disclosure, and use of prescriber-identifying information. *** For example, those who wish to engage in certain "educational communications," § 4631(e)(4), may purchase the information. The measure then bars any disclosure when recipient speakers will use the information for marketing. Finally, the provision's second sentence prohibits pharmaceutical manufacturers from using the information for marketing. The statute thus disfavors marketing, that is, speech with a particular content. More than that, the statute disfavors specific speakers, namely pharmaceutical manufacturers. As a result of these content- and speaker-based rules, detailers cannot obtain prescriber-identifying information, even though the information may be purchased or acquired by other speakers with diverse purposes and viewpoints. ***

Vermont's law thus has the effect of preventing detailers—and only detailers—from communicating with physicians in an effective and informative manner. *** Given the legislature's expressed statement of purpose, it is apparent that § 4631(d) imposes burdens that are based on the content of speech and that are aimed at a particular viewpoint. *** There is thus a strong argument that prescriber-identifying information is speech for First Amendment purposes. The State has imposed content and speaker-based restrictions on the availability and use of prescriber-identifying information. ***

B. In the ordinary case it is all but dispositive to conclude that a law is content-based and, in practice, viewpoint-discriminatory. *** Under a commercial speech inquiry, it is the State's burden to justify its content-based law as consistent with the First Amendment. *Thompson v. Western States Medical Center,* 535 U.S. 357, 373, 122 S.Ct. 1497, 152 L.Ed.2d 563 (2002). To sustain the targeted, content-based burden § 4631(d) imposes on protected expression, the State must show at least that the statute directly advances a substantial governmental interest and that the measure is drawn to achieve that interest. *** Given the information's widespread availability and many permissible uses, the State's asserted interest in physician confidentiality does not justify the burden that § 4631(d) places on protected expression. ***

The State also contends that § 4631(d) protects doctors from "harassing sales behaviors." "Some doctors in Vermont are experiencing an undesired increase in the aggressiveness of pharmaceutical sales representatives," the Vermont Legislature found, "and a few have reported that they felt coerced and harassed." § 1(20). It is doubtful that concern for "a few" physicians who may have "felt coerced and harassed" by pharmaceutical marketers can sustain a broad content-based rule like § 4631(d). *** Doctors who wish to forgo detailing altogether are free to give "No Solicitation" or "No Detailing" instructions to their office managers or to receptionists at their places of work. Personal privacy even in one's own home receives "ample protection" from the "resident's unquestioned right to refuse to engage in conversation with unwelcome visitors." *Watchtower Bible & Tract Soc. of N. Y., Inc. v. Village of Stratton,* 536 U.S. 150, 168, 122 S.Ct. 2080, 153 L.Ed.2d 205 (2002); ***

Vermont argues that detailers' use of prescriber-identifying information undermines the doctor-patient relationship by allowing detailers to influence treatment decisions. According to the State, "unwanted pressure occurs" when doctors learn that their prescription decisions are being "monitored" by detailers. 2007 Vt. Laws No. 80, § 1(27). *** The State contends that § 4631(d) advances important public policy goals by lowering the costs of medical services and promoting public health.*** While Vermont's stated policy goals may be proper, § 4631(d) does not advance them in a permissible way. *** The defect in Vermont's law is made clear by the fact that many listeners find detailing instructive. Indeed, the record demonstrates that some Vermont doctors view targeted detailing based on prescriber-identifying information as "very helpful" because it allows detailers to shape their messages to each doctor's practice. *** Vermont may be displeased that detailers who use prescriber-identifying information are effective in promoting brand-name drugs. *** It is true that content-based restrictions on protected expression are sometimes permissible, and that principle applies to commercial speech. *** Here, however, Vermont has not shown that its law has a neutral justification. *** The State nowhere contends that detailing is false or misleading within the meaning of this Court's First Amendment precedents. See *Thompson*, 535 U.S., at 373, 122 S.Ct. 1497. Nor does the State argue that the provision challenged here will prevent false or misleading speech. *** The State has burdened a form of protected expression that it found too persuasive. At the same time, the State has left unburdened those speakers whose messages are in accord with its own views. This the State cannot do. The judgment of the Court of Appeals is affirmed.

Justice BREYER, with whom Justice GINSBURG and Justice KAGAN join, dissenting.

The Vermont statute before us adversely affects expression in one, and only one, way. It deprives pharmaceutical and data-mining companies of data, collected pursuant to the government's regulatory mandate, that could help pharmaceutical companies create better sales messages. *** The First Amendment does not require courts to apply a special "heightened" standard of review when reviewing such an effort. And, in any event, the statute meets the First Amendment standard this Court has previously applied when the government seeks to regulate commercial speech. For any or all of these reasons, the Court should uphold the statute as constitutional. ***

The statute threatens only modest harm to commercial speech. *** The legitimate state interests that the statute serves are "substantial." *Central Hudson*, 447 U.S., at 564, 100 S.Ct. 2343. Vermont enacted its statute "to advance the state's interest in protecting the public health of Vermonters, protecting the privacy of prescribers and prescribing information, and to ensure costs are contained in the private health care sector, as well as for state purchasers of prescription drugs, through the promotion of less costly drugs and ensuring prescribers receive unbiased information." § 4631(a). *** The Court reaches its conclusion through the use of important First Amendment categories—"content-based," "speaker-based," and "neutral"—but without taking full account of the regulatory context, the nature of the speech effects, the values these First Amendment categories seek to promote, and prior precedent. At best the Court opens a Pandora's Box of First Amendment challenges to many ordinary regulatory practices that may only incidentally affect a commercial message. At worst, it reawakens *Lochner's* pre-New Deal threat of substituting judicial for democratic decision making where ordinary economic regulation is at issue. *** And with respect, I dissent.

CRITICAL ANALYSIS: Evaluate why the majority ruled as it did in *Sorrell* and whether you agree with the analysis.

Corporate Accountability—*Purdue*

Should corporate officials be held liable for FDCA violations by their subordinates? This issue remains debatable. Even if a corporate officer is not convicted of any wrongdoing, the Office of Inspector General (OIG) could institute proceedings to exclude corporate officers from doing business with the federal government. This is so despite the fact that a corporate official is not convicted of any wrongdoing. Obviously, this has ramifications for corporate officials because it sends a message of corporate accountability. OIG issued a guidance as to factors it will consider in bringing such a proceeding as following.

➢ Circumstances of the misconduct and seriousness of the offense;
➢ Individual's role in the company;
➢ Individual's actions in response to the misconduct; and
➢ Information about the company.

Purdue Frederick Company

Back in 2007, the Purdue Frederick Company (Purdue) agreed to settle allegations by FDA's Office of Criminal Investigations and the United States Department of Justice of improper marketing in terms of sales and promotion of its pain reliever product OxyContin. Superiority claims articulated the product was less addictive and less subject to abuse than other pain medications.

Purdue pled guilty to felony charges and three Purdue officials pled guilty to strict liability misdemeanor charges as "responsible corporate officers". The amount the defendants agreed to pay was $634,515,475. Of this amount, the individuals agreed to pay over $34 million. Purdue agreed to pay $600 million, forfeiture of over $276 million as well as a criminal fine of $500,000. There was no order of restitution nor incarceration.

NOTE: See discussion Opioids, this *Volume*.

United States v. The Purdue Frederick Co., Inc.,
495 F. Supp.2d 569 (W. D. Va. 2007)

Opinion and Order—James P. Jones Chief United States District Judge. The Purdue Frederick Company, Inc. ("Purdue") has pleaded guilty to misbranding OxyContin, a prescription opioid pain medication, with the intent to defraud or mislead, a felony under the federal Food, Drug, and Cosmetic Act. 21 U.S.C.A. §§ 331(a), 333(a)(2) (West 1999). The individual defendants, Michael Friedman, [former President and CEO] Howard R. Udell, [executive vice president and chief legal officer] and Paul D. Goldenheim, [former chief scientific officer] have pleaded guilty to the misdemeanor charge of misbranding, solely as responsible corporate officers. 21 U.S.C.A. § 333(a)(1) (West 1999); *see United States v. Park,* 421 U.S. 658, 676, 95 S. Ct. 1903, 44 L. Ed. 2d 489 (1975). The individual defendants are not charged with personal knowledge of the misbranding or with any personal intent to defraud. *** Beginning on or about December 12, 1995, and continuing until on or about June 30, 2001, certain PURDUE supervisors and employees, with the intent to defraud or mislead, marketed and promoted OxyContin as less addictive, less subject to abuse and diversion, and less likely to cause tolerance and withdrawal than other pain medications as follows:

a. Trained PURDUE sales representatives told some health care providers that it was more difficult to extract the oxycodone from an OxyContin tablet for the purpose of intravenous abuse, although PURDUE's own study showed that a drug abuser could extract approximately 68% of the oxycodone from a single 10mg OxyContin tablet by crushing the tablet, stirring it in water, and drawing the solution through cotton into a syringe;

b. Told PURDUE sales representatives they could tell health care providers that OxyContin potentially creates less chance for addiction than immediate-release opioids;

c. Sponsored training that taught PURDUE sales supervisors that OxyContin had fewer "peak and trough" blood level effects than immediate-release opioids resulting in less euphoria and less potential for abuse than short-acting opioids;

d. Told certain health care providers that patients could stop therapy abruptly without experiencing withdrawal symptoms and that patients who took OxyContin would not develop tolerance to the drug; and

e. Told certain health care providers that OxyContin did not cause a "buzz" or euphoria, caused less euphoria, had less addiction potential, had less abuse potential, was less likely to be diverted than immediate-release opioids, and could be used to "weed out" addicts and drug seekers.

Purdue has agreed that these facts are true, and the individual defendants, while they do not agree that they had knowledge of these things, have agreed that the court may accept these facts in support of their guilty pleas. *** Under the law, Purdue is subject to a penalty of five years probation and a fine of up to $500,000. In its plea agreement, Purdue has agreed to substantial additional monetary sanctions totaling $600 million, reported to be one of the largest in the history of the pharmaceutical industry. The amount includes the following:

1. $100,615,797.25 payable to federal government health care agencies;
2. $59,384,202.75 in escrow for those states that elect to settle their claims against Purdue. These civil settlements to the federal and state government total $160 million, of which the federal government is receiving sixty percent;
3. $3,471,220.68 to Medicaid programs for improperly calculated rebates;
4. $500,000 fine to the United States;
5. $20 million in trust to the Virginia Prescription Monitoring Program;
6. $5.3 million to the Virginia Medicaid Fraud Control Unit's Program Income Fund;
7. $276.1 million forfeiture to the United States;
8. $130 million to settle private civil claims related to OxyContin; and
9. $4,628,779.32 for monitoring costs for a Corporate Integrity Agreement.

The individual defendants are subject to a punishment of twelve months imprisonment and a fine of up to $100,000. In their plea agreements, they have agreed to pay a total of $34.5 million to the Virginia Medicaid Fraud Unit's Program Income Fund. In return, the government has agreed to sentences for them without any imprisonment.

There have been several reasons suggested why the court should reject the plea agreements.
Lack of Restitution. The plea agreements preclude restitution other than as set forth in the agreements and a number of alleged victims object to this provision, contending that the amounts allocated to private parties are insufficient, compared to the recovery by governmental victims. Blue-Cross BlueShield of Tennessee has filed a Request for Notice, an Opportunity to be Heard at Sentencing, and an Order of Restitution. Other third-party health care payors have joined in this motion. In addition, an individual who considers herself a victim because of her addiction to OxyContin has objected to the plea agreements and has filed a formal Motion to Assert Victim's Rights, in which she complains about restitution, as well as other matters. ***

Purdue agrees to pay at least $130 million to settle private claims, but no maximum limit is imposed. I do not find that the plea agreements are inherently unfair in this regard. *** I would have preferred that the plea agreements had allocated some amount of the money for the education of those at risk from the improper use of prescription drugs, and the treatment of those who have succumbed to such use. *** On the other hand, I am forbidden by law to participate in plea discussions, Fed. R. Crim. P. 11(c)(1), and I will not reject these agreements simply because they do not contain provisions that I would have preferred. ***

Political Interference. It has been suggested that Purdue may have received a favorable deal from the government solely because of politics. I have had long experience with the United States Attorney for this district, and I am convinced that neither he nor the career prosecutors who handled this case would have permitted any political interference. ***

Lack of Incarceration. The plea agreements provide for no incarceration for the individual defendants. The government points out that a sentence of incarceration under the federal sentencing guidelines would be unusual based on the facts of the case. The government is also convinced that the nature of the convictions of the individual defendants—based on strict liability for mis-branding—will send a strong deterrent message to the pharmaceutical industry. *** However, while the question is a close one, I find that in the absence of government proof of knowledge by the individual defendants of the wrongdoing, prison sentences are not appropriate.

Summary. In summary, I find that the plea agreements are supported by the facts and the law and impose adequate punishment on the defendants and I accept them. ***

NOTE: The Office of Inspector General (OIG) in the Department of Health and Human Services (HHS) excluded the three former Purdue executives in 2007 from federal healthcare programs due to their convictions for misbranding under FDCA responsible corporate officer (RCO) doctrine. Originally, the individuals were excluded for 20 years and through administrative appeals

the exclusion was reduced to 12 years. In 2012, in *Friedman v. Sebelius*, (11-5028) the Court of Appeals upheld their exclusions; however, the Court of Appeals remanded the case back to the district court concerning the length of the exclusion due to lack of an explanation. That is, HHS failed to explain why the penalty was much longer (three times) than comparable cases and longer than the presumptive baseline in the statute (four times).

CRITICAL ANALYSIS: Discuss how the outcome might be different if decided today in terms of incarceration of the corporate executives.

Direct-to-Consumer Promotion and "Puffery"

New Jersey Citizen Action v. Schering Plough Corp. et.al.,
842 A.2d 174 (N.J. Super. 2003)

OPINION: The opinion of the court was delivered by HOENS, J.A.D. Plaintiffs are not-for-profit organizations and individuals seeking to assert, on behalf of a nationwide class, consumer fraud claims against defendants Schering-Plough Corp. (Schering), a pharmaceutical manufacturer, and two companies that assisted it in advertising and marketing certain of its Claritin products. Plaintiffs appeal from the decision of the trial judge dismissing their complaint. *** Schering manufactures the proprietary pharmaceutical product Claritin, an allergy medication marketed in a variety of forms. *** Defendants Quantum Group and Commonhealth L.P. are marketing and advertising agencies that worked for Schering in connection with its direct-to-consumer (DTC) sales strategy for its Claritin products. Plaintiffs contend that they are representatives of a class of consumers of these products who have been damaged by false claims about the efficacy of the products in Schering's DTC advertising. *** The central contention of plaintiffs is that statements in DTC advertisements which used such phrases as "you can lead a normal nearly symptom-free life again" were intended to be understood by consumers as a guarantee of total and universal effectiveness of the product. That contention is meritless. This and similar statements in Schering's DTC advertising for these products are, simply put, not statements of fact, but are merely expressions in the nature of puffery and thus are not actionable. *** Our Supreme Court has recognized, in an analogous context, that a pharmaceutical manufacturer's compliance with FDA regulations including regulations relating to DTC marketing campaigns may shield it in a failure to warn case. *Perez v. Wyeth Labs, Inc.*, 161 N.J. 1, 24, 734 A.2d 1245 (1999). ***

Moreover, as a practical matter, the products remain available only through a physician's prescription. While our Supreme Court has held that the learned intermediary doctrine will not shield the manufacturer from a duty to warn claim arising in the DTC context, *Perez v. Wyeth Labs, Inc.*, supra, 161 N.J. at 21-22, nonetheless, the intervention by a physician in the decision-making process necessitated by his or her exercise of judgment whether or not to prescribe a particular medication protects consumers in ways respecting efficacy that are lacking in advertising campaigns for other products. In this context, that is, within a highly regulated industry in which the ultimate consumer is not in fact free to act on claims made in advertising in any event, the relationship between words used in the advertising and purchase of the product is at best an attenuated one. *** We further conclude that plaintiffs cannot demonstrate that any loss that they may have suffered was caused by defendants' allegedly misleading DTC advertisements. *** As defendants aptly note, however, the theory on which plaintiffs seek to rely would virtually eliminate the requirement that there be a connection between the misdeed complained of and the loss suffered. Affirmed.

CRITICAL ANALYSIS: Why did the court rule in favor of the pharmaceutical company?

Direct-to-Consumer Promotion—Learned Intermediary Doctrine
Perez, Hamilton, **and** *Johnson & Johnson*

When a pharmaceutical company directly advertises its product to a consumer does the learned intermediary doctrine still apply? Courts throughout the United States have addressed and decided this issue with varied results. For example, the New Jersey Supreme Court in *Perez v. Wyeth Laboratories* articulated an exception to the learned intermediary doctrine whereas the Texas Supreme Court in *Centocor v. Hamilton* ruled otherwise. Finally, the West Virginia Supreme Court in *Johnson* court refused to adopt the learned intermediary doctrine. These decisions follow.

Perez v. Wyeth Laboratories, 734 A.2d 1245 (NJ 1999)

OPINION: O'HERN, J: Our medical-legal jurisprudence is based on images of health care that no longer exist. At an earlier time, medical advice was received in the doctor's office from a physician who most likely made house calls if needed. The patient usually paid a small sum of money to the doctor. Neighborhood pharmacists compounded prescribed medicines. Without being pejorative, it is safe to say that the prevailing attitude of law and medicine was that the "doctor knows best." *Logan v. Greenwich Hosp. Ass'n*, 191 Conn. 282, 465 A.2d 294, 299 (Conn. 1983). Pharmaceutical manufacturers never advertised their products to patients, but rather directed all sales efforts at physicians. In this comforting setting, the law created an exception to the traditional duty of manufacturers to warn consumers directly of risks associated with the product as long as they warned health-care providers of those risks. For good or ill, that has all changed. *** Drug manufacturers now directly advertise products to consumers on the radio, television, the Internet, billboards on public transportation, and in magazines. For example, a recent magazine advertisement for a seasonal allergy medicine in which a person is standing in a pastoral field filled with grass and goldenrod, attests that to "TAKE [THE PRODUCT]" is to "TAKE CLEAR CONTROL." Another recent ad features a former presidential candidate, encouraging the consumer to "take a little courage" to speak with "your physician."

The question in this case, broadly stated, is whether our law should follow these changes in the marketplace or reflect the images of the past. We believe that when mass marketing of prescription drugs seeks to influence a patient's choice of a drug, a pharmaceutical manufacturer that makes direct claims to consumers for the efficacy of its product should not be unqualifiedly relieved of a duty to provide proper warnings of the dangers or side effects of the product. *** This appeal concerns Norplant, a Food and Drug Administration (FDA)-approved, reversible contraceptive that prevents pregnancy for up to five years. *** According to plaintiffs, Wyeth began a massive advertising campaign for Norplant in 1991, which it directed at women rather than at their doctors. Wyeth advertised on television and in women's magazines such as Glamour, Mademoiselle and Cosmopolitan. According to plaintiffs, none of the advertisements warned of any inherent danger posed by Norplant; rather, all praised its simplicity and convenience. None warned of side effects including pain and permanent scarring attendant to removal of the implants. Wyeth also sent a letter to physicians advising them that it was about to launch a national advertising program in magazines that the physicians' patients may read. *** Side effects complained of by plaintiffs included weight gain, headaches, dizziness, nausea, diarrhea, acne, vomiting, fatigue, facial hair growth, numbness in the arms and legs, irregular menstruation, hair loss, leg cramps, anxiety and nervousness, vision problems, anemia, mood swings and depression, high blood pressure, and removal complications that resulted in scarring. *** The trial court dismissed plaintiffs' complaints, concluding that even when a manufacturer advertises directly to the public, and a woman is influenced by the advertising campaign, "a physician is not simply relegated to the role of prescribing the drug according to the woman's wishes." Id. at 658. *** The Appellate Division affirmed the trial court's grant of summary judgment in favor of defendants and its determination that the learned intermediary doctrine applied. 313 N.J. Super. 511, 713 A.2d 520 (1998). ***

Direct-to-Consumer Advertising It is paradoxical that so pedestrian a concern as male-pattern baldness should have signaled the beginning of direct-to-consumer marketing of prescription drugs. Upjohn Company became the first drug manufacturer to advertise directly to consumers when it advertised for Rogaine, a hair-loss treatment. Jon D. Hanson & Douglas A. Kysar, Taking Behaviorism Seriously: Some Evidence of Market Manipulation, 112 Harv. L. Rev. 1420, 1456 (1999).

The ad targeted male consumers by posing the question, "Can an emerging bald spot . . . damage your ability to get along with others, influence your chance of obtaining a job or date or even interfere with your job performance?" Ibid. (footnotes omitted). A related ad featured an attractive woman asserting suggestively, "I know that a man who can afford Rogaine is a man who can afford me." Ibid. Advertising for Rogaine was the tip of the iceberg. Since drug manufacturers began marketing directly to consumers for products such as prescription drugs in the 1980s, "almost all pharmaceutical companies have engaged in this direct marketing practice." Consider the following example: A hot-air balloon floats lazily across the backdrop of a beautiful, cloudless, sunny sky. Cole Porter sings in the background, "Blue skies smiling at me[.] Nothing but blue skies do I see." A kind voice instructs the viewer to "see your doctor about Claritin (R)" because a "clear answer is out there." This advertisement for Claritin (R), a nondrowsy prescription antihistamine, aired prior to the . . . (FDA's) release of new direct-to-consumer (DTC) broadcast advertising guidelines in August 1997. The viewer often was bewildered because the "clear answer" about what Claritin (R) treated was not in the otherwise well-produced thirty-second television advertisement. *** The marketing gimmick used by the drug manufacturer often provides the consumer with a diluted variation of the risks associated with the drug product. Even without such manipulation, "television spots lasting 30 or 60 seconds are not conducive to 'fair balance' [in presentation of risks]." *** Consumers often interpret such warnings as a "general reassurance" that their condition can be treated, rather than as a requirement that "specific vigilance" is needed to protect them from product risks.

How Has the Law Responded to These Changes?

A. The new Restatement (Third) of Torts has left the issue to "developing case law." *** Despite the early effort to provide an exception to the doctrine in the case of direct marketing of pharmaceuticals to consumers, the drafters left the resolution of that issue to "developing case law." ***

B. The New Jersey Products Liability Act does not legislate the boundaries of the learned intermediary doctrine. *** An adequate product warning or instruction is one that a reasonably prudent person in the same or similar circumstances would have provided with respect to the danger and that communicates adequate information on the dangers and safe use of the product, taking into account the characteristics of, and the ordinary knowledge common to, the persons by whom the product is intended to be used, or in the case of prescription drugs, taking into account the characteristics of, and the ordinary knowledge common to, the prescribing physician. ***

C. Direct advertising of drugs to consumers alters the calculus of the learned intermediary doctrine. Prescription drugs are likely to be complex medicines, esoteric in formula and varied in effect. As a medical expert, the prescribing physician can take into account the propensities of the drug, as well as the susceptibilities of [the] patient. [The physician's] task [is to weigh] the benefits of any medication against its potential dangers. The choice [the physician] makes is an informed one, an individualized medical judgment bottomed on a knowledge of both patient and palliative. *** First, the fact that manufacturers are advertising their drugs and devices to consumers suggests that consumers are active participants in their health care decisions, invalidating the concept that it is the doctor, not the patient, who decides whether a drug or device should be used. Second, it is illogical that requiring manufacturers to provide direct warnings to a consumer will undermine the patient-physician relationship, when, by its very nature, consumer-directed advertising encroaches on that relationship by encouraging consumers to ask for advertised products by name. Finally, consumer-directed advertising rebuts the notion that prescription drugs and devices and their potential adverse effects are too complex to be effectively communicated to lay consumers. *** When all of its premises are absent, as when direct warnings to consumers are mandatory, the learned intermediary doctrine, "itself an exception to the manufacturer's traditional duty to warn consumers directly of the risk associated with any product, simply drops out of the calculus, leaving the duty of the manufacturer to be determined in accordance with general principles of tort law." *Edwards* *v. Basel Pharms.*, 116 F.3d 1341, 1343 (10th Cir. 1997) (discussing question of adequacy of nicotine patch warning under Texas law certified in *Edwards v. Basel Pharms.*, 933 P.2d 298 (Okla. 1997)). *** Concerns regarding patients' communication with and access to physicians are magnified in the context of medicines and medical devices furnished to women for reproductive decisions. In *MacDonald v. Ortho Pharmaceutical Corp.*, 394 Mass. 131, 475 N.E.2d 65 (Mass.), cert. denied, 474 U.S. 920, 106 S. Ct. 250, 88 L. Ed. 2d 258 (1985), the plaintiff's use of oral contraceptives allegedly resulted in a stroke. The Massachusetts Supreme Court explained several reasons why contraceptives differ from other prescription drugs and thus "warrant the imposition of a common law duty on the manufacturer to warn users directly of associated risks." 394 Mass. at 136-37. For example, after the patient receives the prescription, she consults with the physician to receive a prescription annually, leaving her an infrequent opportunity to "explore her questions and concerns about the medication with the prescribing physician." 394 Mass. at 137. *** The court also explained that because oral contraceptives are drugs personally selected by the patient, a prescription is often not the result of a physician's skilled balancing of individual benefits and risks but originates, instead, as a product of patient choice. 394 Mass. at 137. Thus, "the physician is relegated to a passive role." ***

It is one thing not to inform a patient about the potential side effects of a product; it is another thing to misinform the patient by deliberately withholding potential side effects while marketing the product as an efficacious solution to a serious health problem. Further, when one considers that many of these "life-style" drugs or elective treatments cause significant side effects without any curative effect, increased consumer protection becomes imperative, because these drugs are, by definition, not medically necessary. ***

D. Prescription drug manufacturers that market their products directly to consumers should be subject to claims by consumers if their advertising fails to provide an adequate warning of the product's dangerous propensities. In reaching the conclusion that the learned intermediary doctrine does not apply to the direct marketing of drugs to consumers, we must necessarily consider that when prescription drugs are marketed and labeled in accordance with FDA specifications, the pharmaceutical manufacturers should not have to confront "state tort liability premised on theories of design defect or warning inadequacy." Note, A Question of Competence: The Judicial Role in the Regulation of Pharmaceuticals, 103 Harv. L. Rev. 773, 773 (1990). Section 352(n) of the Act contains the "brief summary requirement," which is a misnomer considering that the summary is anything but brief. Accordingly, all advertisements must include a description of "side effects, contraindications, and effectiveness as shall be required in regulations." 21 U.S.C.A. § 352(n)(3). ***

To sum up, the dramatic shift in pharmaceutical marketing to consumers is based in large part on significant changes in the health-care system from fee-for-service to managed care. Managed care companies negotiate directly with pharmaceutical companies and then inform prescribers which medications are covered by the respective plans. Because managed care has made it more difficult for pharmaceutical companies to communicate with prescribers, the manufacturers have developed a different strategy, marketing to consumers. *** Pharmaceutical companies are already seeing results in strong sales growth, due to DTC advertising. *** The judgment of the Appellate Division is reversed and the matter is remanded to the Law Division for further proceedings.

CRITICAL ANALYSIS: Why should the manufacturer be liable when the prescription drugs product is directly advertised to the consumer?

Centocor, Inc. v. Hamilton,
372 S.W.3d 140 (Tex. 2012), reh'g denied **(Aug. 17, 2012)**

Centocor v. Hamilton focused on the failure to warn and the learned intermediary doctrine and the exception to the learned doctrine due to direct-to-consumer marketing. Hamilton and her husband filed a lawsuit against the drug manufacturer for fraud, negligence, gross negligence, and misrepresentation. The trial court entered judgment, in favor of Hamilton for $4,687,461.70, and in favor of her husband for $120,833.71 which included both actual and punitive damages. The appeals court affirmed on all counts except for the future physical pain and mental anguish award of $1million dollars. That is, the appeals court held that the direct-to-consumer promotion exception to the learned intermediary doctrine applied in this case and held that there was sufficient evidence that the manufacturer intended for patients to rely on the marketing video and which omitted risk information. The Supreme Court reversed and ruled in favor of Centocor.

Opinion: Justice GREEN delivered the Opinion of the Court.

Under the learned intermediary doctrine, the manufacturer of a pharmaceutical product satisfies its duty to warn the end user of its product's potential risks by providing an adequate warning to a "learned intermediary," who then assumes the duty to pass on the necessary warnings to the end user. *See, e.g., Gravis v. Parke–Davis & Co.,* 502 S.W.2d 863, 870 (Tex.Civ.App.-Corpus Christi 1973, writ ref'd n.r.e.). *** We hold that the doctrine generally applies within the context of a physician-patient relationship and allows a prescription drug manufacturer to fulfill its duty to warn end users of its product's potential risks by providing an adequate warning to the prescribing physician. We further hold that the court of appeals erred by creating an exception to the learned intermediary doctrine for direct-to-consumer (DTC) advertising. *** Therefore, the learned intermediary doctrine applies to all of the patient's claims, and the patient was required to show that an inadequate warning to the prescribing physicians caused the patient's injuries. *** Accordingly, we reverse the court of appeals' judgment in part and render judgment that the plaintiffs take nothing.

I. Background In March 2003, Patricia and Thomas Hamilton sued Centocor, Inc., a prescription drug manufacturer and subsidiary of Johnson & Johnson, claiming that Centocor provided "inadequate and inappropriate warnings and instruction for use" of its prescription drug Remicade, which made Remicade "defective and unreasonably dangerous," and seeking damages for injuries that Patricia allegedly incurred from using the drug. *** They claimed that Centocor was liable for, among other things, (1) "manufacturing, promoting, distributing and/or selling Remicade®," which was "defective and unreasonably dangerous" because of "inadequate and inappropriate warnings and instructions for use"; (2) negligence; (3) gross negligence; (4) fraud; and (5) malice. *** In the course of her prescribed treatments, Patricia's treating physician, Michael Bullen, M.D., showed her an informational video that he received from Centocor. The Hamiltons alleged that Centocor's video over-emphasized the benefits of Remicade and intentionally omitted warnings about the potential side effect of lupus-like syndrome. They argued that the video bypassed the physician-patient relationship and required Centocor to warn Patricia directly of Remicade's potential risks and side effects, thereby making Centocor liable for Patricia's injuries. The jury found in favor of the Hamiltons, and the trial court entered judgment for approximately $4.6 million. The court of appeals reversed the award of future pain and mental anguish damages but affirmed the remainder of the trial court's judgment, adopted a DTC advertising exception to the learned intermediary doctrine, and held that the record contained sufficient expert evidence to prove that Centocor's actions caused Patricia's injuries.

A. Patricia's Medical History Prior to 2001 Patricia Hamilton has a complicated medical history. For more than two decades, she has suffered from Crohn's disease, recurring joint pain, arthritis, and several other ailments. ***

B. Dr. Hauptman Treats Patricia's Crohn's Disease *** Based in part on Patricia's desire to avoid steroid treatments, which had previously caused severe adverse effects, Dr. Hauptman prescribed three treatments of Remicade, a relatively new drug that had been developed since Patricia's surgery in 1997, administered at six-week intervals of 400 milligrams each.

C. Remicade *** An immunomodulator medication, Remicade is designed to suppress the immune system's inflammatory response to the affected bowel. Patients receive Remicade treatments through intravenous infusions—the medication is injected through an IV catheter in the patient's arm.

1. The FDA Approval Process *** Because the FDA requires continuing studies of the safety and efficacy of the prescription drug, it is common for the package insert to undergo revisions as new information becomes available.

2. The 2001 Remicade Package Insert At the time of Patricia's initial Remicade prescription in December 2001, Centocor provided Patricia's doctors with a package insert that warned Remicade's use could lead to certain adverse reactions. The package insert included the following warning information regarding lupus-like syndrome:

> **PRECAUTIONS: Autoimmunity** Treatment with REMICADE may result in the formation of autoantibodies and, rarely, in the development of a lupus-like syndrome. If a patient develops symptoms suggestive of a lupus-like syndrome following treatment with REMICADE, treatment should be discontinued. ***

> **ADVERSE REACTIONS:** A total of 771 patients were treated with REMICADE in clinical studies. In both rheumatoid arthritis and Crohn's disease studies, approximately 6% of patients discontinued REMICADE because of adverse experiences. ***

D. Lupus–Like Syndrome According to Mary Olsen, M.D., an expert witness hired by Centocor but called by the Hamiltons, lupus-like syndrome, also called drug-induced lupus, has similar characteristics to the autoimmune disorder systemic lupus erythematosus (SLE), except that lupus-like syndrome is caused by a drug. ***

E. Dr. Bullen and the Remicade Infusions Dr. Hauptman prescribed three infusions of Remicade over a six-week period from December 2001 to January 2002 and referred Patricia to Dr. Bullen for treatment. *** As the non-prescribing, treating physician, neither Dr. Bullen nor his staff discussed with Patricia the risks inherent in Remicade, but they informed her of the potential risks directly associated with the infusion process. *** Dr. Bullen stated that he was aware that Remicade could cause lupus-like syndrome, but admitted that he probably did not give Patricia any warnings or instructions concerning the risk of developing lupus-like syndrome. ***

F. Centocor's Informational Video The video, titled "Patient Guide to Remicade® (infliximab) IV Administration," was viewed by the jury during trial. *** [T]he video provides several written warnings and disclaimers at the end of the production. ***

G. Dr. Pop–Moody Treats Patricia's Arthritis Dr. Pop–Moody informed Patricia that she may have lupus-like syndrome, but Patricia's medical records indicate that, despite this risk, Patricia desired to continue taking Remicade. ***

H. The Houston Doctors The Houston Doctors stopped Patricia's Remicade treatments and, instead, prescribed steroids for her joint pains. *** Within a few months of ceasing the Remicade infusions, Patricia's lupus-like symptoms subsided. Patricia's arthritic symptoms also improved dramatically after she ceased taking Remicade.

II. Procedural Background A. Trial Court Proceedings *** Before the trial court submitted the charge to the jury, the court granted a directed verdict in favor of Dr. Bullen and his infusion clinic, finding that Dr. Bullen and his staff had no duty to warn Patricia of the risks associated with Remicade because Dr. Bullen was not the prescribing physician. ***

B. Court of Appeals *** Relying on reasoning from the New Jersey Supreme Court's opinion in *Perez v. Wyeth Laboratories,* 161 N.J. 1, 734 A.2d 1245, 1246–47 (1999), the court of appeals adopted "an exception to the learned intermediary doctrine when a drug manufacturer directly advertises to its consumers in a fraudulent manner." 310 S.W.3d at 480–81. ***

III. Learned Intermediary Doctrine *** Centocor argues that the learned intermediary doctrine applies and therefore it had no duty to warn Patricia directly of the risks and potential side effects associated with Remicade. *** Centocor claims that DTC advertising does not threaten the physician-patient relationship, but helps educate consumers about available medications—sometimes causing patients to seek treatment for ailments they otherwise would not have treated or sometimes even discovered. ***

A. The Learned Intermediary Doctrine in Texas Jurisprudence The learned intermediary doctrine has been part of Texas jurisprudence for many years. *See, e.g., Gravis v. Parke–Davis & Co.,* 502 S.W.2d 863, 870. *** Our decision to apply the learned intermediary doctrine in the context of prescription drugs, prescribed through a physician-patient relationship, not only comports with our prior references to the doctrine and many years of Texas case law, but it places us alongside the vast majority of other jurisdictions that have considered the issue. Our sister states have overwhelmingly adopted the learned intermediary doctrine in this context and, to date, only one state has rejected the doctrine altogether. *See State ex rel. Johnson & Johnson Corp. v. Karl,* 220 W.Va. 463, 647 S.E.2d 899, 913–14 (2007). ***

B. Recognized Exceptions to the Learned Intermediary Doctrine Having concluded that the learned intermediary doctrine generally applies in the prescription drug context, we next consider whether some exception to the doctrine is warranted here, so that, despite the doctrine, Centocor retained a duty to warn the patient directly. *** In 1997, the Oklahoma Supreme Court recognized a marketing exception to the learned intermediary doctrine when the FDA mandated that the manufacturers, through their product labels, must communicate warnings directly to patients. *Edwards v. Basel Pharm.,* 933 P.2d 298, 301 (Okla.1997). While this decision did not abrogate the learned intermediary doctrine on the basis of DTC advertising, soon thereafter, the New Jersey Supreme Court adopted a sweeping DTC advertising exception to the learned intermediary doctrine in *Perez v. Wyeth Laboratories Inc.,* 161 N.J. 1, 734 A.2d 1245, 1246–47 (1999). *Perez* involved a prescription contraceptive called Norplant—a "hybrid" medical device that consists of a drug capsule that is surgically implanted in the patient's arm. *Id.* at 1247. *** As a result, the court held that the learned intermediary doctrine no longer provided complete protection to pharmaceutical manufacturers that provided adequate warnings to physicians on the risks and benefits of a drug when that company chose to market directly to consumers. *Id.* The *Perez* court did, however, recognize that a drug manufacturer's compliance with "FDA advertising, labeling, and warning requirements" created a "rebuttable presumption that the [manufacturer's] duty to consumers is met." *Id.* at 1259. *** To date, West Virginia is the only state whose highest court has followed the New Jersey Supreme Court's holding in *Perez. See Karl,* 647 S.E.2d at 912–13.20 In *State ex rel. Johnson & Johnson Corp. v. Karl,* the West Virginia Supreme Court relied on the *Perez* court's reasoning to reject the learned intermediary doctrine entirely: "Given the plethora of exceptions to the learned intermediary doctrine, we ascertain no benefit in adopting a doctrine that would require the simultaneous adoption of numerous exceptions in order to be justly utilized." *Id.* at 910–11, 913. ***

C. The DTC Advertising Exception Does Not Apply *** Here, the alleged harm was not caused by Centocor's direct advertising to Patricia. At trial, the Hamiltons admitted that the first time they heard of Remicade was when Patricia's husband, Thomas, saw a textual banner displayed on the bottom ticker of the CNN news channel, which stated that the FDA had approved Remicade for the treatment of Crohn's disease. This innocuous news report is a far cry from the basis for the *Perez* court's adoption of a DTC advertising exception where the pharmaceutical company "ma [de] direct claims to consumers for the efficacy of its product" through prescription drug advertisements. *Cf. Perez,* 734 A.2d at 1247. Instead of DTC advertising prompting her to request Remicade from her doctors, Patricia's claims rest on the video that she viewed after her doctor had prescribed Remicade and after the infusion process had begun. ***

IV. The Learned Intermediary Doctrine Within the Prescription Drug Context Is Not a Common–Law Affirmative Defense *** We agree with Centocor that, within the prescription drug context, the learned intermediary doctrine is more akin to a common-law rule rather than an affirmative defense. ***

V. The Non–Prescribing Physician Had No Duty to Warn *** As a matter of both necessity and practicality, the duty to warn the patient of the potential risks and possible alternatives to any prescribed course of action rests with the prescribing physician. *** While Dr. Bullen owed a duty to inform Patricia of the relevant risks associated with the treatment process, including the infusion method of delivery, and to obtain her informed consent to the treatment, which he properly performed, he owed no further duty to explain all of the potential risks associated with Remicade nor was he required to second-guess the professional judgment of Dr. Hauptman. ***

VI. The Learned Intermediary Doctrine Applies to All of the Hamiltons' Claims *** We hold that when a patient alleges a fraud-by-omission claim against a prescription drug manufacturer for alleged omissions about a prescription drug's potential side effects, (1) the patient cannot plead around the basic requirements of a failure-to-warn claim, and (2) the learned intermediary doctrine applies. ***

VII. The Hamiltons' Presented No Evidence That the Allegedly Inadequate Warning Was the Producing Cause of Patricia's Injuries *** Because Patricia's prescribing physicians were aware of the potential risk of contracting lupus-like syndrome but chose to prescribe it in spite of those risks, and because the Hamiltons failed to present any evidence that including additional post-approval reports in the warning would have caused Patricia's physicians to change their prescription, the Hamiltons failed to meet their burden of proof. ***

VIII. CONCLUSION *** In sum, we hold that: (1) the learned intermediary doctrine generally applies within the context of the physician-patient relationship, and a prescription drug manufacturer fulfills its duty to warn its product's end users by providing an adequate warning to the prescribing physician; (2) the court of appeals erred by adopting a DTC advertising exception to the doctrine; (3) the learned intermediary doctrine is not a common-law affirmative defense, but a common-law rule and its applicability was not waived by Centocor; (4) Dr. Bullen, as the non-prescribing, treating physician, owed no duty to warn Patricia of the risks associated with Remicade beyond the risks directly attributable to the infusion process; (5) because all of the Hamiltons' claims are premised on Centocor's alleged failure to warn, the learned intermediary doctrine applies to all of their claims; and (6) the Hamiltons failed to introduce any evidence that the allegedly inadequate warning was the producing cause of Patricia's purported injuries. Accordingly, we reverse the portions of the court of appeals' judgment that are inconsistent with this opinion and render judgment that the Hamiltons take nothing.

CRITICAL ANALYSIS: Why did the court reverse? Was this case about the failure to warn by the prescribing physician or the failure to warn directly to the patient by the drug manufacturer or perhaps both? Incorporate the learned intermediary doctrine in your response.

State ex. rel. Johnson & Johnson Corp. v. Karl,
647 S.E.2d 899 (W. Vir. 2007)

DAVIS, Chief Justice: In this action invoking the original jurisdiction of this Court in prohibition, a drug manufacturer asks this Court to adopt the learned intermediary doctrine as an exception to the general duty of manufacturers to warn consumers of the dangerous propensities of their products. After thorough consideration of the learned intermediary doctrine in light of the current state of the prescription drug industry and physician/patient relationships, we decline to adopt this doctrine. Accordingly, the requested writ of prohibition is denied.

FACTUAL AND PROCEDURAL HISTORY

[I]t appears to be undisputed that on May 19, 1999, Mrs. Nancy J. Gellner was prescribed the drug Propulsid® by her primary care physician, Daniel J. Wilson, M.D., a respondent to this proceeding (hereinafter referred to as "Dr. Wilson"). Petitioner Janssen Pharmaceutica, Inc, is a wholly-owned subsidiary of petitioner Johnson & Johnson Corporation (hereinafter collectively referred to as "Janssen"). Propulsid® was manufactured and distributed by Janssen. In addition to prescribing Propulsid®, Dr. Wilson also provided Mrs. Gellner with samples of the prescription drug, which samples had been provided to Dr. Wilson by representatives of Janssen. Mrs. Gellner died suddenly on the third day after she began taking Propulsid®. ***

DISCUSSION

"The learned intermediary doctrine provides an exception to the general rule imposing a duty on manufacturers to warn consumers about the risks of their products." *In re Norplant Contraceptive Prods. Liab. Litig.,* 215 F.Supp.2d 795, 803 (E.D.Tex.2002) (citing *Reyes v. Wyeth Labs.,* 498 F.2d 1264, 1276 (5ᵗʰ Cir.1974); *Sterling Drug, Inc. v. Cornish,* 370 F.2d 82, 85 (8ᵗʰ Cir.1966)). The learned intermediary doctrine stands for the proposition that a drug "manufacturer is excused from warning each patient who receives the product when the manufacturer properly warns the prescribing physician of the product's dangers." *In re Norplant,* 215 F.Supp.2d at 803.

Considering decisions of only the highest state courts, we find that a mere twenty-one states have expressly adopted the learned intermediary doctrine. In one additional state, North Carolina, the doctrine has been adopted by statute. *See* N.C. Gen.Stat. § 99B-5I (1995). Thus, the total number of jurisdictions recognizing the learned intermediary doctrine, either by decision of the highest court or by statute, is only twenty-two. *** On the other hand, the highest courts of the remaining twenty-two states, Arizona, Colorado, Idaho, Indiana, Iowa, Louisiana, Maine, Maryland, Michigan, Minnesota, Nevada, New Hampshire, New Mexico, North Dakota, Rhode Island, South Carolina, South Dakota, Vermont, Wisconsin, West Virginia, and Wyoming, have not adopted the learned intermediary doctrine. Likewise, the District of Columbia Court of Appeals and the Supreme Court of Puerto Rico have not adopted the learned intermediary doctrine. Thus, while the doctrine is widely applied among lower courts, the number of high courts who have followed suit and expressly adopted the doctrine, while admittedly in the majority, do not make up the *overwhelming majority* that has often been suggested by courts and commentators.

Among the primary justifications that have been advanced for the learned intermediary doctrine are (1) the difficulty manufacturers would encounter in attempting to provide warnings to the ultimate users of prescription drugs; (2) patients' reliance on their treating physicians' judgment in selecting appropriate prescription drugs; (3) the fact that it is physicians who exercise their professional judgment in selecting appropriate drugs; (4) the belief that physicians are in the best position to provide appropriate warnings to their patients; and (5) the concern that direct warnings to ultimate users would interfere with doctor/patient relationships. *** We find these justifications for the learned intermediary doctrine to be largely outdated and unpersuasive. At the outset, we note that the learned intermediary doctrine is not a modern doctrine. Rather, its origins may be traced as far back as 1925. *** When the learned intermediary doctrine was developed, direct-to-consumer advertising of prescription drugs was utterly unknown. ***

Drug manufacturers now directly advertise products to consumers on the radio, television, the Internet, billboards on public transportation, and in magazines. *Perez v. Wyeth Labs., Inc.,* 161 N.J. 1, 4, 734 A.2d 1245, 1246-47 (1999). *** Studies show that DTC advertising generates an increased patient load and often causes physicians to spend more time reviewing the benefits and risks of a specific brand with each patient and explaining formulary restrictions when patients request a brand that is outside the health plan's drug formulary. *** The doctor-patient relationship may suffer when physicians must justify decisions to patients concerning which product they will prescribe. Physicians also believe that superficial and misleading advertisements create unreasonable or inappropriate patient expectations for product effectiveness and often lead patients to request inappropriate products for their medical needs. *Tamar v. Terzian*, Note, *Direct-to-Consumer Prescription Drug Advertising,* 25 Am. J.L. & Med. 149, 157-58 (1999) *** [One doctor] says that direct-to-consumer advertising 'has created more conflict between the doctor and the patient where the doctor is seen as a barrier to the drug the patient wants.' ...[Another] says that if a doctor feels that the requested prescription is not right for the patient, doctors find their credibility at issue, not the manufacturer. ***

In rejecting the application of the learned intermediary doctrine to drugs that had been the subject of direct-to-consumer advertising, the Supreme Court of New Jersey opined, and we agree, that such advertising obviates each of the premises upon which the doctrine rests: These premises: (1) reluctance to undermine the doctor patient-relationship; (2) absence in the era of "doctor knows best" of need for the patient's informed consent; (3) inability of drug manufacturer to communicate with patients; and (4) complexity of the subject; are all (with the possible exception of the last) absent in the direct-to-consumer advertising of prescription drugs. ***

Given the plethora of exceptions to the learned intermediary doctrine, we ascertain no benefit in adopting a doctrine that would require the simultaneous adoption of numerous exceptions in order to be justly utilized. *** Finally, because it is the prescription drug manufacturers who benefit financially from the sales of prescription drugs and possess the knowledge regarding potential harms, and the ultimate consumers who bear the significant health risks of using those drugs, it is not unreasonable that prescription drug manufacturers should provide appropriate warnings to the ultimate users of their products. *** Pharmaceutical manufacturers spend millions to make millions more. They are pushing their products onto the general public like never before. Consequently, consumers need more protection. As a response to the changing times, courts have diminished the manufacturer's shield of the learned intermediary doctrine. *** Based upon the foregoing, we now hold that, under West Virginia products liability law, manufacturers of prescription drugs are subject to the same duty to warn consumers about the risks of their products as other manufacturers. We decline to adopt the learned intermediary exception to this general rule.

CRITICAL ANALYSIS: The *Johnson* court held that under West Virginia products liability law, manufacturers of prescription drugs are subject to the identical duty to warn as other manufacturers. Assess whether the *Johnson* court was correct in declining to apply the learned intermediary doctrine.

Chapter 6: Duty to Warn and Preemption

Preemption and State Court Actions
Cerveny v. Adventis, In re: Fosamax, Wyeth v. Levine, Pliva v. Mensing and Mutual v. Bartlett

The doctrine of preemption emanates from the Supremacy Clause (Article VI, Clause 2) of the United States Constitution. Article VI, Clause 2 prohibits states from enacting laws that conflict with federal law unless the federal law contains explicit preemption language. Preemption is a complex legal issue. The federal court of appeals in *Cerveny v. Aventis, Inc.* set forth the following. There are three types of preemption: "(1) express preemption, which occurs when the language of the federal statute reveals an express congressional intent to preempt state law . . . ; (2) field preemption, which occurs when the federal scheme of regulation is so pervasive that Congress must have intended to leave no room for a State to supplement it; and (3) conflict preemption, which occurs either when compliance with both the federal and state laws is a physical impossibility, or when the state law stands as an obstacle to the accomplishment and execution of the full purposes and objectives of Congress." *Cerveny v. Aventis, Inc.*, 855 F.3d 1091 (10th Cir. 2017) quoting *Mount Olivet Cemetery Ass'n v. Salt Lake City*, 164 F.3d 480, 486 (10th Cir. 1998). In *Cerveny*, the Court affirmed the district court's ruling that the brand drug manufacturer was not liable for failing to warn about birth defect risks associated with pre-pregnancy use of Clomid. FDA had disallowed a 2009 citizen petition regarding such warnings. Interestingly, the district court relied on the "conflict preemption" and held it would have been impossible for Aventis to comply with both FDA regulations and state law.

In re Fosamax (Alendronate Sodium) Prods. Liab. Litig., the appeals court decided that what FDA would have done had the plaintiffs' requested warnings been presented was a question of fact for a jury. *In re Fosamax Prods. Liab. Litig.,* focused on allegations that the label warnings with respect to an increased risk of femur fractures was inadequate. The district court ruled that the plaintiffs' claims were preempted due to the interpretation of a 2009 FDA denial of the manufacturer's attempt to add language regarding the risk of femur fractures to the warnings and precautions section of the drug's label. The court of appeals reversed, and the United Supreme Court agreed to hear the appeal by Merck. *Merck Sharp & Dohme Corp. v. Doris Albrecht et al.,* No. 17-290.

Congress has not amended the FDCA in terms of express preemptive language except for the Medical Device Amendments. FDA, attempted to assert preemption in a preamble to its final rule about package inserts (January 18, 2006; effective June 30, 2006) In the preamble, FDA set forth that drug manufacturers of FDA approved drugs should have immunity from certain product-liability and false-claims lawsuits in state courts. The preemption stance by FDA would have affected state claims for example against drug manufacturers and claims against health care professionals related to risk information that is disseminated and to print drug advertising that reprints the warning information from drug labels. However, the United States Supreme Court in *Wyeth v. Levine* declined to give deference to FDAs "policy".

Is there a distinction between generic and branded drugs in terms of state tort liability and failure to warn? The United States Supreme Court, faced with this issue in 2011 in *Pliva v. Mensing*, decided that there is a distinction and applied federal preemption principles to generic drug products. This contravenes the brand name drug decision in *Wyeth v. Levine*. In *Pliva*, the Court applied preemption to generic drugs effectively barring plaintiffs from bringing a failure to warn action in state court. Finally, in *Mutual Pharmaceutical v. Bartlett*, the Court applied preemption again in a generic drug design defect action based on the reasoning of *Pliva v. Mensing*.

Generic Proposed Rule "Changes Being Effected"
Supplemental Applications Proposing Labeling Changes for Approved Drugs and Biological
Products

To remedy the disparity and contradictory result in *Wyeth, Pliva* and *Mutual,* FDA issued a proposed rule that would permit generic drug manufacturers to use the same process as brand drug manufacturers to update safety information in product labeling and ultimately speed the dissemination of new safety information about generic drugs to health professionals and patients. The proposed rule provides that like brand manufacturers, generic drug manufacturers could independently update product labeling (also known as prescribing information or package inserts) with newly acquired safety information prior to review of the change by FDA. Generic manufacturers would be required to notify the brand name manufacturer about the change. The proposal has met with resistance. (78 FR 67985 Nov. 13, 2013); (Docket No. FDA-2013-N-0500).

CRITICAL ANALYSIS: The proposed rule has been stalled for several years. Include a discussion about patient safety, politics, public health and costs.

Failure to Warn Brand Drugs—*Wyeth v. Levine*

The United States Supreme Court was faced with deciding whether the FDA's drug labeling judgments "preempt state law product liability claims premised on the theory that different labeling judgments were necessary to make drugs reasonably safe for use." The Court decided in *Wyeth v. Levine* that federal law does not preempt state tort claims.

Wyeth v. Levine, 129 S. Ct. 1187 (2009)

STEVENS, J., delivered the opinion of the Court, in which KENNEDY, SOUTER, GINSBURG, and BREYER, JJ., joined. BREYER, J., filed a concurring opinion. THOMAS, J., filed an opinion concurring in the judgment. ALITO, J., filed a dissenting opinion, in which ROBERTS, C.J., and SCALIA, J., joined.

Directly injecting the drug Phenergan into a patient's vein creates a significant risk of catastrophic consequences. A Vermont jury found that petitioner Wyeth, the manufacturer of the drug, had failed to provide an adequate warning of that risk and awarded damages to respondent Diana Levine to compensate her for the amputation of her arm. The warnings on Phenergan's label had been deemed sufficient by the federal Food and Drug Administration (FDA) when it approved Wyeth's new drug application in 1955 and when it later approved changes in the drug's labeling. The question we must decide is whether the FDA's approvals provide Wyeth with a complete defense to Levine's tort claims. We conclude that they do not.

Phenergan is Wyeth's brand name for promethazine hydrochloride, an antihistamine used to treat nausea. The injectable form of Phenergan can be administered intramuscularly or intravenously, and it can be administered intravenously through either the "IV-push" method, whereby the drug is injected directly into a patient's vein, or the "IV-drip" method, whereby the drug is introduced into a saline solution in a hanging intravenous bag and slowly descends through a catheter inserted in a patient's vein. The drug is corrosive and causes irreversible gangrene if it enters a patient's artery. Levine's injury resulted from an IV-push injection of Phenergan. *** This time, the physician assistant administered the drugs by the IV-push method, and Phenergan entered Levine's artery, either because the needle penetrated an artery directly or because the drug escaped from the vein into surrounding tissue (a phenomenon called "perivascular extravasation") where it came in contact with arterial blood. As a result, Levine developed gangrene, and doctors amputated first her right hand and then her entire forearm. In addition to her pain and suffering, Levine incurred substantial medical expenses and the loss of her livelihood as a professional musician. ***

The evidence presented during the 5-day jury trial showed that the risk of intra-arterial injection or perivascular extravasation can be almost entirely eliminated through the use of IV-drip, rather than IV-push, administration. *** While Phenergan's labeling warned against intra-arterial injection and perivascular extravasation and advised that "[w]hen administering any irritant drug intravenously it is usually preferable to inject it through the tubing of an intravenous infusion set that is known to be functioning satisfactorily," *id.,* at 390, the labeling did not contain a specific warning about the risks of IV-push administration. ***

The narrower question presented is whether federal law pre-empts Levine's claim that Phenergan's label did not contain an adequate warning about using the IV-push method of administration. *** In 2007, after Levine's injury and lawsuit, Congress again amended the FDCA, 121 Stat. 823. For the first time, it granted the FDA statutory authority to require a manufacturer to change its drug label based on safety information that becomes available after a drug's initial approval. § 901(a). ***

Wyeth first argues that Levine's state-law claims are pre-empted because it is impossible for it to comply with both the state-law duties underlying those claims and its federal labeling duties. The FDA's premarket approval of a new drug application includes the approval of the exact text in the proposed label. See 21 U.S.C. § 355; 21 CFR § 314.105(b) (2008). *** There is, however, an FDA regulation that permits a manufacturer to make certain changes to its label before receiving the agency's approval. Among other things, this "changes being effected" (CBE) regulation provides that if a manufacturer is changing a label to "add or strengthen a contraindication, warning, precaution, or adverse reaction" or to "add or strengthen an instruction about dosage and administration that is intended to increase the safe use of the drug product," it may make the labeling change upon filing its supplemental application with the FDA; it need not wait for FDA approval. §§ 314.70(c)(6)(iii)(A), (C). *** As the FDA explained in its notice of the final rule, 'newly acquired information' is not limited to new data, but also encompasses "new analyses of previously submitted data." [73 Fed.Reg.] *Id.,* at 49604. The rule accounts for the fact that risk information accumulates over time and that the same data may take on a different meaning in light of subsequent developments: "[I]f the sponsor submits adverse event information to FDA, and then later conducts a new analysis of data showing risks of a different type or of greater severity or frequency than did reports previously submitted to FDA, the sponsor meets the requirement for 'newly acquired information." *Id.,* at 49607; see also *id.,* at 49606. *** Thus, when the risk of gangrene from IV-push injection of Phenergan became apparent, Wyeth had a duty to provide a warning that adequately described that risk, and the CBE regulation permitted it to provide such a warning before receiving the FDA's approval. *** On the record before us, Wyeth has failed to demonstrate that it was impossible for it to comply with both federal and state requirements. The CBE regulation permitted Wyeth to unilaterally strengthen its warning, and the mere fact that the FDA approved Phenergan's label does not establish that it would have prohibited such a change. ***

Wyeth contends that the FDCA establishes both a floor and a ceiling for drug regulation: Once the FDA has approved a drug's label, a state-law verdict may not deem the label inadequate, regardless of whether there is any evidence that the FDA has considered the stronger warning at issue. *** Building on its 1906 Act, Congress enacted the FDCA to bolster consumer protection against harmful products. See *Kordel v. United States,* 335 U.S. 345, 349, 69 S.Ct. 106, 93 L.Ed. 52 (1948); *United States v. Sullivan,* 332 U.S. 689, 696, 68 S.Ct. 331, 92 L.Ed. 297 (1948). Congress did not provide a federal remedy for consumers harmed by unsafe or ineffective drugs in the 1938 statute or in any subsequent amendment. *** If Congress thought state-law suits posed an obstacle to its objectives, it surely would have enacted an express pre-emption provision at some point during the FDCA's 70-year history. But despite its 1976 enactment of an express pre-emption provision for medical devices, see § 521, 90 Stat. 574 (codified at 21 U.S.C. § 360k(a)), Congress has not enacted such a provision for prescription drugs. See *Riegel,* 552 U.S., at ___, 128 S.Ct., at 1009 ("Congress could have applied the pre-emption clause to the entire FDCA. It did not do so, but instead wrote a pre-emption clause that applies only to medical devices"). *** This Court has recognized that an agency regulation with the force of law can preempt conflicting state requirements. See, *e.g., Geier v. American Honda Motor Co.,* 529 U.S. 861, 120 S.Ct. 1913, 146 L.Ed.2d 914 (2000); *Hillsborough County v. Automated Medical Laboratories, Inc.,* 471 U.S. 707, 713, 105 S.Ct. 2371, 85 L.Ed.2d 714 (1985). In such cases, the Court has performed its own conflict determination, relying on the substance of state and federal law and not on agency proclamations of pre-emption. *** Because Congress has not authorized the FDA to preempt state law directly, cf. 21 U.S.C. § 360k (authorizing the FDA to determine the scope of the Medical Devices Amendments' pre-emption clause), the question is what weight we should accord the FDA's opinion. Under this standard, the FDA's 2006 preamble does not merit deference. When the FDA issued its notice of proposed rulemaking in December 2000, it explained that the rule would "not contain policies that have federalism implications or that preempt State law." 65 Fed.Reg. 81103; see also 71 *id.,* at 3969 (noting that the "proposed rule did not propose to preempt state law"). In 2006, the agency finalized the rule and, without offering States or other interested parties notice or opportunity for comment, articulated a sweeping position on the FDCA's pre-emptive effect in the regulatory preamble. *** The FDA has limited resources to monitor the 11,000 drugs on the market, and manufacturers have superior access to information about their drugs, especially in the postmarketing phase as new risks emerge. State tort suits uncover unknown drug hazards and provide incentives for drug manufacturers to disclose safety risks promptly. *** Failure-to-warn actions, in particular, lend force to the FDCA's premise that manufacturers, not the FDA, bear primary responsibility for their drug labeling at all times. Thus, the FDA long maintained that state law offers an additional, and important, layer of consumer protection that complements FDA regulation. *** In short, Wyeth has not persuaded us that failure-to-warn claims like Levine's obstruct the federal regulation of drug labeling. Congress has repeatedly declined to preempt state law, and the FDA's recently adopted position that state tort suits interfere with its statutory mandate is entitled to no weight. ***

We conclude that it is not impossible for Wyeth to comply with its state and federal law obligations and that Levine's common-law claims do not stand as an obstacle to the accomplishment of Congress' purposes in the FDCA. Accordingly, the judgment of the Vermont Supreme Court is affirmed. *It is so ordered.*

NOTE: The concurring and dissenting opinions, in part, are included below.

Justice BREYER, concurring. I write separately to emphasize the Court's statement that "we have no occasion in this case to consider the pre-emptive effect of a specific agency regulation bearing the force of law." ***

Justice THOMAS, concurring in the judgment. I agree with the Court that the fact that the Food and Drug Administration (FDA) approved the label for petitioner Wyeth's drug Phenergan does not pre-empt the state-law judgment before the Court. That judgment was based on a jury finding that the label did not adequately warn of the risk involved in administering Phenergan through the IV-push injection method. *** The federal statute and regulations neither prohibited the stronger warning label required by the state judgment, nor insulated Wyeth from the risk of state-law liability. ***

Justice ALITO, with whom THE CHIEF JUSTICE and Justice SCALIA join, dissenting.

This case illustrates that tragic facts make bad law. The Court holds that a state tort jury, rather than the Food and Drug Administration (FDA), is ultimately responsible for regulating warning labels for prescription drugs. *** Indeed, that result follows directly from our conclusion in *Geier.* Alexis Geier drove her 1987 Honda Accord into a tree, and although she was wearing her seatbelt, she nonetheless suffered serious injuries. She then sued Honda under state tort law, alleging that her car was negligently and defectively designed because it lacked a driver's-side airbag. She argued that Congress had empowered the Secretary to set only "minimum standard[s]" for vehicle safety. 15 U.S.C. § 1391(2). *** Notwithstanding the statute's saving clause, and notwithstanding the fact that Congress gave the Secretary authority to set only "minimum" safety standards, we held Geier's state tort suit pre-empted. *** When respondent was injured in 2000, Phenergan's label specifically addressed IV push in several passages (sometimes in lieu of and sometimes in addition to those discussed above). *** While Phenergan's label very clearly authorized the use of IV push, it also made clear that IV push is the delivery method of last resort. *** Therefore, I would reverse the judgment of the Supreme Court of Vermont.

CRITICAL ANALYSIS: Evaluate why the majority ruled as it did in *Wyeth* and whether you agree with the analysis. Incorporate the analysis by the dissent.

Failure to Warn Generic Drugs—*Pliva v. Mensing*

Pliva, Inc., et al. v. Mensing, 131 S. Ct. 2567 (2011)

THOMAS, J., delivered the opinion of the Court, except as to Part III–B–2. ROBERTS, C.J., and SCALIA and ALITO, JJ., joined that opinion in full, and KENNEDY, J., joined as to all but Part III–B 2. SOTOMAYOR, J., filed a dissenting opinion, in which GINSBURG, BREYER, and KAGAN, JJ., joined.

These consolidated lawsuits involve state tort-law claims based on certain drug manufacturers' alleged failure to provide adequate warning labels for generic metoclopramide. The question presented is whether federal drug regulations applicable to generic drug manufacturers directly conflict with, and thus pre-empt, these state-law claims. We hold that they do.

III.   Metoclopramide is a drug designed to speed the movement of food through the digestive system. The Food and Drug Administration (FDA) first approved metoclopramide tablets, under the brand name Reglan, in 1980. Five years later, generic manufacturers also began producing metoclopramide. The drug is commonly used to treat digestive tract problems such as diabetic gastroparesis and gastroesophageal reflux disorder. ***

Accordingly, warning labels for the drug have been strengthened and clarified several times. In 1985, the label was modified to warn that "tardive dyskinesia. May develop in patients treated with metoclopramide," and the drug's package insert added that "[t]herapy longer than 12 weeks has not been evaluated and cannot be recommended." In 2004, the brand-name Reglan manufacturer requested, and the FDA approved, a label change to add that "[t]herapy should not exceed 12 weeks in duration." And in 2009, the FDA ordered a black box warning—its strongest—which states: "Treatment with metoclopramide can cause tardive dyskinesia, a serious movement disorder that is often irreversible. Treatment with metoclopramide for longer than 12 weeks should be avoided in all but rare cases." ***

Gladys Mensing and Julie Demahy, the plaintiffs in these consolidated cases, were prescribed Reglan in 2001 and 2002, respectively. Both received generic metoclopramide from their pharmacists. After taking the drug as prescribed for several years, both women developed tardive dyskinesia. In separate suits, Mensing and Demahy sued the generic drug manufacturers that produced the metoclopramide they took (Manufacturers). Each alleged that long-term metoclopramide use caused her tardive dyskinesia and that the Manufacturers were liable under state tort law (specifically, that of Minnesota and Louisiana) for failing to provide adequate warning labels.

The Courts of Appeals for the Fifth and Eighth Circuits rejected the Manufacturers' arguments and held that Mensing and Demahy's claims were not pre-empted. See 588 F.3d, at 614, 593 F.3d, at 449. We granted certiorari, 562 U.S. ——, 131 S.Ct. 817, 178 L.Ed.2d 550 (2010), consolidated the cases, and now reverse each.

II. A. It is undisputed that Minnesota and Louisiana tort law require a drug manufacturer that is or should be aware of its product's danger to label that product in a way that renders it reasonably safe. Under Minnesota law, which applies to Mensing's lawsuit, "where the manufacturer ... of a product has actual or constructive knowledge of danger to users, the ... manufacturer has a duty to give warning of such dangers." Similarly, under Louisiana law applicable to Demahy's lawsuit, "a manufacturer's duty to warn includes a duty to provide adequate instructions for safe use of a product." *Stahl v. Novartis Pharmaceuticals Corp.*, 283 F.3d 254, 269–270 (C.A.5 2002); see also

La.Rev.Stat. Ann. § 9:2800.57 (West 2009). In both States, a duty to warn falls specifically on the manufacturer. ***

B. Federal law imposes far more complex drug labeling requirements. *** In 1984, however, Congress passed the Drug Price Competition and Patent Term Restoration Act, 98 Stat. 1585, commonly called the Hatch–Waxman Amendments. Under this law, "generic drugs" can gain FDA approval simply by showing equivalence to a reference listed drug that has already been approved by the FDA. 21 U.S.C. § 355(j)(2)(A). *** A generic drug application must also "show that the [safety and efficacy] labeling proposed.....is the same as the labeling approved for the [brand-name] drug." § 355(j)(2)(A)(v); see also § 355(j)(4)(G); Beers §§ 3.01, 3.03[A].

As a result, brand-name and generic drug manufacturers have different federal drug labeling duties. A brand-name manufacturer seeking new drug approval is responsible for the accuracy and adequacy of its label. See, *e.g.,* 21 U.S.C. §§ 355(b)(1), (d); *Wyeth, supra,* at 570–571, 129 S.Ct. 1187. A manufacturer seeking generic drug approval, on the other hand, is responsible for ensuring that its warning label is the same as the brand name. See, *e.g.,* § 355(j)(2)(A)(v); § 355(j)(4)(G); 21 CFR §§ 314.94(a)(8), 314.127(a)(7). ***

First, Mensing and Demahy urge that the FDA's "changes-being-effected" (CBE) process allowed the Manufacturers to change their labels when necessary. *** The CBE process permits drug manufacturers to "add or strengthen a contraindication, warning, [or] precaution," 21 CFR § 314.70I(6)(iii)(A) (2006), or to "add or strengthen an instruction about dosage and administration that is intended to increase the safe use of the drug product," § 314.70(c)(6)(iii)(C). When making labeling changes using the CBE process, drug manufacturers need not wait for preapproval by the FDA, which ordinarily is necessary to change a label. *Wyeth, supra,* at 568, 129 S.Ct. 1187. They need only simultaneously file a supplemental application with the FDA. 21 CFR § 314.70(c)(6).

Next, Mensing and Demahy contend that the Manufacturers could have used "Dear Doctor" letters to send additional warnings to prescribing physicians and other healthcare professionals. *** A Dear Doctor letter that contained substantial new warning information would not be consistent with the drug's approved labeling. Moreover, if generic drug manufacturers, but not the brand-name manufacturer, sent such letters, that would inaccurately imply a therapeutic difference between the brand and generic drugs and thus could be impermissibly "misleading." *** As with the CBE regulation, we defer to the FDA. *** Accordingly, we conclude that federal law did not permit the Manufacturers to issue additional warnings through Dear Doctor letters. ***

According to the FDA, the Manufacturers could have proposed—indeed, were required to propose—stronger warning labels to the agency if they believed such warnings were needed. If the FDA had agreed that a label change was necessary, it would have worked with the brand-name manufacturer to create a new label for both the brand-name and generic drug. ***

C. To summarize, the relevant state and federal requirements are these: State tort law places a duty directly on all drug manufacturers to adequately and safely label their products. Taking Mensing and Demahy's allegations as true, this duty required the Manufacturers to use a different, stronger label than the label they actually used. Federal drug regulations, as interpreted by the FDA, prevented the Manufacturers from independently changing their generic drugs' safety labels. But, we assume, federal law also required the Manufacturers to ask for FDA assistance in convincing the brand-name manufacturer to adopt a stronger label, so that all corresponding generic drug manufacturers could do so as well. We turn now to the question of pre-emption.

III. The Supremacy Clause establishes that federal law "shall be the supreme Law of the Land any Thing in the Constitution or Laws of any State to the Contrary notwithstanding." U.S. Const., Art. VI, cl. 2. Where state and federal law "directly conflict," state law must give way. *Wyeth, supra,* at 583, 129 S.Ct. 1187 (THOMAS, J., concurring in judgment);

We find impossibility here. *** If the Manufacturers had independently changed their labels to satisfy their state-law duty, they would have violated federal law. Taking Mensing and Demahy's allegations as true, state law imposed on the Manufacturers a duty to attach a safer label to their generic metoclopramide. Federal law, however, demanded that generic drug labels be the same at all times as the corresponding brand-name drug labels. See, *e.g.,* 21 CFR § 314.150(b)(10). ***

B.1. Mensing and Demahy argue that if the Manufacturers had asked the FDA for help in changing the corresponding brand-name label, they might eventually have been able to accomplish under federal law what state law requires. ***

2. Moreover, the text of the Clause—that federal law shall be supreme, "any Thing in the Constitution or Laws of any State to the Contrary notwithstanding"—plainly contemplates conflict preemption by describing federal law as effectively repealing contrary state law. ***

3. Here, state law imposed a duty on the Manufacturers to take a certain action, and federal law barred them from taking that action. Mensing and Demahy's tort claims are pre-empted.

C. *Wyeth* is not to the contrary. In that case, as here, the plaintiff contended that a drug manufacturer had breached a state tort-law duty to provide an adequate warning label. 555 U.S., at 559–560, 129 S.Ct. 1187. The Court held that the lawsuit was not pre-empted because it was possible for Wyeth, a brand-name drug manufacturer, to comply with both state and federal law. *Id.,* at 572–573, 129 S.Ct. 1187. Specifically, the CBE regulation, 21 CFR § 314.70I(6)(iii), permitted a brand-name drug manufacturer like Wyeth "to unilaterally strengthen its warning" without prior FDA approval. 555 U.S., at 573, 129 S.Ct. 1187. ***

We recognize that from the perspective of Mensing and Demahy, finding pre-emption here but not in *Wyeth* makes little sense. Had Mensing and Demahy taken Reglan, the brand-name drug prescribed by their doctors, *Wyeth* would control and their lawsuits would not be pre-empted. But because pharmacists, acting in full accord with state law, substituted generic metoclopramide instead, federal law pre-empts these lawsuits. *** As always, Congress and the FDA retain the authority to change the law and regulations if they so desire. * * * The judgments of the Fifth and Eighth Circuits are reversed, and the cases are remanded for further proceedings consistent with this opinion. *It is so ordered.*

Justice SOTOMAYOR, with whom Justice GINSBURG, Justice BREYER, and Justice KAGAN join, dissenting.

The Court today invokes the doctrine of impossibility pre-emption to hold that federal law immunizes generic-drug manufacturers from all state-law failure-to-warn claims because they cannot unilaterally change their labels. I cannot agree. We have traditionally held defendants claiming impossibility to a demanding standard: Until today, the mere possibility of impossibility had not been enough to establish pre-emption. The Food and Drug Administration (FDA) permits—and, the Court assumes, requires—generic-drug manufacturers to propose a label change to the FDA when they believe that their labels are inadequate. If it agrees that the labels are inadequate, the FDA can initiate a change to the brand-name label, triggering a corresponding change to the generic labels. *** As a result of today's decision, whether a consumer harmed by inadequate warnings can obtain relief turns solely on the happenstance of whether her pharmacist filled her prescription with a brand-name or generic drug. *** This outcome "makes little sense."

I. A. Today's decision affects 75 percent of all prescription drugs dispensed in this country. The dominant position of generic drugs in the prescription drug market is the result of a series of legislative measures, both federal and state. ***

B. Under federal law, generic manufacturers must "develop written procedures for the surveillance, receipt, evaluation, and reporting of postmarketing adverse drug experiences" to the FDA. 21 CFR § 314.80(b); see also § 314.98 (making § 314.80 applicable to generic manufacturers); *** FDA regulations require that labeling "be revised to include a warning as soon as there is reasonable evidence of an association of a serious hazard with a drug." 21 CFR § 201.57I (2006), currently codified at 21 CFR § 201.80I (2010); see also *Wyeth,* 555 U.S., at 570–571, 129 S.Ct. 1187. The FDA construes this regulation to oblige generic manufacturers "to seek to revise their labeling and provide FDA with supporting information about risks" when they believe that additional warnings are necessary. ***

II. A. Two principles guide all pre-emption analysis. First, "the purpose of Congress is the ultimate touchstone in every pre-emption case." ***

B. *** It was not necessarily impossible for the Manufacturers to comply with both federal and state law because, had they approached the FDA, the FDA may well have agreed that a label change was necessary. Accordingly, as in *Wyeth,* I would require the Manufacturers to show that the FDA would not have approved a proposed label change. They have not made such a showing.

This is not to say that generic manufacturers could never show impossibility. If a generic-manufacturer defendant proposed a label change to the FDA but the FDA rejected the proposal, it would be impossible for that defendant to comply with a state-law duty to warn. Likewise, impossibility would be established if the FDA had not yet responded to a generic manufacturer's request for a label change at the time a plaintiff's injuries arose. A generic manufacturer might also show that the FDA had itself considered whether to request enhanced warnings in light of the evidence on which a plaintiff's claim rests but had decided to leave the warnings as is. ***

C. ***As discussed above, however, *Wyeth* does not stand for the proposition that it is impossible to comply with both federal and state law whenever federal agency approval is required. ***
III. Today's decision leads to so many absurd consequences that I cannot fathom that Congress would have intended to pre-empt state law in these cases. ***

As the majority itself admits, a drug consumer's right to compensation for inadequate warnings now turns on the happenstance of whether her pharmacist filled her prescription with a brand-name drug or a generic. If a consumer takes a brand-name drug, she can sue the manufacturer for inadequate warnings under our opinion in *Wyeth.* *** Even when consumers can request brand-name drugs, the price of the brand-name drug or the consumers' insurance plans may make it impossible to do so. As a result, in many cases, consumers will have no ability to preserve their state-law right to recover for injuries caused by inadequate warnings.

*** When a generic drug has a brand-name equivalent on the market, the brand-name manufacturer will remain incentivized to uncover safety risks. But brand-name manufacturers often leave the market once generic versions are available, meaning that there will be no manufacturer subject to failure-to-warn liability. *** Today's decision introduces a critical distinction between brand-name and generic drugs. Consumers of brand-name drugs can sue manufacturers for inadequate warnings; consumers of generic drugs cannot. These divergent liability rules threaten to reduce consumer demand for generics, at least among consumers who can afford brand-name drugs. ***
With respect, I dissent.

CRITICAL ANALYSIS: Compare and contrast with *Wyeth v. Levine*. See proposed rule "*Changes Being Effected*" for generic drugs above.

Generic Drug Company—Failure to Update Labeling

The California Appeals Court in *Teva Pharmaceuticals USA, Inc. et al. v. Superior Court of California* (2013) *(Pikerie real party in interest)*, allowed the plaintiff to proceed with its lawsuit against the generic companies for the failure to warn of potential safety issues because of the failure to update labeling to match the brand-name equivalent version of the osteoporosis drug Fosamax. The court found the claims were not preempted by the United States Supreme Court's *Mensing* decision. See: *Teva Pharmaceuticals USA, Inc. v. Superior Court of California (Pickerie).* The United States Supreme Court denied the certiorari petition (Dec. 14, 2014 13-956) that Teva Pharmaceuticals had filed (Cert. Denied, Jan. 20, 2015). Similarly, in *Pliva v. Huck* (U.S., No 14-544, cert. denied 3/30/15) the U.S. Supreme Court refused to reconsider the Iowa Supreme Court ruling that permitted generic-drug makers to face failure-to-update labeling claims. Yet, the success of these cases at trial is questionable since the plaintiffs would have to prove that an updated warning would have influenced their doctors not to prescribe the generic drug.

CRITICAL ANALYSIS: Evaluate the impact of cases such as *Pickerie* and *Huck*. Will the "floodgates" open the door to failure to update labeling actions? Distinguish *Pliva v. Mensing*.

Generic Drugs Design Defects—*Mutual Pharmaceutical v. Bartlett*

The United States Supreme Court held in *Mutual Pharmaceutical, Inc. v. Bartlett* that generic drug manufacturers could not be sued in state court by patients who alleged that drugs they took were defectively designed. The basis of the decision was due to the fact that the generic company, Mutual Pharmaceutical, a division of Sun Pharmaceutical Industries in India, had to comply with FDA federal law under the FDCA to make a copy of the brand-name drug, Clinoril.

The decision overturned a New Hampshire state court award of $21 million to the plaintiff. The plaintiff (Ms. Bartlett) developed a horrific skin disease after taking a generic version of the pain medication sulindac and lost nearly two-thirds of her skin. She was placed in a medically induced coma and is legally blind after suffering a reaction to the medication she took for a sore shoulder. The decision comports with *Pliva v. Mensing* where the Court found that generic drug makers could not be held liable for failing to warn about a drug's dangers because they must use the same safety label as the brand-name version. Generic drug manufacturers hailed the decision, arguing that the decisions of state courts should not supplant the authority of the FDA.

NOTE: As previously discussed, legislative efforts are underway to permit generic drug companies to change their labels when they become aware of a safety risk. Brand name companies already have the ability to do so. This is critical as there may no longer be any brand name products in the marketplace. According to an advocacy group, there were 11 such occasions over the last five years where serious safety warnings were added to drug labeling where there are no longer any brand-name products available in the marketplace. See 78 FR67985.

Mutual Pharmaceutical Co., Inc. v. Bartlett,
133 S. Ct. 2466, 186 L. Ed. 2d 607 (2013)

Opinion Justice ALITO delivered the opinion of the Court. We must decide whether federal law pre-empts the New Hampshire design-defect claim under which respondent Karen Bartlett recovered damages from petitioner Mutual Pharmaceutical, the manufacturer of sulindac, a generic non-steroidal anti-inflammatory drug (NSAID). New Hampshire law imposes a duty on manufacturers to ensure that the drugs they market are not unreasonably unsafe, and a drug's safety is evaluated by reference to both its chemical properties and the adequacy of its warnings. Because Mutual was unable to change sulindac's composition as a matter of both federal law and basic chemistry, New Hampshire's design-defect cause of action effectively required Mutual to change sulindac's labeling to provide stronger warnings. But, as this Court recognized just two Terms ago in *PLIVA, Inc. v. Mensing,* 564 U.S. —— (2011), federal law prohibits generic drug manufacturers from independently changing their drugs' labels. ***. The Court of Appeals' solution—that Mutual should simply have pulled sulindac from the market in order to comply with both state and federal law—is no solution. *** Accordingly, we hold that state-law design-defect claims that turn on the adequacy of a drug's warnings are pre-empted by federal law under *PLIVA.* We thus reverse the decision of the Court of Appeals below.

I. *** First, the proposed generic drug must be chemically equivalent to the approved brand-name drug: it must have the same "active ingredient" or "active ingredients," "route of administration," "dosage form," and "strength" as its brand-name counterpart. 21 U.S.C. §§ 355(j)(2)(A)(ii) and (iii). Second, a proposed generic must be "bioequivalent" to an approved brand-name drug. § 355(j)(2)(A)(iv). That is, it must have the same "rate and extent of absorption" as the brand-name drug. § 355(j)(8)(B). Third, the generic drug manufacturer must show that "the labeling proposed for the new drug is the same as the labeling approved for the [approved brand-name] drug." § 355(j)(2)(A)(v). *** Generic manufacturers are also prohibited from making any unilateral changes to a drug's label. See §§ 314.94(a)(8)(iii), 314.150(b)(10) (approval for a generic drug may be withdrawn if the generic drug's label "is no longer consistent with that for [the brand-name] drug").

II. In 1978, the FDA approved a nonsteroidal anti-inflammatory pain reliever called "sulindac" under the brand name Clinoril. When Clinoril's patent expired, the FDA approved several generic sulindacs, including one manufactured by Mutual Pharmaceutical. *** In December 2004, respondent Karen L. Bartlett was prescribed Clinoril for shoulder pain. Her pharmacist dispensed a generic form of sulindac, which was manufactured by petitioner Mutual Pharmaceutical. Respondent soon developed an acute case of toxic epidermal necrolysis. The results were horrific. Sixty to sixty-five percent of the surface of respondent's body deteriorated, was burned off, or turned into an open wound. She spent months in a medically induced coma, underwent 12 eye surgeries, and was tube-fed for a year. She is now severely disfigured, has a number of physical disabilities, and is nearly blind. *** At the time respondent was prescribed sulindac, the drug's label did not specifically refer to Stevens–Johnson Syndrome or toxic epidermal necrolysis, but did warn that the drug could cause "severe skin reactions" and "[f]atalities." *** However, Stevens–Johnson Syndrome and toxic epidermal necrolysis were listed as potential adverse reactions on the drug's package insert. *** FDA completed a "comprehensive review of the risks and benefits, [including the risk of toxic epidermal necrolysis], of all approved NSAID products." Decision Letter, FDA Docket No. 2005P–0072/CP1, p. 2 (June 22, 2006) *** As a result of that review, the FDA recommended changes to the labeling of all NSAIDs, including sulindac, to more explicitly warn against toxic epidermal necrolysis. [A] jury found Mutual liable and awarded respondent over $21 million in damages. The Court of Appeals affirmed. 678 F.3d 30. *** We granted certiorari.

III. The Supremacy Clause provides that the laws and treaties of the United States "shall be the supreme Law of the Land ... any Thing in the Constitution or Laws of any State to the Contrary notwithstanding." U.S. Const., Art. VI, cl. 2. *** In the instant case, it was impossible for Mutual to comply with both its state-law duty to strengthen the warnings on sulindac's label and its federal-law duty not to alter sulindac's label. Accordingly, the state law is pre-empted.

A. *** As discussed below in greater detail, New Hampshire requires manufacturers to ensure that the products they design, manufacture, and sell are not "unreasonably dangerous." The New Hampshire Supreme Court has recognized that this duty can be satisfied either by changing a drug's design or by changing its labeling. *** In the present case, however, redesign was not possible for two reasons. First, the FDCA requires a generic drug to have the same active ingredients, route of administration, dosage form, strength, and labeling as the brand-name drug on which it is based. 21 U.S.C. §§ 355(j)(2)(A)(ii)-(v) and (8)(B); 21 CFR § 320.1(c). *** Second, because of sulindac's simple composition, the drug is chemically incapable of being redesigned. *** Given the impossibility of redesigning sulindac, the only way for Mutual to ameliorate the drug's "risk-utility" profile—and thus to escape liability—was to strengthen "the presence and efficacy of [sulindac's] warning" in such a way that the warning "avoid[ed] an unreasonable risk of harm from hidden dangers or from foreseeable uses." ***

C. *** As *PLIVA* made clear, federal law prevents generic drug manufacturers from changing their labels. *** Thus, federal law prohibited Mutual from taking the remedial action required to avoid liability under New Hampshire law. ***

D. *** Because it is impossible for Mutual and other similarly situated manufacturers to comply with both state and federal law, New Hampshire's warning-based design-defect cause of action is pre-empted with respect to FDA-approved drugs sold in interstate commerce.

IV. The Court of Appeals reasoned that Mutual could escape the impossibility of complying with both its federal- and state-law duties by "choos[ing] not to make [sulindac] at all." 678 F.3d, at 37.

V. *** Respondent's situation is tragic and evokes deep sympathy, but a straightforward application of pre-emption law requires that the judgment below be reversed. *It is so ordered.*

Justice BREYER, with whom Justice KAGAN joins, dissenting. It is not literally impossible here for a company like petitioner to comply with conflicting state and federal law. *** Moreover, unlike the federal statute at issue in *Medtronic,* the statute before us contains no general pre-emption clause. See 518 U.S., at 481–482. *Wyeth, supra,* at 574 (presence of pre-emption clause could show that "Congress thought state-law suits posed an obstacle to its objectives"). ***

Justice SOTOMAYOR, with whom Justice GINSBURG joins, dissenting. In *PLIVA, Inc. v.*

Mensing, 564 U.S. —— (2011), this Court expanded the scope of impossibility pre-emption to immunize generic drug manufacturers from state-law failure-to-warn claims. Today, the Court unnecessarily and unwisely extends its holding in *Mensing* to pre-empt New Hampshire's law governing design-defects with respect to generic drugs. ***

I. *** First, " 'the purpose of Congress is the ultimate touchstone' in every pre-emption case." *Ibid.* (quoting *Medtronic, Inc. v. Lohr,* 518 U.S. 470, 485 (1996)). ***

II. The majority nevertheless accepts Mutual's argument that "compliance with both federal and state [law was] a physical impossibility." *Florida Lime & Avocado Growers, Inc. v. Paul,* 373 U.S. 132, 142–143, 83 S.Ct. 1210, 10 L.Ed.2d 248 (1963). But if state and federal law are properly understood, it is clear that New Hampshire's design-defect claim did not impose a legal obligation that Mutual had to violate federal law to satisfy.

A. Impossibility pre-emption "is a demanding defense," *Levine,* 555 U.S., at 573, that requires the defendant to show an "irreconcilable conflict" between federal and state legal obligations, *Silkwood,* 464 U.S., at 256. ***

B. The majority insists that Mutual was required by New Hampshire's design-defect law to strengthen its warning label. In taking this position, the majority effectively recharacterizes Bartlett's design-defect claim as a *de facto* failure-to-warn claim. *** But just as New Hampshire's design-defect law did not impose a legal obligation for Mutual to change its label, it also did not mandate that Mutual change the drug's design.

1. a. Following blackletter products liability law under § 402A of the Restatement (Second) *** New Hampshire recognizes strict liability for three different types of product defects: manufacturing defects, design defects, and warning defects. ***

  b. *** Specifically, and contrary to the majority, see *ante,* at 11, New Hampshire's design-defect law did not require Mutual to change its warning label. *** New Hampshire's design-defect law did not require Mutual to do anything other than to compensate consumers who were injured by an unreasonably dangerous drug. ***

C. A manufacturer of a drug that is unreasonably dangerous under New Hampshire law has multiple options: It can change the drug's design or label in an effort to alter its risk-benefit profile, remove the drug from the market, or pay compensation as a cost of doing business. *** New Hampshire's design-defect cause of action thus does no more than provide an impetus for an action that is permitted and sometimes encouraged or even required by federal law.

D. New Hampshire, through its design-defect law, has made a judgment that some drugs that were initially approved for distribution turn out to be inherently and unreasonably dangerous and should therefore not be sold unless the manufacturer is willing to compensate injured consumers.

III. While the majority never addresses obstacle pre-emption, Mutual did argue in the alternative that Bartlett's design-defect cause of action is pre-empted because it conflicts with the purposes and objectives of the FDCA, as supplemented by the Hatch–Waxman Act, 98 Stat. 1585. Though it presents a closer question than the impossibility argument on which the majority relies, I would reject Mutual's obstacle pre-emption defense as well. *** Given the FDCA's core purpose of protecting consumers, our recognition in *Levine* that state tort law generally complements the statute's safety goals, the practical limits on the FDA's ability to monitor and promptly address concerns about drug safety once a drug is in the market, and the absence of any federal remedy for injured consumers, I would reject this broad obstacle pre-emption argument as well. ***

IV. If manufacturers of products that require preapproval are given *de facto* immunity from design-defect liability, then the public will have to rely exclusively on imperfect federal agencies with limited resources and sometimes limited legal authority to recall approved products. ***As a result, the Court has left a seriously injured consumer without any remedy despite Congress' explicit efforts to preserve state common-law liability.

CRITICAL ANALYSIS: Evaluate why the majority ruled as it did and whether you agree.

Include the impact of *Pliva*. See beginning of this chapter for rulemaking proceedings and *Volume IV: Medical Devices* for the Court decisions about preemption pertaining to Medical Devices—*Medtronic*, *Riegel*, and *Buckman*.

Concealment of Material Facts and Preemption—*Desiano*

In *Desiano v. Warner-Lambert*, the Court of Appeals determined that federal law did not preempt traditional common law claims. That is, preemption did not apply despite the FDA statement in the preamble to the prescription drug labeling rule. The lawsuit involved the drug Rezulin® that has since been withdrawn. The United States Supreme Court decided to hear the appeal; however, an equally divided Supreme Court in 2008 in a *per curiam* four to four ruling affirmed the Michigan Second Circuit without an opinion. United States Supreme Court Chief Justice Roberts did not participate in the decision. The Michigan plaintiffs alleged that the drug company knowingly concealed material facts from FDA about the drug Rezulin® causing liver damage. The four to four ruling did not establish a precedent in drug preemption cases. The ruling permitted Michigan residents to pursue their claim in Michigan state court.

Desiano v. Warner-Lambert, 467 F.3d 85 (2nd Cir. 2006)

CALABRESI, Circuit Judge: In 1995, the State of Michigan enacted legislation immunizing drugmakers from products liability claims so long as the Food and Drug Administration ("FDA") approved the pharmaceutical product at issue. *See* Mich. Comp. Laws § 600.2946(5) (hereinafter "M.C.L. § 2946(5)"). Michigan's immunity scheme contains an exception that preserves liability if the pharmaceutical company withheld or misrepresented information that would have altered the FDA's decision to approve the drug. In 2001, in a case dealing with different legal rules and a different jurisdiction, the Supreme Court held that state "fraud-on-the-FDA" claims were impliedly preempted by federal law. *Buckman Co. v. Plaintiffs' Legal Comm.*, 531 U.S. 341, 348, 121 S.Ct. 1012 (2001). The question presented by this appeal is whether, under the rationale of *Buckman*, federal law also preempts traditional common law claims that survive a state's legislative narrowing of common law liability through a fraud exception to that statutory limitation. For the reasons below, we conclude that federal law does not preempt these state claims.

Procedural History Appellants in this case are all Michigan residents alleging injuries caused by Rezulin, a drug marketed and sold by Appellees for the treatment of Type-2 diabetes. The FDA originally approved Rezulin in 1997. After adverse liver-related effects were documented in patients taking Rezulin, Appellees agreed to a series of label changes, which were authorized by the FDA on four occasions between November 1997 and June 1999. In March 2000, apparently at the FDA's request, *see Desiano v. Warner-Lambert Co.*, 326 F.3d 339, 344 (2d Cir.2003), Appellees withdrew Rezulin from the United States market. ***

DISCUSSION Accordingly, the central question presented by this appeal—*i.e.*, whether federal law preempts Michigan's immunity exception—is controlled by the decision in *Garcia* only to the extent that the Sixth Circuit's conclusion rested solely on findings as to state law. *** The Michigan legislature has provided a general immunity for drug manufacturers with a specific exception for circumstances involving, *inter alia*, fraud on the FDA rather than a specific cause of action for fraud on the FDA. *Garcia*, 385 F.3d at 965-66. ***

In *Buckman*, the Supreme Court considered whether federal law— specifically, the FDCA and the MDA—preempted state "fraud-on-the-FDA" claims. The plaintiffs in *Buckman* contended that a medical device manufacturer had obtained FDA approval for its product only after making fraudulent misrepresentations to the federal agency. *** In the absence of any presumption against preemption, the Court found that fraud-on-the-FDA claims conflicted with, and were therefore impliedly preempted by, federal law. *** The *Buckman* Court went on to express its concern that the potential conflict between federal law and the competing regulatory regimes of 50 states would unduly burden drug companies seeking to obtain FDA approval for their products. *** But the Court ended by emphasizing that the plaintiffs' claims before it were not rooted in traditional state law, and were instead derivative of federal law: *** For these reasons, the Court invalidated the plaintiffs' fraud-on-the-FDA claims as impliedly preempted by federal law.

A. Presumption Against Preemption *** In *Medtronic,* the Supreme Court explained that "because the States are independent sovereigns in our federal system, we have long presumed that Congress does not cavalierly pre-empt state-law causes of action." *Medtronic,* 518 U.S. at 485, 116 S.Ct. 2240. In *Buckman,* the Court held that this presumption did not apply *because "[p]olicing fraud against federal agencies is hardly a field which the States have traditionally occupied." Buckman,* 121 S.Ct. 1012. *** The Michigan legislature's desire to rein in state-based tort liability falls squarely within its prerogative to "regulat[e] matters of health and safety," which is a sphere in which the presumption against preemption applies, indeed, stands at its strongest. ***

B. Traditional Common Law Liability Second, Appellants here are not pressing "fraud-on-the-FDA" claims, as the plaintiffs in *Buckman* were understood by the Supreme Court to be doing. They are, rather, asserting claims that sound in traditional state tort law. *** The second difference between common law actions and "fraud-on-the-FDA" claims, suggested in *Buckman,* is that in FDA-fraud cases, proof of fraud against the FDA is *alone sufficient* to impose liability. In *Buckman,* there were no freestanding allegations of wrongdoing apart from the defendant's purported failure to comply with FDA disclosure requirements. And *Buckman* explicitly distinguished *Medtronic* on this ground. *Medtronic,* the *Buckman* Court said, involved a "common-law negligence action against the manufacturer of an allegedly defective" product.

As in *Medtronic,* the plaintiffs' claims in the case before us "parallel federal safety requirements" but are not premised principally (let alone exclusively) on a drug maker's failure to comply with federal disclosure requirements. *** These pre-existing common law claims survive under M.C.L. § 2946(5) because there is also evidence of fraud in FDA disclosures. But, unlike the claims in *Buckman,* they are anything but based *solely* on the wrong of defrauding the FDA. Given *Buckman's* explanation of *Medtronic, Buckman* cannot be read as precluding such preexisting common law liability based on other wrongs, even when such liability survives only because there was *also* evidence of fraud against the FDA. ***

C. Immunity as Affirmative Defense *** Finding preemption of traditional common law claims where fraud is not even a required element—but may be submitted to neutralize a drugmaker's use of an affirmative defense available under state law—would result in preemption of a scope that would go far beyond anything that has been applied in the past. ***

Because of its important role in state regulation of matters of health and safety, common law liability cannot be easily displaced in our federal system. *Buckman* underscored this fact, finding implied preemption of a newly-fashioned state cause of action only where (1) no presumption against federal preemption obtained, and (2) the cause of action, by assigning liability *solely* on the basis of fraud against the FDA, imposed significant and distinctive burdens on the FDA and the entities it regulates. The appeal before us presents a very different set of circumstances, one in which there is a clear presumption against preemption of long-standing common law claims. In the presence of this presumption, because Michigan law does not in fact implicate the concerns that animated the Supreme Court's decision in *Buckman,* and because Appellants' lawsuits depend primarily on traditional and preexisting tort sources, not at all on a "fraud-on-the-FDA" cause of action created by state law, and only incidentally on evidence of such fraud, we conclude that the Michigan immunity exception is not prohibited through preemption. It follows that common law liability is not foreclosed by federal law, and Appellants' claims should not have been dismissed.

CRITICAL ANALYSIS: Compare and contrast *Buckman* in *Volume IV* to *Desiano.*

Federal Compliance and Common Law Duty to Warn—*Edwards*

Does compliance with federal mandates excuse the manufacturer from the duty to warn? Does the duty to warn depend on the type of product? The *Edwards* decision illustrates that a duty does exist under state law despite federal compliance. More recently, the *Wyeth v. Rowatt* decision hinged on "known risks" and affirmed the duty to warn prevailed despite federal compliance.

Edwards v. Basel Pharmaceuticals,
116 F. 3d 1341 (10th Cir. 1997)

Plaintiff Alpha Edwards brought this wrongful death action after her husband suffered a fatal heart attack while smoking cigarettes and wearing two of Basel's "Habitrol" nicotine patches. Her theory of liability was Basel's failure to warn of the risks of nicotine overdose resulting from smoking and (over) use of the patch. While a relatively thorough warning, specifically noting the fatal risk realized here, was included in materials intended for the prescribing physician, a package insert addressed to the patient failed to mention the possibility of any fatal reaction to nicotine overdose, cautioning only that "[a]n overdose might cause you to faint." Appellant's Appendix (App.) at 45. *** Although Oklahoma courts have acknowledged the FDA-mandate exception, they have never had the occasion to consider the effect of the manufacturer's compliance with the very agency mandate on which the exception rests. ***

Some courts have held that the LIR, [learned intermediary rule] itself an exception to the manufacturer's traditional duty to warn consumers directly of the risks associated with any product, simply drops out of the calculus, leaving the duty of the manufacturer to be determined in accordance with general principles of tort law. See, e.g., *Odgers v. Ortho Pharmaceutical Corp.*, 609 F.Supp. 867, 877-79 (E.D.Mich.1985); *Martin ex rel. Martin v. Ortho Pharmaceuticals,* 645 N.E.2d 431, 436-37 (Ill.Ct.App.1994); *MacDonald v. Ortho Pharmaceutical Corp.*, 475 N.E.2d 65, 69-71 (Mass.), cert. denied, 474 U.S. 920 (1985). Pursuant to such principles, traditional standards involving reasonableness govern the adequacy of warnings and, hence, compliance with a non-preemptive and "minimal" FDA mandate (in particular, the one negating the LIR) is at most inconclusive evidence of adequacy. *Odgers*, 609 F.Supp. at 879; *Martin*, 645 N.E.2d at 437; *MacDonald*, 475 N.E.2d at 70.

Other courts have held that the LIR remains operative, thus barring reversion to general duty principles, and yields only to the extent of the FDA mandate, which carves out—and thereby delimits—an exceptional, exclusive duty owed directly to the consumer. *** Under Oklahoma law, what determines the scope or extent of the prescription drug manufacturer's duty to warn the consumer when FDA recognition of the need for direct warnings has undercut application of the learned intermediary rule? More specifically, what is the effect of the manufacturer's compliance with the very FDA requirements invoking this exception to the rule?

*** We hold that when the FDA requires warnings be given directly to the patient with a prescribed drug, an exception to the "learned intermediary doctrine" has occurred, and the manufacturer is not automatically shielded from liability by properly warning the prescribing physician. When this happens the manufacturer's duty to warn the consumer is not necessarily satisfied by compliance with FDA minimum warning requirements. The required warnings must not be misleading and must be adequate to explain to the user the possible dangers associated with the product. Whether that duty has been satisfied is governed by the common law of the state. *** *Edwards v. Basel Pharmaceuticals* 933 P.2d 298, 303 (Okla.1997). Implementing this definitive pronouncement of controlling state law, we issued an order and judgment reversing the district court insofar as it had granted summary judgment for Basel on plaintiff's consumer warning claim: "The district court has never considered the adequacy of Basel's consumer warnings under the common law of Oklahoma. Accordingly, summary judgment must be reversed and the case remanded for further proceedings on that issue, consistent with the principles expressed by the state supreme court." *Edwards v. Basel Pharmaceuticals*, No. 95-6176, 1997 WL, 158134 at 1 (10th Cir. Apr. 2, 1997). With respect to "plaintiff's analytically separate claim that Basel also did not adequately warn the decedent's prescribing physician," however, we affirmed, agreeing with the district court that plaintiff had offered no affirmative evidence to dispute Basel's showing that the information provided to the prescribing physician was accurate, appropriate, and complete. Id. *** The thrust of that duty analysis may be further clarified in response to two objections advanced by amicus Pharmaceutical Research and Manufacturers of America (PRMA). *** Specifically, PRMA is concerned about preserving the independence between state tort warning standards and particular patient labels or inserts the FDA has mandated/approved. *** Indeed, the Oklahoma Supreme Court's answer—that the duty recognized here is not necessarily satisfied by compliance with the FDA mandate triggering it—effectuates precisely the content-independence referred to in the quoted passage. PRMA displays a similar confusion in arguing that we have mistaken the Habitrol patient insert for a "comprehensive warning" when it is just a "lay" admonition meant merely to complement the more exhaustive information provided to the prescribing physician. *** Again, PRMA confuses the conditions creating Basel's duty to warn with considerations relating to the content/satisfaction of that duty, a matter that simply has not been reached yet. See id. at 303 (recognizing Basel's duty to warn consumer, but explaining "[w]hether that duty has been satisfied [under] the common law of the state ... [is] beyond our assignment in response to this certified question"); Edwards, 1997 WL 158134, at 1 (this court's order and judgment remanding to the district court, which "has never considered the adequacy of Basel's consumer warnings under the common law of Oklahoma"). Thus, some of what PRMA has to say may be relevant to assessing the adequacy of Basel's consumer warnings, but it is not pertinent to the analytically prior decision, dispositive of this appeal, that Basel had a common law duty to provide such warnings.

CRITICAL ANALYSIS: Discuss the duty to warn in terms of manufacturer liability despite federal compliance.

Duty to Warn and Known Risks—Hormone Replacement Therapy
Wyeth v. Rowatt

The *Wyeth v. Rowatt* decision detailed the evolution of hormone replacement therapeutic drugs. Succinctly stated, before 1995, many patients combined Premarin, Wyeth's estrogen-based drug, with progestin-laden Provera, manufactured by Pfizer's Pharmacia & Upjohn unit. Wyeth, now part of Pfizer, combined the two hormones in Prempro. Over 6 million women used Prempro and related menopause drugs to treat symptoms such as mood swings and hot flashes. However, a 2002 study highlighted the link to cancer. Over 10,000 lawsuits were filed.

The *Rowatt* lawsuit against Wyeth pharmaceutical company and its subsidiaries, was instituted by consumers who developed invasive breast cancer due to Wyeth's combined estrogen-progestin hormone therapy. The Supreme Court of Nevada determined that compliance with regulations promulgated by the Food and Drug Administration (FDA) pertaining to labeling and drug testing did not absolve Wyeth of punitive damages and that Wyeth acted with malice as a basis for the punitive damage award. Substantial evidence supported the $23 million award of compensatory damages; the punitive damages award of $57,778,909 was not impermissibly excessive.

Wyeth v. Rowatt, 244 P.3d 765 (Nev. Sup. Ct. 2010)
Cert. Denied, *Wyeth v. Scofield*, 131 S. Ct. 3028 (2011)

By the Court, CHERRY, J.: This case arises from personal injury and strict products liability actions filed by respondents against appellants after respondents took appellants' [Wyeth's] drugs for years and were subsequently diagnosed with breast cancer. *** Because we perceive no reversible errors in the issues raised on appeal, we affirm the district court's judgment.

Respondents Arlene Rowatt, Pamela Forrester, and Jeraldine Scofield all took hormone replacement therapy drugs for a number of years and later developed breast cancer. The specific hormone replacement drugs prescribed to respondents were in one of two forms: two pills—one estrogen pill and one progestin pill, or a single pill that combined both hormones. Appellants Wyeth and Wyeth Pharmaceutical, Inc., manufactured and sold the estrogen pill known as Premarin, which was combined with a progestin pill manufactured by a different pharmaceutical company. Wyeth also manufactured the combination hormone pill known as Prempro. ***

Wyeth had knowledge that hormone-receptive organs, such as breast tissue, responded to the introduction of additional hormones in the body, and Wyeth allegedly failed to reasonably test the estrogen-progestin combination based on that knowledge. Second, respondents argued that Wyeth failed to adequately warn them and their physicians about the breast cancer risk associated with the estrogen-progestin combination. Third, respondents alleged that Wyeth's drugs were unreasonably dangerous because they could cause breast cancer and respondents purportedly developed breast cancer as a result of taking the estrogen-progestin combination. ***

The development of hormone replacement therapy

In 1942, Wyeth introduced Premarin, an estrogen hormone used to treat menopausal symptoms. By the 1970s, the medical community had recognized a potential link between the use of estrogen and endometrial cancer. Wyeth's Premarin sales dropped. In 1976, Wyeth's internal documents show that its researchers knew that the presence of both estrogen and progestin in a tumor indicates that the tumor had responded to hormones. In the late 1970s, a published scientific article recommended adding progestin to an estrogen regimen to avoid the risk of developing endometrial cancer. Consequently, physicians began prescribing estrogen and progestin. ***

In 1983, Wyeth sought approval from the FDA to study and market the combination of estrogen and progestin. The FDA allowed Wyeth to study the drugs' combination, but rejected its application to market the drugs together. The FDA specifically told Wyeth that a large, long-term study was first needed to evaluate the drug combination's safety. *** In fact, Wyeth's documents showed that it had a company policy of not supporting breast cancer studies.

Starting in the late 1980s and early 1990s, independent studies were published that linked an increase in breast cancer risk to the estrogen-progestin hormone therapy regimen. For example, in 1989, a study was published in the New England Journal of Medicine that showed a 4.4 relative risk of breast cancer in premenopausal women. The study characterized the risk as a "slightly increased risk of breast cancer" among women who took estrogen plus progestin for a long time. The 1989 study was followed by another study shortly thereafter confirming those results. In 1990, another independent study showed an increased risk of developing breast cancer when the hormone therapy regimen was estrogen plus progestin. Internal Wyeth documents show that it responded to studies suggesting a possible breast cancer risk by downplaying the risk through public relations campaigns and its sales representatives' interactions with physicians. Wyeth also created an internal task force to counteract such findings.

In 1992, the FDA's advisory committee noted that there was insufficient data to determine whether adding progestin to estrogen increased the breast cancer risk. *** That same year, Wyeth provided its drug to the National Institutes of Health, which was conducting a study called the Women's Health Initiative (WHI). *** This long-term study was halted in 2002 because a significant number of women on the estrogen-progestin combination had developed cancer.

In 1994, Wyeth sought approval from the FDA to market Prempro. Along with its request, Wyeth submitted at least 14 different breast cancer studies, including a quantitative statistical analysis of 31 breast cancer studies performed at Wyeth's request. The FDA, relying on the studies, approved Prempro as safe and effective. Its approval, however, was conditioned on Wyeth conducting a large-scale clinical trial on bone mineral density and the breast cancer risk to obtain comprehensive answers about breast cancer. ***

The FDA modified Wyeth's proposed warning label. The modified warning informed readers that "[s]ome studies have reported a moderately increased risk of breast cancer." The label noted that "[t]he effect of added progestins on the risk of breast cancer is unknown, although a moderately increased risk in those taking combination estrogen/progestin therapy has been reported." The label also stated that the rate of breast cancer that showed up in Wyeth's own human study did "not exceed that expected in the general population." Wyeth, however, never conducted its own human study. With the launch of Prempro, Wyeth became the first pharmaceutical company to combine estrogen and progestin into one pill. Although Wyeth knew there were no long-term studies on the safety of estrogen plus progestin, it recommended Prempro's use for "all women for life."

A 1996 published European study showed that the estrogen-progestin combination increased the breast cancer risk for thin or lean women. Following that study, Wyeth updated its European label warning, but did not update its warning label in the United States. Wyeth specifically cautioned its "Breast Cancer Working Group" to keep the article "confidential, [and] not discuss [it] with anyone outside of Wyeth." Testimony indicated that Wyeth developed a plan to minimize the study and divert attention from it. ***

By 1997, Wyeth had not begun a comprehensive clinical trial, as required by the FDA. *** By 2000, a number of published scientific articles linked hormone replacement drugs to an increased risk for breast cancer. Evidence showed that Wyeth responded to these articles by creating a task force and adding $40.4 million to its large yearly marketing budget to counter rising consumer awareness about the relationship between breast cancer risk and hormone replacement therapy. Wyeth also began promoting Prempro's unproven, and later debunked, heart and mental health benefits in television advertisements and informational pamphlets, guides, and textbooks. The promotional materials failed to mention any breast cancer risk. The FDA admonished Wyeth for recommending its drugs for unapproved benefits as a violation of FDA regulations. As it pertained to those promotional materials, Wyeth disregarded the admonition, and the FDA never sanctioned Wyeth for the improper practices. In another situation involving different promotional materials that Wyeth intended to send to its hormone therapy consumers, Wyeth complied with the FDA's warnings to omit information about unapproved benefits.

Over the years, Wyeth sponsored 51 medical articles by selecting different physicians to author the articles, when in fact Wyeth personnel wrote the articles or provided the substance for the articles. Wyeth's involvement with those articles was never identified. Published under independent doctors' names, the 51 ghostwritten medical articles touted the benefits of hormone replacement therapy while minimizing the breast cancer risk. ***

After the WHI study results were released, prescriptions for the standard dose of estrogen plus progestin dropped by 80 percent. Similarly, the number of diagnosed hormone-receptor-positive breast cancers—cancers in which tumors show an active hormone receptor—also fell.

Following the WHI study, Wyeth introduced a new, lower dose estrogen-progestin pill called Prempro Low. This lower-dose treatment is recommended only as a second-line treatment and for the shortest duration necessary. It also carries the strongest warning possible—a "black box" warning— and informs the consumer that the risk of breast cancer increases with prolonged use.

Trial testimony

The parties' causation theories: Respondents argued and presented evidence that, but for ingesting estrogen plus progestin, they would not have developed cancer. ***

Respondents' hormone replacement therapy history: *** All three women testified that if they had known of the risk of breast cancer, they would not have taken the medication. Each of their health care providers testified that when they prescribed the hormone therapy drugs, they believed that the benefits outweighed the risks. Following the WHI study, their opinions changed.

The jury's verdict: *** The jury returned verdicts in favor of respondents totaling $134.6 million in compensatory damages. The jury also found that Wyeth had acted with malice or fraud. Because the jury made this last finding, the court ordered the jury to return for a trial on punitive damages. *** Evidence was presented regarding Wyeth's financial condition and following deliberations the jury returned three punitive damages awards totaling $99 million. It reduced the compensatory damages to $23 million and the punitive damages to $57,778,909.

The district court properly concluded that Nevada law applied: *** Their cancer was not detected while they lived in other states, even though the cancerous tumors may have been developing while they lived in those states.

The district court did not abuse its discretion when it modified the causation instruction, but the evidence supported a but-for causation instruction: *** Respondents presented evidence that Wyeth's drugs were the sole cause of their injuries. ***

Compensatory and punitive damages awards

Compliance with applicable regulatory standards does not automatically insulate a defendant from punitive damages: *** Wyeth urges this court to follow a line of cases that hold that compliance with FDA regulations negates malice such that punitive damages should not be awarded. We decline to do so.

While the cases cited by Wyeth allowed the defendants to avoid punitive damages by complying with federal standards, those cases' holdings are inapplicable to the facts presented in this case. *** Other courts have recognized that FDA regulations for drug manufacturers are generally viewed as establishing minimum standards for product design and warning. *** The United States Supreme Court has recognized that under the FDA's regulations, a drug manufacturer is responsible for the content of its drug label and ensuring that the warning remains adequate as long as the drug is on the market. *Wyeth v. Levine,* 555 U.S. 555, __, 129 S.Ct. 1187, 1197–98, 173 L.Ed.2d 51 (2009). Thus, if a drug manufacturer knows, or has reason to know, of increased dangers that are not already identified in its drug's label, compliance with the FDA's minimal standard may not satisfy its duty to warn.

Although Wyeth presented evidence that its drug label warned women and physicians that there was a risk of breast cancer, these warnings were inadequate because they were misleading. Evidence was presented that Wyeth financed and manipulated scientific studies and sponsored medical articles to downplay the risk of cancer while promoting certain unproven benefits. The evidence demonstrated that Wyeth used these same publications to mislead respondents' physicians. *** The studies that were developed over the years demonstrated that the breast cancer risk increased over time. While estrogen-progestin hormone therapy remains approved by the FDA and is still available on the market, Wyeth's particular drug, Prempro, is in a new lower dosage and carries a more serious warning that recommends its use only as a second-line treatment and for short durations. Therefore, we reject Wyeth's contention that compliance with FDA standards negates its liability for punitive damages, as Wyeth should not be able to benefit from its malicious and deceptive practices.

The compensatory and punitive damages awards are supported by substantial evidence and are not excessive—The jury found that Wyeth was negligent, its products were defective, and that Wyeth concealed material facts about its products' safety. *** The jury also found that respondents established by clear and convincing evidence that Wyeth acted with malice or fraud. Because of this last finding, the jury returned for a second trial regarding punitive damages. ***

The jury received subsequent instructions on assessing punitive damages for the second phase of trial. Evidence was presented regarding Wyeth's financial condition. After deliberating, the jury returned punitive damages awards that totaled $99 million. *** With regard to reducing the punitive damages awards, the district court abated those verdicts from $31 to $10 million for respondent Rowatt, $33 to $12 million for respondent Scofield, and $35 to $13 million for respondent Forrester. This decision was based on evidence that Wyeth provided a breast cancer warning, although arguably inadequate, and that it sponsored some limited testing.

Compensatory damages awards—Wyeth argues that the compensatory damages awards are not supported by substantial evidence as respondents presented little evidence of actual past and future damages, and thus, the awards are excessive as they are disproportionate to the injuries suffered. Based on our review of the appellate record, we conclude that substantial evidence supports the compensatory damages awards and that the reduced awards are not excessive.*** Respondents all developed a debilitating disease, breast cancer, as a result of Wyeth's actions, or lack thereof. The evidence supported the jury's finding that Wyeth was negligent in failing to conduct appropriate studies on breast cancer and that it concealed material facts about its products' safety. The evidence showed that Wyeth knew in the mid–1970s that certain body organs, such as breast tissue, responded negatively to hormones. Yet Wyeth failed to conduct or participate in any meaningful study of the estrogen-progestin drug combination until it gave its drug to the WHI study in 1992.

Wyeth knew also, by the late 1970s, that physicians were commonly prescribing the drug combination to treat menopause and prevent osteoporosis. And when published medical studies linked estrogen-progestin hormone therapy to an increased breast cancer risk, Wyeth sought to downplay the studies' results and divert attention from the information.

Punitive damages awards—Substantial evidence supports the jury's finding of malice: The evidence shows that while the words "breast cancer" appear ten times in the Prempro label, in many instances the term appeared in reassuring statements. *** Testimony showed that Wyeth spent $200 million each year marketing these drugs, but did not perform sufficient drug testing regarding breast cancer and its products to determine whether they were safe to use.

Evidence further demonstrated that Wyeth financed and manipulated scientific studies and sponsored articles that deliberately minimized the risk of breast cancer while promoting other unproven benefits. It also implemented a policy to dismiss scientific studies that showed any link between breast cancer and hormone therapy drugs and to distract the public and medical professionals from the information as well.

Over the years, Wyeth organized task forces to contain any negative publicity about hormone therapy and breast cancer. Wyeth's strategy to undermine scientific studies linking an increased risk of breast cancer to estrogen-progestin hormone therapy included ghostwriting multiple articles. The evidence further showed that Wyeth worked to keep a European study that exposed the unusually high breast cancer risk for thin women confidential. As a result of the study, Wyeth updated its European warnings, but never updated its United States labels. *** Based on the warning's language and Wyeth's actions, we conclude that a jury could reasonably determine that while Wyeth warned of breast cancer, it also tried to hide any potential harmful consequences of its products. Thus, substantial evidence supports the jury's conclusion that Wyeth acted with malice when it had knowledge of the probable harmful consequences of its wrongful acts and willfully and deliberately failed to act to avoid those consequences such that punitive damages were warranted.

The punitive damages awards are not excessive—*** Wyeth's misrepresentations and concealment of data showed reckless disregard for the health and safety of the users of its drugs. *** The harm suffered by respondents was the result of Wyeth's malicious activities and deceit. ***

The jury's improper deliberations were cured—*** When the district court learned that the jury awarded punitive damages in the trial's first phase, the court reinstructed the jury and sent them back to deliberate compensatory damages a second time. ***

Conclusion—The district court did not err or abuse its discretion in denying Wyeth's motions for judgment as a matter of law or its motion for a new trial, and therefore, we affirm the district court on all issues presented.

CRITICAL ANALYSIS: Evaluate the court ruling despite federal compliance and assess manufacturer liability if any.

NOTE: The Superior Court of Pennsylvania, in *Singleton v. Pfizer*, affirmed a lower court decision that Pfizer should pay $10.4 million in compensatory and punitive damages to the plaintiff due to risks involved and contraction of breast cancer attributed to taking the drug Prempro. Similar to the *Rowatt* decision, the court held that the drug company misled physicians about Prempro's risks.

Adequacy of Warnings—*Banner v. Hoffmann-LaRoche, Inc.*

The *Banner* decision illustrates that a court will review in detail the adequacy of warnings. In this case, the court was reluctant to impose liability on the manufacturer. The *Banner* court reviewed several factors illustrated below in this determination.

Banner v. Hoffmann-La Roche, Inc.,
383 NJ Super 364, 891 A.2d 1229 (2006)

WEFING, P.J.A.D. Plaintiffs Debbie and Kevin Banner appeal from trial court orders granting the motion of defendants Hoffmann-La Roche Inc. and Roche Laboratories Inc. ("Roche") to dismiss plaintiffs' complaint for failure to state a claim, *R.* 4:6-2(e), and subsequently denying their motion for reconsideration. After reviewing the record in light of the contentions advanced on appeal, we affirm. *** Accutane is a prescription medication developed by Roche and approved by the Food and Drug Administration; it is intended for the treatment of severe disfiguring nodular acne that has been recalcitrant to standard therapies. Accutane is known to be a teratogen, that is, there is an extremely high risk that if the drug is taken by a woman while she is pregnant, her child will be born with severe abnormalities. *** Because of the risks involved if a woman of child-bearing age were to take Accutane, Roche had developed a Pregnancy Prevention Program for physicians to use while discussing with their patients whether Accutane would be an appropriate therapy. Part of this Pregnancy Prevention Program involved having the patient complete a document titled in large, bold type "Patient Information/Consent and Survey Enrollment Form." Roche's protocol called for a physician to review this consent form with the patient and have the patient complete it prior to writing a prescription for Accutane. Ms. Banner's physician utilized this form in connection with reviewing with her the risks attendant to the use of Accutane.

On the top right-hand corner of this form is the silhouette of a pregnant woman, upon which is superimposed a circle, with an angular line descending to the right, the universal pictograph to depict a warning, together with the words, "Pregnancy Prevention Program for Women on Accutane." These words are in bold type and all capital letters. Beneath that, in large italic type, is written "Accutane must not be used by females who are pregnant or who may become pregnant while undergoing treatment." We set forth the pertinent provisions of this consent form in detail.

My treatment with Accutane has been personally explained to me by Dr. ___.
The following points of information, among others, have been specifically discussed and made clear:

1. I, ___, understand that Accutane is a very powerful medicine used to treat severe nodular acne that did not get better with other treatments, including oral antibiotics. Initials: ___

2. I understand that I must not take Accutane if I am or may become pregnant during treatment. Initials: ___

3. I understand that severe birth defects have occurred in babies of women who took Accutane during pregnancy. I have been warned by my doctor that there is an extremely high risk of severe damage to my unborn baby if I am or become pregnant while taking Accutane.
Initials: ___

4. I have been told by my doctor that effective birth control (contraception) must be used for at least 1 month before starting Accutane, all during Accutane therapy and for at least 1 month after Accutane treatment has stopped. My doctor has recommended that I either abstain from sexual intercourse or use two reliable kinds of birth control at the same time. I have also been told that any method of birth control can fail. I must use two forms of reliable birth control simultaneously even if I think I cannot become pregnant, unless I abstain from sexual intercourse or have had a hysterectomy. INITIALS: ___

5. I know that I must have a blood or urine test done by my doctor that shows I am not pregnant within 1 week before starting Accutane, and I understand that I must wait until the second or third day of my next normal menstrual period before starting Accutane. INITIALS: ___

6. My doctor has told me that I can participate in the "Patient Referral" program for an initial free pregnancy test and birth control counseling session by a consulting physician. INITIALS: ___

7. I also know that I must immediately stop taking Accutane if I become pregnant while taking the drug and immediately contact my doctor to discuss the desirability of continuing the pregnancy. I also know that I must immediately contact my doctor if I become pregnant during the month after stopping Accutane. INITIALS: ___

8. I have carefully read the Accutane patient brochure, "Important Information Concerning Your Treatment With Accutane (isotretinoin)," given to me by my doctor. I understand all of its contents and have talked over any questions I have with my doctor. INITIALS: ___

9. I am not now pregnant, nor do I plan to become pregnant for at least 30 days after I have completely finished taking Accutane. INITIALS: ___

10. My doctor has told me that I can participate in a survey concerning Accutane use in women by completing an additional form. INITIALS: ___

Ms. Banner completed this form, placing her initials after each statement, indicating she had reviewed and understood each section. Accutane's accompanying package insert began in the following manner: **CONTRAINDICATION AND WARNING:** Accutane must not be used by females who are pregnant or who may become pregnant while undergoing treatment. Although not every fetus exposed to Accutane has resulted in a deformed child, there is an extremely high risk that a deformed infant can result if pregnancy occurs while taking Accutane in any amount even for short periods of time. Potentially any fetus exposed during pregnancy can be affected. Presently there is no accurate means of determining after Accutane exposure which fetus has been affected and which fetus has not been affected. Accutane is contraindicated in females of childbearing potential unless the *patient meets all of the following conditions:*

✓ Is reliable in understanding and carrying out instructions;

✓ Is capable of complying with the mandatory contraceptive measures;

✓ Has received both oral and written warnings of the hazards of taking Accutane during pregnancy and exposing a fetus to the drug;

✓ Has received both oral and written warnings of the risk of possible contraception failure and of the need to use two reliable forms of contraception simultaneously, unless abstinence is the chosen method, or the patient has undergone a hysterectomy and has acknowledged in writing her understanding of these warnings and of the need for using dual contraceptive methods;

✓ Has had a negative serum or urine pregnancy test with a sensitivity of at least 56 mIU/mL within 1 week prior to beginning therapy; and

✓ Will begin therapy only on the second or third day of the next normal menstrual period.

The package insert also listed the abnormalities that had been reported in babies who had been exposed to Accutane during their mothers' pregnancies. Major human fetal abnormalities related to Accutane administration have been documented: CNS abnormalities (including cerebral abnormalities, cerebellar malformation, hydrocephalus, microcephaly, cranial nerve deficit); skull abnormality; external ear abnormalities (including anolia, micropinna, small or absent external auditory canals); eye abnormalities (including microphthalmia); cardiovascular abnormalities; facial dysmorphia; cleft palate; thymus gland abnormality; parathyroid hormone deficiency. In some cases death has occurred with certain of the abnormalities previously noted. Cases of IQ scores less than 85 with or without obvious CNS abnormalities have also been reported. There is an increased risk of spontaneous abortion. In addition, premature births have been reported. ***

According to plaintiff's initial complaint, she, for religious reasons, elected not to use birth control in any form to prevent a pregnancy. *** Ms. Banner, however, did not remain abstinent. She and her husband did engage in unprotected sexual relations. She became pregnant, and their child was born profoundly disabled. *** As the appellants have framed the question before us, the critical issue is the trial court's determination that the warnings provided by Roche in connection with Accutane were adequate as a matter of law. *** Product liability actions in New Jersey are governed by our Products Liability Act, *N.J.S.A.* 2A:58C-1 to -11. *** The statute provides that a manufacturer or seller of a product is liable for harm caused by a product that is "not reasonably fit, suitable or safe for its intended purpose" as a result of a manufacturing defect, a design defect or a failure "to contain adequate warnings or instructions." ***

The only exception to the learned intermediary doctrine in New Jersey arises when a pharmaceutical company has advertised its drug directly to the consuming public. *Perez v. Wyeth Lab., Inc.*, 161 N.J. 1, 734 A.2d 1245 (1999). Plaintiffs contend that the learned intermediary rule does not apply to this matter. They point to Roche's alleged practice of supplying brochures to doctors' offices and placement of non-branded ads in magazines. They also point to Roche having developed the Pregnancy Prevention Program. Plaintiffs assert these activities constitute direct-to-consumer advertising under *Perez,* thus imposing upon Roche a duty to supply adequate warnings not only to Ms. Banner's physician but also to Ms. Banner herself. ***

The Court in *Perez* considered whether the defendant, which manufactured and distributed Norplant, an implanted, reversible contraceptive designed to prevent pregnancy for up to five years, could invoke the learned intermediary doctrine to defend against claims it had failed to provide adequate warnings of Norplant's side effects. *Id.* at 5, 734 A.2d 1245. *** In our judgment, the placement of informational brochures in a physician's office cannot fairly be equated with a course of mass advertising or be deemed direct-to-consumer advertising so as to remove the predicates of the learned intermediary doctrine. Our conclusion in this regard is bolstered by 21 *C.F.R.* § 202.1(k)(2), which does not treat such material as advertising, but as labeling. ***

In our judgment, the warnings given to Debbie Banner in 1995 were "accurate, clear, and unambiguous," and were, therefore, adequate as a matter of law. The Accutane package insert and the Patient Information/Consent and Survey Enrollment Form clearly indicated that birth defects would very likely result if an unborn child was exposed to the drug. These warnings also clearly state that a woman of child-bearing age undergoing Accutane treatment must avoid becoming pregnant. *** The warnings in Ms. Banner's case were even more clear, accurate and unambiguous than those discussed in earlier cases. Roche adequately warned both the physician and Ms. Banner that pregnancy must be avoided during Accutane treatment, and that if pregnancy occurred, the unborn child would very likely suffer severe birth defects as a result of exposure to the drug. *** Roche fulfilled its duty by advising of the risks associated with Accutane therapy and advising of the need for either effective contraception or abstinence. The choice was plaintiffs' to elect. The orders under review are affirmed.

CRITICAL ANALYSIS: Evaluate the adequacy of the warnings in *Banner* and determine if the court decided this case correctly.

The Pharmacist Duty to Warn—*Kowalski* and *Allberry*

Does a pharmacist have a duty to warn a consumer about a dangerous mix of prescription medicines? The Arkansas Supreme Court determined that the pharmacist had no duty to warn and upheld a lower court ruling that a pharmacist has no general duty to warn a customer about a dangerous mix of prescription medicines, no duty to refuse to fill dangerous prescriptions and no duty to inquire about the physicians who prescribed them. The cause of death was ruled "mixed drug intoxication" combined with alcohol. In *Allberry,* the facts presented differently, yet the court declined to extend the duty to warn to the pharmacist.

Kowalski v. Rose Drugs of Dardanelle, Inc.,
378 S.W.3d 109 (Ark. 2011)

DONALD L. CORBIN, Justice. Appellant Virginia Kowalski, individually and as special administratrix of the Estate of Kevin Allen Curry, deceased, and on behalf of the statutory beneficiaries of the Estate of Kevin Allen Curry ("the Estate"), appeals from the circuit court's order granting summary judgment to Appellee Rose Drugs of Dardanelle, Inc. ("Rose Drugs"). On appeal, the Estate argues that the circuit court erred in concluding that Rose Drugs, as a pharmacy, had no general duty to warn, to not fill dangerous prescriptions, and to inquire of a prescribing physician. We find no error and affirm.

The facts as alleged in the complaint reveal the following. On August 24, 2005, Kevin Allen Curry was found dead in his home in Dardanelle, Arkansas. Following an autopsy, his cause of death was ruled "mixed drug intoxication" combined with alcohol. Four days prior to his death, Curry saw Dr. Randeep Mann for generalized facial pain resulting from a blast to the face. Dr. Mann prescribed Curry several medications, including Norflex, Zoloft, Valium, Oxycontin,

Percocet, Lorazepam, Methadone, Propoxyphene, and Doxepin . At the time that Curry saw Dr. Mann, he was already taking Percocet, Valium, Ambien, Trazodone, Norflex, Zoloft, Effexor, and Oxycontin. Curry had the prescriptions written by Dr. Mann filled at Rose Drug, a pharmacy owned by Appellee Rose Drugs, on August 22, 2005., Dr. Mann admitted only to prescribing Norflex, Valium, Percocet, and Methadone for Curry on August 20, 2005. Rose Drugs did not specify in its answer which drugs it filled. But, attached as exhibits to a brief in support of a motion for summary judgment were pharmacy records showing that Curry had prescriptions filled for Oxycodone, Methadone, Diazepam, Trazodone, Norflex, and Lunesta.

The Estate filed a wrongful-death action against Rose Drugs and Dr. Mann. It asserted therein that Dr. Mann was liable for wrongful death by his "failure to properly treat Kevin Curry and negligent prescribing of numerous medications without regard to the ramifications of those multiple prescription medications." The Estate further asserted a wrongful-death action against Rose Drugs for its "failure to properly monitor and negligent filling of numerous medications without regard to the ramifications of the multiple prescriptions." ***

In seeking summary judgment, Rose Drugs relied on the decision in *Kohl v. American Home Products Corp.,* 78 F.Supp.2d 885, 893 (W.D.Ark.1999), wherein the Arkansas federal district court held that "pharmacies generally have no common-law or statutory duty to warn customers of the risks associated with the prescription drugs they purchase." *** According to the Estate, the question of duty is dependent upon the foreseeability of injury and, here, Rose Drugs had a duty to foresee injury to Curry from improper dispensation of medications that were contraindicated. In advancing its argument, the Estate asserts that Rose Drugs owed Curry a duty to warn him about the dangers of the medications prescribed or should have refused to fill them because certain regulations governing pharmacies established such a duty, otherwise known as a duty by regulation. ***

I. Duty: The question of what is a pharmacist's duty in Arkansas is an issue of first impression for this court. *** Thus, the law of negligence requires as an essential element that the plaintiff show that a duty of care was owed. *Young v. Paxton,* 316 Ark. 655, 873 S.W.2d 546 (1994). ***

A. Controlled Substances: The first regulation relied upon by the Estate to demonstrate that Rose Drugs had a duty to warn or to refuse to fill the prescriptions is the Controlled Substances Act (CSA), codified at 21 U.S.C. §§ 801-971 (1970). *** In short, the CSA is a statutory framework for punishing individuals, including doctors or pharmacists, who engage in the distribution of certain controlled substances outside the ordinary scope of their professional practice. *** The Estate's argument that it imposes a duty that required Rose Drugs to warn Curry about the medications prescribed by Dr. Mann is without merit.

B. OBRA: Next, the Estate points to the Omnibus Budget Reconciliation Act of 1990 (OBRA), and states that this federal act, codified at 42 U.S .C. § 1396r-8, requires states to establish programs, including counseling customers concerning drug interactions and requirements for maintaining patient information and, thus, created a duty that required Rose Drugs to warn Curry. ***

C. Arkansas's Statutory & Regulatory Framework: *** First, the Estate points to Ark.Code Ann. § 17-92-101(13) (Repl.2010), which sets forth the definition for "pharmacy care" and provides that it means the process by which a pharmacist in consultation with the prescribing practitioner identifies, resolves, and prevents potential and actual drug-related problems and optimizes patient therapy outcomes through the responsible provision of drug therapy or disease state management for the purpose of achieving any of the following definite outcomes that improve a patient's quality of life: (A) Cure of disease, (B) Elimination or reduction of a patient's symptomology, (C) Arresting or slowing a disease process or (D) Preventing a disease or symptomology.

In sum, the Estate can point to no statutory or regulatory framework that imposes on a pharmacist a duty to warn, to refuse to fill a legally written prescription, or to consult with a physician. *** Physicians exercising sound medical judgment act as intermediaries in the chain of distribution, preempting, as it were, the exercise of discretion by the supplier-pharmacist, and, within limits, by the patient-consumer. *** In support, the Estate relies on cases from a minority of the jurisdictions that have recognized that a pharmacist has a duty beyond merely filling a prescription accurately. *See, e.g., Hooks SuperX, Inc. v. McLaughlin,* 642 N.E .2d 514 (Ind.1994) (rejecting applicability of the learned-intermediary doctrine and holding that a pharmacist had a duty to refuse to fill a prescription); *Spalitto,* 1 S.W.3d 519 (holding that in some cases a pharmacist's duty will never extend beyond accurately filling a prescription but, in other cases, a pharmacist's education and expertise will require that he or she do more to help protect their patrons from risks that pharmacists can reasonably foresee). ***

We believe, however, that the better approach is that adopted by the majority of jurisdictions that there is no general duty to warn imposed on pharmacists. *See, e.g., Walls v. Alpharma USPD, Inc.,* 887 So.2d 881 (Ala.2004) (holding that to the extent that the learned-intermediary doctrine applies, the duty to determine whether the medication as prescribed is dangerously defective is owed by the prescribing physician and not by the pharmacist filling the prescription); *Cottam v. CVS Pharmacy,* 764 N.E.2d 814 (Mass.2002) (holding that generally a pharmacy has no duty to warn its customers of the side effects of prescription drugs); *** Arkansas adopted the learned-intermediary doctrine in *West v. Searle & Co.,* 305 Ark. 33, 806 S.W.2d 608 (1991). That doctrine provides an exception to the general rule that a manufacturer has a duty to warn the ultimate user of the risks of its products. *** The physician acts as the "learned intermediary" between the manufacturer and the ultimate consumer. *Id.* at 42, 806 S.W.2d at 613.

We cannot say that Rose Drugs had a general duty to warn, to refuse to fill the prescriptions, or to inquire of Dr. Mann. The duty to warn of the medications' dangers was with Dr. Mann, who prescribed the drugs. We therefore affirm the circuit court's order granting summary judgment in favor of Rose Drugs.

JIM HANNAH, Chief Justice, dissenting I respectfully dissent. Rose Drugs of Dardanelle, Inc. moved for summary judgment asserting that its duty to Kevin Curry "required no more" than to fill Curry's prescriptions as ordered by Dr. Mann. The circuit court found that *Kohl v. American Home Products Corp.,* 78 F.Supp.2d 885 (W.D.Ark.1999) was persuasive on this issue and was a decision that would likely be adopted by this court. *** The court in *Kohl* concluded that, "absent the presence of some contraindication," a pharmacist's duty does not include a general duty to warn. *Kohl,* 78 F.Supp.2d at 892. Plaintiff's expert, Dr. Michael Horseman, testified that the prescriptions given by Dr. Mann would have resulted in multiple warnings of drug interactions on the store computer software. In other words, contraindications were present. ***

There is more at issue in this case than just the pharmacist's duty to accurately fill and properly label a prescription. This case also presents the issue of whether a duty arises where a pharmacist has reason to believe that (1) the physician issuing the prescription has made an error, or (2) the prescription has been altered. Under such facts, there may be a duty on the part of the pharmacist to clarify the prescription with the doctor or to warn of contraindications. ***

ROBERT L. BROWN, Justice, dissenting The majority holds today that pharmacists owe *no* duty to their customers to warn them of fatal prescriptions. This conclusion is totally at odds with the Regulations of the Arkansas Board of Pharmacy and does a disservice to the pharmaceutical profession in general by failing to recognize the high standards observed within the profession itself. ***

I. The Issue: Four days before his death, Kevin Allen Curry was prescribed heavy dosages of Oxycodone, Methadone, Diazepam, Trazodone, Orphenadrine, and Lunesta by Dr. Randeep Mann of Russellville. Several of these drugs were central nervous system depressants, and Methadone was a controlled substance. Curry filled these prescriptions at Rose Drugs in Dardanelle as a first-time patient. *** Hence, the issue before this court on appeal is whether a pharmacist *ever* has a duty to consult with the physician or warn a customer regarding a suspect prescription. The majority thinks not. I could not disagree more.

II. Legal Duty of Care in Arkansas: Arkansas statutory law makes it clear that pharmacists owe a duty of ordinary care and diligence to their customers. For example, the Pharmacy Code defines "pharmacy care" as "the process by which a pharmacist *in consultation with the prescribing practitioner* identifies, resolves, and prevents potential and actual drug-related *problems* and optimizes patient therapy outcomes through the responsible provision of drug therapy or disease state management." Ark.Code Ann. § 17-92-101(13) (Supp.2009) (emphasis added). ***

III. Exceptions to the General Rule: The rationale advanced by Rose Drugs and adopted by the majority for no duty to warn is that the physician acts as the "informed intermediary" in the chain of distribution of the drugs between the manufacturer and the patient, preempting any discretion on the part of the pharmacist. ***

In several of the cases cited by the majority from other jurisdictions, exceptions are noted to the general rule. *See Cottam v. CVS Pharmacy,* 764 N.E.2d 814 (Mass.2002) (court expressly did not rule on the situation where pharmacist has specific knowledge of increased danger to customer); *Moore v. Mem'l Hosp. of Gulfport,* 825 So.2d 658 (Miss.2002) (recognizing that there are exceptions to the learned-intermediary doctrine, as applied to pharmacists, where it was undisputed that the plaintiff had informed the pharmacy of health problems which contraindicated the use of the drug in question or where the pharmacist filled prescriptions in quantities inconsistent with the recommended dosage guidelines); *McKee v. Am. Home Prods. Corp.,* 782 P.2d 1045 (Wash.1989) (court noted that under certain circumstances where there is a patent error on the prescription such as an obvious lethal dose, inadequacy of the instructions, known contraindication, or incompatible prescriptions, the pharmacist should take corrective measures); *Morgan v. Wal-Mart Stores, Inc.,* 30 S.W.3d 455 (Tx.Ct. App.2000) (recognizing that the courts that have held that pharmacists owe their customers a duty beyond accurately filing prescriptions do so based on the presence of additional factors, such as known contraindications, that would alert a reasonably prudent pharmacist to a potential problem and not disputing that a pharmacist may be held liable for negligently filling a prescription in such situations).

Furthermore, several jurisdictions have explicitly held that in certain circumstances, a duty to warn exists. *See, e.g., Riff v. Morgan Pharmacy,* 508 A.2d 1247, 1252 (Pa.Super.Ct.1986) (holding that the pharmacy had a legal duty to exercise due care and diligence, and that the pharmacy breached this duty "by failing to warn the patient or notify the prescribing physician of the obvious inadequacies appearing on the face of the prescription which created a substantial risk of serious harm to the plaintiff."). ***

IV. Standard of Care: Several states have endorsed a standard of care for pharmacists that, under certain circumstances, includes a duty to warn. For example, in *Dooley v. Everett,* 805 S.W.2d 380 (Tenn.Ct.App.1990), the Tennessee Court of Appeals was presented with the question of whether a pharmacist had a duty to warn a customer of the potential interaction between two different prescription drugs which were prescribed for asthma. The *Dooley* court concluded that "the pharmacist has a duty to act with due, ordinary, care and diligence in compounding and selling drugs." *Id.* at 384. *** Also, in *Lasley v. Shrake's Country Club Pharmacy, Inc.,* 880 P.2d 1129 (Ariz.Ct.App.1994), the Arizona Court of Appeals initially recognized that a pharmacy owed the customer a duty of reasonable care and then stated that the next question was whether the pharmacy breached the standard of care established because of that duty. ***

V. Arkansas Standard of Care-Board Regulations: The Arkansas State Board of Pharmacy has adopted a comprehensive regulation on patient care and patient counseling for pharmacists. *** This regulation requires the pharmacist to evaluate prescriptions and engage in "effective communication" with the customer concerning the dosage, times of administration, significant side effects, and other questions that the patient might have. Regulation 09-00-0001(a)-(d). Regulation 09-00-0001(e) also requires the pharmacy to "maintain a computer program which will identify significant drug interactions". The pharmacist will be responsible for counseling the patient on these interactions with verbal and, where appropriate, written information. *** However, "[i]t is the pharmacist's responsibility to monitor the patient's medication therapy in the areas addressed in this regulation and to inform the physician of a suspected problem." *Id.* *** Thus, our own statutes and Board regulations define the role of pharmacists as more than mere order fillers and specifically provide that pharmacists should work with physicians to identify, resolve, and prevent potential and actual drug-related problems and also counsel with their customers about the dosages and side effects. *** Regulation 9, in particular, provides the standard of care pharmacists must provide to their customers and imposes in certain situations a duty to warn the customer and alert the prescribing physician of a serious, potentially lethal problem. ***

VI. Expert Testimony: In the deposition of Dr. Michael Horseman, Kowalski's expert and a pharmacist from Corpus Christi, Texas, he testified that the number of prescriptions of central nervous system depressants in the instant case and the combined large dosages more likely than not caused Curry's death. *** Dr. Horseman emphasized that Curry was a first-time customer and added that in this situation, the standard of care required the pharmacist at Rose Drugs to question Curry about whether he had taken these drugs before and whether he was aware that these drugs in combination are particularly dangerous drugs.

Dr. Horseman added that the pharmacist should have recognized the fact that there was a contraindication in filling these combined prescriptions and should have called Dr. Randeep Mann to confirm what was prescribed and the combination in which they were prescribed. If Dr. Mann confirmed the prescriptions, then the pharmacist at Rose Drugs had a choice of either filling them or not filling them. *** Dr. Horseman added that the required computer system, which alerts a pharmacist to potential drug interactions, should have "red flagged" the pharmacist about the interactions involved with the multiple prescriptions.*** Dr. Harvey Ham, a pharmacist at Rose Drugs who worked the day that Curry's prescriptions were filled, testified that he did not remember filling Curry's prescriptions. He did say that Rose Drugs has a computer program that flags interactions, contraindications, and other problems with regard to prescriptions. ***

Dr. Lee Roy Parker, the other pharmacist working at Rose Drugs when Curry filled his prescriptions, testified that he counseled Curry for about five minutes about whether he was familiar with the medications since they were potent and advised Curry not to take the prescriptions with other medications or alcohol. He acknowledged that he had the authority to refuse to fill prescriptions. He did not recall any conversation with Dr. Mann on that day. ***

VII. Conclusion: The majority opinion fails to recognize that, far from being a robot, the pharmacist is a critical link in the prescription chain who owes a duty of due care to customers. ***

CRITICAL ANALYSIS: Assess the majority and dissenting opinions and determine whether the majority was correct.

Allberry v. Parkmor Drug, Inc.,
834 N.E.2d 199 (Ind. App. 2005)

BAILEY, Judge ***Issue: *Allberry* raises two issues on appeal, which we consolidate and restate as whether Parkmor owed a duty to Allberry to either warn him of the potential side effects associated with a particular prescription drug or, in the alternative, provide Allberry with the manufacturer's product information.

Facts and Procedural History: On or before June 1, 2002, Allberry purchased the prescription drug Caverject—which is generally used to treat impotence—from Parkmor. At the time, Parkmor did not give Allberry "any product information" from the drug's manufacturer or any "drug information, leaflets, [or] pamphlets." In particular, Parkmor did not advise Allberry to seek medical attention if, after using the drug, he had an erection for more than four hours. On June 1, 2002, after injecting Caverject into his penis, Allberry experienced a "severely painful erection which lasted for almost 72 hours." *** After his surgery and upon inquiry to Parkmor, Allberry's wife received the "patient information leaflet," which contains the following, pertinent information: "The erection should last about one hour. If an erection lasts more than 4 hours, seek immediate medical attention. If you notice other effects not listed above, contact your doctor or pharmacist." As a result of the incident, Allberry developed "priapism and later became impotent." On July 28, 2004, Allberry filed an amended complaint against Parkmor, alleging, in part, that the pharmacy had failed to provide him with any warnings regarding the adverse side effects of the prescription drug Caverject. *** On February 9, 2004, the trial court granted summary judgment to Parkmor with respect to Allberry's failure to warn claim. ***Allberry now appeals.

Discussion and Decision

II. Analysis On appeal, Allberry argues that the trial court erroneously granted summary judgment to Parkmor because, as his pharmacist, Parkmor owed a duty of care to warn him of the adverse side effects of Caverject. *** Here, the undisputed evidence demonstrates that the relationship between Parkmor and Allberry was that of a pharmacy and its customer. The designated evidence also reveals that the drug in question, i.e., Caverject, was prescribed to Allberry by his physician and, further, that the prescription itself contained only the following language: "Caverject 40 mg[,] use as directed[,] 1 bottle."

In Ingram, 476 N.E.2d at 885, another panel of this Court determined that a pharmacist has no duty to warn a consumer of the possible side effects associated with a prescription drug prescribed by a physician. The Ingram court concluded that physicians, not pharmacists, are in the better position to weigh the potential risks and rewards of particular medications for specific patients and, thus, declined to impose a duty upon pharmacists to warn customers about the potential side effects of medication unless such warnings were included in the prescription received from the physician. Id. at 886-87; see also *Hooks SuperX, Inc. v. McLaughlin*, 642 N.E.2d 514, 518 (Ind. 1994) (affirming that the responsibility of warning patients about drug side effects lies with physicians but imposing a duty where the pharmacist had personal knowledge that the customer was taking medication more quickly than prescribed). *** The rationale expressed in Ingram is consistent with the majority of other jurisdictions that have addressed this issue and refused to impose a duty to warn on pharmacists. These jurisdictions generally reason that imposing such a duty on the pharmacist would place the pharmacist between the physician—who knows the patient's physical condition—and the patient and could lead to harmful interference in the patient-physician relationship. *** By contrast, a few jurisdictions have imposed a duty on pharmacies that goes beyond merely filling prescriptions accurately. See, e.g., *Horner v. Spalitto*, 1 S.W.3d 519, 523-24 (Mo. Ct. App. 1999) (holding that a pharmacy could be found negligent for filling a prescription for what the pharmacist knew to be a lethal dose), reh'g denied, trans. denied; *Lasley v. Shrake's Country Club Pharmacy, Inc.*, 179 Ariz. 583, 880 P.2d 1129, 1132-34 (Ariz. Ct. App. 1994) (imposing a duty for failing to warn the customer when filling two prescriptions that adversely interacted with one another). *** Because we find the majority view to be more persuasive, today, we reaffirm our holding in Ingram. As such, Parkmor had no duty to warn Allberry of the side effects associated with Caverject. Parkmor also had no duty to give Allberry the manufacturer's product information, which contained certain warnings about the use of Caverject, as such information was not included in the prescription itself. Accordingly, under these circumstances, the trial court properly granted summary judgment to Parkmor. Accordingly, if the legislature wanted to require pharmacists to warn customers of the side effects associated with prescription drugs, it would have done so by statute. We will not impose such a duty absent clear legislative intent.

CRITICAL ANALYSIS: This case, along with *Kowalski,* held the pharmacist did not have a duty to warn. Discuss under what circumstances a pharmacist should have a duty to warn.

The Pharmacist Duty to Warn Revisited
The Changing Role of Pharmacy in Health Care and the Resultant Impact on the Obligation of a Pharmacist to Warn
Roseann B. Termini, Ohio Northern University Law Review, Used with Permission; modified in part (2018).
I. Introduction

Gone are the days when the sole duty of a pharmacist consisted of accurately filling and dispensing prescription drugs. [1] Today, the role of the pharmacist in the health care system has taken on a greater significance. Traditionally, the physician had the sole responsibility to monitor and counsel the drug consumption of a patient. [2] However, recent changes in the education of the pharmacist, technology, direct-to-consumer advertising, and the competitive nature of the pharmaceutical market[3] has altered the scope of liability on the part of the pharmacist.

Most courts found pharmacists owed no duty to warn. [4] The consensus among the majority of courts centered on the physician as the conduit to convey information to the patient and to assess the risks involved with the adverse effects of a prescription drug. [5] The physician, as the learned intermediary between the manufacturer and the patient, was the proper medical professional to warn a patient of possible risks associated with drug consumption. [6] Thus, the sole obligation of the pharmacist centered on the accurate dispensing of pharmaceuticals. [7] Over the years, the view of pharmacy has evolved into greater recognition of pharmacists as proactive professionals in the health care field. [8] Advances in technology also expanded the capabilities and role of pharmacists. Computer systems that maintain patient profiles and warn of drug interactions are now commonly utilized within the pharmaceutical market. Changes within the pharmaceutical industry resulted in direct-to-consumer advertising and increased competition between pharmacies. [9]

This article focuses on past and present cases and how recent changes in the pharmaceutical and health care industry altered the traditional view that a pharmacist owned no duty to warn his customer. The article concludes by recognizing that the minority position that encompasses both a duty to warn and a duty to refuse to fill a validly issued prescription might in the future become the majority prevailing view.

II. The Learned Intermediary Doctrine Prevails

Generally, the physician is still viewed as the professional with the obligation to warn. For example, the Michigan courts view the physician as the professional to impart information to the patient and to monitor the prescription status. In the case of *Adkins v. Mong*, [10] the plaintiff alleged negligence and malpractice on the part the pharmacist for filling excessive amounts of addictive substances. [11] The plaintiff claimed that the failure of the pharmacist to warn of the possibility of addiction resulted in his drug addiction; however, all of the prescriptions filled by the pharmacist were valid. [12]

In addressing the issue of whether a pharmacist owes this duty, the Adkins court looked to the decisions from other jurisdictions. [13] The Adkins court concluded that other jurisdictions faced with the same issue overwhelmingly rejected the idea that a pharmacist owes this duty to a customer. [14] Other decisions by the Michigan courts have consistently held that a pharmacist owes no duty to warn, hence refusing to expand the obligation of a pharmacist beyond that of accurately filling a prescription. As a result, the Adkins court held that "there exists no legal duty on the part of a pharmacist to monitor and intervene with a customer's reliance on drugs prescribed by a licensed treating physician." [15] The Adkins court was unpersuaded. [16]Although Michigan courts have held pharmacists to a high standard of care in filling prescriptions, a pharmacist fulfills this high standard of care once a prescription is accurately filled. [17] For example, the Stebbins court concluded a pharmacist owes no duty to warn of possible side effects of prescription drugs. [18] Where the prescription is proper on its face and neither the physician nor the manufacturer required the pharmacist to provide a customer with a warning directly, the pharmacist owes no duty to warn of possible side effects of a prescribed medication. [19]

Similarly, in *Kintigh v. Abbott Pharmacy*, [20] the plaintiff alleged that the pharmacist continued to fill a codeine-based cough syrup prescription which perpetuated a substance abuse problem. [21] However, the court found no duty on the part of the pharmacist to discover an addictive status of a customer and, furthermore, no duty to refuse to fill a valid prescription for a controlled substance. [22]

Legislative policy could play a major role in determining the duty to warn. For example, in Illinois, the legislative policy is against expanding the liability risks of health professionals. [23] At least one court focused on the legislative policy in deciding the duty to warn issue. As an example, in *Leesley v. West*, [24] the pharmacist failed to directly warn a customer or ensure that the relevant

214

warnings reached the ultimate consumers of the drug. [25] The plaintiff contended that the pharmacist had a duty to provide the package inserts about the known risks and side effects that the drug manufacturer provided to the pharmacist. [26] The *Leesley* court relied on the "learned intermediary theory" in determining that the pharmacist owed no duty to warn. [27] Under the "learned intermediary theory" the drug manufacturer only has a duty to provide warnings directly to physicians. [28] Thus, the court found it illogical and inequitable to impose a duty on the pharmacist to also provide warnings. [29] However, the customer still contended that the pharmacy had an independent duty to warn because of the dangerous side effects. [30] The court recognized foreseeability of harm, burden on the pharmacist, and public policy to determine if a duty existed for a pharmacist to warn of dangerous side effects. [31] The *Leesley* court concluded that requiring a pharmacist to convey the warnings it receives to its customers would be very burdensome, even though it did receive a package insert of the relevant cautionary information from the manufacturer. [32] That is, the court refused to impose liability when warnings were not ordered by the prescribing physician. [33] The *Leesley* court unequivocally determined that a pharmacist has no independent duty to warn a consumer of dangerous side effects. [34]

The Tennessee case of *Laws v. Johnson* [35] examined the liability of a pharmacist who removed the printed package insert containing the manufacturer information and warnings before dispensing eye medication. [36] The insert included a section concerning adverse effects on the cardiovascular system. [37] The plaintiff in Laws suffered several heart attacks while taking the eye medication. [38] The plaintiff, who inadvertently received the package insert, read the package insert and became concerned that the use of his eye medication contributed to his heart problems. [39] Upon consultation, his doctor explained in rare cases the eye medication could cause heart problems. [40] The plaintiff argued that the pharmacist had a duty to provide the package inserts to the customer. [41] The Laws court applied the "learned intermediary theory," [42] and held that the drug manufacturer owes the responsibility to supply package inserts to the physician and not the pharmacist. [43] Once the physician is provided with adequate warnings by the manufacturer, the physician has the duty to provide the warnings to the patient. [44] The court held the plaintiff was not entitled to receive the warnings, in any form, directly from the manufacturer or the pharmacist. [45]

The reasoning in Laws was also based on a variety of public policy justifications. [46] The court determined that total disclosure may not be in the best interest of the patient. [47] The court pointed out that the technical information in the warnings probably could not be understood by a lay person. [48] Further, the technical information could possibly confuse a patient who may discontinue using the medication. [49] The court also addressed the claim that removal of the warnings violated a standard of practice among pharmacists. [50] The plaintiff argued the pharmacist failed to dispense the medication within the requirements of a Tennessee statute, which required the drug be dispensed with strict conformity to a physician's orders. [51] The plaintiff asserted that removal of the package insert violated the integrity of the drug to the point the drug was no longer dispensed in accordance with physician's orders. [52] The court, however, found no authority to support this contention. [53] Furthermore, the court found nothing in the record to support any claim that the pharmacist did not dispense the prescription in accordance with the orders of the physician. [54]

III. Pharmacists Owe a Duty of Due Care to the Patient Only

Although the physician is still deemed as the professional who warns the patient, pharmacists still owe a duty to exercise due care and diligence in the performance of their professional duties. For example, in *Riff v. Morgan Pharmacy*, [55] the court held that the pharmacy failed to exercise due care and diligence because they did not warn about the maximum dosage. [56] The failure to specify the maximum dosage resulted in an overdose of suppositories and caused permanent damage. [57] Expert testimony from a pharmacist and pharmacologist focused on the fact that a pharmacist who receives inadequate instructions as to the maximum dosage has a duty to ascertain if the patient is aware of the limitation concerning the use of the medication or alternatively, to contact the prescribing physician as to the inadequacy of the prescription. [58] These experts testified that a reasonably prudent pharmacist under the facts of this case would have corrected the inadequacies appearing on the face of the prescription. [59]

As a professional, a pharmacist is held to the standard of care within the profession. [60] The *Riff* court held that the defendant pharmacy owed a legal duty to exercise due care and due diligence. [61] The pharmacist breached that duty in failing to warn the patient or notify the physician of the inadequacies of the prescription, which created a substantial risk of serious harm to the plaintiff. [62] The Riff court further explained that public policy dictates that pharmacists who dispense prescription drugs be held accountable when their conduct falls below the level of reasonable conduct in the practice of pharmacy and, as a consequence, injury results. [63]

Thus far, the cases addressed suggest that a pharmacist owes a legal duty of due care and diligence. Courts have been unwilling to impose a duty to warn of the possible adverse side effects of prescribed medications. [64] In *Lasley v. Shrake's Country Club Pharmacy*, [65] the pharmacy dispensed a prescription drug for several years without any warnings about its addictive nature. [66] It was alleged that by not warning the customer, the pharmacy failed in its duty to exercise a reasonable standard of care expected from pharmacists in the profession. [67] The *Lasley* court determined that a question existed as to whether a duty to warn of the adverse side effects was included as part of a pharmacist's reasonable standard of care. [68] Arizona courts had not determined whether a pharmacist's duty to provide reasonable care included a duty to warn. [69] As a result, the *Lasley* court turned to other jurisdictions for guidance and determined that many jurisdictions find no duty to warn for two reasons. [70] First, imposition of a duty on pharmacists would lead to interference with the physician-patient relationship. [71] Second, burdening pharmacists with this duty would cause them to second guess every prescription. [72] This court, however, rejected both approaches and instead chose to follow the analysis in *Dooley v. Everett*, [73] which found a distinction between duty and standard of care. [74] Similarly, the court in *Lasley* determined that a breach of care might exist because of an obligation to warn. [75]

Baker v. Arbor Drugs, Inc. illustrates a court imposing a duty of care when a pharmacist voluntarily assumed a duty. [76] What is significant, in *Baker*, [77] is the scope of a duty to a customer. In *Baker*, three different prescriptions were prescribed by the same physician. Prescriptions for all three of the patient's medications were filled at the same pharmacy. [78] The pharmacy maintained a computer system which detected drug interactions. [79] The customer contended that the pharmacy, in implementing a computer system, voluntarily assumed a duty to monitor for adverse drug interactions. [80] The pharmacy implemented, used, and advertised to consumers that they could, through the use of a special computer monitoring system, provide a medication profile of a customer for adverse drug interactions. [81] The Baker court concluded that because the pharmacy advertised and used this computer system to monitor the medications of a customer, the pharmacist voluntarily assumed a duty of care. [82] Therefore, the pharmacy voluntarily assumed a duty to detect the harmful drug interaction. [83]

Tennessee courts have been faced with the issue of whether to extend the duty to warn to a non-customer. [84] The case of *Pittman v. Upjohn Co.* [85] concerned whether a pharmacist owed a duty to warn third party non-customers of foreseeable dangers in taking a prescription drug. [86] The plaintiff in Pittman sustained injuries as a result of ingesting a drug that had been prescribed for his grandmother. [87] Pittman recognized that a pharmacist has a duty to exercise the standard of care required of the profession in the same or similar communities. [88] The State Board of Pharmacy for Tennessee requires a pharmacist to explain to the patient or the agent for the patient the directions for the use and significant and/or potential effects of the medication. [89] The Pittman court also found that "[a] significant factor affecting the pharmacy's duty was the knowledge that no warning had been given by the physician." [90] The court held that under the circumstances of this case "it was reasonably foreseeable that the customer was at risk of injury." [91] Thus, the pharmacist had a duty to warn. [92]

However, the Pittman court also decided whether the duty to warn extended to a non-customer third party. [93] The customer was the grandmother, not the plaintiff, and the consumption of the drug was not foreseeable to a non-customer third party. Therefore, the pharmacy was not liable to a third party. [94] Pittman clarified that a duty or obligation of a pharmacist pertains solely to a customer patient or agent to warn against foreseeable consequences. [95] Although the court in Pittman recognized a duty to warn the customer, the refusal to extend the duty to a non-patient third party hinged on the foreseeability test. [96] Pittman refused to extend the duty to warn beyond that of the customer patient. [97] Perhaps the court could have extended the duty to warn to immediate family members of the customer. Yet, the Pittman court recognized that a plethora of litigation would follow if the duty was extended to a non-customer third party. [98]

Finally, should the pharmacist warn of the addictive nature of a drug? That is, a special exception be created exclusively for addictive type drugs? In *Pysz v. Henry's Drug Store*, [99] an action against a retail druggist for the failure to warn of addictive propensities of a prescription, the court determined the pharmacist owed no duty to warn. [100] The plaintiff in Pysz further argued that filling his prescription for more than nine years constituted negligence because the defendant pharmacy knew or should have known that use of this drug over an extended period of time would subject him to physical and psychological dependence resulting in addiction. [101] However, the court concluded that the failure to warn the user or to notify the physician was not a failure to exercise due care on the part of the pharmacist. [102]

The plaintiff in Psyz sought to convince the court that the pharmacist should take responsibility. [103] That is, the plaintiff argued that the pharmacist rather than the physician possessed the greater knowledge about the propensity of drugs. [104] The plaintiff requested the court view the duty of the druggist to either warn the customer of the dangerous propensities of a drug prescribed by a licensed physician or in the alternative, to notify the physician of the dangerous propensities of the drug and the effect on the patient. [105] The Pysz court concluded that the physician still owes the duty to know the drug prescribed and to properly monitor the patient. [106] Thus, the Pysz court held that where the prescribing physician knew the quantity prescribed over the nine year span, and also knew of the addiction, the pharmacist owed no duty to warn the patient of the addictive qualities of the drug or to notify the physician. [107]

IV. Pharmacists Duty of Care Extended to Warn About the Addictive Nature Drug and Refusal to Fill a Valid Prescription

In *Hooks SuperX v. McLaughlin*, [108] the Supreme Court of Indiana determined a pharmacist had a duty to refuse to refill prescriptions at an unreasonably faster rate than prescribed pending direct and explicit directions from the prescribing physician. [109] Furthermore, the duty of the pharmacist to provide a standard of care includes a duty to refuse to refill the prescriptions. [110] In Hooks, the customer was injured while working and his physician prescribed medication to relieve the pain. [111] The customer became addicted to this medication and was treated for this addiction on numerous occasions. [112] His prescriptions were filled at the same pharmacy for a period of about one and a half years. [113] Although all of the prescriptions were valid, the customer had them refilled at a rate considerably faster than the rate prescribed. [114]

The Supreme Court of Indiana applied three factors in concluding a duty exists between a pharmacist and a customer: relationship between the parties, foreseeability of harm, and public policy. [115] The court focused on what constitutes a relationship. [116] The court found the relationship between a pharmacist and a customer was based on contract principles and was independent of the physician-patient relationship. [117] The Hooks court found the existence of privity of contract between the parties and the expertise of the pharmacist sufficiently close to justify the imposition of a duty. [118] Second, the Hooks court examined the foreseeability of the harm. [119] The court held it is reasonably foreseeable that consumption of large quantities of addictive substances can give rise to an addiction and that addiction carries foreseeable consequences. [120] Therefore, for the purpose of determining the existence of a duty, the court was satisfied that the addiction was foreseeable from the series of events that occurred. [121] Third, the Hooks court analyzed the three public policy considerations present: preventing intentional and unintentional drug abuse, not jeopardizing the

217

physician-patient relationship, and avoiding unnecessary health costs. [122] The court determined that the public policy of Indiana requires the imposition of a duty on the pharmacist. [123] The court examined the Indiana Pharmacy Code which provides immunity for a pharmacist who refuses to honor prescriptions. [124]

The Indiana Code, provides in relevant part, "[t]he pharmacist is immune from criminal prosecution or civil liability if he, in good faith, refuses to honor a prescription because, in his professional judgment, the honoring of the prescription would . . . (3) [a]id or abet an addiction of habit." [125] Although the statute does not create a duty on the part of the pharmacist, the Hooks court found the statute demonstrates the state's significant interest in preventing drug addiction. [126] Moreover, the Hooks court concluded that establishing this duty for pharmacists would not interfere with the physician-patient relationship. [127] The Supreme Court of Indiana distinguished the situation of a pharmacist managing the rate at which a customer is consuming drugs from the situation in *Ingram v. Hook's Drugs, Inc.* [128] In Ingram, the court found that the physician was responsible to warn patients about drug side effects and the court refused to impose this duty on pharmacists. [129] However, the situation in *Hooks*, discussed above, involved the rate at which the customer was consuming drugs. [130] A pharmacist monitoring the rate of consumption of a customer will not interfere with the physician-patient relationship because in Indiana, pharmacists possess that authority by statute and physicians remain ultimately responsible for prescribing medications. [131]

Thus, all three factors for determining the imposition of a duty indicate this obligation should be recognized. [132] This duty requires a pharmacist to "exercise that degree of care that an ordinarily prudent pharmacist would under the same or similar circumstances." [133] What is required in each case is a question of fact depending upon the circumstances of each case. [134] Perhaps the three factors relied on by the Hooks court, which are relationship, foreseeability, and public policy, all evidence the beginning of recognition of an independent duty on the part of the pharmacist separate from that of the physician. [135]

V. Conclusion

The traditional role of the pharmacist in drug distribution has focused on the accurate dispensing of medication to the customer in accordance with a physician's order. [136] The majority view remains that a licensed pharmacist owes no legal duty to warn of the dangerous propensities of a prescription drug. [137] One objection to expanding the duty to warn on the part of physicians is the interference with the physician-patient relationship. [138] The issue to consider should center on the point at which a court will recognize a legal duty to perform an act that pharmacy practitioners regard as a professional responsibility. [139] Previously, a physician was deemed as the only professional with access to a patient's health history. Hence, the pharmacist owed no duty to warn. However, with the advent of the high-tech computer era, pharmacists now have access to patient drug histories, such as the type of drug, frequency of refills, and drug interactions. [140] A pharmacist, with advanced computer systems, now undertakes a responsibility to warn customers about drug interactions, including the addictive nature of drugs. A pharmacist who voluntarily undertakes to provide this information to a patient must do so accurately. [141]

Courts remain reluctant to impose a legal duty on a pharmacist to provide unsolicited information to patients.[142] The *Hooks* court is the minority position finding that a pharmacist owes a duty to refuse to fill a valid prescription for an addictive drug. [143] This duty is different from a mere warning of the dangerous nature of a drug or possible drug interactions [144] Is *Hooks* an aberration from well settled law? [145] The unequivocal answer is yes. However, the issue now becomes whether other jurisdictions will adopt the Hooks rule and rationale. [146] Is *Hooks* an exception due to the addictive qualities of the pharmaceutical? [147.] Perhaps, because the Indiana Appeals Court in *Allberry v. Parkmour Drug* held that the duty to warn is part of the physician-patient relationship as did the Arkansas Supreme Court in the *Rose v. Kowalski Drugs*.

However, in *Happel v. Wal-Mart Stores*, Inc., 199 Ill. 2d 179, 766 N.E.2d 1118 (2002), the Illinois Supreme Court determined that the pharmacy owed a duty to warn of the possibility of a dangerous reaction to a certain anti-inflammatory medication because the pharmacy knew about the allergic condition of the individual. The court in *Happel*, clarified that the "learned intermediary doctrine" and the doctor patient relationship would not be impinged. Similarly, the Supreme Court of Massachusetts determined that a pharmacist owes no duty to inform a customer of potential side effects of a prescribed drug, lacking particular knowledge of an increased danger to a specific customer. In *Cottam v. CVS Pharmacy* 764 N.E. 2d 814 (Mass. 2002), the court held that when a pharmacist voluntarily assumes a duty to warn of the potential side effects of prescription drugs, then it may be held liable for negligence. The *Cottam* court focused on the fact that the pharmacy implemented a computer system to make available to its customers written information about the risks and side effects of prescription drugs.

Today although the role of the pharmacist has indeed changed from that of counting and pouring to one of a professional with an active role, most courts and state laws do not impose a duty to warn as illustrated in the *Kowalski* decision. [148] The advent of the active role encompasses greater responsibilities. Ultimately, there could be less litigation. Furthermore, the pharmacist will finally achieve the professional recognition deserved.

CRITICAL ANALYSIS: Does imposing a duty to warn possibly interfere with or possibly complement the physician duty to warn? Will expanding the duty to warn to pharmacists impinge on the doctor-patient relationship or possibly enhance it?

Endnotes

[1] See David B. Brushwood & Larry M. Simonsmeier, Drug Information for Patients: Duties of the Manufacturer, Pharmacist, Physician, and Hospital, 7 J. Legal Med. 279 (1986); see also David B. Brushwood, The Pharmacist's Duty to Warn: Toward a Knowledge-Based Model of Professional Responsibility, 40 Drake L. Rev. 1 (1991).

[2] See, e.g., Baker v. Arbor Drugs, 544 N.W.2d 727 (Mich. Ct. App. 1996); Lasley v. Shrake's Country Club Pharmacy, 880 P.2d 1129 (Ariz. Ct. App. 1994); Pittman v. Upjohn Co., 890 S.W.2d 425 (Tenn. 1994); Hooks SuperX v. McLaughlin, 642 N.E.2d 514 (Ind. 1994); Stebbins v. Concord Wrigley Drugs, Inc., 416 N.W.2d 381 (Mich. Ct. App. 1987); Dooley v. Everett, 805 S.W. 2d 380 (Tenn. Ct. App. 1991); Laws v. Johnson, 799 S.W.2d 249 (Tenn. Ct. App. 1990); Adkins v. Mong, 425 N.W.2d 151 (Mich. Ct. App. 1988); Leesley v. West, 518 N.E.2d 758 (Ill. Ct. App. 1988); Riff v. Morgan Pharmacy, 508 A.2d 1247 (Pa. Super. Ct. 1986); Pysz v. Henry's Drug Store, 457 So. 2d 561 (Fla. Dist. Ct. App. 1984).

[3] See FDA Alters Rules for TV Drug Ads, The Philadelphia Inquirer, Aug. 9, 1997, at A01; Pharmacies Health Plans Battle Over Fees on Drugs, The Philadelphia Inquirer, Aug. 3, 1997, at D01.

[4] See, e.g., Kintigh v. Abbott Pharmacy, 503 N.W.2d 657, 661 (Mich. Ct. App. 1993) (concluding pharmacist owed only a duty to dispense controlled drugs with reasonable care and in accordance with all applicable statutes and regulations); Laws, 799 S.W.2d at 254 (pharmacists only function was to fill the prescription in strict conformity with any directions by the physician); Adkins, 425 N.W.2d 154 (concluding that there exists no legal duty on the part of a pharmacist to monitor and intervene with reliance by customer on drugs prescribed by a licensed treating physician); Leesley, 518 N.E.2d at 763 (refusing to subject pharmacists to liability for failure to give warnings which the physician had not requested); Stebbins, 416 N.W.2d at 387-88 (holding pharmacist owes no duty to warn the patient of possible side effects of a prescribed medication where the prescription is proper on its face and neither the physician nor the manufacturer has required that any warning be given to the patient by the pharmacist); Pysz, 457 So. 2d 561 (holding that the physician and not the pharmacist has the duty to know the drug he is prescribing and properly monitor the patient).

[5] Psyz, 457 So. 2d at 562.

[6] Adkins, 425 N.W.2d at 155.

[7] Stebbins, 416 N.W.2d at 387-88.

[8] See supra note 4; see also Kathy Laughter Laizure, The Pharmacist's Duty to Warn When Dispensing Prescription Drugs: Recent Tennessee Developments, 22 U. Mem. L. Rev. 517, 535 (1992) (professionals are held to a higher standard of care in their fields because they have superior knowledge and pharmacists, as trained professionals, are held to this professional standard of care).

[9] See supra note 3.

[10] 425 N.W.2d 151.

[11] Id. at 152. The pharmacy filled 116 prescriptions for several narcotic substances over a course of six years. Id.

[12] Id.

[13] Id. at 152-53.

[14] Id. at 152.

[15] Id. at 154. The court concluded that pharmacists have no duty to monitor or intervene with a customer's reliance on drugs prescribed by a licensed treating physician.

[16] Id. at 153. The plaintiff in Adkins relied on the standards of practice adopted by the American Pharmaceutical Association (APA) in 1979 and upon an article published in a professional journal. Id. The court specifically dismissed these as authorities, in part due to the overwhelming precedent in Michigan and other jurisdictions. Id. However, an Arizona court explicitly pointed to the APA's standards of practice as evidence that a duty to warn may exist as part of the standard of care by the pharmacist. Lasley v. Shrake's

Country Club Pharmacy, 880 P.2d 1129 (Ariz. Ct. App. 1994).

[17] Stebbins v. Concord Wrigley Drugs, Inc., 416 N.W.2d 381 (Mich. Ct. App. 1987).

[18] Id.

[19] Id.

[20] 503 N.W.2d 657.

[21] Id. at 658.

[22] Id.

[23] Leesley v. West, 518 N.E.2d 758 (Ill. Ct. App. 1998).

[24] Id.

[25] Id. at 759.

[26] Id. at 761. The pharmacy received the pills in a bulk container with a "package insert" describing the chemical properties and potential hazards. Id. The pharmacy did not convey any of that information to plaintiff, nor was the pharmacist instructed to do so by the physician. Id.

[27] Id. at 762.

[28] See, e.g., id. at 760.

[29] Id. at 762.

[30] Id.

[31] Id. Factors the Leesley court considered in making a determination of whether a legal duty existed included: 1) the foreseeability of injury to the plaintiff; 2) the magnitude of the burden to the pharmacy of guarding against the injury and the consequences of placing that burden on the pharmacist; and 3) the currently prevailing public policies and social attitudes of the community. Id.

[32] Id. The court ascertained the burden on pharmacists to obtain the cautionary materials, reproduce them, catalogue them, and distribute every document with each appropriate drug would be too great to impose. Id. at 763. The court conceded that there were ways to reduce the burden on pharmacists but that placing any type of burden on a pharmacist to distribute warnings to customers would still be inconsistent with the learned intermediary doctrine. Id.

[33] Id.

[34] Id.

[35] 799 S.W.2d 249 (Tenn. Ct. App. 1990).

[36] Id.

[37] Id. at 249. The warnings contained a section which stated that: "The following additional adverse effects have been reported in clinical experience with oral timolol maleate, and may be considered potential effects of ophthaimic timolol maleate: Cardiovascular: . . . cardiac failure, worsening of angina pectoris, worsening of arterial insufficiency . . . ." Id. at 253.

[38] Laws, 799 S.W.2d at 250.

[39] Id.

[40] Id. at 250.

[41] Id. The plaintiff claimed that the pharmacist had a common law duty to use ordinary care in dispensing the prescription and removal of the insert breached this duty and was the proximate cause of the plaintiff's heart problems. Id.

[42] For a discussion of the learned intermediary doctrine see infra note 17.

[43] Laws, 799 S.W.2d at 253. The court relied on Reyes v. Wyeth Lab., 498 F.2d 1264 (5th Cir. 1974), which held the manufacturer's duty to warn was limited to advising the prescribing physician of any potential dangers from the drug's usage. Laws, 799 S.W.2d at 253. It is the physician that acts as a 'learned intermediary' between the manufacturer and the patient. Id.

[44] Id. The court found, though, the physician was not required to provide all the warnings they received from the manufacturer. Id. The physician was allowed to give only the warnings deemed appropriate or necessary.

[45] Id. at 254.

[46] Id. at 253.

[47] Id. at 254. The court reasoned that the physician is in a better position to take into account all the propensities of the drug, as well as the specific needs or susceptibilities of a given patient. Id. The physician's duty is to balance the dangers of a drug against the potential benefits a patient may receive from taking the drug. Id. Thus, it is their choice about which warnings to give a patient. Id. Furthermore, the court found it is an individual choice based on knowledge of both the patient and the drug and should not involve a pharmacist. Id.

[48] Id. at 251.

[49] Id. In this case, the physician was aware of the information contained in the package inserts and all possible side effects. Id.

[50] Id.

[51] Id. at 254 (citing Tenn. Code Ann. § 63-10-207(1): "(1) All prescriptions shall be filled in strict conformity with any directions of the prescribing physician, dentist, or veterinarian as are contained on the prescriptions.").

[52] Laws, 799 S.W.2d at 254. The plaintiff contended that the prescription given by the physician for Timoptic not only meant the drug itself but also the entirety of the package supplied by the manufacturer, which included the package insert. Id.

[53] Id.

[54] Id. at 255. The court relied on the pharmacist's affidavits which asserted the drug Timoptic was dispensed in accordance with the physician's orders and found nothing in the record to dispute this contention. Id.

[55] 508 A.2d 1247 (Pa. Super. Ct. 1986).

[56] Id. at 1251-52.

[57] Id.

[58] Id. at 1250. Pharmacists are required to maintain the latest editions of the National Formulary and the United States Pharmacopoeia. In addition, they must also have reference publication such as the Physician's Desk Reference, which lists proper dosage and warnings. Id. at

1250 n.3.

[59] Id. at 1250. This court rejected the argument that the only function and duty of the pharmacist was to supply the medication. Id. at 1250.

[60] Id.

[61] Id. at 1251.

[62] Id. at 1251-52. The court found that causation was established because had defendant pharmacy warned the plaintiff or notified the physician, the injuries would not have occurred. Id.

[63] Id. at 1253.

[64] See supra notes 4-7 and accompanying text.

[65] 880 P.2d 1129 (Ariz. Ct. App. 1994).

[66] Id. at 1131. The plaintiff alleged he filled the majority of his prescriptions from 1960-1990 for addictive drugs from the defendant pharmacy. Id. The pharmacy never gave any warnings to the plaintiff about the possibility of addiction. Id. The plaintiff required in-patient detoxification and psychiatric treatment for his long term addiction to both drugs. Id. He also suffered major clinical depression and related disorders. Id.

[67] Id.

[68] Id. at 1132. The case revolved around the issue of summary judgment and whether a material question of fact existed. Id. The pharmacy admitted that it owed a duty to the plaintiff to comply with the applicable standard of care, therefore, the case became a question of whether the standard of care included a duty to warn. Id.

[69] Id. at 1133.

[70] Id.

[71] Id. The court cites several cases that follow this rational: Leesley v. West, 518 N.E.2d 758 (Ill. Ct. App. 1998), Ramirez v. Richardson-Merrell, Inc., 628 F. Supp. 85 (E.D. Pa. 1986), alleging that pharmacist failed to warn a pregnant woman of the side effects of Bendectin on the fetus, and Stebbins v. Concord Wrigley Drugs, Inc., 416 N.W.2d 381 (Mich. Ct. App. 1987). See supra notes 17-19 and accompanying text.

[72] Lasley v. Shrakes Country Club Pharmacy, 880 P.2d 1129 (Ariz. Ct. App. 1994). See, e.g., Pysz v. Henry's Drug Store, 457 So. 2d 561 (Fla. Dist. Ct. App. 1984); Farkhouri v. Taylor, 618 N.E.2d 518 (Ill. Ct. App. 1993), appeal denied, 622 N.E.2d 1204 (Ill. 1993) (holding pharmacist negligently filled prescriptions for quantities beyond the normal without warning patient or physician).

[73] 805 S.W.2d 380, 384 (Tenn. Ct. App. 1991). The Dooley court noted the distinction between duty and standard of care and determined that the pharmacy owed its customers the obligation to use due care.

[74] Id.

[75] Lasley, 880 P.2d 1129.

[76] 544 N.W.2d 727 (Mich. Ct. App. 1996).

[77] Id.

[78] Id.

[79] Id.

[80] Id. The defendant pharmacy's motion for summary judgment was granted by the trial court and trial court held that the pharmacy owed no duty of care to decedent. Id.

[81] Id. at 731. The pharmacy advertised that the special computer monitoring system could detect adverse drug interactions. Id.

[82] Id.

[83] Id. There is also evidence that not only did defendant pharmacy advertise about their computer system, they did so with the intent that customers would rely on it. Id. at 733.

[84] Pittman v. Upjohn Co., 890 S.W.2d 425, 435 (Tenn. 1994).

[85] Id.

[86] Id. at 434. The trial court granted summary judgment for the drug manufacturer and the pharmacy.

[87] Id. at 427. The only instruction on the label was to take one Micronase tablet before breakfast, and to keep all medicine out of the reach of children. Id. Micronase is known to cause severe hypoglycemia, a condition resulting in abnormally low blood sugar. Id. If not treated properly, severe hypoglycemia can cause coma, seizures and other neurological impairments. Id.

[88] Id. at 434. A pharmacist's duty to its customers extends beyond accurately filling the prescriptions. Id.

[89] The Board of Pharmacy of the State of Tennessee has promulgated certain rules and standards of practice. These rules provide: A pharmacist should, on dispensing a new prescription, explain to the patient or the patient's agent the directions for the use and a warning of all side effects of the medication or device that are significant and/or potentially harmful. This communication should be performed in such a manner that will assure the proper use of the medication or device prescribed. Id. at 435 (citing Tenn. Comp. R. & Regs. 1140-3-.03(13) (1991)).

[90] Pittman, 890 S.W.2d at 435.

[91] Id. The pharmacy had been advised by the manufacturer of the potential dangers of Micronase. Id.

[92] Id.

[93] Id.

[94] Id.

[95] Id.

[96] Id. at 435.

[97] Id.

[98] Id.

[99] 457 So. 2d 561 (Fla. Dist. Ct. App. 1984).

[100] Id. The prescription was for Quaalude, a controlled substance available by prescription only. Id.

[101] Id. at 562.

[102] Id.

[103] Id. at 561.

[104] Id.

[105] Id. at 562.

[106] Id.

[107] Id. However, the court did limit their decision to the facts of this case only and recognized that a factual situation could exist that would support an action for negligence against a druggist who had lawfully filled a prescription issued by a licensed physician. Id.

[108] 642 N.E.2d 514 (Ind. 1994).

[109] Id. at 515.

[110] Id. at 519.

[111] Id. at 516.

[112] Id. at 516.

[113] Id.

[114] Id.

[115] Id. at 517. The court used these three factors from Webb v. Jarvis, 575 N.E.2d 992 (Ind. 1991), which used this analysis to determine if a duty exists between parties. Id.

[116] Hooks, 642 N.E.2d at 517. In Indiana, it is well established that there exists a relationship between a pharmacist and customer. Forbes v. Walgreen Co., 566 N.E.2d 90, 91 (Ind. Ct. App. 1991).

[117] Hooks, 642 N.E.2d at 517.

[118] Id.

[119] Id.

[120] Id.

[121] Id. at 518. The question for this court was whether a foreseeable victim suffered a foreseeable harm. Id. at 517. The answer for this court was in the affirmative. Id. at 518.

[122] Id.

[123] Id. at 519.

[124] Id. at 518. See also Ind. Code 25-26-13 16(b) (1993): The pharmacist is immune from criminal prosecution or civil liability if he, in good faith, refuses to honor a prescription because, in his professional judgment, the honoring of the prescription would1) Be contrary to law;
2) Be against the best interest of the patient;
3) Aid or abet an addiction or habit; or
4) Be contrary to the health and safety of the patient.

[125] Ind. Code § 25-26-13-16(b)(3) (1993).

[126] Hooks, 642 N.E.2d at 519.

[127] Id.

[128] Id. at 518. See Ingram v. Hook's Drugs, Inc., 476 N.E.2d 881 (Ind. Ct. App. 1985).

[129] Ingram, 476 N.E.2d at 886-87.

[130] Hooks, 642 N.E.2d at 519.

[131] Id. at 514.

[132] Id.

[133] Id. at 519.

[134] Id. See also Miller v. Griesel, 308 N.E.2d 701, 707 (Ind. 1974).

[135] Hooks, 642 N.E.2d at 517.

[136] See supra note 1 and accompanying text.

[137] See, e.g., Pysz v. Henry's Drug Store, 457 So. 2d 561 (Fla. Dist. Ct. App. 1984).

[138] Laws v. Johnson, 799 S.W.2d 249 (Tenn. Ct. App. 1990).

[139] Brushwood & Simonsmeier; supra note 1, at 320.

[140] Baker v. Arbor Drugs, 544 N.W.2d 727 (Mich. Ct. App. 1996).

[141] See Brushwood & Simonsmeier, supra note 1, at 325.

[142] Id. at 324.

[143] Hooks SuperX v. McLaughlin, 642 N.E.2d 514 (Ind. 1994).

[144] See, e.g., Lasley v. Shrake's Country Club Pharmacy, 880 P.2d 1129 (Ariz. Ct. App. 1994); Pittman v. Upjohn, 890 S.W.2d 425 (Tenn. 1994). See also Riff v. Morgan Pharmacy, 508 A.2d 1247 (Pa. Super. Ct. 1986); Dooley v. Everett, 805 S.W.2d 380 (Tenn. Ct. App. 1990).

[145] Hooks, 642 N.E.2d 514.

[146] Id.

[147] Id. See Rose v. Kowaski, —- S.W.3d ——, 2011 Ark. 44, 2011 WL 478601 (Ark.)

[148] Id.;Terence C. Green, Licking, Sticking, Counting, and Pouring Is That All Pharmacists Do? McKee v. American Home Products Corp., 24 Creighton L. Rev. 1449, 1476 (1991).

Chapter 7: Off-Label Dissemination

Off-Label Background—*Washington Legal Foundation*

Prior to the Food and Drug Administration Modernization Act (FDMA), FDA issued Guidance documents concerning the dissemination of information for "off-label" uses. The court, in *Washington Legal Foundation v. Henney,* invalidated the restrictions imposed by FDA on off-label uses due to First Amendment violations. The court concluded that the FDAMA and Guidance were "contrary to the rights secured by the United States Constitution," specifically the First Amendment. *Washington Legal Foundation v. Henney*, 56 F. Supp. 2d 81, 87 (D.D.C. 1999) ("WLF III"), aff'd *Washington Legal Foundation v. Henney*, 340 U.S. App. D.C. 108, 202 F.3d 331, 335 (D.C. Cir. 2000) ("WLF IV"). The court opined that *Washington Legal Foundation v. Henney*, (128 F. Supp. 2d 11 (DC DC (Nov. 30) 2000)), spanned over six years where the parties argued over the extent to which the federal government can regulate speech regarding the "off-label" uses of prescription drugs. In 2009, FDA issued a Guidance document about *Good Reprint Practices* for unapproved or off-label uses which was revised in 2014.

Distributing Scientific and Medical Publications on Unapproved New Uses—Recommended Practices

http://www.gpo.gov/fdsys/pkg/FR-2014-03-03/html/2014-04560.htm (edited)

FDA issued a revised draft guidance 79 FR 11793 (March 3, 2014) entitled *"Distributing Scientific and Medical Publications on Unapproved New Uses—Recommended Practices."* This draft guidance revised the guidance titled *"Good Reprint Practices for the Distribution of Medical Journal Articles and Medical or Scientific Reference Publications on Unapproved New Uses of Approved Drugs and Approved or Cleared Medical Devices"* published in January 2009 which permitted drug and device companies in some instances to provide information such as journal articles to doctors about unapproved uses for approved products.

The impetus for the 2014 draft guidance stemmed from citizen petitions on behalf of drug and device manufacturers requesting less ambiguity of off-label requirements as well as a reexamination of the regulations. According to FDA, approximately 400 companies distribute scientific and medical publications that discuss unapproved new uses. The 2014 draft guidance describes recommended practices for drug or medical device manufacturers or their representatives to follow when distributing scientific and medical publications that discuss unapproved new uses of approved drugs or approved or cleared medical devices. The draft guidance provides suggestions about the characteristics of scientific and medical publications that companies may elect to distribute as well as recommendations for additional information.

Publication characteristics:

> ➤ *From journals, scientific or medical reference texts, and clinical practice guidelines (CPGs) that are produced by independent sources and satisfy criteria for professional/peer review;*
> ➤ *Based on specified types of scientific evidence; and be*
> ➤ *Complete, unabridged, and without highlighting or characterization by the manufacturer.*

The draft guidance includes separate but related recommendations for the three types of publications: scientific or medical journal articles, scientific or medical texts and CPGs.

In general, the draft guidance recommends that the information have a *"prominently displayed and permanently affixed statement that some of the uses for the drugs and/or devices being distributed might not have FDA approval or clearance."*

The statement also must include any financial interest disclosures, whether they stem from the authors who wrote the information being distributed, or from the drug or device manufacturer. For the front page of the CPG or the textbook, the FDA said this statement should be on a stamp, sticker "or other similar means."

The FDA draft guidance recommends that for all three information sources, the manufacturer disclose all significant risks or safety concerns associated with the unapproved use.

Publication-Specific Recommendations for science or medical journals:
The information should be distributed with
- ✓ Approved labeling;
- ✓ A bibliography, when such information exists, of publications discussing adequate and well-controlled clinical studies published in scientific journals, medical journals or scientific texts about the use of the drug or medical device covered by the information; and
- ✓ A representative publication, when such information exists, that reaches contrary or different conclusions regarding the unapproved use especially when the conclusions of articles to be distributed have been specifically called into question in another publication.

Publication-Specific Recommendations for medical or scientific texts:
The recommendations are based on whether the manufacturer was distributing the reference text in its entirety or only using specific chapters.
- ✓ According to FDA "In situations where a reference text is distributed in its entirety but one or more individual chapters of that reference text devote primary substantive discussion to an individual product or products of the manufacturer distributing it," this information should be "disseminated with the approved product labeling for each such product or, in the case of a medical device reviewed under section 510(k) of the FDCA [Federal Food, Drug, and Cosmetic Act], labeling for the indications in the product's cleared indications for use statement."
- ✓ When a manufacturer distributes an individual chapter or chapters, the context should be provided "with other unaltered/unabridged chapters extracted directly from the same scientific or medical reference text, such as chapters which provide related or supportive information."

Clinical practice guidelines (CPG):
- ✓ A CPG that is distributed in its entirety yet one or more individual sections of that CPG devotes "primary substantive discussion" to an individual product or products of the manufacturer who distributes it, the information should "be disseminated with the approved product labeling for each product or for a medical device reviewed under section 510(k) of the FDCA, labeling for the indications in the product's cleared indications for use statement."
- ✓ If a manufacturer distributes an individual section or sections of the CPG that includes information on unapproved/uncleared uses of the manufacturer's product(s), the section or sections should, when necessary to provide context, be disseminated with other unaltered/unabridged sections extracted directly from the same CPG.

"Off-Label" Promotion—Enforcement and Whistleblower Actions
Amarin Pharma and *Caronia* Impact

The FDA Office of Prescription Drug Promotion (OPDP) directs that drug company sales representatives may promote their products for approved uses only. However, the U. S. District Court for the Southern District, New York, determined that there is a First Amendment free speech right to promote off-label uses as long as the statements are true and non-misleading.
Amarin Pharma, Inc. v. United States FDA (No. 15 Civ. 3588 2nd Cir. 2015) (off-label promotion of Vascepa®) to healthcare professionals and *United States v. Caronia* (No. 09-5006 2nd Cir. 2012) (off-label promotion of Zyrem by drug representative who worked for Orphan Medical now Jazz Pharmaceuticals.) In *Caronia*, the Court of Appeals vacated the conviction of Alfred Caronia for promoting a drug to physicians for off-label use based on First Amendment grounds. That is, the court held that penalizing the drug representative for off-label statements to physicians solely on off-label speech was unconstitutional. The court acknowledged that the First Amendment does not protect false or misleading speech. Further, the *Caronia* court noted that the holding did not speak to whether off-label speech could be used as evidence of intent concerning product misbranding.

In *Amarin*, a settlement was reached where the company can engage in truthful and non-misleading speech promoting the off-label use of Vascepa®. *Amarin* had filed a complaint against FDA proactively; that is, prior to disseminating the off-label information relating to its hypertriglyceridemia drug, Vascepa®, indicated for the decrease of triglyceride levels in adults with severe hypertriglyceridemia. The settlement provides an optional preclearance provision where the company may submit to FDA "up to two proposed communications per calendar year about the off-label use of Vascepa before communicating them in promotion to doctors to determine if FDA has concerns". FDA has 60 days to respond with any concerns. Despite *Amarin* and *Caronia*, where the 2nd Circuit applied First Amendment protections to "off-label" promotion, the Justice Department and FDA continue to aggressively combat health fraud and specifically off-label promotion and has recovered billions of dollars. Undoubtedly, this issue remains controversial.

The FDCA deems a drug misbranded if the label does not contain "adequate directions for use". 21 U.S.C. section 325(f). Compliance requires that the label must reveal "all conditions, purposes or uses for which a drug is intended, including suggested [uses] in oral, written, printed or graphic advertising." 21 C.F.R. section 201.5(a). FDA approves all labeling of prescription drugs and the use of a drug for any purpose(s) other than that stated on the label is known as an "off-label" use and hence prohibited. The cases below are based on how companies promoted "off-label" uses. However, physicians are not prohibited from prescribing drugs for "off-label" use. See: 21 U.S.C. Section 396 "Practice of Medicine".

The False Claims Act under 31 U.S.C. section 3729 pertains to lawsuits brought by private citizens commonly referred to as *qui tam* actions under the False Claims Act (FCA) to address allegations of violations under federal law such as the FDCA (Food, Drug and Cosmetic Act). A portion of the monetary recovery is awarded to the "whistleblower" and part to the United States government. Frequently, whistleblower actions are filed by current or former employees. The initial lawsuit filed by the "whistleblower" is not served on the defendant. However, the plaintiff "whistleblower" must give notice to the government and then the government determines whether to take over the case. Violations of the FDCA and related law such as the False Claims Act in connection with "off-label promotion" have far-reaching effects in terms of company liability.

CRITICAL ANALYSIS: Are *Caronia* and *Amarin* aberrations or a harbinger of the future?

Off-Label Federal and Multistate Settlements
See *https://www.ncbi.nlm.nih.gov/pmc/articles/PMC5384770/* See also: *Volume III.*
Federal Off-Label Settlements
Abbott Laboratories—25 million to end a whistleblower's False Claims Act case alleging off-label promotion of triglyceride drug TriCor and unlawful kickbacks in gift baskets and gift cards. *U.S. ex rel. Bergman v. Abbott Laboratories*, 2:09-cv-04264, (D. C. Eastern District PA)-$25

Celgene—$280 million settlement in 2017. Former sales manager alleged that Celgene promoted the cancer drugs Thalomid and Revlimid for unapproved off-label uses.

Genentech and OSI Pharmaceuticals LLC—$67 million FCA settlement in 2016 with the federal and state governments. Qui tam lawsuit that alleged that Genentech make misleading statements to health care providers concerning the effectiveness of the cancer drug Tarceva.

Genzyme Corp. (*U.S. v. Genzyme Corp.*, U.S. District Court, Middle District of Florida, No. 15-cr-00352) agreed to pay $32.59 million in 2015, admit wrongdoing and enter a two-year deferred prosecution agreement to resolve criminal charge under the FDCA from 2005-2011 over its marketing of the surgical implant Seprafilm, a clear film used in laparotomies to reduce abnormal scarring; however it was promoted as a "slurry" for laparoscopic surgery. Sanofi acquired Genzyme in 2011. According to the Justice Department, sales representatives trained surgeons how to turn Seprafilm into a "slurry", an unapproved use.

NOTE: In 2013, Genzyme reached a $22.28 million civil agreement to resolve claims related to Seprafilm under the federal False Claims Act.

Johnson & Johnson—**$2.2 Billion** settlement in 2013 Johnson & Johnson (J&J) and its subsidiaries a $2.2 billion settlement to resolve criminal and civil liability arising from allegations relating to the prescription drugs Risperdal, Invega and Natrecor for off-label marketing of uses not approved as safe and effective by FDA and payments of kickbacks to physicians and pharmacists. The global resolution is one of the largest health care fraud settlements in United States history. The settlement included criminal fines and forfeiture totaling $485 million and civil settlements with the federal government and states totaling $1.72 billion.

NOTE: See this Chapter, Multistate Litigation and State Consumer Protection Laws regarding Rapamune and Risperdal.

Wyeth Pharmaceuticals—**$490.9 Million** settlement in 2013 to resolve its criminal and civil liability arising from the unlawful marketing of the prescription drug Rapamune for unapproved uses. Rapamune is an "immunosuppressive" drug that prevents the body's immune system from rejecting a transplanted organ. **NOTE:** Pfizer, Inc. acquired Wyeth Pharmaceuticals Inc. in 2009. *See: http://www.justice.gov/opa/pr/2013/July/13-civ-860.html*

Par Pharmaceuticals—**$45 Million** settlement in 2013 where Par Pharmaceutical Companies Inc. pleaded guilty in 2013 and agreed to pay $45 million to resolve its criminal and civil liability in promotion of its prescription drug Megace ES for uses not approved as safe and effective by FDA. Chief Executive Officer Paul V. Campanelli pleaded guilty on behalf of the company. Par was fined $18 million and $4.5 million in criminal forfeiture. Par also agreed to pay $22.5 million to resolve its civil liability. *http://www.justice.gov/opa/pr/2013/March/13-civ-270.html*

GlaxoSmith Kline—**$3 Billion** settlement in 2012 where GlaxoSmithKline pled guilty and agreed to pay $3 billion to resolve criminal and civil allegations involving off-label marketing the diabetes medication, Avandia and other medications, failure to report safety data and false price reporting. Additionally, GlaxoSmithKline agreed to pay $90 million to settle claims by 37 states and the District of Columbia concerning the illegal promotion of Avandia.

NOTE: Glaxo announced in Dec. 2013 that the company would stop paying physicians to attend medical meetings or to speak about its drugs and the diseases that Glaxo drugs treat.

In 2016, GlaxoSmithKline Plc was fined 37.6 million pounds ($54.3 million) by the U.K. antitrust over pay-for-delay deals that held back sales of cheaper, generic versions of its anti-depressant Seroxat.

Abbott Laboratories—**$1.5 Billion** settlement in 2012 concerning the off-label marketing of the anti-seizure drug Depakote. The allegations involved misbranding and the settlement resolved criminal and civil allegations involving misbranding the drug to the elderly.

Merck, Sharp & Dohme—**$950 Million** settlement in 2012 to resolve criminal charges and civil claims related to its promotion and marketing of the painkiller Vioxx® (rofecoxib). Vioxx®, approved by FDA in 1999 was subsequently withdrawn from the marketplace in 2004. *http://www.justice.gov/opa/pr/2011/November/11-civ-1524.html*

NOTE: In 2016, a settlement was reached in *Merck & Co. Inc. Securities Litigation*, D.N.J., MDL-1651, 1/15/16) where the company agreed to pay $830 million to settle investor litigation alleging misleading statements about safety. This means over $8.5 billion in total payments including lawsuits and the government.

Cypress Pharmaceuticals, Inc., Hawthorn Pharmaceuticals Inc.—**$2.8 Million** settlement in 2012. Cypress Pharmaceutical Inc., its subsidiary Hawthorn Pharmaceuticals Inc. and its CEO, Max Draughn, agreed to pay $2.8 million to resolve civil allegations under the False Claims Act. The government alleged that between 2003 and 2009, Cypress, Hawthorn and Draughn were responsible for marketing three pharmaceutical products that were not approved as safe and effective by (FDA). The products were Hylira, a gel used for the treatment of dry skin, Zaclir, an acne treatment and Zacare, another acne treatment. The settlement resolves a False Claims Act lawsuit filed by Robert Heiden, a former district sales manager for Hawthorn. The whistleblower, or *qui tam*, provisions of the False Claims Act permitted the relator, Heiden, to receive over $300,000 which was a portion of the proceeds obtained by the federal government.

http://www.justice.gov/opa/pr/2012/March/12-civ-389.html

***AstraZenecaLP and AstraZeneca Pharmaceuticals LP*—$68.5 Million** multistate settlement in 2011 involving 36 states and $520 million settlement in 2010 for off-label promotion of the antipsychotic drug Seroquel (quetiapine). The Company signed a civil settlement to resolve allegations that by marketing Seroquel for unapproved uses, the company caused false claims for payment to be submitted to federal insurance. The allegations were originally brought in a lawsuit under the *qui tam* or whistleblower provisions of the False Claims Act and various state False Claims Act statutes. The whistleblower, James Wetta, received over $45 million from the federal share of the civil recovery. The resolution included a five Corporate Integrity Agreement (CIA) between AstraZeneca and the Office of Inspector General. The CIA requires, annual review and certification of the company's compliance by a board of directors committee; managers annual certification of compliance; notification to physicians by AstraZeneca about the settlement; company website information about payments to doctors, such as honoraria, travel or lodging. AstraZeneca is subject to exclusion from Federal health care programs, including Medicare and Medicaid, for a material breach of the CIA and subject to monetary penalties for less significant breaches.

***U.S. ex rel. Cheryl Eckard v. GlaxoSmithKline*—$750 Million** settlement of which $150 million dollars was for criminal fines and forfeitures and the remaining account was to settle civil claims. This whistleblower action was brought by Cheryl Eckard, a former GSK employee. The allegations stemmed from Good Manufacturing Practices (GMP) compliance at a GDK plant in Puerto Rico. **See: Gardener Harris and Duff Wilson, *Glaxo to Pay $750 Million for Sale of Bad Products*, N.Y. Times, Oct. 26, A1 (2010).**

***Novartis*—$422.5 Million** in 2011 to pay both the federal government and whistleblowers to resolve both criminal and civil charges concerning how Trileptal, (oxcarbazepine), a drug to treat epilepsy along with five other drugs were marketed. Trileptal, an epilepsy drug, is approved only to treat partial seizures; however, it was marketed to treat psychiatric and pain uses. Four separate whistleblower actions were filed against Novartis as follows: *United* States ex rel. *Garrity v. Novartis Pharmaceuticals Corp.*, E.D. Pa., No. 08-CV-2588); *United States ex rel. McKee v. Novartis Pharmaceuticals Corp.*, E.D. Pa., No. 06-1664; *United States ex rel. Copeland v. Novartis Pharmaceuticals Corp.*, E.D. Pa., No. 06-1630 and *United States ex rel. Austin v. Novartis Pharmaceuticals Corp.*, M.D. Fla., No. 8:03-CV-1551.

Criminal Violations and Forfeiture—Novartis agreed to pay $185 million for marketing Trileptal for unapproved or "off-label" uses, in violation of the FDCA. The FDCA does not prohibit "off-label" use by health care providers. However, the FDCA prohibits manufacturers from promoting their products for off-label uses.

Civil Settlement—Additionally, Novartis paid $237.5 million to settle contentions that it illegally promoted Trileptal and five other drugs Diovan (valsartan), Exforge (amlodipine and valsartan), Sandostatin (octreotide), Tekturna (aliskiren), and Zelnorm (tegaserod) for various unapproved or off-label uses which resulted in false claims submissions to both federal and state health care programs. The civil settlement resolves accusations that Novartis paid kickbacks to doctors. The federal government received $149.2 million from the civil settlement and state Medicaid programs received $88.2 million.

Corporate Integrity Agreement—Novartis executed a five-year corporate integrity agreement with the Office of Inspector General, Department of Health and Human Services. Novartis senior executives must certify on an annual basis departmental compliance.

***Pfizer*—$14.5 Million** settlement in 2011 of a *qui tam* lawsuit that alleged False Claims Act violations by marketing the urinary incontinence drugs Detrol and Detrol LA for unapproved uses. **$142 Million** settlement in 2010 for the illegal off-label marketing of Neurontin. **NOTE: The U.S. Supreme Court declined to review the RICO case against Pfizer related to its allegedly deceptive marketing of Neurontin.**

$2.3 Billion settlement in 2009 to settle civil and criminal charges about how the company marketed some of its drugs including the arthritis drug Bextra withdrawn in 2005. Other drugs involved in the settlement included the cholesterol drug Lipitor, Lyrica treatment for nerve pain, and Zoloft, an antidepressant. This amount surpassed the $1.42 billion dollars Eli Lilly and Company settlement agreement to resolve allegations of off-label promotion of the antipsychotic drug Zyprexa to the elderly for unapproved uses.

Forest Laboratories—**$313 Million** settlement in 2010 for off-label promotion of Celexa and Lexapro.

Eli Lily—**$1.4 Billion** settlement agreement in 2009 with the United States Department of Justice for the off-label promotion of Zyprexa®. In 2005, Lily agreed to a **$36 million** settlement which involved both criminal fines and civil liabilities along with implementation of training programs for the off-label marketing of Evista®.

Cephalon—**$425 Million** settlement in off-label marketing in 2008 for off-label marketing of Actiq, Provigil and Gabitril.

Purdue—**$634.5 Million** settlement in 2007 for off-label marketing of Oxycontin.

Bristol Myers Squibb—**$515 Million** settlement in 2007 for off-label marketing of Abilify.

Schering Plough—**$435 Million** settlement in 2006 to settle charges concerning "off-label" marketing. The Justice Department alleged that Schering illegally promoted drugs for certain types of cancer that had not been approved by FDA.

Parke Davis Company—**$430 Million (Warner Lambert parent company) (acquired by Pfizer Corporation)** *Franklin v. Parke Davis* settlement in 2004, concerned a whistleblower action by an employee due to non-compliance with FDA regulations for off-label promotion. The basis of the action alleged that the company engaged in unlawful activities such as an aggressive illegal marketing plan, kickbacks and questionable research related to the promotion of "off-label uses" such as bi-polar disorder and other illnesses for Neurontin, an anti-convulsant drug approved to treat epilepsy. The company agreed to enter a plea of guilty and pay a fine.

NOTE: This action served as the catalyst for several lawsuits for off-label marketing of neurontin. See: The Neurontin Legacy—Marketing through Misinformation and Manipulation, *Seth Landefeld, Michael A. Steinman,* **360 The New England Journal of Medicine. 103 (Jan. 8, 2009).**

Multistate and State Off-Label Settlements
State Consumer Protection Regulation—State Unfair Trade Practice Laws

Shire Subsidiaries—In 2017 for $350 million-global resolution under the civil FCA with federal and state governments. Allegations concerned that the companies marketed Dermagraft® for off-label uses and kickbacks the companies paid to physicians.

Bristol-Myers Squibb (BMS)—In 2016, BMS agreed to pay $19.5 million to resolve a consumer protection investigation involving claims that BMS improperly marketed the antipsychotic drug Abilify.

Amgen $71 million settlement—In 2015, Amgen agreed to settle claims with 48 states and the District of Columbia concerning the promotion of the anemia drug Aranesp and psoriasis treatment Enbrel. Allegations involved that Amgen marketed Aranesp for dosing frequencies that surpassed the FDA approved levels and for non-approved conditions. The multistate allegations claimed Enbrel was marketed to patients with mild plaque psoriasis when it was only approved for moderate to severe cases.

Pfizer (Wyeth Pharmaceuticals) $35 million Multistate settlement—In 2014, Pfizer agreed to pay $35 million to 41 states and Washington, D.C. to settle claims that its Wyeth unit illegally marketed the drug Rapamune, and encouraged doctors and hospitals to prescribe it for off-label uses. Rapamune is an "immunosuppressive" drug that prevents the body's immune system from rejecting a transplanted organ.

GlaxoSmithKline (GSK)—In June 2014, the District of Columbia along with 44 states shared $105 million that GSK agreed to pay to resolve improper marketing allegations under state consumer protection laws concerning its asthma drug Advair® and its antidepressants Paxil® and Wellbutrin® for unapproved off-label uses. The states alleged that GSK promoted the antidepressant Wellbutrin® for weight loss and sexual dysfunction and that Advair® was promoted for mild asthma when the FDA approval was for severe asthma. Further, the states alleged that GSK concealed studies of teen suicidal thoughts concerning Paxil®.

NOTE: West Virginia GSK $22 million settlement—The lawsuit alleged that GSK failed to disclose the side effects of Avandia, Avandamet and Avandaryl when it was marketing as a drug to lower patients' blood sugar and reducing diabetics' cardiovascular risks.

Risperdal® Johnson & Johnson (J&J) Ortho-McNeil-Janssen Pharmaceuticals—Multi-State

District of Columbia—In 2012, there was a $181 million settlement with 36 other states that Johnson & Johnson (J&J) Ortho-McNeil-Janssen Pharmaceuticals agreed to pay to resolve improper marketing allegations off-label allegations concerning Risperdal®, an antipsychotic drug.

North Carolina—In 2013, there was a $38.8 million recovery as part of a multi-state and federal settlement with Johnson & Johnson and its subsidiary Janssen Pharmaceuticals Inc. to resolve allegations of improper drug marketing of the atypical antipsychotic drugs Risperdal® and Invega. Allegations included promotion and marketing of Risperdal® and Invega for unapproved uses including the treatment of hyperactive children and elderly dementia patients.

Risperdal®—Individual State Jury Decision Illustrations

Pennsylvania— *Pledger et al. v. Janssen Pharmaceuticals et al.,* (Case No. 2088 2016)
The Pennsylvania Superior Court upheld a $2.5 million jury verdict against Johnson & Johnson over allegations its antipsychotic drug Risperdal caused an Alabama boy with autism to grow breasts; remanded to lower court to determine punitive damage award if any.

$70 million verdict in Philadelphia where the jury found that the antipsychotic drug Risperdal had caused an adolescent boy to grow female breasts. *A.Y. v. Janssen Pharm., Inc.*, Pa. Ct. Com. Pl., No. 130402094, verdict 7/1/16).

South Carolina—Jurors found that J&J Ortho-McNeil-Janssen Pharmaceuticals engaged in "unfair and deceptive acts" when the company sent a letter in 2003 to over 7,000 physicians in South Carolina claiming that Risperdal®, an antipsychotic drug, was better and safer than competing drugs. FDA had sent the company a warning letter about the misleading claims that minimized side effects and raised superiority issues. Johnson & Johnson was ordered to pay, in 2011, $327 million in penalties for deceptively marketing the medicine which the court reduced to $136 million due to a three-year statute of limitation on claims and then further reduced to $124.3 million due to a mathematical error.

See: ***State ex rel. Wilson v. Ortho-McNeil-Janssen Pharm., Inc.,*** S.C., No. 27502, 7/8/15. *http://www.judicial.state.sc.us/opinions/HTMLFiles/SC/27502.pdf*

Louisiana—Similarly, a Louisiana jury in 2011 ordered Janssen to pay $257.7 million in damages for misleading claims about Risperdal® as well as $73.3 million in attorney's fees and costs. The court of appeals upheld the jury verdict of $257.7 million (2012).

NOTE: The Arkansas Supreme Court, in 2014, in another Risperdal® case, reversed a $1.26 billion judgment against J&J Ortho-McNeil-Janssen Pharmaceuticals.

CRITICAL ANALYSIS: Evaluate and discuss the ramifications of the federal and multistate off-label settlements above. Include Risperdal® and the reduction to $124.3 million by the South Carolina Supreme Court and $1.26 billion reversal by the Arkansas Supreme Court.

Ghostwriting

"Medical ghostwriting" occurs when professional writers are compensated by pharmaceutical companies to produce the manuscript. Physicians and scientists sign off as the author(s) of the article. The articles are used in a variety of situations such as in published journals that are provided to patients and health providers and as marketing tools. Additionally, ghostwriting occurs in academic institutions. This practice has ramifications for off-label use. Physicians are not prohibited from prescribing drugs for "off-label" use and FDA does not regulate the practice of medicine. See: 21 U.S.C. section 396 Practice of Medicine.

The Ghostwriting Report enumerated the following significant findings.

1. Despite acknowledgment of medical writers for "editorial assistance," the role of pharmaceutical companies in medical publications remains veiled or undisclosed.

2. Some medical schools explicitly prohibit ghostwriting in their policies.

3. Detection of ghostwriting by medical schools is limited.

4. Strengthening journal authorship policies appears to have limited effect on ghostwriting and disclosure of industry financing of medical articles.

5. National Institutes of Health does not have explicit policies on disclosure of industry financing of ghostwritten articles.

CRITICAL ANALYSIS: The Ghostwriting report discusses how the role of pharmaceutical companies in medical publications remains "veiled or undisclosed". Provide specific recommendations to remedy this as well as suggestions about transparency in ghostwriting in terms of disclosure.

Open Payments Disclosure Drug Companies

https://openpaymentsdata.cms.gov

According to the Centers for Medicare and Medicaid Services' Open Payments program, 1,444 drug and device companies paid providers $8.40 billion in payments in 2017. This includes physicians and teaching hospitals.

Background—Senator Grassley co-sponsored section 6002, *"Physician Payments Sunshine Act"*, of the Patient Protection and Affordable Care Act (P.L. 111-148) of 2009. Section 6002, requires all drug, device and biologic and medical supply manufacturers to report annually every payment or transfer of value in excess of $10.00 or $100.00 in the annual aggregate made to physicians and teaching hospitals. Examples of reportable payments and transfers of value may very well include: Cash or cash equivalent; Stock; consulting fees; entertainment; food; and travel. Penalties for failure to submit an annual report include civil monetary penalties that range from $10,000 to $100,000. See 78 Fed. Reg. at 9466.

SUMMARY: This final rule requires applicable manufacturers of drugs, devices, biologicals, or medical supplies and group purchasing organizations covered by Medicare, Medicaid or the Children's Health Insurance Program (CHIP) to report annually to the Secretary certain payments or transfers of value provided to physicians or teaching hospitals ("covered recipients"). In addition, applicable manufacturers and applicable group purchasing organizations (GPOs) are required to report annually certain physician ownership or investment interests.

NOTE: Peter Loftus, *Doctors Net Billions from Drug Firms*, Wall St. J. B1 (Oct. 1, 2014); Payments of $3.5 billion to physicians and teaching hospitals for last five months of 2013. See also: Tom Avril, *Study: Most Patients are Treated by Industry-Paid Docs*, Phila. Inq. G1 (March 19, 2017); 65 percent of patients in the United States were treated by doctors who received industry money.

CRITICAL ANALYSIS: What impact does the payment disclosure have on physicians and the regulated medical device and pharmaceutical industries? Include a discussion about conflict of interest.

Chapter 8: Pharmacy Compounding

Milestone Legislation—Drug Quality and Security Act

Pharmacy compounding was initially limited to small-scale production; however, that has changed dramatically to one of a large-scale production system. FDA was forced to confront this issue in the later part of 2012. This was due to several deaths associated with compounded drug products linked to fungal meningitis that involved the New England Compounding Center (NECC) where thousands of doses of drugs were shipped to several states. The NECC distributed contaminated pain injections that caused serious adverse events including approximately 32 deaths. Back in 2002, an FDA inspection revealed contamination issues with the same steroid; however, FDA had to defer to Massachusetts state authorities. In 2014, the owners of New England Compounding Pharmacy Inc. agreed to a settlement providing $100 million toward compensation for victims (*In re New England Compounding Pharmacy, Inc.*, Bankr. D. Mass., No. 12-bk-19882, 5/6/14). In December 2014, the owner and lead pharmacist Barry Cadden and supervisory pharmacist Glenn Chin were charged with racketeering and 25 acts of second-degree murder in seven states in the 2012 meningitis outbreak which resulted in several deaths. Others, mostly pharmacists, faced allegations in a 131-count indictment. Cadden was found guilty (March 22, 2017) of racketeering, and mail fraud that pertained to the shipments of the substandard drugs (untested and sold without prescriptions) and included the shipment of contaminated steroids. Cadden was not found guilty of murder, some mail fraud racketeering, selling adulterated drugs and conspiracy to defraud the FDA. Cadden was sentenced to a nine-year term of imprisonment.

http://www.justice.gov/opa/pr/14-indicted-connection-new-england-compounding-center-and-nationwide-fungal-meningitis

Other companies have been involved where deaths and serious adverse events have occurred. For example, Gary Osborn and his compounding corporation, ApothéCure Inc., pled guilty in 2012 in the U.S. District Court for the Northern District of Texas to two misdemeanor criminal violations of the Food, Drug and Cosmetic Act (FDCA). The pleas were in connection with ApothéCure's interstate shipment of two lots of misbranded colchicine injectable solution that led to three deaths. Osborne was ordered to pay $400,000 in fines to settle complaints by Oregon, Texas and the Department of Justice. See: Kimberly Kindy, Lena H. Sun and Alice Crites, *Problems Cited for Years at Drug Firms*, The Washington Post, A1 (Feb. 8, 2013).

http://www.fda.gov/ICECI/CriminalInvestigations/ucm302326.htm

Traditionally, state pharmacy boards have maintained regulatory oversight over pharmacy compounding. In Congressional testimony, former FDA Commissioner Hamburg proposed a two-tier system in which traditional compounding pharmacies continue to be regulated at the state level, and larger pharmacies would be subject to FDA oversight. Besides registration, these large-scale compounding pharmacies would be obligated to meet the more rigorous manufacturing standards required of pharmaceutical companies. See: *Drug Quality and Security Act* below.

As background, after the *Thompson v. Western States* decision decided in 2002, FDA clarified that the agency would continue to use enforcement action against those who compounded drugs that are actually attempts to illegally manufacture drugs. FDA issued a Compliance Policy Guide (CPG) section 460.200 [CPG] on May 29, 2002, following the *Thompson* Supreme Court decision. *Medical Center v. Mukasey*, 536 F.3d 383 (5th Cir. 2008) challenged FDA's authority to regulate compounded drugs and inspect state-licensed pharmacies. In 2004, ten pharmacies brought suit in the U.S. District Court for the Western District of Texas in 2004 *Medical Center Pharmacy v. Ashcroft* (changed to *Medical Center v. Gonzalez* and then *Medical Center v. Mukasey*) where the court of Appeals held that compounded drugs are "new drugs" and "new animal drugs" within the meaning of the FDCA and therefore subject to regulation by FDA. *Mukasey* ruled on the severability of advertising prohibitions in section 503A, which were found unconstitutional in the *Thompson v. Western States Med. Ctr.* Supreme Court decision reported below. The Fifth Circuit found that these prohibitions could be severed from section 503A, leaving the remaining parts of that section valid and effective. The *Drug Quality and Security Act* discussed below, settles that promotion is not prohibited and FDA has inspection authority.

Finally, in late 2013, the *Drug Quality and Security Act* was enacted (DQSA). P. L. No: 113-54. The DQSA marks the culmination of nearly a decade long effort by FDA as well as industry stakeholders to clarify and strengthen both the regulatory framework for compounding pharmacies and the security of the pharmaceutical supply chain. The DQSA attempts to address the responsibilities of FDA in terms of regulatory oversight of mass compounded pharmaceuticals. The Act defines the distinction between traditional compounding and compounding manufacturers that make large volumes of drugs without individual prescriptions. Mass compounding pharmacies can choose to register as "outsourcing" facilities and approximately 60 outsourcing facilities have done so. Detailed labeling of compounded drugs is required. Of importance is the enhanced communication with State Pharmacy Boards.

NOTE: See Chapter 9 this *Volume* for Title II of the *Drug Quality and Security Act* (DQSA), *Drug Supply Chain Security Act*, (DSCSA) the "track and trace" provisions throughout the pharmaceutical supply distribution chain.

Final Guidance: Interim Policy on Compounding Bulk Substances under section 503 A and 503 B of the FDCA (Issued in 2016).
http://www.fda.gov/downloads/Drugs/GuidanceComplianceRegulatoryInformation/Guidances/UCM469120.pdf
http://www.fda.gov/downloads/Drugs/GuidanceComplianceRegulatoryInformation/Guidances/UCM469122.pdf
Draft Guidance documents:
Prescription Requirements Under Section 503A of the Federal Food, Drug, and Cosmetic Act (Docket No. FDA-2016-D-0269) (2016);

Hospital and Health System Compounding Under the Federal Food, Drug, and Cosmetic Act (Docket No. FDA-2016-D-0271) (2016); *and*

Facility Definition Under Section 503B of the Federal Food, Drug, and Cosmetic Act (Docket No. FDA–2016–D–0238) (2016).

Final Guidance Documents and draft released concerned pharmacy compounding, and registration of and fees for human drug outsourcing compounding facilities. A draft guidance detailing electronic reporting all issued in 2014. The direct links are as follows:
Final Guidance: Pharmacy Compounding
http://www.fda.gov/downloads/drugs/guidancecomplianceregulatoryinformation/guidances/ucm377052.pdf
Final Guidance: Registration of Human Drug Outsourcing Compounding Facilities
http://www.fda.gov/downloads/Drugs/GuidanceComplianceRegulatoryInformation/Guidances/UCM377051.pdf
Final Guidance: Fees for Human Drug Compounding Outsourcing Facilities
http://www.fda.gov/downloads/Drugs/GuidanceComplianceRegulatoryInformation/Guidances/UCM391102.pdf
Draft Guidance: Electronic Drug Product Reporting for Human Drug Compounding Outsourcing Facilities
https://www.fda.gov/downloads/Drugs/NewsEvents/UCM424303.pdf

CRITICAL ANALYSIS: How does the 2013 *Drug Quality and Security Act* tackle the problems associated with large-scale compounding?

Enforcement

FDA has stepped up enforcement and has issued warning letters under the DQSA if a company does not have a valid prescription for each individually identified patient. Consequently, the drug is deemed both unapproved and misbranded. The Abbott example details a voluntary recall subsequent to an FDA inspection and resultant issuance of a 483 post inspection findings. *http://www.fda.gov/Drugs/GuidanceComplianceRegulatoryInformation/PharmacyCompounding/ucm339771.htm*

Abbott's Compounding Pharmacy Inc., Berkeley, CA
483 Issued 01/08/2016 (PDF - 2MB) Warning Letter 04/04/2017
Firm Press Release: Abbott's Compounding Pharmacy Issues Voluntary Recall of All Lots of Unexpired Sterile Human and Animal Compounded Products Due to Lack of Sterility Assurance (01/16/2016). *https://www.fda.gov/Drugs/ucm339771.htm*

CRITICAL ANALYSIS: Suppose you represent Abbott. Advise your client of compliance issues. See link above.

Promotion and First Amendment Application
Thompson v. Western States

The United States Supreme Court decision of *Thompson v. Western States Med. Ctr.* involved a challenge by a group of licensed pharmacies who based their claims on constitutional principles that the 1997 FDAMA provisions under 21 U.S.C. sections 353a (a) and (c) violated the First Amendment. These sections of FDAMA restricted the advertisement of drug compounding.

The Court of Appeals, 238 F.3d 1090 (9th Cir. 2001) determined that FDAMA's limitations on advertisements for compounded prescriptions were unconstitutional because the restrictions were overly broad and violated the free speech clause of the First Amendment. FDA had argued that the restrictions were necessary to prevent pharmacists from engaging in the major manufacture of unapproved drugs. The United States Supreme Court affirmed. The *Drug Quality and Security Act* comports with the *Thompson* decision reported below. That is, the Act does not prohibit promotion and section 503A of FDMA pertaining to promotion is still unconstitutional.

Thompson v. Western States Medical Center,
122 S. Ct. 1497 (2002)

Justice O'Connor delivered the opinion of the Court. Section 503A of the Food and Drug Administration Modernization Act of 1997 (FDAMA or Act), 111 Stat. 2328, 21 U. S. C. §353a, exempts "compounded drugs" from the Food and Drug Administration's standard drug approval requirements as long as the providers of those drugs abide by several restrictions, including that they refrain from advertising or promoting particular compounded drugs. Respondents, a group of licensed pharmacies that specialize in compounding drugs, sought to enjoin enforcement of the subsections of the Act dealing with advertising and solicitation arguing that those provisions violate the First Amendment's free speech guarantee. The District Court agreed with respondents and granted their motion for summary judgment, holding that the provisions do not meet the test for acceptable government regulation of commercial speech set forth in *Central Hudson Gas & Elec. Corp. v. Public Serv. Comm'n of N. Y.,* 447 U. S. 557, 566 (1980). The court invalidated the relevant provisions, severing them from the rest of § 503A. ***

Compounding is typically used to prepare medications that are not commercially available, such as medication for a patient who is allergic to an ingredient in a mass-produced product. *** For approximately the first 50 years after the enactment of the FDCA, the FDA generally left regulation of compounding to the States. Pharmacists continued to provide patients with compounded drugs without applying for FDA approval of those drugs. *** In 1992, in response to this concern, the FDA issued a Compliance Policy Guide, which announced that the "FDA may, in the exercise of its enforcement discretion, initiate federal enforcement actions when the scope and nature of a pharmacy's activities raises the kinds of concerns normally associated with a manufacturer and results in significant violations of the new drug, adulteration, or misbranding provisions of the Act." Compliance Policy Guide 7132.16 . *** It stated that the "FDA believes that an increasing number of establishments with retail pharmacy licenses are engaged in manufacturing, distributing, and promoting unapproved new drugs for human use in a manner that is clearly outside the bounds of traditional pharmacy practice and that constitute violations of the [FDCA]." Ibid. The Guide expressed concern that drug products "manufactured and distributed in commercial amounts without [the] FDA's prior approval" could harm the public health. ***

The Guide listed nine examples of activities that the FDA believed raised such concerns and that would therefore be considered by the agency in determining whether to bring an enforcement action. These activities included: "[s]oliciting business (e.g., promoting, advertising, or using salespersons) to compound specific drug products, product classes, or therapeutic classes of drug products"; "[c]ompounding, regularly, or in inordinate amounts, drug products that are commercially available ... and that are essentially generic copies of commercially available, FDA-approved drug products"; using commercial scale manufacturing or testing equipment to compound drugs; offering compounded drugs at wholesale [.] Id., at 76a to 77a.

Congress turned portions of this policy into law when it enacted the FDAMA in 1997. *** Finally, and most relevant for this litigation, the prescription must be "unsolicited," § 353a(a), and the pharmacy, licensed pharmacist, or licensed physician compounding the drug may "not advertise or promote the compounding of any particular drug, class of drug, or type of drug." § 353a(c). The pharmacy, licensed pharmacist, or licensed physician may, however, "advertise and promote the compounding service." Respondents are a group of licensed pharmacies that specialize in drug compounding. They have prepared promotional materials that they distribute by mail and at medical conferences to inform patients and physicians of the use and effectiveness of specific compounded drugs. ***

If the Government's failure to justify its decision to regulate speech were not enough to convince us that the FDAMA's advertising provisions were unconstitutional, the amount of beneficial speech prohibited by the FDAMA would be. *** It would prevent pharmacists with no interest in mass-producing medications, but who serve clienteles with special medical needs, from telling the doctors treating those clients about the alternative drugs available through compounding. *** Forbidding advertising of particular compounded drugs would also prohibit a pharmacist from posting a notice informing customers that if their children refuse to take medications because of the taste, the pharmacist could change the flavor, and giving examples of medications where flavoring is possible. The fact that the FDAMA would prohibit such seemingly useful speech even though doing so does not appear to directly further any asserted governmental objective confirms our belief that the prohibition is unconstitutional. *** [W]e affirm the Court of Appeals' judgment that the speech-related provisions of FDAMA § 503A are unconstitutional.

Inspection—*Wedgewood Pharmacy*

The enactment of the *Drug Quality and Security Act* (Act) provides direction and regulatory authority. Still, prior to this Act, courts have ruled in favor of FDA in terms of inspection authority. For example, in *Wedgewood Pharmacy* reported below, the court held that *Wedgewood Pharmacy* was not exempt from inspection by FDA.

Wedgewood Pharmacy v. United States,
421 F.3d 263 (3rd Cir. 2005)

OPINION: McKee, Circuit Judge: Wedgewood Village Pharmacy appeals the District Court's order affirming the Magistrate Judge's denial of Wedgewood's motion to quash an administrative warrant issued to agents of the Food and Drug Administration. Wedgewood argues that it is exempt from FDA inspection under provisions of the Food, Drug, and Cosmetic Act (the "FDCA"), 21 U.S.C. §301 *et seq.* Wedgewood also contends that it was denied procedural due process. For the reasons that follow, we hold that Wedgewood was not exempt from FDA inspection under the FDCA, and that issuance of the warrant did not deny Wedgewood procedural due process. Accordingly, we will affirm the decision of the District Court.

I. Background: Wedgewood is a pharmacy specializing in compounding drugs used for treating humans and animals. "Compounding" refers to the process of modifying prescription drugs to meet the specific needs of individual patients.

> *Drug compounding is a process by which a pharmacist or doctor combines, mixes, or alters ingredients to create a medication tailored to the needs of an individual patient. Compounding is typically used to prepare medications that are not commercially available, such as medication for a patient who is allergic to an ingredient in a mass-produced product. It is a traditional component of the practice of pharmacy, and is taught as part of the standard curriculum at most pharmacy schools...*

Thompson v. W. States Med. Ctr., 535 U.S. 357, 360-61, 152 L. Ed. 2d 563, 122 S. Ct. 1497 (2002) (internal citation omitted).

Drug compounding is frequently regulated by states "as part of their regulation of pharmacies," and the FDA was content to allow the states to regulate compounding for "approximately 50 years after the enactment of the FDCA." *Id.* at 361. However, the FDA eventually became concerned that some pharmacies were "manufacturing and selling drugs under the guise of compounding, thereby avoiding the FDCA's [regulation of new drugs]." *Id.* at 362. Accordingly, in 1992, the FDA issued a Compliance Policy Guide (the "CPG"), "which announced that the 'FDA may, in the exercise of its enforcement discretion, initiate enforcement actions ...when the scope and nature of a pharmacy's activities raises the kinds of concerns normally associated with a manufacturer and ... results in significant violations of the new drug, adulteration, or misbranding provisions of the [FDCA]. *** The application asserted that: in early 1998, Wedgewood had shipped over 1,000 vials of Poison Ivy Extract without receiving the requisite prescriptions for specific patients; in May 2002, Wedgewood had acquired an encapsulation machine which could be used for large-scale drug manufacturing; in 2001 and 2002, it had purchased bulk quantities of substances in excess of the amounts normally associated with a retail pharmacy, including enough diazepam (the active ingredient in Valium) to manufacture over one million 10 mg doses during a six-month period, an amount "typical of a commercial drug manufacturer"; and it routinely produced veterinary drugs in bulk, without receiving specific veterinary prescriptions. ***

II. Jurisdiction: *** Under 21 U.S.C. §§ 331(e), (f) and 333(a)(1), refusing to permit an inspection authorized by the FDCA is a criminal offense punishable by up to one year of imprisonment and a fine of up to $1,000.

III. Discussion

A. Wedgewood Is Not Exempt from Inspection Under the FDCA—Wedgewood argues that it is exempt from all FDA inspections under 21 U.S.C. § 374(a). That section provides that employees and agents designated by the Secretary are permitted to "enter, at reasonable times, any factory, warehouse, or establishment in which food, drugs, devices, or cosmetics are manufactured, processed, packed, or held, for introduction into interstate commerce" and "to inspect, at reasonable times and within reasonable limits and in a reasonable manner, such factory, warehouse, establishment ... and all pertinent equipment, finished and unfinished materials, containers, and labeling therein." *Id.* § 374(a)(1). In the case of "any factory, warehouse, establishment, or consulting laboratory in which prescription drugs, nonprescription drugs intended for human use, or restricted devices are manufactured, processed, packed, or held" the section also provides:

> *The inspection shall extend to all things therein (including records, files, papers, processes, controls, and facilities) bearing on whether prescription drugs, nonprescription drugs intended for human use, or restricted devices which are adulterated or misbranded within the meaning of this chapter, or which may not be manufactured, introduced into interstate commerce, or sold, or offered for sale by reason of any provision of this chapter, have been or are being manufactured, processed, packed, transported, or held in any such place, or otherwise bearing on violation of this chapter. Id.*

However, the statute specifically exempts certain types of pharmacies from this enhanced inspection authority (the enhanced inspection authority set forth above is hereafter referred to as the "records provision"). The exemption provides as follows:

> *(2) The provisions of the third sentence of paragraph (1) [the records provision] shall not apply to—*
>
> *(A) pharmacies which maintain establishments in conformance with any applicable local laws regulating the practice of pharmacy and medicine and which are regularly engaged in dispensing prescription drugs or devices, upon prescriptions of practitioners licensed to administer such drugs or devices to patients under the care of such practitioners in the course of their professional practice, and which do not, either through a subsidiary or otherwise, manufacture, prepare, propagate, compound, or process drugs or devices for sale other than in the regular course of their business of dispensing or selling drugs or devices at retail ...*
>
> *Id. § 374(a).*

Wedgewood's reading of the statute is inconsistent with the text of § 374(a). ***Rather, the exemption granted to pharmacies under § 374(a)(2)(A) only applies, by its own terms, to the "third sentence of paragraph (1)," *i. e.*, the records provision. The general inspection authority contained in the first sentence is not circumscribed by that exemption. *** We therefore conclude that Wedgewood is not exempt from FDA inspection.

B. Wedgewood Is Not Entitled To The Record Exemption—Our conclusion that the FDA possesses some authority to inspect pharmacies such as Wedgewood does not end our inquiry because the inspection authority contained in the first sentence of § 374(a)(1) is quite limited and clearly does not extend to a pharmacy's books and records. *** Wedgewood admits that it engages in compounding but asserts that it does so "in the regular course of [its] business of dispensing or selling drugs or devices at retail." *** Under the language of FDAMA [1997], pharmacies were permitted to compound only "for an identified individual patient based on the unsolicited receipt of a valid prescription order or a notation or in limited quantities before the receipt of a valid prescription for such individual patient." *Id.* The provision did not remain law for long. As a result of two court decisions, Section 127 of the statute, which contained the compounding language, was invalidated on unrelated grounds. *See Western States*, 535 U.S. at 377; *Western States Med. Ctr. v. Shalala*, 238 F.3d 1090 (9th Cir. 2001). ***

II. Conclusion: For the reasons set forth above, we hold that Magistrate Judge Rosen correctly found that probable cause existed to conclude that Wedgewood did not satisfy the requirements of the exemption contained in § 374(a)(2)(A), and he therefore correctly denied Wedgewood's motion to quash. Accordingly, we will affirm the District Court's decision upholding Magistrate Judge Rosen's order.

CRITICAL ANALYSIS: Discuss the exemption under § 374(a)(2)(A) and why the court ruled that Wedgewood did not satisfy the requirement of the exemption.

Chapter 9: Supply Chain, Counterfeit Products and Reimportation

FDA Safety and Innovation Act—Drug Supply Provisions

Approximately 40 percent of finished drugs are imported and approximately 80 percent of active ingredients are from overseas. Title VII of the 2012 *Food and Drug Administration Safety and Innovation Act* Public Law No: 112-144 (FDASIA) contains drug supply chain provisions to address the challenges presented by the increase of the global drug supply. Commercial importers must register specifying a unique facility identifier system (UFI). Further importers are required to submit documentation that their drug complies with FDCA requisites. To that end, other significant FDA actions include the following.

FDA issued a final rule to extend FDA's administrative detention authority to include drugs, in addition to the authority that is already in place for foods and devices. 79 FR 30716 (May 29, 2014)
https://www.federalregister.gov/articles/2014/05/29/2014-12458/administrative-detention-of-drugs-intended-for-human-or-animal-use

FDA issued a final guidance defining conduct FDA considers delaying, denying, limiting or refusing inspection, resulting in a drug being deemed adulterated.
http://www.fda.gov/downloads/RegulatoryInformation/Guidances/UCM360484.pdf

FDA attained higher penalties for adulterated and counterfeit drugs.
http://www.ussc.gov/sites/default/files/pdf/amendment-process/reader-friendly-amendments/20130430_RF_Amendments.pdf

FDA issued a final rule regarding administrative destruction of imported drugs refused U.S. entry. 80 FR 55237 (September 15, 2015)
https://www.gpo.gov/fdsys/pkg/FR-2015-09-15/pdf/2015-23124.pdf

CRITICAL ANALYSIS: Evaluate the Drug Supply Provisions in the *FDA Safety and Innovation Act* and action that FDA has taken such as issuance of the final rules above and higher penalties provision. Evaluate whether these measures are adequate.

"Track and Trace"—Drug Supply Chain Security Act

The *Drug Quality and Security Act* (DQSA), passed in late 2013, P.L. 113-54, 127 Stat. 587 was enacted to further address supply chain issues as well as counterfeiting. Title II of the DQSA contains the *Drug Supply Chain Security Act*, (DSCSA) the "track and trace" provisions throughout the drug supply chain. The *Drug Supply Chain Security Act* addresses drug product protections including regulatory oversight including penalties, movement through the drug distribution chain and track and trace technology.

The "track-and-trace" requirements are intended to prevent counterfeit or contaminated drugs from entering the market in the supply chain and to permit speedier product. Every package of drugs will be electronically traceable throughout the supply chain. The track-and-trace system gradually phases in over a period of 10 years with specific deadlines for all of those operating within the distribution supply chain. The Act was authorized in response to both effective counterfeit measures and inconsistencies in regulation.

http://www.fda.gov/Drugs/DrugSafety/DrugIntegrityandSupplyChainSecurity/DrugSupplyChainSecurityAct/

NOTE: See *Food and Drug Admin. v. RxUSA Wholesale* 285 Fed. Appx. 809 (2ⁿᵈ Cir. 2008) which provides historical analysis. Court enjoined FDA due to inconsistencies in regulation and compliance impossibility; See also, 75 FR 41434-01 (July 14, 2011) which removed a section of the Prescription Drug Marketing Act regulations and pedigree rule inconsistency, 21 C.F.R. section 203.50(a).

CRITICAL ANALYSIS: Evaluate if the *Drug Supply Chain Security Act* adequately resolves the problems associated with contaminated and counterfeit drugs entering the marketplace.

Drug Reimportation

Controversy about drug reimportation resurfaced due to proliferation of products on the Internet. Further, traditional mail order has revolutionized the access to prescription medicines for United States consumers. For example, some Canadian drugs are less expensive than the same drug in the United States mainly because of price controls and government subsidies in Canada. Direct promotion by the Internet has created easy access to foreign drugs beyond Canada. Over the years, there have been attempts to pass legislation for access such as the proposed Prescription Drug Affordability Act of 2015 H.R.3513—114th Congress (2015-2016) and Pharmaceutical Market Access and Drug Safety Act of 2011 (S.319 112th Congress 2011-2012). Despite the Medicine Equity and Safety Act and the Prescription Drug Import Fairness, Act 114 Stat. 1549 Title VII sec. 746(a) (2000), which was not allotted resources, to date legislation has not been enacted. FDA maintains that the sale of imported drugs to United Sates residents is illegal. The intent of proposed legislation to afford reimportation is to permit United States residents to purchase drugs outside of the United States from FDA approved laboratories in designated countries. Reimportation of United States manufactured drugs is only permitted by the drug manufacturer or through authorization by the Secretary of HHS for emergency medical care. 21 U.S.C. section 381 (d).

Concerns expressed by FDA are that of safety; yet this stance has proved contentious. State and local politicians have become active in the drug reimportation debate and want their constituents to have access to "reimported drugs" for cost control reasons. The legality of obtaining prescription drugs across the border remains highly controversial. According to FDA, Americans could possibly pay more for drugs in Canada than if they purchased generic drugs in the United States. FDA has issued warning letters and has coordinated the United States Customs and Border Protection agency "import blitzes". In *RxDepot*, the court granted FDA's Request for a preliminary injunction to stop the company from drug reimportation. The court found that FDA had warned RxDepot that the violations would subject them to enforcement action.

NOTE: *See United States v. RxDepot, Inc.*, **290 F.Supp. 2d 1238 (DC OK 2003).**

Drug reimportation practices in the United States https://www.ncbi.nlm.nih.gov/pubmed/18360614

CRITICAL ANALYSIS: Discuss drug reimportation and consider product safety, politics and economics.

Counterfeit Drugs

Counterfeit drugs pose potentially serious health and safety concerns. Those opposed to drug reimportation claim that a major concern involves counterfeit products. Counterfeit products, contrived to resemble legitimate finished drug products, may contain only inactive ingredients, incorrect ingredients, improper doses, dangerous subpotent or superpotent ingredients or other contaminants or be adulterated and or misbranded in other aspects. The FDCA is applicable and specifically defines what constitutes a counterfeit drug under 21 U.S.C. section 321(g) (2) and counterfeiting under the prohibited acts section, 21 U.S.C. section 331(i);

The prevalence of counterfeit drugs is worldwide; yet, sophisticated techniques make it difficult to investigate and detect these products. The motive to manufacture counterfeit products appears to be one of profit; however, Homeland Security is involved in efforts to combat counterfeit drugs. Besides Homeland Security, FDA and other federal and state agencies and the World Health Organization (WHO) are involved as well. WHO maintains a database on counterfeit drugs and created guidelines for instituting procedures to prevent counterfeit drug products. WHO has a specific form for reporting counterfeit drugs. The FDA report on counterfeit drugs details explicit steps to maintain a safe United States drug supply against increasingly complicated criminal attempts to introduce counterfeit drugs. Counterfeit medicines are not solely a United States problem as other countries are affected as well. A World Health Organization Report about Counterfeit Medicines

worldwide includes: Avastin (for cancer treatment) in the United States; Viagra and Cialis (for erectile dysfunction) in the United Kingdom, Turvada and Viread (for HIV/AIDS) and the United Kingdom, and Zidolan-N (for HIV/AIDS) in Kenya.
http://www.who.int/mediacentre/factsheets/fs275/en/

FDA and other government agencies formed a counterfeit task force in 2003 to address the public threats from counterfeit medications that enter the United States drug distribution system. Security experts, federal and state law enforcement officials, technology developers, manufacturers, wholesalers, retailers, consumer groups, and the general public were all involved in this effort. The task force developed methodologies to assure that the nation's drug distribution system protects Americans from counterfeit drugs. This came to fruition with enactment of the 2013 *Drug Quality and Security Act* discussed above.

CRITICAL ANALYSIS: Manufacturers, distributors, wholesalers, retailers, repackagers and pharmacists have a role in the identification and prevention of counterfeit drug products. Who in the drug distribution chain should be liable for injuries that result from a counterfeit and/or contaminated drugs?

Chapter 10: Adverse Events and PostMarket Surveillance

The overriding goal of FDA is to protect the public health and safety of the consumer. What does postmarket surveillance mean in terms of risk assessment and safety? Our society demands FDA approved medical products without delay; however, the question remains at what cost? The responsibility for risk assessment involves effective communication and collaboration encompassing many participants including the regulated industry, health care providers, the consumer and FDA. Postmarket surveillance in the forefront includes: New drug safety provisions; An Institute for Biomedical Research; Enhanced clinical trials registry; Adverse event reporting timeframes; and Conflict of interest issues. CDER conducts post marketing surveillance to identify safety problems and to take corrective action such as:

> *Medical alerts; Labeling changes; Boxed warnings; and Product withdrawals.*

For example, since 1995, due to safety reasons, approximately 22 drugs have been withdrawn from the United States marketplace. Of the drug withdrawals, over a dozen have been withdrawn since 2000 with the popular drug Vioxx in 2004, and Meridia and Darvon/Darvocet (propoxyphene) in 2010. To that end, the FDA Amendments Act (FDAAA) established risk identification, evaluation and mitigation actions. FDAAA contains several provisions that address postmarket safety. These issues involve a cost benefit analysis in terms of a "best approach" to postmarket co-vigilance. In carrying out the mandate of the Food and Drug Administration Amendments Act of 2007, Section 915 (FDAAA), FDA has created Internet links to postmarket drug safety information. This serves as a starting point and provides direct links for drug safety information such as MedWatch and Drug Safety Podcasts. For instance, pursuant to FDAAA, FDA created a Drug Safety Oversight Board (DSB). The DSB is composed of FDA employees and medical experts from other Health and Human Services agencies.

FDA remains the gatekeeper for safety of all medical products in the United States whether manufactured in the United States or abroad. In fiscal year 2009, drugs manufactured outside the United States in over 100 countries were offered for importation into the United States. The oversight of medical drug products was added to the Government Accounting Office (GAO's) High-Risk list in 2009 due to evolving safety issues in foreign establishment inspection, post-market monitoring and clinical trial oversight. The GAO recommended that FDA:

> *Develop performance-based standards that are results oriented on public safety;*
> *Respond effectively to globalization; and*
> *Expand the scope of postmarket safety.*

http://www.fda.gov/Drugs/DrugSafety/PostmarketDrugSafetyInformationforPatientsandProviders/default.htm

FDA Amendments Act Postmarket Safety

Title IX- Enhanced Authorities Regarding Postmarket Safety of Drugs

Postmarket Studies and Clinical Trials—Section 505(0) strengthens FDA's authority to require and monitor postmarket studies, clinical trials and postmarket labeling changes.

Safety Labeling Changes—Provides a mechanism for FDA to require safety labeling changes if there is new safety information that should be included in the labeling of a drug or biologic. The NDA or Biologic License Holder must submit within 30 days either a supplement to FDA with proposed changes to the labeling to reflect the new safety information or provide a detailed explanation as to why a labeling change would not be warranted. Further 505(0)(4)(I) clarifies that the enhanced safety labeling mechanism does not affect the obligation of a company to maintain a drug product's labeling.

Risk Evaluation and Mitigation Strategy (REM)—FDA has the authority to require a REMS to assure that the benefits outweigh the risks at 18 and 36 month intervals and the seventh year after the drug approval.

Pre-review of Television Advertisement—Section 503B provides a procedure for pre-review of television drug advertisements.

Citizen Petitions and Drug Approvals—FDA cannot delay approval of a generic drug application on the basis of a citizen petition. The only exception is for public protection reasons.

Drug Safety Communication

http://www.fda.gov/downloads/Drugs/GuidanceComplianceRegulatoryInformation/Guidances/UCM295217.pdf (Revision1 issued March 2012)

FDA developed a guidance document as to how the agency develops and disseminates information to the public about important drug safety issues including emerging drug safety information. According to the guidance, in addition to written communications, FDA uses communication tools, such as webinars, broadcasts, and conference calls, to disseminate drug safety information. Additionally, electronic social media to communicate some safety issues is used. Other mechanisms to disseminate drug safety information to the public include concise advisories and other Internet postings; more detailed short articles; articles in trade and professional journals; a standardized, one-document solution for patient medication information (PMI) as well as background papers. The Table below details whom FDA communicates drug safety information to and the type of communication.

Table: Summary of Selected Methods for FDA Communication of Drug Safety Information

Communication Type	Content	Target Audience
Professional labeling for prescription drugs	Summary of essential information needed for safe and effective use of the drug.	Healthcare providers
Patient-directed labeling for prescription drugs (patient package inserts and Medication Guides)	Summary of essential information needed for safe and effective use of the drug.	Patients
OTC "Drug Facts" labeling	Summary of essential information needed for safe and effective use of the drug.	Consumers
Public Health Advisory	Information and advice regarding an emerging drug safety issue or other important public health information.	General public
Patient Information Sheet	Concise summary in plain language of the most important information about a particular drug. Includes an Alert when appropriate to communicate an important, and often emerging, drug safety issue.	Patients and/or consumers, lay caregivers, and interested members of the general public
Healthcare Professional Sheet	Concise summary of an important, and often emerging, drug safety issue, with background information about the detection of the issue and points to consider for clinical decision making.	Healthcare professionals
Alerts on Patient Information and Healthcare Professional Sheets	Summary of an important, and often emerging, drug safety issue. Alerts are tailored to the needs of the primary target audience for each type of information sheet.	Healthcare professionals, patients and/or consumers, lay caregivers, and interested members of the general public

Toll Free Number for Adverse Event Reporting

A final rule was promulgated for compliance concerning the listing of a Toll-Free number for reporting adverse events for human drug products. 21 CFR Parts 201, 208, and 209, 73 FR 63886 (October 28, 2008) Compliance: July 1, 2009.

Final Rule Highlights: One substantive change was made to the regulatory provisions published in the proposed rule: Section 201.66(c)(5)(vii) (21 CFR 201.66(c)(5)(vii)) has been modified to require that only approved application OTC drug products whose packaging does not include a toll-free number through which consumers can report complaints to the manufacturer or distributor of the drug product are required to include the side effects statement in labeling.

PART 201—LABELING OTC Drug Product Labeling

§ 201.66 (c)(5)(vii): Format and content requirements for over-the-counter (OTC) drug product labeling. For all OTC drug products under an approved drug application whose packaging does not include a toll-free number through which consumers can report complaints to the manufac-turer or distributor of the drug product, the following text shall immediately follow the subheading (in a minimum 6–point bold letter height or type size.): **"[Bullet] side effects occur. You may report side effects to FDA at 1–800–FDA–1088."**

PART 208—MEDICATION GUIDES FOR PRESCRIPTION DRUG PRODUCTS

21 CFR § 208.20 (b)(7) (iii): Content and format of a Medication Guide. *"Call your doctor for medical advice about side effects. You may report side effects to FDA at 1–800–FDA–1088."*

§ 209.10 Content and format of the side effects statement.

(a) *Content.* The side effects statement provided with each prescription drug product approved under section 505 of the act must read: *"Call your doctor for medical advice about side effects. You may report side effects to FDA at 1–800–FDA–1088."*

§ 209.11 Dispensing and distributing the side effects statement.

(a) Each authorized dispenser or pharmacy must distribute the side effects statement with each prescription drug product approved under section 505 of the act and dispensed. The side effects statement must be distributed with new and refill prescriptions.

(b) An authorized dispenser or pharmacy must choose one or more of the following options to distribute the side effects statement:

(1) Distribute the side effects statement on a sticker attached to the unit package, vial, or container of the drug product;

(2) Distribute the side effects statement on a preprinted pharmacy prescription vial cap;

(3) Distribute the side effects statement on a separate sheet of paper;

(4) Distribute the side effects statement in consumer medication information; or

(5) Distribute the appropriate FDA-approved Medication Guide that contains the side effects statement.

Adverse Event Reporting MedWatch

The FDA Adverse Event Reporting System database (FAERS) formerly (AERS) is comprised of information on adverse event and medication error reports that are submitted to FDA. FAERS is part of FDA's post-marketing safety surveillance program. Based on the FAERS information, FDA could institute several types of regulatory actions such as updating labeling product infor-mation, drug use restrictions, communication of new safety information and possibly product with-drawal from the market. The latter is utilized in rare circumstances; however, it has been done with Vioxx as a prime example.

Adverse event reporting and medication errors by healthcare professionals (ex. physicians, phar-macists, nurses) and consumers (ex. patients, family, attorneys) is voluntary; yet, FDA does receive adverse event and medication error reports directly from healthcare professionals and consumers. However, if healthcare professionals and consumers report adverse events and/or medication errors to a manufacturer, then the manufacturer is required to send the report to FDA. These reports re-ceived from healthcare professionals, consumers and manufacturers are inputted into the FAERS database. MedWatch provides information on reporting.

Even though FDA conducts one of the most stringent approval processes in the world, it is virtually impossible to identify all probable problems during the premarketing stages. Limitations premarket with human clinical trials include the size, scope and duration of the human clinical trials. Once a medical product is marketed, the size and nature of the population that uses the product changes thus necessitating the need for adverse event reporting by health professionals. Post market surveillance has been under FDA jurisdiction since the early 1960s with a multiple form reporting system. In 1993, the MedWatch program was inaugurated with the intent to streamline the reporting process. An important MedWatch goal is to better inform health professionals about regulatory actions taken by FDA in response to reports of adverse events and product quality problems. Purposes of MedWatch consist of an explanation of what should and should not be reported; improved awareness of serious reactions caused by drugs or medical devices; better feedback to the health community and a simpler reporting process.

Besides prescription drugs, MedWatch reporting applies to OTC products marketed under an approved NDA including prescription drugs that are switched to OTC status. Biological products such as vaccines and blood products are covered under a separate reporting system termed VAERS or the Vaccine Adverse Event Reporting System. MedWatch reports to FDA can be accomplished online, by mail and by fax. Individual health professionals are permitted to use the voluntary Med-Watch form to report adverse events. Health professionals that work in hospitals or other user facilities such as a nursing home or an outpatient treatment facility have mandatory reporting for medical devices. Termed spontaneous reports, both voluntary and mandatory reporting are results outside of formal clinical studies. Limitations and disadvantages do exist when using spontaneous type reporting. Examples of limitations comprise underreporting, biases, and quality of the report in an uncontrolled environment. Yet, the advantages of MedWatch include the relatively inexpensive cost and large-scale surveillance. Adverse reporting by hospitals is connected to the Joint Commission on Accreditation of Healthcare Organizations (JCAHO) standards. JCAHO obligates hospitals to monitor adverse events for pharmaceuticals and medical devices. Similar to JCAHO, the American Society of Health System Pharmacists (ASHP) guiding principles consist of identification of a serious adverse event with specification that reports be made to FDA, the manufacturer or both. The purpose of MedWatch is to enhance the effectiveness of postmarket surveillance of medical products and to pinpoint important health hazards. Health professionals are essential to the effectiveness of MedWatch. MedWatch depends on doctors, dentists, nurses, pharmacists and other health professionals to inform FDA about serious adverse reactions and problems with medical problems. CDER conducts post marketing surveillance to identify any safety problems and takes corrective action such as an FDA Alert and boxed Warnings. http://www.fda.gov/medwatch.

Reporting by individual healthcare providers is voluntary; however, pharmaceutical manufacturers and distributors and packers have mandatory requirements. FDA requires "15-day Alert Reports" for serious and unexpected events that are not in the product labeling. Periodic adverse event reports are required on a quarterly basis for the first three years after approval and then on an annual basis. Reporting requirements are stipulated under 21 CFR 318.80 and 600.80. Serious adverse events are reported by using the MedWatch Form. MedWatch depends on collaboration with health professionals and trade organizations. For instance, FDA MedWatch has partnered with ePocrates, an organization of physicians, to disseminate critical drug safety alerts to physicians and other health care professionals in the ePocrates network. The ePocrates network consists of healthcare professionals including pharmacists and nurses and physicians who use the ePocrates electronic drug source, which contains information on important safety topics such as indication-specific dosing, adverse reactions and multiple drug interactions. The FDA goal in partnering with ePocrates is to make clinically important safety information both easy to use and timely accessible to health care professionals who are then in a better position to discuss treatment with patients. Part of the ePocrates system involves DocAlerts, which are messages sent directly to the physician. According to FDA, the MedWatch/ePocrates partnering is a good example of leveraging technology with the goal to improve public health.
http://www.fda.gov/Drugs/GuidanceComplianceRegulatoryInformation/Surveillance/AdverseDrugEffects/default.htm

Non-Prescription Drug Serious Adverse Event Reporting

The Dietary Supplement and Nonprescription Drug Consumer Protection Act requires dietary supplements and labeling of over-the-counter (OTC) drugs with a domestic address and phone number for adverse event reporting. A mandatory 15 day reporting requirement for manufacturers, packers and distributors of over the counter drugs and dietary supplements is required for reporting a "serious adverse event" to FDA. A Serious Adverse Event is defined as follows:

SEC. 760. SERIOUS ADVERSE EVENT REPORTING FOR NONPRESCRIPTION DRUGS.

(a) Definitions-In this section:

ADVERSE EVENT—The term 'adverse event' means any health-related event associated with the use of a nonprescription drug that is adverse, including—

(A) an event occurring from an overdose of the drug, whether accidental or intentional;

(B) an event occurring from abuse of the drug;

(C) an event occurring from withdrawal from the drug; and

(D) any failure of expected pharmacological action of the drug.

SERIOUS ADVERSE EVENT—The term 'serious adverse event' is an adverse event that—

(A) results in—

    (i) death;

    (ii) a life-threatening experience;

    (iii) inpatient hospitalization;

    (iv) a persistent or significant disability or incapacity; or

    (v) a congenital anomaly or birth defect; or

(B) requires, based on reasonable medical judgment, a medical or surgical intervention to prevent an outcome described under subparagraph (A).

Reports of serious adverse reactions or problems with products can be made directly to the manufacturer who is legally required to report the adverse information to FDA. The key is to understand what a serious adverse event constitutes. A serious adverse event consists of:

> **Death from use of the medical product;**
> **A life-threatening hazard such as failure of an intravenous IV pump that could result in disproportionate drug dosing;**
> **Hospitalization due to the serious reaction; disability such as a permanent change in physical activities; birth defects, miscarriage, stillbirth, or birth with disease; or**
> **Intercession to avoid permanent damage.**

Consumer Product Safety Improvement Act

www.SaferProducts.gov

The Consumer Product Safety Commission (CPSC) regulates product packaging for poison prevention aspects for products required to be in child resistant packaging and for senior adult use. Examples include pain relievers, iron containing medicine and prescription drugs. See 16CFR section 1700.14. Yet, it appears that there is a jurisdictional overlap as various consumer products are jointly regulated by CPSC and FDA. Examples include teething rings, heating pads and infant sleep positioners. The Consumer Safety Improvement Act (CPSIA) Pub. L. 110-314 (2008) amended the Consumer Product Safety Act (CPSA) and added new section 6A. The relevancy for food and drug law concerns the establishment of a database about:

> *Reports of harm;*
> *Manufacturer/Importer or Private Labeler comments regarding reports of harm; and*
> *Information from mandatory recall notices and notices of voluntary corrective action by manufacturers.*

CRITICAL ANALYSIS: CPSC forwards misdirected reports to FDA; however, discuss whether confusion could still result with both FDA and the CPSC regulating some of the same products. Provide recommendations such as a Memorandum of Understanding as to jurisdiction and CPSC links to FDA's MedWatch.

Opioids—Access, Lawsuits, Deterrents, Warnings, Withdrawals

President Trump reaffirmed his declaration of the opioid crisis as a National Emergency and signed the *"Substance Use–Disorder Prevention that Promotes Opioid Recovery and Treatment for Patients and Communities Act"* in 2018. According to the U.S. Department of Justice, the federal government has endorsed litigation by states and local government. Additionally, they will seek reimbursement from drug companies and distributors to recover costs it has incurred from the opioid epidemic. A key element is how these products are promoted.

Suffice to state there are many victims in this epidemic—young children, legitimate users, and workers such as postal employees and customs and border control personnel. In 2016, there were approximately 64,000 drug related deaths. Statistics for 2015 indicate 33,000 deaths from opioids. Further, there are diametrically opposed concerns pertaining to the use of opioids. The *Ensuring Patient Access and Effective Drug Enforcement Act*, 114th Congress (2015-2016) (4/19/16) concerns access to prescription painkillers and collaboration and coordination among federal, state, local and tribal law enforcement agencies. FDA and CDC are accountable to identify both impediments to lawful patient access to controlled substances and as well as diversion of controlled substances. In 2016, Congress enacted a federal law to permit a pharmacist, at the request of a physician, to partially fill a prescription. Further, collaboration between government agencies and the pharmaceutical industry in terms of both patient access and abuse of controlled substances remains critical. Other legislation directed to this issue includes the Cures Act and the Comprehensive Addiction and Recovery Act.

Government Actions—Federal oversight includes for example, the Drug Enforcement Administration (DEA), Centers for Disease Control (CDC), the Food and Drug Administration (FDA), Customs and Border Control, the Federal Trade Commission, (FTC) and the United States Postal System (USPS).

DEA—The Drug Enforcement Administration (DEA) proposed a rule on April 19, 2018, 83 Federal Register 17329 (No. 76) to address the opioid crisis. Under this proposed new rule, if DEA believes that a company's opioids are being diverted for misuse, then the DEA will decrease the number of opioids that a company can manufacture.
https://www.gpo.gov/fdsys/pkg/FR-2018-04-19/pdf/2018-08111.pdf

FDA—Black box warnings, reformulation, steering committees, "dark web" agents, expanded risk management, fast track for non-addictive pain medications, and training are examples of FDA involvement. Further, in 2018 (April 20) FDA released a draft guidance describing techniques drug companies can advance for new medications to treat opioid addiction by submission under section 505 (b)(2) (streamlined pathway) of the FDCA. According to the guidance, the focus is to design modified-release drugs that are either implanted or injected. The guidance details how companies can develop sustained-released "depot" buprenorphine drug products.
https://www.fda.gov/downloads/Drugs/GuidanceComplianceRegulatoryInformation/Guidances/UCM579751.pdf (Guidance discusses ANDA or Sec. 505 (b)(2) Submissions).

Black Box Warnings
http://www.fda.gov/Drugs/DrugSafety/InformationbyDrugClass/ucm363722.htm
Immediate Release Opioids—Postmarket Black Box Warning—In 2016, FDA issued safety-labeling changes for immediate-release opioid pain medications. A black box warning is mandatory concerning the serious risks of misuse, abuse, addiction, overdose and death.
Extended Release Opioids—Postmarket Boxed Box Warning—In 2013, FDA issued new drug labeling standards and safety labeling changes as well as new postmarket study requirements for all extended-release and long-acting (ER/LA) opioid analgesics intended to treat pain. The boxed warning requirement emphasizes risks of use while pregnant which includes neonatal opioid withdrawal syndrome. Additionally, new language denotes that the drugs should be used for severe pain.

Warning—In 2017, FDA issued warnings about the dangers of combining medication to treat opioid addiction (such as methadone) with anti-anxiety (such as Ambien and Lunesta), insomnia (Xanax) and muscle relaxers medications.

Market Withdrawal—In 2017, per FDA request, Endo International Plc removed the painkiller, Opana ER *https://www.fda.gov/NewsEvents/Newsroom/PressAnnouncements/ucm562401.htm*

Liability—Who is liable for the epidemic? Drug companies who manufacture opioid products include, Purdue Pharma, Endo, Janssen, Teva and Allergan; Distributors such as McKesson, Physicians; Dentists, Patients, Pharmacists, Health Care Providers and Lobbyists. See for example *Pennsylvania v. Bruce Lief,* (2018) Chester County- allegations of 25,000 Oxycodone, OnyContin and Methadone pills; *Com. V. Delbaggio*, MJ24103-CR-0000097-2018 (former lover prescribed 1,000 Oxycodone and Xanax pills to heroin-addicted lover for him to sell as a method to repay a $50,000.00 loan.

Manufacturers include Purdue who manufactures opioids including OxyContin and Dilaudid, Endo brands Percocet and Percodan, and Janssen produces Duragesic and Nucynta. Teva manufacturers Actiq and Fentora. Allergan manufactures Kadian, Norco and generic opioids.

Lawsuits—**State Attorney Generals, State and Local Lawsuits**—Several states in 2018 such as California, Illinois, Massachusetts, New Jersey, and New York, have accused companies that manufacture and distribute opioids of increasing health insurance costs due to the over-prescribing of opioids stemming back to 1996 when Purdue Pharma introduced its opioid painkiller OxyContin. Several state Attorney General's for example, Texas, Florida, Nevada, North Carolina, North Dakota and Tennessee have filed lawsuits against Purdue Pharma under state Deceptive Trade Practices Acts based on aggressive marketing with knowledge of the addiction risk. Other state examples include—Alaska, Mississippi, Oklahoma and Washington, New Jersey, Illinois, Massachusetts and Pennsylvania). However, townships, cities, counties and a Native American tribe are instituting lawsuits against pharmaceutical companies, distributors and pharmacies. For example, the city Chicago instituted a lawsuit in 2014 alleging payment for unnecessary prescriptions for city employees due to drug sales representations. In 2017, Bensalem township (PA), Delaware County (PA), several counties in West Virginia and the cities of Birmingham (Alabama) of Dayton (Ohio) sued several pharmaceutical companies, pharmacies, distributors and pain specialists with allegations that they caused the opioid crisis and exhausted public resources, wasted taxpayer monies and ultimately killed thousands of residents. Distributors include AmerisourceBergen, Cardinal Health and McKesson Corporation. Claims are modeled similar to the "Big Tobacco" lawsuits. Allegations include how the drug was promoted and misrepresentation of the addictive risk of opioids. Suffice to state there are many victims in this epidemic—young children, legitimate users, and workers such as postal employees and customs and border control personnel. Defenses include federal preemption, knowledge at the time and impossibility. Lawsuit examples:

Tribal Court—Cherokee Nation, in Oklahoma, filed a lawsuit (2017) against CVS Health, Walgreens Boots Alliance, Inc., McKesson and others (distributors). *The Cherokee Nation v. McKesson Corp. et al.*, CV-2017-203, Dist.Ct. Cherokee Nation.

Missouri (Attorney General) filed a lawsuit in 2017 alleging a complex scheme to misrepresent the addictive risk of opioids. See: *Missouri v. Purdue Pharma LP et al.*, # 1722-CC10626, Circuit Ct. of the City of St. Louis.

Ohio (Attorney General) sued several drug companies including Janssen, Allergan, Purdue, Endo Health Solutions and Teva unit Cephalon Inc for violation of the Ohio Consumer Sales Practices Act by disseminating false and misleading statements by sales representatives and advertising regarding the risks and benefits of opioids. See: *Ohio v. Purdue Pharma et al.*, # 17CI000261, Ross Cty Court of Common Pleas. See also *New Hampshire v. Purdue Pharma LP et al.*, 1:17-cv-00427, U.S. D. Ct; *Oklahoma v. Purdue Pharma LP et al.*, CJ-2017-816.

NOTE: See, for example:
https://www.clarionledger.com/story/news/2017/06/11/mississippi-sets-tone-opioid-drugmakers-face-rising-tide-lawsuits/346518001/
https://www.usnews.com/news/best-states/oklahoma/articles/2017-06-30/oklahoma-ad-sues-4-drug-manufacturers-over-opioid-addiction (June 30, 2017).

See also: Opioid drug makers sued over rising health insurance costs.

https://www.washingtonexaminer.com/policy/healthcare/opioid-drugmakers-sued-over-rising-health-insurance-costs

Insys Therapeutics, Inc.— In 2018, Insys Therapeutics Inc. agreed to pay at least $150 million to resolve the United States Department of Justice criminal and civil investigation concerning allegations of bribery to prescribe its fentanyl spray. States have sued Insys as well. *Commonwealth of Massachusetts v. Insys Therapeutics, Inc.*, Mass. Super. Ct., No. 17-3207D, (consent judgment 10/5/17). Insys Therapeutics paid Massachusetts $500,000 to settle charges concerning the off-label marketing of its fentanyl spray and kickbacks to physicians (speaking fees to health professionals about the drug) to prescribe the opioid. A lawsuit was also filed by the New Jersey Attorney General who alleged the company improperly promoted its opioid for off-label uses to treat minor pain. FDA approval indication was for substantial pain from cancer. Finally, Insys Pharmaceuticals settled with the state of Illinois for $4.45 million to settle a 2016 lawsuit over allegations about the deceptive opioid marketing.

NOTE: See also *U. S. v. Babich et al.,* **case number 1:16-cr-10343, (U.S. District Ct. Massachusetts), where the CEO and other executives of Insys were charged with racketeering, bribery and kickbacks under federal law.**

CRITICAL ANALYSIS: How are these lawsuits similar and dissimilar to the lawsuits against tobacco companies?

Recommendations—The opioid epidemic is huge and multifaceted. Those involved in health care and manufacturers should do the following:

➢ *Develop additional abuse deterrent products. See ex. Arymo ER approved early 2017 extended release tablets with no alternative options. The product manufactured by Egalet Corp., has an increased resistance to being cut, crushed or ground*
➢ *Utilize standard procedures for truthful non-misleading statements by drug representatives by including the dangers of combination drugs ex. medication for opioid addiction and anti-anxiety medications;*
➢ *Utilize existing laws such as partial refill;*
➢ *Develop non-addictive formulations;*
➢ *Establish nationwide network to identify patients who could misuse opioids;*
➢ *Utilize alternative treatments;*
➢ *Train health care providers about the unintentional overdoses of valid prescriptions; and*
➢ *Educate health care providers concerning the gateway to other drugs such as heroin and fentanyl.*

CRITICAL ANALYSIS: How and who should handle the opioid crisis? Discuss the impact of liability of drug company executives.

Gabapentin and Gabapentinoids—Off-Label as Opioid Alternative

In 2018 FDA commenced review of whether gabapentinoids are an addiction threat. Gabapentin (Neurontin) and gabapentinoids like pregabalin (Lyrica) are approved to treat a variety of conditions, including post-herpetic neuralgia, fibromyalgia, and neuropathic pain associated with diabetes. The issue is whether these drugs are being prescribed off-label as alternatives to opioids. Preliminary research does not appear widespread yet FDA plans to continue monitoring abuse and misuse which could result in respiratory depression and death.

Antipsychotic Drugs and Dementia

http://www.fda.gov/drugs/drugsafety/postmarketdrugsafetyinformationforpatientsandprovid-
ers/ucm124830.htm (edited)

Antipsychotics are not indicated for the treatment of dementia-related psychosis.

As early as 2005, FDA notified healthcare professionals that conventional and atypical anti-psychotics are connected to an increased risk of mortality in elderly patients treated for dementia-related psychosis. In 2008, FDA clarified that antipsychotics are not indicated nor approved for the treatment of dementia-related psychosis. Further, physicians who prescribe antipsychotics to elderly patients with dementia-related psychosis should detail the increased mortality risk with their patients, their families and caregivers.

Boxed Warning Requirement—to the drugs' prescribing information about the risk of mortality in elderly patients treated for dementia-related psychosis similar to the *Boxed Warning* and *Warning* added to the prescribing information of the atypical antipsychotic drugs in 2005.

CRITICAL ANALYSIS: Evaluate whether using a black box warning has adequately addressed this problem. What else could be used on the outside label and/or the immediate container?

Labeling Changes and Dosage Limit—*Acetaminophen*

Acetaminophen overdoses in the United States have resulted in approximately 500 deaths annually which are attributed to acetaminophen overdoses. Back in 2011, FDA requested that manufacturers of prescription combination products that contain acetaminophen to limit the amount of acetaminophen to no more than 325 milligrams (mg) in each tablet, capsule or other dosage unit.

In 2014, FDA recommended that health care professionals discontinue prescribing and dispensing prescription combination drug products that contain more than 325 milligrams (mg) per tablet, capsule, or other dosage unit. Further, FDA required manufacturers to update labels of all prescription combination acetaminophen products to warn of the potential risk for severe liver injury. See: *http://www.fda.gov/Drugs/DrugSafety/ucm381644.htm*

http://livertox.nih.gov/Acetaminophen.htm

http://www.regulations.gov/#!documentDetail;D=FDA-2011-N-0021-0001

Drug Withdrawal—*Darvon/Darvocet*

The marketplace withdrawal of Opana ER in 2017 illustrated that despite preventive attempts a marketplace withdrawal is necessary. Another excellent illustration is the withdrawal of Darvon/Darvocet (propoxyphene) in 2010. Propoxyphene, an opioid type drug had been in the marketplace since 1957; however, there was increased concerns as far back as the late 1970's. It was not until 2009 that FDA determined the risks outweighed the benefits. The FDA received new clinical data concerning potential serious or even fatal heart rhythm abnormalities. Further, in 2009 the European Medicines Agency recommended a withdrawal throughout the European Union. Xanodyne Pharmaceuticals, Inc. manufacturer of Darvon and Darvocet (combination with acetaminophen), the brand version of the prescription pain medication propoxyphene, withdrew the medication from the U.S. market at the request of the FDA. The generic manufacturers of propoxyphene-containing products were notified and requested that they voluntarily remove their products as well.

Drug Errors—Bar Code Regulation

A final rule titled: *"Bar Code Label Requirements for Human Drug Products and Biological Products"* was promulgated to improve patient safety and error reduction by requiring the use of bar codes in hospitals on human drugs and biological products. Besides patient safety, other benefits include: reduced litigation and malpractice liability insurance and more efficiency in inventory, ordering and billing. FDA estimated that the bar code labeling rule prevents approximately 500,000 adverse events and transfusion errors which computes to $93 billion in health costs savings over the next 20 years. The rule applies to most prescription drugs, some over the counter products and container labels for blood and blood components for transfusion purposes.

The National Drug Code (NDC) number (linear bar code) affords health care professionals to utilize the bar code scanning to confirm that the appropriate drug is provided to the correct patient. The bar-coded identification bracelet links the patient to his or her computerized medical record. Prior to dispensing a drug, the drug(s) for the patient is scanned to compare against the patient's medical record to the drug(s) being administered.

See: 69 FR 9120 (February 26, 2004) link to Bar Code Label Requirements Guidance as follows: *https://www.fda.gov/downloads/BiologicsBloodVaccines/GuidanceComplianceRegulatoryInformation/Guidances/UCM267392.pdf*

CRITICAL ANALYSIS: Review and evaluate the various postmarket surveillance mechanisms and propose improvements.

Approved Drugs—Distribution of New Risk Information

Draft Guidance for Industry on Distributing Scientific and Medical Publications on Risk Information for Approved Prescription Drugs and Biological Products

This draft guidance *"Approved Drugs and Distribution of New Risk Information"* concerns dissemination of new risk information is related to already *Approved Uses* of a Drug. The guidance above clarifies FDA's position on manufacturer dissemination of new risk information regarding lawfully marketed drugs for approved uses to health care professionals or health care entities. This issue is distinct from the dissemination of information on *Unapproved New Uses of **Approved Drugs**.*

http://www.fda.gov/downloads/drugs/guidancecomplianceregulatoryinformation/guidances/ucm400104.pdf

DEPARTMENT OF HEALTH AND HUMAN SERVICES Food and Drug Administration 79 FR 33569-01 NOTICES [Docket No. FDA-2014-D-0758] Wednesday, June 11, 2014

The draft guidance details recommended practices for drug manufacturers to follow when distributing to health care professionals or health care entities scientific or medical journal articles that discuss new risk information for approved prescription drugs for human use, including drugs licensed as biological products, and approved animal drugs. The recommendations address issues specific to the distribution of new information about risks associated with a drug that further characterizes risks identified in the approved labeling. If firms choose to distribute new risk information that rebuts, mitigates, or refines risk information in the approved labeling, and the information is in the form of a reprint or digital copy of a published study, the guidance provides recommendations regarding the characteristics of those publications.

Specifically, with respect to the data source the draft guidance details that:

"The study or analysis should meet accepted design and other methodological standards for the type of study or analysis (e.g., provides a clear description of the hypothesis tested, acknowledges and accounts for potential bias and multiplicity) and should be sufficiently well-designed and informative to merit consideration in assessing the implications of a risk."

"To rebut a prior determination (reflected in the approved labeling) that there is some basis to believe there is causal relationship between the drug and the occurrence of an adverse event, or to otherwise mitigate a described risk, the study or analysis should also be at least as persuasive as the data sources that underlie the existing risk assessment of causality, severity, and/or incidence of the adverse reaction as reflected in approved labeling (e.g., data from a new controlled trial designed to estimate the relative risk of the event, a pharmacoepidemiologic study that is capable of reliably estimating the relative risk, or a rigorous meta-analysis of all relevant data from new and existing controlled trials)."

"The conclusions of the study or analysis should give appropriate weight and consideration to, and should be a fair characterization of, all relevant information in the safety database, including contrary or otherwise inconsistent findings. There is a broad spectrum of potential data sources that can contribute in some way to characterization of a product's safety; new risk information should be considered in light of relevant existing information and integrated with that data."

"The study or analysis should be published in an independent, peer-reviewed journal."

The draft guidance makes recommendations with respect to the distribution of the reprint or digital copy, including the recommendation that a cover sheet accompany the reprint or digital copy that clearly and prominently discloses the following:

"The study design, critical findings, and significant methodological or other limitations of the study or analysis that may limit the persuasiveness or scope of findings that rebut, mitigate, or refine risk information in the approved labeling. Limitations should be discussed in relation to the specific circumstances of the study and its conclusions about a risk."

"The information is not consistent with certain risk information in the approved labeling (should specifically identify the inconsistent information)."

"FDA has not reviewed the data."

"Any financial interests or affiliations between the study author(s) and the firm."

The reprint or digital copy should have the approved labeling for the product, and when distributed, should be separate from any promotional material. Additionally, FDA notes in the draft guidance that the recommendations in the guidance do not change a firm's existing obligations to revise its approved labeling in accordance with 21 CFR 201.56(a)(2), 314.70, 514.8(c) and 601.12. FDA estimates that approximately 500 firms annually distribute scientific and medical publications that discuss new risk information for approved prescription drugs. FDA also estimates that each firm would include some or all of the additional information described previously when distributing annually a total of approximately 4,250 scientific or medical journal articles that discuss new risk information for approved prescription drugs.

CRITICAL ANALYSIS: Evaluate the draft guidance on the *"Distribution of New Risk Information for Approved Drugs"* including the effectiveness of dissemination of the new risk information. Incorporate legal liability and responsibilities of the drug manufacturer and the health care provider. This draft guidance pertains to already FDA *Approved Drug Uses*.

NOTE: FDA issued a draft guidance in February 2014, entitled *"Distributing Scientific and Medical Publications on Unapproved New Uses—Recommended Practices"* to clarify FDA's position on manufacturer dissemination of scientific or medical publications including scientific or medical journal articles, scientific or medical reference texts, and clinical practice guidelines that includes information on *Unapproved New Uses* of the manufacturer's products. See: this *Volume, Chapter 7 Off-Label Dissemination*.

VOLUME VI

Volume VI: Biotechnology and Biologics Regulation—Biosimilars, Allergenics, Tissue, Blood, Vaccines and Gene Therapy Products

This volume focuses on major issues concerning the proliferation of biologics. Biotech products including bioengineered vaccines and biologics have increased significantly according to a recent Congressional Research Report. Biosimilars have become a multibillion-dollar market. This volume includes a strategic goal plan for the Food and Drug Administration's Center for Biologics Evaluation and Research (CBER). The authority of CBER stems from the Public Health Services Act (PHSA) and specific sections of the United States Food, Drug and Cosmetic Act (FDCA). The PHSA and FDCA impact on these regulated products. Critical parameters in the regulation of these products remains science based to assure purity, potency, safety, efficacy, and availability. Biologics result from living sources such as humans, animals and microorganisms. They are unlike conventional drugs, which are chemically synthesized. Biologics involve complicated mixtures and are produced using biotechnology. Biologics include a wide range of products such as vaccines, blood and blood components, allergenics, somatic cells, gene therapy, tissues, and recombinant therapeutic proteins. Biologics can be composed of sugars, proteins, or nucleic acids or complex combinations of these substances, or living entities such as cells and tissues.

Special topics besides biosimilars include bioterrorism and botulinum Toxin Type A "Botox". Examples of voluntary recalls, gene therapy initiatives and warning letters are included. Each chapter contains critical analysis issues to explore. The United States Supreme Court pronouncement in Association for Molecular Pathology v. Myriad Genetics, hinged on whether naturally occurring human genes and/or isolating those genes from the body were a patentable invention. Another Ebola outbreak occurred in 2018 and earlier the Zika virus in 2015. Coordination amongst United States agencies such as the National Institutes of Health (NIH), Centers for Disease Control (CDC) and the Food and Drug Administration (FDA) and global efforts, prevented an epidemic. The first confirmed Zika virus infection occurred in 2015 in Brazil. In early 2016, the World Health Organization (WHO) classified the Zika virus as an international public health emergency. As the biosimilar market increases, issues concerning these products continue. Increased competition, naming, high costs, transition to the PHSA licensing and attempts to stymie the market by brand companies. The United States Supreme Court settled the issue of notice of commercial marketing in Sandoz, Inc. v. Amgen Inc.

Congress passed the Biologics Price Competition and Innovation Act (BPCI or Biosimilars) Act, in Title VII of the 2010 Patient Protection and Affordable Care Act, Pub.L. 111-148, amended by the Health Care and Reconciliation Act of 2010 (Healthcare Reform Act). The BPCI Act established a 12-year exclusivity period before biosimilars can be approved for marketing in the United States. FDA approved the first biosimilar in 2015 and continues to do so throughout the ensuing years. Generic versions of biotech drugs referred to as biosimilars or follow-on biologics present an interesting and complex issue for both industry and FDA. In 2018, FDA established a biosimilar action plan that addresses innovation and competition. See: https://www.fda.gov/ucm/groups/fdagov-public/@fdagov-drugs-gen/documents/document/ucm613761.pdf

Chapter 1: Biologic Products Regulation

Center for Biologics Evaluation and Research Mission and Vision

Key Websites: *https://www.fda.gov/BiologicsBloodVaccines/default.htm*
http://www.fda.gov/downloads/AboutFDA/WhatWeDo/History/ProductRegulation/100Years-ofBiologicsRegulation/UCM070313.pdf

This chapter includes a strategic goal plan for the Center for Biologics Evaluation and Research (CBER). The authority of CBER stems from section 351 of the Public Health Services Act (PHS Act) and specific sections of the FDCA. The mission of CBER is to protect and enhance the public health through the regulation of biological and related products for human use under the FDCA and the Public Health Service Act (PHSA). That has become a huge mission as projections are that 50% of the top drugs will be the result of biotechnology. According to a Congressional Research Report (CRS 7-5700) about "Follow-on Biologics", biotechnology products including bioengineered vaccines and biologics are predicted to increase. Critical parameters in the regulation of these products remains science based in order to assure purity, potency, safety and efficacy in accordance with statutory authority. CBER conducts inspections prior to approval as well as after approval. CBER monitors ongoing safety and stability of biological products and conducts research as a critical aspect of science-based decision-making. The vision of CBER is to use sound science and regulatory expertise to: *protect public health; provide access to safe and effective products; and encourage novel technologies.*

Guidance Documents—The issuance of guidance documents has been valuable to both the regulated industry and FDA. CBER has issued several guidance documents specific to biologics as follows: *General Biologics, Allergenics, Blood, Cellular and Gene Therapy ,Tissue , Vaccine and Related Biological Products , and Xenotransplantation Guidances.* The following link contains the list of guidance documents.

http://www.fda.gov/BiologicsBloodVaccines/GuidanceComplianceRegulatoryInformation/Guidances/default.htm

Bioterrorism—CBER has a vital role in countering bioterrorism. CBER has developed new regulatory models, new protocols and procedures for preparedness in the event of an attack. For example, the development of products to diagnose, treat or prevent outbreaks from exposure to pathogens documented as bioterrorist agents remains in the forefront. CBER reviews and approves these products prior to any major production for stock piling purposes. The process for approval involves many stages. Further, CBER must monitor manufacturing practices. The procedures involved with preparedness for and response to an attack involving biological agents are extremely complex. For instance, since biological agents could have long incubation periods, the onset of the disease could be delayed. Further, there is a proliferation of possible biological agents, some of which are hardly ever encountered.

However, according to CBER, specific pathogens recognized as potential biological warfare agents include those that cause smallpox, anthrax, plague, botulism, tularaemia and hemorrhagic fevers. CBER has addressed several specialized issues surrounding anthrax and smallpox vaccine. Further, CBER has prepared initiatives for potential bioterrorism threats, performed ongoing increased bioterrorism research and conducted specialized programs.

NOTE: See *Volume IX: Food Law Regulation* for additional information on bioterrorism.

Biologics Differentiation

Unlike conventional drugs, which are chemically synthesized, biologics result from living sources such as humans, animals and microorganisms. Biologics involve complicated mixtures and are produced using biotechnology. CBER anticipates that eventually, biologics will provide an effective methodology to treat medical conditions and illnesses where no other viable treatment option exists. However, CBER maintains the serious responsibility and task of evaluation and determination of whether biologic products fulfill approval requirements. Similar to the drug approval process, the PHS Act requires a license for those who manufacture biological products. Prior to release, a manufacturer must perform tests on each lot and if CBER officially releases the product, then samples must be submitted along with the release protocol.

Biologics defined—The term "biologics" refers to a category of medical treatments derived from living organisms. Biologics more specifically consist of: *"a virus, therapeutic serum, toxin, antitoxin, vaccine, blood, blood component or derivative, allergenic product, or analogous product ... applicable to the prevention, treatment, or cure of a disease or condition of human beings."* 42 U.S.C. §262(i).

Biological Product—Includes an extensive range of products such as vaccines, blood and blood components, allergenics, somatic cells, gene therapy, tissues, and recombinant therapeutic proteins. Biologics can be composed of sugars, proteins, or nucleic acids or complex combinations of these substances, or may be living entities such as cells and tissues. Biologics are isolated from a variety of natural sources, human, animal, or microorganism and may be produced by biotechnology methods and other cutting-edge technologies. Gene-based and cellular biologics, for example, often are at the forefront of biomedical research, to treat a variety of medical conditions for which no other treatments are available. Generally, the term "drug" includes therapeutic biological products.

Biosimilar Market—The market for biosimilars suggests vast possibilities and is a multi-billion dollar industry. The biosimilars market is expected to reach 23.63 billion by 2023 from 4.49 billion in 2017. Examples of the top biologics and their sales (2017) include: Humira rheumatoid arthritis, $18.4 billion; Rituxan $9.2 million; Enbrel rheumatoid arthritis, $7.9 billion; Herceptin breast cancer, $7.4 billion; Remicade rheumatoid arthritis, $7.1 billion; Avastin cancers, $7.1 billion; Lantus, $5.7 billion; Neulasta chemotherapy infections, $4.7 billion; Avonex $2.1 billion; Lucentis $1.5 billion.

https://www.thebalance.com/top-biologic-drugs-2663233

Biologics Price Competition and Innovation Act—Biosimilars

Generic versions of biotech drugs referred to as biosimilars or follow-on biologics, present an interesting and complex issue for both industry and FDA. Most innovator "biotech" and "biopharmaceutical" products are approved under the *Public Health Services Act* (PHS Act). The biotech industry is relatively new and has not faced much competition from generic companies. Biotech drugs are used to treat a variety of serious illness such as cancer and autoimmune diseases. Biosimilar drugs are more expensive and complex than traditional chemical drugs because they are composed of living organisms. Generally, biologics exhibit high molecular complexity and sensitivity to manufacturing process changes. Yet, the basic concerns for generic biopharmaceuticals remain the same; that is, safety and efficacy are paramount and generic biopharmaceuticals must be held to those standards.

Ultimately, Congress passed the *Biologics Price Competition and Innovation Act* of 2009 enacted in 2010 (BPCI or Biosimilars). The BPCI was included as Title VII of the Patient Protection and Affordable Care Act of 2010 Pub.L. 111-148 as amended by the Health Care and Reconciliation Act of 2010 (Healthcare Reform Act known as "Obama Care"). The Healthcare Reform Act or the (Affordable Care Act) was upheld in 2012 by the United States Supreme Court in: *Nat'l Fed'n of Indep. Bus. v. Sebelius*, 132 S. Ct. 2566, 183 L. Ed. 2d 450 (2012). The Biosimilars Act established a 12-year exclusivity period before biosimilars can be approved for marketing in the United States. Additionally, section 351 of Public Health Services Act, 42 U.S.C. section 262 was amended to include a new abbreviated licensure approval pathway for biosimilar biological products. FDA will only accept a Biosimilar Biological Product Application (BBPA) four years after the referenced product was approved. Significant aspects include a pathway, exclusivity, infringement lawsuits timeframe and forfeiture as follows:

Pathway for Biosimilar Products—permits manufacturers to gain approval without duplicating the innovator's safety and efficacy data in a Biosimilar Biological Product Application (BBPA).

Proposed products must have the:
> *Same mechanism of use; the same route of administration; and the same dosage form and strength as the referenced products.*

Exclusivity Provisions—Innovator Exclusivity—12 years of exclusivity after the reference product was originally approved. Generics—1 year after commercial launch.

NOTE: Trans-Pacific Partnership (TPP) agreement provides for an eight-year limit for a brand-name biologic drug maker's data exclusivity rights yet has provisions that would permit some countries to protect the data and only keep generics off the market for five years.

Infringement Lawsuits and Forfeiture Provisions—FDA approval:
> *18 months after final court decision or dismissal; or if litigation persists, 42 months following approval of first interchangeable product. See: Biosimilars Act, § 351(k)(6)(C)(i).*

FDA evaluation has focused on biotech drugs that replace or supplement natural human proteins rather than more complicated biotech drugs such as antibody-based cancer treatments. A critical issue that remains is what constitutes "bioequivalence". Apparently, the type of the protein impacts and this might necessitate clinical evidence of the therapeutic qualities of a final product. Perhaps a comparability assessment might suffice. Yet, the basic concerns for generic biosimilars remain the same; that is, safety and efficacy are paramount and generic follow-on biologics must be held to those standards. Regulatory guidance from FDA continues to evolve and undoubtedly necessitates a lengthy process, due to the complexity involved. Perhaps FDA can learn from the European Union and other countries that have developed guidelines. The European Union spearheaded a regulatory framework for approval of biosimilars. See: Committee for Medicinal Products for Human Use, Guideline on Similar Biological Medicinal Products, CHMP/437/04 Oct. 30,2005 (EU Guidelines); See also: *Biotech Drugs Still Won't Copy*, Christopher Weaver, Jeanne Whalen and Jonathan D. Rockoff, The Wall St. J. B1 (Feb. 27, 2013).

Guidance Documents—FDA issued several guidance documents which detail what a company must do in order to obtain approval. For example, a revised guidance (2015) originally issued (2012), addresses the 2009 Biologics Price Competition and Innovation Act. FDA issued: *Scientific and Quality Considerations in Demonstrating Biosimilarity to a Reference Product* (finalized 2015) and a draft guidance in 2013 on *Formal Meetings Between the FDA and Biosimilar Biological Product Sponsors or Applicants* (2013); *Biosimilars: Additional Questions and Answers Regarding Implementation of the Biologics Price Competition and Innovation Act of 2009* (2015).

http://www.fda.gov/downloads/Drugs/GuidanceComplianceRegulatoryInformation/Guidances/UCM273001.pdf

Clinical Pharmacology Data to Support a Demonstration of Biosimilarity to a Reference Product (2014).

http://www.fda.gov/downloads/Drugs/GuidanceComplianceRegulatoryInformation/Guidances/UCM273001.pdf

Citizen Petition

Abbott Laboratories ("Abbott") submitted a citizen petition to FDA regarding biosimilars under the *Biologics Price Competition and Innovation Act* of 2009 ("BPCIA" or Biosimilars). The citizen petition requested that FDA not accept for filing, file, approve, or discuss with any company any application or any investigational new drug application ("IND") for any biosimilar that cites as its reference product any product for which the biologics license application ("BLA") was submitted to FDA prior to the date on which the BPCIA was enacted. The citizen petition focused on Abbott's approved BLA for Humira® (adalimumab), yet it requests the same treatment for all BLAs submitted to FDA prior to the enactment of the BPCIA.

NOTE: See In re REMICADE ANTITRUST LITIGATION: *Walgreen Co. and Kroger Co., v. Johnson & Johnson and Janssen Biotech, Inc.* Civil Action No.2:17-cv-4326-JCJ (June 2018).

CRITICAL ANALYSIS: Increased competition, naming, high costs, transition to the PHSA licensing and attempts to stymie the market by brand companies exist. Assess these issues and provide recommendations.

Sunshine Payment Provisions Physicians and Teaching Hospitals

Section 6002 of the Patient Protection and Affordable Health Care Act contains provisions for annual disclosure (effective 2013) of payments to physicians and teaching hospitals by drug, device, biologic and medical supply manufacturers. In 2017, there were $8.40 billion payments. *https://openpaymentsdata.cms.gov*

Marketing Notice, Approvals, Naming and Labeling
Sandoz, Inc. v. Amgen Inc.,
137 S. Ct. 1664 Nos. 15–1039, 15–1195 (2017)

Syllabus (edited)—The Biologics Price Competition and Innovation Act of 2009 (BPCIA or Act) provides an abbreviated pathway for acquiring FDA approval of a drug that is biosimilar to an already licensed biological product termed the reference product. 42 U.S.C. § 262(k). Under § 262(*l*)(2)(A), an applicant seeking FDA approval of a biosimilar must provide its application and manufacturing information to the sponsor within 20 days of the date the FDA notifies the applicant that it has accepted the application for review. There are two levels of patent litigation. First, the parties collaborate to identify patents on the lists for immediate litigation. The second phase is triggered when the applicant, under § 262(*l*)(8)(A), gives the sponsor notice at least 180 days before commercial marketing the biosimilar. *** Under § 262(*l*)(9)(C), if an applicant fails to provide its application and manufacturing information to the sponsor under § 262(*l*)(2)(A), then the sponsor may immediately bring an action "for a declaration of infringement, validity, or enforceability of any patent that claims the biological product or a use of the biological product."

Neupogen a filgrastim product marketed by Amgen, which claims to hold patents on methods of manufacturing and using filgrastim. Sandoz sought FDA approval to market a biosimilar filgrastim product under the brand name Zarxio, with Neupogen as the licensed reference product. A day after the FDA informed Sandoz that its application had been accepted for review, Sandoz notified Amgen that it had submitted an application and that it intended to market Zarxio immediately upon receiving FDA approval. It later informed Amgen that it did not intend to provide the application and manufacturing information required by § 262(*l*)(2)(A) and that Amgen could sue immediately for infringement under § 262(*l*)(9)(C). Amgen sued Sandoz for patent infringement and also asserted that Sandoz engaged in "unlawful" conduct in violation of California's unfair competition law. This latter claim was predicated on two alleged violations of the BPCIA: Sandoz's failure to provide its application and manufacturing information under § 262(*l*)(2)(A), and its provision of notice of commercial marketing under § 262(*l*)(8)(A) prior to obtaining licensure from the FDA. Amgen sought injunctions to enforce both BPCIA requirements.

Subsequently, FDA licensed Zarxio, and Sandoz provided Amgen further notice of commercial marketing. The District Court subsequently granted partial judgment on the pleadings to Sandoz on its BPCIA counterclaims and dismissed Amgen's unfair competition claims with prejudice. ***
The [Federal Circuit] court affirmed the dismissal of Amgen's state-law claim based on Sandoz's alleged violation of § 262(*l*)(2)(A), holding that Sandoz did not violate the BPCIA in failing to disclose its application and manufacturing information and that the BPCIA provides the exclusive remedies for failure to comply with this requirement. The court also held that under § 262(*l*)(8)(A) an applicant must provide notice of commercial marketing after obtaining licensure, and that this requirement is mandatory. It thus enjoined Sandoz from marketing Zarxio until 180 days after the date it provided its second notice.

Key Holdings: Section 262(*l*)(2)(A) is not enforceable by injunction under federal law, but the

Federal Circuit on remand should determine whether a state-law injunction is available. An applicant may provide notice under § 262(*l*)(8)(A) prior to obtaining licensure.

(a) Section 262(*l*)(2)(A)'s requirement that an applicant provide the sponsor with its application and manufacturing information is not enforceable by an injunction under federal law. The Federal Circuit reached the proper result on this issue. *** Another provision, § 262(*l*)(9)(C), provides a remedy for an applicant's failure to turn over its application and manufacturing information. It authorizes the sponsor, but not the applicant, to bring an immediate declaratory-judgment action for artificial infringement ***. The presence of this remedy, coupled with the absence of any other textually specified remedies, indicates that Congress did not intend sponsors to have access to injunctive relief, at least as a matter of federal law, to enforce the disclosure requirement.

(b) The Federal Circuit should determine on remand whether an injunction is available under state law to enforce § 262(*l*)(2)(A). The court on remand should determine whether California law would treat noncompliance with § 262(*l*)(2)(A) as "unlawful," and whether the BPCIA pre-empts any additional state-law remedy for failure to comply with § 262(*l*)(2)(A).

(c) An applicant may provide notice of commercial marketing before obtaining a license. Section 262(*l*)(8)(A) states that the applicant "shall provide notice to the reference product sponsor not later than 180 days before the date of the first commercial marketing of the biological product licensed under subsection (k)." Because the phrase "of the biological product licensed under subsection (k)" modifies "commercial marketing" rather than "notice," "commercial marketing" is the point in time by which the biosimilar must be "licensed." [T]he applicant may provide notice either before or after receiving FDA approval. 794 F.3d 1347, vacated in part, reversed in part, and remanded.

Opinion—THOMAS, J., delivered the opinion for a unanimous Court. BREYER, J., filed a concurring opinion. These cases involve 42 U.S.C. § 262(*l*), which was enacted as part of the Biologics Price Competition and Innovation Act of 2009 (BPCIA), 124 Stat. 808. The BPCIA governs a type of drug called a biosimilar, which is a biologic product that is highly similar to a biologic product that has already been approved by the Food and Drug Administration (FDA). Under § 262(*l*), an applicant that seeks FDA approval of a biosimilar must provide its application materials and manufacturing information to the manufacturer of the corresponding biologic within 20 days of the date the FDA notifies the applicant that it has accepted the application for review. The applicant then must give notice to the manufacturer at least 180 days before marketing the biosimilar commercially.

The first question presented by these cases is whether the requirement that an applicant provide its application and manufacturing information to the manufacturer of the biologic is enforceable by injunction. We conclude that an injunction is not available under federal law, but we remand for the court below to decide whether an injunction is available under state law. The second question is whether the applicant must give notice to the manufacturer after, rather than before, obtaining a license from the FDA for its biosimilar. We conclude that an applicant may provide notice before obtaining a license.

I. A. A biologic is a type of drug derived from natural, biological sources such as animals or microorganisms. Biologics thus differ from traditional drugs, which are typically synthesized from chemicals. A manufacturer of a biologic may market the drug only if the FDA has licensed it pursuant to either of two review processes set forth in § 262. Under that subsection [§ 262(a)], the FDA may license a new biologic if, among other things, the manufacturer demonstrates that it is "safe, pure, and potent." § 262(a)(2)(C)(i)(I). *** To obtain approval through the BPCIA's abbreviated process, the manufacturer of a biosimilar (applicant) does not need to show that the product is "safe, pure, and potent." Instead, the applicant may piggyback on the showing made by the manufacturer (sponsor) of a previously licensed biologic (reference product). See § 262(k)(2)(A)(iii). *** An applicant may not submit an application until 4 years after the reference product is first licensed, and the FDA may not license a biosimilar until 12 years after the reference product is first licensed. §§ 262(k)(7)(A), (B). As a result, the manufacturer of a new biologic enjoys a 12–year period *** without competition from biosimilars.

B. The BPCIA facilitates litigation during the period preceding FDA approval so that the parties do not have to wait until commercial marketing to resolve their patent disputes. *** Specifically, it provides that the mere submission of a biosimilar application constitutes an act of infringement. §§ 271(e)(2)(C)(i), (ii). We will refer to this kind of preapproval infringement as "artificial" infringement. Section 271(e)(4) provides remedies for artificial infringement, including injunctive relief and damages.

C. The BPCIA sets forth a carefully calibrated scheme for preparing to adjudicate, and then adjudicating, claims of infringement. See 42 U.S.C. § 262(*l*). When the FDA accepts an application for review, it notifies the applicant, who within 20 days "shall provide" to the sponsor a copy of the application and information about how the biosimilar is manufactured. § 262(*l*)(2)(A). *** These disclosures enable the sponsor to evaluate the biosimilar for possible infringement of patents it holds on the reference product ***. § 262(*l*) (1)(D). *** **The first question presented by these cases is whether § 262(*l*)(2)(A)'s requirement—that the applicant provide its application and manufacturing information to the sponsor is itself enforceable by injunction (emphasis added).** After the applicant makes the requisite disclosures, the parties exchange information to identify relevant patents and to flesh out the legal arguments that they might raise in future litigation. Within 60 days of receiving the application and manufacturing information, the sponsor "shall provide" to the applicant "a list of patents" for which it believes it could assert an infringement claim if a person without a license made, used, offered to sell, sold, or imported "the biological product that is the subject of the [biosimilar] application." § 262(*l*)(3)(A)(i). The sponsor must also identify any patents on the list that it would be willing to license. § 262(*l*)(3)(A)(ii).

Next, within 60 days of receiving the sponsor's list, the applicant may provide to the sponsor a list of patents that the applicant believes are relevant but that the sponsor omitted from its own list, § 262(*l*)(3)(B)(i), and "shall provide" to the sponsor reasons why it could not be held liable for infringing the relevant patents, § 262(*l*)(3)(B)(ii). The applicant may argue that the relevant patents are invalid, unenforceable, or not infringed, or the applicant may agree not to market the biosimilar until a particular patent has expired. *** Following this exchange, the BPCIA channels the parties into two phases of patent litigation. In the first phase, the parties collaborate to identify patents that they would like to litigate immediately. The second phase is triggered by the applicant's notice of commercial marketing and involves any patents that were included on the parties' § 262(*l*)(3) lists but not litigated in the first phase. *** The applicant "shall notify" the sponsor of the number of patents it intends to list for litigation, § 262(*l*)(5)(A), and, within five days, the parties "shall simultaneously exchange" lists of the patents they would like to litigate immediately. § 262(*l*)(5)(B)(i). *** Section 271(e)(2)(C)(i) facilitates this first phase of litigation by making it an act of artificial infringement, with respect to any patent included on the parties' § 262(*l*)(3) lists, to submit an application for a license from the FDA ***

The second phase of litigation involves patents that were included on the original § 262(*l*)(3) lists but not litigated in the first phase (and any patents that the sponsor acquired after the § 262(*l*)(3) exchange occurred and added to the lists, see § 262(*l*)(7)). The second phase is commenced by the applicant's notice of commercial marketing, which the applicant "shall provide" to the sponsor "not later than 180 days before the date of the first commercial marketing of the biological product licensed under subsection (k)." § 262(*l*)(8)(A). *** **The second question presented is whether notice is effective if an applicant provides it prior to the FDA's decision to license the biosimilar (emphasis added).** In this second phase of litigation, *either* party may sue for declaratory relief. See § 262(*l*)(9)(A). In addition, prior to the date of first commercial marketing, the sponsor may "seek a preliminary injunction prohibiting the [biosimilar] applicant from engaging in the commercial manufacture or sale of [the biosimilar] until the court decides the issue of patent validity, enforcement, and infringement with respect to any patent that" was included on the § 262(*l*)(3) lists but not litigated in the first phase. § 262(*l*)(8)(B).

D. If the parties comply with each step outlined in the BPCIA, they will have the opportunity to litigate the relevant patents before the biosimilar is marketed. *** Two of the BPCIA's remedial provisions are at issue here. Under § 262(*l*)(9)(C), if an applicant fails to provide its application and manufacturing information to the sponsor *** then the sponsor, but not the applicant, may immediately bring an action "for a declaration of infringement, validity, or enforceability of any patent that claims the biological product or a use of the biological product." ***

II. These cases concern filgrastim, a biologic used to stimulate the production of white blood cells. Amgen *** has marketed a filgrastim product called Neupogen since 1991 and claims to hold patents on methods of manufacturing and using filgrastim. In May 2014, Sandoz, the petitioner in No. 15–1039 and the respondent in No. 15–1195, filed an application with the FDA seeking approval to market a filgrastim biosimilar under the brand name Zarxio, with Neupogen as the reference product. The FDA informed Sandoz on July 7, 2014, that it had accepted the application for review. One day later, Sandoz notified Amgen both that it had submitted an application and that it intended to begin marketing Zarxio immediately upon receiving FDA approval, which it expected in the first half of 2015. Sandoz later confirmed that it did not intend to provide the requisite application and manufacturing information under § 262(*l*)(2)(A) and informed Amgen that Amgen could sue for infringement immediately under § 262(*l*)(9)(C). In October 2014, Amgen sued Sandoz for patent infringement. *** Amgen alleged that Sandoz engaged in "unlawful" conduct when it failed to provide its application and manufacturing information under § 262(*l*)(2)(A), and when it provided notice of commercial marketing under § 262(*l*)(8)(A) before, rather than after, the FDA licensed its biosimilar.

While the case was pending in the District Court, the FDA licensed Zarxio, and Sandoz provided Amgen a further notice of commercial marketing. The District Court subsequently granted partial judgment on the pleadings to Sandoz on its BPCIA counterclaims and dismissed Amgen's unfair competition claims with prejudice. (N.D.Cal., Mar. 19, 2015). After the District Court entered final judgment as to these claims, Amgen appealed to the Federal Circuit, which granted an injunction pending appeal against the commercial marketing of Zarxio. First, the court affirmed the dismissal of Amgen's state-law claim based on Sandoz's alleged violation of § 262(*l*)(2)(A). It held that Sandoz did not violate the BPCIA in failing to disclose its application and manufacturing information. ***

Second, the court held that an applicant may provide effective notice of commercial marketing only *after* the FDA has licensed the biosimilar.

III. The first question we must answer is whether § 262(*l*)(2)(A)'s requirement that an applicant provide the sponsor with its application and manufacturing information is enforceable by an injunction under either federal or state law.

A. We agree with the Federal Circuit that an injunction under federal law is not available to enforce § 262(*l*)(2)(A), though for slightly different reasons than those provided by the court below. *** The flaw in the Federal Circuit's reasoning is that Sandoz's failure to disclose its application and manufacturing information was not an act of artificial infringement, and thus was not remediable under § 271(e)(4). Submitting an application constitutes an act of artificial infringement. See §§ 271(e)(2)(C)(i), (ii) ("It shall be an act of infringement to submit ... an application seeking approval of a biological product"). Failing to disclose the application and manufacturing information under § 262(*l*)(2)(A) does not.

A separate provision of § 262, however, does provide a remedy for an applicant's failure to turn over its application and manufacturing information. When an applicant fails to comply with § 262(*l*)(2)(A), § 262(*l*)(9)(C) authorizes the sponsor, but not the applicant, to bring an immediate declaratory-judgment action for artificial infringement as defined in § 271(e)(2)(C)(ii). Section 262(*l*)(9)(C) thus vests in the sponsor the control that the applicant would otherwise have exercised over the scope and timing of the patent litigation. *** The remedy provided by § 262(*l*)(9)(C) excludes all other federal remedies, including injunctive relief. Where, as here, "a statute expressly provides a remedy, courts must be especially reluctant to provide additional remedies." *Karahalios v. Federal Employees,* 489 U.S. 527, 533, 109 S.Ct. 1282, 103 L.Ed.2d 539 (1989). The BPCIA's "carefully crafted and detailed enforcement scheme provides strong evidence that Congress did *not* intend to authorize other remedies that it simply forgot to incorporate expressly." *Great–West Life & Annuity Ins. Co. v. Knudson,* 534 U.S. 204, 209, 122 S.Ct. 708, 151 L.Ed.2d 635 (2002) (internal quotation marks omitted). The presence of § 262(*l*)(9)(C), coupled with the absence of any other textually specified remedies, indicates that Congress did not intend sponsors to have access to injunctive relief, at least as a matter of federal law, to enforce the disclosure requirement.

B. We decline to resolve this particular dispute definitively because it does not present a question of federal law. *** If the applicant failed to provide that information, then the sponsor, but not the applicant, could bring an immediate declaratory-judgment action pursuant to § 262(*l*)(9)(C). The parties in these cases agree—as did the Federal Circuit—that Sandoz failed to comply with § 262(*l*)(2)(A), thus subjecting itself to that consequence. *** Whether Sandoz's conduct was "unlawful" under the unfair competition law is a state-law question, and the court below erred in attempting to answer that question by referring to the BPCIA alone.

On remand, the Federal Circuit should determine whether California law would treat noncompliance with § 262(*l*)(2)(A) as "unlawful." ***

IV. The second question at issue in these cases is whether an applicant must provide notice *after* the FDA licenses its biosimilar, or if it may also provide effective notice before licensure. Section 262(*l*)(8)(A) states that the applicant "shall provide notice to the reference product sponsor not later than 180 days before the date of the first commercial marketing of the biological product licensed under subsection (k)." *** The applicant must give "notice" at least 180 days "before the date of the first commercial marketing." "[C]ommercial marketing," in turn, must be "of the biological product licensed under subsection (k)." § 262(*l*) (8)(A). Because this latter phrase modifies "commercial marketing" rather than "notice," "commercial marketing" is the point in time by which the biosimilar must be "licensed." ***Accordingly, the applicant may provide notice either before or after receiving FDA approval. *** In sum, because Sandoz fully complied with § 262(*l*)(8)(A) when it first gave notice (before licensure) in July 2014, the Federal Circuit erred in issuing a federal injunction prohibiting Sandoz from marketing Zarxio until 180 days after licensure. ***We accordingly reverse the Federal Circuit's judgment as to the notice provision.

For the foregoing reasons, the judgment of the Court of Appeals is vacated in part and reversed in part, and the cases are remanded for further proceedings consistent with this opinion. *It is so ordered. https://www.supremecourt.gov/opinions/16pdf/15-1039_1b8e.pdf*

NOTE: On remand, the Court of Appeals held it had discretion to address the preemption issue; field preemption barred sponsor's state law unfair competition claims; and conflict preemption barred sponsor's state law unfair competition claims. *Amgen v. Sandoz* **Fed. Cir. Ct. Ap. 2015-1499 (2017).**

CRITICAL ANALYSIS: Evaluate this case and the implications for the innovator and biosimilar applicant.

Other Approvals

Besides Zarxio, FDAs approvals of biosimilars continue. A novel gene therapy was approved for the treatment of hereditary retinal disorder. Another approval CAR T-cell is indicated to treat blood cancers. Pfizer, Inc. and Celltrion, Inc. received FDA approval to market Inflectra, a low-cost biosimilar to Johnson & Johnson's arthritis treatment, Remicade. FDA approved the intravenous infusion for seven conditions treated by Remicade, including rheumatoid arthritis and plaque psoriasis. FDA approved the biosimilar Erelzi, (2016) (etanercept-szzs) for multiple inflammatory diseases. Enbrel (etanercept) was originally licensed in 1998. Erelzi is administered by injection for the treatment of moderate to severe rheumatoid arthritis. Amgen, Inc.'s Amjevita, was approved 2016 a biosimilar of AbbVie, Inc.'s immunosuppressant Humira. In 2017 five additional biosimilars were approved and several in 2018.

Naming—The active ingredient in Neupogen is filgrastim and FDA determined that Zarxio's name is filgrastim-sndz. FDA issued a guidance titled: "Nonproprietary Naming of Biological Products." The nonproprietary name includes a suffix of four lowercase letters. Each suffix will be incorporated in the nonproprietary name of the product. This naming convention is applicable to biological products previously licensed and newly licensed under sections 351(a) and 351(k) of the Public Health Services Act (PHS).

Label Must State Product Is Biosimilar—Biosimilar product labels must include a statement that the product is a biosimilar and may rely on the data submitted for FDA approval by the originator biologic maker.

CRITICAL ANALYSIS: Evaluate the FDA naming decision for biosimilars and any legal implications regarding this issue.

Products CBER Regulates

http://www.fda.gov/BiologicsBloodVaccines/default.htm
- ➢ Allergenics;
- ➢ Blood and its derivatives;
- ➢ Human tissue and cellular products;
- ➢ Xenotransplatation product;
- ➢ Gene therapy;
- ➢ Biological therapeutics;
- ➢ Medical devices related to biologics such as blood storage refrigerators; and
- ➢ Vaccines.

Allergenics Regulation

www.fda.gov/BiologicsBloodVaccines/Allergenics/default.htm

CBER maintains regulatory responsibility for allergenic products. The types of allergenic products licensed for use consist of allergen patch tests and allergenic extracts.

- ✓ **Allergenic patch tests** are manufactured from known contact dermatitis sources such as nickel, rubber and fragrance mixes. Physicians use patch tests as a diagnostic tool to ascertain the basis for contact dermatitis.
- ✓ **Allergenic extracts** are used to diagnose and treat allergic diseases such as sinusitis, allergenic conjunctivitis, allergic rhinitis or hay fever, bee venom allergy and food allergies. These extracts are prepared from natural sources such as molds, pollens, insect venoms, animal hair, food, and food extracts. Manufactured forms of allergenic extracts are either standardized or non-standardized. CBER makes use of reference standards to assess allergenic extract potency; hence, the term standardized is applied. The term non-standardized extracts means that no reference standard exists for comparison purposes.

Blood Regulation

www.fda.gov/cber/blood.htm

CBER supervision involves the safety of the United States blood supply. CBER has strengthened blood donation procedures to safeguard patient recipients. In so doing, FDA promulgates standards for blood collection and the manufacture of blood products including transfusible components of whole blood. Blood donations are tested for several different infectious agents. Related products such as cell separation devices, blood collection containers, and HIV screening tests are used to assure blood supply safety and to prepare blood products. The tasks of CBER consist of the enforcement of standards for both blood collection and the manufacture of blood products; the inspection of blood firms and the monitoring of reports associated with accidents, errors and adverse events. CBER continues to work with industry on issues such as irradiating and/or freezing blood components collected and stored in anticoagulant/preservative solutions. Blood facilities are inspected at least biennially and more frequently if warranted.

✓ **Blood Establishment Registration and Product Listing:** All owners or operators of establishments that manufacture blood products are required to register with FDA, in accordance with section 510 of the Federal Food, Drug, and Cosmetic Act, unless exempt under 21 CFR 607.65. A list of every blood product manufactured, prepared, or processed for commercial distribution must also be submitted and products must be registered and listed within 5 days of beginning operation as well as annually between November 15 and December 31. Blood product listings require updated information every June and December. Even if a blood establishment is located outside of the United States, registration is still required for import purposes.

✓ **Bar Code Label Requirements for Blood and Blood Components:** Blood and blood components must be labeled with specific machine-readable bar code information to decrease transfusion errors and increase patient safety. The *Bar Code Label Requirement for Human Drug Products and Biological Products* rule became effective April 26, 2006. The regulation for blood and blood components is found in 21 CFR 606.121(c)(13).

✓ **Machine-readable requirement:** The information must show encoded information in a format that is machine-readable and approved for use by the Director, Center for Biologics Evaluation and Research. 21 CFR 606.121(c)(13)(ii-iii).

✓ **Compliance:** FDA determines compliance during routine inspections.

✓ **Blood Action Plan:** CBER works closely with other FDA offices such as the Centers for Disease Control and Prevention, the National Institutes of Health and the Health Care Financing Administration in the carrying out a Blood Action Plan (Plan). The goals of the Plan are to increase the effectiveness of regulatory oversight as well as increased coordination with other federal agencies.

Tissue Regulation

www.fda.gov/cber/tiss.htm

CBER regulates human tissue intended for transplantation which does not change tissue function or characteristics. 21 CFR Part 1270 and 1271 governs human tissue transplants. Parts 1270 and 1271 of 21 CFR requires tissue establishment to screen and test donors, to prepare and to follow procedures regarding the spread of communicable disease. Examples of tissue include bone, skin, corneas, ligament and tendon. Tissue facilities are required by regulation to screen and test donors, to develop and adhere to written procedures to preclude contagious disease increase and to keep records. However, CBER does not oversee human organ transplants such as kidney, liver, heart, lung or pancreas. Rather, the Health Resources Services Administration is the federal agency that oversees and provides funding assistance for the United States organ procurement allocation and transplantation system.

Xenotransplantation

http://www.fda.gov/BiologicsBloodVaccines/Xenotransplantation/default.htm

Xenotransplantation is a procedure that involves the transplantation, implantation or infusion into a human recipient of either (a) live cells, tissues, or organs from a nonhuman animal source, or (b) human body fluids, cells, tissues or organs that have had ex vivo contact with live nonhuman animal cells, tissues or organs. In the United States, approximately, ten patients die each day while on the waiting list to receive lifesaving vital organ transplants. Evidence has detailed that transplantation of cells and tissues may be therapeutic for certain diseases such as neurodegenerative disorders and diabetes, where, again human materials are not usually available.

Although the potential benefits are considerable, the use of xenotransplantation raises concerns regarding the potential infection of recipients with both recognized and unrecognized infectious agents and the possible subsequent transmission to their close contacts and into the general human population. Of public health concern is the potential for cross-species infection by retroviruses, which may be latent and lead to disease years after infection. Moreover, new infectious agents may not be readily identifiable with current techniques.

Cellular and Gene Therapy Regulation

www.fda.gov/cber/gene.htm

Human gene therapy product regulation falls within the responsibility of CBER. Gene therapy works by the introduction of genetic matter into the body substituting for defective or missing genetic matter. FDA details that "Cellular therapy products include cellular immunotherapies, cancer vaccines, and other autologous and allogeneic cells for certain therapeutic indications, including hematopoetic stem cells and adult and embryonic stem cells." Research in gene therapy can lead to gene-based treatments for cancer, cystic fibrosis, heart disease, hemophilia, wounds and infectious diseases. The enabling laws include the Public Health Services Act as well as the Food, Drug and Cosmetic Act.

The Gene Therapy Clinical Trial Monitoring Plan

FDA requires that sponsors of gene therapy trials regularly submit their monitoring plans to FDA for review and modification if necessary. FDA conducts surveillance clinical trials to assess whether the plans are being followed. Those who monitor a trial must substantiate: Protection of human subjects; Trial agreement with the protocol; Regulatory requirements; Good clinical practices and; Correct data and safety reporting to IRB, FDA, and NIH.

National Institutes of Health (NIH) Collaboration

FDA and the National Institutes of Health (NIH) continue their collaborative mission of patient safety for those individuals enrolled in gene therapy clinical studies. Initiatives have included the Gene Therapy Clinical Trial Monitoring Plan, the Gene Transfer Safety Symposia, and the Human Gene Transfer Research Data System.

Genetic Modification Clinical Research Information System

http://www.gemcris.od.nih.gov/Contents/GC_HOME.asp

The Genetic Modification Clinical Research Information System GeMCRIS system, launched in 2004 by NIH and FDA, offers greater ability to monitor adverse events in human gene therapy transfer trials. Information available to GeMCRIS users such as patients, research participants, scientists and sponsors include investigational approaches, specific trials and disease studies. GeMCRIS, serves as a unique public information resource and important electronic method to make possible the reporting and analysis of adverse events. GeMCRIS contains special security features to protect patient privacy and confidential commercial information. GeMCRIS improves the ability of NIH and FDA to analyze adverse events in gene transfer research.

Approved Cellular and Gene Therapy Products

FDA approved Luxturna, a novel therapy for a rare form of inherited vision loss. Approved in 2017, it is the first gene therapy approved in the United States to target a disease caused by mutations in a specific gene. Also in 2017, FDA approved a type of immunotherapy called CAR T-cell therapy children and young adults with a form of acute lymphoblastic leukemia (ALL). The treatment, tisagenlecleucel (Kymriah™) *https://www.cancer.gov/news-events/cancer-currents-blog/2017/tisagenlecleucel-fda-childhood-leukemia*
FDA maintains a list of approved products-see link below.
https://www.fda.gov/BiologicsBloodVaccines/CellularGeneTherapyProducts/ApprovedProducts/default.htm

CRITICAL ANALYSIS: Evaluate how these gene therapy approvals have altered disease management. Consider the cost in your analysis.

Vaccine Regulation

http://www.fda.gov/BiologicsBloodVaccines/Vaccines/default.htm

Vaccines safeguard individuals from serious illnesses. According to CBER, many childhood vaccines have eliminated polio and rubella and considerably decreased certain diseases such as measles, pertussis and chicken pox. By way of illustration, CBER approved the first vaccine to prevent invasive pneumococcal disease in infants and toddlers. The vaccine prevents invasive diseases caused by the organism Streptococcus pneumoniae or pneumococcus including bacteremia, an infection of the bloodstream, and meningitis, an infection of the brain or spinal cord lining. FDA approved the first human Avian Flu vaccine in 2007. Further, CBER completed its evaluation of the use of thimerosal in vaccines under the Food and Drug Administration Modernization Act (FDAMA) of 1997, Section 413, "FDA Study of Mercury Compounds in Drugs and Food" and concluded that the reduction or elimination of thimerosal from vaccines was necessary. The approval for a new indication for Gardasil® is included.

The Vaccine Event Adverse Reporting System (VAERS) is a collaborative effort with the Centers for Disease Control and Prevention (CDC). VAERS is a post-marketing safety surveillance program. VAERS collect information about adverse events that occur as a result of administration of an approved vaccine. Patients, parents, health care providers, pharmacists and vaccine manufacturers may all submit reports to VAERS.

NOTE: Recently, the safety of vaccines has been questioned and well-known celebrities and politicians are being used to promote this message. See: Paul A. Offit M.D., *Bad Advice or Why Celebrities, Politicians and Activists Aren't Your Best Source of Health Information***, Columbia (2018); Cynthia Gorney,** *Why Vaccines Matter***, National Geographic, 120 (Nov. 2017).**

CRITICAL ANALYSIS: The shift in vaccine development has focused on therapies for non-communicable diseases (NCD) such as cancer, hypertension, asthma, arthritis, psoriasis, multiple sclerosis to name a few. How should FDA evaluate NCD vaccine therapies, that is, as traditional vaccines with a new indication(s) or as a new biologic drug(s)? Would the National Childhood Vaccine Injury Compensation Act, which provides immunity and compensates injured patients, apply to NCD vaccine therapies?

Outbreaks— Zika and Ebola
Zika

http://www.cdc.gov/zika/about/index.html

The Zika virus disease (Zika) is transmitted to people principally through the bite of an infected Aedes species mosquito. The illness has mild symptoms such as fever, rash, joint pain, and conjunctivitis and usually does not require hospitalization nor do people normally die from the zika virus. People usually do not get sick enough to seek hospital treatment, and they very rarely die. Yet, there is a very serious problem with Zika virus infection during pregnancy as it can cause a serious birth defect called microcephaly (smaller head size and usually smaller brain), and other serious fetal brain defects. The World Health Organization (WHO) 66 countries and territories have reported transmission of Zika virus since January 2007. The first confirmed Zika virus infection occurred in 2015 in Brazil. In early 2016, the WHO classified the Zika virus as an international public health emergency.

Emergency Use Authorization—In 2016 (April), Quest Diagnostics received FDA approval of the first commercially developed RNA Qualitative Real-Time RT-PCR test to screen for the Zika virus under an emergency use authorization. The test is available to physicians for patient testing. The emergency authorization permits laboratories selected by Focus Diagnostics, Inc.(a subsidiary of Quest), certified under the Clinical Laboratory Improvement Amendments of 1988 (CLIA), to perform the RNA test. (See link below).

Investigational New Animal Drug—Oxitec, Ltd. filed an Investigational New Animal Drug (INAD) pertaining to its genetically engineered mosquitoes. The Oxitec company has created a genetically engineered mosquito *Aedes aegypti* (OX513A) in order to destroy the population of that mosquito at the release site(s).

NOTE: *http://www.questdiagnostics.com/home/physicians/testing-services/condition/infectious-diseases/zika* **(Quest Diagnostics)**
https://www.cdc.gov/zika/geo/index.html

Ebola

https://www.cdc.gov/vhf/ebola/index.html

Perhaps the extensive Ebola outbreak in West Africa afforded the impetus for expedient action. Democratic Republic of Congo (DRC) experienced an outbreak of Ebola virus disease in 2018. Currently, the standard treatment for patients infected with the Ebola virus is supportive therapy. However, that could change in the near future. NIH reported in late 2014 that an experimental vaccine to prevent Ebola virus disease proved successful in a Phase I clinical trial in all 20 healthy adults who received it. The vaccine is being developed by the NIH's National Institute of Allergy and Infectious Diseases and GlaxoSmithKline. The experimental drug ZMapp has been used to treat a few patients infected with Ebola; however, it is still uncertain to ascertain the effectiveness of ZMapp. Besides Mapp Biopharmaceutical, Inc., Tekmira, Chimerix and BioCryst Pharmaceuticals have therapeutic products in early developmental stages for clinical trials. FDA provided fast track designation status to Zmapp in 2015.

NOTE: See, Peter Loftus and Betsy McKay, *Race is On for Ebola Drug*, Wall St. J. A1 (Oct. 18-19, 2014);

http://www.cdc.gov/vhf/ebola/outbreaks/guinea/qa-experimental-treatments.html
http://www.nytimes.com/2014/08/07/business/an-obscure-biotech-firm-hurries-ebola-treatment.html

CRITICAL ANALYSIS: What other recommendations would spur development besides the voucher program for expedited priority track review as well as immunity?

Vaccine Licensing Action—Product Approval Gardasil 9®

*https://www.fda.gov/BiologicsBloodVaccines/Vaccines/ApprovedProducts/ucm426445.htm*FDA

FDA approved Gardasil® 9 (Human Papillomavirus 9-valent Vaccine, Recombinant) (December 10, 2014) for the prevention of certain diseases caused by nine types of Human Papillomavirus (HPV). Gardasil 9 covers five more HPV types than Gardasil® (previously approved by the FDA in 2006), Gardasil 9® has the potential to prevent approximately 90 percent of cervical, vulvar, vaginal and anal cancers. Gardasil 9® is a vaccine approved for use in females ages 9 through 26 and males ages 9 through 15 and in 2018 for use in women and men ages 27-45. It is approved for the prevention of cervical, vulvar, vaginal and anal cancers caused by HPV types 16, 18, 31, 33, 45, 52 and 58, and for the prevention of genital warts caused by HPV types 6 or 11. Gardasil 9® adds protection against five additional HPV types—31, 33, 45, 52 and 58—which cause approximately 20 percent of cervical cancers and are not covered by previously FDA-approved HPV vaccines.

Proper Name: Human Papillomavirus 9-valent Vaccine, Recombinant STN: 125508

Trade-name: Gardasil 9 **Manufacturer:** Merck & CO., Inc.

Indications:

Girls and women 9 through 26 years of age for the prevention of the following diseases:

Cervical, vulvar, vaginal, and anal cancer caused by Human Papillomavirus (HPV) types 16, 18, 31, 33, 45, 52, and 58. (1.1);

Genital warts (condyloma acuminata) caused by HPV types 6 and 11. (1.1);

Precancerous or dysplastic lesions caused by HPV types 6, 11, 16, 18, 31, 33, 45, 52, and 58:

Cervical intraepithelial neoplasia (CIN) grade 2/3 and cervical adenocarcinoma *in situ* (AIS). (1.1)

Cervical intraepithelial neoplasia (CIN) grade 1. (1.1)

Vulvar intraepithelial neoplasia (VIN) grade 2 and grade 3. (1.1)

Vaginal intraepithelial neoplasia (VaIN) grade 2 and grade 3. (1.1)

Anal intraepithelial neoplasia (AIN) grades 1, 2, and 3. (1.1)

Boys 9 through 15 years of age (extended to age 26) for the prevention of these diseases:

Anal cancer caused by HPV types 16, 18, 31, 33, 45, 52, and 58. (1.2)

Genital warts (condyloma acuminata) caused by HPV types 6 and 11. (1.2)

Precancerous or dysplastic lesions caused by HPV types 6, 11, 16, 18, 31, 33, 45, 52, and 58:

Anal intraepithelial neoplasia (AIN) grades 1, 2, and 3. (1.2).

NOTE: In 2018, FDA approved a supplemental application for GARDASIL 9 (human papillomavirus 9-valent vaccine, recombinant) for use in women and men ages 27-45.

https://www.fda.gov/NewsEvents/Newsroom/PressAnnouncements/UCM622715.htm?utm_cam-
paign=10052018_PR_FDA%20approves%20expanded%20use%20of%20Gar-
dasil%209%20to%20include%20individuals%2027%20through%2045%20years%20old&utm_me-
dium=email&utm_source=Eloquahttps://www.cdc.gov/mmWr/preview/mmwrhtml/mm5920a5.htm
https://www.ncbi.nlm.nih.gov/pmc/articles/PMC4149036/
https://www.cdc.gov/features/hpvvaccineboys/index.html

CRITICAL ANALYSIS: The approval has not been without controversy. Some physicians and parent groups have objected to the vaccine because it protects against a sexually transmitted disease and inoculation should not be a mandate in order to attend school. Evaluate whether this vaccine should be mandatory and if so, at what age?

Landmark Decision—*Molecular Pathology v. Myriad Genetics, Inc.*
Human DNA Genes Not Patenable and Synthetic cDNA Patenable

The issue before the United States Supreme Court in *Association for Molecular Pathology v. Myriad Genetics* hinged on whether naturally occurring human genes and/or isolating those genes from the body were a patentable invention. Medical organizations, researchers, genetic counselors, and patients instituted the lawsuit against Myriad Genetics, the patentee and the Patent and Trademark Office (PTO). In a unanimous decision, the Court held that a naturally occurring deoxyribonucleic acid (DNA) segment is a product of nature and hence is not patent eligible simply because it has been isolated. The patents at issue in *Myriad* involved mutations linked to increased risk of breast and ovarian cancer. However, the Court further found that cDNA is patent eligible because cDNA does not occur in nature. Rather, cDNA is a synthetic form of DNA, which omits certain non-functional portions of naturally occurring DNA. Under United States patent law, inventions that claim "any new and useful process, machine, manufacture, or composition of matter, or any new and useful improvement thereof" are patentable; however, unpatentable subject matter includes "laws of nature, physical phenomena and abstract ideas." Interestingly, Justice Thomas further advised that the Court did not consider the patentability of DNA in which the order of the nucleotides; that is, the building blocks of DNA, is altered relative to the naturally occurring state. Nevertheless, the impact of this case on biotech and gene-testing companies is extensive.

Ass'n for Molecular Pathology v. Myriad Genetics, Inc.,
133 S. Ct. 2107, 186 L. Ed. 2d 124 (2013)

Syllabus—The syllabus constitutes no part of the opinion of the Court but has been prepared by the Reporter of Decisions for the convenience of the reader. See *United States v. Detroit Timber & Lumber Co.,* 200 U.S. 321, 337, 26 S.Ct. 282, 50 L.Ed. 499.

Myriad Genetics, Inc. (Myriad), obtained several patents after discovering the precise location and sequence of the BRCA1 and BRCA2 genes, mutations of which can dramatically increase the risk of breast and ovarian cancer. This knowledge allowed Myriad to determine the genes' typical nucleotide sequence, which, in turn, enabled it to develop medical tests useful for detecting mutations in these genes in a particular patient to assess the patient's cancer risk. If valid, Myriad's patents would give it the exclusive right to isolate an individual's BRCA1 and BRCA2 genes and would give Myriad the exclusive right to synthetically create BRCA cDNA. Petitioners filed suit, seeking declaration that Myriad's patents are invalid under 35 U.S.C. § 101.

Held: A naturally occurring DNA segment is a product of nature and not patent eligible merely because it has been isolated, but cDNA is patent eligible because it is not naturally occurring.

(a) The Patent Act permits patents to be issued to "[w]hoever invents or discovers any new and useful ... composition of matter," § 101, but "laws of nature, natural phenomena, and abstract ideas are basic tools of scientific and technological work that lie beyond the domain of patent protection."

(b) Myriad's DNA claim falls within the law of nature exception.

c) cDNA is not a "product of nature," so it is patent eligible under § 101.

(d) This case, it is important to note, does not involve method claims, patents on new applications of knowledge about the BRCA1 and BRCA2 genes, or the patentability of DNA in which the order of the naturally occurring nucleotides has been altered.

Opinion Justice THOMAS. Respondent Myriad Genetics, Inc. (Myriad), discovered the precise location and sequence of two human genes, mutations of which can substantially increase the risks of breast and ovarian cancer. Myriad obtained a number of patents based upon its discovery. *** For the reasons that follow, we hold that a naturally occurring DNA segment is a product of nature and not patent eligible merely because it has been isolated, but that cDNA is patent eligible because it is not naturally occurring. ***

I. A. Genes form the basis for hereditary traits in living organisms. See generally *Association for Molecular Pathology v. United States Patent and Trademark Office,* 702 F.Supp.2d 181, 192–211 (S.D.N.Y.2010). The human genome consists of approximately 22,000 genes packed into 23 pairs of chromosomes. Each gene is encoded as DNA, which takes the shape of the familiar "double helix" that Doctors James Watson and Francis *** Sequences of DNA nucleotides contain the information necessary to create strings of amino acids, which in turn are used in the body to build proteins. Only some DNA nucleotides, however, code for amino acids; these nucleotides are known as "exons." *** Scientists can, however, extract DNA from cells using well known laboratory methods. *** This synthetic DNA created in the laboratory from mRNA is known as complementary DNA (cDNA). ***

B. This case involves patents filed by Myriad after it made one such medical breakthrough. Myriad discovered the precise location and sequence of what are now known as the BRCA1 and BRCA2 genes. Mutations in these genes can dramatically increase an individual's risk of developing breast and ovarian cancer. *** Before Myriad's discovery of the BRCA1 and BRCA2 genes, scientists knew that heredity played a role in establishing a woman's risk of developing breast and ovarian cancer, but they did not know which genes were associated with those cancers.

Myriad identified the exact location of the BRCA1 and BRCA2 genes on chromosomes 17 and 13. *** Knowledge of the location of the BRCA1 and BRCA2 genes allowed Myriad to determine their typical nucleotide sequence. That information, in turn, enabled Myriad to develop medical tests that are useful for detecting mutations in a patient's BRCA1 and BRCA2 genes and thereby assessing whether the patient has an increased risk of cancer.

Once it found the location and sequence of the BRCA1 and BRCA2 genes, Myriad sought and obtained a number of patents. Nine composition claims from three of those patents are at issue in this case. Claims 1, 2, 5, and 6 from the 282 patent are representative. The first claim asserts a patent on "[a]n isolated DNA coding for a BRCA1 polypeptide," which has "the amino acid sequence set forth in SEQ ID NO:2." App. 822. ***

Claim 2 of the 282 patent operates similarly. It claims "[t]he isolated DNA of claim 1, wherein said DNA has the nucleotide sequence set forth in SEQ ID NO:1." *Id.,* at 822. ***

Claim 5 of the 282 patent claims a subset of the data in claim 1. In particular, it claims "[a]n isolated DNA having at least 15 nucleotides of the DNA of claim 1." *** Similarly, Claim 6 of the 282 patent claims "[a]n isolated DNA having at least 15 nucleotides of the DNA of claim 2."

C. Myriad's patents would, if valid, give it the exclusive right to isolate an individual's BRCA1 and BRCA2 genes (or any strand of 15 or more nucleotides within the genes) by breaking the covalent bonds that connect the DNA to the rest of the individual's genome. The patents would also give Myriad the exclusive right to synthetically create BRCA cDNA. ***

But isolation is necessary to conduct genetic testing, and Myriad was not the only entity to offer BRCA testing after it discovered the genes. The University of Pennsylvania's Genetic Diagnostic Laboratory (GDL) and others provided genetic testing services to women. Petitioner Dr. Harry Ostrer, then a researcher at New York University School of Medicine, routinely sent his patients' DNA samples to GDL for testing. After learning of GDL's testing and Ostrer's activities, Myriad sent letters to them asserting that the genetic testing infringed Myriad's patents. App. 94–95 (Ostrer letter). *** Myriad also filed patent infringement suits against other entities that performed BRCA testing, resulting in settlements in which the defendants agreed to cease all allegedly infringing activity. 689 F.3d, at 1315. Myriad, thus, solidified its position as the only entity providing BRCA testing. Some years later, petitioner Ostrer, along with medical patients, advocacy groups, and other doctors, filed this lawsuit seeking a declaration that Myriad's patents are invalid under 35 U.S.C. § 101. 702 F.Supp.2d, at 186.***

With respect to the merits, the court held that both isolated DNA and cDNA were patent eligible under § 101. The central dispute among the panel members was whether the act of *isolating* DNA—separating a specific gene or sequence of nucleotides from the rest of the chromosome—is an inventive act that entitles the individual who first isolates it to a patent. ***

II. A. "Whoever invents or discovers any new and useful ... composition of matter, or any new and useful improvement thereof, may obtain a patent therefor, subject to the conditions and requirements of this title." 35 U.S.C. § 101. We have "long held that this provision contains an important implicit exception[:] Laws of nature, natural phenomena, and abstract ideas are not patentable." *Mayo,* 566 U.S., at —— (slip op., at 1) (internal quotation marks and brackets omitted). Rather, "they are the basic tools of scientific and technological work that lie beyond the domain of patent protection." *Id.,* at —— (slip op., at 2). ***

B. It is undisputed that Myriad did not create or alter any of the genetic information encoded in the BRCA1 and BRCA2 genes. The location and order of the nucleotides existed in nature before Myriad found them. Nor did Myriad create or alter the genetic structure of DNA. Instead, Myriad's principal contribution was uncovering the precise location and genetic sequence of the BRCA1 and BRCA2 genes within chromosomes 17 and 13. The question is whether this renders the genes patentable.*** Groundbreaking, innovative, or even brilliant discovery does not by itself satisfy the § 101 inquiry. *** Myriad's claims are simply not expressed in terms of chemical composition, nor do they rely in any way on the chemical changes that result from the isolation of a particular section of DNA. Instead, the claims understandably focus on the genetic information encoded in the BRCA1 and BRCA2 genes. ***

C. cDNA does not present the same obstacles to patentability as naturally occurring, isolated DNA segments. As already explained, creation of a cDNA sequence from mRNA results in an exons-only molecule that is not naturally occurring. *** As a result, cDNA is not a "product of nature" and is patent eligible under § 101, except insofar as very short series of DNA may have no intervening introns to remove when creating cDNA.

III. It is important to note what is *not* implicated by this decision. First, there are no *method claims* [emphasis added] before this Court. Had Myriad created an innovative method of manipulating genes while searching for the BRCA1 and BRCA2 genes, it could possibly have sought a method patent. *** Similarly, this case does not involve patents on new *applications* of knowledge about the BRCA1 and BRCA2 genes. *** Nor do we consider the patentability of DNA in which the order of the naturally occurring nucleotides has been altered. *** We merely hold that genes and the information they encode are not patent eligible under § 101 simply because they have been isolated from the surrounding genetic material.

CRITICAL ANALYSIS: Evaluate *Myriad* and incorporate a discussion about the viability to patent DNA, that is, not genes that are simply isolates and extracts from the body.

Chapter 2: Post Market Vaccine Adverse Events and Compensation

Vaccine Adverse Event Reporting System

Key Websites— https://vaers.hhs.gov (edited)
https://www.cdc.gov/vaccinesafety/ensuringsafety/monitoring/vaers/ (edited)

The Vaccine Adverse Event Reporting System or VAERS is a national vaccine safety surveillance program created as an outgrowth of the National Childhood Vaccine Injury Act of 1986 (NCVIA) and is administered by the Food and Drug Administration (FDA) and Centers for Disease Control and Prevention (CDC). VAERS collects and analyzes data adverse events reports. According to CDC and FDA, serious adverse events following immunization are rare. VAERS reports are usually submitted by health care providers, vaccine manufacturers, vaccine recipients (or their parents/guardians) and state immunization programs. Patients, parents, and guardians are encouraged to seek the help of a health-care professional in reporting to VAERS. Serious adverse event that occur after the administration of any vaccine licensed in the United States should be reported. The NCVIA requires health care providers to report:

✓ *Any event listed by the vaccine manufacturer as a contraindication to subsequent doses of the vaccine; and*

✓ *Any event listed in the Reportable Events Table that occurs within the specified time after vaccination.*

CDC and the FDA review data reported to VAERS to evaluate whether a reported event is adequately reflected in product labeling, and monitors reporting trends for individual vaccine lots. Approximately 85% of the reports describe mild events such as fever, local reactions, episodes of crying or mild irritability, and other less serious experiences. The remaining 15% of the reports reflect serious adverse events involving life-threatening conditions, hospitalization, permanent disability, or death, which may or may not have been caused by an immunization. VAERS data cannot be used to prove a causal association between the vaccine and the adverse event. The only association between the adverse event and vaccination is temporal, meaning that the adverse event occurred sometime after vaccination. Therefore, the adverse event may be coincidental or it may have been caused by the vaccination. Yet, FDA has the authority to recall a vaccine.

The National Childhood Vaccine Injury Act created the Vaccine Injury Compensation Program (VICP) to compensate individuals whose injuries may have been caused by vaccines recommended by the CDC for routine use. VICP is separate from the VAERS program. Reporting an event to VAERS does not file a claim for compensation to the VICP. A petition must be filed with VICP to start a claim for compensation. See: *http://www.hrsa.gov/Vaccinecompensation/*

Adverse Event Example—Gardasil® and Cervarix®

Reports of Health Concerns Following HPV Vaccination

http://www.cdc.gov/mmwr/preview/mmwrhtml/mm6229a4.htm?s_cid=mm6229a4_w
http://www.cdc.gov/vaccinesafety/vaccines/HPV/Index.html

Licensed HPV vaccines, Gardasil® and Cervarix® are available to protect against the types of HPV infection that cause most cervical cancers. Gardasil® was licensed for use in females, age 9-26 years in June 2006 and for males age 9-26 years in Oct 2009. Cervarix® was licensed for use in females age 10-25 in October 2009. The safety of HPV vaccines was studied in clinical trials worldwide before licensure. For Gardasil®, over 29,000 males and females participated in these trials. For Cervarix®, over 30,000 females participated in several clinical trials. Since licensure, CDC and FDA have been closely monitoring the safety of HPV vaccines. Three systems used to monitor the safety of vaccines after licensure in the United States:

➢ *The Vaccine Adverse Event Reporting System (VAERS)—a useful early warning public health system that helps CDC and FDA detect possible side effects or adverse events following vaccination;*

> ➤ *The Vaccine Safety Datalink (VSD) Project—collaboration between CDC and 10 health care organizations, which monitors and evaluates adverse events following vaccination; and;*
> ➤ *The Clinical Immunization Safety Assessment (CISA) Network—a collaboration between academic centers in the U.S. that conduct research on adverse events that might be caused by vaccines.*

VAERS Reports—Gardasil® Approximately 35 million doses of Gardasil® were distributed in the United States since the summer of 2011. During June 2006–March 2013, VAERS received over 21,500 reports of adverse events following Gardasil® vaccination: 21,194 reports among females and 346 reports for males, of which 285 reports were received after the vaccine was licensed for males in October 2009. VAERS has received 423 reports were of unknown gender. Of the total number of VAERS reports following Gardasil®, 92% were considered to be non-serious, and 8% were considered serious.

Gardasil® Non-Serious Adverse Event Reports—VAERS defines non-serious adverse events as those other than hospitalization, death, permanent disability, or life-threatening illness. The vast majority (92%) of the adverse events reports following Gardasil® vaccination have included fainting, pain, and swelling at the injection site (the arm), headache, nausea, and fever. Syncope (fainting) is common after injections and vaccinations, especially in adolescents. Falls after fainting may sometimes cause serious injuries, such as head injuries, which can be prevented by closely observing the person for 15 minutes after vaccination.

Gardasil® Serious Adverse Event Reports—Any VAERS report that indicated hospitalization, permanent disability, life-threatening illness, congenital anomaly or death is classified as serious. As with all VAERS reports, serious events may or may not have been caused by the vaccine.

Guillain-Barré Syndrome (GBS): Guillain-Barré syndrome (GBS) has been reported after vaccination with Gardasil®. GBS is a rare neurologic disorder that causes muscle weakness. It occurs in 1-2 out of every 100,000 people in their teens. A number of infections have been associated with GBS. There has been no indication that Gardasil® increases the rate of GBS above the rate expected in the general population, whether or not they were vaccinated.

Blood Clots: There have been some reports of blood clots in females after receiving Gardasil®. These clots have occurred in the heart, lungs, and legs. Most of these people had a risk of getting blood clots, such as taking oral contraceptives, smoking, obesity, and other risk factors.

Deaths: There were 68 VAERS reports of death among those who have received Gardasil® as of June 22, 2011. There were 54 reports among females, 3 were among males, and 11 were reports of unknown gender. Thirty-two of the total death reports have been confirmed and 36 remain unconfirmed due to no identifiable patient information in the report such as a name and contact information to confirm the report. A death report is confirmed (verified) after a medical doctor reviews the report and any associated records. In the 32 reports confirmed, there was no unusual pattern or clustering to the deaths that would suggest that they were caused by the vaccine and some reports indicated a cause of death unrelated to vaccination.

VAERS Reports—Cervarix®: There have been 39 VAERS reports of adverse events following Cervarix® vaccination in the United States as of June 2011. The majority of these reports (97%) were considered non-serious. Cervarix® has also been in use in other countries such as England and Europe prior to licensing from the FDA.

Recommendation and Summary: Based on all of the information, CDC recommends HPV vaccination for the prevention of most types of cervical cancer. As with all approved vaccines, CDC and FDA will continue to closely monitor the safety of HPV vaccines. Any problems detected with these vaccines will be reported to health officials, healthcare providers, and the public and needed action will be taken to ensure the public's health and safety.

NOTE: See also, *Chapter 1 This Volume,* for approval of Gardasil9®.

CRITICAL ANALYSIS: Is the post licensure safety monitoring including adverse event reports sufficient? (See link below).
http://www.cdc.gov/mmwr/preview/mmwrhtml/mm6229a4.htm?s_cid=mm6229a4_w

Vaccine Injury Compensation, Liability and Immunity

The *Public Readiness and Emergency Preparedness Act* of 2005 (PREP) provides for liability protections with respect to pandemic flu and other countermeasures. The 2004 *Bioshield Act* exempts certain federal contractors from federal and state tort liability. The Homeland Security Act of 2002 immunizes smallpox vaccine manufacturers and administrators from tort liability. The United States Supreme Court decision of *Bruesewitz v. Wyeth, Inc.* pertains to the National Childhood Vaccine Injury Act and addresses liability.

NOTE: VAERS is not involved in the Vaccine Injury Compensation Program (VICP) and reporting an event to VAERS does not automatically mean a claim for compensation. A petition must be filed with VICP to start a claim for compensation. The National Childhood Vaccine Injury Act created the VICP to compensate individuals whose injuries may have been caused by vaccines recommended by the CDC for routine use.
http://www.hrsa.gov/Vaccinecompensation/

Countermeasures Injury Immunity and Compensation Program
http://www.hrsa.gov/vaccinecompensation/index.html
https://www.phe.gov/Preparedness/legal/prepact/Pages/default.aspx

The Public Readiness and Emergency Preparedness Act (PREP Act) (section 319F-3(b) of the *Public Health Service Act* (PHS Act) (42 U.S.C. 247d-6d)) authorizes (PREP Act declaration) immunity from liability (except for willful misconduct) for claims of loss caused, arising out of, relating to, or resulting from administration or use of countermeasures to diseases, threats and conditions determined by the Secretary to constitute a present, or credible risk of a future public health emergency to entities and individuals involved in the development, manufacture, testing, distribution, administration, and use of such countermeasures. A PREP Act declaration is specifically for the purpose of providing immunity from liability, and is different from, and not dependent on, other emergency declarations.

Current Declarations
➤ Nerve Agents and Certain Insecticides (Organophosphorus and/or Carbamate) Countermeasures (effective April 11, 2017)
➤ Zika Virus Vaccines (effective August 1, 2016)
➤ Ebola Virus Disease Therapeutics (amended effective February 27, 2017)
➤ Ebola Virus Disease Vaccines (amended effective December 3, 2016)
➤ Pandemic Influenza Medical Countermeasures (amended effective January 1, 2016)
➤ Anthrax Medical Countermeasures (amended effective January 1, 2016)
➤ Acute Radiation Syndrome Medical Countermeasures (amended effective January 1, 2016)
➤ Botulinum Toxin Medical Countermeasures (amended effective January 1, 2016)
➤ Smallpox Medical Countermeasures (amended effective January 1, 2016)

NOTE: The PREP Act authorized a "Covered Countermeasures Process Fund" to compensate eligible individuals who suffer injuries due to a countermeasure administered or used under the Declaration.

CRITICAL ANALYSIS: Discuss the ramifications of granting immunity from tort liability.

National Childhood Injury Act—*Bruesewitz v. Wyeth*
Liability Issues—Design Defects

The Supreme Court, in *Bruesewitz v. Wyeth*, Inc., 131 S.Ct. 1068 (2011) held that the National Childhood Vaccine Injury Act of 1986 (NCVIA) preempts all design-defect claims against vaccine manufacturers by plaintiffs who seek compensation for injury or death caused by vaccine side effects. The purpose of the NCVIA is to encourage vaccine production and limit lawsuits. Complaints are handled through a "no-fault" mechanism that offers limited payments for injuries that are proven to be caused by a particular vaccine product. Since 1988, the no-fault process has led to almost $2 billion in compensation to more than 2,500 families. Hannah Bruesewitz, an infant, received the DTP vaccine in 1992. DTP protects against diphtheria, tetanus, and pertussis commonly known as whooping cough. However, since receiving the vaccine, Hannah has suffered seizures and developmental problems. The Bruesewitz's petition under the NCVIA's compensation system was not successful based on lack of proof that the vaccine caused their daughter's injuries. The NCVIA has a lower evidentiary threshold than required by civil courts; however, the Bruesewitz's filed a lawsuit in civil court where they alleged that Wyeth should have sold a safer vaccine formulation. The Supreme Court held that the NCVIA's 'silence' regarding design defect liability was not inadvertent. Rather, according to the Court, it reflects the decision to leave complex epidemiological judgments about vaccine design to the FDA and the National Vaccine Program rather than to juries.

Bruesewitz v. Wyeth, Inc., **131 S. Ct. 1068 (2011)**

SCALIA, J., delivered the opinion of the Court, in which ROBERTS, C.J., and KENNEDY, THOMAS, BREYER, and ALITO, JJ., joined. BREYER, J., filed a concurring opinion. SOTOMAYOR, J., filed a dissenting opinion, in which GINSBURG, J., joined. KAGAN, J., took no part in the consideration or decision of the case.

Justice SCALIA We consider whether a preemption provision enacted in the National Childhood Vaccine Injury Act of 1986 (NCVIA) [42 U.S.C. § 300aa-22(b)(1)] bars state-law design-defect claims against vaccine manufacturers. For the last 66 years, vaccines have been subject to the same federal premarket approval process as prescription drugs, and compensation for vaccine-related injuries has been left largely to the States.

Much of the concern centered around vaccines against diphtheria, tetanus, and pertussis (DTP), which were blamed for children's disabilities and developmental delays. This led to a massive increase in vaccine-related tort litigation. Whereas between 1978 and 1981 only nine product-liability suits were filed against DTP manufacturers, by the mid-1980's the suits numbered more than 200 each year. *** To stabilize the vaccine market and facilitate compensation, Congress enacted the NCVIA in 1986. *** A person injured by a vaccine, or his legal guardian, may file a petition for compensation in the United States Court of Federal Claims. A special master then makes an informal adjudication of the petition within (except for two limited exceptions) 240 days. The Court of Federal Claims must review objections to the special master's decision and enter final judgment under a similarly tight statutory deadline. At that point, a claimant has two options: to accept the court's judgment and forgo a traditional tort suit for damages, or to reject the judgment and seek tort relief from the vaccine manufacturer. Fast, informal adjudication is made possible by the Act's Vaccine Injury Table, which lists the vaccines covered under the Act; describes each vaccine's compensable, adverse side effects; and indicates how soon after vaccination those side effects should first manifest themselves. Claimants who show that a listed injury first manifested itself at the appropriate time are prima facie entitled to compensation. No showing of causation is necessary; the Secretary bears the burden of disproving causation. A claimant may also recover for unlisted side effects, and for listed side effects that occur at times other than those specified in the Table, but for those the claimant must prove causation. Unlike in tort suits, claimants under the Act are not required to show that the administered vaccine was defectively manufactured, labeled, or designed. Successful claimants receive compensation for medical, rehabilitation, counseling, special education, and vocational training expenses; diminished earning capacity; pain and suffering; and $250,000 for vaccine-related deaths. *** The [NCVIA] requires claimants to seek relief through the compensation program before filing suit for more than $1,000. Manufacturers are generally immunized from liability for failure to warn if they have complied with all regulatory requirements (including but not limited to warning requirements) and have given the warning either to the claimant or the claimant's physician. They are immunized from liability for punitive damages absent failure to comply with regulatory requirements, "fraud," "intentional and wrongful with-holding of information," or other "criminal or illegal activity." And most relevant to the present case, the Act expressly eliminates liability for a vaccine's unavoidable, adverse side effects. ***

The vaccine at issue here is a DTP vaccine manufactured by Lederle Laboratories. It first received federal approval in 1948 and received supplemental approvals in 1953 and 1970. Respondent Wyeth purchased Lederle in 1994 and stopped manufacturing the vaccine in 1998. Hannah Bruesewitz was born on October 20, 1991. Her pediatrician administered doses of the DTP vaccine according to the Center for Disease Control's recommended childhood immunization schedule. Within 24 hours of her April 1992 vaccination, Hannah started to experience seizures. She suffered over 100 seizures during the next month, and her doctors eventually diagnosed her with "residual seizure disorder" and "developmental delay." Hannah, now a teenager, is still diagnosed with both conditions. In April 1995, Hannah's parents, filed a vaccine injury petition in the United States Court of Federal Claims, alleging that Hannah suffered from "On-Table" residual seizure disorder and encephalopathy injuries. A Special Master denied their claims on various grounds, though they were awarded $126,800 in attorney's fees and costs. The Bruesewitzes elected to reject the unfavorable judgment, and in October 2005 filed this lawsuit in Pennsylvania state court. Their complaint alleged (as relevant here) that defective design of Lederle's DTP vaccine caused Hannah's disabilities, and that Lederle was subject to strict liability, and liability for negligent design, under Pennsylvania common law. *** We set forth again the statutory text at issue:

"No vaccine manufacturer shall be liable in a civil action for damages arising from a vaccine-related injury or death associated with the administration of a vaccine after October 1, 1988, if the injury or death resulted from side effects that were unavoidable even though the vaccine was properly prepared and was accompanied by proper directions and warnings."

Provided that there was proper manufacture and warning, any remaining side effects, including those resulting from design defects, are deemed to have been unavoidable. State-law design-defect claims are therefore preempted. *** Design defects, in contrast, do not merit a single mention in the NCVIA or the FDA's regulations. Indeed, the FDA has never even spelled out in regulations the criteria it uses to decide whether a vaccine is safe and effective for its intended use. And the decision is surely not an easy one. Drug manufacturers often could trade a little less efficacy for a little more safety, but the safest design is not always the best one. Striking the right balance between safety and efficacy is especially difficult with respect to vaccines, which affect public as well as individual health. Yet the Act, which in every other respect micromanages manufacturers, is silent on how to evaluate competing designs. *** For the foregoing reasons, we hold that the National Childhood Vaccine Injury Act preempts all design-defect claims against vaccine manufacturers brought by plaintiffs who seek compensation for injury or death caused by vaccine side effects. The judgment of the Court of Appeals is affirmed.

Justice SOTOMAYOR, with whom **Justice GINSBURG** joins, dissenting.

Vaccine manufacturers have long been subject to a legal duty, rooted in basic principles of products liability law, to improve the designs of their vaccines in light of advances in science and technology. Until today, that duty was enforceable through a traditional state-law tort action for defective design. In holding that § 22(b)(1) of the National Childhood Vaccine Injury Act of 1986 (Vaccine Act or Act), 42 U.S.C. § 300aa-22(b)(1), pre-empts all design defect claims for injuries stemming from vaccines covered under the Act, the Court imposes its own bare policy preference over the considered judgment of Congress. Its decision leaves a regulatory vacuum in which no one ensures that vaccine manufacturers adequately take account of scientific and technological advancements when designing or distributing their products.

CRITICAL ANALYSIS: The *Bruesewitz* decision hinged on a design-defect claim. However, discuss whether vaccine manufacturers could still be liable for manufacturing defects and/or the failure to include accurate directions or warnings.

Chapter 3: Enforcement

Just as other FDA Centers, CBER has the legal authority to institute various enforcement actions such as sending a regulatory action letter to a biological product manufacturer for violations and for corrective action. Another form of regulatory action could include a seizure action if a company does not voluntarily recall a product.

Regulatory Actions

✓ *Warning Letters;*
✓ *Notice of Initiation of Disqualification Proceedings and Opportunity to Explain (NIDPOE);*
✓ *Untitled Letters;*
✓ *Administrative License Action Letters;*
✓ *Orders of Retention, Recall, Destruction, and Cessation of Manufacturing Related to Human Cell, Tissue, and Cellular and Tissue-Based Products (HCT/Ps);*
✓ *Fines; and*
✓ *Injunctions.*

Warning Letter: A warning letter is an informal advisory correspondence issued to achieve voluntary compliance. It also serves as notice to the responsible individual or firm that one or more products, practices, processes, or other activities are in violation of the FDCA, its implementing regulations and or other federal statutes.

Notice of Initiation of Disqualification Proceedings and Opportunity to Explain (NIDPOE) A NIDPOE letter informs the recipient clinical investigator that FDA is initiating an administrative proceeding to determine whether the clinical investigator should be disqualified from receiving investigational products pursuant to the Food and Drug Administration's regulations. Generally, FDA issues a NIDPOE letter when it believes it has evidence that the clinical investigator repeatedly or deliberately violated FDA's regulations about conducting clinical studies involving investigational products or submitted false information to the sponsor.

Untitled Letters: An untitled letter is an initial correspondence with regulated industry that cites violations that do not meet the threshold of regulatory significance for a Warning Letter. Examples when CBER has issued an Untitled Letter include after its review of a manufacturer's advertising and promotional labeling, after an inspection under CBER's bioresearch monitoring program or by Team Biologics, and as a result of Internet website surveillance.

Administrative License Action Letters

License Revocation is the cancellation of a license and the withdrawal of the authorization to introduce or deliver for introduction, biological products into interstate commerce. Unless in the cases of license suspension (see below) or willful violations, CBER will issue a Notice of Intent to Revoke License letter and will provide an opportunity for the manufacturer to demonstrate or achieve compliance before initiating revocation proceedings and issuing a License Revocation letter.

License Suspension is a summary action and provides for the immediate withdrawal of the authorization to introduce or deliver for introduction, biological products into interstate commerce when there are reasonable grounds to believe that any of the grounds for revocation exist and that by reason thereof there is a danger to health. In such cases, CBER will issue a License Suspension letter to the licensed manufacturer notifying them of the suspension of license.

Orders of Retention, Recall, Destruction, and Cessation of Manufacturing Related to Human Cell, Tissue, and Cellular and Tissue-Based Products (HCT/Ps)

An Order of Retention, Recall, Destruction, or Cessation of Manufacturing may be issued when any of the following conditions exist:

There are reasonable grounds to believe that an HCT/P is a violative HCT/P because it was manufactured in violation of the regulations in this part and, therefore, the conditions of manufacture of the HCT/P do not provide adequate protections against the risk of communicable disease transmission;

The HCT/P is infected or contaminated so as to be a source of dangerous infection to humans; or
An establishment is in violation of the regulations in this part and, therefore does not provide adequate
protections against the risks of communicable disease transmission.

An Order to Cease Manufacturing is issued where violations create an urgent situation involving a communicable disease, because an establishment is in violation of the regulations and, therefore, does not provide adequate protections against the risks of communicable disease transmission. *http://www.fda.gov/BiologicsBloodVaccines/GuidanceComplianceRegulatoryInformation/ComplianceActivities/Enforcement/default.htm* (edited in part).

Consent Enforcement—Fine
American Red Cross

The American Red Cross (ARC) was fined over $9 million in 2012 after FDA found that 16 of its facilities failed to comply with blood-safety rules. According to FDA, inspectors found "significant violations" from April 2010 to October 2010, including inadequate "managerial control," record-keeping and quality assurance. In 2010, the American Red Cross was fined $16 million for prior failures to comply with Federal laws and regulations related to the collection and manufacture of blood products. FDA assessed fines totaling $16.18 million. Of the fine, $9.79 million was for violations related to mismanagement of certain blood products including red cells, plasma and platelets and $6.39 million for Good Manufacturing Practice violations. Blood products included red cells, plasma and platelets. In October 2009, the agency notified the ARC that FDA inspections conducted during fiscal years 2008 and 2009 revealed violations that included failure to identify problems that occur during manufacturing and failure to adequately investigate identified problems. FDA previously sent 12 similar letters to the ARC and imposed more than $21 million in fines under terms of the amended 2003 consent decree.

http://www.fda.gov/downloads/AboutFDA/CentersOffices/OfficeofGlobalRegulatoryOperationsandPolicy/ORA/ORAElectronicReadingRoom/UCM287834.pdf
http://www.fda.gov/NewsEvents/Newsroom/PressAnnouncements/ucm216156.htm

NOTE: Several years transpired before the consent decree was lifted. The blood services operation of the (ARC) is no longer under a consent decree with oversight by the federal government. The original 1993 court order was amended in 2003. The ARC had to demonstrate five years of sustained compliance with FDA regulations.

CRITICAL ANALYSIS: Assess additional enforcement methods appropriate in this case since these issues transpired for numerous years.

Botulinum Toxin Products
https://www.fda.gov/downloads/drugs/drugsafety/ucm176360.pdf
What is BOTOX® and BOTOX Cosmetic®?

Botulinum Toxin Type A, known as "BOTOX®" and BOTOX Cosmetic® is a purified form of the poison botulinum and is given as an injection. The prescription medicine is promoted for cosmetic purposes and other uses. Botulinum Toxin Type A, or "BOTOX®" was approved for use in the late 1980s to treat eye-muscle disorders. However, over the years BOTOX® was used "off-label" for cosmetic purposes to reduce facial frown lines between the eyebrows. With approval by FDA, Allergen who manufactures Botox®, is permitted to promote these approved uses. The following are the approved uses noted in the medication guide (link above).

BOTOX® is a prescription medicine that is injected into muscles and used:
- ✓ to treat overactive bladder symptoms such as a strong need to urinate with leaking or wetting accidents (urge urinary incontinence), a strong need to urinate right away (urgency) and urinating often (frequency) in adults when another type of medicine (anticholinergic) does not work well enough or cannot be taken.
- ✓ to treat leakage of urine (incontinence) in adults with overactive bladder due to neurologic disease when another type of medicine (anticholinergic) does not work well enough or cannot be taken.

✓ to prevent headaches in adults with chronic migraine who have 15 or more days each month with headache lasting 4 or more hours each day.

✓ to treat increased muscle stiffness in elbow, wrist, and finger muscles in adults with upper limb spasticity.

✓ to treat increased muscle stiffness (2010) in ankle and toe muscles in adults with lower limb spasticity (2016).

✓ to treat the abnormal head position and neck pain that happens with cervical dystonia (CD) in adults.

✓ to treat certain types of eye muscle problems (strabismus) or abnormal spasm of the eyelids (blepharospasm) in people 12 years and older.

BOTOX® is also injected into the skin to treat the symptoms of severe underarm sweating (severe primary axillary hyperhidrosis) when medicines used on the skin (topical) do not work well enough.

BOTOX Cosmetic® is a prescription medicine that is injected into muscles and used to improve the look of moderate to severe frown lines between the eyebrows (2002) (glabellar lines), forehead lines (2017) in adults for a short period of time (temporary).

BOTOX® Cosmetic is a prescription medicine that is injected into the area around the side of the eyes to improve the look of crow's feet lines in adults for a short period of time (temporary).

Boxed Warnings, REMS, Drug Name —Botulinum Toxin "Botox®" Products

FDA initiated a safety review of botulinum toxin products in 2008 (Botox®) which resulted in notification to healthcare professionals in April 2009 that manufacturers of licensed botulinum toxin products had to strengthen warnings in product labeling and add a boxed warning concerning the risk of adverse events when the toxin's effects extend past the place where it was injected. FDA approved the following revisions to the prescribing information of Botox/Botox Cosmetic® and Myobloc:

➢ A *Boxed Warning* highlighting the possibility of experiencing potentially life-threatening distant spread of toxin effect from the injection site after local injection.

➢ A Risk Evaluation and Mitigation Strategy (REMS) that includes a *Medication Guide* to help patients understand the risks and benefits of botulinum toxin products.

➢ Changes to the established drug names to reinforce individual potencies and prevent medication errors. The potency units are specific to each botulinum toxin product, and the doses or units of biological activity cannot be compared or converted from one product to any other botulinum toxin product. The new established names reinforce these differences and the lack of interchangeability among products. The other botulinum toxin product in this class, AbobotulinumtoxinA (marketed as Dysport), was approved on April 29, 2009 and included the *Boxed Warning*, REMS, and new established name at the time of approval.

CBER issued Allergan a "Violative Advertising and Promotional Labeling Letter" in 2002 because the website for physicians, www.botoxcosmetic.net, presented confusing information about the dilution table. A Warning Letter, issued in 2003, resulted from routine monitoring and surveillance by FDA's Advertising and Promotional Labeling Branch of CBER.

NOTE: In the first quarter of 2018 GAAP Net Revenues, Botox generated 3.7 billion in sales. Another Allergan product Juvederm Vollure™ xc, was approved by FDA in 2017 and indicated for adults age 21 for the correction of moderate to severe facial wrinkles and folds, such as nasolabial folds.

CRITICAL ANALYSIS: Discuss the various uses for BOTOX® and evaluate the legal liabilities involved in "BOTOX®" events. Include a discussion about what the product name "Botox Cosmetic®" implies as well as informed consent.

Failure to Warn About Side Effects—*Ray v. Allergan, Inc.*

In *Ray v. Allergan, Inc.,* 3:10-cv-00136, (U.S. District Court, E. D. Virginia) a federal jury originally awarded $212 million verdict to Douglas M. Ray due to permanent brain damage from Botox injections. Mr. Ray alleged that Allergan, the drug manufacturer, failed to warn him that the

Botox injections could trigger an autoimmune reaction leading to permanent brain damage. Mr. Ray received the Botox injections for tremors and writer's cramp in his right hand.

The jury awarded the plaintiff, Mr. Ray $12 million in compensatory damages and $200 million in punitive damages; though, under Virginia law, punitive damages are capped at $350,000. However, on June 1, 2012, the court ordered a new trial because of the prohibition on the reference to the "Golden Rule" implying that the jurors should put themselves in the shoes of Mr. Ray, the plaintiff. Additionally, counsel for Ray used hand gestures according to counsel for Allergan resembling black box warnings.

NOTE: By stipulation, the case was dismissed with prejudice on August 10, 2012.

CRITICAL ANALYSIS: Discuss the impact of the "Golden Rule" reference and hand gestures on the outcome of this case.

Practice of Medicine or Drug/Biologic—*Regenerative Sciences*

United States v. Regenerative Sciences LLC,
741 F.3d 1314 (D.C. Cir. 2014)

Regenerative Sciences, LLC vigorously defended its position that FDA could not regulate the practice of medicine in its Regenexx™ treatment or Regenexx-C™ cultured treatment which uses Mesenchymal adult stem cells (MSCs) that originate primarily from bone marrow. The majority of shareholders of Regenerative Sciences, LLC are physicians and the company promotes the Regenexx™ treatment as a "non-surgical" treatment option for joint or bone pain in the hip, knee, shoulder, back or ankle as well as non-union fractures. The dispute with FDA has been ongoing since at least 2008 when FDA sent correspondence to Regenerative Sciences depicting the cell treatment as a drug or biologic. FDA conducted an inspection and found violations of current Good Manufacturing Practices (cGMPs). Thereafter Regenerative Sciences filed an injunction to prevent FDA from regulating the product as a drug. However, the court dismissed the matter as FDA has not yet taken regulatory action.

Subsequently, the court granted FDA the motion for summary judgment and issued a permanent injunction against the use of the Regenexx™ procedure and deemed the product a drug/biologic. Further, the court opined that this was not the practice of medicine. 21 U.S.C. section 396 "Practice of Medicine". *United States v. Regenerative Sciences., LLC*, 878 F. Supp. 2d 248 (D.D.C. 2012). An appeal was filed and the Court of Appeals affirmed. (Feb. 4, 2014 No. 12-5254, 741 F.3d 1314 (D.C. Cir. 2014)

See: *http://www.regenexx.com* and *http://fortipublications.com/blog/*

NOTE: See *Volume V: Human Drug Regulation,* for the reported decision.

CRITICAL ANALYSIS: Do you agree with the determination by the court that the product is properly regulated as a drug (see 21 U.S. C. Sec. 321 (g)(1)(D)) and biologic (see 42 U.S. C. Sec. 262(i) and does not fall under "Practice of Medicine"? Include safety and efficacy considerations as well as a discussion about innovative therapies.

VOLUME VII

Volume VII: Veterinary Products Regulation

FDA's Center of Veterinary Medicine (CVM) is detailed in this volume. Interestingly, Benjamin Rush, one of the signers of the Declaration of Independence, was a leader in Veterinary medicine. Dr. Rush, a physician, held a vision for veterinary science. That vision eventually led to the founding of the University of Pennsylvania Veterinary School. Fast forward from the 1800s to the 1900s for the FDA appointment of the first veterinarian.

Additionally, this volume focuses on issues concerning animal drugs, feeds, foods and animal health products that are regulated through (CVM). Animal drugs are regulated under specific sections of the Food Drug and Cosmetic Act. They are regulated as either new animal drugs under 21 U.S.C. § 360b or as antibiotics and, if used in feed or drinking water for food producing animals, they are regulated as food additives. The terms "new animal drug" and "animal feed" are defined under 21 U.S.C. § 321(v) and (w). A "new animal drug" is "any drug intended for use in animals or in animal feed". Similar to the drug approval process for human drugs, new animal drugs must also go through the drug approval process to establish safety and efficacy. Before a new animal drug can be marketed, it must be approved by CVM using quality, safety and efficacy as a basis. Section 512 of the FDCA or 21 U.S.C. § 352, applies to misbranded animal drugs and devices.

The concept of new animal drugs is detailed in the decision of United States v. Articles of Drug for Veterinary Use. A new animal drug is deemed unsafe unless the drug received FDA approval. Further, the new animal drug must be used in conformity with the approved labeling. The FDCA does not contain a preapproval provision for pet food. However, pet food can nevertheless be deemed "adulterated" and "misbranded" under the FDCA as illustrated in the decision of United States v. Strauss. Pet foods are prohibited from containing poisonous or deleterious substances or pesticide residues in excess of established tolerances. Recalls do occur and the largest in United States history was the nationwide pet food recall due to tainted imported wheat gluten.

The fiercely contested issue of the use of antimicrobials in food producing animals was addressed in late 2013 and reaffirmed in 2014. The outcome was the issuance of a final guidance pertaining to a voluntary phase out antimicrobial program in animals for food production purposes. A companion veterinary feed directive involves the "switch" from over-the-counter to prescription drug product necessitating a veterinary feed directive rule finalized in 2015. Pharmacy compounding is explored in the Frank's decision where the court detailed state versus federal jurisdiction.

The milestone Food Safety Modernization Act (FSMA) has impacted as well. Several rules under the FSMA focus on preserving the integrity of the food supply. Specific targeted rules include preventive controls for animal feed, third party accreditation of auditors, and supplier verification for imported food for animals.

Chapter 1: The Evolution of the Center for Veterinary Medicine

Key website: *http://www.fda.gov/AnimalVeterinary/default.htm*

Center for Veterinary Medicine Mission

http://www.fda.gov/AboutFDA/CentersOffices/OfficeofFoods/CVM/CVMVisionandMission/default.htm

Animal drugs, feeds, foods and animal health products are regulated through FDA's Center of Veterinary Medicine (CVM). CVM is responsible for ensuring that animal drugs and medicated feeds are safe and effective for their intended uses and that food from treated animals is safe for human consumption. In its mission statement, CVM set forth:

> *"The Center for Veterinary Medicine is a consumer protection organization. We foster public and animal health by approving safe and effective products for animals and by enforcing other applicable provisions of the Federal Food, Drug, and Cosmetic Act and other authorities."*

CVM does not regulate the practice of veterinary medicine nor does CVM regulate vaccines for animals. The United States Department of Agriculture (USDA) regulates animal vaccines. CVM monitors the use of veterinary products through postmarket surveillance and compliance programs. A significant priority of CVM is assurance of food safety through elimination of violative residues in meat and milk. CVM strives to:

- ➢ *Monitor safety and effective prior to approval;*
- ➢ *Evaluate data on proposed veterinary products prior to market clearance;*
- ➢ *Discover violative marketed products through post market surveillance programs;*
- ➢ *Initiate legal action to bring violators into compliance with the law; and*
- ➢ *Conduct research to assist CVM scientists in the review process for veterinary products.*

CVM ensures that animal drugs and medicated feeds are safe and effective for their intended use. In addition, food from treated animals must be safe for human consumption. Before a new animal drug can be marketed, it must be approved by CVM based on quality, safety and efficacy. Drugs utilized in food-producing animals must be safe not only for the animals but also for the food-product derived from the treated animal. After approval, CVM then monitors the use of the product through both surveillance and compliance programs. CVM has a direct impact on the human food supply and on the safety of veterinary products. CVM is involved in approving animal drugs, marketing animal products and conducting research. Overall, the goal of CVM, in fulfillment of the intent of the FDCA, is to protect animal and human health throughout the United States. Through the authority to approve new animal drug applications and their supplements (NADAs) and to approve abbreviated new drug applications for generic drugs (ANDAs), CVM may issue proposals, notices and orders related to the refusal to approve and to withdraw approved new animal drug applications. CVM approves the use of animal food additives as well.

Finally, CVM insures that new animal drug applications for food-producing animals are reviewed and evaluated with respect to any possible effects on human health. For example, the use of diethylstilbestrol (DES) in animal feed was very controversial. The use of DES in food animal production was banned in 1979 and new animal drug approvals for the use of DES in food-producing animals were withdrawn as well. The United States Department of Agriculture's Food Safety and Inspection Service (FSIS) assumes responsibility for the inspection of meat and poultry products in federally inspected establishments. FSIS reports violative residues of drugs in meat and poultry to FDA for regulatory follow-up.

NOTE: CVM regulates some flea and tick products while the Environmental Protection Agency (EPA) regulates others. An EPA regulated product label would contain an EPA registration number ("EPA reg. No."). An FDA approved product contains the statement "Approved by FDA" and is followed by a six-digit New Animal Drug Application (NADA) or Abbreviated New Animal Drug Application (ANDA) on the labeling.

See: *http://www.fda.gov/AboutFDA/CentersOffices/OfficeofFoods/CVM/default.htm*

Legislative Milestones

Interestingly, as far back as the early 1800s, Benjamin Rush, a signer of the Declaration of Independence, advocated for the study of animals and remedies for animals. Dr. Rush, a Philadelphian, inspired the founding of the University of Pennsylvania Veterinary School. The historical overview of the Center for Veterinary Medicine (CVM) is detailed below as well as a discussion about the responsibilities of CVM.

1927: A separate law enforcement agency was formed, known first as the Food, Drug, and Insecticide Administration, and later as the Food and Drug Administration. The agency employed its first veterinarian, Dr. Henry Moskey, to evaluate vitamins and minerals in light of their claimed nutritional and treatment uses.

1938: *The Federal Food, Drug, and Cosmetic Act (FDCA)* was enacted. For the first time, manufacturers were required to provide evidence of product safety before distributing new drugs. The Act also granted FDA explicit authority to conduct factory inspections and to use court injunctions as enforcement tools, in addition to seizure and prosecution. Other provisions stipulated the establishment of acceptable tolerances for unavoidable poisonous substances. FDA was transferred in 1940 from USDA to the Federal Security Agency, and the Office of Commissioner of Food and Drugs was established.

1950s: The Veterinary Medical Branch, established in the 1950s, occurred when the Food and Drug Administration (FDA) was organized into separate bureaus. The main function was to determine the safety of animal drugs for animals and consumers of food derived from treated animals. During this time, the development and use of animal drugs and medicated foods increased.

The Durham-Humphrey Amendment (1951) required that human drugs which cannot be safely used without medical supervision must be dispensed only by a prescription of a licensed practitioner and must bear the Rx legend. The veterinary prescription legend was subsequently achieved through a rulemaking procedure. In 1953, the Federal Security Agency became part of the Department of Health, Education and Welfare (DHEW), and the following year FDA was organized into five Bureaus, including a Bureau of Medicine. With the establishment of this Bureau, a Veterinary Medical Branch was created with Dr. John Collins as the first chief. The Branch's primary function was to determine the safety of animal drugs, both for animals and for consumers of food derived from treated animals. The great expansion in the development and use of animal drugs and medicated feeds during this period was a preview to the increasingly prominent role that veterinary medicine was to play in FDA and in animal and human health.

The Food Additive Amendments (1958) expanded regulatory authority over animal food additives and drug residues in animal-derived foods. By 1959, the Veterinary Medical Branch had developed into a Division headed by Dr. Charles G. Durbin.

1960s: *The Kefauver-Harris Drug Amendments* (1962) brought the most important changes to the Food, Drug and Cosmetic Act. These amendments authorized FDA to monitor clinical trials of investigational drugs and strengthen inspection authority. Manufacturers are required to test new drugs for effectiveness as well as safety before entering the marketplace. The amendments required manufacturers to report to FDA any adverse effects and other clinical experiments related to the safety and efficacy of any drug already in the marketplace. Revisions in the Kefauver-Harris Drug Amendments set forth that new drugs may not be cleared for marketing if the labeling is false or misleading. Animal drugs were regulated under three sections of the Act. They were first regulated either as new drugs under Section 505, or as antibiotics under Section 507. If used in the feed for drinking water of food-producing animals they were, in addition, regulated as food additives under Section 409. It was not until the late 1960s, that the Bureau of Veterinary Medicine was established.

1980s: The Bureau of Veterinary Medicine became known as The Center for Veterinary Medicine (CVM) in 1984.

The Generic Animal Drugs and the Generic Animal Drug and Patent Term Restoration Act (Pub. L. 100-670 November 16, 1988 102 Stat. 3971). This Act extended to veterinary products the benefits given to human drugs under the 1984 Drug Price Competition and Patent Term Restoration Act. This led companies to produce and sell generic versions of animal drugs approved without duplicating research done previously to prove them both safe and effective. This Act also authorizes the extension of animal drug patents.

1990s: The Animal Medicinal Drug Use Clarification Act was enacted to allow veterinarians to prescribe extra-labeled use of veterinary drugs for animals under specific circumstances. In addition, this legislation allows licensed veterinarians to prescribe human drugs for use in animals under specific conditions.

1996: The Animal Drug Availability Act (ADAA Pub. L. 104-250) enacted in the late 1990s, allows greater flexibility in the animal drug approval process and provides for flexible labeling and more direct communication between drug sponsors and the FDA. The ADAA established a veterinary feed directive (VFD) permitting veterinarians to order the use of VFD drugs in feed without pharmacist involvement. A veterinarian examines, provides a diagnosis and if necessary prescribes the use of a VFD. This affords a practical solution because some states require a licensed pharmacist to dispense the drugs while other states prohibit feed manufacturers from dispensing prescription drugs. The VFD permits shipment of the VFD feed directly to the animal feeding establishment. In 1997, CVM implemented a rule to prevent the spread of BSE, commonly known as "mad cow disease".

2000s: Animal Drug User Fee Act (2003) Considered milestone legislation, the 2003 Animal Drug User Fee Act (ADUFA), Public Law 108-130, provides user fees for animal drug review. This law permits FDA to collect user fees for selected animal drug applications, on particular animal drug products and establishments where these products are manufactured. The fees are applicable to sponsors of the animal drug applications and or investigational animal drug submissions. The rates and payment procedures for product, establishment and sponsor fees are published in the *Federal Register*. For example, user fee rates are established for an animal drug application, a supplemental animal drug application which requires safety and efficacy data, an annual product fee, an annual establishment fee and an annual sponsor fee. There was a sunset provision date of 2013; however, reauthorization occurred under the ADUFA (2014).

Minor Use-Minor Species Animal Health Act (MUMS) (2004) Provides for more medication availability to veterinarians and animal owners to treat minor species such as zoo animals and uncommon diseases in major animal species. MUMS regulations: 21 CFR section 516.

Food and Drug Administration Amendments Act (FDAAA) (2007) The FDA Consumer Complaint Reporting System (CCRS) mandated by the FDAAA is the Early Warning System for pet food; FDA encourages the use of the CCRS to the veterinary profession through American Veterinary Medical Association and Veterinary Information Network (VIN).

Food Safety Modernization Act (FSMA) (2011) The FSMA applies to food for animals as well as pets. Several proposed rules issued in 2013 were finalized in 2016.

Drug Quality and Security Act (DQSA) (2013) The DQSA addresses compounding and Title II of the DQSA contains the *Drug Supply Chain Security Act* tracking provisions.

CRITICAL ANALYSIS: Suggest additional legislation and a regulatory approach that provides more uniformity and less confusion. See: for example, the regulation of flea and tick products in NOTE above.

Chapter 2: Special Topics—Modernization Act, Feed Controls, Mad Cow Disease, Antibiotics, Antimicrobials, Genetic Engineering, Cloning, Flavorings, Turtles and Geckos

Food Safety Modernization Act Final Rules—Detention, Prior Notice, Preventive Controls, Foreign Supplier Verification, Accreditation, Sanitary Transport

FDA has instituted several regulations under the Food Safety Modernization Act which are applicable to veterinary products. The following detail the final rules.

Final Rule—Administrative Detention of Food (2013)

Criteria Used to Order Administrative Detention of Food for Human or Animal Consumption
This final rule amended the criteria for administrative detention to prevent potentially unsafe food from reaching the marketplace. The final rule issued February 2013 adopts the interim final rule, *"Criteria Used to Order Administrative Detention of Food for Human or Animal Consumption,"* published in May 2011, without change.

Guidance For Industry on Administrative Detention—On March 27, 2013 FDA released a revised guidance on administrative detention entitled "Guidance for Industry: What You Need to Know About Administrative Detention of Foods; Small Entity Compliance Guide." http://www.fda.gov/Food/GuidanceRegulation/GuidanceDocumentsRegulatoryInformation/FoodDefense/ucm342588.htm

Final Rule—Information Required in Prior Notice of Imported Food (2013)

This rule requires when submitting prior notice of imported food, including food for animals, to report the name of any country to which the article has been refused entry.

Final Rule—Preventive Controls for Animal Food (2015)

http://www.fda.gov/Food/GuidanceRegulation/FSMA/ucm366510.htm
FSMA Final Rule for Preventive Controls for Animal Food Finalized
Current Good Manufacturing Practice, Hazard Analysis and Risk-Based Preventive Controls for Food for Animals 80 FR 56170-01 (Sept. 17, 2015).
https://www.federalregister.gov/articles/2015/09/17/2015-21921/current-good-manufacturing-practice-hazard-analysis-and-risk-based-preventive-controls-for-food-for#h-10
Preventive Controls Major Provisions Summary: The FDA published the original rule on October 29, 2013; however, FDA issued a supplemental proposed rule in 2014 to comport with animal feed as well as business size and sales. The rule was finalized September 17, 2015.
Summary of Key Revisions
http://www.fda.gov/Food/GuidanceRegulation/FSMA/ucm366510.htm
1. Current Good Manufacturing Practice (CGMPs) regulations applicable to animal food production.
2. Establish and Implement a Food Safety System that includes analysis of hazards and risk-based preventive controls. The written food safety plan must include:
   - ➢ *Hazard analysis;*
   - ➢ *Preventive controls;*
   - ➢ *Oversight and management including monitoring and verification; and a*
   - ➢ *Recall plan.*
3. Supply chain program more flexible with separate compliance dates. Ex, Definition of very small business proposed at less than $2.5 million in sales.
4. Farm definition clarified—two types of farm operations:
   - ➢ *Primary Production Farm and*
   - ➢ *Secondary Activities Farm*
5. Feed mills associated with farms (vertically integrated operations) not covered.
Compliance Dates—dependent of business size as follows:

CGMP—Current Good Manufacturing Practices and PC-Preventive Controls
Businesses Other than Small and Very Small—a business that is not small or very small and does not qualify for an exemption: 1 year for CGMP compliance and 2 years for PC compliance.
Small business— fewer than 500 persons and that does not qualify for an exemption 2 years CGMP and 3 years for PC and to comply after final rule publication.
Very small business—a business having less than $2.5 million in total annual sales of animal food, adjusted for inflation-3 years for CGMP compliance and 4 years for PC after final rule publication to comply.

Final Rule—Foreign Supplier Verification Programs (FSVP) for Importers of Food for Humans and Animals (2015)
http://www.fda.gov/Food/GuidanceRegulation/FSMA/ucm361902.htm
http://www.fda.gov/Food/GuidanceRegulation/FSMA/ucm361902.htm#fact_sheet-Food%20for%20Humans%20and%20Animals

Foreign Supplier Verification Program Summary: On July 29, 2013, FDA issued proposed regulations and a revised supplemental proposed rule on September 29, 2014 and finalized in November 2015 that strengthens the oversight of foods imported for consumers. Under the Foreign Supplier Verification Program (FSVP) regulations, importers are required to perform certain risk-based activities to verify that food imported into the United States has been produced in a manner that provides the same level of public health protection as that required of domestic food producers. The FSVP regulations implement section 301. Under the final FSVP regulations, an importer is required to develop, maintain, and follow an FSVP for each food it imports, which, in general, would need to include the following:

> ➢ *Compliance Status Review,*
> ➢ *Hazard Analysis,*
> ➢ *Verification Activities,*
> ➢ *Corrective Actions,*
> ➢ *Periodic Reassessment of the FSVP,*
> ➢ *Supplier and Importer Identification,*
> ➢ *Recordkeeping and*
> ➢ *Consistency with other FSMA rules (no more than $1million in annual food sales).*

NOTE: Imported Food Expedited Review- FDA established a voluntary fee-based program commencing in January 2018 for the expedited review of food imported into the United States. Importers must demonstrate a proven food safety track record of supply chain management.

Final Rule—Third Party Accreditation Auditors or "Certification Bodies" (2015)
http://www.fda.gov/Food/GuidanceRegulation/FSMA/ucm361903.htm

Third Party Accreditation Summary: FDA published its proposed rule in 2013 to establish a program for accreditation of third-party auditors to conduct food safety audits and issue certifications of foreign facilities. The final rule (2015) implements Section 307 of the FDA Food Safety Modernization Act (FSMA). FDA would identify accreditation bodies based on criteria such as competency and impartiality. The accreditation bodies could be foreign government agencies or private companies and would in turn accredit third party auditors to audit and issue certifications for foreign food facilities. The final rule contains requirements relating to auditing and certification of foreign food facilities and food under the program and for notifying the FDA of conditions in an audited facility that could cause or contribute to a serious public health risk.
Model Accreditation Standards: The standards would specify what qualifications a certification body must have to qualify for accreditation, such as the minimum requirements for education and experience for third-party auditors and their audit agents.

Final Rule—Sanitary Transportation (2016)

Requires those who transport food to use sanitary practices to ensure the safety of food. Proposed January 2014; Final rule issued on April 5, 2016. With the passage of the updated 2005 Sanitary Food Transportation Act (SFTA), Congress reallocated lead authority for food transportation safety to FDA; however, both the Department of Transportation and the U.S. Department of Agriculture (USDA) remain as partners with FDA. This rule implements the requirement in section 111 of the FDA Food Safety Modernization Act (FSMA) that instructed FDA to issue SFTA regulations.

https://www.federalregister.gov/articles/2016/04/06/2016-07330/sanitary-transportation-of-human-and-animal-food

http://www.fda.gov/Food/GuidanceRegulation/FSMA/ucm247559.htm#Sanitary_Transportation

CRITICAL ANALYSIS: How should FDA ensure industry compliance?

Animal Feed

http://www.fda.gov/ForConsumers/ConsumerUpdates/ucm164473.htm (modified in part)

FDA regulates food for animals, including animal feed for millions of chickens, turkeys, cows, pigs, sheep, and fish. Furthermore, FDA regulates pet food for America's over 177 million dogs, cats, and horses. Animal feed must be pure and wholesome; produced under sanitary conditions; truthfully labeled; and without any harmful substances. FDA carries out its animal feed regulatory responsibilities in cooperation with state and local partners and with the Association of American Feed Control Officials (AAFCO) on uniform feed ingredient definitions and proper labeling.

Improvements to Feed Safety—FDA is improving its Animal Feed Safety System, a program first established in 2003 to protect human and animal health by ensuring safe feeds. The system covers a broad range of agency activities from pre-approving additives for use in feed, to establishing limits on feed contaminants, providing education and training to federal and state feed regulatory personnel, conducting inspections, and taking enforcement actions to ensure compliance with agency regulations. FDA is also taking action to improve the safety of pet food and ingredients used to make pet food, such as establishing:

> *Ingredient standards, definitions, processing standards, and labeling standards for pet food;*
> *An early warning system to identify pet food in violation of regulations, to identify illness outbreaks, and to notify veterinarians and others of pet food recalls;*
> *A searchable database of recalled human and pet foods to ensure effective communications during a recall;*
> *A "reportable food registry" for animal feed as well as human food. Reportable food is any food that carries a reasonable probability that its use or exposure to it will cause serious health consequences or death to humans or animals; and*
> *Collaborating with state regulators and academic partners to set up a network for reporting and investigating unexpected and undesirable signs (adverse events) in pets.*

No Premarket Approval: The FDCA does not require preapproval of animal feed and pet food prior to marketing. However, FDA can take enforcement action post market. Animal feed manufacturers are responsible for ensuring that:

> *Feed is truthfully labeled;*
> *Feed does not contain unsafe additives or contaminants;*
> *If the feed contains drugs, the drugs are approved by FDA for use in animal feeds; and*
> *Federal and state agencies work cooperatively to provide rules and guidance.*

Medicated Feed: Drugs may be added to some animal feeds to prevent or treat diseases. For example, coccidiosis is a disease that commonly infects chickens and can cause death if untreated. The parasites responsible, coccidia, are passed in the droppings and can infect other chickens housed near the sick chickens. Providing medication through the feed or drinking water eliminates the stress to the animals. Medicated feed to treat all the chickens is necessary for good animal health, and ultimately to the health of humans who consume the chicken products. Types of drugs that may be used in feed include the following:

> *Antimicrobials (such as antibacterial drugs) to fight infections;*
> *Anticoccidials to fight coccidial parasites;*
> *Hormonals to suppress estrus (the female "heat" cycle) in cattle;*
> *Anthelmintics to fight parasitic worms;*
> *Sulfonamidics to fight certain types of infections;*
> *Beta agonists to promote leanness in animals raised for meat; and*
> *Anti-bloating drugs to prevent swelling of the stomach compartments or intestinal tract of cows caused by excessive gas.*

NOTE: See "Antimicrobial Phase Out" discussed below.

Antimicrobial Resistance and Residues

FDA is responsible for assuring that animal drugs and medicated feeds are not only safe and effective for animals, but that food products from treated animals are safe for humans to consume. FDA issued a final rule in 2015 originally proposed in 2013. FDA determined to use a phase out of these drugs. Over the years, FDA responded to concerns about antimicrobial resistance and drug residues. There was coordination of the National Antimicrobial Resistance Monitoring System (NARMS), with USDA and the Centers for Disease Control and Prevention (CDC). FDA issued several guidance documents throughout the years. For example, in 2009 FDA issued: *Final Guidance for Industry Studies to Evaluate the Safety of Residues of Veterinary Drugs in Human Food: General Approach to Establish a Microbiological ADI VICH GL-36* and a guidance titled: *Final Guidance for Industry Studies to Evaluate the Safety of Residues of Veterinary Drugs in Human Food: General Approach to Testing VICH GL33* (March 17, 2009.) This final guidance replaced a 2006 guidance and outlined a testing approach to assure human food safety following the consumption of food products derived from animals treated with veterinary drugs. The guidance combines developmental toxicity testing proposals of the European Union, Japan and the United States for the safety of veterinary drug residues in human food.

FDA finalized a guidance document entitled *"The Judicious Use of Medically Important Antimicrobial Drugs in Food-Producing Animals"* (GFI #209 April 13, 2012). GFI #209 discusses FDA's concerns regarding the development of antimicrobial resistance in human and animal bacterial pathogens when medically important antimicrobial drugs are used in food-producing animals in an injudicious manner. In addition, GFI #209 provides two recommended principles regarding the appropriate or judicious use of medically important antimicrobial drugs: (1) Limit medically important antimicrobial drugs to uses in animals that are considered necessary for assuring animal health and (2) Limit medically important antimicrobial drugs to uses in animals that include veterinary oversight or consultation.

Yet, although FDA actively tackled the issue of antimicrobial resistance since 1996 it was not until late 2013 when FDA issued GFI #213 (see note below) that outlined more proactive steps. Previously, FDA addressed antimicrobial resistance through a variety of initiatives, principally through surveillance; product development; education; and research.

NOTE: See below for Final Rule and FDA Guidance issued December 2013 "New Animal Drugs and New Animal Drug Combination Products Administered in or on Medicated Feed or Drinking Water of Food-Producing Animals: Recommendations for Drug Sponsors for Voluntarily Aligning Product Use Conditions with GFI #209 (Guidance #213)".

CRITICAL ANALYSIS: Injunctions have been issued for drug residues due to the effect on the United States food supply. Further a court may issue contempt of injunctions. Choose a contempt injunction from the following link and evaluate why the court issues this type of order. See link: *https://www.fda.gov/AnimalVeterinary/GuidanceComplianceEnforcement/ComplianceEnforcement/ucm290235.htm*

Impetus—*Natural Resources Defense Council, Inc.*

FDA denied petitions to ban medically important antibiotics used in animals. However, in

June 2012, federal District Court Judge Katz in *Natural Resources Defense Council, Inc.* No. 11 Civ. 3562 (March 22, 2012) ordered that FDA must reconsider the denied petitions. The Court of Appeals (July 24, 2014) reversed the District Court's determination that FDA was required by 21 U.S.C. § 360b(e)(1) to proceed with hearings to determine whether to withdraw approval for the use of penicillin and tetracyclines in animal feed and that the FDA's decision denying two citizen petitions urging it to hold such hearings was arbitrary or capricious within the meaning of 5 U.S.C. § 706(2). Specifically, the Court of Appeals concluded that the "decision whether to institute or terminate a hearing process that may lead to a finding requiring withdrawal of approval for an animal drug is a discretionary determination left to the prudent choice of the FDA." The Appeals Court agreed with FDA's determination that its "preferred program of voluntary compliance offers greater prospect for immediate and significant reductions in animal antibiotic use than the pursuit of a potentially contentious withdrawal hearing."

Further, the Court of Appeals opined that they could not conclude that it is "arbitrary or capricious" for the FDA to follow polices intended to reduce the use of animal feed containing antibiotics through various phases "short of withdrawing approval for the use of antibiotics in feed via a protracted administrative process and likely litigation." In 2013 (Dec. 2013) FDA issued a guidance and proposed rule about a phase out of antimicrobial drugs in animals used for food production purposes. According to FDA, the agency issued voluntary guidance that promotes the judicious use of antibiotics in food animal production is preferable because of resource limitations; that is, according to FDA, the agency would use fewer resources compared to withdrawing the animal drugs on an individual basis.

NOTE: FDA used a collaborative approach and worked with stakeholders including animal pharmaceutical companies for compliance purposes.

CRITICAL ANALYSIS: Should rulemaking have been instituted to withdraw the antibiotics as the district court determined or did the court of appeals decide this case correctly?

Antimicrobial Voluntary Phase Out

http://www.fda.gov/AnimalVeterinary/GuidanceComplianceEnforcement/GuidanceforIndustry/ucm216939.htm (edited)

Definition—Antimicrobial drugs: Include all drugs that work against a variety of microorganisms, such as bacteria, viruses, fungi, and parasites.

Distinction—Antibiotic and Antimicrobial: An antibiotic drug is effective against bacteria. All antibiotics are antimicrobials, however, not all antimicrobials are antibiotics.

What is antimicrobial resistance? Antimicrobial resistance is when bacteria or other microbes become resistant to the effects of a drug after being exposed to it. This means that the drug, and similar drugs, will no longer be effective against those microbes. Historically, antimicrobials have been used in the feed or drinking water of cattle, poultry, hogs, and other food animals for production purposes such as using less food to gain weight. However, some of these antimicrobials are important drugs used to treat human infection. Increasingly, the concern has been about the ability of bacteria and other microbes to resist the effects of a drug. Due to antimicrobial resistance, a drug may no longer be as effective in treating various illnesses or infections. According to FDA, it is important to use these drugs only when medically necessary. The plan focuses on those antimicrobial drugs that are considered medically important, that is, those that are important for treating human infection and are approved for use in feed and water of food animals. FDA announced implementation of a plan to help phase out the use of medically important antimicrobials in food animals for food production purposes for growth enhancement or improvement of feed efficiency. The plan phases in veterinary oversight of the remaining appropriate therapeutic uses of these drugs. The phase in program would require animal pharmaceutical companies to notify FDA of their intent to participate. These companies that voluntarily agree to do so would then have a three-year transition process. To that end, as mentioned above, FDA issued a final guidance document in 2013 and a veterinary feed directive final rule in 2015.

Final Guidance—*New Animal Drugs and New Animal Drug Combination Products Administered in or on Medicated Feed or Drinking Water of Food-Producing Animals: Recommendations for Drug Sponsors for Voluntarily Aligning Product Use Conditions with GFI #209 (Guidance #213)* **(Issued December 2013)**

http://www.fda.gov/downloads/AnimalVeterinary/GuidanceComplianceEnforcement/Guidance-forIndustry/UCM299624.pdf

The final guidance provides direction to animal pharmaceutical companies to voluntarily revise the FDA-approved labeled use conditions to:

(a) Remove the use of antimicrobial drugs for production purposes;

(b) Add, where appropriate, scientifically-supported disease treatment, control or prevention uses; and

(c) Change the marketing status from over-the-counter to Veterinary Feed Directive for drugs administered through feed or to prescription status for drugs administered through water in order to provide for veterinary oversight or consultation.

Implementation of GFI 213—Judicious Use of Antimicrobials
Voluntary Withdrawal of 16 Antimicrobials for Use in Food-Producing Animals and Antimicrobials in Treating Human Illnesses.

Drug sponsors holding animal drug applications affected by the **Guidance For Industry (GFI) #213** requested in 2014 that FDA withdraw approval of a collective 19 animal drug applications because the products are no longer manufactured or marketed. Of these 19 applications, 16 are antimicrobials affected by GFI #213 that details the phase out of the use of medically important antimicrobials in food-producing animals for production purposes.

http://www.fda.gov/AnimalVeteri-nary/NewsEvents/CVMUpdates/ucm392461.htm?source=govdelivery&utm_me-dium=email&utm_source=govdelivery

Besides the withdrawal, FDA at the end of 2016, focused on medically important antimicrobials; that is, those critical for treating human disease used in animal feed or water that, according to FDA, have at least one therapeutic indication without a defined duration of use.

Veterinary Feed Directive Final Rule

Once a manufacturer voluntarily makes these changes, its medically important antimicrobial drugs can no longer be used for production purposes, and their use to treat, control, or prevent disease in animals will require veterinary oversight. Therefore, besides the final guidance, FDA issued a final rule effective June 2015. The use of VFD drugs in feed requires specific authorization by a licensed veterinarian based on procedures outlined in the agency's VFD regulations. The VFD proposed rule is intended to update the existing VFD process to clarify and increase the flexibility of the administrative requirements for the distribution and use of VFD drugs. Such updates to the VFD process will assist in the transition of OTC products to their new VFD status. The proposed rule addresses shortages as well.

Further, once product labeling is voluntarily changed, it will be a violation of the FDCA to use these products in feed for production purposes. In addition, FDA's regulations on extralabel use do not permit drugs to be used in an extralabel manner for production purposes, whether administered through feed or otherwise, since the regulations do not permit extralabel use for non-therapeutic purposes. The products affected by this plan have over-the-counter (OTC) product status. A key component of FDA's plan is to transition these products from their current OTC status to one that will require producers to have a prescription or order from a licensed veterinarian to obtain these products. **See: NOTE-Final Rule link below.**

NOTE: Veterinary Feed Directive (Final Rule June 3, 2015 effective October 1, 2015).
https://www.federalregister.gov/articles/2015/06/03/2015-13393/veterinary-feed-directive

Tyson Foods pledged to eliminate the use of human antibiotics for its chickens and instead is using alternative products such as the bacteria in yogurt. *https://www.tysonfoods.com/sustainability/animal-well-being/antibiotics-hormones-steroids*

CRITICAL ANALYSIS: Evaluate whether the phase out and veterinary feed directive rule solves the indiscriminate use of antimicrobials in food producing animals and protect human and animal health.

Mad Cow Disease—BSE Final Rule Cattle Materials Prohibition

Final Rule FDA—Bovine Spongiform Encephalopathy (2016)

http://www.fda.gov/Food/NewsEvents/ConstituentUpdates/ucm490542.htm

As the regulator of animal feed, FDA plays a key role in protecting United States cattle from bovine spongiform encephalopathy (BSE), also referred to as "mad cow" disease. In order to diminish the possible risk of bovine spongiform encephalopathy (BSE), or more commonly referred to as "mad cow disease," in human food, FDA issued a final rule in 2016 that finalized three interim final rules from 2004, 2005 and 2008. The final rule specifies definitions for prohibited cattle materials and bars their use in human food, dietary supplements, and cosmetics. These materials include:

➤ *Specified risk materials (SRMs): brain, skull, eyes, trigeminal ganglia, spinal cord, vertebral column (excluding the vertebrae of the tail, the transverse processes of the thoracic and lumbar vertebrae, and the wings of the sacrum), and dorsal root ganglia (DRG) of cattle 30 months of age and older, and tonsils and distal ileum of the small intestine from all cattle;*

➤ *The small intestine from all cattle unless the distal ileum has been properly removed;*

➤ *Material from non-ambulatory disabled cattle; and*

➤ *Material from cattle not inspected and passed, or mechanically separated (MS) (Beef).*

The rule clarifies that milk and milk products, hides and hide-derived products, tallow that contains no more than 0.15 percent insoluble impurities, and tallow derivatives are not prohibited cattle materials. The FDA also finalized the process for designating a country as not subject to BSE-related restrictions applicable to FDA regulated human food and cosmetics. Although gelatin was never considered a prohibited cattle material, nevertheless, the rule defines gelatin and explains that gelatin is not considered a prohibited cattle material if it is manufactured using customary stipulated industry processes.

Final Rule USDA— Cattle Material Prohibition in Food, Cosmetics and Supplements

A final rule issued by FSIS on July 12, 2007 prohibits the slaughter of downer cattle when presented for pre-slaughter inspection. The final rule affirms two interim final rules published on January 12, 2004. 69 Fed. Reg. 1862, 1885. The ban on bovine-derived material goes beyond human food and applies to cosmetics and dietary supplements as indicated below. In an unusual administrative step, USDA's interim final rules were published in January 2004 and by FDA in July 2004, Prohibited Cattle Materials Docket No. 2004N-0081. Specifically, the interim and now final rule prohibits the following materials from FDA regulated human food, cosmetics and dietary supplements.

➤ *Any material from "Downer" cattle (cattle that cannot walk);*

➤ *Any material from "Dead" cattle (cattle that die on the farm before reaching a slaughter plant);*

➤ *Specified Risk Materials or SRM's such as the brain, skull, eyes, trigeminal ganglia, spinal cord, vertebral column, and dorsal root ganglia from cattle 30 months or older and the distal ileum, a part of the small intestine and tonsils from all cattle despite age or health;*

➤ *Restrictions on techniques to mechanically remove meat from bones and*

➤ *Prohibits the use of "air-injection" stunning.*

NOTE: See *"Prohibition of the Use of Specified Risk Materials for Human Food and Requirements for the Disposition of Non-Ambulatory Disabled Cattle"; "Prohibition of the Use of Certain Stunning Devices Used to Immobilize Cattle During Slaughter"*, **72 Fed. Reg. 38,700 (July 13, 2007) (codified at 9 C.F.R. pts. 309, 310, and 318).**

Another USDA FSIS rule finalized in 2007, is designed to lower the risk that cattle could be inadvertently fed prohibited protein, which led to the BSE epidemic in United Kingdom cattle in the 1980's and 1990's. This rule addresses the following:

➢ *Bans mammalian blood and blood products as a protein source;*

➢ *Bans the use of "poultry litter" as a feed ingredient for ruminant animals;*

➢ *Bans the use of "plate waste" that is, meat scraps and uneaten meat collected from large restaurants; and*

➢ *Requires equipment, facilities or production lines to be dedicated to non-ruminant animal feeds if protein is used that is prohibited in ruminant feed.*

CRITICAL ANYALYSIS: Evaluate the final FDA 2016 rule about BSE and Cattle Material (link above) and postulate why there was such a lengthy time for this rule to become final.

Pet Food Regulation

Pet food, including dry and canned food and pet treats, is considered animal feed. Like other animal feed, FDA regulates pet food and establishes standards for labeling. Pet food labeling is regulated at two levels: federal and state. The federal regulations, enforced by FDA's Center for Veterinary Medicine, establish standards that apply to all animal feeds as follows: Proper identification of the product; Net quantity statement; Manufacturer's address; and Proper listing of ingredients.

Additionally, some states enforce their own labeling regulations. Many of these follow the model pet food regulations of the Association of American Feed Control Officials (AAFCO), a non-government advisory body with representative regulatory officials from all the states. These model regulations are more specific than federal regulations, covering aspects of labeling such as product name, nutritional adequacy statement, feeding directions, and calorie statements.

Turtles, Geckos and Salmonella

FDA enforces a regulation regarding a turtle ban based on the regulation: *Turtles Intrastate and Interstate Requirements* under 21 C.F.R. sec. 1240.62 which bans the sale of turtles with a carapace (upper shell) length of less than 4 inches. This regulation falls under the Public Health Service Act and is enforced by FDA in collaboration with state and local health jurisdictions. The reason for the ban, in effect since 1975, is due to turtle-associated salmonellosis. However, in 2013 FDA published a direct final rule that amended this regulation concerning the ban on the sale and distribution of small turtles in intrastate and interstate commerce. The direct final rule removes the provisions making viable turtle eggs and live turtles with a carapace length of less than four inches held for sale or offered for any other type of commercial distribution in violation of the ban routinely subject to destruction by or under the supervision of FDA. Yet, the 2013 direct final rule does not change the substantive provisions of the regulations, which make it still illegal to sell or distribute viable turtle eggs and turtles with a carapace length of less than four inches. The 1975 regulation contained a procedure for FDA to mandate destruction of violative turtle eggs and turtles. Alternatives to destruction include: raising turtles until they reach a carapace length of four inches or greater; donation to a scientific, educational, or exporting the turtles in compliance with applicable laws.

https://www.ecfr.gov/cgi-bin/text-idx?SID=8682eadcdc9d6079d0a71bd809502a58&mc=true&tpl=/ecfrbrowse/Title21/21cfr1240_main_02.tpl

http://www.cdc.gov/Features/SalmonellaFrogTurtle/

NOTE: See CDC report *http://www.cdc.gov/salmonella/small-turtles-10-15/*

According to the CDC and FDA Geckos also can be the source of a *Salmonella* **outbreak.**

CRITICAL ANALYSIS: A salmonella outbreak was linked to frozen rodents for use in feeding reptiles. Reptile Industry Inc.'s Arctic Mice brand frozen rodents were available at PetSmart, were linked to an outbreak of *Salmonella* Typhimurium illnesses in people. The product was used as reptile and amphibian food. PetSmart stopped selling the product from Reptile Industries Suppose you represent PetSmart, what other preventive measures would you advise?

Genetically Engineered Animals and Cloning

http://www.fda.gov/AnimalVeterinary/DevelopmentApprovalProcess/GeneticEngineering/Genetically EngineeredAnimals/default.htm

Genetically engineered (GE) animals (modified in part)

Genetically engineered (GE) animals were first developed in the 1980s. Genetic engineering generally refers to the use of recombinant DNA (rDNA) techniques to introduce new characteristics or traits into an organism. When scientists splice together pieces of DNA and introduce a spliced DNA segment into an organism to give the organism new properties, it is called rDNA technology. The spliced piece of DNA is called the rDNA construct. A GE animal is one that contains an rDNA construct intended to give the animal a new trait or characteristic. Genetic engineering already is widely used in agriculture to make crops like corn and soy resistant to pests or herbicides. In medicine, genetic engineering is used to develop microbes that can produce pharmaceuticals. In food processing, genetic engineering is used to produce microorganisms that more efficiently aid in baking, brewing, and cheese making. FDA pre-market approval requirements apply to GE animals. According to FDA, scientists are developing GE animals for a variety of applications, such as to:

> ➢ *Produce pharmaceuticals to be used for other animals and humans;*
> ➢ *Decrease the environmental impact of large-scale agricultural practices by decreasing the amount of chemicals such as phosphate in manure, thereby reducing water pollution;*
> ➢ *Serve as a source of cells, tissue, and organs closely matched to humans so that they may be able to be transplanted into humans without rejection;*
> ➢ *Produce high value materials such as those used for surgical sutures and personal protection devices such as body armor for military and law enforcement use;*
> ➢ *Produce highly specific antimicrobials that target disease-causing bacteria such as E. coli 0157:H7 or Salmonella; and*
> ➢ *Provide more healthful or more efficiently produced food.*

GE animals that produce pharmaceuticals provide natural production systems for therapeutic proteins previously available only through purification from human cadavers or animal carcasses. Those opportunities include production of growth factors and inhibitors used to treat metabolic diseases, and cancer. The biological similarity to humans could make GE animals an excellent choice for producing therapeutic proteins, and could boost the manufacturing capacity for critically important pharmaceuticals in short supply. GE animals with new traits for disease resistance, or drought and heat tolerance, may allow for high quality food to be produced in parts of the world where disease, climate, or accessibility of forage material have previously limited the ability to raise food animals.

Cloning

According to FDA, meat and milk from clones of cattle, swine, goats and the offspring of clones from species customarily eaten is safe. FDA, through the Center for Veterinary Medicine, issued a risk assessment plan and guidance on animal cloning. The guidance titled: *Use of Animal Clones and Clone Progeny for Human Food and Animal Feed* addresses risk identified in the assessment and establishes risk management methods.

CRITICAL ANALYSIS: Despite safety assurances, assess the legal issues related to cloning as well as genetically engineered animals.

Labeling and Claims

A feed label should contain information describing the feed product and any details necessary for the safe and effective use of the feed. The federal regulations concerning the labeling of animal feeds are published in Part 501 of the 21 CFR. The FDCA defines "labeling" as all labels and other written, printed or graphic matter upon any article or any of its containers or wrappers, or accompanying such articles. Courts have interpreted labeling to include promotional brochures, promotional pamphlets, testimonials, product information sheets, and books by way of illustration. In addition, promotion of an animal product on the Internet for unapproved drug claims can cause the product to be misbranded under the FDCA, if the product label fails to bear adequate directions for the uses promoted on the Internet. In addition to meeting federal labeling requirements, animal feed products are also subject to individual state laws. Under many state regulations, the feed label must include the following information:

> ➢ Brand Name, if any; Product Name; Purpose Statement; Guaranteed Analysis; List of Ingredients; Directions for Use; Warning or Caution Statements; Name and Address of Manufacturer; and Quantity Statement.

Health Claims under the Nutrition Labeling and Education Act

Under the FDCA, expressed or implied claims that establish the intended use to cure, treat, prevent or mitigate disease, or affect the structure/function of the body in a manner other than food (nutrition, aroma, or taste), identify an intent to offer the product as a "drug." Unless the safety and efficacy was established for its intended use by approval of a New Animal Drug Application (NADA), it could be subject to regulatory action as an adulterated drug. CVM has incorporated the philosophy of Nutrition Labeling and Education Act (NLEA) of 1990 in its policies in order to permit meaningful health information on pet foods. Examples are:

> ➢ *Maintains health of urinary tract; Low magnesium; Reduces plaque and tartar; Reduces hairballs in cats; and Improved digestibility.*
> ➢ *CVM follows the Association of American Feed Control Officials (AAFCO) regulations for terms such as:*
> ➢ *Light; Lean;*
> ➢ *Less or reduced calories; and Less or reduced fat.*
> ➢ *Feed manufacturers provide substantiation that the desired statement is truthful and not misleading. Such a claim is reviewed by CVM prior to its use on product labeling.*

Dietary Supplement Promotion for Animals

http://www.fda.gov/AnimalVeterinary/Products/AnimalFoodFeeds/ucm050223.htm (edited)

The marketing and promotion of dietary supplements products for animals continues to escalate. However, the Center for Veterinary Medicine (CVM) considers the Dietary Supplement Health and Education Act of 1994 (DSHEA) inapplicable and has safety concerns with using dietary supplements intended for humans. Some dietary supplements products marketed for animals contain ingredients that could be unsafe food additives or unapproved new animal drugs, making the products unsafe for the animals. Animal food does not require preapproval prior to marketing, although the ingredients must be either "generally recognized as safe" for the intended use or be an approved food additive. FDA issued a notice in the Federal Register, 61 Fed. Reg. 17706 (April 22, 1996) titled *Inapplicability of the Dietary Supplement Health and Education Act to Animal Products.*

Products marketed as dietary supplements or "feed supplements" for animals still fall under the Food, Drug and Cosmetic Act (FDCA) prior to DSHEA. That is, they are considered "foods" or "new animal drugs" depending on the intended use. The regulatory status of a product is determined on a case-by-case basis employing standards in Guide 1240.3605 in Program Policy and Procedures Manual. Dietary supplements for animals such as vitamin and mineral products have been marketed for many years. Most of these products include ingredients that are approved food additives, generally recognized as safe (GRAS) substances, or ingredients listed in the Official Publication of the Association of American Feed Control Officials (AAFCO).

CVM Authority—CVM is responsible for ensuring that animal drugs are safe, effective, and can be manufactured to a consistent standard. Safety includes drug safety for the animals, environment, and for people who consume animal-derived products. Animal dietary supplements can fit under the definition of food, drug, food additive, or GRAS substance.

Food—There is no requirement that animal foods have pre-market approval by CVM. The FDCA requires that animal foods, like human foods, be pure, wholesome, contain no harmful or deleterious substances, and truthfully labeled.

Drug—The FDCA defines a drug, in part, as "an article intended for use in the diagnosis, cure, mitigation, treatment, or prevention of disease, or an article intended to affect the structure or function of the body other than food." When a substance, including one considered food, is intended to be used for the treatment or prevention of disease or for a "non-food" structure/function effect, FDA considers it a drug. Under the Act, a new animal drug must be shown to be safe and effective for its intended use by adequate data from controlled scientific studies as part of a New Animal Drug Application (NADA).

Food Additive—In 1958, Congress amended the Act to require the pre-market clearance of additives whose safety was not generally recognized. The Act was also amended to deem food unsafe and adulterated if it contains an unapproved food additive. A food additive petition must be filed with FDA that establishes that a food additive is beneficial and safe for its intended use.

Gras Substance—The Act also states that substances added to food that qualified scientists generally recognize as safe (GRAS) under the conditions of the intended use are not "food additives" and as such are exempt from pre-clearance approval. A GRAS substance is GRAS only for an intended purpose. For example, sodium aluminosilicate is GRAS as an anticaking agent. It has been purported to bind mycotoxins and prevent absorption from the intestinal tract, but is not GRAS for this use. A food substance also cannot be GRAS for the prevention, treatment, or mitigation of a disease. Therefore, chondroitin sulfate cannot be GRAS to prevent or treat arthritis. For this use, this ingredient would be a drug. CVM has used regulatory discretion and has not required food additive petitions for some substances that do not raise any safety concerns.

AAFCO Ingredient Definition—This ingredient definition process is done to conserve CVM resources, as food additive approval is time-consuming. Although ingredients used under regulatory discretion are still unapproved food additives, CVM agrees that it will not take regulatory action as long as the labeling is consistent with the accepted intended use, the labeling or advertising does not make drug claims, and that new data are not received that raise questions concerning safety or suitability.

DSHEA Does Not Apply to Animal Supplements—When Congress enacted the DSHEA in 1994, it created a new category of substances and new regulatory scheme. The Act was amended to define a dietary supplement as a product intended to supplement the diet and that contains at least one or more of the following ingredients: a vitamin; a mineral; a herb or other botanical; an amino acid; a dietary substance for use to supplement the diet by increasing total dietary intake; or a concentrate, metabolite, constituent, extract or combination of any of the previously mentioned ingredients. The main effect of DSHEA was to remove certain dietary ingredients from regulation as food additives, which require pre-market approval.

Products marketed as dietary supplements for humans still fall under the pre-DSHEA regulatory scheme when marketed for animals; that is, they are considered food, food additives, new animal drugs, or GRAS depending on the intended use. Most of these types of products on the market would be considered unapproved and unsafe food additives or new animal drugs based on current intended uses. While these products are technically in violation of the law, they are of low enforcement priority except for when public or animal health concerns arise.

CVM's concerns about certain dietary supplements focus on three main areas:

> *Human food safety—supplements that are used in food animals, including horses that are used for food, must be shown to be safe for people who consume products from the animals. Without these data, there is no assurance that animal-derived food is safe.*
> *Animal safety—supplements must be shown to be safe to the animals. CVM and AAFCO have not received data showing that these products have actually been tested on animals to show that a particular level is appropriate or safe for the animals.*
> *Manufacturing quality—supplements must be shown to be manufactured to a consistent standard (for example, shown to contain a given amount of the ingredient).*
> *In addition, some of these products are being marketed to treat or prevent disease. This moves them from the supplement category into the drug category. CVM is concerned that these products have not been shown to be safe and effective. In addition, some owners may be using these products instead of obtaining appropriate veterinary treatment for their animals.*
> *How can companies legally market animal dietary supplement products?*
> *Check the list of approved food additives and GRAS substances in Title 21, Part 570 - 584 of the Code of Federal Regulations.*
> *Check the list of ingredient definitions in the Official Publication of the Association of American Feed Control Officials.*

If the ingredient they propose to use in their product is not on either list, they can submit a Food Additive Petition or the information needed to list the ingredient in the AAFCO Official Publication. Companies may visit the AAFCO web site and contact the appropriate AAFCO investigator. Another option would be for them to contact the control officials within their State. Contact information for the AAFCO investigators and State Feed Control Officials may be found on the AAFCO website. If companies wish to market a new animal drug, they can submit a New Animal Drug Application (NADA) with CVM.

CRITICAL ANALYSIS: How should FDA handle the use of dietary supplements for animals including pets? Discuss the inapplicability of the Dietary Supplement and Health Education Act, safety and enforcement.

Flavorings and Colorings

The promotion of flavorings in pet food has proliferated. There are flavorings intended for animal use as well as flavorings intended for human use. Who is responsible in terms of safety issues associated with flavorings? Besides CVM, the Flavor and Extract Manufacturers Association (FEMS) as well the Association of American Feed Control Officials (AAFCO) are accountable for safety of flavorings added to products for animals. State departments of agriculture utilize the AAFCO "Official Publication Listing" of safe ingredients for animal use.

FDA safety determination is usually based on the "Generally Recognized as Safe" (GRAS) listing 21 C.F. R. Parts 182 and 184 or by a food additive petition. 21 C.F. R. Part 172, subpart F includes food additives approved flavorings for human use. There are no flavorings approved as food additives for use in animal food. Substances such as minerals, vitamins or other nutrients, flavorings, preservatives, or processing aids may be generally recognized as safe (GRAS) for an intended use (21 CFR 582 and 584) or must have approval as food additives (21 CFR 570, 571 and 573). Colorings must have approvals for that use as specified in 21 CFR 70 and be listed in Parts 73, 74, or 81.

CRITICAL ANALYSIS: Similar to the proliferation of dietary supplements for animal use, likewise the use of flavorings for animals has spiraled. Discuss safety issues.

Chapter 3: Postmarket Surveillance and Enforcement, Adverse Events, Compounding, Misbranding and Product Classification

CVM conducts postmarket surveillance through the Office of Surveillance and Compliance (OSC) by monitoring marketed animal drugs, food additives, and veterinary devices for both safety and efficacy. The appraisal of the safety of a new drug is done on a continuous basis through this office. Part of the Post-Approval Monitoring Programs (PAMP) involves submission of information by the drug sponsor to the OSC. PAMPs give FDA information related to antimicrobial susceptibility of foodborne pathogens in animals. State agencies, under inspection agreements with FDA, perform follow-up inspections of those involved in either the production or marketing of food animals or poultry for tissue residue violations. CVM's Tissue Residue Program objective is to do away with violative drug residues in edible tissue of food animals. OSCs objective is continued teamwork with USDA and FSIS on drugs and chemicals in meat and poultry products. Other responsibilities include:

> *Monitoring marketed animal drugs, food additives, and veterinary devices;*
> *Approval of food additive petitions after determining their safety and utility;*
> *Approval of Medicated Feed Mill Licenses after ensuring the sponsoring firm is operating in compliance with good manufacturing practice;*
> *Monitoring animal feeds for safety to the animals which receive them, to the public who consume the food products derived from treated animals, and to the environment;*
> *Monitoring approved veterinary drugs and food additives for safety and effectiveness;*
> *Enforcing industry compliance with the FDCA;*
> *Reviewing labels and provide assessment of their status;*
> *Withdrawal of drugs and food additives from the market when conditions warrant removal, based on scientific fact concerning a lack of safety and/or effectiveness;*
> *Monitoring laboratory investigators who conduct studies as part of the NADA approval;*
> *Monitoring the conduct of clinical investigators and sponsors of clinical investigations;*
> *Monitoring and evaluation of reports of adverse drug experiences for animal safety and public health issues;*
> *Collaborating with USDA/FSIS on drugs and chemicals in meat and poultry; and*
> *Developing and implementing policies that affect marketed products.*

Adverse Event Reports

Under section 514.80 (b) (21 CFR 514.80(b)) approved new animal drug applicants (NADAs) and approved abbreviated new animal drug applications (ANADAs) are required to report ADEs, as well as product and manufacturing defects. FDA Form 1932, for adverse event reporting, is the mandatory form used by manufacturers of animal drugs or the Marketing Authorization Holder (MAH). See: (OMB No. 0910-0645). FDA Form 1932a, *"Veterinary Adverse Experience Lack of Effectiveness or Product Defect Report"* is used to report adverse experiences intended for veterinarians and animal owners. According to CVM, the possibility of product failures is understandable due to inherent limitations imposed on pre-testing the product on a limited number of animals. The United States Department of Agriculture monitors reports for animal biologics, vaccines, bacterins and diagnostic kits while the United States Environmental Protection Agency handles pesticides involving topically applied external parasiticides.

https://www.fda.gov/animalveterinary/safetyhealth/reportaproblem/ucm212682.htm

Postmarket Surveillance—Jerky Pet Treats

http://www.fda.gov/animalveterinary/safetyhealth/productsafetyinformation/ucm360951.htm (modified)
https://www.fda.gov/AnimalVeterinary/NewsEvents/CVMUpdates/ucm500776.htm

FDA details there is no defined link yet continues to investigate the cause of reported pet illnesses associated with jerky pet treat products, the majority imported from China.

Case numbers—FDA received approximately 5,200 complaints of illness in pets that ate chicken, duck, or sweet potato jerky treats, nearly all of which are imported from China (December 31,

2015). The reports involve more than 5,600 dogs, 24 cats, three people, and include more than 1,140 canine deaths. Symptoms are similar to earlier reports: approximately 60 percent of the cases report gastrointestinal/liver disease, 30 percent kidney or urinary disease, with the remaining 10 percent of complaints including various other signs such as neurologic, dermatologic, and immunologic symptoms. About 15 percent of kidney or urinary cases tested positive for Fanconi syndrome, a rare kidney disease associated with the investigation.

Response to Dear Veterinarian Letter—FDA received many well-documented case reports that have and continue to provide valuable information for investigation purposes.

Testing—for contaminants in jerky pet treats has not disclosed a root cause for the reported symptoms in pets. As of Dec 31, 2015, FDA and Vet-LIRN collected approximately 530 jerky treat samples related to more than 290 consumer-related complaints, plus more than 450 retail samples (unopened bags from a store or shipment) and performed a number of tests on these samples.

CRITICAL ANALYSIS: Discuss the reluctance of FDA to recommend a recall or institute a seizure action. *http://www.fda.gov/AnimalVeterinary/SafetyHealth/ProductSafetyInformation/ucm360951.htm*

Nationwide Recalls—Wheat Gluten Melamine Contamination

Pet food products are also voluntarily recalled similar to other FDA regulated products. FDA posts press releases, notices of recalls and market withdrawals from the firms involved. One of the largest nationwide recalls in FDA history involved contaminated pet food. The recall involved over 150 brands of dog and cat food. Menu Foods, Inc. voluntarily recalled dog and cat foods produced at two of its facilities and sold under a number of different brand names. Other companies voluntarily withdrew products as well. Reports received by FDA suggested that approximately 1,950 cats and 2,200 dogs died after eating pet food contaminated with melamine. Over 800 metric tons of tainted wheat gluten was imported into the United States from China with invoices totaling nearly near $850,000. Those indicted included two Chinese nationals and the businesses they operate, a U.S. company and its president and chief executive officer. Sally Qing Miller, controlling owner and president, Chemnutra, and her husband, Stephen S. Miller, owner and chief executive officer of Chemnutra and their company, Chemnutra, Inc., pleaded guilty. The Chemnutra company bought food and food components in China and imported those items into the United States to sell to companies in the food industry. Each of the three co-defendants pleaded guilty to one count of selling adulterated food and one count of selling misbranded food. The shipments of wheat gluten, tainted with melamine, were sold and shipped throughout the United States. The defendants admitted that the labeling of the wheat gluten was false and misleading because the wheat gluten was represented to have a minimum protein level of 75 percent, when in fact it did not. The labeling was also false and misleading because melamine was not listed on the label as an ingredient. Wheat gluten is the natural protein derived from wheat or wheat flour, which is extracted and dried to yield a powder of high protein content. Pet food manufacturers use wheat gluten as a binding agent in the manufacture of certain types of pet food to thicken pet food "gravy." Melamine has no approved use as an ingredient in human or animal food in the United States. Melamine is used to create products such as plastics, cleaning products, counter tops, glues, inks and fertilizers. Mixing melamine with wheat gluten made the wheat gluten appear to have a higher protein level than was actually present. The Millers were subject to a sentence of up to two years in federal prison without parole, plus a fine up to $200,000 and an order of restitution. ChemNutra was subject to a fine up to $400,000 and an order of restitution. The defendants were sentenced as follows:

CHEMNUTRA, Inc. Judgment Count(s) 1, 14. The defendant pleaded guilty to Counts 1 and 14 of the Indictment on 6/16/09. **PROBATION:** The defendant organization is hereby sentenced to probation for a term of 3 years on each count, terms to run concurrently with each other. STANDARD AND SPECIAL CONDITIONS OF PROBATION IMPOSED. MSA: $250.00.
FINE: $25,000.00. No restitution. (Feb. 10, 2010).

SALLY MLLER Judgment Count(s) 1, 14. The defendant pleaded guilty to Counts 1 and 14 of the Indictment on 6/16/09. **PROBATION:** The defendant is hereby placed on probation for a term of 3 years on each count, terms to run concurrent. STANDARD AND SPECIAL CONDITIONS OF PROBATION IMPOSED. MSA: $50.00; FINE: $5,000.00. No restitution.

STEPHEN S. MILLER Judgment Count(s) 1, 14. The defendant pleaded guilty to Counts 1 and 14 of the Indictment on 6/16/09. **PROBATION:** The defendant is hereby placed on probation for a term of 3 years on each count, term to run concurrent. STANDARD AND SPECIAL CONDITIONS OF PROBATION. MSA: $50.00. FINE: $5,000.00. No restitution. Signed on 2/10/2010 by Magistrate Judge John T. Maughmer. (Feb. 10, 2010).

http://www.fda.gov/AnimalVeterinary/SafetyHealth/RecallsWithdrawals/ucm129575.htm

CRITICAL ANALYSIS: Evaluate the sentences imposed. Include a discussion about the magnitude of the recall. *http://www.justice.gov/usao/mow/news2009/miller.ple.htm* (edited)

Seizure Action—Unsanitary Conditions

The FDCA permits the seizure and condemnation of food, including food for animals, shipped in interstate commerce that has been "adulterated," or held for sale under unsanitary conditions where it might have been contaminated with filth as illustrated in the Petco seizure action below. According to FDA, the company had been warned of unsanitary conditions and a follow-up inspection revealed live and dead birds and rodents in the pet food warehouse.

U.S. Seizure at Petco Warehouse—Rodent and Bird Infestation

http://www.fda.gov/NewsEvents/Newsroom/PressAnnouncements/2008/ucm116915.htm

United States Marshals, seized various animal food products stored under allegedly unsanitary conditions, including widespread and active rodent and bird infestation, at a PETCO Animal Supplies, Inc., distribution center in Joliet (Chicago). The action was taken after the United States filed a civil lawsuit and obtained a warrant from a federal judge to seize the products at the warehouse operated by the San Diego-based animal food and supply company. According to the complaint, the FDA inspected the warehouse in April 2008, and found live and dead rodents and birds on or around the containers of pet food, as well as rodent excreta pellets and bird droppings throughout the facility. Inspectors allegedly found holes and gaps in the warehouse allowing entry for the birds and rodents, and they observed debris outside the building that can harbor rodents. FDA investigators informed PETCO management in late April of their findings, but a follow-up inspection last month confirmed continuing, widespread rodent and bird infestation, according to the complaint. Investigators at the May inspection continued to see live and dead rodents and birds on or around the food containers, some of which had been gnawed and defiled by excrement, the lawsuit alleged. The Federal Food, Drug and Cosmetic Act permits the seizure and condemnation of food, including food for animals, shipped in interstate commerce that has been "adulterated," or held for sale under unsanitary conditions where it might have been contaminated with filth. Officials emphasized that there are no known immediate public health risks posed by the seized pet food and that no incidents of human or animal illness have been traced to products stored at the warehouse.

CRITICAL ANALYSIS: Why was the product was seized?

Warning and Advisory Action Letters

An action advisory letter provides an opportunity for a company or firm to correct deficiencies prior to FDA initiating enforcement action. CVM will inform a company of correction action needed in the form of an advisory action letter which include both "Titled" and "Untitled" Warning Letters. Titled warning letters are addressed to the President or CEO. For example, in 2018 an advisory letter was issued to Elanco Animal Health, Inc. for Promotional Claims NADA 141-455 GALLIPRANT® (grapiprant tablets)

https://www.fda.gov/downloads/AnimalVeterinary/GuidanceComplianceEnforcement/ComplianceEnforcement/UCM608419.pdf

NOTE: Elanco was issued a similar advisory letter related to promotional claims concerning CVM NADA 141-361, Pulmotil AC (tilmicosin phosphate) back in 2016. **See link below.**
https://www.fda.gov/AnimalVeterinary/GuidanceComplianceEnforcement/ComplianceEnforcement/ucm042132.htm

Arrow Reliance, Inc. dba Darwin's Natural Pet Products

OVERNIGHT DELIVERY SIGNATURE REQUIRED In reply, refer to: WL CMS 547381
https://www.fda.gov/ICECI/EnforcementActions/WarningLetters/ucm603589.htm
Gary T. Tashjian, President Arrow Reliance, Inc. dba Darwin's Natural Pet Products
350 Treck Drive
Tukwila, Washington 98188

WARNING LETTER

Dear Mr. Tashjian:

The U.S. Food and Drug Administration (FDA) conducted an inspection of your raw pet food manufacturing facility in Tukwila, Washington, on December 6 through 7, 2017, and January 25, 2018, following customer complaints regarding your products. In response to these customer complaints and during and after our inspection, FDA investigators collected samples of a number of raw pet food products from your customers and your manufacturing facility. Analysis of these raw pet food products revealed they were contaminated with *Salmonella, Listeria*, and/or Shiga toxin-producing *Escherichia coli* O128. Your raw pet food products are food under section 201(f) of the Federal Food, Drug, and Cosmetic Act (the Act) [21 U.S.C. § 321(f)], because they are articles used for food for animals. Based on the analytical results, these products are adulterated under section 402(a)(1) of the Act, which states that food is deemed to be adulterated if it bears or contains a poisonous or deleterious substance which may render it injurious to health. The introduction or delivery for introduction into interstate commerce of an adulterated food violates section 301(a) of the Act [21 U.S.C. § 331(a)].

Adulterated Animal Food —Based on a consumer complaint received by FDA and your firm's recall history, an unopened sample of Darwin's Natural Selections Turkey with Organic Vegetables Meals for Dogs, lot 40507, manufactured on September 20, 2017, (FDA sample 441268) was collected by FDA on November 15, 2017, from one of your customers. The sample was analyzed by an FDA laboratory on November 29, 2017, and was found positive for *Salmonella*. An unopened sample of Darwin's Natural Selections Chicken with Organic Vegetables Meals for Dogs, lot 40727, manufactured on September 26, 2017, (FDA sample 441270) was collected on November 15, 2017, from the same customer. That sample was analyzed by an FDA laboratory on November 27, 2017, and was found positive for Salmonella and Listeria monocytogenes. An unopened sample of Darwin's Natural Selections Duck with Organic Vegetables Meals for Dogs, lot 40487, manufactured on September 29, 2017, (FDA sample 441269) was collected on November 15, 2017, from the same customer. That sample was analyzed by an FDA laboratory on November 29, 2017, and was found positive for Salmonella. You initiated a nationwide recall of these specific lots of products after FDA notified you of the sample results. The FDA classified your recall as Class I, based on *Salmonella* and *Listeria monocytogenes* posing acute, life-threatening hazards to health. Also, an unopened sample of Darwin's ZooLogics Chicken Meals for Dogs, lot 41567, manufactured on November 2, 2017, (FDA sample 1031923) was collected by FDA on January 24, 2018, from one of your customers. That sample was analyzed by an FDA laboratory on February 1, 2018, and was found positive for *Salmonella*. An unopened sample of Darwin's ZooLogics Duck Meals for Dogs, lot 41957, manufactured on November 16, 2017, (FDA sample 1031921) was collected by FDA on January 24, 2018, from the same customer. That sample was analyzed by an FDA laboratory on February 6, 2018, and was found positive for Salmonella. You initiated a nationwide recall of these specific lots of these products after FDA notified you of the sample results. The FDA classified your recall as Class I, based on *Salmonella* posing an acute, life-threatening hazard to health. Further, an unopened sample of Darwin's Natural Selections Chicken with Organic Vegetables Meals for Dogs, lot 43887, manufactured on January 30, 2018, (FDA sample 1042721) was collected by FDA on February 28, 2018, from one of your customers. That sample was analyzed by an FDA laboratory on March 19, 2018, and was found positive for

296

Salmonella. An unopened sample of Darwin's ZooLogics Turkey Meals for Dogs, lot 44127, manufactured on February 4, 2018, (FDA sample 1042727) was collected by FDA on February 28, 2018, from one of your customers. That sample was analyzed by an FDA laboratory on March 20, 2018, and was found positive for *Salmonella* and Shiga toxin-producing *Escherichia coli* O128. An unopened sample of Darwin's Natural Selections Duck with Organic Vegetables Meals for Dogs, lot 44147, manufactured on February 5, 2018, (FDA sample 1042728) was collected by FDA on February 28, 2018, from one of your customers. That sample was analyzed by an FDA laboratory on March 16, 2018 and was found positive for *Salmonella*. An unopened sample of Darwin's ZooLogics Chicken Meals for Dogs, lot 44037, manufactured on February 7, 2018, (FDA sample 1042723) was collected by FDA on February 28, 2018, from one of your customers. That sample was analyzed by an FDA laboratory on March 16, 2018 and was found positive for *Salmonella*. You initiated a nationwide recall of these specific lots of these products after FDA notified you of the sample results.

Public Health Impact of Pathogens *** In July 2013, FDA issued a Compliance Policy Guide (CPG) addressing the presence of *Salmonella* in Food for Animals, CPG 690.800, *https://www.fda.gov/downloads/iceci/compliancemanuals/compliancepolicyguidance-manual/ucm361105.pdf Listeria monocytogenes* is a pathogenic bacterium that is a known animal and human food pathogen posing an acute danger to human and animal health. It can proliferate in animal food processing facilities without proper controls. Handling or consuming these contaminated raw pet foods can lead to a severe, sometimes life-threatening illness called listeriosis, an atypical foodborne illness of major public health concern due to the severity of the disease, its high case-fatality rate, long incubation, and predilection for individuals with underlying conditions. *** Shiga toxin-producing *Escherichia coli* O128 (STEC) is a pathogenic bacterium that can cause serious illness in humans. Handling or consuming raw pet foods contaminated with this pathogenic bacterium can lead to *Escherichia coli (E. coli)* infections.

Food Safety System—Unlike other human and pet foods which are heat-treated or are intended to be cooked, raw pet food has the potential to pose a significant risk to human and animal health because raw pet food is produced with minimal processing and is intended to be handled by humans and fed to animals without cooking, which would kill potentially harmful pathogens. It is therefore essential that your firm has a food safety system in place to prevent and control contamination of your products and facility. Aspects of such a system may include: proper implementation and review of cleaning and sanitization procedures, review and/or testing of your incoming materials and outgoing products, review and/or testing of your facility and environment for possible contamination, a kill step to destroy microorganism contamination, and root cause investigation and corrective action procedures when problems arise. ***

Additional Recalls and Sample Results—In September 2016, in response to a customer complaint of dog illnesses, you analyzed three lots of your raw pet food. ***You initiated a nationwide recall of these specific lots of these products. The FDA classified your recall as Class I, based on *Listeria monocytogenes* posing an acute, life-threatening hazard to health.Also, in September 2017, in response to a customer complaint of a kitten death, you analyzed one lot of your raw pet food, Darwin's Natural Selections Duck Meals for Cats, lot 38277, manufactured on June 1, 2017. This product was analyzed by your contract laboratory on September 19, 2017, and was found positive for *Salmonella*. You initiated a nationwide recall of this specific lot of this product. The FDA classified your recall as Class I, based on *Salmonella* posing an acute, life-threatening hazard to health. ***

Whole Genome Sequencing—In addition to these lots of your raw pet foods being contaminated with a variety of bacterial organisms, a customer provided information to FDA that *Salmonella* was isolated from both a deceased kitten and from an unopened package from the same lot of the raw cat food consumed by the kitten, specifically Darwin's Natural Selections Duck Meals for Cats, lot 38277, manufactured on June 1, 2017. The kitten necropsy indicated a severe systemic *Salmonella* infection, and *Salmonella* was isolated from the kitten's liver. Whole Genome Sequencing (WGS) analysis was conducted on these *Salmonella* isolates from the kitten and the unopened raw pet food package, as well as other *Salmonella* isolates obtained from your raw pet foods. *** This analysis indicates that your product may have caused the illness and death of the kitten.

Use of Bacteriophage—During a conference call between FDA and your firm on February 7, 2018, you indicated that your firm uses bacteriophage to reduce the pathogens in your raw pet foods. You stated that you have changed your protocol for applying the bacteriophage to your product; specifically, that you have increased your application of the bacteriophage. FDA notes that controls implemented should have scientifically based validation to ensure they effectively eliminate the pathogens in pet foods intended for distribution. These validated controls should also ensure the control of pathogens in the facility in which the controls are implemented. In addition, we have concerns about the use of these bacteriophage because we are unaware that they are generally recognized as safe, as described in Title 21, Code of Federal Regulations (21 CFR) 570.30, or the subject of a food additive regulation published in 21 CFR Part 573, describing food additives permitted in animal foods.

Please notify this office in writing within fifteen (15) business days from the date you receive this letter describing the specific steps you have taken to correct the noted violations, and to prevent these violations from recurring or other similar violations from occurring. You should include documentation of corrective actions you have taken to date. If your firm will not be able to complete corrective actions before you respond, please state the reason for the delay and include a timetable for implementation of those corrections. Your written response should be sent to:

U.S. Food and Drug Administration, 22215 26th Avenue SE, Suite 210, Bothell, Washington 98021, to the attention of LCDR Cynthia White, Compliance Officer. If you have questions, you may contact LCDR White at (425) 302-0422.

Sincerely, /s/ Miriam R. Burbach, District Director, Program Division Director (April 2, 2018)
cc: Washington State Department of Agriculture Food Safety Program

CRITICAL ANALYSIS: Review the warning letter. How would you advise your client in responding to FDA?

Permanent Injunction— Syfrett Feed Company, Inc.

https://www.justice.gov/opa/pr/district-court-enters-permanent-injunction-against-florida-company-and-senior-managers-stop

The U.S. District Court (Southern District Florida) entered a consent decree of permanent injunction against Syfrett Feed Company, Inc. , its owner and President Charles B. Syfrett I; Vice President Melissa S. Montes De Oca; and Operations Manager Charles B. Syfrett II (Okeechobee, Florida 2017). Under the consent decree the company must adequately control medicated animal feeds production. The Syfrett company was inspected three times and findings indicated multiple violations of the current good manufacturing practice (cGMP) regulations for medicated feeds. FDA inspectors determined that Syfrett Feed failed to: institute and maintain adequate procedures for the identification, storage and inventory control of drugs intended for use in medicated feeds; establish and use adequate procedures for all equipment used in the production and distribution of medicated feeds to avoid unsafe contamination of medicated and non-medicated feeds; and ensure that correct labels are used for all manufactured medicated feeds. A warning letter was issued following the January 2014, citing the cGMP violations. In 2014, Syfrett Feed informed the FDA that the company had received complaints relating to its horse pellet product and the subsequent euthanasia of 17 horses. The company agreed to suspend the production of the horse feed connected to this incident. The consent decree prohibited Syfrett Feed from processing, manufacturing, preparing, packing and distributing the medicated animal feed it produces until an expert was hired to confirm that all cGMP regulations are adhered to in the manufacture of medicated feed.

Consent Decree—T&T Cattle and T&T Cattle Pearl

https://www.fda.gov/AnimalVeterinary/ucm248601.htm#Idaho

The U.S. District Court for the District of Idaho entered a consent decree of permanent injunction against owner Gregory T. Troost, doing business as T&T Cattle and T&T Cattle Pearl, and manager Mark A. Mourton of Parma, Idaho for violations including illegally administering animal drugs for uses that are not approved by the Food and Drug Administration. During FDA inspections in January 2002, January 2006, September 2010, and October through November 2012, investigators determined that the defendants had violated several provisions of the Federal Food, Drug, and Cosmetic Act. The violations included failure to keep adequate medication records to prevent unsafe drug residues in cattle offered for slaughter, failure to review treatment records prior to offering an animal for slaughter, and the use of medications for unapproved uses not specified on the drug label and in a manner that does not comply with FDA regulatory requirements. The defendants offered for slaughter seven dairy cows with illegal levels of drug residues. These included cows with tissues that tested positive for elevated levels of penicillin and sulfadimethoxine. Ingesting food containing excessive amounts of antibiotics and other drugs can cause severe adverse reactions among the general population even at very low levels and can harm consumers who are sensitive to antibiotics. To date, no illnesses have been reported.

The decree prohibits the defendants from selling animals for slaughter for human consumption until they have implemented record-keeping systems to identify and track animals that have been treated with drugs. These records must also note the drug used, dosage, time of administration and how long before slaughter the drug needs to be discontinued. If the defendants offer any animals for sale or slaughter, they also must provide written information about the animals' drug treatment status to the recipient of the animals. The FDA may order the defendants to cease operations if they fail to comply with any provisions of the consent decree, the Act, or FDA regulations. Failure to obey the terms of the consent decree could result in civil or criminal penalties.

CRITICAL ANALYSIS: Advise your client as to future possible proceedings concerning the above cases. Review the guidance document and Veterinary Feed Directive about antimicrobials and drug residues. See: This *Volume*, Chapter 2.

Pharmacy Compounding—*Franck's Lab., Inc.*

Is there a difference in drug compounding intended for humans and compounding for food producing animals versus compounding products for non-food producing animals? The animal compounding case of *Franck's* below provides that distinction.

Human Drug Compounding—Consent Decree of Permanent Injunction

In *United States v. Franck*, M.D. Fla., 5:16-cv-00085-CEM-PRL, a consent order of permanent injunction was issued (4/29/16) that effectively banned compounding pharmacy owner Paul W. Franck (DBA Trinity Care Solutions) from continuing to manufacture and distribute sterile drugs until the facility is in compliance with current good manufacturing practice standards. This means that Mr. Franck must hire an independent expert to certify that the facility has implemented the requisite corrective actions. Mr. Franck must also institute a reporting system to FDA of all adverse drug experiences associated with his drugs.

Animal Drug Compounding—Non-Food Producing Animals

Franck's Lab., originally decided in 2011, concerned pharmacy compounding for non-food producing animals. Franck's Lab., subsequently acquired by Wells Pharmacy Network, LLC, no longer engages in such compounding. A Joint Motion to Vacate the District Court's Judgment and Dismiss the Appeal by the government as Moot was granted Oct. 18, 2012. *The opinion was therefore withdrawn; however, it provides an excellent illustration of state versus federal regulatory authority of pharmacy compounding. The Drug Quality and Security Act, enacted in 2013, provides more direction as to regulatory authority.*

NOTE: The opinion that follows is included only for purpose of understanding the complexity of jurisdictional authority.

United States v. Franck's Lab., Inc.,
No. 5:10–cv–147–Oc–32TBS (Sept. 12, 2011)

TIMOTHY J. CORRIGAN, District Judge. In the seventy-plus years since Congress created the Food and Drug Administration, the FDA has never before sought to enjoin a state-licensed pharmacist from engaging in the traditional practice of bulk compounding of animal drugs. Here, the FDA seeks just such an injunction. ***

I. Facts and Procedural Posture: Mr. Franck, a Florida-licensed pharmacist in good standing since 1981, opened an independent pharmacy practice in Archer, Florida in 1983. *** That same year, Franck began to compound medications at the Ocala location for humans and "non-food-producing animals" (such as horses). Animal and veterinary drug compounding comprises roughly 40 percent of Franck's Lab's business, while human drug compounding accounts for the remaining 60 percent. Franck's compounds the majority of its animal medications from "bulk" active ingredients, which it receives from suppliers outside the state of Florida. *** Franck's holds a valid pharmacy license in each of the 47 states in which it is required to do so, and, nationwide, fills approximately 37,000 animal drug prescriptions per year. The FDA first inspected Franck's compounding facilities between September 29 and October 4, 2004 and, in January 2005, issued a warning. *** Franck's responded by letter dated January 27, 2005, asserting its intention to be in full compliance with all FDA requirements. However, Franck's also expressed disagreement with the FDA's position that bulk compounding of animal drugs was *per se* unlawful and noted that "[s]tate law and good compounding practices allow bulk compounding as long as there is a valid patient physician (veterinarian) relationship." *** In April 2009, a veterinarian commissioned Franck's to compound an injectable solution of the prescription drug Biodyl for the Venezuelan national polo team. Due to a mathematical error in the conversion of an ingredient (which went unnoticed by the prescribing veterinarian), the compounded medication was too potent and 21 polo horses died. The incident was thoroughly investigated by the Florida Board of Pharmacy, which imposed fines and reprimanded Franck's for the misfilled prescription. *** Though the Florida Board of Pharmacy had investigated and resolved the matter to its satisfaction, the Venezuelan polo pony incident prompted the FDA to reinspect Franck's facilities three times: May 4–20, 2009; June 18–23, 2009; and December 1–4, 2009. Subsequent to the May inspection, the FDA issued Franck's a Form FDA 483 which contained five specific observations, none of which identified bulk compounding of animal drugs as a concern. Franck's responded to the Form 483 by letter dated June 12, 2009. *** However, Franck's noted that: the observations that FDA has outlined involve pharmacy practices that we must strenuously assert are regulated by the Florida Department of Health and Board of Pharmacy. *** Without further response or discussion, FDA initiated this action in April of 2010, seeking to enjoin Franck's practice of distributing animal drugs compounded from bulk substances.

II. The Record Allows for Disposition on Cross–Motions for Summary Judgment: *** Rather, the FDA has taken the bright-line position that *any* compounding of animal medications from bulk substances violates its enabling statute, the Federal Food, Drug, and Cosmetic Act, 21 U.S.C. § 301, *et seq.* ("FDCA"), even when conducted by a state-licensed pharmacist for an individual animal patient pursuant to a valid veterinary prescription. ***

III. Background

A. Compounding and Compounding from Bulk Substances Compounding is a process by which a pharmacist combines, mixes, or alters ingredients to create a medication tailored to the needs of an individual human or animal patient. *** Under Florida law, pharmacists may compound medications when they are prescribed for individual patients by a licensed medical practitioner (i.e., a veterinarian). ***

B. The FDA's Regulation of Compounding

1. From 1938 to 1992: *** *For approximately the first 50 years after the enactment of the FDCA, the FDA generally left regulation of compounding to the States.* *** In 1992, in response to this concern, the FDA issued a Compliance Policy Guide, which announced that the *"FDA may, in the exercise of its enforcement discretion, initiate federal enforcement actions ... when the scope and nature of a pharmacy's activities raises the kinds of concerns normally associated with a manufacturer and ... results in significant violations of the new drug, adulteration, or misbranding provisions of the Act."* Compliance Policy Guide 7132.16 ([1992] Guide). ***

2. AMDUCA: In 1994, Congress passed the Animal Medicinal Drug Use Clarification Act ("AM-DUCA"), which amended the FDCA to permit certain off-label uses of FDA-approved human and animal drugs in the treatment of animals. 21 U.S.C. §§ 360b(a)(4) and (a)(5).***

3. The 1996 Guide: The 1996 Guide noted that the FDCA "does not distinguish compounding from manufacturing or other processing of drugs for use in animals," nor does it exempt pharmacists and veterinarians from the FDCA's new drug approval provisions. ***

4. FDAMA & Western States: In 1997, "in a move the Pharmacies call a reaction to the FDA's 1992 [Guide] and the FDA characterizes as a confirmation of it, Congress amended the FDCA by enacting the Food and Drug Modernization Act of 1997 ("FDAMA"), Pub.L. No. 105–115, 111 Stat. 2296 (codified as amended at 21 U.S.C. § 353a (2000))." *** In 2002, in *Western States,* 535 U.S. at 368–77, 122 S.Ct. 1497, 152 L.Ed.2d 563, the Court invalidated the advertising-related provisions of FDAMA, affirming the Ninth Circuit's holding that those portions were unconstitutional restrictions on commercial speech."***

5. The 2002 and 2003 Guides and Beyond: In the wake of *Western States,* the FDA issued revised Compliance Policy Guides addressing compounding of human and animal drugs. *** And despite the 2002 Guide's allowance of compounding from bulk for human drugs so long as the bulk ingredients are FDA-approved, the 2003 Guide lists "[c]om-pounding finished drugs [for animals] ... from bulk substances" among the factors which "raise[ ] the kind[ ] of concern normally associated with a manufacturer." ***

IV. The Court's Decision

A. Introduction: The FDA says this is a simple case: the literal, plain language of the original FDCA, enacted in 1938, gives it the enforcement authority to prevent pharmacists from bulk compounding medications for non-food-producing animals. ***

B. Discussion

1. The FDCA's Language and the New Animal Drug Approval Process: The FDCA broadly defines "drug" to include "articles intended for use in the diagnosis, cure, mitigation, treatment, or prevention of disease in man or other animals." 21 U.S.C. § 321(g)(1)(B). ***

2. Algon, 9/1 Kg. Containers, and Medical Center: *** Both cases were enforcement actions against *suppliers* to prohibit them from supplying unapproved bulk ingredients to *veterinarians* for use in compounding. Neither case mentioned pharmacists or the practice of pharmacy. ***

3. Chevron Step One: Whether Congress Intended to Grant the FDA Authority to Regulate Traditional Compounding:

a. Elephants-in-mouse holes doctrine: *** The elephant-in-mouse holes doctrine is equally applicable: it is not at all clear that Congress meant to hide the elephant of the FDA's regulation of traditional pharmacy compounding in the mouse hole of FDCA's new drug approval process. ***

b. Statutory structure, legislative history and the FDCA's purpose: *** The Florida Drug and Cosmetic Act, Fla. Stat. §§ 499.001 *et seq.,* which was enacted to "provide uniform legislation *to be administered so far as practicable in conformity with the provisions of, and regulations issued under the authority of, the Federal Food, Drug, and Cosmetic Act,"* id. § 499.002(b) (emphasis added), defines "manufacture" as "the preparation, deriving, *compounding,* propagation, producing, or fabrication of any drug, device, or cosmetic," *id.* § 499.003(30) (emphasis added), and "manufacturer" as, *inter alia,* "[a] person who prepares, derives, *manufactures,* or produces a drug, device or cosmetic," *id.* § 499.003(31) (emphasis added). *** Rather, utilizing this first-of-its-kind enforcement action, the FDA seeks to expand its statutory authority by enjoining an individual pharmacy which is engaged in traditional pharmacy compounding of animal drugs in compliance with state law. In so doing, the FDA overreaches. ***

4. Chevron Step Two: *** There is yet another troubling ramification of FDA's position in this case: because the FDCA provides for both criminal and civil penalties for any act prohibited by 21 U.S.C. § 331, *see id.* § 333(a), the compounding of *one* non-food-producing animal medication from bulk ingredients subjects a state-licensed pharmacist—whether the pharmacist's practice consists of a "large, interstate operation" or a "Mom–and–Pop" shop—to the criminal penalties of the FDCA. ***

V. Conclusion: The Court appreciates the FDA's difficult task in protecting the health of both humans and animals. *** The Court holds that, in enacting the FDCA in 1938, Congress did not intend to give the FDA *per se* authority to enjoin the long-standing, widespread, state-regulated practice of pharmacists filling a veterinarian's prescription for a non-food-producing animal by compounding from bulk substances.

CRITICAL ANALYSIS: Why do you think the court denied the injunction and do you agree that pharmacy compounding is best left to the states as the court detailed? See the 2013 *Drug Quality and Security Act*.

Misbranding—*Strauss*

The decision of *United States v. Strauss* provides an excellent example of a prosecution and ultimate conviction for selling adulterated and misbranded animal food. Section 343(a)(1) provides that food is misbranded if "its labeling [is] false or misleading in any particular."

United States v. Strauss, 999 F.2d 692 (2d Cir. 1993)

OPINION: MINER, Circuit Judge: The Strausses were convicted, following a jury trial, on one count of conspiring to hold for sale misbranded and adulterated dog food, in violation of 21 U.S.C. §§ 343(a)(1) and 342(a)(1) and 18 U.S.C. § 371 and on twelve counts of causing false labels to be affixed to dog food with the intent to defraud and mislead, in violation of 21 U.S.C. §§ 331(k), 333(a)(2) and 343(a)(1). Jerome was sentenced to a term of imprisonment of twenty-seven months to be followed by three years of supervised release. Adam was sentenced to a one-year term of probation, four months of which were to be served under house arrest. For the reasons that follow, the judgments of conviction are affirmed.

BACKGROUND: Bow Wow Meow Pet Food Stores ("BWM") was a chain of eleven pet food and pet accessory stores located throughout Nassau County, New York. Jerome was BWM's owner and president, and his son Adam became vice-president in 1991 after graduating from college. BWM sold a variety of nationally advertised baked kibble (crushed or broken up dry dog food), as well as its own brand of kibble called "Professional Choice," which it purchased from Triumph Pet Industries, Inc. ("Triumph"), a leading producer of kibble located in Hillburn, New York. Jerome began purchasing kibble from Triumph around 1980. The kibble was packaged at Triumph's plant in bags designed by Jerome. Triumph manufactured twelve kinds of kibble. Eight kinds of kibble were formulated for particular ages, sizes or activity levels of dogs and included: (1) "Standard"; (2) "Lite & Lean"; (3) "Natural"; (4) "High Protein"; (5) "Original"; (6) "Special Puppy Blend"; (7) "Special Adult Blend"; and (8) "Special Senior Blend." Four kinds of kibble were artificially flavored and colored varieties of the Standard kibble and included: (9) "Milk-Beef-Liver"; (10) "Chicken-Beef-Cheese"; (11) "Egg-Beef-Cheese"; and (12) "Supreme Stew." *** Lite & Lean kibble was less expensive than Standard kibble because it contained less protein and was made from broken biscuits rejected by another customer of Triumph. High Protein kibble was the most expensive due to the additional protein.   ***

From 1985 to 1988, in addition to the Standard kibbles, he purchased High Protein kibble, Natural kibble and Lite & Lean kibble. In 1989 and 1990, Jerome bought only three varieties of kibble: unflavored Standard kibble; the Chicken-Beef-Cheese variation of Standard kibble; and Lite & Lean kibble. By 1991, he was purchasing only the unflavored Standard kibble and the Lite & Lean kibble. At no time did Jerome purchase any Special Puppy Blend, Special Adult Blend or Special Senior Blend kibble. *** A label was affixed to each bag indicating the age, size or activity level of the dog for which that particular kibble was manufactured. Until 1988 or 1989, Triumph would attach the labels prior to shipping the bags to BWM. Labels would be affixed to the bags once they arrived at BWM's warehouse. Gary Evers, a BWM store manager, testified that, under Jerome's supervision, he instructed BWM's warehousemen on the procedure for labeling the bags.

As directed by Jerome, the warehousemen generally disregarded the type of kibble actually in the bags and affixed labels according to the weekly requests received from BWM stores for particular varieties of Professional Choice. Kibble that was identified by Triumph as "Original" would be labeled "Original," "High Protein," "Jumbo" and "All Natural." The kibble Triumph identified as "Chicken-Beef-Cheese" would be labeled "Chicken-Beef-Cheese," "Egg-Beef-Cheese" or "Milk-Beef-Liver." Finally, the kibble designated by Triumph as "Lite & Lean" was labeled "Lite & Lean," "Supreme Stew," "Special Puppy Blend," "Special Adult Blend" or "Special Senior Blend." Several former employees of BWM testified at trial that Jerome instructed them to ascertain the type, age and activity level of a customer's dog and then to recommend the Professional Choice kibble appropriate for that particular canine. The government introduced testimony that, on at least one occasion, when an employee could not fill a customer's request, the store supervisor simply removed the label from a Professional Choice bag in stock and relabeled the bag as the variety requested by the customer. Indeed, when questioned by an employee regarding this practice, Adam allegedly responded that "it was just a marketing technique and basically people didn't know the difference." In each case, after discerning the size, age or activity level of the dog allegedly owned by the undercover agent, the BWM employee would recommend Professional Choice as the food best suited for that canine. Finally, when the kibble became bug infested, store managers were instructed to return the bags to the BWM warehouse. There, the Strausses would remove the kibble, spray the food with Zema Home and Kennel Spray, let it dry, rebag the food and then return it to stock. Testimony by former employees of BWM revealed that hundreds of twenty- and forty-pound bags of kibble were treated in this manner. Marcia Van Gemert, Chief of Toxicology in the Health Effects Division of the Environmental Protection Agency, an expert on the effects of pesticides on animals, testified that the active ingredient in Zema is chlorpyrifos, a "very, very toxic chemical" in the chemical family of organophosphates. ***

DISCUSSION *

1. Mislabeling the Dog Food: Section 343(a)(1) provides that food is misbranded if "its labeling [is] false or misleading in any particular." See *United States v. Hoxsey Cancer Clinic*, 198 F.2d 273, 281 (5th Cir. 1952) (government not required to prove that each and every representation was false or misleading). Even if Professional Choice were nutritionally proper for all dogs, "the appropriate inquiry is whether the ultimate purchaser will be misled." *Libby, McNeill & Libby v. United States*, 148 F.2d 71, 74 (2d Cir. 1945). It also is irrelevant that a reasonable consumer reading the labels would realize that all Professional Choice varieties, and indeed all other dog foods, contain roughly the same ingredients and that the artificial flavoring adds no nutritional value to the dog food. We have construed section 343 broadly, since the test is not the effect of the label on a reasonable consumer, but upon "the ignorant, the unthinking and the credulous" consumer. *United States v. An Article . . . Sudden Change*, 409 F.2d 734, 740 (2d Cir. 1969) (quoting *Florence Mfg. Co. v. J.C. Dowd & Co.*, 178 F. 73, 75 (2d Cir. 1910)). Here, an ignorant, unthinking and credulous consumer would be misled into believing that he or she was purchasing a product designed especially for a dog of a particular age, size or activity level due to the Strausses' misbranding of the Professional Choice bags.

Finally, the "Guaranteed Analysis" (accurately listing the percentages of protein, fat, fiber and moisture content of the kibble) found on the Professional Choice bags does not detract from the deception caused by the Strausses' misbranding. Despite the fact that one part of the label was accurate, the other part was not, and the label as a whole falsely represented that, the kibble was manufactured specifically for a particular type of canine. In *United States v. An Article of Food . "Manischewitz . . . Diet Thins"*, 377 F. Supp. 746 (E.D.N.Y. 1974), the defendant marketed matzoh crackers with a label bearing the name "Diet-Thins." In fact, the crackers in these boxes were no different from the defendant's "regular crackers." The defendant argued that it had not mislabeled its product because any customer who read the ingredients would see that the crackers were the same and because both kinds of crackers were appropriate for someone on a diet. The district court rejected these arguments, finding that "it [was] not necessary to show that anyone was actually misled or deceived" and that "a technically accurate description of a food or drug's content may violate" the statute "if the description is misleading in other respects." ***

2. Adulteration of the Kibble: The Strausses also argue that there was insufficient evidence to show that they violated 21 U.S.C. §§ 331(k) and 342(a)(1). Section 331(k) provides, in relevant part, that adulterated food may not be "held for sale." Section 342(a)(1) provides, in relevant part, that "[a] food shall be deemed to be adulterated . . . if it bears or contains any poisonous or deleterious substance which may render it injurious to health." *** Section 343 is a substantive offense under the Federal Food, Drug, and Cosmetic Act, 21 U.S.C. §§ 301-394 (the "FFDCA"). The Strausses' acts of affixing false labels to the Professional Choice bags violated both section 343(a)(1) and section 331, which lists the acts prohibited under the FFDCA. *** Accordingly, this claim also is without merit.

CRITICAL ANALYSIS: Review the cases such as *Diet Thins* in *Volume IX* and *Sudden Change* in *Volume XII*. Evaluate why the court applied the "ignorant, unthinking and credulous consumer" test instead of a "reasonable person" standard.

Classification—*"Pets Smellfree"*

Pets Smellfree provides an excellent illustration of the term "intended use" as well as product classification. *Pets Smell Free* hinged on whether the product was a drug or simply a deodorant. Product classification determination has far reaching consequences.

United States v. "Pets Smellfree" or "Fresh Pet",
22 F.3d 235 (10th Cir. 1994)

OPINION: HOLLOWAY, Circuit Judge. This case requires us to decide whether a compound sold as an internal pet "deodorant," whose only active ingredient is the antibiotic chlortetracycline, is a "drug" as defined by the Federal Food, Drug, and Cosmetic Act, 21 U.S.C. 301,*et seq.*

I. Pets Smellfree ("PSF" and/or "Smellfree") is a food additive for animals which purports to diminish pet odors. Its only active ingredient is chlortetracycline calcium complex ("CTC"), an antibiotic compound. Smellfree was advertised as being able to stop pet odors associated with feces, urine, gas, and bad breath. Such odors are typically caused by bacteria. ***

II. A. The central question presented by this appeal is whether Smellfree is a drug under 21 U.S.C. 321(g)(1). For reasons that follow, we hold that it is. *** PSF produced Smellfree in batches of 70 pounds at a time. To make one 70-pound batch, PSF mixed one 50-pound package of CtC-50 chlortetracycline premix with 20 pounds of "other" inactive ingredients. CtC-50 is an "antibacterial feed premix for use in the manufacture of feeds" which contains 50 grams of CTC per pound. See R. at 186-90 (manufacturer's description and directions for use). Therefore, each pound of Smellfree made in this way contained approximately 35.7 grams of CTC, so that Smellfree consists of approximately 7.6% - 7.7% CTC, while the remainder of its ingredients are inactive. 21 U.S.C. 321(g)(1) defines "drugs" as: *(A) articles recognized in the official United States Pharmacopoeia, official Homoeopathic Pharmacopoeia of the United States, or official National Formulary, or any supplement to any of them; and (B) articles intended for use in the diagnosis, cure, mitigation, treatment, or prevention of disease in man or other animals; and (C) articles (other than food) intended to affect the structure or any function of the body of man or other animals.*

In reviewing the FDA's determination that Smellfree is a drug, we must be guided by the directives regarding judicial review of administrative agency interpretations of their organic statutes laid down by the Supreme Court in *Chevron U.S.A., Inc. v. Natural Resources Defense Council, Inc.*, 467 U.S. 837, 81 L. Ed. 2d 694, 104 S. Ct. 2778 (1984). Those directives require that we first determine whether Congress has directly spoken to the precise question at issue. If the congressional intent is clear, we must give effect to that intent. If the statute is silent or ambiguous on that specific issue, we must determine whether the agency's answer is based on a permissible construction of the statute. See 467 U.S. at 842-43; *N.L.R.B. v. Viola Industries - Elevator Div.*,

Inc., 979 F.2d 1384, 1393 (10th Cir. 1992) (en banc). Remedial legislation such as the Food, Drug, and Cosmetic Act is to be given a liberal construction consistent with the Act's overriding purpose to protect the public health. *United States v. An Article of Drug Bacto-Unidisk*, 394 U.S. 784, 798, 22 L. Ed. 2d 726, 89 S. Ct. 1410 (1969). ***

B. PSF argues that the district judge properly ruled that Smellfree was not intended to cure, mitigate or prevent disease. *** Essentially, PSF argues that the dosage of CTC contained in Smellfree is too small to have any therapeutic action, i.e. it is "subtherapeutic," and therefore Smellfree cannot be classified as a drug. We cannot agree.

It has been noted that "subtherapeutic, long-term application of antibiotics in animals is usually intended to promote faster growth, improve feeding efficiency, and limit disease outbreaks." See *United States v. An Article of Drug Consisting of 4,680 Pails*, 725 F.2d 976, 988 n.27 (5th Cir. 1984) (emphasis added). *** However, even if a factual issue is presented on that theory concerning Smellfree, the government argues that the labeling and marketing claims made by PSF make the substance a drug under 321(g)(1)(B) in any event. We must agree. *** Mr. Beaston attached one advertisement stating: "We know it works because it cured our 'smelly beast.'" Dr. Parkhie's Affidavit stated that pet odors are usually associated with dermatological disorders, otic and perineal infections, metabolic diseases, and oral/dental diseases, such as decay, plaque and gingivitis. "These pet odors therefore are due to bacterial contamination. Removal of these bacteria to stop pet odors constitutes prevention or treatment of a disease." In sum, we are convinced that Smellfree was intended for use in the cure, mitigation, treatment or prevention of disease in animals. There being no issue of material fact on this question, we hold that the summary judgment in favor of PSF under 321(g)(1)(B) was error and that instead summary judgment on this issue should have been entered for the government.

C. PSF also maintains that the government's evidence does not show that Smellfree was intended to affect the structure or function of animals. *** As noted, Dr. Parkhie's Affidavit stated that the therapeutic or subtherapeutic doses of Smellfree are likely to reduce the number of bacteria in the digestive system and oral cavities of the animal. "Elimination of the 'normal' bacterial flora will affect the function of the animal's body." *** We are persuaded that the record clearly establishes that Smellfree is intended to affect a bodily function of animals, their digestion and elimination function. Again, we note the labeling claims, such as that PSF stops "odors at the source," and that it is "an absolute revolution in pet odor control." See *Nutrilab v. Schweiker*, 713 F.2d 335, 339 (7th Cir. 1983) (Starch blockers indisputably satisfy [321(g) (1)(C)'s] requirement for they are intended to affect digestion in the people who take them.") *** In sum, we feel the showing of intent to alter a function of the animal's body by the use of Smellfree is clearly demonstrated by the record. Hence, Smellfree is also a drug within the meaning of 321(g)(1)(C).

III. We hold that PSF comes within the drug definition of 21 U.S.C. 321(g)(1)(B) since it is intended to cure, mitigate, treat or prevent disease in animals. Further, we hold PSF is within the drug definition of 321(g)(1)(C) because it is intended to affect a function of the body of animals—digestion and elimination. Since there is no issue of material raised regarding the question of Smellfree's status as a drug, the government was entitled to summary judgments as a matter of law. Hence, PSF's motion for summary judgment should have been denied and that of the government should have been granted. Accordingly, the summary judgment in favor of PSF is REVERSED. The case is REMANDED with directions to enter summary judgment in favor of the United States, determining that Pets Smellfree is a drug under the Act, and to conduct further proceedings consistent with this opinion to consider whether the product is an adulterated or misbranded drug.

CRITICAL ANALYSIS: Evaluate whether the court decision regarding drug classification for *Pets Smellfree* was correct.

VOLUME VIII

Volume VIII: Personal Care Products Regulation—Cosmetic Safety, Terminology, Product Classification and Enforcement

The Office of Cosmetics and Colors (OCAC) within the United States Food and Drug Administration (FDA), regulates personal care products such as cosmetics. This volume focuses on those personal care cosmetic products regulated by OCAC. The majority of personal care cosmetic products are regulated by OCAC; however, it depends on the specific product. For example, the Center for Drug Evaluation and Research regulates over-the-counter personal care products such as sunscreens. Further, the Consumer Product Safety Commission regulates some soaps. Today, more than ever, consumers turn to personal care products for reasons beyond that of grooming. Increasingly, personal care products are used for health purposes. Did you know that the United States is at the forefront in terms of market sales of personal care cosmetic products in the entire world? Suffice it to state, revenue from personal care cosmetics is in the billions. The goals of this Volume are as follows:

> ➤ *Discuss the regulatory authority of FDA over personal cosmetic care products;*
> ➤ *Explain issues involved in product classification;*
> ➤ *Detail specific terminology related to cosmetics;*
> ➤ *Provide information on the cosmetic registration program;*
> ➤ *Detail specific enforcement actions; and*
> ➤ *Discuss the "quest for beauty" in culture.*

Safety issues remain paramount especially with ingredients used and harmonization of ingredient nomenclature. Issues related to harmonization, such as varied regulatory rules, remain complicated. For example, only colors approved for use in the United States are permitted in cosmetics and safety substantiation is required. The critical issue that remains is the authority of the United States Food and Drug Administration in terms of pre-market approval rather than the current system of post market enforcement. Perhaps a mandatory cosmetic registration program is in order. Perhaps FDAs OCAC should revisit how these products are regulated to keep in step with the 21st century. Stakeholder collaboration from industry could prove valuable. However, more needs to be done to protect the public in fulfilling the mandate of the Food, Drug and Cosmetic Act such as enforcement of the proliferation of claims concerning personal care cosmetic products and classification.

Legislative proposals to strengthen regulation have failed to pass except for the Microbead-Free Waters Act legislation which was enacted during the 114th Congress (2015-2016) effective in 2018-2019. The Micro-Free Waters Act bans rinse-off cosmetics that contain intentionally-added plastic microbeads. https://www.congress.gov/bill/114th-congress/house-bill/1321

Chapter 1: FDA Authority, Registration, Terminology, and Product Classification

Food and Drug Administration Legal Authority
Key Website: *http://www.fda.gov/Cosmetics/default.htm*
http://www.fda.gov/Cosmetics/GuidanceRegulation/LawsRegulations/ucm074162.htm#Can_FDA_order

The regulation of personal care cosmetic products occurred with passage of the 1938 Food Drug and Cosmetic Act (FDCA). The FDCA details specific sections about cosmetic personal care products, including the definition of a "cosmetic" under 21 U.S.C.§ 321(i) and particular sections on the misbranding and adulteration of a cosmetic personal care product, §§ 361 and 362 respectively. FDA does not pre-approve personal care cosmetic products pre-marketplace entry. Except for color additives and a few prohibited ingredients, a cosmetics manufacturer may use any ingredient and market the final product without governmental approval. FDA lacks the legal authority to require companies to perform pre-market safety testing on cosmetic products.

The Office of Cosmetics and Colors (OCAC) within the Center for Food Safety and Applied Nutrition (CFSAN) regulates cosmetics. However, it is important to emphasize that FDA authority to regulate cosmetics is post-market. Safety issues remain paramount especially with ingredients used and harmonization of ingredient nomenclature. Issues related to harmonization, such as varied regulatory rules, remain complicated. For example, only colors approved for use in the United States are permitted in cosmetics and safety substantiation is required. A warning must be issued directly on the label if the safety of its ingredients is unsubstantiated.

FDA has an *Intercenter Agreement* between the Center for Drug Evaluation and Research (CDER) and the OCAC within CFSAN. The purpose is to regulate those products that claim to be cosmetics yet are actually drugs as defined under the FDCA. According to FDA and under the FDCA definition of "drug", if a product claiming to be a cosmetic is intended to affect the structure, or any function of the human body or is intended for use in the diagnosis, cure, mitigation, treatment, or prevention of disease in man, that product is subject to regulation as a drug. The key is intended use. FDA clarifies that intent may be demonstrated by labeling claims, advertising, or oral or written statements by such persons or their representative. See 21 C.F.R. § 201.128.

CRITICAL ANALYSIS: Proposals to revamp the regulation of cosmetics have been introduced yet have remained dormant. Why? See link below.
https://www.congress.gov/search?searchResultViewType=expanded&q=%7B%22source%22%3A%22legislation%22%2C%22search%22%3A%22cosmetics%22%2C%22congress%22%3A%22115%22%7D

Definition—The FDCA defines cosmetics as follows: *21 U.S.C. § 321(i)*
> *"(1) articles intended to be rubbed, poured, sprinkled, or sprayed on, introduced into, or otherwise applied to the human body or any part thereof for cleansing, beautifying, promoting attractiveness, or altering the appearance, and (2) articles intended for use as a component of any such articles; except that such term shall not include soap."*

Categories—Specific categories include the following: Skin care (creams, lotions, powders, and sprays); Fragrances; Eye makeup; Makeup other than eye (e.g., lipstick, foundation and blush); Manicure products; Hair preparations coloring and non-coloring; Shampoos, permanent waves, and other hair products; Deodorants; Shaving products; Baby products (e.g., shampoos, lotions and powders); Bath oils and bubble baths; Mouthwashes; and Suntan preparations and tanning products.

Code of Federal Regulations—The rules that govern cosmetic regulation are found under the relevant parts of the Code of Regulations (CFR) as follows:
http://www.accessdata.fda.gov/scripts/cdrh/cfdocs/cfcfr/CFRSearch.cfm?CFRPart=700
https://www.accessdata.fda.gov/scripts/cdrh/cfdocs/cfcfr/CFRSearch.cfm?CFRPart=701
https://www.accessdata.fda.gov/scripts/cdrh/cfdocs/cfcfr/CFRSearch.cfm?CFRPart=740

- ➤ General enforcement regulations 21 CFR Part 1; General administrative rulings and decisions 21 CFR Part 2; Public information 21 CFR Part 20;
- ➤ Cosmetics—General provisions 21 CFR Part 700 Subpart A (Section 700.3) 21 CFR Part 250 Section 250.250; Requirements for specific cosmetic products (Sections 700.11 through 700.35) 21 CFR Part 700 Subpart B;
- ➤ Cosmetic labeling General provisions (Sections 701.1 - 701.9) 21 CFR Part 701 Subpart A;
- ➤ Package Form 21 CFR Part 701 Subpart B (Sections 701.10 through 701.19);
- ➤ Labeling of specific ingredients 21 CFR Part 701 Subpart C (Sections 701.20 - 701.30);
- ➤ Voluntary registration of cosmetic product establishments 21 CFR Part 710;
- ➤ Voluntary filing of cosmetic product ingredient and cosmetic raw material composition statements 21 CFR Part 720; and
- ➤ Cosmetic product warning statements 21 CFR Part 740.

Voluntary Product Registration Program

http://www.fda.gov/Cosmetics/GuidanceComplianceRegulatoryInformation/VoluntaryCosmeticsRegistrationProgramVCRP/ (edited)

FDA encourages voluntary cosmetic registration of product ingredient listing and manufacturing facilities. Yet, as indicated, cosmetic registration is voluntary and not mandated by law. Registration is especially significant in the event of a recall since these products are regulated post market. However, FDA's Office of Cosmetics and Colors (OCAC) maintains the Cosmetic Voluntary Registration Program (CVRP), established at the request of the cosmetics industry. The Establishment Registration and Ingredient Listing program consists of voluntary registration of cosmetic manufacturing establishments and the voluntary filing of cosmetic product ingredient (formulations) statements. See: 21 CFR, parts 710 and 720. Voluntary registration and assignment of a registration number does not signify approval of a firm or its products and it is prohibited to use CVRP participation or an assigned registration or listing number for promotional use (see Title 21 of the CFR, parts 710.8 and 720.9).

Yet, registration in the CVRP allows manufacturers to receive important information about cosmetic ingredients. The information received by FDA from the CVRP is entered into a computer database. If it is determined that a cosmetic ingredient presently being used is harmful and should be removed from product use, FDA can notify the product's manufacturer or distributor by using a mailing list generated from the CVRP database. Participating in the CVRP, helps avoid problem ingredients before they result in product recalls or import detentions. If a cosmetic manufacturer files a product formulation with the CVRP, FDA can advise the manufacturer in the event of an inadvertent use of a non-permitted color additive or other prohibited or restricted ingredients. Manufacturers have the opportunity to correct their formulations before attempting to import or distribute them, thus avoiding the risk of a recall or detention due to ingredient related violations.

The CVRP helps retailers identify safety-conscious manufacturers. Retailers sometimes contact FDA to learn whether a cosmetic company is registered with the agency. Although registration does not represent FDA approval, it does indicate that the products have been reviewed by FDA and entered into the Agency's database. The cosmetic manufacturer, packer, or distributor should file a statement for each product the firm markets. Further, a private labeler or packer may file as long as the distributor provides permission to do so.

CRITICAL ANALYSIS: Should registration be mandatory?

Product Classification—Cosmetic, Drug or Medical Device

How is product classification determined? Is a facial cream promoted on the label to reverse the aging process a drug, a cosmetic or both? The key terminology is "intended use." This is determined by the intent of the product. Objective intent is the controlling factor in product classification and is determined by the label, labeling, advertising, product claims and oral representations made. If the product is intended to affect the structure or function of the body of man or intended for use in the diagnosis, cure mitigation, treatment, or prevention of disease, under 21 U.S.C. section

321(g), then the product is considered a drug and subject to the drug approval process. A statutory distinction exists between a cosmetic and a drug. Even as far back as the case *In Estee Lauder v. United States*, 727 F. Supp. 1 (1989), the issue involved whether the labeling of the facial cream would cause the product to become a drug under the FDCA. FDA advised the company about the necessity of a labeling and promotion change. Otherwise, the product would have to go through the drug approval process. The court discussed the issue of intended use and product classification and noted that courts have held that the ultimate decision concerning product classification depends on intended use.

Some products regulated as cosmetics in Europe, such as sunscreens, are regulated as drugs in the United States. There are differences regarding prohibited and restricted ingredients, particularly color additives. Unlike the United states, some countries may require cosmetic companies to register their establishments and list products and ingredients with the government.

NOTE: See *Volume V* for sunscreen regulation and *Volume XII* for the decision of *United States v. An Article Line Away*, 415 F. 2d 369, 371-72 (3d. Cir. 1969). *Line Away* and the other cases in *Volume XII* illustrate the complexity of product classification and intended use.

Cosmetic, Drug or Soap

https://www.fda.gov/Cosmetics/GuidanceRegulation/LawsRegulations/ucm074201.htm (edited)
Is it a Cosmetic, a Drug, or Both? Or Is It Soap? The legal difference between a cosmetic and a drug is determined by a product's intended use. The definitions below are critical.

Definition of cosmetic*—The term "cosmetic", under 21 U.S. C. section 321 (p), is defined in part as "(1) articles intended to be rubbed, poured, sprinkled, or sprayed on, introduced into, or otherwise applied to the human body or any part thereof for cleansing, beautifying, promoting attractiveness, or altering the appearance, and (2) articles intended for use as a component of any such articles..." Sometimes a product falls into dual classification. For example, this could occur when a product has two intended uses, such as shampoo, intended to cleanse the hair. Yet, an anti-dandruff shampoo is a drug, since it is intended to affect the structure of the human body, that is, treat dandruff.*

Definition of drug*— The FDCA defines drugs by their intended use, as "(A) articles intended for use in the diagnosis, cure, mitigation, treatment, or prevention of disease and (B) articles (other than food) intended to affect the structure or any function of the body of man or other animals" [FDCA, sec. 201(g)(1)]. Over-the-counter (OTC) drugs are drugs that can be purchased without a doctor's prescription. OTC drugs must meet the requirements of the appropriate class once that rule is published as a final regulation. If an OTC drug does not meet the requirements of the appropriate final rule, it is considered a misbranded drug and a "new drug." A "new drug" must have an approved New Drug Application (NDA) before it may be introduced into interstate commerce. In addition, drug manufacturers must comply with Good Manufacturing Practices regulations. Certain claims may cause a product to qualify as a drug, even if the product is marketed as if it were a cosmetic. Intended use controls. When the intended use is to treat or prevent disease or otherwise affect the structure or functions of the human body, the products are deemed a drug. Examples are claims that products will restore hair growth, reduce cellulite, treat varicose veins, or revitalize cells.*

Could a product be both a cosmetic and a drug? Some products meet the definitions of both cosmetics and drugs because the product has two intended uses. For example, a shampoo is a cosmetic because its intended use is to cleanse the hair. An antidandruff treatment is a drug because its intended use is to treat dandruff. Consequently, an antidandruff shampoo is both a cosmetic and a drug. Other cosmetic/drug combination examples are toothpastes that contains fluoride, deodorants that are also antiperspirants, and moisturizers and makeup marketed with sun-protection claims. These product types must comply with requirements for cosmetics and drugs.

How intended use is established*—* Intended use may be established by:
> ➢ *Claims stated on the product labeling, in advertising, on the Internet, or in other promotional materials. Certain claims may cause a product to be considered a drug, even if the product is marketed as if it were a cosmetic. Such claims establish the product as a drug because the*

intended use is to treat or prevent disease or otherwise affect the structure or functions of the
human body such as claims that products will restore hair growth or reduce cellulite.

➢ *Consumer perception, which may be established through the product's reputation.*

➢ *Ingredients that may cause a product to be considered a drug because they have a well- known*
(to the public and industry) therapeutic use. An example is fluoride in toothpaste.

How approval requirements are different— FDA does not have a premarket approval system
for cosmetic products or ingredients, with the important exception of color additives. Drugs, however, are subject to FDA approval. Drugs must either receive premarket approval by FDA or conform to final regulations specifying conditions where they are recognized as safe and effective, and
not misbranded. Once a final regulation is promulgated pertaining to a specific class of OTC drugs
is final, those drugs must either:

➢ *Be the subject of an approved New Drug Application, or*

➢ *Comply with the appropriate* monograph, or rule, for an OTC drug.

NDA and OTC Monograph— A drug sponsor files an NDA for FDA approval of a new pharmaceutical detailing safety and effectiveness for its proposed use and that its benefits outweigh the
risks. The NDA system is also used for new ingredients entering the OTC marketplace for the first
time. For example, the newer OTC products (previously available only by prescription) are first
approved through the NDA system and their 'switch' to OTC status is approved via the NDA system. FDA has published monographs, or rules, for a number of OTC drug categories. These monographs, published in the Federal Register detail requirements for categories of non-prescription
drugs, such as what ingredients may be used and for what intended use. Examples of the non-
prescription drug categories covered by OTC monographs are as follows: Acne medications; Treatments for dandruff, seborrheic dermatitis, and psoriasis; and Sunscreens.

"New drugs"—Despite the word "new," a "new drug" may have been in use for many years. If a
product is intended for use as a drug, no matter how ancient or "traditional" its use may be, once
the agency has made a final determination on the status of an OTC drug product it must have an
approved NDA or comply with the appropriate OTC monograph to be legally marketed.

How good manufacturing practice (GMPs) requirements are different—Good manufacturing
practice (GMP) is an important factor in assuring that your cosmetic products are neither adulterated nor misbranded. However, no regulations set forth specific GMP requirements for cosmetics.
In contrast, the law requires strict adherence to GMP requirements for drugs, and there are regulations specifying minimum current GMP requirements for drugs [Title 21 of the Code of Federal
Regulations (CFR), parts 210 and 211]. Failure to follow GMP requirements causes a drug to be
adulterated [FD&C Act, sec. 501(a)(2)(B)].

How registration requirements are different—FDA maintains the Voluntary Cosmetic Registration Program, or VCRP, for cosmetic establishments and formulations [21 CFR 710 and 720]. It is
mandatory for drug firms to register their establishments and list their drug products with FDA
[FD&C Act, sec. 510; 21 CFR 207].

How labeling requirements are different—A cosmetic product must be labeled according to cosmetic labeling regulations. See the Cosmetic Labeling Manual for guidance on cosmetic labeling.
OTC drugs must be labeled according to OTC drug regulations, including the "Drug Facts" labeling, as described in 21 CFR 201.63. Combination OTC drug/cosmetic products must have combination OTC drug/cosmetic labeling. For example, the drug ingredients must be listed alpha-
betically as "Active Ingredients," followed by cosmetic ingredients, listed in order of predominance
as "Inactive Ingredients."

What if it is "soap"? Soap is a category that needs special explanation. That is because the regulatory definition of "soap" is different from the way in which people commonly use the word. Products that meet the definition of "soap" are exempt from the provisions of the FDCA because—even
though Section 201(i)(1) of the FDCA includes "articles ... for cleansing" in the definition of a
cosmetic—Section 201(i)(2) excludes soap from the definition of a cosmetic.

How FDA defines "soap" Not every product marketed as soap meets FDA's definition of the term. Products that meet the following definition are regulated by the Consumer Product Safety Commission. FDA interprets the term "soap" to apply only when:

> ➢ *The bulk of the nonvolatile matter in the product consists of an alkali salt of fatty acids and the product's detergent properties are due to the alkali-fatty acid compounds, and*
> ➢ *The product is labeled, sold, and represented solely as soap.* [21 CFR 701.20].

If a product intended to cleanse the human body does not meet all the criteria for soap, as listed above, it is either a cosmetic or a drug.

A product is regulated as a cosmetic if it: Consists of detergents; or primarily of alkali salts of fatty acids, and is intended not only for cleansing but also for other cosmetic uses, such as beautifying or moisturizing.

A product is regulated as a drug if it: Consists of detergents; or primarily of alkali salts of fatty acids, and is intended not only for cleansing but also to cure, treat, or prevent disease or to affect the structure or any function of the human body.

Final Rules—Health Care and Consumer Antiseptic Wash Products

Health Care Antiseptics—Safety and Effectiveness of Topical Antimicrobial Drug Products for Over-the-Counter Human Use

https://www.federalregister.gov/documents/2017/12/20/2017-27317/safety-and-effectiveness-of-health-care-antiseptics-topical-antimicrobial-drug-products-for

Purpose—FDA issued this final rule, 82 FR 60474, effective Dec. 20, 2018 establishing that certain active ingredients used in nonprescription or commonly known as over-the-counter or OTC antiseptic products intended for use by health care professionals in a hospital setting or other health care situations outside the hospital are not generally recognized as safe and effective (GRAS/GRAE). Health care antiseptic products include health care personnel hand washes, health care personnel hand rubs, surgical hand scrubs, surgical hand rubs, and patient antiseptic skin preparations (*i.e.,* patient preoperative and pre-injection skin preparations).

Background—FDA considered the recommendations of the Nonprescription Drugs Advisory Committee (NDAC); public comments on the and all data and information on OTC health care antiseptic products that have come to the Agency's attention. This final rule finalizes the 1994 tentative final monograph (TFM) for OTC health care antiseptic drug products that published in the Federal Register of June 17, 1994 (the 1994 TFM) as amended by the proposed rule published in the Federal Register (FR) of May 1, 2015 (2015 Health Care Antiseptic Proposed Rule (PR)). This rule in finalizing the 2015 Health Care Antiseptic PR, finds that 24 health care antiseptic active ingredients are not GRAS/GRAE for use as OTC health care antiseptics and therefore are considered new drugs under (21 U.S.C. 321(p)) for which approved applications under section 505 of the FD&C Act (21 U.S.C. 355).

Additional Ingredients—However, FDA has deferred further rulemaking on six active ingredients used in OTC health care antiseptic products to allow for the development and submission to the record of new safety and effectiveness data for these ingredients. The deferred active ingredients are benzalkonium chloride, benzethonium chloride, chloroxylenol, alcohol (also referred to as ethanol or ethyl alcohol), isopropyl alcohol, and povidone-iodine. FDA does not make a GRAS/GRAE determination in this final rule for these six active ingredients for use as OTC health care antiseptics until further data is evaluated.

Consumer Antiseptics—Safety and Effectiveness of Topical Antimicrobial Drug Products for Over-the-Counter Human Use

https://www.federalregister.gov/articles/2016/09/06/2016-21337/safety-and-effectiveness-of-consumer-antiseptics-topical-antimicrobial-drug-products-for

Purpose—FDA issued this final rule in 2016, 81 FR 61106 (Sept. 6, 2016) establishing that over-the-counter (OTC) consumer antiseptic wash products that contain certain active ingredients cannot be marketed anymore. The reason for the rule is because manufacturers failed to demonstrate that the ingredients are both safe for long-term daily use and more effective than plain soap and water in preventing illness and decreasing the spread of certain infections. This rule pertains to antiseptic wash products that contain one or more of 19 specific active ingredients. The most commonly used ingredients triclosan (liquid soaps) and triclocarban (bar soaps) are included in this rule. See: 21 U.S.C. 352 new drugs; 21 U.S.C. 321(p); 21 U.S.C. 355 and part 314, 21 CFR part 314. Effective date September 6, 2017.

Background—Proposed rule published (78 FR 76444) (Dec. 17, 2013 Consumer Wash Proposed Rule (PR)) and amends the 1994 TFM for OTC antiseptic drug products of June 17, 1994 (59 FR 31402). Data suggested that long-term exposure to certain active ingredients used in antibacterial products such as triclosan (liquid soaps) and triclocarban could present health risks, such as bacterial resistance or hormonal effects. Antibacterial hand and body wash manufacturers did not provide the necessary data to establish safety and effectiveness for the 19 active ingredients addressed in the final rule. For these ingredients, either no additional data were submitted or the data and information that were submitted were not sufficient for the agency to find that these ingredients are Generally Recognized as Safe and Effective (GRAS/GRAE).

Additional Ingredients—FDA deferred rulemaking for one year for the following ingredients: benzalkonium chloride, benzethonium chloride, and chloroxylenol (PCMX) to permit submission of new safety and effectiveness data. This means that consumer antibacterial washes products with these specific ingredients may be marketed until the data is submitted and evaluated.

NOTE: *https://www.fda.gov/Drugs/DrugSafety/InformationbyDrugClass/ucm444681.htm*

CRITICAL ANALYSIS: Evaluate why these rules were promulgated.

Tooth Whiteners—Cosmetic or Drug

The American Dental Association (ADA) filed Citizen's Petition in 2009 (Petition) for FDA to "review and establish an appropriate regulatory classification" for peroxide-containing whitening products. The ADA expressed concerns about the safe use of tooth-whitening products without a professional consultation or examination. FDA denied the Petition (April 22, 2014), ruling peroxide-containing tooth whiteners would fall within the definition of cosmetic under 21 U.S.C. sec. 321(i) as they are *"intended to be...applied to the human body....for cleansing, beautifying, promoting attractiveness, or altering the appearance."* FDA set forth that the mechanisms of action, conditions of use, safety and formulation of specific peroxide-containing tooth whitener products is required to determine whether these products also fall within the definition of drug. FDA examined the adverse events reports and determined that there is a very small number of complaints related to peroxide-containing tooth whiteners. Docket No. FDA-2009-P-0566

CRITICAL ANALYSIS: Evaluate whether FDA was correct in deciding product was a cosmetic and evaluate implications of products classification under the FDCA. How should a multivitamin toothpaste be classified?

Cosmetic or Medical Device

http://www.fda.gov/Cosmetics/ComplianceEnforcement/WarningLetters/ucm081141.htm

There is a legal distinction between the definition of a cosmetic and the definition of a medical device. The significant factor is intent; that is, intent to affect appearance falls into the cosmetic classification. If the intent is to diagnose, cure, treat a medical condition or affect the structure or function of the body then, the product is therefore classified as a medical device and would be required under the FDCA to obtain premarket clearance. Furthermore, medical devices are subject to the Quality System Regulation (QSR) (21 CFR part 820) and cosmetics are not subject to this (QSR) regulation. The Consumer Product Safety Commission has the legal authority or jurisdiction over various non-medical devices that people use to affect their appearance. Examples include manicure tools, hair dryers, cotton-tipped swabs, razors and electric shavers.

Cosmetic Defined—*"... (1) articles intended to be rubbed, poured, sprinkled, or sprayed on, introduced into, or otherwise applied to the human body or any part thereof for cleansing, beautifying, promoting attractiveness, or altering the appearance, and (2) articles intended for use as a component of any such articles; except that such term shall not include soap." 21 U.S.C. section 321(i)]*

Medical Device Defined—*"... an instrument, apparatus, implement, machine, contrivance, implant, in vitro reagent, or other similar or related article, including any component, part, or accessory, which is (1) recognized in the official National Formulary, or the United States Pharmacopeia, or any supplement to them, (2) intended for use in the diagnosis of disease or other conditions, or in the cure, mitigation, treatment, or prevention of disease, in man or other animals, or (3) intended to affect the structure or any function of the body of man or other animals, and which does not achieve its primary intended purposes through chemical action within or on the body of man or other animals and which is not dependent upon being metabolized for the achievement of its primary intended purposes." FDCA, section 201 (h)].*

CRITICAL ANALYSIS: Review the list of Import Alert Examples (link below). How should products such as fat burners and hand-held lasers for hair regrowth be classified, that is, as cosmetics or medical devices or combination and which FDA Center should have primary authority to regulate these products?

http://www.accessdata.fda.gov/cms_ia/importalert_244.html

Enforcement—Warning Letters

FDA issued several Warning Letters to companies who alleged drug claims associated with topical skin care, hair care, eyelash and eyebrow preparations, noted on both product labeling and Web sites. FDA's position is that claims about hair restoration or hair loss are drug claims and require a New Drug Application. Further, drug claim assertions include: acne treatment, cellulite reduction, stretch marks reduction, wrinkle removal, blemish and scar removal, dandruff treatment, hair restoration, and eyelash growth.

> *Warning Letters Address Drug Claims Made for Products Marketed as Cosmetics*
> *Warning Letters Cite Cosmetics as Adulterated Due to Microbial Contamination*
> *Warning Letters Highlight Differences Between Cosmetics and Medical Devices*
> *Warning Letter Cites Lime Crime, Inc. Regarding Color Additives*
> *Warning Letter Cites Van Tibolli Beauty Corp. GK Hair Taming System for Safety and Labeling Violations*
> *Warning Letter Cites Brazilian Blowout for Safety and Labeling Violations*
> *Warning Letter to Black Henna Ink, Inc. Cites Illegal Use of Color Additive*

CRITICAL ANALYSIS: Choose one warning letter from the links below and prepare a response to FDA.

http://www.fda.gov/Cosmetics/ComplianceEnforcement/WarningLetters/ucm2005169.htm
http://www.fda.gov/Cosmetics/ComplianceEnforcement/WarningLetters/ucm081086.htm?source=govdelivery&utm_medium=email&utm_source=govdelivery
http://www.fda.gov/Cosmetics/ComplianceEnforcement/WarningLetters/default.htm

Terminology and Labeling Claims

https://www.fda.gov/Cosmetics/Labeling/Claims/default.htm (edited)

Specific terminology includes animal grooming aids, aromatherapy, alcohol free, cruelty free and not tested on animals; fragrance free; and hypoallergenic cosmetics. There are no legal requirements for manufacturers to print an expiration date on cosmetic labels. Cosmetic manufacturers have the responsibility to establish product safety including shelf life for products.

Alcohol Free—Cosmetic manufacturers have marketed certain cosmetic products as "alcohol free." "Alcohols" are a large and diverse family of chemicals, with different names and a variety of effects on the skin. In cosmetic labeling, the term "alcohol," used by itself, refers to ethyl alcohol. Cosmetic products, including those labeled "alcohol free," may contain other alcohols, such as cetyl, stearyl, cetearyl, or lanolin alcohol. These are known as fatty alcohols, and their effects on the skin are quite different from those of ethyl alcohol. Isopropyl alcohol, which some consumers may think of as drying the skin, is rarely used in cosmetics. To prevent the ethyl alcohol from being diverted illegally for use as an alcoholic beverage, it may be "denatured."

Denatured ethyl alcohol may appear in the ingredient listing under several different names. The abbreviation SD Alcohol (which stands for "specially denatured alcohol"), is followed by a number or a number-letter combination that indicates how the alcohol was denatured. Specially denatured alcohols acceptable for use in various cosmetics are SD Alcohol 23-A, SD Alcohol 40, and SD Alcohol 40-B. The term "Alcohol Denat." was introduced in Europe as a generic term for denatured alcohol in the interest of harmonizing ingredient names internationally.

Animal Grooming Aids—FDA recognizes various products originally developed for use on horses and other animals are promoted as cosmetics for human use. However, such products must comply with FDA regulatory requirements for cosmetics.

Aromatherapy—Fragrance products are sometimes marketed with claims or implications that their use will improve personal well-being, such as "strengthening the body's self-defense mechanisms." A claim that a perfume's aroma makes a person feel more attractive, in general, is a cosmetic claim not requiring FDA approval before a product is sold. However, if someone tries to market a scent suggesting effectiveness as an aid in quitting smoking, as a sleeping aid, or to treat or prevent any other condition or disease, or otherwise affect the body's structure or function, such a claim may cause the product to be regulated as a drug, requiring premarket approval. Advertising claims can be used to establish a product's intended use. Room fragrances, such as deodorizers and odor control products, are regulated by the Consumer Product Safety Commission.

"Cosmeceutical"—The Food, Drug, and Cosmetic Act (FDCA) does not define this term; yet, the cosmetic industry uses this word to refer to cosmetic products that have medicinal or drug-like benefits. The FDCA defines drugs as those products that cure, treat, mitigate or prevent disease or that affect the structure or function of the human body and must be approved as a drug.

Cruelty Free Not Tested on Animals—Some cosmetic companies promote their products with claims such as "CRUELTY-FREE" or "NOT TESTED ON ANIMALS" in their labeling or advertising. The unrestricted use of these phrases by cosmetic companies is possible because there are no legal definitions for these terms. Some companies may apply such claims solely to their finished cosmetic products. However, these companies may rely on raw material suppliers or contract laboratories to perform any animal testing necessary to substantiate product or ingredient safety. Other cosmetic companies may rely on combinations of scientific literature, non-animal testing, raw material safety testing, or controlled human-use testing to substantiate their product safety. A cosmetic manufacturer might only use those raw materials and base their "cruelty-free" claims on the fact that the materials or products are not "currently" tested on animals. The European Union ban on animal testing became effective in March 2009.

Fragrance Free and Unscented—The terms "fragrance free" and "unscented" used by the cosmetic industry are virtually without restriction, since there are no legal definitions. Many raw materials used in the manufacture of cosmetics have characteristic odors that may be considered offensive to consumers. In the case of products labeled as "fragrance free" or "unscented," manufacturers generally add fragrance ingredients to cover the offensive odor, yet less than what is needed to impart a noticeable scent. While most ingredients must be listed by their chemical names, fragrances or flavors may be listed simply as "fragrance" or "flavor". The cosmetic regulations do not require the listing of fragrance ingredients present at low levels to cover the off-odor of other ingredients, yet most manufacturers list them on the label.

Hypoallergenic Cosmetics—Hypoallergenic cosmetics are products that manufacturers claim produce fewer allergenic reactions than other cosmetic products. There are no Federal standards or definitions that govern the use of the term "hypoallergenic." The term means whatever a particular company wants it to mean. Manufacturers of these cosmetics are not required to submit substantiation of their hypoallergenic claims to FDA.

"Organic" Cosmetics—There is no legal definition under the Food, Drug and Cosmetic Act for the term "organic". However, The Agricultural Marketing Service of the United States Department of Agriculture (USDA) oversees the National Organic Program (NOP). The NOP regulations include a definition of "organic" and provide for certification that agricultural ingredients have been produced under conditions that would meet the definition.

According to USDA, if a cosmetic is labeled "organic", it is still subject to the laws and regulations enforced by FDA. The USDA requirements for the use of the term "organic" are separate from the laws and regulations that FDA enforces for cosmetics. Cosmetic products labeled with organic claims must comply with both USDA regulations for the organic claim and FDA regulations for labeling and safety requirements for cosmetics. Cosmetics made with "organic" ingredients are not necessarily safer for consumers than those made with ingredients from other sources. An ingredient's source does not determine its safety. Numerous plants, whether or not organically grown, contain substances that may be toxic or allergenic. Companies who market "organic" cosmetics have a legal duty to ensure their products and ingredients are safe for the intended use.

Thigh or Cellulite Creams—FDA recognizes that products have been promoted in the skin care market as thigh and stomach slammers. Advertising claims promise the reduction of "cellulite", waffle like or orange-peel type skin caused by fatty deposits. Aminophylline, an approved prescription drug used in the treatment of asthma, is an ingredient used in many of these thigh cream products that marketers claim will dissolve the fat and smooth the skin. Since some individuals suffer from allergic reactions to ethylenediamine, a component of aminophylline, the FDA is concerned about the use of this ingredient in cosmetics. Thigh creams may more appropriately be classified as drugs under the Food, Drug, and Cosmetic Act since removal or reduction of cellulite affects the "structure or function" of the body.

Wrinkle Treatments and Other Anti-aging Products—If a product is intended to make lines and wrinkles less noticeable, simply by moisturizing, it is a cosmetic. Makeup or "primers" intended to make aging less noticeable just by hiding them are also cosmetics. However, products intended to affect the structure or function of the body, such as the skin, are drugs, or sometimes medical devices, even if they affect the appearance. If a product is intended to remove wrinkles or increase the skin's production of collagen, it is a drug or a medical device.

Shelf Life Expiration Date—There are no regulations or requirements under current United States law that requires cosmetic manufacturers to print expiration dates on the labels of cosmetic products. Manufacturers have the responsibility to determine shelf life for products, as part of their responsibility to substantiate product safety. Voluntary shelf-life guidelines developed by the cosmetic industry vary depending on the product and its intended use. The shelf life for eye-area cosmetics is more limited than for other products due to repeated microbial exposure and the risk of eye infections. "All natural" products that may contain plant-derived substances have an unusually short shelf life as well.

Nanotechnology

http://www.fda.gov/Cosmetics/GuidanceRegulation/GuidanceDocuments/ucm300886.htm

Nanotechnology is an emerging technology that allows scientists to create, explore, and manipulate materials on a scale measured in nanometers – particles so small that they cannot be seen with a regular microscope. The technology has an extensive range of conceivable applications, such as altering the look and feel of cosmetics.

FDA issued a final guidance document in 2014 (June) addressing the use of nanotechnology in the area of cosmetics: *Final Guidance for Industry: Safety of Nanomaterials in Cosmetics.*
The final cosmetics guidance discusses the safety assessment of nanomaterials when used in cosmetic products including the recommendation that manufacturers consult with FDA on test methods and data needed to support the product safety substantiation.

CRITICAL ANALYSIS: How should FDA handle the proliferation of claims that contain the above terminology? Should FDA define these terms and, if so, how? Could FDA still institute enforcement actions despite the fact that there is no specific legal definition under the FDCA for these terms? Incorporate a discussion about nanotechnology and "GMO Free" claims.

Chapter 2: Safety, Records, Inspection, Ingredients and Adverse Events

Adverse Events

Adverse event reporting, which is similar to other FDA regulated products, is accomplished through MedWatch. The Office of Cosmetics and Colors (OCAC) devised an inclusive system for tracking and evaluating adverse events related to cosmetics. The Adverse Events Reporting System (CAERS) utilizes the system as a unified monitoring method. The purpose of CAERS is to recognize potential public health problems that could be related with the use of a particular cosmetic. CAERS is a postmarketing tool used to formulate postmarketing policies. This adverse event program provides public notification through the Internet. Additionally, CFSAN notifies companies about a report(s) of an illness or injury related to the use of the product.

Final Rule—Bovine Spongiform Encephalopathy

http://www.fda.gov/Food/NewsEvents/ConstituentUpdates/ucm490542.htm

FDA issued a rule (March 17, 2016) which finalized three previously-issued interim final rules intended to further decrease the possible risk of bovine spongiform encephalopathy (BSE), commonly referred to as "mad cow disease," in human food. The final rule specifies definitions for prohibited cattle materials and excludes their use in human food, dietary supplements, and cosmetics. The materials include:

✓ *Specified risk materials (SRMs): brain, skull, eyes, trigeminal ganglia, spinal cord, vertebral column (excluding the vertebrae of the tail, the transverse processes of the thoracic and lumbar vertebrae, and the wings of the sacrum), and dorsal root ganglia (DRG) of cattle 30 months of age and older, and the tonsils and distal ileum of the small intestine from all cattle;*

✓ *The small intestine from all cattle unless the distal ileum has been properly removed;*

✓ *Material from nonambulatory disabled cattle; and*

✓ *Material from cattle not inspected and passed, or mechanically separated (MS) (Beef).*

Record Keeping—Cosmetics Containing Cattle Material

http://www.fda.gov/Cosmetics/ProductsIngredients/PotentialContaminants/ucm136786.htm

Manufacturers and processors of cosmetics that are manufactured or processed with or contain material from cattle have to maintain records that establish the cosmetic is not manufactured, processed with or contains prohibited cattle materials. The recordkeeping mandate rule titled: *"Recordkeeping Requirements for Human Food and Cosmetics Manufactured From, Processed With, or Otherwise Containing, Material From Cattle"* was published July 14, 2006 (69 FR 42275) and permits electronic recordkeeping. In addition to the prohibited cattle material recordkeeping requirement, the rule amends the FDCA as follows:

✓ Two year record retention;

✓ Record availability to FDA; and providing

✓ Records within 5 days when filing entry with U.S. Customs.

Inspection

https://www.fda.gov/Cosmetics/ComplianceEnforcement/ucm136455.htm

Despite postmarket regulation, FDA retains the legal authority to inspect laboratories of cosmetic manufacturers, collect samples for examination, follow up with complaints about products, and take action through the United States Department of Justice in order to remove adulterated or misbranded cosmetics from the marketplace. Although FDA collects samples, FDA does not serve as a private testing laboratory. Foreign manufacturers are subject to the same regulations as domestic manufacturers and cosmetics may be prohibited from United States entry.

Security Measures Guidance for Processors and Transporters

http://www.fda.gov/food/guidanceregulation/ucm082716.htm

FDA issued a guidance directed toward security issues related to cosmetics which identifies the types of preventive procedures that cosmetic establishments may take to lessen the risks of cosmetic tampering or other malicious, criminal, or terrorist actions. Additionally, cosmetic companies may register through FDA's Voluntary Cosmetic Registration Program (VCRP).

If a cosmetic manufacturer files a product formulation with the VCRP, FDA can advise the company if it is inadvertently using a non-permitted color additive or other prohibited or restricted ingredients. Manufacturers have the opportunity to correct their formulations prior to marketing them in the United States. In this manner, a manufacturer avoids the risk of having their products detained and denied entry into the United States because of a prohibited ingredient.

CRITICAL ANALYSIS: Evaluate whether the Food, Drug, and Cosmetic Act should be amended to provide FDA with the authority to recall personal care cosmetic products.
http://www.fda.gov/Cosmetics/ComplianceEnforcement/Re-callsAlerts/ucm173559.htm#What_is_FDA_s_role

Prohibited and Restricted Ingredients

http://www.fda.gov/cosmetics/guidanceregulation/lawsregulations/ucm127406.htm (edited)

FDA does not have the legal authority to pre-approve cosmetic products or ingredients with the exception of color additives. However, regulations prohibit or restrict the use of several ingredients due to safety concerns. Additionally, cosmetic and fragrance trade associations have recommended avoiding or limiting the use of some substances. Contaminants raise additional concerns.

Substantiation of safety: It is the responsibility of the manufacturer and distributor to assure the safety of each ingredient and finished product. Without substantiation of safety, Title 21 of the Code of Federal Regulations (21 CFR), Part 740.10 requires that the product carry the following warning on the label: *"Warning: The safety of this product has not been determined."*

Prohibited Ingredients by Regulation

Regulations specifically prohibit the use of the following ingredients in cosmetics. (21 CFR, Parts 250.250 and 700.11 through 700.35).

Bithionol—The use of bithionol is prohibited because it may cause photo-contact sensitization (21 CFR 700.11).

Chlorofluorocarbon propellants—The use of chlorofluorocarbon propellants (fully halogenated chlorofluoroalkanes) in cosmetic aerosol products intended for domestic consumption is prohibited (21 CFR 700.23).

Chloroform—The use of chloroform in cosmetic products is prohibited because of its animal carcinogenicity and likely hazard to human health. The regulation makes an exception for residual amounts from its use as a processing solvent during manufacture, or as a byproduct from the synthesis of an ingredient (21 CFR 700.18).

Halogenated salicylanilides (di-, tri-, metabromsalan and tetrachlorosalicylanilide)—These are prohibited in cosmetic products because they may cause photocontact sensitization (21 CFR 700.15).

Methylene chloride—The use of this substance in cosmetic products is prohibited because of its animal carcinogenicity and likely hazard to human health (21 CFR 700.19).

Vinyl chloride—The use of vinyl chloride is prohibited as an ingredient of aerosol products, because of its carcinogenicity [21 CFR 700.14].

Zirconium-containing complexes—The use of zirconium-containing complexes in aerosol cosmetic products is prohibited because of their toxic effect on lungs, including the formation of granulomas [21 CFR 700.16].

Prohibited cattle materials—To protect against bovine spongiform encephalopathy (BSE), also known as "mad cow disease," cosmetics may not be manufactured from, processed with, or otherwise contain, prohibited cattle materials. These materials include specified risk materials, material from nonambulatory cattle, material from cattle not inspected and passed, or mechanically separated beef. Prohibited cattle materials do not include tallow that contains no more than 0.15 percent insoluble impurities, tallow derivatives, and hides and hide-derived products, and milk and milk products. [21 CFR 700.27, as amended].

Restricted Ingredients by Regulation

Some ingredients may be used in cosmetics, with the restrictions stated in the regulations as follows:

Hexachlorophene—Because of its toxic effect and ability to penetrate human skin, hexachlorophene (HCP) may be used only when an alternative preservative has not been shown to be as effective. The HCP concentration of the cosmetic may not exceed 0.1 percent. HCP may not be used in cosmetics that in normal use may be applied to mucous membranes, such as the lips [21 CFR 250.250].

Mercury compounds—Mercury compounds are readily absorbed through the skin on topical application and tend to accumulate in the body. They may cause allergic reactions, skin irritation, or neurotoxic manifestations. The use of mercury compounds as cosmetic ingredients is limited to eye area cosmetics at concentrations not exceeding 65 parts per million (0.0065 percent) of mercury calculated as the metal (about 100 ppm or 0.01 percent phenylmercuric acetate or nitrate) and is permitted only if no other effective and safe preservative is available for use. All other cosmetics containing mercury are adulterated and subject to regulatory action unless it occurs in a trace amount of less than 1 part per million (0.0001 percent) calculated as the metal and its presence is unavoidable under conditions of good manufacturing practice [21 CFR 700.13].

Contaminants

https://www.fda.gov/cosmetics/resourcesforyou/consumers/ucm290083.htm

The risk of introducing contaminants into a product is always a concern in cosmetic manufacture, whether they are introduced through contaminated raw ingredients or from the manufacturing process. Nitrosamines and dioxane are among those contaminants that may form during the manufacturing process and raise safety issues. Research also has raised safety questions about diethanolamine (DEA) and related ingredients that may contain residual levels of this substance.

Nitrosamines—Many nitrosamines have been determined to cause cancer in laboratory animals. They also have been shown to penetrate the skin. Amines and their derivatives are mostly present in creams, cream lotions, hair shampoos, and cream hair conditioners. Nitrosamines are avoidable by proper formulation: by not using amines or amino derivatives in combination with a nitrosating agent and by testing the product under use conditions to make sure that nitrosamines do not form under customary conditions of use.

Dioxane—In rodent feeding studies conducted for the National Cancer Institute, 1,4-dioxane was found to produce cancer of the liver and the nasal turbinates. It also caused systemic cancer in a skin painting study. Skin absorption studies demonstrated that dioxane readily penetrates animal and human skin from various types of vehicles, although it is uncertain how much is available for absorption and how much evaporates instead of penetrating the skin. Cosmetics containing ethoxylated surface active agents, including detergents, foaming agents, emulsifiers and certain solvents identifiable by the prefix, word, or syllable "PEG," "Polyethylene," "Polyethylene glycol," "Polyoxyethylene," "-eth-," or "-oxynol-," may be contaminated with 1,4-dioxane. It may be removed from ethoxylated compounds by vacuum stripping at the end of the polymerization process without an unreasonable increase in raw material cost.

Sunscreens

The use of the term "sunscreen" or similar sun protection terminology in a product's labeling generally causes the product to be subject to regulation as a drug. However, sunscreen ingredients may also be used in some products for nontherapeutic, nonphysiologic uses (for example, as a color additive or to protect the color of the product). To avoid consumer misunderstanding, if a cosmetic product contains a sunscreen ingredient and uses the term "sunscreen" or similar sun protection terminology anywhere in its labeling, the term must be qualified, in accordance with 21 CFR

700.35(b), by describing the benefit to the cosmetic product provided by the sunscreen ingredient (for example, "Contains a sunscreen to protect product color."). Otherwise, the product may be subject to regulation as a drug [21 CFR 700.35].

Ingredient Review Panel

http://www.cir-safety.org/ingredients

The Cosmetic Ingredient Review (CIR) Expert Panel, an independent panel of scientific experts, regularly assesses the safety of numerous cosmetic ingredients and publishes its findings. The CIR was established by the Personal Care Products Association formerly the Cosmetic, Toiletry, and Fragrance Association. For example, CIR found the following ingredients unsafe:

- **Chloroacetamide** (a preservative), because of sensitization (development of allergic reactions);
- **Ethoxyethanol** and **Ethoxyethanol Acetate** (a solvent), because of reproductive and developmental toxicity;
- **HC Blue No. 1** (a hair coloring ingredient), because of possible carcinogenicity;
- **p-Hydroxyanisole** (an antioxidant), because of skin depigmentation;
- **4-Methoxy-m-Phenylenediamine, 4-Methoxy-m-Phenylenediamine HCl, and 4- Methoxy-m-Phenylenediamine Sulfate** (hair dye ingredients), because of possible carcinogenicity; and
- **Pyrocatechol** (used in hair dyes and skin care preparations), because of carcinogenic and co-carcinogenic potential. (CIR describes this substance as unsafe for leave-on products and considers available data insufficient to assure safety for use in hair dyes.)

International Fragrance Association

http://www.ifraorg.org

Similarly, the International Fragrance Association (IFRA) establishes usage guidelines for fragrance materials. The IFRA member organization in the United States is named the Fragrance Materials Association (FMA). IFRA's Code of Practice currently recommends against the use of more than 30 substances as fragrance materials and advises limiting the use of several more. Among the many that IFRA recommends avoiding are:

- **Acetyl ethyl tetramethyl tetralin (AETT)**, because of neurotoxicity.
- **Musk Ambrette**, because of photocontact sensitization.
- **6-Methylcoumarin (6-MC)**, because of photocontact sensitization.

Color Additives

FDA strictly regulates color additives. In order to protect consumers from harmful contaminants, many cannot be used unless the color comes from a batch certified by FDA and that batch is provided with its own individual certification lot number. The addition of uncertified color to a product will make the entire product adulterated. While colors exempt from certification are not subject to such testing, manufacturers must assure that each color additive complies with the identity, specifications, labeling requirements, use, and restrictions of color additive regulations. With the exception of coal-tar hair dyes, all color additives regardless of whether or not they are subject to certification must be approved by FDA for their intended use. See: 21 U.S.C. sec. 379e. Except in the case of coal-tar hair dyes, a cosmetic product could be deemed adulterated requirements under 601(e); 21 U.S.C sec. 361(e) for failure to meet color additive requirements. This applies to imported cosmetic products as well. United States entry could be denied based on color additive violations.

http://www.fda.gov/ForIndustry/ColorAdditives/ColorAdditivesinSpecificProducts/InCosmetics/ucm110032.htm (edited and modified in part)

Basic Requirements—If the product (except coal-tar hair dyes) contains a color additive, the FDCA under section 721; 21 U.S.C. 379e; 21 CFR Parts 70 and 80 requires:

- **Approval.** All color additives used in cosmetics (or any other FDA-regulated product) must be approved by FDA. There must be a regulation specifically addressing a substance's use as a color additive, specifications, and restrictions.

- **Certification.** In addition to approval, a number of color additives must be batch certified by FDA if they are to be used in cosmetics (or any other FDA-regulated product) marketed in the U.S.
- **Identity and specifications.** All color additives must meet the requirements for identity and specifications stated in the Code of Federal Regulations (CFR).
- **Use and restrictions.** Color additives may be used only for the intended uses stated in the regulations that pertain to them. The regulations also specify other restrictions for certain colors, such as the maximum permissible concentration in the finished product.

Categories—The FDCA section 721(c) [21 U.S. C. 379e(c)] and color additive regulations [21 CFR Parts 70 and 80] separate approved color additives into two main categories: those subject to certification also known as "certifiable" and those exempt from certification. In addition, the regulations refer to other classifications, such as straight colors and lakes.

- **Colors subject to certification.** These color additives are derived primarily from petroleum and are sometimes known as "coal-tar dyes" or "synthetic-organic" colors. (**NOTE:** Coal-tar colors are materials consisting of one or more substances that either are made from coal-tar or can be derived from intermediates of the same identity as coal-tar intermediates. They may also include diluents or substrata. (*Federal Register*, May 9, 1939, page 1922.) Today, most are made from petroleum.) Except in the case of coal-tar hair dyes, these colors must not be used unless FDA has certified that the batch in question has passed analysis of its composition and purity in FDA's own labs. If the batch is not FDA-certified, do not use it. These certified colors generally have three-part names. The names include a prefix FD&C, D&C, or External D&C; a color; and a number. An example is "FD&C Yellow No. 5." Certified colors also may be identified in cosmetic ingredient declarations by color and number alone, without a prefix (such as "Yellow 5").
- **Colors exempt from certification.** These color additives are obtained primarily from mineral, plant, or animal sources. They are not subject to batch certification requirements. However, they still are considered artificial colors, and when used in cosmetics or other FDA-regulated products, they must comply with the identity, specifications, uses, restrictions, and labeling requirements stated in the regulations [21 CFR 73].

Other Classifications

- **Straight color.** "Straight color" refers to any color additive listed in 21 CFR 73, 74, and 81 [21 CFR 70.3(j)].
- **Lake.** A lake is a straight color extended on a substratum by adsorption, coprecipitation, or chemical combination that does not include any combination of ingredients made by a simple mixing process [21 CFR 70.3(l)]. Because lakes are not soluble in water, they often are used when it is important to keep a color from "bleeding," as in lipstick. In some cases, special restrictions apply to their use. As with any color additive, it is important to check the Summary of Color Additives Listed for Use in the United States in Foods, Drugs, Cosmetics and Medical Devices and the regulations themselves [21 CFR 82, Subparts B and C] to be sure you are using lakes only for their approved uses.

Safeguards against color additive violations

- **Do not confuse certified colors with their uncertified counterparts.** For example, FD&C Yellow No. 5 is the certified form of tartrazine, and is approved for use in cosmetics generally. However, tartrazine, which has not undergone FDA analysis and FDA certification, must not be substituted for or identified in an ingredient declaration as FD&C Yellow No. 5.
- **Do not confuse certified colors with colors identified only by a Colour Index (CI) number, or by the E number sometimes used in European color identification.** A color subject to certification cannot be used unless FDA has certified the batch [FD&C Act, sec. 721(a)(1)(A). A CI or E number does not indicate FDA certification.

- **When purchasing color additives subject to certification, check the label.** If the lot is certified, the color's label must state the legal name for the color (such as "FD&C Yellow No. 5"), or, if it is a mixture, the name of each ingredient; the FDA lot certification number; and the color's uses and restrictions as stated in the CFR [21 CFR 70.25).
- **Check the Summary of Color Additives on FDA's Web site.** Although this table is not a substitute for the regulations, it is an easy-to-use reference that introduces you to FDA-approved color additives and directs you to the regulations addressing specific color additives.
- **Become familiar with the regulations themselves.** The color additive regulations are in 21 CFR Parts 70 through 82. Specific color additives are addressed in Parts 73, 74, and 82. The color additive regulations are posted on FDA's Web site.
- **Confirm the status of color additives before use.** There may be changes in color additive approvals and changes in the uses and restrictions that apply to a color additive. Such changes may affect colors subject to certification as well as colors exempt from certification.
- **When purchasing colors subject to certification, confirm that the manufacturer has requested certification.** For example, choose a manufacturer from FDA's list of companies that have requested color certification within the past two years.

The color additives must be used in conjunction with intended use. Whether a particular color is subject to certification or exempt from certification, the FDCA prohibits its use in cosmetics (or any other FDA-regulated product) unless it is approved specifically for the intended use [FD&C Act, sec. 721(a)(1)(A); 21 U.S.C. 379e(a)(1)(A)]. The regulations restrict intended use as follows:

- **Eye-area use:** A color additive cannot be used in the area of the eye unless the regulation for that additive specifically permits such use [21 CFR 70.5(a)]. The "area of the eye" includes "the area enclosed within the circumference of the supra-orbital ridge and the infra-orbital ridge, including the eyebrow, the skin below the eyebrow, the eyelids and the eyelashes, and conjunctival sac of the eye, the eyeball, and the soft areolar tissue that lies within the perimeter of the infra-orbital ridge" [21 CFR 70.3(s)]. There are color additives approved for use in products, for instance, mascara and eyebrow pencils, yet none is approved for dyeing the eyebrows or eyelashes.
- **Externally applied cosmetics:** This term does not apply to the lips or any body surface covered by mucous membrane. For instance, if a color additive is approved for use in externally applied cosmetics, you may not use it in products such as lipsticks unless the regulation specifically permits this use [21 CFR 70.3 (v)].
- **Injection:** No color additive may be used in injections unless its listing in the regulations specifically provides for such use. This includes injection into the skin for tattooing or permanent makeup. The fact that a color additive is listed for any other use does not mean that it may be used for injections [21 CFR 70.5(b)]. There are no color additives listed in the regulations as approved for injections.

Novelty use and special effects does not matter and the regulations apply. The following are examples of out-of-the-ordinary color additives.
- **Color-changing pigments:** Colors that change in response to such factors as change in pH or exposure to oxygen or temperature are subject to the same regulations as all other color additives.
- **Composite pigments:** Color additives used in combination to achieve variable effects, such as those found in pearlescent products, are subject to the same regulations as all other color additives. Some color additives, when used in combination, may form new pigments, which may not be approved for the intended use. Example—"holographic" glitter, consisting of aluminum, an approved color additive bonded to an etched plastic film.
- **Fluorescent colors:** Only the following fluorescent colors are approved for use in cosmetics, and there are limits on their intended uses: D&C Orange No. 5, No. 10, and No. 11; and D&C Red No. 21, No. 22, No. 27, and No. 28 [21 CFR 74.2254, 74.2260, 74.2261, 74.2321, 74.2322, 74.2327, and 74.2328].

- **Glow-in-the-dark colors:** Luminescent zinc sulfide is the only approved glow-in-the-dark color additive [21 CFR 73.2995].
- **Halloween makeup:** These products are considered cosmetics [FD&C Act, sec. 201(i); 21 U.S.C. 321(i)] and are therefore subject to the same regulations as other cosmetics, including the same restrictions on color additives.
- **Liquid crystal colors:** These additives, which produce color motifs in a product through diffraction, are unapproved color additives. Their use in cosmetics is therefore illegal [FD&C Act, sec. 601(e); 21 U.S.C. 361(e)].
- **Tattoo pigments:** As noted above, no color additives are approved for injection into the skin, as in tattoos and permanent makeup.
- **Theatrical makeup:** Like Halloween makeup, these products are considered cosmetics [FD&C Act, sec. 201(i); 21 U.S.C. 321(i)] and are therefore subject to the same regulations as other cosmetics, including the same restrictions on color additives.

Labeling Example—Cochineal Extract and Carmine

http://www.fda.gov/ForIndustry/ColorAdditives/GuidanceComplianceRegulatoryInformation/ucm153038.htm

Carmine is a color additive that comes from dried and ground female bodies of the scale insect *Dactylopius coccus costa*. Carmine is used in hundreds of cosmetics such as lipstick, blush, eye shadow, eyeliner, nail polish, hair colors and suntan products. FDA published a final rule January 5, 2009 in the Federal Register (74 FR 207), effective January 5, 2011, that amended its regulations to require the declaration by name of the color additives cochineal extract and carmine on the label of all food and cosmetic products in the United States. The reason for the regulation is that some people experience an allergic reaction to this color additive. Cosmetics that contain carmine must specifically declare the presence of carmine "prominently and conspicuously at least once in the labeling" such as:

"Contains carmine as a color additive."

CRITICAL ANALYSIS: Does the FDCA provide sufficient safeguards in keeping with the legislative mission of the Food, Drug and Cosmetic Act? Suggest an alternative approach to post-market regulation of personal care products.

Adverse Event Example—*Cleansing Conditioners*

Investigation of WEN by Chaz Dean Cleansing Conditioners

http://www.fda.gov/Cosmetics/ProductsIngredients/Products/ucm511626.htm (edited)

FDA has been investigating reports of hair loss, hair breakage, balding, itching, and rash correlated to the use of WEN by Chaz Dean Cleansing Conditioner (WEN) products. FDA received 127 adverse event reports as of July 7, 2016 directly from consumers about WEN products. This is the highest number of reports ever associated with any cosmetic hair cleansing product, incorporating cleansing conditioners. There were over 21,000 complaints reported directly to Chaz Dean, Inc. and Guthy Renker, LLC, determined by FDA during inspections of manufacturing and distribution facilities. The FDA contacted physicians and other health care providers by sending a "Dear Physician letter requesting that they notify their patients of hair loss and other complaints linked to the use of these products. Further, FDA encourages reporting of adverse events to FDA.

CRITICAL ANALYSIS: Discuss the legal implications of FDA discovering the 21,000 complaints during the inspection.

Chapter 3: International Endeavors

http://www.fda.gov/Cosmetics/InternationalActivities/default.htm (edited)

The Office of Cosmetics and Colors (OCAC) role in international issues that pertain to cosmetics has intensified due to globalization. The International Cooperation on Cosmetics Regulation (ICCR) is an international group of cosmetic regulatory authorities from the following countries and their respective governmental agencies: United States—Food and Drug Administration; Japan—Ministry of Health, Labour, and Welfare; European Union—European Commission, DG Enterprise; and Canada-Health Canada. OCACs involvement with other regulatory agencies and the regulated industry to facilitate international trade includes:

> ➤ *Increased communication to government agencies in other countries to differentiate differences between their regulatory approach and the United States;*
> ➤ *Input to industry inquiries regarding the harmonization of ingredient nomenclature; and*
> ➤ *Determining similarities with other countries for harmonization.*

Ingredient Nomenclature—As the European Union (E.U.) has worked toward agreement on ingredient terms to ease marketing across the borders in countries representing nine different languages, the cosmetic industry has requested that FDA permit similar changes in ingredient labeling for cosmetics marketed in the United States. OCAC considers requests on a case-by-case basis, along with its legal responsibilities under the Fair Packaging and Labeling Act to promulgate necessary regulations to prevent consumer deception or to facilitate value comparisons.

Color Additives—Harmonization of ingredient labeling for color additives is a complicated issue. This is due to factors such as the requirements that only colors approved for use in the United States (U.S.) by FDA are allowed to be added to cosmetics and that, for some of these "approved" colors, only those specifically tested and certified in FDA laboratories may be used. Although the lists of approved colors in the U.S. and other countries share some common ingredients, there are also differences that complicate formulation of products for the different markets.

Animal Testing and the Development of Alternatives. Although U.S. law does not prescribe the methods used by cosmetic firms to test their ingredients or finished products for safety, regulations require a product to bear a warning statement if the safety of the product or its ingredients is not substantiated. That leads to the question of what constitutes "adequate substantiation of safety", a question that becomes especially important in light of an E.U. ban on animal testing.

Ultraviolet (UV) Filters (Sunscreens). Sunscreens pose a special challenge in international harmonization because they are considered drugs under U.S. law and cosmetics according to the E.U. There is continued interest in exploring the approval processes in different countries for sunscreen active ingredients and test procedures for measuring Sun Protection Factor (SPF).

International Cooperation on Cosmetic Regulation

http://www.fda.gov/Cosmetics/InternationalActivities/ICCR/ucm2005211.htm and *www.iccrnet.org*

The International Cooperation on Cosmetics Regulation (ICCR) is an international group of regulatory authorities for cosmetics whose members are from Canada, the European Union, the United States, Brazil and Japan. The ICCR met in 2016 in the United States to discuss issues related to personal care and cosmetic-like drug/quasi-drug products. This multilateral framework maintains the highest level of global consumer protection, while minimizing barriers to international trade. Regulators and industry focused on the following issues:

Alternatives to Animal Testing;
Allergens;
In silico/Quantitative Structure-Activity Relationship;
Microbial Contaminants;
Trace Impurities; and
Governance.

FDA International Efforts—Over-the-Counter Sunscreens

http://www.fda.gov/ForConsumers/ConsumerUpdates/ucm258416.htm (edited)

Sunscreens provide an excellent example of how these products are regulated in the United States and in the European Union. FDA notified the international personal care products community of requirements for over-the-counter (OTC) sunscreen products marketed in the United States. In the United States, these products are regulated as pharmaceutical products and not as cosmetics products as they are in many other countries. The requirements, and several proposed changes, are outlined in four regulatory documents including (1) a Final Rule, (2) a Proposed Rule, (3) an Advanced Notice of Proposed Rulemaking (ANPR), and (4) a Draft Guidance for Industry. These regulations do not address the safety of sunscreen active ingredients and do not specifically address other dosage forms.

> ➤ The Final Rule allows sunscreen products that are in compliance with FDA's requirements for protection against both ultraviolet A (UVA) and ultraviolet B (UVB) rays to be labeled as "Broad Spectrum." Products that have SPF values between 2 and 14 may be labeled as Broad Spectrum if they pass the required test, but only products that are labeled both as Broad Spectrum, with SPF values of 15 or higher, may state that they reduce the risk of skin cancer and early skin aging, when used as directed. This new rule also bans the use of the term "sun block" and requires that these products all be called "sunscreens".

> ➤ The Proposed Rule would limit the maximum SPF value on sunscreen labels to "50 +", because FDA does not deem there is sufficient data to show that products with SPF values higher than 50 provide greater protection for users than products with SPF values of 50. The proposal creates the opportunity for the submission of data to support including higher SPF values in the final rule.

> ➤ The ANPR will allow the public a period of time to submit requested data addressing the effectiveness and the safety of sunscreen sprays and to comment on possible directions and warnings for sprays that the FDA may pursue in the future, among other issues regarding dosage forms for sunscreens.

> ➤ The Draft Enforcement Guidance for Industry outlines information to help sunscreen product manufacturers understand how to label and test their products in light of the new final rule and other regulatory initiatives.

To ensure that sunscreen products meet modern safety standards, FDA is re-examining the safety information available for active ingredients included in sunscreens marketed today. These ingredients have been used for many years. If, following its review of the available relevant safety data, FDA determines that any of the active ingredients in the sunscreen products do not meet required safety standards; the agency will notify the public and work to remove that ingredient from the market promptly. The new regulations became effective for most manufacturers in one year. Manufacturers with annual sales less than $25,000 were provided more time to comply.

NOTE: See *Volume V Human Drugs*, Chapter 4 Over-the-Counter Products: Sunscreen Drug Products.

CRITICAL ANALYSIS: Discuss international implications with the FDA requirements for sunscreen products. See sunscreen final rule above and proposed rule.

Importation

Personal care cosmetic products are subject to examination when they are being imported or offered for import into the United States. FDA works with the United States Customs and Border Protection (CBP) to monitor imports. Cosmetics that may be adulterated or misbranded could be refused entry into the United States. Prior to entry they must be brought into compliance, destroyed, or re-exported. FDA maintains a list of "Import Cosmetic Refusals" updated monthly.

It is important to recognize that cosmetic products imported into the United States are subject to the same laws and regulations as those manufactured in the United States. Safety is paramount and the cosmetic must be safe for its intended use. For example, the cosmetic product must comply with all labeling requirement, must not contain any prohibited ingredients and color additives must be FDA approved. It is impossible to inspect every single personal care cosmetic product for entry into the United States; however, compliance with the FDCA and related laws is paramount. FDA issues Import Alerts that focus on cosmetic-type products marketed with therapeutic claims which are: Unapproved new drugs; adulterated cosmetics due to microbial contamination; those that fail to meet United States requirements for color additives; and bulk shipments of high-risk bovine tissue from BSE (bovine spongiform encephalopathy) countries. FDA surveillance includes issuance of "Import Alerts" related and import refusals.

CRITICAL ANALYSIS: Review the import alerts and refusals (links below). Discuss other regulatory measures that could be used to prevent entry of cosmetic products that do not comply with United States laws.

http://www.accessdata.fda.gov/cms_ia/industry_53.html
http://www.fda.gov/Cosmetics/InternationalActivities/

Exporting Cosmetics

http://www.fda.gov/Cosmetics/InternationalActivities/Exporters/default.htm (edited)

FDA does not require an export certificate nor is the agency legally obligated to issue a "certificate" for export purposes. It is the responsibility of a company to follow U.S. laws and regulations and to know the cosmetics requirements of those countries where a company is exporting to. However, foreign governments and customers may request a "certificate" for cosmetic importation into their country. The following summary is based on FDAs export certificate information. Firms exporting products from the United States are often asked by foreign governments or customers to supply a "certificate" as a requisite to import a product into their country.

➤ FDA does not require an export certificate.
➤ FDA is not required by law to issue certificates for cosmetics.
➤ FDA does not issue certificates for cosmetics manufactured outside the U.S.

Those who request a cosmetic certificate have the responsibility to ensure that their products are cosmetics as defined under U.S. law.

➤ The term "drug" includes articles intended for use in the diagnosis, cure, mitigation, treatment, or prevention of disease in man or other animals and articles (other than foods and dietary supplements) intended to affect the structure or any function of the body.

➤ The term "device" includes an instrument, apparatus, implement, machine, contrivance, implant, in vitro reagent, or other similar or related article, including any component, part, or accessory, intended for use in the diagnosis of disease or other conditions, or in the cure, mitigation, treatment, or prevention of disease, in man or other animals, or intended to affect the structure or any function of the body, and which does not achieve its primary intended purposes through chemical action within or on the body and which is not dependent upon being metabolized for the achievement of its primary intended purposes.

➤ The term "cosmetic" means articles intended to be rubbed, poured, sprinkled, or sprayed on, introduced into, or otherwise applied to the human body or any part thereof for cleansing, beautifying, promoting attractiveness, or altering the appearance, and articles intended for use as a component of any such articles; except that such term shall not include soap (soap is defined in the Code of Federal Regulations at 21 CFR 701.20).

The intended use of a product is determined by claims made on the product label, in collateral labeling, and in other promotional materials. Information on the company's Internet site is also considered when evaluating intended use. Specific and implied drug or device claims are not appropriate for products marketed solely as cosmetics. Some examples of intended use that may cause a product to be regulated as a drug are claims for sun protection, including use of a sun protection factor (SPF) rating; prevention and treatment of dandruff or acne; hair restoration; skin bleaching;

325

immune and circulatory system improvement; and skin lesion healing. Sometimes you may need to request certificates from different FDA Centers for different items of the same kit you wish to export. An example of this would be a dental kit that includes an anticaries toothpaste (drug), a mouthwash for cleansing and fresh breath (cosmetic), and a toothbrush and dental floss (devices). The title of FDA issued export certificates for cosmetics is "CERTIFICATE". There are two types of certificates as follows:

> **General "CERTIFICATE"**—A General Certificate does not list any specific products by name. It states that FDA has on file a letter "regarding the status of products exported from the United States."

> **Product-Specific "CERTIFICATE"**—A Product-Specific Certificate states that FDA has on file a letter regarding specific product(s), listed by name in a supplied product list, which FDA attaches to the Product-Specific Certificate.

There are other sources of cosmetic certificates, besides FDA. Some foreign governments may accept certificates issued by a state or local agency, such as a health department or board of trade, or by a trade association. Some trade associations provide export certificates. Some states that provide export certificates include: Florida, New Jersey, and Texas.

The laws of other countries are different from United States, and there may be situations when a product for export does not comply with the FDCA or Fair Packaging and Labeling Act (FPLA). A product intended for export will not be considered adulterated or misbranded under the FD&C Act (Section 801(e); U.S. Code, Title 21, sec. 381(e)) if it:

> Meets the specifications of the foreign purchaser,

> Is not in conflict with the laws of the country to which it is intended for export,

> Is labeled on the outside of the shipping package that it is intended for export, and

> Is not sold or offered for sale in domestic commerce.

A certificate does not mean FDA approval. The issuance of a certificate does not suggest or imply that FDA approves or sanctions the labels and labeling of the firm's products or that the firm's products comply with the requirements of the FD&C Act and/or the FPLA and related regulations. The issuance of a certificate does not preclude the Agency from taking regulatory action against such products in the future, if such action is warranted. Further, a certificate does not constitute an admission, or agreement, or determination by FDA that a product is a cosmetic as defined in section 201(i) of the FD&C Act.

Chapter 4: Enforcement Mechanisms and Litigation

FDA does not have legal authority under the Food, Drug, and Cosmetic Act (FDCA) for FDA to pre-approve cosmetic products as there is for drugs. That is, pursuant to the FDCA, FDA cosmetic regulatory enforcement occurs only after a product enters the marketplace. However, FDA can exercise postmarket enforcement authority including the issuance of warning letters, nationwide alerts, seizures and court actions.

Usually, a firm will voluntarily recall a product if necessary and FDA will monitor the recall progress. For example, under 21 CFR 7.53, FDA can monitor the progress of a recall and conduct audit checks to verify the effectiveness of a recall. FDA can evaluate the health hazard under 21 CFR 7.41 associated with the product and provide a classification to point to the level of hazard created by a product under recall. See: 21 CFR 7.3(m). Classes of recalls include:

➢ *Class I, a situation in which there is a reasonable probability that the use of or exposure to a violative product will cause serious adverse health consequences or death;*

➢ *Class II, a situation in which use of, or exposure to, a violative product may cause temporary or medically reversible adverse health consequences or where the probability of serious adverse health consequences is remote; and*

➢ *Class III, a situation in which use of, or exposure to, a violative product is not likely to cause adverse health consequences.*

Besides voluntary company initiated recalls, FDA issues warning letters, alerts and can seize cosmetic personal care products. Examples are illustrated below.

NOTE: See this Volume, Chapter 1, for warning letters regarding product classification.

Recalls, Warnings and Alerts

https://www.fda.gov/Cosmetics/ComplianceEnforcement/RecallsAlerts/ucm2005156.htm
Recall Illustrations

➢ INTENZE Products, Inc. recalls Bright Red (Lot SS264) and Royal Blue (Lot SS258) 2 oz. tattoo ink bottles because of microbial organisms (bacillus halosaccharovorans, brachybacterium conglomeratum, and pseudomonas andersonii and pseudomonas balearica) in the inks.

➢ Saje Natural Business, Inc. recalls Saje Natural Wellness Splish Splash Gentle Baby Wash 8.5 fl. oz. and 1.7 fl. oz. bottles for potential contamination with Pseudomonas aeruginosa.

➢ Bath and Body Works recalls Pure Simplicity Body Acai Berry 8 fluid oz products due to potential contamination with Enterobacter aerogenes and/or Enterobacter gergoviae.

➢ Bath and Body Works recalls Pure Simplicity Body Fragrance Free 8 fluid oz products due to potential contamination with Enterobacter aerogenes and/or Enterobacter gergoviae.

➢ Solid Ink recalls SOLID INK ORANGE, 2 oz, Batch #8297, EXP DATE 8/21 because FDA's National Center for Toxicological Research (NCTR) analyzed a sample of Solid Ink Orange (tattoo ink) (Batch #8297) which resulted positive for Bacillus pumilus, Bacillus licheniformis, and Pseudomonas sp. The Office of Cosmetics and Colors concluded that the product appears to be adulterated because it contains microorganisms at a level that exceeds acceptable limits for cosmetics.

CRITICAL ANALYSIS: Review the recalls above. Should FDA have mandatory recall authority for these types of products?

Warning Letters

https://www.fda.gov/Cosmetics/ComplianceEnforcement/WarningLetters/ucm081086.htm

CRITICAL ANALYIS: Choose a warning letter from the above link and prepare a response to FDA.

Jurisdiction—*Brazilian Blowout*

FDA received several inquiries from consumers and salon professionals concerning the safety of "Brazilian Blowout" and similar "professional use only" hair smoothing products. The U.S. Occupational Safety and Health Administration (OSHA) issued a Hazard Alert in 2011 to hair salon owners and workers about potential formaldehyde exposure from these products. FDA issued a Warning Letter also in 2011 citing Brazilian Blowout for safety and labeling violations.

The warning letter lists health risks associated with inhaling formaldehyde and reactions that have been reported when people used the product as directed. Reported reactions included eye problems, nervous system problems such as headaches and dizziness, respiratory tract problems, nausea, chest pain, vomiting, and rash. The warning letter stated that the labeling was misleading because it called the product "formaldehyde free", even though people were exposed to formaldehyde when using it as intended. The labeling failed to disclose likely consequences of using the product under the conditions prescribed in the labels or labeling.

See: *http://www.fda.gov/ICECI/EnforcementActions/WarningLetters/2011/ucm270809.htm*

NOTE: FDA does not have legal authority over salon operations; salons are usually subject to state and local regulation. Further, FDA does not have legal authority over the practice of cosmetology. OSHA regulates workplace safety that includes air quality.

See: Hazard Alert: Hair-Smoothing Products That Could Release Formaldehyde. *https://www.osha.gov/SLTC/formaldehyde/hazard_alert.html*

However, see *Envtl. Working Grp. v. FDA*, 16-2435 (D.D.C., filed December 13, 2016). The complaint alleged that FDA failed, in violation of its statutory mandate under the Food, Drug and Cosmetic Act, 21 U.S.C. § 301, *et seq.* (the "FDCA"), as well as its own regulations, to act on a citizen petition filed *over five years ago*, on or about April 12, 2011 which called on the FDA to investigate and regulate keratin hair straighteners -- cosmetic products routinely used in beauty salons across the nation to smooth, protect, soften and relax hair -- that contain formaldehyde and formaldehyde-releasing chemicals. The case was dismissed on jurisdictional grounds.

CRITICAL ANALYSIS: Review the warning letter (link above) and research any further enforcement action(s). For example, were there any seizure actions? Is the product still in the marketplace and if so, does it comply with the mandates under the FDCA?

Warning—Lead Poisoning Risks
Kohl, Kajal, Al-Kahal, or Surma and "Litargirio"

In this warning update, FDA advised that many people may be unaware of the risk of lead poisoning, in both adults and children, from an easily avoidable source: the traditional eye cosmetic known variously as kohl, kajal, al-kahl, or surma. Samples tested often contain significant amounts of lead. Lead sometimes accounts for more than half the weight of a sample of kohl, usually in the form of lead sulfide. Kohl may also contain a variety of other materials, such as aluminum, antimony, carbon, iron, and zinc compounds, as well as camphor and menthol. Kohl is not legal in the United States. Kohl is a color additive and there is no regulation permitting its use in a cosmetic or in any other FDA-regulated product.

FDA issued a public warning not to use "LITARGIRIO" for any health-related or personal purposes. Litargirio is a yellow- or peach-colored powder manufactured by Roldan, Ferreira, and possibly other laboratories in the Dominican Republic. It has no proven health benefits and, because of its high lead content, poses health risks when used in contact with the skin or ingested. These risks are particularly serious for children. The powder has been used as a deodorant, a foot fungicide, a treatment for burns and wound healing, and for other purposes as a traditional remedy, particularly by people from the Dominican Republic. It contains up to 79 per cent lead—a highly toxic substance that can cause permanent neurological damage in children.

CRITICAL ANALYSIS: Except for most color additives and some prohibited ingredients, personal care cosmetic products are not subject to FDA premarket approval under the FDCA. Despite enforcement authority, over recent years, enforcement appears inadequate. Perhaps this is due to a lack of resources. Review the post-market actions above and determine whether the FDCA should be amended to permit premarket approval authority.

Talcum Powder Litigation

https://www.fda.gov/Cosmetics/ProductsIngredients/Ingredients/ucm293184.htm

The talcum powder cases have proliferated to over 9,000 lawsuits albeit with mixed results. For example, one case in point is the Johnson & Johnson (J&J) case with the allegation that talcum powder caused ovarian cancer. Initially, the plaintiff prevailed where the jury award was $417 million; however, the court declared that there was insufficient evidence and the verdict was overturned. See: *Charmaine Lloyd, et al. v. Johnson & Johnson, et al.*, BC628228, Plaintiff *Eva Echeverria. In re Johnson & Johnson Talcum Powder Cases* (2017). The court granted a new trial to the defendants by order dated 10/20/17:

(1) The motions for JNOV by Johnson & Johnson and JCCI are granted;

(2) The motions for new trial by Johnson & Johnson and JCCI on grounds of (1) insufficiency of the evidence as to causation as to both defendants (Cal. Code of Civ. Pro. 657(6)); (2) error in law occurring at trial and excepted to by defendants (Cal. Code of Civ. Pro. 657(7); (3) misconduct of the jury (Cal. Code of Civ. Pro. 657(2); Civ. Pro. 657(2); and (4) excessive compensatory damages (as to Johnson & Johnson) and excessive punitive damages (as to both defendants) (Cal. Code of Civ. Pro. 657(5) are granted.

However, in 2018 decision, a jury in Missouri ordered J&J to pay $4.69 billion to 22 women who alleged that J&Js talcum powder products caused ovarian cancer. Compensatory damages were $550 million to cover costs of chemotherapy treatment and $4.14 billion in punitive damages.

NOTE: See Johnathan D. Rockoff and Sara Randazzo, *J&J Hit by $4.7 Billion Verdict*, Wall St. J., B3 (July 13, 2018).

Chapter 5: The Quest for Beauty

Tanning Salons and the Tan Tax

http://www.fda.gov/ForConsumers/ConsumerUpdates/ucm186687.htm
http://www.ncsl.org/research/health/indoor-tanning-restrictions.aspx

FDA regulates tanning beds as medical devices. The use of tanning beds or booths including sunlamps continues to raise safety concerns. There is widespread consensus and studies concerning the increased risk of skin cancer due to the regular use of tanning beds. The 2010 Patient Protection and Affordable Care Act contains a tax on "indoor tanning". Additionally, some states have laws with restrictions on tanning booths. The number of states that regulate the use of tanning facilities by minors is at least 42. Further, Some states such as California, Delaware, District of Columbia, Hawaii, Illinois, Louisiana, Minnesota, Nevada, New Hampshire, North Carolina, Oregon, Texas and Vermont have banned the use of tanning beds for all minors under 18.

Those who use tanning booths receive an application of the color additive dihydroxyacetone (DHA) in mist or spray form. DHA is listed as a color additive for use to impart color to the external part of the human body with certain exclusion such as: the lips, body surfaces covered by mucous membrane or the eye area. Similarly, the use of "tanning pills" has become more popular over the years and creates safety issues. Tanning pills, which are not approved by FDA, contain canthaxanthin. Although canthaxanthin is an FDA-approved color additive for foods when used in very small amounts, it does not have FDA approval for any use in large quantities. The legal decision of *French Bronze Tablets* expands on this point.

The Food, Drug, and Cosmetic Act (FD&C Act), Section 721 authorizes the regulation of color additives, including their uses and restrictions. These regulations are found in Title 21, Code of Federal Regulations (21 CFR), beginning at Part 70. If a color additive is not permitted by regulation or is used in a way that does not comply with the specific regulation(s) authorizing its use, it is considered unsafe under the law. Such misuse of color additives causes a cosmetic to be adulterated. DHA is listed in the regulations as a color additive for use in imparting color to the human body. However, its use in cosmetics—including sunless "tanning" products—is restricted to external application (21 CFR 73.2150). According to the CFR, "externally applied" cosmetics are those "applied only to external parts of the body and not to the lips or any body surface covered by mucous membrane" (21 CFR 70.3v). In addition, no color additive may be used in cosmetics intended for use in the area of the eye unless the color additive is permitted specifically for such use (21 CFR 70.5a). The CFR defines "area of the eye" as follows: "the area enclosed within the circumference of the supra-orbital ridge, including the eyebrow, the skin below the eyebrow, the eyelids and the eyelashes, and conjunctival sac of the eye, the eyeball, and the soft areolar tissue that lies within the perimeter of the infra-orbital ridge." (21 CFR 70.3s)

What does this mean for DHA spray "tanning" booths? When using DHA-containing products as an all-over spray or mist in a commercial spray "tanning" booth, it may be difficult to avoid exposure in a manner for which DHA is not approved, including the area of the eyes, lips, or mucous membrane, or even internally. Consequently, FDA advises asking the following questions when considering commercial facilities where DHA is applied by spraying or misting. Are consumers protected from exposure in *the entire eye area, on the lips and all parts of the body covered by mucous membrane and internal exposure caused by inhaling or ingesting the product?*

CRITICAL ANALYSIS: The federal 10% "Tan Tax" See: 26 U.S.C. section 5000B (2010) applies to indoor tanning salons. Evaluate whether this tax dissuades those from using "tanning booths" and hence possibly decrease melanoma and other skins cancers related to artificial indoor tanning? Discuss whether you agree or disagree and recommend other regulatory measures. See: state regulations noted below.

http://www.ncsl.org/research/health/indoor-tanning-restrictions.aspx

Tanning Pills, Bronzers and Sunless Tanners

http://www.fda.gov/Cosmetics/ProductsIngredients/Products/ucm134217.htm (edited)

There is no FDA approved "magic pill" for a "magic tan". Yet, these types of unapproved products nevertheless appear in the marketplace. For example, there are tanning pills promoted for *Tinting the Skin.* This is accomplished by consuming massive doses of color additives, usually canthaxanthin. FDA approved canthaxanthin for use as a color additive in foods in minute amounts; however, it is not approved in tanning pills.

NOTE: Sunless Tanners and Bronzers—There is no legal definition under the FDCA for the terms "sunless tanners" or "bronzers". Sunless tanner products are marketed for consumers for a tanned appearance without exposure to the sun or ultraviolet radiation. Usually, dihydroxyacetone (DHA), a color additive that darkens the skin is contained in the product. DHA reacts with amino acids in the surface of the skin. Similarly, the intent of "bronzers" is to darken the skin on a temporary basis. They are usually marketed in tinted moisturizers and brush-on powders.

French Bronze Tablets

United States v. Eight Unlabeled Cases, More or Less, of an Article of Cosmetic French Bronze Tablets FBNH Enterprises, Inc.,
888 F.2d 945 (2nd Cir. 1989)

KAUFMAN, Circuit Judge: Although the pursuit of an even suntan has long been fashionable, only lately has it been attained through pharmaceutical products. Manufacturers have begun marketing cosmetic products which impart color to the skin without the traditional exposure to the natural and perhaps dangerous rays of the sun. French Bronze Tablets, one such product, is the subject of this appeal. The facts in this case are not in dispute. The United States, on behalf of the Food and Drug Administration ("F.D.A."), commenced a lawsuit on June 16, 1988, by filing a complaint *in rem* seeking the forfeiture and condemnation of a quantity of a product labeled "FRENCH BRONZE TABLETS," in the possession of the Claimant-Appellant, FBNH Enterprises, Inc. ("FBNH"). The complaint alleged that the tablets are "adulterated" cosmetics within the meaning of 21 U.S.C. § 361(e) because they contain canthaxanthin and beta-carotene, allegedly unsafe color additives as defined by 21 U.S.C. § 376(a). *** On appeal, we must decide whether Judge Glasser correctly held that, a cosmetic tanning product which contains a color additive approved for use in food and drugs but unapproved for use in cosmetics must be banned from the marketplace. As a matter of statutory interpretation and simple logic, we agree with the lower court and affirm.

We now commence our tortuous journey through the Food, Drug, and Cosmetic Act (the "Act"). Congress has delegated to the Secretary of Health and Human Services the authority to regulate food, drugs and cosmetics for the purpose of safeguarding the public health from deleterious, adulterated and misbranded articles. *See United States v. Walsh*, 331 U.S. 432, 434, 91 L. Ed. 1585, 67 S. Ct. 1283 (1947); *see also United States v. Diapulse Corp.*, 457 F.2d 25, 28 (2d Cir. 1972) (purpose of Food, Drug and Cosmetic Act is to protect public from products not proven safe and effective). The Secretary of Health and Human Services has redelegated his authority under the Act to the Commissioner of the Food and Drug Administration. *See* 21 C.F.R. § 5.10. Among other powers, the F.D.A. has been given the authority to regulate the use of color additives in food, drugs, and cosmetics. In particular, § 376(b) instructs:

(1) The Secretary shall, by regulation, provide for separately listing color additives for use in or on food, color additives for use in or on drugs, or devices, and color additives for use in or on cosmetics, if and to the extent that such additives are suitable and safe for any such use when employed in accordance with such regulations.

Thus, the F.D.A. is required to issue separate regulations approving color additives specifically for use in food, drugs and cosmetics to the extent an additive is suitable and safe for its intended use. As a means of protecting the public health, 21 U.S.C. § 376(a) creates a presumption that a color additive is "unsafe" if the F.D.A. has not issued a regulation approving its use in a food, drug or cosmetic. Any product that contains the presumptively unsafe color additive is deemed "adulterated" under 21 U.S.C. § 361(e) and is subject to seizure and condemnation pursuant to 21 U.S.C. § 334. Specifically, 21 U.S.C. § 376(a) provides:

> *A color additive shall, with respect to any particular use (for which it is being used or intended to be used or is represented as suitable) in or on food or drugs or devices or cosmetics, be deemed unsafe for the purposes of the application of section . . . 361(e) of this title, as the case may be, unless—(1)(A) there is in effect, and such additive and such use are in conformity with, a regulation issued under subsection (b) of this section.*

Under 21 U.S.C. § 361(e), a cosmetic is deemed adulterated "if it is not a hair dye and it is, or it bears or contains, a color additive which is unsafe within the meaning of section 376(a) of this title." Title 21 U.S.C. § 334, states that any food, drug or cosmetic product which is adulterated while in interstate commerce or held for sale after interstate shipment may be seized, condemned, and destroyed. FBNH does not deny that the defendant French Bronze Tablets are "cosmetics other than hair dye" within the meaning of 21 U.S.C. § 361(e). Further, it concedes that each tablet contains 30 milligrams of canthaxanthin, a color additive that has not been approved for use in a cosmetic under 21 U.S.C. § 376(b). It argues, however, that the existence of regulations permitting the use of canthaxanthin in food or drugs makes it inappropriate to ban the cosmetic product French Bronze Tablets on the ground that it contains the same color additive. ***

Thus, Claimant insists that the existence of regulations permitting the use of canthaxanthin in food and drugs renders its use in a cosmetic product "safe" so that the defendant FRENCH BRONZE TABLETS are exempt from a finding of adulteration under 21 U.S.C. § 361(e). Only such an interpretation, FBNH asserts, makes logical sense of the statutory language. We disagree. *** Both the language and the legislative history of 21 U.S.C. § 376 indicate that its last paragraph was intended to provide that a food or cosmetic product which uses a color additive in accordance with an existing regulation shall not be deemed adulterated on the ground that the color additive may be found "poisonous or deleterious" within the meaning of the food and cosmetic provisions 21 U.S.C. §§ 342(a) and 361(a), respectively. In sum, 21 U.S.C. § 376(a) provides that the F.D.A. may not ban through forfeiture and condemnation proceedings cosmetics that contain color additives which have been approved for use in cosmetics, despite the fact that those color additives may be harmful when used in concentrations or in situations differing from those prescribed as safe by regulation. ***

As long as a color additive present in a food or cosmetic is used in accordance with a prescribed regulation, the product may not be condemned as adulterated because the additive proves harmful in other circumstances. The final provision of 21 U.S.C. § 376(a) therefore acts as a limitation on the scope and application of §§ 361(a) and 342(a) of Title 21. It does not, however, assist in overcoming the presumption that an unapproved additive in a cosmetic is unsafe within the meaning of 21 U.S.C. § 361(e), the section relevant to this appeal. ***

> *We now arrive at the end of our journey through the thicket of the Food, Drug and Cosmetic Act. We are mindful of Learned Hand's consoling words on his foray through the Internal Revenue Act: "cross-reference to cross-reference, exception upon exception—couched in abstract terms . . . but successfully concealed, . . . which it is my duty to extract, but . . . only after the most inordinate expenditure of time." I. Dilliard, The Spirit of Liberty 236 (3rd ed. 1960) [emphasis added].*

We affirm the judgment of the district court that Claimant's FRENCH BRONZE TABLETS are adulterated pursuant to 21 U.S.C. § 361(e) and forfeitable pursuant to 21 U.S.C. § 334(a).

CRITICAL ANALYSIS: Review post *French Bronze Tablets* enforcement below and integrate into an assessment of this case. Evaluate whether the judge ruled correctly.

Post *French Bronze Tablets* Enforcement

http://www.fda.gov/cosmetics/productsingredients/products/ucm134217.htm

What has happened since the *French Bronze Tablets* decision? Has the FDA altered its position? A personal care cosmetic product can be deemed adulterated if it contains a color additive that is unsafe within the meaning of section 721(a) of the FDCA, Sec. 601(e). FDA issued warning letters to the following firms, deeming the personal care cosmetic products adulterated due to the violative use of a color additive. The products contained canthaxanthin and were marketed for use as a tanning product. According to FDA, this is not a permitted use for this color additive. For example, USA Chemicals received a warning letter about this unapproved use. See link below.

http://www.fda.gov/Cosmetics/ComplianceEnforcement/WarningLetters/ucm085155.htm

Import Alert: "Oral Tanning Tablets"

http://www.accessdata.fda.gov/cms_ia/importalert_127.html

Reason for Alert: Import Alert #53-03, originally issued in 1981 and more recently in 2011, was in response to a number of inquiries concerning the status of oral tanning tablets. Recently inquires about these tablets have surfaced again. These products are classified as cosmetics. Canthaxanthin, the major ingredient, is a color additive that has not been approved by the agency for this or any other cosmetic use. Therefore this product contains an unsafe color additive and is deemed adulterated and subject to regulatory action.

Guidance: Districts may detain, without physical examination, all shipments of oral tanning tablets that contain canthaxanthin from all manufacturers. For questions or issues concerning science, science policy, sample collection, analysis, preparation, or analytical methodology, contact the Division of Field Science at (301) 796-5992.

Product Description: Oral Tanning tablets which contain the ingredient canthaxanthin (Alternate names: C.I. 40850 Canthaxanthin (C.I. Food Orange 8).

Charge: "The article is subject to refusal of admission pursuant to Section 801(a)(3) in that it appears to contain a color additive (canthaxanthin) which is unsafe within the meaning of Section 706(a) [Adulteration, Section 601(e)]."

Countries: MULTIPLE COUNTRIES (53 M L - 99) Other Suntan Preparations (not Sunscreen), N.E.C.

Description: Oral tanning tablets which contain canthaxanthin

Problems: 40850-CANTHAXANTHIN (C.I. FOOD ORANGE 8) (03/18/2011)

Future Direction—American Beauty

American Beauty: An Analytical View of the Past and Current Effectiveness of Cosmetic Safety Regulations and the Potential Direction of Future Regulation (edited)

Roseann B. Termini and Leah Tressler (Used with permission, Food and Drug Law Institute).

Virtually every American in our current society uses cosmetics on a daily basis. What was once an industry of products that were developed at home or sold door to door has become a mass market of ubiquitous items used in every American household. Concern for cosmetic safety arose in the early 1900's as consumers faced adverse health effects from dangerous ingredients included in product formulations. Along with the rise of commercial cosmetic sales came a strong public outcry for measures to safeguard consumers against cosmetic hazards.

Public concern influenced the inclusion of cosmetic regulation in the Food, Drug and Cosmetic Act of 1938[1]. The language in the Food, Drug and Cosmetic Act of 1938 concerning cosmetics has not changed substantially over the years. There is ongoing debate as to whether the FDA should exercise greater control over testing, monitoring and approval aspects of cosmetic manufacturing, distribution and sales. Despite voluntarily adoption of more stringent standards by some manufacturers, the question remains as to whether the FDA will also adopt more stringent regulation.

Societal Mores of the Early 1900's and the Beginning of Commercial Cosmetics

---

[1] Federal Food, Drug and Cosmetic Act of 1938, ch. 675, 52 Stat. 1040 (1938) codified at 21 U.S.C. § 301 *et seq.*

During the late 1800's, cosmetics were mainly concocted in private homes with ingredients purchased from pharmacies.[2] During this time period, it was socially unacceptable to wear visible makeup; therefore, many women restricted their use of cosmetics to powders, fragrances and rouge.[3] The recipes used to make the cosmetics sometimes contained hazardous ingredients such as lead, mercury, copper, tin, arsenic and bismuth.[4] In some cases, women used these ingredients although there were warnings about the potential health hazards such ingredients presented.[5]

At the time the Food and Drugs Act of 1906 was enacted, cosmetic sales in the United States were minimal. This insignificant impact on the economy was likely to have played some role in Congress' choice to ignore regulation of cosmetic products. Companies including The Harriet Hubbard Ayer Company and the California Perfume Company (Avon), as well as individuals such as Madam C.J. Walker, began selling products door to door to customers who wished to purchase products and thereby alleviate the time consumed in making the products themselves.[6] This increase in availability of manufactured products, when coupled with the changing social views around the time of World War One, shifted the views of cosmetic use. As younger generations began demanding cosmetics, a mass market quickly erupted so that by 1915 there were annual cosmetic sales of $50 million dollars.[7]

The expanding cosmetic market brought about many safety concerns that had not previously affected a sizeable number of Americans. As more products became available throughout the market, citizens openly relied on advertisements and purchased products intending to receive the advertised benefits. Adverse effects of cosmetic formulations gained public recognition as larger numbers of women suffered from dangerous ingredients. One of the earliest accounts of a cosmetic hazard involved Koremlu cream. Koremlu Cream was a depilatory cream containing thallium acetate, a poison that can cause selective forms of paralysis in customers using products containing one percent of thallium.[8] The American Medical Association's Bureau of Investigation found that Koremlu cream contained an ingredient that could poison the nervous system.[9] Despite these health hazards, Koremlu cream remained available on the market with press or word of mouth being the source of warning to consumers.[10] A second type of product that raised public concerns in the 1930's was eyebrow and lash tint containing color additives, nitrate, ammonia and pyrogallic acid.[11] The high content levels of these ingredients caused permanent eye injuries to numerous purchasers.[12]

---

[2] Gwen Kay, Dying to be Beautiful: The Fight for Safe Cosmetics, 10-12 (The Ohio State University Press, 2005).

[3] *Id.* at 10.

[4] *Id.* at 11.

[5] This may beg the question as to the true effectiveness of warnings and labels; however, Americans seem to demand an informed consumer market where the consumer decides whether he or she is willing to accept potential hazards.

[6] On February 6, 2007, Congress enacted a concurrent resolution expressing the opinion that Madame C.J. Walker, who invented a hair relaxing treatment in 1905 and was one of the first American women to amass a personal net worth exceeding one million dollars, should be recognized as one of history's greatest female business women and role models. H.R.J. Res. 58, 110th Cong. (2007).

[7] Flappers began changing the popularity and use of visible makeup. *See* Kay, *supra* note 2, at 39.

[8] *Smith v. Denholm & McKay Co.*, 192 N.E. 631, 632 (Mass. 1934).

[9] The American Medical Association created The Propaganda Department in 1906. The Department was later re-named the Bureau of Investigation in 1925. The purpose of the Bureau was to collect and disseminate information about health quackery and fraud. Kay, *supra* note 1, at 70-71; *see also* American Medical Association, *Chronology of AMA History*, http://www.ama-assn.org/ama/pub/category/1922.html (last visited Nov. 19, 2007).

[10] The product manufacturer eventually went bankrupt and ceased selling Koremlu Cream. *Id.*

[11] *Bundy v. Ey-Teb, Inc.*, 160 Misc. 325, 326 (N.Y. Misc. 1935 (finding the manufacturer liable for personal injuries suffered by a customer who used a lash tint according to instructions and relied on the label stating that the preparation contained no poisonous metals).

[12] *Id.*

While the FDA continued to receive requests, demands and inquiries concerning these hazardous cosmetics on the market, the FDA reiterated that it lacked the authority to regulate cosmetics.[13] Although injured consumers were able to bring civil actions against the manufacturers, there remained a concern that the dangerous products should not be readily available to consumers who were unaware of such dangers.[14] The increase in harmful effects of Koremlu cream and Lash Lure gained the attention of government officials, who began to realize the void of needed regulation concerning this relatively new mass commodities market.[15]

Legislative Struggles to Enact Regulations Concerning the Cosmetic Industry

Increased manufacturing and use of cosmetics created a greater need for cosmetic regulation in order to safeguard consumers from potential harm. The Food and Drugs Act of 1906 did not regulate cosmetics.[16] By 1917, it had become clear that there was a lack of control in regulating injurious cosmetics due to the inability to fit cosmetics within the definition of a drug.[17]

As consumer injuries from cosmetic ingredients became known, the issue of cosmetic regulation entered the political arena. In 1933, District of New York Senator Royal Copeland introduced legislation that included cosmetic regulation under the FDA.[18] The proposal cited the recent injuries sustained by consumers using Koremlu cream, which had been on the market at the time.[19] This proposed law was met by strong opposition, particularly with respect to the regulation of false advertising.[20] The ever-present cosmetic injuries grew to such an extent that in 1935, President Roosevelt declared that more careful enforcement was needed.[21] The House of Representatives passed the measure with thirty-nine amendments, particularly applying to the issue of advertising; however, due to the Senate's disagreement with these amendments, the proposed legislation was ultimately rejected.[22] Reintroduced of the proposal occurred in 1937, raising the issue of whether ingredients should be required to be listed on cosmetics.[23] In 1938, following five years of numerous amendments and reintroduction, President Roosevelt signed S.5, the Federal Food, Drug and Cosmetic Act of 1938.[24]

The United States Federal Food, Drug and Cosmetic Act of 1938: How is the Term Cosmetic Defined and to What Extent are Cosmetics Regulated?

Cosmetics are defined as "articles intended to be rubbed, poured, sprinkled or sprayed on, introduced into, or otherwise applied to the human body or any part thereof for cleansing, beautifying, promoting attractiveness, or altering the appearance, and articles intended for use as a component

---

[13] *See* Kay, *supra* note 2, at 97 *citing* "*Cosmetics labeled with therapeutic claims subject to action under food and drug laws,*" May 13, 1932, Press Notices, PR Manuscripts (021.1); General Correspondence 1932, NACP 88.

[14] This concern continues to be a debated issue today.

[15] S.B. Forbes & W.C. Blake, *Fatality Resulting from the Use of Lash-Lure on the Eyebrow and Eyelashes*, 103 JAMA 1441-42 (1934).

[16] While an 1897 version of the 1906 Act included cosmetics within the drug definition, this was dropped from the 1906 version, apparently due to an interest in increasing political support. Gary L. Yingling & Suzan Onel, *Cosmetic Regulation Revisited*, Fundamentals of Law and Regulation Vol. I, 316 (Robert P. Brady ed., FDLI 1997), *citing* Anderson, *Pioneer Statutes: The Pure Food and Drugs Act of 1906*, 13 J. Pub. Law 189 (1964).

[17] *See* Yingling, *supra* note 16, at 316-317 *citing* Federal Food, Drug and Cosmetic Act: A Statement of Its Legislative Record 24-25 (Charles Wesley Dunn ed. 1938).

[18] S. 1944, 73d Cong., 1st Sess., *reprinted in* 77 Cong. Rec. 5721-23 (1933).

[19] 1933 USDA, FDA Annual Report 1, 13-16 (1934).

[20] *See* Yingling, *supra* note 16, at 317.

[21] *Id.* at 319.

[22] *Id.* at 319-320.

[23] Additional changes to the bill included the definition of what would constitute an adulterated cosmetic. The original language that included a product as being adulterated "if it was or could be injurious to the user under usual or prescribed conditions" was rejected, with the substitute bill limiting an adulterated product to one that "bears or contains any poisonous or deleterious substance that may render it injurious to the user under the usual or prescribed conditions of use." Laura A. Heymann, *The Cosmetic/Drug Dilemma: FDA Regulation of Alpha-Hydroxy Acids*, 52 Food Drug L.J. 357, 362 (1997).

[24] *See* Yingling, *supra* note 16, at 320 *citing* 83 Cong. Rec. 13,183 (1938).

of any such articles; except that such term shall not include soap."[25] Cosmetics have been classified into several categories: skincare, fragrances, eye and other makeup, manicure products, hair coloring preparations, shampoos, deodorants, shaving products, baby products, bath oils and bubble-baths, mouthwashes and tanning products.[26]

Under the Food, Drug and Cosmetic Act of 1938, a cosmetic shall not be adulterated or misbranded. Cosmetics are considered adulterated if:

> "(a) it bears or contains any poisonous or deleterious substance which may render it injurious to users under the conditions of use prescribed in the labeling thereof, or under such conditions of use as are customary or usual, except that this provision shall not apply to coal-tar hair dye . . .(b) if it consists in whole or in part of any filthy, putrid, or decomposed substance, (c) if it has been prepared, packed, or held under insanitary conditions whereby it may have become contaminated with filth, or whereby it may have been rendered injurious to health, (d) if its container is composed, in whole or in part, of any poisonous or deleterious substance which may render the contents injurious to health, or (e) if it is not a hair dye and it is, or it bears or contains, a color additive which is unsafe within the meaning of section 379e(a)."[27]

This definition does not apply to coal tar hair dyes that include adequate warning labels and instructions.[28] A cosmetic is deemed misbranded if:

> "(a) its labeling is false or misleading in any particular, (b) if in package form unless it bears a label containing (1) the name and place of business of the manufacturer, packer, or distributor; and (2) an accurate statement of the quantity of the contents in terms of weight, measure, or numerical count: *Provided,* That under clause (2) of this paragraph reasonable variations shall be permitted, and exemptions as to small packages shall be established, by regulations prescribed by the Secretary, (c) if any word, statement, or other information required by or under authority of this chapter to appear on the label or labeling is not prominently placed thereon with such conspicuousness (as compared with other words, statements, designs, or devices, in the labeling) and in such terms as to render it likely to be read and understood by the ordinary individual under customary conditions of purchase and use, (d) if its container is so made, formed, or filled as to be misleading, (e) if it is a color additive, unless its packaging and labeling are in conformity with such packaging and labeling requirements, applicable to such color additive, as may be contained in regulations issued under section 379e of this title. This paragraph shall not apply to packages of color additives which, with respect to their use for cosmetics, are marketed and intended for use only in or on hair dyes (as defined in the last sentence of section 361(a) of this title). (f) If its packaging or labeling is in violation of an applicable regulation issued pursuant to section 1472 or 1473 of Title 15." [29]

Unlike drugs, cosmetics are not subject to pre-approval processes prior to placing a cosmetic in the market. Although the FDA is limited to monitoring cosmetic products that are already on the market, the FDA does provide industry manufacturers, distributors and packagers with recommended draft guidances to assist people within the industry in developing systems that decrease the

---

[25] 21 U.S.C. § 321(i) (2006).

[26] Roseann B. Termini, Health Law: Federal Regulations of Drugs, Biologics, Medical Devices, Food and Dietary Supplements 3rd Ed., 415 (Forti Publications 2007).

[27] 21 U.S.C. § 361 (2006).

[28] Products containing coal tar dyes must include: "Caution—This product contains ingredients which may cause skin irritation on certain individuals and a preliminary test according to accompanying directions should first be made. This product must not be used for dyeing the eyelashes or eyebrows; to do so may cause blindness." The label must bear adequate directions for preliminary testing. The term "hair dye" in subsections (a) and (e) shall not include eyelash dyes or eyebrow dyes. 21 U.S.C. § 361(a) (2006).

[29] 21 U.S.C. § 362 (2006).

probability of selling adulterated and or misbranded cosmetics.[30] Due to the lack of pre-market approval processes for cosmetics, the FDA has also developed the Voluntary Cosmetic Regulation Program (VCRP) to act as a post market reporting system.[31] This reporting system is available to manufacturers, packagers and distributors of cosmetics.[32] Parties who wish to participate in the program have the option of choosing to register their establishment on the system or to file a cosmetic product ingredient statement for each product in commercial distribution.[33] By gaining information about commonly used cosmetic ingredients, the FDA's Center for Food Safety and Nutrition (FDA-CFSAN), which oversees the VCRP database, is able to work with the Cosmetic Ingredient Review Board (CIR) in determining which ingredients should receive testing priorities.

An additional benefit of widespread participation in the VCRP is an increased likelihood of consumer protection because the program provides notification to all program participants of ingredients that are determined to be harmful. These warnings are then taken into consideration by manufacturers, who will often reformulate products so that the potentially hazardous ingredient is not included. Although manufacturers, distributors and packagers who do not volunteer and participate gain notice of potentially harmful ingredients through guidance documents and public release statements, the VCRP offers direct communication and ensures that notice is timely.

Mechanisms and Programs Developed to Support Cosmetic Safety
Regulation of Color Additives

Unlike the limited FDA regulation offered for the general cosmetic category, color additives have been stringently regulated since 1960.[34] Regulations have been enacted that specify allowable color additive compositions, restricted additives and conditions for use of additives. The Delaney Clause prohibits the FDA from listing as safe any color additive found to induce cancer in animals or humans.[35] Additives that have been found suitable for food and drug purposes are not automatically considered suitable for cosmetics.[36]

In the past, courts have applied a zero-tolerance level to the Delaney clause. The Court of Appeals for the District of Columbia circuit held that the Delaney Clause has no *de minimis* exception; therefore, a color additive found to have a minimal potential of causing cancer is not able to be added to the list of safe color additives.[37] In applying this zero tolerance level, the court stated that changes to the zero tolerance level should be made as an amendment through legislation rather than decided by the court.[38] A zero tolerance has been maintained by the FDA and is codified in 21 C.F.R. § 70.50 and 21 C.F.R. § 81.10.[39] This stringent tolerance level is likely due to the lack of scientific evidence proving that low levels of carcinogenic color additives are safe.

In contrast, the Sixth Circuit rejected a claim that a color additive should not be listed on the permanent list of safe color additives.[40] Although the additive in question included a minute amount of a second additive independently found to be carcinogenic, the court determined that the additive in question did not cause cancer, thus, the Delaney Clause did not apply to bar the additive from

---

[30] Ctr. for Food Safety & Applied Nutrition Office of Compliance, *Final Guidance for Industry Cosmetics Processors and Transporters: Cosmetics Security Preventative Measures Guidance*, Dec. 17, 2003.
[31] 21 C.F.R. § 710.1 (2007).
[32] 21 C.F.R. § 710, § 720.1 (2007).
[33] FDA, *Voluntary Cosmetic Registration Program*, June 6, 2000, http://www.cfsan.fda.gov/~dms/cos-regn.html (last visited Oct.24, 2007).
[34] 21 U.S.C. § 379e (2006).
[35] 21 U.S.C. § 379e (2006); 21 C.F.R. 70.50 (2007); *Public Citizen, et al. v. Dept. of Health & Human Servs., et al.*, 831 F.2d 1108, 1110-13 (D.C. Cir. 1987) (describing the history and implications of the Delaney Clause.)
[36] *United States v. Eight Unlabeled Cases*, 888 F.2d 945, 947-48 (2d. Cir. 1989 (finding that although the color additive canthaxanthin was approved for use in foods or drugs, this did not automatically render it safe for use in cosmetics).
[37] *Public Citizen, et al.*, 831 F.2d at 1110-13.
[38] *Id.*
[39] 21 C.F.R. § 70.50; § 81.10 (2007).
[40] *Scott v. FDA*, 728 F.2d 322, 324-25 (6th Cir. 1984).

remaining on the permanent list.[41] These cases provide two possibilities; either the FDA and courts have accepted a risk assessment standard rather than a zero tolerance standard, or, zero tolerance applies only to color additives in their final form as opposed to each separate compound ingredient included in the formula of a color additive.

The stringent regulation of color additives stops short of being applied to hair dyes. Hair dyes may contain un-certified dyes.[42] Coal-tar dyes found in hair dyes are an exemption to the safety regulations concerning color additives.[43] Several coal-tar ingredients have been found to cause cancer in laboratory animals.[44] Despite this finding, these dyes are not subject to zero tolerance; rather, the FDA requires warning labels to inform the consumer of the potential harm that may be caused by products containing such dyes.[45] It is important to distinguish that this exemption does not apply to dyes intended for use on eyelashes or eyebrows. Although manufacturers may sell these products on the market as long as warning labels are employed, several United States manufacturers have voluntarily removed coal-tar dyes from product formulations. FDA inaction in providing further regulation for coal-tar in hair dyes seems to be due in part to the lack of both scientific evidence and sound medical studies supporting a link between hair dyes containing coal-tar dyes and adverse health effects.

Labeling-Safety and Duty to Warn

The Fair Packaging and Labeling Act of 1973 applies to cosmetics and requires cosmetic manufacturers to include ingredient statement labels on all products that are intended to be sold to consumers.[46] FDA regulations require specific information to be included on the outside and/or inside of the package.[47] Specific information required includes the cosmetic name, quantity, name and place of business of the manufacturer and ingredients listed in order of predominance.[48] A rare exception to listing ingredients applies in the case of a trade secret.[49] When a company is able to prove that certain ingredients are not well known by competitors and qualify as a trade secret, the company need only list "and other ingredients" rather than including the specific ingredients that make up the trade secret.[50] The Tariff Act of 1930 applies to cosmetics and requires that imported products list the country that the product was manufactured in.[51] Products that may qualify as both cosmetics and drugs must include "active ingredients" prior to listing other ingredients in predominant order.[52] Although cosmetic manufacturers are not required to test the safety of products before placing the products on the market, all products that have not been tested for safety must include a warning label.[53] In order to assist with increased consumer safety, the Cosmetic Product Ingredient

---

[41] *Id.*

[42] In addition to FDA approval, numerous color additives derived primarily from petroleum must be batch certified by the FDA prior to being used in cosmetic formulations. Certification is granted after the additives have passed composition and purity testing. CFSAN, Color Additives and Cosmetics, April 2007, http://www.cfsan.fda.gov/~dms/cos-col.html (last visited January 28, 2008).

[43] 21 C.F.R. 70.3 (2007); CFSAN, *Hair Dye Products*, Nov. 1997, http://www.cfsan.fda.gov/~dms/cos-hdye.html (last visited Oct. 24, 2007).

[44] *Id.*

[45] In the 1970's, the FDA requested that Congress repeal the exemption. Industry representatives and lobbyists vigorously opposed a repeal of the exemption. No changes came to pass. James T. O'Reilly, Food and Drug Administration, 2d. Ed., 17:3 (Thomson/West 2005), *citing* Letter of FDA Director of the Office of the Commissioner on Human Resources, at 4 (Dec. 12, 1977) (re: S. 1681) and 37 F-D-C Reports at TG-1 (Mar. 24, 1975).

[46] Fact Sheet, Cosmetic Labeling, March 26, 2003; *see also* FDA, *Fair Package and Label Act*, www.fda.gov/opacom/laws/fplact.htm.

[47] 21 C.F.R. § 701.10 (2007).

[48] 21 C.F.R. § 701.10; § 701.12 (2007).

[49] 21 C.F.R. § 20.61 (2007).

[50] 21 C.F.R. §701.3; 720.8 (2007).

[51] CFSAN; Office of Cosmetics & Colors, *Cosmetic Labeling Manual*, Oct. 1991, *available at* 1991 WL 11250880 (F.D.A.).

[52] 21 C.F.R. § 701.3(d) (2007).

[53] 21 C.F.R. § 740.10 (2007).

Label Program was developed in 1975.[54] The purpose of this program was to assist in offering adequate substantiation of each ingredient listed on products to prove the safety of products.[55] Unsubstantiated products continue to require warning labels identifying the products as not having been tested for safety. The FDA has also developed a Cosmetic Labeling Manual in order to educate the industry on labeling requirements in order to assist in self-regulated compliance.[56]

Does a cosmetic manufacturer owe a duty to warn consumers about potential harms that may occur from use of a product?[57] A rebuttable presumption may be applied in a case to presume that a client would have read instructions if they had been provided on a product.[58] As an illustration, where a woman was burned by a vapor fire caused by nail polish being applied close to a lit cigarette, the reviewing court held that an insufficient warning is in effect no warning at all.[59] The court stated that the adequacy of the 5.5 point bold face red lettered warning on a .5 ounce nail polish bottle was a question for the jury to determine.[60] Thus, although labeling that may be sufficient FDA compliance may not necessarily provide sufficient warnings to overcome personal tort claims brought by injured consumers. The decision of *Jack v. Alberto-Culver USA, Inc.*, 949 So. 2d 1256 (La. 2007) concerned allegations by the plaintiff that a hair relaxer product made by the defendant was unreasonably dangerous because the product's warning statement did not instruct the user to conduct a scalp test prior to use.[61] The court found that the plaintiff presented no factual evidence to satisfy her burden of proof that the manufacturer failed to use reasonable care in providing an adequate warning.[62] In order to decrease potential law suits arising from allegations of poor warning labels, manufacturers should make efforts to ensure that product label warnings are clearly understood by consumers

Courts have supported the FDA Commissioner's authority to require the placement of where warnings are located on a product container or package as illustrated by the United States District Court for the District of Columbia where the court held that the Commissioner had authority to require a warning on all aerosol cosmetics and allowed the specific requirement that such warning be on the hairspray container.[63] In affirming the Commissioner's rule, the court found the requirements to be supported by consumer and environmental safety concerns.[64] Although it may seem problematic to take remedial steps rather than using pro-active measures, awareness of the need for a warning sometimes only becomes apparent after harm occurs.

In the interest of educating manufacturers to ensure that labeling is not false or misleading, the FDA has drafted guidance documents on industry labeling for all cosmetic products containing alpha hydroxy ingredients.[65] The guidance was developed following an increase in the number of adverse dermatologic experience reports between 1989 and 2000. Testing conducted as a result of

---

[54] F. Alan Andersen, *Approaching 30 Years–The Cosmetic Ingredient Review Program*, FDLI Update, 13 (Nov./Dec. 2005).

[55] *Id.*

[56] *See* CFSAN, *supra* 51.

[57] 42 Am. Jur. Proof of Facts 2d. 97 § 22 (2007).

[58] 63A Am. Jur. 2d. Products Liability § 1108; 1244 (2007).

[59] *Whitehurst v. Revlon, Inc.*, 307 F. Supp. 918, 919-21 (E.D.Va. 1969), *citing Daniel v. Ben E. Keith Co.*, 97 F.3d 1329 (10th Cir. 1996)

[60] *Id.*

[61] *Jack v. Alberto-Culver USA, Inc.*, 949 So. 2d 1256, 1257 (La. 2007).

[62] The court noted that the product warning did satisfy the Louisiana statute requirements for an adequate warning. *Id.* at 1259.

[63] *Cosmetic, Toiletry & Fragrance Ass'n v. Schmidt*, 409 F. Supp. 57, 59-60, 64 (D.D.C. 1976).

[64] *Id.* at 64 (finding this requirement following a suit in which a child punctured a hairspray can and was subsequently burned when a fire erupted).

[65] Office of Cosmetics & Colors, *Draft Guidance for Industry Labeling for Topically Applied Cosmetic Products Containing Alpha Hydroxy Acids as Ingredients*, December 2, 2002, *available at* www.cfsan.fda.gov/~dms/ahaguide.html.

these reports found that alpha hydroxy ingredients caused increased skin sensitivity to UV radiation, thereby increasing a product user's chances of becoming sunburned.[66] The FDA's recommended labeling statement provides a reminder to consumers about product safety information. Because studies have found that test group participants generally believe that cosmetics are safe for their intended uses, it is important for the FDA to recommend that a manufacturer make consumers aware of potential risks of using these products.[67] Because consumers are found to rely on product labels, manufacturers should utilize FDA regulations in order to safeguard against potential failure to warn claims.

Safety Issues Associated with Cosmetic Ingredients—Does Substantiation Really Work as Intended?

With the exception of color additives, ingredient safety has been left to the responsibility of manufacturers. Manufacturers retain the option of substantiating the safety of product ingredients or warning about the lack of safety testing. The Cosmetic Ingredient Review Program (CIR) was adopted in 1976 as an industry-self-regulation panel funded by the Cosmetic, Toiletries and Fragrance Association (CTFA).[68] The program conducts tests on cosmetic ingredients to determine the safety of those ingredients.[69] CIR test results are then published in peer reviewed scientific literature.[70] Cosmetic ingredients listed in the International Cosmetic Ingredient Dictionary and Handbook will not be tested if they have been recently tested and there is no new information questioning the safety of the ingredient, or if the ingredients are in the process of current review.[71] In the case that insufficient evidence is found pertaining to an ingredient, further tests and the opportunity for public comment are granted. The final assessment of the CIR's findings on a particular ingredient is discussed in the International Journal of Toxicology.[72] Ingredients are applicable for repeated review if they have not been reviewed within the past fifteen years.[73]

Until 2004, the effectiveness of CIR had not been challenged. In 2004, a study conducted by the Environmental Working Group issued a report questioning the safety of most skin care product ingredients and alleging that eighty-nine percent of ingredients used in cosmetic products had not been reviewed by CIR.[74] The CTFA defended the CIR as having experts from both the FDA and the Consumer Federation of America.[75]

Current Debates and Concerns of Cosmetic Safety in the United States Marketplace
Hazardous ingredients in product formulations

As stated previously, manufacturers have the general responsibility of ensuring the safety of the products they develop and sell to consumers. Although the FDA has developed labeling requirements, over the years, the agency has banned very few ingredients. FDA labeling requirements, color additive restrictions and manufacturer testing aid in diminishing the likelihood that cosmetics will cause harm to consumers; however, some adverse effects continue to occur. In 2003, 9.3% of human exposures that necessitated calls to poison centers were due to personal care products.[76] Out

---

[66] *Id.*

[67] *Id.*

[68] *See* Andersen, *supra* note 54, at 13.

[69] *Id.*

[70] *Id.*

[71] *Id.*

[72] *Id.*

[73] *Id.*

[74] *Report Criticizes Lack of Regulation for Cosmetics: 89% of Ingredients Not Evaluated, Impurities High*, Warning Letter Bulletin Vol. 12 Issue 12, June 14, 2004, *available at* 2004 WLNR 6598802.

[75] *Id.*

[76] Out of the 2,395,582 human exposure calls made to poison centers during 2003, 223,189 were associated with personal care products. Of these 223,189 calls, 2,356 were judged moderate, 120 were judged major and 8 resulted in death. Phillip L. Casterton, *Benefits From the Scientific Side of Cosmetics*, FDLI Update, 21 (Nov./Dec. 2005), *citing* W.A. Watson et al., *2003 Annual Report of the Am. Ass'n of Poison Control Ctrs. Toxic Effects Surveillance System*, 22 Am. J. Emergency Med., 335-392 (2003).

of this 9%, over 1% was judged to have moderate, major or deadly effects.[77] While these figures may seem low, it is unclear whether these statistics provide a true indication of the number of adverse effects caused by cosmetics. Many adverse effects from cosmetics are minor effects that would not require help from a poison center. Further, these figures do not answer the question as to whether long term cosmetic exposure pose health risks.

Because manufacturers are given the option of marketing products that have not been tested for safety, many state legislatures have begun taking their own measures to protect consumers against potentially harmful ingredients included in products. By way of illustration, in January 2007, the California Cosmetics Safety Act went into effect, requiring manufacturers to disclose to the state health department all ingredients known or suspected to include carcinogenic agents or agents that may cause reproductive damage.[78] The State of Washington proposed a similar act.[79] The concept behind these state measures is to increase consumer knowledge of potential cosmetic hazards by allowing a state department to investigate products and gain data on health effects caused by certain chemicals.[80] State concerns have increased as some new medical findings support the link between cosmetic ingredients and health problems, an example being the link arguably found between dibutyl phthalate and developmental problems in male genitals.[81] Although the FDA has not banned the existence of this chemical compound in cosmetics, most manufacturers have voluntarily removed the ingredient from products, particularly nail polishes.

Customers have the ability to recover monetary recompense in civil court for personal injuries allegedly sustained by cosmetics; however, the lack of solid scientific evidence correlating cosmetic ingredients with harm often leaves the injured party with no way to prove causation. In *Coratti v. Wella Corp. et al.*, 2006 WL 3718247 (N.Y.S.2d), the court found that the plaintiff failed to provide relevant scientific and medical studies, reports or literature to support expert opinions that his multiple chemical sensitivity, inclusion body myositis and chronic obstructive pulmonary disease were caused by his occupational use of the defendants' hair color products.[82] The court found the plaintiff's expert opinions to be speculative and unreliable because there was no scientific support that chemical ingredients in the hair color products were linked to the plaintiff's health problems.[83]

Similarly, a purchaser of a male hair coloring product was unable to recover damages in a suit against the manufacturer for an allegedly defective and unsafe product.[84] Within hours of applying the hair color, the plaintiff suffered a severe allergic reaction that caused him to be hospitalized for several days.[85] The court rejected the claim that the caution warning was inadequate.[86] In so holding, the court cited that the plaintiff had not completed the recommended patch test, that this was the only anaphylactic reaction reported out of 7.7 million units shipped by the manufacturer since 2000, and because the plaintiff lacked any expert report linking the product or the color additive to the injury.[87]

---

[77] *Id.*

[78] Because these state acts do not impose requirements on labeling and packaging of cosmetics, the acts do not violate the federal preemption of state labeling under 21 U.S.C. § 379s (2006). Natasha Singer, *Should You Trust Your Makeup?*, N.Y. Times, Feb. 15, 2007, at G1, *available at* 2007 WLNR 2956300.

[79] Lisa Stiffler, *State Mulls Cosmetic Safety Bill Based on California Measure*, Seattle Post Intelligencer (WA), Feb. 20, 2007, at B1, *available at* 2007 WLNR 3389055.

[80] *Id.*

[81] The test group linking this plasticizer to developmental defects included only eighty-five participants. Janet Raloff & Ben Harder, *Gender Measure: Pollutant Appears to Alter Boys' Genitals*, 167 Science News, No. 23, 355 (2005).

[82] *Coratti v. Wella Corp.*, 2006 WL 3718247, *6-9 (N.Y.S.2d).

[83] *Id.*

[84] *Smallwood v. Clairol, Inc.*, 2005 U.S. Dist. LEXIS 2726, *1 (S.D.N.Y. 2005).

[85] *Id.* at 1-2.

[86] *Id.* at 8.

[87] *Id.* at 3-7.

One reason for the lack of increased FDA regulation of cosmetics may be the same issue discussed by these courts, that is, the lack of evidence supporting the claim that cosmetic products are harmful. Because the purpose of the FDA is to protect and safeguard consumers, it is expected that congress would increase regulation if medical evidence showed adverse health effects from cosmetics.[88] In such a case, increased cosmetic regulation such as pre-approval requirements, if added by congress and funded by new appropriations, would be expected to decrease overall product liability cases. Currently, the lack of scientific evidence, as well as the low incidence of successful product liability suits, has not necessitated such change.

Product Classification: The fine line between a cosmetic and drug

One main concern that continues to require FDA monitoring is whether a product should be considered a cosmetic or a drug. Classification determination is a very serious concern for manufacturers who may not wish to have their product subject to pre-approval by the FDA. There is also a concern to consumers, who may wish to ensure that new drugs are truly safe for use. The distinction between cosmetics and drugs is usually not determined by the ingredients included in a product formulation; rather, the intended use generally controls product classification.[89] Any product that is marketed as changing the structure or function of the body is subject to drug classification and, if not already in a drug monograph requires pre-approval before entering the market.[90] In addition to meeting drug requirements, dually classified products must also meet cosmetic ingredient labeling requirements and list "active ingredients" prior to the predominant order of other products.[91]

The distinction between cosmetics and drugs is sometimes unapparent to consumers. Many household cosmetic items like antiperspirants and toothpastes are found to fit under the drug category. Products that are alleged to or do have the potential of altering the functions of the body present increased health risks that demand FDA scrutiny. Regular cosmetics need not undergo pre-approval because cosmetics are considered strictly topical without having chemical effects on the body, therefore, they are considered much safer. Some products, such as bleaching creams and hormone creams, were previously labeled as cosmetics although they included chemical ingredients that changed the structure of the skin.[92]

Because drugs are not simply topical and are more easily ingested in the body, there are increased chances of physical harm to the consumer. An example of the potential hazards of new drugs that are incorrectly categorized as cosmetics was seen in Global Esthetics, Incorporated's product "PeelAway."[93] The product contained high levels of Alpha Hydroxy Ingredients that caused skin peeling and was advertised as assisting users in the removal of wrinkles, blemishes and blotches.[94] After receiving numerous reports of consumers suffering skin burns from the product, the FDA sent a warning letter to Global Esthetics informing the company that PeelAway was an unapproved new drug that created a significant health hazard.[95] Although the PeelAway concern occurred in 2002, the FDA continues to monitor and contact manufacturers about misbranded products. On February 25, 2007, the FDA informed BioForm Medical Incorporated that the company's

---

[88] While the press often cites scientific findings that arguably show links between physical injury and cosmetic ingredients, there are many scientific studies disproving these causal links. *See Hair Straightening Chemicals Not Linked to Breast Cancer Risk in African-Americans*, Women's Health Weekly, May 31, 2007, *available at* 2007 WLNR 9759057.

[89] *See* Termini, *supra* note 26 at 422.

[90] Robert G. Pinco, *Implications of FDA's Proposal to Include Foreign Marketing Experience in the Over-the-Counter Drug Review Process*, 53 Food Drug L.J. 105, 109 (1998).

[91] 21 C.F.R. § 701.3(d) (2007).

[92] Many bleaching creams contain hydroquinone, a bleaching chemical. Hormonal skin creams contain estrogens that can penetrate the epidermis and cause plumping of the skin. The FDA has voiced concern over the safety and effectiveness of these products and has stated that labeling such as cosmetics constitutes misbranding. 42 Am. Jur. Proof of Facts 2d. 97, § 8 (2006); *see also* Straus, *Hormones in Cosmetics*, 186 JAMA 759 (1963).

[93] *See* Heymann, *supra* note 23, at 361, *citing* Skin Peelers, U.S. Dept. of Health & Human Servs., Food and Drugs Admin., P92-13 (May 21, 1992).

[94] *Id.*

[95] *Id.*

labeling claims pertaining to its Cutanix skin products caused the products to be categorized as drugs because the product was claiming to cure, mitigate, treat and/or prevent disease.[96] The FDA informed BioForm that Cutanix products were not considered safe and effective for curing diseases without first being subject to pre-approval.[97]

The term drug is defined differently than cosmetic and to ensure that cosmetics with drug properties do not slip through the pre-approval process, FDA usually issues a warning letter. However, FDA will institute enforcement proceedings if necessary. Warning letters by FDA alert manufacturers who represent their products as affecting the structure or function of the body. Courts usually defer to FDA decision making in the drug/cosmetic categorization. In *Upjohn Co. v. Riahom Corp.*, 641 F. Supp. 1209 (D. Del. 1986), the court stated that a product's status as a drug or cosmetic was not an issue before the court; however, the court stated that the product Rivixil should not be marketed as a cosmetic without completing tests to ensure that the product did not have qualities causing it to be classified as a drug.[98]

Globalization: Will the United States Provide Better Protection by Coordinating with and Adopting International Regulations?

Variations in cosmetic regulations undoubtedly affect international trade and the creation of a global market. Such regulations also affect the degree of safety provided to consumers within different countries. Under the European Union Directive, all manufacturers must have a full technical file on all cosmetic products that includes, but is not necessarily limited to, information on the product formulation specifications, the manufacturing process, proof of safety and package claims and record of consumer health-related claims.[99] Similar files are not required by the United States. The European Scientific Committee on Consumer Products is similar to the United States' CIR, which tests all special and active cosmetic ingredients.

Unlike the United States, the European Union does not require warning labels to be placed on cosmetic products because ingredients found to be unsafe are systematically listed as banned ingredients.[100] While the United States FDA has banned a small number of ingredients for cosmetic use, the European Union lists have banned well over one thousand ingredients.[101] The European Union requires more specific labeling of fragrances than is required by the United States FDA, which only requires that the general term "fragrance" be listed as an ingredient regardless of how many types of fragrances may be included in a product's formula.[102]

Although several proponents for increased FDA regulation of cosmetics cite the European Union's Directive as providing greater safety to consumers, it has been noted that the stringent cosmetic/drug classifications applied by the United States require many products to undergo pre-clearance procedures, even when the drug is intended to offer only minor structure or function claims.[103]

---

[96] Letter from Dept. of Health & Human Servs. to BioForm Medical Inc. (Feb. 15, 2007), *available at* http://www.fda.gov/foi/warning_letters/g6265d.htm.

[97] *Id.; see also* Letter from Dept. of Health & Human Servs. to Fusion Brands International SRL (April 24, 2007), *available at* http://www.fda.gov/foi/warning_letters/s6371c.htm (finding the company was advertising Lift-Fusion brand products as cosmetics although the associated claims placed the products within the definition of a drug).

[98] This claim involved a patent infringement suit pertaining to a compound, minoxidil, found to promote hair growth. Defendants sold a product that contained minoxidil as a cosmetic without receiving pre-approval by the FDA. Although the defendants claimed that the product did not cause hair growth, no testing had been done to support the contention that the product was a cosmetic rather than a drug. In addition to potential dangers of an untested drug, the court noted potential misleading as a problem since promotional materials implied hair growth. *Upjohn Co. v. Riahom Corp. et al.*, 641 F. Supp. 1209, 1225-26 (D. Del. 1986).

[99] *Cosmetics Introduction*, European Commission (Jan. 23, 2006), http://ec.europa.eu/enterprise/cosmetics/index_en.htm (last visited Oct. 24, 2007).

[100] *Id.*

[101] *Id.*

[102] *Id.*

[103] *See* Pinco, *supra* note 90, at 109.

The United States system requires many products that are considered cosmetics in Europe to undergo pre-approval clearance before being marketable.

Japan has revoked its prior requirement that each cosmetic ingredient be registered and approved individually and now only requires certain ingredients to be registered and approved prior to being used.[104] By relaxing pre-approval standards, Japan's regulation of cosmetics is much more harmonious with that of the United States and the European Union. Similarly, Japan's previous product registration requirements are now notification processes that are much more similar to the voluntary program of the United States and the Dossier system of the European Union.[105] Further harmonization in global regulations is evident by the CTFA's Cosmetic Ingredient Dictionary evolving into the International Nomenclature of Cosmetic Ingredients, which now includes ingredient listing systems in European, United States, and Japanese ingredient names.[106] Even with some variation between countries with respect to methods and extent of cosmetic regulation, it is apparent that most scientific research completed on cosmetic ingredients tends to have similar findings, regardless of where the research was conducted.

An example of similarities in international studies pertains to nanoparticles titanium dioxide and zinc oxide.[107] These color additives are known to be efficacious sunscreen filters and are found in cosmetics and sunscreens.[108] The Scientific Committee for Cosmetic Products in the European Union considered more than one hundred studies and agreed that nanoparticles were safe for cosmetic use.[109] Both Australian and German studies found that the form or size of nanoparticles did not create health risks to consumers.[110] The international consensus on the safety of these ingredients proves that varying regulations does not necessarily provide a void in safeguarding consumers.

A disparity exists between how countries regulate cosmetics. An example of the impact of disparate regulations was seen in 2003 when the FDA issued a warning to United States citizens about the potential hazards of using Litargirio.[111] Litargirio is a cosmetic manufactured in the Dominican Republic.[112] The product has numerous uses, one of the most common being a deodorant. After learning that several children who had been using the product had lead levels as much as four times the normal levels known to cause neurological and behavioral problems, the FDA warned that the product should not be used because the seventy-nine percent lead content posed health risks, particularly for children.[113] One ongoing concern is that even with increased FDA regulatory authority, FDA may nevertheless still be unable to regulate some international "cosmetics" such as Litargirio due to the lack of resources to effectively halt entry of these products into the United States.[114]

Traversing the Ethical and Professional Battlegrounds of the Beauty Industry

A leading issue that has been raised by many special interest groups and entertained by several manufacturers is the issue of animal testing, which extends human safety concerns to the safety of animals. The United States is the one of largest users of laboratory animals for product testing.[115]

---

[104] Janet Winter Blaschke, *Globalization of Cosmetic Regulations*, 60 Food Drug L.J. 413, 415-17 (2005).

[105] *Id.*

[106] *Id.* at 417-18.

[107] *Cosmetic Industry Filed FDA Comments on Use of Nanoparticles in Personal Care Products*, Global News Wire – PR News Wire, Sept. 19, 2006.

[108] *Id.*

[109] *Id.*

[110] *Id.*

[111] *FDA Warns Consumers About Use of "Litargirio,"* FDA Talk Paper, Oct. 2, 2003, http://www.fda.gov/bbs/topics/ANSWERS/2003/ANS01253.html (last visited Oct. 24, 2007).

[112] *Id.*

[113] *Id.*

[114] For example, a shipment of toothpaste made in China was found to contain an antifreeze ingredient, diethylene glycol, which can be poisonous. Although a shipment was found at the U.S. border before the product reached United States stores, two retail stores within the United States were found to be selling the contaminated product. *FDA Says to Avoid Chinese Toothpaste*, St. Louis Post-Dispatch (MO), June 2, 2007, at A18, *available at* 2007 WLNR 10333402.

[115] The European Union has taken a very different approach from the United States and recently considered a directive amendment that would effectively ban the sale of products if animal testing was used to ensure the safety of the product.

While final cosmetics may not require animal testing, most ingredients that are used in the cosmetic formulations are tested on animals. Many tests are conducted on laboratory rabbits. The draize eye test includes particular ingredients or formulations being dropped into the eyes of laboratory rabbits to document any adverse reactions that the animal may have.[116] Other tests include ingredients and formulas being applied to the rabbit's skin after the fur has been removed.[117]

The concern of many animal testing opponents is caused by the inhumane treatment of the laboratory animals combined with alternative methods of testing that are available without significant increased expense to the manufacturer. Some manufacturers have taken a proactive approach to this ethical concern without the recommendation or requirement by the FDA. L'Oreal, one of the largest cosmetic manufacturers within the United States, now conducts research on reconstructed skin rather than utilizing laboratory animals for testing.[118]

Another concern prevalent pertaining to animal testing is to present truth in labeling communication to the consumer. Consumers who do not agree with animal testing may take this view into consideration in making cosmetic purchases. In doing so, consumers are likely to review cosmetic packaging for any statements evidencing whether the manufacturer conducts product testing on animals. Because labeling claims pertaining to animal testing are currently unregulated, manufacturers have the choice of imparting truthful information to consumers about whether animal testing was completed.

In addition to the concern of ethical product testing, excessive prices and costs of products have been questioned as detrimental to consumers. From a consumer standpoint, high priced cosmetics seem to signify better, more effective products yet are they?[119] Doctors have considered this a misinterpretation often accepted by consumers.[120] While high priced cosmetics may include more expensive packaging or rare ingredients, the effectiveness of the product is unlikely to be significantly greater than a less expensive product. A study conducted in December 2006 by Consumer Reports found no correlation between the price and effectiveness of wrinkle creams.[121] While these prices may be justified if a company is spending more money on research and development of ingredients and formulas, perhaps this raises ethical and professional credibility issues of whether companies who inflate product prices might mislead consumers about product effectiveness whether deliberately or unintentionally.[122]

From a consumer protection standpoint, cosmetic manufacturers may be in the best position to recall products because of their ability to trace product location and pay to retrieve the products. Currently FDA does not have the power to require recalls for cosmetics. While FDA may monitor and check effectiveness of the recalls, as well as issue press releases concerning recalls, only the

---

Azalea O. Rosholt, *The Seventh Amendment Directive—An Unnecessary Measure to a Necessary End*, 60 Food Drug L.J. 421, 422 (2005); *see also* Kate Phillips, *New Methods to Eliminate Animal Testing*, Chemical Week, May 16, 2007, *available at* 2007 WLNR 9299075 (stating that five new in-vitro tests have been endorsed and may eliminate the practice of using rabbits in skin and eye irritancy testing for cosmetics).

[116] Delcianna J. Winders, *Combining Reflexive Law and False Advertising Law to Standardize "Cruelty-Free" Labeling of Cosmetics*, 81 N.Y.U.L. Rev. 454, 454-57 (2006).

[117] *Id.* at 455.

[118] L'Oreal USA, http://www.lorealusa.com/_en/_us/index.aspx?from=ww-dispatch-loreal-corporate (last visited Oct. 24, 2007).

[119] Dr. Diane Madfes of Mount Sinai School of Medicine states that a counter argument to the issue of high prices is that expensive product purchases may cause customers to use cleansers and creams more often, thereby potentially benefiting their skin. *The Skinny on Skin: It Might Make You Smile but the Efficacy of That Cosmetic is Doubtful*, Financial Post, Global News Wire–Europe Intelligence Wire, Jan. 5, 2007.

[120] *Id.*

[121] Natasha Singer, *The Cosmetics Restriction Diet*, N.Y. Times, Jan. 4, 2007, at G1, *available at* 2007 WLNR 134283.

[122] A secondary concern raised by high cosmetic prices is the presence, particularly within international countries, of counterfeit cosmetics that may expose the public to products potentially containing hazardous ingredients such as mercury. *See Counterfeit Cosmetics Still Widely Available*, Jakarta Post (Indonesia), May 26, 2007, *available at* 2007 WLNR 9873979.

manufacturer may decide to voluntarily recall a product.[123] This practice may raise the question whether corporations would voluntarily recall a product and risk bad publicity if they were not requested to do so by the FDA; however, if a manufacturer is aware that a product currently on the market is potentially harmful, the liability concerns seem to provide sufficient reason to voluntarily recall the product.

There continue to be numerous recalls concerning cosmetic products on the market. The importance of such recalls should never be underestimated because many of the recalls relate to bacteria and could have the potential to cause very serious harm to consumers.[124] One such bacterium, pseudomonas aeruginosa, found in Anastasia Diabetic Skin Care Therapy Hand and Body Treatment, has the potential of causing blindness if it happens to enter a scratch in the cornea of the eye.[125] There was nationwide recall for this product.[126] Additionally, the same bacterium was located in Woodbridge Laboratory's DermaFreeze365 Instant Line Relax Formulas during one of the manufacturer's routine testing processes.[127] Concern over the effectiveness of this recall is very important because some of the DermaFreeze products may be applied to the eye area.[128] These recalls demonstrate that there are not only ethical and professional concerns about the dangers of ingredients included in product formulations, but also concerns about the reliability of manufacturer testing to ensure safety.

The Future Face of the Cosmetic Industry: What Safety Regulations May We Expect?

The FDA continues to maintain its traditional purpose of monitoring consumer products under the jurisdiction of the agency in order to protect and safeguard consumers against potential harms. The agency has had regulatory authority of cosmetics for nearly eighty years, and while some regulatory developments have occurred, the cosmetic industry varies from the food and drug industries by being largely self-regulated. In 1989, FDA Commissioner F. Young stated "adverse reactions to cosmetics are [usually] of lesser consequence [and are] reported less frequently … risk to human health is usually less because of the nature of the customary cosmetic use and the substances used as cosmetic ingredients."[129] The lack of change or expanse in FDA regulation of cosmetics appears to illustrate that there has not been much deviation from this prior view. Yet, times have changed since the 1980s and consumers groups continue to call for more strict regulation.

Current changes in the globalization of cosmetic regulations seem likely to provide answers about whether the United States should adopt more stringent standards. The argument that the United States should accept more stringent standards used by the European Union may happen as several countries continue to work at developing a unified system. Several cosmetic industries including the United States, Japan, China and the European Union signed and proposed to regulators a regulatory harmonization initiative.[130] Proponents of such a system expect this type of forum to

---

[123] 21 C.F.R. § 7.53 (2007).

[124] Palmer's Baby Butter Massage Lotion was found contaminated with Enterobacter Gergoviae, a pathogen that may cause several infections including, but not limited to, lower respiratory tract infections, skin and soft tissue infections and urinary tract infections. 46 FDA Enf. Rep. 4 (2006), *available at* 2006 WL 3309388 (F.D.A). This same bacteria was found by manufacturers of Alpine Extreme Evergreen Forest Body Wash. *Vi-Jon Issues Nationwide Consumer Recall*, Apr. 19, 2007, http://www.fda.gov/oc/po/firmrecalls/vijon04_07.html (last visited Oct. 24, 2007); *see also* Susan L. Fraser, *Enterobacter Infections*, Wed MD, January 8, 2007, http://www.emedicine.com/med/topic678.htm (last visited Oct. 24, 2007).

[125] 01 FDA Enf. Rep. 2 (2001), *available at* 2007 WL 29841 (F.D.A.).

[126] *Id.*

[127] FDA, *Woodridge Labs Recalls Certain Dermafreeze365 Products Because of Possible Health Risk*, Mar. 23, 2007, http://www.fda.gov/oc/po/firmrecalls/woodridge03_07.html (last visited Oct. 24, 2007).

[128] *Id.*

[129] O'Reilly, *supra* note 45, at 17:1-17:2, *citing* Letter of FDA Comm'r F. Young to Congressman R. Wyden (July 5, 1989).

[130] Annual Meeting Speech by Pamela Bailey, CEO of Cosmetic, Toiletries & Fragrance Association, Mar. 1, 2007, http://www.ctfa.org/Content/NavigationMenu/CTFA_News/Speeches/Pamela_Bailey_Speech_at_the_CTFA_2007_Annual_Meeting.htm (last visited Oct. 24, 2007).

offer consumers safe products that are consistently regulated. In addition to the potential integration of global regulations, the Cosmetic, Toiletries and Fragrance Association intends to assist the FDA in developing a new consumer-based information website where comprehensive information on cosmetic products and ingredients will be available.[131] Not only will the website include credible information, it will also educate consumers on the processes used to assess the safety of cosmetic ingredients.[132] The purpose of this website is to facilitate educated consumer purchase and use of cosmetic products.[133] The website will help qualm concerns that consumers are unaware or uneducated about the existing or potential risks that cosmetic ingredients may cause.

Further, industry-developed programs such as CTFA and CIR have assisted in lobbying for congress to provide over six million dollars per year to the FDA's Office of Cosmetics and Color in order to increase the number of staff available to oversee compliance, research and reporting within the cosmetic industry.[134] In January 2007, environmentalists began a safe cosmetics campaign that has caused more than five hundred cosmetic companies to voluntarily register and pledge to replace potentially harmful ingredients.[135] Nevertheless, even large companies who do not choose to participate in the voluntary pledge campaign have adopted standards that exceed FDA requirements. The continued industry support for the FDA, paired with the voluntary compliance with FDA recommendations, seems to create little need for significant regulatory changes that would impose more stringent requirements.

Yet, the sales of cosmetic products remain astounding, approximately eleven billion personal care products were sold within the United States, causing annual cosmetic sales to reach sixty-two billion dollars.[136] Even with this impressive amount of cosmetics sold, only one-hundred and fifty adverse reactions were reported to the FDA in 2006.[137] This adverse reaction figure is even less than the two hundred cosmetic adverse effect reports received by the FDA back in 1994.[138] The considerably minor number of adverse health effects are related to cosmetics lends support to view that the current post-market FDA regulation of cosmetics is sufficient. Unless more substantiated scientific evidence is developed showing a link between health hazards and cosmetic ingredients, and unless the cosmetic industry fails to accurately rectify such concerns, it is unlikely that Congress will alter FDA's current regulatory authority.

CRITICAL ANALYSIS: Assess whether Congress should enact legislation to encompass stricter regulation of personal care cosmetic products.

---

[131] *Id.*

[132] *Id.*

[133] *Id.*

[134] *Id.*

[135] The purpose of the Campaign for Safe Cosmetics is a coalition aimed at educating consumers on cosmetic products containing potentially harmful ingredients as well as working with manufacturers in an attempt to decrease these ingredients. Judy Foreman, *Scrutinizing the Safety of Cosmetic Ingredients*, Balt. Sun, April 13, 2007, at 3D, *available at* 2007 WLNR 7123742; *see also* Robert Cohen, *Cosmetics Safety Comes Under Fire*, Olympian, June 3, 2007, *available at* 2007 WLNR 10360041 (citing a quote made by an Estee Lauder representative who stated that the company removed dibutyl phthalate from its nail polishes in order to meet European Union marketing requirements, not because of activist groups who "do not rely on sound, peer-reviewed science in their reports").

[136] *See* Annual Meeting Speech by Pamela Bailey, *supra* note 131; *see also* Melissa Suggit, *Global Cosmetics and Toiletries Sales Reach Five Year High in 2006*, Euromonitor International, Apr. 16, 2007, http://www.euromonitor.com/Global_cosmetics_and_toiletries_sales_reach_five_year_high_in_2006 (finding that overall cosmetic sales in the United States increased three percent in 2006) (last visited Oct. 24, 2007).

[137] *Id.*

[138] Dori Stehlin, *Cosmetic Safety: More Complex Than at First Blush*, FDA Consumer, Nov. 1991, rev. May 1995, http://www.cfsan.fda.gov/~dms/cos-safe.html (last visited Oct. 24, 2007).

VOLUME IX

Volume IX: Food Regulation—Safety, Pathogens, Recalls, Claims, Additives, Allergens and Biotechnology

The United States Food and Drug Administration (FDA) and the United States Department of Agriculture (USDA) perform a significant role in the regulation of the United States food supply. Accomplishments of the (USDA's) Food Safety and Inspection Service and FDA's Center for Food Safety and Applied Nutrition are noted in this volume as well as specific legislation. This volume focuses on food safety, recalls, health claims, and other significant topics.

This volume details the collaborative approach to food safety initiatives by governmental agencies and the continued debate about a single food safety agency. Hailed as the most significant overhaul of food safety regulation, the Food Safety Modernization Act (FSMA) became law in early 2011. The United States food safety system was revamped with enactment of the FSMA which grants FDA the legal authority to order food recalls, increase inspections of domestic and foreign processing plants and the authority to establish standards for how fruits and vegetables are grown abroad. Significant aspects of the FSMA and other pertinent food safety legislation are detailed. Yet, despite legislative measures, foodborne illness remains problematic. Specific foodborne pathogens such as Listeria monocytogenes, E. coli O157:H7 and Salmonella are discussed with illustrative firm-initiated recalls such as the recall of 206 million shell eggs in 2018.

Health claims on food labeling and the impact of the Nutrition Labeling and Education Act (NLEA) of 1990 are detailed along with trans-fat disclosure requirements and the declaratory order concerning the phase out of hydrogenated trans fats supported by the World Health Organization. An updated nutrition label was released in 2016 and implementation several years later. Front-of-Package labeling by industry remains in the forefront as FDA considers how to best address this issue for consumer comprehension and protection. Health claims continue to proliferate. Qualified health claims on food labeling remains controversial. FDA continues to both approve and deny qualified claims. Misbranding, terminology and caloric disclosure are discussed in the legal cases of Farinella, Manischewitz Diet Thins and Gerber. Besides NLEA, allegations of deceptive business practices under the Unfair Trade Practices Act were permitted to proceed in Pom LLC v. Coke-Cola, Inc. In response to the obesity crisis, the Patient Protection and Affordable Care Act of 2010 mandated caloric disclosure and towards the end of 2014, FDA issued the long-awaited rules on calorie disclosure for foods sold in vending machines and in some restaurants effective January 1, 2020 for manufacturers with $10 million or more in annual food sale; however, manufacturers with less than $10 million in annual food sales have until January 1, 2021 to comply.

Threats of bioterrorism continue and the safety of the United States food supply including food imports is crucial. Enacted in response to the events of September 11, 2001, the 2002 Bioterrorism Act, specifically Title III, applies to protecting the safety and security of the food and drug supply. The 2007 Food and Drug Administration Amendments Act (FDAAA) mandated an electronic reportable food registry system. Specific measures include registration of food facilities with FDA and prior notice of imported food.

Congress enacted the Bioengineered Food Disclosure legislation in 2016 perhaps in response to state legislative enactments. A case discussion of specific duties of a food manufacturer is included. Trade issues are addressed by review of the country of origin labeling. Special topics such as obesity, arsenic, bovine spongiform encephalopathy (BSE), hydrogenated and trans fatty acids and biotechnology are reviewed. Finally, FDA is reviewing the terms "healthy" and "natural".

Chapter 1: Pathogens, Food Safety Modernization Act, Bioterrorism, Hazard Analysis *and* Enforcement

Coordinated Safety Programs

Key Websites: *https://www.fda.gov/Food/default.htm https://www.fsis.usda.gov/wps/portal/fsis/home*

Multifaced initiatives have been instituted to improve food safety and to combat the many outbreaks of foodborne illness. The Food Safety Working Group chaired by the Secretaries of the Department of Health and Human Services and the Department of Agriculture have focused on the following: *21st Century Food Safety Laws; Increased Government Coordination; and Public Protection Initiatives.* These efforts remain paramount for federal, state, tribal and local governments as well as industry. Yet, endeavors involve a team approach. Government partnerships have been formed with academic institutions and industry. The following are illustrative examples of programs involving representatives from federal, state and local governments, academic institutions, and industry with the unified goal of protecting the United States food supply:

> * *FoodSafety.gov* "Gateway to Federal Food Safety Information";
> * *Food Protection Task Force; grant program;*
> * *PulseNet A Nationwide Network coordinated by the CDC;*
> * *FDA Coordinated Outbreak Response and Evaluation (CORE);*
> * *FoodNet Foodborne Diseases Active Surveillance Network CDC;*
> * *JIFSAN Joint Institute for Food Safety and Applied Nutrition;*
> * *ELEXNET Electronic Laboratory Exchange Network;*
> * *NARMS National Antibiotic Resistance Monitoring; and*
> * *FERN Food Emergency Response Network (Federal, State and Local).*

Single Food Agency and GAO Reports

Should there be a single food agency or alternatively a more collaborative approach with unification at federal, state and local governmental agencies? Approximately 15 federal agencies administer approximately 35 food related laws. Advocates of a single food agency contend that the "system" is antiquated allowing for miscommunication. Coordinated governmental efforts include the White House Homeland Security Council, FDA and the Food Safety and Inspection Service (FSIS) and Agricultural Research Service of USDA. Although the discussion remains as to whether there should be a single independent food safety agency, teamwork approaches used by various agencies are evident. For example, EdNet, an electronic newsletter from FDA, FSIS, and the CDC provide updates on food safety activities to educators and others concerned about food safety. FSIS is committed to strengthening partnerships with federal, state and local agencies. This includes strengthening traditional cooperative programs and other partnerships with state and local agencies to reduce food safety hazards. The Government Accounting Office (GAO) recognized the fractured approach to food safety.

The GAO added food safety to the high-risk list in 2007 and in 2011 issued a report to Congressional Committees *"High Risk Series, An Update"*. The GAO found that the Food Safety Working Group evidenced a commitment to protecting the food supply. Yet, the GAO recommended a results-oriented system wide government performance plan and measures. The GAO suggested Congressional action in enacting uniform risk-based food safety legislation and a commission for alternative organizational configurations. It appears that the GAO approach presents a viable and realistic solution since the single food agency concept does not appear probable.

CRITICAL ANALYSIS: Will Congress enact legislation to authorize a single federal food agency and it is feasible to do so? Incorporate GAO recommendations.
http://www.gao.gov/key_issues/food_safety/issue_summary
See also: *http://www.gao.gov/key_issues/food_safety/issue_summary#t=1*

Federal Food Safety Regulation—USDA and FDA
USDA Food Safety and Inspection Service

The Food Safety and Inspection Service of the United States Department of Agriculture (USDA) (FSIS) strives to achieve its major objective of assuring a safe food supply. This federal regulatory agency protects the public by ascertaining that food products within its legal authority or jurisdiction are safe, wholesome and labeled accurately.

> *Mission Statement: "The Food Safety and Inspection Service (FSIS) is the public health agency in the U.S. Department of Agriculture responsible for ensuring that the nation's commercial supply of meat, poultry, and egg products is safe, wholesome, and correctly labeled and packaged."*

Foods within FSIS jurisdiction include meat, poultry and egg products, raw beef, pork, lamb, turkey, processed meat and poultry products, pizzas, frozen dinners, (generally, products that contain 2% or more cooked meat and poultry or 3% or more raw meat and poultry). Examples of processed egg products regulated by FSIS are dried egg yolks, scrambled egg mix, dried egg powder, and liquid eggs. The specific laws that provide USDA with authority to regulate these products are as follows:

> ➤ *Federal Meat Inspection Act;*
> ➤ *Poultry Products Inspection Act; and the*
> ➤ *Egg Products Inspection Act.*

FSIS is responsible for inspecting all products sold in interstate commerce as well as imported food within its jurisdiction. Additionally, FSIS is responsible for evaluating whether state regulatory meat and poultry inspection programs are at least equal to the Federal standards. In addition to inspection responsibilities, other responsibilities entail label requirements; tests for various types of contamination such as microbiological or chemical contagions; epidemiological investigations and enforcement activities. Risk assessments for *Salmonella enteritidis* in eggs and egg products, *E.coli* 0157:H7 in ground beef, and *Listeria monocytogenes* in an assortment of foods remains a top priority. Using a farm-to-table model, FSIS aims to continue the implementation of a science-based strategy to advance the safety of meat, poultry and egg products. Microbial contamination remains the most serious food safety problem. In early 2016, USDA started to evaluate whether plants are complying with the new pathogen reduction standards for *Salmonella* and *Campylobacter* in raw chicken parts, ground chicken and turkey products. USDA posts sampling results on its website detailing compliance.

FDA Center for Food Safety and Applied Nutrition

Besides USDA, the Center for Food Safety and Applied Nutrition (CFSAN) within the Food and Drug Administration is involved in food safety initiatives. Strategic priorities encompass food defense and security; imported foods; obesity; HACCP inspections for seafood and juices; prevention measures for food-borne pathogens; health and nutrient-content claims, biotechnology and an adverse event reporting system. Regulatory responsibility for state and local retail establishments occurs with state and local jurisdictions. However, FDA issued *"Voluntary National Retail Food Regulatory Program Standards"* to assist state and local regulators to develop food regulatory programs to reduce the risk for foodborne illness. Essential elements include the following: regulatory basis; trained staff; HACCP based inspection program; uniform inspection program; preparedness and response to foodborne illness and food security; enforcement and compliance; industry and community communication; resources; and program evaluation.

Foodborne Pathogens

Despite food safety measures, food-borne pathogens continue to emerge. Importing foods has become a widespread practice and it is critical to control these food-borne pathogens, such as *Listeria, E. coli* and *Salmonella. United States v. Quality Egg and Peanut Corporation of America* involved nationwide salmonella contamination. *United States v. Jensen, United States Neptune Fish, United States v. Blue Ribbon Smoked Fish, Inc., and United States v. Portland Seafood, Inc.*

involved the contamination of food with *Listeria monocytogenes* (L.mono) and are reported below. Besides HACCP, discussed below, there are additional minimum safeguards and measures as follows: *Water supply sources; Training and providing personnel for personal hygiene facilities; Sanitation SOPs; and Accurate traceback.*

Pathogen Prevention Examples Shell Eggs and Mechanically Tenderized Beef
Shell Egg Rule
http://www.gpo.gov/fdsys/pkg/FR-2009-07-09/pdf/E9-16119.pdf
http://www.fda.gov/food/guidanceregulation/guidancedocumentsregulatoryinformation/eggs/ucm170615.htm

FDA and USDA instituted joint agency plans to improve egg safety. FDA issued a final rule titled: *Prevention of Salmonella Enteritidis in Shell Eggs During Production, Storage, and Transportation* 74 FR 33030 in 2009 concerning the prevention of *Salmonella Enteritidis* in connection with shell eggs. The "Egg Rule" applies to egg producers that have from 3,000 to 50,000 laying hens and whose shell eggs are not processed with a treatment such as pasteurization. The rule does not apply to producers who sell all their eggs directly to consumers or have less than 3,000 hens. Compliance records must be maintained along with a written prevention plan. FDA has an inspection program to ensure compliance.

Mechanically Tenderized Beef Products Labeling Rule
http://www.fsis.usda.gov/wps/wcm/connect/a95ea535-a983-45f5-be7c-bed7bdff15ae/2008-0017F.htm?MOD=AJPERES

The Food Safety and Inspection Service (FSIS) issued new labeling requirements in 2015 effective May 18, 2016 for raw or partially cooked beef products that have been mechanically tenderized. These products must include labels that state that they have been mechanically, blade or needle tenderized. The purpose of the new rule is to provide additional information to consumers, restaurants, and other food service facilities about the products such as safe cooking instructions. The labeling must include validated cooking instructions so that consumers know how to safely prepare them. The instructions detail the minimum internal temperatures and any hold or "dwell" times for the products to ensure that they are fully cooked.

CRITICAL ANALYSIS: Review the shell egg rule and the mechanically tenderized beef rule (links above) and discuss in terms of pathogen prevention.

FDA Food Safety Modernization Act—FSMA
http://www.fda.gov/Food/GuidanceRegulation/FSMA/default.htm

A significant amount of the food that Americans consume originate from countries outside of the United States. The FDA Food Safety Modernization Act (FSMA), signed into law back in January 2011, addresses imported food as well as food produced in the United States. The impetus for this legislation concerned data from the Centers for Disease Control and Prevention (CDC), that approximately 48 million people are sickened from foodborne illness. According to the CDC approximately 128,000 people are hospitalized and 3,000 annually from foodborne illness. One of the key milestones of the FSMA is the mandatory recall authority under Sec. 423 or 21 USC section 350(1) as well as increased authority concerning records and inspection. The process for implementation is complex and requires, for example, implementation of rules for fresh produce and preventive controls. The following details key titles and final rules.

CRITICAL ANALYSIS: Contrast the Safe Food for Canadians Act (2012) which modernized food safety in Canada with the United States Food Safety Modernization Act below.
http://www.inspection.gc.ca/eng/1297964599443/1297965645317

Title I Prevention—Improving Capacity to Prevent Food Safety Problems
Inspection of records authority; registration; and registration suspension.
Title II Detection—Detecting and Responding to Food Safety Problems

High-risk facilities—Inspections once every five years and then at least once every three years. Non-high-risk facilities—Inspections at least once in seven years and then no less than every five years.

Tracking and Trace Back: Identify food recipients to prevent/mitigate an outbreak.

Mandatory Recall Authority: Available if the firm refuses or fails to voluntarily stop distribution of products (other than infant formula) that are adulterated or misbranded.

Reportable Food Registry Improvements: Critical information for a reportable food.

Title III Imports—Improving Safety of Imported Food

Foreign Supplier Verification: For imported food safety including HACCP for produce safety.

Voluntary Qualified Importer Program: Voluntary program for expedited review of imported food by participating importers.

Import Certification: Third party certification.

Foreign Offices: To aid foreign governments concerning food safety measures.

Title IV—Whistleblower Protection and Staff Administration

Staff increases: Minimum of 5,000 staff to fulfill the food safety mandates.

Whistleblower protections: Provided to workers involved in the manufacture, processing, packing, transporting, distribution, reception, holding, or importation of food from dismissal or discrimination.

Final Rules—Food Safety Modernization Act

http://www.fda.gov/Food/GuidanceRegulation/FSMA/ucm253380.htm#rules

Major accomplishments include final rules as well as foreign facilities inspections and in-state partnership inspection of domestic facilities as mandated. The following provides a synopsis and assessment of the final rules.

Final Rule—*Administrative Detention of Food* (2013)
Criteria Used to Order Administrative Detention of Food for Human or Animal Consumption

This final rule amended the criteria for administrative detention to prevent potentially unsafe food from reaching the marketplace. The final rule issued February 2013 adopts the interim final rule, *"Criteria Used to Order Administrative Detention of Food for Human or Animal Consumption,"* published in May 2011, without change. Revised guidance was issued (March 27, 2013) on administrative detention entitled ***"Guidance for Industry: What You Need to Know About Administrative Detention of Foods; Small Entity Compliance Guide."***

Final Rule—*Information Required in Prior Notice of Imported Food* (2013)

This rule requires when submitting prior notice of imported food, including food for animals, to report the name of any country to which the article has been refused entry.

Final Rule—*Current Good Manufacturing Practice, Hazard Analysis, and Risk-Based Preventive Controls for Human Food* (2015)
https://www.federalregister.gov/articles/2015/09/17/2015-21920/current-good-manufacturing-practice-hazard-analysis-and-risk-based-preventive-controls-for-human

 Preventive Controls Major Provisions Summary: **Final Rule issued (2015).** The proposed rule issued January 2013, supplemental proposed rule issued September 2014 and finalized September 17, 2015 (See 21CFR 117, effective Sept. 18, 2017) implements the requirements of FSMA for covered facilities to establish and implement a food safety system that includes a hazard analysis and risk-based preventive controls. ***Key Elements of the final rule are as follows.***
http://www.fda.gov/Food/GuidanceRegulation/FSMA/ucm334115.htm

1. A written food safety plan that includes hazard analysis.
 ✓ Preventive controls for process, food allergens, sanitation controls, supply chain controls and a recall plan;
 ✓ Oversight and management of preventive controls: monitoring and corrective actions; and
 ✓ Verification (Possible verification includes product testing and environmental monitoring).

2. Farm definition (expanded in supplemental proposed and final rule) clarified to cover two types of farm operations as follows.

- ✓ Primary Production Farm (under one management); and
- ✓ Secondary Activities Farm (pack or hold food from other farms are not subject to the preventive controls rule).

3. Supply-chain program more flexible with separate compliance dates established.

4. Current Good Manufacturing Practices (CGMPs) are updated and clarified.

5. Compliance Dates dependent on sales: Very Small businesses (sales-less than $1 million) 3 years; Small businesses 2 years (fewer than 500 full-time employees); All other businesses 1 year.

Final Rule—*Produce Safety* (2015)

http://www.fda.gov/Food/GuidanceRegulation/FSMA/ucm334114.htm

https://www.federalregister.gov/documents/2014/09/29/2014-22447/standards-for-the-growing-harvesting-packing-and-holding-of-produce-for-human-consumption

Produce Safety Major Provisions Summary: FDA issued a proposed rule on January 16, 2013 and a supplemental proposed rule September 29, 2014 due to significant public comment. The final rule still established science-based minimum standards for the safe growing, harvesting, packing, and holding of produce on farms. The following are the new final rule standards:

- ✓ Worker Training and Health and Hygiene
- ✓ Equipment, Tools, and Buildings
- ✓ Agricultural Water (proposed supplemental rule water quality testing more flexible)
- ✓ Manure strategy (proposed supplemental more study)
- ✓ Covered farms better defined (proposed supplemental rule)
- ✓ Domesticated and wild animals standards clarified (proposed supplemental rule)
- ✓ Qualified exemption process clarified (proposed supplemental rule)

Final Rule—*Foreign Supplier Verification Programs (FSVP) for Importers of Food for Humans and Animals* (2015)

http://www.fda.gov/Food/GuidanceRegulation/FSMA/ucm361902.htm

http://www.fda.gov/Food/GuidanceRegulation/FSMA/ucm361902.htm#fact_sheet-Food%20for%20Humans%20and%20Animals

Foreign Supplier Verification Program Summary: On July 29, 2013, FDA issued proposed regulations and a revised supplemental proposed rule on September 29, 2014 and finalized in November 2015 to strengthen the oversight of foods imported for U.S. consumers. Under the Foreign Supplier Verification Program (FSVP) regulations, importers would be required to perform certain risk-based activities to verify that food imported into the United States has been produced in a manner that provides the same level of public health protection as that required of domestic food producers. The FSVP regulations would implement section 301.

Under the final FSVP regulations, an importer is required to develop, maintain, and follow an FSVP for each food it imports, which, in general, would need to include the following:

- ✓ Compliance Status Review,
- ✓ Hazard Analysis,
- ✓ Verification Activities,
- ✓ Corrective Actions,
- ✓ Periodic Reassessment of the FSVP,
- ✓ Supplier and Importer Identification,
- ✓ Recordkeeping and
- ✓ Consistency with other FSMA rules concerning no more than $1million in annual food sales.

NOTE: Imported Food Expedited Review—FDA established a voluntary fee-based program which started January 2018 for the expedited review of food imported into the United States. Importers must demonstrate a proven food safety track record of supply chain management.

Final Rule—*Third Party Accreditation of Auditors or "Certification Bodies"* (2015)

http://www.fda.gov/Food/GuidanceRegulation/FSMA/ucm361903.htm

Third Party Accreditation Summary: This final rule, issued in November 2015 implements Section 307 of the FDA Food Safety Modernization Act (FSMA). FDA would identify third party auditors known as accreditation bodies based on criteria such as competency and impartiality. The accreditation bodies could be foreign government agencies or private companies and would in turn accredit third party auditors to audit and issue certifications for foreign food facilities. The final rule contains requirements relating to auditing and certification of foreign food facilities and food under the program and for notifying the FDA of conditions in an audited facility that could cause or contribute to a serious risk to the public health.

Model Accreditation Standards: FDA release of "Model Accreditation Standards" detailing qualifications a certification body must have to qualify for accreditation, such as the minimum requirements for education and experience for third-party auditors and their audit agents.

Final Rule—*Sanitary Transportation* (2016)

https://www.federalregister.gov/articles/2016/04/06/2016-07330/sanitary-transportation-of-human-and-animal-food

http://www.fda.gov/Food/GuidanceRegulation/FSMA/ucm247559.htm#Sanitary_Transportation

Requires those who transport food to use sanitary practices to ensure the safety of food. Final rule issued on April 5, 2016. With the passage of the updated 2005 Sanitary Food Transportation Act (SFTA), Congress reallocated lead authority for food transportation safety to FDA; however, both the Department of Transportation and the U.S. Department of Agriculture (USDA) remain as partners with FDA. This rule implements the requirement in section 111 of the FDA Food Safety Modernization Act (FSMA) that instructed FDA to issue SFTA regulations.

Final Rule—*Focused Mitigation Strategies to Protect Food Against Intentional Adulteration* (2016)

http://www.fda.gov/Food/GuidanceRegulation/FSMA/ucm378628.htm#summary

Mitigation Strategies Summary: On May 27, 2016 FDA issued a final rule that requires the food businesses in the United States and abroad to take measures to prevent facilities from being the target of intentional attempts to contaminate the food supply (Docket Number: FDA-2013-N-1425 (proposed Dec. 24, 2013). Under the rule, a food facility is required to have a written food defense plan that addresses significant vulnerabilities in its food production process. These food facilities would have to identify and implement strategies to address these weaknesses, establish monitoring procedures and corrective actions, substantiate that the system is working, certify that personnel assigned to the vulnerable areas are trained and maintain certain records. The rule does not apply to farms and food for animals. Tiered compliance dates based on facility size.

Final Rule—*Reportable Electronic Food Registry* (2016)

https://www.federalregister.gov/articles/2016/07/14/2016-16531/amendments-to-registration-of-food-facilities

http://www.fda.gov/Food/ComplianceEnforcement/RFR/default.htm

The Food Safety Modernization Act section 211 contains further amendments to improve the registry and FDA issued a final rule in July 2016. Initially, the Food Safety provision of FDAAA of 2007 (Pub. L. 110-085) mandated a provision for FDA to establish an electronic portal Food Reportable Registry (RFR) to which industry must submit reports about a "reportable food". See 21 USC sections 350(d) Registration of Food Facilities and 350(f) Reportable Food Registry. Further, the "Enhanced Authorities Regarding Postmarket Safety of Drugs" applies as well to food as follows. Title IX of FDAAA section 912 added section 310(ll) to the FDCA which prohibits the marketing of food to which has been added an approved drug, a licensed biological product or a "drug" or "biological" product where extensive clinical investigations have been launched and made public. See: 21 USC 350f.

Who must report: Facilities that manufacture, process or hold food for consumption in the United States now must tell the FDA within 24 hours if they find a reasonable probability that an article of food will cause severe health problems or death to a person or an animal.

***Application*:** The reporting requirement applies to all foods and animal feed regulated by the FDA, except infant formula and dietary supplements, which are covered by other regulatory requirements. Some examples of reasons a food may be reportable include bacterial contamination, allergen mislabeling or elevated levels of certain chemical components. The requirements apply to any person who has to submit registration information to the FDA for a food facility that manufactures, processes, packs, or holds food for human or animal consumption in the United States. Reporting is inapplicable if the problem was found before the food was shipped, and the problem was corrected or the food destroyed.

***Responsible party*:** Must investigate the cause of the adulteration if the adulteration of food may have originated with the responsible party; and submit initial information followed by supplemental reports; and work with the FDA authorities to follow up as needed.

NOTE: FDA issued guidances for clarification about exemptions pertaining to the following as HACCP requirements have been in place for years pre-enactment of the FSMA.
https://www.fda.gov/Food/GuidanceRegulation/GuidanceDocumentsRegulatoryInformation/ucm569789.htm

> ✓ *Low-Acid Canned Foods and FSMA*
> ✓ *Juice HACCP and FSMA*
> ✓ *Seafood HACCP and FSMA*

CRITICAL ANALYSIS: Evaluate the FSMA final rules above and the impact on both the regulated industry and FDA.

Recall Mechanisms—USDA and FDA

The following are considerations as to how to handle a recall:
- ✓ Plan in advance;
- ✓ Ensure that your recall plan is updated regularly;
- ✓ Decide whether a recall is necessary;
- ✓ Assess all options;
- ✓ Act expediently;
- ✓ Communicate with government and consumers and anyone else involved in the distribution chain;
- ✓ Maintain written records; and
- ✓ Reassess effectiveness and revamp when warranted.

United States Department of Agriculture Food Safety and Inspection Service Recalls
http://www.fsis.usda.gov/wps/portal/fsis/topics/recalls-and-public-health-alerts

A food recall is a voluntary action by a manufacturer or distributor. However, FSIS has the legal authority to detain and seize those products if a company refuses to recall its products. FSIS oversees all recall activities at official meat and poultry establishments. FSIS evaluates the public health concerns and classifies the recall as follows:

Class I Recalls portray the most serious health situation because of the reasonable probability that use of the product will cause serious adverse health consequences or even death. An example of a Class I recall is the presence of pathogens in a ready-to-eat product or the presence of *E. coli* 0157: H7 in ground beef;

Class II Recalls involve a health hazard where there is a chance of adverse health consequences from the use of a product, such as the presence of undeclared allergens; and

Class III Recalls involve a situation where the use of the product will not cause adverse health consequences, where for example, excess water exists in a product.

Once FSIS discovers such a problem, it uses a Crisis Management Response system. Though, with the implementation of HACCP, plants assume greater accountability. Under the HACCP rationale, a plant is responsible for determining the recall scope and for public notification. Important considerations in a recall include the depth of the recall and the level of product distribution to which the recall is extended, that is, the consumer, retail or restaurant levels. The disposition of the product in terms of action the firm will take to correct the situation is crucial. Product recall procedures for firms should include a recall plan. A person in a firm should be identified to prepare and coordinate all activities related to recalls. A recall plan should identify the personnel, recall procedures, the health hazard evaluation and the scope. Product identification is an important part of the recall process. Public notification can occur by a press release through the general news media, either national or local, depending on the extent. FSIS must be notified even when a firm takes the initiative to recall a product.

Despite best efforts at food safety, recalls do occur. By way of illustration, Quay Corporation, Skokie, Ill. recalled approximately 258,121 pounds of pork lard products that were produced without the benefit of federal inspection (2018).
https://www.fsis.usda.gov/wps/portal/fsis/topics/recalls-and-public-health-alerts/recall-case-archive/archive/2018/recall-053-2018-release

CRITICAL ANALYSIS: Notwithstanding HACCP, recalls continue to occur. There were 131 recalls in calendar year 2017 which involved 20,880,574 pounds of products. What more should be done by industry and USDA in terms of preventive measures to avoid nationwide recalls? *https://www.fsis.usda.gov/wps/portal/fsis/topics/recalls-and-public-health-alerts/recall-summaries*

United States Food and Drug Administration Recall Classifications
http://www.fda.gov/safety/recalls/default.htm

Companies usually voluntarily cooperate with FDA in recalling its own product; however, the Food Safety Modernization Act provides recall authority. FDA has designated three recall classifications as follows:

Class I—Reasonable probability that the use of the product will cause serious, adverse health consequences or death;

Class II—Remote probability of adverse health consequences from the use of the product; and

Class III—Use of the product will not cause adverse health consequences.

Notable Nationwide Recalls

Instant Coffee— The AMPT Life, LLC Recall of AMPT Coffee due to the Presence of Undeclared Active Pharmaceutical Ingredients and Undeclared Milk (Sildenafil and Tadalafil active ingredient in Viagra. which is FDA approved prescription drug for erectile dysfunction (2017). *https://www.fda.gov/safety/recalls/ucm569558.htm*

Dried Milk—Valley Milk Productions LLC: Milk powder and sweet cream buttermilk powder due to *Salmonella* detection during inspection (2016). *https://www.fda.gov/Safety/Recalls/ucm532828.htm*

Eggs—206 million shells eggs (2018)-Rose Acre Farms, Inc., second-largest egg producer in the United States involved 10-state outbreak of Salmonella braenderup (FDA warning letter issued Sept. 2018). DeCoster (Quality Egg) salmonella contamination from two egg farms in Iowa (2010); $6.8 million fine and three-month jail terms for two former executives in 2015.

Cantaloupe—Jensen Farms deadly listeria outbreak (2011). In 2014, the two farmers received probation and $150,000 in restitution.

Peanut Butter—ConAgra ConAgra agreed (May 20, 2015) to pay $11.2 million to settle federal charges from a 2007 salmonella outbreak and from peanut butter produced in a plant in Georgia. Over 600 people in 47 states became ill and triggering a massive recall eight years ago. The misdemeanor charge against the Omaha, Nebraska, based company was due to shipping adulterated food. The company agreed to pay $8 million in criminal fines, as well as an additional $3.2 million in forfeitures. Company executives were not charged.

Peanut Butter and Peanut Paste—unsanitary conditions led to salmonella outbreak caused nine deaths and ultimate closure of Peanut Corporation of America * (2008-2009);

Cookie Dough— (2009);

Peppers—Originally, tomatoes were thought to be the source (2008); and
Spinach—*E. coli O157:H7* (2006).

*NOTE: The corporate executives and others were convicted and sentenced to lengthy terms of imprisonment. See *Volume III: Enforcement*.

CRITICAL ANALYSIS: Review the FDA Food Safety Modernization Act with recall provisions and recommend additional preventive measures to avoid nationwide recalls.

Consent Decree of Condemnation and Permanent Injunction
Permanent Injunction Against Virginia Company and Employees to Prevent Distribution of Adulterated Milk Powder Products (edited). See links below.
https://www.justice.gov/opa/press-release/file/948191/download
https://www.justice.gov/opa/pr/district-court-enters-permanent-injunction-against-virginia-company-and-employees-prevent

The U.S. District Court (March 15, 2017 Western District of Virginia) entered a consent decree of condemnation and permanent injunction against Valley Milk Products LLC, Michael W. Curtis, Robert D. Schroeder, and Jennifer J. Funkhouser (defendants), the Department of Justice announced today. The consent decree also orders the condemnation of certain seized milk powder products and prevents the further distribution of adulterated milk powder products. A seizure action filed on November 18, 2016 alleged that certain milk powder products of the defendants were manufactured under insanitary conditions whereby they may have become contaminated with filth, and/or whereby they may have been rendered injurious to health. That complaint sought to seize and condemn certain adulterated milk powder products at Valley Milk Products' Strasburg, Virginia facility. As alleged in the complaint, during a 2016 inspection of Valley Milk, FDA confirmed the presence of Salmonella meleagridis in the Strasburg facility. Salmonella strains were nearly identical to Salmonella strains found at the firm in 2010, 2011, and 2013. The complaint alleged that Salmonella meleagridis was also present in the firm's undistributed finished product samples. The complaint also alleges that, in addition to the presence of Salmonella, the defendants' milk processing facility had insanitary conditions, including dripping brown fluids and old product residue within the processing equipment. The complaint alleges that this evidence demonstrates that the firm's sanitation practices were inadequate to control or eliminate Salmonella meleagridis in their processing environment.

The defendants have also agreed to be bound by a permanent injunction that prohibits them from resuming the manufacture of milk powder products at the Strasburg facility without implementing effective corrective action. If the defendants wish to resume manufacturing milk powder products at their Strasburg facility, the defendants must notify FDA in advance, and comply with certain remedial provisions set forth in the Decree. Among other things, the remedial provisions require that the defendants establish and implement a written sanitation control program, which shall set out the details for sanitation control over the manufacturing and storage processes for the facilities used to receive, manufacture, prepare, pack, hold, or distribute milk powder products, and all food handling and storage equipment therein.

Bioterrorism Act
http://www.fda.gov/RegulatoryInformation/Legislation/ucm148797.htm

Safeguarding the United States food supply remains a priority especially because of terrorist threats and attacks. Both FDA and USDA have responsibility to ensure a safe food supply and combat threats of bioterrorism. The Public Health Security and Bioterrorism Preparedness and Response Act of 2002, (Bioterrorism Act) was enacted to protect the United States food supply from increased terrorist activity. The terrorist attacks on the United States on September 11, 2001 served as the impetus for this legislation. The Bioterrorism Act under Title III pertains to the Safety of Food and Drug Supply. Specific requirements related to food imports are as follows:

✓ Prior Notice electronically to FDA of every food article arriving at a U.S. port;
✓ Facility Registration for food intended for U.S. consumption;
✓ Recordkeeping (Rule finalized December 9, 2004);
✓ Administrative Detention (Rule finalized May 27, 2004); and
✓ Marking requirements for refused food.

Importers or brokers usually provide the prior notice requirement to the Bureau of Customs and Border Protection (CBP) when foods arrive in the United States. However, the Bioterrorism Act obliges importers or brokers to provide this information to FDA prior to United States arrival. FDA and CBP have worked in partnership on the implementation of the Bioterrorism Act requisites and signed a memorandum of understanding to that effect. The advance information in the "prior notice" requirement, started in December 2003, permits FDA to assess the information and decide whether to inspect the imported food. Compliance is through the CBP's Automated Broker Interface of the Automated Commercial System (ABI/ACS). Prior notice can be submitted through ABI/ACS or FDA's Prior Notice (PN) System Interface by brokers, importers, U.S. agents and any individual with knowledge of the information that is required. It is important to understand what is considered "food" under the FDCA and therefore subject to the prior notice requirement. Examples of "food" encompass:

✓ Dietary supplements and dietary ingredients;
✓ Infant formula;
✓ Beverages (including alcoholic beverages and bottled water);
✓ Fruits and vegetables;
✓ Fish and seafood;
✓ Dairy products and shell eggs;
✓ Raw agricultural commodities for use as food or components of food;
✓ Canned and frozen foods;
✓ Bakery goods, snack food, and candy (including chewing gum);
✓ Live food animals; and
✓ Animal feeds and pet food.

Specific requirements that must be included in the prior notice are detailed below. A new prior notice must be submitted if the information changes.

✓ "Identification of submitter, including name, telephone and fax numbers, email address, and firm name and address";
✓ "Identification of the transmitter (if different from the submitter), including name, telephone and fax numbers, email address, and firm name and address";
✓ "Entry type and CBP identifier";
✓ "The identification of the food article, including complete FDA product code, common or usual name or market name, estimated quantity described from the smallest package size to the largest container, and the lot or code numbers or other identifier (if applicable)";
✓ "The identification of the manufacturer";
✓ "The identification of the grower, if known";
✓ "The FDA Country of Production";
✓ "The identification of the shipper, except for food imported by international mail";
✓ "The country from which the article of food is shipped or, if the food is imported by international mail, the anticipated mailing date and country from which the food is mailed";
✓ "The anticipated arrival information (location, date, and time) or, if the food is imported by international mail, the U.S. recipient (name and address)";
✓ "The identification of the importer, owner, and ultimate consignee, except for food imported by international mail or transshipped through the United States";
✓ "The identification of the carrier and mode of transportation, except for food imported by international mail"; and
✓ "Planned shipment information, except for food imported by international mail".

Specific exclusions from the prior notice requirement as follows:

✓ Food intended for individual personal use; that is "food carried by or otherwise accompanying an individual arriving in the United States for that individual's personal use (i.e., for consumption by themselves, family, or friends, and not for sale or other distribution)";

✓ "Food that is exported without leaving the port of arrival until export";

✓ "Meat food products, poultry products and egg products that are subject to the exclusive jurisdiction of the U.S. Department of Agriculture under the Federal Meat Inspection Act, the Poultry Products Inspection Act, or the Egg Products Inspection Act; and

✓ "Food that was made by an individual in his/her personal residence and sent by that individual as a personal gift (i.e., for non-business reasons) to an individual in the U.S.".

Furthermore, FDA issued a rule that covers the use of private sampling services and laboratories. Titled: *"Requirements Pertaining to Sampling Services and Private Laboratories Used in Connection with Imported Foods."* (Title 21 CFR new part 59). The regulation details proper identification, collection and maintenance of samples as well as mandate private laboratories to use recognized analytical standards. FDA can utilize enforcement mechanisms such as seizure, injunction, prosecution and even institute debarment proceedings for noncompliance.

Bioterrorism—United States Department of Agriculture and Homeland Security

Homeland Security Presidential Directive 9 mandates that the United States Department of Agriculture's Food Safety and Inspection Service ensure foods under their jurisdiction are prepared for an intentional attack. These foods include meat, poultry and egg products. This is accomplished through principles developed by the United States Department of Defense. USDA utilizes the **CARVER** principles as follows: *Critical; Accessibility; Recuperation after an attack; Vulnerability; Effect on the food system; and Recognition of the target.*

CRITICAL ANALYSIS: Earlier in this chapter, the concept of a single food agency was discussed. Would a single federal food agency serve to thwart intentional threats to the food supply? See: GAO Report to Congressional Committees *"FOOD SAFETY Agencies Need to Address Gaps in Enforcement and Collaboration to Enhance Safety of Imported Food"* **GAO-09.**

Bovine Spongiform Encephalopathy (BSE)

BSE, generally known as "mad cow disease," is a progressive neurological fatal degenerative disease that affects the central nervous system of cattle. BSE falls within a class of diseases known as transmissible spongiform encephalopathy (TSEs). The precise cause of BSE is unknown; BSE is caused by infectious forms of a type of prion protein. BSE presence in tissues is ascertained by injecting animals such as mice with samples. Included in the family of illnesses is the human disease, a variant Creutzfeldt-Jakob Disease (vCJD), which is thought to be caused by eating neural tissue, such as brain and spinal cord, from BSE-affected cattle. Detecting a BSE agent is difficult in terms of an accurate assessment. Testing for prion disease is normally performed postmortem; however new technologies are underway to test live animals as well as humans. Particular staining procedures are applied to observe abnormal prion protein in tissue; yet, this might not give an accurate measurement in terms of the contagion.

BSE has occurred mainly in the United Kingdom; however, the disease has been discovered in other countries as well. Federal agencies adopted special measures to prevent BSE in the United States. Although FDA and USDA safeguards were in place, stricter surveillance became necessary due to the discovery of a BSE positive cow in the United Sates in December 2003. These protections include:

✓ *Import controls;*

✓ *U.S. cattle surveillance;*

✓ *Feed prohibitions in terms of mammalian protein to ruminant animals;*

✓ *Prohibition of high-risk bovine tissues known to carry the BSE agent from the human food supply; and*

✓ *Swift and effective response to contain damage from a BSE positive animal.*

Final Rule FDA—Bovine Spongiform Encephalopathy

http://www.fda.gov/Food/NewsEvents/ConstituentUpdates/ucm490542.htm

FDA issued a rule (March 18, 2016) which finalized three previously issued interim final rules intended to further decrease the possible risk of bovine spongiform encephalopathy (BSE), commonly referred to as "mad cow disease," in human food. This rule finalizes three interim rules from 2004, 2005, and 2008. The final rule specifies definitions for prohibited cattle materials and excludes their use in human food, dietary supplements, and cosmetics. These materials include:

✓ *Specified risk materials (SRMs): brain, skull, eyes, trigeminal ganglia, spinal cord, vertebral column (excluding the vertebrae of the tail, the transverse processes of the thoracic and lumbar vertebrae, and the wings of the sacrum), and dorsal root ganglia (DRG) of cattle 30 months of age and older, and the tonsils and distal ileum of the small intestine from all cattle;*

✓ *The small intestine from all cattle unless the distal ileum has been properly removed;*

✓ *Material from nonambulatory disabled cattle; and*

✓ *Material from cattle not inspected and passed, or mechanically separated (MS) (Beef).*

Final Rule USDA— Cattle Material Prohibition in Food, Cosmetics and Supplements

A final rule issued by FSIS on July 12, 2007 prohibits the slaughter of downer cattle when presented for pre-slaughter inspection. The final rule affirms two interim final rules published on January 12, 2004. 69 Fed. Reg. 1862, 1885. The ban on bovine-derived material goes beyond human food and applies to cosmetics and dietary supplements as indicated below. In an unusual administrative step, USDA's interim final rules were published in January 2004 and by FDA in July 2004, Prohibited Cattle Materials Docket No. 2004N-0081. Specifically, the interim and now final rule prohibits the following materials from FDA regulated human food, cosmetics and dietary supplements.

✓ *Any material from "Downer" cattle (cattle that cannot walk);*

✓ *Any material from "Dead" cattle (cattle that die on the farm before reaching a slaughter plant);*

✓ *Specified Risk Materials or SRM's such as the brain, skull, eyes, trigeminal ganglia, spinal cord, vertebral column, and dorsal root ganglia from cattle 30 months or older and the distal ileum, a part of the small intestine and tonsils from all cattle despite age or health;*

✓ *Restrictions on techniques to mechanically remove meat from bones; and*

✓ *Prohibits the use of "air-injection" stunning.*

NOTE: See *"Prohibition of the Use of Specified Risk Materials for Human Food and Requirements for the Disposition of Non-Ambulatory Disabled Cattle"; "Prohibition of the Use of Certain Stunning Devices Used to Immobilize Cattle During Slaughter"*, 72 Fed. Reg. 38,700 (July 13, 2007) (codified at 9 C.F.R. pts. 309, 310, and 318).

Another USDA FSIS rule finalized in 2007, is designed to lower the risk that cattle could be inadvertently fed prohibited protein, which led to the BSE epidemic in United Kingdom cattle in the 1980's and 1990's. This rule addresses the following:

✓ *Bans mammalian blood and blood products as a protein source;*

✓ *Bans the use of "poultry litter" as a feed ingredient for ruminant animals;*

✓ *Bans the use of "plate waste" that is, meat scraps and uneaten meat collected from large restaurants; and*

✓ *Requires equipment, facilities or production lines to be dedicated to non-ruminant animal feeds if protein is used that is prohibited in ruminant feed.*

Record Keeping—Human Food

https://www.gpo.gov/fdsys/pkg/FR-2006-10-11/html/E6-16830.htm

Manufacturers and processors have to maintain records that establish the cosmetic is not manufactured, processed with or contains prohibited cattle materials. The recordkeeping mandate rule titled: *"Recordkeeping Requirements for Human Food and Cosmetics Manufactured From, Processed With, or Otherwise Containing, Material From Cattle"* was published July 14, 2006 (69 FR 42275) and permits electronic recordkeeping. In addition to the prohibited cattle material recordkeeping requirement, the rule amends the FDCA as follows:

✓ *Two-year record retention;*
✓ *Record availability to FDA; and providing*
✓ *Records within 5 days when filing entry with U.S. Customs.*

Hazard Analysis and Critical Control Points System

http://www.fda.gov/Food/GuidanceRegulation/HACCP/

Foodborne illness is a serious problem in the United States and can be life threatening. Protecting the nation's food supply remains a challenge and a priority. The most common pathogens associated with meat and poultry products include Campylobacter jejuni/coli, *E.coli* 0157H:7, *Salmonella* and *Listeria monocytogeners*. For example, bacteria such as *Salmonella* enteritidis and *Escherichia coli* (*E.coli*) 0157:H7 have become more prevalent, harder to detect and more resistant. Chemical and biological contamination remains important considerations as well. Federal agencies such as USDA and FDA adopted a program developed several years ago for astronauts, known as the Hazard Analysis Critical Control Points (HACCP) systems 61 FR 38805 (1996). HACCP systems are preventive in nature rather than traditional reactive checks of final products. USDA has established HACCP requirements for meat and poultry processing plants. FDA has HACCP programs for the regulated industry for retail and food service, seafood and juices. The HACCP rule:

✓ *Requires all meat and poultry plants to develop and implement a system of preventive controls, known as HACCP, to improve the safety of their products;*
✓ *Sets pathogen reduction performance standards for Salmonella that slaughter plants and plants producing raw ground products must meet;*
✓ *Requires all meat and poultry plants to develop and implement written standard operating procedures (SSOPs) for sanitation; and*
✓ *Requires meat and poultry slaughter plants to conduct microbial testing for Generic E. coli to verify the adequacy of process controls for the prevention of fecal contamination.*

HACCP involves these seven principles:

✓ **Conduct a hazard analysis.** Identify both the possible hazards associated with a food such as chemical, toxin, microbe or physical such as glass or metal fragments and identify measures to control those hazards;

✓ **Determine critical control points.** Detect the critical control points involved in a food's production to ultimate consumption by the consumer at which the potential hazard can be controlled or eliminated;

✓ **Institute critical limits.** For each critical control point, crucial limits should be determined. For example, in cooked food, this might include establishing the minimum cooking temperature and time required to ensure the elimination of any harmful microbes;

✓ **Establish procedures.** Monitor the critical control points by establishing procedures such as determining how and by whom cooking time and temperature should be monitored;

✓ **Create corrective actions.** Determine corrective action to be taken when monitoring shows that a critical limit has not been met. For example if the minimum cooking temperature is not met, then the food would have to be reprocessed or disposed.

✓ **Ascertain verification procedures.** Use a verification system to ensure that the system is working properly. For example, make sure temperature recording equipment works properly; and

✓ **Create recordkeeping to document the HACCP** system. This includes records of hazards and their control methods, the monitoring of safety requirements and action taken to correct potential problems.

HACCP provides a science-based focus on prevention, industry responsibility, and efficient government oversight. FSIS reevaluates HACCP through the HACCP Inspection Models Project (HIMP). The focus of HIMP is to improve use of slaughter inspectors and to ensure the reduction and elimination of problems associated with foodborne pathogens. The HIMP project is ongoing and regulations could be adopted based on the research and results of HIMP.

Enforcement under HACCP

The major distinction between pre-HACCP inspection and inspection under HACCP is that HACCP is preventive in nature. This means if HACCP controls are not performing as they should, then regulatory action may be taken. Responsibility is placed on the plant to ensure that HACCP works as intended. Traditional inspections prior to HACCP focused on sight, touch and smell, animal diseases, and sanitation. For example, before HACCP, FSIS could suspend or withdraw an inspection based on unsanitary conditions, inhumane livestock slaughtering, failure to destroy a condemned product, intrusion with inspection personnel or unfitness due to convictions from violating the law. FSIS may refuse, suspend or withdraw inspection for these reasons:

✓ Failure to develop or implement SSOPs;

✓ Failure to collect and analyze samples for generic *E.coli* and record those results;

✓ Failure to design and implement a preventive HACCP plan; and

✓ Failure to fulfill Salmonella performance standard requirements.

FSIS has the authority to file a complaint with the intent to withdraw the grant of inspection. The company is entitled to have the case heard before an administrative law judge and the right to appeal to federal court if the inspection is withdrawn. The case may be referred to federal prosecutors for criminal prosecution and if found guilty there is a possibility of fines, imprisonment and or both. Despite these safeguards, see cases below.

CRITICAL ANALYSIS: Discuss the significance of HACCP and propose improvements.

HACCP Noncompliance—*Floppers, Neptune and Portland*

United States v. BEK Catering, LLC, d/b/a FLOPPERS Foods, and Stembridge and Huxan **Civil Action No. 16-0348-CG-N (So. Dist. Alabama July 5, 2016).**

Complaint for Permanent Injunction against BEK Catering, LLC, doing business as Floppers Foods, and Billy B. Stembridge, Jr., and Kyle D. Huxen, individuals (collectively, "Defendants"), and having consented to this Decree.

IT IS HEREBY ORDERED, ADJUDGED, AND DECREED as follows: Defendants violated 21 U.S.C. § 331(k) by causing articles of food within the meaning of 21 U.S.C. § 321(f), namely fish and fishery products, that are held for sale after shipment of one or more components in interstate commerce to become adulterated under 21 U.S.C. § 342(a)(4) in that they have been prepared, packed, or held under insanitary conditions whereby they may have been rendered injurious to health. Defendants violated 21 U.S.C. § 331(k) by causing articles of food within the meaning of 21 U.S.C. § 321(f), namely fish and fishery products that are held for sale after shipment of one or more components in interstate commerce to become misbranded under 21 U.S.C.: § 343(w) in that they contain a major food allergen (crustacean shellfish, milk or wheat) that is not declared on the product label; § 343(i)(2) in that their label does not bear the common or usual name of each ingredient in accordance with 21 C.F.R. § 101.4; § 343(q) in that the product labeling does not bear nutrition information that provides a declaration of trans fat content in the manner required by 21 C.F.R. § 101.9(2)(2)(ii); § 343(i)(1) in that their label does not bear the common or usual name of the food or an appropriately descriptive term, in accordance with 21 C.F.R. § 101.3; and § 343(e)(1) in that the product, in package form, bears a label that does not contain the place of business (city, state, ZIP) of the manufacturer, packer, or distributor. Defendants represent to the Court that, as of June 1, 2016, they are not engaged in processing, packing, or holding (except for activities incidental to finished product transport and delivery) fish and fishery products at or from any location. If Defendants intend to resume processing, packing, or holding (i.e., operations that are beyond the scope of activities incidental to finished product transport and delivery) fish and fishery products at or from any facility at any time in the future, they must first notify FDA in writing at least ninety

(90) calendar days in advance of resuming operations. *** If Defendants now or in the future directly or indirectly receive, prepare, process, pack, label, hold, and/or distribute articles of food (referred to as "Defendants' Facility" or "the Facility") they must:

Retain an independent person (the "HACCP Expert") who is without any personal or financial ties (other than a retention agreement) to Defendants or their families, and who, is qualified to determine whether Defendants' methods, processes, and controls are operated and administered in conformity with regulations for fish and fishery products, including seafood hazard analysis critical control point (HACCP) requirements, 21 C.F.R. Part 123, and current good manufacturing practice (cGMP) requirements for food, 21 C.F.R. Part 110;

Conduct hazard analyses and develops, to FDA's satisfaction, an adequate written HACCP plan, as required by 21 C.F.R. 123.6, for each type of fish or fishery product received, prepared, processed, packed, labeled, held, and/or distributed by Defendants;

Develop written corrective action plans and verification procedures plans to be taken whenever there is a deviation from a critical limit, as described in 21 C.F.R. 123.7(b);

Develop written verification procedures as part of Defendants' HACCP plans, 21 C.F.R. 123.8;

Develop written sanitation standard operating procedures (SSOPs) specific to Defendants' Facility and operations and that shall conform with the procedures set forth at 21 C.F.R. § 123.11, and shall ensure compliance with the Act and 21 C.F.R. Part 110;

Develop an employee training program;

At their expense, clean and sanitize their Facility and equipment and make improvements to render the Facility and equipment suitable for receiving, preparing, processing, packing, holding, labeling, and distributing articles of food in accordance with this Decree, the Act, and its implementing regulations; and Destroy, under FDA's supervision, all fish or fishery products in Defendants' custody, control, or possession as of the date this Decree is signed by the parties; The HACCP Expert shall conduct a comprehensive inspection of Defendants' Facility;

Defendants have paid all costs of inspection, analysis, review, investigation, examination, and supervision for FDA's oversight.

FDA, as it deems necessary to evaluate Defendants' compliance with the terms of this Decree, the Act, and its implementing regulations, conducts inspections of Defendants' distribution operations and/or Defendants' facilities, including the buildings, sanitation-related systems, equipment, utensils, labeling, and all articles of food and relevant records contained therein;

Recall, at Defendants' expense, all articles of food that have been distributed and/or are under the custody and control of Defendants' agents, distributors, customers, or consumers;

Revise, modify, expand, or continue to submit any reports, plans, procedures, or other records prepared pursuant to this Decree;

Submit samples to a qualified laboratory for analysis;

Issue a safety alert; and/or

Take any other corrective actions as FDA deems necessary to protect the public health or bring Defendants into compliance with this Decree, the Act, or its implementing regulations.

United States v. Neptune Manufacturing Co., Inc. and individuals Alexander Goldring, Peter Oyrekh, and Semyon Krutovsk (collectively, "Defendants").
Permanent Injunction Against Neptune Manufacturing, Inc. and Senior Officers to Stop Distribution of Adulterated Products (No. 2:14-CV-09028-SJO-AS)
http://www.justice.gov/opa/pr/district-court-enters-permanent-injunction-against-los-angeles-seafood-company-and-senior

The U.S. District Court (Central District of California) entered a consent decree of permanent injunction (December 1, 2014) against Neptune Manufacturing, Inc. of Los Angeles and its corporate officers, Alexander Goldring, Peter Oyrekh and Semyon Krutovsky, to prevent the distribution of adulterated seafood products. The complaint alleged that Neptune prepares, processes, packs, holds and distributes ready-to-eat smoked and salt-cured seafood including pickled herring, smoked steelhead trout, smoked halibut, smoked whitefish, smoked salmon and smoked mackerel. *** The defendants agreed to settle the litigation and be bound by a consent decree of permanent injunction that prohibits them from committing violations of the federal Food, Drug, and Cosmetic Act. The consent decree requires Neptune to cease all manufacturing operations and requires that, in order for defendants to resume distributing seafood products, the FDA first must determine that Neptune's manufacturing practices have come into compliance with the law. According to the complaint, since 2006, FDA inspections documented a pattern of continuing conduct of insanitary conditions resulting in the persistent presence of *Listeria monocytogenes* (*L. mono*). These insanitary conditions were the result of deviations from current good manufacturing practices such as not adequately cleaning surfaces and utensils used for cutting fish. Further, according to the complaint, the FDA's most recent inspection in December 2013 documented the defendants' failure to have and comply with adequate Hazard Analysis and Critical Control Point (HACCP) plans that control for *Clostridium botulinum* (*C. bot*) and *L. mono* hazards. *L. mono* is the bacterium that causes listeriosis, a serious and sometimes fatal infection for vulnerable groups such as newborns, the elderly and those with an impaired immune system. Ingestion of the neurotoxin *C. bot* can cause botulism. ***

The complaint alleged that these inspections revealed that the products were adulterated within the meaning of the Food, Drug, and Cosmetic Act. As alleged in the complaint, the company was told to take certain precautions while brining fish to control potential *C. bot* hazards but failed to take appropriate corrective action. Further, according to the complaint, cutting utensils were seen with dried pieces of fish on them, and exposed cracks, pits and crevices on the floor allowed water to pool in them, increasing the risk of *L. mono* contamination. FDA environmental samples taken around the facility tested positive for *L. mono* in critical areas such as the brining room, smoking/drying room and the walk-in cooler where finished products are stored.

United States v. Portland Shellfish Co., Inc., Jeffrey D. Holden, Satyavan Singh and John A. Maloney (DC Maine Civil No. 2:11-CV-00001)

The following, in relevant part, is from the consent decree (January 20, 2011). Plaintiff, the United States of America, for the District of Maine, having filed a complaint for injunctive relief against Portland Shellfish Company, Inc. ("Portland Shellfish"), Jeffrey D. Holden, Satyavan Singh, and John A. Maloney (collectively, "Defendants"), and Defendants having appeared and having consented to entry of this Decree without contest, without admitting any of the allegations in the Complaint and disclaiming any liability.

IT IS HEREBY ORDERED, ADJUDGED, AND DECREED that: Defendants have violated the Act, 21 U.S.C. § 331(a), by introducing into interstate commerce articles of food, as defined by 21 U.S.C. § 321(f), namely ready-to eat, cooked fish and fishery products, that are adulterated within the meaning of 21 U.S.C. §§ 342(a)(1) and (a)(4); and 21 U.S.C. § 331(k), by causing articles of food, namely ready-to-eat, cooked fish and fishery products, to become adulterated within the meaning of 21 U.S.C. §§ 342(a)(1) and (a)(4) after shipment in interstate commerce.

Defendants are perpetually restrained and enjoined under the provisions of 21 U.S.C. § 332(a) from receiving, processing, preparing, packing, holding, or distributing, unless and until:

A. Defendants have thoroughly cleaned and sanitized the facilities and equipment therein and made improvements. ***

B. Defendants have selected a person or persons ("Listeria expert"), other than an employee of Portland Shellfish, who by reason of background, experience, and education is qualified to develop a Hazard Analysis Critical Control Point ("HACCP") plan, a finished product testing program, a Sanitation Standard Operation Procedure ("SSOP"), an employee training program on sanitary food handling techniques and personal hygiene practices, and an environmental microbial monitoring program for all species of the genus Listeria ("L. spp.") for the processing of ready-to-eat, cooked fish and fishery products.

C. The Listeria expert has developed a written finished product testing program for Listeria monocytogenes ("L. mono"), an SSOP, an employee training program, and an environmental microbial monitoring program.

D. The United States Food and Drug Administration ("FDA") has reviewed and approved in writing the finished product testing program, SSOP, training program, environmental microbial monitoring program. ***

E. Defendants, under the supervision of and in accordance with methods acceptable to FDA, have tested for L. mono all ready-to-eat, cooked fish and fishery products. ***

F. Defendants, along with their Listeria expert, have conducted appropriate hazard analyses and have prepared HACCP plans as required by 21 C.F.R. § 123.6(b) for all foods. ***

G. Defendants, along with their Listeria expert, develop and implement an ongoing program of adequate measures to control L. Mono. ***

H. FDA, as it deems necessary to evaluate Defendants' compliances.

I. Portland Shellfish pays inspection costs, supervision, analyses, and FDA examination.

J. FDA has notified Defendants in writing that Defendants appear to be in compliance.

K. During inspections, Defendants shall cooperate fully with FDA, by, among other things, promptly providing FDA investigators with requested documents and materials. ***

No sooner than five (5) years after entry of this Decree, Defendants may petition this Court for an order dissolving the Decree.

NOTE: See: *United States v. Blue Ribbon Smoked Fish, Inc.*, 179 F. Supp. 2d 30 (E.D.N.Y. 2001) CV-01-3887, aff'd 56 F. App'x 542 (2d Cir. 2003). *Blue Ribbon* is one of the earliest cases where the government sought an injunction for insanitary plan conditions, inadequacy and or lack of a HACCP plan and the presence of L. Monocytogenes. The court ordered the defendants to comply with the inadequacies. Using established precedent. The Court opined that the "FDCA's "overriding purpose [is] to protect the public health." *United States v. An Article of Drug, [B]acto-Unidisk*, 394 U.S. 784, 798 (1969).

CRITICAL ANALYSIS: Review *Floppers, Neptune* and *Portland Seafood*. How should you counsel your client if you represented any of these companies?

Salmonella Testing—*Supreme Beef Processors*

The decision of *Supreme Beef Processors v. United States Department of Agriculture* presents many interesting legal issues. The question in this case involved whether the USDA could use Salmonella tests to evaluate the sanitation of a processing plant. The district court held that performance standards and Salmonella tests do not necessarily evaluate the conditions of a processing plant and therefore cannot serve as a basis for deciding whether the product is adulterated under § 601(m)(4). Therefore, the court reasoned that because the defendant's Salmonella tests did not necessarily evaluate the conditions of *Supreme Beef's* processing plant, the results of those tests could not be used as the basis to withdraw inspectors. Under 21 U.S.C. § 601(m)(4), USDA is permitted to withdraw inspectors from a processing plant only if the plant is first found to be unsanitary. The court found problematic USDA's science-based testing of a processor's product to evaluate the conditions of its plant.

United States v. Supreme Beef Processors, Inc.
275 F3d.432 (5th Cir. 2001)

PATRICK E. HIGGINBOTHAM, Circuit Judge: Certain meat inspection regulations promulgated by the Secretary of Agriculture, which deal with the levels of *Salmonella* in raw meat product, were challenged as beyond the statutory authority granted to the Secretary by the Federal Meat Inspection Act. The district court struck down the regulations. We hold that the regulations fall outside of the statutory grant of rulemaking authority and affirm. ***

After four weeks of testing, FSIS notified Supreme that it would likely fail the Salmonella tests. Pursuant to the final test results, which found 47 percent of the samples taken from Supreme contaminated with Salmonella, FSIS issued a Noncompliance Report, advising Supreme that it had not met the performance standard. *** The third set of tests began on August 27, 1999, and after only five weeks, FSIS advised Supreme that it would again fall short of the ground beef performance standard. *** Although Supreme Beef promised to achieve the 7.5 percent performance standard in 180 days, it failed to provide any specific information explaining how it would accomplish that goal, and FSIS decided to suspend inspection of Supreme's plant. ***

The USDA directs us to 21 U.S.C. § 601(m)(4), which provides that a meat product is adulterated if it has been prepared, packed or held under insanitary conditions whereby it may have become contaminated with filth, or whereby it may have been rendered injurious to health. This statutory definition is broader than that provided in 21 U.S.C. § 601(m)(1), which provides that a meat product is adulterated if it bears or contains any poisonous or deleterious substance which may render it injurious to health; but in case the substance is not an added substance, such article shall not be considered adulterated under this clause if the quantity of such substance in or on such article does not ordinarily render it injurious to health. ***

We must decide two issues in order to determine whether the Salmonella performance standard is authorized rulemaking under the FMIA: a) whether the statute allows the USDA to regulate characteristics of raw materials that are "prepared, packed or held" at the plant, such as Salmonella infection; and b) whether § 601(m)(4)'s "insanitary conditions" such that product "may have been rendered injurious to health" includes the presence of Salmonella-infected beef in a plant or the increased likelihood of cross-contamination with Salmonella that results from grinding such infected beef. Since we are persuaded that the Salmonella performance standard improperly regulates the Salmonella levels of incoming meat and that Salmonella cross-contamination cannot be an insanitary condition such that product may be rendered "injurious to health," we conclude that the Salmonella performance standard falls outside of the ambit of § 601(m)(4). ***

Moreover, the USDA has not asserted that there is any correlation between the presence of Salmonella and the presence of § 601(m)(1) adulterant pathogens. The rationale offered by the USDA for the Salmonella performance standard—that "intervention strategies aimed at reducing fecal contamination and other sources of Salmonella on raw product should be effective against other pathogens"—does not imply that the presence of Salmonella indicates the presence of these other, presumably § 601(m)(1) adulterant, pathogens. ***

NOTE: Supreme Beef was successful; however, the company lost its National School Lunch contracts and eventually filed for bankruptcy. See: *Supreme Beef Processors, Inc. v. United States Dept. of Agriculture,* 468 F3d. 248 (5th Cir. 2006).

CRITICAL ANALYSIS: Evaluate why the court ruled in favor of the Supreme Beef Company and rejected the performance standard rationale used by USDA.

Corporate Executive Liability Food Safety—Criminal Convictions
Peanut Corporation of America —Salmonella and Felony Prosecution
http://www.justice.gov/opa/pr/peanut-corporation-america-former-officials-and-broker-convicted-criminal-charges-related
http://www.justice.gov/opa/pr/former-peanut-company-president-receives-largest-criminal-sentence-food-safety-case-two

Corporate executives have been charged with misdemeanor offenses under the strict criminal liability theory known as the *Park* doctrine; however, Peanut Corporation of America (PCA) is distinguishable due to the felony prosecution. Former President and Owner Stewart Parnell received a criminal prison sentence of 28 years in connection with the 2009 salmonella poisoning outbreak of 700 reported cases in 46 states. Expert evidence presented at trial detailed that there were nine deaths linked to PCAs tainted products. Parnell's brother Michael received a 20-year prison sentence. The Quality Assurance employee received a five-year sentence. They were sentenced based on their roles at PCA by shipping salmonella-positive peanut products and by falsifying microbiological test results. A federal jury convicted the Parnell brothers in September 2014 on several counts of conspiracy, mail and wire fraud as well as selling misbranded food. Stewart Parnell was also convicted for introducing adulterated food into interstate commerce. Stewart Parnell and Quality Assurance Manager Mary Wilkerson were also convicted of obstruction of justice. Other former PCA employees previously pleaded guilty to multiple charges.

The prosecutors alleged that PCA defrauded customers as well as defrauded several national food companies by failing to inform them about the presence of food-borne pathogens in laboratory tests, including salmonella. According to prosecutors, despite these results, Peanut Corp. officials falsified lab results, maintaining peanut products were safe for consumption. Further, at times, the Peanut Corp. failed to perform testing. **Judgment Affirmed (No. 15-14400, 11ᵗʰ Cir. January 23, 2018). PCA filed for Chapter 7 bankruptcy protection.**

Jensen Farms—Listeria and Executive Liability Misdemeanor
United States v. Jensen et al., Docket No. 1:13-mj-01138 (D. Colo. Jan. 2014)

A federal judge on January 30, 2014 sentenced Eric and Ryan Jensen, owners of Jensen Farms, a cantaloupe farm in Colorado, which was linked to a deadly Listeria outbreak in 2011. There were 30 deaths associated with the listeria outbreak, which also sickened 147 people. Each owner was sentenced to five years' probation, six months home detention, and $150,000 each in restitution fees to victims. The Jensens could have received a maximum of six years in jail and $1.5 million each in fines on six counts of introducing contaminated food into interstate commerce. The Jensens filed a lawsuit against food safety auditor Primus Labs, which gave the farm's processing facilities a safety rating of 96% shortly prior to when the outbreak occurred.

See: *http://www.cdc.gov/listeria/outbreaks/cantaloupes-jensen-farms/index.html?s_cid=cs_654*
http://www.fda.gov/ICECI/EnforcementActions/WarningLetters/ucm276249.htm

Quality Egg and Decosters Executive Criminal Liability—Misdemeanor

In *United States v. Quality Egg, LLC* there were 2,000 cases of a *Salmonella* poisoning outbreak. The company's fine amounted to $6.79 million and $7.8 million in compensation for damages caused by the contaminated eggs shipment. Former executives, Jack DeCoster and Peter DeCoster, who pled guilty, received prison sentences (three months each and a $100,000 criminal fine, restitution and probation). Court deemed prison sentences appropriate due to company's prior problems of disregard for food safety standards and practices, bribery of a government inspector and disregarded high positive *Salmonella* test results. The DeCosters appeal centered on the allegation of "cruel and unusual punishment". The 8ᵗʰ Circuit Court of Appeals affirmed the three-month term of imprisonment. Excerpts of the opinion follow.

United States v. Austin DeCoster and United States v. Peter DeCoster, Nat'l Assn of Manufacturers, Cato Institute, Washington Legal Foundation, Amici No. 15-1890, No. 15-1891 (July 6, 2016)

Austin "Jack" DeCoster and Peter DeCoster both pled guilty, as "responsible corporate officers" of Quality Egg, LLC, to misdemeanor violations of 21 U.S.C. § 331(a) for introducing eggs that had been adulterated with *salmonella* enteritidis into interstate commerce. The district court sentenced Jack and Peter to three months imprisonment. The DeCosters appeal, arguing that their prison sentences and 21 U.S.C. § 333(a)(1) are unconstitutional, and claiming in the alternative that their prison sentences were procedurally and substantively unreasonable. We affirm.

Jack DeCoster owned Quality Egg, LLC, an Iowa egg production company. Jack's son Peter DeCoster served as the company's chief operating officer. *** Other than conducting the single egg test in April 2009, Quality Egg did not test or divert eggs from the market before July 2010 despite receiving multiple positive environmental and hen test results. *** The FDA inspected the Quality Egg operations in Iowa from August 12–30, 2010. Investigators discovered live and dead rodents and frogs in the laying areas, feed areas, conveyer belts, and outside the buildings. They also found holes in the walls and baseboards of the feed and laying buildings. The investigators discovered that some rodent traps were broken, and others had dead rodents in them. In one building near the laying hens, manure was found piled to the rafters; it had pushed a screen out of the door which allowed rodents into the building. Investigators also observed employees not wearing or changing protective clothing and not cleaning or sanitizing equipment.

The FDA concluded that Quality Egg had failed to comply with its written plans for biosecurity and salmonella prevention. *** The investigation revealed that Quality Egg previously had falsified records about food safety measures and had lied to auditors for several years about pest control measures and sanitation practices. ***

The elimination of a mens rea requirement does not violate the Due Process Clause for a public welfare offense where the penalty is "relatively small," the conviction does not gravely damage the defendant's reputation, and congressional intent supports the imposition of the penalty. The three month prison sentences the DeCosters received were relatively short. ***

Moreover, the DeCosters' three month prison sentences fell at the low end of the prescribed statutory range of 21 U.S.C. § 333(a) (one year maximum), and we have "never held a sentence within the statutory range to violate the Eighth Amendment," *United States v. Vanhorn* 740 F.3d 1166, 1170 (8th Cir. 2014). We decline to do so here as well. We conclude that the district court's sentences in this case do not violate the Eighth Amendment.

NOTE: The ConAgra company agreed to pay $11.2 million ($8 million in criminal fines and $3.2 million in forfeitures) in 2015 to settle federal charges from a 2007 salmonella outbreak due to the tainted peanut butter produced in a plant in Georgia. Over 600 people in 47 states became ill and triggering a massive recall eight years ago. The misdemeanor charge against the Omaha, Nebraska, based company was due to shipping adulterated food.

CRITICAL ANALYSIS: *DeCoster (Quality Egg), Jensen Farms, Peanut Corporation of America* **(PCA) serve as a warning and wake up call to the food industry in terms of corporate executive liability. Yet, in the ConAgra case, company executives were not charged. Why were the ConAgra executives not charged and should they have been? (See also** *Volume III—Enforcement* **for the** *DeCoster salmonella* **egg case).**

Sanitation and Filth Levels—Molded Coffee, Capital City Foods and Nashoba Brook Bakery

This section contains a discussion about tolerance levels, adulteration and misbranding. *United States v. 484 Bags* concerned whether molded green coffee was adulterated within the meaning of Adulteration under § 342 of the FDCA. On remand, the district court adopted the FDA tolerance levels and determined that the coffee beans were within permissible tolerance levels. Subsequently, FDA issued a regulatory action guidance which directly addressed the issue by establishing explicit tolerance levels. In so doing, the guidance put the regulated industry on notice as to acceptable tolerance levels. See Reg. Action Guidance, sec. 510.500 Green Coffee Beans-Adulteration with Insects; Mold (CPG 7101.06) (1980). *Capital City Foods* provides an excellent discussion on zero tolerance levels and filth under 21 U.S.C. § 342(a) (3) and the lack of established tolerance levels. Nashoba Brook Bakery focuses on Good Manufacturing Practices, inspection and remediation.

United States v. 484 Bags, More or Less,
423 F.2d 839 (5th Cir. 1970) [Molded Green Coffee]

GODBOLD, Circuit Judge: This case concerns whether molded green coffee is adulterated, within the meaning of the Food, Drug and Cosmetic Act, 21 U.S.C. § 342(a)(3). These 484 bags of coffee beans have been the subject of this litigation for more than four years. The coffee was imported from Brazil, admitted to the United States, and stored in a warehouse in New Orleans. Three or four days after arrival in September 1965, it was damaged by water during Hurricane Betsy. In an effort to impede the growth of mold on the beans the consignee had them run through a dryer and resacked. Almost three years later the District Court granted summary judgment for the government on the issue of adulteration and ordered the coffee condemned.

The beans were burnished, or brushed, in an effort to remove the mold. The government was dissatisfied with the result and filed a motion that the coffee be destroyed. After an evidentiary hearing the District Court found that the beans were fit for food, under the standards of the New

York Coffee Exchange, and were neither contaminated nor injurious to health. The court concluded, relying upon *United States v. 1500 Cases, Etc..*, 236 F.2d 208 (7th Cir. 1956), that the degree of decomposition made unlawful by § 342(a)(3) is 'one which would, with reasonable certainty, render the article unfit for food.' The District Judge ordered that the coffee be exported to a non-coffee producing country, pursuant to 21 U.S.C. § 381(d), and that it not be returned to the United States. *** 21 U.S.C. § 342(a)(3) provides that a food is deemed adulterated 'if it consists in whole or in part of any filthy, putrid or decomposed substance, or if it is otherwise unfit for food.' The District Court read the first clause of the quoted provision as being elucidated by the second so that the amount of decomposition made unlawful thereby is that 'which would, with reasonable certainty, render the article unfit for food.' 297 F.Supp. at 673. This court, along with others, has long held that the two clauses are independent and complementary, so that a food substance may be condemned as decomposed, filthy, or putrid even though it is not unfit for food, *Bruce's Juices v. United States*, 194 F.2d 935 (5th Cir. 1952); *** The single case relied upon by the District Court, *United States v. 1500 Cases, Etc.*, 236 F.2d 208 (7th Cir. 1956), adopts the accepted interpretation reached in the above-cited cases, albeit reluctantly. *** We recognize that 'It (the first phrase of § 342(a)(3)) sets a standard that if strictly enforced, would ban all processed food from interstate commerce. ***

Part of the government's evidence at the evidentiary hearing, after the claimant had sought to bring the coffee into compliance with the Act, was that it permitted a tolerance of ten per cent moldy beans in coffee, and that the percentage in tested samples of this coffee averaged 15.1. It is undisputed that the claimant had no actual notice of the administrative tolerance and that it had not been published in the Federal Register. The claimant insists that the government may not employ in support of condemnation an unpublished standard of allowable tolerances, known only to itself and sprung upon the unsuspecting merchant at a condemnation hearing and after efforts to rehabilitate the food substance. *** We remand the case to the District Court for it to determine under a correct reading of the statute whether the coffee is adulterated. It may accept as a judicial standard the allowable tolerances now permitted by the Secretary, whether published or not. ***For all future purposes of this case the claimant is entitled to be told what the allowable tolerances are. ***
NOTE: On remand, the court held that the coffee was not adulterated.

CRITICAL ANALYIS: Evaluate the decision by the Court. Include due process issues.

United States v. Capital City Foods,
345 F. Supp. 277 (DC ND 1972)

MEMORANDUM AND DECISION: VAN SICKLE: This is a criminal prosecution by information, based on a claimed violation of 21 U.S.C. § 301 et seq. (The Federal Food, Drug and Cosmetic Act). Specifically, the defendants are charged with having introduced, or delivered for introduction, into interstate commerce, food that was adulterated (21 U.S.C. § 331(a)). The food is claimed to be adulterated because it consisted in part of a filthy substance, i. e., insect fragments. 21 U.S.C. § 342(a) (3). Section 342(a) (3) provides that the food is adulterated if it consists in whole or in part of any filthy, substance, or if it is otherwise unfit for food. Insect fragments in other than infinitesimal quantity are filth.***

1. Since the Food and Drug Administration has not promulgated standards of allowable foreign matter in butter, is that not in itself a standard of zero allowance of foreign matter?

2. If the standard is zero allowance of foreign matter, is such a standard reasonable?

3. In any event, has the government proved sufficient foreign matter to raise its proof above the objection of the maxim *de minimis lex*?

The facts show that miniscule insect fragments were discovered in the butter, and these fragments were identifiable under a 470-power microscope. *** Thus, we can assume any fatty substance reasonably related to the miniscule insect fragments was cooked and distributed into the finished butter. *** As shown by the analysis of evidence, which I present later, my concern in this case is the claim of the government that:

a) The failure of the government to establish under 21 U.S.C. § 346, a standard of permissible deleterious substance which may be tolerably added to butter when, in the manufacturing process it cannot be avoided, establishes as reasonable a standard of zero allowance, and

b) Therefore, in effect, the maxim of "*de minimis non curat lex*" has no application in butter cases.

But, in its "Notice of Proposed Rule Making on Natural or Unavoidable Defects in Food for Human Use that Present No Health Hazard", of the Food and Drug Administration, published in the Federal Register, Volume 37, No. 62, March 30, 1972, the introduction language includes this:

"Few foods contain no natural or unavoidable defects. Even with modern technology, all defects in foods cannot be eliminated. Foreign material cannot be wholly processed out of foods, and many containments introduced into foods through the environment can be reduced only by reducing their occurrence in the environment." "Indeed, if the section were interpreted literally, almost every food manufacturer in the country could be prosecuted since the statute bans products contaminated "in whole or in part". This undesirable result indicates that the section should not receive so expansive a reading. In fact, in several cases judicial common sense has led to recognition that the presence of a minimal amount of filth may be insufficient for condemnation."

The foreign matter found was mainly miniscule fragments of insect parts. They consisted of 12 particles of fly hair (seta), 11 unidentified insect fragments, 2 moth scales, 2 feather barbules, and 1 particle of rabbit hair. The evidence showed that some of these particles were visible to the naked eye, and some, the fly hair, would require a 30x microscope to see. They were identifiable with the aid of a 470x microscope. The only evidence as to size showed that there was one hair, 1 1/2 millimeters long, and one unidentified insect fragments 0.02 millimeters by 0.2 millimeters.

In all, 4125 grams (9.1 lbs.) of butter were checked and 28 miniscule particles were found. This is an overall ratio of 3 miniscule particles of insect fragments per pound of butter. Thus, there having been no standard established, and no showing that this number of miniscule fragments is excludable in the manufacturing process, I find that this contamination is a trifle, not a matter of concern to the law. The defendants are found not guilty. Judgment will be entered accordingly.

CRITICAL ANALYIS: FDA developed a draft risk profile on pathogens and filth in spices at the end of 2013 and updated in 2017. This was due to the questionable effectiveness of current control measures to reduce or prevent illness from spice consumption in the United States. Is it possible to adopt a zero-tolerance level for filth with the sophisticated technology utilized today?

Draft Risk Assessment *https://www.fda.gov/downloads/Food/FoodScienceResearch/RiskSafetyAssessment/UCM367337*

Draft Risk Assessment update 2017: Pathogens and Filth in Spices *https://wayback.archive-it.org/7993/20180425060911/https://www.fda.gov/downloads/Food/FoodScienceResearch/RiskSafetyAssessment/UCM581362.pdf*

WARNING LETTER—Does FDA Regulate Love?
https://www.fda.gov/ICECI/EnforcementActions/WarningLetters/2017/ucm577393.htm
NASHOBA BROOK BAKERY, LLC. CMS# 532236 United Parcel Service Signature Required
John D. Gates, CEO/Co-Owner Stuart J. Witt, Head Baker/ Co-Owner
Nashoba Brook Bakery, LLC. 152 Commonwealth Ave.
Concord, MA 01742-2990

Dear Mr. Gates and Mr. Witt:

The United States Food and Drug Administration (FDA) inspected your ready-to-eat manufacturing facility located at 152 Commonwealth Ave. Concord, MA, 01742 from May 25 through June 8, 2017. During the inspection, FDA investigators observed serious violations of the Current Good Manufacturing Practice (CGMP) regulation for foods, Title 21, Code of Federal Regulations (CFR), Part 110 [21 CFR Part 110]. At the conclusion of the inspection, you were issued a Form FDA-483, Inspectional Observations, which documented insanitary conditions in your facility at the time of the inspection. To date we have not received a written response to the FDA Form 483, List of Inspectional Observations which was issued. Failure to manufacture foods in accordance with the CGMP requirements in 21 CFR Part 110 renders your firm's food products adulterated within the meaning of Section 402(a)(4) of the Federal Food, Drug, and Cosmetic Act (the Act) [21 U.S.C. § 342(a)(4)], in that they have been prepared, packed, or held under insanitary conditions whereby they may have become contaminated with filth, or whereby they may have been rendered injurious to heath. Additionally, during the inspection our investigators obtained the labels that your firm uses for your Nashoba Granola product. We have reviewed your labels and identified violations of the food labeling regulations, 21 CFR Part 101, which causes the products discussed below to be misbranded within the meaning of Section 403 of the Act [21 U.S.C. § 343]. Your significant violations are as follows:

Adulterated Foods:

1. Your firm failed to conduct all food manufacturing, including packaging and storage, under such conditions and controls as are necessary to minimize the potential for the growth of microorganisms, or for the contamination of food, as required by 21 CFR 110.80(b)(2). Specifically, on May 25 and 26, 2017, our investigator observed the following:

a. On May 26, 2017, remnants of Pepper Jack dough (dairy allergen) were observed on the inside, the lip, and the outside edges of the "**(b)(4)**" stainless steel mixing bowl that an operator stated was cleaned, sanitized and ready for use prior to the production of non-dairy Sourdough dough. *** We acknowledge that on May 26, 2017 your firm re-cleaned and sanitized the "**(b)(4)**" stainless steel mixing bowl and on June 8, 2017 your firm promised to retrain employees on proper cleaning and sanitizing of the dough mixers and to create a daily cleaning log which would be checked by a supervisor. However, no FDA-483 response has been provided to show employees have been retrained or systems of verification have been implemented to prevent recurrence.

2. Your firm failed to maintain equipment and utensils and finished product containers in an acceptable condition through appropriate cleaning and sanitizing, as necessary, as required by 21 CFR 110.80(b)(1). On May 25 and 26, 2017, our investigator observed the following:

a. What appeared to be an encrusted buildup of brown colored debris on the metal screen of the "**(b)(4)**" dough mixer that is positioned over all raw dough mixed during its operation.

b. Plastic barrels, barrel lids, totes and tote lids used to hold and transport raw dough with apparent dough residue buildup. One barrel had an approximate 1" dough clump from a different day's production still stuck in a crack. These barrels had previously been pressure washed and were considered ready for use. We acknowledge that during the inspection, your firm promised the cleaning schedule for barrels, totes and their lids would change from **(b)(4)** to being cleaned and sanitized **(b)(4)** and that your firm stated they will now be monitored for crack formation. However, no FDA-483 response has been provided to show implementation of a new cleaning schedule or how your firm is monitoring barrels for crack formation.

3. Your firm failed to maintain buildings, fixtures, and other physical facilities in a sanitary condition and keep in sufficient repair to prevent food from becoming adulterated within the meaning of the Act, as required by 21 CFR 110.35(a).

a. Two ceiling air intake vents adjacent to the bread ovens and above racks of ready-to-eat foods were caked with apparent debris. *** We acknowledge that during the inspection, your firm hired a new employee who will be responsible for cleaning the facility and that your firm promised to replace missing and damaged ceiling tiles and flooring. However, no FDA-483 response has been provided to document corrective and preventative actions have been taken or implemented.

4. Your firm failed to ensure equipment, containers, and utensils used to convey, hold, or store raw materials, work-in-process, rework, or food shall be constructed, handled, and maintained during manufacturing or storage in a manner that protects against contamination, as required by 21 CFR 110.80(b)(1). Specifically, on May 25 and 26, 2017, our investigator observed cracked and damaged barrels were used to hold and transport raw dough.

We acknowledge that during the inspection, your firm began purchasing new barrels to replace cracked ones and have replaced **(b)(4)** cracked or damaged barrels. However, no FDA-483 response has been provided to demonstrate all barrels have been replaced or detailing how your firm will prevent the use of cracked or damaged barrels from recurring in the future.

5. Your firm failed to provide, where necessary, adequate screening or other protection against pests, as required by 21 CFR 110.20(b)(7).

a. Approximately five flies in the ready-to-eat cooling area and processing area of the facility, all near or on food.

b. One approximately 1" long crawling insect underneath exposed ready-to-eat foods in the pastry area, including focaccia breads, 7-Grain rolls, and brioche rolls. ***

We acknowledge on May 25, 2017, that once alerted by our investigator that a fly was observed crawling on raw Brioche dough, your firm removed the dough and separated it into a designated animal food area. However, no FDA-483 response has been provided that details corrections for preventing future recurrence.

6. All persons working in direct contact with food, food-contact surfaces, and food-packaging materials must conform to hygienic practices while on duty to the extent necessary to protect against contamination of food, as required by 21 CFR 110.10(b).

a. Your firm failed to have employees remove unsecured jewelry or other objects which might fall into food, equipment, or containers, as required by 21 CFR 110.10(b)(4). Specifically, on May 25 and 26, 2017, our investigator observed the following:

   1. The mixing employee was wearing a blue plastic bracelet while working with raw dough. The bracelet came into repeated contact with raw dough and dough varieties.

   2. A production employee wore a nose ring and earrings while handling and shaping raw dough. *** We acknowledge that during the inspection, your firm promised to provide re-training to employees and to remove the water cooler from the production area. However, no FDA-483 response has been provided detailing any corrective or preventative actions that may have been implemented.

7. Your firm failed to properly store equipment that may constitute an attractant, breeding place, or harborage area for pests, within the immediate vicinity of the plant buildings or structures, as required by 21 CFR 110.20(a)(1). Specifically, on June 2, 2017, our investigator observed plastic bread trays stacked outside and partially covered with a tarp, up against the facility wall that your firm stated were in long-term storage. ***

Misbranded Foods:

1. Your Nashoba Granola and Whole Wheat Bread (wholesale and retail) products are misbranded within the meaning of section 403(i)(2) of the Act [21 U.S.C. § 343(i)(2)] because they are fabricated from two or more ingredients, but the labels fail to bear a complete list of all the ingredients by common or usual name in descending order of predominance by weight as well as all sub-ingredients, as required by 21 CFR 101.4. For example, Your Nashoba Granola label lists ingredient **"Love"**. Ingredients required to be declared on the label or labeling of food must be listed by their common or usual name [21 CFR 101.4(a)(1). **"Love" is not a common or usual name of an ingredient and is considered to be intervening material because it is not part of the common or usual name of the ingredient.**

Your Whole Wheat Bread label lists the ingredient "Natural Sourdough Starter" but fails to list the sub-ingredients in predominance by weight. ***

2. Your Nashoba Granola product is misbranded within the meaning of Section 403(q) of the Act [21 U.S. C. 343(q)] because it fails to bear a nutrition facts label in accordance with 21 CFR 101.9.

3. Your Whole Wheat Bread (retail) product is misbranded within the meaning of section 403(g)(1) of the Act [21 U.S.C. 343(g)(1)] because it is a food for which a definition and standard of identity has been prescribed by regulation, but it fails to conform to such definition and standard. The label states "whole wheat" and "slow rise breads from . . . ." Therefore, it is represented as

whole wheat bread for which a standard of identity exists under 21 CFR 136.180. Under the standard, the dough must be made exclusively from whole wheat flour. This product contains wheat flour and corn meal.

4. Your Whole Wheat Bread (wholesale) product is misbranded within the meaning of Section 403(i)(1) of the Act [21 U.S.C. 343(i)(1)] because the wholesale label fails to include an appropriate statement of identity in accordance with 21 CFR 101.3. Specifically, the label states "Whole Wheat" however, this is not an appropriate name for a baked good. If this product is a bread, roll, or bun, we note that the product does not meet the standard under 21 CFR 136.180 for whole wheat bread, rolls, and buns. Under the standard, the dough must be made exclusively from whole wheat flour. This product contains wheat flour and corn meal. ***

This letter is not intended to be an all-inclusive list of violations at your facility or in connection with your products. You are responsible for ensuring that your facility operates in compliance with the Act and other applicable laws. You should take prompt action to correct the violations noted in this letter. Failure to do so may result in regulatory action by FDA without further notice, including, without limitation, seizure and injunction. ***Please notify this office in writing within fifteen (15) working days of the receipt of this letter as to the specific steps you have taken to correct the stated violations, including an explanation of each step being taken to identify violations and make corrections to ensure that similar violations will not recur. In your response, you should include documentation, including photographs or other useful information that would assist us in evaluating your corrections. If the corrective action cannot be completed within fifteen working days, state the reason for the delay and the time frame within which the corrections will be implemented.

Sincerely, /S/ Ronald Pace   September 22, 2017

Program Division Director, Office of Human and Animal Food Operations East – Division 1

CRITICAL ANALYSIS: This warning letter generated media attention because of the word "Love". Discuss the reasons why FDA issued the warning letter. Further, if you represented the Nashoba Bakery how would respond to FDA?

Chapter 2: Food Regulation, Labeling

Evolution of United States Food Laws

The development of food regulation in the United States dates from colonial times. The first food laws in the United States, known as "Bread Assizes," approximated those of England. Bread inspectors, appointed for enforcement purposes, entered establishments and seized unmarked or improperly weighed bread. Laws enacted by the American colonies related to industries within the colonies. Virginia enacted the first legislation aimed at curbing both adulteration and misbranding. The laws of colonial Virginia pertained to the accuracy of weights and measures; however, they also regulated the adulteration of food. Another Virginia regulation established lawful measures for corn and provided a penalty for using unsealed barrels or bushels. Massachusetts enacted the first general food law aimed toward protecting consumers against adulteration. Other states soon followed the example of Massachusetts, such as Virginia's general law concerning unwholesome bread, meat, and beverages.

Due to growing public concern during the latter part of the nineteenth century, Congress considered enacting federal food regulation statutes. Federal laws enacted prior to the Pure Food and Drugs Act of 1906 (1906 Act) focused on specific food commodities. For example, in 1883, Congress enacted a statute pertaining to the adulteration of tea. Another federal law focused on the manufacture of oleomargarine. The "oleomargarine law" authorized the Commissioner of the Internal Revenue Service to determine if the "imitation butter" contained deleterious ingredients. If the product contained deleterious ingredients, the product was forfeited to the United States.

Significant events that spurred the passage of the 1906 Act included Industrialization, New Nationalism, and the formation of the United States Department of Agriculture. In response to the proliferation of misbranded and adulterated food, Congress enacted the 1906 Act. The 1906 Act established the necessity of government intervention to protect both the public and the honest manufacturer. The 1906 Act specifically contained a section concerning misbranding.

As early as 1914, the United States Supreme Court, in *United States v. Lexington Mill Elevator Co.*, set forth the purpose of the 1906 Act. The Court stated that "the consumer should know that an article purchased was what it purported to be; that it might be bought for what it really was and not upon misrepresentations as to character and quality." Similarly, the Supreme Court, in *United States v. Ninety-Five Barrels, More or Less, Alleged Apple Cider Vinegar (Apple Cider Vinegar)*, stated that the intent of the 1906 Act pertained to the prohibition of every statement, design and device which may mislead or deceive. The Court, in *Apple Cider Vinegar*, emphasized that "the aim of the 1906 Act is to prevent ... indirection and ambiguity, as well as ... statements which are false." Although the 1906 Act contained specific provisions regarding deceptive labeling, the primary focus centered on unsafe adulteration rather than economic adulteration.

The United States Department of Agriculture's Bureau of Chemistry acknowledged the proliferation of misleading food label claims and economic adulteration that spurred affirmative action by Congress. As a result, the Food, Drug and Cosmetic Act (FDCA) of 1938 was enacted. The purposes of the FDCA included the economic regulation of food and the prohibition of any false or misleading statement on food labels and labeling. The United States Supreme Court, in *Kordel v. United States*, enunciated: *The high purpose of the Act to protect consumers who under present conditions are largely unable to protect themselves in this field would then be easily defeated. The administrative agency charged with its enforcement has not given the Act any such restricted construction. The textual structure of the Act is not agreeable to it.* The court in *United States v. Bradshaw*, followed *Kordel* and concluded that " the general scheme of the FDCA and its legislative history indicate that the overriding congressional purpose is consumer protection—the protection of the public against any misbranded or adulterated food, drug, device, or cosmetic."

A major objective of the FDCA pertained to the prohibition of false or misleading statements on food labels. Under Section 343, food is misbranded if "its labeling is false or misleading...." Under the FDCA, "the adulteration or misbranding of any food, drug, device or cosmetic in interstate commerce is prohibited." The FDCA contains criminal penalties for misbranding food. The FDCA also defines specific terminology pertaining to food labeling. The term "label" is defined as "a display of written, printed, or graphic matter upon the immediate container of any article." The term "labeling" is defined as:

> *[A]ll labels and other written, printed, or graphic matter (1) upon any article or any of its containers or wrappers, or (2) accompanying such article.*
>
> *If an article is alleged to be misbranded because the labeling or advertising is misleading, then in determining whether the labeling or advertising is misleading there shall be taken into account (among other things) not only representations made or suggested by statement, word, design, device, or any combination thereof, but also the extent to which the labeling or advertising fails to reveal facts material in the light of such representations or material with respect to consequences which may result from the use of the articles to which the labeling or advertising relates under the conditions of use prescribed in the labeling or advertising thereof or under such conditions of use as are customary or usual.*

By definition, "labeling" includes more than the label itself, because it encompasses all labels and other written, printed, or graphic matter on the article, its containers, wrappers or accompanying materials. Historically, courts applied a liberal construction to the labeling provisions of the FDCA. The majority of complaints against false or misleading claims have been uniformly successful. The seminal case is *United States v. Kordel*, where the Court determined in construing the word "accompany" stated, "one article or thing is accompanied by another when it supplements or explains it, in the manner that a committee report of Congress accompanies a bill. No physical attachment one to the other is necessary. It is the textual relationship that is significant." The Supreme Court in *Kordel* concluded that booklets containing price lists for drugs constituted labeling because the booklets were part of an integrated distribution scheme.

Similarly, in *United States v. Eight Cartons, Containing Plantation 'The Original' etc. Molasses* (*Plantation Molasses*), the court held that a book constitutes labeling. In this case, the book was prominently displayed in the establishment's store window alongside the molasses. Customers received a copy of the book "Look Younger, Live Longer" which, in part, pertained to the uses and purposes of blackstrap molasses. In deciding that the book constituted "labeling," the court determined that the association with the article triggered the application of the FDCA. The *Plantation Molasses* decision, based on the precise wording of the definition of the term "labeling," demonstrates a literal interpretation in keeping with the explicit purpose of the FDCA.

The decision of *United States v. An Article of Drug Consisting of 250 Jars of United States Fancy Pure Honey* (*Pure Honey*) demonstrated that a newspaper leaflet and booklet promoting the sale of honey constituted "labeling" in accordance with the FDCA. The booklets, entitled "About Honey," were displayed atop the shelves adjacent to the honey. The newspaper leaflets were located in another section of the store. The court found that both displays constituted labeling. The court specifically stated: "The word 'accompany' has been given a very broad interpretation by the Supreme Court in *Kordel*." "The claimant cannot escape the conclusion that the literature was 'labeling,' even though the booklets were held for sale, and that the newspaper leaflets constituted 'advertising.'" The court in the *Pure Honey* decision relied on *Kordel* for the proposition that the materials constituted an integrated distribution scheme. The *Kordel* court stated:

> *[T]he fact that some of the booklets carried a selling price is immaterial on the facts shown here. As stated by the [c]ourt of [a]ppeals, the booklets and drugs were nonetheless interdependent; they were parts of an integrated distribution program. The Act cannot be circumvented by the easy device of a "sale" of the advertising matter where the advertising performs the function of labeling.*

The *Pure Honey* and *Kordel* decisions illustrate a liberal and literal interpretation of the FDCA as well as a common sense approach toward consumer protection. As the court in the *Pure Honey* case stated: *"[The] Act [FDCA] was passed for the purpose of protecting unwary customers in vital matters of health and, consequently, it must be given a liberal interpretation to effectuate this high purpose."* In the landmark decision of *United States v. Dotterweich,* Justice Frankfurter articulated: *The purposes of this legislation thus touch[es] phases of the lives and health of people which in the circumstances of modern industrialism, are largely beyond self-protection. Regard for these purposes should infuse construction of the legislation ... as a working instrument of government and not merely as a collection of English words.*

Yet, over the years, some courts have reached different results. One case was *United States v. 46 Cases, More or Less, Welch's Nut Caramels.* The court held that the label "Nut Caramels" was not false or misleading even though peanuts constituted the sole nut ingredient. The FDA argued that the label statement "Nut Caramels" was misleading because the ingredient statement was not highly visible. According to the court, the label designation sufficiently placed consumers on notice that the ingredients contained nuts. Furthermore, the court indicated that the government did not present evidence which demonstrated that ordinary consumers were misled by the labeling. This analysis appears to contravene the intent and purpose of the FDCA. The literal reading of the misbranding section of the FDCA states "false or misleading in any particular manner," and it is immaterial whether any consumers were actually misled.

In "Fortified Sugar", the court determined that statements on the labels of *Dextra Brand "Fortified" Sugar* were not false or misleading. The government contended that the sugar was misbranded under the FDCA because the false or misleading label statements were inherently deceptive to the consumer. The government's major assertions included that the label contained statements which represented that Dextra sugar, when used in the ordinary diet, is significantly more nutritious than any other sugar. The label contained the following statement: "Almost any diet can be nutritionally improved by the use of DEXTRA Fortified Cane Sugar in place of sweetening agents containing only "empty" calories—calories unaccompanied by nutrients." The court rejected all of the government's allegations and concluded that the labels were not false or misleading. The "fortified" sugar label, therefore, was not misbranded within the meaning of the FDCA. *Dextra Brand Sugar* and *Welch's Nut Caramels* were decided prior to the Nutrition Labeling and Education Act of 1990 (NLEA). Perhaps today a different result would be reached. Yet, the *Farinella* decision, hinged on terminology— "best when purchased by" reveals otherwise in terms of consumer protection.

Overall, truthful and non-deceptive labeling remains critical to the integrity of the food supply. This is especially relevant in the current climate of increased public interest in the relationship of diet and health issues. The enactment of NLEA is milestone legislation in defining parameters, health claims and providing uniformity; however, with increased science about health-related conditions, NLEA continue to remain ripe for amendment. Part of that occurred in 2010 with the caloric disclosure mandate reported below and at the end of this chapter.

CRITICAL ANALYSIS: The NLEA does not contain a provision for a private right of action. Should there be a provision to include a citizen lawsuit?

Caloric Disclosure—Restaurant Menus and Vending Machines

The Affordable Care Act mandated disclosure of caloric requirement on some restaurant menus and vending machines. The federal final rules for caloric disclosure for foods in vending machines and menu disclosure were issued in late 2014, and enforcement was originally delayed until one year after Level I guidance issued (May 5, 2016) *A Labeling Guide for Restaurants and Retail Establishments Selling Away-From-Home Foods—Part II (Menu Labeling Requirements in Accordance with the Patient Protection Affordable Care Act of 2010); Guidance for Industry; Availability* (81 FR 27067-01). See: 21 U.S.C. 343(q)(5)(H). However, Compliance date extensions: The compliance date for covered establishments in the final rule published December 1, 2014 (79 FR 71156), was extended in final rules published on July 10, 2015 (80 FR 39675), December 30, 2016 (81 FR 96364) and

May 4, 2017. Compliance was further extended to May 7, 2018 (82 FR 20825-01). 21 CFR § 11.1; 21 CFR § 101.921 CFR § 101.1021 CFR § 101.11.

See: *http://www.fda.gov/Food/IngredientsPackagingLabeling/LabelingNutrition/ucm217762.htm*

Vending Machines Final Rule—Food Labeling; Calorie Labeling of Articles of Food
Applies to Operators of 20 or more vending machines. **See: 79 FR 71259.**

NOTE: Trade associations requested compliance date extension for certain foods sold from glass-front vending machines due to the requirements for front-of-package font size.

Menu Labeling Final Rule—Applies to restaurants and similar retail food establishments if they are part of a chain of 20 or more locations, doing business under the same name, offering for sale substantially the same menu items and offering for sale restaurant-type foods. **See: 79 FR 71156; See also, this *Volume*, at the end of this Chapter.**

Front of Package Labeling

http://www.fda.gov/Food/IngredientsPackagingLabeling/LabelingNutrition/ucm202726.htm

The food industry developed a Front of Labeling Program (FOP) dubbed "Smart Choices" or "Facts Up Front" back in 2009. The intent of the FOP is to provide a logo and scoring program that rates the nutritional profile of foods. In 2010, FDA and USDA jointly issued a statement to the administrators of the FOP expressing concern mainly of consumer confusion. In 2011, the Food Marketing Institute and Grocery Manufacturers Association, announced plans to develop a new FOP program yet this has not been without controversy. Opponents argue that FOP or "Smart Choices" is simply a marketing ploy while proponents claim the information provided is valuable to consumers. A study conducted by the Institute of Medicine (IOM) report concluded that Front of Package Labeling would be helpful to consumers.

Ultimately, FDA issued strategic priorities that included "Front of Package Initiatives" (FOP). Perhaps a "Front of Package Nutrition Facts Panel" with more consumer-oriented disclosure would help resolve some of the criticism garnered toward industry. To that end, FDA conducted an experimental study concerning nutrition facts label improvements. *See: Agency Information Collection Activities; Submission for Office of Management and Budget Review; Comment Request; Experimental Study on Consumer Responses to Nutrition Facts Labels With Various Footnote Formats and Declaration of Amount of Added Sugars,* 78 FR 32394-01 (May 13, 2013);*http://www.reginfo.gov/public/jsp/EO/eoDashboard.jsp?agency_cd=0900&agency_nm=HHS&stage_cd=2&from_page=index.jsp&sub_index=0*

**NOTE: See William Neuman, *Food Industry Devise Own Label Plan*, NY Times (Jan. 24, 2011). http://www.nytimes.com/2011/01/25/business/25label.html?_r=1&*Nutrition Keys Not so Smart* (July 11, 2011*) http://www.saladbowlbranding.com/front-of-package-labeling/nutrition-keys-front-of-package-labeling-not-so-smart/*

Nutrition Facts Panel Updated—Final Rule

FDA issued a proposed rule which was finalized in 2016 to update the Nutrition Facts Panel. ***Proposed Rule***—*Revision of the Nutrition and Supplement Facts Labels*, 79 FR 11880-01 (2014). *Serving Sizes of Foods That Can Reasonably Be Consumed at One-Eating Occasion; Dual-Column Labeling; Updating, Modifying, and Establishing Certain Reference Amounts Customarily Consumed* (2014). In July 2015 issued a **supplemental proposed rule** to: (1) require declaration of the percent daily value (%DV) for added sugars; and (2) change the current footnote on the Nutrition Facts label to assist consumers to understand the meaning of percent daily value.

Final Rule—The final rule updates serving size, provides a clearer visual image, and reflects updated science as to added sugars and certain vitamins. Compliance date extended to January 1, 2020 except manufacturers with less than $10 million in annual food sales have an additional year to comply (January 1, 2021). The Label Format follows (Pre-2016 Rule left side and Updated Label on right side).

Food Labeling: Serving Sizes of Foods That Can Reasonably Be Consumed at One Eating Occasion; Dual-Column Labeling; Updating, Modifying, and Establishing Certain Reference Amounts Customarily Consumed; Serving Size for Breath Mints; and Technical Amendments

ORIGINAL LABEL PRE-2016 RULE **2016 UPDATED LABEL Jan. 1, 2020-2021**

Nutrition Facts	
Serving Size 2/3 cup (55g)	
Servings Per Container About 8	

Amount Per Serving

Calories 230	Calories from Fat 72
	% Daily Value*
Total Fat 8g	**12%**
Saturated Fat 1g	**5%**
Trans Fat 0g	
Cholesterol 0mg	**0%**
Sodium 160mg	**7%**
Total Carbohydrate 37g	**12%**
Dietary Fiber 4g	**16%**
Sugars 1g	
Protein 3g	
Vitamin A	10%
Vitamin C	8%
Calcium	20%
Iron	45%

* Percent Daily Values are based on a 2,000 calorie diet. Your daily value may be higher or lower depending on your calorie needs.

	Calories:	2,000	2,500
Total Fat	Less than	65g	80g
Sat Fat	Less than	20g	25g
Cholesterol	Less than	300mg	300mg
Sodium	Less than	2,400mg	2,400mg
Total Carbohydrate		300g	375g
Dietary Fiber		25g	30g

Nutrition Facts	
8 servings per container	
Serving size	**2/3 cup (55g)**

Amount per serving

Calories	**230**
	% Daily Value*
Total Fat 8g	**10%**
Saturated Fat 1g	**5%**
Trans Fat 0g	
Cholesterol 0mg	**0%**
Sodium 160mg	**7%**
Total Carbohydrate 37g	**13%**
Dietary Fiber 4g	**14%**
Total Sugars 12g	
Includes 10g Added Sugars	**20%**
Protein 3g	
Vitamin D 2mcg	10%
Calcium 260mg	20%
Iron 8mg	45%
Potassium 235mg	6%

* The % Daily Value (DV) tells you how much a nutrient in a serving of food contributes to a daily diet. 2,000 calories a day is used for general nutrition advice.

http://tinyurl.com/preview.php?num=jkvln98

NOTE: Original Compliance Date: July 26, 2018 for manufacturers with $10 million or more in annual food sales, and July 26, 2019 for manufacturers with less than $10 million in annual food sales; extended to January 1, 2020 and January 1, 2021 respectively.

FDA Health and Diet Telephone Survey—2,480 participants. Key findings included: 77% of U.S. adults use Nutrition Facts label. Two thirds expressed concern about the amount of salt in their diet.

http://www.fda.gov/downloads/Food/FoodScienceResearch/ConsumerBehaviorResearch/UCM497251.pdf?source=govdelivery&utm_medium=email&utm_source=govdelivery

CRITICAL ANALYSIS: The FDA final rule includes more realistic serving sizes, bolder caloric disclosure, sugar breakdown and understandable measurements. Postulate the delay in compliance and whether the new updated FDA "*Nutrition Facts Panel*" provides the solution to consumer comprehension. See Note below about salt.

Salt in Processed Foods—The Center for Science in the Public Interest (CSPI) filed a lawsuit in 2015 against FDA for inaction on the CSPI's 2005 Citizen Petition. The petition requested that FDA withdraw the Generally Recognized as Safe (GRAS) status of salt, as well as require reduced levels of salt in processed foods and "health messages" to be displayed on retail salt packages. The case was voluntarily dismissed on June 3, 2016. *http://cspinet.org/new/pdf/sodium-complaint-final-10-8-15.pdf and https://www.regulations.gov/document?D=FDA-2005-P-0196-0056*

NOTE: FDA issued a Draft Guidance in 2016 titled: *Voluntary Sodium Reduction Goals: Target Mean and Upper Bound Concentrations for Sodium in Commercially Processed, Packaged, and Prepared Foods.* **The guidance specifies that the 10-year targets aims to reduce sodium intake to 2,300 milligrams per day. See: (81 FR 35363 (June 2, 2016))** *http://www.fda.gov/Food/GuidanceRegulation/GuidanceDocumentsRegulatoryInformation/ucm494732.htm?source=govdelivery&utm_medium=email&utm_source=govdelivery*

NOTE: Local Ordinances—The City of Philadelphia enacted an ordinance in 2018 requiring fast food establishments with 15 or more locations to place warnings on menus for items that contain more than 2,300 milligrams of sodium. This amount is the maximum recommended daily intake. New York City has had such an ordinance in place since 2015.

CRITICAL ANALYSIS: Evaluate the impact of the guidance issued June 2, 2016 and the voluntary dismissal of the CSPI lawsuit June 3, 2016.

Landmark Labeling Decision—*95 Barrels*

United States v. Ninety-Five Barrels Alleged Apple Cider Vinegar,
244 S. Ct. 529 (1924)

Mr. Justice BUTLER delivered the opinion of the Court. This case arises under Food and Drugs Act June 30, 1906, c. 3915, 34 Stat. 768. (Comp. St. § 8717 et seq.). *** Every barrel seized was labeled: 'Douglas Packing Company Excelsior Brand Apple Cider Vinegar Made from Selected Apples Reduced to 4 Percentum Rochester, N. Y.' The information alleged that the vinegar was adulterated, in violation of section 7 of the act. It also alleged that the vinegar was made from dried or evaporated apples, and was misbranded, in that the statements on the label were false and misleading, and in that it was an imitation of and offered for sale under the distinctive name of another article, namely, apple cider vinegar. *** The question for decision is whether the vinegar was misbranded. During the apple season, from about September 25 to December 15, it makes apple cider and apple cider vinegar from fresh or unevaporated apples. During the balance of the year, it makes products which it designates as 'apple cider' and 'apple cider vinegar' from evaporated apples. *** A heavy weight is placed on top of the apples and a stream of water is introduced at the top of the receptacle through a pipe and is applied until the liquid, released through a vent at the bottom, has carried off in solution such of the constituents of the evaporated apples as are soluble in cold water and useful in the manufacture of vinegar. Such liquid, which is substantially equivalent in quantity to that which would have been obtained had unevaporated apples been used, carries a small and entirely harmless quantity of sulphur dioxide, which is removed during the process of fining and filtration by the addition of barium carbonate or some other proper chemical agent. The liquid is then subjected to alcoholic and subsequent acetic fermentation in the same manner as that followed by the manufacturer of apple cider vinegar made from the liquid content of unevaporated apples. Claimant employs the same receptacles, equipment and process of manufacturing for evaporated as for unevaporated apples, except that, in the case of evaporated apples, pure water is added as above described, and in the process of fining and filtration an additional chemical is used to precipitate any sulphur compounds present and resulting from dehydration. Vinegar so made is similar in taste and in composition to the vinegar made from unevaporated apples, except that the vinegar made from evaporated apples contains a trace of barium incident to the process of manufacture. ***

That the term 'misbranded,' as used herein, shall apply to all *** articles of food, or articles which enter into the composition of food, the package or label of which shall bear any statement, design, or device regarding such article, or the ingredients or substances contained therein which shall be false or misleading in any particular. *** The statute is plain and direct. Its comprehensive terms condemn every statement, design, and device which may mislead or deceive. Deception may result from the use of statements not technically false or which may be literally true. The aim of the statute is to prevent that resulting from indirection and ambiguity, as well as from statements which are false. It is not difficult to choose statements, designs, and devices which will not deceive. The vinegar made from dried apples was not the same as that which would have been produced from the apples without dehydration. The dehydration took from them about 80 per cent of the water content—an amount in excess of two-thirds of the total of their constituent elements. The substance removed was a part of their juice from which cider and vinegar would have been made if the apples had been used in their natural state. Samples of cider fermented and unfermented made from fresh and evaporated apples, and vinegar made from both kinds of cider were submitted to and examined by the District Judge who tried the case.

If an article is not the identical thing that the brand indicates it to be, it is misbranded. The vinegar in question was not the identical thing that the statement, 'Excelsior Brand Apple Cider Vinegar made from selected apples,' indicated it to be. The words 'Excelsior Brand,' calculated to give the impression of superiority, may be put to one side at not liable to mislead. But the words, 'apple cider vinegar made from selected apples' are misleading. *** The vinegar in question was not the same as if made from apples without dehydration. The name 'apple cider vinegar' included in the brand did not represent the article to be what it really was, and, in effect, did represent it to be what it was not—vinegar made from fresh or unevaporated apples. The words 'made from selected apples' indicate that the apples used were chosen with special regard to their fitness for the purpose of making apple cider vinegar. They give no hint that the vinegar was made from dried apples, or that the larger part of the moisture content of the apples was eliminated and water substituted therefor. *** The label was misleading as to the vinegar, its substance and ingredients. The facts admitted sustain the charge of misbranding.

CRITICAL ANALYSIS: Evaluate this decision and assess whether the court would reach the same conclusion today.

Misbranded Labeling Federal Decisions—*Farinella* and *"Diet Thins"*

The *Farinella* case raises issues of evidence and statements by the prosecutor deemed improper by the appeals court. The defendant, Mr. Farinella, was criminally prosecuted for introducing into interstate commerce a misbranded food, that is, salad dressing, with intent to defraud or mislead. The prosecution was based on defendant's sale of salad dressing after altering the label "best when purchased by" date. The appellate court reversed the conviction due to statements by the prosecutor that constituted misconduct. According to the court, the comments by the prosecutor implied that FDA required that "best when purchased by" date not be altered. Further, the court found problematic the prosecutor's assertions about food safety and the implication that the salad dressing was decayed, which was never established.

United States v. An Article of Food... Manischewitz... Diet Thins focused on the package labeling and the meaning that a consumer connotes from words such as *"Diet Thins"*. The critical concept in this case centered on the application of the proper test and requisite proof. The court held that: (1) The government was not required to prove that all the label representations were both false and misleading; (2) a demonstration that any individual was actually misled or deceived was unnecessary; and (3) proof of any intent to deceive was not required. The court opined that "[p]urchasers of diet products are often 'pathetically eager' to obtain a more slender figure." The *Manischewitz* court ascertained "that the weight conscious consumer may be led to believe *Diet Thins* Matzos are lower in calories than ordinary matzo crackers."

United States v. Farinella, 558 F.3ʳᵈ 695 (7ᵗʰ Cir. 2009)

POSNER, Circuit Judge. The defendant was convicted by a jury of wire fraud, 18 U.S.C. § 1343, and of introducing into interstate commerce a misbranded food with intent to defraud or mislead. 21 U.S.C. §§ 331(a), 333(a)(2). The [trial] judge sentenced him to five years' probation (including six months of home confinement) and to pay a $75,000 fine and forfeit the net gain from the offense, which was in excess of $400,000. *** In May 2003, the defendant bought 1.6 million bottles of "Henri's Salad Dressing" from ACH Foods, which in turn had bought it from Unilever, the manufacturer. The label on each bottle said "best when purchased by" followed by a date, which had been picked by Unilever, ranging from January to June 2003. ACH had purchased Henri's Salad Dressing from Unilever when the "best when purchased by" date was approaching. ***The defendant accordingly resold the salad dressing he bought from ACH to "dollar stores," which are discount stores, but before doing so he pasted on each bottle, over the part of the label that contains the "best when purchased by" date, a new label changing the date to May or July 2004. ***[T]he principal prosecutor said that "it's a case about taking nearly two million bottles of old, expired salad dressing and relabeling it with new expiration dates to pass it off as new and fresh.... [N]obody wants to eat foul, rancid food." The term "expiration date" (or "sell by" date, another date that the government's brief confuses with "best when purchased by" date) on a food product, unlike a "best when purchased by" date, has a generally understood meaning: it is the date after which you shouldn't eat the product. ***

ACH had faxed the defendant that it would guarantee the freshness of the salad dressing for up to 180 days past the "best when purchased by" date, but the dates that he had affixed to them were more than 180 days after the dates that Unilever had picked. *** That charge, upon which as we said the government's entire case depends, is limited to the change of the "best when purchased by" dates on the labels. It is important to understand what else this case does not involve, and also what is not in the record—the omissions are more interesting than the scanty contents of the government's threadbare case. There is no suggestion that selling salad dressing after the "best when purchased by" date endangers human health; so far as appears, Henri's Salad Dressing is edible a decade or more after it is manufactured. There is no evidence that the taste of any of the 1.6 million bottles of Henri's Salad Dressing sold by the defendant had deteriorated by the time of trial-four years after the latest original "best when purchased by" date—let alone by the latest relabeled "best when purchased by" date, which was 18 months after Unilever's original "best when purchased by" date. The term "misbranded food" is defined in some detail in 21 U.S.C. § 343, but there is nothing there about dates on labels, so that the defendant's conduct if illegal is so only if it can be said to be "false or misleading in any particular." § 343(a)(1). No regulation issued by the Food and Drug Administration, or, so far as we are informed, by the Federal Trade Commission or any other body, official or unofficial, defines "best when purchased by" or forbids a wholesaler (as here) or retailer to change the date. *** No evidence was presented that "best when purchased by" has a uniform meaning in the food industry. *** But well-off consumers prefer to buy before that date, and after the date passes the product will be sold at a discount in dollar stores or their equivalent, catering to less well-off consumers. ***

So was the defendant ripping off the consumer by selling salad dressing after its "best when purchased by" date had passed, without disclosing the fact? Apparently not, because it sold the salad dressing to dollar stores rather than to stores that cater to consumers who would not buy a product after its "best when purchased by" date. Still another possibility is that "best when purchased by" is just a guarantee by the seller, in this case by the defendant-a time-limited warranty. *** It is a denial of due process of law to convict a person of a crime because he violated some bureaucrat's secret understanding of the law. *** Because the government presented insufficient evidence that the defendant engaged in misbranding, he is entitled to be acquitted. But since there was insufficient evidence, why did the jury convict? Perhaps because of a series of improper statements by prosecutor Juliet Sorensen in her rebuttal closing argument, for which the government in its brief (which she signed) belatedly apologizes (belatedly because the government defended the remarks emphatically in the district court). *** After the court sustained the defendant's objection to the first statement—"Ladies and gentlemen, don't let the defendant and his high-paid lawyer buy his way out of this"—she said to the jury: "Black and white in our system of justice, ladies and gentlemen. You have to earn justice. You can't buy it." The judge sustained an objection to this statement too. *** The prosecutor told the jury that the "best when purchased by" date "allows a manufacturer to trace the product if there is a consumer complaint, if there is illness, if there is a need to recall the product." *** If that were true, the FDA presumably would require that the date not be altered, and it does not require that; in any event there was no evidence that a bottle of Henri's Salad Dressing consumed before or for that matter after the altered "best when purchased by" date could make anybody ill.

That was a veiled reference to the nonexistent issue of safety, which she pressed further when she said that "in spite of all this talk about the quality of the dressing, I don't see them opening any of these bottles and taking a whiff." *** She told the jury that the defendant was indifferent to "safety" and that "the harm caused by the fraud was to public confidence in the safety of the food supply." *** She also called the bottles of salad dressing "truckfulls of nasty, expired salad dressing," which was another groundless comment about quality and safety. She said that after the "expiration date" the salad dressing was no longer "fresh" and that the defendant "had to convert the expired dressing into new, fresh product," a proposition that is not completely intelligible, but sounds ominous. In her closing argument the prosecutor 14 times substituted "expiration date" or "expires" for "best when purchased by"; further improprieties, which grew to 20 in the government's main appeal brief by virtue of its using "sell-by date" as a synonym for "expiration date." [I]n this case, had the government presented enough evidence to sustain a conviction, we would have reversed the judgment and ordered a new trial on the basis of the prosecutor's misconduct. *** Since we are directing an acquittal on all counts, the sentencing issues are academic and we do not address them, beyond expressing our surprise that the government would complain about the leniency of the sentence for a crime it had failed to prove. REVERSED.

CRITICAL ANALYSIS: Except for infant formulas, product dating is not required under Federal regulations. However, food manufacturers use a variety of terms such as "Best if Used By", "Best By", "Sell By" and "Use By". Examine whether the court of appeals decision is correct and what really occurred in this case. Include a discussion of terminology above such as "Best By", "Sell By" and consumer protection. See link below.

https://www.fsis.usda.gov/wps/portal/fsis/topics/food-safety-education/get-answers/food-safety-fact-sheets/food-labeling/food-product-dating/food-product-dating

United States v. An Article of Food… Manischewitz… Diet Thins,
377 F. Supp. 746 (D.C. E.D. 1974)

JUDD, District Judge Plaintiff [government] has moved for summary judgment in this action to condemn food as misbranded. *** The proceeding relates to a food product labeled 'Diet-Thins Matzo Crackers.' (Diet-Thins). Claimant B. Manischewitz Co., Inc. has manufactured Diet-Thins under that name since about 1959. The government initiated this action in 1972 when 423 cases of Diet Thins were seized in Baltimore, Maryland. The government contended that the name Diet-Thins prominently displayed on the label's front panel conveyed to consumers the misleading impression that the matzos were lower in caloric content than other matzos and were useful in weight control diets. *** Originally, the Diet-Thins were thinner than the regular matzos manufactured and marketed by the claimant. Sometime during the mid-60's, however, the thickness of the regular matzos was reduced, so that at the time of the seizure the Diet-Thins were identical with other matzo crackers made by claimant, except that the Diet-Thins were made with enriched flour rather than ordinary flour. The Diet-Thins furnish the same number of calories as plain matzo crackers and have no greater value in weight control diets than claimant's ordinary matzo crackers. The words 'Diet-Thins' on the label of the seized article are displayed across the entire front panel in print 1 ¾" high. In the corner of the front panel, a sunburst contains the words 'enriched with vitamins and minerals, wheat germ added' in letters approximately 3/16" high. These legends suggest to the consumer that Diet-Thins are useful in a balanced weight control program and are significantly lower in calories than ordinary matzos. Although matzos contain less calories than many other crackers on the market, their caloric content is substantially the same as Melba toast, whole wheat crackers, and certain other crackers. The side panel also states, 'perfect for low salt, low sugar, no food dyes' and 'No salt, no sugar, shortening, spices or artificial sweeteners added.' *** 21 U.S.C. § 343, provides that: *A food shall be deemed to be misbranded (a) If its labeling is false or misleading in any particular.* ***

A food is misbranded if it appears that any one representation is false or misleading. *United States v. Hoxsey Cancer Clinic*, 198 F.2d 273, 281 (5th Cir. 1952), cert. denied, 344 U.S. 928, 73 S.Ct. 496, 97 L.Ed. 714 (1953). *** It is not necessary to show that anyone was actually misled or deceived, or that there was any intent to deceive. As the Supreme Court stated in *United States v. 95 Barrels-Cider Vinegar*, 265 U.S. 438, 442-443, 44 S.Ct. 529 (1924), at p. 531.

The same principle has been applied in this circuit *United States v. An Article—Sudden Change*, 409 F.2d 734, 740 (2d Cir. 1969). In the *Sudden Change* case, the court said that the test is not the effect of the label on a 'reasonable consumer,' but upon 'the ignorant, the unthinking and the credulous' consumer. Even a technically accurate description of a food or drug's content may violate 21 U.S.C. § 343 if the description is misleading in other respects. *United States v. An Article—Nuclomin*, 482 F.2d 581 (8th Cir. 1973). Thus, whether or not the side panel of the Diet-Thins label may accurately describe its virtues for certain special diets which do not appear to involve weight control, the misleading nature of the front panel still justifies condemnation of the seized articles. *** Purchasers of diet products are often 'pathetically eager' to obtain a more slender figure. See, e.g. *V. E. Irons Inc. v. United States,* 244 F.2d 34, 39 (1st Cir), cert. denied, 354 U.S. 923, 77 S.Ct. 1383, 1 L.Ed.2d 1437 (1957); *United States v. 38 Dozen Bottles . . . Tryptacin,* 114 F.Supp. 461, 462 (D.Minn.1953). There can be no doubt that the weight-conscious consumer may be led to believe that Diet-Thin Matzos are lower in calories than ordinary matzo crackers. *** It is ordered that the government's motion for summary judgment be granted, and that a decree of condemnation be entered, and that defendants' motions be denied.

CRITICAL ANALYSIS: Why did the court utilize "ignorant unthinking consumer" test instead of the reasonable consumer test? Is this test used for other FDA regulated products?

Misbranded Labeling State Action—*Williams v. Gerber Products Co.*

In an interesting state action, parents filed a class action against the manufacturer of "fruit juice" snacks for toddlers and alleged that the packaging contained misleading, deceptive, and false statements. The California Court of Appeals found that sufficient facts were alleged to state a claim that a reasonable consumer would be deceived by packaging that contained pictures of "real fruit" and terminology such as "natural" on the label for Toddler Fruit Juice Snacks. The Court of Appeals reversed the lower court that had determined the pictures and statements amounted to puffery even though the product was mostly corn syrup and sugar. *Williams v. Gerber Products Company* 439 F.Supp.2d 1112 (D.C. S.D. CA 2006). Ultimately, the case settled.

Williams v. Gerber Products Company,
552 F.3d 934 (2008) (Rehearing denied)

PREGERSON, Circuit Judge: Named class members parents of small children, brought a class action against Gerber Products Company ("Gerber"). An amended complaint alleged that Gerber deceptively marketed its "Fruit Juice Snacks" ("Snacks") a food product developed for toddlers. The district court granted Gerber's motion to dismiss. [W]e reverse.

BACKGROUND—Fruit Juice Snacks are sold as part of Gerber's "Graduates for Toddlers" product line. *** First, Appellants challenged the use of the words "Fruit Juice" juxtaposed alongside images of fruits such as oranges, peaches, strawberries, and cherries. Appellants contended that this juxtaposition was deceptive because the product contained no fruit juice from any of the fruits pictured on the packaging and because the only juice contained in the product was white grape juice from concentrate. Second, Appellants challenged a statement on the side panel of the packaging describing the product as made "with real fruit juice and other all-natural ingredients," even though the two most prominent ingredients were corn syrup and sugar. Third, Appellants challenged a separate statement on the side panel; namely, that Snacks was "one of a variety of nutritious Gerber Graduates foods and juices." *** The district court found that Gerber's statements were not likely to deceive a reasonable consumer, particularly given that the ingredient list was printed on the side of the box and that the "nutritious" claim was non-actionable puffery.

DISCUSSION—The district court granted Gerber's motion to dismiss all of Appellants' claims. *Williams v. Gerber Products Co.,* 439 F.Supp.2d 1112, 1117 (S.D.Cal.2006). It similarly dismissed the fraud and warranty claims, holding that "the challenged statements and images, viewed in context, are truthful or constitute non-actionable puffery." *** Under the reasonable consumer standard, Appellants must "show that members of the public are likely to be deceived." The product is called "fruit juice snacks" and the packaging pictures a number of different fruits, potentially suggesting (falsely) that those fruits or their juices are contained in the product. Further, the statement that Fruit Juice Snacks was made with "fruit juice and other all-natural ingredients" could easily be interpreted by consumers as a claim that all the ingredients in the product were natural, which appears to be false. And finally, the claim that Snacks is "just one of a variety of nutritious Gerber Graduates foods and juices that have been specifically designed to help toddlers grow up strong and healthy" adds to the potential deception. *** We disagree with the district court that reasonable consumers should be expected to look beyond misleading representations on the front of the box to discover the truth from the ingredient list in small print on the side of the box. *** We do not, however, think that a busy parent walking through the aisles of a grocery store should be expected to verify that the representations on the front of the box are confirmed in the ingredient list. Instead, reasonable consumers expect that the ingredient list contains more detailed information about the product that confirms other representations on the packaging.

CONCLUSION—The district court erred in determining as a matter of law that the Snacks packaging was not deceptive. The decision of the district court is therefore REVERSED.

NOTE: Similarly, in *Lam v. General Mills, Inc.* 3:11-cv-05056-SC. (2012), consumer allegations concerned General Mills' advertising of "Fruit by the Foot" and "Fruit Roll-Ups" on the packaging as deceptive because the claim "made with real fruit" could mislead consumers. Ultimately, the parties settled, and the case was dismissed by Order January 3, 2013.

CRITICAL ANALYSIS: Evaluate whether sufficient facts were alleged to state a claim that a reasonable consumer would be deceived by packaging that contained pictures of "real fruit" and terminology such as "natural" on the label for the "Fruit Juice Snacks".

State Example—New York City Board of Health

Prior to the federal caloric disclosure legislation in the Affordable Health Care Act, various state and local governments required restaurants to provide nutritional labeling beyond calorie disclosure. For example, the New York Board of Health required disclosure under certain parameters such as type (primarily fast food) and size of restaurant. The New York State Restaurant Association (NYSRA), a trade association comprising of approximately 7,000 restaurants, challenged a local New York City Board of Health rule about disclosure of nutrition information by restaurants. The United States Court of Appeals held that a local regulation which required approximately 10 percent of local restaurants to post caloric content information on their menus was not preempted by federal law. Further, applying the rational basis test, the court determined that the New York Municipal Regulation did not impermissibly impinge on the restaurants' First Amendment speech rights. Other cities and states adopted rules similar to the New York City rule. For example, California enacted legislation similar to the New York City rule and cities such as Philadelphia, San Francisco, and Seattle followed. Conversely, states such as Georgia and Ohio opposed this type of regulation. See: *New York State Restaurant Assn. vs. New York Board of Health* 556 F.3d 114 (2nd Cir. 2009).

CRITICAL ANALYSIS: See the New York City Board of Health Rule Sec. 81.50 of the New York City Health Code and compare and contrast to the federal mandate below.

Federal Caloric Disclosure—Restaurant Menus and Vending Machines

The Patient Protection and Affordable Care Act of 2010 (Affordable Care Act) established changes for fast food menus and vending machines. Section 4205 of the ACA established new federal requirements for foods sold at certain restaurants, coffee shops, delis, ice cream shops, and vending machines. The federal law requires chain restaurants with 20 or more locations that offer substantially the equivalent menu items to list calorie content information on menus and menu boards. Upon request, other nutrient information such as total calories, total fat, saturated fat, cholesterol, sodium, total carbohydrates, complex carbohydrates, sugars, dietary fiber and total protein must be provided in writing. The "menu disclosure law" preempts state and local requirements; however, a petition for an exemption may be filed and FDA may grant an exemption. Section 4205 required FDA to issue proposed regulations by March 23, 2011; however, it was delayed and a proposed rule was issued in April 2011. Food Labeling; Nutrition Labeling of Standard Menu Items in Restaurants and Similar Retail Food Establishments. **Final Rule: 79 FR 71259.** The link to both rules is below. Compliance date May 7, 2018. See note below.

Final Rules under Section 4205 Vending Machines and Restaurant Menus

Food Labeling; Calorie Labeling of Articles of Food in Vending Machines. The intent of the final rule published December 1, 2014 is to assist consumers by requiring the availability of point of purchase nutrition caloric information prior to purchasing the food item. See: 79 FR 71259. **NOTE: Certain foods sold from glass-front vending machines compliance date is July 26, 2018. Trade associations requested the extension due to the requirements for front-of-package font size.**

Food Labeling; Nutrition Labeling of Standard Menu Items in Restaurants and Similar Retail Food Establishments, **21 U.S.C. 343(q)(5)(H).** The purpose of this final rule published December 1, 2014 is to implement the menu labeling provisions of the Affordable Care Act. The requirements concern providing certain nutrition information for standard menu items in certain chain restaurants and similar retail food establishments. The Affordable Care Act, in part, amended the FDCA to

385

require restaurants and similar retail food establishments that are part of a chain with 20 or more locations and doing business under the same name and offering for sale substantially the same menu items to provide calorie and other nutrition information for standard menu items. This includes food on display and self-service food. The Affordable Care Act provides that restaurants and similar retail food establishments not otherwise covered by the law may elect to become subject to the Federal requirements by registering biennially with the FDA.

Compliance Date: Originally, the compliance date was December 1, 2015, then extended to December 1, 2016; 79 FR 71156; compliance was again delayed until one year after a Level I guidance was published in the federal register May 5, 2016 (See: 81 FR 96364-01; however, compliance was further postponed until May 7, 2018. See: 82 FR 20825.

A Labeling Guide for Restaurants and Retail Establishments Selling Away- From-Home Foods – Part II (Menu Labeling Requirements in Accordance with 21 CFR 101.11): Guidance for Industry. http://www.fda.gov/downloads/Food/GuidanceRegulation/GuidanceDocumentsRegulatoryInformation/UCM461963.pdf

NOTE: *"A Labeling Guide for Restaurants and Other Retail Establishments Selling Away-From-Home Foods–Part I"* was previously issued on other nutrition-related information that must be provided to customers of restaurants or similar establishments not covered by the guidance (Part II above) yet choose to make claims about nutrients in the food it serves or about positive health effects that can be gained from the food.

See: Jane E. Brody, *The Heartbreakers at Chain Restaurants*, N.Y. Times, D5 (Aug. 28, 2018); David S. Ludwig and Kenneth S. Rogoff, *The Toll of America's Obesity*, A21 Col. 2 NY Times (Aug.10, 2018).

CRITICAL ANALYSIS: Are the federal rules for calorie disclosure for vending machines and restaurant menus sufficient in terms of "the consumer right to know"? Incorporate a discussion about the compliance date delays. Further, with the continued rise of obesity and diet related diseases, should other disclosures be required as well?

Labeling—Nondairy Plant Based Products Labeled "Milk"

https://www.fda.gov/NewsEvents/Newsroom/PressAnnouncements/ucm621824.htm

Recently, controversy has developed concerning the labeling of nondairy plant based beverages. The "Dairy Pride Act" was introduced to consider nondairy products such as almond, soy, and coconut labelled milk as a misbranded product.

FDA has initiated proceedings which would bar nondairy products from calling nonanimal products milk by issuing a request for information (RFI) in the Federal Register 83 FR 49103 (2018). The FDA solicited comments on the labeling of plant-based products with names that include the names of dairy foods such as "milk," "cultured milk," "yogurt," and "cheese." Further, as part of the Nutrition Innovation Strategy, Commissioner Gottlieb issued a statement concerning modernizing standards of identity and the use of daily names for plant-based substitutes (link above).

CRITICAL ANALYSIS: Discuss how these types of products should be labelled in terms of consumer right-to-know.

Chapter 3: Claims—Health, Structure-Function, Nutrient Content, Qualified and Functional Foods

Claims—Conventional Foods

FDA regulates claim validity on labeling while FTC regulates product advertising. The crucial element is substantiation; that is, manufacturers must have adequate support for the claims on their products. For example, an FDA guidance document details that structure function claims must be supported by competent and reliable scientific evidence.

The European Union (EU) definition of "health claim" is considerably broader than the definition under the FDCA. The EU defines "health claim" as "any claim that states, suggests or implies that a relationship exists between a food category, a food or one of its constituents and health". Regulation (EC) (No. 1924/2006), Official J. of the EU L 12/3 Jan. 2007. Submission is required for any new health claim not on the EU list of approved claims. As illustrated below, the United States approval process is complicated. A simpler approach is needed.
NOTE: See *http://ec.europa.eu/nuhclaims/*

CRITICAL ANALYSIS: Discuss whether the EU definition would serve as a better definition in terms of clarity or would a broader claim be a disservice in terms of consumer confusion.

Categories—The categories below are based on specific laws detailed as follows:
Health Claims;
Structure Function Claims;
Nutrient Content Claims; and
Dietary Guidance Statements.
https://www.fda.gov/Food/LabelingNutrition/ucm111447.htm

Health Claims

A health claim describes the relationship between a substance (food or food component) and a disease or health-related condition (21 CFR 101.14(a) (1)). Health claims are limited to claims about disease risk reduction and cannot be claims about the cure, mitigation, treatment or prevention of disease. The latter claims are drug claims under section 201(g) of the Federal Food, Drug, and Cosmetic Act. The following methods are used by FDA to determine which health claims may be used on a label or in labeling for a food—Significant Scientific Agreement (under NELA), Authoritative Statement (under FDAMA) and Qualified Claims.

Health Claims—*Significant Scientific Agreement NLEA Basis*

FDA authorized health claim that meets the significant scientific agreement standard in the 1990 Nutrition Labeling and Education Act (NLEA) as follows.

Calcium, Vitamin D, and Osteoporosis
21 CFR 101.72 Health claims: calcium and osteoporosis
Final Rule: Food Labeling: Health Claims; Calcium and Osteoporosis, and Calcium, Vitamin D, and Osteoporosis September 29, 2008

Dietary Lipids (Fat) and Cancer
21 CFR 101.73 Health claims: dietary lipids and cancer

Dietary Saturated Fat and Cholesterol and Risk of Coronary Heart Disease
21 CFR 101.75 Health claims: dietary saturated fat and cholesterol and risk of coronary heart disease

Dietary Non-cariogenic Carbohydrate Sweeteners and Dental Caries
21 CFR 101.80 Health claims: dietary noncariogenic carbohydrate sweeteners and dental caries
Final Rule: Food Labeling: Health Claims; Dietary Noncariogenic Carbohydrate Sweeteners and Dental Caries May 27, 2008
Final Rule: Food Labeling: Health Claims; D-tagatose and Dental Caries July 3, 2003

Final Rule: Food Labeling: Health Claims; Dietary Sugar Alcohols and Dental Caries December 2, 1997

Final Rule: Food Labeling: Health Claims; Sugar Alcohols and Dental Caries August 23, 1996

Fiber-containing Grain Products, Fruits and Vegetables and Cancer

21 CFR 101.76 Health claims: fiber-containing grain products, fruits, and vegetables and cancer

Folic Acid and Neural Tube Defects

21 CFR 101.79 Health claims: Folate and neural tube defects

Final Rule: Food Labeling: Health Claims; Folate and Neural Tube Defects March 5, 1996

Final Rule: Revoking January 4, 1994 Regulation That Became Final By Operation of Law September 24, 1996

Fruits and Vegetables and Cancer

21 CFR 101.78 Health claims: fruits and vegetables and cancer

Fruits, Vegetables and Grain Products that contain Fiber, particularly Soluble fiber, and Risk of Coronary Heart Disease

21 CFR 101.77 Health claims: fruits, vegetables, and grain products that contain fiber, particularly soluble fiber, and risk of coronary heart disease

Sodium and Hypertension

21 CFR 101.74 Health claims: sodium and hypertension

Soluble Fiber from Certain Foods and Risk of Coronary Heart Disease

21 CFR 101.81 Health claims: Soluble fiber from certain foods and risk of coronary heart disease (CHD)

Final Rule: Food Labeling: Health Claims; Soluble Fiber from Certain Foods and Risk of Coronary Heart Disease (Barley Betafiber) August 15, 2008

Final Rule: Food Labeling: Health Claims; Soluble Fiber from Certain Foods and Risk of Coronary Heart Disease May 1, 2008

Final Rule: Health Claims; Soluble Dietary Fiber from Certain Foods and Coronary Heart Disease (CHD) (Barley) May 22, 2006

Final Rule: Health Claims; Soluble Dietary Fiber From Certain Foods and Coronary Heart Disease (Oatrim) July 28, 2003

Final rule: correction: Food Labeling: Health Claims; Soluble Fiber From Certain Foods and Coronary Heart Disease; Correction (Psyllium husk) April 9, 1998

Final Rule: Food Labeling; Health Claims; Soluble Fiber from Certain Foods and Risk of Coronary Heart Disease (Psyllium husk) February 18, 1998

Final Rule: Food Labeling: Health Claims; Soluble Fiber From Whole Oats and Risk of Coronary Heart Disease Amended March 31, 1997

Final Rule: Food Labeling: Health Claims; Oats and Coronary Heart Disease January 23, 1997

*Soy Protein and Risk of Coronary Heart Disease

21 CFR 101.82 Health claims: Soy protein and risk of coronary heart disease (CHD)

Final Rule: Food Labeling: Health Claims; Soy Protein and Coronary Heart Disease October 26, 1999

* NOTE: FDA issued a proposed rule (82 FR 50324 Oct. 31, 2017) to revoke this claim due to the totality of the evidence as inconsistent and not conclusive. Docket No. FDA-2017-N-0763.

If the claim is revoked, then FDA would permit companies to use a qualified claim which requires a lower scientific standard of evidence.

https://www.federalregister.gov/documents/2017/10/31/2017-23629/food-labeling-health-claims-soy-protein-and-coronary-heart-disease

Stanols/Sterols and Risk of Coronary Heart Disease

Proposed Rule: Food Labeling: Health Claim; Phytosterols and Risk of Coronary Heart Disease December 8, 2010

FDA Letter Regarding Enforcement Discretion With Respect to Expanded Use of an Interim Health Claim Rule About Plant Sterol/Stanol Esters and Reduced Risk of Coronary Heart Disease February 14, 2003

21 CFR 101.83 Health claims: plant sterol/stanol esters and risk of coronary heart disease (CHD)

Health Claims—*Authoritative Statement FDAMA Basis*

The Food and Drug Administration Modernization Act of 1997 (FDAMA) provides a second way for the use of a health claim on foods to be authorized. FDAMA allows certain health claims to be made as a result of a successful notification to FDA of a health claim based on an "authoritative statement" from a scientific body of the U.S. Government or the National Academy of Sciences.

https://www.fda.gov/Food/LabelingNutrition/ucm111447.htm

Linoleic Acid: Nutrient Content Claims Notification for Foods and Dietary Supplements Containing Linoleic Acid December 23, 2014

Choline: Nutrient Content Claims Notification for Choline Containing Foods August 30, 2001

Fluoride and the Risk of Dental Caries:

Health Claim Notification for Fluoridated Water October 14, 2006

Potassium and the Risk of High Blood Pressure and Stroke:

Health Claim Notification for Potassium Containing Foods October 31, 2000

Saturated Fat, Cholesterol, and *Trans* Fat, and the Risk of Heart Disease:

Health Claim Notification for Saturated Fat, Cholesterol, and *Trans* Fat and Reduced Risk of Heart Disease November 15, 2006

Substitution of Saturated Fat with Unsaturated Fatty Acids and Risk of Heart Disease:

Health Claim Notification for the Substitution of Saturated Fat in the Diet with Unsaturated Fatty Acids and Reduced Risk of Heart Disease May 25, 2007

Whole Grain Foods and the Risk of Heart Disease and Certain Cancers:

Health Claim Notification for Whole Grain Foods with Moderate Fat Content December 9, 2003

Health Claim Notification for Whole Grain Foods July 8, 1999

Health Claims—*Qualified*

http://www.fda.gov/Food/IngredientsPackagingLabeling/LabelingNutrition/ucm2006877.htm

FDA's *Consumer Health Information for Better Nutrition Initiative* provides for the use of qualified health claims when there is emerging evidence for a relationship between a food, food component, or dietary supplement and the reduced risk of a disease or health-related condition. In this case, the evidence is not well enough established to meet the significant scientific agreement standard required for FDA to issue an authorizing regulation. Qualifying language is included as part of the claim to indicate that the evidence supporting the claim is limited. Both conventional foods and dietary supplements may use qualified health claims. FDA uses its enforcement discretion for qualified health claims after evaluating and ranking the quality and strength of the totality of the scientific evidence.

NOTE: See *Health Claims Unpacking their Language on Food Labels,* Mary L. Klatt and Roseann B. Termini, 1 Update 33 (Used with Permission, Food and Drug Law Institute) (2008).

Standardized Qualifying Language for Qualified Health Claims

Scientific Ranking*	FDA Category	Appropriate Qualifying Language**
Second Level	B	"although there is scientific evidence supporting the claim, the evidence is not conclusive."
Third Level	C	"Some scientific evidence suggests ... however, FDA has determined that this evidence is limited and not conclusive."
Fourth Level	D	"Very limited and preliminary scientific research suggests... FDA concludes that there is little scientific evidence supporting this claim."

> **NOTE: FDA Category A— are approved claims.**
>
> *From Guidance for Industry and FDA: Interim Evidence-based Ranking System for Scientific Data. ** Language reflects wording used in qualified health claims FDA has previously exercised enforcement discretion for certain dietary supplements. During this interim period, the precise language as to which the agency considers exercising enforcement discretion may vary depending on the specific circumstances of each case.

Qualified Health Claims: Enforcement Discretion
Whole Grain Consumption and Reduced Risk of Type 2 Diabetes

ConAgra Foods, Inc. petitioned FDA in 2012 (FDA-2012-Q-0242-0001) for a qualified health claim relating to whole grain consumption and a reduced risk of type 2 diabetes; however, not all whole grain food products would qualify as ConAgra proposed that products bearing the claim contain at least 12 grams of whole grains per Reference Amount Customarily Consumed (RACC). The Kellogg Company filed comments in opposition to this petition. FDA granted the petition in a September 2013 letter to ConAgra, with the following qualified health claims.

> *"Whole grains may reduce the risk of type 2 diabetes, although the FDA has concluded that there is very limited scientific evidence for this claim."*

> *"Whole grains may reduce the risk of type 2 diabetes. FDA has concluded that there is very limited scientific evidence for this claim."*

Atopic Dermatitis

100% Whey-Protein Partially Hydrolyzed Infant Formula and Reduced Risk of Atopic Dermatitis May 24, 2011

Cardiovascular Disease

Macadamia Nuts *https://www.fda.gov/Food/NewsEvents/ConstituentUpdates/ucm568052.htm* "Supportive but not conclusive research shows that eating 1.5 ounces per day of macadamia nuts, as part of a diet low in saturated fat and cholesterol and not resulting in increased intake of saturated fat or calories may reduce the risk of coronary heart disease. See nutrition information for fat [and calorie] content." (Petition filed by Royal Hawaiian Macadamia Nut, Inc.).

Folic Acid, Vitamin B6, and Vitamin B12 and Vascular Disease

Settlement Health Claim Relating B Vitamins and Vascular Disease May 15, 2001

Folic Acid, Vitamin B6, and Vitamin B12 and Vascular Disease November 28, 2000

Nuts and Coronary Heart Disease

Walnuts and Coronary Heart Disease March 9, 2004

Nuts and Coronary Heart Disease July 14, 2003 Omega-3 Fatty Acids

Omega-3 Fatty Acids and Reduced Risk of Coronary Heart Disease (Martek Petition) September 8, 2004

Omega-3 Fatty Acids and Reduced Risk of Coronary Heart Disease (Wellness Petition) September 8, 2004

Unsaturated Fatty Acids

Corn Oil and Corn Oil-Containing Products—Reduced Risk of Heart Disease March 26, 2007

Unsaturated Fatty Acids from Canola Oil—Reduced Risk of Coronary Heart Disease October 6, 2006

Monounsaturated Fatty Acids from Olive Oil and Coronary Heart Disease November 1, 2004

Cognitive Function

Letter Updating the Phosphatidylserine and Cognitive Function and Dementia Qualified Health Claim November 24, 2004

Phosphatidylserine and Cognitive Dysfunction and Dementia, May 13, 2003

Phosphatidylserine and Cognitive Dysfunction and Dementia February 24, 2003

Diabetes

Approved Psyllium statements:

Psyllium husk may reduce the risk of type 2 diabetes, although the FDA has concluded that there is very little scientific evidence for this claim.

Psyllium husk may reduce the risk of type 2 diabetes. FDA has concluded that there is very little scientific evidence for this claim.

http://www.fda.gov/downloads/Food/IngredientsPackagingLabeling/LabelingNutrition/UCM403090.pdf (June 23, 2014).

Whole Grains and a Reduced Risk of Diabetes Mellitus Type 2 (PDF - 564KB) September 11, 2013

Chromium Picolinate

Reduced Risk of Insulin Resistance, Type 2 Diabetes August 25, 2005

Hypertension

Calcium and Hypertension, Pregnancy-Induced Hypertension, and Preeclampsia

Neural Tube Defects

Folic Acid and Neural Tube Defects April 3, 2001

Folic Acid and Neural Tube Defects October 10, 2000

Cancer

Selenium and a Reduced Risk of Site-specific Cancers June 19, 2009

Antioxidant Vitamins C and E and Reduction in the Risk of Site-Specific Cancers June 19, 2009

Tomatoes and Prostate, Ovarian, Gastric, and Pancreatic Cancers (American Longevity Petition) November 8, 2005

Tomatoes and Prostate Cancer (Lycopene Heath Claim Coalition Petition) November 8, 2005

Calcium and Colon/Rectal Cancer and Calcium and Colon/Rectal Polyps October 12, 2005

Letter Updating the Green Tea and Risk of Breast Cancer and Prostate Cancer Health Claim April 17, 2012

Green Tea and Risk of Breast Cancer and Prostate Cancer February 24, 2011

Selenium and Certain Cancers April 28, 2003

Selenium and Certain Cancers February 21, 2003

Antioxidant Vitamins and Risk of Certain Cancers April 1, 2003

NOTE: See: In *Fleminger, Inc. v. United States Dept. of Health and Human Services,* **Civ. Action 854 F. Supp.2d 192 No. 3:10 855 (DC D. Conn. Feb. 23, 2012) the plaintiff filed a lawsuit against FDA and objected in First Amendment principles due to the FDA qualifying language requirement as follows:**

"Green tea may reduce the risk of breast or prostate cancers. FDA does not agree that green tea may reduce that risk because there is very little scientific evidence for the claim."

The federal district court agreed that this language did not impart a reasonable fit between FDA's end and the agency's means used to achieve that end. In remanding the case to the FDA to reconsider the language "FDA does not agree that green tea may reduce that risk because there is very little scientific evidence for the claim, the court opined that the following language would be appropriate and still fulfill the agency's interest to protect the public.

"Green tea may reduce the risk of breast or prostate cancer although the FDA has concluded that there is very little scientific evidence to support the claim."

Qualified Health Claims: Letters of Denial

Cancer

Lycopene and Various Cancers (American Longevity Petition) November 8, 2005

Lycopene and Prostate Cancer (Lycopene Heath Claim Coalition Petition) November 8, 2005

Calcium and Risk of Breast and Prostate Cancers October 12, 2005

Green Tea and Risk of: Gastric Cancer; Lung Cancer; Colon/Rectal Cancer; Esophageal Cancer;

Pancreatic Cancer; Ovarian Cancer; Liver Cancer; Bladder Cancer; and Skin Cancer, as well as Total Cancers Combined June 30, 2005

Fiber and Colorectal Cancer October 10, 2000

Cardiovascular Disease

Green Tea and Reduced Risk of Cardiovascular Disease May 9, 2006

Eggs with Enhanced Omega-3 Fatty Acid Content and Balanced 1:1 Ratio of Omega-3/Omega-6 Fatty Acids and Reduced Risk of Heart Disease and Sudden Fatal Heart Attack April 5, 2005

Vitamin E and Heart Disease February 9, 2001

Diabetes

Chromium Picolinate and a Reduced Risk of: Cardiovascular Disease When Caused by Insulin Resistance; Cardiovascular Disease When Caused by Abnormally Elevated Blood Sugar Levels; Cardiovascular Disease When Caused by Type 2 Diabetes; Retinopathy When Caused by Abnormally High Blood Sugar Levels; and Kidney Disease When Caused by Abnormally High Blood Sugar Levels August 25, 2005

Eye Diseases

Xangold® Lutein Esters, Lutein, or Zeaxanthin and Reduced Risk of Age-related Macular Degeneration or Cataract Formation December 19, 2005

Food Allergy

100 Percent Partially Hydrolyzed Whey Protein in Infant Formula and Reduced Risk of Food Allergy in Infants May 11, 2006

Kidney Stones/Urinary Stones

Calcium and Kidney/Urinary Stones October 12, 2005

Menstrual Disorders

Calcium and a Reduced Risk of Menstrual Disorders September 12, 2005

Osteoarthritis

Glucosamine and/or Chondroitin Sulfate and a Reduced Risk of: Osteoarthritis; Osteoarthritis-related Joint Pain, Joint Tenderness, and Joint Swelling; Joint Degeneration; and Cartilage Deterioration October 7, 2004

Crystalline Glucosamine Sulfate and a Reduced Risk of Osteoarthritis October 7, 2004

CRITICAL ANALYSIS: Discuss the approval mechanisms for health claims, particularly that of qualified claims and determine whether health claims could be evaluated differently.

Structure-Function Claims

https://www.fda.gov/Food/LabelingNutrition/ucm111447.htm

Structure function claims describe the role of substances intended to affect the normal structure or function in humans (21 CFR 101.93), for example, "calcium builds strong bones." In addition, structure-function claims may characterize the means by which substances act to maintain such structure or function, for example, "fiber maintains bowel regularity" or they may describe general well-being from consumption of a nutrient or dietary ingredient. Structure function claims may also describe a benefit related to a nutrient deficiency disease (like Vitamin C and scurvy), as long as the statement also tells how widespread such disease is in the U.S. Such claims may not explicitly or implicitly link the relationship to a disease or health-related condition. Structure-function claims on conventional foods can be made without FDA review or authorization before use, but they must be truthful and not misleading and the claims must derive from the nutritional value of the product.

Nutrient Content Claims

https://www.fda.gov/Food/LabelingNutrition/ucm111447.htm

The Nutrition Labeling and Education Act of 1990 (NLEA) permits the use of label claims that characterize the level of a nutrient in a food, known as nutrient content claims as long as the claim complies with FDA's regulations for Nutrient Content Claims under 21 CFR 101.13. A nutrient content claim describe the level of a nutrient in a food using terms such as *free*, *high* and *low*, or they compare the level of a nutrient in a food to that of another food, using terms such as *more*, *reduced* and *lite*. Most nutrient content claim regulations apply only to those nutrients or substances that have an established Daily Value (DV). The requirements that govern the use of nutrient content claims help ensure that descriptive terms, such as *high* or *low*, are used consistently for all types of food products and are meaningful to consumers. The term *Healthy* has been defined by a regulation (21 CFR 101.65(d)) as an implied nutrient content claim that characterizes a food that has "healthy" levels of total fat, saturated fat, cholesterol, other nutrients and sodium.

FDA exercises its oversight in determining nutrient content claims that may be used on a label or in labeling: (1) FDA issues a regulation authorizing a nutrient content claim after FDA's careful review of the scientific evidence submitted in a nutrient content claim petition, and (2) FDA prohibits or modifies, by regulation, a nutrient content claim within 120 days after it has received a nutrient content claim notification under FDAMA, which provides for nutrient content claims based on an authoritative statement from a scientific body by the U.S. government with official responsibility for public health protection or research directly related to human nutrition or the National Academy of Sciences or any of its subdivisions (in the alternative, a U.S. district court may find that the requirements of sections 303 or 304 of FDAMA have not been met).

Final Rule Food Labeling—Omega-3 Fatty Acids: DHA, EPA and ALA Nutrient Content Claims Prohibition
Food Labeling: Nutrient Content Claims; Alpha-Linolenic Acid, Eicosapentaenoic Acid, and Docosahexaenoic Acid Omega-3 Fatty Acids

FDA published a final rule prohibiting certain nutrient content claims for foods that contain the omega-3 fatty acids docosahexaenoic acid (DHA), eicosapentaenoic acid (EPA) and alpha-linolenic acid (ALA).   (72 FR 66103). The final rule, published April 28, 2014 effective January 1, 2016 prohibits statements on the labels of food products, including dietary supplements, that claim the products are "high in" DHA or EPA, and synonyms such as "rich in" and "excellent source of." Nutrient content claims such as "high in" are allowed only for nutrients for which a reference level to which the claim refers has been set. FDA can establish such nutrient levels by regulation, or in some instances, if the requirements of the FDCA have been met, such nutrient levels can be based on authoritative statements published by certain types of scientific bodies such as the Institute of Medicine of the National Academies (IOM).

FDA has not established nutrient levels that can serve as the basis for nutrient content claims for DHA, EPA, or ALA. FDA received notifications in 2004 and 2005 asserting that the IOM had issued authoritative statements that identified such nutrient levels for DHA, EPA, and ALA. According to FDA, there were several notifications that identified multiple, sometimes conflicting nutrient levels for these three omega-3 fatty acids. With respect to all of the nutrient content claims for DHA and EPA that were identified in the notifications, FDA has determined that none of these claims meets the requirements of the FDCA. The final rule prohibits all of these claims. With respect to the two sets of nutrient content claims for ALA that were identified in the notifications, FDA determined that one of these sets of claims did not meet the requirements of the Act. The final rule prohibits that set of claims.

https://www.federalregister.gov/documents/2014/04/28/2014-09492/food-labeling-nutrient-content-claims-alpha-linolenic-acid-eicosapentaenoic-acid-and-docosahexaenoic?source=govdelivery&utm_medium=email&utm_source=govdelivery

Dietary Guidance Statements
www.fda.gov/Food/GuidanceRegulation/GuidanceDocumentsRegulatoryInformation/LabelingNutrition/ucm053425.htm

Dietary guidance statements can also be made on food labels. While health claims describe the relationship between a substance that is a specific food or food component and a disease or health-related condition, dietary guidance statements do not contain both elements see 58 FR 2478 at 2487,

January 6, 1993. Dietary Guidance statements center on general dietary patterns, practices and recommendations that promote health. Typically, "dietary guidance" statements refer to a category of foods and not a specific substance. Dietary guidance statements can be made without FDA review or authorization before use; however, the statements must be truthful and not misleading. Example: *"Carrots are good for your health."*

Functional Food Claims

What are functional foods? The FDCA does not have a specific definition as to what constitutes a "functional food"; however, FDA has regulatory authority pertaining to claims. The Institute of Food Technologists deems "functional foods" as those foods and food components that provide a health benefit or a psychological effect. Food companies do market foods with claims that advocate wellness.

https://www.fda.gov/Food/LabelingNutrition/ucm111447.htm

CRITICAL ANALYSIS: Consider whether functional foods should be classified as perhaps drugs, medical foods or dietary supplements? What data should be necessary to demonstrate that functional foods are both safe and effective as promoted? See: This *Volume*, Chapter 4.

Enforcement of Health Claims

Health claims must be supported by scientific evidence and must not be false and or deceptive in any particular manner. The Federal Trade Commission (FTC) administrative complaint below charged the POM Wonderful LLC and principals with deceptive advertising concerning claims made about POM juice and supplements. For example, FTC charged that claims such as: prevents or treats heart disease, prostate cancer, and erectile dysfunction were false and unsubstantiated.

FTC Deceptive Advertising Charge—POM Wonderful

http://www.ftc.gov/opa/2010/09/pom.shtm

A complaint by the FTC charged that POM Wonderful LLC, sister corporation Roll International Corp., and principals Stewart Resnick, Lynda Resnick, and Matthew Tupper violated federal law by making deceptive disease prevention and treatment claims. The advertisements in question appeared in national publications such as *Parade, Fitness, The New York Times*, and *Prevention* magazines; on Internet sites such as pomtruth.com, pomwonderful.com, and pompills.com; on bus stops and billboards; in newsletters to customers; and on tags attached to the product. POM Wonderful Pomegranate Juice is widely available at grocery stores nationwide, and a 16 oz. bottle retails for approximately $3.99. POMx pills and liquid extract are sold via direct mail, with a one-month supply costing approximately $30. Contrary to POM Wonderful's advertising, the available scientific information does not prove that POM Juice or POMx effectively treats or prevents these illnesses." The advertisements touted POM Juice and POMx supplements with statements such as:

✓ "SUPER HEALTH POWERS! 100% PURE POMEGRANATE JUICE ... Backed by $25 million in medical research. Proven to fight for cardiovascular, prostate and erectile health."

✓ "NEW RESEARCH OFFERS FURTHER PROOF OF THE HEART-HEALTHY BENEFITS OF POM WONDERFUL JUICE. 30% DECREASE IN ARTERIAL PLAQUE ... 17% IMPROVED BLOOD FLOW ... PROMOTES HEALTHY BLOOD VESSELS ..."

✓ **Prostate health**—Prostate cancer is the most commonly diagnosed cancer among men in the United States and the second-leading cause of cancer death in men after lung cancer.

✓ **Time pill**—Stable levels of prostate-specific antigens (or PSA levels) are critical for men with prostate cancer. Patients with quick PSA doubling times are more likely to die from their cancer. According to a UCLA study of 46 men age 65 to 70 with advanced prostate cancer, drinking an 8 oz glass of POM Wonderful 100% Pomegranate Juice every day slowed their PSA doubling time by nearly 350%. ... 83% of those who participated in the study showed a significant decrease in their cancer regrowth rate.

✓ "You have to be on pomegranate juice. You have a 50 percent chance of getting [prostate cancer]. Listen to me. It is the one thing that will keep your PSA normal. You have to drink pomegranate juice. There is nothing else we know of that will keep your PSA in check. ... It's also 40 percent as effective as Viagra." The FTC's administrative complaint against POM Wonderful alleges that these claims are false and unsubstantiated.

✓ Clinical studies prove that POM Juice and POMx prevent, reduce the risk of, and treat heart disease, including by decreasing arterial plaque, lowering blood pressure, and improving blood flow to the heart.

✓ Clinical studies prove that POM Juice and POMx prevent, reduce the risk of, and treat prostate cancer, including by prolonging prostate-specific antigen doubling time.

✓ Clinical studies prove that POM Juice prevents, reduces the risk of, and treats, erectile dysfunction.

The FTC complaint detailed that POM Wonderful's heart disease claims are false and unsubstantiated because many of the scientific studies conducted by POM Wonderful did not show heart disease benefit from use of its products. It alleged that the prostate cancer claims are false and unsubstantiated because, among other reasons, the study POM Wonderful relied on was neither "blinded" nor controlled. Finally, it alleged that the erectile dysfunction claims are false and unsubstantiated because the study on which the company relied did not show that POM Juice was any more effective than a placebo. The complaint set forth an order that would prevent future law violations by POM Wonderful. In part, it required that future claims that any pomegranate-based product cures, prevents, treats, or reduces the risk of any disease not be misleading and comply with Food and Drug Administration regulations for the claim. Although FDA approval of health claims generally is not required for compliance with the FTC Act, the proposed order would require FDA pre-approval before POM Wonderful makes future claims that certain products prevent or treat serious diseases, in order to provide clearer guidance for the company, facilitate POM Wonderful's compliance with the order, and make it easier to enforce. See link below:

Administrative Law Judge Upholds FTC's Complaint that POM Deceptively Advertised Its Products as Treating, Preventing, or Reducing the Risk of Heart Disease, Prostate Cancer, and Erectile Dysfunction

https://www.ftc.gov/news-events/press-releases/2012/05/administrative-law-judge-upholds-ftcs-complaint-pom-deceptively

In a related case, below Mark Dreher, POM Wonderful's former head of scientific and regulatory affairs and expert endorser, agreed to a settlement that bars him from making any disease treatment or prevention claims in advertising for a POM Wonderful product unless the claim is not misleading and comports with FDA requirements for the claim. The settlement prohibits Dreher from making other health claims for a food, drug, or dietary supplement for human use without competent and reliable scientific evidence to support the claim. See:

FTC Commissioners Uphold Trial Judge Decision that POM Wonderful, LLC; Stewart and Lynda Resnick; Others Deceptively Advertised Pomegranate Products by Making Unsupported Health Claims

https://www.ftc.gov/news-events/press-releases/2013/01/ftc-commissioners-uphold-trial-judge-decision-pom-wonderful-llc

NOTE: See *Volume X: Dietary Supplements* for additional enforcement actions. See also *Volume III: Enforcement,* Lanham Act litigation by POM Wonderful LLC against the Coca-Cola Company.

CRITICAL ANALYSIS: Evaluate whether the FTC was correct in filing the complaint against POM Wonderful LLC.

Chapter 4: Terminology—Medical Foods, Country of Origin, Natural, Organic, Hormones, Antibiotics, Nanotechnology and Honey

Medical Foods

Medical foods are intended for a specific dietary management of a disease or condition and are physician supervised. A medical food, under 21 U.S.C. 360ee (b)(3), is defined as follows:

"a food which is formulated to be consumed or administered enterally under the supervision of a physician and which is intended for the specific dietary management of a disease or condition for which distinctive nutritional requirements, based on recognized scientific principles, are established by medical evaluation."

They are specifically formulated and processed for a patient who has a reduced or compromised capacity to ingest, digest, absorb, or metabolize ordinary food or certain nutrients, or who has other special medically determined nutrient requirements that cannot be met by modification of a normal diet alone. Medical foods are not foods merely suggested by a physician as part of a general diet to manage the symptoms or reduce a disease such as for example, diabetes.

http://www.fda.gov/Food/GuidanceRegulation/GuidanceDocumentsRegulatoryInformation/MedicalFoods/ucm054048.htm (2016).

Country of Origin Labeling

The Farm Security and Rural Investment Act (2002 Farm Bill) and related laws amended the 1946 Agricultural Marketing Act (AMA) to include country of origin labeling (COOL) regulations. Shellfish and fish notification requirement started in April 2005 pursuant to the "Seafood Rule of 2005". Retailer notification effective September 30, 2008 required notification to consumers of the country of origin for certain covered commodities such as peanuts, pecans, macadamia nuts, fruits and vegetables and ginseng. The 2008 Farm Bill expanded the food commodities. The final rule effective March 16, 2009 was amended May 23, 2013 (78 FR 31367). The final rule contains definitions, consumer notification requirements and product marking, and recordkeeping responsibilities for retailers and suppliers of these are covered commodities: Beef, Lamb, Chicken, Pork, Goat Meat, Wild and Farm Raised Fish, Shellfish, Peanuts, Pecans, Macadamia Nuts, Perishable Agricultural Commodities, and Ginseng. Disclosure is not required if the covered commodity is an ingredient in a processed food item. Even domestically produced commodities must comply with COOL. The 2013 rule amended the definition of "retailer" to include any person subject to be licensed as a retailer under the Agricultural Commodities Act (ACA) and changed the labeling provisions for muscle cut covered commodities to provide consumers with more specific information. Notification formats include the following: ***Label, Sticker, twist tie, Product of the United States,*** or ***Grown in (specific country name).***

The WTO Appellate Body found that the COOL requirements for muscle cut meat commodities were inconsistent with U.S. obligations under the WTO agreement on Technical Barriers to Trade. The American Meat Institute (AMI), and other meat processors filed a lawsuit to prevent the 2013 COOL regulations from going into effect which the Court denied. However, as detailed below, the spending bill eliminated the requirement. In an ongoing clash primarily with Canada and Mexico, the WTO rejected the revised United States "country of origin" labeling rules for packaged meat cuts including ribs and steaks deeming it unfair. (Oct. 20, 2014; May 18, 2015). Finally, part of the 2016 Consolidated Appropriations Act eliminated the country of origin labeling for beef and pork. H.R. 2029 114th (2015-2016). Subsequently the *Ranchers-Cattlemen Action Legal Fund et al vs. United States Department of Agriculture (USDA) et al.,* filed a lawsuit (2:17-cv-00223 U.S. D.Ct. E.D. DC 2017). The court granted summary judgement for USDA.

https://www.congress.gov/bill/114th-congress/house-bill/2029/text

http://www.wto.org/english/tratop_e/dispu_e/cases_e/ds384_e.htm

CRITICAL ANALYSIS: Discuss the WTO decision for beef and pork products and the *Ranchers-Cattlemen Action Legal Fund* decision. Why did Congress eliminate COOL for beef and pork? Was the court correct in granting summary judgment in favor of USDA?

Natural Defined

According to FDA, for years the term 'natural' has meant that "nothing artificial or synthetic (including color additives) has been included in, or has been added to, a food that would not normally be expected to be in that food." Since 1993 FDA has declined to regulate natural and there is no specific definition. However, this may be changing as FDA published a notice in 2015 (See: 80 FR 69905, Nov. 12, 2015) regarding solicitation of comments on the use of "natural" claims on food labels. Possibly the reason, in part, is due to the use of the word "Natural" on labels in genetically modified (GM) products. Advocacy groups have argued that using "natural" on the label is misleading on products that have GM ingredients. Vermont enacted legislation to prevent the use of "Natural" on food labels that contains GM ingredients. FDA's policy was not intended to address food production methods, including pesticide use, food processing or manufacturing methods, such as thermal technologies, pasteurization, or irradiation.

The United States Department of Agriculture (USDA) does define natural as follows:

"A product containing no artificial ingredient or added color and is only minimally processed. Minimal processing means that the product was processed in a manner that does not fundamentally alter the product." The label must include a statement explaining the meaning of the term natural (such as "no artificial ingredients; minimally processed").

http://www.fda.gov/Food/GuidanceRegulation/GuidanceDocumentsRegulatoryInformation/LabelingNutrition/ucm456090.htm

USDA Standards for Livestock and Meat Marketing Claims, Naturally Raised Claim for Livestock and the Meat and Meat Products Derived from Such Livestock *Federal Register Online via GPO Access wais.access.gpo.gov, January 21, 2009 (Volume 74, Number 12) Notices Page 3541-3545 Authority: 7 U.S.C. 1621-1627.*

Claim and Standard *Naturally Raised—Livestock used for the production of meat and meat products that have been raised entirely without growth promotants, antibiotics (except for iono-phores used as coccidiostats for parasite control), and have never been fed animal (mammalian, avian, or aquatic) by-products derived from the slaughter/harvest processes, including meat and fat, animal waste materials (e.g., manure and litter), and aquatic by-products (e.g., fishmeal and fish oil). All products labeled with a naturally raised marketing claim must incorporate information explicitly stating that animals have been raised in a manner that meets the following conditions: (1) No growth promotants were administered to the animals; (2) no antibiotics (other than ionophores used to prevent parasitism) were administered to the animal; and (3) no animal by-products were fed to the animals. If ionophores used only to prevent parasitism were administered to the animals, they may be labeled with the naturally raised marketing claims if that fact is explicitly noted.*

NOTE: ***In re Frito-Lay N. Am., Inc. All Nat. Litig., No. 12-MD-2413 RRM RLM (E.D.N.Y. Aug. 29, 2013).*** **In the settlement, the company agreed to eliminate claims that the products are made with all-natural ingredients and has agreed not to label them as "all natural" if the product includes GMO ingredients. Further, during the next five years, Frito-Lay will not market them as "all natural" for any reason unless federal regulations permit the ingredients for use in "natural" products. Any "non-GMO" claim requires certification by an independent organization.**

CRITICAL ANALYSIS: How should FDA define the term "Natural" and under what circumstances should this term be permitted on labeling? Draft such a rule.

Healthy

Recently, perhaps due in part to the Kind® warning letter (March 2015) and subsequent close out letter by FDA (2016), the FDA is evaluating the term *healthy.* Specifically, FDA stated:
"In our discussions with KIND, we understood the company's position as wanting to use "healthy and tasty" as part of its corporate philosophy, as opposed to using "healthy" in the context of a nutrient

content claim. The FDA evaluates the label as a whole and has indicated that in this instance it does not object." *http://www.fda.gov/Food/IngredientsPackagingLabeling/LabelingNutrition/ucm500184.htm*

The current regulations are linked below; however, this could change based on FDA's stance. See: PART 101 -- FOOD LABELING Subpart D--Specific Requirements for Nutrient Content Claims Sec. 101.65 Implied nutrient content claims and related label statements. 21 C.F.R. 101.65(d) (2) (i) (use of the term healthy on food labeling) and Sec. 101.62 (b) (2) (B). Nutrient content claims for fat, fatty acid, and cholesterol content of foods (related to the Kind warning letter).
https://www.accessdata.fda.gov/scripts/cdrh/cfdocs/cfcfr/CFRSearch.cfm?fr=101.65
CRITICAL ANALYSIS: Detail how FDA should address this issue especially in terms of preventing consumer deception in accordance with the FDCA.

Organic

The Organic Food Production Act of 1990 established national standards for agricultural products labeled as organic. See: 7 U.S.C. section 6501-22. A product must consist of 95% organic ingredients if a seller wants to use a claim that the product is "organic".

USDA Pasture Rule for Organic Farms—The Department of Agriculture's National Organic Program issued a rule in 2010 that farm animals must spend a minimum of 120 days per year in pastures in order to be considered organic.

CRITICAL ANALYSIS: Using USDA as an example, should the FDCA be amended to specifically define and therefore regulate organic?

Claims—"GMO-free", Hormones and Antibiotics

"GMO-free"—USDA developed a program in 2015 for food companies that wish to label products as free of genetically modified ingredients or *"GMO-free"*. Companies would voluntarily request verification of a "GMO-free" marketing claim through the USDA Agriculture Marketing Service (AMS) that oversees the Process Verified Program (PVP).

No Hormones—Pork or Poultry: Hormones are not allowed in raising hogs or poultry Therefore, the claim *"no hormones added"* cannot be used on the labels of pork or poultry unless it is followed by a statement that says *"Federal regulations prohibit the use of hormones."*

No Hormones—Beef: The term *"no hormones administered"* may be approved for use on the label of beef products if sufficient documentation is provided to the Agency by the producer showing no hormones have been used in raising the animals.

Antibiotics—Red Meat and Poultry: The terms *"no antibiotics added"* may be used on labels for meat or poultry products if sufficient documentation is provided by the producer to USDA demonstrating that the animals were raised without antibiotics.

CRITICAL ANALYSIS: How should USDA's Food Safety and Inspection Service enforce these claims statements? What is "sufficient documentation"?
http://www.foodsafetynews.com/2012/07/usda-looking-at-antibiotics-claims-on-meat-labels/.

Nanotechnology—Guidance
http://www.fda.gov/Food/GuidanceRegulation/GuidanceDocumentsRegulatoryInformation/IngredientsAdditivesGRASPackaging/ucm300661.htm

The term nanotechnology has become increasingly popular in the life sciences regulated community. Nanotechnology material is extremely small matter and cannot be seen with a regular microscope. FDA issued a final guidance: *Final Guidance for Industry: Assessing the Effects of Significant Manufacturing Process Changes, Including Emerging Technologies, on the Safety and Regulatory Status of Food Ingredients and Food Contact Substances, Including Food Ingredients that Are Color Additives* (2014). The final guidance document addresses the use of nanotechnology and alerts manufacturers to the potential impact of any significant manufacturing process change, including changes involving nanotechnology, regarding the safety and regulatory status of food substances. The guidance explains considerations for determining whether a significant man-ufacturing process change for a food substance already in the market affects the identity, safety, or regulatory status of the use of the food substance, and possibly warrants a regulatory submission to FDA. In terms of regulation, FDA still has regulatory authority to ensure purity and safety of the food supply. Yet, the question remains as to the role of FTC in enforcement regarding advertising issues.

CRITICAL ANALYSIS: What role should FTC have in the regulation of advertising for food products that contain nanomaterial? Is disclosure warranted despite the lack of a specific regulation?

Labeling Guidance Example—Honey

http://www.fda.gov/Food/GuidanceRegulation/GuidanceDocumentsRegulatoryInfor-mation/LabelingNutrtion/ucm389501.htm?source=govdelivery&utm_me-dium=email&utm_source=govdelivery#intro

Possibly due to the adulteration of honey from foreign countries and/or perhaps due to increased use of other sweeteners, FDA issued a draft guidance in February 2014 for industry entitled "Proper Labeling of Honey and Honey Products" to help ensure that honey and honey products are not adulterated or misbranded under sections 402 and 403 of the Federal Food, Drug, and Cosmetic Act (21 U.S.C. secs. 342 and 343, respectively). Back in 2006 (March 8, 2006), the American Beekeeping Federation and several other honey-related associations sub-mitted a citizen petition requesting that FDA adopt a U.S. standard of identity for honey based on the 2001 Revised Codex Alimentarius Commission's Standard for Honey. The petitioners asserted that a U.S. standard of identity for honey would achieve the following goals: "(1) Clarify what the term "honey" means with respect to the food's composition and therefore promote honesty and fair dealing in the interest of consumers; (2) combat economic adultera-tion of honey by aiding enforcement and industry compliance; and (3) promote honesty and fair dealing within the food trade in general, where pure honey is used as an ingredient in other food." FDA denied the petition by letter dated October 5, 2011, because the petition did not provide reasonable grounds for FDA to adopt the Codex standard for honey. A product that is blend or a mixture of honey and another sweetener cannot be labeled with the common or usual name "honey." The name of the food on the label must be sufficiently described to distinguish it from simply "honey" (21 CFR 102.5(a)).

NOTE: See *Volume III: Enforcement*—"Honeygate".

CRITICAL ANALYSIS: Review the "Proper Labeling of Honey and Honey Products" guidance and determine if the guidance adequately addresses adulteration and misbrand-ing under 21 U.S. C. sec. 342 and sec. 343. See link below.

http://www.fda.gov/Food/GuidanceRegulation/GuidanceDocumentsRegulatoryInfor-mation/LabelingNutrtion/ucm389501.htm?source=govdelivery&utm_me-dium=email&utm_source=govdelivery#intro

Chapter 5: Hydrogenated Fat, *Trans* Fat, Additives, Arsenic, BPA, Acrylamide, Irradiation, and Botanicals

Partially Hydrogenated Oil and *Trans* Fatty Acids—GRAS Removal

http://www.fda.gov/Food/IngredientsPackagingLabeling/FoodAdditivesIngredients/ucm449162.htm
https://www.federalregister.gov/documents/2015/06/17/2015-14883/final-determination-regarding-partially-hydrogenated-oils

FDA issued a milestone determination in 2015 that partially hydrogenated oils (PHOs) are not "generally recognized as safe" (GRAS) for use in food. See: 80 FR 34650 (June 17, 2015). A "declaratory order", (which has the "force and effect" of a rule), was issued pursuant to 5 U.S.C. 554(e) (section 5(d) of the Administrative Procedure Act (APA)). PHOs are the primary dietary source of artificial *trans* fat in processed foods. There is a phase out program over use of these oils in the food supply and removal from the United States food supply. FDA estimates that annually approximately 7,000 deaths from heart disease will be prevented. The *Federal Register* notice concerning hydrogenated fat was published November 8, 2013 (78 FR 67169) and the comment period was extended until March 8, 2014. FDA received 6000 comments and 4500 letters in response to the November 2013 notice about the FDA tentative determination regarding the GRAS elimination. FDA found that there is no longer agreement that partially hydrogenated oils (PHOs), the main dietary source of industrially-produced *trans* fatty acids (IP-TFA) are generally recognized as safe (GRAS) for any use in human food.

Years ago, studies revealed that the consumption of *trans* fatty acids contribute to increased blood LDL cholesterol, known as the "bad" cholesterol, thereby raising the risk of coronary heart disease. *Trans* fatty acids or *trans* fat are made through the process of hydrogenation that solidifies liquid oils. Types of foods that may contain *trans* fatty acids include vegetable shortenings, some margarines, some cookies and some snack foods. The Center for Science in the Public Interest (CSPI) filed a citizen's petition in 1994 (docket number 94-P0036/CP1), which addressed the issue of dietary *trans* fats and the link to coronary heart disease. A proposed rule was published in the Federal Register (64 FR 62746 November 17, 1999) with comment extension to April 17, 2000 (65 FR 7806); however, the comment period was reopened until January 19, 2001 (65 FR 75887 December 5, 2000). The final rule, (68 FR 41434 July 11, 2003) effective January 1, 2006, required the declaration of *trans fatty acids* or *trans fats* on nutrition labels of conventional foods and dietary supplements. However, since implementation of the *trans* fat regulation, FDA found a significant number of products still contained PHOs.

The FDA Order specific to PHO ban means that food manufacturers would no longer be permitted to sell PHOs, either directly or as ingredients in another food product, without prior FDA approval for use as a food additive. A three-year phase-out period for reformulation and product relabeling was permitted with compliance by June 18, 2018.

https://www.fda.gov/Food/IngredientsPackagingLabeling/FoodAdditivesIngredients/ucm449162.htm?source=govdelivery&utm_medium=email&utm_source=govdelivery

NOTE: The World Health Organization (WHO) urged a global ban on trans-fats. *http://www.who.int/news-room/detail/14-05-2018-who-plan-to-eliminate-industrially-produced-trans-fatty-acids-from-global-food-supply*. See also, See: NY Times, A8 (May 15, 2018).

CRITICAL ANALYSIS: Evaluate why FDA determined that PHOs are "Not Generally Recognized as Safe" (NOT GRAS) effectively banning the sale of PHOs directly or as an ingredient(s) in food products. *https://www.regulations.gov/docket?D=FDA-2013-N-1317*

Food Additives Regulation

http://www.fda.gov/food/ingredientspackaginglabeling/foodadditivesingredients/ucm094211.htm (edited)

The authority for the FDA to regulate additives originates from the Federal Food, Drug and Cosmetic Act (FDCA) of 1938. The Food Additives Amendment to the FDCA, passed in 1958, obligates food manufacturers to prove the safety of an additive. The term "food additive", in part, includes "any substance the intended use which results or may reasonably be expected to result directly or indirectly in its becoming a component or otherwise affecting the characteristics of any food." Under the FDCA, "food additive" is defined under § 201(s), 21 U.S.C. § 321(s).

The Food Additives Amendment requires FDA approval for the use of an additive prior to its inclusion in food. It also requires the manufacturer to prove an additive's safety for the intended use. The Food Additives Amendment exempted two groups of substances from the food additive regulation process:

- ✓ *Prior-sanctioned substances* <u>and</u>
- ✓ *GRAS substances.*

All substances that FDA or the USDA had determined were safe for use in specific food prior to the 1958 amendment were designated as prior-sanctioned substances. Examples of prior-sanctioned substances are sodium nitrite and potassium nitrite used to preserve luncheon meats. A second category of substances excluded from the food additive regulation process are generally recognized as safe or GRAS substances. GRAS substances are those whose use is generally recognized by experts as safe, based on their extensive history of use in food before 1958 or based on published scientific evidence. Salt, sugar, spices, vitamins and monosodium glutamate are classified as GRAS substances, along with several hundred other substances. Manufacturers may request FDA to review the use of a substance to determine if it is GRAS. Since 1958, FDA and USDA have continued to monitor all prior sanctioned and GRAS substances in light of new scientific information. If new evidence suggests that a GRAS or prior sanctioned substance may be unsafe, FDA can prohibit its use or require further studies to determine its safety. Under sections 201(s) and 409 of the Act, and FDA's implementing regulations in 21 CFR 170.3 and 21 CFR 170.30, the use of a food substance may be GRAS either through scientific procedures or, for a substance used in food before 1958, through experience based on common use in food.

- ✓ Under 21 CFR 170.30(b), general recognition of safety through scientific procedures requires the same quantity and quality of scientific evidence as is required to obtain approval of the substance as a food additive and ordinarily is based upon published studies, which may be corroborated by unpublished studies and other data and information.
- ✓ Under 21 CFR 170.30(c) and 170.3(f), general recognition of safety through experience based on common use in foods requires a substantial history of consumption for food use by a significant number of consumers.

The Food Additives Amendment includes a provision that prohibits the approval of an additive if it is found to cause cancer in humans or animals. This clause is often referred to as the *Delaney Clause*, named for its Congressional sponsor, Representative James Delaney. Good Manufacturing Practices regulations (GMP) limit the amount of food and color additives used in foods.

http://www.fda.gov/food/ingredientspackaginglabeling/foodadditivesingredients/ucm094211.htm

Unsafe Food Additives-Flavorings and Caffeine in Malt Beverages
Flavorings
https://www.federalregister.gov/documents/2018/10/09/2018-21807/food-additive-regulations-synthetic-flavoring-agents-and-adjuvants

FDA amended the food additives regulations in 2018 (83 FR 50490 effective Oct. 9, 2018) to no longer the use of benzophenone, ethyl acrylate, eugenyl methyl ether, myrcene, pulegone, and pyridine as synthetic flavoring substances for use in food. According to FDA, the petitioners, provided data which demonstrated the additives induced cancer in animals. Further, FDA amended the food additive regulations to no longer permit the use of benzophenone as a plasticizer in rubber articles intended for repeated use in contact with food. Since the use of styrene as a synthetic flavoring substance has been permanently and completely abandoned the FDA denied that part of the petition as it is a moot issue.

See: 21 CFR 172.515 https://www.gpo.gov/fdsys/pkg/CFR-2018-title21-vol3/xml/CFR-2018-title21-vol3-sec172-515.xml

CRITICAL ANALYSIS: Review the petition and evaluate why FDA agreed to prohibit the use of these additives. *https://www.federalregister.gov/documents/2018/10/09/2018-21807/food-additive-regulations-synthetic-flavoring-agents-and-adjuvants*

Caffeine in Alcoholic Malt Beverages

http://www.fda.gov/Food/IngredientsPackagingLabeling/FoodAdditivesIngredients/ucm190366.htm

FDA warned four companies that the caffeine added to their alcoholic malt beverages is an "unsafe food additive". According to FDA, some manufacturers failed to demonstrate that the direct addition of caffeine to the malt beverages is "generally recognized as safe" or GRAS and warning letters were sent to:

Charge Beverages Corp.—Core High Gravity HG Green, Core High Gravity HG Orange, and Lemon Lime Core Spiked; New Century Brewing Co., LLC—Moonshot; United Brands Company, Inc.—Joose and Maxand Phusion Projects, LLC (doing business as Drink Four Brewing Co.)—Four Loko.

See: ***Companies stop shipping 7 caffeine-alcohol drinks***

discussing removal: *http://www.cnn.com/2010/HEALTH/11/24/alcohol.caffeine.drinks/index.html*

NOTE: See *Volume X* for further discussion of Caffeine; Highly Concentrated Caffeine in Dietary Supplements: Guidance for Industry (April 2018).

https://www.fda.gov/downloads/Food/GuidanceRegulation/GuidanceDocumentsRegulatoryInformation/UCM604319.pdf

See also: FTC legal actions and modified Order 02/12/2013: *FTC Requires Packaging Changes for Fruit-Flavored Four Loko Malt Beverage 10/03/2011*

https://www.ftc.gov/news-events/press-releases/2014/07/ftc-approves-modified-final-order-four-loko-deceptive-advertising Final Order 2014

https://www.ftc.gov/system/files/documents/cases/140725phusionorder.pdf FTC Opinion\

See also: Assurance of Voluntary Compliance and Voluntary Discontinuance AOD No. 14-075 *http://www.ag.ny.gov/pdfs/Phusioin%20Projects,%20LLC%20AOD.PDF*

CRITICAL ANALYSIS: According to FDA, the manufacturers of these products failed to demonstrate that the direct addition of caffeine to the malt beverages is "generally recognized as safe". Do you agree with this assessment? Read the FTC order link above and integrate.

Color Additives

http://www.fda.gov/forindustry/coloradditives/default.htm (edited)

Color additives date as far back as 5000 B.C. FDA considers a color additive as "any dye, pigment or substance that can impart color when added or applied to a food, drug, cosmetic or to the human body." The only substances that may be used to color foods, drugs, cosmetics and medical devices are those that are approved. The FDCA stipulated mandatory color additive certification. FDA classifies color additives in two specific categories: colors from petroleum (coal tar), and colors that are exempted from certification which are obtained principally from mineral, plant or animal sources. In 1960, the Color Additive Amendments to the FDCA placed color additives on a "provisional" list and required further testing using up-to-date procedures. Under the FDCA, color additives, except for coal tar hair dyes, are subject to FDA approval prior to use in food, drugs, or cosmetics, or in medical devices that come in contact with human and animals bodies for a significant time period. Color additives exempt from certification are required to pass stringent safety standards prior to being permitted for use in foods.

Known as the *Delaney Amendment* as referenced above, the addition of adding any food substance that has been shown to cause cancer in animals or man regardless of the dose is prohibited under the FDCA. FDA requires foreign and domestic manufacturers of certain colors to submit samples from each batch of color produced. Scientists then test each sample to confirm that each batch of the color is within established specifications. Manufacturers are required to remit a user fee for each pound of color the agency certifies.

Color Additives Regulation Under 21 CFR

The term color additive is defined under 21 U.S.C. § 321(t) under the FDCA; however, there are specific parts and sections of 21 CFR that pertain to color additives:

- ➤ CFR 21 Part 70 Color Additives;
- ➤ CFR 21 Part 71 Color Additive Petitions;
- ➤ CFR 21 Part 73 Listing of Color Additives Exempt from Certification;
- ➤ CFR 21 Part 74 Listing of Color Additives Subject to Certification;
- ➤ CFR 21 Part 80 Color Additive Certification;
- ➤ CFR 21 Part 81 General Specifications and General Restrictions for Provisional Color Additives for Use in Foods, Drugs, and Cosmetics; and
- ➤ CFR 21 Part 82 Listing of Certified Provisionally Listed Colors and Specifications.

Color Additive Terminology

- ➤ Allura Red AC—the common name for uncertified FD&C Red No. 40.
- ➤ Certifiable color additives—colors manufactured from petroleum and coal sources listed in the CFR for use in foods, drugs, cosmetics, and medical devices.
- ➤ Coal-tar dyes—coloring agents originally derived from coal sources.
- ➤ D&C—a prefix designating that a certifiable color has been approved for use in drugs and cosmetics.
- ➤ Erythrosine—the common name of FD&C Red No. 3.
- ➤ Exempt color additives—colors derived primarily from plant, animal and mineral (other than coal and petroleum) sources that are exempt from FDA certification.
- ➤ Ext. D&C—a prefix designating that a certifiable color may be used only in externally applied drugs and cosmetics.
- ➤ FD&C—a prefix designating that a certified color can be used in foods, drugs or cosmetics.
- ➤ Indigotine—the common name for uncertified FD&C Blue No. 2.
- ➤ Lakes—water-insoluble forms of certifiable colors that are more stable than straight dyes and ideal for a product in which leaching of the color is undesirable (coated tablets and hard candies, for example).
- ➤ Permanent listing—a list of allowable colors determined by tests to be safe for human consumption under regulatory provisions.
- ➤ Provisional listing—a list of colors, originally numbering about 200, that FDA allows to continue to be used pending acceptable safety data;
- ➤ Straight dye—certifiable colors that dissolve in water and are manufactured as powders, granules, liquids, or other special forms (used in beverages, baked goods, and confections, for example); and
- ➤ Tartrazine—a common name for uncertified FD&C Yellow No. 5.

Arsenic

Arsenic is found in some food as either inorganic or organic. Inorganic forms of arsenic are the harmful types and organic forms of arsenic are basically harmless. Both forms of arsenic have been found in soil; therefore, there may be arsenic in certain food and beverage products such as apple juice and rice. Until 1970 arsenic-based pesticides were regularly used in United States agricultural production. Trace levels of organic and inorganic forms of arsenic can be detected in some agribusiness settings. Consequently, there could be arsenic in certain food and beverage products such as apple juice and rice. Although FDA has been monitoring the levels of arsenic in foods for several years, testing has increased. Testing is a step in the right direction to understand possible arsenic-related risks associated with the consumption of certain foods and remediate if necessary. FDA needs to issue regulatory measures to address possible arsenic-related risks associated with the consumption of these foods.

Proposed "Action Level" for Arsenic in Apple Juice—Consumer advocates have rallied for regulation of arsenic in apple juice. After years of debate, dialog and testing FDA issued a guidance albeit in draft format in 2013 about acceptable levels in apple juice. According to FDA, the agency does not have clear data that demonstrates organic juice is better than non-organic apple juice in terms of arsenic levels. This is due to the soil where apple juice is grown. FDA published a draft guidance in the Federal Register July 15, 2013 (78 FR 42086). The draft guidance proposes an action level of 10 parts per billion (ppb) for inorganic arsenic in apple juice, which is the same level set by the U.S. Environmental Protection Agency for arsenic in drinking water.

Rice and Rice Products—Arsenic Levels

http://www.fda.gov/Food/FoodborneIllnessContaminants/Metals/ucm319870.htm?source=govdelivery&utm_medium=email&utm_source=govdelivery

http://www.fda.gov/Food/FoodborneIllnessContaminants/Metals/ucm319870.htm

The FDA proposed an action level or limit of 100 parts per billion (ppb) for inorganic arsenic in infant rice cereal based on FDA's evaluation of scientific information and aims to lessen infant exposure to inorganic arsenic in 2106. Future plans concern assessment of the potential health risk from long-term exposure to the arsenic in rice and foods made with this grain.

CRITICAL ANALYSIS: Arsenic in foods remains controversial yet should FDA institute rule-making? Would a guidance document suffice in the interim?

http://www.foodsafety.gov/blog/2016/04/arsenic-in-rice.html?utm_source=GovDelivery&utm_medium=Email&utm_campaign=FoodSafetySL

Food Packaging and "Bisphenol A"

Controversy issues such as bisphenol A, more commonly known as BPA, a chemical used in food packaging developed over the years. For example, the Natural Resources Defense Council petitioned FDA to amend its regulations on its use in plastic bottles and linings of cans. In 2012, FDA determined that the agency would not ban the use of BPA in food packaging.

A final rule was published in 2013, 21 CFR 175.300, amended the food additive regulations to prohibit the use of bisphenol A or BPA-based epoxy resins as coatings in infant formula packaging because this use had been abandoned. This was a formality as FDA clarified that the action was based solely on a determination of abandonment and unrelated to the safety of BPA.

http://www.accessdata.fda.gov/scripts/cdrh/cfdocs/cfcfr/cfrsearch.cfm?fr=175.300

https://www.niehs.nih.gov/health/topics/agents/sya-bpa/index.cfm

Acrylamide

Acrylamide in food is a concern due to the human carcinogen potential. It is present as a by-product of high temperature cooking that is greater than 120°C or 248°F. The World Health Organization and the Food and Agriculture Organization convened an expert panel in 2002 to study acrylamide. In 2003, FDA finalized a plan for acrylamide assessment and in 2004 devised an action plan concerning acrylamide. FDA published a request for comments in the Federal Register Notice: *Acrylamide in Food; Request for Comments and for Scientific Data and Information* (74 FR 43134 August 26, 2009). Due to overriding concern, in 2016, FDA issued a final guidance on **How to Reduce Acrylamide in Certain Foods** to help the food industry decrease levels of acrylamide in certain foods.

NOTE: See: Acrylamide in Food and Cancer Risk *http://www.cancer.gov/cancertopics/factsheet/Risk/acrylamide-in-food*

CRITICAL ANALYSIS: Should FDA be more proactive concerning acrylamide and BHA (bisphenol A)? Is the final guidance issued concerning Acrylamide sufficient?

See: *http://www.fda.gov/Food/NewsEvents/ConstituentUpdates/ucm374601.htm*

Food Irradiation

http://www.fda.gov/food/ingredientspackaginglabeling/irradiatedfoodpackaging/ucm261680.htm

Food irradiation, a process in which food is exposed to a specific amount of radiant energy to kill harmful bacteria products such as E. coli *O157:H7*, campylo-bacter, and salmonella is controversial in terms of food safety concerns. The irradiation process controls insects and parasites, reduces spoilage, and inhibits ripening and sprouting. According to FDA, the agency has evaluated the safety of this technology for more than 40 years and has found irradiation safe under a variety of conditions. Consequently, FDA has approved its use for many foods such as meat, poultry, fresh vegetables and spices. FDA requires that irradiated foods include labeling with either the statement "treated with radiation" or "treated by irradiation" as well as the symbol for irradiation. The following are the FDA approved foods for irradiation:

> *Beef and Pork, Poultry, Molluscan Shellfish, (e.g., oysters, clams, mussels, scallops, crab, shrimp, lobster, crayfish and prawns) *, Shell Eggs, Fresh Fruits and Vegetables, Lettuce and Spinach, Spices and Seasonings, and Seeds for Sprouting (e.g., for alfalfa sprouts).*

NOTE: * Final Rule—*Irradiation in the Production, Processing and Handling of Food*
FDA amended the food additive regulations in April 2014 to permit the safe use of ionizing radiation on crustaceans (e.g., crab, shrimp, lobster, crayfish, and prawns) to control food-borne pathogens and extend the shelf life. This action was in response to a food additive petition submitted by the National Fisheries Institute.

FDA regulates sources of irradiation (the equipment used) for foods as "food additives" that require approval before being allowed on the market. FDA approves a source of irradiation for use on food only after it has determined that irradiating the food is safe at a maximum dose specified by FDA. FDA continues to evaluate the safe use of irradiation in additional foods. A final rule was issued in 2008 which permits the use of irradiation to make fresh iceberg lettuce and fresh spinach safer and last longer without spoiling. Despite proactive efforts, multi-state outbreaks of Listeria, Salmonella and *E coli* O157:H7 illnesses linked to prepackaged salad meals has occurred as recent as 2018. FDA along with USDA's Food Safety and Inspection Service (FSIS), the Centers for Disease Control and Prevention (CDC), and state and local officials investigated the outbreak.

CRITICAL ANALYSIS: See links below concerning outbreaks. Will the regulations under the *Food Safety Modernization Act* preventive controls for produce for example solve these food safety difficulties? Recommend other regulatory measures.
See: Salmonella outbreaks *https://www.cdc.gov/salmonella/outbreaks-2018.html*
See: *EColi* Romaine Lettuce Outbreak *https://www.cdc.gov/ecoli/2018/o157h7-04-18/index.html*

Botanicals

Are botanicals added to foods deemed "unsafe additives"? Further, are botanicals added to conventional food the end result of a product classification conversion from a food to a drug which would then necessitate pre-approval? This issue remains complex and controversial. The FDA's concern is that some herbal and other botanical ingredients added to conventional foods may cause the food to be adulterated because these added ingredients are not being used in accordance with an approved food additive regulation and may not be generally recognized as safe (GRAS) for their intended use.

A substance is exempt from the definition of a food additive and consequently from pre-market approval, if, among other reasons, it is GRAS by qualified experts under the conditions that the substance is safe for its intended use. Several years ago, FDA sent a letter to manufacturers about the addition of botanicals added to conventional food. The link to the FDA correspondence to manufacturers is below.

http://www.fda.gov/Food/GuidanceRegulation/GuidanceDocumentsRegulatoryInformation/DietarySupplements/ucm103443.htm

http://www.fda.gov/Food/RecallsOutbreaksEmergencies/SafetyAlertsAdvisories/ucm111188.htm
NOTE: FDA issued a guidance titled: *Considerations Regarding Substances Added to Foods, Including Beverages and Dietary Supplements* in 2014 due to concerns about.
http://www.fda.gov/Food/GuidanceRegulation/GuidanceDocumentsRegulatoryInformation/IngredientsAdditivesGRASPackaging/ucm381315.htm#_Toc358003922

CRITICAL ANALYSIS: Review the guidance above. How should products termed "botanical" be classified and regulated—as a food, dietary supplement, drug or perhaps dual classification? See *Volume V Human Drugs Regulation*, Chapter 2.

Chapter 6: Food Allergens, Gluten-Free, and Biotechnology GMO's

Food Allergens

Over the years, undeclared allergens in foods have presented a serious public health risk and their presence has become more prevalent. Further, the ingestion of food allergens could be life-threatening to certain people. According to FDA, the number of recalls has risen significantly. In response, the Food Allergen Labeling and Consumer Protection Act of 2004 (Allergen Labeling Act) (FALCPA) (Pub. L. 108-282) was enacted. The Allergen Labeling Act requires a plain English listing of any ingredients that contain protein from the following foods: milk, eggs, fish, crustacean shellfish, tree nuts peanuts, wheat or soybeans. FDA issued a final guidance (see below) concerning labeling of food allergens such as soybeans, eggs, meat, fish and poultry.

Final Guidance Document—Food Allergen Labeling

http://www.fda.gov/food/guidanceregulation/guidancedocumentsregulatoryinformation/allergens/ucm059116.htm (4th ed. 2004) (edited and modified in part)

The FDCA requires that a food containing two or more ingredients must state each ingredient by its common or usual name (except that spices, flavorings, and colors could be declared as a class.) However, consumers might not recognize the common or usual name of an ingredient and might not recognize that certain ingredients contain or are derived from a food allergen. This situation led, at least in part, to the enactment of the Food Allergen Labeling and Consumer Protection Act of 2004 (FALCPA) (Pub. L.108-282). A company and its management may be subject to civil sanctions, criminal penalties, or both under the FDCA for noncompliance.

Definition of "Major food allergen"—an ingredient that is one of the following five foods or from one of the following three food groups or is an ingredient that contains protein from one of the following: Milk, Egg, Fish, Crustacean shellfish, Tree nuts, Wheat, Peanuts and Soybeans.

Declaration of ingredients from the three food groups designated as "major food allergens (i.e., tree nuts, fish, and Crustacean shellfish"). The specific type of nut must be declared (e.g., almonds, pecans, or walnuts), the type of fish must be declared for fish (e.g., bass, flounder, or cod) and Crustacean shellfish (crab, lobster, or shrimp).

"Contains" statement—If a "Contains" statement is used on a food label, the statement must include the names of the food sources of all major food allergens used as ingredients in the packaged food. For example, if "sodium caseinate," "whey," "egg yolks," and "natural peanut flavor" are declared in a product's ingredients list, any "Contains" statement appearing on the label immediately after or next to that statement is required to identify all three sources of the major food allergens present—"Contains milk, egg, peanuts" in the same type (i.e., print or font) size as that used for the ingredient list.

Advisory Statements—The FALCPA does not require food manufacturers to label their products with advisory statements, such as "may contain [allergen]" or "processed in a facility that also processes [allergen]." FALCPA does not address the use of advisory labeling, including statements describing the potential presence of unintentional ingredients in food products resulting from the food manufacturing process. Yet, any advisory statement such as "may contain [allergen]" must be truthful and not misleading.

Unintentional addition to a food as the result of cross-contact—FALCPA's labeling requirements do not apply to major food allergens that are unintentionally added to a food as the result of cross-contact. "Cross-contact" occurs when a residue or other trace amount of an allergenic food is unintentionally incorporated into another food that is not intended to contain that allergenic food. Cross-contact could occur from growing and harvesting crops, shared storage, transportation, or production equipment.

Section 201(qq) of the FDCA defines the term "major food allergen" to include "tree nuts." In addition to the three examples provided in section 201(qq) (almonds, pecans, and walnuts), the following are considered "tree nuts" for purposes of section 201(qq). The "common or usual name" should be used to declare the specific type of nut as required by section 403(w)(2).

Common or usual name	Scientific name
Almond	*Prunus dulcis* (Rosaceae)
Beech nut	*Fagus* spp.(Fagaceae)
Brazil nut	*Bertholletia excels* (Lecythidaceae)
Butternut	*Juglans cinerea*(Juglandaceae)
Cashew	*Anacardium occidentale* (Anacardiaceae)
Chestnut (Chinese, American, European, Seguin)	*Castanea* spp (Fagaceae)
Chinquapin	*Castanea pumila* (Fagaceae)
Coconut	*Cocos nucifera* L.(Arecaceae (alt. Palmae))
Filbert/Hazelnut	*Corylus* spp.(Betulaceae)
Ginko nut	*Ginkgo biloba* L. (Ginkgoaceae)
Hickory nut	*Carya* spp.(Juglandaceae)
Lichee nut	*Litchi chinensis* Sonn. Sapindaceae
Macadamia nut/Bush nut	*Macadamia* spp.(Proteaceae)
Pecan	*Carya illinoensis* (Juglandaceae)
Pine nut/Pinon nut	*Pinus* spp.(Pineaceae)
Pili nut	*Canarium ovatum* Engl. in A. DC.(Burseraceae)
Pistachio	*Pistacia vera* L.(Anacardiaceae)
Sheanut	*Vitellaria paradoxa* C.F. Gaertn.(Sapotaceae)
Walnut (English, Persian, Black, Japanese, California), Heartnut, Butternut	*Juglans* spp.(Juglandaceae)

Food Allergy Management—Educational Setting

Improving Capacity to Prevent Food Safety Problems, under the Food Safety Modernization Act, Subchapter I, explicitly addresses food allergy management in the educational setting, 21 U.S. C. § 2205 (effective January 4, 2011). Section 2205, *Food allergy and Anaphylaxis Management* provides for the following voluntary guidelines:

(i) develop voluntary guidelines to design plans for individuals to manage the risk of food allergy and anaphylaxis in schools and early childhood education programs; and

(ii) availability of the voluntary guidelines to local educational agencies, schools, early childhood education programs, and other interested persons.

Gluten-Free Food Labeling Final Rule

https://www.federalregister.gov/articles/2013/08/05/2013-18813/food-labeling-gluten-free-labeling-of-foods

FDA issued a final rule on *"Gluten-Free Labeling of Foods"* (GF) on July 30, 2013 (proposed rule 2007) that defines the term "gluten-free" for the voluntary use in food labeling. Prior to the final rule, in 2011 FDA issued—*"Health Hazard Assessment for Gluten Exposure in Individuals with Celiac Disease: Determination of Tolerable Daily Intake Levels and Levels of Concern for Gluten"*. According to FDA, approximately one percent of the United States population is estimated to have Celiac Disease (CD), which is a type of digestive disorder that involves an abnormal immune response to the consumption of gluten. Eating foods that contain gluten triggers the production of antibodies in persons who have CD, which then attack the lining of the small intestine resulting in damage. Over time, with continual exposure to gluten, the body is unable to properly absorb nutrients from foods, which can lead to vitamin and mineral deficiencies. Persons with CD are also at higher risk of developing other serious health problems such as growth issues, short stature, infertility, and intestinal cancers. Below are excerpts of the final rule.

Final Rule—Food and Drug Administration 21 CFR Part 101[Docket No. FDA-2005-N-0404] RIN 0910-AG84; **Compliance Date:** Final Rule Compliance Aug. 5, 2014.

SUMMARY: The Food and Drug Administration (FDA) issued a final rule to define the term "gluten-free" for voluntary use in the labeling of foods. The final rule defines the term "gluten-free" to mean that the food bearing the claim does not contain an ingredient that is a gluten-containing grain (e.g., spelt wheat); an ingredient that is derived from a gluten-containing grain and that has not been processed to remove gluten (e.g., wheat flour); or an ingredient that is derived from a gluten-containing grain and that has been processed to remove gluten (e.g., wheat starch), if the use of that ingredient results in the presence of 20 parts per million (ppm) or more gluten in the food (i.e., 20 milligrams (mg) or more gluten per kilogram (kg) of food); or inherently does not contain gluten; and that any unavoidable presence of gluten in the food is below 20 ppm gluten (i.e., below 20 mg gluten per kg of food). A food that bears the claim "no gluten," "free of gluten," or "without gluten" in its labeling and fails to meet the requirements for a "gluten-free" claim will be deemed to be misbranded. In addition, a food whose labeling includes the term "wheat" in the ingredient list or in a separate "Contains wheat" statement as required by a section of the Federal Food, Drug, and Cosmetic Act (the FD&C Act) and also bears the claim "gluten-free" will be deemed to be misbranded unless its labeling also bears additional language clarifying that the wheat has been processed to allow the food to meet FDA requirements for a "gluten-free" claim. Establishing a definition of the term "gluten-free" and uniform conditions for its use in food labeling will help ensure that individuals with celiac disease are not misled and are provided with truthful and accurate information with respect to foods so labeled. Final Rule issued under the Food Allergen Labeling and Consumer Protection Act of 2004 (FALCPA).

The final rule defines and sets conditions on the use of the term "gluten-free" as follows:

• Foods that inherently do not contain gluten (e.g., raw carrots or grapefruit juice) may use the "gluten-free" claim.

• Foods with any whole, gluten-containing grains (e.g., spelt wheat) as ingredients may not use the claim;

• Foods with ingredients that are gluten-containing grains that are refined but still contain gluten (e.g., wheat flour) may not use the claim;

• Foods with ingredients that are gluten-containing grains that have been refined in such a way to remove the gluten may use the claim, so long as the food contains less than 20 ppm gluten/has less than 20 mg gluten per kg (e.g. wheat starch);

• Foods may not use the claim if they contain 20 ppm or more gluten as a result of cross-contact with gluten containing grains.

In addition, the final rule provides that:

• A food that bears the claim "no gluten," "free of gluten," or "without gluten" in its labeling and fails to meet the requirements for a "gluten-free" claim is misbranded.

• A food whose labeling includes the term "wheat" in the ingredient list or in a separate "Contains wheat" statement as required by FALCPA and also bears the claim "gluten-free" will be deemed to be misbranded unless its labeling also bears additional language clarifying that the wheat has been processed to allow the food to meet FDA requirements for a "gluten-free" claim.

NOTE: Beer—FDA intends to exercise enforcement discretion with respect to the requirements for "gluten-free" labeling for FDA regulated beers that currently make a "gluten-free" claim and that are: (1) Made from a non-gluten-containing grain or (2) made from a gluten-containing grain, where the beer has been subject to processing that the manufacturer has determined will remove gluten below a 20 ppm threshold.

Fermented or Hydrolyzed Foods—FDA compliance verification for fermented or hydrolyzed foods labeled "gluten-free" based on manufacturer records.

http://www.fda.gov/Food/GuidanceRegulation/GuidanceDocumentsRegulatoryInformation/Allergens/ucm472735.htm?source=govdelivery&utm_medium=email&utm_source=govdelivery

CRITICAL ANALYSIS: FDA can institute an action against companies that cannot support claims that their products are "gluten-free". As indicated, foods marketed as gluten-free and those labeled "free of gluten," "without gluten" or "no gluten" should have gluten content of less than 20 parts per million. Discuss the voluntary "Gluten-Free" labeling disclosure rule. Evaluate whether this rule is sufficient in terms of the "right to know".

Bioengineered Federal Food Disclosure Standard

https://www.congress.gov/bill/114th-congress/senate-bill/764/text?resultIndex=1

The National Bioengineered Food Disclosure Standard (*Bioengineered Food Disclosure or GMO*), PL 114–216, codified in 7 USC § 1639, passed July 29, 2016 amended the Agricultural Marketing Act by adding Subtitles E and F. Subtitle F concerns establishing the National Bioengineered Food Disclosure Standard. The Agricultural Marketing Service proposed a rule that would require food manufacturers and other entities to disclose bioengineered food and bioengineered food ingredient content. See: 83 FR 19860 (May 4, 2018).

The *Bioengineered Food Disclosure* law, was enacted partly in response to state GMO legislation such as the Vermont GMO law, which became effective July 1, 2016. USDA is tasked with the responsibility of promulgating regulations to implement the *Bioengineered Food Disclosure*. This law permits producers with a U.S. Department of Agriculture "certified organic" designation to display an additional "non-GMO" label on their products. Consumer advocates assert that the federal GMO law is industry based and fails to protect the consumer. Yet, prior to the *Bioengineered Food Disclosure* some companies had started to eliminate GMO ingredients or disclose GMO ingredients. For example, in July 2016, Dannon removed GMO ingredients in some products and disclose GMO ingredients in the labeling of other products by December 2017. See: *http://www.dannon.com/the-dannon-pledge-on-sustainable-agriculture-naturality-and-transparency/*

Companies are required to print on the packaging any of the following: text, a symbol such as a QR code, a digital link or telephone contact that directs consumers for more information. Bioengineered food is defined as follows: "(A) that contains genetic material that has been modified through *in vitro* recombinant [DNA] techniques; and (B) for which the modification could not otherwise be obtained through conventional breeding or found in nature."

Specific requirements are as follows:

✓ *Prohibit a food derived from an animal to be considered a bioengineered food merely because the animal consumed feed produced from, containing, or consisting of a bioengineered substance;*

✓ *Determine the amounts of a bioengineered substance that may be present in food for the food to be a bioengineered food;*

✓ *Establish a process for requesting and granting a determination by the Secretary regarding other factors and conditions under which a food is considered a bioengineered food;*

✓ *Provide alternate disclosure options for food contained in small or very small packages; and*

✓ *Devise measures specific to small food manufacturers.*

NOTE: See Jennifer A. Staman, *Legal Issues with Federal Labeling of Genetically Engineered Food: In Brief*, Congressional Research Service, (March 11, 2016). *http://nationalaglawcenter.org/wp-content/uploads/assets/crs/R43705.pdf*

National Bioengineered Food Disclosure Standard—"Subtitle E
ESTABLISHMENT OF NATIONAL BIOENGINEERED FOOD DISCLOSURE STANDARD 7
USC 1639b

SEC. 293—(e) State Food Labeling Standards—Notwithstanding section 295, no State or political subdivision of a State may directly or indirectly establish under any authority or continue in effect as to any food in interstate commerce any requirement relating to the labeling or disclosure of whether a food is bioengineered or was developed or produced using bioengineering for a food that is the subject of the national bioengineered food disclosure standard under this section that is not identical to the mandatory disclosure requirement under that standard.

Preemption: "Subtitle F—Labeling of Certain Food"

SEC. 295. FEDERAL PREEMPTION 7 USC 1639i

"(a) Definition Of Food—In this subtitle, the term 'food' has the meaning given the term in section 201 of the Federal Food, Drug, and Cosmetic Act (21 U.S.C. 321)."

"(b) Federal Preemption—No State or a political subdivision of a State may directly or indirectly establish under any authority or continue in effect as to any food or seed in interstate commerce any requirement relating to the labeling of whether a food (including food served in a restaurant or similar establishment) or seed is genetically engineered (which shall include such other similar terms as determined by the Secretary of Agriculture) or was developed or produced using genetic engineering, including any requirement for claims that a food or seed is or contains an ingredient that was developed or produced using genetic engineering."

SEC. 296. EXCLUSION FROM FEDERAL PREEMPTION 7 USC 1639j

"Nothing in this subtitle, subtitle E, or any regulation, rule, or requirement promulgated in accordance with this subtitle or subtitle E shall be construed to preempt any remedy created by a State or Federal statutory or common law right."

Federal Import Alert—Genetically Engineered Salmon 99-40

http://www.accessdata.fda.gov/CMS_IA/importalert_1152.html

President Trump signed the Fiscal Year (FY) 2018 Consolidated Appropriations Act which includes funding of the federal government during fiscal year 2018 (FY18) on March 23, 2018 (Public Law 115-141). Specific to salmon, this law directs that during FY18, the FDA shall not allow the introduction or delivery for introduction into interstate commerce of any food that contains genetically engineered salmon, until FDA publishes final labeling guidelines for informing consumers of such content. This language was in the FY16 and FY17 Omnibus Appropriations Acts. Further, when FDA reviews the 2019 Omnibus Appropriations Act or FDA finalizes the guidelines as directed, the "Import Alert" will be either revised or deactivated.

Chronological Background of GMOs

FDA and USDA Efforts Prior to the 2016 Federal Legislation

http://www.fda.gov/Food/FoodScienceResearch/Biotechnology/ucm346858.htm

"Biotech" debates continue about the use of biotechnology and transcends global issues in terms of health, the environment, and agricultural integrity. Biotechnology, specifically the use of genetically modified organisms (GMOs), remains controversial. Scientists have tried to improve plant quality by changing their genetic composition. The safety of genetically engineered crops, such as soybeans, corn and their byproducts continue as an ongoing discussion. In 2016, The National Academies of Sciences, Engineering, and Medicine issued a report on the impact of genetically engineered crops. The report concluded that genetically engineered crops do not pose immediate threat to the public health or to the environment. Yet, the report concluded that there are advantages to labeling genetically modified (GMO) foods. Food developed through biotechnology raises "right to know" issues such as labeling food that contains GMOs.

In *United States, Alliance for Bio-Integrity v. Shalala*, (DC 1998) the court dismissed the challenge to FDA's GMO policies. FDA published its "Statement of Policy: Foods Derived from New

Plant Varieties", 57 FR 22984 (May 29, 1992). Yet, this policy did not mandate special labeling for bioengineered foods. In 1993, FDA requested information on labeling issues concerning the 1992 policy, 58 FR 25837 (April 28, 1993). Based on the written comments and responses at the public meetings, FDA issued a proposed rule 66 FR 4706 (January 18, 2001) requiring data submission and information at least 120 days before commercial distribution of the food about plants derived from bioengineered foods that would be eaten by humans or animals. FDA had issued a guidance in 2015 concerning voluntary labeling of foods. However, the 2016 federal legislation supersedes the guidance.

The USDA Advisory Committee on Biotechnology and 21st Century Agriculture (AC21) originally established in 2003 has been reactivated to address national and international concerns. Further, USDA developed a program in 2015 for food companies that desire to label products as free of genetically modified ingredients or "GMO-free".

http://www.usda.gov/wps/portal/usda/usdahome?contentidonly=true&contentid=AC21Main.xml

State GMO Legislation

Prior to the federal law, Maine passed a GMO labeling law in 2013 that required foods containing genetically modified organisms (GMOs) to be labeled as such however it contained a "trigger clause" as the law would only go into effect if four other nearby states also pass GMO labeling laws. Similarly, Connecticut passed a law with a "trigger clause". In 2015, the Maine legislature proposed a new law that would remove the trigger clause requirement that relies on other states. New York State is also considering legislation to label GMOs, which would not include a trigger.

Vermont took the lead in enacting the Nation's first GMO labeling law in 2014 (H112 May 8, 2014) without a trigger clause. The Vermont GMO labeling law and promulgated "Rule 121", became effective July 1, 2016, applied to foods retailed in Vermont that contain genetically modified ingredients that total greater than 0.9 percent of the product's weight. Such products must carry the statement on the labeling that states: "may be partially produced with genetic engineering". Restaurant food and meat, milk and raw agricultural commodities not grown with genetically modified seed are exempt from the labeling requirement. Violators face fines of up to $1,000 per day. Other states such as California and Pennsylvania initiated legislative proposals for GMO labeling disclosure. Opponents have spent millions of dollars to defeat such efforts.

See: *http://www.leg.state.vt.us/docs/2014/journal/HJ140508.pdf#page=60*

CRITICAL ANALYSIS: The GMO labeling issue has proved controversial both in the United States and around the world. Therefore, does the 2016 federal legislation provide for the consumer right to know, uniformity and comport in terms of international trade? Incorporate a discussion about preemption.

Chapter 7: Bottled Water

Key Website: *http://www.fda.gov/Food/ResourcesForYou/Consumers/ucm046894.htm*

Regulatory Authority

The safety of drinking water is regulated by FDA and the Environmental Protection Agency (EPA). FDA regulates bottled drinking water and EPA regulates public drinking or tap water. The popularity of bottled drinking water is continually on the rise due to safety concerns about terrorist attacks on the food supply and due to the promotion of health benefits by companies that manufacture bottled water. General food labeling requirements apply to bottled drinking water. Usually, commercially prepared bottled water includes an expiration date; however, FDA does not require an expiration date on the label or labeling. Under FDA authority to regulate this product, the agency instituted standards of quality, Current Good Manufacturing Practices (CGMPs) and a guidance for industry for bottled drinking water.

Bottled water is regulated as a food and the labeling must comply with food labeling regulations contained in 21 CFR 101. Nutrition labeling must be provided on the label of any bottled water product that contains more than insignificant amounts of any of the nutrients or food components that are required to be listed under the nutrition labeling requirements, or whose label, labeling, or advertising contains a nutrient content claim or any other nutrition information in any context. Furthermore, any health claims made on bottled water products must comply with the requirements that FDA has established for the use of health claims that characterize the relationship of a food component to a disease or health related condition on the labels and in labeling of foods under 21 CFR 101. Bottled water includes products labeled:

Bottled water; Drinking water; Artesian water; Mineral water; Sparkling bottled water; Spring water; and Purified water—distilled, demineralized, deionized and reverse osmosis water.

NOTE: Waters with added carbonation, soda water or club soda, tonic water and seltzer are regulated by FDA as soft drinks.

Flavored Water and Nutrient-Added Water Beverages

Bottled water has proliferated the market in a variety of flavors and or added nutrients such as vitamins, electrolytes like sodium and potassium, and amino acids. The same bottled water requirements apply to these bottled water beverages if the term "water" is highlighted on the label. Additionally, the added flavorings and nutrients must be listed in the ingredients on the label. Further, these water beverages must comply with FDA safety requirements.

Standards of Quality

Standards of quality for bottled drinking water are contained under 21 CFR section 165. Bottled water is defined as water that is intended for human consumption sealed in bottles or other containers with no added ingredients except that it may optionally contain safe and suitable antimicrobial agents. Fluoride may be optionally added within the limitations established in Sec. 165.110(b)(4)(ii). FDA has established maximum allowable levels for physical, chemical, microbiological, and radiological contaminants in the bottled water quality standard regulations. All bottled water products that meet the bottled water definition must comply with the quality standard.

Coliform Testing Rule

Bottled water regulations were amended, 74 Fed. Reg. 25651 (December 1, 2009), 21 CFR part 165 to require that bottled water manufacturers test source water for total coliform, as is required for finished bottled water products, and to require, if any coliform organisms are detected in source water, that bottled water manufacturers determine whether any of the coliform organisms are Escherichia coli (E. coli), an indicator of fecal contamination. FDA also amended its bottled water regulations to require, if any coliform organisms are detected in finished bottled water products, that bottled water manufacturers determine whether any of the coliform organisms are E. coli. Finally, FDA amended the adulteration provision of the bottled water standard to reflect the possibility of adulteration caused by the presence of filth. Bottled water containing E. coli is considered adulterated, and source water containing E. coli will not be considered to be of a safe, sanitary quality and will be prohibited from use in the production of bottled water. The regulations require that, before a bottler can use source water from a source that has tested positive for E. coli, the bottler must take appropriate measures to rectify or eliminate the cause of E. coli contamination of that source. The bottler is subject to recordkeeping requirements. This final rule ensures that FDA's standards for the minimum quality of bottled water, as affected by fecal contamination, protects the public health as those established by EPA for public drinking water.

Chemical Levels in Bottled Water Rule

FDA issued a final rule concerning allowable chemical levels in bottled water, published at 76 FR 64810 (effective April 16, 2012). The allowable level for DEHP in the bottled water quality standard, which includes allowable levels for pesticides and other synthetic organic chemicals established by FDA is 0.006 mg/L. The bottled water quality standard regulations were amended to institute an allowable level for the chemical di(2-ethylhexyl)phthalate (DEHP) to correspond to those levels established by the Environmental Protection Agency. This means that bottled water manufacturers will be required to monitor their finished bottled water products for DEHP on an annual basis at a minimum under the current good manufacturing practice (CGMP) regulations for bottled water. Manufacturers must monitor their source water for DEHP annually. Manufacturers are exempt if they meet the criteria for source water monitoring exemptions under the CGMP regulations.

Current Good Manufacturing Practices

FDA has established Current Good Manufacturing Practices (CGMPs) 21 CFR 129 specifically for bottled water which require bottled water producers to:
  ➢ Process, bottle, hold and transport bottled water under sanitary conditions;
  ➢ Protect water sources from bacteria, chemicals and other contaminants;
  ➢ Use quality control processes to ensure the bacteriological and chemical safety of water; and,
  ➢ Sample and test both source water and the final product for contaminants.

Inspection

FDA monitors and inspects bottled water products and processing plants under its food safety program. When FDA inspects plants, the Agency verifies that the plant's product water and operational water supply are obtained from an approved source; inspects washing and sanitizing procedures; inspects bottling operations; and determines whether the companies analyze their source water and product water for contaminants.

CRITICAL ANALYSIS: Discuss product classification and claims on bottled water. How should FDA regulate these claims? Provide examples of claims on bottled water that may be classified as a drug or dietary supplement. Should FDA and FTC increase enforcement in terms of the claims on the labeling?

Chapter 8: Obesity in the United States

Obesity Epidemic in the United States

http://www.who.int/mediacentre/factsheets/fs311/en/
http://www.fda.gov/Food/FoodScienceResearch/ConsumerBehaviorResearch/ucm082094.htm

The "obesity epidemic" both in the United States and globally remains a major concern for several reasons including obesity related deaths, healthcare costs and related links to life threatening diseases. Most recently, scientists have linked body fat to certain cancers, Type 2 diabetes and cardiovascular disease. Additionally, Americans who are obese have an increased risk of hypertension, stroke, asthma, sleep apnea and osteoarthritis. Obesity presents a complex plethora of issues and FDA has coined the obesity problem as the "nation's obesity epidemic". It is multifaceted in terms of social, cultural, genetic, physiological, and psychological issues. Estimates vary; however, according to FDA, approximately 65% of Americans are overweight and over 30% are obese. Obesity is not limited to a certain age group. Roughly 17% or 12.5 million children and adolescents aged 2-19 years are obese which is triple the rate from the 1980s. This is problematic as obesity in the early years can lead to high blood pressure, heart disease, Type 2 diabetes, sleep apnea and asthma, heartburn and other digestive problems, and mental health conditions, into adult life. Obesity is not limited to gender either as both males and females are affected. Several executive initiatives have spearheaded efforts to curtail the obesity "crisis". Former President Obama initiated the Obesity Task Force on Childhood Obesity in 2010 (Task Force) and prior to that, an Obesity Working Group (Working Group), was established. The Working Group findings are reported below. Besides the Task Force and Working Group, other governmental agencies along with FDA are involved in addressing the "obesity epidemic". These include the Centers for Disease Control (CDC), the Federal Trade Commission (FTC), the United States Postal Service (USPS), and the United States Attorney's Office to name a few.

The question becomes what has led to the increase of obesity and the answer has become apparent. Lifestyle changes over the years in our ultra-modern society are partly to blame for the epidemic. Modernization has resulted in an increased sedentary lifestyle and a contributing factor in the escalation of obesity. Along with modernization, economics has played a role. Consumers with more disposable income have spent billions on weight related products that range from "diet foods" to weight loss cessation programs and aids. The economic affluence has led to increased work with less time to cook with a greater amount of disposable income to spend on fast foods and highly processed convenience type foods. A documentary *"Supersize Me"* evolved over this issue. *Supersize Me* centered on the effects of fast food consumption over a specified time frame.

Lawsuits alleging fast food consumption as the cause of serious health problems have increased against fast food manufacturers, yet lawsuits of this nature have not been successful. Claims have linked the marketing of fast foods aimed at young children and years of fast food consumption to obesity and other related illnesses. A lawsuit *In Liberty v. District of Columbia Police and Firemens's Retirement and Relief Board* (452 A. 2d 1187 (D.C. D.C. 1982), the court of appeals affirmed a decision that the patrolman's coronary artery condition was not caused nor aggravated by his "fast foods" consumption during shift work. In *Pelman v. McDonald's Corp,* the original lawsuit, filed in 2002 was dismissed; however, subsequently, the court permitted the complaint to be amended. On remand, the District Court granted McDonald's motion for a more definite statement as to the specific misleading advertisements that the plaintiffs asserted were misleading. The Court of Appeals reinstated the lawsuit as to the deceptive trade practices claim. See: *Pelman v. McDonalds's Corp.* 396 F. 3d 508 (2nd Cir. 2005). Eventually, the complaint was voluntarily dismissed in 2011.

Over the years, Congress introduced legislation apparently aimed at protecting fast food manufacturers, distributors or sellers from frivolous lawsuits related to "fast foods". For example, proposed legislation titled: *"Commonsense Consumption Act"* and *"Personal Responsibility in Food*

Consumption Act", dubbed the *"Cheeseburger Bills"*, places responsibility on fast food consumption on the individual consumer rather than on food manufacturers, advertisers, marketers, distributors and sellers. Yet, in an effort to deter civil liability lawsuits, approximately 26 states have enacted such legislation. See: Cara L. Wilking and Richard A. Daynard, *Beyond Cheeseburgers: The Impact of Commonsense Consumption Acts on Future Obesity-Related Lawsuits* 68 Food and Drug Institute J. 229 (2013); *"Do 'cheeseburger bills' work? Effects of tort reform for* fast food", by Christopher Carpenter and Sebastian Tello-Trillo (2015).
http://www.nber.org/papers/w21170
http://www.phaionline.org/wp-content/uploads/2013/08/WilkingDaynardFDLJAug13.pdf

NOTE: See Discussion about Caloric disclosure pp. 385-386; See also Roseann B. Termini, Thomas G. Roberto and Shelby G. Hostettler, *Food Advertising and Childhood Obesity: A Call to Action for Proactive Solutions***, Minnesota J. of Law, Science and Technology, 12 (2) 619-651 (2011) and** *Should Congress Pass Legislation to Regulate Child-Directed Food Advertising?* **Vol. 1, No. 9 FDLI Policy Forum (2011).**
http://www.foodanddrugpolicyforum.org/2011/05/vol-1-no-9-should-congress-pass.html
Discussion about Caloric disclosure pp. 385-386
See also: David S. Ludwig and Kenneth S. Rogoff, *The Toll of America's Obesity***, NY Times A21 (Aug. 10., 2018) authors discuss the economic costs of diet-related illness.**

CRITICAL ANALYSIS: Regulations in Britain prohibit advertising of high fat, high sugar and high salt foods during prime-time programming for children. For example, the Kellogg Company was prohibited from advertising its Coco Pops. What lessons could the United States learn from Britain? See: Happy Meal Ad is O.K. But Coco Pops Ad Isn't , B2, Wall St. J. (August 9, 2018).

Obesity Working Group

http://wayback.archive-it.org/7993/20180424211133/https://www.fda.gov/Food/FoodScienceRe-search/ConsumerBehaviorResearch/ucm081696.htm#trans

The FDA Obesity Working Group (OWG) issued a final report which relates to food labeling, consumer education, nutritional information provided by restaurants, enforcement, obesity drugs and collaboration. These proposals consist of:

➢ Improvement of the food label to show calorie count more prominently and to use meaningful serving sizes;
➢ Initiation of a consumer education campaign focusing on the "Calories Count" message;
➢ Recommendation that restaurants provide nutritional information to consumers;
➢ Increased enforcement actions about accurate food labels;
➢ Modification of FDA guidance for developing drugs to treat obesity; and
➢ Collaboration with other government agencies, non-profits, industry, and academia on obesity research.

CRITICAL ANALYSIS: FDA issued two final rules in late 2014 about caloric disclosure in accordance with the Affordable Care Act and in 2016, FDA revised the Nutrition Facts Panel Label. Further, FDA designated partially hydrogenated fat (PHOs) as Not GRAS (not generally recognized as safe) and thereby eliminated them from the United States food supply. FDA issued a voluntary guidance about sodium reduction in 2016. What more should be done in terms of the obesity crisis in the United States?

"Miracles"— Diet Coffee and Caffeine-Infused Shapewear

The advertisement of deceptive "miracle weight loss products" that provide no benefit remains problematic. In terms of the "obesity epidemic" and product marketing, the main mission of FTC is to oversee the advertising and marketing of foods, non-prescription products and cosmetics that promote weight loss. Advertisements on television, radio, the Internet, in magazines, flyers and posters must be truthful as well as not misleading. Product claims must be substantiated as well. Yet, false or deceptive advertising of weight loss products continues to escalate. Over the years,

FTC instituted several actions against companies for deceptive advertising this issue remains a top FTC enforcement priority such as the examples below illustrate from Diet Coffee to Coffee Infused clothing promoting weight loss.

Federal Trade Commission v. Diet Coffee, Inc.—Slim Coffee

http://www.ftc.gov/os/caselist/0723052/080104dietcoffeestipfinal.pdf

Judge Rakoff: 08 CV 0094 Stipulated Final Judgement and Order for Permanent Injunction and Other Equitable Relief as to Diet Coffee, Inc. Plaintiff, the Federal Trade Commission ("Commission" or "FTC"), filed a Complaint for Permanent Injunction and Other Equitable Relief against defendants Diet Coffee, Inc. ("DCI"), a corporation; David Stocknoff, individually and as President, Chief Financial Officer, and a Director of DCI; and David Attarian, individually and as a Secretary and Director DCI ("defendants") pursuant to Section 13(b) of the Federal Trade Commission Act ("FTC Act"), 15 U.S. § 53(b), alleging deceptive acts or practices and false advertisements in violation of Sections 5(a) and 12 of the FTC Act, 15 U.S.C. §§ 45(a) and 52. The Commission and defendant DCI stipulate to the entry of this Order in settlement of the Commission's allegations against defendant DCI. The Court, being advised in the premises, finds:

I. FALSE WEIGHT-LOSS REPRESENTATIONS PROHIBITED—IT IS ORDERED that defendant DCI *** are hereby permanently restrained and enjoined from making, or assisting others in making, directly or by implication, including through the use of a product name or endorsement, any representation that such product enables users to lose substantial weight without reducing caloric intake or increasing physical activity.

II. PROHIBITED REPRESENTATIONS FOR COVERED PRODUCTS OR SERVICES

IT IS FURTHER ORDERED Regarding the health benefits, performance, efficacy, safety, or side effects of any such product, service, or program; unless the representation is true, not misleading, and, at the time it is made, defendant DCI possesses and relies upon competent and reliable scientific evidence that substantiates the representation.

III. MISREPRESENTATION OF TESTS OR STUDIES—IT IS FURTHER ORDERED that defendant DCI *** are permanently restrained and enjoined from misrepresenting, in any manner, expressly or by implication, including through the use of any product name or endorsement, the existence, contents, validity, results, conclusions, or interpretations of any test or study.

IV. FDA APPROVED CLAIMS—IT IS FURTHER ORDERED that nothing in this Order shall prohibit defendant DCI from making any representation for any drug that is permitted in labeling for such drug under any tentative final or final standard promulgated by the Food and Drug Administration, or under any new drug application approved by the Food and Drug Administration; and Nothing in this Order shall prohibit defendant DCI from making any representation for any product that is specifically permitted in labeling for such product by regulations promulgated by the FDA pursuant to the Nutrition Labeling and Education Act.

V. MONETARY JUDGMENT AND REDRESS TO CONSUMERS

IT IS FURTHER ORDERED that judgment is hereby entered in favor of the Commission and against defendant DCI in the amount of nine hundred twenty-three thousand nine hundred ten dollars ($923,910) for redress to consumers.

GOVERNMENT-ORDERED DISCLOSURE

Dear Slim Coffee Reseller or Distributor: [on Diet Coffee, Inc. letterhead]

The Federal Trade Commission (FTC) has sued Diet Coffee, Inc. for misleading advertising. According to the FTC, we deceptively claimed that Slim Coffee would cause weight loss without diet or exercise. To settle this lawsuit, we have agreed to stop claiming that Slim Coffee will cause substantial weight loss without reducing calories or increasing exercise. In addition, we are prohibited from claiming that Slim Coffee can reduce fat, curb the appetite, or increase metabolism unless we have adequate scientific support for these claims. Our agreement also requires that we notify you to stop making claims that Slim Coffee: causes substantial weight loss without reducing calories or increasing exercise; or reduces fat, curbs the appetite, or increases metabolism, unless you have adequate scientific support for these claims.

You cannot make these claims either expressly or by implication, including in conjunction with the use of the Slim Coffee product name. Thank you for your cooperation. If you have any questions, please call [insert name and telephone number].

Sincerely, [name]   President, Diet Coffee, Inc.

CRITICAL ANALYSIS: Suppose you represent Diet Coffee. Determine requisite proactive measures to ensure compliance.

Norm Thompson Outfitters and Wacoal America Settle FTC Charges Over Weight-Loss Claims for Caffeine-Infused Shapewear

More recently, the Federal Trade Commission approved two final orders settling charges that two companies, *Norm Thompson Outfitters. Inc., and Wacoal America, Inc.*, misled consumers regarding the ability of their caffeine-infused shapewear undergarments to reshape the wearer's body and reduce cellulite. According to the FTC's *complaints, the two companies' marketing claims for their caffeine-infused products were false and not substantiated by scientific evidence.*

The FTC's complaint against Norm Thompson Outfitters alleged the company deceptively advertised, marketed, and sold women's undergarments infused with microencapsulated caffeine, retinol, and other ingredients, claiming the "shapewear" would slim and reshape the wearer's body and reduce cellulite. The products, made with Lytess brand fabrics, were sold via mail order and on the company's Norm Thompson Outfitters, Sahalie, Body Solutions, and Body Belle websites. Specifically, the FTC alleged that the company made claims that wearing its shapewear would eliminate or substantially reduce cellulite; reduce the wearer's hip measurements by up to two inches and their thigh measurements by one inch; and reduce thigh and hip measurements "without any effort." The complaint against Wacoal America contained similar allegations. It charged that the company's iPants supposedly slimmed the body and reduced cellulite. Specifically, the company made false and unsubstantiated claims that wearing iPants would: substantially reduce cellulite; cause a substantial reduction in the wearer's thigh measurements; and destroy fat cells, resulting in substantial slimming.

In settling the charges, the companies are banned from claiming that any garment that contains any drug or cosmetic causes substantial weight or fat loss or a substantial reduction in body size. The companies also are prohibited from making claims that any drug or cosmetic reduces or eliminates cellulite or reduces body fat, unless they are not misleading and can be substantiated by competent and reliable scientific evidence. The final orders also require the companies to pay $230,000 and $1.3 million, respectively, that the FTC can use to provide refunds to consumers. (FTC File Nos. 132-3094 and 132-3095; the staff contact is David Newman, FTC Western Region, San Francisco, 415-848-5123). *http://www.ftc.gov/enforcement/cases-proceedings/132-3095/wacoal-america-inc-matter*

CRITICAL ANALYSIS: Discuss these miracle weight loss cases, that is Diet Coffee and the "Caffeine-Infused Sleepwear" legal order (link above). Discuss why courts would utilize the "unthinking ignorant consumer test" in weight loss cases such as these rather than test rather than the "reasonable person" test. How would you advise one of these companies?

NOTE: See *this Volume III Notable Recalls—*Libido Booster-Instant Coffee Containing Libido *and Volume X, Dietary Supplements, Herbs and Botanicals Regulation* for additional FTC Enforcement of Weight Loss Products.

Chapter 9: Food Supplier and Manufacturer Liability

Supplier and Manufacturer Liability—Caban and Jackson

What are the legal duties of a food manufacturer and food supplier? Does a food manufacturer owe a duty beyond that of reasonable care? In *Caban v. JR Seafood*, the court grappled with the application of the strict liability doctrine. In *Jackson v. Nestle-Beich*, 589 N.E.2d 547 (1992), the court had to determine the proper test in determining legal duties; that is, whether the foreign but natural test applied or the reasonable consumer test applied.

Caban v. JR Seafood,
132 F. Supp. 3d 274 (2015), 285 F. Supp. 3d 502 (2018)

Luis González Cabán ("González") filed a lawsuit and alleged that he was stricken with paralytic shellfish poisoning after consuming a toxic shrimp at Restaurante El Nuevo Amanecer, in Coamo, Puerto Rico which permanently caused incomplete quadriplegia and is wheelchair bound. The court detailed that: Paralytic Shellfish poisoning is an "[i]llness caused by consuming shellfish contaminated with certain dinoflagellates that produce saxitoxin and other toxins." Some of its symptoms include: "numbness or tingling in the face, lips, tongue, and extremities. There may also be a headache, fever, rash, nausea, and vomiting, with impaired coordination, changes in mental status, incoherent speech, and difficulty in swallowing, flaccid paralysis, and respiratory failure in severe cases. Death can occur within two hours of ingestion of the contaminated fish." See: J.E. Schmidt, Attorneys' Dictionary of Medicine and Word Finder, vol. 4 M-PQ, 63 (2013). The district court certified the following questions to the Supreme Court of Puerto Rico

Under the principles of product liability, is a supplier/seller strictly liable for the damages caused by human consumption of an extremely poisonous natural toxin found in a shrimp, even if said food product (and its "defect") are not a result of manufacturing or fabrication process?

If the previous question is answered in the affirmative, would it make a difference if the "defect" of the food product is readily discoverable scientifically or otherwise?

The Supreme Court held that the strict liability doctrine was inapplicable. The shrimp contaminated with saxitoxin became contaminated without human intervention and was not manufactured. The Supreme Court of Puerto Rico determined that the case at bar falls outside of the scope of the strict liability doctrine's protection. Ultimately, the lower court dismissed the strict liability claim.

Jackson v. Nestle-Beich,
589 N.E.2d 547 (Ill. 1992)

FACTUAL BACKGROUND Jackson purchased a sealed can of Katydids, chocolate-covered, pecan and caramel candies manufactured by Nestle. Shortly thereafter, Jackson bit into one of the candies and allegedly broke a tooth on a pecan shell embedded in the candy. As a result, Jackson filed a complaint asserting breach of implied warranty (count I) and strict products liability (count II) against Nestle. Nestle moved for summary judgment on the basis of the foreign-natural doctrine. That doctrine provides that, if a substance in a manufactured food product is natural to any of the ingredients of the product, there is no liability for injuries caused thereby; whereas, if the substance is foreign to any of the ingredients, the manufacturer will be liable for any injury caused thereby. *Mix v. Ingersoll Candy Co.* (1936), 6 Cal.2d 674, 59 P.2d 144 (chicken bone in chicken pie); *Goodwin v. Country Club of Peoria* (1944), 323 Ill.App. 1, 54 N.E.2d 612 (turkey bone in creamed turkey dish). *** We agree with the appellate court's conclusion that the foreign-natural doctrine is unsound and should be abandoned.

NESTLE'S ARGUMENTS In appealing the appellate court's decision, Nestle first asserts that the decision "has, in practice, created a strict liability situation[ ]" because the court "failed to change the general test" for determining the existence of a breach of warranty with respect to food products, viz., the presence of foreign matter in the food or its diseased, decayed or otherwise spoiled and poisonous condition. *** That test is the reasonable expectation of the consumer with respect to the ingredients of the food product involved. *** The crux of Nestle's arguments on appeal is that we should adopt the Louisiana version of the foreign-natural doctrine. In Louisiana, if injury is caused by a foreign substance in a food product, the manufacturer is subject to being held strictly liable. In contrast, if the substance causing injury is natural to the product or its ingredients, the manufacturer may be held liable only if the presence of the substance resulted from its negligence in the manufacture of the product. *Title v. Pontchartrain Hotel (La.App.1984), 449 So.2d 677; Musso v. Picadilly Cafeterias, Inc. (La.App.1965), 178 So.2d 421.*

We decline Nestle's invitation to adopt the Louisiana version of the foreign-natural doctrine in place of the reasonable expectation test. We agree with Jackson that the Louisiana approach comes too close to the outdated and discredited doctrine of caveat emptor. ***

In this regard, we believe the consumer's reasonable expectation as to the contents of food products, as the gauge of strict liability, adequately balances consumers' interest in defect-free products and such manufacturers' interest in reasonable costs of doing business. Would a reasonable consumer expect that a given product might contain the substance or matter causing a particular injury? *** Similarly, with an awareness of that test, manufacturers can act accordingly with respect to their means of production. *** The test thus provides a reasonable and concrete standard to govern actions of this sort. ***

In Nestle's case, that aspect would be that the meat of pecans, an ingredient of Katydids, is found inside a hard shell. That Nestle actually processes the ingredients in its product before placing it in the stream of commerce and thereby has some opportunity to discover and eliminate the risk of injury posed by its ingredients, unlike the seller of poisonous mushrooms, actually militates in favor of, rather than against, imposing strict liability against Nestle. ***

Rather than imposing an obligation upon consumers of Nestle's product to protect themselves by "think[ing] and chew[ing] carefully," we believe that the obligation of protection is better placed on Nestle and like manufacturers. In this regard, we agree with the following observation: "With the prevalence of processed foods on the market today and the development of technology in the food industry, consumers increasingly rely upon food processors to inspect and purify the foods they consume. *** One might imagine a consumer in a jurisdiction that applies the foreign-natural test tearing away the crust from a beef pot pie to search for tiny bones, or picking apart a cherry-nut ice cream cone to remove stray shells or pits.

In an era of consumerism, the foreign-natural standard is an anachronism. It flatly and unjustifiably protects food processors and sellers from liability even when the technology may be readily available to remove injurious natural objects from foods. The consumer expectation test, on the other hand, imposes no greater burden upon processors or sellers than to guarantee that their food products meet the standards of safety that consumers customarily and reasonably have come to expect from the food industry." Note, Products Liability—The Test of Consumer Expectation for "Natural" Defects in Food Products, 37 Ohio St.L.J. 634, 651-52 (1976). With respect to Nestle's argument that it is in no better position than consumers of its Katydids to identify the risks associated therewith, we disagree that the common knowledge that pecans are hard-shelled nuts makes it common knowledge that processed foods containing pecan meats may also contain pecan shell. *** As a result, we do not believe that consumers of its Katydids must be required to "think and chew carefully" when consuming them. *** Specifically, they can place an adequate warning to the consumer on their product's container of the possibility or risk of injury posed thereby. In this regard, we note that, even if we agreed with Nestle that its Katydids merit classification as an unavoidably unsafe product, we would nonetheless find it ubject to strict liability due to the absence of a warning of the unavoidable risk of injury it posed. For all of the reasons stated herein, we affirm the judgment of the appellate court.

NOTE: See *Newton v. Standard Candy Co., Inc. v. Jimbo's Jumbos*, Inc. No. 8:06CV242. March 19, 2008 (court discussed reasonable expectation test in connection with injury from ingesting a peanut Goo Goo Cluster candy bar).

CRITICAL ANALYSIS: Review *Caban* and *Jackson*. What are the legal duties of a food manufacturer? Evaluate the reasonable expectation test versus the foreign natural test and the application of strict liability.

VOLUME X

Volume X: Dietary Supplements, Herbs and Botanicals

This volume details the regulation of dietary supplements, herbs and botanical products. This industry continues to burgeon and has become a multibillion-dollar industry. Interestingly, as early as 1944, in Barnes v. United States, the court held that the label on vitamins was false and misleading. The product label implied that the tablets consisted of a significant quantity of vitamins when in fact the product was deficient in vitamins A, B, and D. In a later decision, the court focused again on consumer protection, as exemplified in United States v. Aangamik 15 Calcium Pangamate. The court held that the vitamin product was misbranded under the FDCA.

Fifty years after Barnes, the Dietary Supplement Health and Education Act of 1994 (DSHEA), was enacted which has over 25 years later, proved both significant yet controversial. Approximately 4,000 supplements were in the marketplace when DSHEA was enacted in 1994. That has drastically escalated to well over 75,000 available dietary supplement, herb and botanical products. Back in 1996, consumers spent $6.5 billion dollars annually, in 2004 the dollar expenditure jumped to $20 billion and according to NIH $36 billion in 2014. Industry reports indicated that in 2017 supplement sales reached $43.4 billion and are projected to rise.

DSHEA amended the Food Drug and Cosmetic Act (FDCA) with provisions applicable to dietary supplements and the ingredients of dietary supplements. For example, the term "dietary supplement" under DSHEA is defined along with the term "dietary ingredients". Dietary supplement products include vitamins, minerals, amino acids, herbs or other botanicals and substances such as enzymes, organ tissues, glandular and metabolites as well as extracts or concentrates. Dietary supplement forms include tablets, capsules, softgels, gelcaps, liquids, or powders. Other forms such as a bar could qualify as a dietary supplement; however, the label cannot represent the product as a conventional food or a sole item of a meal or diet. Importantly, DSHEA established a framework for safety including claims and nutritional support statements; ingredient and nutrition labeling; and granted FDA the authority to establish Good Manufacturing Practice (GMP) regulations.

This volume details landmark court decisions, namely Nutraceutical Corp. v. Eshenbach, Pearson v. Shalala, Alliance for Natural Health, Whitaker v. Thompson and Pharmanex, Inc. v. Shalala. Other topics include an explanation of good manufacturing practices for dietary supplements, claims on dietary supplements, selected enforcement actions and advertising. DSHEA does not provide FDA with authority to approve dietary supplements prior to marketing; therefore, safety and efficacy considerations remain contentious. However, FTC and FDA exercise post market regulatory authority through court actions, nationwide alerts, traditional warning and cyber letters, advisories and product bans. Further, there is adverse reporting specific to dietary supplements. Yet, a Government Accounting Office Report (GAO) recommendation calls for Congress to provide FDA with additional regulatory oversight. This is essential as the multibillion dietary supplement industry continues to escalate. Towards the end of 2015, FDA created the Office of Dietary Supplement Programs (ODSP) that elevated the program status. The critical issue moving forward is whether Congress should strengthen government oversight to protect the public health.

Chapter 1: Legislation, Regulation, GMPS's and Adverse Events

FDA Office of Dietary Supplement Programs

Key Websites*: http://www.fda.gov/food/dietarysupplements/* (edited)
http://ods.od.nih.gov/factsheets/DietarySupplements-HealthProfessional/ (edited)

The Dietary Supplement Health Education Act of 1994 (DSHEA) altered how FDA regulates dietary supplements, herbs, and botanical products. The Office of Dietary Supplement Programs (ODSP) within the Center for Food Safety and Applied Nutrition (CFSAN) is responsible for regulation. The ODSP is the central point for dietary supplement policy, reviews, and regulations. To that end, a ten-year strategic plan issued in 2000 (Plan) included adverse reporting, enhanced mechanisms for health hazard evaluation; a safety database; pre-market review notifications for new dietary supplement ingredients; Internet surveillance, and claims clarification. The Plan involved specifying boundaries between dietary supplements and foods by defining significant terms, such as "intended for ingestion" and "represented for use as a conventional food."

Despite the legal authority to regulate pre-market, FDA continues to identify the highest priority safety issues and take regulatory action against unsafe products through enforcement legal actions. Yet, the recurring critical issue is whether more proactive enforcement is necessary for this multibillion-dollar industry in the United States where continued sales growth is predicted.

Significant Events in the Regulation of Dietary Supplements

Year	Key events in the Regulation of Dietary Supplements
1990	The Nutrition Labeling and Education Act of 1990 amended the Federal Food, Drug, and Cosmetic Act to require most foods, including dietary supplements, to bear nutrition labeling.
1994	DSHEA amended the Federal Food, Drug, and Cosmetic Act to create a new regulatory category, safety standard, labeling requirements, and other rules for dietary supplements. Under DSHEA, dietary supplements are generally presumed to be safe.
2002	The Public Health Security and Bioterrorism Preparedness and Response Act of 2002 amended the Federal Food, Drug, and Cosmetic Act to require all food companies, including dietary supplement companies, to register with FDA no later than December 12, 2003, to provide information on the name and address of the facility and, to some extent, the types of products they manufacture or sell.
2004	FDA was successful in banning ephedra after thousands of adverse events, including a number of deaths, and a lengthy legal process.
2006	The Dietary Supplement and Nonprescription Drug Consumer Protection Act amended the Federal Food, Drug, and Cosmetic Act to require dietary supplement companies that receive a serious adverse event report to submit information about the event to FDA.
2007	FDA finalized its Current Good Manufacturing Practice regulations to establish quality control standards for dietary supplements. The final rule became effective on August 24, 2007, and companies had 10, 22, or 34 months from the effective date of the rule to comply, depending on company size.
	Serious adverse event reporting requirements for supplement companies effective.
2009	GAO Adverse Event Report (see below). See also 2013 GAO Report later in this chapter.
2014	Distinguishing Liquid Dietary Supplements from Beverages (Guidance).
2017	Memory Supplements—Clarifying FDA and FTC Roles Could Strengthen Oversight GAO-17-416 (Released June 15, 2017). https://www.gao.gov/products/GAO-17-416.

Dietary Supplement Health and Education Act
http://www.fda.gov/food/dietarysupplements/ (edited)

The Dietary Supplement Health and Education Act of 1994, (DSHEA) signed by former President Clinton on October 25, 1994, amended the FDCA by incorporating several provisions applicable to dietary supplements including ingredients. To that end, DSHEA:

> *Defines "dietary supplement" and "dietary ingredients";*
> *Furnishes a framework for safety;*
> *Outlines guidelines for literature display where supplements are sold;*
> *Provides for the use of claims and nutritional support statements;*
> *Requires ingredient and nutrition labeling;*
> *Authorized FDA to establish Good Manufacturing Practice (GMP) regulations; and*
> *Requires an executive level Commission and an Office of Dietary Supplements in NIH.*

Section 321(ff) establishes a formal definition of a dietary supplement. Controversy remains as to regulation and the exact criteria for defining a dietary supplement. Congress enacted DSHEA to provide greater consumer access to safe dietary supplements and to remove unreasonable regulatory barriers that could impede the availability of dietary supplements. DSHEA places the burden on FDA to prove a dietary supplement is unsafe prior to any marketplace removal.

Premarket Approval Not Required—Dietary supplements present a completely different regulatory scheme than drug approvals. In order for a new drug to enter the marketplace, safety and efficacy must be documented through the extensive process of submitting a new drug application to FDA. Unlike drugs, DSHEA does not require premarket approval for dietary supplements.

New Dietary Ingredients—There is a 75-day **pre-market notification** requirement for manufacturers or distributors of dietary supplements that contain "new dietary ingredients" not marketed in the United States prior to October 15, 1994. That is, manufacturers or distributors are only required to notify FDA of a product intended for marketing only if the product contains "a new dietary ingredient". The term "new dietary supplement" means that it must fall within the definition of dietary supplement under DSHEA and not sold as a dietary supplement in the United States before October 15, 1994. The 75-notice requirement applies unless the supplement contains only ingredients that have been present without chemical alteration in the food supply as an article used for food. A manufacturer and distributor must prove that the new ingredient is safe for use unless previously recognized as a food substance and already present in the food supply.

Dietary Supplement Defined—Dietary supplements were traditionally regulated as foods and considered to be composed only of essential nutrients, such as vitamins, minerals, and proteins. However, the Nutrition Labeling and Education Act of 1990 added "herbs, or similar nutritional substances," to the term "dietary supplement." DSHEA expanded the meaning of the term "dietary supplements" beyond essential nutrients to include such substances as ginseng, garlic, fish oils, psyllium, enzymes, glandulars, and mixtures of these; however, it does not include the term "Neutraceutical". Hence, FDA does not recognize "neutraceuticals" as dietary supplements. Dietary supplement defined under Section 201 (f)(f)(3) of DSHEA, 21 U.S.C. section 321 (f)(f)(3), contains several criteria in its formal definition. Significant elements of this definition, 21 U.S.C. section 321 (f)(f)(3), provide that a dietary supplement:

> *Is a product (other than tobacco) that is intended to supplement the diet that bears or contains one or more of the following dietary ingredients: a vitamin, a mineral, an herb or other botanical, an amino acid, a dietary substance for use by man to supplement the diet by increasing the total daily intake, or a concentrate, metabolite, constituent, extract, or combinations of these ingredients;*
> *Is intended for ingestion in pill, capsule, tablet, or liquid form;*
> *Is not represented for use as a conventional food or as the sole item of a meal or diet;*
> *Is labeled as a "dietary supplement"; and*
> *Includes products such as an approved new drug, certified antibiotic, or licensed biologic that was marketed as a dietary supplement or food before approval, certification, or license*

In terms of regulatory authority, FDA's postmarket rather than premarket authority as stipulated under DSHEA remains controversial. That is, under DSHEA, dietary supplements do not go through the comprehensive and complicated approval processes as drugs do. It is up to the manufacturer to provide a safe product prior to marketplace entry.

Safety—Under DSHEA a dietary supplement is adulterated if it or one of its ingredients presents *"a significant or unreasonable risk of illness or injury"* when used as directed on the label, or under normal conditions of use if there are no directions. A dietary supplement that contains a new dietary ingredient, that is, an ingredient not marketed for dietary supplement use in the United States prior to October 15, 1994 may be adulterated when there is inadequate information to provide reasonable assurance that the ingredient will not present a significant or unreasonable risk of illness or injury. FDA has the legal authority to ban a dietary supplement if a dietary supplement or dietary ingredient poses an imminent hazard to public health or safety. The rule prohibiting the use of ephedrine alkaloids serves as an example.

Literature—DSHEA permits retail outlets to have "third-party" materials available for consumers. The information must not be false or misleading, must be displayed separate from the supplements, must be displayed with other literature and cannot promote a specific brand of supplement. Examples include the following: articles; book chapters; scientific abstracts; and other third-party publications.

Statements on Labels—DSHEA provides for the use of various types of statements on the label of dietary supplements, although claims may not be made about the use of a dietary supplement to diagnose, prevent, mitigate, treat, or cure a specific disease unless approved under the new drug provisions of the FDCA. For example, a product may not carry the claim *"cures cancer"* or *"treats arthritis."* Appropriate health claims authorized by FDA such as the claim linking folic acid and reduced risk of neural tube birth defects and the claim that calcium may reduce the risk of osteoporosis may be made in supplement labeling if the product qualifies to bear the claim. Under DSHEA, firms can make statements about classical nutrient deficiency diseases—as long as these statements disclose the prevalence of the disease in the United States. In addition, manufacturers may describe the supplement's effects on the *"structure or function"* of the body or the *"well-being"* achieved by consuming the dietary ingredient. To use these claims, manufacturers must have substantiation that the statements are truthful and not misleading, and the product label must bear the following statement: ***"This statement has not been evaluated by the Food and Drug Administration. This product is not intended to diagnose, treat, cure, or prevent any disease."***

Unlike health claims, nutritional support statements need not be approved by FDA before manufacturers market products bearing the statements, however, FDA must be notified no later than 30 days after a product that bears the claim is first marketed.

Labeling—A dietary supplement label must contain:

A statement of identity (product name) that identifies the product as a dietary supplement;
Nutrition information in the form of a Supplement Facts panel;
A list of any ingredients not listed in the Supplement Facts panel;
The name and address of the manufacturer, packager, or distributor; and the
Net quantity of the contents.

Per Day Labeling—FDA's nutrition labeling regulations for dietary supplements provide the quantitative amount and the percent of Daily Value of a dietary ingredient may be voluntarily presented on a "per day" basis in addition to the required "per serving" basis when a recommendation is made on the label that the dietary supplement be consumed more than once per day. The rule affords dietary supplement manufacturers or distributors if the distributor does the labeling, the option to present nutrition information of dietary supplements on a "per day" basis. A parenthetical statement in the Supplement Facts label that provides directions for calculating the "per day" amount when there is a recommendation or directions for use in other parts of the label that the dietary supplement be consumed more than once per day is permitted (21 CFR Sec. 101.36(e)(9). As mentioned, certain claims are permissible under DSHEA with an appropriate disclaimer. For example, if the labeling includes a claim to affect the structure or function of the body, a well-being claim of a general nature, or a health claim, the product label must contain a disclaimer stating that FDA has not evaluated the claim and that the product is not intended to diagnose, treat, cure, or prevent any disease. Additionally, any claims made must have substantiation that the claim is truthful and not misleading. FDA must receive notification that the product includes such a claim within 30-days of product marketing with the claim. Products that contain herbs and botanical ingredients must disclose the specific part of the plant from which the ingredient is derived. Supplements represented as complying with specifications in an official compendium are deemed misbranded if it does not conform to those specifications. Examples of official compendia include the United States Pharmacopeia, the United States Homeopathic Pharmacopeia, or the National Formulary. Supplements not covered by a compendium must be the product identified on the label.

Good Manufacturing Practices and Verification

Dietary Supplement Current Good Manufacturing Practices (cGMPs) establish minimum parameters that pertain to preparation, packaging and holding dietary supplements or dietary ingredients under conditions that ensure their safety. The cGMPs address identity, purity, quality, consistency and product composition and requires a written operation plan. Testing of incoming ingredients and finished product specification testing is required. That is, the focus of cGMPs is to help ensure that dietary supplements are not adulterated, free from contaminants or other impurities and properly labeled. Finalized in 2007, they became effective based on company size.

NIH Office of Dietary Supplements

http://ods.od.nih.gov

The Office of Dietary Supplements (ODS), within the National Institutes of Health (NIH), performs a significant role. The Dietary Supplement Health and Education Act of 1994 (Public Law 103-417, DSHEA) authorized the establishment of the Office of Dietary Supplements (ODS) at the NIH. DSHEA specifically defined the purpose and responsibilities of ODS as follows:

> ➢ *To explore more fully the potential role of dietary supplements as a significant part of the efforts of the United States to improve health care;*
> ➢ *To promote scientific study of the benefits of dietary supplements in maintaining health and preventing chronic disease and other health-related conditions;*
> ➢ *To conduct and coordinate scientific research within NIH relating to dietary supplements;*
> ➢ *To collect and compile the results of scientific research relating to dietary supplements, including scientific data from foreign sources; and*
> ➢ *To serve as the principal advisor to the Secretary and to the Assistant Secretary for Health and provide advice to the Director of NIH, the Director of the Centers for Disease Control and Prevention, and the Commissioner of the Food and Drug Administration on issues relating to dietary supplements.*

Supplements have been available for years yet scientific research has lagged. This is in contrast to other countries such as Asia and Europe where research has been conducted for years about the effects of botanical and herbal dietary supplements. Perhaps due to cultural mores, in countries such as Asia and Europe these products have been used for years. Yet, because supplement use in the United States continues to gain unprecedented popularity, valid scientific study by the ODS remains imperative.

NIH Computer Access to Research

http://ods.od.nih.gov/Research/CARDS_Database.aspx

The Computer Access to Research on Dietary Supplements Program (CARDS) within NIH is a database of federally funded research projects specific to dietary supplements. CARDS was developed in fulfilling the Congressional mandate under DSHEA to "compile a database of scientific research on dietary supplements and individual nutrients". CARDS provides research information and direction to Congress, federal agencies, researchers, health providers and consumers. Projects comprise of those funded by the National Institute of Health. The computer system affords the opportunity to determine if the federal government is supporting a particular type of research. The CARDS program provides information about: *specific dietary supplement research such as Vitamin E; type of study such as an animal study; and health outcomes such as antioxidant function.*

United States Pharmacopeia Verification

www.uspverified.org

The United States Pharmacopeia (USP) created a certification program to verify the contents of dietary supplements. USP's Dietary Supplement Verification Program launched in 2002 (DSVP) provides an example of industry self-regulation since it is an independent non-government organization. USP developed standards for thousands of prescription and over-the-counter products and monograph standards for nearly one thousand nutritional and dietary supplement products. The significant aspect of this voluntary program is for dietary supplement standardization. In other words, the label of one brand can state the same quality as a competing brand; however, the consumer has no method of determining whether the product is standard.

Under the DSVP, USP assesses and substantiates dietary supplements for several factors that include product purity, label accuracy for ingredients and correct manufacturing practices. USP awards a "DSVP certification mark" if the product fulfills USP established criteria. This means that the dietary supplement product contains the ingredients as indicated on the label in the stated amount and strength; that the dietary supplement product meets established purity standards; and that the product complies with good manufacturing practices. USP assesses dietary supplement certification submissions based on extensive laboratory testing, an all-encompassing review of quality control and manufacturing documentation and assessment of manufacturing practices. The DSVP certification program entails post-certification in the form of annual internal audits by the manufacturer, DSVP conducted on site audits and DSVP conducted post-certification sampling.

Adverse Event Reporting

The Dietary Supplement and Nonprescription Drug Consumer Protection Act (Dietary Supplement Adverse Event Act) addresses adverse event reporting. FDA issued a guidance titled: *Guidance for Industry: Questions and Answers Regarding Adverse Event Reporting and Recordkeeping for Dietary Supplements as Required by the Dietary Supplement and Nonprescription Drug Consumer Protection Act.* Although not legally binding, the guidance provides details about adverse event reporting.

There is a mandatory 15-day reporting requirement for manufacturers, packers and distributors of over the counter drugs and dietary supplements to report to FDA a "serious adverse event" through Med Watch. Section 403(y) and 502(x) of the FDCA requires all dietary supplement labels to contain a domestic address and phone number through which a responsible person may receive adverse event reports. A responsible person means manufacturer, packer or distributor whose name appears on the label. A retailer specified on the label as a distributor may agree to have the manufacturer or packer submit the reports as long as the retailer informs either the manufacturer or packer of all adverse event reports whether or not deemed serious. The Dietary Supplement Adverse Event Act does not require adverse event reporting by consumers; however, 21 U.S.C. sections 403(y) and 502(x) requires all dietary supplement labels to contain a domestic address and phone number through which a responsible person may receive adverse event reports.

SEC. 761. SERIOUS ADVERSE EVENT REPORTING FOR DIETARY SUPPLEMENTS (21 U.S.C. 379aa-1(a)(1)).

(a) Definitions- In this section:

(1) ADVERSE EVENT— The term "adverse event" means any health-related event associated with the use of a dietary supplement that is adverse.

(2) SERIOUS ADVERSE EVENT- The term "serious adverse event" is an adverse event that—(A) results in—

(i) death

(ii) a life-threatening experience

(iii) inpatient hospitalization

(iv) a persistent or significant disability or incapacity

(v) a congenital anomaly or birth defect

(B) requires, based on reasonable medical judgment, a medical or surgical intervention to prevent an outcome described under subparagraph (A).

CRITICAL ANALYSIS: Should the definition of "serious adverse event" be expanded?

GAO Reports—Dietary Supplements and FDA Oversight

The Government Accounting Office Report (GAO) titled *DIETARY SUPPLEMENTS FDA Should Take Further Actions to Improve Oversight and Consumer Understanding* (2009) provides valuable insights specifically about adverse event reporting, FDA surveillance and international comparison. According to the GAO report, since mandatory reporting went into effect, FDA received 596 mandatory reports of adverse events that included serious cardiac, respiratory, and gastrointestinal disorders. Other adverse events involved 9 deaths, 64 life-threatening illnesses, and 234 patient hospitalizations. Table 2 reveals that 66 percent of serious adverse event reports were associated with dietary supplements that either contained product combinations, for instance, a product containing both vitamins and herbals, or could not be categorized under one of FDA's other product classifications. Forty percent pertained to vitamins. However, according to FDA, due to the variability in the quality and detail of information in reports and the lack of a control group, FDA cannot necessarily determine a causal relationship between an adverse event and the dietary supplement associated with the event. Significant GAO Report Tables follow. **Table 2: Number of Cases with Mandatory Reported Adverse Event Outcomes by Dietary Supplement Product Classification, from 12/22/07 through 10/31/08**

Dietary supplement product classification	Number of serious adverse events reported, from December 22, 2007, through October 31, 2008	Percentage of all serious adverse events reported
Combination products and products not elsewhere classified	391	65.6
Vitamin	240	40.3
Mineral	111	18.6
Fats and lipid substances	55	9.2
Herbal and botanical (other than tea)	24	4.0
Fiber	20	3.4
Herbal and botanical teas	15	2.5
Protein	9	1.5
Animal by-products and extracts	1	0.2%
Total	**596[a]**	

Note a: Total does not add because some adverse event reports involved more than one product and are counted in more than one subcategory. For example, according to FDA, if a consumer was taking both a vitamin C supplement and an echinacea supplement when the adverse event took place, the event would be classified under both "vitamin" and "herbal and botanical." If the consumer was taking a single product containing both vitamin C and echinacea, the event would be classified under "combination products."

Appendix III Table 7: Number of Dietary Supplement-Related Adverse Event Cases Characterized as Serious, January 1, 2003, through October 31, 2008

Description	2003	2004	2005	2006	2007	2008	Total
Cases characterized as serious	510[a]	483	364	213	213	759	**2,542**
Total number of dietary supplement related cases	**739**	**657**	**491**	**317**	**350**	**948**	**3,502**

Table 3: Examples of FDA Surveillance to Identify Safety Concerns

Surveillance actions	
Monitoring adverse events	FDA received 3,502 adverse event reports related to dietary supplements from January 1, 2003 through October 31, 2008. The top three outcomes associated with these cases were hospitalization (32 percent), nonserious illness or injury (28 percent), and serious illness or injury (25 percent).
Monitoring consumer complaints	FDA received 1,018 consumer complaints from fiscal year 2001 through July 3, 2008. Forty-two percent of these complaints involved adverse symptoms. Consumer complaints involving adverse symptoms triggered 236 active surveillance operations, including inspections and sample collections.
Screening imports	FDA reviewed 616,464 import entry lines of dietary supplements from fiscal year 2002 through March 24, 2008, and either sampled or examined, on average, approximately 3 to 5 percent of the imported entry lines entering the country.
Conducting inspections	FDA conducted 804 inspections, and state partners conducted 105 inspections, of domestic dietary supplement firms from fiscal years 2002 through 2008. Investigators identified potential problems, such as a lack of quality control and unsanitary conditions, in 49 percent of these inspections.

Table 4: Examples of FDA Actions in Response to Identified Safety Concerns

Advisory actions	
Hold regulatory meeting with the firm	FDA officials may meet with firm representatives to discuss concerns and request voluntary action; however, FDA does not collect agency wide data on these meetings.
Issue firm a warning	FDA issued 293 warning letters citing 534 violations regarding dietary supplements from fiscal years 2002 through 2007. Seventy percent of these violations related to dietary supplements that FDA determined were either unapproved new drugs or misbranded drugs.
Issue consumer alerts	FDA had posted 12 consumer alerts on its Web site since 1999, including warnings for kava, aristolochic acid, and St. John's wort, among others, as of November 21, 2008.
Issue advisory to industry	FDA had posted letters to industry advising against the marketing of products containing aristolochic acid, comfrey, androstenedione, Lipokinetix, and ephedra, as of November 21, 2008.
Administrative and judicial enforcement actions to remove a product from the market	
Work with company on a voluntary product recall	At least 45 recalls related to dangerous or defective dietary supplement products that posed a serious health concern were initiated from fiscal years 2003 through 2008. Of these recalls, 27 were due to the unapproved presence of pharmaceutical ingredients in the supplement products.
Detain/refuse the product if imported	FDA detained 3,225 dietary supplement import entry lines from fiscal year 2002 through March 24, 2008. Fifty percent of the detentions were due to the potential presence of a poisonous or unsafe substance. Over this same period, FDA refused 3,604 lines of dietary supplements, citing 5,560 violations. Twenty-five percent of the violations were due to the potential presence of an unsafe substance.
Pursue legal action against the firm	FDA initiated action for 27 seizures and 6 injunctions from fiscal year 2002 through July 18, 2008. Nineteen of the seizures and 6 of the injunctions regarded products promoted to treat, cure, or prevent diseases. FDA had filed criminal charges or won convictions in 19 cases since fiscal year 2002, as of July 31, 2008.
Ban ingredient	FDA banned one ingredient—ephedra—in 2004, almost 10 years after issuing its first advisory. FDA has not banned any other dietary supplement ingredients.

Table 5: Examples of FDA Actions Taken on Dietary Supplement Ingredients Banned in Other Countries

Ingredient	Reported uses	Dangers	Regulatory actions in other countries	FDA actions
Aristolochic acid	Aphrodisiac, immune stimulant	Kidney damage, cancers, deaths reported.	Banned in seven European countries, Japan, Venezuela, and Egypt.	In 2000 and 2001, FDA listed aristolochic acid as a "Botanical Ingredient of Concern" and issued letters to industry and health care professionals. In 2001, FDA issued an "Import Alert" for products containing the ingredient and issued a consumer advisory. FDA has also taken some enforcement or advisory actions against individual products.
Kava	Anxiety, stress	Abnormal liver function or damage, deaths reported.	Banned in Canada, Germany, Singapore, South Africa, and Switzerland.	FDA issued letters to health care professionals in 2001 and 2002 and a consumer advisory in 2002.
Lobelia	Asthma, bronchitis	Tremor, overdose may cause coma and possibly death.	Banned in Bangladesh and Italy.	No action.

Appendix III: Comparison of Selected Foreign Countries' Regulation of Dietary Supplements with the United States

In comparison with the United States, Canada and Japan have more regulatory requirements in place for dietary supplements and related products. Table 23 compares the regulatory framework for dietary supplement products in these countries with the United States regulatory system.

Table 23: Comparison of Dietary Supplement Regulations: United States, Canada, United Kingdom, and Japan

The comparison of the United States and other countries follows in Table 23.

Country	Product registration	Manufacturer registration	Premarket approval of products	Specific good manufacturing practices	Serious mandatory adverse event reporting by industry
United States		X (limited)		X	X
Canada	X	X[a]	X	X	X
United Kingdom		X	X[b] (limited)		X[c]
Japan[d]	X	X	X	X[e]	

Source: GAO.

Note: GAO did not independently verify descriptions of foreign laws.

[a]Manufacturers, packagers, labelers, and importers of natural health products must obtain a site license to perform these activities.

[b]Under European Community (E.C.) law, novel supplements without a history of consumption in the European Union prior to May 1997, or foods containing genetically-modified ingredients are subject to premarket approval for safety.

[c]According to a U.K. official, under E.C. law, firms must report any problems with products to the local and national authorities.

[d]Foods for Specified Health Uses (FOSHU) products only.

[e]According to a Japanese official, Japan does not have separate good manufacturing practice regulations for dietary supplement products; however, firms applying to use a FOSHU claim on a product must provide evidence that quality control procedures are in place for that particular product.

Canada: Companies in Canada are required to obtain a product license to market natural health products, such as vitamin and mineral supplements, herbal remedies, and other products, based upon their medicinal ingredients and intended uses. The product licensing application must include detailed information about the product, ingredients, potency, intended use, and evidence supporting the product's safety and efficacy. A license number is assigned for approved products and placed on the product label. Manufacturers, packagers, labelers, and importers of natural health products must obtain a site license to perform these activities. A firm must provide evidence of quality control procedures that meet government standards for good manufacturing practices in order to procure a site license. Similar to the United States, a firm must report serious adverse reactions associated with their products within 15 days and must provide information summarizing all adverse reactions, including mild or moderate events, on an annual basis. (edited).

United Kingdom: In the United Kingdom (U.K.), dietary supplements are legally termed "food supplements" and are regulated under food law and based on European Community (E.C.) legislation implemented at the national level. Food supplements are generally not subject to premarket approval. For example, any supplement that either meets the guidelines established under E.U. law for specific vitamins and minerals or does not include a new or genetically modified ingredient, does not require approval prior to marketing. Direct oversight of the dietary supplement industry in the U.K. is with the local government. For example, all investigations, enforcement actions, and monitoring activities such as inspections are undertaken at the local level. Food supplement firms are required to register with local authorities and should detail the specific activities undertaken at each establishment as part of this process. Interestingly, there is no centralized registry of food supplement products in the U.K. Although government standards for food good manufacturing practices apply to food supplement manufacturing, there are no good manufacturing practice guidelines specific for food supplements. Under E.C. law, firms are required to report any problems with food products to the local and national authorities and, if the product is injurious to health, the firm must remove it from the market. (edited).

Japan: Products are regulated based on their claims: *Food with Nutrient Function Claims (FNFC)*, which are standardized, preapproved claim statements for certain vitamins and minerals with established benefits, and *Food for Specified Health Uses (FOSHU)* claims, which require government approval for safety and efficacy prior to marketing a product advertised as having a physiological effect on the body. FNFC claims are standardized and preapproved, firms do not need to notify the government prior to marketing a product using an approved FNFC claim, provided the product meets established ingredient content specifications. Prior to marketing, to use a FOSHU claim on a product, a company must provide the government with evidence supporting the product's physiological effect and safety. Company information must be submitted along with evidence of quality control processes. (edited).

CRITICAL ANALYSIS: As noted, unlike the United States regulatory classification, Canada typically classifies dietary supplements as drugs. Companies are required to obtain a product license to market natural health products, which include a range of products, such as vitamin and mineral supplements, herbal remedies, and other products, based upon their medicinal ingredients and intended uses. Discuss the impact of Canadian companies exporting dietary supplements to the United States and United States companies exporting dietary supplements to Canada.

GAO Report 2013—Dietary Supplements and Adverse Events
Dietary Supplements—FDA May Have Opportunities to Expand Its Use of Reported Health Problems to Oversee Products
http://www.gao.gov/products/GAO-13-244

The GAO report issued in 2013 (GAO-13-244, Mar 18, 2013) concerned adverse reports and followed the 2009 report referenced above.

Figure 3: The Number of Voluntary and Mandatory Industry AERs Related to Dietary Supplements FDA Received, 2008 through 2011

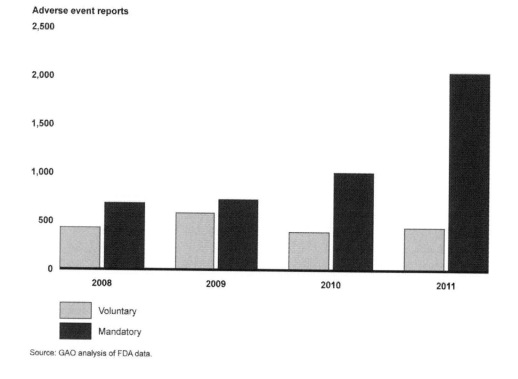

Source: GAO analysis of FDA data.

The 6,307 adverse event reports (AERs) for dietary supplements from 2008-2011reported the following serious outcomes:

- 53 percent (3,370) resulted in unspecified important medical events of a serious nature,
- 29 percent (1,836) resulted in hospitalization,
- 20 percent (1,272) resulted in serious injuries or illnesses,
- 8 percent (512) resulted in a life-threatening condition, and
- 2 percent (92) resulted in death.

NOTE: Each AER can report multiple outcomes; therefore, numbers and percentages of outcomes should not be totaled.

The AERs were associated with supplements containing a combination of ingredients, such as vitamins and minerals or were otherwise not classified within FDA's product categories. Of the AERs, 71 percent were from industry as serious adverse events. The AERs were associated with supplements containing a combination of ingredients, such as vitamins and minerals or were otherwise not classified within FDA's product categories. The GAO 2013 report found that FDA may not be receiving information on all adverse events because consumers and others may not be voluntarily reporting these events to FDA. Consumers may be contacting poison centers. For example, from 2008 to 2010 these centers received over 1,000 more reports of adverse events connected to dietary supplements. GAO found that FDA increased its inspections of supplement firms from 120 in 2008 to 410 for the first nine months in 2012. Regulatory action involved issuance of warning letters, an injunction and 15 import refusals associated with AER violations, such as not including contact information on the product label or failure to submit serious AER.

Although more needs to be done, this GAO 2013 report found that FDA partially implemented all of the GAO's 2009 recommendations, such as issuing guidance for new dietary ingredients, clarifying the boundary between dietary supplements and conventional foods, and increasing partnerships.

CRITICAL ANALYSIS: Note the escalation of adverse reports. Should Congress revisit DSHEA and enact stronger legislation similar to the Canadian system of regulation? Include a discussion about the following: *"This statement has not been evaluated by the Food and Drug Administration. This product is not intended to diagnose, treat, cure, or prevent any disease."* Is this statement adequate for consumer comprehension?

Memory Supplements
Clarifying FDA and FTC Roles Could Strengthen Oversight and Enhance Consumer Awareness
GAO-17-416: Published: May 16, 2017. Publicly Released: Jun 15, 2017.
https://www.gao.gov/products/GAO-17-416 (edited)
Summation of Report

GAO's market review consisted of 490 memory supplements products and found that approximately 96 percent of marketing was through the Internet. GAO found 28 examples of advertisements that linked supplement use to treatment or prevention of memory-related diseases, prohibited by the FDCA. FDA determined that 27 of these examples appeared to violate federal law.

FDA's has authority to regulate dietary supplements and their labeling, and the Federal Trade Commission's (FTC) authority is to enforce the prohibitions against deceptive advertising. The agencies coordinate enforcement actions. In prioritizing enforcement and outreach efforts, the agencies focus on safety, egregiousness of deception, and impact of marketing.

CRITICAL ANALYSIS: According to FDA, the agency understands it needs to improve its oversight while FTC considers its oversight is sufficient. GAO recommended that both FDA and FTC have to do better in terms of communication and clarification of the respective role of FTC and FDA. This is critical as both FDA and FTC take consumer complaints very seriously. Propose how FDA and FTC should better communicate in terms of enforcement roles.

Chapter 2: Specific Claims for Dietary Supplements

Key Website: *https://www.fda.gov/Food/LabelingNutrition/ucm111447.htm*

FDA regulates claim validity while FTC regulates product advertising. The key is substantiation; that is, manufacturers must have adequate support for product claims.

Categories include:

> ➢ *Health,*
> ➢ *Structure Function, and*
> ➢ *Nutrient Content.*

Specific types of health claims and approved health claims are detailed below and depend on the specific law noted below. Additionally, FDA uses what is termed *"Enforcement Discretion"* for several health claims termed "qualified claims". Qualified claims and the FDA methodology for "enforcement discretion" are detailed. Finally, structure-function and nutrient content claims are discussed as well.

Health Claims—Specific Types

A health claim describes the relationship between a substance and a disease or health-related condition (21 CFR 101.14(a)(1)). Health claims are limited to claims about disease risk reduction and cannot be claims about the cure, mitigation, or treatment of disease. The latter claims are drug claims under section 201(g) of the FDCA.

Types of health claims include the following:

> ➢ *Significant Scientific Agreement (NLEA);*
> ➢ *Authoritative Statement (FDAMA); and*
> ➢ *Qualified Claims.*

Health Claims—Significant Scientific Agreement (SSA)

The Nutrition Labeling and Education Act (NLEA) of 1990, the Dietary Supplement Act of 1992, and the Dietary Supplement Health and Education Act of 1994 (DSHEA), provide for health claims used on labels that characterize a relationship between a food, a food component, dietary ingredient, or dietary supplement and risk of a disease for example, "diets high in calcium may reduce the risk of osteoporosis", provided the claims meet certain criteria and are authorized by an FDA regulation. FDA authorizes these types of health claims based on an extensive review of the scientific literature. For an explanation of the significant scientific agreement standard. See: link for list of approved claims under the significant scientific agreement (SSA) standard.

Approved Health Claims under NELA Applying the SSA Standard

FDA authorized health claim that meets the significant scientific agreement standard in the 1990 Nutrition Labeling and Education Act (NLEA) as follows. The following link contains the approved claims.

Calcium, Vitamin D, and Osteoporosis

21 CFR 101.72 Health claims: calcium and osteoporosis

Final Rule: Food Labeling: Health Claims; Calcium and Osteoporosis, and Calcium, Vitamin D, and Osteoporosis September 29, 2008

Dietary Lipids (Fat) and Cancer

21 CFR 101.73 Health claims: dietary lipids and cancer

Dietary Saturated Fat and Cholesterol and Risk of Coronary Heart Disease

21 CFR 101.75 Health claims: dietary saturated fat and cholesterol and risk of coronary heart disease

Dietary Non-cariogenic Carbohydrate Sweeteners and Dental Caries

21 CFR 101.80 Health claims: dietary noncariogenic carbohydrate sweeteners and dental caries

Final Rule: Food Labeling: Health Claims Dietary Noncariogenic Carbohydrate Sweeteners and dental caries May 27, 2008

Final Rule: Food Labeling: Health Claims; D-tagatose and Dental Caries July 3, 2003

Final Rule: Food Labeling: Health Claims; Dietary Sugar Alcohols and Dental Caries December 2, 1997

Final Rule: Food Labeling: Health Claims; Sugar Alcohols and Dental Caries August 23, 1996

Fiber-containing Grain Products, Fruits and Vegetables and Cancer

21 CFR 101.76 Health claims: fiber-containing grain products, fruits, and vegetables and cancer

Folic Acid and Neural Tube Defects

21 CFR 101.79 Health claims: Folate and neural tube defects

Final Rule: Food Labeling: Health Claims; Folate and Neural Tube Defects March 5, 1996

Final Rule: Revoking January 4, 1994 Regulation That Became Final By Operation of Law September 24, 1996

Fruits and Vegetables and Cancer

21 CFR 101.78 Health claims: fruits and vegetables and cancer

Fruits, Vegetables and Grain Products that contain Fiber, Particularly Soluble Fiber, and Risk of Coronary Heart Disease

21 CFR 101.77 Health claims: fruits, vegetables, and grain products that contain fiber, particularly soluble fiber, and risk of coronary heart disease

Sodium and Hypertension

21 CFR 101.74 Health claims: sodium and hypertension

Soluble Fiber from Certain Foods and Risk of Coronary Heart Disease

21 CFR 101.81 Health claims: Soluble fiber from certain foods and risk of coronary heart disease (CHD)

Final Rule: Food Labeling: Health Claims; Soluble Fiber from Certain Foods and Risk of Coronary Heart Disease (Barley Betafiber) August 15, 2008

Final Rule: Food Labeling: Health Claims; Soluble Fiber from Certain Foods and Risk of Coronary Heart Disease May 1, 2008

Final Rule: Health Claims; Soluble Dietary Fiber from Certain Foods and Coronary Heart Disease (CHD) (Barley) May 22, 2006

Final Rule: Health Claims; Soluble Dietary Fiber From Certain Foods and Coronary Heart Disease (Oatrim) July 28, 2003

Final rule: correction: Food Labeling: Health Claims; Soluble Fiber From Certain Foods and Coronary Heart Disease; Correction (Psyllium husk) April 9, 1998

Final Rule: Food Labeling; Health Claims; Soluble Fiber from Certain Foods and Risk of Coronary Heart Disease (Psyllium husk) February 18, 1998.

Final Rule: Food Labeling: Health Claims; Soluble Fiber From Whole Oats and Risk of Coronary Heart Disease Amended March 31, 1997

Final Rule: Food Labeling: Health Claims; Oats and Coronary Heart Disease Jan. 23, 1997

Soy Protein and Risk of Coronary Heart Disease

21 CFR 101.82 Health claims: Soy protein and risk of coronary heart disease (CHD)

Final Rule: Food Labeling: Health Claims; Soy Protein and Coronary Heart Disease October 26, 1999

NOTE: FDA issued a proposed rule to revoke this regulation authorizing the use of health claims on the relationship between soy protein and coronary heart disease on the label or in the labeling of foods due to a lack of scientific consensus. 82 FR 50324 (October 31, 2017). If the proposed rule becomes final the regulation would be classified as a qualified claim.

CRITICAL ANALYSIS: Evaluate whether FDA will be successful in recategorizing this claim.

Stanols/Sterols and Risk of Coronary Heart Disease

Proposed Rule: Food Labeling: Health Claim; Phytosterols and Risk of Coronary Heart Disease December 8, 2010

FDA Letter Regarding Enforcement Discretion With Respect to Expanded Use of an Interim Health Claim Rule About Plant Sterol/Stanol Esters and Reduced Risk of Coronary Heart Disease February 14, 2003

21 CFR 101.83 Health claims: plant sterol/stanol esters and risk of coronary heart disease (CHD)

Health Claims—Authoritative Statement FDAMA

The Food and Drug Administration Modernization Act of 1997 (FDAMA) provides a second way for the use of a health claim on foods to be authorized. FDAMA allows certain health claims to be made as a result of a successful notification to FDA of a health claim based on an "authoritative statement from a scientific body of the U.S. Government or the National Academy of Sciences. The following link provides access to the approved health claims.

http://www.fda.gov/food/ingredientspackaginglabeling/labelingnutrition/ucm2006874.htm

https://www.fda.gov/Food/GuidanceRegulation/GuidanceDocumentsRegulatoryInformation/ucm056975.htm

Approved Health Claims Under FDAMA Using the Authoritative Statement

Linoleic Acid: Nutrient Content Claims Notification for Foods and Dietary Supplements Containing Linoleic Acid December 23, 2014

Choline: Nutrient Content Claims Notification for Choline Containing Foods August 30, 2001

Fluoride and the Risk of Dental Caries: Health Claim Notification for Fluoridated Water October 14, 2006

Potassium and the Risk of High Blood Pressure and Stroke: Health Claim Notification for Potassium Containing Foods October 31, 2000

Saturated Fat, Cholesterol, and *Trans* Fat, and the Risk of Heart Disease: Health Claim Notification for Saturated Fat, Cholesterol, and *Trans* Fat and Reduced Risk of Heart Disease November 15, 2006

Substitution of Saturated Fat with Unsaturated Fatty Acids and Risk of Heart Disease: Health Claim Notification for the Substitution of Saturated Fat in the Diet with Unsaturated Fatty Acids and Reduced Risk of Heart Disease May 25, 2007

Whole Grain Foods and the Risk of Heart Disease and Certain Cancers: Health Claim Notification for Whole Grain Foods with Moderate Fat Content December 9, 2003

Health Claim Notification for Whole Grain Foods July 8, 1999

Health Claims—Qualified

https://www.fda.gov/Food/LabelingNutrition/ucm111447.htm

FDA's *Consumer Health Information for Better Nutrition Initiative* provides for the use of qualified health claims when there is emerging evidence for a relationship between a food, food component, or dietary supplement and the reduced risk of a disease or health-related condition. In this case, the evidence is not well enough established to meet the significant scientific agreement standard required for FDA to issue an authorizing regulation. Qualifying language is included as part of the claim to indicate that the evidence supporting the claim is limited. Both conventional foods and dietary supplements may use qualified health claims. FDA uses its enforcement discretion for qualified health claims after evaluating and ranking the quality and strength of the totality of the scientific evidence.

NOTE: See *Health Claims Unpacking their Language on Food Labels,* Mary L. Klatt and Roseann B. Termini, 1 Update 33 (2008) (Used with Permission, Food and Drug Law Institute).

Standardized Qualifying Language for Qualified Health Claims

http://www.fda.gov/Food/GuidanceRegulation/GuidanceDocumentsRegulatoryInformation/LabelingNutrition/ucm053832.htm

The following chart lists the Scientific Ranking, FDA Category and Appropriate Qualifying Language.

Scientific Ranking*	FDA Category	Appropriate Qualifying Language**
Second Level	B	"although there is scientific evidence supporting the claim, the evidence is not conclusive."
Third Level	C	"Some scientific evidence suggests ... however, FDA has determined that this evidence is limited and not conclusive."
Fourth Level	D	"Very limited and preliminary scientific research suggests... FDA concludes that there is little scientific evidence supporting this claim."

NOTE: FDA Category A—are approved claims. *From Guidance for Industry and FDA: Interim Evidence-based Ranking System for Scientific Data. **Language reflects wording used in qualified health claims as to which the FDA has previously exercised enforcement discretion for certain dietary supplements. During this interim period, the precise language as to which the agency considers exercising enforcement discretion may vary depending on the specific circumstances of each case.

Qualified Health Claims—Enforcement Discretion

The following link provides a list of qualified claims and their status.

https://www.fda.gov/Food/LabelingNutrition/ucm2006877.htm (edited)

Atopic Dermatitis

100% Whey-Protein Partially Hydrolyzed Infant Formula and Reduced Risk of Atopic Dermatitis May 24, 2011

Cancer

Selenium and a Reduced Risk of Site-specific Cancers June 19, 2009

Antioxidant Vitamins C and E and Reduction in the Risk of Site-Specific Cancers June 19, 2009

Tomatoes and Prostate, Ovarian, Gastric, and Pancreatic Cancers (American Longevity Petition) November 8, 2005

Tomatoes and Prostate Cancer (Lycopene Heath Claim Coalition Petition) November 8, 2005

Calcium and Colon/Rectal Cancer and Calcium and Colon/Rectal Polyps October 12, 2005

Letter Updating the Green Tea and Risk of Breast Cancer and Prostate Cancer Health Claim April 17, 2012

Green Tea and Risk of Breast Cancer and Prostate Cancer February 24, 2011

Selenium and Certain Cancers April 28, 2003

Selenium and Certain Cancers February 21, 2003

Antioxidant Vitamins and Risk of Certain Cancers April 1, 2003

NOTE: Selenium—See Chapter 3 This Volume— *Alliance for Natural Health US, et al. v. Sebelius*

First Amendment—In *Fleminger, Inc. v. United States Dept. of Health and Human Services*, Civ. Action 854 F. Supp.2d 192 No. 3:10 855 (DC D. Conn. Feb. 23, 2012),

the plaintiff filed a lawsuit against FDA and objected in First Amendment principles due to the FDA qualifying language requirement as follows: *"Green tea may reduce the risk of breast or prostate cancers. FDA does not agree that green tea may reduce that risk because there is very little scientific evidence for the claim."*

The federal district court agreed that the above language did not impart a reasonable fit between FDA's end and the agency's means used to achieve that end. The court deemed the following language appropriate and still fulfill the agency's interest to protect the public.

"Green tea may reduce the risk of breast or prostate cancer although the FDA has concluded that there is very little scientific evidence to support the claim."

Cardiovascular Disease

Folic Acid, Vitamin B6, and Vitamin B12 and Vascular Disease: Settlement Health Claim B Vitamins and Vascular Disease May 15, 2001

Folic Acid, Vitamin B6, and Vitamin B12 and Vascular Disease November 28, 2000

Nuts and Coronary Heart Disease

Walnuts and Coronary Heart Disease March 9, 2004

Nuts and Coronary Heart Disease July 14, 2003

Omega-3 Fatty Acids

Omega-3 Fatty Acids and Reduced Risk of Coronary Heart Disease (Martek Petition) September 8, 2004

Omega-3 Fatty Acids and Reduced Risk of Coronary Heart Disease (Wellness Petition) September 8, 2004

Unsaturated Fatty Acids

Corn Oil and Corn Oil-Containing Products and a Reduced Risk of Heart Disease March 26, 2007

Unsaturated Fatty Acids from Canola Oil and Reduced Risk of Coronary Heart Disease October 6, 2006

Monounsaturated Fatty Acids from Olive Oil and Coronary Heart Disease Nov. 1, 2004

Cognitive Function

Letter Updating the Phosphatidylserine and Cognitive Function and Dementia Qualified Health Claim November 24, 2004

Phosphatidylserine and Cognitive Dysfunction and Dementia, May 13, 2003

Phosphatidylserine and Cognitive Dysfunction and Dementia February 24, 2003

Diabetes

Approved Psyllium statements:

Psyllium husk may reduce the risk of type 2 diabetes, although the FDA has concluded that there is very little scientific evidence for this claim.

Psyllium husk may reduce the risk of type 2 diabetes. FDA has concluded that there is very little scientific evidence for this claim.

http://www.fda.gov/downloads/Food/IngredientsPackagingLabeling/LabelingNutrition/UCM403090.pdf (June 23, 2014).

Whole Grains and a Reduced Risk of Diabetes Mellitus Type 2 (PDF - 564KB) September 11, 2013

Chromium Picolinate

Reduced Risk of Insulin Resistance, Type 2 Diabetes August 25, 2005.

Hypertension

Calcium and Hypertension, Pregnancy-Induced Hypertension Preeclampsia Oct. 12, 2005.

Neural Tube Defects

Folic Acid and Neural Tube Defects April 3, 2001 and October 10, 2000.

Peanut Allergy

Ground Peanuts and Reduced Risk of Developing Peanut Allergy (Docket No. FDA-2016-Q-0274)

Qualified Health Claims: Letters of Denial

Cancer

Lycopene and Various Cancers (American Longevity Petition) November 8, 2005

Lycopene and Prostate Cancer (Lycopene Heath Claim Coalition Petition) November 8, 2005.

Calcium and Risk of Breast and Prostate Cancers October 12, 2005

Green Tea and Risk of: Gastric Cancer; Lung Cancer; Colon/Rectal Cancer; Esophageal Cancer; Pancreatic Cancer; Ovarian Cancer; Liver Cancer; Bladder Cancer; and Skin Cancer, as well as Total Cancers Combined June 30, 2005

Fiber and Colorectal Cancer October 10, 2000

Cardiovascular Disease

Green Tea and Reduced Risk of Cardiovascular Disease May 9, 2006

Eggs with Enhanced Omega-3 Fatty Acid Content and a Balanced 1:1 Ratio of Omega-3/Omega-6 Fatty Acids and Reduced Risk of Heart Disease and Sudden Fatal Heart Attack April 5, 2005

Vitamin E and Heart Disease February 9, 2001

Diabetes

Chromium Picolinate and a Reduced Risk of: Cardiovascular Disease When Caused by Insulin Resistance; Cardiovascular Disease When Caused by Abnormally Elevated Blood Sugar Levels; Cardiovascular Disease When Caused by Type 2 Diabetes; Retinopathy When Caused by Abnormally High Blood Sugar Levels; and Kidney Disease When Caused by Abnormally High Blood Sugar Levels August 25, 2005

Eye Diseases

Xangold® Lutein Esters, Lutein, or Zeaxanthin and Reduced Risk of Age-related Macular Degeneration or Cataract Formation December 19, 2005

Food Allergy

100 Percent Partially Hydrolyzed Whey Protein in Infant Formula and Reduced Risk of Food Allergy in Infants May 11, 2006

Kidney Stones/Urinary Stones

Calcium and Kidney/Urinary Stones October 12, 2005

Menstrual Disorders

Calcium and a Reduced Risk of Menstrual Disorders September 12, 2005

Osteoarthritis

Glucosamine and/or Chondroitin Sulfate and a Reduced Risk of: Osteoarthritis; Osteoarthritis-related Joint Pain, Joint Tenderness, and Joint Swelling; Joint Degeneration; and Cartilage Deterioration October 7, 2004

Crystalline Glucosamine Sulfate and a Reduced Risk of Osteoarthritis October 7, 2004

NOTE: The National Institutes of Health, National Center for Alternative and Complementary Medicine conducted a large-scale study of Glucosamine/chondroitin Arthritis Intervention Trial (GAIT) to determine the effects of the dietary supplements glucosamine hydrochloride (glucosamine) and sodium chondroitin sulfate (chondroitin sulfate) for the treatment of knee osteoarthritis. The GAIT study tested whether glucosamine and chondroitin sulfate used either separately or in combination alleviated pain in study participants with knee osteoarthritis.

See: *http://nccam.nih.gov/research/results/gait*

CRITICAL ANALYSIS: Evaluate the "approval process" for qualified claims and latitude of FDA including enforcement discretion.

Structure-Function and Related Dietary Supplement Claims

https://www.fda.gov/Food/LabelingNutrition/ucm111447.htm (edited)

Structure-function claims have historically appeared on the labels of conventional foods and dietary supplements as well as drugs. However, the Dietary Supplement Health and Education Act of 1994 (DSHEA) established some special regulatory procedures for such claims for dietary supplement labels. Structure/function claims describe the role of a nutrient or dietary ingredient intended to affect normal structure or function in humans, for example, "calcium builds strong bones." In addition, they may characterize the means by which a nutrient or dietary ingredient acts to maintain such structure or function, for example, "fiber maintains bowel regularity," or "antioxidants maintain cell integrity," or they may describe general well-being from consumption of a nutrient or dietary ingredient. Structure/function claims may also describe a benefit related to a nutrient deficiency disease (like vitamin C and scurvy), as long as the statement also tells how widespread such a disease is in the United States.

The manufacturer is responsible for ensuring the accuracy of these claims; they are not pre-approved by FDA yet must be truthful and not misleading. If a dietary supplement label includes such a claim, it must state in a "disclaimer" that FDA has not evaluated the claim. The disclaimer must also state that the dietary supplement product is not intended to "diagnose, treat, cure or prevent any disease," because only a drug can legally make such a claim. Manufacturers of dietary supplements that make structure/function claims on labels or in labeling must submit a notification to FDA no later than 30 days after marketing the dietary supplement that includes the text of the structure/function claim. See 21 CFR 101.93 entitled "Certain Types of Statements for Dietary Supplements," and the January 6, 2000 Federal Register (65 FR 1000) that describes the types of claims that can and cannot be made for dietary supplements.

NOTE: Structure/function claims for conventional foods focus on effects derived from nutritive value, while structure/function claims for dietary supplements may focus on non-nutritive as well as nutritive effects. FDA does not require conventional food manufacturers to notify FDA about their structure/function claims, and disclaimers are not required for claims on conventional foods.

Nutrient Content Claims

https://www.fda.gov/Food/LabelingNutrition/ucm111447.htm (edited)

The Nutrition Labeling and Education Act of 1990 (NLEA) permits the use of label claims that characterize the level of a nutrient in a food. Nutrient content claims describe the level of a nutrient or dietary substance in the product, using terms such as *free*, *high*, and *low*, or they compare the level of a nutrient in a food to that of another food, using terms such as *more*, *reduced*, and *lite*. An accurate quantitative statement (e.g., 200 mg of sodium) that does not "characterize" the nutrient level may be used to describe any amount of a nutrient present. However, a statement such as "only 200 mg of sodium" characterizes the level of sodium as being low and would therefore need to conform to the criteria of an appropriate nutrient content claim or carry a disclosure statement that it does not comply with the claim.

The requirements that govern the use of nutrient content claims help ensure that descriptive terms, such as *high* or *low*, are used consistently for all types of food products and are thus meaningful to consumers. *Healthy* has been defined by a regulation as an implied nutrient content claim that characterizes a food that has "healthy" levels of total fat, saturated fat, cholesterol and sodium. Percentage claims for dietary supplements are another category of nutrient content claims. These claims are used to describe a percentage level of a dietary ingredient for which there is no established Daily Value. Examples include simple percentage statements such as "40% omega-3 fatty acids, 10 mg per capsule," and comparative percentage claims, e.g., "twice the omega-3 fatty acids per capsule (80 mg) as in 100 mg of menhaden oil (40 mg)." (See 21 CFR 101.13(q)(3)(ii)).

NOTE: HEALTHY— Perhaps due in part to the Kind® warning letter (March 2015) and subsequent close out letter by FDA (2016), the agency evaluated the term *healthy*. Specifically, FDA stated: "*In our discussions with KIND, we understood the company's position as wanting to use "healthy and tasty" as part of its corporate philosophy, as opposed to using "healthy" in the context of a nutrient content claim. The FDA evaluates the label as a whole and has indicated that in this instance it does not object.*" The current regulations links are below; however, this could change based on FDA's stance.

https://www.accessdata.fda.gov/scripts/cdrh/cfdocs/cfcfr/CFRSearch.cfm?fr=101.65
https://www.accessdata.fda.gov/scripts/cdrh/cfdocs/cfcfr/CFRSearch.cfm?fr=101.62

Chapter 3: Milestone Dietary Supplement Court Decisions

Noteworthy court decisions important to the dietary supplement industry and FDA are detailed. *Pearson v. Shalala* is the seminal case that changed the landscape for how FDA approves claims. Another principal decision, *Alliance for Natural Health,* involved selenium and qualified claims. *Whitaker v. Thompson* concerned saw palmetto extract. *Pharmanex Inc. v. Shalala,* involved a cholesterol product classified as a dietary supplement. The *Nutraceutical Corp.* decision concerning the ban of ephedrine alkaloids is in Chapter 4, Enforcement.

Pearson v. Shalala

FDA's general health claim regulations for dietary supplements as well as the denial by FDA of certain health claims were legally challenged in 1998 in *Pearson [Pearson I].* On January 15, 1999, the U.S. Court of Appeals for the D.C. Circuit invalidated the regulations that prohibited the use of four health claims at issue listed in the court decision below. The court, in *Pearson v. Shalala,* directed FDA to reconsider authorization of the claims required FDA to clarify the "significant scientific agreement" standard (SSA) for authorizing health claims, either by issuing a regulatory definition of SSA or by a case-by-case basis. Rehearing petition denied.

Pearson [Pearson I] v. Shalala,
164 F.3d 650 (D.C. Cir.1999)

SILBERMAN, Circuit Judge: Marketers of dietary supplements must, before including on their labels a claim characterizing the relationship of the supplement to a disease or health-related condition, submit the claim to the Food and Drug Administration for preapproval. The FDA authorizes a claim only if it finds "significant scientific agreement" among experts that the claim is supported by the available evidence. Appellants failed to persuade the FDA to authorize four such claims and sought relief in the district court, where their various constitutional and statutory challenges were rejected. We reverse.

Dietary supplement marketers Durk Pearson and Sandy Shaw, presumably hoping to bolster sales by increasing the allure of their supplements' labels, asked the FDA to authorize four separate health claims. A "health claim" is a "claim made on the label or in labeling of ... a dietary supplement that expressly or by implication ... characterizes the relationship of any substance to a disease or health-related condition." 21 C.F.R. § 101.14(a)(1) (1998). Each claim links the consumption of a particular supplement to the reduction in risk of a particular disease:

(1) "Consumption of antioxidant vitamins may reduce the risk of certain kinds of cancers."

(2) "Consumption of fiber may reduce the risk of colorectal cancer."

(3) "Consumption of omega-3 fatty acids may reduce the risk of coronary heart disease."

(4) ".8 mg of folic acid in a dietary supplement is more effective in reducing the risk of neural tube defects than a lower amount in foods in common form."

The problem with these claims, according to the FDA, was not a dearth of supporting evidence; rather, the agency concluded that the evidence was inconclusive for one reason or another and thus failed to give rise to "significant scientific agreement." But the FDA never explained just how it measured "significant" or otherwise defined the phrase. *** We invert the normal order here to discuss first appellants' most powerful constitutional claim, that the government has violated the First Amendment by declining to employ a less draconian method—the use of disclaimers—to serve the government's interests, because the requested remedy stands apart from appellants' request under the APA that the FDA flesh out its standards. *** Under *Central Hudson,* we are obliged to evaluate a government scheme to regulate potentially misleading commercial speech by applying a three-part test. First, we ask whether the asserted government interest is substantial. *Central Hudson,* 447 U.S. at 566, 100 S.Ct. 2343. The FDA advanced two general concerns: protection of public health and prevention of consumer fraud. *** The agency could require the label to state that "The FDA does not approve this claim." *** Accordingly, on remand, the FDA must

440

explain what it means by significant scientific agreement or, at minimum, what it does not mean. *** For the foregoing reasons, we hold invalid the four sub-regulations, 21 C.F.R. § 101.71(a), (c), (e); § 101.79(c)(2)(i)(G), and the FDA's interpretation of its general regulation, id. § 101.14. The decision of the district court is reversed, and the case is remanded to the district court with instructions to remand in turn to the FDA for reconsideration of appellants' health claims.

FDA Reconsideration of Claims after *Pearson I*—FDA's strategy for implementing *Pearson* included: a review of the scientific evidence on the four claims involved; issuance of a guidance to explain the "significant scientific agreement" standard; rulemaking proceedings to reconsider the general health claims regulations and rulemaking proceedings on the four Pearson health claims. The outcome was as follows:

"Consumption of antioxidant vitamins may reduce the risk of certain kinds of cancer."
Required Claim Statement(s).

(1) Some scientific evidence suggests that consumption of antioxidant vitamins may reduce the risk of certain forms of cancer. However, FDA has determined that this evidence is limited and not conclusive.

(2) Some scientific evidence suggests that consumption of antioxidant vitamins may reduce the risk of certain forms of cancer. However, FDA does not endorse this claim because this evidence is limited and not conclusive.

(3) FDA has determined that although some scientific evidence suggests that consumption of antioxidant vitamins may reduce the risk of certain forms of cancer, this evidence is limited and not conclusive.

"Consumption of omega-3 fatty acids may reduce the risk of coronary heart disease."
Required Claim Statement(s) *Consumption of omega-3 fatty acids may reduce the risk of coronary heart disease. FDA evaluated the data and determined that although there is scientific evidence supporting the claim, the evidence is not conclusive.*

"0.8 mg of folic acid in a dietary supplement is more effective in reducing the risk of neural tube defects than a lower amount in foods in common form."
Required Claim Statement(s) *0.8 mg folic acid in a dietary supplement is more effective in reducing the risk of neural tube defects than a lower amount in foods in common form. FDA does not endorse this claim. Public health authorities recommend that women consume 0.4 mg folic acid daily from fortified foods or dietary supplements or both to reduce the risk of neural tube defects.*

"Consumption of fiber may reduce the risk of colorectal cancer." FDA determined that the proposed health claim about dietary fiber and reduced risk of colorectal cancer could not be authorized because studies revealed an insufficient relationship between dietary fiber supplements and the risk of colorectal cancer. Furthermore, this claim could not be qualified because the evidence against the claim outweighed the evidence for it.

CRITICAL ANALYSIS: Evaluate this case and explain why the court ruling as it did and how FDA adhered to the ruling.

Selenium—*Alliance for Natural Health*

Several dietary supplement manufacturers challenged the denial of qualified health claims about selenium-containing dietary supplements on First Amendment principles. The District Court, in *Alliance for Natural Health,* held that FDA was required to consider whether inclusion of appropriate disclaimers would negate the possibility of misleading claims as well as FDA's substitute claim concerning prostate cancer risk and selenium intake was inconsistent with the First Amendment.

Alliance for Natural Health US, et al. v. Sebelius,
714 F. Supp. 2d 48 (2010)
District Judge Ellen Segal Huvelle: Plaintiffs Alliance for Natural Health US, Durk Pearson,

Sandy Shaw, and Coalition to End FDA and FTC Censorship have sued the Food and Drug Administration ("FDA" or "Agency") sought review of FDA's decision to deny plaintiffs' petition for authorization of qualified health claims regarding selenium-containing dietary supplements.

I. STATUTORY AND REGULATORY FRAMEWORK—A "dietary supplement" is a "product (other than tobacco) intended to supplement the diet that bears or contains" one or more of certain dietary ingredients, including vitamins, minerals, herbs or botanicals, amino acids, concentrates, metabolites, constituents, or extracts. 21 U.S.C. § 321(ff)(1)(A)-(F). A dietary supplement is deemed to be "food," *id.* § 321(ff), which is defined in part as "articles used for food or drink for man or other animals," *id.* § 321(f)(1), except when it meets the definition of a "drug," which is defined in part as "articles intended for use in the diagnosis, cure, mitigation, treatment, or prevention of disease in man or other animals." *Id.* § 321(g)(1)(B). A "health claim" is "any claim made on the label or in labeling of a food, including a dietary supplement, that expressly or by implication *** characterizes the relationship of any substance to a disease or health-related condition." 21 C.F.R. § 101.14(a)(1); *see also* 21 U.S.C. § 343(r)(1)(A)-(B). ***

II. *PEARSON V. SHALALA* AND SUBSEQUENT CASE LAW
A. Introduction Plaintiffs' lawsuit is the latest in a series of disputes between dietary supplement designers and the FDA regarding the Agency's regulation of health claims regarding dietary supplements after the passage of the NLEA. Pearson, Shaw, and other individuals and groups affiliated with the production, sale, and use of dietary supplements have, since 1995, sought judicial review of FDA decisions denying a variety of proposed health claims. The first of these lawsuits, challenging the FDA's rejection of the plaintiffs' proposed claims on First Amendment grounds, resulted in an invalidation of the Agency's regulations regarding health claim review by the D.C. Circuit. Pearson I, 164 F.3d at 661. FDA has struggled to balance its concerns for consumer protection and dietary supplement manufacturers' First Amendment commercial speech rights.
B. *Pearson I [see reported decision Pearson I above]* In 1995, a group of dietary supplement manufacturers filed suit against the FDA and other defendants under the First Amendment, challenging the FDA's rejection of four health claims that the manufacturers sought to include on certain dietary supplements. *Pearson v. Shalala,* 14 F.Supp.2d 10, 14 (D.D.C.1998) [*Pearson I*]
C. *Pearson II [Folic Acid—See also Pearson I "FDA Reconsideration"]* After the decision in *Pearson I,* the FDA published a notice requesting submission of scientific data concerning the four health claims at issue in that case, including the folic acid claim. *Id.* at 110. *** The district court agreed with the plaintiffs, finding that the FDA "failed to comply with the constitutional guidelines outlined in *Pearson [I]* "when it concluded, without explanation, that the "weight of the evidence is *against* both aspects of the proposed [folic acid] claim" and that the claim was therefore "inherently misleading" and not susceptible to correction by disclaimer. *** The court remanded the case to the FDA to "draft one or more appropriately short, succinct, and accurate disclaimers." *Id.* at 120.
D. *Pearson III [FDA's Motion for Reconsideration Denied]* After the preliminary injunction was entered in *Pearson II,* the FDA filed a motion for reconsideration, arguing that the district court had "assign[ed] undue weight to a particular clinical study and fail[ed] to consider the relevant scientific evidence in totality" and "creat[ed] a legal standard which is inconsistent with [*Pearson I*]." *Pearson v. Thompson,* 141 F.Supp.2d 105, 108 (D.D.C.2001) ("*Pearson III*"). The district denied the motion, pointing to the FDA's "fail[ure] to fully and accurately describe the record evidence" and "speculative" arguments. *Id.* at 109.
E. *Whitaker v. Thompson* [Selenium Antioxidant Claim] Another lawsuit was filed to challenge the Agency's decision not to authorize the antioxidant claim at issue in *Pearson I*. The plaintiffs in *Whitaker* were Julian M. Whitaker, M.D.; Durk Pearson; Sandy Shaw; American Association for Health Freedom; Wellness Lifestyles, Inc.; and Pure Encapsulations, Inc. *Whitaker v. Thompson,* 248 F.Supp.2d 1, (D.D.C.2002). The claim at issue was that "Consumption of antioxidant vitamins may reduce the risk of certain kinds of cancers." *Whitaker,* 248 F.Supp.2d at 2; *see also*

Pearson I, 164 F.3d at 652. The Agency, after reviewing the antioxidant-cancer relationship studies submitted at its request subsequent to *Pearson I,* "found a lack of significant scientific agreement as to the relationship between antioxidant vitamin intake and reduction in the risk of developing cancer." *** Citing the Supreme Court's then-recent decision in *Western States,* the court held that the Agency had not met its "burden *** to prove that its method of regulating speech [wa]s the least restrictive means of achieving its goals." *Id.* at 9 (citing *Western States,* 535 U.S. at 371-73, 122 S.Ct. 1497). *** As a result, the court granted a preliminary injunction after concluding that the Agency's decision to suppress the claim did not "comport with the First Amendment's clear preference for disclosure over suppression of commercial speech." (remanded case to FDA to draft "short, succinct, and accurate alternative disclaimers").

THIS CASE

III. FACTUAL AND PROCEDURAL HISTORY—Wellness Lifestyles, Inc., one of the plaintiffs in *Whitaker,* submitted to the FDA two proposed health claims regarding the relationship between selenium and cancer risk. On February 21, 2003, the FDA exercised enforcement discretion with respect to two "qualified" versions of the health claims. *** The original proposed health claims were 1) "Selenium may reduce the risk of certain cancers;" and 2) "Selenium may produce anticarcinogenic effects in the body." The FDA concluded that the petition "d[id] not meet the 'significant scientific agreement standard'" but ultimately exercised enforcement discretion with respect to qualified versions of the claims that stated as follows: 1) "Selenium may reduce the risk of certain cancers. Some scientific evidence suggests that consumption of selenium may reduce the risk of certain forms of cancer. However, FDA has determined that this evidence is limited and not conclusive;" and 2) "Selenium may produce anticarcinogenic effects in the body. Some scientific evidence suggests that consumption of selenium may produce anticarcinogenic effects in the body. However, FDA has determined that this evidence is limited and not conclusive." In addition to opposing the FDA's planned re-evaluation of the qualified selenium health claims, plaintiffs submitted a health claim petition seeking authorization of ten new qualified health claims (collectively, "qualified selenium health claims") concerning the purported relationship between selenium and cancer. Plaintiffs proposed the following claims:

1. Selenium may reduce the risk of certain cancers. Scientific evidence supporting this claim is convincing but not yet conclusive.

2. Selenium may produce anticarcinogenic effects in the body. Scientific evidence supporting this claim is convincing but not yet conclusive.

3. Selenium may reduce the risk of prostate cancer. Scientific evidence supporting this claim is convincing but not yet conclusive.

4. Selenium may reduce the risk of bladder and urinary tract cancers. Scientific evidence supporting this claim is convincing but not yet conclusive.

5. Selenium may reduce the risk of lung and respiratory tract cancers. Scientific evidence supporting this claim is convincing but not yet conclusive.

6. Selenium may reduce the risk of colon and digestive tract cancers. Scientific evidence supporting this claim is convincing but not yet conclusive.

7. Selenium may reduce the risk of thyroid cancer. Scientific evidence supporting this claim is convincing but not yet conclusive.

8. Selenium may reduce the risk of brain cancer. Scientific evidence supporting this claim is convincing but not yet conclusive.

9. Selenium may reduce the risk of liver cancer. Scientific evidence supporting this claim is limited and applies only to hepatitis B virus-induced forms of the disease.

10. Selenium may reduce the risk of breast cancer. Scientific evidence supporting this claim is convincing but not yet conclusive.

Accordingly, the FDA denied Claims 1, 2, 5, 6, 8, 9, and 10 and stated that it would exercise enforcement discretion with respect to modified versions of Claims 3, 4, and 7.

ANALYSIS

I. LEGAL STANDARD

A. Scope of Review *** The Court concludes that it is obligated to conduct an independent review of the record and must do so without reliance on the Agency's determinations as to constitutional questions. ***

B. Regulation of Commercial Speech Because the qualified selenium health claims are commercial speech, the FDA's refusal to authorize them must be evaluated under the analytical framework established in *Central Hudson,* discussed by the D.C. Circuit in *Pearson I,* and elaborated upon by the Supreme Court in *Western States. Central Hudson* established a multi-step analysis of speech regulation. "As a threshold matter," the Court must determine "whether the commercial speech [being regulated] concerns unlawful activity or is misleading." *Western States,* 535 U.S. at 367, 122 S.Ct. 1497. If so, the speech is not protected. *Id.* But if the speech is lawful and not misleading, or is only potentially misleading, the Court must ask "whether the asserted governmental interest in regulating the speech is substantial." *Id.* (quoting *Central Hudson,* 447 U.S. at 566, 100 S.Ct. 2343). If it is, the Court then ascertains "whether the regulation [at issue] directly advances the governmental interest asserted" and "whether [the regulation] is not more extensive than is necessary to serve that interest." *Id.* (quoting *Central Hudson,* 447 U.S. at 566, 100 S.Ct. 2343.) This last step requires the Court to evaluate "whether the fit between the government's ends and the means chosen to accomplish those ends is reasonable."

II. FDA'S COMPLETE BAN OF PLAINTIFFS' CLAIMS

Claims 1 and 2: Plaintiffs' "Certain Cancers and Anticarcinogenic Effects" Claims *** [T]he Court will remand the claims relating to certain cancers and anticarcinogenic effects to the FDA for the purpose of drafting one or more disclaimers or, alternatively, setting forth empirical evidence that any disclaimer would fail to correct the claims' purported misleadingness.

Claim 5: Plaintiffs' Lung and Respiratory Tract Claim In contrast to the certain cancers and anticarcinogenic effects claims, the FDA considered the scientific evidence proffered by plaintiffs and concluded that it could draw scientific conclusions from only four of those studies concerning plaintiffs' lung/respiratory tract claim. *** [T]he Agency rejected the SU.VI.MAX study because the study "did not confirm that all subjects were free of the cancers of interest prior to the intervention" and therefore may have involved subjects who already had cancer at the time the study began. *** Accordingly, the Court remands the lung/respiratory tract claim to the Agency to determine an appropriate disclaimer in light of the SU.VI.MAX study.

Claim 6: Plaintiffs' Colon and Digestive Tract Claim As with the lung/respiratory tract claim, the FDA concluded that there is no credible evidence for a claim about selenium supplements and reduced risk of colon or other digestive tract cancers. *** The Agency excluded several studies because they are "retrospective," meaning that they measured selenium intake after the subjects "had already been diagnosed with the disease." *** In sum, based on its examination of the scientific literature and the FDA's response to plaintiffs' petition, the Court finds that the FDA's decision to ban plaintiffs' colon and digestive tract claim because there is no credible evidence in support of it "is unreasonable because it is not supported by a review of the available evidence or the FDA's own Guidance Report." *** The Court will remand this claim to the Agency for reconsideration and, if needed, appropriate qualifying language.

Claim 3: FDA'S Qualification of Plaintiffs' Prostate Claim After reviewing the scientific literature submitted with plaintiffs' petition, the FDA concluded that it could draw scientific conclusions regarding plaintiffs' prostate claim from eight observational studies and one intervention study. *** However, the FDA rejected plaintiffs' proposed claim because it found the characterization of the evidence in support of the claim as "convincing but not yet conclusive" to be false and misleading. *** In short, the FDA's replacement of plaintiffs' claim with different and contradictory language is inconsistent with the spirit, if not the letter, of *Pearson I.* The FDA has failed to justify the complete substitution of new language for plaintiffs' proposed claim, especially since it appears that the Agency's central objection to the claim concerns the nature of the qualifying language, not the underlying relationship claim. *** As such, the Court will remand plaintiffs' prostate claim to the FDA for the purpose of reconsidering the scientific literature and drafting one or more short, succinct, and accurate disclaimers in light of that review.

CONCLUSION—This case is remanded to the FDA for the purpose of 1) drafting one or more disclaimers to accompany plaintiffs' certain cancers, anticarcinogenic, and prostate claims, or, alternatively, setting forth empirical evidence that any disclaimer would fail to correct the claims' purported misleadingness; 2) determining an appropriate disclaimer to accompany plaintiffs' lung and respiratory tract claim in light of the SU.VI.MAX study; and 3) reevaluating plaintiffs' colon and digestive tract claim and drafting one or more disclaimers.

NOTE: FDA and the plaintiffs reached a settlement consistent with the opinion of the district court. The revised claims are listed below.

SELENIUM REVISED CLAIMS

Selenium may reduce the risk of colorectal cancer. Scientific evidence concerning this claim is inconclusive. Based on its review, FDA does not agree that selenium may reduce the risk of colorectal cancer.

Selenium may reduce the risk of colon and rectal cancer. Scientific evidence concerning this claim is inconclusive. Based on its review, FDA does not agree that selenium may reduce the risk of colon and rectal cancer.

Selenium may reduce the risk of colon cancer. Scientific evidence concerning this claim is inconclusive. Based on its review, FDA does not agree that selenium may reduce the risk of colon cancer.

Selenium may reduce the risk of prostate cancer. Scientific evidence concerning this claim is inconclusive. Based on its review, FDA does not agree that selenium may reduce the risk of prostate cancer.

Selenium may reduce the risk of bladder, colon, prostate, rectal and thyroid cancers. Scientific evidence concerning this claim is inconclusive. Based on its review, FDA does not agree that selenium may reduce the risk of these cancers.

CRITICAL ANALYSIS: Considering both First Amendment safeguards and public protection, evaluate the above milestone cases and determine whether there is a less complex legal solution to claims evaluation.

Saw Palmetto Extract Claim Denial—*Whitaker v. Thompson*

The Court of Appeals in affirming the District Court decision in *Whitaker v. Thompson* upheld the FDA's action in its denial of the health claim petition regarding Saw Palmetto. FDA found that the Saw Palmetto claim a "treatment" health claim. The FDA denied the following claim relating to the consumption of saw palmetto extract and mild benign prostatic hyperplasia. *"Consumption of 320 mg daily of saw palmetto extract may improve urine flow, reduce nocturia and reduce voiding urgency associated with mild benign prostatic hyperplasia (BHP)."* The *Whitaker* appellate decision follows.

Whitaker v. Thompson,
353 F.3d 947 (D.C. Cir. 2004)

WILLIAMS, *Senior Circuit Judge*: When substances aimed at the treatment or prevention of disease are marketed, their regulation by the Food and Drug Administration ("FDA") commonly turns on the nature of the claims made about the substance. Items to be sold with "drug claims," including foods and dietary supplements, are subject to extensive testing; foods or dietary supplements that merely make "health claims" pass muster far more easily. This case turns primarily on whether the FDA faithfully applied the Federal Food, Drug and Cosmetic Act ("FFDCA"), 21 U.S.C. § 301 *et seq.*, in its analysis of a petition by Dr. Julian Whitaker and others (for simplicity's sake, "Whitaker") to approve their intended marketing of "saw palmetto," an extract from the pulp and seed of the dwarf American palm, *Serenoa repens*, under a label that they argued was a "health claim." Whitaker proposed a label stating: 'Consumption of 320 mg daily of Saw Palmetto extract may improve urine flow, reduce nocturia and reduce voiding urgency associated with mild benign prostatic hyperplasia (BPH)." The FDA denied the petition. In explaining the decision, it drew a distinction between claims regarding use of a product to maintain health and to "prevent" disease, on the one hand, and claims that a product could "treat" a disease, on the other. The former could qualify as "health claims," but the latter would always be considered "drug claims." Whitaker challenged the FDA's decision in district court on statutory and First Amendment grounds. The district court granted the FDA's motion to dismiss, *Whitaker v. Thompson*, 239 F. Supp. 2d 43 (D.D.C. 2003). We affirm. ***

The statutory claim—The FFDCA definition of "drug" includes "articles intended for use in the diagnosis, cure, mitigation, treatment, or prevention of disease," 21 U.S.C. § 321(g)(1)(B), which would seem by its plain terms to cover the marketing of a substance intended to mitigate the symptoms associated with BPH. But that apparent simplicity is undermined by language added in 1990 by the Nutrition Labeling and Education Act ("NLEA"), Pub. L. No. 101–535, 104 Stat. 2353, which created a separate procedure authorizing "health claims" for food (or for dietary supplements classified as food). ***

The FDA gave several reasons for classifying claims regarding cure, mitigation, or treatment of an existing disease ("treatment claims") as drug claims and for exempting only health claims that concern reducing the risk of contracting a disease ("prevention claims"). *** FDA invoked policy concerns to support a distinction between treatment and prevention claims. It argued that, because the health of diseased populations is particularly vulnerable, greater regulation may be justified for products intended for their consumption. Moreover, it argued that treatment claims for symptoms of a disease might lull people with those symptoms into a "false sense of security," leading them to delay a visit to a doctor that might result, for example, in a diagnosis of prostate cancer rather than BPH. ***

The constitutional claim—Whitaker argues that the FDA's refusal to allow marketing of saw palmetto extract under the proposed label, which he describes as a true and non-misleading statement about its salutary effects on BPH symptoms, violates the First Amendment's limits on restrictions of commercial speech. Under *Central Hudson Gas & Electric Corp. v. Public Service Commission*, 447 U.S. 557 (1980), commercial speech enjoys First Amendment protection only if it concerns a lawful activity and is not misleading. ***

The district court upheld the FDA's decision under the first step of *Central Hudson*. "Because the FDA determined that the saw palmetto claim was a drug claim for disease treatment, it concluded that the claim was an *unlawful* health claim" *Whitaker v. Thompson*, 239 F. Supp. 2d at 54. Accordingly, the proposed label constituted speech about unlawful activities. *Id.* *** Thus it is constitutionally permissible for the FDA to use speech, in the form of labeling, to infer intent for purposes of determining that Whitaker's proposed sale of saw palmetto extract would constitute the forbidden sale of an unapproved drug. *** The judgment of the district court dismissing plaintiffs' claim is *affirmed.*

NOTE: Whitaker's petition for a rehearing *en banc* was denied (March 9, 2004) No.03-5020.

CRITICAL ANALYSIS: Contrast *Whitaker* with the *Pearson* and *Alliance* decisions.

Product Classification—Drug or Dietary Supplement

Initially dietary supplement manufacturers in *Pharmanex* were successful when the United States District Court held that red yeast rice capsules manufactured by the *Pharmanex* Company constituted a dietary supplement rather than a drug. The district court's decision focused on the meaning of the term "article" found in the definition of a dietary supplement. The district court ultimately found that "article" refers to finished drug products rather than components of drug products. However, the court of appeals reached an opposite result, holding that "article" is not limited to finished products and remanded the case to the district court. Thereafter, upon remand, on March 30, 2001, the district court decided that the product did not fall within the classification of a dietary supplement, and hence could not be marketed as such. The holding arguably has affected future regulation by FDA in the quest to ensure public protection.

Pharmanex, Inc. v. Shalala,
Case No. 2:97CV262K (D. Ct. Utah 2001)

DALE A. KIMBALL, United States District Judge. MEMORANDUM DECISION AND ORDER: This matter is before the court on remand from the Tenth Circuit Court of Appeals. Previously, defendants ("FDA") had filed a Motion to Affirm Administrative Decision, and Plaintiff ("Pharmanex") had filed a Motion to Hold Unlawful and Set Aside FDA's Decision of May 20, 1998. In February 1998, this court granted Pharmanex's motion and set aside FDA's determination that Pharmanex's product, Cholestin, was a drug. This court found that Cholestin is a "dietary supplement" within the definition set forth in 21 U.S.C. 321(ff), based on the determination that section 321(ff)(3)(B) refers unambiguously to finished drug products, rather than their individual constituents. Because of that ruling, it was unnecessary to reach the other issues raised by the parties. The Tenth Circuit reversed this court's decision in July 2000 [.] Thus, the active ingredients of approved new drugs, such as lovastatin, could be articles that are approved as new drugs and, as such, are excluded from the definition of dietary supplement under 321(ff)(3). Consequently, the Tenth Circuit remanded the case for consideration of the record-based issues not previously reached by this court. ***

I. BACKGROUND— The background *** is set forth in the Tenth Circuit's decision and need not be repeated here. See *Pharmanex v. Shalala*, 221 F.3d 1151 (10th Cir. 2000). The parties agree that the remaining issues on remand are the following: whether FDA was arbitrary and capricious in determining (1) that Pharmanex, in manufacturing and marketing Cholestin, was actually manufacturing and marketing lovastatin; and (2) that lovastatin had not been "marketed as a dietary supplement or as a food" prior to its approval as a "new drug." The relevant statutory provision regarding these two issues is the exclusionary clause found at 21 U.S.C. section 321(ff)(3)(B), which provides in pertinent part that the term "dietary supplement":

> *"(B) [does not include] an article that is approved as a new drug under Section 355 of this title [21 U.S.C. section 355] . . . which was not before such approval . . . marketed as a dietary supplement or as a food . . . ." 21 U.S.C. section 321(ff)(3)(B).*

In its Decision, FDA determined that Cholestin is excluded from the definition of dietary supplement under 321(ff)(3) because it includes an article, lovastatin, which was approved as a new drug under 21 U.S.C. section 355 and because lovastatin was not "marketed as a dietary supplement or as a food" before FDA approved lovastatin as a new drug in 1987. FDA determined that the relevant "article" for purposes of section 321(ff)(3) is lovastatin based on evidence that (1) Pharmanex manufactures Cholestin in a manner designed to ensure that the product contains significant amounts of lovastatin, and (2) Pharmanex promotes Cholestin for its lovastatin content.

III. DISCUSSION
A. ANALYSIS OF FDA'S DETERMINATION THAT THE RELEVANT "ARTICLE" FOR PURPOSES OF 321(FF)(3)(B) IS LOVASTATIN BECAUSE PHARMANEX, IN MANUFACTURING AND MARKETING CHOLESTIN, IS MANUFACTURING AND MARKETING LOVASTATIN
1. Pharmanex's Arguments: Pharmanex argues that FDA's determination that the relevant "article" for purposes of section 321(ff)(3)(B) is lovastatin is arbitrary and capricious. ***
Pharmanex argues that the administrative record does not support FDA's factual determinations that traditional red yeast rice does not contain lovastatin, that Phaukrmanex's use of one specific strain of red yeast fungus supports the conclusion that it is manufacturing lovastatin, that it controls temperatures to ensure production of lovastatin during the manufacture of Cholestin, that Pharmanex's tracking of the levels of HMG-CoA reductase inhibitors is a surrogate for monitoring the total quantity of lovastatin in red yeast rice, and that Pharmanex markets lovastatin. ***
2. FDA's Arguments: FDA argues that its determination that Pharmanex, in manufacturing and marketing Cholestin, is manufacturing and marketing lovastatin is fully supported by the record.

FDA cites to significant evidence that Pharmanex is manufacturing lovastatin, not traditional red yeast rice. Among other things, it points to several studies that demonstrate that traditional red yeast rice does not contain significant amounts of lovastatin, whereas Cholestin does. It points to evidence that Pharmanex's manufacturing processes produce a high amount of lovastatin and that, if Pharmanex's production processes were really not materially different that the traditional process for making red yeast rice, it would not have applied for a patent for an improved red yeast rice product that, Pharmanex asserted, was unlike traditional red yeast rice with respect to the lovastatin content and its use to treat high cholesterol. ***

3. Analysis: Significantly, FDA determined that traditional red yeast rice does not contain lovastatin, that Cholestin contains lovastatin, and that Cholestin is a carefully manufactured, non-traditional product designed to contain specific levels of lovastatin, the active ingredient of the approved prescription drug Mevacor, intended to reduce cholesterol and treat heart disease. ***

Accordingly, the court affirms FDA's determination that the relevant "article" for purposes of section 321(ff)(3)(B) is lovastatin because Pharmanex, in manufacturing and marketing Cholestin, is manufacturing and marketing lovastatin.

B. ANALYSIS OF FDA'S DECISION THAT LOVASTATIN WAS NOT MARKETED AS A DIETARY SUPPLEMENT OR AS A FOOD PRIOR TO 1987

1. Pharmanex's Arguments: Pharmanex claims that, even if the relevant article is lovastatin, it was "marketed as a dietary supplement or as a food" prior to its approval as a new drug, and thus qualifies as a dietary supplement. Pharmanex argues that lovastatin was present in red rice yeast, oyster mushrooms, and other foods that were marketed in the United States and East Asia before lovastatin was approved as a new drug in 1987. It argues that FDA has misinterpreted the second portion of the exclusionary clause, reading into the "prior market clause" an extra-statutory requirement: that, for a food constituent to have been "marketed as a dietary supplement or as a food," the manufacturer of the food containing the constituent must have promoted the food based on the properties of the food constituent at issue, or in some way must have increased or optimized the concentration of the constituent as issue, prior to the constituent's approval as a "new drug."

2. FDA's Arguments: FDA argues that its determination that lovastatin was not marketed as a dietary supplement prior to its approval as a new drug is not arbitrary and capricious. It claims that Pharmanex has failed to show that lovastatin was previously marketed as a dietary sup-plement, food, or component of a food, and therefore, Cholestin does not qualify as a dietary supplement.

3. Analysis: Having found that, even if it were appropriate to reach the question of whether FDA properly interpreted the "marketed as" language found in section 321(ff)(3)(B), FDA's interpretation merits Chevron deference and is a rational interpretation, the only questions remaining are whether FDA's conclusions that (1) the red yeast rice in Cholestin is not traditional red rice, and (2) traditional red yeast rice did not and does not contain lovastatin, are arbitrary and capricious. *** Accordingly, FDA's conclusion that lovastatin was not marketed as a dietary supplement or as a food prior to 1987 is affirmed.

CRITICAL ANALYSIS: The District Court in *Pharmanex* flip-flopped from the original decision to the judgment on remand. Evaluate *Pharmanex* in terms of whether the final outcome was correct.

A Wake-Up Call for Congress and a Not So Bitter Pill for FDA

Roseann B. Termini, Ohio Northern University Law Review, Used with permission. (modified and edited 2018).

Introduction: In 1994, Congress, through specific legislation, enacted the Dietary Supplement and Education Act (DSHEA), for the Federal Food and Drug Administration (FDA) to regulate dietary supplements which seemingly puzzled food and drug practitioners for years. FDA officials and critics have debated back and forth over whether dietary supplements constitute food or drugs and the proper procedure for regulating these products. Yet, controversy still remains over exactly how

a dietary supplement should be regulated.

DSHEA redefined dietary supplements so currently, FDA regulates dietary supplements like food products, meaning FDA must prove a supplement is unsafe prior to removing it from the marketplace. The new definition of dietary supplement is an attempt by Congress to ensure consumer access to supplements. Congress did not desire stringent FDA regulation of dietary supplements which would unnecessarily limit consumer access. Thus, the aim of DSHEA appears to be more focused on consumer convenience rather than product safety.

Another controversy surrounding dietary supplements is the regulatory scheme itself. Many question if problems are being addressed in a manner that protects consumers from potential harm. In enacting DSHEA, Congress recognized the valuable role played by dietary supplements in improving health, preventing disease and reducing health care costs. Congress specifically enacted DSHEA to "protect the right of access of consumers to safe dietary supplements" and to remove "unreasonable regulatory barriers limiting or slowing the flow of safe products and accurate information to consumers" imposed by FDA. DSHEA places the burden on FDA to prove a dietary supplement is unsafe prior to any removal from the marketplace. Dietary supplements present a completely different regulatory scheme than drug approvals. That is, in order for a new drug to enter the marketplace safety and efficiency must be documented through the extensive process of submitting an NDA or new drug application to FDA. On the other hand, DSHEA does not require pre-market approval by FDA for dietary supplements. In so doing, FDA does not have the authority to regulate dietary supplements prior to dissemination into the marketplace.

This article focuses on the regulatory procedure for dietary supplements through an examination of *Pharmanex, Inc. v. Shalala* which dissects both the definition of dietary supplements and predicts the regulatory outcome of a finding by the district court that a product conforms to DSHEA criteria. Yet, the court of appeals in *Pharmanex* found linguistic ambiguity existed. The article examines the expanding variety and proliferation of dietary supplements and products touting various health benefits and injuries attributed to dietary supplement ingestion. The pros and cons of dietary supplements have pushed both courts and FDA to attempt to determine the legal treatment of dietary supplements and the proper control tactics to better assist consumers who depend on dietary supplements for their "well-being."

An Examination of *Pharmanex v. Shalala*: Initially, dietary supplement makers won a huge victory when the United States District Court of Utah held that red yeast rice capsules manufactured by Pharmanex constitute a dietary supplement rather than a drug. The district court's decision focused on the meaning of the term "article" found in the definition of a dietary supplement. The district court initially found that "article" refers to finished drug products rather than components of drug products. However, the court of appeals reached an opposite result, holding that "article" is not limited to finished products. The holding arguably will have long term effects on the type and manner of products regulated by FDA in the agency's quest to ensure consumer safety, because different products under FDA control encounter regulation at different stages of their intended use. Upon remand, the district court agreed with the court of appeals

An examination of *Pharmanex* should begin with a review of DSHEA's definition of dietary supplement under 21 U.S.C. § 321(ff)(3) which states:

The term "dietary supplement"

(1) means a product (other than tobacco) intended to supplement the diet that bears or contains one or more of the following dietary ingredients: (A) a vitamin; (B) a mineral; (C) an herb or other botanical; (D) an amino acid; (E) a dietary substance for use by man to supplement the diet by increasing the total dietary intake; or (F) a concentrate, metabolite, constituent, extract, or combination of any ingredient described in clause (A), (B), (C), (D), or (E).

(2) means a product that—(A)(i) is intended for ingestion in a form described in section 350(c)(1)(B)(i) of this title; or (ii) Complies with section 350(c)(1)(B)(ii) of this title; is not represented for use as a conventional food or as a sole item of a meal or the diet; and is labeled as a dietary supplement.

(3) Does—(A) include an article that is approved as a new drug under section 355 of this title, or licensed as a biologic under section 262 of Title 42, and was, prior to such approval, certification, or license, marketed as a dietary supplement or as a food unless the Secretary has issued a regulation, after notice and comment, finding that the article, when used as or in a dietary supplement under the conditions of use and dosages set forth in the labeling for such dietary supplement, is unlawful under section 342 (f) of this title.

(B) not include—(i) an article that is approved as a new drug under section 355 of this title, certified as an antibiotic under section 357 of this title, or licensed as a biologic under section 262 of Title 42, or (ii). An article authorized for investigation as a new drug, antibiotic, or biological for which substantial clinical investigations have been instituted and for which the existence of such investigations has been made public, which was not before such approval, certification, licensing, or authorization marketed as a dietary supplement or as a food unless the Secretary, in the Secretary's discretion, has issued a regulation, after notice and comment, finding that the article would be lawful under this chapter.

Pharmanex produces a product called Cholestin which is a capsule containing milled red yeast rice as a dietary supplement. Traditionally, red yeast rice has been eaten and appreciated for its health benefits in China and other parts of East Asia for hundreds of years. Cholestin has nutritive value because it contains red yeast and is intended, with diet and exercise, to aid in maintaining a healthy cholesterol method. Specifically, Pharmanex advertises the benefits of Cholestin as promoting healthy cholesterol levels, supported by clinical research, is 100% natural, a patent pending formula and a natural complement to diet and exercise.

Cholestin contains a range of enzymes which act to reduce serum cholesterol methods. Among the enzymes that Cholestin contains is mevinolin a substance FDA determined is "chemically indistinguishable" from the active ingredient in the prescription drug Mevacor. FDA specifically argued that mevinolin is "chemically indistinguishable from lovastatin, a pure, crystallized, and synthesized substance, which is the active ingredient in Mevacor." Mevacor is indicated for treatment of high blood serum cholesterol and triglyceride levels, atherosclerotic disease and coronary heart disease. Pharmanex had been marketing Cholestin since November 1996; however in April 1997, FDA informally notified Pharmanex that it considered Cholestin a drug requiring preapproval for marketing purposes. Then, in May of 1998, FDA formally announced that Cholestin, although promoted as a dietary supplement, was not a dietary supplement, but instead an unapproved drug. FDA banned the importation of the red yeast rice. This meant that it was illegal to sell Cholestin in the United States.

FDA essentially determined that the word "article" as used in 21 U.S.C. § 321(ff)(3)(B) can refer to a finished drug product or an individual component of a drug product. Thus, the district court was required to interpret DSHEA's statutory scheme to determine the outcome of the decision. To determine the validity of FDA's statutory construction, the district court tracked FDA's regulatory reasoning as follows:

> *lovastatin is an article that was approved as a new drug in 1987, (ii) Cholestin is manufactured and marketed with a sufficiently great emphasis on its lovastatin content that Cholestin is to be equated with lovastatin, and (iii), therefore, Cholestin is excluded from the category of*
> *dietary supplements because it was not marketed as a dietary supplement of food before 1987, when lovastatin was approved.*

The Supreme Court in *Chevron, U.S.A., Inc. v. Natural Resources Defense Council, Inc.* sets forth the criteria for determining whether agency statutory construction conflicts with congressional intent. Chevron sets forth a two-prong test for analyzing congressional intent. The first prong is an examination to determine if Congress has spoken clearly on the issue at hand and if so, then that ends the matter. Second, if Congress leaves a gap in the statutory interpretation, or if the intent of Congress is ambiguous, then the agency may fill this void and deference to the agency is permissible unless they are arbitrary, capricious, or manifestly contrary to the statute. A court may not substitute its own statutory interpretation if the agency's construction is reasonable.

FDA urged that 21 U.S.C. § 321(ff)(3)(B) is unambiguous because under the Federal Food, Drug and Cosmetic Act (FDCA), the term "article" includes both a finished product and its components. According to FDA the term "article" means both a finished product and its components. For example, the definition of food uses article to mean both a component of a whole product and a completed product. Likewise, the definition of drug employs both interpretations of the word "article," again adding to the confusion of the meaning of the word "article" as it is used in the FDCA. FDA advanced the argument that "article approved as a new drug" may refer to a finished drug product like Medvacor or a component part of a finished product like lovastatin.

The court of appeals determined that the disclaimed Senate Report relied on by the district court did not support the conclusion that Congress intended § 321 (ff)(3)(B) to apply solely to finished drug products. Furthermore, the court of appeals found that the policies underlying DSHEA did not support such a finding that Congress clearly intended that § 321 (ff)(3)(B) apply only to finished drug products. Such a result, according to the appeals court, would undermine a primary purpose of the Federal, Food, Drug and Cosmetic Act, which is to ensure safe and effective products.

FDA and *Pharmanex* set forth various examples of why their statutory interpretation has merit, including evaluation of prior judicial decisions, agency regulations and previous statutory authority. Alternatively, *Pharmanex* argued that previous case law has defined "article" within the purview of the definition of new drug to mean the entire drug product. This argument was rejected by the court of appeals. The conflicting authority cited by both parties seemingly indicates the regulatory confusion presented by DSHEA and the agency charged with the regulatory authority to enforce DSHEA. Yet, the court of appeals specifically held that the interpretation by FDA of §321 (ff)(3)(B) was not arbitrary, capricious or manifestly contrary to the statute.

FDA's Lack of Authority to Regulate Dietary Supplements: FDA is constrained in its regulatory enforcement and may only utilize its regulatory powers for dietary supplements after the product is on the marketplace.

Congress' enactment of the Federal Food Drug and Cosmetic Act (FDCA) in 1938 began FDA's relationship with dietary supplements. Prior to FDCA's amendment in 1962, the definition of drug also included that of dietary supplements. The inclusion of dietary supplement within the definition of a drug was intended to "bring certain potentially dangerous products that had physiological effects unrelated to diseases within the regulatory authority of FDA." In 1962 dietary supplements became classified as food additives. As food additives, dietary supplements no longer had to endure pre-market screening process. The pre-market approval process required that if nutritional experts could not agree that a dietary supplement was safe, a manufacturer had to prove the safety of the product. In the 1960s, false and misleading claims about dietary supplements forced FDA to seek greater regulatory control over supplements. FDA requested stricter regulations which backfired with the passage of the "Proxmire Amendments" that prohibited FDA from placing maximum limits on potency of vitamins and minerals in food. Eventually, largely in response to industry pressure, Congress passed DSHEA in 1994.

Prior to passage of DSHEA, Congress entertained including dietary supplements within the Nutrition Labeling and Education Act of 1990 (NLEA), therefore creating strict labeling requirements for all dietary supplements and products such as vitamins, minerals, herbs, or other similar nutritional substances. However, dietary supplement regulation did not become part of the NLEA. DSHEA effectively created a new class of products under FDA jurisdiction. Though dietary supplements may look like or even act like drugs, unlike drugs, DSHEA does not require clinical safety and efficiency trials. Rather, FDA bears the burden of showing that dietary supplements are dangerous before they can be removed from store shelves.

Now the preventive techniques used by FDA for drugs to ensure consumer safety have been replaced by a wait and see regulatory practice. In the face of dietary supplement injuries and regulatory confusion regarding dietary supplements, is the new legislation really helping consumers or rather does DSHEA advance the interest of manufacturers in product advancement?

Outcome of *Pharmanex* and DSHEA: The initial victory by dietary supplement manufacturers after the Utah District Court's favorable decision in *Pharmanex,* dismayed many critics of DSHEA. Representatives of the National Consumers League maintained that "[t]he [district] court decision [*Pharmanex*] permitted a dangerous situation to continue." Now any firm can process a plant substance into a supplement as potent as a drug and sell it without proof of safety or efficiency. FDA retains the authority to seize any supplement that has caused serious harm; however, for some people that protection could be too little, too late. This criticism of the initial district court decision stands as one indication of concern that surrounds both the implementation of DSHEA and its interpretation. Nutritional supplement pills or liquids, unlike a drug, may have the appearance of an approved drug, yet do not undergo rigorous premarket approval including confirmation of the product's claims.

Questionable Aspects of Dietary Supplements: Congress has exhibited extreme confidence in the dietary supplement industry as evidenced by the lack of explicit authority for FDA to fully regulate. DSHEA prohibits the federal government from taking any actions that impose an "unreasonable regulatory barrier limiting or slowing the flow of safe products and accurate information to the consumers." Congress noted that "dietary supplements are safe within a broad range of intake, and safety problems with the supplements are relatively rare." However, confidence has been undermined on several instances of dietary supplement disaster.

Shortly after the district court decision in *Pharmanex,* four college students were admitted to a healthcare facility due to an adverse reaction from ingesting dietary supplements containing gamma butyrolactone (GBL). The reports indicated that the students had trouble breathing after ingesting the supplement. This outcome probably did not surprise FDA, because in correspondence to healthcare providers and consumers the agency cataloged the problems caused by supplements containing GBL. However, despite FDA warnings that supplements containing GBL caused adverse effects, including reports of loss of consciousness and resulting comas due to the ingestion of GBL products, the number of adverse events occurring after the warnings is believed to have risen significantly. Perhaps the GBL tragedies are yet another example of the failings of post incident intervention by FDA. Other products have also caused serious side effects. For instance, an analysis of FDA records found over 2,500 reports of side effects such as dizziness, nausea, and heart palpitations and 79 deaths associated with dietary supplements. Another example of supplement disaster concerns the ingestion of herbal ephedrine tablets. The product was advertised as "producing euphoria, increasing sexual sensations, heightening awareness, and increasing energy." The question remains as to not just efficacy but safety considerations as well.

Dietary Supplement Reform: Safety and Efficacy Issues: DSHEA is a liberal law designed to promote supplement manufacturers freedom in marketing. However, unanswered questions about safety and efficiency remain a concern. Congress designed DSHEA to improve the health of Americans by making dietary supplements readily available without unduly burdensome regulatory constraint. However, in reality, confusion over the properties of products and dangerous consumer reliance on absent pre-market testing has resulted. Some notion of common ground between the supplement industry and FDA must be found to ensure safety and efficacy of supplements for the consumer.

The broad language of DSHEA must be interpreted to ensure that confusion over product proliferation must be reconciled so that dangerous drugs do not infiltrate the marketplace. It appears that the interpretation as advanced by FDA and by the court of appeals better advances the goals of Congress concerning consumer health rather than a confusing stance that permits untested and questionable products to enter the marketplace. Despite DSHEA's apparent result of a consumer base who appear to rely on dietary supplements because of dietary supplement marketing techniques, it does not appear that Congress intended this effect. Industry and FDA have worked together to provide more complete information on labels of dietary supplement products. For example, one improvement while not necessarily ensuring safety and efficacy, entails that all dietary supplements contain nutrition information entitled "Supplement Facts." The "Supplement Facts" panel is similar to the "Nutrition Facts" panel that appears on most processed food products. Many manufacturers complied with the new labeling requirements even before the mandatory deadline was reached. FDA continues to educate consumers on how to use the "supplement facts" panel and to survey the marketplace to ensure manufacturer compliance with the new regulations. However, it is arguable that these labeling regulations will have little effect because FDA cannot investigate a dietary supplement until an adverse event situation occurs.

Another method for informed dietary supplement information concerns the use of health claims based on authoritative statements for dietary supplements. This follows the FDA Modernization Act which allows health claims based on authoritative statements on conventional food products. FDA proposed the authoritative statement regulation hoping to place dietary supplements on the same stance as conventional food. However, for the authoritative statement rules to be successful and not abused by manufacturers, it is essential that the Federal Trade Commission continue to vigilantly evaluate supplement advertisements.

FDA encountered a major stumbling block in its quest to regulate dietary supplement labeling. In *Pearson*, dietary supplement manufacturers, distributors and consumer organizations brought suit against FDA because of their requirement to have agency authorization before placing health claims on nutritional supplements. The United States Court of Appeals for the District of Columbia, found that FDA violated the Administrative Procedures Act by failing to define "significant scientific agreement." *Pearson* indicates yet another problem by FDA in interpreting the vague directions of DSHEA and the confusing message transmitted by the goals of Congress for easy access to nutritional supplements while at the same time ensuring consumer safety.

DSHEA critics maintain that the regulatory allowance of statements of nutritional support and health claims give supplement manufacturers a way to "suggest miracle health benefits without quite promising them." Critics also suggest that there are no standards for the kind of substantiation FDA may demand and FDA notice requirements are not complied with most of the time. Thus, despite regulations concerning the distribution of dietary supplements, enforcement is difficult. The latitude in DSHEA allowed to supplement makers makes it difficult for FDA to successfully assert its regulatory authority over supplements. One option in terms of regulatory action for safety and efficacy purposes is premarket approval with controlled clinical studies and submission of a dietary supplement application to FDA similar to new drug applications. This suggestion would require legislation because DSHEA contains no mandate for premarket approval. This recommendation would obviously require a monetary expense to the dietary supplement industry and to FDA in terms of available resources.

However, because premarket approval by FDA of a dietary supplement is not required, FDA monitors through post-incident reporting. An example of FDA's post-incident report occurred when FDA issued a Talk Paper alerting consumers not to purchase or consume products containing gamma butyrolactone (GBL). FDA maintained that though the GBL containing products were marketed as dietary supplements they are really "illegally marketed unapproved new drugs." FDA reported at least fifty-five adverse health reports and at least one death attributed to GBL based products. Unfortunately, FDA could not act to prevent the products from entering the marketplace, but rather had to wait for the adverse effects. Rather, FDA must rely on consumer and medical professionals to report adverse events to FDA's MedWatch program. Of course, this reporting occurs after the adverse health problems from consumer ingestion of the product.

Consumer advocates suggest that supplement makers contribute to a fund according to each company's market share of the dietary supplement industry to be used for clinical trials that no one company can afford on their own. This proposal is similar to the Prescription Drug User Fee Act. In suggesting a monetary fund, consumer advocates point out that the National Institutes of Health Office of Dietary Supplements budgets to study dietary supplements, and the National Center for Complementary and Alternative Medicine at the National Institutes of Health budget to study dietary supplements and other non-traditional medical practices. The medical profession weighs in on the side of those critical of DSHEA. For example, medical professionals complain that DSHEA provides only a procedural framework for supplement regulation without any pre-clearance authority for FDA. Specifically, DSHEA permits an inadequate determination of whether the product falls within the safe harbor. In addition, DSHEA does not allow for any scheme for adverse reports of supplement reactions. In other words, there is no statutory scheme that directs consumers on the proper method to inform FDA of adverse effects of dietary supplement use. Thus, in the only instance FDA can assert its authority over supplements, adverse events, Congress has not provided a scheme to inform FDA to intervene to protect public health and safety.

In *Pharmanex*, FDA successfully attempted to construe the term "article" narrowly in a manner that conflicted with the liberal views of DSHEA, evidencing their discomfort with the statutory scheme. The confusion of conflicting and confusing claims could potentially subject consumers to a wide variety of supplement information. Physicians must become knowledgeable about supplements and the manner in which consumers are using them. Medical commentators therefore request various educational materials on both industry trends and consumer use, as managed care now dictates how patients self-care for themselves. Commentators suggest, "People within the medical profession have to become aware of the potential adverse short-term and long-term side effects [of dietary supplements]. Nobody's taught about herbs in medical school." Perhaps with the proliferation of dietary supplements and the lack of regulatory controls, even physicians will not be able to properly assess the properties of dietary supplements and the manner in which consumers are using them. Perhaps if FDA was afforded minimal pre-market regulatory authority aimed toward safety and efficacy, both consumers and medical professionals might be better equipped to handle the newly emerging supplement trend.

The *Pharmanex* appeals court correctly decided this case based on the traditional tools of statutory interpretation, namely the purpose of Congress for enacting DSHEA and the statutory language of 21 U.S.C. § 321(ff). However, any problems associated with dietary supplement regulation stems from DSHEA itself. The broad and ambiguous language set forth by Congress and FDA's inability to regulate products within DSHEA's protective umbrella indicates more and more products will slip through the statutory loop-holes and out into the marketplace for consumer consumption. Essentially, *Pharmanex* begs the question of how far supplement manufacturers can go in creating products that mimic drugs.

Industry and regulators must both assume proactive roles to address the problems that exist in the multibillion-dollar supplement industry before consumer tragedy reaches even higher levels. Federal agencies such as FTC and FDA and industry simply cannot function in a vacuum; rather, they must work together to fashion a clear plan for implementing the "real" DHSEA goals of consumer convenience and safety without bowing to the regulatory confusion it has created.

CRITICAL ANALYSIS: Due to the proliferation of dietary supplements and the lack of pre-approval, discuss regulatory mechanisms government agencies should use in terms of greater enforcement.

Chapter 4: Enforcement

Federal Trade Commission and the Food and Drug Administration

The Federal Trade Commission (FTC) and the Food and Drug Administration (FDA) and other agencies such as the National Institutes of Health (NIH) coordinate efforts and resources in enforcement actions. An excellent example is the action against *Seasilver USA, Inc.* for marketing a supplement purported to treat or cure cancer, AIDS, diabetes, and 650 other diseases. **See: *FTC v. Seasilver USA, Inc.*, No. CV-S-0676-RHL-LRL (D. Nev. Final order 03/04/2004),** where FTC obtained a temporary restraining order and asset freeze and FDA seized the defendants' product. The FTC settlement included $4.5 million in consumer redress. The FDA companion settlement included destruction of $5.3 million worth of the misbranded supplement.

FTC Enforcement

Billions of dollars are spent annually on supplements perhaps searching for a miracle cure. The FDA regulates claims made in labeling including packaging, and inserts; however, the FTC regulates the advertising of dietary supplements for example: Internet, broadcast advertising, print advertisements, infomercials and catalogs. The role of FTC is to protect the consumer in the prevention of fraudulent, deceptive, and unfair business practices. A complaint filed by the FTC is done in the public interest because FTC has "reason to believe" that the law has been or is being violated. The complaint is an initial legal proceeding and does not mean that the defendant in fact violated the law. A stipulated final order is for settlement reasons only and requires court approval. Further, it is not an admission by the defendants. A court approved stipulated final order when signed by the judge has the force of law. FTC complaints are logged in an online database. According to FTC, this database is available to approximately 1,800 civil and criminal law enforcement agencies in the United States and abroad. The FTC remains aggressive in instituting actions against dietary supplement companies for product promotions that violate the Federal Trade Commission Act. Selected enforcement examples include: testimonials, "clinically proven", weight loss, children's products,

Endorsements and Testimonials: Substantiation and Disclosure

https://www.ftc.gov/tips-advice/business-center/guidance/ftcs-endorsement-guides-what-people-are-asking

What does FTC require for substantiation of health claims? FTC requires "competent and reliable scientific evidence" that substantiates product claim(s). FTC published revisions to the guidance *"FTC's Guide Concerning the Use of Endorsements and Testimonials in Advertising" (Endorsements and Testimonials Guide).* The changes affect Testimonial Advertisements, Bloggers and Celebrity Endorsements. The 2009 *Endorsements and Testimonials Guide* addresses endorsements by consumers, experts, organizations, and celebrities, as well as the disclosure of important connections between advertisers and endorsers. The following are key requirements.

Clear disclosure of the results that consumer can generally expect; and
Clear disclosure of "material connections".

1. Example: *The post of a blogger who receives cash or in-kind payment to review a product is considered an endorsement.*
2. Example: *If a company refers to findings of research in an advertisement, the advertisement must disclose the connection between the advertiser and the research organization if any.*

The *Endorsements and Testimonials Guide* clarifies that advertisers and endorsers may be liable for false or unsubstantiated claims made in an endorsement as well as the failure to disclose material connections between the advertiser and endorsers. Further, the revised *Endorsements and Testimonials Guide* explains that celebrities have a duty to disclose their relationships with advertisers when making endorsements. This includes traditional advertisements as well as appearances on talk shows and other social media.

FTC and State Joint Enforcement—Testimonials

The FTC and State of Maine charged nine defendants with making false and misleading claims about CogniPrin and FlexiPrin. The claims include that CogniPrin: 1) *reverses mental decline by 12 years*; 2) *improves memory by 44 percent*; and 3) *improves memory in as little as three weeks* and is *clinically proven to improve memory*; and that FlexiPrin: 1) *reduces joint and back pain, inflammation*, and *stiffness in as little as two hours*; 2) *rebuilds damaged joints and cartilage*; and 3) *has been clinically proven to reduce the need for medication in 80 percent of users* and *to reduce morning joint stiffness in all users*. According to the complaint, Synergixx and Fusco promoted CogniPrin and FlexiPrin through 30-minute radio ads that were deceptively formatted to sound like educational talk shows. The complaint also alleged that Synergixx and Fusco created inbound call scripts that deceptively claimed that consumers could try the supplements "risk-free" with an unconditional 90-day money-back guarantee, without disclosing burdensome requirements for obtaining refunds and making product returns.

See: *https://www.ftc.gov/system/files/documents/cases/1523024_xxl_impressions_complaint.pdf*

CRITICAL ANALYSIS: Review the Testimonial action above. Should pre-approval of advertising claims be a mandate?

Supplements Targeted for Children—Notable FTC Actions

Examples of FTC actions concerning advertising supplements for children are detailed below. FTC charged NBTY, Inc. and two subsidiaries, NatureSmart LLC and Rexall Sundown, Inc., with making deceptive claims about the amount of DHA, an Omega-3 fatty acid used in their line of Disney and Marvel Heroes licensed children's multivitamin gummies and tablets. According to the FTC complaint, these companies made unsupported claims that a daily serving of the products promoted healthy brain and eye development in children. The companies agreed to pay $2.1 million to provide refunds to purchases of certain Disney and Marvel Heroes multivitamins. The following details advertising supplement cases targeted for children:

Company That Touted Products' Ability to Treat Children's Speech Disorders Settles FTC Charges It Deceived Consumers

In the Matter of NBTY, Inc., a corporation, Naturesmart LLC, a limited liability company, and Rexall Sundown, Inc., FTC File No. 1023080

Disney or Marvel Hero-themed Children's Vitamins – 08/08/2013

https://www.ftc.gov/news-events/press-releases/2010/12/ftc-settlement-prohibits-marketers-childrens-vitamins-making– 12/13/2010

https://www.ftc.gov/news-events/press-releases/2015/01/company-touted-products-ability-treat-childrens-speech-disorders

Height Max-Discovery of Hidden Assets: Sunny Health Nutrition Technology & Products, Inc. The U.S. District Court for the Middle District of Florida entered a Judgment that ordered Sunny Health Nutrition Technology & Products, Inc. to pay $375,000 based on sworn financial statements. The Judgement included a clause that required payment of $1.9 million if the financial statements were inaccurate. Subsequently, FTC located $1.8 million in an undisclosed account. A new final order was entered into and the defendants were required to pay $1.9 million. FTC instituted a refund program for HeightMax purchasers. Stipulated Order Feb. 22, 2007.

Pedia Loss: Sellers of Children's Weight-Loss Product Settle FTC Charges The FTC's complaint alleged that the defendants could not support claims that Pedia Loss causes weight loss in overweight or obese children ages six and over, and that when taken by overweight or obese children, Pedia Loss suppresses appetite, increases fat burning, and slows carbohydrate absorption. The order prohibits the defendants from making unsubstantiated benefits, performance, or efficacy claims for any dietary supplement, food, or drug, and prohibits the defendants from misrepresenting any test or study. File No. 042-30022006 No. 9317.

Marketers of the Supplements Focus Factor and V-Factor Agree to Settle FTC Charges and Pay $1 Million

Creative Health Institute, Inc., and Kyl L. Smith, C-4108 (Apr. 26, 2004) Consent Order alleged unsubstantiated efficacy claims for the dietary supplement "Focus Factor." Dr. Smith developed Focus Factor and advertised and sold it through CHI at least from 1997 to 2000. Consumer redress of $60,000 required by the Order.

CRITICAL ANALYIS: Should there be more scrutiny of advertisements specifically targeted to children and if so, what should be done in terms of regulation? Integrate cases above.

Weight Control Products—Notable FTC Actions

The advertisement of "miracle weight loss products" that provide little or no benefit remains problematic. In terms of the "obesity epidemic" and product marketing FTC oversees the advertising and marketing of foods, non-prescription products and cosmetics that promote weight loss. According to FTC, advertisements on television, radio, the Internet, in magazines, flyers and posters must be both truthful and not misleading. Product claims must be substantiated as well.

Yet, false or deceptive advertising of weight loss products continues to escalate. FTC instituted several actions against companies for deceptive advertising illustrated by the FTC action against several weight loss product marketers. For example, the Acai Berry was touted as a weight loss miracle product. Derived from acai palm trees that are native to Central and South America, acai berry supplements are often marketed to consumers who hope to lose weight. In 2010, the FTC filed an action against acai berry marketer Central Coast Nutraceuticals for deceptively marketing acai berry supplements as weight-loss products and "colon cleansers" as cancer prevention aid. The following are examples of FTC enforcement.

District Court Ruling Allowed FTC to Attempt to Collect Up To $3.2 Million From Marketers Who Deceptively Advertised Homeopathic HCG Diet Direct Drops

https://www.ftc.gov/news-events/press-releases/2016/02/district-court-ruling-allows-ftc-attempt-collect-32-million

Sensa and Three Other Marketers of Fad Weight-Loss Products Settle FTC Charges in Crackdown on Deceptive Advertising

http://www.ftc.gov/news-events/press-releases/2014/01/sensa-three-other-marketers-fad-weight-loss-products-settle-ftc

This FTC enforcement action focused on national marketers that used deceptive advertising claims to market fad weight-loss products such as food additives, skin cream and dietary supplements.

"Operation Failed Resolution" is part of the FTC's ongoing effort to stop misleading claims for products promoting easy weight loss and slimmer bodies. The marketers of Sensa, encouraged consumers to *"sprinkle, eat, and lose weight"* —$26.5 million to settle FTC charges that they deceived consumers with unfounded weight-loss claims and misleading endorsements. The FTC will make these funds available for refunds to consumers who bought Sensa. Charges were filed against the marketers of two other products that made unfounded promises: **L'Occitane** which claimed that its skin cream would slim users' bodies but had no science to back up that claim, and **HCG Diet Direct** which marketed an unproven human hormone that has been touted by hucksters for more than half a century as a weight-loss treatment.

There was a partial settlement in a fourth case, LeanSpa, LLC, an operation that allegedly deceptively promoted acai berry and "colon cleanse" weight-loss supplements through fake news websites. In total, the weight-loss marketers will pay approximately $34 million for consumer redress. In addition to the $26.5 million to be paid by Sensa, L'Occitane, Inc. will pay $450,000, and the LeanSpa settling defendants will surrender assets totalling an estimated $7.3 million. The judgment against the HCG Diet Direct defendants is suspended due to their inability to pay.

Acai Berry Weight Loss Products
FTC Permanently Stopped Six Operators from Using Fake News Sites that Allegedly Deceived Consumers about Acai Berry Weight-Loss Products – 01/25/2012
https://www.ftc.gov/news-events/press-releases/2012/01/ftc-permanently-stops-six-operators-using-fake-news-sites

Six online marketers agreed to settlements with the Federal Trade Commission to permanently halt their allegedly deceptive practice of using fake news websites to market acai berry supplements and other weight-loss products. As part of its ongoing crackdown on bogus health claims, the proposed settlements will require that the six operations make clear when their commercial messages are advertisements rather than objective journalism, and will bar the defendants from further deceptive claims about health-related products such as the acai berry weight-loss supplements and colon cleansers that they marketed. The defendants also are required to disclose any material connections they have with merchants and will be barred from making deceptive claims about other products, such as the work-at-home schemes or penny auctions that most of them promoted. The settlements also require that these defendants collectively pay roughly $500,000 to the Commission because their advertisements violated federal law. This money amounts to most of their assets.

At the request of the FTC, federal courts temporarily halted these operations and four others. In its sweep last year against marketers who allegedly used fake news sites to promote weight-loss products, the FTC alleged that their websites were designed to falsely appear as if they were part of legitimate news organizations but were actually nothing more than advertisements deceptively enticing consumers to buy the featured acai berry weight-loss products from online merchants. With titles such as "News 6 News Alerts," "Health News Health Alerts," or "Health 5 Beat Health News," the sites often falsely represented that the reports they carried had been seen on major media outlets such as ABC, Fox News, CBS, CNN, *USA Today*, and Consumer Reports. Investigative-sounding headlines presented stories that purported to document a reporter's first-hand experience with acai berry supplements – typically claiming to have lost 25 pounds in four weeks, according to the FTC complaints. The proposed settlements impose monetary judgments in the full amount of the commissions the defendants received for deceptive marketing through their fake news sites. Due to the defendants' financial condition, the judgments will be suspended when the FTC receives the following assets from them. In all cases, if it is later determined that the financial information the defendants provided the FTC was false, the full amount of their judgments would become due.

Xenadrine EFX, CortiSlim, CortiStress, Trim Spa, One-A-Day Weight Smart—FTC $25 Million to Settle Allegations of Deceptive Marketing
http://www.ftc.gov/opa/2009/04/xenadrine.shtm
Federal Trade Commission, Plaintiff, v. Robert Chinery, Jr.; Tracy A. Chinery; and RTC Research & Development, LLC, Defendants (United States District Court for the District of New Jersey), Civil Action No. 05-3460

FTC filed complaints in 2007 in four separate cases alleging that weight-loss and weight-control claims were not supported by competent and reliable scientific evidence. Marketers of the four products—Xenadrine EFX, CortiSlim, TrimSpa, and One-A-Day WeightSmart—have settled with the FTC, surrendered cash and other assets worth at least $25 million, and agreed to limit their future advertising claims. The Federal Trade Commission's case against the marketers of Xenadrine EFX, a purported weight-loss product, ended in 2009 with the final defendant in the case settling charges of false and unsubstantiated advertising.

Xenadrine EFX: Two marketers of Xenadrine EFX a minimum settlement of at least $8 million and as much as $12.8 million to settle FTC allegations that Xenadrine EFX's weight-loss claims were false and unsubstantiated. The funds will be used for consumer redress. In a bankruptcy case not involving the Commission, the defendants have also agreed to pay at least an additional $22.75 million to settle claims brought by creditors and consumers, including personal injury claims for an earlier ephedra-based product. Xenadrine EFX, which contains, among other ingredients, green tea extract (EGCG), caffeine, and bitter orange (Citrus aurantium), was advertised heavily in print and on television, including in such publications as People, TV Guide, Cosmopolitan, and Men's Fitness. Xenadrine EFX advertising also appeared in Spanish-language publications. The FTC's complaint alleged that the defendants made false or unsubstantiated claims for Xenadrine EFX, including that it was clinically proven to cause rapid and substantial weight loss and clinically proven to be more effective than leading ephedrine-based diet products. According to the complaint, Robert Chinery commissioned several studies of Xenadrine EFX, none of which showed substantial weight loss. The complaint alleged that in one of these studies, subjects taking Xenadrine EFX lost an average of only 1.5 pounds over the 10-week study, while a control group taking a placebo lost an average of 2.5 pounds over the same period.

The complaint also alleged that Xenadrine EFX advertisements falsely represented that persons appearing in the ads achieved the reported weight loss solely by using Xenadrine EFX. According to the FTC complaint, consumer endorsers lost weight by engaging in rigorous diet and/or exercise programs. In addition, the endorsers were paid from $1,000 to $20,000 in connection with their testimonials; according to the complaint, Xenadrine EFX advertisements failed to disclose those payments. The stipulated federal court order with Robert Chinery, Jr. and RTC Research & Development, LLC ("RTC") prohibits certain claims regarding Xenadrine EFX and prohibits all claims regarding the health benefits, performance, efficacy, safety, or side effects of any weight-loss product, dietary supplement, food, drug, or device, unless the representation is true, not misleading, and substantiated by competent and reliable scientific evidence. The settlement also prohibits misrepresentations about any test or study. In addition, the order prohibits misrepresentations of the actual experience of any user or endorser and requires clear and prominent disclosure of any relationship that would materially affect the weight or credibility given to a user testimonial or endorsement. Finally, Robert Chinery and RTC cannot use their settlement with the Commission as a basis for seeking a cash refund of Xenadrine EFX-related income taxes that they previously reported as paid.

CortiSlim and CortiStress: The seven marketers of CortiSlim and CortiStress surrendered, in total, assets worth at least $12 million to settle FTC charges that they made false and unsubstantiated claims that their products can cause weight loss and reduce the risk of, or prevent, serious health conditions. In the final three settlement agreements, the FTC recovery included $8.4 million in cash, along with proceeds from the sale of a residence acquired with CortiSlim profits. The settlements also require the two individual defendants to liquidate tax shelters and transfer to the Commission any funds that remain after paying taxes and penalties. In two earlier settlement agreements, the defendants turned over $1.5 million in cash, a boat, a truck, a real estate interest, and proceeds from a tax shelter. The funds recovered from the seven defendants will be used for consumer redress. The advertising campaign for CortiSlim ran nationwide, including ads on broadcast and cable television, radio, print media, and the Internet. The FTC's complaint alleged that advertising claims about CortiSlim's ability to cause rapid, substantial, and permanent weight loss in all users were false or unsubstantiated, as were claims about CortiStress's ability to reduce the risk of osteoporosis, obesity, diabetes, Alzheimer's disease, cancer, and cardiovascular disease. The FTC also alleged that CortiSlim and CortiStress infomercials were deceptively formatted to appear as talk shows rather than advertisements.

TrimSpa: The marketers of TrimSpa paid $1.5 million to settle FTC allegations that their weight-loss claims were unsubstantiated. According to the FTC's complaint, the marketers had inadequate scientific evidence to support their advertising claims that TrimSpa causes rapid and substantial weight loss and that one of its ingredients, Hoodia gordonii, enables users to lose substantial amounts of weight by suppressing appetite. Many ads for "TrimSpa Completely Ephedra Free Formula X32" featured testimonials. Celebrity Anna Nicole Smith claimed to have lost 69 pounds in eight months by using TrimSpa. Other advertising claims included "Your high speed dream body diet pill" and "It makes losing 30, 50, even 70 pounds (or however many pounds you need to lose) painless." TrimSpa ads appeared on television, in magazines, on radio, and in local newspapers. TrimSpa was also promoted on a Web site, at NASCAR and other live events.

One-A-Day WeightSmart: The Bayer Corporation paid a $3.2 million civil penalty to settle FTC allegations that advertisements for One-A-Day WeightSmart multivitamins violated an earlier Commission order requiring all health claims for One-A-Day brand vitamins to be supported by competent and reliable scientific evidence. Bayer ran a national advertising campaign for One-A-Day WeightSmart, which contains EGCG (epigallocatechin gallate), a green tea extract. Bayer also advertised on television, radio, and the Internet, and in newspapers and magazines, such as RedBook, Family Circle, and TV Guide. Advertising claims included statements such as:

"Just in! Most women over 30 can gain 10 pounds a decade, due in part to slowing metabolism.... So eat right, exercise, and take One-A-Day WeightSmart. The complete multi-vitamin with EGCG to enhance metabolism."

The FTC alleged that these unsubstantiated claims violate a 1991 Commission order against Bayer's predecessor, Miles, Inc., that require all claims about the benefits of One-A-Day brand products to be substantiated by competent and reliable scientific evidence.

CRITICAL ANALYSIS: Evaluate the above weight control cases and determine what should be done in terms of a more proactive stance. In some cases, such as *Diet Thins*, the court utilized the stricter standard of the "unthinking, ignorant consumer" rather than the reasonable person standard. Should a stricter standard apply to these types of cases as well?

"Clinically Proven" and Scientific Evidence

FTC v. CellMark Biopharma, LLC, Derek E. Vest, individually and as the owner of CellMark Biopharma, 2:18-cv-00014-JES-CM LLC

Florida dietary supplement company CellMark Biopharma LLC and owner agreed to stop advertising that two products were "clinically proven" to fight cancer-related malnutrition and cognitive impairment 1/11/2018. The former president (Derek E. Vest) of Gentech Pharmaceutical was sentenced to 18 months in prison and fined $2.5 million over supplements AddTabz, PhenTabz and PhenTabz-Teen. Products were deemed misbranded as they contained an unlisted ingredient, DMAA an amphetamine derivative.
https://www.ftc.gov/enforcement/cases-proceedings/162-3134/cellmark-biopharma-derek-e-vest

AdvaCal-Fertile Male—FTC v. Lane Labs-USA

The Federal Trade Commission (FTC) appealed to the Court of Appeals because of the District Court ruling which had denied the FTC's motion to hold the Lane defendants in contempt for violation of the consent decree judgments entered back in 2000. The consent judgments required that Lane could not make claims about its products without possessing competent and reliable scientific evidence. The products involved calcium supplements and a male fertility product. The Court of Appeals decision is reported below.

FTC v. Lane Labs-USA,
 624 F.3d 575 (3rd Cir. 2010)

Circuit Judges Sloviter, Barry and Smith. Opinion by Circuit Judge Smith

The Federal Trade Commission ("FTC") appeals from an order of the United States District Court for the District of New Jersey denying its motion to hold Lane Labs-USA, Inc., I. William Lane, and Andrew J. Lane in contempt for violation of consent judgments entered by the District Court on July 6, 2000 and September 26, 2000. For the reasons set forth below, we conclude that the District Court committed clear error. Lane Labs-USA, Inc. ("Lane Labs") is a manufacturing distributor of specialty dietary supplements and cosmetic products. The company was founded in 1994 by its current president and sole shareholder, Andrew J. Lane ("Lane"). In June of 2000, the FTC charged the Lane defendants with deceptive acts in violation of § 5 of the Federal Trade Commission Act ("FTC Act") [Section 5 of the FTC Act prohibits "[u]nfair methods of competition in or affecting commerce, and unfair or deceptive acts or practices in or affecting commerce." 15 U.S.C. § 45(a)(1)

The FTC's complaint focused upon unsubstantiated representations pertaining to two products: BeneFin, a dietary supplement, and SkinAnswer, a cosmetic cream. Shortly after the litigation was commenced, however, each of the Lane defendants reached a settlement with the FTC and agreed to the terms of a consent decree. The District Court entered the decree as a stipulated final order for permanent injunction (hereinafter, the "Final Order"), and adjudged Lane Labs liable for the sum of $1 million.

Two provisions of the Final Order are pertinent to this appeal. In Section III, the Lane defendants agreed that "in connection with the manufacturing, labeling, advertising, promotion, offering for sale, or distribution of any food, dietary supplement, or drug," they would refrain from mak[ing] any representation, in any manner, … expressly or by implication, about the effect of [a] product on any disease or disorder, or the effect of such product on the structure or function of the human body, or about any other health benefits of such product, unless, at the time the representation is made, [they] possess[ed] and rel[ied] upon competent and reliable scientific evidence that substantiates the representation. "Competent and reliable scientific evidence" was defined as "tests, analyses, research, studies, or other evidence based on the expertise of professionals in the relevant area, that have been conducted and evaluated in an objective manner by persons qualified to do so, using procedures generally accepted in the profession to yield accurate and reliable results." Section IV of the Final Order forbade express or implied misrepresentations regarding "the existence, contents, validity, results, conclusions, or interpretations of any test, study or research" in connection with "the manufacturing, labeling, advertising, promotion, offering for sale, sale, or distribution of any food, dietary supplement, or drug." Two other provisos, Sections IX and XIV, imposed record keeping and periodic reporting requirements, respectively. Two products are at issue: AdvaCal, a calcium supplement, and Fertil Male, which, as the name suggests, purports to improve male fertility.

AdvaCal—The product primarily consists of calcium hydroxide derived from oyster shells smelted at extremely high temperatures. Once the smelting process is complete, the calcium component is combined with a heated algae ingredient ("HAI") extracted from Hijiki seaweed. This combination of active ingredients purportedly yields a calcium hydroxide product that is significantly more absorbable by the human body than competing calcium supplements. Lane Labs began marketing AdvaCal in 2000 as a means to increase bone strength and combat osteoporosis. *** Typical among the claims appearing in AdvaCal marketing materials were assertions that the supplement (1) was unique in its ability to increase bone mineral density, (2) was clinically proven to be more absorbable than other calcium supplements, and (3) was clinically shown to increase bone density in the hip. In addition, Lane Labs distributed literature promoting AdvaCal as comparable or superior to prescription osteoporosis medicine, and Lane told at least one prospective retail purchaser that the calcium supplement was "on par with" prescription pharmaceuticals.

Fertil Male— is derived from a Peruvian plant known as "maca." After it is 461peciose461ed and heated, the plant is combined with HAI. *** One advertisement featured a customer who proclaimed that Fertil Male caused his sperm count to "skyrocket" within one month.

The Contempt Proceeding—On July 12, 2006, the FTC notified Lane Labs that certain Fertil Male advertisements contained misrepresentations which amounted to violations of the Final Order. *** Thus, on January 12, 2007, the FTC filed a motion with the District Court to hold the Lane defendants in contempt for violating Sections III and IV of the Final Order. To remedy these purported violations, the FTC requested $24 million in monetary damages. *** [T]he District Court denied the FTC's motion for contempt. *** The [District Court] Court also characterized Lane's testimony in a favorable fashion, stating that it "found Mr. Lane to be forthcoming and credible, and consider[ed] his testimony to be evidence of the efforts undertaken by Defendants [Lane]to comply with the [Final Order]." ***

461

Absent from the decision, however, was any detailed examination of the particular representations challenged by the FTC. Rather, the Court simply set forth, in a series of bullet points, a "representative selection" of the challenged assertions, eschewing an analysis of whether each claim found support in the record. *** The Court further concluded that even if the Lane defendants violated the Final Order, they were entitled to a defense of substantial compliance. The FTC timely appealed. ****

The FTC argues that the Lane defendants disobeyed Sections III and IV of the Final Order, and that the District Court erred in holding otherwise. Section III requires that each of Lane Labs' marketing claims find substantiation in competent or reliable scientific research. According to the FTC, the District Court failed to consider the specific marketing claims challenged during the contempt proceeding. *** The FTC also challenges the assertion that Fertil Male can cause sperm count to "skyrocket" in as little as one month. Finally, the government argues that it proved Lane Labs violated Section IV of the Final Order by distorting research regarding AdvaCal and other forms of calcium. We will address each of these contentions in turn.

A. Only AdvaCal Can Increase Bone Density—In various marketing, the Lane defendants claimed that AdvaCal was unique in its ability to increase bone density. One full-page print advertisement proclaimed, "Clinical studies show that AdvaCal does what no other calcium does: actually increases bone density in women." A direct mail circular asserted, "Other calcium supplements cannot increase bone mass. AdvaCal can." Yet another print publication explains, "When LaneLabs introduced AdvaCal and AdvaCal Ultra in the mid-1990s, the scientific view of calcium changed forever. Up until then, calcium supplements, at best, could only PREVENT bone loss. AdvaCal was different. AdvaCal demonstrated in multiple clinical studies that it could actually BUILD bone density quickly, naturally and safely." In a 2003 infomercial, William Lane described AdvaCal as "the only calcium that I know of where you can actually increase bone density." Finally, on two occasions in 2005, Lane wrote to a book publisher to promote AdvaCal. In a February 9, 2005 email, Lane portrayed AdvaCal as "the one calcium clinically shown to build bone density in multiple human clinical studies. No other calcium can make that claim." ***

The record is devoid of credible evidence to contradict the government's proffer. *** The District Court ruled that the Lane defendants "offered support and substantiation" for the claim that AdvaCal was unique in its ability to increase human bone density. The Court's finding is not plausible in view of the entire record. The Lane defendants were not merely asserting that AdvaCal produced beneficial bone-building results or outcomes that were superior to other calcium supplements; rather, the claims indicated that other supplements did not build bone at all. *** We are thus left with the definite conviction that the District Court's finding is clearly erroneous and must be reversed.

B. AdvaCal Has Been Shown in Clinical Tests to Increase Bone Density in the Hip—The FTC moved into evidence two print documents—one a direct mailing, the other a two-page advertisement—in which Lane Labs touts clinical research exhibiting AdvaCal's ability to increase bone density in the hip. It is undisputed that no such clinical research exists, a fact that the District Court did not address in its memorandum. In spite of this omission, our review of the record leaves us satisfied that the Court did not clearly err by finding that these representations were in accord with Section III of the Final Order. Dr. Holick pointed to two clinical studies supportive of Lane Labs' claims. Both appeared in peer-reviewed journals, and both showed that calcium increased bone density in the human hip. *** The District Court was entitled to rely upon this testimony, to credit Dr. Holick's reliance on data "extrapolated" from generic calcium studies, and to find that the Lane defendants did not violate the Final Order by making the claims in question. Accordingly, we will affirm the District Court's finding.

C. AdvaCal is Three to Four Times More Absorbable Than Other Calcium Supplements
In direct mailers, print advertisements, and in an infomercial, the Lane defendants represented that AdvaCal was three to four times more absorbable than other calcium supplements. One assertion

characteristic of these claims appeared in a direct mail article distributed to Lane Labs' customers. In it, AdvaCal was described as "an extremely high-potency calcium supplement that is absorbed *four times better* than typical calcium-carbonate supplements."

Dr. Heaney characterized such a contention as "not physically possible." He explained that the typical calcium carbonate supplement is absorbed at a rate of 30-35%; were AdvaCal capable of performing at the advertised rate, its absorption value would rise to 120%. Dr. Heaney testified that this is physiologically-and mathematically-unattainable. *** The Lane defendants argue that AdvaCal was not marketed to the average individual, but rather to elderly females, a substantial number of who suffer from conditions of achlorhydria and osteoporosis. Achlorhydric individuals cannot produce stomach acid and, as a result, absorb calcium at a rate significantly below average. In some patients, this rate is as low as 4%. Dr. Holick explained that it would not be unusual for an achlorhydric individual, whose calcium absorption rate is far below 30-35%, to absorb AdvaCal three to four times more effectively than calcium carbonate. ***

Lane Labs' marketing did not include phraseology limiting its claims to elderly females suffering conditions of achlorhydria. A 2003 infomercial was typical: "Osteo-porosis now strikes women and men of all ages, races and nationalities. But osteoporosis can be prevented. A key is taking the right calcium and the right calcium supplement is AdvaCal.... AdvaCal has been clinically shown to be three times more absorbable than other calciums." *** We consider it appropriate to remand so that the District Court may address these particular claims more exhaustively.

D. AdvaCal is Comparable or Superior to Prescription Osteoporosis Medicine—In 1999, Lane sent a "pitch letter" to Monica Reinagel, who was then the editor of the Health Sciences Institute ("HSI") newsletter. In this correspondence, Lane lauded AdvaCal's potential, describing it as "a revolutionary calcium supplement … that has been clinically shown to actually build postmenopausal bone density, without the side effects of hormonal drugs or supplements." HSI published an article praising AdvaCal shortly thereafter. *** Lane himself acknowledged that Lane Labs paid for the right to distribute the article, and then did so "extensively." *** In either event, the District Court's finding was clearly erroneous; there is no dispute that the comparability/superiority claim was unsupported by competent or reliable scientific evidence and, by their own admission, the Lane defendants used this claim to market AdvaCal. [T]his claim violates Section III of the Final Order and the District Court's holding to the contrary is clear error.

E. Fertil Male Can Cause Sperm Count to "Skyrocket" in as Little as One Month—Lane Labs published an advertisement for Fertil Male which claims, *inter alia,* that the supplement caused a male customer's sperm count to "skyrocket" after one month's use. This is the sole Fertil Male representation challenged by the FTC on appeal. *** Dr. Seibel testified unequivocally that there was competent or reliable scientific research to substantiate the claim that Fertil Male increased sperm count. The FTC declined to delve further into this inquiry when it had the opportunity, but now asks that we set aside the District Court's factual findings on the basis of testimony that is ambiguous at best. *** The finding of the District Court with respect to this marketing claim will stand.

F. Distortion of Research—According to the FTC, the District Court committed error by finding that Lane Labs did not violate Section IV of the Final Order. Section IV forbids express or implied misrepresentations regarding "the existence, contents, validity, results, conclusions, or interpretations of any test, study or research" pertaining to "the manufacturing, labeling, advertising, promotion, offering for sale, sale, or distribution of any food, dietary supplement, or drug." *** The District Court's analysis is problematic. Section IV of the Final Order prohibits the Lane defendants from misrepresenting the results of research and data; it is simply unconcerned with a product's overall salutary effects. *** The District Court's failure to provide us with a reasoned basis for concluding that Lane Labs did not violate Section IV prevents us from exercising meaningful review. Many of the challenged representations appear misleading on their face, and the District Court provides no rationale for its conclusion that they are not. For example, a direct mailing advertisement asserted, "In clinical tests [AdvaCal] has been shown to actually increase bone density—even in the critical hip bones...." *** Even Lane conceded, "There are no clinical studies on AdvaCal in the hip.... [W]e can't verify that statement." Without any explanation from the District Court, we are unable to determine if this claim was even considered in its Section IV analysis. *** Other challenged representations appear equally misleading. Rather than speculate as to the factual basis underlying the District Court's ultimate conclusions, we will return this matter to the District Court so that it may make findings that are more specific than those presently before us.

G. Substantial Compliance—The District Court held that even if the Lane defendants violated Sections III and IV of the Final Order, they were entitled to a defense of substantial compliance. We have never explicitly recognized the validity of the substantial compliance defense, *see Robin Woods,* 28 F.3d at 399, but we note that several of our sister circuits have done so, *see Morales-Feliciano v. Parole Bd. Of P.R.,* 887 F.2d 1, 4-5 (1st Cir.1989). *** In *Robin Woods,* we favorably referenced a decision of the Court of Appeals for the Ninth Circuit and set forth the two-part substantial compliance defense adopted therein. The rule permits a party cited for contempt to assert the defense if it (1) has taken all reasonable steps to comply with the court order at issue, and (2) has violated the order in a manner that is merely 'technical' or 'inadvertent.' ***

The impossibility defense necessarily requires the defending party to assert a present inability to comply with the relevant court order. *** Substantial compliance evokes a standard somewhat less demanding. A party substantially complies when it takes all reasonable steps to do so, but nonetheless contravenes the court order by good faith mistake or excusable oversight. The distinction is important, for a party that substantially complies is physically capable of doing so; it has simply erred in a manner for which it would be inequitable to impose contempt sanctions.

Recognizing that we did not formally adopt the defense of substantial compliance in *Robin Woods,* we do so here. In order to avail oneself of the defense, a party must show that it (1) has taken all reasonable steps to comply with the valid court order, and (2) has violated the order in a manner that is merely "technical" or "inadvertent." *** It [District Court] did not explicitly address the extent to which violations of the Final Order were "technical" or "inadvertent." *** Moreover, although the [District] Court implicitly recognized that some violations occurred, it neither identified this misconduct nor explained why the conduct qualified as a "technical" or "inadvertent" violation of the Final Order. *** Accordingly, we will vacate the District Court's finding that the Lane defendants substantially complied with the Final Order, and will remand for reconsideration consistent with the discussion set forth above. *** Rather, the FTC contended that specific marketing claims were violations of two previously entered consent decrees. Unfortunately, the able District Judge did not provide sufficiently detailed findings or sufficient rationale to allow us to perform effective appellate review. For the reasons set forth above, we will remand this matter to the District Court for further proceedings consistent with this opinion.

NOTE: On remand, the District Court granted the FTC Motion for Contempt and found that the defendants were not entitled to the defense of substantial compliance and that the violation of the consent decree was not "technical" or "inadvertent". (Civ. Action No. 00-cv-3174, Nov. 18, 2011). In *United States v. Lane Labs-USA, Inc.,* 427 F.3d 219 (3d Cir.2005), FDA filed a complaint against Lane Labs alleging violations of the Federal Food, Drug, and Cosmetic Act ("FDCA"), 21 U.S.C. § 301 *et seq.* FDA alleged that BeneFin, SkinAnswer, and MGN-3 were misbranded and falsely advertised. The District Court issued a permanent injunction and ordered payment of restitution to consumers who purchased these products. *United States v. Lane Labs-USA, Inc.,* 324 F.Supp.2d 547 (D.C. N.J. 2004). The Court of Appeals affirmed the District Court's decision. See: *Volume III,* for *United States v. Lane Labs-USA, Inc.,* 427 F.3d 219 (3d Cir.2005) (discussing restitution as an equitable remedy concerning BeneFin, SkinAnswer and MGN-3).

CRITICAL ANALYSIS: This particular *Lane Labs* decision involving AdvaCal and Fertile Male raised the issues of substantial compliance and sufficiency of evidence. Discuss these concepts.

FDA Enforcement

Warnings, Product Destruction, Recalls, Seizures, Consent Decrees and Criminal Actions, Public Notifications

FDA regulates dietary supplements products post market and does not have legal premarket approval authority. Inspections, warning letters, recalls, seizures are all within the purview of FDA. FDA regulates the safety, manufacturing and labeling of dietary supplements while the Federal Trade Commission (FTC) regulates advertising as detailed above.

Regulatory enforcement actions by FDA have included voluntary recalls, warning letters, seizures, in junctions and criminal enforcement as well as joint action with FTC and the Department of Justice. For example, FDA obtained a court ordered seizure, 21 U.S.C. section 331, of a dietary supplement due to product claims because the product promoted a treatment for autism. Examples of specific types of dietary supplements and associated problems include DMAA, OxyElite Pro, Ephedrine alkaloids, Seasilver, Erectile Dysfunction Supplements, Herbal Phenterrnine and androstenedione commonly known as "Andro" used to enhance athletic performance and marketed to stimulate testosterone and muscle growth yet have anabolic steroid effects in the body. Other FDA warnings have focused on body building and weight loss products. FDA has used its regulatory authority to issue public warnings and alerts about the safety of various dietary supplements. Listed below are FDA enforcement actions, consumer warnings and public notifications.

Tainted Sexual Enhancement, Body Building, and Weight Loss Products

Medication health fraud remains rampant and a top FDA priority is the increased enforcement of products touted as dietary supplements, when in reality, these products contain hidden drugs. These products are an example of economic fraud as well as the potential for serious injuries. In 2010, FDA issued a letter to dietary supplement manufacturers detailed, in part, below. Yet, as the public notifications reveal, drugs concealed in dietary supplements remain.
http://www.fda.gov/Drugs/ResourcesForYou/Consumers/BuyingUsingMedicineSafely/MedicationHealthFraud/default.htm

FDA Letter to Manufacturers

Dear Dietary Supplement Manufacturer:

Where FDA investigations have discovered products marketed as dietary supplements that contain the same active ingredients as in FDA-approved drug products, analogs of such drug ingredients, or other compounds of concern, such as novel synthetic steroids, FDA has issued warning letters and conducted seizures and criminal prosecutions. The Agency has also issued consumer alerts and press announcements to warn consumers about such products. FDA established a RSS feed on its website to alert consumers more rapidly when FDA finds that a product marketed as a dietary supplement is tainted.

In addition to the actions listed above, responsible individuals and companies should be aware that the government may initiate criminal investigations to hold accountable those who violate the Federal Food, Drug, and Cosmetic Act (the Act) and endanger the public health. Responsible individuals, even if the individual did not participate in, encourage, or have personal knowledge of the violation, can be criminally prosecuted under the Act, pursuant to 21 U.S.C. § 331. See *United States v. Park*, 421 U.S. 658 (1975). When the evidence warrants, felony charges may be appropriate. Actions that pose a risk to public health should expect a swift and strong agency response. Manufacturers, distributors, importers and others in the supply chain of dietary supplements are responsible for ensuring that their products comply with the statutes and regulations FDA enforces. Therefore, responsible individuals should take appropriate steps to ensure that their products do not contain active ingredients that may cause the product to be an unapproved new drug, a misbranded drug and/or an adulterated or misbranded dietary supplement, such as: those in FDA-approved drugs, analogs of approved drugs, active pharmaceutical ingredients removed from the market for safety reasons, new chemical ingredients that have not been studied adequately in humans, or controlled substances. In addition, companies that manufacture, process, pack or hold dietary supplements are required to register their facilities under 21 U.S.C.§ 350d and 21 CFR 1.225-1.243. Products in the weight loss, sexual enhancement, and body building categories should receive extra attention and scrutiny from their manufacturers and distributors.

Manufacturers and distributors of dietary supplements must comply with all applicable dietary supplement Current Good Manufacturing Practice (CGMP) requirements in 21 CFR Parts 111 and 110 and are subject to FDA inspection. A dietary supplement manufacturer must have proper controls in place to ensure the quality of the dietary supplement and to ensure that the supplement is processed in a consistent manner. The CGMP requirements in Parts 111 and, as applicable, 110 apply to all domestic and foreign companies that manufacture, package, label, or hold dietary supplements for the U.S. market. Specifically, dietary supplement manufacturers must implement processes to ensure the integrity of their supply chain. For example, a firm that manufactures a dietary supplement must establish specifications for components used in the manufacture of the supplement. These specifications must include limits on those types of contamination that may adulterate or lead to adulteration of the finished batch of dietary supplement, as required by 21 CFR 111.70(b). The firm must verify that such component specifications are met, as required by 21 CFR 111.75(a). A firm must maintain records, including documentation that dietary supplements were manufactured in conformance with written procedures (21 CFR 111.375), that dietary supplement components conform to established product specifications, and, as appropriate, documentation of the qualification of a supplier for the purpose of relying on a supplier's certificate of analysis (21 CFR 111.95). Raw ingredients arriving at a manufacturer's facility may already be tainted with undisclosed and illegal ingredients that, if present in a finished dietary supplement, would adulterate the dietary supplement, or cause it to be an unapproved and misbranded drug. A manufacturer must qualify its supplier and establish specifications for raw ingredients used in the manufacture of a dietary supplement to ensure that such ingredients are not a source of contamination. A strong program of qualifying your suppliers, testing incoming ingredients, and verifying the contents of finished products—all of which are required by the CGMP regulations—can help minimize those risks. FDA encourages industry to report any suspected tainted supplement ingredients or finished products and the manufacturers or distributors who market these products to FDA. We have created two tools to receive this information via email to TaintedProducts@fda. hhs.gov and/or via our anonymous reporting form "Report Suspected Criminal Activity" located at: *http://www.fda.gov/oci.*We are asking the dietary supplement industry's trade associations to share this letter widely. FDA is also seeking continued input and collaboration from the trade associations to educate the industry about this problem and to develop strategies to combat it. *http://www.fda.gov/downloads/Drugs/ResourcesForYou/Consumers/BuyingUsingMedicineSafely/MedicationHealthFraud/UCM236985.pdf* (edited)

CRITICAL ANALYSIS: Does this letter suffice in terms of thwarting adulterated and misbranded products? Should Congress revisit Dietary Supplement regulation and perhaps require pre-market approval? See Sexual Enhancement Products, DMAA Body Building and Weight Loss and Kratom below.

Public Notification—Tainted Sexual Enhancement Products

The following are examples of FDA public notifications of tainted sexual enhancement products that contained hidden drugs in the dietary supplement labeled products.
Online access link:
Wonder-Erect Male Pills contains hidden drug ingredient
Wonder-Erect Male Gum contains hidden drug ingredient
http://www.fda.gov/Drugs/ResourcesForYou/Consumers/BuyingUsingMedicineSafely/MedicationHealthFraud/ucm234539.htm

Consumer Warning—Sexual Enhancement Man Up Now Capsules

http://www.fda.gov/NewsEvents/Newsroom/PressAnnouncements/ucm236538.htm (edited)

The U.S. Food and Drug Administration issued a warning to consumers not to use *Man Up Now* capsules, marketed as a dietary supplement for sexual enhancement, because they contain a variation of an active drug ingredient found in Viagra that can dangerously lower blood pressure. *Man Up Now* claims to be "herbal" and "all natural," and consumers may mistakenly assume the product is harmless and poses no health risk. The FDA analyzed *Man Up Now* and determined that it contains sulfoaildenafil, a chemical similar to sildenafil, the active ingredient in Viagra. Like sildenafil, this chemical may interact with prescription drugs such as nitrates, including nitroglycerin, and cause dangerously low blood pressure. When blood pressure drops suddenly, the brain is deprived of an adequate blood supply that can lead to dizziness or lightheadedness.

Man Up Now, distributed by Synergy Distribution LLC, is sold on Internet sites, online marketplaces, and possibly in retail outlets in single, double, and triple blister packs, and in six-, 12-, and 30-count capsule bottles. Sexual enhancement products that claim to work as well as prescription products, but that contain prescription strength drugs, are likely to expose unknowing consumers to unpredictable risks and the potential for injury or death.

The FDA has found many products marketed as dietary supplements for sexual enhancement during the past several years that can be harmful because they contain active ingredients in FDA-approved drugs or variations of these ingredients. Sexual enhancement products promising rapid effects such as working in minutes to hours, or long-lasting effects such as 24 hours to 72 hours, are likely to contain ingredients in FDA-approved drugs or variations of those ingredients. The FDA advises consumers who have experienced any negative side effects from sexual enhancement products to consult a health care professional and to safely discard the product. Consumers and health care professionals should report adverse events to the FDA's MedWatch Adverse Event Reporting program.

Warning Letters—Dimethylamylamine DMAA

Dimethylamylamine commonly known as (DMAA) provides an excellent illustration example of issues related to post-market enforcement. Legally, the process to force removal of dietary supplements for safety reasons is lengthy and arduous. DMAA, a stimulant is used in supplements, promotes weight loss, muscle building and performance enhancement. Medical issues associated with DMAA include elevated blood pressure, potential cardiovascular problems such as heart attack, shortness of breath and tightening of the chest. DMAA, known as 1,3-dimethylamylamine, methylhexanamine or geranium extract, is an ingredient found illegally in some dietary supplements and often advertised as a "natural" stimulant. DMAA, especially in combination with other ingredients such as caffeine, can be a health risk to consumers. Ingestion of DMAA can elevate blood pressure and lead to cardiovascular problems ranging from shortness of breath and tightening in the chest to heart attack. By mid 2013, FDA received 86 reports of illnesses and death associated with supplements containing DMAA. The majority are voluntary reports from consumers and healthcare practitioners. The illnesses reported include heart problems and nervous system or psychiatric disorders.

FDA sent 11 warning letters in 2012 to the companies that use DMAA in its products. Ten of the companies agreed to remove the products from the marketplace. FDA notified the companies that DMAA needs to be taken off the market or reformulated to remove this substance. Most companies warned are no longer distributing products with DMAA. However, USPLabs, responded to FDA's warning by submitting published studies that purport to challenge FDA's conclusions. However, after reviewing the studies provided by USPLabs, FDA found the information insufficient to defend the use of DMAA as an ingredient in dietary supplements. FDA followed up with a warning letter to the company. USPLabs decided to phase out use of DMAA. Dietary supplements containing DMAA, is referred to on different product labels by 10 possible names.

NOTE: The first link contains the FDA warning letters and the second link contains the response letter from FDA to USPlabs.
http://www.fda.gov/Food/DietarySupplements/QADietarySupplements/ucm346576.htm
http://www.fda.gov/AboutFDA/CentersOffices/OfficeofFoods/CFSAN/CFSANFOIAElectronicReadingRoom/ucm350199.htm

Product Destruction— DMAA Jack3d and OxyElite Pro

USPlabs, a dietary supplement company, voluntarily destroyed its DMAA containing products located at its facility in Dallas, Texas (On July 2, 2013). USPlabs OxyElite Pro and Jack3d are estimated to have been worth more than $8 million at the retail level. USPlabs agreed to stop manufacturing dietary supplements containing DMAA. USPlabs agreed to destroy the products after FDA administratively detained them under the Federal Food, Drug and Cosmetic Act, recently amended by the Food Safety Modernization Act (FSMA). Under its administrative detention authority, FDA can detain a food or dietary supplement product if the agency has reason to believe the product is adulterated or misbranded. FDA is permitted to detain products and keep them out of the marketplace for a maximum of 30 days while it determines whether to take further enforcement action, such as seizure. Under FDA regulations, detained articles can be voluntarily destroyed by their owner.

In late 2013, under FDA supervision, USPLabs again destroyed certain other products termed **"OxyElite Pro"** linked to several cases of acute liver failure and hepatitis. There was at least one death and several patients required liver transplants. The supplement was advertised as an aid to losing weight and building muscles. FDA warned the company on Oct. 11, 2013, that certain OxyElite Pro products and another supplement, VERSA-1, are considered adulterated because they contain a new dietary ingredient, aegeline, for which the company did not provide evidence of safety. In late 2013, there were over 56 cases of acute liver failure or acute hepatitis linked to OxyPro Elite, 43 of them in Hawaii. Earlier in 2013, another formulation of OxyElite Pro was destroyed after being held through an FDA administrative detention order. A stimulant included in those products, DMAA, or dimethylamylamine, can cause high blood pressure and lead to heart attacks, seizures, psychiatric disorders and death.

Companies are required to provide evidence of safety of the new dietary ingredient 75 days before the product goes to market. This notification was not made by USPLabs before it began using DMAA, a new dietary ingredient, in OxyElite Pro. After removing DMAA from its products, USPLabs substituted aegeline, among other ingredients, in certain OxyElite Pro products without informing FDA. Non-synthetic aegeline is an alkaloid extract from leaves of the Asian bael tree (Agele marmelos). *http://www.fda.gov/forconsumers/consumerupdates/ucm374742.htm*

CRITICAL ANALYSIS: The Food Safety Modernization Act provided FDA with the authority to detain products such as those above as well as the Kratom example below. Recommend other enforcement measures for these types of products.

Mandatory Recall, Seizure and Import Alert—Kratom

https://www.fda.gov/NewsEvents/Newsroom/PressAnnouncements/ucm603517.htm
http://www.fda.gov/NewsEvents/Newsroom/PressAnnouncements/ucm480344.htm
https://www.fda.gov/Safety/Recalls/ucm617098.htm

FDA concluded in 2018 that numerous kratom-containing products have been linked to a large outbreak of salmonellosis and mandatory recall was ordered in 2018. For example, Zakah Life, LLC of Ankeny, Iowa, voluntarily recalled the following Kratom products: Super Green Maeng Da Premium Kratom powder, Powerful Red Vein Bali Premium Kratom powder, Super Green Maeng Da Premium Kratom capsules, and Powerful Red Vein Bali Premium Kratom capsules due to the possible *Salmonella* contamination. Previously, United States Marshals, seized nearly 90,000 bottles of dietary supplements labeled as containing kratom. The product, manufactured for and held by Dordoniz Natural Products LLC, located in South Beloit, Illinois, is marketed under the brand name RelaKzpro and worth more than $400,000. *Mitragyna 468peciose*, commonly known as kratom, is a botanical substance that grows naturally in Thailand, Malaysia, Indonesia and Papua New Guinea. Serious concerns exist regarding the toxicity of kratom in multiple organ systems. Consumption of kratom can lead to a number of health impacts, including, among others, respiratory depression, vomiting, nervousness, weight loss and constipation. Kratom has been indicated to have both narcotic and stimulant-like effects and withdrawal symptoms may include hostility, aggression, excessive tearing, aching of muscles and bones and jerky limb movements. In 2014, the FDA issued an import alert that allows U.S. officials to detain imported dietary supplements and bulk dietary ingredients that are, or contain, kratom without physical examination. FDA administratively detained RelaKzpro in January 2016. Detained products can be kept out of the marketplace for a maximum of 30 days while it determines whether to take further enforcement action, such as seizure. In obtaining the court authorized seizure action, the U.S. Department of Justice, on behalf of FDA, filed a complaint in the U.S. District Court for the Northern District of Illinois alleging, among other things, that kratom is a new dietary ingredient for which there is inadequate information to provide reasonable assurance that it does not present a significant or unreasonable risk of illness or injury; therefore, dietary supplements containing kratom are adulterated. In 2018, FDA Commissioner Gottlieb

warned that Kratom should not be used as an alternative to opioids.
https://www.fda.gov/NewsEvents/Newsroom/PressAnnouncements/ucm595622.htm
See Statement by Commissioner Gottlieb linking Kratom ad Salmonella.
https://www.fda.gov/NewsEvents/Newsroom/PressAnnouncements/ucm612420.htm
NOTE: See *Volume III* Kratom Seizure

CRITICAL ANALYSIS: Kratom is very controversial and to date seizure has occurred with the product touted as a food and/or a dietary supplement. Discuss the issues associated with Kratom and whether the product is a food and/or dietary supplement or a drug.

Weight Loss Products Voluntary Recall and Failure to Comply
Voluntary Recall—Dream Body Weight Loss
http://www.fda.gov/Safety/Recalls/ucm509727.htm?source=govdelivery&utm_medium=email&utm_source=govdelivery

Dream Body Weight Loss voluntarily recalled (July 2016) all lots of Dream Body Extreme Gold 800mg 30 gold capsules, Dream Body 450mg 30 white capsules, and Dream Body Advanced 400mg 30 purple capsules to the consumer level. The Dream Body Extreme 800mg Gold, Dream Body 450mg and Dream Body Advanced 400mg have been found to contain sibutramine after FDA sampling and testing. See link above.

Failure to Comply With Recall Order—Hi-Tech Pharmaceuticals
Hi-tech pharmaceuticals executives were arrested after a Georgia federal court found that they failed to comply with an order to recall their weight-loss supplements. *FTC v. Nat'l Urological Grp. Inc.*, no. 4-3294 (D. Ct. N.D. Ga. Sept. 2, 2014). Earlier, the court ordered the company to pay $40 million to the Federal Trade Commission (FTC) and recall several products, including Fastin, lipodrene, benzedrine, and stimerex-es. The court found that Hi-Tech delayed the beginning of the recall. For example, the recall notice was not mailed until 50 days after the order was entered and the scope was inaccurate as the company mailed 2,402 notices yet advised the court that it had more than 3,700 retailers and distributors. Further, Hi-tech's recall notice was in nature a "legal brief" rather than a recall notice. The envelope that contained the recall notice did not identify the contents as a recall notice and depicted product advertisements. Hi-tech's Website failed to depict a prominent notice; rather, it contained a small link labeled "recall," and did not appear on the product purchasing page. Further, the court found the follow-up recordkeeping problematic. Finally, only eight companies returned a total of less than 3,000 bottles.

CRITICAL ANALYSIS: Using Hi-Tech and Dream Body Weight Loss as illustrations, how would you advise your client in terms of compliance?

Caffeine Products—Warning Letters, Recalls and Consent Decrees
Powdered Caffeine

https://www.fda.gov/Food/GuidanceRegulation/GuidanceDocumentsRegulatoryInformation/ucm604318.htm

Dietary Supplements that contain pure caffeine have been problematic and linked to at least two deaths. In 2018, FDA issued a guidance titled: **Highly Concentrated Caffeine in Dietary Supplements; Guidance for Industry.** The FDA guidance details the significant risk of illness with these pure or highly concentrated caffeine products marketed as dietary supplements. According to FDA, one teaspoon of pure powdered caffeine is equivalent to the amount of caffeine in about 28 cups of regular coffee. In 2015, FDA issued warning letters to Bridge City Bulk, Hard Eight Nutrition, Kreativ Health, Inc. dba Natural Food Supplements, Purebulk, Inc. and SPN LLC dba Smartpowders about selling pure powdered caffeine as a dietary supplement.

CRITICAL ANALYSIS: FDA could seize the product or obtain a court injunction if the manufacturer continues to market this product. What other enforcement and preventive actions would you recommend?

Nationwide Recalls—*Magic Power Coffee*

According to FDA, Magic Power Coffee, an instant coffee product marketed as a dietary supplement for sexual enhancement, contains the drug ingredient hydroxythiohomosildenafil, a chemical similar to sildenafil, the active ingredient in Viagra. Hydroxythiohomosildenafil, like sildenafil, may interact with prescription drugs known as nitrates, including nitroglycerin, and cause dangerously low blood pressure. The product is distributed on Internet sites and online auctions by multiple independent distributors participating in an online multi-level marketing scheme.

http://www.fda.gov/Safety/MedWatch/SafetyInformation/SafetyAlertsforHumanMedicalProducts/ucm216355.htm

INZ Distributors, Inc. Magic Power Coffee, Inc. Conducts a Voluntary Nationwide Recall of Magic Power Coffee Dietary Supplement

http://www.fda.gov/Safety/Recalls/ucm217482.htm   http://www.magicpowercoffeepro.com/

INZ of Brooklyn, NY announced a voluntary nationwide recall of the dietary supplement product sold under the name, Magic Power Coffee. The Company has been informed by representatives of the Food and Drug Administration (FDA) that lab analysis of one lot of the product by the FDA found that the product contains undeclared hydroxythiohomosildenafil, similar in structure to Sildenafil, an FDA-approved drug used for the treatment of male Erectile Dysfunction (ED), making Magic Power Coffee an unapproved drug. The hydroxythiohomosildenafil drug ingredient is not listed on the product label. Hydroxythiohomosildenafil may interact with nitrates found in some prescription drugs such as nitroglycerin and may lower blood pressure to dangerous levels. Consumers with diabetes, high blood pressure, high cholesterol or heart disease often take nitrates. Magic Power Coffee is distributed nationwide on Internet sites and online auctions by multiple independent distributors participating in an online multi-level marketing program. It is sold in a 2-serving box with UPC 718122686872 and a 12-serving carton containing six 2-serving boxes with UPC 718122686773. Customers were advised to stop using it immediately and contact their physician if they have experienced any problems that may be related to taking this product as well as return any unused product to the place of purchase for full refund or contact INZ Distributors, Inc./Magic Power Coffee, Inc. at (718) 313-1579.

CRITICAL ANALYSIS: Compare and contrast how INZ Distributors, Inc. Magic Power Coffee, Inc. handled the recall as opposed to Hi-Tech Pharmaceuticals.

Consent Decree—*Caffeine Infused Shapewear*
Norm Thompson Outfitters and Wacoal America Settle FTC Charges Over Weight-Loss Claims for Caffeine-Infused Shapewear

The Federal Trade Commission approved two final orders settling charges that two companies, *Norm Thompson Outfitters, Inc., and Wacoal America, Inc.*, misled consumers regarding the ability of their caffeine-infused shapewear undergarments to reshape the wearer's body and reduce cellulite. According to the FTC's *complaints, the two companies' marketing claims for their caffeine-infused products were false and not substantiated by scientific evidence.*

The FTC's complaint against Norm Thompson Outfitters alleged the company deceptively advertised, marketed, and sold women's undergarments infused with microencapsulated caffeine, retinol, and other ingredients, claiming the "shapewear" would slim and reshape the wearer's body and reduce cellulite. The products, made with Lytess brand fabrics, were sold via mail order and on the company's Norm Thompson Outfitters, Sahalie, Body Solutions, and Body Belle websites. Specifically, the FTC alleged that the company made claims that wearing its shapewear would eliminate or substantially reduce cellulite; reduce the wearer's hip measurements by up to two inches and their thigh measurements by one inch; and reduce thigh and hip measurements "without any effort." The complaint against Wacoal America contained similar allegations. It charged that the company's iPants supposedly slimmed the body and reduced cellulite. Specifically, the company made false and unsubstantiated claims that wearing iPants would: substantially reduce cellulite; cause a substantial reduction in the wearer's thigh measurements; and destroy fat cells, resulting in substantial slimming.

In settling the charges, the companies are banned from claiming that any garment that contains any drug or cosmetic causes substantial weight or fat loss or a substantial reduction in body size. The companies also are prohibited from making claims that any drug or cosmetic reduces or eliminates cellulite or reduces body fat, unless they are not misleading and can be substantiated by competent and reliable scientific evidence. The final orders also require the companies to pay $230,000 and $1.3 million, respectively, that the FTC can use to provide refunds to consumers. (FTC File Nos. 132-3094 and 132-3095; the staff contact is David Newman, FTC Western Region, San Francisco, 415-848-5123*). http://www.ftc.gov/enforcement/cases-proceedings/132-3095/wacoal-america-inc-matter* (Dec. 2014).

CRITICAL ANALYSIS: Courts have utilized the "unthinking ignorant consumer test" in weight loss cases such as this. Consider the above FTC action and evaluate why this test protects the consumer. Contrast this test with the "reasonable person" test.

Permanent Injunction—*EonNutra LLC, CDSM LLC, and HABW LLC*
Colorado Companies to Stop Adulterated and Misbranded Dietary Supplements Distribution and Unapproved and Misbranded Drugs
https://www.justice.gov/opa/pr/district-court-enters-permanent-injunction-against-colorado-companies-stop-distribution

The U.S. District Court for the District of Colorado entered a permanent injunction against EonNutra LLC, two related companies, CDSM LLC and HABW LLC, and their owner, Michael Floren, to prevent the sale and distribution of adulterated and misbranded dietary supplements and unapproved and misbranded drugs. The Justice Department filed a complaint (March 10, 2017) in the U.S. District Court for the District of Colorado, alleging that the defendants, who sell some 150 dietary supplement products, violated the Federal Food, Drug, and Cosmetic Act (FDCA). Although labelled as dietary supplements, several of the defendants' products were, according to the complaint, marketed as drugs, with claims that the products could help treat or prevent a host of serious conditions or diseases, including heart disease, diabetes, depression, hypertension, osteoporosis, and liver and kidney disorders without FDA approval. Some of the specific products identified in the complaint as unapproved drugs were 4NOx2, HGH Night Time, rHGH Drops Black Label, Primal Rage Levo 5 GH Mass and Deer Antler Velvet Extract. The defendants sold these supplements without implementing the requisite procedures to validate the supplements' composition. The complaint further alleges that, despite repeated warnings from FDA, the defendants continued to post statements on their websites claiming that their products cured, mitigated, treated, or prevented a number of serious diseases. According to the complaint, these claims were unsupported by any well-controlled clinical studies or other credible scientific substantiation. In addition, the complaint alleges that the defendants' products did not contain adequate directions for such uses. In addition to claims related to sales of unapproved drugs, the complaint further alleges that the defendants' products were adulterated dietary supplements because they were not manufactured in compliance with federal good manufacturing practice regulations. According to the complaint, a 2016 FDA inspection of the defendants' manufacturing facility revealed, among other things, that the defendants failed to establish specifications for the identity, purity, strength, and composition of their finished products or the components in their products, or prepare and follow their manufacturing plans. The complaint alleges, for example, that some of the defendants' supplement labels did not list all of the products' ingredients, indicate the correct serving size, or indicate the number of servings in a bottle.

The defendants agreed to settle the litigation and be bound by a consent decree of permanent injunction. The consent decree requires that if the defendants wish to resume manufacturing drugs or dietary supplements in the future, they must implement the remedial measures set forth in the consent decree, notify the FDA of the measures they have taken, and obtain written approval from the FDA that they appear to be in compliance with both the terms of the consent decree and the provisions of the FDCA.

Consent Decree—*Scilabs Nutraceuticals Adulterated Products*

http://www.justice.gov/opa/pr/district-court-enters-permanent-injunction-against-california-dietary-supplement-company-and

The U.S. District Court for the Central District of California entered a consent decree of permanent injunction against Scilabs Nutraceuticals, Inc. of Irvine, California, and its board chairman and chief executive officer (CEO), Paul P. Edalat, to prevent the distribution of adulterated dietary supplements. SciLabs Nutraceuticals, Inc. is a contract manufacturer of dietary supplements distributed under the brand name All Pro Science, including Complete Immune + capsules and various flavored powders called Complete, Recovery and Precharge. In conjunction with the filing of the complaint, the defendants agreed to settle the litigation and be bound by a consent decree of permanent injunction that prohibits them from committing violations of the Federal Food, Drug, and Cosmetic Act. The consent decree requires the dietary supplement manufacturer to cease all operations and requires that, in order for defendants to resume manufacturing dietary supplements, the FDA first must determine that Scilabs' manufacturing practices are compliant with Good Manufacturing Practices. According to the complaint, FDA inspections performed in 2012, 2013 and 2014 revealed that the company's dietary supplements are adulterated within the meaning of the Food, Drug, and Cosmetic Act. The complaint alleges, for example, that the company failed to conduct at least one appropriate test or examination to verify the identity of every dietary ingredient before using them. The complaint also alleges that the company failed to establish product specifications for the identity, purity, strength and composition of finished batches of dietary supplements. In addition, defendants failed to document equipment use, maintenance, cleaning and sanitization in individual equipment logs as required by law.

NOTE: See also—*United States v. Mira Health Products Ltd.*

http://www.justice.gov/iso/opa/resources/5542014711431442328.pdf

Consent Decree Violation—*Seasilver*

Original Consent Decree— *Seasilver USA, Inc., and Americaloe, Inc., Consent Decree With FDA To Stop Selling Product Claiming To Cure "Over 650" Diseases*

Back in 2004, FDA had announced that Seasilver USA, Inc., and Americaloe, Inc., Carlsbad, California, and their principals, Bela Berkes and Jason Berkes, signed a consent decree of permanent injunction in which they agreed to stop manufacturing and distributing violative products, including "Seasilver" a purported cure-all liquid supplement. This action is the culmination of coordinated efforts by FDA and the Federal Trade Commission (FTC) to act against the marketing of these violative products. The consent decree gives FDA the authority to order the firm to discontinue the marketing of and recall any products that violate the law in the future. The liquidated damages provision of the consent decree requires the companies and their principals to pay $1,000.00 for each article distributed in interstate commerce in violation of the consent decree, the retail value of each lot manufactured in violation of the consent decree, but not distributed in interstate commerce, and $10,000.00 per day, per violation for any other consent decree violation.

U.S. Marshals seized 132,480 bottles of Seasilver, worth nearly $5.3 million, from Seasilver USA's San Diego headquarters (June 16, 2003). The Government's complaint alleged that, the companies promote it on the Internet and in marketing materials sent with the product as a treatment for "over 650" diseases including, for example, cancer, heart disease, stroke, diabetes, hepatitis, arthritis, depression and other diseases. These claims cause Seasilver to be an unapproved new drug under the Federal Food, Drug, and Cosmetic Act (FD&C Act). Seasilver's labeling also contains claims such as "cleanses your vital organs" and "oxygenates your body's cells." These claims show that Sea-silver is intended to affect the structure or function of the body. The FTC, alleged, in part, that the defendants promoted Seasilver through false claims that it was clinically proven to treat or cure 650 diseases, including cancer and AIDS. Under a settlement with the FTC, entered on March 4, 2004, the Seasilver defendants and the individual distributors agreed to pay $4.5 million in consumer redress.

Seasilver Consent Decree Violation— The Ninth Circuit Court of Appeals issued a Memorandum and Order (2008) that affirmed the District Court's Grant of the FTC Commissioner's Motion to Enforcea Stipulated Judgment. The Order filed allowed the FTC to recover judgment against Seasilver USA, Inc., and Americaloe, Inc., Bela Berkes and Jason Berkes in the amount of $119,237,000.00. Seasivler and Americaloe, Inc. had signed a consent decree in March 2004 of permanent injunction in which they agreed to stop manufacturing and distributing violative cure all products including "Seasilver". The consent decree provided FDA with the authority to order to discontinue the marketing as well as recall any products that violate the law in the future. The decree encompassed liquidated damages for any further violations. The liquidated damages provision required the companies and their principals to pay $1,000.00 for each article distributed in interstate commerce in violation of the consent decree. Damages were based on the retail value of each lot manufactured in violation of the consent decree and a $10,000.00 per day, per violation for any other violations.

NOTE: See *Seasilver* coordinated efforts by FTC and FDA earlier in this Chapter.

CRITICAL ANALYSIS: Review the consent decrees—*Caffeine-Infused Shapewear, SciLabs* and *Seasilver*. Evaluate the impact of a consent decree violation(s).

Additional Dietary Supplement Alerts and Recalls
Butala Emporium, Inc. Ayurvedic Dietary Supplements Recall—Elevated levels of lead and mercury which may cause health problems to consumers, particularly infants, small children, pregnant women, and those with underlying kidney disorders (2015).

Androstenedione Warnings—Focused on companies that manufacture, market, and distribute products containing androstenedione, or, "andro." These products act like a steroid once metabolized by the body and pose health risks. Andro products are generally advertised as dietary supplements that enhance athletic performance based on their claimed anabolic and androgenic properties to stimulate muscle growth and increase production of testosterone. FDA issued several warning letters to companies asking them to cease distributing of such products.

NOTE: In 2016, FDA approved class-wide labeling changes for all prescription testosterone products, adding a new Warning and updating the Abuse and Dependence section to include new safety information from published literature and case reports regarding the risks associated with abuse and dependence of testosterone and other anabolic androgenic steroids (AAS). See: *http://www.fda.gov/Drugs/DrugSafety/ucm526206.htm*

DDS Probiotic Products—warning letter in 2005 to UAS Laboratories due to claims for its probiotic supplements that products prevented diseases, including cold, flu, and yeast infections, resulted in the products to be illegal drug products. An inspection in 2007 indicated that UAS did remove the identified claims from its website. However, in a subsequent inspection in 2011 (March 2011), FDA found out the UAS Laboratories website again contained disease claims for the products. FDA filed a complaint for seizure of the products because the claims were not removed and UAS responded to FDA's Complaint by denying that its products are drugs.

NOTE: See *Volume III*, Enforcement—FDA Seizure.

Germanium Sesqioxide—Entry of 20 kilograms of bulk germanium sesquioxide valued at $16,500 destined for use in human dietary supplements. Germanium has caused nephrotoxicity (kidney injury) and death when used chronically by humans, even at recommended levels of use.

Aristolochic Acid—FDA Concerns About Botanical Products, Including Dietary Supplements, Containing Aristolochic Acid April 11, 2001.

Botanical Dietary Supplements—Concerns About Botanicals and Other Novel Ingredients in Conventional Foods; Letter to Health Professionals Regarding Safety Concerns Related to the Use of Botanical Products Containing Aristolochic Acid Adverse Events with Ephedra and Other Botanical Dietary Supplements.

Colloidal Silver—Consumer Advisory: Dietary Supplements Containing Silver May Cause Permanent Discoloration of Skin and Mucous Membranes (Argyria) October 6, 2009

Letter to Health Care Professionals: FDA Consumer Advisory Regarding Dietary Supplements that Contain Silver October 6, 2009

Comfrey—FDA Advises Dietary Supplement Manufacturers to Remove Comfrey Products From the Market July 6, 2001.

Kava—Hepatic Toxicity Possibly Associated with Kava-Containing Products CDC MMWR Report, November 29, 2002.

Consumer Advisory: Kava-Containing Dietary Supplements May be Associated With Severe Liver Injury March 25, 2002.

Red Yeast Rice—FDA Warned Consumers to Avoid Red Yeast Rice Products Promoted on the Internet as Treatments for High Cholesterol August 9, 2007.

St. John's Wort and Indinavir—FDA Public Health Advisory: Risk of Drug Interactions with St. John's Wort and Indinavir and Other Drugs February 10, 2000.

CRITICAL ANALYSIS: Evaluate all of the above actions such as, Scilabs, DMAA, OxyElite Pro, Magic Power Coffee, Man Up Now, DDS Probiotic Products, Seasilver, and the other alerts above. Determine what should be done in terms of proactive action.

Ban Ephedrine Alkaloids—*Nutraceutical Corp.*

Ephedra, also called Ma huang and primarily used for weight loss has been linked to deaths, strokes and heart attacks. How did FDA arrive at the decision to ban ephedrine alkaloids? Ultimately, FDA published a final rule on February 11, 2004 prohibiting the sale of dietary supplements containing ephedrine alkaloids, effective April 12, 2004. An FDA proposed rule in 1997 and modified in 2000, called for a warning statement to appear on ephedrine dietary supplements. However, with additional scientific evidence, FDA published a notice in 2003 outlining FDA's concerns and reopening of the comment period culminating in a final rule on February 11, 2004. In *Hi-Tech Pharmaceuticals, Inc. v. Crawford* (N.D. FL 2007), the court held that FDA complied with the requirements of the Administrative Procedures Act and the Dietary Supplement Health and Education Act. FDA concluded that dietary supplements containing ephedrine alkaloids present an unreasonable risk of illness or injury under the conditions of use specified in the labeling or in ordinary use and therefore adulterated under section 342(f)(1)(A) of the FDCA.

In 2006, the U.S. Court of Appeals for the Tenth Circuit upheld the Food and Drug Administration's (FDA) final rule declaring all dietary supplements containing ephedrine alkaloids adulterated, and therefore illegal for marketing in the United States, reversing a decision by the District Court of Utah. The court found that the 133,000-page administrative record compiled by FDA supported FDA's conclusion that dietary supplements containing ephedrine alkaloids create an unreasonable risk of illness or injury especially those who suffer from heart disease and high blood pressure. As maintained by FDA, dietary supplements containing ephedrine alkaloids are unsafe and the sale of these products in the United States is illegal.

NOTE: The results of a study of deaths and poisonings from ephedra revealed a decrease by over 98% after the FDA 2004 ban.

Nutraceutical Corp. v. Von Eschenbach,
459 F.3d 1033 (10th Cir. 2006)

EAGAN, District Judge. Defendants-appellants, Andrew von Eschenbach, M.D., Acting Commissioner of the U.S. Food and Drug Administration, the United States Food and Drug Administration ("FDA" or "the agency"), Michael O. Leavitt, Secretary of the Department of Health and Human Services, the Department of Health and Human Services, and the United States, appeal from a judgment of the district court denying their motion for summary judgment and granting the cross-motion of plaintiffs-appellees for summary judgment. *Nutraceutical Corp. v. Crawford*, 364 F. Supp. 2d 1310 (D. Utah 2005). Plaintiffs-appellees, Nutraceutical Corporation and its wholly-owned subsidiary, Solaray Corporation (collectively, "Nutraceutical"), manufacture and sell Ephedra, a product containing ephedrine-alkaloid dietary supplements ("EDS"). In 2004, the FDA issued a regulation which banned all EDS sales in the United States market. Nutraceutical brought this action challenging the regulation as unlawful. The district court agreed with Nutraceutical. Id. at 1321. Our jurisdiction arises under 28 U.S.C. § 1291, and we reverse.

Background—In its published decision, the district court determined that the risk-benefit analysis employed by FDA to support an EDS ban was contrary to the intent of Congress and that the FDA had failed to prove by a preponderance of the evidence that EDS pose an unreasonable risk of illness or injury at 10 milligrams ("mg") or less a day. Nutraceutical, 364 F. Supp. 2d 1310. It accordingly entered summary judgment in favor of Nutraceutical, enjoined the FDA from enforcing its proscription against Nutraceutical for the sale of products with a recommended daily dosage of 10 mg or less of EDS, and remanded to the FDA for new rule-making. ***

The issues raised by this appeal are: (1) whether the FDA correctly interpreted the relevant statute to require a risk-benefit analysis in determining if a dietary supplement presents an "unreasonable risk of illness or injury"; and (2) whether the FDA satisfied its burden of proving that dietary supplements containing EDS present an unreasonable risk of illness or injury when doses of 10 mg or less per day are suggested or recommended in labeling. *** Ephedrine alkaloids are a class of structurally-related chemical stimulants that occur naturally in some botanicals. In the 1980s and 1990s, manufacturers promoted the sale of EDS for weight loss and athletic performance enhancement. In the 1990s, the FDA received numerous Adverse Event Reports ("AERs") which documented harmful side effects, including heart attacks, strokes, seizures, and death, associated with EDS intake. *** The FDA's 1997 proposed regulation of EDS faced substantial opposition, including from the General Accounting Office ("GAO"). FDA's Proposed Rule on Ephedrine Alkaloids 11 (1999). Responding to the GAO's concerns, the FDA withdrew the 1997 proposed regulation. 65 Fed. Reg. 17,474 (Apr. 3, 2000).

The FDA continued to receive AERs and compile scientific literature regarding EDS. Given the fact that dietary supplement manufacturers are not required to submit scientific data on their products, the body of scientific literature on EDS was limited. *** The administrative record grew to over 130,000 pages, approximately 19,000 AERs were collected, and extensive public notice and comment resulted in over 48,000 comments.

After seven years of investigating EDS, the FDA adopted a regulation which banned EDS at all dosage levels from the national market. Final Rule Declaring Dietary Supplements Containing

Ephedrine Alkaloids Adulterated Because They Present an Unreasonable Risk, 69 Fed. Reg. 6788 (Feb. 11, 2004) ("Final Rule"). In the Final Rule, the FDA concluded that "[t]he best clinical evidence for a benefit supports only a modest short-term weight loss, insufficient to positively affect cardiovascular risk factors or health conditions associated with being overweight or obese." Id. at 6789. Based on this risk-benefit analysis, the FDA determined that all EDS present an "unreasonable risk of illness or injury" under all ordinary or recommended conditions of use. Id. at 6788.

Standard of Review Courts are to review agency actions under DSHEA using the "traditional tools of statutory construction." *Pharmanex v. Shalala*, 221 F.3d 1151, 1154 (10th Cir. 2000). The de novo standard, under section 342(f), applies to enforcement actions by the United States against manufacturers of dietary supplements. ***

"Unreasonable Risk" *** We nevertheless reverse the district court after finding that Congress unambiguously required the FDA to conduct a risk-benefit analysis under DSHEA. *** The FDCA should not be read too restrictively but in manner consistent with the statute's overriding purpose to protect public health. See 21 U.S.C.A. § 301 et seq.; *United States v. Rx Depot, Inc.*, 438 F.3d 1052, 1061 (10th Cir. 2006) ("The FDCA's primary purpose is to protect the public health.") (citing *United States v. An Article of Drug . . . Bacto-Unidisk*, 394 U.S. 784, 798, 89 S. Ct. 1410, 22 L. Ed. 2d 726 (1969)). Accordingly, DSHEA should receive a liberal construction where the FDA has taken remedial steps in response to a perceived public health problem. *** Congress expressly placed the burden of proof on the government to determine whether a dietary supplement is adulterated. Accordingly, EDS were allowed to enter the market without findings of safety or effectiveness. The FDA did not impose a pre-market requirement for the sale of EDS. For example, Nutraceutical has been selling EDS since 1988. As dictated by the statutory scheme, the FDA assumed the duty of post-market surveillance and imposed the EDS ban following numerous AERs, public notice and comment, and significant scientific review. See 69 Fed. Reg. 6788. Based on the record, we disagree with the district court and find that the FDA did not shift the burden of proof to manufacturers. ***

"Conditions of Use" Under DSHEA, the government bears the burden of proof to show that, "under conditions of use recommended or suggested in labeling," a dietary supplement is adulterated. 21 U.S.C. § 342(f)(1)(A)(i). *** The evidence relied on by the FDA to enact its ban of EDS covers over seven years of agency review, public notice and comment, peer-reviewed literature, and scientific data. It is the purview of the FDA to weigh the evidence, including the evidence submitted by Nutraceutical and other manufacturers during public notice and comment.

It is noteworthy that Nutraceutical relies on the 1999 GAO report to support its contention that the Final Rule lacks support. However, the GAO has since updated its findings and arrived at conclusions in support of the Final Rule. See GAO, Dietary Supplements: Review of Health-Related Call Records for Users of Metabolife 356 (GAO-03-494) (2003). Based on scientific data and AERs, the GAO concluded that EDS pose a significant risk of cardiovascular and nervous system effects among consumers who are young to middle-aged. See GAO, Dietary Supplements Containing Ephedra (July 23, 2003).; 69 Fed. Reg. at 6818 (GAO found that AERs "were consistent with . . . the scientifically documented pharmacological and physiological effects of ephedrine alkoids."). *** The majority of data in the administrative record suggests that EDS pose an unreasonable threat to the public's health. The FDA looked at the seriousness of the risks and the quality and persuasiveness of the totality of the evidence to support the presence of those risks. *** The evidence in the administrative record was sufficiently probative to demonstrate by a preponderance of the evidence that EDS at any dose level pose an unreasonable risk. *** The FDA's extensive research identified the dose level at which ephedrine alkaloids present unreasonable risk of illness or injury to be so minuscule that no amount of EDS is reasonably safe. The FDA reasonably concluded that there is no recommended dose of EDS that does not present an unreasonable risk. Id. at 6829 ("dose limitations cannot change the unfavorable risk-benefit ratio of [EDS]"). The FDA was not arbitrary or capricious in its Final Rule; the FDA met its statutory burden of justifying a total ban of EDS by a preponderance of the evidence. We find that the FDA correctly followed the congressional directive to analyze the risks and benefits of EDS in determining that there is no dosage level of EDS acceptable for the market. *** Accordingly, the district court's decision is reversed, and we remand for entry of judgment in favor of defendants [Defendants-appellants, Andrew von Eschenbach, M.D., Acting Commissioner of the U.S. Food and Drug Administration]. REVERSED And REMANDED.

NOTE: A rehearing before the entire Court of Appeals was denied.

Nutraceutical Corp. and Solaray, Inc. v. Von Eschenbach
Case No. 2:04-CV-00409 PGC (2007)

OPINION: MEMORANDUM DECISION GRANTING DEFENDANTS' (FDA) MOTION FOR SUMMARY JUDGMENT: In 2004, the Food and Drug Administration promulgated a rule that banned ephedrine-alkaloid dietary supplements ("EDS") at any dosage level from the United States market. Before the effective date of this rule, the plaintiffs, Nutraceutical Corporation and Solaray, Inc. (collectively, "Nutraceutical"), marketed EDS in the United States. *** The Tenth Circuit already addressed a different portion of this case on appeal upholding the validity of the FDA's final rule on EDS pursuant to the Food, Drug, and Cosmetic Act (FDCA), as amended by the Dietary Supplement Health and Education Act (DSHEA). [*See Nutraceutical v. Von Eschenbach*, 459 F.3d 1033 (10th Cir. 2006)].

Nutraceutical now claims the final rule on EDS is invalid because the FDA gave insufficient statutory notice and opportunity to comment on its use of a risk-benefit analysis to determine that EDS are adulterated. Nutraceutical also alleges the FDA acted in an arbitrary and capricious manner when it prohibited the marketing of EDS but failed to ban other products containing ephedrine alkaloids, such as conventional foods and traditional Asian medicines. While Nutraceutical's counsel has ably presented Nutraceutical's case, the case is simply unpersuasive. The defendants have successfully shown the FDA's process and its final rule comply with the notice-and-comment requirements of the Administrative Procedures Act. *** Accordingly, the court finds Nutraceutical has failed to meet its burden in challenging the FDA's action under the APA. *** In whole, the administrative record on EDS comprises more than 132,000 pages. The FDA received more than 48,000 comments during its notice-and-comment periods, and the FDA collected information on about 19,000 complaints or adverse events from EDS use.

Procedural Background *** On August 17, 2006, the Tenth Circuit reversed this court's decision and directed the court to enter summary judgment for the defendants and against Nutra-ceutical. Specifically, the Tenth Circuit held that "Congress unambiguously required the FDA to conduct a risk-benefit analysis under DSHEA." According to the Tenth Circuit, the FDA had demonstrated that *any dose* of EDS posed an unreasonable risk of illness or injury, so the FDA's decision to ban EDS completely was justified. In accordance with the Tenth Circuit's mandate, this court entered summary judgment for the defendants with regard to Nutraceutical's statutory challenge to the FDA's ban of EDS. *** These extensive notice-and-comment efforts easily meet APA requirements, even though the FDA's final rule differed from the proposed rule, because the final rule was a logical outgrowth of the 1997 proposal. Indeed, it would seem odd for the FDA to continue to endorse its proposed rule after reviewing such an extensive and long-spanning record. *** Contrary to Nutraceutical's claims, the FDA's separate regulation of EDS is not arbitrary or capricious because it is consistent with the regulatory scheme of the DSHEA. The DSHEA requires the FDA to regulate dietary supplements differently than conventional foods—conven-tional foods and other drug products are subject to their own statutory and regulatory requirements, including some requirements to which dietary supplements are not always subject. *** In its rulemaking, the FDA simply followed Congress' determination that dietary supplements be subject to a standard—the "unreasonable risk" standard—that does not apply to conventional foods. *** In short, the FDA acted in accordance with the statutory scheme by restricting the application of its final rule to EDS and restricting the scope of its regulatory activities to EDS.

CONCLUSION: The court finds the FDA's rulemaking with regard to EDS to be procedurally and substantively proper. Consequently, Nutraceutical's motion for summary judgment / appeal is denied, and the defendants' cross-motion for summary judgment / cross-appeal is granted.

NOTE: *United States v. 5 Unlabeled Boxes...Lipodrene.* **District Court (10/15/07) granted the government's motion for summary judgment finding that Hi-Tech's dietary supplements containing ephedrine alkaloids were adulterated under the Federal Food, Drug and Cosmetic Act because they present a "significant or unreasonable risk of illness or injury" as labeled under ordinary conditions of use.**

CRITICAL ANALYSIS: Discuss the ephedrine ban.

Criminal Sanctions—*Warshak* and *Pugh*

Despite the fact that FDA regulatory authority is post market, FDA has instituted legal actions where courts have imposed criminal sanctions including imprisonment and monetary fines as illustrated in *Warshak* (*Berkelely Premium Nutraceuticals)* and the *Pugh* decisions.

United States v. Warshak, 631 F.3d 266 (6th Cir. 2010)

Nos. 08-3997 Steven Warshak/4085/4087/09-3176; Harriet Warshak 08-3997/4087/ 4429; TCI Media, Inc. 08-3997/4212

Executives of Berkeley Premium Nutraceutical were convicted due to their involvement in a multi-million dollar dietary supplement fraud scheme. The plot involved dietary supplement misbranding and defrauding customers. Berkeley's in-house counsel (*United States v. Kellogg*) was sentenced to a term of one year and one day of imprisonment, followed by three years of supervised release. A jury convicted (February 22, 2008) the in-house attorney, of six counts of conspiracy, including conspiracy to obstruct proceedings before the FDA. Company president and owner, Steven E. Warshak was originally sentenced to a term of 25 years imprisonment, followed by five years of supervised release, with a fine of $93,000. However, upon remand, Warshak was sentenced to a term of 10 years of imprisonment.

The jury also convicted Warshak of five counts of conspiracy to commit money laundering and various types of fraud, conspiracy to obstruct agency proceedings, mail fraud, bank fraud and money laundering. Warshak's mother, Harriet Warshak, was sentenced to 24 months imprisonment, followed by three years supervised release for her part in the scheme; however the Court of Appeals reversed Harriet Warshak's convictions related to money laundering forfeiture judgement. The Warshaks, Berkeley Premium Nutraceuticals, and Kellogg were ordered to forfeit approximately $500 million to the United States Treasury. Other defendants received sentences of imprisonment that ranged from one month to one year and a day, and included the warehouse manager, the accountant, and the vice president of sales. The company was sentenced to five years probation and a fine of $15 million. The warehouse manager (Pugh) was convicted of conspiracy to obstruct proceedings of the FDA, and received a sentence of a year plus a day imprisonment. See: *United States v. Warshak*, 631 F.3d 266 (6th Cir. 2010). *United States v. Warshak*, 09-3321, 2011 WL 2450991 (appeal unreported). (6th Cir. Mar. 30, 2011); *United States v. Warshak* (Petition to Vacate sentence denied April 30, 2013). The conviction of the warehouse manager, reported below, was affirmed.

United States v. Pugh,

404 F. App'x 21 (6th Cir. 2010) (No. 08-4214)

Circuit Judge Boogs: Steven Pugh, a former warehouse manager at Berkeley Premium Nutraceuticals, Inc. ("Berkeley"), was convicted of conspiracy to obstruct a Food and Drug Administration ("FDA") inspection, in violation of 18 U.S.C. §§ 371 and 1505. In this appeal, Pugh argues that his conviction should be reversed, claiming that the government failed to introduce sufficient evidence that he knowingly entered into an agreement to impede the FDA's efforts. *** For the reasons that follow, we affirm Pugh's conviction.

Roy Stephens, an FDA inspector, appeared unannounced at Berkeley's offices in Blue Ash,

Ohio. Berkeley was a distributor of herbal supplements, and Stephens had come to gather information on the company's practices and take samples of its products. Upon entering the company's headquarters, Stephens asked to speak with "the most responsible person" and eventually met with Steven Warshak and Paul Kellogg, the owner and general counsel of Berkeley, respectively. Stephens presented Warshak with a notice of inspection and explained that the FDA would need to take a look around. *** It was agreed that the FDA would inspect the facilities on the following day. *** After Stephens left, Kellogg gathered a number of Berkeley executives to discuss the impending inspection of the warehouses. According to James Teegarden, one of the executives present at the meeting, Kellogg indicated that "the FDA agent was going to go to the warehouse and review all of the products and check labeling and the like." This caused a measure of alarm among the executives, who thought that one of the warehouses contained mislabeled boxes of Rovicid, a supplement that was advertised to promote heart health. Rovicid was originally formulated to promote prostate health. However, lagging sales prompted the company to reformulate it—*i.e.,* change its ingredients—and market it as a heart-health product. *** To avoid simply throwing the old Rovicid away, the company repackaged it as new Rovicid. To ensure that the FDA did not stumble across any of the mislabeled Rovicid, the executives decided "to move [the] Rovicid out of the warehouse and basically hide it somewhere as quickly as possible." ***

Once the group disbanded, Greg Cossman, Berkeley's President, went to the warehouse to speak with Pugh, who was in charge of the facility. According to Cossman, he "informed [Pugh] that there was an FDA inspection coming and [that they] needed to get rid of the Rovicid." Pugh replied, "Okay, I'll take care of it." Following his conversation with Cossman, Pugh instructed several warehouse employees to load the mislabeled Rovicid onto a Penske rental truck before the end of the night. The next morning, Pugh ordered another employee, James Kinmon, to "get the truck out of there and drive it over to [another Berkeley site] and park it in the overflow lot." ***

That same morning, the FDA arrived, collected samples, and subsequently moved on to the remaining facilities. The inspection concluded within the next several days, and the Rovicid-laden rental truck was driven back to the Duff Road warehouse. Cossman, who had told Pugh to dispose of the Rovicid, later visited the warehouse and saw that "the Rovicid that was to be gotten rid of was [back]." According to Cossman, Pugh explained that "he had hidden [the Rovicid] on a rental truck and returned it back to the warehouse." *** On September 27, 2005, Pugh was arrested in the wake of a massive criminal investigation into Berkeley's business practices. On September 20, 2006, a grand jury returned a 112-count indictment against Pugh and several others. Pugh was charged with one count of conspiracy to commit misbranding, one count of misbranding, and one count of conspiracy to obstruct an FDA proceeding. In February 2008, a jury acquitted Pugh of the misbranding charges but convicted him of conspiracy to impede the FDA inspection. *** He was later sentenced to one year and one day of imprisonment, to be followed by three years of supervised release. Pugh argues that the evidence at trial was insufficient to support his conviction for conspiracy to obstruct an agency proceeding. *** To establish that a defendant is guilty of conspiracy under 18 U.S.C. § 371, the government must prove three elements: "(1) the existence of an agreement to violate the law; (2) knowledge and intent to join the conspiracy; and (3) an overt act constituting actual participation in the conspiracy."

Pugh argues that the government failed to prove that he knowingly joined a conspiracy to obstruct the FDA inspection. He argues that he was merely "an unwitting pawn" in the hands of Berkeley executives. He also claims that "there [was] no evidence that [he] had any involvement in conversations, meetings or transactions relating to the illegal criminal activity."… Cossman testified that he told Pugh to get rid of the Rovicid so that the FDA would not find it. Thus, there is competent evidence in the record that Pugh discussed the aims of the conspiracy with Cossman before moving the Rovicid out of the warehouse. Pugh's statement that he would "take care of it" permits the conclusion that he knowingly agreed to advance the criminal aims of the Berkeley executives. There is also the testimony of James Seiter, who stated that Pugh told him "the FDA inspectors were coming and to get the remaining [Rovicid] that hadn't been switched from the old

479

box to the new box out of sight." Seiter also testified that he put Rovicid "in [a] rental truck." Additionally, James Kinmon testified that Pugh instructed him to drive the rental truck to an off-site parking lot. A reasonable juror, when confronted with this testimony, could rationally conclude that Pugh was a knowing participant in the plot to conceal the Rovicid from the FDA.

Pugh's next argument is that the evidence was insufficient because, if anything, it showed only that he attempted to impede a routine FDA inspection. The inspection, he argues, does not qualify as an agency "proceeding" within the meaning of 18 U.S.C. § 1505. It is clear, however, that the FDA inspection was an agency proceeding for purposes of the relevant statute. *** Furthermore, the fact that the FDA inspection was not a "formal administrative action" has no bearing on the conclusion that it was an agency proceeding. *** Pugh's next argument is that the district court erred in failing to instruct the jury on the definition of the term "proceeding" as it is used in 18 U.S.C. § 1505.... In this case, our review of the jury instructions is brief, for the question of whether an agency action constitutes a "proceeding" is a question for the judge, not the jury. *** During that line of questioning, Pugh's attorney asked Cossman whether he told "Steve Pugh to hide the product from the FDA[.]" ***

Pugh's next argument is that the district court erred in admitting certain hearsay statements. At trial, a number of warehouse employees were permitted to testify that they had heard from other employees that the Rovicid was moved to prevent the FDA from discovering it. The district court admitted the testimony over repeated hearsay objections, ruling that the statements were admissible under Federal Rule of Evidence 801(d)(2)(D). In so ruling, the district court stated, "[m]y philosophy is ... that it is [an] exception to the hearsay rule. They're all employees of the company. They're all admissions against interest here." *** Assuming, *arguendo,* that the district court's ruling was improper, there is still no cause for reversal. The record contains unequivocal—and plainly admissible—testimony from several individuals who stated that Pugh knew the FDA was coming. Thus, the hearsay statements at issue were cumulative, rendering any mistake on the part of the district court harmless. *** Pugh's final evidentiary argument is that the district court improperly permitted the government to elicit testimony through leading questions. *** In the words of the district court, all the government's attorney did was "focus[ ] on a particular area of inquiry on cross-examination, so we [did not] have to go around the mulberry bush." Leading is permissible under those circumstances. For the foregoing reasons, Pugh's conviction is AFFIRMED.

NOTE: See also *Volume III, United States v. Pugh,* 6th Cir., No. 08-4214 (12/14/10) FTC action accessible at:

https://www.ftc.gov/enforcement/cases-proceedings/042-3003/berkeley-premium-nutraceuti-cals-inc-et-al

CRITICAL ANALYSIS: Why did the warehouse manager's sufficiency of evidence argument fail? Was the sentence imposed on the manager too harsh?

VOLUME XI

Volume XI: Tobacco Products Regulation

Admittedly, smoking has plagued the United States for generations; however, it was not until the past several years that this issue received more serious scrutiny. FDA determined that over 1,300 people die each day in the United States due to smoking and over 8.6 million Americans have chronic illnesses linked to smoking. According to the CDC in the United States, cigarette smoking is responsible for more than 480,000 deaths annually, including more than 41,000 deaths resulting from secondhand smoke exposure. Based on CDC statistics, about 3,200 youth start smoking and 2,100 youth become day-to-day smokers. This means that using current rates, of smoking among youth, 5.6 million Americans younger than 18 years of age are expected to die prematurely from a smoking-related illness. This denotes about one in every 13 Americans aged 17 years or younger who are alive today. FDA regulates tobacco products by utilization of a public health standard. The Center for Tobacco Products (CTP) within FDA regulates tobacco products with a single focused mission; that is, to diminish tobacco related deaths and diseases. Since its existence, the CTP has maintained a critical focus of prevention of youth smoking. Further, the marketing to and use of e-nicotine products by teens has escalated.

The United States Supreme Court decision of FDA v. Brown and Williamson Tobacco Corp. spurred the impetus for the Family Smoking Prevention and Tobacco Control Act (FSPTCA or Tobacco Control Act). The Supreme Court, in Brown, held that FDA lacked the authority to regulate tobacco products. FDA asserted jurisdiction over tobacco products based on the FDCA definitions of "drug" and "device." Nearly ten years after the United States v. Brown decision, Congress provided FDA with explicit legal authority or jurisdiction to regulate tobacco products. To that end, on June 22, 2009, Former President Obama signed the FSPTCA or Tobacco Control Act. This historic legislation conferred authority to FDA to regulate tobacco products. This law amended the FDCA and other federal laws by permitting FDA regulatory authority over the manufacture, marketing, and distribution of all tobacco products. Initially, this included cigarettes, cigarette tobacco, roll-your-own tobacco, and smokeless tobacco. In May 2016, FDA issued what are known as "deeming regulations" to include regulation of e-cigarettes, as well as other covered tobacco products such as cigars. Covered tobacco product means any tobacco product deemed subject to the Federal Food, Drug, and Cosmetic Act pursuant to § 1100.2. The FSPTCA requires large graphic warnings on cigarette cartons that describe the health consequences of smoking; however, this was met with resistance. However, FDA was ordered in 2018 to redraft the graphic warnings. FDA Commissioner Gottlieb announced in 2018 a further crackdown by initiating age restricted sales and online heightened age verification of flavored tobacco products of electronic nicotine delivery devices (ENDS) to youth except mint, menthol and tobacco flavors. Further, ongoing concern remains about menthol flavored cigarettes and public health impact.

The Progress Report published by the Centers for Disease Control provides a 50 Year review. The Health Consequences of Smoking: 50 Years of Progress. A Report of the Surgeon General: Health and Human Services, Centers for Disease Control and Prevention, National Center for Chronic Disease Prevention and Health Promotion, Office on Smoking and Health. The tobacco industry spends billions of dollars on cigarette and smokeless tobacco advertising. In 2016 alone, approximately $26 million daily was spent on marketing of cigarettes and smokeless tobacco. Finally, the economic costs are astounding with over $300,000 billion a year with a breakdown of nearly $170,000 billion in medical care and $156 billion in lost productivity.

https://www.cdc.gov/tobacco/data_statistics/fact_sheets/fast_facts/index.htm
https://www.ftc.gov/system/files/documents/reports/federal-trade-commission-cigarette-report-2016-federal-trade-commission-smokeless-tobacco-report/ftc_cigarette_report_for_2016_0.pdf

Chapter 1: Food and Drug Administration Regulatory Milieu

The "Why" of Tobacco Products Regulation

The *Family Smoking Prevention and Tobacco Control Act* (FSPTCA or Tobacco Act) became law on June 22, 2009. This historic legislation conferred authority to FDA to regulate tobacco products. The Tobacco Act amended the FDCA and other federal laws by permitting FDA regulatory authority over the manufacture, marketing, and distribution of tobacco products. This includes cigarettes, cigarette tobacco, roll-your-own tobacco, and smokeless tobacco. The requirement, of large graphic warnings on cigarette cartons that describe the health consequences of smoking met with resistance. FDA decided to withdraw the graphic warnings due to legal actions.

Several factors contributed to the impetus of the FSPTCA such as the rise of youth smoking, death associated with smoking and United States Supreme Court decision of *FDA v. Brown and Williamson Tobacco Corp.* The Supreme Court, in *Brown,* held that FDA lacked the authority to regulate tobacco products. FDA asserted jurisdiction over tobacco products based on the FDCA definitions of "drug" and "device." Although the district court agreed with FDA in the decision of *Coyne Beam, Inc. v. FDA*, the court of appeals in *Brown and Williamson Tobacco Corp. v. FDA* reversed. The United States Supreme Court affirmed the court of appeals decision.

The Supreme Court held that FDA lacked jurisdiction over tobacco products because the measure lacked the requisite Congressional intent required to execute the regulatory framework. The Supreme Court denied FDA jurisdiction over tobacco products due to fundamental conflicts and inconsistencies in prior actions by FDA and prior Congressional inaction. Despite the strong showing of compatible existing regulatory provisions and evidence of the danger of nicotine addiction, the Court determined that FDA lacked jurisdiction over tobacco products. Subsequently, Congress provided FDA with explicit legal authority or jurisdiction to regulate tobacco products. The following pre-Tobacco Act article and the Supreme Court *Brown* decision both serve as a backdrop to better comprehend the Congressional intent and the "why" of the Tobacco Act.

Pre-Family Smoking Prevention Act— Milieu and FDA Authority

Roseann B. Termini, St. John's Law Review, (Used with Permission) (modified in part).

Background—The Waffle Effect and the Food and Drug Administration's Change in Policy in Asserting Jurisdiction

As early as 1964, there were indications that tobacco products posed a serious threat to human health surfaced. At that time, the Surgeon General reported that smoking caused cancer in men and could also affect women in the same manner. Congress acted swiftly in response to the report by passing the Federal Cigarette Labeling and Advertising Act in 1965, requiring warning labels on all cigarette packages. Soon thereafter, Congress banned cigarette advertising on television and radio. The Surgeon General then began issuing new, more detailed warnings, which prompted the Federal Trade Commission to refine their labeling criteria to specifically reflect warnings about health consequences. The war on smoking evolved into a full-scale attack when several states enacted indoor clean air laws, such as Pennsylvania's Clean Indoor Air Act, to combat secondhand smoking's adverse effects. For example, in *United States v. 354 Bulk Cartons*, the FDA asserted jurisdiction over cigarettes that promised appetite reduction and subsequent weight loss. The district court found that jurisdiction had been properly asserted where the manufacturer's promises were based upon such weight reduction. The manufacturer intended the cigarettes to be used for therapeutic purposes. The court held that this satisfied the requisite intent of a drug under the FDCA as a product intended to affect the structure and function of the human body.

The FDA also asserted jurisdiction in *United States v. 46 Cartons, Etc.*, when the manufacturer claimed through advertising leaflets that cigarettes were effective in preventing respiratory infections, circulatory disease, and other physical ailments. This advertisement was sufficient to bring the cigarettes under the second statutory meaning of a "drug," which is a product intended to mitigate or prevent diseases. The fact that the FDA only asserted jurisdiction when cigarette manufacturers promised increased health benefits, prompted heated argument from a citizen's group called Action on Smoking and Health (ASH). This group filed suit pushing for the FDA's active assertion of jurisdiction over all tobacco products. The 1980 litigation resulted in the determination that the FDA lacked general jurisdiction over tobacco products. The court found no manifestation of the cigarette manufacturer's intent "to affect the structure or any function of the body of man." The FDA agreed that it lacked general jurisdiction over tobacco products because ASH had presented no evidence proving this requisite intent. The court interpreted the FDA's position against general regulation of tobacco, not as an indefinitely binding decision, but rather one reserved for a time when the proper showing of manufacturer intent could be established. Thus, this decision should be viewed as an indication of how times have changed, rather than as one that bars the FDA from asserting jurisdiction. The FDA asserted general jurisdiction over tobacco products only after the majority of health organizations acted in concert to declare nicotine's harmful effects. In 1996, the FDA issued regulations to control teen smoking, including the prohibition of the sale of cigarettes to persons under age eighteen and the regulation of advertisement geared toward minors. As the FDA has based its jurisdiction on the FDCA's definitions of "drug" and "device," a close examination of these definitions is warranted.

The district court determined in *Coyne Beahm, Inc. v. Food & Drug Administration,* that based on judicial history, legislative intent, and product use, the FDA properly asserted jurisdiction over tobacco products. The *Coyne* court discussed the meaning of "drug" and "device" and applied evidence of foreseeable use, actual use, and manufacturer representations to determine that tobacco products are intended to affect the structure or function of the body. The court also found that congressional intent reinforced their findings, based on Congress' acquiescence to agency interpretation. Manufacturers appealed this ruling, maintaining that nicotine-containing products did not fall under the definition of "drug" or "device" and thus, should escape regulation by the FDA.

Agreeing with the Fourth Circuit in *Brown & Williamson Tobacco Corp. v. Food & Drug Administration,* the United States Supreme Court held that the FDA lacked jurisdiction over tobacco products, because the measure lacked the requisite congressional intent required to execute the regulatory framework. Both the United States Supreme Court and the Fourth Circuit denied the FDA jurisdiction over tobacco products due to "fundamental conflicts" and several "internal inconsistencies" in the FDA's regulatory scheme. Thus, the judiciary determined that the FDA lacked jurisdiction over tobacco products, despite its strong showing of compatible, existing regulatory provisions and convincing evidence of the danger of nicotine addiction.

The United States Supreme Court and the court of appeals in *Coyne* used very different approaches in analyzing the problem of FDA's assertion of jurisdiction over tobacco than did the district court. The appellate courts determined that statutory interpretation was the threshold of the analysis, and if the legislative history did not encourage regulation, the product should not be regulated. The district court found that the FDA's theories of regulation comported with elements such as foreseeable use and actual consumer use, which could not be ignored. The *Coyne* court accepted the FDA's position that relied on foreseeable use, actual consumer use, and manufacturer representations to establish intended use. Furthermore, agency interpretation and judicial decisions do not prohibit the FDA from considering other evidence to prove intended use. According to the district court, the legislative history and the definitions of drug and device do not indicate that Congress meant for the FDA to rely solely on evidence of manufacturer representations to establish intended use. The appellate courts, however, rejected this analysis and narrowed the scope of inquiry to the historical role and actions of the FDA in relation to tobacco regulation and prior congressional actions. Ultimately, it was decided that FDA lacked jurisdiction over tobacco based on legislative intent, choosing to ignore the vital factors of consumer use, foreseeable use and manufacturer memoranda, and information from newly emergent scientific findings concerning tobacco and its effect on the American public.

The Role of Congressional Intent or Congressional Inaction in Affording Explicit Authority to Regulate by the Food and Drug Administration

The Court in *Brown & Williamson* rejected the lower court's analysis in *Coyne*, as well as the FDA's contention that Congress' lack of explicit delegation of authority to regulate tobacco did not negate its jurisdictional authority. The Fourth Circuit stated that both the FDA and the district court used only a "mechanical reading" approach to interpret the definition of "drug" and "device" under the FDCA. The United States Supreme Court and the court of appeals recognized that the FDA was charged with protecting the public health from harmful drugs and devices, but ultimately rejected the FDA's chosen method of regulation. The court determined that the FDA should weigh the risks and benefits of the use of a particular product and not balance the effects of removing that product from the market. The United States Supreme Court and the Fourth Circuit disagreed with the FDA's interpretation of why tobacco falls within its regulatory authority, and also determined that the FDA lacked the power to make this "major policy decision."

The Court further agreed with the contention by tobacco manufacturers that if Congress intended the FDA to regulate tobacco, then acquiescence to the FDA's jurisdiction over tobacco would have been included in either the Cigarette Labeling and Advertising Act, the Comprehensive Smokeless Tobacco Health Education Act, or the Alcohol, Drug Abuse, and Mental Health Reorganization Act of 1992 (the "Acts"). The *Coyne* court found that the FDA's tobacco regulations did not conflict with the text of the Acts. Additionally, the Acts did not evidence congressional intent to withhold jurisdiction from the FDA to regulate tobacco products.

The lack of clear Congressional intent forced the district court in *Coyne* to move to the second prong of the Chevron test. The *Coyne* court examined the FDA's reasoning behind its assertion of jurisdiction over tobacco as a "drug" and "device." Unlike the Fourth Circuit and the United States Supreme Court, the *Coyne* court accepted the FDA's argument that evidence of actual use and foreseeable use constituted an independent basis for "intended use" under the FDCA. The district court also found that though the FDA had changed its position regarding its authority to regulate tobacco products since the 1980 ASH decision, this change was not arbitrary or capricious—the Supreme Court determined otherwise.

The district court in *Coyne* relied on Chevron's reasoning in noting that "[a]n initial agency interpretation is not instantly carved in stone." Rather, "[an] agency, to engage in informed rulemaking, must consider varying interpretations and the wisdom of its policy on a continuing basis." The FDA waited to assert general jurisdiction until new findings of nicotine addiction indicated scant scientific doubt regarding the adverse effects of nicotine in tobacco products on the structure or function of the body. As previously mentioned, "[a]n administrative agency is clearly free to revise its interpretations." The ASH court noted, "[n]othing in this opinion should suggest that [the FDA] is irrevocably bound by any long-standing interpretation and representations thereof to the legislative branch." Although the FDA declined jurisdiction over nicotine containing products in 1980, it had the ability to alter its position if and when evidence appeared that made the FDA's assertion of jurisdiction timely and proper. The *Coyne* court buttressed the FDA's statutory interpretation by clarifying that the FDCA was intended to broaden former food and drug laws. The intent of Congress to broaden the statutory definition of a drug is illustrated in *United States v. Bacto-Unidisk*. The Supreme Court noted, after examining the product at hand and medical definitions of "drug," "we think it plain that Congress intended to define 'drug' far more broadly than does the medical profession." The *Coyne* court noted that another purpose of the FDCA was to protect the public from problematic devices.

Consumer Use as a Factor in the Determination of Whether the Food and Drug Administration has the Legal Authority to Regulate Tobacco

Tobacco companies asserted that the FDA could not consider consumer use in determining whether tobacco products meet the "drug" or "device" criteria. The district court in *Coyne* disagreed, finding that actual consumer use was a vital factor in analyzing whether the FDA has jurisdiction over tobacco products. The *Brown & Williamson* courts agreed with the manufacturers and did not analyze the role of actual consumer use in determining the FDA's jurisdiction over tobacco products. The discrepancy between the appellate and district courts on the issue of actual consumer use plays a major role in the determination of which court has the most persuasive and, perhaps, most politically correct analysis. The determination of the proper analysis of the FDA's jurisdiction over tobacco products now lies with Congress.

Previous courts have found that actual consumer use plays an important role in determining FDA jurisdiction. For example, the court in *United States v. 22 Devices "The Ster-O-Lizer MD-200"* addressed whether a product used to sterilize surgical equipment could be regulated by the FDA as a device. The district court noted, "[t]he objective intent referred to in the regulation may be shown not only by a product's labeling claims, advertising or written statements relating to the circumstances of a product's distribution, but also by a product's actual use." The *Ster-O-Lizer* case illustrated that objective intent looks further than a product's label, into the heart of its purpose. The ASH court noted that statutory intent could be inferred when consumers use a product exclusively and with a specific purpose. A finding that consumers use cigarettes as a drug corroborates the FDA's claims of actual use. The FDA found that 77% to 92% of smokers and 75% of smokeless tobacco users are addicted to nicotine. According to the FDA, one third to one half of young smokers use smoking for weight control, and 50% of young people utilize smokeless tobacco for relaxation. FDA findings also indicate that of those smokers aged ten to twenty-two, 70% use cigarettes for relaxation. Thus, actual consumer use substantiates use that affects the structure or function of the body. *Agnew v. United States* confirmed that "intended for use" could be inferred from one's actions by concluding that "[t]he law presumes that every man intends the legitimate consequence of his own acts." The proposition that one's actions foretell intention has long been a part of this legal theory and should similarly apply to tobacco product regulation.

Foreseeability as a Factor in Granting the FDA the Authority to Regulate

Another factor in the FDA's assertion of jurisdiction to regulate tobacco products was based on the foreseeable effects of tobacco products, which can be used to prove manufacturer's intent. FDA evidence has indicated that the manufacturer's design of cigarettes and smokeless tobacco, combined with a potent dosage of nicotine, show that manufacturers foresaw consumer addiction. The lower court in *Coyne* made clear that, although Congress did not specifically state that foreseeable use could be considered for determining intended use, nothing prohibits it. The court of appeals and the United States Supreme Court did not address foreseeable use in their tightly woven opinions. The lack of discussion of foreseeable use has left the FDA and proponents of the FDA's jurisdiction over tobacco without one of their most powerful and convincing arguments for the assertion of jurisdiction to regulate tobacco. The *Brown & Williamson* appellate courts based their decisions on Congressional inaction to enact tobacco legislation, and its inaction, as applied to the FDA, indicated specific intent to deny the agency regulatory authority.

The foreseeability test that the FDA relied on stems from evidence that nicotine is addictive and causes "significant pharmacological effects." The FDA also noted that nicotine could have mood altering effects and other qualities that parallel those of opiates. Today, findings of the powerful, addictive nature of nicotine emanate from health agencies. Nicotine is identified by all the pertinent expert organizations as one of the few truly dependence-producing drugs, occupying the list with cocaine, heroin, and alcohol. Thus, the "scientific consensus" and consumer use patterns indicate that manufacturers do foresee that their products have addictive qualities and that consumers use tobacco products for their pharmacological properties.

Internal Manufacturer's Memoranda as a Factor in FDA Regulation

Perhaps the most compelling evidence of manufacturer's intent was the manufacturer's memorandum. Even in 1996, when the FDA chose to assert its regulatory jurisdiction over tobacco products, evidence existed which proved manufacturer's knowledge of nicotine's powerful effects.

Since 1996, tobacco litigation has resulted in more company documents surfacing that reveal manufacturer knowledge about the addictive nature of their product. For example, internal memoranda from a cigarette producer revealed that several tests were done in the late 1970's and early

1980's to "[d]etermine the minimum level of nicotine that will allow continued smoking" and also note that "smoking is 'both physiologically and psychologically motivated,' and that when nicotine levels drop too low 'smokers will quit'." Even as litigation continued regarding whether tobacco is a drug or device, these manufacturer documents reveal that they clearly knew their products both affected the structure and function of the body and were used by consumers as drug delivery devices. FDA findings also revealed that tobacco companies specifically designed their products to deliver "a pharmacologically active dose of nicotine to the smoker."

The Complexity of Regulation

Past agency policy regarding tobacco should not be held to dictate all future regulatory schemes. New findings show, unlike past agency information, that smoking affects the structure and function of the body. Secondary findings show manufacturers intend this to be the case. The argument that congressional intent prohibits FDA regulation over tobacco products is also misplaced. The failure of Congress to explicitly extend to the FDA the authority to regulate tobacco does not mean that regulatory activity is barred indefinitely. The regulatory techniques, though controversial, fulfill the overall intent of the FDCA: to protect consumers who are "unable to protect themselves."

If manufacturers discover a formula to make safer cigarettes, should the FDA regulate this type of product? If the FDA can regulate these products, could smoking rise? These are only a few questions regarding FDA regulation. Critics have noted that the best methods of cigarette control are negative advertisements, rather than a ban on specific advertisement forms. Perhaps this is a more realistic answer to regulation. Nevertheless, the answer to regulatory techniques is a complex issue due to the powerful social implications presented by tobacco use. The prevention of smoking must be skillfully handled and in a manner suitable to government objectives and existing regulatory techniques. Tobacco addiction, however, can no longer be ignored. A multifaceted examination of consumer use, foreseeability, and closeted manufacturer findings, must be considered when determining whether tobacco or any other product meets the "drug" or "device" criteria and should hence, be regulated.

These courts focused on historical actions by the FDA and Congressional inaction and concluded that the FDA "exceeded the authority granted to it by Congress." In so doing, the FDA's rulemaking to regulate tobacco as a "drug," "device" or "combination product" could not stand. The Fourth Circuit ignored, and the United States Supreme Court did not reach the issue of, newly acquired evidence regarding the FDA's jurisdiction over tobacco and the Agency's regulatory premise. Although the prior tobacco legislation and Congressional delay remain important considerations, they did not solely justify the conclusion that the FDA lacked authority to regulate tobacco. Undoubtedly, the current regulatory scheme that provided FDA with jurisdiction has aided in curbing America's deadliest preventable killer.

Impetus for Congressional Action—*FDA v. Brown & Williamson*

FDA v. Brown & Williamson, 120 S. Ct. 1291 (2000)

Justice O'Connor delivered the opinion of the Court. This case involves one of the most troubling public health problems facing our Nation today: the thousands of premature deaths that occur each year because of tobacco use. In 1996, the Food and Drug Administration (FDA), after having expressly disavowed any such authority since its inception, asserted jurisdiction to regulate tobacco products. 61 Fed. Reg. 44619-45318. FDA concluded that nicotine is a "drug" within the meaning of the Food, Drug, and Cosmetic Act (FDCA or Act) and that cigarettes and smokeless tobacco are "combination products" that deliver nicotine to the body. 61 Fed. Reg. 44397 (1996). *** The agency believed that, because most tobacco consumers begin their use before reaching the age of 18, curbing tobacco use by minors could substantially reduce the prevalence of addiction in future generations and thus the incidence of tobacco-related death and disease. ***

Having resolved the jurisdictional question, the FDA next explained the policy justifications for its regulations, detailing the deleterious health effects associated with tobacco use. It found that tobacco consumption was "the single leading cause of preventable death in the United States." Id., at 44398. According to the FDA, "[m]ore than 400,000 people die each year from tobacco-related illnesses, such as cancer, respiratory illnesses, and heart disease." Ibid. The agency also determined that the only way to reduce the amount of tobacco-related illness and mortality was to reduce the level of addiction, a goal that could be accomplished only by preventing children and adolescents from starting to use tobacco. Id., at 44398-44399. FDA found that 82% of adult smokers had their first cigarette before the age of 18, and more than half had already become regular smokers by that age. Id., at 44398. It also found that children were beginning to smoke at a younger age, that the prevalence of youth smoking had recently increased, and that similar problems existed with respect to smokeless tobacco. Id., at 44398-44399. FDA accordingly concluded that if "the number of children and adolescents who begin tobacco use can be substantially diminished, tobacco-related illness can be correspondingly reduced because data suggest that anyone who does not begin smoking in childhood or adolescence is unlikely ever to begin." Id., at 44399.

Based on these findings, the FDA promulgated regulations concerning tobacco products' promotion, labeling, and accessibility to children and adolescents. See id., at 44615-44618. The access regulations prohibit the sale of cigarettes or smokeless tobacco to persons younger than 18; require retailers to verify through photo identification the age of all purchasers younger than 27; prohibit the sale of cigarettes in quantities smaller than 20; prohibit the distribution of free samples; and prohibit sales through self-service displays and vending machines except in adult-only locations. Id., at 44616-44617. The promotion regulations require that any print advertising appear in a black-and-white, text-only format unless the publication in which it appears is read almost exclusively by adults; prohibit outdoor advertising within 1,000 feet of any public playground or school; prohibit the distribution of any promotional items, such as T-shirts or hats, bearing the manufacturer's brand name; and prohibit a manufacturer from sponsoring any athletic, musical, artistic, or other social or cultural event using its brand name. Id., at 44617-44618. The labeling regulation requires that the statement, "A Nicotine-Delivery Device for Persons 18 or Older," appear on all tobacco product packages. Id., at 44617. ***

The [District Court] held that the FDCA authorizes the FDA to regulate tobacco products as customarily marketed and that the FDA's access and labeling regulations are permissible, but it also found that the agency's advertising and promotion restrictions exceed its authority under § 360j(e). Id., at 1380-1400. *** The Court of Appeals reversed, holding that Congress has not granted the FDA jurisdiction to regulate tobacco products. See 153 F.3d 155 (1998). *** The FDA's assertion of jurisdiction to regulate tobacco products is founded on its conclusions that nicotine is a "drug" and that cigarettes and smokeless tobacco are "drug delivery devices." ***

With these principles in mind, we find that Congress has directly spoken to the issue here and precluded the FDA's jurisdiction to regulate tobacco products. *** Viewing the FDCA as a whole, it is evident that one of the Act's core objectives is to ensure that any product regulated by the FDA is "safe" and "effective" for its intended use. See 21 U.S.C. § 393(b)(2) (1994 ed., Supp. III) (defining the FDA's mission). *** The Act also requires the FDA to classify all devices into one of three categories. § 360c(b)(1). *** Thus, the Act generally requires the FDA to prevent the marketing of any drug or device where the "potential for inflicting death or physical injury is not offset by the possibility of therapeutic benefit." *United States v. Rutherford*, 442 U.S. 544, 556 (1979). ***

These findings logically imply that, if tobacco products were "devices" under the FDCA, the FDA would be required to remove them from the market. *** The FDA's findings make clear that tobacco products are "dangerous to health" when used in the manner prescribed. Second, a drug or device is misbranded under the Act "[u]nless its labeling bears ... adequate directions for use ... in such manner and form, as are necessary for the protection of users," except where such directions are "not necessary for the protection of the public health." § 352(f)(1). Given the FDA's conclusions concerning the health consequences of tobacco use, there are no directions that could adequately protect consumers. That is, there are no directions that could make tobacco products safe for obtaining their intended effects. Thus, were tobacco products within the FDA's jurisdiction, the Act would deem them misbranded devices that could not be introduced into interstate commerce. Contrary to the dissent's contention, the Act admits no remedial discretion once it is evident that the device is misbranded. *** The FDCA's misbranding and device classification provisions therefore make evident that were the FDA to regulate cigarettes and smokeless tobacco, the Act would require the agency to ban them. In fact, based on these provisions, the FDA itself has previously taken the position that if tobacco products were within its jurisdiction, "they would have to be removed from the market because it would be impossible to prove they were safe for their intended us[e]." Public Health Cigarette Amendments of 1971: Hearings before the Commerce Subcommittee on S. 1454, 92d Cong., 2d Sess., 239 (1972).

Congress, however, has foreclosed the removal of tobacco products from the market. A provision of the United States Code currently in force states that "[t]he marketing of tobacco constitutes one of the greatest basic industries of the United States with ramifying activities which directly affect interstate and foreign commerce at every point, and stable conditions therein are necessary to the general welfare." 7 U.S.C. § 1311(a). More importantly, Congress has directly addressed the problem of tobacco and health through legislation on six occasions since 1965. See Federal Cigarette Labeling and Advertising Act (FCLAA), Pub. L. 89-92, 79 Stat. 282; Public Health Cigarette Smoking Act of 1969, Pub. L. 91-222, 84 Stat. 87; Alcohol and Drug Abuse Amendments of 1983, Pub. L. 98-24, 97 Stat. 175; Comprehensive Smoking Education Act, Pub. L. 98-474, 98 Stat. 2200; Comprehensive Smokeless Tobacco Health Education Act of 1986, Pub. L. 99-252, 100 Stat. 30; Alcohol, Drug Abuse, and Mental Health Administration Reorganization Act, Pub. L. 102-321, § 202, 106 Stat. 394. *** Nonetheless, Congress stopped well short of ordering a ban. Instead, it has generally regulated the labeling and advertisement of tobacco products, expressly providing that it is the policy of Congress that "commerce and the national economy may be ... protected to the maximum extent consistent with" consumers "be[ing] adequately informed about any adverse health effects." 15 U.S.C. § 1331. Congress' decisions to regulate labeling and advertising and to adopt the express policy of protecting "commerce and the national economy to the maximum extent" reveal its intent that tobacco products remain on the market. Indeed, the collective premise of these statutes is that cigarettes and smokeless tobacco will continue to be sold in the United States. A ban of tobacco products by the FDA would therefore plainly contradict congressional policy. ***

In 1977, ASH filed a citizen petition requesting that the FDA regulate cigarettes, citing many of the same grounds that motivated the FDA's rulemaking here. See Citizen Petition, No. 77P-0185 (May 26, 1977), 10 Rec. in No. 97-1604 (CA4), Tab No. 22, pp. 1-10. ASH asserted that nicotine was highly addictive and had strong physiological effects on the body; that those effects were "intended" because consumers use tobacco products precisely to obtain those effects; and that tobacco causes thousands of premature deaths annually. Ibid. In denying ASH's petition, FDA Commissioner Kennedy stated that "[t]he interpretation of the Act by FDA consistently has been that cigarettes are not a drug unless health claims are made by the vendors." ***

In 1983, Congress again considered legislation on the subject of smoking and health. HHS Assistant Secretary Brandt testified that, in addition to being "a major cause of cancer," smoking is a "major cause of heart disease" and other serious illnesses, and can result in "unfavorable pregnancy outcomes." Nonetheless, Assistant Secretary Brandt maintained that "the issue of regulation of tobacco ... is something that Congress has reserved to itself, and we do not within the Department have the authority to regulate nor are we seeking such authority." ***

Against this backdrop, Congress enacted three additional tobacco-specific statutes over the next four years that incrementally expanded its regulatory scheme for tobacco products. In 1983, Congress adopted the Alcohol and Drug Abuse Amendments, Pub. L. 98-24, 97 Stat. 175 (codified at 42 U.S.C. § 290aa et seq.), which require the Secretary of HHS to report to Congress every three years on the "addictive property of tobacco" and to include recommendations for action that the Secretary may deem appropriate. A year later, Congress enacted the Comprehensive Smoking Education Act, Pub. L. 98-474, 98 Stat. 2200, which amended the FCLAA by again modifying the prescribed warning. Notably, during debate on the Senate floor, Senator Hawkins argued that the Act was necessary in part because "[u]nder the Food, Drug and Cosmetic Act, the Congress exempted tobacco products." 130 Cong. Rec. 26953 (1984). And in 1986, Congress enacted the Comprehensive Smokeless Tobacco Health Education Act of 1986 (CSTHEA), Pub. L. 99-252, 100 Stat. 30 (codified at 15 U.S.C. § 4401 et seq.), which essentially extended the regulatory provisions of the FCLAA to smokeless tobacco products. Like the FCLAA, the CSTHEA provided that "[n]o statement relating to the use of smokeless tobacco products and health, other than the statements required by [the Act], shall be required by any Federal agency to appear on any package of a smokeless tobacco product." § 7(a), 100 Stat. 34 (codified at 15 U.S.C. § 4406(a)).

Taken together, these actions by Congress over the past 35 years preclude an interpretation of the FDCA that grants the FDA jurisdiction to regulate tobacco products. We do not rely on Congress' failure to act—its consideration and rejection of bills that would have given the FDA this authority—in reaching this conclusion. Indeed, this is not a case of simple inaction by Congress that purportedly represents its acquiescence in an agency's position. To the contrary, Congress has enacted several statutes addressing the particular subject of tobacco and health, creating a distinct regulatory scheme for cigarettes and smokeless tobacco. In doing so, Congress has been aware of tobacco's health hazards and its pharmacological effects. It has also enacted this legislation against the background of the FDA repeatedly and consistently asserting that it lacks jurisdiction under the FDCA to regulate tobacco products as customarily marketed. ***

By no means do we question the seriousness of the problem that the FDA has sought to address. The agency has amply demonstrated that tobacco use, particularly among children and adolescents, poses perhaps the single most significant threat to public health in the United States. Nonetheless, no matter how "important, conspicuous, and controversial" the issue, and regardless of how likely the public is to hold the Executive Branch politically accountable, an administrative agency's power to regulate in the public interest must always be grounded in a valid grant of authority from Congress. *** Reading the FDCA as a whole, as well as in conjunction with Congress' subsequent tobacco-specific legislation, it is plain that Congress has not given the FDA the authority that it seeks to exercise here. For these reasons, the judgment of the Court of Appeals for the Fourth Circuit is affirmed.

CRITICAL ANALYSIS: Evaluate why in the past, Congress failed to enact legislation to provide FDA with the jurisdiction to regulate tobacco products.

Chapter 2: The Family Smoking Prevention and Tobacco Control Act

Key Websites: *http://www.fda.gov/TobaccoProducts/default.htm*
http://www.fda.gov/downloads/TobaccoProducts/GuidanceComplianceRegulatoryInfor-mation/UCM396614.pdf?source=govdelivery&utm_medium=email&utm_source=govdelivery

The Family Smoking Prevention and Tobacco Control Act (FSPTCA) provides FDA with regulatory authority over the manufacture, marketing, and distribution of tobacco products. FDA cannot ban tobacco under the FSTPCA. In fact, the FSPTCA specifically prohibits FDA from banning an entire category of tobacco products, such as cigarettes. Statistically, on average, adults who smoke cigarettes die 14 years earlier than nonsmokers. Further, over 8.6 million Americans have chronic illnesses related to smoking. Despite those facts, 1 in 4 high school students report current tobacco use. About 3,200 children start smoking and 2,100 children become regular smokers every day. Approximately 9 out of 10 smokers start smoking by age 18. The Centers for Disease Control and Prevention (CDC) estimated that "if smoking continues at the current rate among youth in this country, 5.6 million of today's Americans younger than 18 will die early from a smoking-related illness which is approximately 1 of every 13 Americans aged 17 years or younger that are alive today." See CDC Report Smoking and Tobacco Use.

http://www.cdc.gov/tobacco/data_statistics/fact_sheets/youth_data/tobacco_use/

FDA Center for Tobacco Products

The FSPTCA specifically states that FDA cannot ban an entire category of tobacco products, such as cigarettes. Implementing the FSPTCA involves a recognition of the complexity in terms of the role tobacco has played in the American economy and culture. That aforesaid, FDA must execute its responsibilities in complete recognition of the indisputable facts about tobacco use; it is an addictive product and has profound health effects on users and on the public health of our nation. FDA's regulatory role for drugs and medical devices is normally based on a safety and efficacy standard. The FSPTCA established a new standard; that is, to regulate tobacco products based on a public health and population health standard. To that end, the FDA Center for Tobacco Products (CTP) regulates tobacco products.

Priorities, Goals and Accomplishments

The CTP priorities include the following: *Implementation of restrictions to reduce and prevent youth from using cigarettes and smokeless tobacco; encourage adults who use tobacco to quit; reduce product harms and addictiveness; develop a science based product regulation to reduce the toll of tobacco-related disease, disability and death; use of a public health regulatory standard; tobacco product testing; provide accurate information on the contents of tobacco products ingredients; restriction of advertising and promotion; evaluation of whether a tobacco product can be marketed as a modified risk product; compliance training programs for retailers; establishment of tobacco product performance standards; and use of regulatory enforcement tools to assure adherence to the FSPTCA mandates. Accomplishments include the following:*

- ✓ Issued Final Rule—Clarification of When Products Made or Derived From Tobacco Are Regulated as Drugs, Devices, or Combination Products; Amendments to Regulations Regarding "Intended Uses" (2017); *https://www.gpo.gov/fdsys/pkg/FR-2017-01-09/pdf/2016-31950.pdf*
  NOTE: Final rule only partially implemented.
- ✓ Extended authority to regulation in "deeming" all tobacco products, including E-Cigarettes, Cigars, and Hookah (2016);
- ✓ Issued warning letters to cigarette manufacturers asserting "additive free" or "natural claims" (2016).
- ✓ Focused on efforts to curb marketing of electronic nicotine delivery systems to youth (2018).
- ✓ Use of Investigational Tobacco Products - Draft Guidance *https://www.fda.gov/TobaccoProducts/Labeling/RulesRegulationsGuidance/ucm463951.htm?source=govdelivery&utm_medium=email&utm_source=govdelivery*

✓ Released Final Rule Restricting the Sales and Distribution of Cigarettes and Smokeless Tobacco Products to Children and Adolescents (effective June 22, 2010);

✓ No sales: *to youth under 18, cigarette packs with fewer than 20 cigarettes; vending machines, self-service displays or other impersonal methods of sale except under very limited circumstances*; No sale or distribution of hats, tee shirts or similar items with tobacco brand names, logos or selling messages;

✓ No distribution: of free cigarette samples and smokeless tobacco product restriction; of hats, tee shirts or similar items with tobacco brand names, logos or selling messages;

✓ No tobacco brand name sponsorship of athletic, musical or other social events and of teams and entries in those events;

✓ Implemented and enforced the Flavored Cigarette Ban in the FSPTCA for certain fruit and candy characterizing flavors;

✓ Mandated tobacco industry registration;

✓ Required tobacco company submission of ingredient listing;

✓ Issued Guidance on Registration and Product Listing; and

✓ Prohibition: Misleading Marketing Terms "Light," "Low," and "Mild" (June 22, 2010).

Deeming Regulations and Covered Tobacco Product

The deeming regulations extends FDA's authority to include the regulation of electronic nicotine delivery systems (such as e-cigarettes and vape pens), all cigars, hookah (waterpipe) tobacco, pipe tobacco and nicotine gels. See: 81 FR 28973 prohibits the sale of "covered tobacco products" to individuals under the age of 18 and requires the display of health warnings on cigarette tobacco, roll-your own tobacco, and covered tobacco product packages and in advertisements.

Covered tobacco product—"means any tobacco product deemed to be subject to the Federal Food, Drug, and Cosmetic Act pursuant to § 1100.2, but excludes any component or part that is not made or derived from tobacco." "Products that meet the statutory definition of "tobacco products" include currently marketed products such as dissolvables not already regulated by FDA, gels, waterpipe tobacco, electronic nicotine delivery system (ENDS) (including e-cigarettes, e-hookah, e-cigars, vape pens, advanced refillable personal vaporizers, and electronic pipes), cigars, and pipe tobacco." See also: This Volume Chapter 4.

CRITICAL ANALYSIS: Evaluate the deeming regulations. See link below.

https://www.federalregister.gov/documents/2016/05/10/2016-10685/deeming-tobacco-products-to-be-subject-to-the-federal-food-drug-and-cosmetic-act-as-amended-by-the

Tobacco Product Marketing Orders

http://www.fda.gov/TobaccoProducts/Labeling/TobaccoProductReviewEvaluation/NewTobaccoProductReviewandEvaluation/ucm304506.htm

Tobacco products are regulated so differently than other FDA regulated products due to the fact they are harmful yet still extensively used consumer products and are responsible for severe health problems in both users and non-users, including cancer, lung disease, and heart disease. Therefore, FDA's traditional "safe and effective" standard for evaluating other FDA regulated medical products does not apply to tobacco. Instead, FDA regulates tobacco products based on a public health standard intended to reduce the toll that tobacco use causes. Legally, companies are prohibited from claiming that their products are "FDA approved". A new tobacco product may not be legally marketed in the United States unless FDA has issued an order authorizing marketing. A company who desires to market a new tobacco product has these options available:

➢ *Premarket Tobacco Applications;*
➢ *Substantial Equivalence; and*
➢ *Exemption from Substantial Equivalence.*

Grandfathered Tobacco Products

*https://www.fda.gov/TobaccoProducts/GuidanceComplianceRegulatoryInfor-
mation/ucm416495.htm?source=govdelivery&utm_medium=email&utm_source=govdelivery*

Tobacco products commercially marketed as of February 15, 2007 are identified as "grandfathered tobacco products," and are not considered new tobacco products. Consequently, grandfathered tobacco products are not subject to the premarket requirements under the FDCA. To that end, FDA issued a final guidance that provides information on how manufacturers may demonstrate that a tobacco product was commercially marketed in the United States as of February 15, 2007 which according to the FDA guidance, "as of" means "on" February 15, 2007.

See: Tobacco Product 21 U.S.C. 321(rr) and New Tobacco Product 21 U.S.C. 387j(a)(1).

Premarket Tobacco Application

*http://www.fda.gov/TobaccoProducts/Labeling/TobaccoProductReviewEvaluation/NewTobac-
coProductReviewandEvaluation/ucm304506.htm*

Marketing orders are given to Premarket Tobacco Applications that have demonstrated that the new tobacco product is appropriate for the protection of the public health, which is determined with respect to the risks and benefits to the population as a whole, including users and non-users of tobacco products, and taking into account the following:

> ➤ *The increased or decreased likelihood that existing users of tobacco products will stop using such products; and*
> ➤ *The increased or decreased likelihood that those who do not use tobacco products will start using such products.*

FDA issued its first "marketing order" in 2015 where the manufacturer had to prove that the new tobacco product comports with public protection purposes. This involved a risk benefit analysis and included users and non-users of tobacco products in terms of increased use, decreased use as well as the likelihood of use among non-users. The marketing orders were for eight Swedish Match North America, Inc. snus smokeless tobacco products under the General brand name.

*http://wayback.archive-it.org/7993/20180425120158/https://www.fda.gov/downloads/TobaccoProducts/La-
beling/TobaccoProductReviewEvaluation/UCM472123.pdf*

NOTE: Final Rule—Refuse to Accept Procedures for Premarket Tobacco Product Submissions 81 FR 95863 (effective Jan. 30, 2017).

Prior History—A direct final rule, 81 FR 52329 (August 8, 2016), was withdrawn effective November 16, 2016 due to adverse comments. The final rule considered the comments received on the direct final rule and the companion proposed rule published 81 FR 52371 (August 8, 2016).

Substantial Equivalence

Substantial equivalence is another route manufacturers can utilize to market a new tobacco product under certain circumstances as follows:

> ➤ *It was commercially marketed after February 15, 2007 but before March 22, 2011;* **and**
> ➤ *A Substantial Equivalence Report was submitted by March 22, 2011.*

This means that the new tobacco product may continue to be marketed unless FDA issues an order that the new product is not substantially equivalent to a valid predicate product.

According to FDA, "substantial equivalence means one pathway manufacturers can utilize to market a new tobacco product". In so doing, a manufacturer is required to establish that their product has the same characteristics as a valid previously marketed tobacco or predicate product. Alternatively, if the new product has different characteristics then it must not raise other public health issues. However, unlike other FDA regulated products, it does not mean a tobacco product authorized by substantial equivalence is "FDA approved".

Summary of Substantial Equivalence Final Actions

http://www.fda.gov/TobaccoProducts/Labeling/TobaccoProductReviewEvaluation/ucm339928.htm#2
The following chart details final substantial equivalence actions.

SE Actions	Oct	Nov	Dec	Jan	Feb	Mar	Apr	May	June	July	Aug	Sept	FY2018 Total-To-Date
SE Orders	11	10	21	6	3	10	17	38	64	40	10	25	255
NSE Orders	1	9	26	3	7	0	2	0	0	15	12	0	87
Refuse-To-Accept (RTA)	0	0	0	0	0	0	0	0	0	0	0	0	0
Withdrawals	10	12	18	3	69	28	26	34	1	13	9	3	227
Total Applications Received	2	9	7	0	20	6	25	10	13	6	7	0	104

Note: **Information current as of Dec., 2018.**

A substantial equivalence order means FDA determined that the product is substantially equivalent to the predicate product. Part of FDA decision making is based on company submissions and other scientific evidence that verified that a product does not present further harm to the public health than the predicate product(s). Despite the fact that the new products have different characteristics than the predicate products, the new products must not raise different questions of public health. A SE Marketing Order is not a finding that the product is safe or safer than its predicate product, or less harmful in general. See link below for FDA guidance: Not substantially equivalent (NSE). See: *http://www.fda.gov/downloads/TobaccoProducts/Labeling/MarketingandAdvertising/UCM462409.pdf*

Not Substantially Equivalent Orders

FDA issued orders for products manufactured by R. J. Reynolds Tobacco Company. FDA concluded that Camel Crush Bold, Pall Mall Deep Set Recessed Filter, Pall Mall Deep Set Recessed Filter Menthol and Vantage Tech 13 cigarettes were not substantially equivalent (NSE) to their respective "predicate" products; that is, products that were commercially marketed as of Feb. 15, 2007. FDA determined the products have different characteristics than the predicate products and that the manufacturer failed to show that the new products do not raise different questions of public health when compared to them. For example, in the Camel Crush Bold, the company failed to demonstrate that the addition of a menthol capsule in the filter did not affect consumer perception. Accordingly, the products can no longer be sold, distributed, imported or marketed in interstate commerce. *https://www.fda.gov/TobaccoProducts/Labeling/TobaccoProductReviewEvaluation/ucm371765.htm*

Exemption from Substantial Equivalence

A tobacco product that is altered by adding or deleting a tobacco additive, or increasing or decreasing the quantity of an existing tobacco additive, may be considered for exemption from demonstrating substantial equivalence if:

> *The product is a modification of another tobacco product and the modification is minor;*
> *The modifications are to a tobacco product that may be legally marketed under the FDCA;*
> *A Substantial Equivalence Report is not necessary to ensure that permitting the tobacco*

product to be marketed would be appropriate for the protection of public health;
➤ *The modified tobacco product is marketed by the same organization as the original product; and*
➤ *An exemption is otherwise appropriate.*

Prior to legally marketing of the product, written notification must be obtained that FDA has granted the product an exemption from demonstrating substantial equivalence. Furthermore, a minimum of 90 days before commercial marketing a report must be submitted to FDA of the intent to market as well as establishing that the product is covered by a granted exemption. See: 21 CFR 1107.1 and FDCA Section 905(j).

Use of Investigational Tobacco Products
http://www.fda.gov/TobaccoProducts/Labeling/RulesRegulationsGuidance/ucm463951.htm?source=govdelivery&utm_medium=email&utm_source=govdelivery

FDA has the authority to issue regulations to exempt tobacco products intended for investigational use from the requirements of Chapter IX of the FDCA, including premarket submission requirements. See: Under 21 U.S.C 387j(g)). Thus, investigational tobacco products are not exempt from requirements under the FDCA such as premarket submission requirements. However, although not legally binding, FDA issued a draft guidance in 2015 until regulations are issued and become effective or FDA provides written notice of its intent to change its enforcement policy. The guidance discusses describes the current thinking of FDA regarding the type of information FDA intends to consider regarding enforcement decisions about the use of investigational tobacco products. Previously issued draft guidances that discuss investigational tobacco products include: Applications for Premarket Review of New Tobacco Products (September 2011); and Modified Risk Tobacco Product Applications (March 30, 2012). When finalized, this guidance will reflect the FDA's most detailed recommendations on the use of investigational tobacco products.

Enforcement Emphasis

CTP established the Office of Compliance and Enforcement (OCE); however, enforcement is limited as FDA's regulatory authority is dictated by the FSPTCP. Therefore, enforcement efforts must adhere to the mandates of the FSPTCA. In addition to warning letters, CTP has filed actions for civil monetary penalties mainly for sales to minors. A Civil Money Penalty (CMP) Complaint is used to initiate an administrative legal action against a retailer that can result in the imposition of a fine, termed a Civil Money Penalty. As an example of enforcement efforts, FDA filed approximately 100 civil legal actions. Enforcement focuses on violations of the following: *Sales to minors; Flavored cigarette sales; Advertising/promotion/marketing restrictions (e.g., Describing the tobacco product as "light," "mild," or "low" or claiming that the product is safer or less harmful without an FDA order in effect; distributing t-shirts or other novelty items with brand name of a cigarette or smokeless tobacco product; and event sponsorship in the brand name of a cigarette or smokeless tobacco product); Free samples; Vending machines in prohibited areas/self-service display/direct access to cigarette or smokeless tobacco; and Sale of cigarettes in packs of less than 20.*

NOTE: CTP issued a Compliance and Enforcement Report that details both compliance and enforcement actions from enactment of the FSPTCA in 2009 through Sept. 30, 2013. Total violations: 18, 960. The majority of violations focused on selling tobacco products to a minor and failure to verify age.
http://www.fda.gov/downloads/TobaccoProducts/GuidanceComplianceRegulatoryInformation/UCM396614.pdf

Enforcement Example

https://www.fda.gov/ICECI/EnforcementActions/WarningLetters/Tobacco/ucm613340.htm
U.S. Food & Drug Administration Center for Tobacco Products
10903 New Hampshire Avenue, Silver Spring, MD 20993

WARNING LETTER
June 21, 2018 VIA UPS
Atkinsons' Market Attn: Site Manager
93 East Croy Street, Hailey, ID 83333
Re: **FDA Warning Letter Regarding Tobacco Retailer Inspection Violation**
    Reference Number: 18ID019429A-B

Dear Sir or Madam:

This Warning Letter is notification from the United States Food and Drug Administration (FDA) advising you that Atkinsons' Market was observed to be in violation of federal tobacco laws and regulations. Failure to correct these violations may lead to federal enforcement actions, including monetary penalties. Your response is requested in 15 working days.

On April 28, 2018, an inspector representing the FDA completed a two-part inspection of the establishment located at 93 East Croy Street, Hailey, ID 83333. During this inspection, the establishment was in violation because you or your employee sold cigarettes to a minor.This inspection revealed that the establishment sells, distributes, and/or advertises tobacco products, including cigarettes, which requires that the establishment and its owners comply with federal laws and regulations governing such practices. The violation observed during the April 28, 2018, two-part inspection includes the following:

1. A minor was able to buy a package of Camel Blue 99's cigarettes on April 28, 2018, at approximately 10:45 AM in the establishment. A retailer must NOT sell cigarettes, cigarette tobacco, roll-your-own tobacco, and/or smokeless tobacco to a person younger than 18 years of age. Doing so violates 21 C.F.R. § 1140.14(a)(1) (2016).

The listed violation causes your cigarettes to be "misbranded" under 903 of the FD&C Act (21 U.S.C. § 387c). You should immediately correct the violation listed above. Failure to correct the violation may result in FDA taking regulatory action without further notice. These actions may include, but are not limited to, civil money penalty, no-tobacco-sale order, seizure, and/or injunction.

The violation indicated in this letter may not be a complete list of violations at the establishment.
We will periodically inspect your establishment and review your promotional activities (e.g., website(s)) related to FDA-regulated tobacco products to assess your compliance with all applicable laws and regulations, including access, marketing, labeling, and advertising restrictions.

Please be aware that, effective August 8, 2016, FDA deemed additional products meeting the definition of a tobacco product, except accessories to these newly deemed products, to be subject to regulation under the Act. These products include, but are not limited to, electronic nicotine delivery systems (including e-cigarettes), e-liquids, cigars, and pipe tobacco. See Final Rule, Deeming Tobacco Products To Be Subject to the Federal Food, Drug, and Cosmetic Act, as Amended by the Family Smoking Prevention and Tobacco Control Act; Restrictions on the Sale and Distribution of Tobacco Products and Required Warning Statements for Tobacco Products, 81 Fed. Reg. 28,974 (May 10, 2016), available at https://federalregister.gov/a/2016-10685.

For more information on these requirements, helpful resources for retailers, a database of inspections, and retailer education materials, visit our website at http://www.fda.gov/TobaccoProducts. The following Guidance documents provide additional information on compliance with retailer responsibilities:

Guidance for Industry: Compliance with Regulations Restricting the Sale and Distribution of Cigarettes and Smokeless Tobacco to Protect Children and Adolescents (http://www.fda.gov/TobaccoProducts/ GuidanceComplianceRegulatoryInformation/ucm252758.htm)

Small Entity Compliance Guide: FDA Deems Certain Tobacco Products Subject to FDA Authority, Sales and Distribution Restrictions, and Health Warning Requirements for Packages and Advertisements (http://www.fda.gov/TobaccoProducts/ Labeling/RulesRegulationsGuidance/ucm499353.htm)

You have 15 working days from the date you receive this letter to respond. In your response, explain your plan for correcting the listed violation and preventing future violations. Include a telephone number and address. Note your reference number of 18ID019429A-B in your response and mail it to:

Food and Drug Administration, Center for Tobacco Products
Document Control Center Building 71, Room G335
10903 New Hampshire Avenue
Silver Spring, MD 20993-0002

If you have any questions, contact the Center for Tobacco Products via email at CTP-WL@fda.hhs.gov or via phone at 1-877-CTP-1373, option 6. Have your reference number ready when you call and include it with any email communications.

Sincerely,

/s/

Ann Simoneau, J.D., Director, Office of Compliance and Enforcement, Center for Tobacco Products

CRITICAL ANALYSIS: Suppose you represent Atkinsons' Market. How would you advise your client in responding to the warning letter?

No Tobacco Sales Order—*Breaktime 3028*

Retailers who have committed five (5) or more repeated violations of particular requirements promulgated under Section 906(d) of the Act (21 U.S.C. § 387f(d)) within a 36-month period are subject to a No Tobacco Sales Order (NTSO). See Guidance Document link below. In 2016 (July 1, 2016) FDA filed a second No-Tobacco-Sale Order (NTSO) complaint against the retailer MFA Petroleum Company (dba Break Time 3028 in Columbia, MO). Break Time 3018 has previous violations including sales to minors. FDA issued a previous NTSO complaint against Break Time 3028 in October 2015. In this NTSO complaint, FDA has requested a 6-month restriction from selling tobacco products for violating FDA's tobacco regulations promulgated under Section906(d) of the Federal Food, Drug, and Cosmetic Act (Act) (21 U.S.C. § 387f(d)). Inspectors observed several violations over a 36-month period. CTP respectfully requested that the Court impose a no-tobacco-sale order for a period of 6 months on Respondent.

See Determination of the Period Covered by a No-Tobacco- Sale Order and Compliance With an Order
https://www.fda.gov/downloads/tobaccoproducts/labeling/rulesregulationsguidance/ucm460155.pdf
See Revised Guidance: *Civil Money Penalties and No-Tobacco-Sale Orders For Tobacco Retailers*
(Issued Dec. 2016).
https://www.fda.gov/downloads/TobaccoProducts/Labeling/RulesRegulationsGuid-
ance/UCM252955.pdf

CRITICAL ANALYSIS: How would you advise your client, *Break Time 3028*?

Onserts as Advertising

An FDA warning letter sent to the Altria Group Philip Morris USA, Inc. regarding the use of "onserts" that Marlboro Lights would appear as Marlboro Gold. An "onsert" is a peel-off attachment advertisement affixed to a product container, box, magazine or newspaper.

CRITICAL ANALYSIS: Does the use of an "onsert" violate the FSPTCA and if so, how?

Chapter 3: Warnings, Advertisements, Lawsuits and Bans
FDA's Legal Authority to Issue Graphic and Written Warning

Tobacco use remains a leading cause of both premature yet preventable death in the United States according to FDA and the CDC. More than 25 years has elapsed since warnings were issued on cigarette packaging and advertisements. To that end, the FSPTCA mandated that FDA develop regulations pertaining to warning statements and nine new more noticeable images to appear on cigarette packages and in cigarette advertisements. The FSPTCA directed FDA to issue regulations requiring that color graphic images depicting the negative health consequences of smoking accompany the nine new textual warning statements. Despite the issuance of the nine-cigarette health warnings for all cigarette packaging and advertisements, legal challenges prevailed. Scheduled to commence in September 2012, this issue became legally contentious and eventually FDA withdrew the proposed graphic warnings. The objective of the warnings was to communicate the dangers of smoking while at the same time with the aim to decrease the number of people who smoke. FDA selected the final nine cigarette health warnings based on their ability to effectively communicate the health risks of smoking to the public. In making selections, FDA considered its review of relevant scientific literature, more than 1,700 public comments, and results from its 18,000-person study. Apparently, that was insufficient.

A lawsuit filed in 2011 by tobacco Companies Reynolds American, Inc.'s R.J. Reynolds unit, Lorillard, Inc., Liggett Group LLC, Commonwealth Brands, Inc., owned by Britain's Imperial Tobacco Group Plc., and Santa Fe Natural Tobacco Co. alleged violation of their free speech rights under the First Amendment. See: *R.J. Reynolds Tobacco Co. et al. v. FDA*, (D. Ct., D.C.), No. 11-01482; Preliminary Injunction granted Nov. 7, 2011, which effectively stayed the new graphic warnings from FDA implementation. According to the court, the firms showed a "substantial likelihood" of prevailing "on the merits of their position that these mandatory graphic images unconstitutionally compel speech." Subsequently, the district court decided that the government's rule violated the tobacco companies' rights to free speech. The Court of Appeals (District of Columbia) held that FDA failed to provide substantial evidence that graphic warnings on cigarette advertising would advance the government's interest in smoking reduction to a material degree.
R.J. Reynolds Tobacco Co. et al. v. Food & Drug Administration, No. 11-5332 Consolidated with No. 12-5063, 696 F.3d 1205 (D. C. Cir. 2012).
https://www.cadc.uscourts.gov/internet/opin-
ions.nsf/4C0311C78EB11C5785257A64004EBFB5/$file/11-5332-1391191.pdf

Eventually FDA withdrew the nine graphic warnings and did not appeal nor issue new warnings. See 77 FR 72355-01NOTICES Food and Drug Administration [Docket No FDA-2012-N-0273] Experimental Study of Graphic Cigarette Warning Labels (December 5, 2012). Yet, the *Discount Tobacco* decision noted below and the *American Academy of Pediatrics* lawsuit filed due to delay in issuing graphic warnings and deeming rule all provide guidance. The deeming regulation issued in 2016 clarified that FDA still retains the legal authority to require warnings under the FSPTCA. *Deeming Tobacco Products to Be Subject to the Federal Food, Drug, and Cosmetic Act, as Amended by the Family Smoking Prevention and Tobacco Control Act; Restrictions on the Sale and Distribution of Tobacco Products and Required Warning Statements for Tobacco Products* 81 FR 28973 (May 10, 2016). The Deeming Rule uses the term that the *R. J. Reynolds* decision was "overtaken" by the *American Meat Institute* decision.

In *Discount Tobacco City & Lottery, Inc.* 674 F.3d 509 (2012), the court held that curbing juvenile tobacco use is a substantial government interest that is directly advanced by the FSPTCA's provisions. Further, Discount Tobacco held that graphical and textual warnings on cigarettes and smokeless tobacco products were reasonably related to the government's in preventing consumer deception and were deemed constitutional. The United States Supreme Court denied cert., (Case re-captioned) *Am. Snuff Co., LLC v. United States*. 12-521, 2013 WL 1704718 (U. S. Apr. 22, 2013). See also: *American Meat Institute v. United States Dept. of Agriculture*, 760 F.3d 18 (D.C. Cir. 2014) rev'd *R. J. Reynolds* on other grounds.

The *American Academy of Pediatrics et al. v. United States Food and Drug Administration,* 1:16-cv-11985, (D. C. Mass. 2016). In 2018, the Court ordered the FDA to issue long overdue revamped warnings on an expedited schedule since several years elapsed as follows: May 2019— Complete study on "Experimental Study of Cigarette Warnings"; April 2020—Submit Notice of Proposed Rulemaking to the Office of the Federal Register for publication; December 2020—Internal deadline for review of public comments; May 2021—Submit final rule to the Office of the Federal Register for publication.

CRITICAL ANALYSIS: Discuss the impact of the withdrawal of the graphic warning labels and subsequent court order *American Academy of Pediatrics et al. v. United States Food and Drug Administration,* 1:16-cv-11985, (D. C. Mass. 2016). What does the future hold in terms of warnings on cigarette packaging and cigarette advertisements? Recommend types of warnings that would pass constitutional muster.

Flavored Tobacco Ban

http://www.fda.gov/tobaccoproducts/protectingkidsfromtobacco/flavoredtobacco/default.htm

Ban Parameters—A ban on cigarettes containing certain characterizing flavors such as clove, cinnamon, vanilla authorized by the Family Smoking Prevention and Tobacco Control Act, (FSPTCA) applies to all tobacco products that meet the definition of a "cigarette" in section 900(3) of the FDCA even if not labeled as "cigarettes" (effective September 22, 2009). Specifically, Section 907(a)(1)(A) of the FSPTCA states: a cigarette or any of its component parts (including the tobacco, filter, or paper) shall not contain, as a constituent (including a smoke constituent) or additive, an artificial or natural flavor (other than tobacco or menthol) or an herb or spice, including strawberry, grape, orange, clove, cinnamon, pineapple, vanilla, coconut, licorice, cocoa, chocolate, cherry, or coffee, that is a characterizing flavor of the tobacco product or tobacco smoke. Congress has stated that flavors make cigarettes more appealing to youth and often result in exposure to additional carcinogens and other toxic constituents. The removal from the market of cigarettes that contain certain characterizing flavors is an important step in FDA's efforts to reduce the burden of illness and death caused by tobacco products. Failure to comply means a product is adulterated and the product could be seized. Other sanctions that manufacturers, distributors, and retailers may be subject to include injunctions, civil monetary penalties, and or criminal prosecution.

See: *http://www.cdc.gov/tobacco/data_statistics/fact_sheets/youth_data/tobacco_use/*

Applicability of the flavored tobacco ban to menthol cigarettes and other tobacco products— FDA announced in 2018 that the agency is advancing rulemaking to ban menthol in combustible tobacco products such as cigarettes and cigars as noted below. An important method to reduce the death and disease caused by smoking is to prevent children and adolescents from starting to smoke and prohibit these flavors. See: CDC Tobacco Report:

http://www.cdc.gov/tobacco/data_statistics/fact_sheets/youth_data/tobacco_use/

CRITICAL ANALYSIS: Discuss whether there are other flavored products that should be banned as well and, if so, which flavors. Include a discussion about menthol below. Discuss the impact of the deeming regulations on, for example, cigars in terms of a flavor ban. *http://1.usa.gov/1WbltVX*

Menthol in Cigarettes—Proposed Rulemaking

https://www.regulations.gov/document?D=FDA_FRDOC_0001-4088 (2013)

FDA, HHS 21 CFR Part 1140 Docket No. FDA-2013-N-0521 Advance notice: proposed rulemaking.

SUMMARY: HHS 21 CFR Part 1140 Docket No. FDA-2013-N-0521. FDA issued advanced notice of proposed rulemaking (ANPRM) to obtain information related to the potential regulation of menthol in cigarettes. Preliminary scientific evaluation indicates there is likely a public health impact of menthol in cigarettes. At the close of comment period, 106,273 comments were submitted.

NOTE: See also: *Regulation of Flavors in Tobacco Products* (Advanced Notice of Rulemaking) 83 FR 12294 (March 21, 2018). (Data regarding use of menthol cigarettes and non-cigarette tobacco products among youth indicate widespread appeal of flavored tobacco products).

In 2018, FDA Commissioner Gottlieb reiterated the concern about menthol in cigarettes in terms of a public health issue. *https://www.fda.gov/NewsEvents/Newsroom/PressAnnouncements/ucm625884.htm*

CRITICAL ANALYSIS: FDA asked the following in determining a course of action regarding menthol. Choose at least one question below under A., B., and/or C. and discuss.

A. Tobacco Product Standards

1. Should FDA consider establishing a tobacco product standard for menthol in menthol cigarettes? If so, what allowable level of menthol would be appropriate to protect public health?

2. Rather than a tobacco product standard for menthol in menthol cigarettes, should FDA consider a tobacco product standard for any additive, constituent, artificial or natural flavor, or other ingredient that produces a characterizing flavor of menthol in the tobacco product or its smoke?

3. If a tobacco product standard for menthol in menthol cigarettes were to be established, should FDA consider issuing regulations to address menthol in other tobacco products besides cigarettes?

4. If a product standard prohibiting or limiting menthol were to be established, what length of time should manufacturers be provided to achieve compliance with the standard? If a product standard prohibiting or limiting menthol were to be established, would a stepped approach in which the level of menthol was gradually reduced be appropriate for public health protection?

5. If a product standard limiting menthol were to be established, are there alternatives that could be substituted by manufacturers to maintain the effect or appeal of menthol to menthol cigarette smokers and potential initiators?

B. Sale and Distribution Restrictions

1. Should FDA consider establishing restrictions on the sale and/or distribution of menthol cigarettes? If so, what restrictions would be appropriate and what would be the impact on youth or adult smoking behavior, initiation, and cessation?

2. Should FDA consider establishing restrictions on the advertising and promotion of menthol cigarettes? If so, what restrictions would be appropriate and what would be the impact on youth or adult smoking behavior, initiation, and cessation?

C. Other Actions and Considerations

1. Are there other tobacco product standards, regulatory, or other actions that FDA could implement that would more effectively reduce the harms caused by menthol cigarette smoking and better protect the public health than the tobacco product standards or regulatory actions discussed in the preceding questions?

2. To the extent that you have identified a tobacco product standard or other regulatory action in response to the prior questions, please provide additional information and comments on:

2.1 Is compliance with the tobacco product standard or other regulatory action technically achievable?

2.2 How FDA would structure a corresponding rule to maximize compliance, facilitate enforcement, and otherwise maximize public health benefits?

3. If menthol cigarettes could no longer be legally sold, is there evidence that illicit trade in menthol cigarettes would become a significant problem? If so what would be the impact of any such illicit trade on public health? How would any such illicit trade compare to the existing illicit trade in cigarettes?

4. What additional information and research beyond that described in the evaluation is there on the potential impact of sale and distribution restrictions of menthol cigarettes on specific subpopulations, such as those based on racial, ethnic, socioeconomic status, sexuality/gender identity?

5. To what extent are you aware of current (within the past 5 years) advertising and/or promotion of menthol cigarettes that have targeted specific communities, subpopulations, and locations, beyond that described in the evaluation?

6. Might any current advertising or other marketing or public statements concerning menthol cigarettes, or menthol in other tobacco products, constitute reduced risk claims?

Corrective Statements

In a protracted court case, corrective statements were ordered, yet delay ensued. The case against cigarette manufacturers and other tobacco entities spanned several years as detailed below.

United States, et al., v. Philip Morris USA, Inc., et al., Brown & Williamson Tobacco Corp., directly and as successor by merger to American Tobacco Company, et al., 855 F.3d 321, No. 16-5101 Consolidated with 16-5127 (April 25, 2017).

Background: The government brought suit against cigarette manufacturers and other tobacco-related entities under the Racketeer Influenced and Corrupt Organizations Act (RICO). Defendants by bench trial, were found to have intentionally misled American public (449 F.Supp.2d 1 and 449 F.Supp.2d 988). The United States District Court for the District of Columbia, Gladys Kessler, J., 907 F.Supp.2d 1 and 2014 WL 2506611, required defendants to add two statements to their cigarette packages and advertisements. The Court of Appeals, 801 F.3d 250, affirmed in part, reversed in part, and remanded. On remand, the United States District Court for the District of Columbia, No. 1:99-cv-02496, Gladys Kessler, J., 164 F.Supp.3d 121, held that government's proposed preamble and corrective statements fell within scope of district court's authority. Defendants appealed.

The Court of Appeals, Sentelle, Senior Circuit Judge, held that:

text of proposed preambles that district court required tobacco companies to issue to general public would be modified by removing **"here is the truth"** *language;*

text of modified proposed preambles was permissible under First Amendment; and

text of topic description to preamble that district court required tobacco companies to issue to general public exceeded scope of district court's authority to issue injunctions to prevent and restrain future RICO violations, and would therefore be modified. [emphasis added].

Affirmed in part, reversed in part and remanded.

Opinion—Sentelle, Senior Circuit Judge: In 2006, the district court found that Appellant cigarette manufacturers had for decades conspired to deny the health effects of smoking in violation of RICO. *United States v. Philip Morris USA, Inc.*, 449 F.Supp.2d 1 (D.D.C. 2006) ("*Liability Opinion*"). The district court ordered Appellants to disseminate "corrective statements" relating to the health effects of smoking in newspapers, on television, on cigarette packages, and on websites. *Id.* at 938-41; for over ten years the parties have argued over the precise language of these statements. Appellants claim the most recent language proposed by the government is conduct-focused and beyond the scope of RICO and, violates the First Amendment.

BACKGROUND—In August 2006, a district court found that Appellant cigarette manufacturers ("Defendants") had violated RICO by associating together to misinform the public about smoking. *Liability Opinion*, 449 F.Supp.2d at 851-906. The district court found that "an injunction ordering Defendants to issue corrective statements is appropriate and necessary to prevent and restrain them from making fraudulent public statements on smoking and health matters in the future." *Id.* at 926. *** On appeal, we upheld the concept of a corrective-statements remedy against RICO and First Amendment challenges because "[r]equiring Defendants to reveal the previously hidden truth about their products will prevent and restrain them from disseminating false and misleading statements, thereby violating RICO, in the future." *United States v. Philip Morris USA, Inc.*, 566 F.3d 1095, 1140 (D.C. Cir. 2009) ("*2009 Opinion*"). On remand from the *2009 Opinion*, the district court formulated the text of the corrective statements, including bullet points containing factual statements on each topic preceded by a preamble stating: "A Federal Court has ruled that [Defendants] deliberately deceived the American public about [the topic of the statement], and has ordered those companies to make this statement. Here is the truth[.]" *United States v. Philip Morris USA, Inc.*, 907 F.Supp.2d 1, 8-9 (D.D.C. 2012). Defendants appealed. This Court held that the "district court exceeded its authority under RICO because the preambles reveal nothing about cigarettes; instead, they disclose defendants' prior deceptive *conduct*." *United States v. Philip Morris USA, Inc.*, 801 F.3d 250, 261 (D.C. Cir. 2015) ("*Corrective Statements Opinion*") (emphasis in original). While the bulleted statements "reveal[ed] the previously hidden truth about [Defendants'] *products*," the preambles did not and could "not be justified on grounds of general deterrence." *Id.* at 263 (quoting *2009 Opinion*, 566 F.3d at 1140) (emphasis in original). *** The Court remanded for further proceedings. On remand, the district court ordered the preambles to read as follows:

A Federal Court has ordered [Defendants] to make this statement about [the topic of the statement]. Here is the truth: ....

United States v. Philip Morris USA, Inc., 164 F.Supp.3d 121, 124-25 (D.D.C. 2016) ("*Revised Preamble Opinion*"). The district court explained that the new preambles "do not in any way send a message to the public that Defendants deceived them in the past, nor that Defendants are being punished for their previous conduct." *Id.* at 125-26. The district court also rejected Defendants' First Amendment arguments. *Id.* at 126-27. Defendants appealed.

DISCUSSION

A. Standard of Review—This Court reviews *de novo* the district court's conclusions that the corrective statements comport with RICO and the First Amendment. *2009 Opinion*, 566 F.3d at 1110, 1147.

B. RICO—In a civil RICO action, the statute provides district courts with jurisdiction to impose remedies that "prevent and restrain" future RICO violations, not to punish prior violations. 18 U.S.C. § 1964(a). Thus, the district court's remedy requiring Defendants to issue corrective statements complied with RICO because Defendants would be "impaired in making false and misleading assurances" about cigarettes if simultaneously required to tell the truth. *2009 Opinion*, 566 F.3d at 1140. *** However, the district court's "jurisdiction is limited to forward-looking remedies that are aimed at future violations." *United States v. Philip Morris USA, Inc.*, 396 F.3d 1190, 1198 (D.C. Cir. 2005) ("*Disgorgement Opinion*"). Defendants allege that the preambles approved by the district court exceed its RICO jurisdiction because the preambles "convey the unequivocal message that Defendants previously deceived the American public and, further, that they are being compelled by a court to make the corrective statements as a sanction for prior wrongdoing." Defendants' Br. at 30. Defendants point to five elements that they believe demonstrate the backward-looking nature of the preambles, both individually and cumulatively: (1) the "Here is the truth" tagline; (2) the declaration that "A Federal Court has ordered [Defendants] to make this statement"; (3) that different preambles are permitted for the ITG Entities; (4) the description in the preamble of two of the specific topics; and (5) the district court's rejection of Defendants' proposed alternative preambles.

Defendants assert that the **"Here is the truth"** tagline conveys the unambiguous message that Defendants have previously withheld "the truth" about the effects of smoking because "[n]o one affirms that a message is 'the truth'—or is ordered by a court to tell 'the truth'—for no reason." *** Similarly, Defendants allege that the declaration **"A Federal Court has ordered [Defendants] to make this statement"** is backward-looking. We agree that, read together, these two phrases most naturally suggest prior misconduct by Defendants. Such language "can serve only two purposes: either to attract attention that a correction follows or to humiliate the advertiser," *Warner-Lambert Co. v. FTC*, 562 F.2d 749, 763 (D.C. Cir. 1977), neither of which is a permissible goal under civil RICO, *Corrective Statements Opinion*, 801 F.3d at 262 ("Correcting consumer misinformation, which 'focuse[s] on remedying the effects of past conduct,' is ... an impermissible objective under RICO." (quoting *Disgorgement Opinion*, 396 F.3d at 1198)); *id.* at 256 (noting that RICO's civil-remedy provision does not provide for remedies that "seek to punish prior wrongdoing").

This problem is remedied by simply removing the **"Here is the truth"** line such that the preambles read only:

> *A Federal Court has ordered [Defendants] to make this statement about [the topic of the statement].*

This modified preamble is aimed "toward[ ] thwarting prospective efforts by Defendants" to commit future RICO violations. *2009 Opinion*, 566 F.3d at 1144-45. *** Because we hold that the modified preambles satisfy RICO, it cannot be true, as Defendants argue, that "the only reason to prefer the Government's proposal is to taint Defendants with implications of past wrongdoing." Def. Br. at 39.

C. First Amendment—Although we have determined that the modified preambles do not exceed the statutory authority granted under RICO, the question remains as to whether this compelled speech is violative of Defendants' First Amendment rights. The threshold question for this court is what standard applies to guide us in making that determination.

Traditionally, First Amendment questions arising in the arena of "commercial speech" have occasioned scrutiny under the standard of *Central Hudson Gas & Electric Corp. v. Public Service Commission*, 447 U.S. 557, 100 S.Ct. 2343, 65 L.Ed.2d 341 (1980). Under *Central Hudson*, protected speech may be regulated if the governmental interest is "substantial." *Id.* at 566, 100 S.Ct. 2343. Any such regulation must "directly advance[ ] the governmental interest asserted." *Id.* ***

The government argues that the present controversy is governed by *Zauderer v. Office of Disciplinary Counsel*, 471 U.S. 626, 105 S.Ct. 2265, 85 L.Ed.2d 652 (1985). *Zauderer* teaches that the careful "evidentiary parsing" mandated by *Central Hudson* "is hardly necessary when the government uses a disclosure mandate to achieve a goal of informing consumers about a particular product trait, assuming of course that the reason for informing consumers qualifies as an adequate interest." *AMI*, 760 F.3d at 26 (citing *Zauderer*, 471 U.S. at 650, 105 S.Ct. 2265). "[B]y acting only through a reasonably crafted disclosure mandate, the government meets its burden of showing that the mandate advances its interest in making the 'purely factual and uncontroversial information' accessible to the recipients." *Id.* (quoting *Zauderer*, 471 U.S. at 651, 105 S.Ct. 2265). Under *Zauderer*, then, as long as a disclosure requirement is not "unjustified or unduly burdensome," a company's rights "are adequately protected as long as disclosure requirements are reasonably related to the State's interest in preventing deception of consumers." 471 U.S. at 651, 105 S.Ct. 2265. *** We find that the preamble requirements are "reasonably related to the [government's] interest in preventing deception of consumers." *Zauderer*, 471 U.S. at 651, 105 S.Ct. 2265. The preambles are confined to " 'purely factual and uncontroversial information,' geared toward[ ] thwarting prospective efforts by Defendants to either directly mislead consumers or capitalize on their prior deceptions by continuing to advertise in a manner that builds on consumers' existing misperceptions." *2009 Opinion*, 566 F.3d at 1144-45 (quoting *Zauderer*, 471 U.S. at 651, 105 S.Ct. 2265). ***

D. Statement C and D topic descriptions—Defendants also challenge the topic descriptions in the preambles to Statements C and D, asserting that they exceed the remedial scope of civil RICO because they convey past wrongdoing. The Statement D topic description explains that Defendants are required to make the statement **"about designing cigarettes to enhance the delivery of nicotine."** Defendants cannot challenge the preamble language in Statement D. As this Court previously held, Defendants waived any challenge to language that they "manipulate[d] [the] design of cigarettes in order to enhance the delivery of nicotine" or "intentionally designed cigarettes to make them more addictive." *Corrective Statements Opinion*, 801 F.3d at 258-59 (first alteration added). The Statement C topic description states that Defendants are required to make the following statement **"about selling and advertising low tar and light cigarettes as less harmful than regular cigarettes."** This language was not previously considered and is indeed backward-looking, as it implies that Defendants previously sold and advertised cigarettes in such a way. Alternatively, a topic description requiring Defendants to make the statement "about low tar and light cigarettes being as harmful as regular cigarettes," "the harmfulness of low tar and light cigarettes," or "the lack of significant health benefit from smoking low tar and light cigarettes" would be permissible under both RICO and the First Amendment.

CONCLUSION *** In short, while we remand this matter for further proceedings, we see no reason why extensive proceedings will be required in the district court. With the minor revisions mandated in this opinion, the district court can simply issue an order requiring the corrected statements remedy to go forward.

PART 1: REVISED TEXT FOR CORRECTIVE STATEMENTS

As required by the Court of Appeals in *United States v. Philip Morris USA, Inc.*, 80 I F.3d 250 (D.C. Cir. 2015), and *United States v. Philip Morris USA, Inc.*, 855 F.3d 321 (D.C. Cir. 2017), and the memorandum opinions accompanying Order #62-Remand and Order #67- Remand, the text of the Corrective Statements shall be as follows for Altria, R.J. Reynolds Tobacco, Lorillard, and Philip Morris USA.

The following is from the **SECOND SUPERSEDING CONSENT ORDER IMPLEMENTING THE CORRECTIVE STATEMENTS REMEDY FOR NEWSPAPERS AND TELEVISION** dated October 5, 2017, Civil Action No. 99-CV-2496 (PLF).

A. Adverse Health Effects of Smoking A Federal Court has ordered Altria, R.J. Reynolds Tobacco, Lorillard, and Philip Morris USA to make this statement about the health effects of smoking.

• Smoking kills, on average, 1,200 Americans. Every day.

• More people die every year from smoking than from murder, AIDS, suicide, drugs, car crashes, and alcohol, combined.
• Smoking causes heart disease, emphysema, acute myeloid leukemia, and cancer of ihe mouth, esophagus, larynx, lung, stomach, kidney, bladder; and pancreas.
• Smoking also causes reduced fertility, low birth weight in newborns, and cancer of the cervix.

B. Addictiveness of Smoking and Nicotine A Federal Court has ordered Altria, R.J. Reynolds Tobacco, Lorillard, and Philip MorrisUSA to make this statement about the addictiveness of smoking and nicotine.
• Smoking is highly addictive.   Nicotine is the addictive drug in tobacco.
• Cigarette companies intentionally designed cigarettes with enough nicotine to create and sustain addiction.
• When you smoke, the nicotine actually changes the brain- that's why quitting is so hard.

**C. Lack of Significant Health Benefit from Smoking "Low Tar," "Light," "Ultra
Light," "Mild," and "Natural" Cigarettes** A Federal Court has ordered Altria, R.J. Reynolds Tobacco, Lorillard, and Philip Morris USA to make this statement about low tar and light cigarettes being as harmful as regular cigarettes.
• Many smokers switch to low tar and light cigarettes rather than quitting because they think low tar and light cigarettes are less harmful.   They are not.
• "Low tar" and "light" cigarette smokers inhale essentially the same amount of tar and nicotine as they would from regular cigarettes.
• All cigarettes cause cancer, lung disease, heart attacks, and premature death - lights, low tar, ultra lights, and naturals.   There is no safe cigarette.

**D. Manipulation of Cigarette Design and Composition to Ensure Optimum
Nicotine Delivery** A Federal Court has ordered Altria, R.J. Reynolds Tobacco, Lorillard, and Philip Morris USA to make this statement about designing cigarettes to enhance the delivery of nicotine.
• Altria, R.J. Reynolds Tobacco, Lorillard, and Philip Morris USA intentionally
designed cigarettes to make them more addictive.
• Cigarette companies control the impact and delivery of nicotine in many ways, including designing filters and selecting cigarette paper to maximize the ingestion of nicotine, adding ammonia to make the cigarette taste less harsh, and controlling the physical and chemical make-up of the tobacco blend.
• When you smoke, the nicotine actually changes the brain- that's why quitting is so hard.

E. Adverse Health Effects of Exposure to Secondhand Smoke A Federal Court has ordered Altria, R.J. Reynolds Tobacco, Lorillard, and Philip MorrisUSA to make this statement about the health effects of secondhand smoke.
• Secondhand smoke kills over 38,000 Americans each year.
• Secondhand smoke causes lung cancer and coronary heart disease in adults who do **not** smoke.
• Children exposed to secondhand smoke are at an increased risk for sudden infant death syndrome (SIDS), acute respiratory infections, ear problems, severe asthma, and reduced lung function.
•There is no safe level of exposure to secondhand smoke.

NOTE: The corrective statements appeared in approximately 50 newspapers, online and major television prime time for a one-year duration. *https://www.tobaccofreekids.org/media/2017/corrective-statements.*

CRITICAL ANALYSIS: What was the main reason the defendant companies protracted this litigation? Evaluate the effectiveness of the "corrective statements".

Chapter 4: Deeming Rule—Covered Tobacco Products Regulation: Electronic Nicotine Delivery Systems, Cigars, Pipe Tobacco, Dissolvables

https://www.fda.gov/TobaccoProducts/Labeling/RulesRegulationsGuidance/ucm394909.htm

Where do electronic nicotine systems (ENDS) such as e-cigarettes fit in the scheme of FDA regulation? Previously, FDA argued that e-cigarettes were drug-device combination products and/or drugs rather than tobacco products. For example, in correspondence to the Electronic Cigarette Association, FDA deemed e-cigarettes as combination products with CDER as primary regulator and subject to a new drug application review process (NDA). FDA set forth that despite the legal authority to regulate tobacco products under the 2009 Family Smoking Prevention and Tobacco Control Act (FSPTCA) the e-cigarettes noted in the warning letters and similar products, fell within the definitions under the FDCA as drugs and devices, with a drug primary mode of action. See: 21 USC 321(g), (h), and (p). See also: Office of Combination Products *http://www.fda.gov/CombinationProducts/default.htm.*

Electronic cigarettes are products designed to deliver nicotine or other substances to a user in the form of a vapor. Typically, they are composed of a rechargeable, battery-operated heating element, a replaceable cartridge that may contain nicotine or other chemicals, flavor and an atomizer that, when heated, converts the contents of the cartridge into a vapor. The user can then inhale this vapor. These products are manufactured to appear similar to products such as cigarettes, cigars, and pipes. Sometimes, they are fashioned to look like everyday items such as pens and USB memory sticks. They are available in different flavors such as chocolate and mint. According to FDA, experts opine that e-cigarettes can increase nicotine addiction.

Overall, FDA's concern stemmed from safety issues associated with quality control. For example, in 2009, FDA notified healthcare professionals and patients that a laboratory analysis of electronic cigarette samples found that they contain carcinogens and toxic chemicals such as diethylene glycol, an ingredient used in antifreeze. FDA issued warning letters in 2010 to certain distributors of electronic cigarettes for violations of the (FSPTCA) due to unsubstantiated claims and poor manufacturing practices such as varying amounts of nicotine or cartridges with nicotine yet labeled without nicotine as follows: *Gamucci America (Smokey Bayou, Inc.); E-Cig Technology, Inc.; E-CigaretteDirect, LLC; Johnson Creek Enterprises, LLC; and Ruyan America, Inc.*

Consequently, FDA issued a final rule which includes e-cigarettes within FDA authority to regulate. **See: *Deeming Tobacco Products Subject to the Federal Food, Drug, and Cosmetic Act, as Amended by the Family Smoking Prevention and Tobacco Control Act; Restrictions on the Sale and Distribution of Tobacco Products and Required Warning Statements for Tobacco Products* 81 FR 28973 (May 10, 2016).**

CRITICAL ANALYSIS: Evaluate legal and safety issues of e-cigarettes. See note below and include a discussion about the "heat not burn" product.

NOTE: Phillip Morris Internationl, Ltd., Altria, Inc. (once part of Phillip Morris and now in partnership), applied to FDA for its product called IQOS. British American Tobacco Plc—also sought FDA approval for its electronic tobacco heat not burn device called Glo. According to these tobacco companies, these are healthier alternatives to traditional smoking and imparts a sensation of puffing on a real cigarette. See: Smokers Feel Heat but Not the Burn, Wall St. J. B1 (August 7, 2017). E-cigarettes Heating Device—Advisory Committee Determined Insufficient Evidence that heating device reduces risks of tobacco related disease (Jan. 2018). https://www.regulations.gov/document?D=FDA-2017-D-3001-0002

Background—*Sottera, Inc. v. FDA & Drug Administration*

The court in *Soterra*, originally captioned *Smoking Everywhere*, deemed e-cigarette products as falling within the FSTPCA. In *Smoking Everywhere, Inc.* 680 F. Supp.2d 62 (2010), the District

Court found that electronic cigarettes were tobacco products under FSPTCA. On appeal, the question before the court was as follows: "[W]hether Congress has authorized the Food and Drug Administration ("FDA") to regulate e-cigarettes under the drug/device provisions of the Federal Food, Drug, and Cosmetic Act ("FDCA"), 21 U.S.C. § 351 et seq., or under the Family Smoking Prevention and Tobacco Control Act of 2009" (the "Tobacco Act" or FSPTCA), Pub. L. 111-31, 123 Stat. 1776.

The Court of Appeals, in *Sottera, Inc. v. Food & Drug Administration*, 627 F.3d 891 (D.C. Cir. Dec. 7, 2010) affirmed the lower court decision (originally captioned *Smoking Everywhere*). The court held that e-cigarettes and other products made or derived from tobacco can be regulated as "tobacco products" under the FSPTCA and are not drugs/devices unless they are marketed for therapeutic purposes. The FSPTCA does not provide FDA with the authority to ban tobacco products. The court's reasoning was based on intended use set forth by the manufacturer. The company stated that NJOY is marketed as a "pleasure product" and not for therapeutic purposes. Therefore, according to the court, FDA lacked authority under FDCA's drug/device provisions to regulate tobacco products customarily marketed without claims of therapeutic effect. FDA has authority to regulate tobacco products customarily marketed without claims of therapeutic benefit under the Family Smoking Prevention and Tobacco Control Act or the FSPTCA. The court of appeals decision permitted Sottera, Inc. to market and distribute e-cigarettes under the brand name NJOY.

NOTE: While the appeal was pending, *Smoking Everywhere* voluntarily withdrew its complaint against FDA. Further, *Smoking Everywhere* settled a civil lawsuit brought by the state of California. The settlement involved an agreement by *Smoking Everywhere* not to target sales and advertising to minors.

http://www.fda.gov/NewsEvents/PublicHealthFocus/ucm252360.htm.

Soterra, Inc. DBA as NJOY v. Food and Drug Administration
627 F.3d 891 (2010), Rehearing *En Banc* Denied Jan. 24, 2011

WILLIAMS, Senior Circuit Judge—Sottera, Inc., which does business as NJOY, is an importer and distributor of "electronic cigarettes" or "e-cigarettes," a product that enables users to inhale vaporized nicotine. The question before us is whether Congress has authorized the Food and Drug Administration ("FDA") to regulate e-cigarettes under the drug/device provisions of the Federal Food, Drug, and Cosmetic Act ("FDCA"), 21 U.S.C. § 351 *et seq.*, or under the Family Smoking Prevention and Tobacco Control Act of 2009 (the "Tobacco Act"), Pub.L. 111-31, 123 Stat. 1776. We think that the statutes, properly read in light of the Supreme Court's decision in *FDA v. Brown & Williamson*, 529 U.S. 120, 120 S.Ct. 1291, 146 L.Ed.2d 121 (2000), locate the product under the Tobacco Act.

Electronic cigarettes are battery-powered products that allow users to inhale nicotine vapor without fire, smoke, ash, or carbon monoxide. NJOY Compl. at 2. Designed to look like a traditional cigarette, each e-cigarette consists of three parts: the nicotine cartridge, the atomizer or heating element, and the battery and electronics. The plastic cartridge serves as the mouthpiece and contains liquid nicotine, water, propylene glycol, and glycerol. *Id.* at 5. The atomizer vaporizes the liquid nicotine, and the battery and electronics power the atomizer and monitor air flow. *Id.* When the user inhales, the electronics detect the air flow and activate the atomizer; the liquid nicotine is vaporized, and the user inhales the vapor. *Id.*

NJOY has imported and distributed e-cigarettes since 2007. *Id.* at 2, 4. The liquid nicotine in each e-cigarette is derived from natural tobacco plants, Decl. of John Leadbeater at 2, and NJOY claims that its product is marketed and labeled for "smoking pleasure," rather than as a therapeutic or smoking cessation product. NJOY Compl. at 2; Decl. of John Leadbeater at 2. On April 15, 2009 the FDA ordered that a shipment of NJOY's e-cigarettes be denied entry into the United States, asserting that the e-cigarettes appeared to be adulterated, misbranded, or unapproved drug-device combinations under the FDCA. April 20, 2009 Notice of FDA Action. ***

Smoking Everywhere and NJOY argued that the FDA can regulate electronic cigarettes, as they propose to market them, only under the Tobacco Act, claiming that the Supreme Court's opinion in *Brown & Williamson* foreclosed FDCA drug/device jurisdiction over tobacco products marketed without claims of therapeutic effect. The district court agreed and granted the injunction. While this appeal was pending, Smoking Everywhere voluntarily dismissed its complaint against the FDA, leaving NJOY as the sole appellee. See NJOY Br. at 4. *** When deciding whether to grant a preliminary injunction, a district court must consider four familiar factors: whether "(1) the plaintiff has a substantial likelihood of success on the merits; (2) the plaintiff would suffer irreparable injury were an injunction not granted; (3) an injunction would substantially injure other interested parties; and (4) the grant of an injunction would further the public interest." Under the FDCA, the FDA has authority to regulate articles that are "drugs," "devices," or drug/device combinations. 21 U.S.C. § 321(g)(1) defines drugs to include:

> (B) articles intended for use in the diagnosis, cure, mitigation, treatment, or prevention of disease in man or other animals; and (C) articles (other than food) intended to affect the structure or any function of the body of man or other animals.

21 U.S.C. § 321(g)(1)(B) & (C). The statute defines devices similarly, see 21 U.S.C. § 321(h)(2) & (3); products that are "combination[s] of a drug, device, or biological product" are regulated as combination products, see 21 U.S.C. § 353(g)(1).

Until 1996, the FDA had never attempted to regulate tobacco products under the FDCA (with one exception, irrelevant for reasons discussed below) unless they were sold for therapeutic uses, that is, for use in the "diagnosis, cure, mitigation, treatment, or prevention of disease" under § 321(g)(1)(B). Cf. *Action on Smoking and Health v. Harris,* 655 F.2d 236 (D.C.Cir.1980). But in that year, the FDA changed its long-held position, promulgating regulations affecting tobacco products as customarily marketed, i.e., ones sold without therapeutic claims. See Regulations Restricting the Sale and Distribution of Cigarettes and Smokeless Tobacco to Protect Children and Adolescents, 61 Fed.Reg. 44,396 (Aug. 28, 1996). The agency asserted that nicotine is a drug that affects the structure or function of the body under § 321(g)(1)(C) and that cigarettes and smokeless tobacco were therefore drug/device combinations falling under the FDA's regulatory purview, even absent therapeutic claims. See 61 Fed.Reg. at 44,397, 44,400.

In *FDA v. Brown & Williamson,* the Supreme Court rejected the FDA's claimed FDCA authority to regulate tobacco products as customarily marketed. Looking to the FDCA's "overall regulatory scheme," the "tobacco-specific legislation" enacted since the FDCA, and the FDA's own frequently asserted position, it held that Congress had "ratified ... the FDA's plain and resolute position that the FDCA gives the agency no authority to regulate tobacco products as customarily marketed." 529 U.S. at 126, 159, 120 S.Ct. 1291. *** To fill the regulatory gap identified in *Brown & Williamson,* Congress in 2009 passed the Tobacco Act, Pub.L. No. 111-31, 123 Stat. 1776, 21 U.S.C. §§ 387 *et seq.,* providing the FDA with authority to regulate tobacco products. The act defines tobacco products so as to include all consumption products derived from tobacco *except* articles that qualify as drugs, devices, or drug-device combinations under the FDCA:

> (rr)(1) The term "tobacco product" means any product made or derived from tobacco that is intended for human consumption, including any component, part, or accessory of a tobacco product.
>
> (2) The term "tobacco product" does not mean an article that is a drug under [the FDCA's drug provision], a device under [the FDCA's device provision], or a combination product described in [the FDCA's combination product provision]. 21 U.S.C. § 321(rr).

The Tobacco Act itself states that it does not "affect, expand, or limit" the FDA's jurisdiction to regulate products under the drug/device provisions of the FDCA, 21 U.S.C. § 387a(c)(1), and the district court and parties themselves appear to agree that the Tobacco Act did not expand the category of drugs, devices, and combination products subject to FDCA jurisdiction in the wake of *Brown & Williamson.* See Mem. Op. 9 n. 4. The question before us, therefore, is whether the FDA can regulate electronic cigarettes under the FDCA's drug/device provisions or whether it can regulate them only under the Tobacco Act's provisions.

In *Brown & Williamson* the Supreme Court addressed the FDA's regulation of cigarettes and smokeless tobacco products under the FDCA. It began by noting that the FDCA seeks to ensure that the FDA will approve products only if they are safe and effective for their intended use. 529 U.S. at 133, 120 S.Ct. 1291. Yet the FDA had itself found that tobacco products are "unsafe," "dangerous," and "cause great pain and suffering from illness." *Id.* at 134, 120 S.Ct. 1291 (quoting 61 Fed.Reg. 44,412). If tobacco products were drug/device combinations under the FDCA, the FDA would have no choice but to ban them. *Id.* at 135, 120 S.Ct. 1291. ***

For our purposes, the central question is whether *Brown & Williamson*'s reading of the FDA's authority under the drug/device provisions of the FDCA applies only to tobacco products for which Congress has passed specific regulatory statutes or whether it extends to all tobacco products as customarily marketed. The FDA argues that *Brown & Williamson* takes a statute-specific approach, excluding the FDA from regulating only those tobacco products that at the time of *Brown & Williamson* had been the subject of specific federal legislation. FDA Br. at 14. Though *Brown & Williamson* is not crystal clear, we think the better reading is that the FDA lacks FDCA drug/device authority to regulate all tobacco products marketed without claims of therapeutic effect, i.e., as customarily marketed. ***

Brown & Williamson concentrated overwhelmingly on the unifying theme of historic FDA policy towards tobacco products—a policy that it saw as undifferentiated except with regard to the presence or absence of claims of therapeutic effect. See, e.g., *id.* at 145, 120 S.Ct. 1291 ("[T]obacco marketed for chewing or smoking without accompanying therapeutic claims, does not meet the definitions in the Food, Drug, and Cosmetic Act ..." (citing Letter to Directors of Bureaus, Divisions and Directors of Districts from FDA Bureau of Enforcement (May 24, 1963))); *id.* at 146, 120 S.Ct. 1291 ("In the 73 years since the enactment of the original Food and Drug Act, and in the 41 years since the promulgation of the modern Food, Drug, and Cosmetic Act, the FDA has repeatedly informed Congress that cigarettes are beyond the scope of the statute absent health claims establishing a therapeutic intent on behalf of the manufacturer or vendor" (citing Brief for Appellee (FDA) in *Action on Smoking and Health v. Harris,* 655 F.2d 236 (D.C.Cir.1980))); *id.* at 146, 120 S.Ct. 1291 (noting that the FDA's predecessor agency, the Bureau of Chemistry, stated it lacked authority to regulate tobacco products absent therapeutic claims); *id.* at 155, 120 S.Ct. 1291 (quoting the FDA's General Counsel as defining regulatory scope over tobacco products based on therapeutic purpose); *id.* at 158, 120 S.Ct. 1291 (citing the FDA Deputy Commissioner stating that FDA's jurisdiction was limited to tobacco products bearing "drug claims"); *id.* at 158, 120 S.Ct. 1291 (citing the Commissioner of the FDA stating that FDA's jurisdiction was limited to tobacco products bearing "health claims"). ***

Brown & Williamson therefore did not preclude the FDA from regulating only those products for which Congress had passed specific statutes. Rather, it recognized that Congress had consciously developed a statutory scheme for tobacco and health that distinguished tobacco products as customarily marketed from ones marketed for therapeutic purposes. "Thus, what Congress ratified was the FDA's plain and resolute position that the FDCA gives the agency no authority to regulate tobacco products as customarily marketed." *Id.* at 159, 120 S.Ct. 1291.

The Tobacco Act is wholly consistent with this reading of *Brown & Williamson.* Written to address the regulatory gap that the case identified, the Tobacco Act provides the FDA with regulatory authority over tobacco products without requiring therapeutic claims. Besides leaving the FDA's authority under the drug/device provisions of the FDCA undisturbed, see 21 U.S.C. § 321(rr)(2) & § 387a(c)(1), the act broadly defines tobacco products as extending to "*any* product made *or derived from* tobacco," 21 U.S.C. § 321(rr)(1) (emphasis added). To be sure, this definition could align with a variety of interpretations of *Brown & Williamson's* scope (including the one FDA proffers here), but our reading is squarely within that range. ***

In fact the Tobacco Act gives the FDA broad regulatory authority over tobacco products, including, for instance, authority to impose restrictions on their sale, and on the advertising and promotion of such products, see 21 U.S.C. § 387f(d), to regulate the mode of manufacture of tobacco products, see *id.* § 387f(e), and to establish standards for tobacco products, see *id.* § 387g. To the extent that Congress believed *Brown & Williamson* left an insufficiently regulative environment for cigarettes, smokeless tobacco, cigars, and other tobacco products, it found the Tobacco Act an adequate remedy. Together, *Brown & Williamson* and the Tobacco Act establish that the FDA cannot regulate customarily marketed tobacco products under the FDCA's drug/device provisions, that it can regulate tobacco products marketed for therapeutic purposes under those provisions, and that it can regulate customarily marketed tobacco products under the Tobacco Act. ***

We also find that the district court did not abuse its discretion in finding that the balance of harms tips toward NJOY. *** More significantly, the court rightly found that the FDA has authority under the Tobacco Act to regulate electronic cigarettes, enabling it to mitigate or perhaps extinguish any harm to public health. *Id.* at 31. Given the likelihood of NJOY's success on the merits, the irreparable harm to NJOY's business, and the FDA's unquestioned Tobacco Act authority to mitigate any public harm, the district court did not abuse its discretion in granting the preliminary injunction.

As we have already noted, the FDA has authority to regulate customarily marketed tobacco products including e-cigarettes-under the Tobacco Act. It has authority to regulate therapeutically marketed tobacco products under the FDCA's drug/device provisions. And, as this decision is limited to tobacco products, it does not affect the FDA's ability to regulate other products under the "structure or any function" prong defining drugs and devices in 21 U.S.C. § 321(g) and (h), as to the scope of which—tobacco products aside—we express no opinion. Of course, in the event that Congress prefers that the FDA regulate e-cigarettes under the FDCA's drug/device provisions, it can always so decree. The judgment of the district court is *Affirmed.*

GARLAND, Circuit Judge, concurring in the judgment—Although I join my colleagues in the disposition of this case, I do so based on different reasoning. I do not read *FDA v. Brown & Williamson,* 529 U.S. 120, 120 S.Ct. 1291, 146 L.Ed.2d 121 (2000), as barring the FDA from regulating "electronic cigarettes" under the Food, Drug, and Cosmetic Act (FDCA), 21 U.S.C. § 301 *et seq.,* because I do not believe the Supreme Court intended its use of the term "tobacco products" to extend to products that do not contain tobacco. The Tobacco Control Act of 2009, Pub.L. No. 111-31, 123 Stat. 1776, however, expressly extends to products that are merely "derived from" tobacco. Accordingly, at least in the absence of a contrary agency interpretation entitled to *Chevron* deference, I read the Tobacco Control Act as requiring the FDA to regulate products like electronic cigarettes under that Act, rather than under the FDCA. *** In sum, I see nothing in the words, context, or rationale of *Brown & Williamson* that supports interpreting that case as barring the FDA from regulating electronic cigarettes under the drug/device provisions of the FDCA. *** In the absence of an authoritative agency interpretation, I conclude that, unless a product derived from tobacco is marketed for therapeutic purposes, the FDA may regulate it only under the provisions of the Tobacco Control Act. *** What the result would be were the FDA to offer a contrary statutory interpretation in the form of a regulation, I leave for the day the agency decides to take that step.

CRITICAL ANALYSIS—Product classification remains an important focus across the board for all FDA regulated products. *Soterra* demonstrates that principle. Do you agree with the analysis by the court in *Soterra*? Include a discussion about therapeutic use and the bright line approach used by the court. Does the deeming rule settle this classification issue?
http://1.usa.gov/1WbltVX

E-Cigarettes and Additional Tobacco Products —*Soterra* Impetus

In 2014, FDA issued proposed a proposed rule for e-cigarettes and cigars that was finalized on May 10, 2016 (81 FR 28973). Prior to that, FDA issued correspondence in 2011, which set forth the stance of FDA. Excerpts of the 2011 FDA correspondence follow (edited).

The purpose of this letter is to provide stakeholders and the public with information, in light of a recent court decision, regarding the regulation of products made or derived from tobacco. The Family Smoking Prevention and Tobacco Control Act of 2009 (Tobacco Control Act), which amends *the Federal Food, Drug, and Cosmetic Act (FD&C Act), was enacted on June 22, 2009, and it provides the Food and Drug Administration (FDA) with authority to regulate "tobacco products." The FD&C Act, as amended by the Tobacco Control Act, defines the term "tobacco product," in part, as any product "made or derived from tobacco" that is not a "drug," "device," or combination product under the FD&C Act. *** Between 2008 and 2010, the FDA determined that certain electronic cigarettes (e-cigarettes) were unapproved drug/device combination products and detained and/or refused admission to those offered for import by Sottera, Inc. and other manufacturers. *** The court held that e-cigarettes and other products made or derived from tobacco can be regulated as "tobacco products" under the Act and are not drugs/devices unless they are marketed for therapeutic purposes. Moreover, Chapter IX of the FDCA subjects "tobacco products" to general controls, such as registration, product listing, ingredient listing, good manufacturing practice requirements, user fees for certain products, and adulteration and misbranding provisions. Chapter IX also subjects "new tobacco products" (i.e., products that are first marketed or modified after February 15, 2007) and "modified risk tobacco products" (i.e., products that are "sold or distributed for use to reduce harm or the risk of tobacco-related disease associated with commercially marketed tobacco products") to premarket review. Although the statute places certain "tobacco products" immediately under the general controls and premarket review requirements in Chapter IX (i.e., cigarettes, cigarette tobacco, roll-your-own tobacco, and smokeless tobacco), it also permits FDA, by regulation, to extend those controls to other categories of "tobacco products." FDA has taken the following steps to ensure that appropriate regulatory mechanisms govern all "tobacco products" and all other products made or derived from tobacco after the Sottera decision:*

- *Proposed rule (Issued final rule May 10, 2016 below) (81 FR 28973) extending the FDA's "tobacco product" to other categories of tobacco products that meet the statutory definition of "tobacco product" in Section 201(rr) of the Act. The additional tobacco categories are subject to general controls, such as registration, product listing, ingredient listing, good manufacturing practices, user fees, and the adulteration and misbranding provisions, as well as to the premarket review requirements for "new tobacco products" and "modified risk tobacco products."*

- *The Sottera decision states that products made or derived from tobacco can be regulated under the Tobacco Control Act unless they are "marketed for therapeutic purposes," in which case they are regulated as drugs and/or devices.*

- *Section 201(rr)(4) of the Tobacco Control Act prohibits the marketing of "tobacco products" in combination with other FDA-regulated products.*

- *A "tobacco product" that is not "grandfathered" is considered a "new" tobacco product, and it is adulterated and misbranded under the FD&C Act, and therefore, subject to enforcement action, unless it has received premarket authorization or been found substantially equivalent http://www.fda.gov/newsevents/publichealthfocus/ucm252360.htm (April 25, 2011).*

"Deeming Rule"—Extension of FDA Authority

Deeming Tobacco Products to be Subject to the Federal Food, Drug, and Cosmetic Act, as Amended by the Family Smoking Prevention and Tobacco Control Act; Regulations on the Sale and Distribution of Tobacco Products and Required Warning Statements for Tobacco Products
https://www.federalregister.gov/articles/2016/05/10/2016-10685/deeming-tobacco-products-to-be-subject-to-the-federal-food-drug-and-cosmetic-act-as-amended-by-the

FDA issued a final rule on May 10, 2016 (rule proposed April 25, 2014, 79 FR 23142-0) that extended the agency's authority to cover additional tobacco products. See: 21 U.S.C. 387 through 387u; Pub. L. 111-31, 123 Stat. 1776. FDA previously only regulated cigarettes, cigarette tobacco, roll-your-own tobacco, and smokeless tobacco. Deemed products are those that are now "deemed" to be subject to FDA regulation that meet the definition of a tobacco product. This includes products, such as:

Electronic Nicotine Delivery Systems (ENDS) (including e-cigarettes e-cigars, e-hookah, vape pens, advanced refillable personal vaporizers), Cigars, Pipe tobacco, Nicotine gels, and Dissolvables not already regulated under the FDA's authority.

FDA regulates the manufacture, import, packaging, labeling, advertising, promotion, sale, and distribution of ENDS, including components and parts of ENDS; however, accessories are excluded. Examples of components and parts of ENDS include:

E-liquids, A glass or plastic vial container of e-liquid, Cartridges, Atomizers, Certain batteries, Cartomizers and clearomizers, Digital display or lights to adjust settings, Tank systems, Drip tips, Flavorings for ENDS, and Programmable software.

Under the final rule, manufacturers of deemed tobacco products need to:

➢ Register manufacturing establishments and providing product listings to the FDA;

➢ Report ingredients, and harmful and potentially harmful constituents;

➢ Require premarket review and authorization of new tobacco products by the FDA;

➢ Place health warnings on product packages (see below for cigar warning statements) and advertisements; and

➢ Not sell modified risk tobacco products (including those described as "light," "low," or "mild") unless authorized by the FDA.

In addition, there are several provisions aimed at restricting youth access to tobacco products, including:

✓ Not allowing products to be sold to persons under the age of 18 years (both in-person and online); *

✓ Requiring age verification by photo ID;

✓ Not allowing the selling of tobacco products in vending machines (unless in an adult-only facility); and

✓ Not allowing the distribution of free samples.

Youth Epidemic and FDA Initiatives

The increased use of Electronic Nicotine Delivery Systems (ENDS) such as e-cigarettes by youth has escalated. The FDA and the Centers for Disease Control and Prevention data from the 2018 National Youth Tobacco Survey (NYTS) indicate a significant increase in use of e-cigarettes and other ENDS by youth. For example, from 2017 to 2018, there was a 78 percent increase in current e-cigarette use among high school students and a 48 percent increase among middle school students. The total number of youths including middle and high school students that use e-cigarettes increased to 3.6 million. Suffice it to state, the FDA mandate is that of public health and specific to prevention of youth tobacco addiction. FDA's Comprehensive Plan for Tobacco and Nicotine Regulation issued in 2017 focused on youth tobacco and nicotine prevention. The Youth Prevention Plan purpose is threefold:

✓ Preventing youth **access** to tobacco products;

✓ Curbing **marketing** of tobacco products aimed at youth; and

✓ **Educating** teens about the dangers of using any tobacco product, including e-cigarettes, as well as educating retailers about their key role in protecting youth.

FDA Commissioner Gottlieb issued statements about the youth epidemic of e-cigarettes and a *Youth Tobacco Prevention Plan* was released in 2018. In this realm, enforcement has increased and for example, FDA issued 55 warning letters to tobacco retailers for selling tobacco products, such as e-cigarettes, e-liquids and cigars to minors (see links below). FDA and FTC have joint coordination concerning the promotion of e-liquids that resemble candies, cookies and juice boxes. Further a hearing was held in December 2018 to discuss efforts to eliminate youth e-cigarette use with a focus on the potential role of drug therapies to support cessation. Finally, implementation procedures were announced by FDA Commissioner Gottlieb in 2018 to restrict access of flavored products (except mint, menthol and tobacco flavors) to youth both at retail establishments and online.

See link to Nicotine Regulation
https://www.fda.gov/TobaccoProducts/PublicHealthEducation/ProtectingKidsfromTobacco/ucm608433.htm
See link below to: Statement from FDA Commissioner Scott Gottlieb, M.D., on proposed new steps to protect youth by preventing access to flavored tobacco products and banning menthol in cigarettes
https://www.fda.gov/NewsEvents/Newsroom/PressAnnouncements/ucm625884.htm

Warning letter links below.
https://www.fda.gov/NewsEvents/Newsroom/PressAnnouncements/ucm605507.htm
https://www.fda.gov/NewsEvents/Newsroom/PressAnnouncements/ucm620185.htm
See also, Shelia Kaplan, *FDA Says E-Cigarette Crackdown is Working*, N.Y. Times A16 (Aug. 24, 2018).
NOTE: See *Regulation of Flavors in Tobacco Products* (Advanced Notice of Rulemaking) 83 FR 12294 (March 21, 2018). Data regarding use of menthol cigarettes and non-cigarette tobacco products among youth indicate widespread appeal of flavored tobacco products.

CRITICAL ANALYSIS: Discuss the promotion of e-cigarettes and to minors and the FDA crackdown. *https://www.fda.gov/NewsEvents/Newsroom/PressAnnouncements/ucm620185.htm*
https://www.drugabuse.gov/publications/drugfacts/electronic-cigarettes-e-cigarettes
https://www.fda.gov/NewsEvents/Newsroom/PressAnnouncements/ucm625884.htm

Tobacco Intended Use Rule

FDA issued a Final Rule (82 Fed. Reg. 2193 (Jan. 9, 2017)) titled: *Clarification of When Products Made or Derived from Tobacco Are Regulated as Drugs, Devices, or Combination Products; Amendments to Regulations Regarding "Intended Uses."* Effective date of February 8, 2017 was extended to March 19, 2018 then indefinitely delayed the portion of the rule due to controversy (industry citizen petition filed) as to "totality of the evidence" approach to assessing intended use and off-label use. That is, the portion of the final rule that regulates how manufacturers discuss off-label uses of their products is on hold; however, the other aspects of the rule, which describes the circumstances in which a product derived from tobacco will be subject to regulation as a drug, device, or a combination product, became effective on March 19, 2018. The rule became controversial due to the implications for pharmaceutical and device promotion. The rule purported to apply to tobacco; however, it also proposed to amend FDA's definition of intended use found in 21 CFR Sections 201.128 and 801.4 "the knowledge" clause. Under the clause, FDA is not only able to regulate products based on their intended uses, but on their actual uses based on whether a manufacturer "knows or has knowledge of facts that would give him notice, that a drug or device introduced into interstate commerce ... is to be used for conditions, purposes, or uses other than the ones for which he offers it." However, in the final rule released, FDA amended the knowledge clause to read:

> **"And if the *totality of the evidence* establishes that a manufacturer objectively intends that a drug introduced into interstate commerce by him is to be used for conditions, purposes, or uses other than ones for which it is approved (if any), he is required, in accordance with section 502(f) of the Federal Food, Drug, and Cosmetic Act, or, as applicable, duly promulgated regulations exempting the drug from the requirements of section 502(f)(1), to provide for such drug adequate labeling that accords with such other intended uses." (italics added).**

https://www.federalregister.gov/documents/2017/01/09/2016-31950/clarification-of-when-products-made-or-derived-from-tobacco-are-regulated-as-drugs-devices-or
https://www.gpo.gov/fdsys/pkg/FR-2017-01-09/pdf/2016-31950.pdf

CRITICAL ANALYSIS: Intended use has major implications as noted in the "totality of evidence" standard. Why was that portion of the rule indefinitely placed "on hold"?

Submission of Warning Plans for Cigars

http://www.fda.gov/downloads/TobaccoProducts/Labeling/RulesRegulationsGuidance/UCM517682.pdf (2016)
Packages. [I]t will be unlawful for any person to manufacture, package, sell, offer to sell, distribute, or import for sale or distribution within the United States any cigar unless the product package bears one of the following required warning statements listed in § 1143.5(a):
 WARNING: This product contains nicotine. Nicotine is an addictive chemical.
 WARNING: Cigar smoking can cause cancers of the mouth and throat, even if you do not inhale.

WARNING: Cigar smoking can cause lung cancer and heart disease.
WARNING: Cigars are not a safe alternative to cigarettes.
WARNING: Tobacco smoke increases the risk of lung cancer and heart disease, even in nonsmokers.
WARNING: Cigar use while pregnant can harm you and your baby. Or
SURGEON GENERAL WARNING: Tobacco Use Increases the Risk of Infertility, Stillbirth and Low Birth Weight.

As an optional alternative to the FDA warning, FDA is permitting the use of the reproductive health warning statement as required by the Federal Trade Commission (FTC) consent decrees to the FDA warning, **"WARNING: Cigar use while pregnant can harm you and your baby."**

In certain situations described in § 1143.5(a)(4), retailers of cigars are exempt from this requirement. The retailer will not be in violation of this section for cigar packaging that:
(1) contains a health warning; (2) is supplied to the retailer by the tobacco product manufacturer, importer, or distributor who has the required state, local, or Alcohol and Tobacco Tax and Trade Bureau (TTB)-issued license or permit, if applicable; and (3) is not altered by the retailer in a way that is material to the requirements of § 1143.5(a)(§ 1143.5(a)(4)). However, a retailer must still comply with other applicable requirements relating to cigars, including those in part 1143.

Cigars that are sold individually, without any packaging, are exempt from the packaging requirements. In this circumstance, retailers must post a warning sign that lists all six of the required warning statements at the point-of-sale, in accordance with the requirements set forth in § 1143.5(a)(3). Retailers of cigars sold individually and not in product packaging are not required to submit a warning plan for warnings on packages, because the warning signs posted at the retailer's point-of-sale will include all six warnings applicable to cigars. Cigar retailers are responsible for creating and posting these signs in accordance with § 1143.5(a)(3)(i)-(iv).

Advertisements [I]t will be unlawful for any cigar manufacturer, packager, importer, distributor, or retailer to advertise or cause to be advertised within the United States any cigar unless the advertising bears one of the required warning statements, in accordance with an FDA-approved warning plan (§ 1143.5(b)(1) and (b)(2)). Specifically, the warning statement requirements for advertisements outlined in § 1143.5(b) apply to a retailer only if that retailer is responsible for or directs the required warning statements. However, this does not relieve a retailer of liability if the retailer displays, in a public location, an advertisement that does not contain a health warning or contains an altered health warning by the retailer in a way that is material to the requirements of § 1143.5.

NOTE: *Cigar and Pipe Warnings*—effective date of August 10, 2018 delayed due to an injunction issued which blocked the U.S. Food and Drug Administration from enforcing health warning label requirements for cigars and pipe tobacco. See: *Cigar Association of America, et al*, v. *U.S. Food and Drug Administration*, et al, U.S. District Court for the District of Columbia, No. 16-cv-01460.

***Therapeutic Products*—marketed for therapeutic purposes will continue to be regulated as medical products under the FDA's existing drug and device authorities under the FDCA.**

CRITICAL ANALYSIS: How does the deeming rule regulate ENDS such as e-cigarettes and other tobacco products noted above in conformity with the FDA public health and population standard? Include a discussion about cigars, pipe tobacco, nicotine gels, and waterpipes (or hookah) and dissolvables. See final rule above and links. *http://www.fda.gov/TobaccoProducts/Labeling/ucm388395.htm*
http://1.usa.gov/1WbltVX

VOLUME XII

Volume XII: Politics, Globalization, Foreign Corrupt Practices, Product Classification, Professionalism and the Future

Today the popular term is civility and a lack thereof. Civility, professionalism, accountability and "corporate governance" remain critical for public trust. Cross cutting topics and special issues are detailed in this volume. Over the years, controversy has existed regarding FDA decision-making and referred to as "politically charged" and "morality" based determinations. The Plan B decision provides an excellent illustration of this issue. That decision still advances the question of whether FDA is truly a science based agency. Another issue is that of the revolving door impact on post employment. FDA has post employment restrictions and there is a statutory application to former employees including what is termed "a cooling off" period.

Product classification is a key topic throughout this volume. The intended use rule for tobacco discussed in Volume XI, is an excellent example of the complications of product classification. Legal decisions have illustrated that intended use controls in determining product category. That is, the historical decisions of Line Away and Sudden Beauty still provide judicial guidance for regulatory purposes about whether the product is a food, drug, personal care cosmetic product, medical device, dietary supplement or combination product. The question remains whether product categorization should be revisited with a possible amendment of the Food, Drug and Cosmetic Act.

The Food, Drug and Cosmetic Act expressly details that FDA cannot regulate the practice of medicine. This exact issue arose in the case of Regenerative Medicine, LLC. The Court of Appeals settled that the product in question in Regenerative Medicine was a drug/biologic. The court rejected the practice of medicine argument set forth by Regenerative Medicine.

Counterterrorism remains in the forefront and globalization plays a key role in the regulation of food, drugs, cosmetics, medical devices and biologics. This chapter highlights FDA's role outside of the United States to protect the United States public health from unsafe imported products. Jurisdiction or the authority of FDA to regulate remains imperative. Further the impact of the Foreign Corrupt Practices Act is detailed.

What does the future hold in terms of food and drug regulation? How should FDA regulate tobacco products, food, human and veterinary drugs, biologics, medical devices, personal care cosmetic products and dietary supplements? Think about how the regulation of tobacco products fits in the scheme of traditional FDA regulation. Consider how societal mores and culture impact on regulation. The answer is multifaceted and complex. The major focus necessitates a public protection stance to uphold the tenets of the Federal Food, Drug and Cosmetic Act. Finally, the volume concludes with professional practice pointers.

Chapter 1: Science, Politics and Morality

Intense debate and controversy have escalated in terms of FDA decision-making. By way of illustration, the "Plan B" decision discussed below evidences both "political charged" and "morality" based determinations. Further, in 2009, former President Obama issued a presidential memorandum and a stem cell executive order to the White House Office of Science and Technology Policy to create a plan for restoring scientific integrity to government decision-making.

Yet, in many respects, the issue that FDA must ponder is whether the FDCA evidences societal and moral tones. For example, balancing the risks and benefits to patients in determining the safety of an FDA regulated product has social implications. Additionally, 21 C.F.R section 19.6 pertains to a Code of Ethics for Government Service. The issue centers on the scope of FDA discretion concerning ethical issues that raise moral questions such as the controversy surrounding "Plan B". Perhaps the demarcation and bright line approach is when FDA goes beyond what is stipulated in the FDCA and its public health protection mission.

CRITICAL ANALYSIS: What is FDA's role in public protection as mandated by the FDCA? Should FDA balance science with considerations such as economics, ethics, and morality? How does politics factor in FDA decision making?

Stem Cell Research

Executive Order Challenged

Former President Obama signed an executive order to lift restrictions on embryonic stem cell research which effectively revoked a policy by former President George W. Bush's administration that proscribed the use of public funds for research using embryonic stem cells created after Aug. 9, 2001. The executive order (March 9, 2009) directed NIH to review and issue within 120 days new guidance on stem cell research consistent with the policies of the administration. In so doing, this increased the National Institutes of Health funding for stem cell research and greater access to additional embryonic stem cell lines. Divergent views exist regarding stem cell research. For example, "Research!America", the International Society for Stem Cell Research and the Association of American Medical Colleges applauded the decision to lift the ban on stem cell research by former President Bush. Conversely, there are those who believe that stem cell research is morally wrong. For example, former Senator Sam Brownback (R-Kan.) stated: "The Administration's policy change does not answer the central question—Do human embryos, which are clearly alive, constitute a life or mere property?" Some religious groups vehemently oppose stem cell research.

The United States District Court for the District of Columbia issued a preliminary injunction in 2010 that prevented use of federal funding of research on human embryonic stem cells (hESC). The District Court determined that the two scientists who conduct research using adult and pluripotent stem cells met the standard for issuing a preliminary injunction and would likely succeed on the merits of their claim. Their claim was based on the Dickey-Wicker Amendment Pub. L. No. 104-99, §128, 110 Stat. 26, 34 (1996), which prohibits all federal funding of hESC research on cell lines not in existence before passage of the amendment. The United States Court of Appeals for the District of Columbia Circuit lifted the preliminary injunction, which meant that the National Institutes of Health could continue funding this research pending appeal. *Sherley v. Sebelius*, 644 F. 3d 388 D.C. Cir. No.10-5287 (April 29, 2011). See e.g. *Sherley v. Sebelius* 689 F.3d 776 No. 11–5241 (Aug. 24, 2012), Cert. Denied, 133 S. Ct. 847, 184 L. Ed. 2d 655, (2013).

NOTE: See Roseann B. Termini, *Does Political Science Exist Anymore? Embryonic Stem Cell Research in the New Political Era*, 5 J. Health & Biomedical L. 249 (2009).

CRITICAL ANALYSIS: Evaluate the impact of funding resistance due to lobbying and politics for controversial issues such as embryonic stem cell research. Include examples.

Practice of Medicine or Drug/Biologic—*Regenerative Sciences LLC*
United States v. Regenerative Sciences LLC

Regenerative Sciences, LLC vigorously defended its position that FDA could not regulate the practice of medicine in its Regenexx™ treatment or Regenexx-C™ cultured treatment which uses Mesenchymal adult stem cells (MSCs) that originate primarily from bone marrow. The majority of shareholders of Regenerative Sciences, LLC are physicians and the company promotes the Regen-exx™ treatment as a "non-surgical" treatment option for joint or bone pain in the hip, knee, shoulder, back or ankle as well as non-union fractures. The dispute with FDA has been ongoing since at least 2008 when FDA sent correspondence to Regenerative Sciences depicting the cell treatment as a drug or biologic. FDA conducted an inspection and found violations of current Good Manufacturing Practices (cGMPs). Thereafter Regenerative Sciences filed an injunction to prevent FDA from regulating the product as a drug. However, the court dismissed the matter as FDA had not yet taken regulatory action.

Subsequently, the district court granted FDA the motion for summary judgment and issued a permanent injunction against the use of the Regenexx procedure and deemed the product a biologic/drug. Further, the court opined that this did not fall within the "practice of medicine" argument advanced by Regenerative Sciences LLC. Another argument advanced by Regenerative Sciences was that the product was exempt from FDA approval because it was a compounded product and further it was a minimally manipulated product. The court rejected this argument as well advanced by Regenerative Sciences. *United States v. Regenerative Sciences, LLC*, 878 F. Supp. 2d 248 (D.D.C. 2012). The court of appeals determined that FDA had the authority to regulate the product and affirmed the district court's judgment and the permanent injunction it entered. (Feb. 4, 2014 No. 12-5254, 741 F.3d 1314 (D.C. Cir. 2014) See: *https://www.regenexx.com* and *http://fortipublications.com/blog/*

NOTE: See *Volume V: Human Drugs* and *Volume VI Biologics.*

CRITICAL ANALYSIS: Do you agree with the determination by the court that the product is properly regulated as a drug (see 21 U.S. C. Sec. 321 (g)(1)(D) and biologic (42 U.S. C. Sec. 262(i) and does not fall under the "Practice of Medicine"? Include safety and efficacy considerations as well as a discussion about innovative therapies.

Plan B and Plan B One-Step—*Tummino I and II*

Tummino v. Torti (Tummino I)—For years, FDA resisted the recommendation to approve Plan B (two pill), an oral contraceptive prescription drug, as an over-the-counter or OTC product. Eventually, Plan B was approved for OTC status for females 18 and over. However, In *Tummino v. Torti,* (*Tummino* I) the plaintiffs challenged FDA's denial of OTC status for women of all ages. Years of litigation ensued. Finally, in 2009, the U.S. District Court (E. D. New York) ordered FDA to permit the manufacturer of Plan B to make the emergency contraceptive available to 17-year-old females without a prescription within 30 days of the Order. In the opinion, Judge Korman ordered FDA to reconsider whether minors under the age of 17 also should be permitted nonprescription access to Plan B. Politics played a key role as Judge Korman noted that "political considerations, delays, and implausible justifications for decision-making" were "not the only evidence of a lack of good faith and reasoned agency decision-making" in the Plan B matter.

Tummino v. Hamburg (Tummino II)—Secretary of Health and Human Services, Kathleen Sebelius, in December 2011, overruled the FDA's decision that would have permitted over-the-counter sales to females under 17 for Plan B-One Step, a contraceptive "One-pill" product that helps prevent pregnancy after sexual intercourse. Further, there was restricted access; that is, pharmacies could not place the pills on public shelves.

This was the first time a cabinet member had ever publicly annulled an FDA decision. The issue is not whether politics played a role. Rather, the decision reveals the extent to which politics influences decision making. Perhaps this is just a cautionary tale of viewing the entire landscape of more than science. Yet, how do these types of decisions undermine the expertise of FDA?

In early April 2013, Judge Korman in *Tummino v. Hamburg et al.* (April 2013) ruled against FDA and determined that over the counter access to both Plan B (Two-pill) and Plan B One-Step (One-pill) should be made accessible and available without age restrictions. Additionally, Judge Korman set forth that if FDA found a difference between Plan B (Two-pill) and Plan B One-Step (One-pill), then the agency could limit its over-the-counter approval to the One-pill product. Ultimately, FDA acquiesced, and Plan B One-Step was provided over-the-counter access without age or point-of-sale restrictions. Plan B (Two pill) has over the counter access for those 17 and older and requires a prescription for those younger than 17. Plan B One-Step is available as the Plan B two pill was discontinued. *Tummino v. Hamburg (Tummino* II) (Plan B One-Step One-pill) follows *Tummino v. Torti* (Plan B Two-pill).

Tummino v. Torti,
603 F.Supp.2d 519 (E. D. NY 2009)

KORMAN, J.: Plan B is an emergency contraceptive that can be used to reduce the risk of unwanted pregnancy after sexual intercourse. When used as directed, it can reduce the risk of pregnancy by up to 89 percent. Plan B acts mainly by stopping the release of an egg from an ovary. It may also prevent sperm from fertilizing an egg that has been released or, if fertilization has already occurred, block implantation of the resulting embryo in the uterus. Plan B does not have any known serious or long-term side effects, though it may have some mild and short-term side effects, such as nausea or abdominal pain, in some users. The approved dosage of Plan B is two pills taken 12 hours apart, each containing 0.75 mg of levonorgestrel, a synthetic hormone similar to the naturally occurring hormone progesterone. Because the drug works best when taken within 24 hours of sexual intercourse, it is commonly referred to as a "morning-after pill." Nevertheless, the drug is effective if the first dose is taken within 72 hours of sexual intercourse.

Studies have shown that Plan B is equally effective if the two doses of levonorgestrel are taken less than 12 hours apart or at the same time. Plan B was approved for prescription-only use in the United States in 1999. Plan B and other emergency contraceptives with the same active ingredient are available without a prescription or age restriction in much of the world, including virtually all major industrialized nations. Plaintiffs [are] individuals and organizations advocating wider distribution of and access to emergency contraceptives, as well as parents and their minor children brought this action challenging the denial of a Citizen Petition, which requested that the Food and Drug Administration ("FDA") make Plan B available without a prescription to women of all ages.

The FDA considered the Citizen Petition in tandem with a number of proposals—referred to as supplemental new drug applications ("SNDA")—submitted by Women's Capital Corporation, the drug's original manufacturer. Women's Capital Corporation sold its right to market Plan B to Barr Pharmaceuticals, Inc. during the course of the proceedings described below. *** The first SNDA, like the Citizen Petition, sought non-prescription access to Plan B for women of all ages. After the FDA denied such access, the Plan B sponsor submitted a second SNDA, seeking non-prescription access for women 16 and older. The FDA rejected that application too despite nearly uniform agreement among FDA scientific review staff that women of all ages could use Plan B without a prescription safely and effectively. The Plan B sponsor then submitted a third SNDA, which proposed making Plan B available without a prescription to women 17 and older. *** The FDA repeatedly and unreasonably delayed issuing a decision on Plan B for suspect reasons and, on two occasions, only took action on Plan B to facilitate confirmation of Acting FDA Commissioners, whose confirmation hearings had been held up due to these repeated delays. The first occasion involved the confirmation of then-Acting FDA Commissioner Lester M. Crawford, who froze the review process for seven months in 2005. In order to overcome a hold that had been placed on his nomination by two Senators, the Secretary of Health and Human Services promised that the FDA would act on Plan B by September 2005. After Dr. Crawford was confirmed by the Senate in July

2005, however, he reneged on the promise and, instead, delayed action another eleven months to pursue, and then abandon, a rulemaking with respect to Plan B. There is also evidence that when the FDA finally decided to approve non-prescription use of Plan B for women 18 and older, it did so to facilitate the confirmation of Commissioner Crawford's successor, then-Acting FDA Commissioner Andrew C. von Eschenbach, whose confirmation certain Senators had vowed to block because of the continued delays on Plan B.

These political considerations, delays, and implausible justifications for decision-making are not the only evidence of a lack of good faith and reasoned agency decision-making. Indeed, the record is clear that the FDA's course of conduct regarding Plan B departed in significant ways from the agency's normal procedures regarding similar applications to switch a drug product from prescription to non-prescription use, referred to as a "switch application" or an "over-the-counter switch." For example, FDA upper management, including the Commissioner, wrested control over the decision-making on Plan B from staff that normally would issue the final decision on an over-the-counter switch application; the FDA's denial of non-prescription access without age restriction went against the recommendation of a committee of experts it had empanelled to advise it on Plan B. In light of this evidence, the FDA's denial of the Citizen Petition is vacated and the matter is remanded to the FDA for reconsideration of whether to approve Plan B for over-the-counter status without age or point-of-sale restrictions. While the FDA is free, on remand, to exercise its expertise and discretion regarding the proper disposition of the Citizen Petition, no useful purpose would be served by continuing to deprive 17 year olds access to Plan B without a prescription. Indeed, the record shows that FDA officials and staff both agreed that 17 years olds can use Plan B safely without a prescription. ***

I. Background
A. Statutory and Regulatory Background
*** There are two means by which the FDA can switch a prescription-only drug to nonprescription status. First, it can promulgate a regulation changing the drug's status. See 21 U.S.C. § 353(b)(3). This rulemaking process may be initiated by the Commissioner, 21 C.F.R. § 310.200(b), or by any interested person who files a citizen petition. Id. § 10.25(a). Within 180 days of receipt of the petition, the Commissioner must either approve or deny the petition or provide "a tentative response [to the petitioner], indicating why the agency has been unable to reach a decision on the petition." Id. § 10.30(e)(2)(iii). Alternatively, a drug sponsor may request an over-the-counter switch. Id. § 310.200(b). Unlike the first mechanism, this process does not require rulemaking. See 21 U.S.C. §§ 355(c), (d); 21 C.F.R. § 314.71. ***

B. Factual Background: On July 28, 1999, the FDA approved an NDA for Plan B submitted by the Plan B sponsor on a prescription-only basis.

1. Filing of the Citizen Petition and First OTC Switch Application: On February 14, 2001, one of the named plaintiffs, the Association of Reproductive Health Professionals ("ARHP"), and sixty-five other organizations (together the "petitioners") filed a Citizen Petition, asking the FDA to switch Plan B, and all emergency contraceptives like it, from prescription-only to over-the-counter status without age or point-of-sale restrictions. *** The FDA did not respond for nearly five more years, when it announced, on June 9, 2006, that it had denied the petition.

2. Review of First OTC Switch Application: OTC Access Without Age Restriction: *** Dr. Sandra Kweder, who had been involved in the formation of many advisory committees, testified that the Office of the Commissioner appointed several individuals to the committee "who would [not] normally [be] considered as the kind of people we would be looking for to be on the panel." Id. at 35:3-5. These people had "very limited experience in product development, clinical trials." *** While the Advisory Committee does not have the final say regarding the OTC switch applications, the FDA has followed advisory committee recommendations in every OTC switch application in the last decade: Of the 23 OTC switch applications reviewed by advisory committees from

1994 to 2004, the Plan B over-the-counter switch application was the only one that was not approved after the joint committee voted to recommend its approval. ***

3. Review of Second OTC Switch Application: OTC Access for 16 and Older: After it received the May 6, 2004 Not-Approvable letter, the Plan B sponsor submitted an amended SNDA in July 2004, formally proposing a dual marketing plan for Plan B that would allow non-prescription sales to persons age 16 and over who presented a valid identification to a pharmacist, and prescription-only sales to women 15 years and younger. *** Dr. Galson, Acting Director of the Center for Drug Evaluation and Research, asked Dr. Jenkins to draft an approvable letter for the Plan B OTC switch application approving OTC status for women age 17 and over. *** Nevertheless, in January or February 2005, before Dr. Galson could issue the letter he had instructed Dr. Jenkins to draft, Acting Commissioner Crawford removed Dr. Galson's authority to make a decision on the OTC switch application. **** As a result, the FDA failed, as required by law, to respond to the SNDA filed by the Plan B sponsor within 180 days of its filing. See 21 U.S.C. § 355(c); 21 C.F.R. § 314.100(a). *** Notwithstanding assurances that the FDA would act by September 1, 2005, Commissioner Crawford announced in late August 2005 that he would put off the decision yet again. *** Finally, on August 24, 2006, the FDA approved non-prescription use of Plan B for consumers 18 and older.

4. Denial of Citizen Petition: In June 2006, less than two months before the FDA announced that it would approve non-prescription use of Plan B only for women over the age of 18, the FDA issued a final agency decision denying the Citizen Petition—which had requested non-pre-scription access to Plan B for women of all ages—finding that petitioners had failed to provide sufficient data or information to meet the statutory and regulatory requirements for an OTC switch for any age group, much less the under 16 age group. ***

C. GAO Investigation: *** In reviewing the FDA's decision regarding the OTC switch application, the GAO concluded that four aspects of the FDA's review process were "unusual" and departed from the typical FDA review procedures. First, it noted that "the Directors of the Offices of Drug Evaluation III and V, who would normally have been responsible for signing the Plan B action letter, disagreed with the decision and did not sign the not-approvable letter for Plan B." ***. Third, the GAO noted that "there are conflicting accounts of whether the decision to not approve the application was made before the reviews were completed." *** Finally, the GAO concluded that "the rationale for [Dr. Galson's] decision was novel and did not follow FDA's traditional practices." *** With respect to how the Plan B decision compared to that for other proposed OTC switches, the GAO found that "the Plan B OTC switch application was the only 1 of th[e] 23 [switch applications reviewed by the joint advisory committee from 1994 to 2004] that was not approved after the joint committee voted to recommend approval of the application." ***

D. Litigation History

1. The Complaints: *** Specifically, plaintiffs allege that, in refusing to approve over-the-counter access without age or point-of-sale restriction, the FDA bowed to political pressure from the White House and anti-abortion constituents despite the uniform recommendation of the FDA's scientific review staff to approve over-the-counter access to Plan B without limitation. ***

II. Discussion: The FDA's Decision Was Not the Result of Good Faith and Reasoned Agency Decision-Making. Plaintiffs have presented unrebutted evidence of the FDA's lack of good faith regarding its decisions on the Plan B switch applications. This lack of good faith is evidenced by, among other things, (1) repeated and unreasonable delays, pressure emanating from the White House, and the obvious connection between the confirmation process of two FDA Commissioners and the timing of the FDA's decisions; and (2) significant departures from the FDA's normal procedures and policies in the review of the Plan B switch applications as compared to the review of other switch applications in the past 10 years.

1. Improper Political Influence: *** Plaintiffs have proffered evidence that the Commissioner did not make the decision on his own, but was pressured by the White House and "constituents who would be very unhappy with an over-the-counter Plan B." *** There is also evidence that the Commissioner transmitted this pressure down the chain of command at the FDA pressuring Dr. Galson not to approve over-the-counter use of Plan B without age restriction, and removing Dr. Galson's authority to make any decision on Plan B after he told the Commissioner that he believed Plan B could be used safely by adolescents 17 and older. Indeed, the evidence strongly suggests that even the decision to permit the OTC sale of Plan B to women over the age of 18 was made solely to facilitate the confirmation of Dr. von Eschenbach as Commissioner of the FDA. ***

2. Departures from Its Own Policies: The most glaring procedural departure was the decision to act against the Advisory Committee's recommendation to approve the Plan B OTC switch application without age restriction. While advisory committees do not have the final say on OTC switch applications, the fact remains that in every such application in the last decade, the FDA has followed committee recommendations. *** The second departure was the unusual involvement of the White House in the Plan B decision-making process. *** The third departure concerns the timing of the decision to deny OTC use without age restriction. *** The fourth departure was the FDA's refusal to extrapolate actual use study data from the older age group to the 16 and younger age group. ***

E. The Appropriate Remedy: *** [A] decision whether Plan B, a systemic hormonal contraceptive drug, may be used safely without a prescription by children as young as 11 or 12, is best left to the expertise of the FDA, to which Congress has entrusted this responsibility; it should not be made by a federal district court judge. ***

Conclusion: *The denial of the Citizen Petition is vacated and the matter is remanded to the FDA to reconsider its decisions regarding the Plan B switch to OTC use. The FDA is also ordered to permit Barr Pharmaceuticals, Inc. the Plan B drug sponsor, to make Plan B available to 17-year olds without a prescription, under the same conditions as Plan B is now available to women over the age of 18. The latter order should be complied with within thirty days.* [Italics added].
NOTE: See Roseann B. Termini and Miranda Lee, *Sex, Politics, and Lessons Learned from Plan B: A Review of the FDA's Actions and Future Direction*, **Oklahoma Law Rev. Vol.36, No. 2 (2011).**

CRITICAL ANALYSIS: Evaluate why FDA was reluctant to approve "Plan B" (Two-pill). Incorporate political pressure from special interest groups and personal moral views of FDA.

Tummino v. Hamburg,
936 F. Supp.2d 162 (E. D. NY April 5, 2013) (No. 1:12-cv-763)
MEMORANDUM & ORDER EDWARD R. KORMAN, Senior District Judge.
I. OVERVIEW: Plan B and Plan B One–Step are emergency contraceptives that can be taken to reduce the risk of pregnancy after unprotected intercourse. *** Subsequently, the FDA was ordered to make it available without a prescription to adolescents aged 17. *Tummino v. Torti,* 603 F.Supp.2d 519 (E.D.N.Y.2009). Even for women 17 and older, Plan B can only be purchased at a pharmacy and requires government-issued proof of age. Plan B One–Step was approved by the FDA in 2009 and is available without a prescription subject to the same restrictions. Though Plan B itself is no longer marketed, generic versions are available.

Both contraceptives contain the same total dose of levonorgestrel, a synthetic hormone similar to the naturally occurring hormone progesterone; Plan B consists of two pills containing 0.75 mg each of levonorgestrel that are to be taken 12 hours apart, while Plan B One–Step consists of one pill containing 1.5 mg of levonorgestrel. Studies have shown that combining the two 0.75 mg doses of the hormone into one pill does not decrease its effectiveness; indeed, the two Plan B pills may be taken simultaneously, fewer than 12 hours apart, or up to 24 hours apart, without any adverse consequences. Both Plan B and Plan B One–Step are most effective when taken immediately after intercourse and preferably no later than 24 hours later, though they may retain some effectiveness if taken within 72 hours. Neither drug has any known serious or longterm side effects, though they may have some mild short-term side effects, such as nausea, fatigue, and headache.

Levonorgestrel-based emergency contraception "interferes with prefertilization events. It reduces the number of sperm cells in the uterine cavity, immobilizes sperm, and impedes further passage of sperm cells into the uterine cavity. In addition, levonorgestrel has the capacity to delay or prevent ovulation from occurring." U.S. Gov't Accountability Office, GAO–06–109, *Food and Drug Administration: Decision Process to Deny Initial Application for Over–the–Counter Marketing of the Emergency Contraceptive Drug Plan B Was Unusual* at 12 (November 2005), Case No. 05–cv–366, Doc. No. 68–2 (hereinafter "GAO Report"). ***

Plaintiffs in this case—organizations and individuals concerned with women's health, as well as minors and their parents—seek to expand the availability of Plan B and all emergency contraceptives. This action was originally brought in January 2005 to challenge the FDA's denial of a Citizen Petition seeking over-the-counter ("OTC") access to Plan B for women of all ages. *** In a prior opinion, I concluded that the plaintiffs were right. *Tummino v. Torti,* 603 F.Supp.2d 519 (E.D.N.Y.2009). In light of the overwhelming evidence of political pressure underlying the agency's actions, I vacated the FDA's denial of the Citizen Petition and remanded for the agency to exercise its discretion without impermissible political intrusion. I also directed the FDA to make Plan B available to 17–year–old women without a prescription, because the same evidence relied on by the agency to support over-the-counter access to the drug by 18–year–olds applied equally to 17–year–olds–a holding which the FDA ultimately conceded was "consistent with the scientific findings [the FDA] made in 2005." ***

The FDA did not rule on the remanded Citizen Petition for almost three years. During this time, the agency again considered a proposal—referred to as a supplemental new drug application ("SNDA")—from Plan B's manufacturer; this proposal would have allowed over the-counter access to Plan B One–Step, the one-pill emergency contraceptive product, for all ages. The FDA agreed to approve this SNDA. *** Based on the information submitted to the agency, CDER determined that the product was safe and effective in adolescent females, that adolescent females understood the product was not for routine use, and that the product would not protect them against sexually transmitted diseases. *** Commissioner Hamburg then observed that she had "reviewed and thoughtfully considered the data, clinical information, and analysis provided by CDER," and she expressly agreed that "there is adequate and reasonable, well-supported, and science-based evidence that Plan B One–Step is safe and effective and should be approved for nonprescription use for all females of child-bearing potential." *Id.*

Nevertheless, she explained that Kathleen Sebelius, the Secretary of Health and Human Services, "invoking her authority under the Federal Food, Drug, and Cosmetic Act to execute its provisions," disagreed with the agency's decision "to allow the marketing of Plan B One–Step nonprescription for all females of child-bearing potential" and ordered Commissioner Hamburg to deny the Plan B One–Step SNDA. *** The President endorsed this decision, explaining that "the reason [Secretary Sebelius] made this decision was she could not be confident that a 10–year–old or an 11–year–old go into a drugstore, should be able—alongside bubble gum or batteries—be able to buy a medication that potentially, if not used properly, could end up having an adverse effect." Statement by the President (Dec. 8, 2011), available at:
http://www.whitehouse.gov/the-press-office/2011/12/08/statement-president.

II. DISCUSSION

A. Procedural Posture: Secretary Sebelius's directive to FDA to reject the Plan B One–Step SNDA forced the agency to ride roughshod over the policies and practices that it consistently applied in considering applications for switches in drug status to over-the-counter availability. ***

B. Deviations from Policy:

1. The Unprecedented Intervention of the Secretary: Perhaps the most significant departure from agency practice was the intervention of the Secretary of Health and Human Services. She overruled the FDA in an area which Congress entrusted primarily to the FDA, 21 U.S.C. § 393(d)(2), and which fell within the scope of the authority that the Secretary expressly delegated to the Commissioner. *See* Delegations of Authority to the Commissioner of Food and Drugs, *republished in* FDA Staff Manual Guide § 1410.10.

In my 2009 opinion, I traced the evidence demonstrating that the conduct of the FDA was influenced by the Bush White House, acting through the Office of the Commissioner of the FDA, and I held that this kind of political interference called into serious question the legitimacy of the FDA's decision. In the present circumstances, the political interference came directly from the Secretary of Health and Human Services, a member of the President's Cabinet. ***

a. *The First Sentence:* The Secretary says that "[t]he label comprehension and actual use studies submitted to FDA do not include data on all ages for which the drug would be approved and available over-the-counter." Sebelius Mem. This statement ignores the fact that the FDA waived the requirement that included a minimum number of enrollees between the ages of 11 and 13 in the drug sponsor's studies. ***

b. *The Second Sentence:* The Secretary also observed that there are "significant cognitive and behavioral differences between older adolescent girls and the youngest girls of reproductive age," which she believes "are relevant to making this determination as to non-prescription availability of this product for all ages." Sebelius Mem. *** In response, Dr. John Jenkins, Director of the Office of New Drugs at the FDA, explained that such concerns are beyond the scope of the FDA's review because they are "more applicable to the ability of adolescents to make reasoned decisions about engaging in sexual intercourse, not their ability to understand how to use Plan B safely and effectively as an emergency contraceptive should they engage in unprotected sexual intercourse." ***

c. *The Third Sentence:* The Secretary finally observed that, if the SNDA were granted, Plan B One–Step would be available "without a prescription or other point-of-sale restrictions, even to the youngest girls of reproductive age," including the ten percent of girls who "reach menarche by 11.1 years of age." Sebelius Mem. ***

2. *The Failure to Make Plan B Available to Older Adolescents:* The Secretary did not question the adequacy of the evidence regarding the ability of older adolescents, between the ages of 13 and 16, to understand Plan B One–Step's label and use the drug correctly. ***

3. *Extrapolation:* *** More significantly, the FDA did engage in extrapolation in considering the Plan B One–Step SNDA; otherwise, it would not have announced its intention to approve that SNDA and expand access to Plan B One–Step to all women of childbearing age. *** No conclusions about 11 year olds as a group could be drawn given the incredibly small number of 11 year olds who are users of emergency contraception. ***

4. *Deviations Where Extrapolation Is Not Possible Because Safety Not Established:* *** Again, as Dr. Jenkins testified, age-based labeling restrictions have "been [the FDA's] long-standing way of handling instructing consumers whether they should or should not use a product in a young age group, and [the Plan B marketing regime is] a substantial deviation from that practice." Jenkins Dep. at 113:7–16, Case No. 05–cv–366, Doc. No. 235–9 *** Prilosec OTC was approved for frequent heartburn in 2003 for adults 18 and older. *** Nevertheless, the FDA permitted Prilosec OTC to be sold over-the-counter and without point of sale restrictions with simply a warning on the label that it was not approved for use by children or adolescents.*** While some over-the-counter drugs, such as Prilosec OTC, probably would not be purchased by adolescent consumers without the advice of a doctor, the same cannot be said for drugs such as Alli, a weight-loss drug that is likely to attract teenage purchasers concerned about their physical appearance rather than medical necessity. Nor can it be said of cough syrup containing dextromethorphan, which is regularly abused by teenagers. The FDA's willingness to rely on labeling to make these drugs available for sale over-the-counter without any age or point-of-sale restrictions, even though they are unsafe for unsupervised use by young adolescents, stands in stark contrast to its refusal to make equally available concededly safe and time sensitive levonorgestrel-based emergency contraceptives.

5. *Point–of–Sale Departure from Policy:* *** The regime, which the Secretary forced the FDA to retain, requires that the product be sold only at pharmacies and health clinics and that it be kept behind the counter at pharmacies. *** The central holding of *American Pharmaceutical Ass'n* is that the FDA's authority over nonprescription drugs does not extend to restricting the point-of-sale distribution of drugs that have been found to be safe "when used in the manner intended." *Am. Pharm. Ass'n,* 377 F.Supp. at 828. *** Indeed, rather than rely on § 355(d), it argued that FDA regulations, specifically 21 C.F.R. § 314.520, expressly authorized it to restrict distribution of Plan B to select pharmacies and health clinics. *** Plan B does not fit within the class of drugs § 314.520 was designed to restrict. *** Each of the drugs the FDA mentioned is highly toxic and/or has serious health risks associated with its use: Accutane, which is used to treat severe acne, "may cause birth defects if ingested while pregnant"; Trovan, which treats infections, "can cause serious liver disease". *** This is demonstrated not only by the drugs that were either not shown to be safe or were unsafe for the pediatric population such as Prilosec and Alli, which were dealt with through labeling, not point-of-sale restrictions, but also by the recent express acquiescence of the FDA in a college's provision of Plan B One–Step to its students through a vending machine. *FDA OK with college's Plan B contraceptive vending machine,* MSN News, Jan. 29, 2013 ***. The only condition on access to the vending machine was that students swipe their college ID; the school had previously verified that all of its students were age 17 or over.

C. Standard of Review: *** The only decision subject to review here is the denial of the Citizen Petition; I do not have any authority to review the denial of the Plan B One–Step SNDA for the purpose of granting relief. Nevertheless, as observed earlier, the two were clearly linked together for two reasons. First, once the Secretary directed the FDA to deny the Plan B One–Step SNDA, the FDA had no possible basis on which to approve the Citizen Petition. ***

The applicable standard of review is prescribed by the Administrative Procedure Act ("APA"), which provides that a district court may set aside an agency's findings, conclusions of law or action only if they are "arbitrary, capricious, an abuse of discretion, or otherwise not in accordance with law." 5 U.S.C. § 706(2)(A). *** In apparent recognition of the complexity of this process, the Secretary has delegated to the Commissioner of Food and Drugs, with the authority to re-delegate, "[f]unctions vested in the Secretary under the [FDCA] (21 U.S.C. 301 et seq.)." Delegations of Authority to the Commissioner of Food and Drugs, *republished in* FDA Staff Manual Guide § 1410.10. *** The change in the status of the Commissioner was based on a finding that "the independence and integrity of the Food and Drug Administration need to be enhanced in order to ensure the continuing protection of the public health." Food and Drug Administration Act of 1988, Pub.L. No. 100–607, § 502, 102 Stat. 3048, 3120. One consequence of this change was that the Commissioner was no longer a subordinate of the Secretary. She does not serve at the pleasure of the Secretary, and she cannot be removed from office by the Secretary. Only the President has the power to do so. In this case, if Commissioner Hamburg had refused to follow the directive of Secretary Sebelius, the President would have been faced with the unpalatable choice of either dismissing the Commissioner or overruling the Secretary. ***

D. Citizen Petition Denial: The FDA denied the Citizen Petition almost immediately after it rejected the Plan B OneStep SNDA in December 2011. ***

While these unexplained departures from precedent alone render the denial arbitrary, capricious, and unreasonable, they are not the only reasons for reversing the denial of the Citizen Petition. *** First, the FDA had available the actual use and label comprehension studies submitted by the Plan B sponsor in support of its SNDAs seeking expanded over-the-counter access to Plan B and Plan B One–Step. Specifically, the label comprehension study submitted with the Plan B One–Step SNDA tested participants' understanding of six key concepts, developed with the FDA's input:

(1) The product is used to prevent pregnancy after unprotected sex;

(2) It should be taken as soon as possible after sex;

(3) It does not prevent sexually transmitted disease or HIV/AIDS;

(4) It should not be used instead of regular contraception;

(5) It should be taken within 72 hours after sex; and

(6) It should not be used by women who are already pregnant.

Raymond Decl. ¶ 33, Case No. 12–cv–763, Doc. No. 5. These six key concepts were understood by 83–96% of all subjects. Raymond et al., *Comprehension of a prototype emergency contraception package label by female adolescents,* 79 Contraception 199, 203 (2009), Case No. 12–cv–763, Doc. No. 27–1. As the article publishing the study states: Lower literacy was significantly associated with lower likelihood of understanding of each of the six key concepts. Younger subjects were significantly less likely than older subjects to understand four of the key concepts, although the difference in understanding between 12– to 14–year–olds and 15– to 17–year–olds was no more than 10 percentage points for any one concept. ***

In its letter explaining its reasons for rejecting the Citizen Petition, the FDA provided additional insight into the process by which it found Plan B One–Step to be appropriate for over-the-counter access by all ages. *** Nevertheless, the FDA insisted that the Plan B One–Step actual use study could not be used to support over-the-counter access to Plan B because Plan B involves two pills taken 12 hours apart instead of one pill. Specifically, the FDA said: "[T]he two drugs are not the same product, and all of the data supporting one application cannot automatically be used for the other." *** The approval of Plan B One–Step demonstrates its recognition that there would be no adverse consequences or decrease in effectiveness if the two pills were taken at the same time or less than 12 hours apart. The only consequence that the defendants were able to identify from a failure to follow the label instructions is that "if you miss the timing of the second dose, it reduces effectiveness and that can have unfortunate consequences for someone who is taking the drug to avoid becoming pregnant." ***

In sum, the Citizen Petition denial was inevitable after the Secretary ordered Commissioner Hamburg to deny the Plan B One–Step SNDA. Because the Secretary's action was politically motivated, scientifically unjustified, and contrary to agency precedent, it cannot provide a basis to sustain the denial of the Citizen Petition. The Citizen Petition Denial Letter, which came five days after the denial of the Plan B One–Step SNDA, was clearly prompted by the Secretary's action, despite the FDA's fanciful effort to make it appear that it undertook an independent review of the Citizen Petition. ***

E. Proper Record on Review

1. The Actual Use and Label Comprehension Studies: The defendants argue that the actual use and label comprehension studies submitted with the Plan B One–Step switch application could not have been considered by the FDA in its review of the Citizen Petition and may not be considered here in my review of the Citizen Petition denial. ***

This leaves the FDA with an argument that the use of the studies submitted by the Plan B One–Step sponsor, Teva Women's Health, Inc. ("Teva"), would deprive Teva of the right to three years of exclusive marketing of Plan B One–Step, to which it would have been entitled under the FDCA. *See* 21 U.S.C. § 355(c)(3)(E)(iv) & 355(j)(5)(F)(iv). This exclusivity could only have followed if Teva's application for over-the-counter access had been granted by the FDA based on a finding by the FDA that those studies were "essential" to the approval. The purpose underlying this exclusivity provision, according to both the FDA and Teva, is "to encourage and reward drug manufacturers who devote the time and expense to clinical trials necessary to approve changes to a drug product." *Id.* ***

The defendants' final arrow in their effort to invoke Teva's commercial interests to prevent reliance on the Plan B One–Step studies turns on the fact that Teva has never given its permission for the Citizen Petition proponents to use its studies. Specifically, the defendants argue that "a sponsor's clinical studies cannot be applied to support the approval of another manufacturer's drug product unless the drug sponsor grants a 'right of reference' to those studies." Defs.' Mem. in Opp. to Summ. J. at 34 n.9, Case No. 12–cv–763, Doc. No. 37. They cite one statute, 21 U.S.C. § 355, and one regulation, 21 C.F.R. § 314.3. I decline to consider this argument, upon which even Teva itself does not rely, because it was advanced in a single footnote, it relied on a 20,000+ word statutory section with numerous parts and subparts without any pincite to the relevant language, and the footnote did not in any way develop the legal argument to which the defendants allude. ***

2. The Declarations Submitted in Support of Plaintiffs' Summary Judgment Motion *** My decision, however, would be the same even without reference to the real-life consequences of the Secretary's conduct. Her decision with respect to the Plan B One–Step SNDA, which dictated the denial of the Citizen Petition, was arbitrary, capricious, and unreasonable for the reasons I have already outlined and do not repeat.

3. Administrative Record Rule: The last rule the FDA relies on to preclude consideration of documents unhelpful to its position is the rule that a reviewing court must judge the propriety of administrative agency action "by the grounds invoked by the agency." *** Nevertheless, the law is clear that a reviewing court may consider extra-record materials in certain circumstances. *See Nat'l Audubon,* 132 F.3d at 14–15. Indeed, "a strong showing of bad faith or improper behavior" may justify supplementing the record. *Citizens to Preserve Overton Park v. Volpe,* 401 U.S. 402, 420 (1971). *** Moreover, no meaningful review of the denial of the Citizen Petition would be possible without a review of the administrative record for the SNDAs because the FDA understood the issues presented by the SNDAs and Citizen Petition to be one and the same. *Tummino,* 603 F.Supp.2d at 543. *** The same reasons that justified my consideration of materials outside the administrative record in 2009 apply equally here, including a strong showing of bad faith and improper political influence.

III. CONCLUSION: *The decisions of the Secretary with respect to Plan B One–Step and that of the FDA with respect to the Citizen Petition, which it had no choice but to deny, were arbitrary, capricious, and unreasonable. *** Consequently, the decision of the FDA denying the Citizen Petition is reversed, and the case is remanded to the FDA with the instruction to grant the Citizen Petition and make levonorgestrel-based emergency contraceptives available without a prescription and without point-of-sale or age restrictions within thirty days. On remand, the FDA may determine whether any new labeling is reasonably necessary. Moreover, if the FDA actually believes there is any significant difference between the one and two-pill products, it may limit its over-the-counter approval to the one-pill product.*

I do not grant the application of the FDA to remand for the commencement of administrative rulemaking proceedings. *** More than twelve years have passed since the Citizen Petition was filed and eight years since this lawsuit commenced. The FDA has engaged in intolerable delays in processing the petition. Indeed, it could accurately be described as an administrative agency filibuster. Moreover, one of the devices the FDA has employed to stall proceedings was to seek public comment on whether or not it needed to engage in rulemaking in order to adopt an age-restricted marketing regime. After eating up eleven months, 47,000 public comments, and hundreds of thousands, if not millions, of dollars, it decided that it did not need rulemaking after all. The plaintiffs should not be forced to endure, nor should the agency's misconduct be rewarded by, an exercise that permits the FDA to engage in further delay and obstruction. [Italics added for emphasis].

NOTE: Interestingly, on April 30, 2013, FDA had approved over-the-counter use of the emergency contraceptive Plan B One-Step for women 15 years of age and older.

Aftermath—Politics, FDA and the Court

Judge Korman denied FDA's Motion for a Stay pending appeal. See (936 F.Supp.2d 198 (E.D. NY 2013)). The government appealed Judge Korman's ruling to the Second Circuit. In its motion to stay the district court's ruling pending the government's appeal, the government set forth that the Judge Korman's order exceeded the court's authority. The government argued that the court should have remanded the matter to FDA for further administrative action instead of issuing the order to make Plan B (two-pill) available without age restrictions. Further, the DOJ argued the court's order concerned Plan B One-Step, a drug product that was not the subject of a citizen petition to the Food and Drug Administration. See: *Tummino v. Hamburg* No. 13–1690 2013 WL 2435370 June 5, 2013 (Stay granted One-pill and denied Two-pill).

However, by letter to Judge Korman dated June 10, 2013 (see below), FDA agreed to make Plan B One-Step (One-pill) available without age and point of sale restrictions pending a supplemental application by Teva Pharmaceuticals, the drug sponsor. This was accepted by Judge Korman by Memorandum June 12, 2013.

BY ELECTRONIC COURT FILING Case 1:12-cv-00763-ERK-VVP
Document 103 Filed 06/10/13 Page ID #: 2391
Honorable Edward R. Korman, Senior Judge, Eastern District of New York
U.S. Department of Justice
United States Attorney Eastern District of New York
271 Cadman Plaza East Brooklyn, NY 11201-1820
June 10, 2013

Re: *Tummino v. Hamburg*, No. 12-CV-0763 (ERK/VVP)

Dear Judge Korman:

We write to advise the Court that the Food and Drug Administration (FDA) and the Department of Health and Human Services (HHS) have complied with the Court's April 10, 2013, judgment in the above-referenced case by granting the 2001 Citizen Petition and making Plan B One-Step (PBOS) available over-the-counter (OTC) without age or point-of-sale restrictions as described below. It is the government's understanding that this course of action fully complies with the Court's judgment in this action. Once the Court confirms that the government's understanding is correct, the government intends to file with the Circuit Court notice that it is voluntarily withdrawing its appeal in this matter.

Procedurally, FDA today has invited the sponsor of PBOS, Teva Branded Pharmaceutical Products R&D, Inc. (Teva), to promptly submit a supplemental new drug application (SNDA) with proposed labeling that would permit PBOS to be sold without a prescription and without age or point-of-sale restrictions. Upon receipt of this SNDA, FDA will approve it without delay. After FDA receives and approves Teva's supplement, we expect the sponsors of the generic versions of PBOS to submit appropriate amendments to their abbreviated new drug applications. If FDA grants Teva marketing exclusivity, the scope of that exclusivity may affect the labeling that could be approved for generic equivalents of PBOS. Further to comply with the Court's judgment, FDA today has issued a response to the 2001 Citizen Petition granting the petition by taking the steps with respect to PBOS described in this letter. In accordance with this Court's order and as explained below, FDA will not at this time take steps to change the approval status of the two-pill Plan B or its generic equivalents.

As the Court is aware, the Second Circuit stayed this Court's judgment pending appeal to the extent that this Court required FDA to make PBOS available OTC, but denied a stay to the extent the Court mandated that the two-pill Plan B and its generic equivalents be made available OTC. FDA, however, intends to comply with the Court's order in the manner described in the preceding paragraph because this Court's April 10, 2013, judgment expressly authorized FDA to comply by making PBOS and not Plan B available, if FDA believes that there is a significant difference between Plan B and PBOS. Specifically, while the Court's judgment directed the defendants to "make levonorgestrel-based emergency contraceptives available without a prescription and without point-of-sale or age restrictions within 30 days," it also provided that "FDA may determine whether any new labeling is reasonably necessary" and that "if the FDA actually believes that there is any significant difference between the one- and two- pill products, it may limit its over-the-counter approval to the one-pill product." ECF No. 87, 04/10/13, at 1-2. FDA continues to believe, for the reasons that the government has previously explained in its briefs to this Court, that there are significant differences between Plan B and PBOS under FDA's regulations and the Federal Food, Drug, and Cosmetic Act.

It is, moreover, the PBOS application that contained actual use data specifically addressing the ability of adolescents, including younger adolescents, to understand and follow the directions for safe and effective use as a nonprescription product; there are fewer data available regarding the actual use of Plan B as a nonprescription product by younger adolescents. FDA therefore believes it is appropriate and consistent with this Court's order to comply by making only PBOS (and not the two-pill product) available OTC for younger adolescents.

Respectfully submitted,

cc (by email and ECF notification): Janet Crepps, Andrea H. Costello Kirsten Clanton, Michael Shumsky, Steven Menashi, LORETTA E. LYNCH   United States Attorney Eastern District of New YorkBy: /s/ {FILED ELECTRONICALLY} F. FRANKLIN AMANAT (FA6117) Senior Counsel   (718) 254-6024 *franklin.amanat@usdoj.gov*

Plan B and PlanB One-Step

On June 12, 2013, Judge Korman Court by Memorandum No. 12-CV-763 accepted FDA's acquiescence to permit access for all ages and without restrictions for Plan B One-Step and to permit the drug sponsor, Teva to submit a supplemental for Plan B One-Step for all ages. Judge Korman cautioned about continued exclusivity issues. Plan B (Two pill) and generic versions are available over the counter for ages 17 and over and for those under 17 a prescription is required. Plan B One-Step is available as the Plan B two pill was discontinued.

NOTE: Are emergency contraceptive pills less effective for obese women? This is an important consideration in the United States as according to a CDC report, over 35% of adults are obese. FDA is reviewing research for labeling changes for these types of products. See: *http://win.niddk.nih.gov/publications/PDFs/stat904z.pdf*
http://who.int/mediacentre/factsheets/fs244/en/
https://www.ncbi.nlm.nih.gov/pmc/articles/PMC4079263/

CRITICAL ANALYSIS: Will politicization ever cease? Should public morality be a factor in FDA decision making or should FDA decision making be strictly science based?

NOTE: A proposed rule titled *Protecting Statutory Conscience Rights in Health Care; Delegations of Authority* was published back in January 2018. The intent of the proposed rule is compliance with the Federal laws that protect the rights of conscience and prohibit associated discriminatory policies and practices in such programs and activities. See 83 Fed. Reg. 3880 (Jan. 26, 2018). See link below.

https://www.gpo.gov/fdsys/pkg/FR-2018-01-26/pdf/2018-01226.pdf#page=1

Chapter 2: Globalization and International Considerations

http://www.fda.gov/InternationalPrograms/FDABeyondOurBordersForeignOffices/ucm2016758.htm

The involvement of FDA in the international arena remains crucial. Globalization has provided challenges for FDA with diametrically opposed limited resources and increased imports. Yet, globalization is a 21st Century reality. Significant globalization issues include safety, adequate resources and societal standards and mores. The purpose of the FDCA is to protect the public health, safety and welfare in relationship to the products regulated by FDA. This means that it is the responsibility of FDA to ensure that products that enter the United States comply with FDA agency standards. FDA inspectors review entry documents and employ numerous methods to ensure that product imports meet United States standards prior to entry. Products regulated by FDA manufactured outside of the United States and imported are subject to the identical standards as those manufactured domestically.

FDA identified China, India, Latin America, the Middle East, Europe, North Africa and Sub-Saharan Africa for an in-country presence. According to FDA, greater than 80% of all seafood, 20% of all fresh produce and numerous other FDA regulated products have international origins. Future endeavors need a continuum of FDA international presence along with adequate resources for public safety assurance including that of counterterrorism preparedness.

Counterterrorism Measures

http://www.fda.gov/EmergencyPreparedness/Counterterrorism/default.htm (edited)

The Medical Countermeasures Initiative (MCMi) FDA program coordinates medical countermeasure development, preparedness and response. Specific involvement focuses on regulatory oversight, monitoring infrastructure and responding to terrorist attacks and naturally occurring emerging threats with timely and appropriate countermeasures. FDA advances the expansion of safe and effective medical countermeasures to alleviate the effects of threats by actively engaging industry, other federal, state and local partners. Each FDA Center is involved in FDA's counterterrorism efforts as follows.

***The Center for Biologics and Evaluation and Research* (CBER)** oversees the safety, effectiveness, quality and availability of biologic products, including oversight of vaccines, cells, tissues and the US blood system; works collaboratively to facilitate product development, manufacturing and quality for needed CBRN medical countermeasures.

***The Center for Drug Evaluation and Research* (CDER)** the Counter-Terrorism and Emergency Coordination Staff ensures that safe and effective drugs are available for treating and preventing illness due to CBRN agents; facilitates the development of new drugs and new uses for already-approved drugs that could be used as medical countermeasures.

***The Center for Devices and Radiological Health* (CDRH)** ensures that safe and effective diagnostics and personal protective equipment are available for diagnosing and preventing illness due to CBRN agents; assures that radiation-emitting products meet radiation safety standards.

***The Center for Food Safety and Applied Nutrition* (CFSAN)** protects the Nation's food supply against CBRN agents, prevents the distribution of suspect food imports and minimizes the risk of CBRN contamination of food.

***The Center for Veterinary Medicine* (CVM)** ensures that animal drugs, food additives, animal devices, and medicated feeds are safe and effective and ensures that food from treated animals is safe.

***The National Center for Toxicological Research* (NCTR)** conducts scientific research applicable to CBRN threats including the identification of virulent biomarkers, technologies for intervention, and rapid, field-rugged tests to detect bioterrorism agents.

***The Office of Regulatory Affairs* (ORA)** protects consumers and enhances public health by maximizing compliance of FDA regulated products and minimizing risk associated with those products; inspects regulated products, including food, and facilities; conducts law enforcement activities for tampered and adulterated products.

The Office of Counterterrorism and Emerging Threats **(OCET)** coordinates the portfolio of FDA Counterterrorism (CT) policy initiatives; develops an FDA strategy for CT; promotes CT policy, goals, and needs; facilitates intra- and inter-agency CT communications; coordinates Emergency Use Authorization activities.

The Office of Crisis Management **(OCM)** coordinates emergency/crisis response activities involving FDA regulated products or in situations when FDA regulated products need to be utilized or deployed; works closely with US Department of Health and Human Services, Office of the Assistant Secretary for Preparedness and Response in coordination with the FDA Centers and Offices to develop policies to help FDA respond quickly to emergency or crisis situations; plans/direct activities related to FDA's physical and personnel security programs.

International Programs

http://www.fda.gov/InternationalPrograms/FDABeyondOurBordersForeignOffices/ucm2016758.htm

FDAs Office of International programs serves as the agency's focal point for all international matters. All of the agency's international offices, whether located overseas or in the United States, work to build stronger cooperative relationships around the world. Offices include:

➢ The China Office;
➢ The India Office;
➢ The Africa and Asia Office;
➢ The Latin American Office;
➢ The Europe Office;
➢ The Middle East Office;
➢ The Quadrilateral and Trilateral Office; and the
➢ The Office of Harmonization and Multilateral Relations.

The Office of Harmonization and Multilateral Relations—FDA's Harmonization and Multilateral Relations Office, is responsible for coordinating and collaborating food and drug activities with various international organizations and governments, including the World Health Organization, the international foods standards organization Codex Alimentarius, and the International Conference on Harmonization of Technical Requirements for Registration of Pharmaceuticals for Human Use. The office coordinates and collaborates on similar harmonization initiatives for veterinary drugs, medical devices, and cosmetics. In partnering with these global organizations and regulators, FDA and its counterpart agencies around the world help to promote public health globally. This office also handles various other cross-cutting initiatives and pilot programs such as anti-counterfeiting efforts and harmonizing certain global standards.

The China Office—In 2008, FDA opened its China Office with posts in Beijing, Shanghai, and Guangzhou. FDA specialists include senior technical experts in foods, medicines, and medical devices, along with inspectors. The opening of the office represents a new era in U.S.—China cooperation on the safety of food, animal feed, and medical products. The goals of this office include working in concert with the regulatory authorities in China to strengthen the capacity of Chinese regulatory bodies, increase FDA inspections, and help Chinese industry understand FDA standards and expectations. In 2009, a new food safety law was passed in China, creating a food safety committee and requiring licensure for all food producers, caterers, and retailers, among other provisions. The law also calls for an emergency response plan and a mandatory recall requirement when food doesn't meet standards.

The India Office—FDA's staff in the India Office is located in New Delhi and Mumbai starting in 2008 at the U.S. Embassy in New Delhi. The India Office includes senior technical experts covering medicines, foods, and medical devices. FDA employees in the India Office are developing relations with foreign counterparts, are involved in inspections of many products destined for the

United States, and are actively engaged with other U.S. government entities in India such as the U.S. Department of Agriculture and the Foreign Agricultural Services.

The Africa and Asia Office—FDA's Africa/Asia office is responsible for 71 countries throughout Sub-Saharan Africa and Asia—21 in Asia and 50 in Africa. The office does not include the countries of North Africa, which are part of the Middle East office, or the Asian territories of India, China, Hong Kong, Macau, or Taiwan.

This office seeks to work with the national regulatory authorities to build the regulatory capacity of its countries and gain a better understanding of production and transport of products to U.S. ports. Under the President's Emergency Plan for AIDS Relief (PEPFAR), FDA has been responsible for coordinating a process whereby generic antiretroviral medicines, including formulations for children, have received approvals that certify that they meet the safety and quality standards of products in the United States. Purchasers of products under the PEPFAR program use these so-called "tentative" approvals to guide their purchases. These approvals save many millions of dollars per year and enable millions of people in PEPFAR countries, including those in Africa and Asia, to receive these life-preserving therapies for HIV/AIDS. This approach can dramatically reduce the number and severity of illnesses associated with HIV infection, and can also improve the duration and quality of life.

The Latin American Office—FDA staff arrived at the U.S. Embassy in San Jose, Costa Rica, in April 2009. There is also an FDA office in Santiago, Chile, and Mexico City. The Latin American Office is responsible for FDA's interactions with Mexico and the countries of Central America, South America, and the Caribbean. As with the other international offices, by working with FDA counterpart agencies in the region, along with the local industry and other U.S. government agencies in the region, the Latin American office aims to ensure that FDA-regulated products that are manufactured or processed from this region and exported to the United States meet U.S. standards of quality and safety.

The Europe Office—FDA first arrived at its office in Brussels, Belgium, in May 2009. Other FDA staff members are located at the European Medicines Evaluation Agency (EMEA) in London, with plans for an FDA employee to join the European Food Safety Agency (EFSA) in Parma, Italy, in 2010. FDA has an ongoing, robust collaboration with EMEA in a number of areas. For example, FDA and Europe exchange large amounts of data and reports on various products and firms. A staff person from EMEA will join FDA in the Rockville, Md., location later in the year. The counterpart liaison official from EFSA has already joined FDA.

The Middle East Office—FDA's Middle East Office is currently based in Rockville, Md. Interactions with the Middle East are important because of the sensitivity of products traded between the United States and Middle Eastern countries. The agency plans to open posts in Amman, Jordan, and in Tel Aviv, Israel, but dates are uncertain at this time. The goals of the Middle East Office are to learn more about the region by working with FDA's counterpart agencies in the region and identifying opportunities for capacity building.

The Quadrilateral and Trilateral Office—This office is responsible for FDA's interactions with FDA counterparts in Canada, Australia, and New Zealand. The name of this office comes from two initiatives—the Food Safety Quadrilateral Group between Canada, Australia, New Zealand, and the United States; and the Trilateral Cooperation between Canada, Mexico, and the United States.

International Memoranda of Understanding (MOUs)

A Memorandum of Understanding is a legal document that outlines the terms of an agreement, and permits FDA to accept foreign government information when the foreign agencies have standards similar to FDA. FDA Memoranda of Understanding (MOUs) with foreign governments cover areas such as inspections, good laboratory practices, good manufacturing practices, and food certifications and safety. Products for entry into the United States must still meet United States standards. Examples of countries that FDA has agreements with governments of foreign countries are: Australia, Belgium, Canada, Chile, China, Denmark, European Community, Finland, France, Germany, Iceland, Ireland, Italy, Japan, Korea, Mexico, Netherlands, New Zealand, Norway, Philippines, Russia, Spain, Sweden, Switzerland, Taiwan, and the United Kingdom.

Other systems in place for product imports include training, higher international standards, harmonization of guidelines, and mutual recognition agreements. Training of the agency's regulatory counterparts in exporting countries in U.S. public health requirements remains a priority. FDA assists foreign as well as domestic manufacturers in understanding compliance with FDA's current good manufacturing practices, good clinical practice, good laboratory practice, and Hazard Analysis and Critical Control Point procedures or HACCP for the safe and sanitary processing and importing of fish and fish related products.

FDA, through its contribution in organizations such as Codex Alimentarius and the International Organization for Standards, is another means to raise criterion for food, medical devices, drugs and other products regulated by FDA and made internationally. FDA has forged ahead in harmonization of guidelines such as the International Conference on Harmonization for new drugs, the Global Harmonization Task Force for medical devices and the Veterinary International Conference on Harmonization for veterinary medications. Mutual recognition agreements involve FDA implementation of an agreement where FDA relies on its counterparts in the European Union to inspect European plants that export pharmaceuticals and medical devices to the United States. FDA has become a global leader in protecting public health worldwide. The ultimate goal of FDA remains to protect the United States public health and safety in relationship to the products the agency regulates. The compliance policy guide detailed exemplifies FDA policy for initiating, developing, and monitoring agreements such as memoranda of understanding (MOU's) between FDA and foreign governments. The objective is to foster uniformity in developing MOU's with foreign governments.

Confidentiality Commitments
http://www.fda.gov/InternationalPrograms/Agreements/ConfidentialityCommitments/default.htm

COUNTRY	SUBJECT	SCOPE
Argentina	Information Sharing	Foods, Animal & Veterinary
Australia	Information sharing	Tobacco, Cosmetics, Food, Animal and Veterinary
Australia	Information Sharing	Drugs, Biologics, Medical Devices, Radiation-Emitting Products
Australia / New Zealand	Information Sharing	Foods
Austria	Information Sharing	Drugs, Medical Devices, Animal & Veterinary
Brazil	Information Sharing	Foods, Drugs, Biologics, Medical Devices, Animal & Veterinary, Cosmetics, Radiation-Emitting Products, tobacco products
Belgium	Information Sharing	Foods, Drugs, Biologics, Medical Devices
Belgium	Information Sharing	Drugs, Medical Devices, Animal & Veterinary
Canada	Information Sharing	Tobacco
Canada	Information Sharing	Biologics, Food Safety
Canada	Information Sharing	Foods, Medical Devices, Animal & Veterinary Drugs, Biologics, Radiation-Emitting Products
Chile	Information Sharing	Foods, Drugs, Medical Device, biologics, and Cosmetics
Czech Republic	Information Sharing	Drugs, Biologics and Vaccines
Denmark	Information sharing	Drugs and Medical Devices

Europe - Council of Europe	Information Sharing	Drugs, Biologics, Animal & Veterinary Products
European Union EC, DG Enterprise	Information Sharing related to Medical Devices	N/A, responsibilities transferred to DG SANCO
European Union EC, DG Enterprise	Information Sharing related to Cosmetics	N/A, Responsibilities transferred to DG SANCO
European Union (EFSA)	Information Sharing related to food and feed	Foods
European Union (EMA)	Information Sharing	Drugs, Biologics, Animal & Veterinary Products
European Union (EC, DG SANCO)	Information Sharing	Foods, Drugs, Biologics, Medical Devices, Animal & Veterinary, Cosmetics, Radiation-Emitting Products, tobacco products
France	Information Sharing	Drugs, Biologics, Medical Devices, Cosmetics
France	Information Sharing	Foods, Animal & Veterinary
Germany	Information Sharing	Drugs, Biologics and Animal & Veterinary
Germany	Information Sharing	Foods and Radiation-Emitting Products
Germany	Information Sharing	Drugs, Medical Devices
Germany	Information Sharing	Foods, Animal & Veterinary and Tobacco Products
Germany	Information Sharing	Foods, Drugs, Biologics, Medical Devices, Animal & Veterinary, Cosmetics, Radiation-Emitting Products and Tobacco Products
Ireland	Information Sharing	Drugs, Biologics, Medical Devices, Animal & Veterinary, Cosmetics,
Ireland	Information Sharing	Good laboratory practices
Israel	Information Sharing	Drugs, Medical Devices, Foods, Veterinary Drugs, Cosmetics, Radiation-Emitting Products
Italy	Information Sharing	Drugs
Japan	Information Sharing	Animal Foods and feeds, Veterinary drugs
Japan	Information Sharing	Biologics, Human Drugs, and Medical Devices
Japan	Information Sharing	Biologics, Cosmetics, Human Drugs, Food and Medical Devices
Mexico	Information sharing	Foods, Drugs, Medical Devices, Biologics, Cosmetics, Radiation-Emitting Products, Tobacco Products
Mexico	Information sharing	Foods, Animal & Veterinary
Netherlands	Information sharing	Drugs, Biologics, Medical Devices, Animal & Veterinary, Foods
New Zealand	Information sharing	Tobacco Products
New Zealand	Information sharing	Foods
New Zealand	Information sharing	Drugs, Biologics, Medical Devices, Radiation-Emitting Products
Singapore	Information sharing	Biologics, Cosmetics, Human Drugs, Medical Devices and Tobacco Products
South Africa	Information sharing	Biologics and Human Drugs, and Veterinary Products
Sweden	Information Sharing	Drugs, Biologics, Medical Devices, Cosmetics
Switzerland	Information sharing	Drugs, Biologics, Medical Devices, Animal & Veterinary
Switzerland	Information sharing	Foods & Public Health
United Kingdom	Information Sharing	Biologics
United Kingdom	Information Sharing	Foods

United Kingdom	Information Sharing	Drugs, Biologics, Medical Devices
United Kingdom	Information Sharing	Animal & Veterinary
WHO	Information Sharing	Medical Devices, Drugs, and Biologics
WHO	Information sharing	Tobacco
WHO	Products Approved under PEP-FAR and WHO's Prequalifica-tion Program	Health related products (PEPFAR)
WHO	Information sharing	Drugs, human Biologics

The Foreign Corrupt Practices Act

http://www.justice.gov/criminal/fraud/fcpa/

Globalization has transformed the method of how business is done and increasingly United States companies look to foreign countries for business opportunities. What are the ethical issues involved in payments to, for example, foreign government officials? Payments to foreign government officials to aid in procuring or retaining business are illegal under the Foreign Corrupt Practices Act (FCPA). The FCPA of 1977, as amended, 15 U.S.C. §§ 78dd-1, *et seq.* contains specific anti-bribery provisions that have applied to all United States persons and certain foreign issuers of securities. The 1998 FCPA amendment extended application to foreign firms and persons who "cause, directly or through agents, an act in furtherance of such a corrupt payment to take place within the territory of the United States."

Under the FCPA, it is a crime to pay, offer, or give anything of value to a foreign official, a foreign political party or even a candidate for foreign office if done so to acquire or maintain business or to obtain preferential treatment. It does not have to be a direct payment; rather, under the FCPA the prohibition applies to payments to a third party such as an employee of a government owned health facility. Some countries have explicit laws that prohibit bribes and improper payments. The Department of Justice (DOJ) and the Securities and Exchange Commission (SEC) published *"A Resource Guide to the U.S. Foreign Corrupt Practices Act"* (2012). The FCPA Resource Guide, although not legally binding, is a comprehensive written guidance on enforcement. The FCPA Resource Guide provides significant guidance along with hypothetical examples regarding how DOJ and the SEC would enforce the FCPA including prosecutorial discretion. Significant factors in this regard include the type of compliance program, due diligence, self-regulation, self-reporting, the gravity and length of the violation(s) and recidivism.

The Foreign Corrupt Practices Act (FCPA) applies to FDA regulated products. The United States and foreign governments have stepped-up enforcement due to increased globalization. FDA regulated firms in the United States remain liable if found to have violated the Foreign Corrupt Practices Act as the cases below illustrate. One of the earliest actions involved payments to doctors employed by private and public hospitals in Taiwan over a 17-year person ending in 2002. See: *Securities and Exchange Commission v. Syncor International Corporation*, Case No. 1:02CV02421 (D.C. D.C.) In a related proceeding, the United States Department of Justice filed criminal FCPA charges against Syncor Taiwan, Inc., a subsidiary of Syncor, *United States v. Syncor Taiwan, Inc.* No. 02-CR-1244-ALL (C.D. Cal.). Syncor Taiwan agreed to plead guilty to one count of violating the anti-bribery provisions of the FCPA and to pay a $2 million fine. See: *http://www.sec.gov/litigation/litreleases/lr17887.htm*

Enforcement Illustrations

http://www.justice.gov/criminal/fraud/fcpa/cases/a.html
The following serve as illustrations of recent enforcement actions.
Biomet—Warsaw, Ind. based medical device manufacturer agreed to pay more than $30 million to resolve SEC and Justice Department investigations into the company's anti-bribery violations in Brazil and Mexico (1/12/17).
Bio-Rad Laboratories—California-based medical diagnostics and life sciences manufacturing

and sales company, Bio-Rad Laboratories, Inc. agreed to pay a $14.35 million penalty to resolve allegations that it violated the Foreign Corrupt Practices Act (FCPA) by falsifying its books and records and failing to implement adequate internal controls in connection with sales it made in Russia. (11/04/2014) *http://www.justice.gov/criminal/fraud/fcpa/cases/bio-rad.html*

NOTE: See *Wadler v. Bio-Rad* where Wadler prevailed in his retaliation lawsuit against Bio-Rad and was awarded $2.96 million in back wages and $5 million in punitive damages. Bio-Rad had alleged corporate counsel terminated (2013) due to "abusive conduct" not because corporate counsel reported possible bribes. Bio-Rad appealed (June 8, 2017) 9th Cir. Ct. of Appeals (17-16193).

See also: *Hall v. Teva Pharmaceutical Industries Ltd.*, D.Ct. So. Dist. Florida 0:15-cv-61356. The former finance director at Teva Pharmaceuticals alleged that the firing was due to cooperation with federal authorities concerning possible bribes to officials in Chile; however, according to the court, Teva provided sufficient evidence that Hall's termination was based on other grounds.

Stryker Corporation—SEC charged the Michigan-based medical technology company with violating the FCPA by bribing doctors and other government officials in five countries to obtain or retain business and make $7.5 million in illicit profits. Stryker agreed to pay more than $13.2 million to settle SEC's charges. (10/24/13)

Eli Lilly and Company—SEC charged the Indianapolis-based pharmaceutical company for improper payments to its subsidiaries made to foreign government officials to win business in Russia, Brazil, China, and Poland. Lilly agreed to pay over $29 million to settle the charges. (12/20/12)

Pfizer—SEC charged the pharmaceutical company for illegal payments made by its subsidiaries to foreign officials in Bulgaria, China, Croatia, Czech Republic, Italy, Kazakhstan, Russia, and Serbia to obtain regulatory approvals, sales, and increased prescriptions for its products. Pfizer and recently acquired Wyeth LLC - charged with its own FCPA violations - agreed to pay a combined $60 million in their settlements. (8/7/12) See: Christopher Matthews, *Pfizer Settlement Offers Window Into Pharmaceutical Industry Probe,* (Wall St. J. Nov. 21, 2011) *http://blogs.wsj.com/corruption-currents/2011/11/21/pfizer-settlement-offers-window-into-pharmaceutical-industry-probe/?mod=google_news_blog*

Johnson & Johnson—J&J agreed to pay $70 million to settle cases brought by the SEC and criminal authorities for bribing public doctors in several European countries to win contracts for their products and paying kickbacks to Iraq to illegally obtain business. (4/8/11)

See: SEC Litigation Release No. 21922; See also, Gardiner Harris, *Johnson & Johnson Settles Bribery Complaint for $70 Million in Fines* (NY Times April 8, 2011) *http://www.nytimes.com/2011/04/09/business/09drug.html.* *http://www.justice.gov/opa/pr/2011/April/11-crm-446.html http://www.justice.gov/opa/pr/2012/August/12-crm-980.html*

CRITICAL ANALYSIS: Despite the fact that bribes are a customary method of conducting business in some countries the FCPA precludes this form of business dealings. Incorporating the above cases, how would you advise your client in terms of pro-active measures?

Impact of Culture—Antidepressants

The following article explores the cultural impact on utilization of antidepressants prescribed to children in the United States and Pakistan. The diagnosis and treatment of childhood depression has become more complicated. Furthermore, there are additional antidepressants that have become available in the marketplace. A continuing debate has focused on both efficacy and the potential for serious side effects.

The Influence of Culture, Government and the Law on the Use of Antidepressants for Children in the United States and Pakistan

Roseann B. Termini and Christine A. Kelly-Miller (Used with permission, Food and Drug Law Institute).

Depression in children is a controversial topic in the United States.[1] It is an even more contentious subject when one looks at mental healthcare for children in developing nations, such as Pakistan. The diagnosis and treatment of childhood depression has become more complicated as additional antidepressants become available on the market and their efficacy, as well as their potential for serious side effects, is fiercely debated. American parents struggle with what, if any, medicinal intervention to provide to their children, given the information available regarding potential side effects. The Food and Drug Administration (FDA) provides such information as it is analyzed for validity.[2] FDA has been criticized as falling short of meeting the governmental entity's responsibilities.[3] Failure to disclose has also been at the heart of multiple lawsuits regarding antidepressant usage in children.[4] Despite the lack of agreement on what information should have been disclosed, those in the United States can consider themselves fortunate that they have outlets for receiving and disputing such information. Those who suffer from depression in developing nations not only lack information from the government and from drug manufacturers, they also have centuries of cultural issues that preclude even considering medication as a potential source of helping children with mental health ailments.

Culture, governmental involvement and legal ramifications all play roles in the treatment of childhood mental health ailments no matter what country is studied. Pakistan, for example, is a stark contrast to the United States in terms of economy, religion and government. Pakistan's total population is approximately 160,943,000, compared to the total population of the United States, which is estimated at 302,841,000.[5] The probability of dying under the age of five in Pakistan is 97 per 1,000 births.[6] In the United States, that same probability declines to 8 per 1,000 births.[7] The total expenditure on health per capita in Pakistan is forty-nine dollars ($49.00), whereas in the United States, the amount soars to $6,350 per capita.[8] Pakistani laws are still derived from the Islamic belief system and 97% of Pakistanis are Muslims.[9] In the United States, Christianity is the predominant religion with 71% of the population.[10] The separation of church and state is a founding doctrine of the United States. Given these vast differences, Pakistan and the United States offer a diverse comparative opportunity to look at the impact that culture, government and the law have on the psychological health of our children. Culture impacts all aspects of human life. The culture of the United States is arguably more diverse than Pakistan due to diversity of religions, ethnicities, languages and freedoms experienced in America. However, it is equally arguable that the cultural impact on mental health is much more significant in Pakistan today.[11]

American history of the treatment of those afflicted with mental health disorders, such as depression, is similar to the current status in Pakistan. In the late 17th and early 18th centuries, individuals with mental health disorders experienced harsh treatment by caregivers in the United States.[12] Since depression does not manifest itself visually, the origin of diagnosis has a complex

---

[1] *Hope from a Pill*, The Economist, Feb. 28, 2008, available at http://www.economist.com/science/PrinterFriendly. cfm?story_id=10765331 (last visited January 10, 2014).

[2] Manual of Policies and Procedures, Center for Drug Evaluation and Research (MAPP 4151.3) (Mar. 2, 2007).

[3] Gardiner Harris, FDA Links Drugs to Being Suicidal, N.Y. Times, Sept. 14, 2004.

[4] See for example *Miller v. Pfizer, Inc.* 356 F. 3rd 1326 (10th Cir. 2004).

[5] World Health Organization, http://www.who.int/countries/en/ (last visited June 13, 2008).

[6] Id.

[7] Id.

[8] Id.

[9] Religious Tolerance In Pakistan, http://www.religioustolerance.org/rt_pakis.htm (last visited June 13, 2008).

[10] Religious Practices and Faith Groups, http://www.religioustolerance.org/chr_prac2.htm (last visited June 13, 2008).

[11] Interview with Kalim Ahmed, MBBS, MD, Waynesboro Hospital, in Waynesboro, PA. (June 12, 2008).

[12] *History of Mental Health Movement*, National Mental Health Association, http://www1.nmha.org/about/history.cfm (last visited June 12, 2008).

history. Initially, the American view of mental health disorders was characterized as "demonic." Individuals suffering from mental disorders were once regarded as being "possessed by evil spirits."[13] Others attributed mental disorders to the changes of the moon, which were thought to cause cyclical periods of insanity.[14] The later belief is evidenced by the origin of the word, "lunacy," which is the Latin term for "moon."[15] Americans who were diagnosed with such conditions were commonly treated with physical restraints, including arm and leg chains.[16]

Many in the American and European mental health profession credit Clifford Beers for beginning a cultural shift in the approach to psychological illnesses.[17] Clifford Beers describes his struggle with mental illness in his autobiography, A Mind That Found Itself.[18] Detailing his psychological journey through his ailment, he describes the fear of being arrested for attempting suicide, which was a common punishment in early 18th century America, as well as the "torture" of the physical restraints, which precluded any significant physical movement during his nights of hospitalization.[19] Today's Pakistan is all too similar to 18th century America regarding the stigma and treatment of those who suffer mental health anomalies. Eventually, Pakistan repealed the Lunacy Act of 1912, which was the "most important piece of psychiatric legislation in Pakistan."[20] According to Ahmed Ijaz Gilani, member of the Department of Basic Health Sciences, Shifa College of Medicine, Islamabad, Pakistan, and his colleagues, the statute was "woefully inadequate and obsolete for the needs of a modern state."[21] The Lunacy Act was replaced with the enactment of the Pakistan Mental Health Ordinance.[22] Although the Mental Health Ordinance varies significantly from its predecessor, realistically the impact remains questionable. The new statute was adopted into law on February 20, 2001.[23]

Yet, mental health disorders are mainly viewed with the negative connotations and stigma as "lunacy." According to pediatrician Dr. Fouzia Rishi, who earned her medical degree from Dow Medical College in Karachi, Pakistan, the subject of depression was considered "taboo" and she received nothing in her training specific to the treatment of mental health.[24] Dr. Rishi explained that little emphasis was placed on the study of psychiatric illness and virtually none on the pediatric population.[25] In 2005, Ahmed Ijaz Gilani and several colleagues published an article regarding mental health in Pakistan where they concluded that even in the modern realm of today's world, mental illness is still "attributed to supernatural causes – it is considered to be a curse, a spell, or a test from God."[26] This perception is echoed in multiple publications regarding mental illness in Pakistan. The limited psychiatric services that are available are underutilized due to the "popular misconception" that "mental illnesses are considered to be due to 'possession' or caused by evil…or supernatural evil forces."[27] In fact, Pakistan's official language, Urdu is "devoid of terms"

---

[13] Ann Palmer, *20th Century History of the Treatment of Mental Illness: A Review*, accessed at http://www.mentalhealth world.org/29ap.html (last visited June 10, 2008).

[14] Id.

[15] Origin of word, "lunatic," http://www.askoxford.com/consice_oed/lunatic?view=uk (last visited June 13, 2008).

[16] NMHA and the History of the Mental Health Movement, http://www1nmha.org/about/history.cfm (last visited June 10, 2008).

[17] The Clifford Beers Foundation, Welcome, http://www.cliffordbeersfoundation.co.uk/ (last visited June 13, 2008).

[18] Clifford Whittingham Beers, A Mind That Found Itself (Kessinger Publishing June 17, 2004) (Mar. 1908).

[19] Id.

[20] Ahmed Ijaz Gilani et al., *Psychiatric Health Laws in Pakistan: From Lunacy to Mental Health*, Public Library of Science (Sept. 20, 2005), http://medicine.plosjournals.org/perlserv/?request=get-document&doi=10.1371%2Fjournal. pmed.0020317 (last visited June 7, 2008).

[21] Id.

[22] Government of Pakistan, Mental Health Ordinance (2001), http://www.emro.who.int/MNH/WHD/Pakistan-Ordinance. pdf (last visited June 13, 2008).

[23] Muhammad Iqbal Afridi, *Mental Health: Priorities in Pakistan*, 58 (No. 5) J. Pakistan Med. Ass'n. 225, 226 (May 2008).

[24] Telephone interview with Fouzia Rishi, MD, Pediatric Specialists of Franklin County, Pa. (June 6, 2008) (Dr. Rishi earned her medical degree in 1984).

[25] Id.

[26] Ahmed Ijaz Gilani et al., *Psychiatric Health Laws in Pakistan: From Lunacy to Mental Health*, Public Library of Science (Sept. 20, 2005), http://medicine.plosjournals.org/perlserv/?request=get-document&doi=10.1371%2Fjournal.pmed.0020317 (last visited June 7, 2008).

[27] Muhammad Iqbal Afridi, *Mental Health: Priorities in Pakistan*, 58 (No. 5) J. Pakistan Med. Ass'n. 225 (May 2008).

that generically describe mental health ailments and would be easily understood by lay people.[28] Dr. Kalim Ahmed, who studied medicine at Sind Medical College in Karachi, Pakistan, describes the cultural view of depression as "more accepted now with globalization and the changes in the media."[29] Yet, Pakistan remains "a male chauvinistic society and depression is considered a weakness."[30] Despite a clinical diagnosis of depression, proper treatment remains problematic and this diagnosis is rare in the pediatric population.[31] In contrast to the United States, there is minimal reliance on antidepressants.[32] Treatment for adults continues to consist of being "chained, beaten, burnt and scars are made on [patients' bodies] especially in skulls with serious consequences."[33]

It seems that only limited progress has been made in Pakistan regarding mental health treatment. For example, Dr. Irshad Sethi, a practicing pediatrician in Karachi, Pakistan stated that he prescribes antidepressants to approximately two children per 100 seen, typically in the age range of six to 12.[34] Dr. Sethi said that diagnosing and treating depression is becoming much more common than in the past; though, people still predominantly rely on their faith to deal with childhood depression.[35] In fact, shamans, who is a person "who acts as intermediary between the natural and supernatural worlds, using magic to cure illness,"[36] far outnumber child psychiatrists in Pakistan. According to Malik Hussain Mubashir, Vice-Chancellor of Lahore's University of Health Sciences, there is only one child psychiatrist for every "four million children estimated to be suffering from mental health issues."[37] The number of practicing shamans in Karachi alone numbers approximately four hundred and a popular form of treatment includes amulets, which are charms worn around the neck to guard against evil.[38] Other methods include spiritually treated water or incantations.[39] Shamans also prescribe medication, which is often readily available over the counter and not as controlled as in the United States.[40] The United States in comparison to Pakistan had 8.67 child and adolescent psychiatrists per 100,000 youth in 2001.[41] Yet, the prevalence of child psychiatrists in the United States is considered inadequate to meet the needs of the country's children.[42] Compounding the Pakistani shortage of mental health professionals is the fact that many medical practitioners who train in psychiatric care in Pakistan ultimately end up practicing their specialty in other countries.[43] This is due, in part, to the stigma that is present among Pakistanis and the vast opportunities available in other countries and virtually nonexistent in Pakistan.[44] Further, "only 7.6 percent of third-year medical students from four medical colleges" in Pakistan, "have reported psychiatry to be either their chosen career or a highly likely choice."[45]

---

[28] Id. at 225.

[29] Interview with Kalim Ahmed, MBBS, MD, Waynesboro Hospital, in Waynesboro, Pa. (June 12, 2008).

[30] Id.

[31] Id.

[32] Id.

[33] Muhammad Iqbal Afridi, *Mental Health: Priorities in Pakistan*, 58 (No. 5) J. Pakistan Med. Ass'n. 226, 225 (May 2008).

[34] Telephone interview with Irshad Sethi, MD, Karachi, Pakistan (June 9, 2008).

[35] Id.

[36] http://dictionary.reference.com/browse/shaman (last visited June 23, 2008).

[37] Integrated Regional Information Networks, Pakistan: Millions Lack Access to Mental Healthcare, http://www.irin news.org/Report.aspx?ReportId=75204 (last visited June 13, 2008).

[38] The New Lexicon Webster's Dictionary of the English Language 31 (1989 ed.).

[39] Amin A. Muhammed Gadit, *Psychiatry in Pakistan: 1947-2006: A new balance sheet*, 57 (No. 9) J. Pakistan Med. Ass'n. 455 (Sept. 2007).

[40] Id. at 455.

[41] Aaron Levin, *Rural Counties Suffer from Child Psychiatry Shortage*, 41 (No. 14) Psychiatric News 4 (July 21, 2006).

[42] Id.

[43] *Only 7% of Our Medical Students Want to Become Psychiatrists,* Daily Times Monitor Karachi, Mar. 29, 2008, accessible at http://www.dailytimes.com.pk/default.asp?page=2008\03\29\story_29-3-2008_pg12_10 (last visited June 13, 2008).

[44] Id.

[45] Id.

The current stigma regarding mental health in the United States has begun to be specifically studied in order to provide guidance to initiatives such as the President's New Freedom Commission (Commission) on Mental Health.[46] The Commission emanated from the United States Public Health Service Office of the Surgeon General report that reiterated the findings that stigma is the "most formidable obstacle to future progress in the arena of mental illness and health" in the United States.[47] A group of mental health professionals specifically examined the stigma related to mental healthcare in children.[48] The results illustrate that "the public holds a set of cultural beliefs and attitudes that suggests more recognition of and support for treatment of childhood depression."[49] More respondents in the study viewed depression in children as "serious, as needing treatment, and as resulting from underlying genetic or biological problems."[50] Regardless of any stigma, 1.5 million children in the United States are currently being treated with antidepressants.[51]

While modern United States still has a stigmatized view of mental health, Pakistan's cultural view is similar to 18th Century America in multiple ways. Similar to Clifford Beers' experience in the early 1900's in the United States, today under Pakistani law, which is based on the tenet of Islam, "both suicide and deliberate self-harm are illegal acts," punishable with imprisonment and a financial penalty.[52] Further, when an individual experiences a negative outcome associated with medication use, lawsuits are essentially non-existent in Pakistan.[53] Dr. Kalim Ahmed pointed out that the reasons for this are complicated and deep-rooted.[54] According to Dr. Ahmed, a mistrust of the legal system exists. "People are afraid to get involved so they do not sue."[55] Additionally, to file a lawsuit in Pakistan is costly.[56] This is a significant barrier and deterrent to access to the Pakistani judicial system since the gross national income per capita in Pakistan is $2,500.[57] This pales in comparison to the gross national income per capita in the United States, which is $44,260.[58] An even more entrenched reason for the lack of litigation in Pakistan is described by Dr. Ahmed as follows: "Pakistan is now like the United States used to be 60 years ago. There is a basic belief that a physician will do no harm. People trust the physicians and resist believing that the physician did anything wrong. There is a great deal of trust [between] the patient and the physician."[59] This belief system is very strong according to Dr. Ahmed and consists of the idea that a "cure comes from God and if something negative happens, people believe that God did not want that person to get better."[60] Dr. Amatul Khalid, who studied at the University of Punjab and is now practicing Internal Medicine in the United States, echoed this statement. She revealed that if a negative outcome occurs, it is believed that "it was supposed to happen that way. It is attributed to God."[61] An additional complication to access to one's legal rights in Pakistan is a lack of education and awareness.[62] According

---

[46] Achieving the Promise: Transforming Mental Health Care in America, The President's New Freedom Commission on Mental Health Final Report (July 2003).

[47] U.S. Department of Health & Human Services, Office of the Surgeon General, SAMHSA, Mental Health: Culture, Race and Ethnicity (2001).

[48] Bernice A. Pescosolido, Ph.D., *Culture, Children, and Mental Health Treatment: Special Section on the National Stigma Study – Children,* 58 (No. 5) Psychiatric Services 611 (May 2007).

[49] Id. at 612.

[50] Id. at 612.

[51] *Parent Group Says Public Unaware that Antidepressant Induced Suicides are in the Tens of Thousands,* Ablechild, Nov. 5, 2007, accessible at http://www.prlog.org/10036793-parent-group-says-public-unaware-that-antidepressant-induced-suicides-are-in-the-tens-of-thousands.html (last visited June 13, 2008).

[52] Murad M. Khan, *Suicide Prevention in Pakistan: an impossible challenge?,* 57 (No. 10) J. Pakistan Med. Ass'n. 478 (Oct. 2007).

[53] Interview with Kalim Ahmed, MBBS, MD, Waynesboro Hospital, in Waynesboro, Pa. (June 12, 2008).

[54] Id.

[55] Id.

[56] Id.

[57] World Health Organization, http://www.who.int/countries/en/ (last visited June 13, 2008).

[58] Id.

[59] Interview with Kalim Ahmed, MBBS, MD, Waynesboro Hospital, in Waynesboro, Pa. (June 12, 2008).

[60] Id.

[61] Telephone interview with Amatul Khalid, MD, Chambersburg Medical Associates (June 12, 2008).

[62] Telephone interview with Irshad Sethi, MD, Karachi, Pakistan (June 9, 2008).

to one commentator, less accountability exists for mistakes and less pressure from the general public to take responsibility for errors due to the high illiteracy rate and lack of assertion of one's limited rights.[63] Indeed the adult literacy rate in Pakistan in 2005 was 49.9%.[64]

In contrast to Pakistan, the legal landscape in the United States is replete with lawsuits surrounding prescription medication, which includes antidepressants. For example, a 13 year old had been taking the antidepressant Zoloft for 6 days prior to his death and committed suicide by hanging himself.[65] The parents of the decedent filed suit against the drug manufacturer based on claims which included strict liability and failure to test and to warn.[66] In *Miller v. Pfizer*, the court granted summary judgment to the drug manufacturer on the basis of a lack of evidence of causation.[67] The Court of Appeals upheld the lower court decision.[68] The United States Supreme Court declined to hear this case.[69] Other litigation has produced results similar to *Miller v. Pfizer*.[70] For example, the parents of the decedent minor instituted legal action on behalf of their daughter who also committed suicide.[71] The adolescent was taking the antidepressant Paxil for three months prior to her death.[72] In *White v. SmithKline Beecham*, the drug manufacturer's motion for judgment on the pleadings was granted and the case terminated.[73] According to the court, the plaintiffs failed to demonstrate that the drug manufacturer had misled FDA or bribed an agency official, which was required to satisfy one of the two limited state exceptions to the broad protections afforded drug manufacturers under Michigan state law.[74] Despite unsuccessful lawsuits legal actions against drug manufacturers for the use of antidepressants in children continue to spiral.[75]

FDA impacts the litigation of antidepressants and children in America. A medication receives FDA approval based upon studies of safety and efficacy for specific uses. Once this approval process is complete, FDA has little control over how the approved drug is then prescribed.[76] When a licensed medical professional prescribes an FDA-approved medication for a non-FDA approved use, this is the process known as off-label prescribing.[77] A study in the June 2005 Journal of Clinical Psychiatry indicated that 75% of prescriptive antidepressants known as selective serotonin reuptake inhibitors (SSRIs), which Paxil and Zoloft mentioned previously are categorized as, were prescribed for treatments not approved by FDA.[78] There are reasons touted for support of continuation of off-label prescribing. The first is the time it takes FDA to approve medication for specific use.[79] Without off-label prescriptions, people could be waiting an inordinate amount of time to obtain medication for a particular use. Additionally, some populations that may benefit from drug use may never receive such drugs if they required approval for every ailment and age group because there are not enough people within the afflicted population to perform statistically valid research.[80]

---

[63] *Id.*

[64] Core Health Indicators, World Health Organization, accessible at http://www.who.int/whosis/database/core/core_
select_process.cfm (last visited June 13, 2008).

[65] *Miller v. Pfizer, Inc.*, 196 F.Supp.2d 1062 (D. Kan. Feb. 7, 2002).

[66] Id. at 1062.

[67] Id. at 1063.

[68] *Miller v. Pfizer, Inc.*, 356 F.3d 1326 (10th Cir. 2004).

[69] *Miller v. Pfizer, Inc.* 543 U.S. 917 (2004).

[70] *Miller v. Pfizer, Inc.*, 356 F.3d 1326 (10th Cir. 2004).

[71] *White v. SmithKline Beecham Corp.*, 538 F.Supp.2d 1023 (W.D. Mich. 2008).

[72] Id.

[73] Id.

[74] Id. at 1031 (Michigan law provides immunity whose products are approved by FDA with exceptions of when companies act to misled FDA or bribe or attempt to bribe agency officials).

[75] See for example Vickery & Waldner, LLP Attorneys at Law, story available at http://www.paxildefects.com/Practice
Areas/Paxil-Wrongful-Death.asp (last visited June 23, 2008).

[76] Alexander T. Tabarrok, *Assessing the FDA via the Anomaly of Off-Label Drug Prescribing*, n.1, The Independent Review, Summer 2000, at 25.

[77] Id.

[78] Evelyn Pringle, *Off-Label Sales of SSRIs Leads to More Litigation*, (Feb. 22, 2007), *available at* http://www.
opednews.com/articles/genera_evelyn_p_070222_off_label_sales_of_s.htm (last visited June 13, 2008).

[79] Alexander T. Tabarrok, *Assessing the FDA via the Anomaly of Off-Label Drug Prescribing*, n.1, The Independent Review, Summer 2000, at 25.

[80] Id.

FDA issued a guidance document for drug and medical device manufacturers on "good reprint practices" that are to be used when informing medical professionals about unapproved new uses of drugs.[81] Promotion of off-label uses by drug manufacturers for medication is impermissible.[82] However, FDA "recognizes that the public health can be served when health care professionals receive truthful and non-misleading information on unapproved uses of approved or cleared medical products."[83] Essentially the draft guidance outlines recommendations for dissemination of off-label usage in reputable, scientific or medical references to avoid FDA designation of "unlawful promotion" of a drug.[84] The guidance coincides with the latest allegations surrounding antidepressant drug manufacturers. Iowa Senator Charles Grassley recommended that FDA probe into the potential that GlaxoSmithKline withheld information from FDA during the company's application process for FDA approval of its antidepressant Paxil in 1989.[85] Grassley alleges that the manufacturer should have known then that Paxil could lead to a higher risk of suicide.[86] It was further acknowledged by GlaxoSmithKline that the Justice Departments from Colorado, Boston and Washington were investigating the company's off-label marketing of Paxil.[87]

FDA issued a "black box warning" on all antidepressants for the "increased risk" of suicidal thoughts and behaviors in children and adolescents.[88] Short of a market withdrawal, black box warnings are the "most serious warnings placed in the labeling of a prescription medication.[89] As of 2004, antidepressants were the 11th drug product approved for children to receive a black box warning about their use in children.[90] However, the warning does not disallow prescribing the medication in question; "rather, it warns of the risk of suicidality and encourages prescribers to balance this risk with clinical need."[91] Since FDA's 2004 black box warning, the debate rages on as to the issue of increased risk of suicidality in children. The warning that the FDA issued was based upon drug manufacturers' clinical trials, which are considered the "gold standard" in pharmacological research.[92] The data was collected and analyzed from 24 trials, which included over 4,400 children and adolescents.[93] The results indicated a "greater risk of suicidality during the first few months of treatment in those receiving antidepressants. The average risk of such events on drug was 4%, twice the placebo risk of 2%. No suicides occurred in these trials."[94]

The Journal of the American Medical Association (JAMA) published the results of the pooled trial analysis that indicated the increased risk of suicidality in children was not statistically significant between those receiving an antidepressant and those receiving a placebo.[95] There were no completed suicides and the conclusion of the researchers was the benefit of antidepressant use to

---

[81] Guidance for Industry: Good Reprint Practices for the Distribution of Medical Journal Articles and Medical or Scientific Reference Publications on Unapproved New Uses of Approved Drugs and Approved or Cleared Medical Devices, U.S. Department of Health and Human Services, Food and Drug Administration (Feb. 2008).

[82] David Kailin, Ph.D., M.P.H., L.Ac., *FDA Issues Draft Guidance Document on Good Reprint Practices*, (Mar. 3, 2008), accessible at http://www.convergentmedical.com/images/FDAGoodReprintPractices.pdf (last visited June 23, 2008).

[83] Guidance for Industry: Good Reprint Practices for the Distribution of Medical Journal Articles and Medical or Scientific Reference Publications on Unapproved New Uses of Approved Drugs and Approved or Cleared Medical Devices, U.S. Department of Health and Human Services, Food and Drug Administration (Feb. 2008).

[84] Id. at 6.

[85] Bob Fernandez, *Glaxo's Paxil Faces Scrutiny on the Hill*, accessible at http://www.philly.com/philly/business/20624784.html (last visited June 23, 2008).

[86] Id.

[87] Id.

[88] *FDA Launches a Multi-Pronged Strategy to Strengthen Safeguards for Children Treated with Antidepressant Medications*, U.S. Food and Drug Administration (Oct. 15, 2004), accessible at http://www.fda.gov/bbs/topics/news/2004/NEW01124.html (last visited June 10, 2008).

[89] Id.

[90] Id.

[91] Id.

[92] Alex Berenson & Benedict Carey, *Experts Question Study on Youth Suicide Rates*, N.Y. Times (Sept. 14, 2007).

[93] FDA Public Health Advisory: Suicidality in Children and Adolescents Being Treated with Antidepressant Medication (Oct. 14, 2004), accessible at http://www.fda.gov/cder/drug/antidepressants/SSRIPHA200410.htm (last visited June 23, 2008).

[94] Id.

[95] Jeffrey A. Bridge, Ph.D., et al., *Clinical Response and Risk for Reported Suicidal Ideation and Suicide Attempts in Pediatric Antidepressant Treatment: A Meta-analysis of Randomized Controlled Trials*, 297 J. Am. Med. Ass'n. 1683 (Apr. 2007).

treat pediatric depression outweighed the risk.[96] A report published in the American Journal of Psychiatry, concluded that the 2004 warning led to a decrease in antidepressant prescriptions and those decreased prescriptions "were associated with increases in suicide rates in children and adolescents."[97] According to Dr. Mushtaq Jameel, a child and adolescent psychiatrist who practices in the United States, the "practices of prescribing antidepressants to the child and adolescent population was on the rise specifically during 1995-2003; thereafter, the FDA issued the Black Box Warning."[98] "Since this [warning], there was a sharp decline in antidepressants prescribed to this group."[99] Since Dr. Jameel's patients are "on the moderate to severe spectrum of disorders" he does not "hesitate to prescribe antidepressants" despite the warning and further indicated that a failure to prescribe to the population he treats, if warranted, would be an act of "neglect" and the "risks" of not treating are "higher."[100]

Pakistan's Ministry of Health serves a somewhat similar role as the FDA. The Drug Control Organization (DCO) is the entity within the Ministry of Health that oversees medication regulations within Pakistan.[101] The DCO approves foreign medications prior to marketing within the country. Eighty percent of medications offered within Pakistan are manufactured within the country[102]; however, the majority of prescription drugs are developed in other countries.[103] Dr. Kalim Ahmed noted that there is actually minimal involvement by the Ministry of Health in drug authorization and warnings.[104] Physicians generally rely on information directly from the drug manufacturers and FDA and, unlike the United States, it is not typical to rely on the Ministry of Health for precautions regarding medication prescriptions.[105] A study in the January-March 2007 publication of the Pakistan Journal of Medical Sciences listed tricyclic antidepressants as a treatment for attention deficit hyperactivity disorder in children and the only side effects listed were "drowsiness, sleep disturbances, anxiety, headaches, dry mouth, constipation, may produce arrhythmias."[106] Tricyclic antidepressants were included in the 2004 FDA black box warning regarding the increased risk of suicidality in children and adolescents.[107]

The prevalence of antidepressant usage varies significantly with regard to the country where one resides.[108] Reliance on psychotropic medication is also impacted by the stigma that the societal mores attach to such drugs. Despite the continued cultural stigma that lingers in the United States regarding depression and other mental health issues, it certainly pales in comparison to the negative connotations that attach to mental health disorders in Pakistan. Long-standing, deeply-rooted beliefs in alternative methods of treatment hinder the acceptance to access modern mental health options. Once a negative outcome occurs that is possibly associated with medication usage, the country where a person lives dictates the likelihood of potential litigation against the manufacturer. While a judicial system is available to citizens of Pakistan, apprehension, economic status and entrenched cultural beliefs essentially shut the door on lawsuits. On the other hand, those in the United

---

[96] Id.

[97] Robert D. Gibbons, Ph.D., et al., *Early Evidence on the Effects of Regulators' Suicidality Warnings on SSRI Prescriptions and Suicide in Children and Adolescents*, 164 Am. J. Psychiatry 1356 (Sept. 2007).

[98] E-mail from Mushtaq Jameel, M.D., Child and Adolescent Psychiatrist, Summit Behavioral Health Services, in Chambersburg, Pa. (June 11, 2008, 02:27:55 EST) (on file with author).

[99] Id.

[100] Id.

[101] Our History, Ministry of Health, accessible at http://www.dcomoh.gov.pk/about/history.php (last visited June 23, 2008).

[102] Overview, Ministry of Health, accessible at http://www.dcomoh.gov.pk/about/overview.php (last visited June 23, 2008).

[103] Interview with Kalim Ahmed, MBBS, MD, Waynesboro Hospital, in Waynesboro, Pa. (June 12, 2008).

[104] Id.

[105] Id.

[106] Nazish Imran, *Attention Deficit Hyperactivity Syndrome: An update on assessment and management*, 23 Pakistan J. Med. Sci. 13 (Jan.-Mar. 2007).

[107] FDA Public Health Advisory: Suicidality in Children and Adolescents Being Treated with Antidepressant Medication (Oct. 14, 2004), accessible at http://www.fda.gov/cder/drug/antidepressants/SSRIPHA200410.htm (last visited June 13, 2008).

[108] Psycho-Pharmaceuticals in Europe: Mental Health Policy and Practice across Europe 146-187 (Martin Knapp et al. eds., Milton Keynes: Open University Press, 2007).

States are much more prone to being enticed to bring a lawsuit against a drug manufacturer for potential correlation between ingestion and a negative outcome. Yet, both countries have governmental entities in place to provide oversight to medications.

Finally, the United States is far more advanced than Pakistan in the research conducted on antidepressants and medication in general, including the dissemination of research outcomes through FDA. However, both countries' governments have taken steps to increase awareness in mental health. The United States instituted The President's New Freedom Commission on Mental Health and Pakistan enacted the Mental Health Ordinance. The commonality between the United States and Pakistan is the fact that despite what country a child is from, the largest victim of depression can sometimes be the smallest.

CRITICAL ANALYSIS: Using the above article as an example, evaluate the impact of culture on using medicine to treat, for example, depression. Evaluate any cross-cultural implications in treatment.

Chapter 3: Product Classification—Food, Supplement, Personal Care Product, Drug, Medical Device or Combination

Product Classification under the Food, Drug and Cosmetic Act

One of the most complicated areas in food and drug law regulation is that of accurate product classification. The issues are complex with far reaching effects on the regulated industry. For example, if a product is deemed a dietary supplement rather than a drug for regulation purposes, then no preapproval prior to market entry is necessary. Intended use remains a controlling factor in FDA product categorization. Mandated by the Medical Device User Fee and Modernization Act of 2002, FDA created an Office of Combination Products for those regulated products that fall within more than one category. The regulatory authority involves combination products such as drug-device, drug-biologic, and device-biologic.

Combination Product Defined

As defined in 21 CFR § 3.2(e), the term combination product includes:

(1) A product comprised of two or more regulated components, i.e., drug/device, biologic/device, drug/biologic, or drug/device/biologic, that are physically, chemically, or otherwise combined or mixed and produced as a single entity.

(2) Two or more separate products packaged together in a single package or as a unit and comprised of drug and device products, device and biological products, or biological and drug products.

(3) A drug, device, or biological product packaged separately that according to its investigational plan or proposed labeling is intended for use only with an approved individually specified drug, device, or biological product where both are required to achieve the intended use, indication, or effect and where upon approval of the proposed product the labeling of the approved product would need to be changed, e.g., to reflect a change in intended use, dosage form, strength, route of administration, or significant change in dose.

(4) Any investigational drug, device, or biological product packaged separately that according to its proposed labeling is for use only with another individually specified investigational drug, device, or biological product where both are required to achieve the intended use, indication, or effect.

Classification—Personal Care Cosmetic Product or Drug

Cosmetic, Drug, or Both? Is It Soap?

http://www.fda.gov/Cosmetics/GuidanceRegulation/LawsRegulations/ucm074201.htm (edited)

Definition: How does the law define a cosmetic? The Food, Drug, and Cosmetic Act (FD&C Act) defines cosmetics by their intended use, as "articles intended to be rubbed, poured, sprinkled, or sprayed on, introduced into, or otherwise applied to the human body for cleansing, beautifying, promoting attractiveness, or altering the appearance" [FD&C Act, sec. 201(i)]. Among the products included in this definition are skin moisturizers, perfumes, lipsticks, fingernail polishes, eye and facial makeup preparations, shampoos, permanent waves, hair colors, toothpastes, and deodorants, as well as any material intended for use as a component of a cosmetic product.

Definition: How does the law define a drug? The FD&C Act defines drugs by their intended use, as "(A) articles intended for use in the diagnosis, cure, mitigation, treatment, or prevention of disease. and (B) articles (other than food) intended to affect the structure or any function of the body of man or other animals" [FD&C Act, sec. 201(g)(1)].

Dual Classification: How can a product be both a cosmetic and a drug? Some products meet the definitions of both cosmetics and drugs. This may happen when a product has two intended uses. For example, a shampoo is a cosmetic because its intended use is to cleanse the hair. An antidandruff treatment is a drug because its intended use is to treat dandruff. Consequently, an antidandruff shampoo is both a cosmetic and a drug. Among other cosmetic/drug combinations are toothpastes that contain fluoride, deodorants that are also antiperspirants, and moisturizers and makeup marketed with sun-protection claims. Such products must comply with the requirements for both cosmetics and drugs.

Intended Use: How is a product's intended use established? Intended use may be established in a number of ways. Among them are:

> ➢ *Claims on the product labeling, in advertising, on the Internet, or in other promotional materials.*
> ➢ *Consumer perception, which may be established through the product's reputation. Ingredients that may cause a product to be considered a drug because they have a well known (to the public and industry) therapeutic use.*

Drug-Beverage—Coca-Cola Plus®

http://www.coca-colacompany.com/stories/coca-cola-fortified-with-dietary-fiber-to-launch-in-japan
https://www.wsj.com/articles/things-go-better-with-coke-laxative-edition-1515354223
http://www.mhlw.go.jp/english/topics/foodsafety/fhc/02.html (Foods for Specified Health Uses)

Do things go better with Coke? Apparently, they do in Japan. Each 470-ml bottle of Coca-Cola Plus®, contains five grams of indigestible dextrin which is a type of dietary fiber that is recognized to have a laxative effect.

CRITICAL ANALYSIS: If marketed in the United States, how would the product be classified and why? For example, should Coca-Cola Plus® be regulated as a food or OTC drug product or both.

Cosmetic or Drug—Tooth Whiteners Examples
Docket No. FDA-2009-P-0566

In 2014, FDA denied a Citizen's Petition (Petition) submitted by the American Dental Association (ADA) in 2009. The ADA had requested that FDA "review and establish an appropriate regulatory classification" for peroxide-containing whitening products and expressed concerns about the safe use of tooth-whitening products without a professional consultation or examination. FDA determined that the majority of peroxide-containing tooth whiteners would fall within the definition of cosmetic under 21 U.S.C. sec. 321(i) as they are "intended to be...applied to the human body....for cleansing, beautifying, promoting attractiveness, or altering the appearance."

FDA set forth that the mechanisms of action, conditions of use, safety and formulation of specific peroxide-containing tooth whitener products is required to determine whether these products also fall within the definition of drug. FDA determined that the adverse events reports evidenced very small number of complaints related to peroxide-containing tooth whiteners. FDA concluded that there was insufficient information to conclude that peroxide containing tooth whitening products are over-use or abused.

CRITICAL ANALYSIS: Do you agree with FDA's determination? Why did the American Dental Association submit a Citizen's petition?

Drug or Medical Device Examples—Maggots and Leeches

FDA approved medicinal and maggots leeches as medical devices as Class II with special controls with a detailed guidance document rather than drugs based on the definitions of drug and medical device. See: 21 U.S.C. sec. 321 (g) and (h). Leeches consume blood and FDA categorizes this process as a mechanical rather than a chemical action. For example, clinically leeches have been used to reestablish blood circulation and to decrease postoperative swelling.

Bob Carlson, *Crawling Through the Millennia: Maggots and Leeches Come Full Circle*
See: *https://www.ncbi.nlm.nih.gov/pmc/articles/PMC3571037/*

CRITICAL ANALYSIS: Do you agree with FDA's classification of maggots and leeches as medical devices?

Legal Precedent—*"Sudden Change"* and *"Line Away"*

Influential legal decisions concerning product classification and intended use are detailed below. In the *Sudden Change* and *Line Away* cases, the court had to determine whether the wrinkle smoother product was a drug or cosmetic. Each decision discusses intended use and the promotional claims about the product.

United States v. An Article Consisting of 216 Individually Cartons Bottles, More or Less, of an Article Labeled in part: SUDDEN CHANGE, Hazel Bishop, Inc., 409 F.2d 734 (2d Cir.1969)

OPINION-ANDERSON, Circuit Judge: This is an appeal in a seizure action from an order of the United States District Court for the Eastern District of New York entered on July 30, 1968, denying the Government's motion for summary judgment and granting summary judgment for the claimant. The seizure concerned 216 bottles of a cosmetic product called "Sudden Change" which is a clear liquid lotion consisting primarily of two ingredients: bovine albumen (15%) and distilled water (over 84%). It is meant to be applied externally to the surface of the facial skin, and it is claimed, inter alia, in its labeling and advertising that it will provide a "Face Lift Without Surgery." The court below described the effects of the product as follows: Allowed to dry on the skin, it leaves a film which (1) masks imperfections, making the skin look smoother and (2) acts mechanically to smooth and firm the skin by tightening the surface. Both effects are temporary. There is apparently no absorption by, or changes in, skin tissue resulting from its applications; it washes off. The central issue presented in this appeal is whether Sudden Change is, within the meaning of the Federal Food, Drug and Cosmetic Act, 21 U.S.C. § 321(g) (1), a "drug." That Section, in pertinent part, provides: "The term 'drug' means (C) articles (other than food) intended to affect the structure *** of the body of man ***." The question posed is whether, by reason of its labeling and promotional claims, Sudden Change is to be deemed a drug for purposes of the Act. Claimant also filed a statement of claimed uncontested facts which admits inter alia:

1. That the label for Sudden Change does not specify its ingredients.
2. That the specific ingredients for the article are Bovine Serum, Albumin 15.00%, Sodium Benzoate 0.70%, Ethylmercurithiosalicylate 0.005%, 6 Acetoxy-2, 4 dimethyl-N-diozaul 0.05% and distilled water to make 100.00%.
3. That the article's labeling made the following claims:
    (a) "it gives a face lift without surgery"
    (b) "it lifts the skin"
    (c) "it firms the skin"
    (d) "it tones the skin"
    (e) "it smoothes the skin"
    (f) "it moisturizes the skin"
    (g) "it provides a tingling sensation to indicate the article is working"
    (h) "it lifts puffs under the eyes"
    (i) "it provides the user with beneficial results for hours"
    (j) "it is more effective if applied regularly"
4. Claimant further admits that its labeling claims achieved the foregoing results by the following mechanisms of action:

"When 'Sudden Change' dries on the surface of the skin, the residual solids are deposited as a film. This effect is achieved by the cohesive properties of this substance which cause the particles to be attracted to each other. The film on the surface of the skin thus achieves a dynamic multilateral tensing action and as said deposit ultimately undergoes an isometric process, it smooths the surface of the skin by a virtually invisible masking effect and imparts to the facial tissues a lift, firmness and tone which smooth out the skin surface. In so doing, "the preparation does not enter into the tissues of the skin or bring about any change in the skin's cellular structure or function." *** As the aqueous portion of 'Sudden Change' evaporates after application and the contractile film is formed, the evaporative and contractile processes result in a tactile sensation of tightening that is perceptible to the user. As the film is formed and lines are, in fact, smoothed out, "a visible difference is apparent to the user." Claimant concedes that there is no approved New Drug Application in effect for the article "Sudden Change." ***

The box in which Sudden Change is sold bears the capitalized words " SUDDEN CHANGE"

"THE PERFECTED ANTI-WRINKLE FACE LIFT." Another side of the box bears the following description:

"SUDDEN CHANGE by Lanolin Plus is the new and improved, dramatically different wrinkle smoothing cosmetic. By simple, dynamic contraction, it lifts, firms, tones slack skin, smooths out wrinkles, lifts the puffs under eyes, leaving your contours looking beautifully defined. It acts noticeably, visibly, and so quickly you will see and feel results minutes after you apply it. Not a hormone or chemical astringent, SUDDEN CHANGE is a concentrated purified natural protein, a clear invisible liquid cosmetic that can be used as often as you like. Because there never has been a cosmetic exactly like SUDDEN CHANGE before, we suggest you read the directions carefully before applying. For best results, use SUDDEN CHANGE often. The more you use, the longer your wrinkle-free look will last."

The face of the leaflet insert bears the following words, capitalized and displayed prominently: "FACE LIFT WITHOUT SURGERY"—"The Perfected Anti-Wrinkle Face Lift Acts in Minutes Lasts for Hours." It also repeats the descriptive material that appears on the box and contains directions for use. The advertising claims for Sudden Change (newspaper, magazine, store placard, television) include the prominently displayed capitalized words "Now a face lift without surgery!" together with "before" and "after" poses of a model and the following words:

"'Sudden Change'—the new antiwrinkle face lift—works in minutes *** lasts for hours *** gives you a noticeably smoother younger look. Sudden change is the one cosmetic that can make you look years younger for hours *** although it cannot eliminate wrinkles permanently. Just smooth it on and watch it smooth away crowsfeet, laugh and frown lines—even under-eye puffiness. In minutes. Sudden Change helps keep fatigue lines, wrinkles and 'that tired look' away for hours. Sudden Change is pure natural protein—contains no hormones—does not change the structure or function of your skin in any way. Try Sudden Change. As long as you are using Sudden Change, you have nothing to lose but your wrinkles. 'Sudden Change' by Lanolin Plus $2.95 plus tax." It is well settled that the intended use of a product may be determined from its label, accompanying labeling, promotional material, advertising and any other relevant source. *United States v. Hohensee*, 243 F.2d 367, 370 (3 Cir. 1957), cert. den., 353 U.S. 976, 77 S. Ct. 1058, 1 L. Ed. 2d 1136 (1957) (intended use proved by promotional claims in graphic material as well as oral representations); *United States v. Millpax, Inc.*, 313 F.2d 152, 154 (7 Cir. 1963), cert. den., 373 U.S. 903, 83 S. Ct. 1291, 10 L. Ed. 2d 198 (1963) (intended use proved by form "disclaimer letter" and magazine testimonials implying that iron tonic was a cancer cure); *Nature Food Centers, Inc. v. United States*, 310 F.2d 67, 69 (1 Cir. 1962), cert. den., 371 U.S. 968, 83 S. Ct. 552, 9 L. Ed. 2d 539 (1963) *** Regardless of the actual physical effect of a product, it will be deemed a drug for purposes of the Act where the labeling and promotional claims show intended uses that bring it within the drug definition. *** Thus, Congress has made a judgment that a product is subject to regulation as a drug if certain promotional claims are made for it. The mere statement of this rule poses a crucial issue: by what standards are these claims to be evaluated? Or, to put it another way, what degree of sophistication or vulnerability is to be ascribed to the hypothetical potential consumer in order to understand how these claims are understood by the buying public? The District Court answered this question as follows:

"Such seller's claims [as that of "face lift without surgery"] must be considered in the special context of late twentieth century American mores. The labeling of Sudden Change is directed to women who are potential consumers of the article. Subjected to the incessant advertising campaigns of the cosmetic industry, a potential buyer can be expected to have achieved some immunity to the beautifiers' hyperbole." And further: "Against this background of constant exposure to puffing and extravagant claims, we cannot believe that a prospective purchaser of Sudden Change—faced with instructions advising her that she can repeat the process in a few hours—expects anything other than a possibility that she may look better. She would view the promise of 'face lift' with the same skepticism—or lack of it—as she would view other promises offering her beauty, loveliness, rejuvenation or a young look. She would not expect a structural change of the kind available through plastic surgery." ***

A primary purpose of the Act is the protection of the ultimate consumer's economic interests. See *Federal Security Administrator v. Quaker Oats Co.*, 318 U.S. 218, 230, 63 S. Ct. 589, 87 L. Ed. 724 (1943); *United States v. Two Bags *** Poppy Seeds*, 147 F.2d 123, 126-127 (6 Cir. 1945). Considering the remedial purposes of the Act and particularly of the 1938 amendments, the Supreme Court declared: "The purposes of this legislation thus touch phases of the lives and health of people which, in the circumstances of modern industrialism, are largely beyond self-protection.

Accepting this admonition, we conclude that the purposes of the Act will best be effected by postulating a consuming public which includes "the ignorant, the unthinking and the credulous ***." *Florence Mfg. Co. v. J. C. Dowd & Co.*, 178 F. 73, 75 (2 Cir. 1910). See, *United States v. 62 Packages* See also *United States v. 250 Jars *** "Cal's Tupelo Blossom U.S. Fancy Pure Honey"*, *supra*, 344 F.2d at 289, which held that *** "the Act was passed to protect unwary customers in vital matters of health and, consequently, must be given a liberal construction to effectuate this high purpose, and [this court should] not open a loophole through which those who prey upon the weakness, gullibility, and superstition of human nature can escape the consequences of their actions." While it is not altogether clear what standard the court below applied, the reasoning appears to assume something like a "reasonable woman" standard. *** The references to "face lift" and "surgery" carry distinctly physiological connotations, suggesting, at least to the vulnerable consumer, that the product will "affect the structure *** of the body ***" in some way other than merely temporarily altering the appearance. We do not accept the concept that skepticism toward familiar claims necessarily entails skepticism toward unfamiliar claims; the theory of the legislation is that someone might take the claim literally. In other words, with the exception of those claims which have become so associated with the familiar exaggerations of cosmetics advertising that virtually everyone can be presumed to be capable of discounting them as puffery, the question of whether a product is "intended to affect the structure *** of the body of man ***" is to be answered by considering, first, how the claim might be understood by the "ignorant, unthinking or credulous" consumer, and second, whether the claim as so understood may fairly be said to constitute a representation that the product will affect the structure of the body in some medical—or drug-type fashion, i.e., in some way other than merely "altering the appearance." We hold, therefore, that so long as Sudden Change is claimed to give a "face lift without surgery" and to "lift out puffs" it is to be deemed a drug within the meaning of 21 U.S.C. § 321(g) (1) (C). Reversed and remanded for proceedings not inconsistent with this opinion.

United States v. An Article of Drug Consisting of 36 Boxes, More or Less Line Away Temporary Wrinkle Smoother, 415 F.2d 369 (3rd Cir. 1969)

OPINION OF THE COURT: HASTIE, Chief Judge. This is an appeal from a judgment of condemnation entered in a seizure action under section 304 of the Federal Food, Drug, and Cosmetic Act, 21 U.S.C. § 334. Involved is an article known as "Line Away Temporary Wrinkle Smoother, Coty," or more simply, "Line Away." The sole issue before this court is whether Line Away is a "drug" within the meaning of section 201 of the Food, Drug, and Cosmetic Act. So far as is relevant to this case, section 201 provides:

*"The term 'drug' means *** (C) articles * * * intended to affect the structure *** of the body of man ***" 21 U.S.C. §321(g) (1) (C).*

The district court found that since the admitted effect of Line Away is to smooth, firm, and tighten the skin, it does "affect the structure" of the skin within the literal definition of "drug" contained in section 201. *** For regardless of the actual physical effect of a product, it will be deemed a drug if the labeling, including separate promotional claims, attributes characteristics to the product that would bring it within the Act's definition. *Kordel v. United States*, 1948, 335 U.S. 345, 69 S. Ct. 106, 93 L. Ed. 52; *United States v. Hohensee*, 3d Cir. 1957, 243 F.2d 367, cert. den. 353 U.S. 976, 77 S. Ct. 1058, 1 L. Ed. 2d 1136. See *United States v. Article of Drug*, 3d Cir. 1966, 362 F.2d 923. Nor can it be doubted that the fact that an article is a beautifying agent or "cosmetic," as is claimed here, does not preclude its also being a drug for purposes of the Act. Accordingly, we turn to an examination of the promotional claims made for Line Away. The leaflet packed in each box of Line Away contains application instructions and makes it clear, as does the promotional material, that the effect of the product is temporary, lasting only up to five hours. Prior to the instructions, however, some introductory material is included. Recited prominently in italics is the preface: *"Manufactured exclusively for Coty in the pharmaceutical laboratories of Charles Pfizer & Co., Inc."*

There follows, inter alia:

> *"Line Away is not a face lift, not a treatment. It's a clear protein cosmetic. Contains absolutely no harmful chemicals, no hormones.*
>
> *"To assure superior performance, Line Away is sealed and packaged under biologically aseptic conditions. You can be absolutely certain your protein lotion will stay fresh, superactive."* * * *
>
> *"You'll feel a tingling sensation the instant you smooth Line Away on. It means that Line Away is at work—smoothing, firming, tightening."*

A leaflet entitled "COTY CUES Advance Information for Coty Consultants" contains in part the following information:

> *"LINE AWAY is an amazing new cosmetic * * * manufactured exclusively for Coty in the pharmaceutical laboratories of Chas. Pfizer & Co., Inc."*
>
> *"LINE AWAY is a colorless protein cosmetic in liquid form."*
>
> *"LINE AWAY is not a face lift *** not a treatment *** not a cover up. LINE AWAY contains no harmful drugs."* ***
>
> *"LINE AWAY visibly smoothes out fatigue lines, laugh lines, worry lines, frown lines, tiny age lines, and crows feet while discouraging new lines from forming."*** "LINE AWAY is perfectly harmless to use as often as desired *** two, three or more times a day. LINE AWAY is sealed and packaged under biologically aseptic conditions in the laboratories of Chas. Pfizer and Co., Inc."*

The remainder of this leaflet contains use instructions and selling information. The cover of the leaflet, in addition to the title mentioned above, contains the salutation:

> *"Coty Invites You to Enter the Exciting World of Protein Cosmetics."*

A newspaper advertisement, below three pairs of before and after pictures, contains the following copy: *"Line Away is an amazing protein lotion which contains no hormones or harmful drugs. New Line Away by Coty is the only wrinkle smoother packaged under biologically aseptic conditions in the laboratories of Chas. Pfizer & Co., Inc. ***"*

Another newspaper advertisement, designed to be used over a merchant's name, contains before and after pictures and the following material below them: *"Line Away is an amazing protein liquid. Contains no hormones or harmful drugs. It's the only wrinkle smoother packaged under biologically aseptic conditions in the pharmaceutical laboratories of Chas. Pfizer & Co., Inc."*

Our analysis begins with a preliminary brief examination of the product and its use. The product's critical ingredient is bovine albumin. Albumin is a simple protein found in the tissues of animals and plants. A typical source is egg white, but bovine albumin was employed here since it is more soluble in water. The product is a clear liquid which is applied externally on the face. As it dries, it forms a film and contracts. This results in the skin being smoothed. Beyond this simple mechanical operation, Line Away has no effect upon the skin. In contrast, the promotional material is, for the most part, elaboration of the implications inherent in the description of Line Away as an "amazing protein lotion." Since protein is a principal nutrient, advertising so structured as to emphasize the protein content of the product suggests that the lotion nourishes the skin. In line with this basic suggestion, the repeated statements that Line Away is made in a "pharmaceutical laboratory" and packaged under "biologically aseptic conditions" imply that the product itself is a pharmaceutical. Characterizing the lotion as "super-active" and "amazing", creating a "tingling sensation" when "at work", "tightening" the skin and "discouraging new wrinkles from forming" strongly reinforces the impression that this is a therapeutic product, the protein content of which has a tonic or otherwise wholesome physiological effect upon the skin itself. The impression thus affirmatively created is allowed full play by avoiding any indication, other than to mention that the effect of the lotion is temporary and its frequent application is appropriate, of the exclusively mechanical operation of the film as it dries upon the skin. Even the denial that Line Away is a "hormone" or a "harmful drug", read in the context of the other representations, suggests that it is a harmless drug. *** Some "puffery" may not amount to representation of a cosmetic as a drug, but when "puffery" contains the strong therapeutic implications we find in the Line Away promotional material, we think the dividing line has been crossed. The order of the district court will be affirmed.

NOTE: *See United States v. Article of Drug 47 Shipping Cartons, More or Less, "Helene Curtis Magic Secret", 331 F. Supp. 912 (D. Md. 1971) (Court held claims that Magic Secret was a "pure protein" which caused an "astringent sensation" amounted to puffery and were less exaggerated than in the Line Away and Sudden Beauty cases).*

CRITICAL ANALYSIS: Product classification remains complex and problematic for both industry and FDA. Integrating the above cases, discuss the ramifications of classification of an FDA regulated product as a drug or cosmetic.

Chapter 4: Professionalism, Ethics and the Future of Regulation

Today, more than ever, accountability remains as the mainstay for government, counsel and industry. Transparency initiatives remain critical for reasons beyond due process. Transparency extends to public protection and the "right to know".

NOTE: See e.g. ***Trzaska v. L'Oreal USA, Inc. et al.,*** **865 F.3d 155 (2017) case no. 15-3810 (3rd. Cir.) (court revived lawsuit and denied rehearing). Steven Trzaska, former in-house counsel for L'Oréal alleged he was improperly fired after raising conduct concerns about patent-application quotas. Third Circuit revived suit and denied L'Oréal's rehearing request. Circuit Court held allegations are "more than skin-deep".**

Conflicts of Interest Guidances—Advisory Committees and Gifts

FDA issued two draft guidances on June 29, 2016 concerning conflicts of interest. The first guidance concerns how it evaluates advisory committee members. The second guidance concerns when FDA can accept gifts. The draft guidance on gifts clarifies when the FDA should refuse gifts from external sources and the regulated industry.

Procedures for Evaluating Appearance Issues and Granting Authorizations for Participation in Food and Drug Administration Advisory Committees; Draft Guidance for the Public, Food and Drug Administration Advisory Committee Members, and Food and Drug Administration Staff

This draft guidance clarifies the process that FDA uses for assessing whether an advisory committee member has a conflict of interest issue that should preclude participation. According to FDA, the agency screens committee members for two categories of potentially disqualifying interests. These categories are as follows:

*The committee member's **financial interests** and other interests and relationships that may create an **appearance issue(s)** that the member lacks impartiality.*

Specifically, the draft guidance addresses the FDA's *"process for evaluating whether an advisory committee member has potentially disqualifying interests or affiliations that fall into the second category of interests, which are known as appearance issues".*

FDA details in the guidance the process for determining whether to authorize a member with an appearance issue to participate in an advisory committee meeting. **See 81 Fed. Reg. 42,363** *https://www.gpo.gov/fdsys/pkg/FR-2016-06-29/pdf/2016-15384.pdf* Docket No. FDA-2016-D-1399.

Gifts to the Food and Drug Administration: Evaluation and Acceptance: Draft Guidance for the Public and Food and Drug Administration Staff

https://www.regulations.gov/document?D=FDA-2015-D-4361-0001

The draft guidance defines gifts as "resources of monetary value given to FDA as an institution, including competitive grants awarded to FDA employees as part of their official duties, including: funds for either general or specific purposes, data, materials, items, information, or services." However, FDA specified that gifts do not include "resources of monetary value to which a different authority or financial mechanism applies, such as resources the agency collects or receives in the course of carrying out" its regulatory responsibilities.

Rejection of Gifts—According to FDA there are five reasons for refusing a gift without further assessment, including:

- ✓ The donor imposes conditions that are illegal, are contrary to public policy, are unreasonable to administer, are contrary to the policies and procedures of FDA, or are contrary to generally accepted public standards;
- ✓ The donor requires the agency to provide the donor with some privilege, concession or other present or future benefit in return for the gift;
- ✓ A debarred entity offers the gift;
- ✓ A different authority or financial mechanism applies; or

    ✓   The total costs associated with acceptance are expected to exceed the cost of purchasing a similar item and the cost of normal care and maintenance.

The guidance affirmed that the FDA should not accept gifts from the regulated industry "unless the gift addresses exceptional public health circumstances for which no other solution could be achieved in the time available." Further, the only person who has the authority to identify such exceptional circumstances is the FDA commissioner. **See 81 Fed. Reg. 42,365, Docket No. FDA-2015-D-4361.** *https://www.gpo.gov/fdsys/pkg/FR-2016-06-29/pdf/2016-15385.pdf*

CRITICAL ANALYSIS: Evaluate either the Advisory Committee or Gift draft guidances. See links above.

FDA Post Employment Restrictions

    The following list of post-employment restrictions summarizes restricted employment. The FDA summary provides a breakdown of restrictions applicable to all employees and restrictions applicable to senior level employees. Section 207 of Title 18 details the specific restrictions applicable to former employees.

Post-Employment Summary of Restrictions

http://www.fda.gov/downloads/AboutFDA/WorkingatFDA/Ethics/UCM125319.pdf

    Current employees who have begun seeking or negotiating for subsequent non-federal employment must immediately recuse from participation in any official matter that involves the prospective employer as an identified party, such as a grant, contract, application, audit, investigation, or lawsuit. The recusal also must extend to any particular matter of general applicability that affects the discrete industry, economic sector, or other defined class of organizations in which the prospective employer operates, such as a legislative initiative, regulatory proposal, or policy determination that affects the prospective employer as a member of such class.

    Former employees are subject to the provisions described below. Former government attorneys and public officials with a law license are subject to additional post-employment restrictions under State Rules of Professional Conduct. See: 5 CFR Part 2635, Subpart F.

Restrictions Applicable to All Employees

18 US Code 207(a)(1) Permanent Ban on "Switching Sides." Former employees are subject to a lifetime ban on communicating to or appearing before the Government on behalf of their new employer or anyone else regarding specific party matters in which they participated personally and substantially during their entire government service.

18 US Code 207(a)(2) Two-Year Official Responsibility Provision. For two years after leaving federal employment, former employees cannot make representational communications to or appearances before the Government regarding specific party matters that were pending under their official responsibility during their last year of government service.

18 US Code 207(b) One-Year Ban on Trade or Treaty Negotiation Activities. Former employees who participated in ongoing trade or treaty negotiations on behalf of the United States within the year preceding their departure cannot, for one year, represent, aid, or advise anyone based on information exempt from disclosure to which the employees had access.

18 US Code 203 Compensation Limitation. Former employees who join a law, accounting, or government relations firm cannot share in any bonus, profit sharing, or similar compensation derived from fees earned by the employee's new firm or partnership for representational services before the Government rendered during the former employee's period of government service.

41 US Code 423(a) Disclosure of Procurement Information. Former employees cannot knowingly disclose contractor bid or proposal information or source selection information to anyone not authorized to receive such information.

41 US Code 423(d) One-Year Ban on Contractor Compensation. Employees who worked on a contract in excess of 10 million dollars cannot receive compensation from that contractor within one year after the employee: (1) served as a contracting officer, member of a source selection board, or chief of a technical evaluation team; (2) served as a program manager, deputy program manager, or administrative contracting officer; or (3) personally made certain decisions such as approving an award, modification, task or delivery order, establishing overhead, or settling a claim.

45 CFR Part 2 Testimony and Production of Documents in Proceedings where the United States is Not a Party. Former employees cannot provide testimony or produce documents in a federal, state, local, or tribal judicial or administrative proceeding (or a state, local, or tribal legislative hearing) concerning information acquired during the course of their official duties or because of their former government position, unless authorized by the head of their respective OPDIV or, if a former employee of OS, the ASAM. This requirement applies to requested or subpoenaed oral statements before a court or an adjudicative or investigatory body, as well as statements made in depositions, interrogatories, declarations, affidavits, or other formal participation.

Restrictions Applicable Only to "Senior Employees"

Executive Levels II through V; Uniformed Service Pay Grades O-7 or above; SES and Employees in other Pay Systems with an Annual Rate of Basic Pay (Excluding Locality-Based Adjustments) at or above $155,441.

18 US Code 207(c) One-Year "Cooling-Off" Period. Former employees cannot, for one year after completing service in a "senior" position, knowingly make, with the intent to influence, any communication to or appearance before any officer or employee of their former agency on behalf of anyone seeking official action. Except for Senate confirmed Presidential appointees, who are prohibited from contacting the entire Department, "former agency" means the OPDIV where the employee worked. The restrictions in 18 US Code 207(c) do not apply to acts done in carrying out official duties as an employee of and on behalf of a:

    (1) State or local government
    (2) College or university
    (3) Non-profit hospital or medical research organization

Other exceptions may apply for certain types of testimony, uncompensated statements based on special knowledge, and scientific or technological information, and for certain contacts made on behalf of international organizations or political campaign organizations. 18 US Code 207(f).

One-Year Foreign Entity Provision—Former employees cannot, for one year after completing service in a "senior" position, knowingly represent, aid, or advise a foreign government or foreign political party with the intent to influence any officer or employee of the United States.

NOTE: Cabinet officers paid at Executive Level I, known as "very senior employees," are subject to an additional two-year restriction that precludes representational contact to the appointee's former department, as well as to any Presidential appointee in the entire Executive Branch and any employee paid at Executive Levels I-V. (October 2011).

CRITICAL ANALYSIS: The expression "revolving door" is used to describe those FDA employees who later work in the private, yet FDA regulated sector. Do the above restrictions provide sufficient safeguards? Provide recommendations.

The Future of Regulation

Future regulation is multi-faceted and involves the global sector. Lessons learned from the present and past provides insight into the future. Technology has revamped how regulated companies market their products and the techniques FDA uses to regulate those products. International computerization will apply to all regulated products. In the future, everything will become virtual except the product itself. Federal regulation of foods, human drugs, veterinary products, medical devices, biologics, personal care cosmetic products, dietary supplements and tobacco products have evidenced a long road in terms of FDA standards for safety and efficacy. The future holds the potential of improved products across the board for all FDA regulated products.

Nanotechnology provides an excellent illustration. The term has become increasingly popular in the life sciences regulated community. Nanotechnology material is extremely small matter. This technology can have enormous future implications for food and drug related products such as implants and prosthetics, drug delivery and food processing. What role should FTC have in the regulation of advertising for products that contain nanomaterials such as dietary supplements, over-the-counter products, cosmetics and foods?

NOTE: FDA issued a final guidance in 2014 titled: *"Considering Whether an FDA-Regulated Product Involves the Application of Nanotechnology,"* **to provide greater regulatory clarity for industry about the use of nanotechnology in FDA-regulated products, including drugs, devices, cosmetics and food. See also** *Volume VI: Veterinary Products* **nanotechnology draft guidance in animal feed;** *Volume VIII: Personal Care Products*, **nanotechnology, guidance in cosmetic products and** *Volume IX: Food Regulation*—**Nanotechnology Guidance in Food Ingredients.**
https://www.fda.gov/RegulatoryInformation/Guidances/ucm257698.htm

Public trust remains most significant. Industry and government both have a responsibility to ensure product integrity. According to FDA, critical issues encompass drug post-market safety, nanotechnology, online direct-to-consumer promotion, food additive safety, dietary supplement regulation, foodborne pathogens, biosimilars, gene therapy, vaccines, antibiotic resistance and global concerns.

Due process and First Amendment protections will continue to be preserved and considered. The *Tummino* decisions (Plan B) provided the requisite administrative oversight. The decisions of *Western Medical States, Washington Legal Foundation* and *Sorrell* concerning off-label drug marketing and the tobacco graphic warnings litigation have protected free speech by charting a new course for marketing FDA regulated products.

Has Congress kept pace with the changing landscape such as the opioid crisis and legalization of marijuana? The Food and Drug Administration Amendments Act continued what the Food and Drug Administration Modernization Act started; that is, to legally open the channels of communication between industry and FDA. Finally, the Food and Drug Administration Safety and Innovation Act and the Drug Quality and Security Act serve as recent legislative efforts to provide FDA with the authority to protect the public in keeping with the mission of the FDA in accordance with the Federal, Food, Drug and Cosmetic Act. Whether one is a regulator or part of the regulated industry, the following practice pointers provide a barometer for how to conduct business. Finally, these pointers apply across the board to the regulated industry as well as to regulators, as both have an onerous responsibility to protect the American public.

Professional Practice Pointers

Strive for excellence.

Foster integrity.

Update your knowledge and skills.

Assess all issues thoroughly.

Maintain a sense of pride in quality work.

Keep current on federal and state matters.

Evaluate all possible options.

Insist on a plain language explanation.

Strive for positive change.

Remember your moral compass.

Identify needed policy changes.

Treat people with respect.

Use common sense.

Play tough and play fair.

Listen intensely to all positions.

Utilize logic.

Practice compassion.

Focus on the "big" picture.

Practice civility.

Advocate, advocate, advocate.

CRITICAL ANALYSIS: The obligation by FDA to protect public health remains steadfast. Recommend regulatory reforms for all FDA regulated products—foods, drugs, biologics, medical devices, dietary supplements, personal care cosmetics, veterinary and tobacco products.

Index Key Words

554

Made in the USA
Middletown, DE
12 September 2021